USA TODAY SPORTS

RON SHANDLER'S 2023

BASEBALL FORECASTER

AND ENCYCLOPEDIA OF FANALYTICS

D1401181

TRIUMPH
BOOKS

Triumph Books and colophon are registered trademarks of Random House, Inc.

This book is available in quantity at special discounts for your group or organization. For further information, contact:

Triumph Books LLC
814 North Franklin Street
Chicago, Illinois 60610
(312) 337-0747
www.triumphbooks.com

Printed in U.S.A.
ISBN: 978-1-63727-186-5

Rotisserie League Baseball is a registered trademark of the Rotisserie League Baseball Association, Inc.

Statistics provided by Baseball Info Solutions

Cover design by Brent Hershey
Front cover photograph by Ken Blaze-USATODAY Sports
Author photograph by Kevin Hurley

Ron Shandler's
BASEBALL FORECASTER

Editors

Ray Murphy
Brent Hershey

Associate Editors

Brandon Kruse
Ryan Bloomfield

· · · · · ·

Tech/Data/Charts

Matt Cederholm
Mike Krebs

Graphic Design

Brent Hershey

Player Commentaries

Ryan Bloomfield
Alain de Leonardis
Brent Hershey
Brandon Kruse
Dan Marcus
Ray Murphy
Stephen Nickrand
Kristopher Olson
Greg Pyron
Brian Rudd
Ron Shandler
Paul Sporer
Jock Thompson
Rod Truesdell
Corbin Young

Research and Articles

Ed DeCaria
Cary James
Dan Marcus
Brian Rudd
Steve Weimer

Prospects

Chris Blessing
Jeremy Deloney
Rob Gordon
Tom Mulhall

Injury Chart

Rick Wilton

Acknowledgments

Producing the *Baseball Forecaster* is a team effort; the list of credits to the left is where the heavy lifting gets done. On behalf of Ron, Brent, and Ray, our most sincere thanks to each of those key contributors.

We are just as grateful to the rest of the BaseballHQ.com staff, who do the yeoman's work in populating the website with 12 months of incredible content: Dave Adler, Sarah Allan, Andy Andres, Matt Beagle, Alex Beckey, Bob Berger, Derrick Boyd, Brian Brickley, Tim Cavanaugh, Brant Chesser, Jake Crumpler, Patrick Davitt, Alan Davison, Doug Dennis, Brian Entrekin, Jim Ferretti, Greg Fishwick, Neil FitzGerald, Arik Florimonte, Rick Green, Phil Hertz, Ed Hubbard, Greg Jewett, Brad Johnson, Tom Kephart, Zach Larson, Chris Lee, David Martin, Bill McKnight, Landon Moblad, Matthew Mougalian, Harold Nichols, Doug Otto, Josh Paley, Nick Richards, Peter Sheridan, Adam Sloate, Tanner Smith, Skip Snow, Matthew St-Germain, Jeffrey Tomich, Shelly Verougstraete, Michael Weddell, Ryan Williams and Michael Yachera.

Thank you to all our industry colleagues—you are technically competitors, but also comrades working to grow this industry. That is never more evident than at our First Pitch Forum live events. Hope to see many of you again in person in either Florida or Arizona in 2023.

Thank you to Ryan Bonini and the team at USA Today Sports Media Group, as well as all the support from the folks at Triumph Books and Action Printing.

And of course, thank *you*, readers, for your interest in what we all have to say. Your kind words, support and (respectful) criticism move us forward on the fanalytic continuum more than you know. We are grateful for your readership.

·

From Brent Hershey The pressure of putting together this volume seemed especially acute this year, as the extended season (thank youuuuu, lockout!) tightened the screws on our already-fragile production timeline. All the folks in the box to the left came through and we once again take pride in the final product. Specific shout-outs are due to Brandon and Ryan; every reader benefits from your multi-layered expertise. Thanks to Ron for shepherding this flock each year. And Ray: We've somehow done it again—succinctly capping the past baseball season while providing readers with tools and insights for the next one, all in one entertaining, 288-page package. Thanks for your thoughtful partnership throughout. For Lorie, Dillon and Eden, thanks for supporting me as always during this six-week frenzy. You, more than anyone, can understand my Pete Alonso-like outburst upon finishing this year's book. Love to you all.

From Ray Murphy Due to a major hiring cycle, the list of BaseballHQ.com staff above is a lot longer than last year. New voices and perspectives are invigorating, and I am definitely feeling those positive effects. I'm also filled with gratitude to the staff veterans who carried a significant workload through pandemic- and lockout-created uncertainty of these past few years. Knock on wood, the horizon looks clear, and teaming up with Ron and Brent to meet that future is a prospect as exciting as Julio Rodríguez.

My home life has also overlapped with this space more this year, as now-11-year-olds Bridget and Grace have become avid softball players. They are a developing pitcher/catcher combo, though we haven't assigned prospect ratings to them just yet. As always, my wife Jennifer is the one who makes all of these endeavors possible, and worthwhile.

From Ron Shandler The first edition of this book was published a few weeks before my 28th birthday. Since then, nearly a million of you have read my words and numbers, and I have tracked the years with your league championships. I am honored to have Ray, Brent, Brandon and Ryan, and a group of amazing analysts build upon my early work and create something that keeps you coming back each year.

I have also marked time with a historical work that tracks the beginnings of the fantasy baseball industry and the writers who became its first "experts." Thanks to the folks at Triumph Sports for helping me tell this story. ETA Fall 2023.

And as always, my undying gratitude to Sue, Darielle and Justina who still get excited for the release of each book. And thank you to every cherished reader; there are no words. The idea for this book appeared to me over Thanksgiving dinner in 1985 and I am thrilled that so many of you get to read each year's edition between string bean casserole and pumpkin pie after 37 years.

TABLE OF CONTENTS

Phoenix

by Ron Shandler

In early November, a couple hundred fantasy leaguers descended upon a hotel in Mesa, Arizona for the 27th First Pitch Arizona conference. Many see this annual sojourn as marking the official beginning of the Fantasy Hot Stove season (hence, "first pitch"), and look forward to a long weekend of sun, scouting and socializing.

This year's conference was the first since 2019 that looked ahead to an off-season mostly unaffected by pandemic or labor strife. That alone should have given the event an air of optimism. Instead, there was an undercurrent of uncertainty in the conference program. There was a session that provided a post-mortem analysis of 2022's post-pandemic changes. Other sessions were devoted to projecting the potential impact of the new MLB rules. And dozens participated in fantasy drafts, all facing questions about the future of our cherished statistics. Would they even be recognizable next September?

At the same time, there was also a tempered excitement at the challenge of deconstructing the chaos. Some folks dug in their heels on what would or would not happen. Some conjectured within a wide range of possible outcomes. Some even reveled in the randomness. I love that we're such diehard stat geeks.

So, while we are potentially facing a season of statistical shambles, the best we can do is hunker down and try to figure it all out. This game's foundation is all about gathering and analyzing information, making the best decisions, reviewing the outcomes and repeating the cycle. That's nothing new, but the process becomes more difficult with each new variable added to the equation.

This year presents a different set of challenges. Here are a few we faced in 2022 and the new ones we'll have to deal with in 2023.

Anchored to uncertainty

For over three months last winter, we were flying blind. Baseball owners locked out the players on December 2, 2021, and all MLB roster activity ceased. There were no free agent signings, no trades and no pipeline to the critical news we needed to plan for our 2022 drafts.

There was also no decline in daily talk and speculation. Even though we were sitting blindfolded in dark rooms, tossing darts at targets that were months away, we still drafted teams. In December and January, baseball stopped, but we didn't. We compiled Average Draft Position rankings from that activity, which became source material for subsequent drafts in February into March. And it was all driven by incomplete, perhaps faulty information.

For the record, one certainty was accurately predicted:

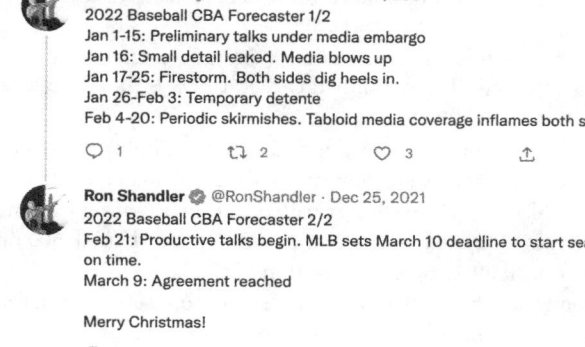

Just wanted to put that out there.

Anyway, when the lockout lifted on March 10 (okay, I was off by a day), we were bombarded with a news deluge. We found out what players had been doing during the winter. Some had spent their downtime in workout rooms; others on buffet lines. We got a first look at some prospects who might have a chance to crack a major league roster. We finally got to see some on-field play. And we started funneling 500 pounds of potential playing time into 162-game bags.

This was sparkling, fresh information. A good deal of it validated what we already assumed, but a fair chunk didn't. One would think this input might have a significant impact on our drafting tendencies. After all, we had spent three months drafting off bad information; now we could see the light. Perhaps it even merited a full reset.

Well, that wasn't the case. Three months of fuzzy information became a firm reference point for all subsequent drafting activity. Was that a good path or a bad path? If nothing else, reliance on the winter ADPs carved an *easier* path.

I looked at the National Fantasy Baseball Championship (NFBC) ADPs of the Top 100 players compiled before March 10 and compared them to those from drafts after March 17 (allowing for a week for the news to filter into the draft results). With few exceptions, drafters dug in their heels on their winter expectations. While most players moved a few spots due to random volatility, virtually none of those shifts reflected any real change in perceived value. There was just a handful who moved by a round or more in the rankings.

As you might expect, six injured players dropped significantly, some out of the Top 100 completely: Fernando Tatis (-79 spots), Jacob deGrom (-60), Chris Sale (-110), Lance Lynn (-41), Jack Flaherty (-124) and Luis Castillo (-44). Zack Wheeler dropped by a little (-10) as a hedge against a balky spring shoulder. No surprises here; we would have expected this, lockout or no lockout. Still, questions remain:

- Would these drops have been deeper had we known about the health issues earlier?
- Or were these drops excessive knee-jerk reactions to the late news? Had we known earlier, perhaps they would have been tempered.

The most significant non-injury drops shifted players by only a round, and there were only two—Cody Bellinger (-12) and Tommy Edman (-17). Bellinger batted .139 in 36 spring training at bats. Edman batted just .083 in 24 AB. Drafters batted .500 on that pair of small-sample overreactions.

Among all the players in or near the Top 100, only seven improved their ADP by a round or more once the lockout ended.

Kenley Jansen's signing to be the Braves' closer netted him one round in the ADPs, moving from 93 to 79. Despite holding the role all year with decent success, he'd finish outside the Top 130.

Jordan Romano's increasing grasp of Toronto's closer role bumped him from 104 to 87. In what could be considered an amazing feat of forecasting fortune, Romano finished at exactly No. 87 in roto earnings.

Byron Buxton once again looked healthy in camp—.469 with 5 HR—netting him a 19-spot bump in the ADPs, from 54 to 35. Despite following up with a career-high 28 HR, he once again finished with fewer than 350 AB and ranked outside the Top 150.

Carlos Rodón jumped 28 spots, from 123 to 95, likely due to his March 11 signing by the 107-win Giants. His 6 spring innings with a 1.35 ERA didn't hurt either. He'd earn it back and more, finishing just inside the Top 50.

Bobby Witt, Jr.'s .406 spring average boosted his chances of making the team, which bought him a 30-spot ADP boost, from 91 to 61. He'd finish inside the Top 30, so the intent was on the money.

Justin Verlander reported healthy to camp and threw 13.2 innings with a 1.32 ERA, earning a 36-spot ADP improvement, from 106 to 70. It wasn't nearly enough; he finished 5th overall in roto earnings.

Kris Bryant was the biggest mover in the post-lockout ADPs. Upon signing with the Rockies, he jumped 37 spots, from 92 to 55. But he got hurt and managed just 160 AB, finishing barely inside the Top 500.

There were likely more multi-round movers further down the ADPs, but honestly, after Round 10 (ADP 150 in a 15-teamer), the ADPs hardly matter at all (read "The Ineptitude of ADPs" in the Encyclopedia). From Rounds 11 to 23, almost 65 percent of our picks have historically been losers, with 57 percent finishing at least *four rounds lower* than where they were drafted. Worse, more than 25 percent of our Round 11-23 picks would be *undraftable* even in a 15-team league with 50-man rosters. We stink at this. That is why it is important to know whether better information might have made better picks.

But the key takeaway from this exercise is not about the particular movers. The important note is that, with few exceptions, our player perceptions were anchored in the winter ADPs, even though those rankings were driven by incomplete, often faulty information.

Was that a flawed decision-making process? Perhaps. But I'd have these remaining questions:

Had Kenley Jansen signed in December and Jordan Romano locked down his closer role earlier, would they have earned better ADPs? Established front-line closers typically go a round or two earlier than they did.

Similarly, if Carlos Rodón and Kris Bryant had signed over the winter, might the hype have pushed their ADPs higher?

If the media had been talking up Bobby Witt, Jr. over the winter and we had gotten our first look at him in February, might he have gone higher than No. 61?

If Byron Buxton had put on his slugging display and Justin Verlander compiled even more elite innings for six weeks' worth of spring games instead of three, might their ADPs have broken into the Top 30?

Had we not anchored our rankings in the winter drafts, it's possible these players would have cost us even more at the draft table in March. But even at their actual ADPs, only four of the seven earned back their investment or turned a profit.

View from 38,000 feet

Since the 2016 edition of this book, I've included annual statistical trend data to provide context for our player valuation decisions. The economics of this game are driven by the knowledge about which statistical categories are plentiful or scarce. Supply and demand. If there are fewer 200-inning pitchers or 40-steals sources, you will have to pay more for them. Lots of home runs? Prices and ADPs go down.

Over the past few years, many trends were heading in the same direction. Well, things seem to be starting to plateau. Let's look:

		Players with		
Year	Tot HR	20+ HR	30+ HR	HR/FB%
2013	4661	70	14	10.5%
2014	4186	57	11	9.5%
2015	4909	64	20	11.4%
2016	5610	111	35	12.8%
2017	6105	118	41	13.7%
2018	5585	100	27	12.7%
2019	6776	130	58	15.3%
*2020	6221	119	53	14.8%
2021	5944	102	43	13.6%
2022	5215	71	23	11.4%

Pro-rated to full season

There is an explanation for this decline in home runs; in fact, there are several. After being put on notice for use of sticky stuff in 2021, pitchers were far less policed and had nearly free reign again in 2022, suppressing power. There was also a huge surge in rookie hitter debuts last year, players who possessed less potent artillery:

Year	Debuts	Batters	Pitchers
2013	230	85	145
2014	234	84	150
2015	255	95	160
2016	257	80	177
2017	262	89	173
2018	247	78	169
2019	261	85	176
2021	265	96	169
2022	303	153	150

That's more than 50 new batters than last year's 96, which was the high water mark up to that point. That accounted for a whole bunch of plate appearances being spread around more than ever. And while Julio Rodríguez and Michael Harris II earned their stripes, there were also the Spencer Torkelsons and Nick Allens eating up PAs and dragging down the numbers.

However, an even larger influence on the decline in homers was the installation of a humidor in every ballpark last year. I could say that this was the year the balls went soggy, but players still hit more bombs than in 2015. If you recall, 2015 was the year they switched to different balls after the All-Star break and we all went nuts about the late power barrage. Seven years later, the current level seems almost sedate.

But the last thing we want is less offense. Thankfully, we may be getting that back in another area:

Year	Singles%	Three True Outcomes%	K%
2013	67.6%	30.3%	18.9%
2014	68.3%	30.3%	19.4%
2015	66.5%	30.7%	19.5%
2016	65.1%	32.3%	20.2%
2017	63.8%	33.5%	20.6%
2018	64.2%	33.7%	21.6%
2019	61.7%	35.1%	22.3%
2020	62.8%	36.1%	22.9%
2021	63.3%	35.1%	23.2%
2022	65.2%	33.4%	22.4%

Extreme defensive shifting and 100 mph heaters were just as prevalent last year as before. Still, singles as a percentage of hits bounced back to their highest level since 2015. The percentage of three true outcomes (BB, K, HR) settled down as well. However, we can't plant a stake in any of these levels or trends. They will be moving the fences on us in 2023 (metaphorically), so nothing here may be real.

	Number of Pitchers with			
Year	200 IP	200 K	15 W	**10 W
2013	36	12	16	82
2014	34	13	25	83
2015	28	18	13	70
2016	15	12	23	70
2017	15	16	17	74
2018	13	18	19	59
2019	15	24	16	74
*2020	6	20	19	70
2021	4	17	5	54
2022	8	11	14	63

*Prorated to full season   **Includes relief pitchers

On the pitching side, the number of 200-inning pitchers rebounded a bit, but 200-strikeout hurlers declined to the lowest level since 2009. Nearly all 11 of those pitchers are going to cost you a ton.

	INNINGS		WINS	
Year	Starters	Relievers	Starters	Relievers
2016	63.3%	36.7%	67.1%	32.9%
2017	61.9	38.1	67.5	32.5
2018	59.9	40.1	62.3	37.7
2019	57.9	42.1	59.7	40.3
2020	55.5	44.5	52.2	47.8
2021	57.3	42.7	55.4	44.6
2022	58.7	41.3	59.4	40.6

Two years ago, it looked like the beginning of a paradigm shift. With the proliferation of game openers and innovative bullpen management, reliever innings and wins were poised to overtake those of starters. Roles would be blurred and tactical in-game situations would drive pitcher usage.

Despite starters winning a larger percentage of games than in the past two years, some teams were a significant drag on that average. Here are the teams whose starters accounted for no more than half of their wins:

Team	Wins	From Starters	Pct.
TAM	86	43	50.0%
CHC	74	37	50.0%
BAL	83	41	49.4%
KC	65	32	49.2%
PIT	62	21	33.9%

The opener-heavy Rays are not surprising, but yikes—Pirates! One might think this list would only include cellar-dwellers, but no. Compare that to the Astros, whose starters accounted for 84 of their 106 wins (79%).

This, too:

Year	IP/GS	CG%
2013	5.90	2.6%
2014	5.97	2.4%
2015	5.81	2.1%
2016	5.65	1.7%
2017	5.51	1.2%
2018	5.36	0.9%
2019	5.18	0.9%
2020	4.78	1.6%
2021	5.02	1.0%
2022	5.20	0.7%

2020 was an aberrant season. Still, I thought it was a terrific direction for the game and I hoped we'd continue that trend. Baseball's caretakers did not, doing all they could to preserve the sanctity of the starter and reliever roles. We see the signs of that trend reversal here. Still, more than one-third of all teams' starting pitchers did average fewer than 5 innings per start in 2022. It's just further justification that we should be chasing high-skilled middle relievers over 5th, 4th and maybe even 3rd starters, and not just for wins.

The definition of insanity

The quotable definition of insanity is "doing the same thing over and over again and expecting different results." This definition has been attributed to various sources, from Albert Einstein, to Sigmund Freud, to Alcoholics Anonymous. For us sports fans, I think it harkens back to cartoonist Charles Schulz.

Picture Lucy. She represents the totality of major league bullpens. Her football represents our quest for saves. And every one of us is Charlie Brown. Each year, Lucy presents us with that ball and goads us into attempting a successful kick, only to pull the ball away every time. Yet, we keep going back, year after year.

From the beginning of time (circa 1980), saves have been the bane of our fantasy existence. The commodity is accumulated by a small core of pitchers, and no matter how much talent they may or may not have, their positioning on a ninth inning mound is left to the fickle whims of a major league manager.

In 1999, I started tracking how well the experts in LABR and Tout Wars could identify the best investments. We did pretty well that first year, with only a 22 percent failure rate (defined as investments that returned less than 50 percent of their draft price). That jumped to 37 percent in 2000 and 59 percent in 2003 before settling into a 35-45 percent range for a good decade.

After a bad year in 2012 (66%), the failure rate settled down again, but breached 50 percent in 2016 and has not abated since. Over the past six years coming into 2022 (not counting 2020), our failure rate has *averaged* 59 percent.

Concurrently, the average draft price for these closers has plummeted from about $20 in the early 2000s to $11.79 in 2021. The riskier the investment, the less we are generally willing to pay. Even five years ago, it was unheard of to draft a potential closer for less than $10; now, at least one-third of our closers cost less than that.

And then there was 2022.

All the draft season talk was about how Liam Hendriks and Josh Hader were getting overdrafted in the second round, or costing owners $25 and up. And why not? Both had earned around $30 for their owners in 2021. But in 2022, Hendriks returned about $21; Hader just $10.

The losses trickled down throughout most of the draft pool. After Emmanuel Clase, Edwin Díaz and Jordan Romano returned fair value, arms like Giovanny Gallegos, Aroldis Chapman and Corey Knebel failed, and most of the sub-$10 speculative picks were losers.

In all, 25 of the 35 pitchers drafted for saves earned back less than 50 percent of their draft value, a record-breaking failure rate of 71 percent. Over the entire draft pool, only 17 of the pitchers even returned positive earnings, and only two turned a profit—Paul Sewald and Devin Williams. In real dollar terms, the $443 spent on saves in 2022 returned just $65. That's less than 15 cents earned for each dollar spent.

What does this mean for 2023?

Year	Saves	Number of pitchers with		
		30+	20+	5+
2013	1266	19	28	41
2014	1264	17	25	46
2015	1292	19	28	44
2016	1276	15	22	52
2017	1179	10	23	51
2018	1244	8	20	50
2019	1180	11	22	53
*2020	1139	9	17	67
2021	1191	9	19	62
2022	1232	10	18	65

Prorated to full season

In 2022, relievers notched the most saves since 2018, but the spread was wider than this chart shows. In 2019, 200 pitchers had at least one save, the first time we ever reached that level. In 2022, that jumped to 223, a new record. So, while more saves are being recorded, more pitchers are getting a piece of them.

Odds are the 2022 studs will continue to command top dollar, because that is what the flawed marketplace does. So Emmanuel Clase and Edwin Díaz will surely cost you a second or third round

pick. You can decide to pay that if you want, but be sure to familiarize yourself with Díaz's 2019 stat line to get a sense of the range of possible outcomes. Clase has yet to have a down year; maybe he's due, maybe not.

But the bigger question is this: Why are we still chasing a stat that returned 15 cents on the dollar last year?

Some argue that we should continue to play within the rules as written; figuring out how to make the best of a challenging situation is just part of the game. I would argue that sticking with an approach that has a 15-cent R.O.I. is a first-level definition of insanity.

So I continue to wave the flag for adding Holds to the process.

Some argue that Holds are a flawed stat. A hold is "awarded when a reliever enters the game in a save situation and maintains his team's lead for the next relief pitcher, while recording at least one out." This opens up potential grey areas, not the least of which is that a pitcher can be awarded a hold and a loss for the same appearance.

I would argue that a closer can be awarded a save for coming into a clean ninth inning with a three-run lead, facing the bottom of the batting order and giving up two runs. There is nothing award-worthy about that performance either. It's just cherry-picking your particular flavor of disaster.

These are all situational considerations, which lend themselves to grey areas. But we should be more concerned with populating our fantasy rosters with *skilled players*, regardless of their situational fates. Some of the best-skilled relief pitchers are on the mound in the highest leverage situations, often earlier than the ninth inning, and our current rules mostly ignore them.

Holds are not perfect; neither are saves. As I've written about eleventeen times over the past decade, "saves and holds together form a reasonable proxy for overall bullpen performance."

In fact, saves, holds and even wins are essentially the same class of statistic. They are **role-based tags that help identify players who are placed in situations that maximize their skills.** The outcomes of those performances—saves, holds, wins—are team-based results. If we treat them as what they are—just placekeepers—we can focus on building our pitching staffs with what's *most* important—rostering skilled pitchers.

In some ways, holds are an even better stat than wins, especially those awarded to relievers. With a hold, the pitcher was deliberately put on the mound with an expectation of a positive outcome, and rewarded if successful. By comparison, if a pitcher happened to be the last man on the mound when the offense put the team ahead, he's rewarded with a win no matter how poorly he pitched.

Some leagues are slowly coming around to the Saves + Holds mindset. Some have dimmed the stigma by calling them Solds, or Shaves. And some have decided to dip their toes in by using a category like "Saves + 1/2 Holds," noting that multiple holds can be awarded in a single game. I'm not sure that's necessary; it's a hedge against full adoption.

But here's the thing… Even with holds in the formula, drafters will still tend to focus on saves acquisition as their default approach—saves are still more plentiful on an individual player basis. Then they'll backfill their staff with prime holds targets who could move into the closer's role. This manner of identifying valuable bullpen arms is how we've always done it, but now with the added benefit of getting to add Holds to our category total. That softens the blow when Raisel Iglesias gets traded into a setup role through no fault of our own, or Aroldis Chapman turns into a pumpkin.

Change is hard; I get it. Maybe you can't imagine tinkering with a core Rotisserie statistic that has been a part of this game for more than four decades. But seriously, we gotta stop chasing a stat with a 15 cent R.O.I. Lucy is teeing up that football again; we already know this will not end well.

The New Rules: Here we go!
We have enough trouble projecting the future without MLB throwing a bunch of new wrinkles into the mix. Beginning in 2023, there will be a new balanced schedule, pitch clock, bigger bases, defensive shackles, and a host of corollaries that likely add 50 pages to an already-bloated rulebook.

When deciding to make changes and close loopholes in a roto constitution, I always advise not to make things too complicated or difficult to administrate. But that's exactly what MLB has done. There are so many accommodations for breakages in play and areas where umpires have the discretion to interpret as they see fit that this can only lead to angst.

I hate angst.

The impact of the new balanced schedule: For the first time since ever, all 30 teams will play the other 29 teams at least once during the season. That will mean 24 fewer games against intra-divisional opponents, which will presumably level the competitive playing field.

For some teams and players, this is good news. A.L. East teams will be able to feast on more Central Division chum. If Aaron Judge can hit 62 homers facing divisional foes 76 times, imagine what he could do shifting 24 of those games to some lesser opponents. And Nick Pivetta is probably throwing a party right now. (Were you invited? I was not. Sad.) He faced the Yankees, Rays and Blue Jays 13 times in 2022, accounting for 64 of his 180 innings, and posted a 7.57 ERA against those divisional opponents. His ERA against every other team was 2.95.

Of course, this is not such good news for other teams and players. The Reds, Pirates, Royals and Tigers won't be able to beat up on each other as much, now facing more games against tougher opponents. Even Shane Bieber becomes a little less desirable—his ERA against divisional opponents was 2.27; against everyone else it was 3.58. I might be less tempted to take a chance on Tarik Skubal, or maybe even Hunter Greene. And N.L. West hitters who used to feast on Rockies pitchers will have fewer visits to Coors Field. I'm talking about guys like Jake Cronenworth, Christian Walker and Mike Yastrzemski, all of whom posted an OPS over 1.000 at Coors in 2022.

At First Pitch Arizona, Todd Zola also reminded us that this change will affect park factors as the mix of road parks will now be different. Given the need for a good three years of data here, it will take awhile for this to provide us with usable intel.

Some analysts believe this change will have a more far-reaching impact than any of the other new rules. I wouldn't go that far. The other rules will affect all games; this change only affects some. Still, select players will see a measurable impact.

Gut Prediction: One of the Central Division winners will have a sub-.500 record. One of the other division winners will make a run at 120 victories.

The impact of the pitch clock: The use of a pitch clock in the minors in 2022 cut the duration of games by about 25 minutes. This is good news for people who want shorter games. Fantasy leaguers don't care if games go seven hours as long as our stats keep accumulating, but the pitch clock could potentially impact those numbers.

Pitchers will only be allowed 15 seconds between pitches when the bases are empty and 20 seconds when there are runners on base. By comparison, last year's pitchers took an average of 18.2 seconds and 23.6 seconds, respectively. Chopping off 3-4 seconds seems like no big deal. But for some pitchers, those precious seconds will feel like trying to catch the 5:09pm PATH train to Hoboken when it's 5:05pm and you're stuck in a crowd at 34th street. (New Yorkers understand.) Basically, *every second counts.*

(Yes, you can always catch the 5:16. You're missing the point.)

Major league pitchers have had mixed reactions to the change. The clock may or may not affect their ability to maintain the rhythm to which they have become accustomed. Some might easily adjust; some might not.

The league-wide average time between pitches, regardless of on-base conditions, has slowly increased over the past few years. Some pitchers are used to lollygagging on the mound way beyond the average, and they might have the most trouble adjusting to the new rule. In 2022, here are the starting pitchers who averaged over 20 seconds between pitches, regardless of on-base conditions. *(All advanced data is from Statcast and Baseball Savant.)*

Pitcher	Seconds
Shohei Ohtani	21.7
Luis Garcia (HOU)	21.2
Corbin Burnes	21.1
Michael Kopech	21.1
Yu Darvish	21.0
Lucas Giolito	20.7
Alek Manoah	20.7
Jordan Montgomery	20.4
Kevin Gausman	20.3
Aaron Nola	20.2
Justin Verlander	20.1

Lollygaggers, all of them.

Perhaps more worrisome are hard-throwing relievers. They occupy higher positions on the ranking list above. Those who routinely throw at triple-digit speed might require a longer recovery time between maximum effort deliveries. Shorten that recovery time and what could happen?

- They throw at a lower velocity, which potentially affects their effectiveness.
- They continue to throw at max effort, which potentially affects their effectiveness *and* risks injury.
- They continue to throw at max effort; nothing bad happens.

In 2022, the worst offenders, each taking 24 seconds or longer between pitches were (in ascending order of down time) Hunter Strickland, Alex Vesia, Aroldis Chapman, Andrew Bellati, Devin Williams, Kyle Finnegan and Kenley Jansen. But the co-winners of the 2022 Mike Hargrove Human Rain Delay Award (Pitchers Division) were Jonathan Loaisiga and Giovanny Gallegos, each clocking 25.8 seconds between pitches and besting all hurlers by at least two tenths of a second. (Again, remember the PATH train.)

In 2021, Chapman led the field at 26.9 seconds; Rafael Dolis led in 2020 with 27.2 seconds. Over the past five years, the lollygaggiest pitchers were Chapman (24.3), Emmanuel Clase (24.4) and Finnegan (25.8). Looking only at the data when runners were on base, the following relievers averaged *over a half a minute* between pitches: Alex Colomé, Devin Williams, Giovanny Gallegos and Kenley Jansen (the worst offender at 31.4 seconds). Heck, grab a seat and do Wordle while you're waiting.

All of this adds some risk to our 2023 pitching picks. However, it's not as easy as just pushing a bunch of hard-throwers down our ranking lists. When the clock was tested in the minors, there were reports that it helped young pitchers maintain focus better. Over several years, it even decreased the incidence of injuries. So we can't respond to this in broad strokes.

One thing I do know for sure: the pitch clock has already had a devastating effect on me personally.

Before this year, my wife Sue and I had a routine that had become near and dear to our relationship. Sue works in the ticket office at Clover Park, the Mets' spring training venue and also home to the St. Lucie Mets of the Florida State League (and 2022 Champions). During the minor league season, I'd attend games and wait for her to get off work and join me, usually around the fifth inning. We'd have a beer and watch the rest of the game together, which would be a nice end to our respective workdays.

But since they started using the clock, the games have been going quicker and Sue hasn't gotten off work until almost the eighth inning, *after they've stopped selling beer.* This has been particularly troublesome since our marriage is fueled by evening alcohol.

Okay, that's hyperbole. But it really stinks that we can't have this nice routine anymore. Two innings to wind down together—sans alcohol—just doesn't cut it.

Some rules don't affect everyone equally; I guess that's the point.

Gut Prediction: Starting pitchers will be mostly unaffected. Bullpen management will become even tougher than it already is, with more underperformances, more injuries and more closer turnover.

The impact of bigger bases: Increasing the size of bases from 15 inches to 18 inches was sold to us as a means to reduce injuries and perhaps to increase base-stealing. According to *Baseball America*, when this was tested in the minors, "the stolen base rate and success rate skyrocketed, but that had much more to do with the other rules tweaks than it had with the larger bases." Regardless, the running distance from first base to second base (and second to third) was shorter by four and one half inches (or

11.43 centimeters for Blue Jays fans). Logic says that must have had *some* effect.

Units of measure can be abstract concepts without some real-world examples. So for perspective and context, here are everyday items that are about 4.5 inches (11.43 cm) long:

- The diameter of a compact disc
- The longer side of a household sponge
- A can of Campbell's Chicken Noodle Soup

And here are things that are slightly longer than 4.5 inches:

- An uncapped Bic pen
- Two stacked baseballs
- My Pete Alonso bobble-head

So, is the length of a soup can enough to make a difference in stolen base attempts and successes? Will it help all runners equally? Will it increase the rate that runners attempt to steal? Or will baserunners whose SB success rate was on the fringes of acceptability get more of a boost? Chicken soup cures all ills, so it could help all of that.

I like to use a rule of thumb that the minimum SB success rate that provides value to a team is 80% (some teams are more lenient). Of the 84 players who had at least 10 SB attempts last year, 55 (65%) met that threshold. But there were another 12 who were successful between 75% and 79% of the time. Perhaps those 12 might see a benefit to larger bases. A closer look:

Player	SB	CS	SB%	SBO%	Spd
Luis Robert	11	3	79%	15%	92
Taylor Walls	10	3	77%	14%	101
Whit Merrifield	16	5	76%	17%	100
Steven Kwan	19	5	79%	13%	151
Aaron Hicks	10	3	77%	10%	134
Victor Robles	15	4	79%	23%	143
Julio Rodríguez	25	7	78%	25%	159
Thairo Estrada	21	6	78%	22%	121
Tyler O'Neill	14	4	78%	20%	109
Cedric Mullins II	34	10	77%	29%	120
Marcus Semien	25	8	76%	21%	140
Adam Engel	12	4	75%	32%	143

I'd filter out the first group of three as their underlying speed skill (Spd) was barely league average or below. Steven Kwan and Aaron Hicks might have some potential to increase their bags, but they'd need to get more of a green light (SBO%). That could come with larger bases, but is not a given.

The final seven have the underlying skill and have been given the opportunity in the past. They might be the best prospects for a bump in stolen bases.

Those with slightly lower success rates, between 70% and 74%, who meet the other two criteria include Luke Williams, Oneil Cruz, Dylan Moore and Jazz Chisholm. They could see a surge in steals too.

Further fueling these numbers will be the fallout from pitchers being limited to only two throws to first base to hold a runner. A third throw has to nail the runner or the pitcher will be charged with a balk. This sets up a cat-and-mouse game, and odds are there will be many more runners taking off for second base, especially as the pitch clock ticks down. According to *BA*, this made more of an impact on the rise of SB in the minors.

Still, all this is good news for our stolen base totals. After a decade-long decline in running…

Year	Tot SB	Players with 20+	30+
2013	2693	40	16
2014	2764	39	15
2015	2505	30	7
2016	2537	28	14
2017	2527	29	6
2018	2474	28	11
2019	2280	21	8
*2020	2387	29	9
2021	2213	19	6
2022	2487	24	6

* Pro-rated to full season

…we started to turn the corner last year. However, that 274-SB increase may not be a cause for celebration. We did see a nice influx of speedy guys in 2022, but they are not necessarily ones you want to chase. The following players stole at least 10 bases in 2022.

Player	SB	BA	xBA	OBP
Jorge Mateo	35	.221	.223	.267
Bobby Witt, Jr.	30	.254	.235	.294
Andrew Velasquez	17	.196	.196	.236
Jose Siri	14	.213	.206	.268
Bryson Stott	12	.234	.239	.295
Eli White	12	.200	.169	.274
Luke Williams	11	.236	.187	.287
Oneil Cruz	11	.233	.232	.294
Jeremy Pena	11	.253	.250	.289
Taylor Walls	10	.172	.209	.268

That's 163 steals from 10 relatively new players, none of whom could crack a .300 OBP. These are among the "huge surge in rookie debuts who possessed less potent artillery" as I noted earlier. The fantasy value of these players might be goosed a bit because of those bags, but it's risky to chase steals from players who have trouble making it to first base.

That's not all. There were also a dozen veterans who swiped at least 10 bags and could not break a .300 OBP last year: Harrison Bader, Cody Bellinger, Adam Engel, Billy Hamilton, Garrett Hampson, Ramon Laureano, Nicky Lopez, Brandon Marsh, Whit Merrifield, Victor Robles, Myles Straw and Joe Wendle. That was another 163 steals.

These 326 stolen bases from sub-par OBP sources represented a disturbing data point:

Players with 10+ SB and sub-.300 OBP

Year	No.	Steals
2016	13	193
2017	11	233
2018	17	293
2019	8	139
2021	16	214
2022	22	326

So, while steals may be getting easier to come by, they also come with a cost. Still, players are running, and that trend will likely increase next season. If the impact of the larger bases in the minors is any indication, the spike in base-stealing could be substantial. If you've decided to hoard steals, that might not be necessary next year. Or in some cases, advisable.

Gut Prediction: League-wide stolen base attempts will rise 20 percent, and at least five players will exceed 50 bags. The supply-demand valuation transition begins.

The impact of banning the shift: This rule will force all four infielders to be positioned on the infield dirt with two on each side of second base. This is a terrible, terrible idea.

Balanced schedule? Makes competitive sense. Larger bases? A tweak at the margins. Pitch clock? Quickening the pace of play doesn't change the rules of the game. But restricting the free movement of defensive players? That alters the very game itself.

Last year I wrote:

"At its core, defensive shifting just seems to be part of the natural batter versus pitcher meta-game. As such, the common argument we keep hearing is, "Well, batters just need to learn to hit the other way," which is obviously as easy as teaching a frog to croak Puccini. If it was that simple, then this wouldn't even be an issue, but 100 mph fastballs test the limits of human reaction time. It's tough enough for hitters to make any contact these days, just like it's tough enough to train frogs to even stay on key."

That hasn't changed. The only thing that surprises me a little is this: Faster pitches beget shorter batter reaction times, which should beget swinging late on pitches, which should beget more opposite field contact. There are too many "shoulds" in that sentence (and too many "begets") but it makes logical sense to me. Lefty hitters should be spraying hits all over left field. Righty hitters should be spraying hits all over right field. Why isn't that happening?

On our fantasy end, what *should* happen with the shift ban is more hits, higher batting averages and higher ERAs. Again, this won't affect all players equally and there are no guarantees. Analysts are speculating that some hitters will over-compensate for the gaps in the defense, open their swings and strike out more often, sacrificing the potential for additional hits. I suppose that could happen.

But baseball remains a game of adjustments and readjustments, and teams will always try to find loopholes to manipulate the system. So, despite the limitations imposed by this new rule, defenses will likely find a way to reposition their fielders—shortstop right at second base, secondbaseman on the edge of the grass, rightfielder moves in, centerfielder moves to hard right center—to cover more of the right side and minimize the impact for lefty hitters. Will it work? Who knows? If it does, someone else will come up with another tactic to combat it.

In the end, we might see virtually no effect on a league-wide basis. Individual players are another story.

It's fair to assume that high contact pitchers might be most affected in a game where more balls-in-play find outfield grass. These low-strikeout hurlers already tend to have higher ERAs. But I'm not worried that a guy like Spenser Watkins—with his 4.70 ERA and 14% strikeout rate—will be harmed by a more open field; I'm not drafting his ilk anyway. I'm more concerned about the downside of starting pitchers like these (2022 stats, maximum 3.99 ERA and 18% strikeout rate):

Starters	ERA	WHIP	K%	GB%	LD%	FB%
Adrian Sampson	3.11	1.23	17	40	20	40
Andre Pallante	3.17	1.42	16	64	19	17
Dean Kremer	3.23	1.25	17	39	21	39
Johnny Cueto	3.35	1.23	16	43	19	38
Cal Quantrill	3.38	1.21	17	42	20	38
Matt Manning	3.43	1.17	18	41	19	40
Zack Greinke	3.68	1.34	12	41	23	35
Adam Wainwright	3.71	1.28	18	43	24	33
Devin Smeltzer	3.71	1.22	14	39	16	46
Chris Flexen	3.73	1.33	16	34	20	46
JP Sears	3.86	1.29	18	40	18	41
Noah Syndergaard	3.94	1.25	17	43	19	38
Cole Irvin	3.98	1.16	17	38	20	42

And these relief pitchers, most of whom are unlikely to be drafted but typically end up on a roster when you're trying to tourniquet a hemorrhaging ERA:

Relievers	ERA	WHIP	K%	GB%	LD%	FB%
Jake Woodford	2.23	1.12	13	52	20	28
Alex Young	2.36	1.50	18	54	20	25
Zach Pop	2.77	1.15	16	57	19	24
Erasmo Ramirez	2.92	1.08	18	45	21	34
Mason Thompson	2.92	1.14	15	53	15	32
Joel Payamps	3.23	1.37	17	53	17	31
Ralph Garza	3.34	1.54	11	41	26	32
Andres Machado	3.34	1.37	18	43	23	34

All those ERAs could spike.

Perhaps targeting hitters is a better approach. Here is a list of last year's highest contact hitters who were shifted against the most in 2022 (minimum 300 PA, 75% shift rate, 75% contact rate):

Hitters	BA	Shift%	ct%	GB%	LD%	FB%
Yordan Alvarez	.306	88	77	39	22	39
Kyle Tucker	.257	91	83	34	19	47
Josh Naylor	.256	77	82	49	17	34
Adley Rutschman	.254	80	78	38	23	38
Salvador Perez	.254	76	76	36	18	46
Keibert Ruiz	.251	82	87	40	23	37
Marcus Semien	.248	75	82	34	19	47
Corey Seager	.245	93	83	40	21	39
Anthony Santander	.240	85	79	31	19	50
Max Kepler	.227	90	83	46	20	34
Jonah Heim	.227	78	79	39	18	43
Anthony Rizzo	.224	83	78	33	18	49
Jesse Winker	.219	76	77	39	21	41
Rowdy Tellez	.219	78	77	39	16	45
Carlos Santana	.202	98	80	39	17	44

If you were to assemble a group of prime candidates for a batting average spike, this is as good a place to start as any. Within this list, a few are particularly interesting—those with high line drive or ground ball rates. Yordan Alvarez is scary. Andy Rutschman and Keibert Ruiz lead a quartet of upwardly mobile backstops. And imagine a healthy Max Kepler and Jesse Winker.

In the end, if you decide to downgrade pitchers or upgrade hitters, just don't treat everyone on the above lists the same. Spend time looking at each one's profile individually. And for those hoping for data to support Joey Gallo hitting .270, sorry to disappoint you.

Gut Prediction: Hitters who had been shifted against the most will see an average 15-point increase in batting average, but some could see a 30-40 point boost. Some pitchers will see a 0.10 increase

in ERA. However, these bumps are just averages and will not affect every player equally.

Chaos theory

Baseball was never perfectly predictable, but we could always count on power hitters slamming balls over fences and bullet throwers keeping runners off the bases. There were patterns to the data, leading indicator skills metrics, and aging curves. We had assembled enough research and rules to project performance within a broad range, and mitigate a good amount of risk. There were always lots of messy moving pieces but we could organize them well enough that playing fantasy baseball wasn't a completely random game.

For 2023, all bets are off.

Credible research requires a control group and, optimally, a single test variable. Once you introduce more variables, it becomes challenging to determine which one impacts the observed results. With MLB introducing *multiple* rule changes, it will be tough to pinpoint the reason for any anomalies—or utter chaos—that occurs in 2023.

If ERAs spike, will it be because the clock messed with pitcher timing? Or will it be because of the new holes in defensive alignments? Or will it be because of an increase in stolen bases? Or a weak division pitcher facing better opponents?

If stolen bases spike, will it be because of the larger bases? Or will it be because the clock has messed with pitcher timing, opening up more opportunities to steal? Or will it be because pitchers can't hold runners on as well with the pickoff limitations? Or maybe runners are taking off more often with the pitch clock ticking down? Or will it be because rising batting averages due to shift restrictions opened up more baserunning opportunities?

If stolen bases dive, will it be because the shift limitations position the shortstop closer to the second base bag than usual? Or will it be because there are more holes on the right side of the infield, which encourage more hit-and-run plays?

If batting averages soar, will it be because of the shift limitations? Or will it be because the clock is messing with pitcher timing? Or will it be because the defense is trying to protect against increased base-stealing, thereby opening up even more holes? Or will it be because strong division hitters are facing more weak division pitchers?

If batting averages decline, will it be because hitters are seduced by the outfield gaps and striking out more? Or will it be because the pitchers are trying to adjust to shorter recovery times by not throwing as hard so batters are trying to go the other way more often, unsuccessfully? Or will it be because weak division hitters are facing more strong division pitchers?

Or if batting averages rise or fall, or ERAs rise or fall, or stolen bases rise or fall, might it be due to normal everyday, run-of-the-mill regression, and have nothing to do with the new rules at all? Yeesh.

There's more.

It is also possible that all the stat lines at the end of 2023 will look no different than those of this year. Perhaps the rule changes will cancel each other out. Or maybe the impacts seen in the minors simply won't carry over to the majors. Or maybe normal regression will effectively offset any impact of the new rules.

But one season is just a sample size of one. It might also be a faux equilibrium that could explode in 2024 if there is a shift in any of the variables. This could be the fluttering of a butterfly's wings that causes a tsunami. If everything looks the same, we just might be sitting on a slowly-igniting powder keg.

Or maybe the explosion happens now. ERAs, stolen bases and batting averages could all spike. Cy Young candidates could all have ERAs over 4.00. Andrew Velasquez could steal 100 bases. Joey Gallo could compete for the batting title. The Tigers and Pirates could meet in the World Series.

And it all could start with a can of soup. Flap those wings, little butterfly!

With these rule changes, so many things could happen. There are too many interrelationships. And we may not be able to parse the data well enough to figure out which specific variable drives any particular result. Because of this massive uncertainty, it was difficult to adjust the player projections in this book. We've made a few tweaks, but nothing truly impactful. Because, well, we just don't know. And when you just don't know, everything becomes more random.

Welcome to our prognosticating nightmare.

Gut Prediction: The theme for next year's introduction will be the fallout from unintended consequences.

But, wait…

Maybe, possibly… everything could go right. If nothing else, this *will* be the first off-season in years with a baseline of normality. Maybe all these changes will provide us with a more fulfilling baseball spectating experience. Maybe that alone will be worth any statistical wreckage left for us analysts to clean up. We are survivors, after all. My cynicism has trouble seeing calm climbing out of chaos, but who knows? It's possible that baseball will once again prove to be an immortal phoenix, rising from the ashes of yet another incarnation.

LIMA 2023

It's been 25 years since I participated in the inaugural Tout Wars NL-only draft and made one of the most notable $1 buys in history. Here is how I describe it in my upcoming historical memoir, *Fantasy Expert* (coming Fall 2023 to a bookseller near you):

About two-thirds of the way into the draft, I had spent a ton on offense but the only pitchers on my staff were two mediocre starters and a closer. Fearing that I would not be able to afford any other decent pitchers, I started looking at the names on my sabermetric speculation list – those guys with great support metrics but lousy surface stats. My Denny Neagle List. It was time to take a dive.

I glanced at my page and saw a 25-year-old right-hander who had just earned the No. 4 starter job in the Houston Astros rotation. His ERAs coming into 1998 were 6.11, 5.70 and 5.28. As the draft passed the three-hour mark, I called out four words that would forever change the course of my fantasy baseball career.

"Jose Lima, one dollar."

I then go on to deconstruct the phenomenon of "crickets" and how everyone thought I was crazy. But Lima went on to win 16 games with a 3.71 ERA, earning me $23 in profit and helping me win the Tout Wars-NL league. The process I used to identify him as a target, and the draft strategy that arose from that became the LIMA Plan: Low Investment Mound Aces.

The plan had a specific set of rules and statistical benchmarks that have been adjusted over time. But we have not been keeping up with the current statistical environment fast enough. I was looking over the definition in last year's book and realized that LIMA has become out of touch with the current game and the way we do analysis now.

So it's time for an update.

The general rules remain unchanged: You start by budgeting $60 of your $260 wallet for your pitching staff, allotting $30 of that to acquire saves. Then you ignore ERA and WHIP, instead targeting pitchers solely by their skills metrics. We've always looked for high strikeout rates and K/BB ratios, and low HR rates. Those skills are still foundation elements, but the metrics and benchmarks need to better reflect how we measure them now. So, the new LIMA filters will advise you to only draft pitchers with:

- a strikeout rate of 25% or greater
- a walk rate of less than 10%
- a home run rate of less than 3.5%

In 2022, these new benchmarks would have yielded about 100 LIMA-worthy pitchers, about 70% of them relievers. About two-thirds of the entire LIMA pool earned less than $10, making them potentially undervalued. It's a classic LIMA pool.

Stud starters like Justin Verlander and Shane McClanahan lead that way, as do lockdown closers like Emmanuel Clase and Edwin Díaz. The magic comes further down the list, with pitchers who will likely be undervalued next spring, like Tyler Mahle, Shawn Armstrong and perhaps Taylor Rogers. All are LIMA-worthy based on their 2022 skills metrics. Our projections in this book yield a new set of candidates for 2023, identifiable by the LIMA grades in their player boxes.

The last part of the Plan are the hitters. Those metrics and benchmarks will remain the same. You can review the complete set of LIMA rules in the Fanalytic Encyclopedia on page 60.

CONSUMER ADVISORY

AN IMPORTANT MESSAGE FOR FANTASY LEAGUERS REGARDING PROPER USAGE OF THE *BASEBALL FORECASTER*

This document is provided in compliance with authorities to outline the prospective risks and hazards possible in the event that the Baseball Forecaster is used incorrectly. Please be aware of these potentially dangerous situations and avoid them. The publisher assumes no risk related to any financial loss or stress-induced illnesses caused by ignoring the items as described below.

1. The statistical projections in this book are intended as general guidelines, not as gospel. It is highly dangerous to use the projected statistics alone, and then live and die by them. That's like going to a ballgame, being given a choice of any seat in the park, and deliberately choosing the last row in the right field corner with an obstructed view. The projections are there, you can look at them, but there are so many better places to sit.

We have to publish those numbers, but they are stagnant, inert pieces of data. This book focuses on a live forecasting process that provides the tools so that you can understand the leading indicators and draw your own conclusions. If you at least attempt your own analyses of the data, and enhance them with the player commentaries, you can paint more robust, colorful pictures of the future.

In other words...

If you bought this book purely for the projected statistics and do not intend to spend at least some time learning about the process, then you might as well just buy an $8 magazine.

2. The player commentaries in this book are written by humans, just like you. These commentaries provide an overall evaluation of performance and likely future direction, but 70-word capsules cannot capture everything. Your greatest value will be to use these as a springboard to your own analysis of the data. Odds are, if you take the time, you'll find hidden indicators that we might have missed. Forecaster veterans say that this self-guided excursion is the best part of owning the book.

3. This book does not attempt to tackle playing time. Rather than making arbitrary decisions about how roles will shake out, the focus is on performance. The playing time projections presented here are merely to help you better evaluate each player's talent. Our online preseason projections update provides more current AB and IP expectations based on how roles are being assigned.

4. The dollar values in this book are intended solely for player-to-player comparisons. They are not driven by a finite pool of playing time—which is required for valuation systems to work properly—so they cannot be used for bid values to be used in your own draft.

There are two reasons for this:

a. The finite pool of players that will generate the finite pool of playing time will not be determined until much closer to Opening Day. And, if we are to be brutally honest, there is really no such thing as a finite pool of players.

b. Your particular league's construction will drive the values; a $10 player in a 10-team mixed league will not be the same as a $10 player in a 12-team NL-only league.

Note that book dollar values also cannot be compared to those published at BaseballHQ.com as the online values are generated by a more finite player pool.

5. Do not pass judgment on the effectiveness of this book based on the performance of a few individual players. The test, rather, is on the collective predictive value of the book's methods. Are players with better base skills more likely to produce good results than bad ones? Years of research suggest that the answer is "yes." Does that mean that every high skilled player will do well? No. But many more of them will perform well than will the average low-skilled player. You should always side with the better percentage plays, but recognize that there are factors we cannot predict. Good decisions that beget bad outcomes do not invalidate the methods.

6. If your copy of this book is not marked up and dog-eared by Draft Day, you probably did not get as much value out of it as you might have.

7. This edition of the Forecaster is not intended to provide absorbency for spills of more than 7.5 ounces.

8. This edition is not intended to provide stabilizing weight for more than 18 sheets of 20 lb. paper in winds of more than 45 mph.

9. The pages of this book are not recommended for avian waste collection. In independent laboratory studies, 87% of migratory water fowl refused to excrete on interior pages, even when coaxed.

10. This book, when rolled into a cylindrical shape, is not intended to be used as a weapon for any purpose, including but not limited to insect extermination, canine training or to influence bidding behavior at a fantasy draft.

Welcome to the 37th Edition

If you are new to the *Baseball Forecaster*, the sheer volume of information in this book may seem a bit daunting. We don't recommend you assess its contents over a single commute to work, particularly if you drive. But do set aside some time this winter; instead of staring out the window, waiting for baseball to begin again, try immersing yourself in all the wisdom contained in this tome. There's a ton of it, and the payoff—Yoo-Hoo or otherwise—is worth it.

But where to begin?

The best place to start is with the Encyclopedia of Fanalytics, which provides the foundation concepts for everything else that appears in these pages. It's our research archive and collective memory, just as valuable for veterans as it is for rookies. Take a cursory read-through, lingering at any section that looks interesting. You'll keep coming back here frequently.

Then just jump in. Close your eyes, flip to a random page, and put your finger down anywhere. Oh, look—Gavin Lux. Power has been disappointing, but contact rate is on the rise and he's just 25. With some consistency and age-related skills growth... maybe there's another level lurking here. See, you've learned something already!

What's New in 2023?

The game on the field is ever-changing; and we strive to keep up:

Updated formulas: we refined a couple of existing formulas to better reflect the trends in today's game:

- LIMA Grades get an adjustment as we shift benchmark levels to better reflect today's walk, strikeout, and HR rates. See the side bar on Ron Shandler's introductory essay (pg. 9) for details.
- Our xHR (and xHR/F) metrics now adjust to the league environment each year, making it more accurate for each individual season's HR output by measuring batted balls that would have been a HR in that season. (Astute readers may notice xHR totals in this book may not match prior editions of this book due to this change.)

A new way to look at playing time is a major research piece that introduces an entirely new way to think about (and measure) playing time. See pages 67 and 275 for more info.

Also, answers to questions, such as: How well does a reliever's first-half performance foretell their second-half performance? How does volume of AB and IP correlate with roto standings points? Is there an ideal structure to your first five draft picks? And much, much more.

Updates

The Baseball Forecaster page at BaseballHQ.com is at www.baseballhq.com/bf2023. This is your headquarters for all information and updates regarding this book. Here you will find links to the following:

Content Updates: In a project of this magnitude, there are occasionally items that need clarification or correction. You can find them here.

Free Projections Update: As a buyer of this book, you get one free 2023 projections update. This is a set of Excel spreadsheet files that will be posted on or about March 1, 2023. Remember to keep the book handy when you visit as the access codes are hidden within these pages.

Electronic book: The complete PDF version of the *Forecaster*—plus Excel versions of most key charts—is available free to those who bought the book directly through the BaseballHQ.com website. These files will be available in January 2023 for most of you; those who have an annual standing order should have received the PDF just before Thanksgiving. Contact us if you do not receive information via e-mail about access. Information about the e-book version can be found through the website.

If you purchased the book online or at a bookstore, or would like these files earlier, you can purchase them from us for $9.95. Reach us at support@baseballhq.com for more information.

Beyond the Forecaster

The *Baseball Forecaster* is just the beginning. The following companion products and services are described in more detail in the back of the book.

BaseballHQ.com is our home website. It provides regular updates to everything in this book, including daily updated statistics and projections. A subscription to BHQ gets you more than 1,000 articles over the course of a year updated daily from spring training through the end of the regular season, customized tools, access to data going back over a decade, plus much more. For a free peek, sign up for our BaseballHQFriday newsletter at www.baseballhq.com/friday.

We take this show on the road twice a year via our *First Pitch Forums* weekend conferences. We just completed our 27th year of our Arizona Fall League symposium, *First Pitch Arizona*. It's the ultimate fantasy baseball getaway, where you can meet top industry analysts and network with fellow fantasy leaguers. There are also plans to return for *First Pitch Florida* in 2023, with three days of baseball talk, spring training games and the legendary LABR expert league drafts. Find out more about these events on page 281 and at BaseballHQ.com.

The 18th edition of the *Minor League Baseball Analyst* is the *Forecaster's* prospect companion, with stat boxes for 900-plus prospects, essays on prospects, lists upon lists, and more. In an era where rookies matter, it's an essential resource and available in January.

RotoLab is the best draft software on the market and comes pre-loaded with our projections. Learn more at www.rotolab.com.

Even further beyond the Forecaster

Visit us on *Facebook* at www.facebook.com/baseballhq. "Like" the BaseballHQ page for updates, photos from events and links to other important stuff.

Follow us on *Twitter.* Site updates are tweeted from @BaseballHQ and many of our writers share their insights from their own personal accounts. We even have a list to follow: www.twitter.com/BaseballHQ/lists/hq-staff.

But back to baseball. Your winter comfort awaits.

—Brent Hershey and Ray Murphy

For new readers...

Everything begins here. The information in the following pages represents the foundation that powers everything we do.

You'll learn about the underlying concepts for our unique mode of analysis. You'll find answers to long-asked questions, interesting insights into what makes players tick, and innovative applications for all this newfound knowledge.

This Encyclopedia is organized into several logical sections:

1. Fundamentals
2. Batters
3. Pitchers
4. Prospects
5. Gaming

Enough talking. Jump in. Remember to breathe.

For veteran readers...

As we do in each edition, this year's ever-expanding Encyclopedia includes relevant research results we've published over the past year. We've added some of the essays from the Research Abstracts section in the 2022 *Forecaster* as well as some other essays from BaseballHQ.com.

And we continue to mold the content to best fit how fantasy leaguers use their information. Many readers consider this their fantasy information bible.

Okay, time to jump-start the analytical process for 2023. Remember to breathe—it's always good advice.

Abbreviations

Fundamentals

What is Fanalytics?

Fanalytics is the scientific approach to fantasy baseball analysis. A contraction of "fantasy" and "analytics," fanalytic gaming might be considered a mode of play that requires a more strategic and quantitative approach to player analysis and game decisions.

The three key elements of fanalytics are:

1. Performance analysis
2. Performance forecasting
3. Gaming analysis

For performance analysis, we tap into the vast knowledge of the sabermetric community. Founded by Bill James, this area of study provides objective and progressive new ways to assess skill. What we do in this book is called "component skills analysis." We break down performance into its component parts, then reverse-engineer it back into the traditional measures with which we are more familiar.

Our forecasting methodology is one part science and one part art. We start with a computer-generated baseline for each player, driven by the performance analysis and a contextual assessment of the player's role and expected playing time. We then make subjective adjustments based on a variety of factors, such as discrepancies in skills indicators and historical guidelines gleaned from more than 30 years of research. We don't rely on a rigid model; our method forces us to get our hands dirty.

You might say that our brand of forecasting is more about finding logical journeys than blind destinations.

Gaming analysis is an integrated approach designed to help us win our fantasy leagues. It takes the knowledge gained from the first two elements and adds the strategic and tactical aspect of each specific fantasy game format.

Component Skills Analysis

Familiar gauges like HR and ERA have long been used to measure skill. In fact, these gauges only measure the outcome of an individual event, or series of events. They represent statistical output. They are "surface stats."

Raw skill is the talent beneath the stats. Players use these skills to create the individual events, or components, that are the building blocks of measures like HR and ERA. Our approach:

1. It's not about batting average; it's about seeing the ball and making contact. We target hitters based on elements such as their batting eye (walks to strikeouts ratio), how often they make contact and the type of contact they make. We then combine these components into an "expected batting average." By comparing each hitter's actual BA to how he should be performing, we can draw conclusions about the future.

2. It's not about home runs; it's about power. From the perspective of a round bat meeting a round ball, it may be only a fraction of an inch at the point of contact that makes the difference between a HR and a long foul ball. When a ball is hit safely, often it is only a few inches that separate a HR from a double or long fly out. We can now measure elements like swing speed, exit velocity and launch angle to provide a more granular perspective.

We must incorporate all these components to paint a complete picture of power.

3. It's not about ERA; it's about getting the ball over the plate and minimizing the damage of contact. Forget ERA. You want to draft pitchers who walk few batters (Control), strike out many (Dominance) and succeed at both in tandem (Command). You generally want pitchers who keep the ball on the ground (because home runs are bad), though some fly ball pitchers can succeed under the right conditions. All of this translates into an "expected ERA" that you can use to validate a pitcher's actual performance.

4. It's never about wins. For pitchers, winning ballgames is less about skill than it is about offensive support. As such, projecting wins is a high-risk exercise and valuing hurlers based on their win history is dangerous. Current trends in pitching usage—which fragment roles and spread innings to more pitchers—dilute our ability to project wins even more. Target skill; wins may or may not come, but it's your best hope. Many leagues are switching to tracking innings instead.

5. It's not about saves; it's about opportunity first and skills second. While the highest-skilled pitchers have the best potential to succeed as closers, they still have to be given the ball with the game on the line in the 9th inning, and that is a decision left to others. Over the past 10 years, about 55% of relievers drafted for saves failed to hold the role for the entire season (that percentage is over 63% since 2018). The lesson: Don't take chances on draft day. There will always be saves in the free agent pool. Or toss out a wider net over the bullpen pool and switch to Saves-plus-Holds.

Accounting for "luck"

Luck has been used as a catch-all term to describe random chance. When we use the term here, we're talking about unexplained variances that shape the statistics. While these variances may be random, they are also often measurable and projectable. To get a better read on "luck," we use formulas that capture the external variability of the data.

Through our research and the work of others, we have learned that when raw skill is separated from statistical output, what's remaining is often unexplained variance. The aggregate totals of many of these variances, for all players, is often a constant. For instance, while a pitcher's ERA might fluctuate, the rate at which his opposition's batted balls fall for hits will tend towards roughly 30%. Large variances can be expected to regress towards 30%.

Why is all this important? Analysts complain about the lack of predictability of many traditional statistical metrics. The reason they find it difficult is that they are trying to project performance using metrics that are loaded with external noise. Raw skills metrics follow better-defined trends during a player's career. Then, as we get a better handle on the variances—explained and unexplained—we can construct a more complete picture of what a player's statistics really mean.

Baseball Forecasting

Forecasting in perspective

The crystal ball aura of "predicting the future" conceals the fact that forecasting is a process. We might define it as "the systematic process of determining likely end results." At its core, it's scientific.

However, the *outcomes* of forecasted events are what are most closely scrutinized, and are used to judge the success or failure of the forecast. That said, as long as the process is sound, the forecast has done the best job it can do. *In the end, forecasting is about analysis, not prophecy.*

Baseball performance forecasting is inherently a high-risk exercise with a very modest accuracy rate. This is because the process involves not only statistics, but also unscientific elements, from random chance to human volatility. And even from within the statistical aspect there are multiple elements that need to be evaluated, from skill to playing time to a host of external variables.

Every system is comprised of the same core elements:

- Players will tend to perform within the framework of past history and/or trends.
- Skills will develop and decline according to age.
- Statistics will be shaped by a player's health, expected role and venue.

While all systems are built from these same elements, they also are constrained by the same limitations. We are all still trying to project a bunch of human beings, each one...

- with his own individual skill set
- with his own rate of growth and decline
- with his own ability to resist and recover from injury
- limited to opportunities determined by other people
- generating a group of statistics largely affected by external noise.

Research has shown that the best accuracy rate that can be attained by any system is about 70%. In fact, a simple system that uses three-year averages adjusted for age ("Marcel") can attain a success rate of 65%. This means all the advanced systems are fighting for occupation of the remaining 5%.

But there is a bigger question... *what exactly are we measuring?* When we search for accuracy, what does that mean? In fact, any quest for accuracy is going to run into a brick wall of paradoxes:

- If a slugging average projection is dead on, but the player hits 10 fewer HRs than expected (and likely, 20 more doubles), is that a success or a failure?
- If a projection of hits and walks allowed by a pitcher is on the mark, but the bullpen and defense implodes, and inflates his ERA by a run, is that a success or a failure?
- If the projection of a speedster's rate of stolen base success is perfect, but his team replaces the manager with one that doesn't run, and the player ends up with half as many SBs as expected, is that a success or a failure?
- If a batter is traded to a hitters' ballpark and all the touts project an increase in production, but he posts a statistical line exactly what would have been projected had he not been traded to that park, is that a success or a failure?
- If the projection for a bullpen closer's ERA, WHIP and peripheral numbers is perfect, but he saves 20 games instead of 40 because the GM decided to bring in a high-priced free agent at the trading deadline, is that a success or a failure?
- If a player is projected to hit .272 in 550 AB and only hits .249, is that a success or failure? Most will say "failure." But wait a minute! The real difference is only two hits per month. That shortfall of 23 points in batting average

is because a fielder might have made a spectacular play, or a screaming liner might have been hit right at someone, or a long shot to the outfield might have been held up by the wind... once every 14 games. Does that constitute "failure"?

Even if we were to isolate a single statistic that measures "overall performance" and run our accuracy tests on it, the results will still be inconclusive.

According to OPS, these players were virtually identical in 2022:

BATTER	HR	RBI	SB	BA	OBA	SLG	OPS
Tellez,R.	35	89	2	.219	.306	.461	.767
Urshela,G	13	64	1	.285	.338	.429	.767

If I projected Rowdy Tellez-caliber stats and ended up with Gio Urshela's numbers, I'd hardly call that an accurate projection. According to Rotisserie dollars, these players were also dead-on in 2022:

BATTER	HR	RBI	Runs	SB	BA	R$
Arenado,N	30	103	73	5	.293	$27
Semien,M	26	83	101	25	.248	$27

It's not so simple for someone to claim they have accurate projections. And so, it is best to focus on the bigger picture, especially when it comes to winning at fantasy baseball.

More on this: "The Great Myths of Projective Accuracy"

http://www.baseballhq.com/great-myths-projective-accuracy

Baseball Forecaster's forecasting process

Our approach is to assemble component skills in such a way that they can be used to validate our observations, analyze their relevance and project a likely future direction.

In a perfect world, if a player's raw skills improve, then so should his surface stats. If his skills decline, then his stats should follow. But, sometimes a player's skill indicators increase while his surface stats decline. These variances may be due to a variety of factors.

Our forecasting process is based on the expectation that events tend to move towards universal order. Surface stats will eventually approach their skill levels. Unexplained variances will regress to a mean. And from this, we can identify players whose performance may potentially change.

For most of us, this process begins with the previous year's numbers. Last season provides us with a point of reference, so it's a natural way to begin the process of looking at the future. Component skills analysis allows us to validate those numbers. A batter with few HRs but elevated power metrics has a good probability of improving his future HR output. A pitcher whose ERA was poor while his pitching support metrics were solid might be a good bet for ERA improvement.

Of course, these leading indicators do not always follow the rules. There are more shades of grey than blacks and whites. When indicators are in conflict—for instance, a pitcher who is displaying both a rising strikeout rate and a rising walk rate—then we have to find ways to sort out what these indicators might be saying.

It is often helpful to look at leading indicators in a hierarchy. A rank of the most important pitching indicators might be: K-BB%, K%, BB% and GB/FB rate. For batters, contact rate tops the list, followed by power, walk rate and speed.

Assimilating additional research

Once we've painted the statistical picture of a player's potential, we then use additional criteria and research results to help us add some color to the analysis. These other criteria include the player's health, age, changes in role, ballpark and a variety of other factors. We also use the research results described in the following pages. This research looks at things like traditional periods of peak performance and breakout profiles.

The final element of the process is assimilating the news into the forecast. This is the element that many fantasy leaguers tend to rely on most since it is the most accessible. However, it is also the element that provides the most noise. Players, management and the media have absolute control over what we are allowed to know. Factors such as hidden injuries, messy divorces and clubhouse unrest are routinely kept from us, while we are fed red herrings and media spam. *We will never know the entire truth.*

Quite often, all you are reading is just other people's opinions... a manager who believes that a player has what it takes to be a regular or a team physician whose diagnosis is that a player is healthy enough to play. These words from experts have some element of truth, but cannot be wholly relied upon to provide an accurate expectation of future events. As such, it is often helpful to develop an appropriate cynicism for what you read.

For instance, if a player is struggling for no apparent reason and there are denials about health issues, don't dismiss the possibility that an injury does exist. There are often motives for such news to be withheld from the public.

And so, as long as we do not know all the facts, we cannot dismiss the possibility that any one fact is true, no matter how often the media assures it, deplores it, or ignores it. Don't believe everything you read; use your own judgment. If your observations conflict with what is being reported, that's powerful insight that should not be ignored.

Also remember that nothing lasts forever in major league baseball. *Reality is fluid.* One decision begets a series of events that lead to other decisions. Any reported action can easily be reversed based on subsequent events. My favorite examples are announcements of a team's new bullpen closer. Those are about the shortest realities known to man.

We need the media to provide us with context for our analyses, and the real news they provide is valuable intelligence. But separating the news from the noise is difficult. In most cases, the only thing you can trust is how that player actually performs.

Embracing imprecision

Precision in baseball prognosticating is a fool's quest. There are far too many unexpected variables and noise that can render our projections useless. The truth is, the best we can ever hope for is to accurately forecast general tendencies and percentage plays.

However, even when you follow an 80 percent play, for instance, you will still lose 20 percent of the time. That 20 percent is what skeptics use as justification to dismiss prognosticators; they conveniently ignore the more prevalent 80 percent. The paradox, of course, is that fantasy league titles are often won or lost by those exceptions. Still, long-term success dictates that you always chase the 80 percent and accept the fact that you will be wrong 20 percent of the time. Or, whatever that percentage play happens to be.

For fantasy purposes, playing the percentages can take on an even less precise spin. The best projections are often the ones that are just far enough away from the field of expectation to alter decision-making. In other words, it doesn't matter if I project Player X to bat .320 and he only bats .295; it matters that I project .320 and everyone else projects .280. Those who follow my less-accurate projection will go the extra dollar to acquire him in their draft.

Or, perhaps we should evaluate the projections based upon their intrinsic value. For instance, coming into 2022 would it have been more important for me to tell you that Trea Turner was going to hit .300 or that Nolan Arenado would improve from a .255 average to hit .275? By season's end, the Turner projection would have been more accurate, but the Arenado projection—even though it was off by nearly 20 points—would have been far more valuable. The Arenado projection might have persuaded you to go an extra buck on Draft Day, yielding more profit.

And that has to be enough. Any tout who projects a player's statistics dead-on will have just been lucky with his dart throws that day.

Perpetuity

Forecasting is not an exercise that produces a single set of numbers. It is dynamic, cyclical and ongoing. Conditions are constantly changing and we must react to those changes by adjusting our expectations. A pre-season projection is just a snapshot in time. Once the first batter steps to the plate on Opening Day, that projection has become obsolete. Its value is merely to provide a starting point, a baseline for what is about to occur.

During the season, if a projection appears to have been invalidated by current performance, the process continues. It is then that we need to ask... What went wrong? What conditions have changed? In fact, has *anything* changed? We need to analyze the situation and revise our expectation, if necessary. This process must be ongoing.

When good projections go bad

All we can control is the process. We simply can't control outcomes. However, one thing we *can* do is analyze the misses to see *why* they occurred. This is always a valuable exercise each year. It puts a proper focus on the variables that were out of our control as well as providing perspective on those players with whom we might have done a better job.

In general, we can organize these forecasting misses into several categories. To demonstrate, here are players whose 2022 Rotisserie earnings varied from our projections.

Performances that exceeded expectation

Development beyond the growth trend: These are young players for whom we knew there was skill. Some of them were prized prospects in the past who have taken their time ascending the growth curve. Others were a surprise only because their performance spike arrived sooner than anyone anticipated... Michael Harris II, Steven Kwan, Josh Rojas, Nico Hoerner, Andrew Vaughn, Taylor Ward, Alec Bohm, Julio Rodríguez, Jeremy Peña, William Contreras, Spencer Strider, Kyle Wright, Jhoan Duran, Nestor Cortes, Brady Singer, Alek Manoah

Skilled players who just had big years: We knew these guys were good too; we just didn't anticipate they'd be this good... Aaron Judge, Adolis García, Andrés Giménez, Tommy Edman, Nate Lowe, Dansby Swanson, Christian Walker, Anthony Santander, Francisco Lindor, Pete Alonso, Nolan Arenado, Randy Arozarena, Miles Mikolas, Merrill Kelly, Tyler Anderson

Unexpected health: We knew these players had the goods; we just didn't know whether they'd be healthy or would stay healthy all year... Josh Naylor, Jeff McNeil, Zac Gallen, Triston McKenzie

Unexpected playing time: These players had the skills—and may have even displayed them at some time in the past—but had questionable playing time potential coming into this season. Some benefited from another player's injury, a rookie who didn't pan out or leveraged a short streak into a regular gig... Luis Rengifo, Luis Arraez, Jose Miranda, Thairo Estrada, Jon Berti, Ross Stripling, Cristian Javier

Unexpected role: This category is reserved for players who played their way into, or backed into, a larger role than anticipated. For most, there was already some previously demonstrated skill: Brandon Drury, Harold Ramirez, Ryan Helsley, Daniel Bard, Jeffrey Springs, Scott Barlow, Camilo Doval, Clay Holmes

Unexpected discovery of the Fountain of Youth: These players should have been done, or nearly done, or at least headed down the far side of the bell curve. That's what the trends were pointing to. The trends were wrong... Paul Goldschmidt, Elvis Andrus, Matt Carpenter, Albert Pujols, José Quintana, Justin Verlander, Johnny Cueto, Yu Darvish, Michael Wacha

Surprise, yes, but not as good as it looked: These are players whose numbers were pretty, but unsupported by their skills metrics. Enjoy them now, but be wary of next year... Eugenio Suárez, Tony Gonsolin, Jorge Mateo

Who the heck knows? Maybe there are reasonable explanations, but this year was so far off the charts for... Martín Pérez

Performances that fell short of expectation

Hobbled masses yearning to breathe free: These are players who got hurt, may not have returned fully healthy, or may have never been fully healthy (whether they'd admit it or not)... Adalberto Mondesi, Kris Bryant, Brandon Lowe, Ozzie Albies, Miguel Sanó, Anthony Rendon, Alex Kirilloff, Wander Franco, Brandon Belt, Austin Meadows, Jonathan India, Avisaíl García, Nick Madrigal, Byron Buxton, Joey Votto, Bryce Harper, Yasmani Grandal, Mitch Haniger, Jorge Polanco, Jazz Chisholm, Wil Myers, David Fletcher, Yoán Moncada, Tim Anderson, Adam Duvall, Mitch Garver, Luis Robert, Trevor Story, Tyler O'Neill, Michael Brantley, Chris Taylor, Walker Buehler, John Means, Frankie Montas, Chris Sale, Shane Baz, Hyun-Jin Ryu, Jack Flaherty, Brandon Woodruff, Lance Lynn, Casey Mize, Jacob deGrom, Luis Severino, Tyler Mahle, Nathan Eovaldi

Accelerated skills erosion: These are players who we knew were on the downside of their careers or had soft peripherals but who we did not think would plummet so quickly. In some cases, there were injuries involved, but all in all, 2022 might have been the beginning of the end for... Lorenzo Cain, Nelson Cruz, Jonathan Schoop, Didi Gregorius, Yuli Gurriel, Aroldis Chapman, Michael Pineda, Patrick Corbin, Kyle Hendricks

Inflated expectations: Here are players who we really should not have expected much more than what they produced. Some had short or spotty track records, others had soft peripherals coming into 2022, and still others were inflated by media hype. Yes, for some of these, it was "What the heck was I thinking?" For others, we've almost come to expect players to ascend the growth curve faster these days. (You're 23 and you haven't broken out yet? What's the problem??) The bottom line is that player performance trends simply don't progress or regress in a straight line; still, the skills trends were intriguing enough to take a leap of faith. We were wrong... Akil Baddoo, Spencer Torkelson, Jarred Kelenic, Javy Báez, Jared Walsh, Ketel Marte, Bobby Dalbec, Sean Manaea, Ian Anderson, Josiah Gray

Unexpected loss of role: This category is reserved for would-be closers who lost the job before they could return profit... Jake McGee, Matt Barnes, Craig Kimbrel, Will Smith, Anthony Bender, Tanner Houck, Taylor Rogers, Mark Melancon, Giovanny Gallegos, Corey Knebel, Lou Trivino, Raisel Iglesias

Surprise, yes, but not as bad as it looked: These are players whose numbers were disappointing, but supported by better skills metrics. Diss them now, but keep an open mind for next year... JD Martinez, Teoscar Hernández, Gerrit Cole

Who the heck knows? Maybe any one of these players could have been slotted into another category, but they still remain head-scratchers... Juan Soto, Whit Merrifield, Trevor Rogers, Lucas Giolito, José Berríos, Josh Hader.

About fantasy baseball touts

As a group, there is a strong tendency for all pundits to provide numbers that are publicly palatable, often at the expense of potential accuracy. That's because committing to either end of the range of expectation poses a high risk. Few touts will put their credibility on the line like that, even though we all know that those outliers are inevitable. Among our projections, you will find no .350 hitters or 70-steal speedsters. *Someone* is going to post a sub-2.50 ERA next year, but damned if any of us will commit to that. So we take an easier road. We'll hedge our numbers or split the difference between two equally possible outcomes.

In the world of prognosticating, this is called the *comfort zone*. This represents the outer tolerances for the public acceptability of a set of numbers. In most circumstances, even if the evidence is outstanding, prognosticators will not stray from within the comfort zone.

As for this book, occasionally we do commit to outlying numbers when we feel the data support it. But on the whole, most of the numbers here can be nearly as cowardly as everyone else's. We get around this by providing "color" to the projections in the capsule commentaries, often listing UPside or DOWNside projections. That is where you will find the players whose projection has the best potential to stray beyond the limits of the comfort zone.

As analyst John Burnson once wrote: "The issue is not the success rate for one player, but the success rate for all players. No system is 100% reliable, and in trying to capture the outliers, you weaken the middle and thereby lose more predictive pull than you gain. At some level, everyone is an exception!"

Validating Performance

Performance validation criteria

The following is a set of support variables that helps determine whether a player's statistical output is an accurate reflection of his skills. From this we can validate or refute stats that vary from expectation, essentially asking, is this performance "fact or fluke?"

1. **Age:** Is the player at the stage of development when we might expect a change in performance?

2. **Health:** Is he coming off an injury, reconditioned and healthy for the first time in years, or a habitual resident of the injured list?

3. **Minor league performance:** Has he shown the potential for greater things at some level of the minors? Or does his minor league history show a poor skill set that might indicate a lower ceiling?

4. **Historical trends:** Have his skill levels over time been on an upswing or downswing?

5. **Component skills indicators:** Looking beyond batting averages and ERAs, what do his support metrics look like?

6. **Ballpark, team, league:** Pitchers going to Colorado will see their ERA spike. Pitchers going to Oakland will see their ERA improve.

7. **Team performance:** Has a player's performance been affected by overall team chemistry or the environment fostered by a winning or losing club?

8. **Batting stance, pitching style/mastery:** Has a change in performance been due to a mechanical adjustment?

9. **Usage pattern, lineup position, role:** Has a change in RBI opportunities been a result of moving further up or down in the batting order? Has pitching effectiveness been impacted by moving from the bullpen to the rotation?

10. **Coaching effects:** Has the coaching staff changed the way a player approaches his conditioning, or how he approaches the game itself?

11. **Off-season activity:** Has the player spent the winter frequenting workout rooms or banquet tables?

12. **Personal factors:** Has the player undergone a family crisis? Experienced spiritual rebirth? Given up red meat? Taken up testosterone?

13. **And in 2023, MLB's new rules:** How will the balanced schedule, defensive shift limitations, larger bases and pitch clock impact a player's numbers?

Skills ownership

Once a player displays a skill, he owns it. That display could occur at any time—earlier in his career, back in the minors, or even in winter ball play. And while that skill may lie dormant after its initial display, the potential is always there for him to tap back into that skill at some point, barring injury or age. That dormant skill can reappear at any time given the right set of circumstances.

Caveats:

1. The initial display of skill must have occurred over an extended period of time. An isolated 1-hit shutout in Single-A ball amidst a 5.00 ERA season is not enough. The shorter the display of skill in the past, the more likely it can be attributed to

random chance. The longer the display, the more likely that any reemergence could be for real.

2. If a player has been suspected of using performance enhancing drugs at any time, all bets are off.

Corollaries:

1. Once a player displays a vulnerability or skills deficiency, he owns that as well. That vulnerability could be an old injury problem, an inability to hit breaking pitches, or just a tendency to go into prolonged slumps.

2. The probability of a player correcting a skills deficiency declines with each year that deficiency continues to exist.

Contract year performance *(Tom Mullooly)*

There is a contention that players step up their game when they are playing for a contract. Research looked at contract year players and their performance during that year as compared to career levels. Of the batters and pitchers studied, 53% of the batters performed as if they were on a salary drive, while only 15% of the pitchers exhibited some level of contract year behavior.

How do players fare *after* signing a large contract (minimum $4M per year)? Research from 2005-2008 revealed that only 30% of pitchers and 22% of hitters exhibited an increase of more than 15% in BPV after signing a large deal either with their new team, or re-signing with the previous team. But nearly half of the pitchers (49%) and nearly half of the hitters (47%) saw a drop in BPV of more than 15% in the year after signing.

Risk Analysis

Risk management and reliability grades

Forecasts are constructed with the best data available, but there are factors that can impact the variability. One way we manage this risk is to assign each player Reliability Grades. The more certainty we see in a data set, the higher the reliability grades assigned to that player. The following variables are evaluated:

Health: Players with a history of staying healthy and off the IL are valuable to own. Unfortunately, while the ability to stay healthy can be considered skill, it is not very projectable. We can track the number of days spent on the injured list and draw rough conclusions. The grades in the player boxes also include an adjustment for older players, who have a higher likelihood of getting hurt. That is the only forward-looking element of the grade.

"A" level players would have accumulated fewer than 30 days on the major league IL over the past five years. "F" grades go to those who've spent more than 120 days on the IL. Recent IL stays are given a heavier weight in the calculation.

Playing Time and Experience (PT/Exp): The greater the pool of MLB history to draw from, the greater our ability to construct a viable forecast. Length of service—and consistent service—is important. So players who bounce up and down from the majors to the minors are higher risk players. And rookies are all high risk.

For batters, we simply track plate appearances. Major league PAs have greater weight than minor league PAs. "A" level players would have averaged at least 550 major league PAs per year over the past three years. "F" graded players averaged fewer than 250 major league PA per year.

For pitchers, workload can be a double-edged sword. On one hand, small IP samples are deceptive in providing a read on a pitcher's true potential. Even a consistent 65-inning reliever can be considered higher risk since it would take just one bad outing to skew an entire season's work.

On the flipside, high workload levels also need to be monitored, especially in the formative years of a pitcher's career. Exceeding those levels elevates the risk of injury, burnout, or breakdown. So, tracking workload must be done within a range of innings. The grades capture this.

Consistency: Consistent performers are easier to project and garner higher reliability grades. Players that mix mediocrity with occasional flashes of brilliance or badness generate higher risk projections. Even those who exhibit a consistent upward or downward trend cannot be considered truly consistent as we do not know whether those trends will continue. Typically, they don't. *(See next: Using 3-year trends as leading indicators)*

"A" level players are those whose runs created per game level (xERA for pitchers) has fluctuated by less than half a run during each of the past three years. "F" grades go to those whose RC/G or xERA has fluctuated by two runs or more.

Remember that these grades have nothing to do with quality of performance; they strictly refer to confidence in our expectations. So a grade of AAA for a bad player only means that there is a high probability he will perform as poorly as we've projected.

Using 3-year trends as leading indicators *(Ed DeCaria)*
It is almost irresistibly tempting to look at three numbers moving in one direction and expect that the fourth will continue that progression. However, for both hitters and pitchers riding positive trends over any consecutive three-year period, not only do most players not continue their positive trend into a fourth year, their Year 4 performance usually regresses significantly. This is true for every metric tested (whether related to playing time, batting skills, pitching skills, running skills, luck indicators, or valuation). Negative trends show similar reversals, but tend to be more "sticky," meaning that rebounds are neither as frequent nor as strong as positive trend regressions.

Reliability and age
Peak batting reliability occurs at ages 29 and 30, followed by a minor decline for four years. So, to draft the most reliable batters, and maximize the odds of returning at least par value on your investments, you should target the age range of 28-34.

The most reliable age range for pitchers is 29-34. While we are forever looking for "sleepers" and hot prospects, it is very risky to draft any pitcher under 27 or over 35.

Evaluating Reliability *(Bill Macey)*
When you head into an upcoming auction or draft, consider the following with regard to risk and reliability:

- Reliability grades do help identify more stable investments: players with "B" grades in both Health and PT/Experience are more likely to return a higher percentage of their projected value.

- While top-end starting pitching may be more reliable than ever, the overall pool of pitchers is fraught with uncertainty and they represent a less reliable investment than batters.

- There does not appear to be a significant market premium for reliability, at least according to the criteria measured by BaseballHQ.com.

- There are only two types of players: risky and riskier. So while it may be worth going the extra buck for a more reliable player, be warned that even the most reliable player can falter—don't go overboard bidding up a AAA-rated player simply due to his Reliability grades.

Normal production variance *(Patrick Davitt)*
Even if we have a perfectly accurate understanding of a player's "normal" performance level, his actual performance can and does vary widely over any particular 150-game span—including the 150-game span we call "a season." A .300 career hitter can perform in a range of .250-.350, a 40-HR hitter from 30-50, and a 3.70/1.15 pitcher from 2.60/0.95 to 6.00/1.55. And all of these results must be considered "normal."

Health Analysis

Injury Primer *(James C. Ferretti, DO)*
Every player injury and recovery process is unique. Still, you can gain a sizable advantage with a better understanding of both injuries and the corresponding medical terms. An overview of the human musculoskeletal system:

- *Bones:* The rigid support framework which is also a foundation for the other moving parts.
- *Cartilage:* Soft tissue that acts as a cushion and prevents wear—usually in areas where bones are close to each other.
- *Muscles:* Bundles of fibers that bend and stretch to perform work.
- *Tendons:* Bundles of (less bendy/stretchy) fibers that attach muscles to bones.
- *Ligaments:* Bundles of (even less bendy/stretchy) fibers that attach bones to other bones.

Some common ailments:

A **fracture** is simply a break in a bone, which means it isn't able to act as a stabilizer or absorb/distribute forces. Time to heal and/or long-term effects? Usually 4-6 weeks, though sometimes longer, though once the new bone has matured, it's as good as new.

Strains/sprains are tears of the fibers of muscles/tendons (strains) and ligaments (sprains). Most doctors categorize them on a Grade 1, 2, 3, scale, from less severe to most.

Time to heal and/or long-term effects? A rough estimate is 2-4 weeks for a Grade 1, 4-8 weeks for a Grade 2, and at least 8 weeks for a Grade 3. There can be long-term effects, notably that the repaired areas contain fibrous ("scar") tissue, which is neither as strong nor as flexible as the original tissue, and is more prone to re-injury.

Inflammation is an irritation of soft tissues, often from overuse or repetitive motion and the structures affected get "angry." Even if they occur for different reasons, inflammation and a Grade 1 strain can behave similarly—and both can keep a player out for weeks. Long-term effects? Injury/pain can recur, or even worsen without adequate time to heal. (So, maybe your player coming back early isn't such good news after all.)

Some widely-used injury terms:

"No structural damage" sounds reassuring, but it's often misleading. When medical imagers unaffiliated with MLB clubs make an injury diagnosis, they might term it a fracture, dislocation, soft tissue tear, or inflammation; all of which are bad news. Or they may call it "normal," or "negative," which is good news. But rarely would they describe an injury in terms of "no structural damage," because it's not an actual diagnosis. Rather, it's a way of saying that whatever body part being imaged is intact, with no broken bone or soft tissue tear. This is not the same as a "normal" or "negative" diagnosis. When you hear "no structural damage", continue to keep a close eye on the situation.

Similarly, **"day-to-day"** sounds reassuring—but really doesn't tell you anything other than "We aren't sure," which can be far more worrisome.

"X-Rays are negative": Imaging a player is usually prompted by sudden or increasing onset of pain. Most baseball injuries, though, are to soft tissue, which is never diagnosed with an X-ray alone. Unless there's suspicion of a broken bone or joint injury, an X-ray probably isn't going to tell you much. We often see writers and analysts use a "negative" X-ray report to justify that the injury is "not believed to be serious." Don't make that mistake—await the results of more definitive imaging/tests, like a CAT scan or MRI.

Injured list statistics

Year	#Players	3yr Avg	IL Days	3yr Avg
2012	409	408	30,408	27,038
2013	442	419	29,551	28,523
2014	422	424	25,839	28,599
2015	454	439	28,982	28,124
2016	478	451	31,329	28,717
2017	533	488	30,913	30,408
2018	574	528	34,284	32,175
2019	563	557	36,394	33,864
2020*	456	-	13,518	-
2021**	835	657	47,693	39,457
2022	726	708	44,389	42,825

*Due to the 60-game season, 2020 data is not included in 3-year averages.
** The 2021 data includes 103 players/1,467 days whose only "injury" loss was due to a COVID-19 quarantine, and another 78 players who had other injuries in addition to a COVID quarantine.

IL days as a leading indicator *(Bill Macey)*

Players who are injured in one year are likely to be injured in a subsequent year:

% IL batters in Year 1 who are also DL in year 2	38%
Under age 30	36%
Age 30 and older	41%
% IL batters in Year 1 and 2 who are also DL in year 3	54%
% IL pitchers in Year 1 who are also DL in year 2	43%
Under age 30	45%
Age 30 and older	41%
% IL pitchers in Yr 1 and 2 who are also DL in year 3	41%

Previously injured players also tend to spend a longer time on the IL. The average number of days on the IL was 51 days for batters and 73 days for pitchers. For the subset of these players who get hurt again the following year, the average number of days on the IL was 58 days for batters and 88 days for pitchers.

How a batter's age affects IL stays *(Jeff Zimmerman)*

Some players seem to get more than their fair share of injuries, but for those hitters with the "injury-prone" tag, it only takes one healthy season to make a difference. After breaking up hitters into three age groups (25 and younger; 26-29; 30 and older), a study examined length and frequency of IL stints. Among the findings:

1. If someone in the youngest group goes on the IL once, they aren't as likely to again the next season. The probability increases after two IL seasons, however, from 33% to 43%.

2. The best health is exhibited by the middle group. It seems this age is the sweet spot for avoiding injuries. The hitters have shown they can hold up to a full season, but their bodies have not started to break down.

3. Not surprisingly, the oldest group takes longer to heal. The IL-related stats hover above the league average, but the IL rate doesn't increase as a player racks up previous injuries.

Do overworked hitters wear down? *(Jeff Zimmerman)*

A study compared the first- and second-half statistics for batters who played the most games over the entire season from 2002-16. These players were continually run out on the field, and one figures that fatigue would show up in their statistics. In actuality, their output improves the more they play. Though this concept goes against conventional wisdom, it is true: If a hitter plays more, the more likely he is healthy and not wearing down.

In-Season Analysis

The weight of early season numbers

Early season strugglers who surge later in the year often get little respect because they have to live with the weight of their early numbers all season long. Conversely, quick starters who fade late get far more accolades than they deserve.

For instance, take Josh Bell's month-by-month batting average in 2022. The perception is that his .266 mark was a solid follow-up to 2021's .261 and within a normal range for his career, but doesn't nearly show how much he struggled in the second half. Bell had a .315 BA at mid-season—and was still batting over .300 on August 6—but batted only .185 over the season's last nine weeks:

Month	BA	Cum BA
Apr	.365	.365
May	.252	.298
June	.358	.319
July	.253	.302
August	.188	.278
Sept-Oct	.199	.266

Courtship period

Any time a player is put into a new situation, he enters into a courtship period. This period might occur when a player switches leagues, or switches teams. It could be the first few games when a minor leaguer is called up. It could occur when a reliever moves into the rotation, or when a lead-off hitter is moved to another spot in the lineup. There is a team-wide courtship period when a manager is replaced. Any external situation that could affect a player's performance sets off a new decision point in evaluating that performance.

During this period, it is difficult to get a true read on how a player is going to ultimately perform. He is adjusting to the new situation. Things could be volatile during this time. For instance, a role change that doesn't work could spur other moves. A rookie hurler might buy himself a few extra starts with a solid debut, even if he has questionable skills.

It is best not to make a roster decision on a player who is going through a courtship period. Wait until his stats stabilize. Don't cut a struggling pitcher in his first few starts after a managerial change. Don't pick up a hitter who smacks a pair of HRs in his first game after having been traded. Unless, of course, talent and track record say otherwise.

Half-season fallacies

A popular exercise is to analyze players who are consistent first half to second half surgers or faders. There are several fallacies with this analytical approach.

1. There are very few players who show consistent changes in performance from one half of the season to the other.

2. Multi-year scans may not show any consistency at all. A player whose 5-year batting average shows a 15-point rise in the 2nd half, for instance, may actually have experienced a BA decline in several of those years, a fact that might have been offset by a huge BA rise in one of the years.

3. The season's midpoint is an arbitrary delineator of performance swings. Some players are slow starters and might be more appropriately evaluated as pre-May and post-May. Others bring up their game in a pennant chase and might see a performance swing with an August 15 cut-off. Each player may have his own individual tendency, if, in fact, one exists at all.

Half-season tendencies

Despite the above, it stands to reason logically that there might be some underlying tendencies on a more global scale, first half to second half. In fact, one would think that the player population as a whole might decline in performance as the season drones on. There are many variables that might contribute to a player wearing down—workload, weather, boredom—and the longer a player is on the field, the higher the likelihood that he is going to get hurt. A recent 5-year study uncovered the following tendencies:

Batting

Overall, batting skills held up pretty well, half to half. There was a 5% erosion of playing time, likely due, in part, to September roster expansion.

Power: First half power studs (20 HRs in 1H) saw a 10% drop-off in the second half. 34% of first half 20+ HR hitters hit 15 or fewer in the second half and only 27% were able to improve on their first half output.

Speed: Second half speed waned as well. About 26% of the 20+ SB speedsters stole *at least 10 fewer bases* in the second half. Only 26% increased their second half SB output at all.

Batting average: 60% of first half .300 hitters failed to hit .300 in the second half. Only 20% showed any second half improvement at all. As for 1H strugglers, managers tended to stick with their full-timers despite poor starts. Nearly one in five of the sub-.250 1H hitters managed to hit *more than* .300 in the second half.

Pitching

Overall, there was some slight erosion in innings and ERA despite marginal improvement in skills metrics.

ERA: For those who pitched at least 100 innings in the first half, ERAs rose an average of 0.40 runs in the 2H. Of those with first half ERAs less than 4.00, only 49% were able to maintain a sub-4.00 ERA in the second half.

Wins: Pitchers who won 18 or more games in a season tended to pitch *more* innings in the 2H and had slightly better skills metrics.

Saves: Of those closers who saved 20 or more games in the first half, only 39% were able to post 20 or more saves in the 2H, and 26% posted fewer than 15 saves. Aggregate ERAs of these pitchers rose from 2.45 to 3.17, half to half.

In-season trends in hitting and pitching *(Zach Larson)*

League-wide baselines not only change each season, but monthly within a season as well, due to a variety of factors (such as weather). A study of the 2021 and 2022 seasons found some general trends, including the fact that hitters do tend to perform better in warmer weather. Some of the variances between the two years can be attributed to post-pandemic and post-lockout factors.

2022 MLB stats by month (per game):

Month	GP	R	HR	RBI	SB	AVG	K	SV	ERA	WHIP
Apr	634	4.03	0.91	3.82	0.48	0.231	8.50	0.27	3.72	1.24
May	839	4.43	1.08	4.22	0.52	0.246	8.21	0.25	4.10	1.28
Jun	808	4.49	1.19	4.30	0.52	0.246	8.32	0.24	4.14	1.29
Jul	780	4.32	1.10	4.12	0.51	0.245	8.46	0.26	3.97	1.27
Aug	840	4.22	1.04	4.07	0.50	0.245	8.33	0.24	3.93	1.27
Sep/Oct	958	4.17	1.09	3.99	0.54	0.240	8.58	0.25	3.91	1.25

2021 MLB stats by month (per game):

Month	GP	R	HR	RBI	SB	AVG	K	SV	ERA	WHIP
Apr	766	4.26	1.14	4.01	0.46	0.232	9.07	0.24	3.98	1.25
May	834	4.41	1.12	4.19	0.46	0.239	8.92	0.25	4.06	1.29
Jun	796	4.66	1.28	4.46	0.45	0.246	8.69	0.24	4.43	1.32
Jul	742	4.62	1.29	4.41	0.44	0.248	8.51	0.23	4.39	1.32
Aug	828	4.54	1.24	4.35	0.45	0.246	8.51	0.25	4.26	1.29
Sep/Oct	892	4.67	1.27	4.49	0.47	0.250	8.38	0.25	4.42	1.32

Can in-season deficiencies in ratio categories be overcome?
(Patrick Davitt)

Many fantasy players think that later in the season, we can't move the decimals (BA, ERA, WHIP) because with the majority of AB/IP in the books, the ratio's large denominators make it too hard. While it's true we can't move as much late as early, we can still gain points. We tested this idea at the two-thirds mark in the season. Using teams and stats in a 15-team mixed expert's league, we built tables to see how much an owner could gain—first just by dropping a poor performer, and then by replacing a poor performer with a good performer.

From a study of a 15-team mixed expert's league, we found that it's still possible to gain points in the ratio categories by replacing a poor performer with a good performer, even at the two-thirds mark of the season. (Obviously, stratification of league standings will vary.)

Batting Average

The BA test projected a team to finish with a .257 BA. With 190 remaining projected AB per batter, we found that by dropping a players and not replacing him:

- Drop a .235 hitter: Team BA .25756
- .225 hitter: .25783
- .215 hitter: .25810

The gains are amplified when the poor hitter is replaced with a high projected BA hitter. Dropping a .215 pBA hitter and adding a .305 guy jumps team pBA to .25927. Dropping a .245 and adding a .265 still gains 57 baseline points. Again, depending on how close your league standings are, this matters.

ERA

Gains in pitching decimals can be greater because the denominator is smaller than BA. This study used a team with a 4.00 final pERA in 1,325 IP. Let's start again by just dropping a poor performer with 55 pIP:

- Dropping a 4.50 pERA pitcher, finished at 3.976
- 5.00 pitcher: 3.954
- 5.50 pitcher: 3.933

And now, by adding a low-pERA replacement: Dropping a 5.50 disaster for a 2.75 stud means a final pERA of 3.885, an improvement of .115.

Again, much depends on how each category is stratified.

Surprisingly Productive Years *(Ed DeCaria)*

Here's a skills-based method of finding productive in-season roster additions:

1. Consider all batters projected for 50% or less playing time, all starting pitchers projected for 10% or less of his team's innings pitched (about 140 IP), and all relief pitchers projected for less than 4% of his team's innings pitched (about 50 IP)

2. Using each player's projected skills—not stats—in the form of his Mayberry scores, include only batters whose sum of three Mayberry skills (power, speed, and hitting) was 7 or higher (8 or higher for mixed leagues). For pitchers, only consider players whose sum of two Mayberry skills (xERA and strikeout rate) was 4 or higher (5 or higher for mixed leagues). For relievers, we also counted Mayberry's saves potential score, so we included only relievers whose sum of three scores was 7 or higher (8 or higher for mixed leagues).

3. Examine the specific situation of each player that met our first two criteria and assign a realistic playing time upside given his skills and injury, consistency, and forecast risk, and that of the player(s) ahead of him on his team's depth chart.

4. Calculate a single number that measured their "projected skill" over their "potential playing time" to arrive at their "potential value."

a. For hitters, take his Mayberry sum and multiply it by his potential playing time (pPT). Then rank batters by this metric and subtract the minimum value of the group from all players, so that the least valuable batter had a marginal score (mSCORE) of zero. Then use mSCORE to calculate each player's "share" of the total, and multiply that by the league's total wasted dollars (using a 65/35 batter/pitcher split) to determine each batter's potential value (pR$).

b. Similarly for pitchers, take the Mayberry sum multiplied by potential innings percentage (pPT) and rank pitchers by this metric. Subtract the minimum value of the group from all pitchers, then use mSCORE to calculate each pitcher's "share" of the total, and multiply that by the league's total wasted dollars (using a 65/35 batter/pitcher split) to determine each pitcher's potential value (pR$).

Use these rankings to produce lists of players who are projected for far less than full playing time despite good or even great skills. A well-timed pick-up of any one of these players could be a boon to most teams' chances of winning their league.

Teams

Johnson Effect *(Bryan Johnson)*: Teams whose actual won/loss record exceeds or falls short of their statistically projected record in one season will tend to revert to the level of their projection in the following season.

Law of Competitive Balance *(Bill James)*: The level at which a team (or player) will address its problems is inversely related to its current level of success. Low performers will tend to make changes to improve; high performers will not. This law explains the existence of the Plexiglass and Whirlpool Principles.

Plexiglass Principle *(Bill James)*: If a player or team improves markedly in one season, it will likely decline in the next. The opposite is true but not as often (because a poor performer gets fewer opportunities to rebound).

Whirlpool Principle *(Bill James)*: All team and player performances are forcefully drawn to the center. For teams, that center is a .500 record. For players, it represents their career average level of performance.

Other Diamonds

The Fanalytic Fundamentals

1. This is not a game of accuracy or precision. It is a game of human beings and tendencies.
2. Draft skills, not stats. Draft skills, not roles.
3. A player's ability to post acceptable stats despite lousy support metrics will eventually run out.
4. Once you display a skill, you own it.
5. Virtually every player is vulnerable to a month of aberrant performance. Or a year.
7. Exercise excruciating patience.

Aging Axioms

1. Age is the only variable for which we can project a rising trend with 100% accuracy. (Or, age never regresses.)

2. The aging process slows down for those who maintain a firm grasp on the strike zone. Plate patience and pitching command can preserve any waning skill they have left.

3. Negatives tend to snowball as you age.

Steve Avery List

Players who hang onto MLB rosters for six years searching for a skill level they only had for three.

Bylaws of Badness

1. Some players are better than an open roster spot, but not by much.

2. Some players have bad years because they are unlucky. Others have *many* bad years because they are bad... and lucky.

Christie Brinkley Law of Statistical Analysis

Never get married to the model.

Employment Standards

1. If you are right-brain dominant, own a catcher's mitt and are under 40, you will always be gainfully employed.

2. Some teams believe that it is better to employ a player with any experience because it has to be better than the devil they don't know.

3. It's not so good to go *pffft* in a contract year.

Brad Fullmer List

Players whose leading indicators indicate upside potential, year after year, but consistently fail to reach that full potential. Players like Byron Buxton, Andrew Heaney and Chris Paddack head the list once again.

Good Luck Truism

Good luck is rare and everyone has more of it than you do. That's the law.

The Gravity Principles

1. It is easier to be crappy than it is to be good.

2. All performance starts at zero, ends at zero and can drop to zero at any time.

3. The odds of a good performer slumping are far greater than the odds of a poor performer surging.

4. Once a player is in a slump, it takes several 3-for-5 days to get out of it. Once he is on a streak, it takes a single 0-for-4 day to begin the downward spiral. *Corollary:* Once a player is in a slump, not only does it take several 3-for-5 days to get out of it, but he also has to get his name back on the lineup card.

5. Eventually all performance comes down to earth. It may take a week, or a month, or may not happen until he's 45, but eventually it's going to happen.

Health Homilies

1. Staying healthy is a skill.

2. A $40 player can get hurt just as easily as a $5 player but is eight times tougher to replace.

3. Chronically injured players never suddenly get healthy.

4. There are two kinds of pitchers: those that are hurt and those that are not hurt... yet.

5. Players with back problems are always worth $10 less.

6. "Opting out of surgery" usually means it's coming anyway, just later.

The Health Hush

Players get hurt and potentially have a lot to lose, so there is an incentive for them to hide injuries. HIPAA laws restrict the disclosure of health information. Team doctors and trainers have been instructed not to talk with the media. So, when it comes to information on a player's health status, we're all pretty much in the dark.

The Livan Level

The point when a player's career Runs Above Replacement level has dropped so far below zero that he has effectively cancelled out any possible remaining future value. (Similarly, the Dontrelle Demarcation.)

The Momentum Maxims

1. A player will post a pattern of positive results until the day you add him to your roster.

2. Patterns of negative results are more likely to snowball than correct.

3. When an unstoppable force meets an immovable object, the wall always wins.

Noise

Irrelevant or meaningless pieces of information that can distort the results of an analysis. In news, this is opinion or rumor. In forecasting, this is random variance or irrelevant data. In ballparks, this is a screaming crowd cheering for a team down 12-3 with two outs and bases empty in the bottom of the ninth.

Paradoxes and Conundrums

1. Is a player's improvement in performance from one year to the next a point in a growth trend, an isolated outlier or a complete anomaly?

2. A player can play through an injury, post rotten numbers and put his job at risk... or... he can admit that he can't play through an injury, allow himself to be taken out of the lineup/rotation, and put his job at risk.

3. Did irregular playing time take its toll on the player's performance or did poor performance force a reduction in his playing time?

4. Is a player only in the game versus right-handers because he has a true skills deficiency versus left-handers? Or is his poor performance versus left-handers because he's never given a chance to face them?

5. The problem with stockpiling bench players in the hope that one pans out is that you end up evaluating performance using data sets that are too small to be reliable.

6. There are players who could give you 20 stolen bases if they got 400 AB. But if they got 400 AB, they would likely be on a bad team that wouldn't let them steal.

Paths to Retirement

1. **The George Brett Path:** Get out while you're still putting up good numbers and the public perception of you is favorable. Like Chipper Jones, Mariano Rivera and David Ortiz.

2. **The Steve Carlton Path:** Hang around the majors long enough for your numbers to become so wretched that people begin to forget your past successes. Recent players who took this path include Jon Lester and Jake Arrieta. Current players who may be on this path are Robinson Canó and Carlos Santana.

3. **The Johan Santana Path:** Stay on the injured list for so long that nobody realizes you've officially retired until your name shows up on a Hall of Fame ballot. Perhaps like Carl Crawford and Jacoby Ellsbury.

Process-Outcome Matrix *(Russo and Schoemaker)*

	Good Outcome	Bad Outcome
Good Process	Deserved Success	Bad Break
Bad Process	Dumb Luck	Poetic Justice

Quack!

An exclamation in response to the educated speculation that a player has used performance enhancing drugs. While it is rare to have absolute proof, there is often enough information to suggest that, "if it looks like a duck and quacks like a duck, then odds are it's a duck."

Rules of Regression

1. The two strongest forces on Earth are regression and gravity.
2. The most accurate forecast is often just a regression to a player's career average.
3. Regression doesn't punch a time clock. *(Todd Zola)*

Surface Stats

All those wonderful statistics we grew up with that those mean bean counters are telling us don't matter anymore. Home runs, RBIs, batting average, won-loss record. Let's go back to the 1960s and make baseball great again! [EDITOR: No.]

Tenets of Optimal Timing

1. If a second half fader had put up his second half stats in the first half and his first half stats in the second half, then he probably wouldn't even have had a second half.

2. Fast starters can often buy six months of playing time out of one month of productivity.

3. Poor 2nd halves don't get recognized until it's too late.

4. "Baseball is like this. Have one good year and you can fool them for five more, because for five more years they expect you to have another good one." — Frankie Frisch

The Three True Outcomes

1. Strikeouts
2. Walks
3. Home runs

The Three True Handicaps

1. Has power but can't make contact.
2. Has speed but can't hit safely.
3. Has potential but is too old.

Zombie

A player who is indestructible, continuing to get work, year-after-year, no matter how dead his skills metrics have become. Players like Dallas Keuchel, Jhoulys Chacin, Chase Anderson, Mike Minor and Tommy Milone are among the walking dead now.

Batters

Batting Eye, Contact and Batting Average

Batting average (BA, or Avg)

This is where it starts. BA is a grand old nugget that has long outgrown its usefulness. We revere .300 hitting superstars and think of .250 hitters as slightly below average, yet the difference between the two is one hit every five games. BA is a poor evaluator of performance in that it neglects the offensive value of the base on balls and assumes that all hits are created equal.

Walk rate (bb%)
(BB / (AB + BB))

A measure of a batter's plate patience. BENCHMARKS: The best batters will have levels more than 10%. Those with poor plate patience will have levels of 5% or less.

On base average (OB)
(H + BB + HBP) / (AB + BB + HBP + Sac Flies)

Addressing a key deficiency with BA, OB gives value to events that get batters on base, but are not hits. An OB of .350 can be read as "this batter gets on base 35% of the time." When a run is scored, there is no distinction made as to how that runner reached base. So, two-thirds of the time—about how often a batter comes to the plate with the bases empty—a walk really is as good as a hit. BENCHMARKS: We know what a .300 hitter is, but what represents "good" for OB? That comparable level would likely be .340, with .290 representing the comparable level of futility.

Ground ball, line drive, fly ball percentages (G/L/F)

The percentage of balls in play that are hit on the ground, as line drives, and in the air. For batters, increased fly ball tendency may foretell a rise in power skills; increased line drive tendency may foretell an improvement in batting average. A study of 2017-2021 batted ball data shows league averages for each:

BIP Type	Total%	Out%
Ground ball	43%	72%
Line drive	21%	28%
Fly ball	37%	85%

Line drives and luck *(Patrick Davitt)*

Given that each individual batter's hit rate sets its own baseline, and that line drives (LD) are the most productive type of batted ball, a study looked at the relationship between the two. Among the findings were that hit rates on LDs are much higher than on FBs or GBs, with individual batters consistently falling into the 72-73% range. Ninety-five percent of all batters fall between the range of 60%-86%; batters outside this range regress very quickly, often within the season.

Note that batters' BAs did not always follow their LD% up or down, because some of them enjoyed higher hit rates on other batted balls, improved their contact rates, or both. Still, it's justifiable to bet that players hitting the ball with authority but getting fewer hits than they should will correct over time.

Batting eye (Eye)
(Walks / Strikeouts)

A measure of a player's strike zone judgment. BENCHMARKS: The best hitters have Eye ratios more than 1.00 (indicating more walks than strikeouts) and are the most likely to be among a league's .300 hitters. Ratios less than 0.30 represent batters who likely also have lower BAs.

Batting eye as a leading indicator

There is a correlation between strike zone judgment and batting average but research shows that this is more descriptive than predictive.

However, we can create percentage plays for the different levels:

For Eye Levels of	Pct who bat .300+	.250-
0.00 - 0.25	7%	39%
0.26 - 0.50	14%	26%
0.51 - 0.75	18%	17%
0.76 - 1.00	32%	14%
1.01 - 1.50	51%	9%
1.51 +	59%	4%

Any batter with an eye ratio more than 1.50 has about a 4% chance of hitting less than .250 over 500 at bats.

Of all .300 hitters, those with ratios of at least 1.00 have a 65% chance of repeating as .300 hitters. Those with ratios less than 1.00 have less than a 50% chance of repeating.

Only 4% of sub-.250 hitters with ratios less than 0.50 will mature into .300 hitters the following year.

In this study, only 37 batters hit .300-plus with a sub-0.50 eye ratio over at least 300 AB in a season. Of this group, 30% were able to accomplish this feat on a consistent basis. For the other 70%, this was a short-term aberration.

Chase rate (Chase%)

A Statcast plate discipline metric defined as the percentage of pitches thrown outside the zone that a batter swings at. BENCHMARKS: The league-wide chase rate in 2022 was 29%. The lower (better) chase rates are typically below 25%, while the free-swingers are above 33%.

Contact rate (ct%)
((AB - K) / AB)

Measures a batter's ability to get wood on the ball and hit it into the field of play. BENCHMARKS: Those batters with the best contact skill will have levels of 80% or better. The hackers will have levels of 70% or less.

Contact rate as a leading indicator

The more often a batter makes contact with the ball, the higher the likelihood that he will hit safely.

		Batting Average			
Contact Rate	2018	2019	2020	2021	2022
0% - 60%	.196	.179	.184	.188	.185
61% - 65%	.223	.223	.212	.222	.216
66% - 70%	.237	.241	.224	.225	.225
71% - 75%	.245	.252	.248	.245	.239
76% - 80%	.258	.264	.261	.261	.249
81% - 85%	.268	.277	.269	.268	.263
Over 85%	.277	.282	.284	.273	.271

Contact rate and walk rate as leading indicators

We looked at seasons from 2000-2021 to see how well both walk rate (BB%) and strikeout rate (K%; loosely inverse to contact rate, ct%) correlate with batting average:

Year	BB%	K%
All	0.01	-0.47
2000	0.14	-0.39
2007	0.00	-0.41
2014	-0.07	-0.53
2021	-0.06	-0.55

A correlation of zero literally means zero correlation, and that's what we see right down the line with walk rate: it doesn't matter to batting average. Strikeouts, however, have quite solid negative correlations: as strikeouts go up, BA goes down, and vice versa.

HCt and HctX *(Patrick Davitt)*

HCt= hard hit ball rate x contact rate
HctX= Player HCt divided by league average Hct, normalized to 100

The combination of making contact and hitting the ball hard might be the most important skills for a batter. HctX correlates very strongly with BA, and at higher BA levels often does so with high accuracy. Its success with HR was somewhat limited, probably due to GB/FB differences. **BENCHMARKS:** The average major-leaguer in a given year has a HctX of 100. Elite batters have an HctX of 135 or above; weakest batters have HctX of 55 or below.

Balls in play (BIP)

(AB – K)

The total number of batted balls that are hit fair, both hits and outs. An analysis of how these balls are hit—on the ground, in the air, hits, outs, etc.—can provide analytical insight, from player skill levels to the impact of luck on statistical output.

Batting average on balls in play *(Voros McCracken)*

(H – HR) / (AB – HR – K)

Or, BABIP. Also called hit rate (h%). The percent of balls hit into the field of play that fall for hits. **BENCHMARK:** Every hitter establishes his own individual hit rate that stabilizes over time. A batter whose seasonal hit rate varies significantly from the h% he has established over the preceding three seasons (variance of at least +/- 3%) is likely to improve or regress to his individual h% mean (with over-performer declines more likely and sharper than under-performer recoveries). Three-year h% levels strongly predict a player's h% the following year.

Pitches/Plate Appearance as a leading indicator for BA *(Paul Petera)*

The deeper a batter works a count (via pitches per plate appearance, or P/PA), the more likely his batting average will fall (e.g., more strikeouts) but his OBA will rise (e.g., more walks):

P/PA	OBA	BA
4.00+	.360	.264
3.75-3.99	.347	.271
3.50-3.74	.334	.274
Under 3.50	.321	.276

Players with an unusually high or low BA for their P/PA in one year tend to regress heavily the next:

YEAR ONE	YEAR TWO	
	BA Improved	BA Declined
Low P/PA and Low BA	77%	23%
High P/PA and High BA	21%	79%

Expected batting average *(John Burnson)*

xCT% * [xH1% + xH2%]
where
$xH1\% = GB\% \times [0.0004\ PX + 0.062\ ln(SX)]$
$\qquad + LD\% \times [0.93 - 0.086\ ln(SX)]$
$\qquad + FB\% \times 0.12$
and
$xH2\% = FB\% \times [0.0013\ PX - 0.0002\ SX - 0.057]$
$\qquad + GB\% \times [0.0006\ PX]$

A hitter's expected batting average as calculated by multiplying the percentage of balls put in play (contact rate) by the chance that a ball in play falls for a hit. The likelihood that a ball in play falls for a hit is a product of the speed of the ball and distance it is hit (PX), the speed of the batter (SX), and distribution of ground balls, fly balls, and line drives. We further split it out by non-homerun hit rate (xH1%) and homerun hit rate (xH2%). **BENCHMARKS:** In general, xBA should approximate batting average fairly closely. Those hitters who have large variances between the two gauges are candidates for further analysis. **LIMITATION:** xBA tends to understate a batter's true value if he is an extreme ground ball hitter (G/F ratio over 3.0) with a low PX. These players are not inherently weak, but choose to take safe singles rather than swing for the fences.

Expected batting average variance

xBA – BA

The variance between a batter's BA and his xBA is a measure of over- or under-achievement. A positive variance indicates the potential for a batter's BA to rise. A negative variance indicates the potential for BA to decline. **BENCHMARK:** Discount variances that are less than 20 points. Any variance more than 30 points is regarded as a strong indicator of future change.

Power

Slugging average (Slg)

(Singles + (2 x Doubles) + (3 x Triples) + (4 x HR)) / AB

A measure of the total number of bases accumulated (or the minimum number of runners' bases advanced) per at bat. It is a misnomer; it is not a true measure of a batter's slugging ability because it includes singles. Slg also assumes that each type of hit has proportionately increasing value (i.e. a double is twice as valuable as a single, etc.) which is not true. For instance, with the bases loaded, a HR always scores four runs, a triple always scores three, but a double could score two or three and a single could score one, or two, or even three. **BENCHMARKS:** Top batters will have levels over .450. The bottom batters will have levels less than .350.

Home runs to fly ball rate (HR/F)

The percent of fly balls that are hit for HRs.

HR/F rate as a leading indicator *(Joshua Randall)*

Each batter establishes an individual home run to fly ball rate that stabilizes over rolling three-year periods; those levels strongly predict the HR/F in the subsequent year. A batter who varies significantly from his HR/F is likely to regress toward his individual HR/F mean, with over-performance decline more likely and more severe than under-performance recovery.

Estimating HR rate for young hitters *(Matt Cederholm)*

Over time, hitters establish a baseline HR/F, but how do we measure the HR output of young hitters with little track record? Since power is a key indicator of HR output, we can look at typical HR/F for various levels of power, as measures by xPX:

xPX	HR/F percentiles				
	10	25	50	75	90
<=70	0.9%	2.0%	3.8%	5.5%	7.4%
71-80	3.3%	5.1%	6.4%	8.1%	10.0%
81-90	3.8%	5.4%	7.4%	9.0%	11.0%
91-100	4.7%	6.6%	8.9%	11.3%	13.0%
101-110	6.6%	8.3%	10.9%	13.0%	16.2%
111-120	7.4%	9.8%	11.9%	14.7%	17.1%
121-130	8.5%	10.9%	12.8%	15.5%	17.4%
131-140	9.7%	11.9%	14.6%	17.1%	20.4%
141-160	11.3%	13.1%	16.5%	19.2%	21.5%
161+	14.4%	16.5%	19.4%	22.0%	25.8%

To predict changes in HR output, look at a player and project his HR as if his HR/F was at the median for his xPX level. For example, if a player with a 125 xPX exceeds a 12.8% HR/F, we would expect a decline in the following season. The greater the deviation from the mean, the greater the probability of an increase or decline.

Expected home run total (xHR) *(Arik Florimonte)*

A study assessing all baseball conditions from 2015-2019 created a model for expected home run rate (xHR) given exit velocity (EV) and launch angle (LA) found in MLB's Statcast system. The model was applied to the entire database of batted balls to calculate the likelihood of each batted ball becoming a home run.

The xHR metric is not a measure of whether a specific batted ball should have been a home run. Rather, it is a measure of how often a ball struck in the way it was turns out to be a home run. By comparing a hitter's actual home run total to xHR over a given year, we can estimate how much of that performance was earned or unearned, and adjust home run expectations for the following season.

Expected home runs to fly ball rate (xHR/F) *(Arik Florimonte)*

A player's xHR divided by his fly balls in a given season. While previous years' HR/F results do have some useful correlation to current year's result, xHR/F does even better in that it has added benefit for shorter periods of time. In predicting the next month's results, xHR/F from one month does as well as two months of HR/F. And for equal samples, a batter's xHR/F is about 15-25% better correlated to the upcoming result over a similar time period. This additional predictive value persists for up to about two years, at which time xHR/F and HR/F are roughly equally valuable.

Is fly ball carry a skill? *(Arik Florimonte)*

Using Statcast data from 2015-17, we determined that "Carry"—how much a fly ball travels compared to its projected distance based on Launch Angle and Exit Velocity—is a repeatable skill for batters. Specific findings from this study include:

- Carry is well-correlated from year-to-year, with Prior Year Carry explaining 47% of Current Year Carry.
- On average, a batter will retain two-thirds of his fly ball Carry from year-to-year.
- Batters with unlucky HR totals in Year 0 tend to see an improvement in Year 1. Of those with high Carry in Year 0, 88% saw improvement in the difference between HR/F and xHR/F (expected HR/F), and the average gain is +0.059 (including non-gainers).

Hard-hit fly balls as a skill *(Arik Florimonte)*

A study of batted ball data from 2002-2020 found we should seek batters that produce hard-hit fly balls. Among the key findings:

- The ability to hit the ball hard is good, the ability to hit fly balls and line drives is also good, and the ability to do both at once is even better.
- All three of these metrics have good correlation year to year, meaning each can reliably be called a "skill".
- When evaluating batters whose xPX, which uses hard-hit fly balls and line drives as inputs, seems out of line with hard-hit rate and FB% or LD%, we should expect some regression, and the real talent level probably lies somewhere in the middle.

Launch angle (LA)

A Statcast metric defined by MLB.com as the vertical angle at which the ball leaves a player's bat after being struck. In other words, it's a precise measure for how high (or low) a ball is hit. BENCHMARKS: The league-wide average launch angle in 2022 was 12.7 degrees. We can convert launch angle ranges into traditional batted ball trajectories as follows:

Batted ball type	Launch angle
Groundball	Less than 10 degrees
Line drive	10-25 degrees
Flyball	25-50 degrees
Pop-up	Greater than 50 degrees

Exit velocity (EV)

A Statcast metric defined by MLB.com as the speed of the baseball as it comes off the bat, immediately after a batter makes contact. In other words, it's a precise measure for how hard a ball is hit. Batters with higher average exit velocities make harder contact and are more likely to see favorable outcomes than those with lower exit velocities. BENCHMARKS: The league-wide average exit velocity in 2022 was 88.6 miles per hour. Top batters will average above 90 mph with bottom batters struggling to reach 87 mph.

Barrel rate (Brl%)

A "barrel" is a Statcast metric defined by MLB.com as a well-struck ball where the combination of exit velocity and launch angle generally leads to a minimum .500 batting average and 1.500 slugging percentage. Barrel rate (Brl% in hitter boxes) is simply the number of barrels divided by the number of batted balls for a given hitter. BENCHMARKS: The league-wide barrel rate in 2022 was 7.5%. A rate of >12% is generally considered top tier.

Quality of batted ball score (QBaB) *(Arik Florimonte)*

For batters, greater exit velocity and greater mean launch angle are better. In addition, we've shown elsewhere that reduced launch angle variability is correlated with better batted ball results. The Quality of Batted Ball score (QBaB) assigns A-F grades for exit velocity, launch angle, and launch angle variability based on percentile groups with the thresholds below:

Percentile	Grade	Exit Velocity (mph)	Launch Angle	Launch Angle Variability
90+	A	> 90.8	> 17.6°	< 23.95°
70-90	B	89.2 – 90.8	14.1° – 17.6°	23.95° – 25.64°
30-70	C	88.6 – 89.2	9.2° – 14.1°	25.64° – 27.91°
10-30	D	84.1 – 88.6	5.7° – 9.2°	27.91° – 29.45°
10-	F	< 84.1	< 5.7°	> 29.45°

These scores can be useful in several ways:
- QBaB is very well correlated with batter output.
- Higher EV grades are always desirable.
- Higher LA grades are good for power, but do not help batting average.
- Smaller Launch Angle Variation is good for batting average, but impact on power is murky.
- QBaB scores are very sticky. It is extremely rare for a great hitter to become terrible and vice versa.
- Batters who have great QBaB scores but underperform tend to recover; the converse is true for those with poor scores.

QBaB appears in our hitter boxes, giving readers and analysts another tool to evaluate hitters, and to know whether appearances are to be believed.

QBaB over short samples—Exit Velocity *(Arik Florimonte)*

Using Statcast data from 2015-2020, we determined that QBaB scores for exit velocity can be meaningful over short sample sizes. Specifically:
- Over any sample size, a QBaB "A" for exit velocity is correlated with improved QBaB scores over the next 25 batted balls (1-2 weeks), and "F" scores portended worse results.
- The magnitude of the differences in outcomes changes steadily and dramatically as sample size increases.
- A single batted ball in the top 10% of all batted balls is a surprisingly good indicator of upcoming exit velocity goodness.

As you make roster decisions throughout the year, be sure to check in on the rolling 100- and 25- batted ball exit velocity trends.

Linear weighted power (LWPwr)

((Doubles x .8) + (Triples x .8) + (HR x 1.4)) / (At bats- K) x 100

A variation of Pete Palmer's linear weights formula that considers only events that are measures of a batter's pure power. BENCHMARKS: Top sluggers typically top the 17 mark. Weak hitters will have a LWPwr level of less than 10.

Linear weighted power index (PX)

(Batter's LWPwr / League LWPwr) x 100

LWPwr is presented in this book in its normalized form to get a better read on a batter's accomplishment in each year. For instance, a 30-HR season today is much less of an accomplishment than 30 HRs hit in a lower offense year like 2014. BENCHMARKS: A level of 100 equals league average power skills. Any player with a value more than 100 has above average power skills, and those more than 150 are the Slugging Elite.

Expected LW power index (xPX) *(Bill Macey)*

2.6 + 269*HHLD% + 724*HHFB%

Previous research has shown that hard-hit balls are more likely to result in hits and hard-hit fly balls are more likely to end up as HRs. As such, we can use hard-hit ball data to calculate an expected skills-based power index. This metric starts with hard-hit ball data, which measures a player's fundamental skill of making solid contact, and then places it on the same scale as PX (xPX). In the above formula, HHLD% is calculated as the number of hard hit-line drives divided by the total number of balls put in play. HHFB% is similarly calculated for fly balls. The variance between PX and xPX can be viewed as a leading indicator for other power metrics.

Pitches/Plate Appearance as a leading indicator for PX *(Paul Petera)*

Batters that work deeper into the count (via pitches per plate appearance, or P/PA) tend to display more power (as measured by PX) than batters who don't:

P/PA	PX
4.00+	123
3.75-3.99	108
3.50-3.74	96
Under 3.50	84

Players with an unusually high or low PX for their P/PA in one year tend to regress heavily the next:

YEAR ONE	YEAR TWO PX Improved	PX Declined
Low P/PA and High PX	11%	89%
High P/PA and Low PX	70%	30%

Doubles as a leading indicator for home runs *(Bill Macey)*

There is little support for the theory that hitting many doubles in year x leads to an increase in HR in year x+1. However, it was shown that batters with high doubles rates (2B/AB) also tend to hit more HR/AB than the league average; oddly, they are unable to sustain the high 2B/AB rate but do sustain their higher HR/AB rates. Batters with high 2B/AB rates and low HR/AB rates are more likely to see HR gains in the following year, but those rates will still typically trail the league average. And, batters who experience a surge in 2B/AB typically give back most of those gains in the following year without any corresponding gain in HR.

Opposite field home runs *(Ed DeCaria)*

Opposite field HRs serve as a strong indicator of overall home run power (AB/HR). Power hitters (smaller AB/HR rates) hit a far higher percentage of their HR to the opposite field or straight away (over 30%). Conversely, non-power hitters hit almost 90% of their home runs to their pull field.

	Performance in Y2-Y4 (% of Group)		
Y1 Trigger	<=30 AB/HR	5.5+ RC/G	$16+ R$
2+ OppHR	69%	46%	33%
<2 OppHR	29%	13%	12%

Players who hit just two or more OppHR in one season were 2-3 times as likely as those who hit zero or one OppHR to sustain strong AB/HR rates, RC/G levels, or R$ values over the following three seasons.

	Y2-Y4 Breakout Performance (% Breakout by Group, Age <=26 Only)		
	AB/HR	RC/G	R$
Y1 Trigger	>35 to <=30	<4.5 to 5.5+	<$8 to $16+
2+ OppHR	32%	21%	30%
<2 OppHR	23%	12%	10%

Roughly one of every 3-4 batters age 26 or younger experiences a *sustained three-year breakout* in AB/HR, RC/G or R$ after a season in which they hit 2+ OppHR, far better odds than the one in 8-10 batters who experience a breakout without the 2+ OppHR trigger.

A 2015 Brad Kullman study that examined hard hit balls of all types (flies, liners, and grounders) by hitters with 100 or more plate appearances offered a broader conclusion. His research found that hitters who can effectively use the whole field are more productive in virtually every facet of hitting than those with an exclusively pull-oriented approach.

Home runs in bunches or droughts *(Patrick Davitt)*
A study from 2010-2012 on HR data showed that batters hit HRs in a random manner, with game-gaps between HRs that correspond roughly to their average days per HR. Hitters do sometimes hit HRs with greater or lesser frequency in short periods, but these periods are not predictive. It appears pointless to try to "time the market" by predicting the beginning or end of a drought or a bunch, or by assuming the end of one presages the beginning of the other, despite what the ex-player in the broadcast booth tells you.

Power breakout profile
It is not easy to predict which batters will experience a power spike. We can categorize power breakouts to determine the likelihood of a player taking a step up or of a surprise performer repeating his feat. Possibilities:
- Increase in playing time
- History of power skills at some time in the past
- Redistribution of already demonstrated extra base hit power
- Normal skills growth
- Situational breakouts, particularly in hitter-friendly venues
- Increased fly ball tendency
- Use of illegal performance-enhancing substances
- Miscellaneous unexplained variables

Speed

Wasted talent on the base paths
We refer to some players as having "wasted talent," a high level skill that is negated by a deficiency in another skill. Among these types are players who have blazing speed that is negated by a sub-.300 on base average.

These players can have short-term value. However, their stolen base totals are tied so tightly to their "green light" that any change in managerial strategy could completely erase that value. A higher OB mitigates that downside; the good news is that plate patience can be taught.

There are always a handful of players who had at least 20 SBs with an OBP less than .300, putting their future SBs at risk. That number has declined in recent years with the drop in SB attempts in general. In 2022, Jorge Mateo (35 SB, .267 OBP), Bobby Witt, Jr. (30, .294) and Myles Straw (21, .291) fit this profile. Adolís García (25, .300) was close, and it's tough to see long-term SB viability for Andrew Velasquez (17, .236).

Stolen base attempt rate (SBA%)
(SB + CS) / (BB + Singles + HBP)
A rough approximation of how often a baserunner attempts a stolen base. Provides a comparative measure for players on a given team and, as a team measure, the propensity of a manager to give a "green light" to his runners.

Stolen base success rate (SB%)
SB / (SB + CS)
The rate at which baserunners are successful in their stolen base attempts. **BENCHMARK:** It is generally accepted that an 80% rate is the minimum required for a runner to be providing value to his team.

Speed score *(Bill James)*
A measure of the various elements that comprise a runner's speed skills. Although this formula (a variation of James' original version) may be used as a leading indicator for stolen base output, SB attempts are controlled by managerial strategy which makes speed score somewhat less valuable.

Speed score is calculated as the mean value of the following four elements:

1. Stolen base efficiency = $(((SB + 3)/(SB + CS + 7)) - .4) \times 20$

2. Stolen base freq. = *Square root of $((SB + CS)/(Singles + BB)) / .07$*

3. Triples rating = $(3B / (AB - HR - K))$ and the result assigned a value based on the following chart:

< 0.001	0	0.0105	6
0.001	1	0.013	7
0.0023	2	0.0158	8
0.0039	3	0.0189	9
0.0058	4	0.0223+	10
0.008	5		

4. Runs scored as a percentage of times on base = $(((R - HR) / (H + BB - HR)) - .1) / .04$

Speed score index (SX)

(Batter's speed score / League speed score) x 100

Normalized speed scores get a better read on a runner's accomplishment in context. A level of 100 equals league average speed skill. Values more than 100 indicate above average skill, more than 200 represent the Fleet of Feet Elite.

Statistically scouted speed (Spd) *(Ed DeCaria)*

(104 + {[(Runs–HR+10*age_wt)/(RBI-HR+10)]/lg_av*100} / 5
+ {[(3B+5*age_wt)/(2B+3B+5)]/lg_av*100} / 5
+ {[(SoftMedGBhits+25*age_wt)/(SoftMedGB+25)]/lg_av*100} / 2
- {[Weight (Lbs)/Height (In)^2 * 703]/lg_av*100}

A skills-based gauge that measures speed without relying on stolen bases. Its components are:

- *(Runs – HR) / (RBI – HR)*: This metric aims to minimize the influence of extra base hit power and team run-scoring rates on perceived speed.
- *3B / (2B + 3B)*: No one can deny that triples are a fast runner's stat; dividing them by 2B+3B instead of all balls in play dampens the power aspect of extra base hits.
- *(Soft + Medium Ground Ball Hits) / (Soft + Medium Ground Balls)*: Faster runners are more likely than slower runners to beat out routine grounders. Hard hit balls are excluded from numerator and denominator.
- *Body Mass Index (BMI)*: Calculated as *Weight (lbs) / Height (in)2 * 703*. All other factors considered, leaner players run faster than heavier ones.

In this book, the formula is scaled with a midpoint of 100.

Expected stolen bases (xSB) *(Ed DeCaria)*

Stolen bases are an unusual fantasy baseball statistic. While most statistics are largely a reflection of skill, context, and luck, stolen bases involve a unique fourth factor: WILL.

Expected stolen bases (xSB) attempts to predict stolen bases given a player's playing time and ability to get on base. To this end, we focus on estimating a player's expected stolen base attempt rate (xSBA%) and success rate (xSBS%), and then apply those to his projected times on base (TOF) to arrive at an expected stolen base total.

xSB = TOF * xSBA% * xSBS%, where:
xSBA% = 0.027 + (Spd - 100) * 0.000545 + y0SBA% * 0.5645 +
y0SBA%^2 * 0.23
xSBS% = 0.6664 + (y0SBS% * 0.1127)

Note that xSBA% is largely driven by last year's actual attempt rate, i.e., the player's demonstrated willingness to run. So to isolate how much of xSB comes from skill vs. will, we created a separate version of xSBA% (xSBA%-Skill) that is unaware of the player's past SB attempt rate. The difference between the version with attempt rate and without attempt rate then represents the player's will (xSBA%-Will):

xSBA%-Skill = 0.049 + y0SBS% * 0.04 + (Spd - 100) * 0.001 +
(Spd - 100)^2 * sign (Spd - 100) * 0.000009576
xSBA%-Will = -0.022 + (Spd - 100) * -0.000455 + y0SBA% *
0.5645 + y0SBA%^2 * 0.23 - y0SBS% * 0.04 - (Spd - 100)^2 *
sign (Spd - 100) * 0.000009576

Fantasy owners may well choose to continue to invest in high-will players, and those players may make good on their willingness to run for yet another season. But always remember: stolen bases come from players' minds as much as they come from their legs.

Roto Speed (RSpd)

(Spd x (SBO + SB%))

An adjustment to the measure for raw speed that takes into account a runner's opportunities to steal and his success rate. This stat is intended to provide a more accurate predictive measure of stolen bases for the Mayberry Method.

Stolen base breakout profile *(Bob Berger)*

To find stolen base breakouts (first 30+ steal season in the majors), look for players that:

- are between 22-27 years old
- have 3-7 years of professional (minors and MLB) experience
- have previous steals at the MLB level
- have averaged 20+ SB in previous three seasons (majors and minors combined)
- have at least one professional season of 30+ SB

Overall Performance Analysis

On base plus slugging average (OPS)

A simple sum of the two gauges, it is considered one of the better evaluators of overall performance. OPS combines the two basic elements of offensive production—the ability to get on base (OB) and the ability to advance baserunners (Slg). **BENCHMARKS:** The game's top batters will have OPS levels more than .850. The worst batters will have levels less than .660.

Adjusted on base plus slugging average (OPS+)

OPS scaled to league average to account for year-to-year fluctuations in league-wide statistical performance. It's a snapshot of a player's overall skills compared to an average player; also used in platoon situations (vL+; vR+). **BENCHMARK:** A level of 100 means a player had a league-average OPS in that given season.

Base Performance Value (BPV)

(Walk rate - 5) x 2) + ((Contact rate - 75) x 4)
+ ((Power Index - 80) x 0.8) + ((Spd - 80) x 0.3)

A single value that describes a player's overall raw skill level. This formula combines the individual raw skills of batting eye, contact rate, power and speed.

Base Performance Index (BPX)

BPV scaled to league average to account for year-to-year fluctuations in league-wide statistical performance. It's a snapshot of a player's overall skills compared to an average player. **BENCHMARK:** A level of 100 means a player had a league-average BPV in that given season.

Linear weights *(Pete Palmer)*

((Singles x .46) + (Doubles x .8) + (Triples x 1.02)
+ (Home runs x 1.4) + (Walks x .33) + (Stolen Bases x .3)
- (Caught Stealing x .6) - ((At bats - Hits) x Normalizing Factor)

(Also referred to as Batting Runs.) Formula whose premise is that all events in baseball are linear; that is, the output (runs) is directly proportional to the input (offensive events). Each of these events is then weighted according to its relative value in producing runs. Positive events—hits, walks, stolen bases—have positive values. Negative events—outs, caught stealing—have negative values.

The normalizing factor, representing the value of an out, is an offset to the level of offense in a given year. It changes every season, growing larger in high offense years and smaller in low offense years. The value is about .26 and varies by league.

LW is not included in the player boxes, but the LW concept is used with the linear weighted power gauge.

Runs above replacement (RAR)

An estimate of the number of runs a player contributes above a "replacement level" player. "Replacement" is defined as the level of performance at which another player can easily be found at little or no cost to a team. What constitutes replacement level is a topic that is hotly debated. There are a variety of formulas and rules of thumb used to determine this level for each position (replacement level for a catcher will be very different from replacement level for an outfielder). Our estimates appear below.

One of the major values of RAR for fantasy applications is that it can be used to assemble an integrated ranking of batters and pitchers for drafting purposes.

To calculate RAR for batters:

- Start with a batter's runs created per game (RC/G).
- Subtract his position's replacement level RC/G.
- Multiply by number of games played: (AB - H + CS) / 25.5.

Replacement levels used in this book:

POS	AL	NL
CA	3.36	3.37
1B	3.90	4.29
2B	3.57	3.87
3B	3.66	3.93
SS	3.76	4.01
LF	3.78	3.85
CF	3.71	3.83
RF	3.85	4.02
DH	4.38	4.08

RAR can also be used to calculate rough projected team won-loss records. *(Roger Miller)* Total the RAR levels for all the players on a team, divide by 10 and add to 53 wins.

Runs created *(Bill James)*

(H + BB – CS) x (Total bases + (.55 x SB)) / (AB + BB)

A formula that converts all offensive events into a total of runs scored. As calculated for individual teams, the result approximates a club's actual run total with great accuracy.

Runs created per game (RC/G)

Runs Created / ((AB - H + CS) / 25.5)

RC expressed on a per-game basis might be considered the hypothetical ERA compiled against a particular batter. Another way to look at it: A batter with a RC/G of 7.00 would be expected to score 7 runs per game if he were cloned nine times and faced an average pitcher in every at bat. Cloning batters is not a practice we recommend. **BENCHMARKS:** Few players surpass the level of a

10.00 RC/G, but any level more than 7.50 can still be considered very good. At the bottom are levels less than 3.00.

Plate Appearances as a leading indicator *(Patrick Davitt)*

While targeting players "age 26 with experience" as potential breakout candidates has become a commonly accepted concept, a study has found that cumulative plate appearances, especially during the first two years of a young player's career, can also have predictive value in assessing a coming spike in production. Three main conclusions:

- When projecting players, MLB experience is more important than age.
- Players who amass 800+ PAs in their first two seasons are highly likely to have double-digit Rotisserie dollar value in Year 3.
- Also target young players in the season where they attain 400 PAs, as they are twice as likely as other players to grow significantly in value.

When do hitters get platooned? *(Jeff Zimmerman)*

We created a talent baseline to determine when a hitter might get platooned by examining 24 actual platoon pairs from the 2017 season. We compared the more extreme hitter's projected OPS splits entering the year. Among the main findings:

- Normally, a spread of ~200 points of OPS is needed to start a platoon. In only two instances did a platoon happen with a projected split under 130 points.
- For most teams to implement a platoon, they need at least one player to have a projected platoon OPS around .830.
- The minimum projected OPS in which teams begin using platoons is around .590. A player could have a 200-point spread, but if the low projected OPS is over .700, teams aren't likely to add another player to make up the difference.

The simple rule of an ".800-.600 OPS spread" works great for an average platoon benchmark. Owners may want to relax the values to snare a few more players with a .775-.625 OPS spread, or an ".800-.600 OPS spread with shrinkage".

Skill-specific aging patterns for batters *(Ed DeCaria)*

Most published aging analyses are done using composite estimates of value such as OPS or linear weights. By contrast, fantasy GMs are typically more concerned with category-specific player value (HR, SB, AVG, etc.). We can better forecast what matters most by analyzing peak age of individual baseball skills rather than overall player value.

For batters, recognized peak age for overall batting value is a player's late 20s. But individual skills do not peak uniformly at the same time:

Contact rate (ct%): Ascends modestly by about a half point of contact per year from age 22 to 26, then holds steady within a half point of peak until age 35, after which players lose a half point of contact per year.

Walk rate (bb%): Trends the opposite way with age compared to contact rate, as batters tend to peak at age 30 and largely remain there until they turn 38.

Stolen Base Opportunity (SBO): Typically, players maintain their SBO through age 27, but then reduce their attempts steadily in each remaining year of their careers.

Stolen base success rate (SB%): Aggressive runners (>14% SBO) tend to lose about 2 points per year as they age. However, less aggressive runners (<=14% SBO) actually improve their SB% by about 2 points per year until age 28, after which they reverse course and give back 1-2 pts every year as they age.

GB%/LD%/FB%: Both GB% and LD% peak at the start of a player's career and then decline as many hitters seemingly learn to elevate the ball more. But at about age 30, hitter GB% ascends toward a second late-career peak while LD% continues to plummet and FB% continues to rise through age 38.

Hit rate (h%): Declines linearly with age. This is a natural result of a loss of speed and change in batted ball trajectory.

Isolated Power (ISO): Typically peaks from age 24-26. Similarly, home runs per fly ball, opposite field HR %, and Hard Hit % all peak by age 25 and decline somewhat linearly from that point on.

Catchers and late-career performance spikes *(Ed Spaulding)*

Many catchers—particularly second line catchers—have their best seasons late in their careers. Some possible reasons why:

1. Catchers often get to the big leagues for defensive reasons and not their offensive skills. These skills take longer to develop.

2. The heavy emphasis on learning the catching/ defense/ pitching side of the game detracts from their time to learn about, and practice, hitting.

3. Injuries often curtail their ability to show offensive skills, though these injuries (typically jammed fingers, bruises on the arms, rib injuries from collisions) often don't lead to time on the injured list.

4. The time spent behind the plate has to impact the ability to recognize, and eventually hit, all kinds of pitches.

In-Season Analysis

Sample size reliability *(Russell Carleton)*

At what sample size do skill and luck each represent 50 percent contributors to a specific metric?

*Measured in plate appearances

60:	Contact rate
120:	Walk rate
160:	ISO (Isolated power)
170:	HR rate
320:	Slg
460:	OBP

*Measured via balls in play:

50:	HR/F
80:	GB%; FB%
600:	LD%
820:	Hit rate (BABIP)

*Unlisted metrics did not stabilize over a full season of play.

How to read: "After 60 plate appearances, the luck-to-skill ratio for contact rate has evened out. If a player with a career 70 percent contact rate has an 85 percent contact rate after 60 PA, we can attribute 50% of that new rate to a new skill and the other 50% to

random chance." These levels represent the point at which these metrics become useful, though not as direct predictors. Their value is as another data point in the forecasting process.

Can we trust in-season sample size? *(Arik Florimonte)*

When a batter's performance deviates from their established history, when can you trust the change? And are there any metrics that are better in short periods than long? Using data from 2010-2017 and filtering for full-time players (≥ 350 PA in a season, or ≥ 75 PA in a month), we were able to answer these questions.

Not surprisingly, there is no magic date for believing the current season's results more than the previous season's; rather, it's more of a continuum. We were able to estimate the point in the season current year-to-date results are more predictive than the prior year's results, noted in the table below by the change from white blocks to black. We also note at which point the previous month alone offers better predictive value than the entire previous year ("PM>PY").

	Months of the Season						PM>PY starting...
Hard%	A	M	J	J	A	S	June
Soft%	A	M	J	J	A	S	May
HR/FB	A	M	J	J	A	S	Never
GB%	A	M	J	J	A	S	Never
LD%	A	M	J	J	A	S	Never
FB%	A	M	J	J	A	S	Never
IFFB%	A	M	J	J	A	S	Never
K%	A	M	J	J	A	S	Never
BB%	A	M	J	J	A	S	Never

Prior Year is Better
Year-to-date is Better

Note that due to the data filters used, a month in the chart above can be equated to roughly 90 plate appearances.

Key takeaways:

- Don't buy hard into early changes in batter plate skills until at least June

- Changes in ground ball and fly ball rates take a while to become firm; true "swing changers" can't really be discerned until mid-summer.

- In both of the above, it might pay to speculate earlier if you can stash a player on reserve.

- Don't expect the prior year's Soft% to continue, but pay attention to the current year's Soft contact rates.

- Generally, projections based on prior years' skills should remain your fallback position but keep moving the needle toward the current year's results as the year goes on.

Batting order facts *(Ed DeCaria)*

Eighty-eight percent of today's leadoff hitters bat leadoff again in their next game, 78% still bat leadoff 10 games later, and 68% still bat leadoff 50 games later. Despite this level of turnover after 50 games, leadoff hitters have the best chance of retaining their role over time. After leadoff, #3 and #4 hitters are the next most likely to retain their lineup slots.

On a season-to-season basis, leadoff hitters are again the most stable, with 69% of last year's primary leadoff hitters retaining the #1 slot next year.

Plate appearances decline linearly by lineup slot. Leadoff batters receive 10-12% more PAs than when batting lower in the lineup. AL #9 batters and NL #8 batters get 9-10% fewer PAs. These results mirror play-by-play data showing a 15-20 PA drop by lineup slot over a full season.

Walk rate is largely unaffected by lineup slot in the AL. Beware strong walk rates by NL #8 hitters, as much of this "skill" will disappear if ever moved from the #8 slot.

Batting order has no discernable effect on contact rate.

Hit rate slopes gently upward as hitters are slotted deeper in the lineup.

As expected, the #3-4-5 slots are ideal for non-HR RBIs, at the expense of #6 hitters. RBIs are worst for players in the #1-2 slots. Batting atop the order sharply increases the probability of scoring runs, especially in the NL.

The leadoff slot easily has the highest stolen base attempt rate. #4-5-6 hitters attempt steals more often when batting out of those slots than they do batting elsewhere. The NL #8 hitter is a SB attempt sinkhole. A change in batting order from #8 to #1 in the NL could nearly double a player's SB output due to lineup slot alone.

DOMination and DISaster rates

Week-to-week consistency is measured using a batter's BPV compiled in each week. A player earns a DOMinant week if his BPV was greater or equal to 50 for that week. A player registers a DISaster if his BPV was less than 0 for that week. The percentage of Dominant weeks, DOM%, is simply calculated as the number of DOM weeks divided by the total number of weeks played.

Is week-to-week consistency a repeatable skill? *(Bill Macey)*

To test whether consistent performance is a repeatable skill for batters, we examined how closely related a player's DOM% was from year to year.

YR1 DOM%	AVG YR2 DOM%
< 35%	37%
35%–45%	40%
46%–55%	45%
56%+	56%

Quality/consistency score (QC)

(DOM% – (2 x DIS%)) x 2

Using the DOM/DIS percentages, this score measures both the quality of performance as well as week–to-week consistency.

	Sample configurations		
DOM%	Neutral	DIS%	QC
100	0	0	200
70	20	10	100
60	30	10	80
50	30	20	20
50	25	25	0
40	30	30	-40
30	20	50	-140
20	20	60	-200
0	100	0	-400

Projecting RBI *(Patrick Davitt)*

Evaluating players in-season for RBI potential is a function of the interplay among four factors:

- Teammates' ability to reach base ahead of him and to run the bases efficiently
- His own ability to drive them in by hitting, especially XBH
- Number of Games Played
- Place in the batting order

3-4-5 Hitters:
$(0.69 x GP x TOB) + (0.30 x ITB) + (0.275 x HR) – (.191 x GP)$

6-7-8 Hitters:
$(0.63 x GP x TOB) + (0.27 x ITB) + (0.250 x HR) – (.191 x GP)$

9-1-2 Hitters:
$(0.57 x GP x TOB) + (0.24 x ITB) + (0.225 x HR) – (.191 x GP)$

...where *GP = games played, TOB = team on-base pct.* and *ITB = individual total bases (ITB)*.

Apply this pRBI formula after 70 games played or so (to reduce the variation from small sample size) to find players more than 9 RBIs over or under their projected RBI. There could be a correction coming.

You should also consider other factors, like injury or trade (involving the player or a top-of-the-order speedster) or team SB philosophy and success rate.

Remember: the player himself has an impact on his TOB. When we first did this study, we excluded the player from his TOB and got better results. The formula overestimates projected RBI for players with high OBP who skew his teams' OBP but can't benefit in RBI from that effect.

Ten-Game hitting streaks as a leading indicator *(Bob Berger)*

Research of hitting streaks from 2011 and 2012 showed that a 10-game streak can reliably predict improved longer-term BA performance during the season. A player who has put together a hitting streak of at least 10 games will improve his BA for the remainder of the season about 60% of the time. This improvement can be significant, on average as much as .020 of BA.

What can foul balls tell us? *(Nick Trojanowski)*

Foul balls, because of their relatively meager influence on in-game outcomes, have been examined far less often than balls in play. Using 2008-17 data for every 500+ pitch season, we found that hitting foul balls is a skill, in that it's repeatable from year to year. Other findings:

1. Hitters who swing at more pitches, regardless of location, hit more foul balls, regardless of contact rate.
2. Routinely fouling off pitches doesn't regularly lead to better outcomes, and in fact tends to make walks less likely.

Other Diamonds

It's a Busy World Shortcut

For marginal utility-type players, scan their PX and Spd history to see if there's anything to mine for. If you see triple digits anywhere, stop and look further. If not, move on.

Chronology of the Classic Free-Swinger with Pop

1. Gets off to a good start.
2. Thinks he's in a groove.
3. Gets lax, careless.
4. Pitchers begin to catch on.
5. Fades down the stretch.

Errant Gust of Wind

A unit of measure used to describe the difference between your home run projection and mine.

Mendoza Line

Named for Mario Mendoza, it represents the benchmark for batting futility. Usually refers to a .200 batting average, but can also be used for low levels of other statistical categories. Note that Mendoza's lifetime batting average was actually a much more robust .215.

Old Player Skills

Power, low batting average, no speed and usually good plate patience. Young players, often those with a larger frame, who possess these "old player skills" tend to decline faster than normal, often in their early 30s.

Power Peak Postulate

A player's career power trend is not a climb up to a single peak and then descent. It is more of a mountain range, with many peaks of varying elevations.

Esix Snead List

Players with excellent speed and sub-.300 on base averages who get a lot of practice running down the line to first base, and then back to the dugout.

Pitchers

Strikeouts and Walks

Fundamental skills

The contention that pitching performance is unreliable is a fallacy driven by the practice of attempting to project pitching stats using gauges that are poor evaluators of skill.

How can we better evaluate pitching skill? We can start with the statistical categories that are generally unaffected by external factors. These stats capture the outcome of an individual pitcher versus batter match-up without regard to supporting offense, defense or bullpen:

Walks Allowed, Strikeouts and Ground/Fly Balls

Even with only these stats to observe, there is a wealth of insight that these measures can provide.

Control rate (Ctl, bb/9), or opposition walks per game
BB allowed x 9 / IP

Measures how many walks a pitcher allows per game equivalent.
BENCHMARK: The best pitchers will have bb/9 of 2.5 or less.

Walk rate (BB%)
(BB / TBF)

Measures how many walks a pitcher allows as a percentage of total batters faced. BB% replaces Control rate (Ctl, or bb/9) in our pitcher boxes as a more precise leading indicator of a pitcher's control.

Approximate Conversions		
Ctl	Ball%	BB%
1.5	<31	4.1
1.7	31	4.8
1.8	32	5.0
2.2	33	5.9
2.3	34	6.1
2.7	35	7.2
2.9	36	7.6
3.2	37	8.3
3.4	38	8.7
3.8	39	9.6
4.1	40	10.5
4.7	41	11.6
5.4	>41	12.8

BENCHMARK: For those who used a Ctl rate of 2.5 or less as a benchmark for potential skills upside, the comparable level on the BB% scale would be about 6.6%. Better (and easier to remember): target pitchers with a rate of 6% or lower. The league-wide BB% in 2022 was 8.2%.

Dominance rate (Dom, k/9), or opposition strikeouts/game
Strikeouts recorded x 9 / IP

Measures how many strikeouts a pitcher allows per game equivalent. BENCHMARK: The best pitchers will have k/9 levels of 9.0 or higher.

Swinging strike rate as leading indicator *(Stephen Nickrand)*
Swinging strike rate (SwK%) measures the percentage of total pitches against which a batter swings and misses. SwK% can help

us validate and forecast a SP's Dominance (K/9) rate, which in turn allows us to identify surgers and faders with greater accuracy. An expected Dominance rate can be estimated from SwK%; and a pitcher's individual SwK% does not regress to league norms.

BENCHMARKS: The few starters per year who have a 12.0% or higher SwK% are near-locks to have a 9.0 Dom or 25% K%. In contrast, starters with a 7.0% or lower SwK% have nearly no chance at posting even an average Dom. Finally, use an 9.5% SwK% as an acceptable threshold when searching for SP based on this metric; raise it to 10.5% to begin to find SwK% difference-makers.

Strikeout rate (K%)
(K / TBF)

Measures how many strikeouts a pitcher produces as a percentage of total batters faced. K% replaces Dominance rate (Dom, or k/9) in our pitcher boxes as a more precise leading indicator of a pitcher's ability to rack up Ks.

Approximate Conversions		
K/9	SwK%	K%
5.4	<6.0	13.2
5.6	6.0	14.1
6.1	7.0	15.2
6.6	8.0	17.5
7.3	9.0	19.1
7.8	10.0	20.5
8.5	11.0	22.2
9.3	12.0	24.8
9.9	13.0	27.1
10.7	14.0	29.2
11.3	15.0	31.6
12.0	16.0	33.5
12.9	>16.0	36.0

BENCHMARK: For those who used a Dominance rate of 9.5 as a benchmark for potential skills upside, the comparable level on the K% scale would be about 25%. The league-wide K% in 2022 was 22.4%.

Command ratio (Cmd)
(Strikeouts / Walks)

A measure of a pitcher's ability to get the ball over the plate. There is no more fundamental a skill than this, and so it is used as a leading indicator to project future rises and falls in other gauges, such as ERA. BENCHMARKS: Baseball's best pitchers will have ratios in excess of 3.0. Pitchers with ratios less than 1.0—indicating that they walk more batters than they strike out—have virtually no potential for long-term success. If you make no other changes in your approach to drafting pitchers, limiting your focus to only pitchers with a command ratio of 2.5 or better will substantially improve your odds of success.

Strikeout rate minus walk rate (K-BB%)
(K% – BB%)

Measures a pitchers' strikeout rate (K%) minus walk rate (BB%) and is a leading indicator for future performance. K-BB% replaces Command ratio (Cmd, or K/BB) in our pitcher boxes as a more precise measurement of a pitcher's command, as it's better correlated to both ERA and xERA, and is stickier year-to-year.

Approx Conversions		Correlated
K/BB	K-BB%	ERA
<1.0	-4%	8.43
1.0-2.0	7%	5.44
2.1-3.0	15%	4.26
3.1-4.0	19%	4.00
4.1-5.0	23%	3.73
>5.0	26%	3.13

BENCHMARK: For those who used a Command ratio of 3.0 as a benchmark for potential skills upside, the comparable level on the K-BB% scale would be about 18%. Better (and easier to remember): target pitchers with a rate of 20% or higher. The league-wide K-BB% in 2022 was 14.2%.

Fastball velocity and Dominance rate *(Stephen Nickrand)*
It is intuitive that an increase in fastball velocity for starting pitchers leads to more strikeouts. But how much?

Research shows that the vast majority of SP with significant fastball velocity gains follow this three-step process:

1. They experience a significant Dom gain during the same season.
2. Most often, they give back those Dom gains during the following season.
3. They are likely to increase their Dom the following season, but the magnitude of the Dom increase usually is small.

By contrast, the vast majority of SP with significant fastball velocity losses are likely to experience a significant Dom decrease during the same season.

Those SP with significant fastball velocity losses from one season to the next are just as likely to experience a fastball velocity or Dom increase as they are to experience a fastball or Dom decrease, and the amounts of the increase/decrease are nearly identical.

How aging affects fastball velocity, swinging strikes and strikeout rate *(Ed DeCaria)*
On average, pitchers lose about 0.2 mph per season off their fastballs. Over time, this coincides with decreases in swinging strike rate (SwK%) and overall strikeout rate (K/PA)—the inevitable effects of aging. But one thing that pitchers can do to delay these effects is to throw more first pitch strikes.

Power/contact rating
(BB + K) / IP
Measures the level by which a pitcher allows balls to be put into play. In general, extreme power pitchers can be successful even with poor defensive teams. Power pitchers tend to have greater longevity in the game. Contact pitchers with poor defenses behind them are high risks to have poor W-L records and ERA.
BENCHMARKS: A level of 1.13+ describes pure throwers. A level of .93 or less describes high contact pitchers.

Balls in Play

Balls after contact (BAC)
(Batters faced – (BB + HBP + SAC)) + H – K
The total number of batted balls that are hit fair, both hits and outs. An analysis of how these balls are hit—on the ground, in the air, hits, outs, etc.—can provide analytical insight, from player skill levels to the impact of luck on statistical output.

Balls in play (BIP)
(Batters faced – (BB + HBP + SAC)) + H – K - HR
The total number of batted balls that are hit into the field of play. Essentially, BAC minus home runs.

Batting average on balls in play *(Voros McCracken)*
(H – HR) / (Batters faced – (BB + HBP + SAC)) + H – K – HR
Abbreviated as BABIP; also called hit rate (H%), this is the percent of balls hit into the field of play that fall for hits. In 2000, Voros McCracken published a study that concluded "there is little if any difference among major league pitchers in their ability to prevent hits on balls hit in the field of play." His assertion was that, while a Johan Santana would have a better ability to prevent a batter from getting wood on a ball, or perhaps keeping the ball in the park, once that ball was hit in the field of play, the probability of it falling for a hit was virtually no different than for any other pitcher.

Among the findings in his study were:

- There is little correlation between what a pitcher does one year in the stat and what he will do the next. This is not true with other significant stats (BB, K, HR).
- You can better predict a pitcher's hits per balls in play from the rate of the rest of the pitcher's team than from the pitcher's own rate.

This last point brings a team's defense into the picture. It begs the question, when a batter gets a hit, is it because the pitcher made a bad pitch, the batter took a good swing, or the defense was not positioned correctly?

BABIP as a leading indicator *(Voros McCracken)*
The league average is 30%, which is also the level that individual performances will regress to on a year to year basis. Any +/- variance of 3% or more can affect a pitcher's ERA.

Pitchers will often post hit rates per balls-in-play that are far off from the league average, but then revert to the mean the following year. As such, we can use that mean to project the direction of a pitcher's ERA.

Subsequent research has shown that ground ball or fly ball propensity has some impact on this rate.

Hit rate *(See Batting average on balls in play)*

Opposition batting average (OBA)
Hits allowed / (Batters faced – (BB + HBP + SAC))
The batting average achieved by opposing batters against a pitcher.
BENCHMARKS: The best pitchers will have levels less than .235; the worst pitchers levels more than .280.

Opposition on base average (OOB)
(Hits allowed + BB) / ((Batters faced – (BB + HBP + SAC)) + Hits allowed + BB)

The on base average achieved by opposing batters against a pitcher. BENCHMARK: The best pitchers will have levels less than .290; the worst pitchers levels more than .350.

Walks plus hits divided by innings pitched (WHIP)

Essentially the same measure as opposition on base average, but used for Rotisserie purposes. BENCHMARKS: A WHIP of less than 1.15 is considered top level; more than 1.50 indicative of poor performance. Levels less than 1.00—allowing fewer runners than IP—represent extraordinary performance and are rarely maintained over time.

Expected walks plus hits divided by innings pitched (xWHIP) *(Arik Florimonte)*

Hit rate luck makes an amplified contribution to WHIP, due to its impact on both the numerator (hits) and denominator (outs). To neutralize the effect, Expected WHIP (xWHIP) assumes that a pitcher's walk rate, strikeout rate, rate of hit batters, and ground-ball-to-flyball ratio reflect their true skill, but assigns league average rates of line drives, hits per batted ball type (xH%), and double plays per ground ball (xDP%). xWHIP better captures a pitcher's true skill, and is therefore more useful for predicting future results.

Ground ball, line drive, fly ball percentages (G/L/F)

The percentage of balls in play that are hit on the ground, as line drives, and in the air. For pitchers, the ability to keep the ball on the ground can contribute to his statistical output exceeding his demonstrated skill level. A study of 2017-2021 batted ball data shows league averages for each:

BIP Type	Total%	Out%
Ground ball	43%	72%
Line drive	21%	28%
Fly ball	37%	85%

Ground ball tendencies *(John Burnson)*

Ground ball pitchers tend to give up fewer HRs than do fly ball pitchers. There is also evidence that GB pitchers have higher hit rates. In other words, a ground ball has a higher chance of being a hit than does a fly ball that is not out of the park.

GB pitchers have lower strikeout rates. We should be more forgiving of a low strikeout rate if it belongs to an extreme ground ball pitcher.

GB pitchers have a lower ERA but a higher WHIP than do fly ball pitchers. On balance, GB pitchers come out ahead, even when considering strikeouts, because a lower ERA also leads to more wins.

Extreme GB/FB pitchers *(Patrick Davitt)*

Among pitchers with normal strikeout levels, extreme GB pitchers (>37% of all batters faced) have ERAs about 0.4 runs lower than normal-GB% pitchers but only slight WHIP advantages. Extreme FB% pitchers (>32% FB) show no ERA benefits.

Among High-K (>=24% of BF), however, extreme GBers have ERAs about 0.5 runs lower than normal-GB pitchers, and WHIPs about five points lower. Extreme FB% pitchers have ERAs about 0.2 runs lower than normal-FB pitchers, and WHIPs about 10 points lower.

Revisiting fly balls *(Jason Collette)*

The increased emphasis on defensive positioning is often associated with infield shifting, but the same data also influences how outfielders are positioned. Some managers are positioning OFs more aggressively than just the customary few steps per a right- or left-handed swinging batter. Five of the top 10 defensive efficiency teams in 2013 —OAK, STL, MIA, LAA and KC—also had parks among the top 10 in HR suppression.

Before dismissing flyball pitchers as toxic assets, pay more attention to park factors and OF defensive talent. In particular, be a little more willing to roster fly ball pitchers who pitch both in front of good defensive OFs and in good pitchers' parks.

Line drive percentage as a leading indicator *(Seth Samuels)*

The percentage of balls-in-play that are line drives is beyond a pitcher's control. Line drives do the most damage; from 2017-2022, here were the expected hit rates and number of total bases per type of BIP.

Trajectory	% of BIP	BABIP	BAC	TB/BIP
Ground balls	43.0%	.240	.240	.260
Line drives	24.8%	.093	.217	.671
Fly balls	30.9%	.615	.633	.930
Bunts	1.3%	.422	.422	.423

Despite the damage done by LDs, pitchers do not have any innate skill to avoid them. There is little relationship between a pitcher's LD% one year and his rate the next year. All rates tend to regress towards the mean of 24.8%.

Home run to fly ball rate (HR/F)

The percent of fly balls that are hit for home runs.

HR/F as a leading indicator *(John Burnson)*

McCracken's work focused on "balls in play," omitting home runs from the study. However, pitchers also do not have much control over the percentage of fly balls that turn into HR. Research shows that there is an underlying rate of HR as a percentage of fly balls which in 2022 was 11.4%. A pitcher's HR/F rate will vary each year but always tends to regress to that mean. The element that pitchers do have control over is the number of fly balls they allow. That is the underlying skill or deficiency that controls their HR rate.

Exit velocity, barrel rate and launch angle for pitchers *(Stephen Nickrand)*

Though primarily used to evaluate batter performance and skill, Statcast metrics such as exit velocity, barrel rate, and launch angle have moderate-to-strong correlations to several pitching indicators:

- There is a modest correlation between the average exit velocity and barrel rate allowed by starting pitchers to both their ERA and HR/9.

- As a pitchers' exit velocity and barrel rate go up, so does their ERA and HR/9; and vice-versa.
- A significant deviation from a pitcher's average exit velocity baseline usually results in a regression towards that prior baseline during the following season.
- Starting pitchers experience a lot of volatility in their Barrel%. There is not a pattern of them regressing to their prior barrel rate baseline, partly because launch angle has been increasing in the game steadily over the past four seasons.

Expected home run total (xHR) *(Arik Florimonte)*

A study assessing all baseball conditions from 2015-2019 created a model for expected home run rate (xHR) given exit velocity (EV) and launch angle (LA) found in MLB's Statcast system. The model was applied to the entire database of batted balls to calculate the likelihood of each batted ball becoming a home run.

The xHR metric is not a measure of whether a specific batted ball should have been a home run. Rather, it is a measure of how often a ball struck in the way it was turns out to be a home run. By comparing a pitcher's actual home runs allowed total to xHR over a given year, we can estimate how much of that performance was earned or unearned, and adjust home runs allowed expectations for the following season.

Expected home runs per fly ball rate (xHR/F) *(Arik Florimonte)*

A pitcher's xHR allowed divided by his fly balls given up in a season. It is well-established that a pitcher's HR/F in one season is not a valid predictor for the pitcher's following year's HR/F. Despite this, biases may linger against pitchers who have "proven" to have acute gopheritis, or in favor of pitchers who managed to avoid surrendering HR. Unfortunately, knowing a pitcher's xHR/F history provides negligible improvement to predictive models. If a pitcher's xHR/F is high, it means that he was hit hard, but it does not mean he will be hit hard again. Once park factors are considered, regression to league average HR/F is still the best predictor.

"Just Enough" home runs as a leading indicator *(Brian Slack)*

Using ESPN's Home Run Tracker data, we analyzed year-to-year consistency of "Just Enough" home runs (those that clear the fence by less than 10 vertical feet or land less than one fence height past the fence). For the 528 starting pitchers who logged enough innings to qualify for the ERA title in consecutive years from 2006 through 2016 season, research showed:

- The percentage of Just Enough home runs that a pitcher gives up gravitates towards league average (32%) the following year.
- There is only a tenuous connection between a pitcher's ability to limit the percentage of Just Enough home runs and a pitcher's HR/FB rate. So we should avoid the assumption that a pitcher with a high percentage of Just Enough home runs will necessarily improve his HR/FB rate (and presumably ERA) the following year, or vice versa.

- This means be careful not to over-draft a pitcher based solely on the idea of HR/FB improvement in the coming year. Conversely, one should not automatically avoid pitchers with perceived HR/FB downside.

What can foul balls tell us? *(Nick Tojanowski)*

Foul balls, because of their relatively meager influence on in-game outcomes, have been examined far less often than balls in play. Using 2008-17 data for every 500+ pitch season, we found that inducing foul balls is a skill, in that it's repeatable from year to year. Other findings:

1. Pitchers who induce more swings at strikes allow more fouls, but pitchers who induce more chases do not.
2. Groundball pitchers tend to give up fewer foul balls than flyball pitchers.

Runs

Expected earned run average (xERA)

Gill and Reeve version: $(.575 \times H \text{ [per 9 IP]}) + (.94 \times HR \text{ [per 9 IP]}) + (.28 \times BB \text{ [per 9 IP]}) - (.01 \times K \text{ [per 9 IP]}) - \text{Normalizing Factor}$

John Burnson version (used in this book):
$(xER \times 9)/IP$, where xER is defined as
$xER\% \times (FB/10) + (1-xS\%) \times [0.3 \times (BIP - FB/10) + BB]$
where $xER\% = 0.96 - (0.0284 \times (GB/FB))$
and
$xS\% = (64.5 + (K/9 \times 1.2) - (BB/9 \times (BB/9 + 1)) / 20) + ((0.0012 \times (GB\%^2)) - (0.001 \times GB\%) - 2.4)$

xERA represents the an equivalent of what a pitcher's real ERA might be, calculated solely with skills-based measures. It is not influenced by situation-dependent factors.

Expected ERA variance

$xERA - ERA$

The variance between a pitcher's ERA and his xERA is a measure of over or underachievement. A positive variance indicates the potential for a pitcher's ERA to rise. A negative variance indicates the potential for ERA improvement. BENCHMARK: Discount variances that are less than 0.50. Any variance more than 1.00 (one run per game) is regarded as a strong indicator of future change.

Projected xERA or projected ERA?

Which should we be using to forecast a pitcher's ERA? Projected xERA is more accurate for looking ahead on a purely skills basis. Projected ERA includes *situation-dependent* events—bullpen support, park factors, etc.—which are reflected better by ERA. The optimal approach is to use both gauges as *a range of expectation* for forecasting purposes.

Strand rate (S%)

$(H + BB - ER) / (H + BB - HR)$

Measures the percentage of allowed runners a pitcher strands (earned runs only), which incorporates both individual pitcher skill and bullpen effectiveness. BENCHMARKS: The most adept at stranding runners will have S% levels over 75%. Those with rates over 80% will have artificially low ERAs which will be prone to relapse. Levels below 65% will inflate ERA but have a high probability of regression.

Expected strand rate *(Michael Weddell)*

$73.935 + K/9 - 0.116 * (BB/9*(BB/9+1))$
$+ (0.0047 * GB\%^2 - 0.3385 * GB\%)$
$+ (MAX(2,MIN(4,IP/G))/2-1)$
$+ (0.82$ if left-handed$)$

This formula is based on three core skills: strikeouts per nine innings, walks per nine innings, and ground balls per balls in play, with adjustments for whether the pitcher is a starter or reliever (measured by IP/G), and his handedness.

Strand rate as a leading indicator *(Ed DeCaria)*

Strand rate often regresses/rebounds toward past rates (usually 69-74%), resulting in Year 2 ERA changes:

% of Pitchers with Year 2 Regression/Rebound

Y1 S%	RP	SP	LR
<60%	100%	94%	94%
65	81%	74%	88%
70	53%	48%	65%
75	55%	85%	100%
80	80%	100%	100%
85	100%	100%	100%

Typical ERA Regression/Rebound in Year 2

Y1 S%	RP	SP	LR
<60%	-2.54	-2.03	-2.79
65	-1.00	-0.64	-0.93
70	-0.10	-0.05	-0.44
75	0.24	0.54	0.75
80	1.15	1.36	2.29
85	1.71	2.21	n/a

Starting pitchers (SP) have a narrower range of strand rate outcomes than do relievers (RP) or swingmen/long relievers (LR). **Relief pitchers** with Y1 strand rates of <=67% or >=78% are likely to experience a +/- ERA regression in Y2. **Starters and swingmen/long relievers** with Y1 strand rates of <=65% or >=75% are likely to experience a +/- ERA regression in Y2. Pitchers with strand rates that deviate more than a few points off of their individual expected strand rates are likely to experience some degree of ERA regression in Y2. Over-performing (or "lucky") pitchers are more likely than underperforming (or "unlucky") pitchers to see such a correction.

Wins

Expected Wins (xW) *(Matt Cederholm)*

$[(Team\ runs\ per\ game)^{1.8}/[(Pitcher\ ERA)^{1.8} + (Team\ runs\ per\ game)^{1.8}] \times 0.72 \times GS$

Starting pitchers' win totals are often at odds with their ERA. Attempts to find a strictly skill-based analysis of this phenomenon haven't worked, but there is a powerful tool in the toolbox: Bill James' Pythagorean Theorem. While usually applied to team outcomes, recent research has shown that its validity holds up when applied to individual starting pitchers.

One key to applying the Pythagorean Theorem is factoring in no-decisions. Research shows that the average no-decision rate is

28% of starts, regardless of the type or quality of the pitcher or his team, with no correlation in ND% from one season to the next.

Overall, 70% of pitchers whose expected wins varied from actual wins showed regression in wins per start in the following year, making variation from Expected Wins a good leading indicator.

Projecting/chasing wins

There are five events that need to occur in order for a pitcher to post a single win...

1. He must pitch well, allowing few runs.
2. The offense must score enough runs.
3. The defense must successfully field all batted balls.
4. The bullpen must hold the lead.
5. The manager must leave the pitcher in for 5 innings, and not remove him if the team is still behind.

Of these five events, only one is within the control of the pitcher. As such, projecting or chasing wins based on skills alone can be an exercise in futility.

Home field advantage and wins *(Ed DeCaria)*

Pitchers starting at home are 7% more likely to earn a Win than when they start on the road. This extra Win potential comes from two sources: 1) home starting pitchers tend to go deeper into games than away starters, and 2) even when home starters only last 5-6 IP, they are more likely to get the Win.

Usage

Batters faced per game *(Craig Wright)*

$((Batters\ faced - (BB + HBP + SAC)) + H + BB) / G$

A measure of pitcher usage and one of the leading indicators for potential pitcher burnout.

Workload

Research suggests that there is a finite number of innings in a pitcher's arm. This number varies by pitcher, by development cycle, and by pitching style and repertoire. We can measure a pitcher's potential for future arm problems and/or reduced effectiveness (burnout):

Sharp increases in usage from one year to the next. Common wisdom has suggested that pitchers who significantly increase their workload from one year to the next are candidates for burnout symptoms. This has often been called the Verducci Effect, after writer Tom Verducci. BaseballHQ.com analyst Michael Weddell tested pitchers with sharp workload increases during the period 1988-2008 and found that no such effect exists.

Starters' overuse. Consistent "batters faced per game" (BF/G) levels of 28.0 or higher, combined with consistent seasonal IP totals of 200 or more may indicate burnout potential, especially with pitchers younger than 25. Within a season, a BF/G of more than 30.0 with a projected IP total of 200 may indicate a late season fade.

Relievers' overuse. Warning flags should be up for relievers who post in excess of 100 IP in a season, while averaging fewer than 2 IP per outing.

When focusing solely on minor league pitchers, research results are striking:

Stamina: Virtually every minor league pitcher who had a BF/G of 28.5 or more in one season experienced a drop-off in BF/G the following year. Many were unable to ever duplicate that previous level of durability.

Performance: Most pitchers experienced an associated drop-off in their BPVs in the years following the 28.5 BF/G season. Some were able to salvage their effectiveness later on by moving to the bullpen.

Effects of short-term workloads on relief pitcher value

(Arik Florimonte)

Using game logs from 2002-17, we studied the effects of recent workload on relief pitcher performance. After accounting for factors such as selection and usage bias—good pitchers get used on short rest more often—we discovered there is almost no measurable performance impact. Pitchers used heavily for several days, including the day before, show perhaps a 5-10% reduction in BPV.

Pitchers who have thrown often in the recent past are less likely to be used, which can significantly reduce their value, with a 36% reduction in saves and a 64% reduction in games pitched when "worn out".

In leagues with daily lineup changes, monitoring RP workloads can help owners decide to start rested closers of lesser quality, and therefore lower cost, over more expensive closers who may be worn out.

Protecting young pitchers *(Craig Wright)*

There is a link between some degree of eventual arm trouble and a history of heavy workloads in a pitcher's formative years. Some recommendations from this research:

Teenagers (A-ball): No 200 IP seasons and no BF/G over 28.5 in any 150 IP span. No starts on three days rest.

Ages 20-22: Average no more than 105 pitches per start with a single game ceiling of 130 pitches.

Ages 23-24: Average no more than 110 pitches per start with a single game ceiling of 140 pitches.

When possible, a young starter should be introduced to the majors in long relief before he goes into the rotation.

Overall Performance Analysis

Base Performance Value (BPV)

((K/9 - 5.0) x 18)
+ ((4.0 - bb/9) x 27))
+ (Ground ball rate as a whole number - 40%)

A single value that describes a player's overall raw skill level. The formula combines the individual raw skills of dominance, control and the ability to keep the ball down in the zone, all characteristics that are unaffected by most external factors. In tandem with a pitcher's strand rate, it provides a more complete picture of the elements that contribute to ERA, and therefore serves as an accurate tool to project likely changes in ERA. Note that the league-normalized version (BPX) is what appears in this book.

Base Performance Index (BPX)

BPV scaled to league average to account for year-to-year fluctuations in league-wide statistical performance. It's a snapshot of a player's overall skills compared to an average player. **BENCHMARK:** A level of 100 means a player had a league-average BPV in that given season.

Runs above replacement (RAR)

An estimate of the number of runs a player contributes above a "replacement level" player.

Batters create runs; pitchers save runs. But are batters and pitchers who have comparable RAR levels truly equal in value? Pitchers might be considered to have higher value. Saving an additional run is more important than producing an additional run. A pitcher who throws a shutout is guaranteed to win that game, whereas no matter how many runs a batter produces, his team can still lose given poor pitching support.

To calculate RAR for pitchers:

1. Start with the replacement level league ERA.
2. Subtract the pitcher's ERA. (To calculate projected RAR, use the pitcher's xERA.)
3. Multiply by number of games played, calculated as plate appearances (IP x 4.34) divided by 38.
4. Multiply the resulting RAR level by 1.08 to account for the variance between earned runs and total runs.

Skill-specific aging patterns for pitchers *(Ed DeCaria)*

Baseball forecasters obsess over "peak age" of player performance because we must understand player ascent toward and decline from that peak to predict future value. Most published aging analyses are done using composite estimates of value such as OPS or linear weights. By contrast, fantasy GMs are typically more concerned with category-specific player value (K, ERA, WHIP, etc.). We can better forecast what matters most by analyzing peak age of individual baseball skills rather than overall player value.

For pitchers, prior research has shown that pitcher value peaks somewhere in the late 20s to early 30s. But how does aging affect each demonstrable pitching skill?

Strikeout rate (k/9): Declines fairly linearly beginning at age 25.

Walk rate (bb/9): Improves until age 25 and holds somewhat steady until age 29, at which point it begins to steadily worsen. Deteriorating k/9 and bb/9 rates result in inefficiency, as it requires far more pitches to get an out. For starting pitchers, this affects the ability to pitch deep into games.

Innings Pitched per game (IP/G): Among starters, it improves slightly until age 27, then tails off considerably with age, costing pitchers nearly one full IP/G by age 33 and one more by age 39.

Hit rate (H%): Among pitchers, H% appears to increase slowly but steadily as pitchers age, to the tune of .002-.003 points per year.

Strand rate (S%): Very similar to hit rate, except strand rate decreases with age rather than increasing. GB%/LD%/FB%: Line drives increase steadily from age 24 onward, and outfield flies increase beginning at age 31. Because 70%+ of line drives fall for hits, and 10%+ of fly balls become home runs, this spells trouble for aging pitchers.

Home runs per fly ball (HR/F): As each year passes, a higher percentage of a pitcher's fly balls become home runs allowed increases with age.

Catchers' effect on pitching *(Thomas Hanrahan)*

A typical catcher handles a pitching staff better after having been with a club for a few years. Research has shown that there is an improvement in team ERA of approximately 0.37 runs from a catcher's rookie season to his prime years with a club. Expect a pitcher's ERA to be higher than expected if he is throwing to a rookie backstop.

First productive season *(Michael Weddell)*

To find those starting pitchers who are about to post their first productive season in the majors (10 wins, 150 IP, ERA of 4.00 or less), look for:

- Pitchers entering their age 23-26 seasons, especially those about to pitch their age 25 season.
- Pitchers who already have good skills, shown by an xERA in the prior year of 4.25 or less.
- Pitchers coming off of at least a partial season in the majors without a major health problem.
- To the extent that one speculates on pitchers who are one skill away, look for pitchers who only need to improve their control (bb/9).

Bounceback fallacy *(Patrick Davitt)*

It is conventional wisdom that a pitcher often follows a bad year (value decline of more than 50%) with a significant "bounceback" that offers profit opportunity for the canny owner. But research showed the owner is extremely unlikely to get a full bounceback, and in fact, is more likely to suffer a further decline or uselessly small recovery than even a partial bounceback. The safest bet is a $30+ pitcher who has a collapse—but even then, bid to only about half of the previous premium value.

Closers

Saves

There are six events that need to occur in order for a relief pitcher to post a single save:

1. The starting pitcher and middle relievers must pitch well.
2. The offense must score enough runs.
3. It must be a reasonably close game.
4. The manager must put the pitcher in for a save opportunity.
5. The pitcher must pitch well and hold the lead.
6. The manager must let him finish the game.

Of these six events, only one is within the control of the relief pitcher. As such, projecting saves for a reliever has less to do with skills than opportunity. However, pitchers with excellent skills may create opportunity for themselves.

Saves conversion rate (Sv%)

Saves / Save Opportunities

The percentage of save opportunities that are successfully converted. **BENCHMARK:** We look for a minimum 80% for long-term success.

Leverage index (LI) *(Tom Tango)*

Leverage index measures the amount of swing in win probability indexed against an average value of 1.00. Thus, relievers who come into games in various situations create a composite score and if that average score is higher than 1.00, then their manager is showing enough confidence in them to try to win games with them. If the average score is below 1.00, then the manager is using them, but not showing nearly as much confidence that they can win games.

Saves chances and wins *(Patrick Davitt)*

Do good teams get more saves because they generate more wins, or do poor teams get more saves because more of their wins are by narrow margins. The "good-team" side is probably on firmer ground, though there are enough exceptions that we should be cautious about drawing broad inferences.

The 2014 study confirmed what Craig Neuman found years earlier: The argument "more wins leads to more saves" is generally correct. Over five studied seasons, the percentage of wins that were saved (Sv%W) was about 50%, and half of all team-seasons fell in the Sv%W range of 48%-56%. As a result, high-saves seasons were more common for high-win teams.

That wins-saves connection for individual team-seasons was much less solid, however, and we observed many outliers. Data for individual team-seasons showed wide ranges of both Sv%W and actual saves.

Finally, higher-win teams do indeed get more blowout wins, but while poorer teams had a higher percentage (73%) of close wins (three runs or fewer) than better teams (56%), good teams' higher number of wins meant they still had more close wins, more save opportunities and more saves, again with many outliers among individual team-seasons.

Origin of closers

History has long maintained that ace closers are not easily recognizable early on in their careers, so that every season does see its share of the unexpected. Clay Holmes, Ryan Helsley, Félix Bautista…who would have thought it a year ago?

Accepted facts, all of which have some element of truth:

- You cannot find major league closers from pitchers who were closers in the minors.
- Closers begin their careers as starters.
- Closers are converted set-up men.
- Closers are pitchers who were unable to develop a third effective pitch.

More simply, closers are a product of circumstance.

Are the minor leagues a place to look at all? In the 41 years from 1990 to 2021, there have been nearly 500 twenty-save seasons recorded in Double-A and Triple-A ball. Only 16 of those pitchers ever saved 20 games in the majors, and only eight had multiple 20-save seasons: John Wetteland, Mark Wohlers, Ricky Bottalico, Braden Looper, Francisco Cordero, Craig Kimbrel, A.J. Ramos and Kirby Yates.

One of the reasons that minor league closers rarely become major league closers is because, in general, they do not get enough innings in the minors to sufficiently develop their arms into big-league caliber. In fact, organizations do not look at minor league closing performance seriously, assigning that role to pitchers who they do not see as legitimate prospects. The average age of minor league closers over the past decade has been 27.5.

Elements of saves success

The task of finding future closing potential comes down to looking at two elements:

Talent: The raw skills to mow down hitters for short periods.

Opportunity: The more important element, yet the one that pitchers have no control over.

There are pitchers that have Talent, but not Opportunity. These pitchers are not given a chance to close for a variety of reasons (e.g. being blocked by a solid front-liner in the pen, being left-handed, etc.), but are good to own because they will not likely hurt your pitching staff. You just can't count on them for saves, at least not in the near term.

There are pitchers that have Opportunity, but not Talent. MLB managers decide who to give the ball to in the 9th inning based on their own perceptions about what skills are required to succeed, even if those perceived "skills" don't translate into acceptable metrics.

Those pitchers without the metrics may have some initial short-term success, but their long-term prognosis is poor and they are high risks to your roster. Recent examples include Sam Dyson, Brad Ziegler, Jeanmar Gómez, Brad Boxberger and Lou Trivino.

Closers' job retention *(Michael Weddell)*

Of pitchers with 20 or more saves in one year, only 67.5% of these closers earned 20 or more saves the following year. The variables that best predicted whether a closer would avoid this attrition:

- *Saves history:* Career saves was the most important factor.
- *Age:* Closers are most likely to keep their jobs at age 27. For long-time closers, their growing career saves totals more than offset the negative impact of their advanced ages. Older closers without a long history of racking up saves tend to be bad candidates for retaining their roles.
- *Performance:* Actual performance, measured by ERA+, was of only minor importance.
- *Being right-handed:* Increased the odds of retaining the closer's role by 9% over left-handers.

Closer volatility history

Year	Closers Drafted	Avg R$	Closers Failed	Failure %	New Sources
2013	29	$15.55	9	31%	13
2014	28	$15.54	11	39%	15
2015	29	$14.79	13	45%	16
2016	33	$13.30	19	58%	17
2017	32	$13.63	17	53%	15
2018	27	$13.22	17	63%	20
2019	31	$13.29	18	58%	14
2020*	27	$14.30	19	70%	26
2021	33	$11.79	21	64%	22
2022	35	$12.66	25	71%	14

The 2020 data should be mostly ignored due to the vagaries of the short season.

Drafted refers to the number of saves sources purchased in both LABR and Tout Wars experts leagues each year. These only include relievers drafted specifically for saves speculation. *Avg R$* refers to the average purchase price of these pitchers in the AL-only and NL-only leagues. *Failed* is the number (and percentage) of saves sources drafted that did not return at least 50% of their value that year. The failures include those that lost their value due to ineffectiveness, injury or managerial decision. *New Sources* are arms that were drafted for less than $5 (if drafted at all) but finished with at least 10 saves.

After 2021's post-COVID reluctance to invest in closers, 2022's drafters opened their wallets a bit, but spread those investments across 35 potential saves sources, the most since we began record-keeping in 1999. Of those sources, 14 (40%) were rostered for less than $10. Over the entire draft pool, 17 of the pitchers returned positive earnings, but only two turned a profit—Paul Sewald and Devin Williams.

In fact, the total of $443 spent on closers returned just $65 overall. The failure rate was record-breaking. Most notable: While there were 25 failures, there were only 14 new sources of saves (of which only nine earned posi-tive value), which meant that some teams were sticking with incumbents even if they were struggling. With the on-going uncertainty around bullpen usage, odds are we will continue to be risk-averse with these investments in 2023.

Closers and multi-year performance *(Patrick Davitt)*

A team having an "established closer"—even a successful one—in a given year does not affect how many of that team's wins are saved in the next year. However, a top closer (40-plus saves) in a given year has a significantly greater chance to retain his role in the subsequent season.

Research of saves and wins data over several seasons found that the percentage of wins that are saved is consistently 50%-54%, irrespective of whether the saves were concentrated in the hands of a "top closer" or passed around to the dreaded "committee" of lesser closers. But it also found that about two-thirds of high-save closers reprised their roles the next season, while three-quarters of low-save closers did not. Moreover, closers who held the role for two or three straight seasons averaged 34 saves per season while closers new to the role averaged 27.

Other Relievers

Reliever efficiency percent (REff%)

(Wins + Saves + Holds) / (Wins + Losses + SaveOpps + Holds)

This is a measure of how often a reliever contributes positively to the outcome of a game. A record of consistent, positive impact on game outcomes breeds managerial confidence, and that confidence could pave the way to save opportunities. For those pitchers suddenly thrust into a closer's role, this formula helps gauge their potential to succeed based on past successes in similar roles. BENCHMARK: Minimum of 80%.

Vulture

A pitcher, typically a middle reliever, who accumulates an unusually high number of wins by preying on other pitchers' misfortunes. More accurately, this is a pitcher typically brought into a game after a starting pitcher has put his team behind, and then pitches well enough and long enough to allow his offense to take the lead, thereby "vulturing" a win from the starter. This concept has been losing its relevance with the rising use of Openers. Today's "vulture" is the bulk inning relief pitcher who follows the one-inning Opener and does not have to pitch five innings to qualify for a Win.

In-Season Analysis

Sample size reliability *(Russell Carleton)*

At what sample size do skill and luck each represent 50 percent contributors to a specific metric?

*Measured in batters faced

60:	K/PA
120:	BB/PA

Note that 120 batters faced is roughly equivalent to just shy of five outings for a starting pitcher.

*Measured via balls in play:

50:	HR/F
80:	GB%; FB%
600:	LD%
820:	Hit rate (BABIP)

*Unlisted metrics did not stabilize over a full season of play.

How to read: "After 50 balls in play, the luck-to-skill ratio for home run to fly ball rate has evened out. If a player with a career HR/F rate of 12 percent has an 8 percent rate after 50 balls in play, we can attribute 50% of that new rate to a new skill and the other 50% to random chance." These levels represent the point at which these metrics become useful, though not as direct predictors. Their value is as another data point in the forecasting process.

Can we trust in-season sample size? *(Arik Florimonte)*

When a pitcher's performance deviates significantly from their established history, when can you trust the change? And are there any metrics that are better in short periods than long? Using data from 2010-2017 and filtering for full-time players (≥ 120 IP in a season, or ≥ 25 IP in a month), we were able to answer these questions.

Not surprisingly, there is no magic date for believing the current season's results more than the previous season's; rather, it's more of a continuum. We were able to estimate the point in the season current year-to-date results are more predictive than the prior year's results, noted in the table below by the change from white blocks to black. We also note at which point the previous month alone offers better predictive value than the entire previous year ("PM>PY").

	Months of the Season							PM>PY starting...
K%	A	M	J	J	A	S		July
BB%	A	M	J	J	A	S		Never
GB%	A	M	J	J	A	S		Never
FB%	A	M	J	J	A	S		Never
Soft%	A	M	J	J	A	S		Always
Hard%	A	M	J	J	A	S		May

Prior Year is Better
Year-to-date is Better

Note that due to the date filters used, a month here is roughly equivalent to 25-35 IP, or around 125 batters faced.

Key takeaways:

- Don't fully buy into a change in GB/FB mix or K/BB until June (although you may still want to speculate earlier if you can stash a player on reserve)
- Don't expect last year's hard and soft contact tendencies to continue into the current year.
- Pay some attention to the current year's Soft% and Hard%— there is useful information there—but remember that at best, future outcomes are still 80% noise and regression.
- There is essentially no month-to-month or year-to-year correlation for HR/FB for pitchers. There may be pitchers with a "homer problem," but it is not possible to identify them by looking at home run rates.
- Generally, projections based on prior years' skills should remain your fallback position but keep moving the needle toward the current year's results as the year goes on.

Pure Quality Starts

Pure Quality Starts (PQS) says that the smallest unit of measure should not be the "event" but instead be the "game." Within that game, we can accumulate all the strikeouts, hits and walks, and evaluate that outing as a whole. After all, when a pitcher takes the mound, he is either "on" or "off" his game; he is either dominant or struggling, or somewhere in between.

In PQS, we give a starting pitcher credit for exhibiting certain skills in each of his starts. Then by tracking his "PQS Score" over time, we can follow his progress. A starter earns one point for each of the following criteria:

1. *The pitcher must go more than 6 innings (record at least one out in the 7th). This measures stamina.*
2. *He must allow fewer hits than innings pitched. This measures hit prevention.*
3. *His number of strikeouts must equal to or more than 5. This measures dominance.*
4. *He must strike out at least three times as many batters as he walks (or have a minimum of three strikeouts if he hasn't walked a batter). This measures command.*
5. *He must not allow a home run. This measures his ability to keep the ball in the park.*

A perfect PQS score is 5. Any pitcher who averages 3 or more over the course of the season is probably performing admirably.

The nice thing about PQS is it allows you to approach each start as more than an all-or-nothing event.

Note the absence of earned runs. No matter how many runs a pitcher allows, if he scores high on the PQS scale, he has hurled a good game in terms of his base skills. The number of runs allowed—a function of not only the pitcher's ability but that of his bullpen and defense—will tend to even out over time.

It doesn't matter if a few extra balls got through the infield, or the pitcher was given the hook in the fourth or sixth inning, or the bullpen was able to strand their inherited baserunners. When we look at performance in the aggregate, those events do matter, and will affect a pitcher's skills metrics and ERA. But with PQS, the minutia is less relevant than the overall performance.

In the end, a dominating performance is a dominating performance, whether Max Scherzer hurls six innings of score-less baseball or gives up two runs while striking out 10 in 6 IP. And a disaster is still a disaster, whether Kris Bubic gets pulled in the second inning after allowing 7 runs, or gets a hook after four innings after giving up 6 runs.

Skill versus consistency

Two pitchers have identical 4.50 ERAs and identical 3.0 PQS averages. Their PQS logs look like this:

```
PITCHER A:   3   3   3   3   3
PITCHER B:   5   0   5   0   5
```

Which pitcher would you rather have on your team? The risk-averse manager would choose Pitcher A as he represents the perfectly known commodity. Many fantasy leaguers might opt for Pitcher B because his occasional dominating starts show that there is an upside. His Achilles Heel is inconsistency—he is unable to sustain that high level. Is there any hope for Pitcher B?

- If a pitcher's inconsistency is characterized by more poor starts than good starts, his upside is limited.
- Pitchers with extreme inconsistency rarely get a full season of starts.
- However, inconsistency is neither chronic nor fatal.

The outlook for Pitcher A is actually worse. Disaster avoidance might buy these pitchers more starts, but history shows that the lack of dominating outings is more telling of future potential. In short, consistent mediocrity is bad.

PQS DOMination and DISaster rates *(Gene McCaffrey)*

DOM% is the percentage of a starting pitcher's outings that rate as a PQS-4 or PQS-5. DIS% is the percentage that rate as a PQS-0 or PQS-1.

DOM/DIS percentages open up a new perspective, providing us with two separate scales of performance. In tandem, they measure consistency.

Quality/consistency score (QC)

(DOM% – (2 x DIS%)) x 2)

Using PQS and DOM/DIS percentages, this score measures both the quality of performance as well as start-to-start consistency.

	Sample configurations		
DOM%	Neutral	DIS%	QC
100	0	0	200
70	20	10	100
60	30	10	80
50	30	20	20
50	25	25	0
40	30	30	-40
30	20	50	-140
20	20	60	-200
0	100	0	-400

The Predictive value of PQS *(Arik Florimonte)*

Using data from 2010-2015, research showed that PQS values can be used to project future starts. A pitcher who even threw only one PQS-DOM start had a slightly better chance of throwing another DOM in his subsequent start. For a pitcher who posts two, three, or even four PQS-DOMs in a row, the streak does portend better results to come. The longer the streak, the better the results.

Fantasy owners best positioned to take advantage are those who can frequently choose from multiple similar SP options, such as in a DFS league, or streaming in traditional leagues. In either case, make your evaluations as you normally would (e.g. talent first, then matchups, ballpark or by using BaseballHQ. com's Pitcher Matchups Tool)—and then give a value bump to the pitcher with the hot streak.

PQS correlation with Quality Starts *(Ed DeCaria)*

PQS	QS%	% of all starts	% of all QS	QS Index
0	4%	14%	1%	11
1	9%	22%	4%	17
2	23%	25%	9%	37
3	46%	20%	18%	91
4	71%	14%	28%	204
5	99%	7%	39%	601

High pitch counts and PQS *(Paul Petera)*

A 2017 study found that high-scoring PQS starters who also ran up high pitch counts continued to thrive in their next start (and beyond). Taking three seasons of PQS and pitch-count data, starts were grouped by pitch count into five cohorts and averaged by PQS. The study then calculated the average PQS scores in the subsequent starts, and found that pitchers with higher pitch counts are safer bets to throw well in their next start (and beyond) than those who throw fewer pitches. Near-term fatigue or other negative symptoms do not appear to be worthy of concern; so do not shy away from these pitchers solely for that reason.

In-season ERA/xERA variance as a leading indicator
(Matt Cederholm)

Pitchers with large first-half ERA/xERA variances will see regression towards their xERA in the second half, if they are allowed (and are able) to finish out the season. Starters have a stronger regression tendency than relievers, which we would expect to see given the larger sample size. In addition, there is substantial attrition among all types of pitchers, but those who are "unlucky" have a much higher rate.

An important corollary: While a pitcher underperforming his xERA is very likely to rebound in the second half, such regression hinges on his ability to hold onto his job long enough to see that regression come to fruition. Healthy veteran pitchers with an established role are more likely to experience the second half boost than a rookie starter trying to make his mark.

Pure Quality Relief *(Patrick Davitt)*

A system for evaluating reliever outings. The scoring :

1. Two points for the first out, and one point for each subsequent out, to a maximum of four points.
2. One point for having at least one strikeout for every four full outs (one K for 1-4 outs, two Ks for 5-8 outs, etc.).
3. One point for zero baserunners, minus one point for each baserunner, though allowing the pitcher one unpenalized runner for each three full outs (one baserunner for 3-5 outs, two for 6-8 outs, three for nine outs)
4. Minus one point for each earned run, though allowing one ER for 8– or 9-out appearances.
5. An automatic PQR-0 for allowing a home run.

Avoiding relief disasters *(Ed DeCaria)*

Relief disasters (defined as ER>=3 and IP<=3), occur in 5%+ of all appearances. The chance of a disaster exceeds 13% in any 7-day period. To minimize the odds of a disaster, we created a model that produced the following list of factors, in order of influence:

1. Strength of opposing offense
2. Park factor of home stadium
3. BB/9 over latest 31 days (more walks is bad)
4. Pitch count over previous 7 days (more pitches is bad)
5. Latest 31 Days ERA>xERA (recent bad luck continues)

Daily league owners who can slot relievers by individual game should also pay attention to days of rest: pitching on less rest than one is accustomed to increases disaster risk.

April ERA as a leading indicator *(Stephen Nickrand)*

A starting pitcher's April ERA can act as a leading indicator for how his ERA is likely to fare during the balance of the season. A study looked at extreme April ERA results to see what kind of in-season forecasting power they may have. From 2010-2012, 42 SP posted an ERA in April that was at least 2.00 ER better than their career ERA. The findings:

- Pitchers who come out of the gates quickly have an excellent chance at finishing the season with an ERA much better than their career ERA.
- While April ERA gems see their in-season ERA regresses towards their career ERA, their May-Sept ERA is still significantly better than their career ERA.
- Those who stumble out of the gates have a strong chance at posting an ERA worse than their career average, but their in-season ERA improves towards their career ERA.
- April ERA disasters tend to have a May-Sept ERA that closely resembles their career ERA.

Using K–BB% to find SP buying opportunities *(Arik Florimonte)*

Research showed that finding pitchers who have seen an uptick in K–BB% over the past 30 days is one way to search for mid-season replacements from the waiver wire. Using 2014-2016 player-seasons and filtering for starting pitchers with ≥ 100 IP, the K–BB% mean is about 13%. The overall MLB mean is approximately 12%, and the top 50 SP tend to be 14% or higher.
The findings:

- Last 30 days K–BB% is useful as a gauge of next 30 days performance.
- Pitchers on the upswing are more likely to climb into the elite ranks than other pitchers of similar YTD numbers; pitchers with a larger uptick show a greater likelihood.
- Last-30 K–BB% surgers could be good mid-season pickups if they are being overlooked by other owners in your league.

Second-half ERA reduction drivers *(Stephen Nickrand)*

It's easy to dismiss first-half-to-second-half improvement among starting pitchers as an unpredictable event. After all, the midpoint of the season is an arbitrary cutoff. Performance swings occur throughout the season.

A study of SP who experienced significant 1H-2H ERA improvement from 2010-2012 examined what indicators drove second-half ERA improvement. Among the findings for those 79 SP with a > 1.00 ERA 1H-2H reduction:

- 97% saw their WHIP decrease, with an average decrease of 0.26
- 97% saw their strand (S%) rate improve, with an average increase of 9%
- 87% saw their BABIP (H%) improve, with an average reduction of 5%
- 75% saw their control (bb/9) rate improve, with an average reduction of 0.8
- 70% saw their HR/9 rate improve, with an average decrease of 0.5
- 68% saw their swinging strike (SwK%) rate improve, with an average increase of 1.4%
- 68% saw their BPV improve, with an average increase of 37
- 67% saw their HR per fly ball rate (HR/F) improve, with an average decrease of 4%
- 53% saw their ground ball (GB%) rate improve, with an average increase of 5%
- 52% saw their dominance (k/9) rate improve, with an average increase of 1.3

These findings highlight the power of H% and S% regression as it relates to ERA and WHIP improvement. In fact, H% and S% are more often correlated with ERA improvement than are improved skills. They also suggest that improved control has a bigger impact on ERA reduction than does increased strikeouts.

Pitcher home/road splits *(Stephen Nickrand)*

One overlooked strategy in leagues that allow frequent transactions is to bench pitchers when they are on the road. Research reveals that several pitching stats and indicators are significantly and consistently worse on the road than at home.

Some home/road rules of thumb for SP:

- If you want to gain significant ground in ERA and WHIP, bench all your average or worse SP on the road.
- A pitcher's win percentage drops by 15% on the road, so don't bank on road starts as a means to catch up in wins.
- Control erodes by 10% on the road, so be especially careful with keeping wild SP in your active lineups when they are away from home.
- NL pitchers at home produce significantly more strikeouts than their AL counterparts and vs. all pitchers on the road.
- HR/9, groundball rate, hit rate, strand rate, and HR/F do not show significant home vs. road variances.

Other Diamonds

The Pitching Postulates

1. Never sign a soft-tosser to a long-term contract.
2. Right-brain dominance has a very long shelf life.
3. A fly ball pitcher who gives up many HRs is expected. A GB pitcher who gives up many HRs is making mistakes.
4. Never draft a contact fly ball pitcher who plays in a hitter's park.
5. Only bad teams ever have a need for an inning-eater.
6. Never chase wins.

Dontrelle Willis List

Pitchers with skills metrics so horrible that you have to wonder how they can possibly draw a major league paycheck year after year.

Chaconian

Having the ability to post many saves despite sub-Mendoza metrics and an ERA in the stratosphere. (See: Shawn Chacón, 2004.)

Coors Chum

Soft-tossing fly ball/line drive contact pitchers in the Colorado system. By rights, they should not be allowed anywhere near Coors Field, not even to buy a hot dog. Like Chad Kuhl and Ashton Goudeau.

ERA Benchmark

A half run of ERA over 200 innings comes out to just one earned run every four starts.

The Knuckleballers Rule

Knuckleballers don't follow no stinkin' rules.

Brad Lidge Lament

When a closer posts a 62% strand rate, he has nobody to blame but himself.

Vin Mazzaro Vindication

Occasional nightmares (2.1 innings, 14 ER) are just a part of the game.

PQS Benchmark

Generally, a single DISaster outing requires two DOMinant outings just to get back to par.

The Five Saves Certainties

1. On every team, there will be save opportunities and someone will get them. At a bare minimum, there will be at least 30 saves to go around, and not unlikely more than 45.

2. Any pitcher could end up being the chief beneficiary. Bullpen management is a fickle endeavor.

3. Relief pitchers are often the ones that require the most time at the start of the season to find a groove. The weather is cold, the schedule is sparse and their usage is erratic.

4. Despite the talk about "bullpens by committee," managers prefer a go-to guy. It makes their job easier.

5. As many as 50% of the saves in any year will come from pitchers who are undrafted.

Soft-tosser land

The place where feebler arms leave their fortunes in the hands of the defense, variable hit and strand rates, and park dimensions. It's a place where many live, but few survive.

Vintage Eck Territory

A BPX of over 300. From 1989-1992, Dennis Eckersely posted sub-2.00 ERAs and 300-plus BPXs three times. He had an ERA of 0.61 in 1990. In 1989 and 1990, he posted K/BB ratios over 18.0.

Prospects

General

Minor league prospecting in perspective

In our perpetual quest to be the genius who uncovers the next Mike Trout when he's still in high school, there is an obsessive fascination with minor league prospects. That's not to say that prospecting is not important. The issue is perspective:

1. From 2006 to 2015, 14% of players selected in the first round of the Major League Baseball First Year Player Draft went on to have at least one $20 season in the Majors. From those in the top 10, 32% posted at least one $20 MLB season. There have no $20 seasons from the 2016 or later classes. It takes time to develop.

2. Some prospects are going to hit the ground running (Julio Rodríguez) and some are going to immediately struggle (Vidal Bruján), no matter what level of hype follows them.

3. Some prospects are going to start fast (since the league is unfamiliar with them) and then fade (as the league figures them out). Others will start slow (since they are unfamiliar with the opposition) and then improve (as they adjust to the competition). So if you make your free agent and roster decisions based on small early samples sizes, you are just as likely to be an idiot as a genius.

4. How any individual player will perform relative to his talent is largely unknown because there is a psychological element that is vastly unexplored. Some make the transition to the majors seamlessly, some not, completely regardless of how talented they are.

5. Still, talent is the best predictor of future success, so major league equivalent base performance indicators still have a valuable role in the process. As do scouting reports, carefully filtered.

6. Follow the player's path to the majors. Did he have to repeat certain levels? Was he allowed to stay at a level long enough to learn how to adjust to the level of competition? A player with only two great months at Double-A is a good bet to struggle if promoted directly to the majors because he was never fully tested at Double-A, let alone Triple-A.

7. Younger players holding their own against older competition is a good thing. Older players reaching their physical peak, regardless of their current address, can be a good thing too. The Seth Browns and Joey Meneses can have some very profitable years.

8. Remember team context. A prospect with superior potential often will not unseat a steady but unspectacular incumbent, especially one with a large contract.

9. Don't try to anticipate how a team is going to manage their talent, both at the major and minor league level. You might think it's time to promote Francisco Álvarez and give him an everyday role. You are not running the Mets.

10. Those who play in shallow, one-year leagues should have little cause to be looking at the minors at all. The risk versus reward is so skewed against you, and there is so much talent available with a track record, that taking a chance on an unproven commodity makes little sense.

11. Decide where your priorities really are. If your goal is to win, prospect analysis is just a *part* of the process, not the entire process.

Factors affecting minor league stats *(Terry Linhart)*

1. Often, there is an exaggerated emphasis on short-term performance in an environment that is supposed to focus on the long-term. Two poor outings don't mean a 21-year-old pitcher is washed up.

2. Ballpark dimensions and altitude create hitters parks and pitchers parks. Also, some parks have inconsistent field quality which can artificially depress defensive statistics while inflating stats like batting average. However, these are now isolated issues affecting only some parks (e.g. Chattanooga, Daytona, Durham). When MLB took over managing the minor leagues, they gave MiLB organizations five years (starting in 2021) to correct issues or risk losing their affiliation agreement.

3. Some players' skills are so superior to the competition at their level that you can't get a true picture of what they're going to do from their stats alone.

4. Many pitchers are told to work on secondary pitches in unorthodox situations just to gain confidence in the pitch. The result is an artificially increased number of walks.

5. The #3, #4, and #5 pitchers in the lower minors are truly longshots to make the majors. They often possess only two pitches and are unable to disguise the off-speed offerings. Hitters can see inflated statistics in these leagues.

6. MLB has experimented with a variety of rule changes in the minor leagues since 2021. This includes the use of automated strike zones in the Pacific Coast League (Triple-A), the International League (Triple-A, Charlotte only) and the Florida State League (Low-A) in 2022. These changes have primarily affected base running stats, strike out rates and walk rates depending on the rules being used in a particular league or level.

Minor league level versus age

When evaluating minor leaguers, look at the age of the prospect in relation to the median age of the league he is in:

Low level A	Between 19-20
*Upper level A	Around 21
*Double-A	22
*Triple-A	23

* The lost 2020 pandemic year, along with the contraction of both the draft and number of minor league teams have effectively advanced the ages by a year over where they used to be.

These are the ideal ages for prospects at the particular level. If a prospect is younger than most and holds his own against older and more experienced players, elevate his status. If he is older than the median, reduce his status.

Triple-A experience as a leading indicator

The probability that a minor leaguer will immediately succeed in the majors can vary depending upon the level of Triple-A experience he has amassed at the time of call-up.

	BATTERS		PITCHERS	
	< 1 Yr	Full	< 1 Yr	Full
Performed well	57%	56%	16%	56%
Performed poorly	21%	38%	77%	33%
2nd half drop-off	21%	7%	6%	10%

The odds of a batter achieving immediate MLB success was slightly more than 50/50. More than 80% of all pitchers promoted with less than a full year at Triple-A struggled in their first year in the majors. Those pitchers with a year in Triple-A succeeded at a level equal to that of batters.

When do Top 100 prospects get promoted? *(Jeff Zimmerman)*

We created a simple procedure to determine if—and when—a player will make it to the majors in the season after being ranked in BaseballHQ.com's HQ100 prospect list (2010-17). We examined only the prospects who had not yet played in the majors, and found that the chances of a major league call-up for a healthy hitter or pitcher who last played in each level to be as follows:

- As a veteran in a foreign league: 100%
- In Triple-A: 90%
- In Double-A: 50%
- In A-ball: 20%
- Other: 0%

Additionally, to increase the odds of a call-up, take the (1) higher-ranked player; (2) the older player; and (3) the player on a contending team.

Major League Equivalency (MLE) *(Bill James)*

A formula that converts a player's minor or foreign league statistics into a comparable performance in the major leagues. These are not projections, but conversions of current performance. MLEs contain adjustments for the level of play in individual leagues and teams. They work best with Triple-A stats, not quite as well with Double-A stats, and hardly at all with the lower levels. Foreign conversions are still a work in process. James' original formula only addressed batting. Our research has devised conversion formulas for pitchers, however, their best use comes when looking at skills metrics, not traditional stats.

Adjusting to the competition

All players must "adjust to the competition" at every level of professional play. Players often get off to fast or slow starts. During their second tour at that level is when we get to see whether the slow starters have caught up or whether the league has figured out the fast starters. That second half "adjustment" period is a good baseline for projecting the subsequent season, in the majors or minors.

Premature major league call-ups often negate the ability for us to accurately evaluate a player due to the lack of this adjustment period. For instance, a hotshot Double-A player might open the season in Triple-A. After putting up solid numbers for a month, he gets a call to the bigs, and struggles. The fact is, we do not have enough evidence that the player has mastered the Triple-A

level. We don't know whether the rest of the league would have caught up to him during his second tour of the league. But now he's labeled as an underperformer in the bigs when in fact he has never truly proven his skills at the lower levels.

Bull Durham prospects

There is some potential talent in older players—age 26, 27 or higher—who, for many reasons (untimely injury, circumstance, bad luck, etc.), don't reach the majors until they have already been downgraded from prospect to suspect. Equating potential with age is an economic reality for major league clubs, but not necessarily a skills reality.

Skills growth and decline is universal, whether it occurs at the major league level or in the minors. So a high-skills journeyman in Triple-A is just as likely to peak at age 27 as a major leaguer of the same age. The question becomes one of opportunity—will the parent club see fit to reap the benefits of that peak performance?

Prospecting these players for your fantasy team is, admittedly, a high risk endeavor, though there are some criteria you can use. Look for a player who is/has:

- Optimally, age 27-28 for overall peak skills, age 30-31 for power skills, or age 28-31 for pitchers.
- At least two seasons of experience at Triple-A. Career Double-A players are generally not good picks.
- Solid base skills levels.
- Shallow organizational depth at their position.
- Notable winter league or spring training performance.

Players who meet these conditions are not typically draftable players, but worthwhile reserve or FAB picks.

Deep-league prospecting primer *(Jock Thompson)*

There's no substitute for having a philosophy, objective, and plan for your fantasy farm system. Here's a prospecting process checklist:

Commit to some prospecting time. Sounds intuitive, but some owners either don't have the time or won't take the time to learn about their league's available prospects.

Have a prospecting framework/philosophy. Such as TINSTAPP—there is no such thing as a pitching prospect. The non-linear rise and development of prospects can be frustrating in general, but much more so with pitchers. Unlike with hitters, you're usually safe in forgoing low-minors pitching, and are better off speculating on near-ready pitching names.

Have objectives. Upside vs. MLB proximity is an ongoing dilemma, but rebuilders will always need to take on some faraway high-ceiling flyers.

Devise a strategy and stick with it. You'll need an idea as to how you'll 1) acquire available talent; and 2) upgrade your roster deficiencies. Above all, play out the year. Your team will improve by making good free agent assessments all season—not by taking off in August and September.

Always account for defense. A plus glove is a real advantage in finding MLB opportunity. Versatility and athleticism are even better, and often feed multi-position eligibility.

Consider all the variables. Things like age, opportunity, organization, venue, and club positional needs should all be factors.

Exercise excruciating patience – with legit hitting prospects. Even the most highly-regarded prospects do not grow to the moon in linear fashion.

Speculate readily and be nimble with your in-season pitching moves. If you see something that looks more promising than what you have, grab it fast. If you don't, someone else will.

Pay attention and dig into in-season minor league developments. All of these lights can flicker on and turn into big edges if you can identify them. For example: a plus hit tool guy suddenly begins tapping into power, a pitcher makes in-season mechanical changes, a hitter makes across-the-board improvement following a position change.

Don't dismiss late bloomers with extended MLB opportunity. Like the more publicized names, plenty of lesser prospects have playable talent, and are just late figuring out how to unlock it.

Batters

Identifying Batting Average-led breakouts *(Chris Blessing)*
Much of the chatter around prospect "breakouts" centers around power, but there is a subset of minor leaguers who can provide batting-average-led value. While minor league swing data is much less accessible than for MLB players, key phrases in scouting reports can hold clues to what type of player could emerge. Players who post elite contact rates and low chase rates, possess a solid spray (or all-fields) approach, and have exemplary bat control can often find success early in their MLB careers. Often, these players exhibit topspin-heavy, line-drive and ground-ball contact characteristics. While profiles such as these have tended to decline in recent years, players with many plate appearances and batting-average-forward results like Jeff McNeil and Luis Arraez can become fantasy assets in the right team construction.

MLE PX as a leading indicator *(Bill Macey)*
Looking at minor league performance (as MLE) in one year and the corresponding MLB performance the subsequent year:

	Year 1 MLE	Year 2 MLB
Observations	496	496
Median PX	95	96
Percent PX > 100	43%	46%

In addition, 53% of the players had a MLB PX in year 2 that exceeded their MLE PX in year 1. A slight bias towards improved performance in year 2 is consistent with general career trajectories.

Year 1 MLE PX	Year 2 MLB PX	Pct. Incr	Pct. MLB PX > 100
<= 50	61	70.3%	5.4%
51-75	85	69.6%	29.4%
76-100	93	55.2%	39.9%
101-125	111	47.4%	62.0%
126-150	119	32.1%	66.1%
> 150	142	28.6%	76.2%

Slicing the numbers by performance level, there is a good amount of regression to the mean.

Players rarely suddenly develop power at the MLB level if they didn't previously display that skill in the minors. However, the relatively large gap between the median MLE PX and MLB PX for these players, 125 to 110, confirms the notion that the best players continue to improve once they reach the major leagues.

MLE contact rate as a leading indicator *(Bill Macey)*
There is a strong positive correlation (0.63) between a player's MLE ct% in Year 1 and his actual ct% at the MLB level in Year 2.

MLE ct%	Year 1 MLE ct%	Year 2 MLB ct%
< 70%	69%	68%
70% - 74%	73%	72%
75% - 79%	77%	75%
80% - 84%	82%	77%
85% - 89%	87%	82%
90% +	91%	86%
TOTAL	**84%**	**79%**

There is very little difference between the median MLE BA in Year 1 and the median MLB BA in Year 2:

MLE ct%	Year 1 MLE BA	Year 2 MLB BA
< 70%	.230	.270
70% - 74%	.257	.248
75% - 79%	.248	.255
80% - 84%	.257	.255
85% - 89%	.266	.270
90% +	.282	.273
TOTAL	.261	.262

Excluding the <70% cohort (which was a tiny sample size), there is a positive relationship between MLE ct% and MLB BA.

Pitchers

Skills metrics as a leading indicator for pitching success
The percentage of hurlers that were good investments in the year that they were called up varied by the level of their historical minor league skills metrics prior to that year.

Pitchers who had:	Fared well	Fared poorly
Good indicators	79%	21%
Marginal or poor indicators	18%	82%

The data used here were MLE levels from the previous two years, not the season in which they were called up. The significance? Solid current performance is what merits a call-up, but this is not a good indicator of short-term MLB success, because a) the performance data set is too small, typically just a few month's worth of statistics, and b) for those putting up good numbers at a new minor league level, there has typically not been enough time for the scouting reports to make their rounds.

East Asia Baseball *(Tom Mulhall)*
There has been a slow but steady influx of MLB-ready players from East Asian professional leagues to Major League Baseball, which is especially important in dynasty leagues with larger reserve or farm clubs. The Japanese major leagues (Nippon Professional Baseball) is generally considered to be equivalent to Triple-A ball, though the pitching is possibly better. The Korean league (Korean Baseball Organization) is considered slightly less competitive with less depth, and is roughly comparable to Double-A ball.

When evaluating the potential of Asian League prospects, the key is not to just identify the best players—the key is to identify impact players who have the desire and opportunity to sign with a MLB team. Opportunity is crucial, since players must have a certain number years of professional experience in order to qualify for international free agency, or hope that their team "posts" them early for full free agency. With the success of players like Ichiro, Darvish and Ohtani, it is easy to overestimate the value of drafting these players. Most don't have that impact. Still, for owners who are allowed to carry a large reserve or farm team at reduced salaries, rostering these players before they sign with a MLB club could be a real windfall, especially if your competitors do not do their homework.

When doing your own research, note that in both Japan and Korea, the family name may be listed first, followed by the given name. The *Forecaster* will "westernize" those names for familiarity and ease of use. Names are sometimes difficult to translate into English so the official NPB or KBO designation will be used.

Japan

Baseball was first introduced in 1872 with professional leagues founded in the 1920s. It reached widespread popularity in the 1930s, partially due to exhibition games against American barnstorming teams that included Babe Ruth, Lou Gehrig, and Jimmie Foxx. Baseball is now considered the most popular spectator and participatory sport in Japan. The Nippon Professional Baseball (NPB) has two leagues, the Central League and Pacific League, each consisting of six teams. The Pacific League is currently considered superior to the more conservative Central League. There is also a strong amateur Industrial League, where players like Hideo Nomo and Kosuke Fukudome were discovered.

Statistics are difficult to compare due to differences in the way the game is played in Japan:

1. While strong on fundamentals, Japanese baseball's guiding philosophy remains risk avoidance. Runners rarely take extra bases, batters focus on making contact rather than driving the ball, and managers play for one run at a time. Bunts are more common. As a result, offenses score fewer runs per number of hits, and pitching stats tend to look better.

2. Stadiums in Japan usually have smaller dimensions and shorter fences. This should mean more HRs, but given the style of play, it is the foreign born players who make up much of Japan's power elite. While a few Japanese power hitters such as Shohei Ohtani and Hideki Matsui made a full equivalent transition to MLB, it is still rare for the power to be duplicated.

3. There are more artificial turf fields, which increases the number of ground ball singles. A few stadiums still use all dirt infields.

4. Teams are limited to having four foreign players on an active roster, and they cannot all be hitters or pitchers.

5. Teams have smaller pitching staffs and use a six-man rotation. Starters usually pitch once a week, typically on the same day since Monday is an off-day for the entire league. Some starters will also occasionally pitch in relief between starts. Managers push for complete games, no matter what the score or situation. Because of the style of offense, higher pitch counts are common. Despite superior conditioning, Japanese pitchers tend to burn out early due to overuse.

6. The ball is smaller and lighter, and the strike zone is slightly closer to the batter. Their ball also has more tack than the current MLB ball, which allows for a better spin rate.

7. There is an automatic ejection for hitting a batter in the area of the head and for arguing a call for more than three minutes.

8. Travel is less exhausting, with much shorter distances between teams.

9. If the score remains even after 12 innings, the game goes into the books as a tie.

10. There are 144 games in a season, as opposed to 162 in MLB.

Players may sign with a MLB team out of high school, but this is a rare occurrence and most players sign with a NPB team. Player movement between players signed to a Japanese team and MLB teams is severely restricted by their "posting" system. Japanese teams have far greater control over player contracts than MLB teams. While domestic free agency usually comes a year sooner, players must have nine years of experience before they obtain international free agency. If a player wishes to play in the ML sooner than that, his team must agree to "post" him for free agency. Posting usually comes in the penultimate year of the player's contract but can come sooner if the club agrees. Some teams are more willing to do that than others, usually those with financial problems. Unfortunately, since not all time spent on Injured Reserve counts towards free agency, some teams manipulate the system to delay the required service time. (For example, the SoftBank Hawks are notorious for manipulated the IR to delay the required service time towards free agency.)

The good news is that under the new posting system, a player may now negotiate with all interested MLB teams, rather than be restricted to the team with the highest posting bid. The Japanese team then receives a "release fee" from the MLB club based on a percentage of the total guaranteed value of the contract, usually around 15-20%. This release fee is received if and only if the player signs with a MLB team.

Korea

Baseball was probably introduced in Korean around 1900. Professional leagues developed long after they did in Japan, with the Korean Baseball Organization (KBO) being founded in 1981. The KBO currently has ten teams in one league with no divisions. While many solid players have come from Korea, their professional league is considered a rung lower than Japan, mostly because of less depth in players.

When comparing statistics, consider:

1. Stadiums were very hitter friendly. For example, Jung-ho Park had 40 HR the year before joining the Pirates, and just 15 in his first ML season. To address this issue, a "dejuiced" ball was introduced in 2019 which has decreased the number of home runs.

2. Since there is just one League, the designated hitter rule is universal.

3. Again, there are much shorter travel times in a smaller country.

4. Like Japan, tie games are allowed.

5. The KBO also uses a "pre-tacked" baseball, like Japan.

6. Ejections are rare, as players and managers seldom argue with calls.

7. Korea also plays fewer games, currently 144 in a season.

The KBO has a very similar posting system to Japan, although a Korean team is allowed to post only one player per off-season while a Japanese team has no limits. However, the requisite experience time is "just" seven years.

China/Taiwan
As with other Asian countries, baseball was introduced long ago to China, possibly in the mid-nineteenth century. Professional baseball is in its infancy, although MLB signed an agreement with the Chinese Baseball Association (CBA) in 2019 to help with development. Baseball in Taiwan is more advanced, with the Chinese Professional Baseball League (CPBL) beginning play in 1990. The best players usually sign with a Japanese team but some players have played MLB ball. Coverage on the Chinese leagues will expand as their impact grows.

A list of Asian League players who could move to the majors appears in the Prospects section of the Forecaster, beginning on page 237.

Other Diamonds

Age 26 Paradox
Age 26 is when a player begins to reach his peak skill, no matter what his address is. If circumstances have him celebrating that birthday in the majors, he is a breakout candidate. If circumstances have him celebrating that birthday in the minors, he is washed up.

A-Rod 10-Step Path to Stardom
Not all well-hyped prospects hit the ground running. More often they follow an alternative path:

1. Prospect puts up phenomenal minor league numbers.
2. The media machine gets oiled up.
3. Prospect gets called up, but struggles, Year 1.
4. Prospect gets demoted.
5. Prospect tears it up in the minors, Year 2.
6. Prospect gets called up, but struggles, Year 2.
7. Prospect gets demoted.
8. The media turns their backs. Fantasy leaguers reduce their expectations.
9. Prospect tears it up in the minors, Year 3. The public shrugs its collective shoulders.
10. Prospect is promoted in Year 3 and explodes. Some lucky fantasy leaguer lands a franchise player for under $5.

Some players that are currently stuck at one of the interim steps, and may or may not ever reach Step 10, include Vidal Bruján, Jo Adell and Jared Kelenic. Lewis Brinson has been stuck in a step 6-7-8-9 loop for three years, like Groundhog's Day gone mad. He might never reach step 10.

Bull Durham Gardening Tip
Late bloomers have fewer flowering seasons.

Developmental Dogmata
1. Defense is what gets a minor league prospect to the majors; offense is what keeps him there. *(Deric McKamey)*
2. The reason why rapidly promoted minor leaguers often fail is that they are never given the opportunity to master the skill of "adjusting to the competition."
3. Rookies who are promoted in-season often perform better than those that make the club out of spring training. Inferior March competition can inflate the latter group's perceived talent level.
4. Young players rarely lose their inherent skills. Pitchers may uncover weaknesses and the players may have difficulty adjusting. These are bumps along the growth curve, but they do not reflect a loss of skill.
5. Late bloomers have smaller windows of opportunity and much less chance for forgiveness.
6. The greatest risk in this game is to pay for performance that a player has never achieved.

Quad-A Player
Some outwardly talented prospects simply have a ceiling that's spelled "A-A-A." They may be highly rated prospects—even minor league stars—but are never able to succeed in the majors. They have names like Franklin Barreto, Danny Hultzen, Andy Marte and Brandon Wood. Perhaps we can add Lewis Brinson to this list.

Rule 5 Reminder
Don't ignore the Rule 5 draft lest you ignore the possibility of players like Jose Bautista, Johan Santana, and Jayson Werth. All were Rule 5 draftees.

The following are players were acquired in the first two rounds of the Rule 5 Draft who became at least serviceable Major Leaguers:

Year	Players who eventually stuck
2012	Héctor Rondón, Ryan Pressly, Ender Inciarte
2014	Mark Canha, Delino Deshields, Odúbel Herrera
2015	Joey Rickard, Jake Cave, Ji-Man Choi
2016	Caleb Smith, Anthony Santander
2017	Nestor Cortes, Victor Reyes, Brad Keller, Elieser Hernandez
2018	Jordan Romano, Connor Joe
2020	Akil Baddoo, Garrett Whitlock

Trout Inflation
The tendency for rookies to go for exorbitant draft prices following a year when there was a very good rookie crop.

Gaming

Standard Rules and Variations

Rotisserie Baseball was invented as an elegant confluence of baseball and economics. Whether by design or accident, the result has lasted for more than four decades. But what would Rotisserie and fantasy have been like if the Founding Fathers knew then what we know now about statistical analysis and game design? You can be sure things would be different.

The world has changed since the original game was introduced yet many leagues use the same rules today. New technologies have opened up opportunities to improve elements of the game that might have been limited by the capabilities of the 1980s. New analytical approaches have revealed areas where the original game falls short.

As such, there are good reasons to tinker and experiment; to find ways to enhance the experience.

Following are the basic elements of fantasy competition, those that provide opportunities for alternative rules and experimentation. This is by no means an exhaustive list, but at minimum provides some interesting food-for-thought.

Player pool

Standard: American League-only, National League-only or Mixed League.

AL/NL-only typically drafts 8-12 teams (pool penetration of 49% to 74%). Mixed leagues draft 10-18 teams (31% to 55% penetration), though 15 teams (46%) is a common number.

Drafting of reserve players will increase the penetration percentages. A 12-team AL/NL-only league adding six reserves onto 23-man rosters would draft 93% of the available pool of players on all teams' 25-man rosters.

The draft penetration level determines which fantasy management skills are most important to your league. The higher the penetration, the more important it is to draft a good team. The lower the penetration, the greater the availability of free agents and the more important in-season roster management becomes.

There is no generally-accepted optimal penetration level, but we have often suggested that 75% (including reserves) provides a good balance between the skills required for both draft prep and in-season management.

Alternative pools: There are many options here. Certain leagues draft from within a small group of major league divisions or teams. Some competitions, like home run leagues, only draft batters.

Positional structure

Standard: 23 players. One at each defensive position (though three outfielders may be from any of LF, CF or RF), plus one additional catcher, one middle infielder (2B or SS), one corner infielder (1B or 3B), two additional outfielders and a utility player/designated hitter (which often can be a batter who qualifies anywhere). Nine pitchers, typically holding any starting or relief role.

Open: 25 players. One at each defensive position (plus DH), 5-man starting rotation and two relief pitchers. Nine additional players at any position, which may be a part of the active roster or constitute a reserve list.

40-man: Standard 23 plus 17 reserves. Used in many keeper and dynasty leagues.

Reapportioned: In recent years, new obstacles are being faced by 12-team AL/NL-only leagues thanks to changes in the real game. The 14/9 split between batters and pitchers no longer reflects how MLB teams structure their rosters. Of the 30 teams, each with 26-man rosters, not one contained 14 batters for any length of time.

For fantasy purposes in AL/NL-only leagues, that left a disproportionate draft penetration into the batter and pitcher pools. Assuming MLB teams rostering 13 batters and 13 pitchers:

	BATTERS	PITCHERS
On all MLB rosters	195	195
Players drafted	168	108
Pct.	86%	55%

These drafts are depleting 31% more batters out of the pool than pitchers. Add in those leagues with reserve lists—perhaps an additional six players per team removing another 72 players—and post-draft free agent pools are very thin, especially on the batting side.

The impact is less in 15-team mixed leagues, though the FA pitching pool is still disproportionately deep.

	BATTERS	PITCHERS
On all rosters	390	390
Drafted	210	135
Pct.	54%	35%

One solution is to reapportion the number of batters and pitchers that are rostered. Adding one pitcher slot and eliminating one batter slot may be enough to provide better balance. The batting slot most often removed is the second catcher, since it is the position with the least depth. However, that only serves to populate the free agent pool with a dozen or more worthless catchers.

Beginning in the 2012 season, the Tout Wars AL/NL-only experts leagues opted to eliminate one of the outfield slots and replace it with a "swingman" position. This position could be any batter or pitcher, depending upon the owner's needs at any given time during the season.

Selecting players

Standard: The three most prevalent methods for stocking fantasy rosters are:

Snake/Straight/Serpentine draft: Players are selected in order with seeds reversed in alternating rounds. This method has become the most popular due to its speed, ease of implementation and ease of automation.

In these drafts, the underlying assumption is that value can be ranked relative to a linear baseline. Pick #1 is better than pick #2, which is better than pick #3, and the difference between each pick is assumed to be somewhat equivalent. While a faulty assumption, we must believe in it to assume a level playing field.

Auction: Players are sold to the highest bidder from a fixed budget, typically $260. Auctions provide the team owner with more control over which players will be on his team, but can take twice as long as snake drafts.

The baseline is $0 at the beginning of each player put up for bid. The final purchase price for each player is shaped by many wildly variable factors, from roster need to geographic location of the draft. A $30 player can mean different things to different drafters.

One option that can help reduce the time commitment of auctions is to force minimum bids at each hour mark. You could mandate $15 openers in hour #1; $10 openers in hour #2, etc. This removes some nominating strategy, however.

Pick-a-player / Salary cap: Players are assigned fixed dollar values and owners assemble their roster within a fixed cap. This type of roster-stocking is an individual exercise which results in teams typically having some of the same players.

In these leagues, "value assessment" is taken out of the hands of the owners. Each player has a fixed cost, pre-assigned based on past season performance and/or future expectation.

Stat categories

Standard: The standard statistical categories for Rotisserie leagues are:

4x4: HR, RBI, SB, BA, W, Sv, ERA, WHIP

5x5: HR, R, RBI, SB, BA, W, Sv, K, ERA, WHIP

6x6: Categories typically added are Holds and OPS.

7x7, etc.: Any number of categories may be added.

In general, the more categories you add, the more complicated it is to isolate individual performance and manage the categorical impact on your roster. There is also the danger of redundancy; with multiple categories measuring like stats, certain skills can get over-valued. For instance, home runs are double-counted when using the categories of both HR and slugging average. (Though note that HRs are actually already triple-counted in standard 5x5—HRs, runs, and RBIs)

If the goal is to have categories that create a more encompassing picture of player performance, it is actually possible to accomplish more with less:

Modified 4x4: HR, (R+RBI-HR), SB, OBA, (W+QS), (Sv+Hld), K, ERA

This provides a better balance between batting and pitching in that each has three counting categories and one ratio category. In fact, the balance is shown to be even more notable here:

	BATTING	PITCHING
Pure skill counting stat	HR	K
Ratio category	OBA	ERA
Dependent upon managerial decision	SB	(Sv+Hold)
Dependent upon team support	(R+RBI-HR)	(W+QS)
Alternative or addition to team support:		
Usage/stamina/health	Plate app	Innings

Replacing saves: The problem with the Saves statistic is that we have a scarce commodity that is centered on a small group of players, thereby creating inflated demand for those players. With the rising failure rate for closers these days, the incentive to pay full value for the commodity decreases. The higher the risk, the lower the prices.

We can increase the value of the commodity by reducing the risk. We might do this by increasing the number of players that contribute to that category, thereby spreading the risk around. One way we can accomplish this is by changing the category to Saves + Holds.

Holds are not perfect, but the typical argument about them being random and arbitrary can apply to saves as well. In fact, many of the pitchers who record holds are far more skilled and valuable than closers; they are often called to the mound in much higher leverage situations (a fact backed up by a scan of each pitcher's Leverage Index).

Neither stat is perfect, but together they form a reasonable proxy for overall bullpen performance.

In tandem, they effectively double the player pool of draftable relievers while also flattening the values allotted to those pitchers. The more players around which we spread the risk, the more control we have in managing our pitching staffs.

Replacing wins: Some have argued for replacing the Wins statistic with W + QS (quality starts). This method of scoring gives value to a starting pitcher who pitches well, but fails to receive the win due to his team's poor offense or poor luck. However, with the decline in the average length of starts, the number of QS outings has dropped sharply. W+QS was a good idea a few years ago; less so now. A replacement stat gaining in popularity is Innings Pitched. Pitchers left on the mound for more innings are more likely to be helping your team, regardless of whether they are in line for a win or quality start.

Keeping score

Standard: These are the most common scoring methods:

Rotisserie: Players are evaluated in several statistical categories. Totals of these statistics are ranked by team. The winner is the team with the highest cumulative ranking.

Points: Players receive points for events that they contribute to in each game. Points are totaled for each team and teams are then ranked.

Head-to-Head (H2H): Using Rotisserie or points scoring, teams are scheduled in daily or weekly matchups. The winner of each matchup is the team that finishes higher in more categories (Rotisserie) or scores the most points.

Free agent acquisition

Standard: Three methods are the most common for acquiring free agent players during the season.

First come first served: Free agents are awarded to the first owner who claims them.

Reverse order of standings: Access to the free agent pool is typically in a snake draft fashion with the last place team getting the first pick, and each successive team higher in the standings picking afterwards.

Free agent budget (FAB): Teams are given a set budget at the beginning of the season (typically $100 or $1000) from which they bid on free agents in a closed auction process.

Vickrey FAB: Research has shown that more than 50% of FAB dollars are lost via overbid on an annual basis. Given that this is a scarce commodity, one would think that a system to better manage these dollars might be desirable. The Vickrey system conducts a closed auction in the same way as standard FAB, but the price of the winning bid is set at the amount of the second highest bid, plus $1. In some cases, gross overbids (at least $10 over) are reduced to the second highest bid plus $5.

This method was designed by William Vickrey, a Professor of Economics at Columbia University. His theory was that this process reveals the true value of the commodity. For his work, Vickrey was awarded the Nobel Prize for Economics (and $1.2 million) in 1996.

The season

Standard: Leagues are played out during the course of the entire Major League Baseball season.

Split-season: Leagues are conducted from Opening Day through the All-Star break, then re-drafted to play from the All-Star break through the end of the season.

50-game split-season: Leagues are divided into three 50-game seasons with one-week break in between.

Monthly: Leagues are divided into six seasons or rolling four-week seasons.

The advantages of these shorter time frames:

- They can help to maintain interest. There would be fewer abandoned teams.
- There would be more shots at a title each year.
- Given that drafting is considered the most fun aspect of the game, these splits multiply the opportunities to participate in some type of draft. Leagues may choose to do complete re-drafts and treat the year as distinct mini-seasons. Or, leagues might allow teams to drop their five worst players and conduct a restocking draft at each break.

Daily games: Participants select a roster of players from one day's MLB schedule. Scoring is based on an aggregate points-based system rather than categories, with cash prizes awarded based on the day's results. The structure and distribution of that prize pool varies across different types of events, and those differences can affect roster construction strategies. Although scoring and prizes are based on one day's play, the season-long element of bankroll management provides a proxy for overall standings.

In terms of projecting outcomes, daily games are drastically different than full-season leagues. Playing time is one key element of any projection, and daily games offer near-100% accuracy in projecting playing time: you can check pre-game lineups to see exactly which players are in the lineup that night. The other key component of any projection is performance, but that is plagued by variance in daily competitions. Even if you roster a team full of the most advantageous matchups, the best hitters can still go 0-for-4 on a given night.

Draft Process

Draft-day cheat sheet *(Patrick Davitt)*

1. Know what players are available, right to the bottom of the pool.
2. Know what every player is worth in your league format.

3. Know why you think each player is worth what you think he's worth.
4. Identify players you believe you value differently from the other owners.
5. Know each player's risks.
6. Know your opponents' patterns.
7. For sure, know the league rules and its history, and what it takes to win.

Draft preparation with a full-season mindset *(Matt Dodge)*

Each of the dimensions of your league setup—player pool, reserve list depth; type and frequency of transactions, scoring categories, etc.—should impact your draft day plan. But it may also be helpful to look at them in combination.

Sources of additional stats after draft day

	League Player Pool	
Reserve List	Mixed 15 team	AL- or NL-only 12 team
Short	free agents	trades, free agents
Long	free agents, trades	trades

Review the prior season's transactions for your league and analyze the successful teams' category contributions from trade acquisitions and free agent pickups. Trades are often necessary to add specific stats in AL/NL-only leagues as the player pool penetration is generally much deeper, and the size of a reserve roster further reduces the help possible from the free agent pool.

Draft strategies related to in-season player acquisition

	Trade Activity	
FA Pool	Low	High
Shallow	solid foundation (STR)	tradable commodoties surplus counting stats
Deep	gamble on upside (S&S)	ultimate flexibility

Trading activity is a function of multiple factors. Keeper leagues provide opportunities for owners to contend this year or play for next year. However, those increased opportunities are often controlled by rules to prevent "dump trading." Stratification of the standings in redraft leagues can cause lower ranked owners to lose interest, reducing the number of effective trading partners as the season goes on.

When deep rosters create a shallow free agent pool in a league with little trading, draft day success becomes paramount. In this case, a Spread the Risk strategy designed to accumulate at bats, innings, and saves is recommended. If the free agent pool is deep, the drafter can take more risks with a Stars and Scrubs approach, acquiring "lottery ticket" players with upside, knowing that replacements are readily available if the upside plays don't hit.

In leagues where trading is prevalent, a shallow free agent pool means you should acquire players on draft day with the intent of trading them. This could mean acquiring a category surplus (frequently saves and/or steals), and then trading it in-season to shore up other categories. In a keeper league, this includes grabbing a few bargains (to interest rebuilding teams) or grabbing top performers to flip in trade (if you are on "the two year plan").

Draft Day Considerations for In-season Roster Management

Reserve List Txn Freq	4 x 4 League Format	5 x 5 League Format
Daily	careful SP management batting platoons positional flexibility	RP (K, ERA, WHIP) batting platoons positional flexibility
Weekly	SP (2 start weeks) cover risky starters	SP (2 start weeks) cover risky starters

Owners must be careful with pitching, due to the negative impact potential of ERA and WHIP. Blindly streaming pitchers on a daily basis can be counter-productive, particularly in 4x4 leagues. In 5x5, the Strikeouts category can make a foundation of high Dom relievers a useful source of mitigation for the invariable starting pitching disappointments.

The degree that these recommendations can be implemented is also dependent on the depth of the reserve list. Those with more reserves can do more than those with fewer, obviously, but the key is deciding up front how you plan to use your reserves, and then tailoring your draft strategy toward that usage.

The value of mock drafts *(Todd Zola)*

Most assume the purpose of a mock draft is to get to know the market value of the player pool. But even more important, mock drafting is general preparation for the environment and process, thereby allowing the drafter to completely focus on the draft when it counts. Mock drafting is more about fine-tuning your strategy than player value. Here are some tips to maximize your mock drafting experience.

1. Make sure you can seamlessly use an on-line drafting room, draft software or your own lists to track your draft or auction. The less time you spend looking, adding and adjusting names, the more time you can spend on thinking about what player is best for your team. This also gives you the opportunity to make sure your draft lists are complete, and assures all the players are listed at the correct position(s).

2. Alter the draft slots of your mocks. The flow of each mock will be different, but if you do a few mocks with an early initial pick, a few in the middle and a few with a late first pick, you may learn you prefer one of the spots more than the others. If you're in a league where you can choose your draft spot, this helps you decide where to select. Once you know your spot, a few mocks from that spot will help you decide how to deal with positional runs.

3. Use non-typical strategies and consider players you rarely target. We all have our favorite players. Intentionally passing on those players not only gives you an idea when others may draft them but it also forces you to research players you normally don't consider. The more players you have researched, the more prepared you'll be for any series of events that occurs during your real draft.

Snake Drafting

Snake draft first round history

The following tables record the comparison between pre-season projected player rankings (using Average Draft Position data from Mock Draft Central and National Fantasy Baseball Championship) and actual end-of-season results. The 18-year

success rate of identifying each season's top talent is only 33.7%. Even if we extend the study to the top two rounds, the hit rate is only around 50%.

2015	ADP		ACTUAL = 4
1	Mike Trout	1	Jake Arrieta
2	Andrew McCutchen	2	Zack Greinke
3	Clayton Kershaw	3	Clayton Kershaw (3)
4	Giancarlo Stanton	4	Paul Goldschmidt (5)
5	Paul Goldschmidt	5	A.J. Pollock
6	Miguel Cabrera	6	Dee Gordon
7	Jose Abreu	7	Bryce Harper
8	Carlos Gomez	8	Josh Donaldson
9	Jose Bautista	9	Jose Altuve (12)
10	Edwin Encarnacion	10	Mike Trout (1)
11	Felix Hernandez	11	Nolan Arenado
12	Jose Altuve	12	Manny Machado
13	Anthony Rizzo	13	Dallas Keuchel
14	Adam Jones	14	Max Scherzer
15	Troy Tulowitzki	15	Nelson Cruz

2016	ADP		ACTUAL = 7
1	Mike Trout	1	Mookie Betts
2	Paul Goldschmidt	2	Jose Altuve (11)
3	Bryce Harper	3	Mike Trout (1)
4	Clayton Kershaw	4	Jonathan Villar
5	Josh Donaldson	5	Jean Segura
6	Carlos Correa	6	Max Scherzer (15)
7	Nolan Arenado	7	Paul Goldschmidt (2)
8	Manny Machado	8	Charlie Blackmon
9	Anthony Rizzo	9	Clayton Kershaw (4)
10	Giancarlo Stanton	10	Nolan Arenado (7)
11	Jose Altuve	11	Daniel Murphy
12	Kris Bryant	12	Kris Bryant (12)
13	Miguel Cabrera	13	Joey Votto
14	Andrew McCutchen	14	Jon Lester
15	Max Scherzer	15	Madison Bumgarner

2017	ADP		ACTUAL = 5
1	Mike Trout	1	Charlie Blackmon
2	Mookie Betts	2	Jose Altuve (4)
3	Clayton Kershaw	3	Corey Kluber
4	Jose Altuve	4	Max Scherzer (12)
5	Kris Bryant	5	Paul Goldschmidt (7)
6	Nolan Arenado	6	Giancarlo Stanton
7	Paul Goldschmidt	7	Chris Sale
8	Manny Machado	8	Aaron Judge
9	Bryce Harper	9	Dee Gordon
10	Trea Turner	10	Clayton Kershaw (3)
11	Josh Donaldson	11	Nolan Arenado (6)
12	Max Scherzer	12	Jose Ramirez
13	Anthony Rizzo	13	Joey Votto
14	Madison Bumgarner	14	Marcell Ozuna
15	Carlos Correa	15	Elvis Andrus

2018	ADP		ACTUAL = 3*
1	Mike Trout	1	Mookie Betts (7)
2	Jose Altuve	2	Christian Yelich
3	Nolan Arenado	3	J.D. Martinez
4	Trea Turner	4	Max Scherzer (11)
5	Clayton Kershaw	5	Jacob deGrom
6	Paul Goldschmidt	6	Jose Ramirez
7	Mookie Betts	7	Francisco Lindor
8	Giancarlo Stanton	8	Trevor Story
9	Charlie Blackmon	9	Justin Verlander
10	Bryce Harper	10	Mike Trout (1)
11	Max Scherzer	11	Blake Snell
12	Chris Sale	12	Javier Baez
13	Corey Kluber	13	Whit Merrifield
14	Carlos Correa	14	Aaron Nola
15	Kris Bryant	15	Manny Machado

2018 represents the lowest first round hit rate in 15 years. However, the next four players on the list would be: 16) Trea Turner (4); 17) Chris Sale (12); 18) Nolan Arenado (3); 19) Corey Kluber (13)

2019	ADP		ACTUAL = 4
1	Mike Trout	1	Justin Verlander
2	Mookie Betts	2	Gerrit Cole
3	Jose Ramirez	3	Christian Yelich (6)
4	Max Scherzer	4	Ronald Acuna (8)
5	J.D. Martinez	5	Cody Bellinger
6	Christian Yelich	6	Rafael Devers
7	Nolan Arenado	7	Anthony Rendon
8	Ronald Acuna	8	Jacob deGrom (10)
9	Trea Turner	9	Jonathan Villar
10	Jacob deGrom	10	Trevor Story
11	Alex Bregman	11	Nolan Arenado (7)
12	Chris Sale	12	Ketel Marte
13	Francisco Lindor	13	D.J. LeMahieu
14	Aaron Judge	14	Zack Greinke
15	Jose Altuve	15	Xander Bogaerts

Similar to 2018, the next players on the 2019 list would be: 16) Alex Bregman (11); 17) Mookie Betts (2); 18) Mike Trout (1); 19) Trea Turner (9)

2020	ADP		ACTUAL = 5
1	Ronald Acuna	1	Shane Bieber
2	Christian Yelich	2	Trea Turner (8)
3	Cody Bellinger	3	Fernando Tatis, Jr.
4	Gerrit Cole	4	Jose Ramirez (11)
5	Mookie Betts	5	Trevor Bauer
6	Mike Trout	6	Mookie Betts (5)
7	Francisco Lindor	7	Freddie Freeman
8	Trea Turner	8	Jose Abreu
9	Jacob deGrom	9	Manny Machado
10	Trevor Story	10	Marcell Ozuna
11	Jose Ramirez	11	Yu Darvish
12	Juan Soto	12	Trevor Story (10)
13	Justin Verlander	13	Adalberto Mondesi
14	Nolan Arenado	14	Juan Soto (12)
15	Max Scherzer	15	Kenta Maeda

2021	ADP		ACTUAL = 3
1	Ronald Acuna	1	Trea Turner (8)
2	Fernando Tatis, Jr.	2	Shohei Ohtani*
3	Juan Soto	3	Bo Bichette
4	Mookie Betts	4	Vladimir Guerrero, Jr.
5	Jacob deGrom	5	Starling Marte
6	Mike Trout	6	Max Scherzer
7	Gerrit Cole	7	Fernando Tatis, Jr. (2)
8	Trea Turner	8	Jose Ramirez (10)
9	Shane Bieber	9	Walker Buehler
10	Jose Ramirez	10	Cedric Mullins III
11	Christian Yelich	11	Marcus Semien
12	Trevor Story	12	Whit Merrifield
13	Freddie Freeman	13	Teoscar Hernandez
14	Trevor Bauer	14	Bryce Harper
15	Cody Bellinger	15	Zack Wheeler

* Includes earnings as both hitter and pitcher. Ohtani ranked 9th overall on his hitting stats alone.

2022	ADP		ACTUAL = 3
1	Trea Turner	1	Aaron Judge
2	Jose Ramirez	2	Shohei Ohtani (7)*
3	Juan Soto	3	Freddie Freeman
4	Vladimir Guerrero, Jr.	4	Paul Goldschmidt
5	Bo Bichette	5	Trea Turner (1)
6	Gerrit Cole	6	Jose Ramirez (2)
7	Shohei Ohtani	7	Justin Verlander
8	Bryce Harper	8	Manny Machado
9	Corbin Burnes	9	Pete Alonso
10	Kyle Tucker	10	Dansby Swanson
11	Mike Trout	11	Francisco Lindor
12	Rafael Devers	12	Julio Rodriguez
13	Ronald Acuna	13	Jose Altuve
14	Mookie Betts	14	Sandy Alcantara
15	Luis Robert	15	Yordan Alvarez

* Includes earnings as both hitter and pitcher. Ohtani ranked outside the top 15 on his hitting or pitching stats alone. So if you are in a league where you can only use Ohtani as batter or pitcher in any given week, he drops out of the ranking here. In that case, move up the players ranked 3-15 and add Mookie Betts (14) at No. 15.

ADP attrition

Why is our success rate so low in identifying what should be the most easy-to-project players each year? We rank and draft players based on the expectation that those ranked higher will return greater value in terms of productivity and playing time, as well as being the safest investments. However, there are many variables affecting where players finish.

Earlier, it was shown that players spend an inordinate number of days on the injured list. In fact, of the players projected to finish in the top 300, the number who were placed on the injury list, demoted or designated for assignment has been extreme:

Year	Pct. of top-ranked 300 players who lost PT
2012	45%
2013	51%
2014	53%
2015	47%
2016	47%
2017	58%
2018	60%
2019	59%
2020*	43%
2021	71%
2022	59%

*In 60 games.

When you consider that well over half of each season's very best players had fewer at-bats or innings pitched than we projected, it shows how tough it is to rank players each year.

The Ineptitude of ADPs

What is our true aptitude in accurately ranking players each year? It's very, very bad. Using the ADPs from a 15-team mixed league (2018 and 2019), we looked at each player, round by round and tagged each one:

- PROFIT: Turned a profit on the round he was drafted in
- PAR: Earned back the exact value of the round he was drafted in
- LOSS: Took a 1-3 round loss on his draft round
- BUST: Took a 4-plus round loss on his draft round
- DISASTER: Returned earnings outside the top 750 players, essentially undraftable in a league with 50-man rosters. Disasters are subsets of Busts.

2018					
Rds	Profit	Par	Loss	Bust	Dis
1-5	21%	8%	27%	44%	4%
6-10	24%	7%	24%	45%	4%
11-15	27%	3%	9%	61%	27%
16-20	37%	1%	8%	53%	25%
21-25	41%	1%	4%	53%	21%
26-30	40%	0%	0%	60%	35%
31-35	15%	0%	0%	85%	76%
36-40	15%	1%	0%	84%	79%
41-45	19%	3%	1%	77%	76%
46-50	28%	0%	3%	69%	68%

2019					
Rds	**Profit**	**Par**	**Loss**	**Bust**	**Dis**
1-5	20%	13%	21%	45%	4%
6-10	28%	8%	12%	52%	5%
11-15	35%	0%	5%	60%	15%
16-20	31%	3%	7%	60%	27%
21-25	37%	3%	4%	56%	39%
26-30	39%	4%	7%	51%	33%
31-35	35%	0%	1%	64%	49%
36-40	32%	0%	3%	65%	55%
41-45	37%	0%	3%	60%	57%
46-50	33%	0%	3%	64%	64%

For starters, there is no such thing as "Player-X is a Y-rounder." We had virtually no ability to identify exactly where a player should be drafted. Over the first five rounds, we got about 90 percent of them wrong and nearly half our picks were full-out busts. Over the rest of the draft, the right answers were blind dart throws.

Our percentage of profitable picks increased as we progressed through the active draft rounds. However, much of that is just probability; the deeper into a draft, the more room for picks to finish higher. In most cases the draft round was random. Rounds 21-30 were the sweet spot for profitable picks. We fared best after the active part of the draft was mostly over.

2018					
Rds	**Profit**	**Par**	**Loss**	**Bust**	**Dis**
1-23	30%	4%	16%	50%	15%
24-50	24%	1%	1%	75%	64%

2019					
Rds	**Profit**	**Par**	**Loss**	**Bust**	**Dis**
1-23	30%	5%	10%	55%	16%
24-50	35%	1%	3%	60%	51%

In the active roster draft, a third of our picks performed at par or better; two thirds performed worse than where we drafted them. Fully half of them could have been considered busts. In other words, *every player we drafted had, at best, only a one-in-three chance of being a good pick.*

Importance of the early rounds *(Bill Macey)*
It's long been said that you can't win your league in the first round, but you can lose it there. An analysis of data from actual drafts reveals that this holds true—those who spend an early round pick on a player that severely under-performs expectations rarely win their league and seldom even finish in the top 3.

At the same time, drafting a player in the first round that actually returns first-round value is no guarantee of success. In fact, those that draft some of the best values still only win their league about a quarter of the time and finish in the top 3 less than half the time. Research also shows that drafting pitchers in the first round is a risky proposition. Even if the pitchers deliver first-round value, the opportunity cost of passing up on an elite batter makes you less likely to win your league.

The Impact of the draft on final statistics *(Todd Zola)*
Which has more impact on your team's final standings—your draft or in-season roster management? The standings correlation based on draft-to-final results ranges from 0.42 to 0.94, with the mean around 0.73. The top hitting counting stat drafted is home runs; the fewest is stolen bases. The top pitching counting stat drafted is saves; the fewest is wins. More hitting is acquired at the draft or auction than pitching. The in-season influx of stats is greatest in Mixed Leagues, suggesting that owners should practice patience with in-season free agents in AL/NL formats while being cautiously aggressive in Mixed formats.

Top teams almost always improve ratio categories from their drafted rosters, despite available free agents sporting poorer aggregate ratios. This is most applicable to improving your pitching staff as the year progresses, but it's easier said than done.

Being top-three in saves is far more important in Mixed leagues than in AL/NL. Most Mixed champions draft the majority of saves while AL/NL winners often acquire saves in season.

What is the best seed to draft from?
Most drafters like mid-round so they never have to wait too long for their next player. Some like the swing pick, suggesting that getting two players at 15 and 16 is better than a 1 and a 30. Many drafters assume that the swing pick means you'd be getting something like two $30 players instead of a $40 and $20.

Equivalent auction dollar values reveal the following facts about the first two snake draft rounds:

In an AL/NL-only league, the top seed would get a $44 player (at #1) and a $24 player (at #24) for a total of $68; the 12th seed would get two $29s (at #12 and #13) for $58.

In a mixed league, the top seed would get a $47 and a $24 ($71); the 15th seed would get two $28s ($56).

Since the talent level flattens out after the 2nd round, low seeds never get a chance to catch up:

$ difference between first player/last player selected		
Round	**12-team**	**15-team**
1	$15	$19
2	$7	$8
3	$5	$4
4	$3	$3
5	$2	$2
6	$2	$1
7-17	$1	$1
18-23	$0	$0

The total value each seed accumulates at the end of the draft is hardly equitable:

Seed	Mixed	AL/NL-only
1	$266	$273
2	$264	$269
3	$263	$261
4	$262	$262
5	$259	$260
6	$261	$260
7	$260	$260
8	$261	$260
9	$261	$258
10	$257	$260
11	$257	$257
12	$258	$257
13	$254	
14	$255	
15	$256	

The counter-argument to this focuses on whether we can reasonably expect "accurate projections" at the top of the draft. Given the snake draft first round history, a case could be made that any seed might potentially do well. In fact, an argument can be made that the last seed is the best spot because it essentially provides two picks from the top 13 players (in a 12-team league) during the part of the draft with the steepest talent decline.

Using ADPs to determine when to select players *(Bill Macey)*

Although average draft position (ADP) data provides a good idea of where in the draft each player is selected, it can be misleading when trying to determine how early to target a player. This chart summarizes the percentage of players drafted within 15 picks of his ADP as well as the average standard deviation by grouping of players.

ADP Rank	% within 15 picks	Standard Deviation
1-25	100%	2.5
26-50	97%	6.1
51-100	87%	9.6
100-150	72%	14.0
150-200	61%	17.4
200-250	53%	20.9

As the draft progresses, the picks for each player become more widely dispersed and less clustered around the average. Most top 100 players will go within one round of their ADP-converted round. However, as you reach the mid-to-late rounds, there is much more uncertainty as to when a player will be selected. Pitchers have slightly smaller standard deviations than do batters (i.e. they tend to be drafted in a narrower range). This suggests that drafters may be more likely to reach for a batter than for a pitcher.

Using the ADP and corresponding standard deviation, we can to estimate the likelihood that a given player will be available at a certain draft pick. We estimate the predicted standard deviation for each player as follows:

Stdev = -0.42 + 0.42*(ADP - Earliest Pick)

(That the figure 0.42 appears twice is pure coincidence; the numbers are not equal past two decimal points.)

If we assume that the picks are normally distributed, we can use a player's ADP and estimated standard deviation to estimate the likelihood that the player is available with a certain pick (MS Excel formula):

=1-normdist(x,ADP,Standard Deviation,True)

where «x» represents the pick number to be evaluated.

We can use this information to prepare for a snake draft by determining how early we may need to reach in order to roster a player. Suppose you had the 8th pick in a 15-team league draft and your target was a player with an ADP of 128.9 and an earliest selection at pick 94. This would yield an estimated standard deviation of 14.2. You could have then entered these values into the formula above to estimate the likelihood that this player was still available at each of the following picks:

Pick	Likelihood Available
83	100%
98	99%
113	87%
128	53%
143	16%
158	2%

ADPs and scarcity *(Bill Macey)*

Most players are selected within a round or two of their ADP with tight clustering around the average. But every draft is unique and every pick in the draft seemingly affects the ordering of subsequent picks. In fact, deviations from "expected" sequences can sometimes start a chain reaction at that position. This is most often seen in runs at scarce positions such as the closer; once the first one goes, the next seems sure to closely follow.

Research also suggests that within each position, there is a correlation within tiers of players. The sooner players within a generally accepted tier are selected, the sooner other players within the same tier will be taken. However, once that tier is exhausted, draft order reverts to normal.

How can we use this information? If you notice a reach pick, you can expect that other drafters may follow suit. If your draft plan is to get a similar player within that tier, you'll need to adjust your picks accordingly.

Mapping ADPs to auction value *(Bill Macey)*

Reliable average auction values (AAV) are often tougher to come by than ADP data for snake drafts. However, we can estimate predicted auction prices as a function of ADP, arriving at the following equation:

y = -9.8ln(x) + 57.8

where ln(x) is the natural log function, x represents the actual ADP, and y represents the predicted AAV.

This equation does an excellent job estimating auction prices ($r2=0.93$), though deviations are unavoidable. The asymptotic nature of the logarithmic function, however, causes the model to predict overly high prices for the top players. So be aware of that, and adjust.

Auction Value Analysis

Auction values (R$) in perspective

R$ is the dollar value placed on a player's statistical performance in a Rotisserie league, and designed to measure the impact that player has on the standings.

There are several methods to calculate a player's value from his projected (or actual) statistics.

One method is Standings Gain Points, described in the book, *How to Value Players for Rotisserie Baseball*, by Art McGee. SGP converts a player's statistics in each Rotisserie category into the number of points those stats will allow you to gain in the standings. These are then converted back into dollars.

Another popular method is the Percentage Valuation Method. In PVM, a least valuable, or replacement performance level is set for each category (in a given league size) and then values are calculated representing the incremental improvement from that base. A player is then awarded value in direct proportion to the level he contributes to each category.

As much as these methods serve to attach a firm number to projected performance, the winning bid for any player is still highly variable depending upon many factors:

- the salary cap limit
- the number of teams in the league
- each team's roster size
- the impact of any protected players
- each team's positional demands at the time of bidding
- the statistical category demands at the time of bidding
- external factors, e.g. media inflation or deflation of value

In other words, a $30 player is only a $30 player if someone in your draft pays $30 for him.

Roster slot valuation *(John Burnson)*

When you draft a player, what have you bought?

"You have bought the stats generated by this player."

No. You have bought the stats generated by his slot. Initially, the drafted player fills the slot, but he need not fill the slot for the season, and he need not contribute from Day One. If you trade the player during the season, then your bid on Draft Day paid for the stats of the original player plus the stats of the new player. If the player misses time due to injury or demotion, then you bought the stats of whoever fills the time while the drafted player is missing. At season's end, there will be more players providing positive value than there are roster slots.

Before the season, the number of players projected for positive value has to equal the total number of roster slots. However, the projected productivity should be adjusted by the potential to capture extra value in the slot. This is especially important for injury-rehab cases and late-season call-ups. For example, if we think that a player will miss half the season, then we would augment his projected stats with a half-year of stats from a replacement-level player at his position. Only then would we calculate prices. Essentially, we want to apportion $260 per team among the slots, not the players.

Average player value by draft round

Rd	AL/NL	Mxd
1	$34	$34
2	$26	$26
3	$23	$23
4	$20	$20
5	$18	$18
6	$17	$16
7	$16	$15
8	$15	$13
9	$13	$12
10	$12	$11
11	$11	$10
12	$10	$9
13	$9	$8
14	$8	$8
15	$7	$7
16	$6	$6
17	$5	$5
18	$4	$4
19	$3	$3
20	$2	$2
21	$1	$2
22	$1	$1
23	$1	$1

Benchmarks for auction players:

- All $30 players will go in the first round.
- All $20-plus players will go in the first four rounds.
- Double-digit value ends pretty much after Round 11.
- The $1 end game starts at about Round 21.

How likely is it that a $30 player will repeat? *(Matt Cederholm)*

From 2003-2008, there were 205 players who earned $30 or more (using single-league 5x5 values). Only 70 of them (34%) earned $30 or more in the next season.

In fact, the odds of repeating a $30 season aren't good. As seen below, the best odds during that period were 42%. And as we would expect, pitchers fare far worse than hitters.

	Total>$30	# Repeat	% Repeat
Hitters	167	64	38%
Pitchers	38	6	16%
Total	205	70	34%
*High-Reliability**			
Hitters	42	16	38%
Pitchers	7	0	0%
Total	49	16	33%
100+ BPV			
Hitters	60	25	42%
Pitchers	31	6	19%
Total	91	31	19%
*High-Reliability and 100+ BPV**			
Hitters	12	5	42%
Pitchers	6	0	0%
Total	18	5	28%

Reliability figures are from 2006-2008

For players with multiple seasons of $30 or more, the numbers get better. Players with consecutive $30 seasons, 2003-2008:

	Total>$30	# Repeat	% Repeat
Two Years	62	29	55%
Three+ Years	29	19	66%

Still, a player with two consecutive seasons at $30 in value is barely a 50/50 proposition. And three consecutive seasons is only a 2/3 shot. Small sample sizes aside, this does illustrate the nature of the beast. Even the most consistent, reliable players fail 1/3 of the time. Of course, this is true whether they are kept or drafted anew, so this alone shouldn't prevent you from keeping a player.

Dollar values: expected projective accuracy

There is a 65% chance that a player projected for a certain dollar value will finish the season with a value within plus-or-minus $5 of that projection. Therefore, if you value a player at $25, you only have about a 2-in-3 shot of him finishing between $20 and $30.

If you want to raise your odds to 80%, the range becomes +/- $9, so your $25 player has to finish somewhere between $16 and $34.

Predicting player value from year 1 performance *(Patrick Davitt)*

Year-1 (Y1, first season >=100AB) batter results predict some—but not all—subsequent-year performance. About half of all Y1players have positive value. Players with higher Y1 value were likelier to get playing time in subsequent seasons. Players with –$6 to –$10 in Y1 got more chances than players +$5 to –$5 and performed better. Batters with Y1 value of $16 or more are excellent bets to at least provide positive value in subsequent seasons, and those above $21 in Y1 value play in all subsequent seasons and return an average of $26. But even a $21 batter is only a 50-50 bet to do better in Y2.

How well do elite pitchers retain their value? *(Michael Weddell)*

An elite pitcher (one who earns at least $24 in a season) on average keeps 80% of his R$ value from year 1 to year 2. This compares to the baseline case of only 52%.

Historically, 36% of elite pitchers improve, returning a greater R$ in the second year than they did the first year. That is an impressive performance considering they already were at an elite level. 17% collapse, returning less than a third of their R$ in the second year. The remaining 47% experience a middling outcome, keeping more than a third but less than all of their R$ from one year to the next.

Valuing closers

Given the high risk associated with the closer's role, it is difficult to determine a fair draft value. Typically, those who have successfully held the role for several seasons will earn the highest draft price, but valuing less stable commodities is troublesome.

A rough rule of thumb is to start by paying $10 for the role alone. Any pitcher tagged the closer on draft day should merit at least $10. Those without a firm appointment may start at less than $10. Then add anywhere from $0 to $15 for support skills.

In this way, the top level talents will draw upwards of $20-$25. Those with moderate skill will draw $15-$20, and those with more questionable skill in the $10-$15 range.

Realistic expectations of $1 end-gamers *(Patrick Davitt)*

Many fantasy articles insist leagues are won or lost with $1 batters, because "that's where the profits are." But are they?

A 2011 analysis showed that when considering $1 players in deep leagues, managing $1 end-gamers should be more about minimizing losses than fishing for profit. In the cohort of batters projected $0 to -$5, 82% returned losses, based on a $1 bid. Two-thirds of the projected $1 cohort returned losses. In addition, when considering $1 players, speculate on speed.

Advanced Drafting Concepts

Stars & Scrubs v. Spread the Risk

Stars & Scrubs (S&S): A Rotisserie auction strategy in which a roster is anchored by a core of high priced stars and the remaining positions filled with low-cost players.

Spread the Risk (STR): An auction strategy in which available dollars are spread evenly among all roster slots.

Both approaches have benefits and risks. An experiment was conducted in 2004 whereby a league was stocked with four teams assembled as S&S, four as STR and four as a control group. Rosters were then frozen for the season.

The Stars & Scrubs teams won all three ratio categories. Those deep investments ensured stability in the categories that are typically most difficult to manage. On the batting side, however, S&S teams amassed the least amount of playing time, which in turn led to bottom-rung finishes in HRs, RBIs and Runs.

One of the arguments for the S&S approach is that it is easier to replace end-game losers (which, in turn, may help resolve the playing time issues). Not only is this true, but the results of this experiment show that replacing those bottom players is critical to success.

The Spread the Risk teams stockpiled playing time, which led to strong finishes in many counting stats, including clear victories in RBIs, wins and strikeouts. This is a key tenet in drafting philosophy; we often say that the team that compiles the most ABs will be among the top teams in RBI and Runs.

The danger is on the pitching side. More innings did yield more wins and Ks, but also destroyed ERA/WHIP.

So, what approach makes the most sense? **The optimal strategy might be to STR on offense and go S&S with your pitching staff.** STR buys more ABs, so you immediately position yourself well in four of the five batting categories. On pitching, it might be more advisable to roster a few core arms, though that immediately elevates your risk exposure. Admittedly, it's a balancing act, which is why we need to pay more attention to risk analysis.

The LIMA Plan

The LIMA Plan is a strategy for Rotisserie leagues (though the underlying concept can be used in other formats) that allows you to target high skills pitchers at very low cost, thereby freeing up dollars for offense. LIMA is an acronym for Low Investment Mound Aces, and also pays tribute to Jose Lima, a $1 pitcher whose $24 breakout in 1998 breakout exemplified the power of the strategy. In a $260 league:

1. Budget a maximum of $60 for your pitching staff.
2. Allot no more than $30 of that budget for acquiring saves.
3. Ignore ERA. Draft only pitchers with:
   - Strikeout rate of 25% or greater.

- Walk rate of less than 10%.
- Home run rate of less than 3.5%.

4. Draft as few innings as your league rules will allow. This is intended to manage risk. For some game formats, this should be a secondary consideration.

5. Maximize your batting slots. Spend $200 on batters who have:
- Contact rate of at least 80%
- Walk rate of at least 10%
- PX or Spd level of at least 100

Spend no more than $29 for any player and try to keep the $1 picks to a minimum.

You'll note that the benchmark metrics have been updated in step 3. The statistical environment in the game has changed and LIMA must change with it.

The goal is to ace the batting categories and carefully pick your pitching staff so that it will finish in the upper third in ERA, WHIP and saves (and Ks in 5x5), and an upside of perhaps 9th in wins. In a competitive league, that should be enough to win, and definitely enough to finish in the money. Worst case, you should have an excess of offense available that you can deal for pitching.

The strategy works because it better allocates resources. Fantasy leaguers who spend a lot for pitching are not only paying for expected performance, they are also paying for better defined roles—#1 and #2 rotation starters, ace closers, etc.—which are expected to translate into more IP, wins and saves. But roles are highly variable. A pitcher's role will usually come down to his skill and performance; if he doesn't perform, he'll lose the role.

The LIMA Plan says, let's invest in skill and let the roles fall where they may. In the long run, better skills should translate into more innings, wins and saves. And as it turns out, pitching skill costs less than pitching roles do.

In *snake draft leagues,* you may be able to delay drafting starting pitchers until Round 6, 7 or 8. In *shallow mixed leagues,* the LIMA Plan may not be necessary; just focus on the support metrics. In *simulation leagues,* build your staff around those metrics.

Variations on the LIMA Plan

LIMA Extrema: Limit your total pitching budget to only $30, or less. This can be particularly effective in shallow leagues where LIMA-caliber starting pitcher free agents are plentiful during the season.

SANTANA Plan: Instead of spending $30 on saves, you spend it on a starting pitcher anchor. In 5x5 leagues, allocating those dollars to a high-end LIMA-caliber starting pitcher can work well as long as you pick the right anchor and can acquire saves during the season.

Total Control Drafting (TCD)

On Draft Day, we make every effort to control as many elements as possible. In reality, the players that end up on our teams are largely controlled by the other owners. Their bidding affects your ability to roster the players you want. In a snake draft, the other owners control your roster even more. We are really only able to get the players we want within the limitations set by others.

However, an optimal roster can be constructed from a fanalytic assessment of skill and risk combined with more assertive draft day demeanor.

Why this makes sense

1. Our obsession with projected player values is holding us back. If a player on your draft list is valued at $20 and you agonize when the bidding hits $23, odds are about two chances in three that he could really earn anywhere from $15 to $25. What this means is, in some cases, and within reason, you should just pay what it takes to get the players you want.

2. There is no such thing as a bargain. Most of us *don't* just pay what it takes because we are always on the lookout for players who go under value. But we really don't know which players will cost less than they will earn because prices are still driven by the draft table. The concept of "bargain" assumes that we even know what a player's true value is.

3. "Control" is there for the taking. Most owners are so focused on their own team that they really don't pay much attention to what you're doing. There are some exceptions, and bidding wars do happen, but in general, other owners will not provide that much resistance.

How it's done

1. Create your optimal draft pool.

2. Get those players.

Start by identifying which players will be draftable based on the LIMA or Mayberry criteria. Then, at the draft, focus solely on your roster. When it's your bid opener, toss a player you need at about 50%-75% of your projected value. Bid aggressively and just pay what you need to pay. Of course, don't spend $40 for a player with $25 market value, but it's okay to exceed your projected value within reason.

From a tactical perspective, mix up the caliber of openers. Drop out early on some bids to prevent other owners from catching on to you.

In the end, it's okay to pay a slight premium to make sure you get the players with the highest potential to provide a good return on your investment. It's no different than the premium you might pay for a player with position flexibility or to get the last valuable shortstop. With TCD, you're just spending those extra dollars up front to ensure you are rostering your targets. As a side benefit, TCD almost assures that you don't leave money on the table.

Mayberry Method

The Mayberry Method (MM) asserts that we really can't project player performance with the level of precision that advanced metrics and modeling systems would like us to believe.

MM is named after the fictional TV village where life was simpler. MM evaluates skill by embracing the imprecision of the forecasting process and projecting performance in broad strokes rather than with hard statistics.

MM reduces every player to a 7-character code. The format of the code is 5555 AAA, where the first four characters describe elements of a player's skill on a scale of 0 to 5. These skills are indexed to the league average so that players are evaluated within the context of the level of offense or pitching in a given year.

The three alpha characters are our reliability grades (Health, Experience and Consistency) on the standard A-to-F scale. The skills numerics are forward-looking; the alpha characters grade reliability based on past history.

Batting

The first character in the MM code measures a batter's power skills. It is assigned using the following table:

Power Index	MM
0 - 49	0
50 - 79	1
80 - 99	2
100 - 119	3
120 - 159	4
160+	5

The second character measures a batter's speed skills. RSpd takes our Statistically Scouted Speed metric (Spd) and adds the elements of opportunity and success rate, to construct the formula of RSpd = Spd x (SBO + SB%).

RSpd	MM
0 - 39	0
40 - 59	1
60 - 79	2
80 - 99	3
100 - 119	4
120+	5

The third character measures expected batting average.

xBA Index	MM
0-87	0
88-92	1
93-97	2
98-102	3
103-107	4
108+	5

The fourth character measures playing time.

Role	PA	MM
Potential full-timers	450+	5
Mid-timers	250-449	3
Fringe/bench	100-249	1
Non-factors	0-99	0

Pitching

The first character in the pitching MM code measures xERA, which captures a pitcher's overall ability and is a proxy for ERA, and even WHIP.

xERA Index	MM
0-80	0
81-90	1
91-100	2
101-110	3
111-120	4
121+	5

The second character measures strikeout ability.

K/9 Index	MM
0-76	0
77-88	1
89-100	2
101-112	3
113-124	4
125+	5

The third character measures saves potential.

Description	Saves est.	MM
No hope for saves; starting pitchers	0	0
Speculative closer	1-9	1
Closer in a pen with alternatives	10-24	2
Frontline closer with firm bullpen role	25+	3

The fourth character measures **playing time**.

Role	IP	MM
Potential #1-2 starters	180+	5
Potential #3-4 starters	130-179	3
#5 starters/swingmen	70-129	1
Relievers	0-69	0

Overall Mayberry Scores

The real value of Mayberry is to provide a skills profile on a player-by-player basis. I want to be able to see this…

Player A	4455 AAB
Player B	5245 BBD
Player C	5255 BAB
Player D	5155 BAF

…and make an objective, unbiased determination about these four players without being swayed by preconceived notions and baggage. But there is a calculation that provides a single, overall value for each player.

This is the calculation for the overall MM batting score:

MM Score =
(PX score + Spd score + xBA score + PA score)
x PA score

An overall MM pitching score is calculated as:

MM Score =
((xERA score x 2) + K/9 score + Saves score + IP score)
x (IP score + Saves score)

The highest score you can get for either is 100. That makes the result of the formula easy to assess.

Adding Reliability Grades to Mayberry *(Patrick Davitt)*

Research shows that players with higher reliability grades met their Mayberry targets more often than their lower-reliability counterparts. Players with all "D" or "F" reliability scores underperform Mayberry projections far more often. Those results can be reflected by multiplying a player's MM Score by each of three reliability bonuses or penalties:"

	Health	Experience	Consistency
A	x 1.10	x 1.10	x 1.10
B	x 1.05	x 1.05	x 1.05
C	x 1.00	x 1.00	x 1.00
D	x 0.90	x 0.95	x 0.95
F	x 0.80	x 0.90	x 0.90

Let's perform the overall calculations for Player A (4455 AAB), using these Reliability adjustments.

Player A: 4455 AAB
= (4+4+5+5) x 5
= 90 x 1.10 x 1.10 x 1.05
= 114.3

Portfolio3 Plan concepts

When it comes to profitability, all players are not created equal. Every player has a different role on your team by virtue of his skill set, dollar value/draft round, position and risk profile. When it comes to a strategy for how to approach a specific player, one size does not fit all.

We need some players to return fair value more than others. A $40/first round player going belly-up is going to hurt you far more than a $1/23rd round bust. End-gamers are easily replaceable.

We rely on some players for profit more than others. First-rounders do not provide the most profit potential; that comes from players further down the value rankings.

We can afford to weather more risk with some players than with others. Since high-priced early-rounders need to return at least fair value, we cannot afford to take on excessive risk. Our risk tolerance opens up with later-round/lower cost picks.

Players have different risk profiles based solely on what roster spot they are going to fill. Catchers are more injury prone. A closer's value is highly dependent on managerial decision. These types of players are high risk even if they have great skills. That needs to affect their draft price or draft round.

For some players, the promise of providing a scarce skill, or productivity at a scarce position, may trump risk. Not always, but sometimes. The determining factor is usually price.

Previously, we created a model that integrated these types of players into a roster planning tool, called the Portfolio3 Plan. However, over time, variables like baseball's changing statistical environment and the shifting MLB roster construction affected the utility of the model. The rigid player allocation framework of the tiers began to erode, and no fudging could retain the integrity of the model. So we have retired it. The Mayberry Method includes the relevant player evaluators that Portfolio3 used; you can rely on those to create your own roster plan that balances skill and risk.

Head-to-Head Leagues

Consistency in Head-to-Head leagues *(Dylan Hedges)*

Few things are as valuable to H2H league success as filling your roster with players who can produce a solid baseline of stats, week in and week out. In traditional leagues, while consistency is not as important—all we care about are aggregate numbers—filling your team with consistent players can make roster management easier.

Consistent batters have good plate discipline, walk rates and on base percentages. These are foundation skills. Those who add power to the mix are obviously more valuable, however, the ability to hit home runs consistently is rare.

Consistent pitchers demonstrate similar skills in each outing; if they also produce similar results, they are even more valuable.

We can track consistency but predicting it is difficult. Many fantasy leaguers try to predict a batter's hot or cold streaks, or individual pitcher starts, but that is typically a fool's errand. The best we can do is find players who demonstrate seasonal consistency; in-season, we must manage players and consistency tactically.

Building a consistent Head-to-Head team *(David Martin)*

Teams in head-to-head leagues need batters who are consistent. Focusing on certain metrics helps build consistency, which is the roster holy grail for H2H players. Our filters for such success are:

- Contact rate = minimum 80%
- xBA = minimum .280
- PX (or Spd) = minimum 120
- RC/G = minimum 5.00

Ratio insulation in Head-to-Head leagues *(David Martin)*

On a week-to-week basis, inequities are inherent in the head-to-head game. One way to eliminate your competitor's advantage in the pure numbers game is to build your team's pitching foundation around the ratio categories.

One should normally insulate at the end of a draft, once your hitters are in place. To obtain several ratio insulators, target pitchers that have:

- K-BB% greater than 19%
- K% greater than 20%
- xERA less than 3.30

While adopting this strategy may compromise wins, research has shown that wins come at a cost to ERA and WHIP. Roster space permitting, adding two to four insulators to your team will improve your team's weekly ERA and WHIP.

A Head-to-Head approach to the Mayberry Method *(David Martin)*

Though the Mayberry Method was designed for use in Rotisserie leagues, a skill set analysis about whether a player is head-to-head league material is built into each seven-digit Mayberry code. By "decoding" Mayberry and incorporating quality-consistency (QC) scores, one can assemble a team that has the characteristics of a successful H2H squad.

In reviewing the MM skills scores, we can correlate the power and contact skills as follows:

- PX > 4 or 5 = PX of 120 or higher
- xBA > 4 or 5 = xBA index of 103 or higher

Only full-time players will have an opportunity to produce the counting statistics required, so to create a top tier of players, we need to limit our search to those who earn a 5 for playing time. This top tier should be sorted by QC scores so that the more consistent players are ranked higher.

To create the second tier of players, lower the power index to 3, but keep all other skill requirements intact:

PWR	SPD	BA	PT	HLTH
3	N/A	4/5	5	A/B

The interplay between tiers is important; use Tier 2 in conjunction with Tier 1 and not simply after the top tier options are exhausted. For example, it might make sense to dip into Tier 2 if there is a player available with a higher QC score.

Additionally, while the H2H MM codes do not target players based on their speed skills, the second column of the MM codes contains this information. Though you are de-prioritizing the speed skill, you do not need to punt the steals category. You will typically find that the tiers nonetheless contain multiple players with a MM speed score of 3 or higher, so you can still be competitive in the steal category most weeks applying this approach.

Consistency in points leagues *(Bill Macey)*

Previous research has demonstrated that week-to-week statistical consistency is important for Rotisserie-based head-to-head play. But one can use the same foundation in points-based games. A study showed that not only do players with better skills post more overall points in this format, but that the format caters to consistent performances on a week-to-week basis, even after accounting for differences in total points scored and playing-time.

Therefore, when drafting your batters in points-based head-to-head leagues, ct% and bb% make excellent tiebreakers if you are having trouble deciding between two players with similarly projected point totals. Likewise, when rostering pitchers, favor those who tend not to give up home runs.

In-Season Roster Management

Rotisserie category management tips *(Todd Zola)*

1. Disregard whether you are near the top or the bottom of a category; focus instead on the gaps directly above and below your squad.
2. Prorate the difference in stats between teams.
3. ERA tends to move towards WHIP.
4. As the season progresses, the number of AB/IP do not preclude a gain/loss in the ratio categories.
5. An opponent's point lost is your point gained.
6. *Most important!* Come crunch time, forget value, forget names, and forget reputation. It's all about stats and where you are situated within each category.

Sitting stars and starting scrubs *(Ed DeCaria)*

In setting your pitching rotation, conventional wisdom suggests sticking with trusted stars despite difficult matchups. But does this hold up? And can you carefully start inferior pitchers against weaker opponents? Here are the ERAs posted by varying skilled pitchers facing a range of different strength offenses:

	OPPOSING OFFENSE (RC/G)				
Pitcher (ERA)	5.25+	5.00	4.25	4.00	<4.00
3.00-	3.46	3.04	3.04	2.50	2.20
3.50	3.98	3.94	3.44	3.17	2.87
4.00	4.72	4.57	3.96	3.66	3.24
4.50	5.37	4.92	4.47	4.07	3.66
5.00+	6.02	5.41	5.15	4.94	4.42

Recommendations:

1. Never start below replacement-level pitchers.
2. Always start elite pitchers.
3. Other than that, never say never or always.

Playing matchups can pay off when the difference in opposing offense is severe.

Two-start pitcher weeks *(Ed DeCaria)*

A two-start pitcher is a prized possession. But those starts can mean two DOMinant outings, two DISasters, or anything else in between, as shown by these results:

PQS Pair	% Weeks	ERA	WHIP	Win/Wk	K/Wk
DOM-DOM	20%	2.53	1.02	1.1	12.0
DOM-AVG	28%	3.60	1.25	0.8	9.2
AVG-AVG	14%	4.44	1.45	0.7	6.8
DOM-DIS	15%	5.24	1.48	0.6	7.9
AVG-DIS	17%	6.58	1.74	0.5	5.7
DIS-DIS	6%	8.85	2.07	0.3	5.0

Weeks that include even one DISaster start produce terrible results. Unfortunately, avoiding such disasters is much easier in hindsight. But what is the actual impact of this decision on the stat categories?

ERA and WHIP: When the difference between opponents is extreme, inferior pitchers can be a better percentage play. This is true both for 1-start pitchers and 2-start pitchers, and for choosing inferior one-start pitchers over superior two-start pitchers.

Strikeouts per Week: Unlike the two rate stats, there is a massive shift in the balance of power between one-start and two-start pitchers in the strikeout category. Even stars with easy one-start matchups can only barely keep pace with two-start replacement-level arms in strikeouts per week.

Wins per week are also dominated by the two-start pitchers. Even the very worst two-start pitchers will earn a half of a win on average, which is the same rate as the very best one-start pitchers.

The bottom line: If strikeouts and wins are the strategic priority, use as many two-start weeks as the rules allow, even if it means using a replacement-level pitcher with two tough starts instead of a mid-level arm with a single easy start. But if ERA and/or WHIP management are the priority, two-start pitchers can be very powerful, as a single week might impact the standings by over 1.5 points in ERA/WHIP, positively or negatively.

Top 12 trading tips *(Fred Zinkie)*

We all need to make trades to win our leagues. And while every negotiation is unique, here are some quick tips that should make anyone more effective on the trade market.

1. Learn how the other owner wishes to communicate. Some owners prefer email, others like the league website, some prefer a Twitter DM, and texting is often a desirable option. And there are even some who still want a phone call. The easy way to figure this out is to send your initial contact in multiple ways. Generally, the other owner's preferred method is the one they use to send their initial reply.

2. All negotiations start with an offer. Don't beat around the bush—give the other owner something concrete to work with. You can start with your best deal or merely a respectable proposal, but you should get the ball rolling with a firm offer.

3. Check your ego at the door. You should enter trade talks with low expectations and a willingness to accept a different point of view. The other owner is not necessarily wrong when they disagree with your opinions on player values or what makes sense for their roster.

4. Be willing to unbalance your roster. Owners who draft a balanced team and then only seek out deals that maintain that balance are going to miss out on buying opportunities. To improve your roster—especially during the first half—you should be

Daily Fantasy Baseball

Daily Fantasy Sports (DFS) is an offshoot of traditional fantasy sports. Many of the same analytic methods that are integral to seasonal fantasy baseball are just as relevant for DFS.

General Format

1. The overwhelming majority of DFS contests are pay-for-play where the winners are compensated a percentage of their entry fee, in accordance with the rules of that game.

2. DFS baseball contests are generally based on a single day's slate of games, or a subset of the day's games (i.e., all afternoon games or all evening games)

3. Most DFS formats are points-based salary cap games.

Most Popular Contests

1. Cash Games: Three variants (50/50, Multipliers, and Head-to-Head) all pay out a flat prize to a portion of the entries.

2. GPP (Guaranteed prize pool) Tournaments: The overall winner earns the largest prize and prizes scale downward.

3. Survivor: A survivor contest is a multiple-slate format where a portion of the entries survives to play the following day.

4. Qualifiers/Satellites: Tournaments where the prize(s) consist of entry tickets to a larger tournament.

DFS Analysis

1. Predicting single-day performance entails adjusting a baseline projection based on that day's match-up. This adjusted expectation is considered in context with a player's salary to determine his potential contributions relative to the other players.

2. Weighted on base average (wOBA) is a souped-up version of OBP, and is a favorite metric to help evaluate both hitters and pitchers. (For more useful DFS metrics, see next section)

3. Pitching: In DFS, innings and strikeouts are the two chief means of accruing points, so they need to be weighed heavily in pitching evaluation.

Tips for Players New to DFS

1. Start slow and be prepared to lose: While cogent analysis can increase your chances of winning, the variance associated with a single day's worth of outcomes doesn't assure success. Short-term losing streaks are inevitable, so start with low cost cash games before embarking on tournament play.

2. Minimize the number of sites you play: The DFS space is dominated by two sites but there are other options. At the beginning, stick to one or two. Once you're comfortable, consider expanding to others.

3. Bankroll management: The recommended means to manage your bankroll is to risk no more than 10% on a given day in cash games, or 2% in tournaments.

4. General Strategies

   A. Cash Games: Conventional wisdom preaches to be conservative in cash games. Upper level starting pitchers make excellent cash game options. For hitters, it's best to spread your choices among several teams. In general, you're looking for players with a high floor rather than a high ceiling.

   B: GPP Tournaments: In tournaments (with a larger number of entrants), a common ploy is to select a lesser priced, though risky, pitcher with a favorable match-up. It's also very common to overload—or

stack—several batters from the same team, hoping that squad scores a bunch of runs.

5. Miscellaneous Tips

   A. Pay extra attention to games threatened by weather, as well as players who are not a lock to be in the lineup.

   B. Avoid playing head-to-head against strangers until you're comfortable and have enjoyed some success.

   C. Stay disciplined. The worst thing you can do is eat up your bankroll quickly by entering into tournaments.

   D. Most importantly, have fun. Obviously, you want to win, but hopefully you're also in it for the challenge of mastering the unique skills intrinsic to DFS.

Using BaseballHQ Tools in DFS

Here are some of the additional skill metrics to consider:

Cash Game Metrics

bb%: This simple indicator may receive only a quick glance when building lineups, but it is imperative in providing insight on a batter's underlying approach and plate discipline. Walks also equal points in all DFS scoring structures.

ct%: Another byproduct of good plate discipline, reflecting the percentage of balls put in play. Players with strong contact rates tend to provide a higher floor, and less chance of a negative score from a free swinger with a high strikeout rate.

xBA: Measures a hitter's BA by multiplying his contact rate by the chance that a ball in play falls for a hit. Hitters whose BA is far below their xBA may be "due" for some hits.

Tournament / GPP Metrics

PX / xPX: Home runs are the single greatest multi-point event. Using PX (power index) and xPX (expected power index) together can help identify underperformers who are due in the power category.

Choosing Pitchers in DFS

The criteria for choosing a pitcher(s) may be more narrow than for full-season league, but the skills focus should remain.

Major Considerations

• Overall skills. Look for the following minimums: BB% under 7%, K% over 23%, K-BB% over 16%, and max 1.0 hr/9.

• Home/Away. In 2022, MLB pitchers logged a 3.82 ERA, 7.9% BB%, 22.9% K% (15.0% K-BB%) at home; 4.13 ERA, 8.4% BB%, 21.9% K% (13.5% K-BB%) on the road.

• Is he pitching at Coors Field? (Even the best pitchers are a risky start there.)

Moderate Considerations

• Recent performance. Examine Ks and BBs over last 4-5 starts.

• Strength of opponent. Refer to opposing team's OPS for the season, as well as more recent performance.

Minor Considerations

• L/R issues. Does the pitcher/opponent have wide platoon splits?

• Park. Is the game at a hitter's/pitcher's/neutral park?

• Previous outings. Has he faced this team already this season? If so, how did he fare? (Skills; not just his ERA.)

You should be left with a tiered list of pitching options, ripe for comparing individual risk/reward level against their price point.

willing to have stretches with weak hitting, poor starting pitching, or a lack of saves. The goal is to acquire value.

5. Proofread. Always take the extra minute to proofread your communication and ensure your thoughts are clear. Beyond looking for typos, be sure that all players mentioned are the ones you intend to mention. Keep your initial communication to a couple sentences.

6. Be prompt. Trading can be inconvenient, but an active trader makes time when the opportunity arises. Don't get yourself fired or abandon your children in search of the perfect trade, but in general, you should be willing to work around your competitor's schedule.

7. Send multiple offers. Submitting multiple offers lets the other owner pick the proposal they like best. If you don't want to take the time to send multiple offers, you can at least mention that you would be willing to trade Player X, Y, or Z to get your desired return.

8. Be clear about all the players who interest you on the other team. An easy way to start negotiations is to mention all players who interest you on the other team. Again, this gives some control to the other owner, who can now tell you which players are most available.

9. The message board is your last resort. Trade messages can make you appear desperate. This is especially true when trying to unload a certain player. Like a house that sits on the market, the asking price on your player tends to drop once a couple days have passed.

10. Look for owners who may be desperate. Because most owners seek to achieve roster balance, you can find value by helping those who have an immediate need. And you can always help since you are the rare owner willing to unbalance their roster to obtain value. Look at the standings, as owners who are low in a roto category are likely to trade away value in order to address their weakness.

11. Look for owners who have a surplus. On the opposite end of the spectrum, owners can be willing to make deals when they have a surplus of a position or skill. Targeting the owner who is running away with the steals category could get you SB at a reasonable price.

12. Have the guts to trade away overachievers. This is one of the hardest tips to put into practice, but experience tells us that most players who have surprising stretches return to normal at some point. If it sometimes seems too good to be true, it probably is.

Other Diamonds

The Universal Tenets of Fantasy Economics

- This is not a game of projections. It is a game of market value versus real value.
- We don't need precisely accurate projections. All we need are projections accurate enough to tell us when the marketplace is wrong.
- The marketplace is generally wrong, so we don't have to buy into anything it tells us.

- The variance between market cost and real value (in dollars or draft rounds) is far more important than the accuracy of any player projection.
- The market cost of a veteran player is driven more by the certainty of past performance than the uncertainty of future potential.
- The market cost of a young player is driven more by the promise of future potential than the questionable validity of past performance.
- Your greatest competitive advantage is to leverage the variance between market cost and real value.

Cellar value
The dollar value at which a player cannot help but earn more than he costs. Always profit here.

Crickets
The sound heard when someone's opening draft bid on a player is also the only bid.

End-game wasteland
Home for players undraftable in the deepest of leagues, who stay in the free agent pool all year. It's the place where even crickets keep quiet when a name is called at the draft.

FAB Forewarnings
1. Spend early and often.
2. Emptying your budget for one prime league-crosser is a tactic that should be reserved for the desperate.
3. If you chase two rabbits, you will lose them both.

The Hope Hypothesis
- Hope can keep you interested, but will have no effect on how a player performs.
- Hope is sometimes referred to as "wishcasting" and may sound more scientific, but really it's just plain old hope with a random number attached.
- In the end, hope has virtually no intrinsic value and you can't win with it alone.
- Yet, hope will cost you about $5 over market value at the draft table.

Professional Free Agent (PFA)
Player whose name will never come up on draft day but will always end up on a roster at some point during the season as an injury replacement.

Seasonal Assessment Standard
If you still have reason to be reading the boxscores during the last weekend of the season, then your year has to be considered a success.

The Three Cardinal Rules for Winners
If you cherish this hobby, you will live by them or die by them...
1. Revel in your success; fame is fleeting.
2. Exercise excruciating humility.
3. 100% of winnings must be spent on significant others.

The Future of playing time measurement starts now

by Ed DeCaria

"Volume" may be the biggest buzzword in fantasy baseball today—and with good reason. It's experts' secret code word for "accumulating more playing time," which we advise doing because playing time leads to higher counting stats and, the theory goes, more fantasy championships.

But chasing volume isn't easy. Not only is it hard to predict which players will accumulate the most playing time *in the future*, we still have only the most rudimentary metrics to understand how players have even accumulated playing time *in the past*.

As metrics in every other aspect of our game have become dazzlingly more sophisticated, the parallel progression of playing time metrics has been almost comically insufficient. For position players specifically, the top-level metrics to measure volume are Plate Appearances (PA) and Games (G). Neither is particularly informative as a standalone metric, nor particularly well aligned with how or when fantasy managers make decisions.

Let's look at two example players: Player A and Player B. What can fantasy managers really infer from the fact that Player A had 558 PAs in 2022 and Player B had 542? On the surface, it seems like Player A is slightly better positioned to deliver volume heading into 2023. But then we might look at Games instead, and find that Player A played in 136 games and Player B in 140. Do we now prefer Player B? Or do we just shrug and decide they're about the same? We could do the only other possible thing and divide PA by G to get PA/G, which would tell us that Player A netted 4.10 PA per G compared to Player B's 3.87 PA per G. So, do we now prefer Player A again?

It's impossible to say. It's not until we know their names—Player A is Nick Castellanos, Player B is Mark Canha—and take the time to study their seasons in detail that we can begin to understand what's driving those differences. But doing that for not just two but 250 or even all 500+ position players would be far too inefficient and subjective, because we have literally ZERO metrics that truly, accurately represent what's happening on managers' lineup cards and in the GM's office.

It's time for an upgrade.

After years of tinkering, we are finally ready to unveil a simple yet revolutionary new set of playing time metrics that give us a complete picture of every player's playing time situation without requiring fantasy managers to click a single link or read a single word. Just numbers, telling a story.

Our new playing time metrics are:
- Active Weeks (AW)
- Plate Appearances per Active Week (PAAW)
- Starts per Active Week (SAW)
- Plate Appearances per Start (PAS)
- Extra Plate Appearances per Active Week (EAW)
- "Ghost" Plate Appearances as % of Total PA (GPA%)

Now, instead of combing through detailed player pages to understand what might have been going on during Castellanos' or Canha's 2022 seasons, you'll be able to see playing time profiles like this:

Name	PA	AW	PAAW	SAW	PAS	EAW	GPA%
Castellanos, Nick	558	23 ◗	23.3 ●	5.6 ●	4.15 ◗	0.1 ○	4%
Canha, Mark	542	26 ●	20.3 ◗	4.6 ◗	4.21 ●	0.7 ◓	3%

Which tells you everything you need to know about...
- how often each player was available (AW: Canha > Castellanos)
- how much playing time they earned when available (PAAW: Castellanos > Canha)
- how often they started (SAW: Castellanos > Canha)
- how often they came to the plate when they started (PAS: Canha > Castellanos)
- how often they came off the bench (EAW: Canha > Castellanos)
- and how many times they earned real-life playing time from which you, as a fantasy manager, likely never benefitted (GPA%: Castellanos > Canha).

It's all there. And it's beautiful.

These six new metrics relate to each other and to Total PA as follows:

$$PAAW = SAW * PAS + EAW; \text{ and}$$
$$Total\ PA = AW * PAAW / (1 - GPA\%)$$

Let's review each metric in detail, and officially welcome playing time measurement to the 21st century!

Active Weeks per Season (AW)

Explanation: Number of weeks during which the player was active on an MLB roster at the start of the week (Opening Day plus Mondays).

Scale: Players can accumulate anywhere from 0 to 27 Active Weeks (or as many weeks as the season is long).

Usefulness: Active Weeks is useful for lots of reasons:
- It directly correlates to fantasy decisions, i.e., How often did I have the opportunity to use this player?
- It normalizes playing time across players with different usage patterns (e.g., total PA for players with 27 Active Weeks ranged from 725 all the way to 121)
- It factors in all reasons for missing time equally. Injuries, suspensions, late call-ups, frequent shuttling back and forth between the majors and minors, etc.
- It enables us to credit players for the value of their fantasy roster slot during inactive weeks, both historically and in projections
- It can serve as the denominator for other playing time metrics and *literally any other volume metric* (e.g., HR per active week)

Using this method, we can now easily see Active Weeks for every MLB player. Here's a breakdown of Active Weeks across all batters with positive value in 2022 ($5x5), for both mixed leagues and "only" leagues:

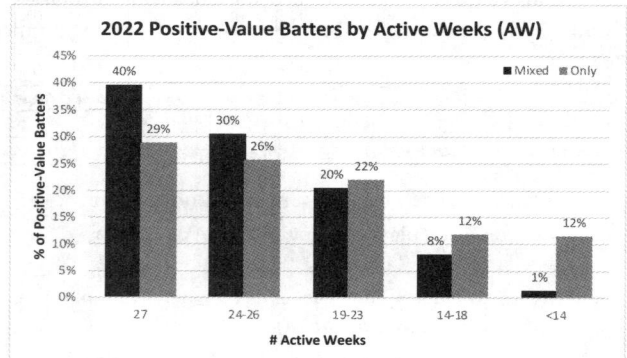

2022 Positive-Value Batters by Active Weeks (AW)

Depending on league type, 30-40% of all positive-value 5x5 batters were active for all 27 weeks. Another 25-30% were active for all but 1-3 weeks (90%+ of the season). Another ~20% were active for 19-23 weeks (70-85% of the season). About 10% were active for 14-18 weeks (50-65% of the season). And the remaining positive-value players were active for fewer than 14 weeks (<50% of the season).

Active Weeks serves as the backbone for the rest of our new playing time metrics.

Plate Appearances per Active Week (PAAW)

Explanation: Average number of PAs by the player per week, during weeks that he was available.

Calculation: Divide Adjusted Total PA* by Active Weeks. *MLB teams can activate players any day of the week, meaning players can enter games on days during non-Active Weeks. We call these "Ghost Days," and any PAs on these days "Ghost PAs," because they accumulate while the player is on most fantasy managers' benches, and are therefore only an illusion of volume. To calculate PAAW, we back out Ghost PAs from the numerator to align it with the Active Weeks denominator to get Adjusted Total PA.*

Scale: Elite accumulators max out at 25-27 PAAW. Median PAAW for positive-value players was 21.4 in 15-team mixed leagues, and 19.7 in -only leagues.

Usefulness: It measures total volume accumulation within the unit of time (i.e., one week) that best aligns with fantasy decision-making.

Here are two examples of how PAAW can help identify "hidden" full-time players, specifically those who missed chunks of time throughout the season for one reason or another. First, a list of close-to-full-time players (21+ PAAW) who were active for 50-75% of the year:

Name	PA	AW	PAAW	SAW	PAS	EAW	GPA%
Greene, Riley	418	16	25.6	5.7	4.49	0.0	2%
Gonzalez, Oscar	382	14	24.5	5.7	4.26	0.2	10%
Harper, Bryce	426	18	23.0	5.3	4.34	0.1	3%
Laureano, Ramon	383	15	22.9	5.5	4.12	0.2	10%
Harris II, Michael	441	19	22.8	5.9	3.87	0.0	2%
Cruz, Oneil	361	16	22.5	5.3	4.22	0.1	0%
Anderson, Tim	351	15	22.4	5.0	4.44	0.0	4%
Hernandez, Enrique	402	17	22.4	5.1	4.38	0.2	5%
Franco, Wander	344	15	21.9	5.1	4.25	0.3	4%
Garcia, Luis	377	16	21.9	5.3	4.12	0.1	7%
Moncada, Yoan	433	19	21.6	4.9	4.37	0.3	5%
Polanco, Jorge	445	19	21.6	5.0	4.30	0.1	8%
India, Jonathan	431	19	21.6	4.9	4.35	0.3	5%
McCarthy, Jake	354	16	21.3	4.9	4.17	0.7	4%
Bader, Harrison	313	14	21.0	5.2	3.95	0.6	6%

Second, a list of close-to-full-time players (21+ PAAW) who were active for less than 50% of the year:

Name	PA	AW	PAAW	SAW	PAS	EAW	GPA%
Meneses, Joey	240	9	24.3	5.6	4.35	0.1	9%
Soler, Jorge	306	13	23.5	5.4	4.33	0.2	0%
Brantley, Michael	277	12	23.1	5.3	4.33	0.0	0%
Henderson, Gunnar	132	5	23.0	5.2	4.13	1.4	13%
Jung, Josh	102	4	22.9	5.8	3.92	0.0	10%
Castro, Rodolfo	278	11	22.2	5.4	4.04	0.2	12%
Albies, Ozzie	269	11	22.1	5.2	4.24	0.2	10%
Cabrera, Oswaldo	171	7	22.1	5.3	4.05	0.6	10%
Pasquantino, Vinnie	298	13	22.0	5.3	4.14	0.0	4%
Bleday, J.J.	238	11	21.0	4.9	4.05	1.0	3%

With PAAW, full-time players in small sample sizes will zoom right to the top of playing time leaderboards in a way that was never possible without controlling for Active Weeks.

Starts per Active Week (SAW)

Explanation: Average number of games started by the player per week, during weeks he was available.

Calculation: Divide Adjusted Games Started* by Active Weeks. *As with PAAW, "Adjusted" Games do not include "Ghost Starts" in the total.*

Scale: Players earn 0-6 Starts per Active Week. Median SAW for positive-value players was 5.0 in 15-team mixed leagues, and 4.7 in -only leagues.

Usefulness: It elegantly quantifies a player's high-level role with his team, e.g., everyday stalwart, rested regular, platoon partner, bench bat.

Seeing SAW as a metric in a table is fascinating, because you can instantly recognize when players are getting less than true full-time playing time relative to others, and more easily understand different teams' philosophies and their impact on fantasy. Let's take a quick look at two teams, the 2022 Houston Astros and 2022 San Francisco Giants, listing all players with 2+ SAW on average, in descending order:

2022 Houston Astros

Name	PA	AW	PAAW	SAW	PAS	EAW	GPA%
Bregman, Alex	656	26 ◑	24.4 ●	5.7 ●	4.27 ◑	0.1 ○	3%
Tucker, Kyle	609	27 ●	22.6 ●	5.5 ●	4.10 ◑	0.1 ○	0%
Brantley, Michael	277	12 ○	23.1 ●	5.3 ●	4.33 ●	0.0 ○	0%
Altuve, Jose	604	26 ◑	23.2 ●	5.3 ◑	4.38 ●	0.2 ○	0%
Gurriel, Yulieski	584	27 ●	21.6 ●	5.2 ◑	4.11 ◑	0.1 ○	0%
Alvarez, Yordan	561	26 ◑	21.5 ●	5.1 ●	4.20 ◑	0.1 ○	0%
Pena, Jeremy	558	26 ◑	21.3 ●	5.0 ●	4.20 ◑	0.1 ○	1%
Mancini, Trey	587	27 ●	21.7 ●	5.0 ●	4.25 ◑	0.3 ○	0%
Maldonado, Martin	379	27 ●	14.0 ●	4.1 ◑	3.45 ○	0.0 ○	0%
Meyers, Jake	160	10 ○	14.5 ◑	4.0 ◑	3.50 ○	0.6 ◑	10%
Vazquez, Christian	426	27 ●	15.8 ◑	3.8 ◑	4.03 ◑	0.6 ◑	0%
McCormick, Chas	407	26 ◑	15.1 ◑	3.7 ◑	3.97 ◑	0.5 ◑	3%
Diaz, Aledmys	327	23 ◑	13.7 ◑	3.2 ◑	4.05 ◑	0.8 ◑	4%
Dubon, Mauricio	265	27 ●	9.8 ○	2.2 ○	3.83 ◑	1.4 ◑	0%

2022 San Francisco Giants

Name	PA	AW	PAAW	SAW	PAS	EAW	GPA%
Estrada, Thairo	541	25 ◑	21.1 ◑	5.0 ◑	4.09 ◑	0.5 ◑	3%
Machado, Dixon	17	1 ○	17.0 ◑	5.0 ◑	3.40 ○	0.0 ○	0%
Yastrzemski, Mike	558	25 ◑	21.7 ●	4.9 ◑	4.10 ◑	1.6 ●	3%
Flores, Wilmer	602	27 ●	22.3 ●	4.9 ◑	4.31 ◑	1.2 ◑	0%
Crawford, Brandon	458	22 ◑	19.7 ◑	4.9 ◑	4.00 ◑	0.3 ○	5%
Villar, David	181	10 ○	17.0 ◑	4.4 ◑	3.70 ○	0.7 ◑	6%
Gonzalez, Luis	350	18 ◑	17.1 ◑	4.4 ◑	3.76 ○	0.7 ◑	12%
Belt, Brandon	298	15 ◑	18.3 ◑	4.1 ◑	4.21 ●	1.0 ◑	8%
Pederson, Joc	433	26 ◑	16.5 ◑	4.0 ◑	3.70 ○	1.7 ●	1%
Wade, LaMonte	251	16 ◑	14.6 ◑	3.6 ◑	3.74 ○	1.1 ◑	7%
Longoria, Evan	298	17 ◑	15.9 ◑	3.6 ◑	4.04 ◑	1.5 ◑	9%
Bart, Joey	291	22 ◑	12.2 ◑	3.5 ◑	3.43 ○	0.3 ○	7%
Calhoun, Willie	62	5 ○	12.3 ◑	3.4 ◑	3.12 ○	1.8 ●	1%
Walker, Steele	16	1 ○	12.8 ◑	3.2 ◑	3.50 ○	1.7 ●	20%
Vosler, Jason	111	5 ○	12.2 ◑	3.1 ○	3.59 ○	0.9 ◑	45%
Davis, J.D.	365	27 ●	13.5 ◑	3.0 ○	3.95 ◑	1.5 ◑	0%
La Stella, Tommy	195	14 ◑	12.5 ◑	3.0 ○	3.72 ◑	1.3 ◑	10%
Wynns, Austin	177	17 ◑	10.4 ○	2.8 ○	3.40 ○	0.8 ◑	0%
Mercedes, Yermin	83	6 ○	11.8 ○	2.8 ○	3.45 ○	2.1 ●	15%
Slater, Austin	325	23 ◑	13.9 ◑	2.6 ○	3.92 ◑	3.7 ●	1%
Proctor, Ford	22	2 ○	9.5 ○	2.6 ○	3.50 ○	0.4 ○	14%
Brinson, Lewis	39	3 ○	10.6 ○	2.4 ○	3.22 ○	2.9 ●	19%
Walton, Donnie	78	7 ○	8.1 ○	2.1 ○	3.50 ○	0.9 ◑	27%

The Astros consistently ran out the same lineup with eight different players having 5+ SAW and 13 with 2+ SAW. The Giants, on the other hand, had only two players with 5+ SAW, and 23 (!) with 2+ SAW in their time with the team. The Giants' mix-and-match platoon strategy is on *direct* display in these metrics.

Plate Appearances per Start (PAS)

Explanation: Average number of times the player came to bat in games that they started.

Calculation: Divide Adjusted Plate Appearances in Games Started by Adjusted Games Started.

Scale: Elite accumulators max out at 4.50-4.65 PAS. Median 2022 PAS for positive-value players was 4.20 in 15-team mixed leagues, and 4.09 in -only leagues.

Usefulness: It is a strong proxy for lineup position, strength of surrounding lineup, and the likelihood of the player to be substituted out of the game.

Small differences in PAS make a big difference to cumulative PA over the course of a season. Let's look at three players from 2022, each with 27 Active Weeks and 5.5 Starts per Active Week:

Name	PA	AW	PAAW	SAW	PAS	EAW	GPA%
Yelich, Christian	671	27 ●	24.9 ●	5.5 ●	4.48 ●	0.1 ○	0%
Machado, Manny	644	27 ●	23.9 ●	5.5 ●	4.34 ◑	0.1 ○	0%
Tucker, Kyle	609	27 ●	22.6 ●	5.5 ◑	4.10 ◑	0.1 ○	0%

The primary difference in cumulative 2022 PA between Yelich, Machado, and Tucker was Plate Appearances per Start. Yelich's 4.48 PAS as the Brewers' leadoff or #3 hitter drove his 671 PA, outpacing Machado's 644 PAs on his 4.34 PAS, and dwarfing Tucker's 609 PA on his 4.10 PAS. The +0.38 PAS difference between Yelich and Tucker was enough to yield an additional 62 PA over the entire season, the equivalent of more than two entire weeks of additional playing time.

Extra Plate Appearances per Active Week (EAW)

Explanation: Average number of times per week that the player came off the bench to hit.

Calculation: Divide Adjusted Plate Appearances in Non-Starts by Active Weeks.

Scale: Players can earn roughly 0.0-5.0 Extra Plate Appearances per Week.

Usefulness: EAW rounds out the playing time picture, high-lighting borderline players who may not start as often as we'd like but seem to be favored by managers for additional opportunities.

By definition, the players with the highest EAW are those with low SAW, but it is precisely EAW that makes a certain class of players still viable in deeper leagues by enabling them to accumulate just enough total plate appearances to pop a HR, steal a base, and produce/score a handful of runs by the end of the week. Here are 14 players from 2022 whose EAW made them more interesting pickups than they otherwise would have been:

Name	PA	AW	PAAW	SAW	PAS	EAW	GPA%
Slater, Austin	325	23 ◑	13.9 ○	2.6 ○	3.92 ◑	3.7 ●	1%
Ruf, Darin	388	25 ◑	14.7 ◑	3.1 ◑	4.01 ◑	2.4 ●	5%
Velazquez, Nelson	206	17 ◑	12.1 ○	2.8 ○	3.53 ○	2.3 ●	0%
Sosa, Edmundo	190	12 ○	14.8 ◑	3.5 ◑	3.67 ○	2.0 ●	6%
Peterson, Jace	328	22 ◑	14.6 ◑	3.6 ◑	3.52 ○	1.9 ◑	2%
Dalbec, Bobby	353	24 ◑	14.4 ◑	3.3 ◑	3.86 ◑	1.8 ◑	2%
Miller, Bradley	241	18 ◑	12.7 ○	3.1 ◑	3.59 ○	1.8 ◑	5%
Pederson, Joc	433	26 ◑	16.5 ◑	4.0 ◑	3.70 ○	1.7 ◑	1%
Thompson, Trayce	255	19 ◑	13.0 ○	3.0 ○	3.84 ◑	1.6 ◑	3%
Celestino, Gilberto	347	24 ◑	13.7 ◑	3.4 ◑	3.53 ○	1.6 ◑	5%
Yastrzemski, Mike	558	25 ◑	21.7 ●	4.9 ◑	4.10 ◑	1.6 ◑	3%
Fraley, Jake	247	14 ◑	17.1 ◑	3.9 ◑	4.00 ◑	1.6 ◑	3%
Ortega, Rafael	371	24 ◑	15.5 ◑	3.5 ◑	3.92 ◑	1.6 ◑	0%
Pujols, Albert	351	27 ●	13.0 ○	3.0 ○	3.86 ◑	1.6 ◑	0%

EAW accounts for 10-20% of total playing time for these kinds of players. While you may not necessarily target high-EAW players, it's a good second metric to check (after PAS) for players with borderline SAW.

Ghost Plate Appearances as % of Total (GPA%)

Explanation: Playing time earned during weeks when the player wasn't active at the start of the week, but was subsequently activated later in the week.

Calculation: Divide Ghost PAs by total Plate Appearances.

Scale: Typically 0-10% for most fantasy-relevant players, but outliers can be much higher. The more times a player shifts between active and inactive, the higher the likelihood of Ghost PAs.

Usefulness: GPA% quantifies how much of a player's surface-level volume likely went unrealized by fantasy managers who kept the player on their bench until officially activated.

Here's a list of players in 2022 who technically accumulated 400+ plate appearances, but from whom fantasy managers received substantially less volume:

Name	PA	AW	PAAW	SAW	PAS	EAW	GPA%
Robert, Luis	401	22 ◑	16.3 ◑	3.7 ◑	4.36 ●	0.0 ○	11%
Renfroe, Hunter	522	22 ◑	21.9 ◑	5.2 ◕	4.18 ◑	0.0 ○	8%
Cooper, Garrett	469	24 ◕	18.0 ◑	4.3 ◑	4.13 ◑	0.3 ○	8%
Polanco, Jorge	445	19 ◑	21.6 ◑	5.0 ◕	4.30 ●	0.1 ○	8%
Correa, Carlos	590	24 ◕	23.1 ●	5.2 ◕	4.41 ●	0.2 ○	6%
Aguilar, Jesus	507	25 ◕	19.1 ◑	4.4 ◑	4.17 ◑	0.6 ◔	6%
Crawford, Brandon	458	22 ◑	19.7 ◑	4.9 ◑	4.00 ◑	0.3 ○	5%
Hernandez, Enrique	402	17 ◔	22.4 ◕	5.1 ◕	4.38 ●	0.2 ○	5%
Ward, Taylor	564	23 ◑	23.3 ●	5.4 ◕	4.28 ●	0.3 ○	5%
Moncada, Yoan	433	19 ◑	21.6 ◑	4.9 ◑	4.37 ●	0.3 ○	5%
India, Jonathan	431	19 ◑	21.6 ◑	4.9 ◑	4.35 ●	0.3 ○	5%
Suzuki, Seiya	446	20 ◑	21.3 ◑	5.0 ◕	4.20 ◕	0.2 ○	5%
Berti, Jon	404	20 ◑	19.3 ◑	4.4 ◑	4.32 ◕	0.3 ○	5%

For example, not only did Luis Robert fail to deliver on his 2022 early Round 2 price with his underwhelming production in 401 PA, his actual return for fantasy managers was more like 358 PA once factoring in his 11% GPA%. In general, a GPA in the 5-10% range for otherwise active, full-time players equates to 1-2 full weeks' worth of PAs over the course of the season where fantasy managers likely earned replacement level stats—or risked taking zeroes—during weeks where they kept that player on the bench awaiting their activation.

Benchmarks and Application

In the tables above, next to most of the numbers is a circle filled in to 100%, 75%, 50%, 25%, or 0%. These symbols serve as a guide to help interpret each new metric relative to the fantasy-relevant player pool. Here are the minimums needed to achieve each level of fill in each metric:

Group *(% of all batters)*	AW	PAAW	SAW	PAS	EAW
Elite *(5-10%)*	27 ●	24.0 ●	5.5 ●	4.35 ●	2.0 ●
Great *(10-20%)*	24 ◕	22.0 ◕	4.9 ◕	4.20 ◕	1.5 ◕
Good *(10-20%)*	19 ◑	18.0 ◑	4.0 ◑	4.00 ◑	1.0 ◑
Borderline *(10-20%)*	14 ◔	14.0 ◔	3.0 ◔	3.80 ◔	0.5 ◔
Bad *(40-50%)*	0 ○	0.0 ○	0.0 ○	0.00 ○	0.0 ○

If you think about each metric in real baseball terms, particularly AW, SAW, and PAS, you'll find that these benchmarks are quite intuitive:

- *Elite:* 27 AW means they missed almost no time except maybe a day-to-day injury; 5.5+ SAW means they

start nearly every game; and 4.35+ PAS means they're likely a top-third-of-the-order hitter; combining these benchmarks, elite playing time batters will accumulate 650+ PAs

- *Great:* 24-26 AW means they had only a brief IL stint or short stay in the minors; 4.9-5.4 SAW means they only get 1 day off every 1-2 weeks; and 4.20-4.34 PAS often means they're a middle-third-of-the-order hitter; combining these benchmarks, great playing time batters will accumulate 500-600 PAs

- *Good:* 19-23 AW means they missed a chunk of time but nothing season-ending; 4.0-4.8 SAW means they sit out one game every team series; and 4.00-4.19 PAS means they're a middle-to-bottom-third hitter or in a weak lineup; combining these benchmarks, good playing time batters will accumulate 300-450 PAs

- *Borderline:* 14-18 AW means something major likely impacted their availability or readiness to play; 3.0-3.9 SAW means they're likely in a platoon/utility role; and 3.80-3.99 PAS means they're likely a bottom-third-of-the-order hitter in a weak lineup or often taken out of games early; combining these benchmarks, borderline playing time batters will accumulate 160-280 PAs

Note, however, that very few players achieve elite status across the board. In 2022, only 16 players were classified as elite in AW, SAW, and PAS:

Name	PA	AW	PAAW	SAW	PAS	EAW	GPA%
Semien, Marcus*	724	27 ●	26.8 ●	6.0 ●	4.50 ●	0.0 ○	0%
Freeman, Freddie*	708	27 ●	26.2 ●	5.9 ●	4.45 ●	0.0 ○	0%
Turner, Trea	708	27 ●	26.2 ●	5.9 ●	4.43 ●	0.0 ○	0%
Guerrero Jr., Vlad	706	27 ●	26.1 ●	5.9 ●	4.45 ●	0.1 ○	0%
Lindor, Francisco	706	27 ●	26.1 ●	6.0 ●	4.39 ●	0.0 ○	0%
Bichette, Bo	697	27 ●	25.8 ●	5.9 ●	4.41 ●	0.0 ○	0%
Judge, Aaron	696	27 ●	25.8 ●	5.7 ●	4.52 ●	0.1 ○	0%
Riley, Austin	693	27 ●	25.7 ●	5.9 ●	4.38 ●	0.0 ○	0%
Ramirez, Jose	685	27 ●	25.4 ●	5.8 ●	4.36 ●	0.0 ○	0%
Cronenworth, Jake	684	27 ●	25.3 ●	5.7 ●	4.39 ●	0.1 ○	0%
Hoskins, Rhys	672	27 ●	24.9 ●	5.7 ●	4.35 ●	0.1 ○	0%
Yelich, Christian	671	27 ●	24.9 ●	5.5 ●	4.48 ●	0.1 ○	0%
Rosario, Amed	670	27 ●	24.8 ●	5.6 ●	4.42 ●	0.1 ○	0%
Schwarber, Kyle	669	27 ●	24.8 ●	5.7 ●	4.36 ●	0.1 ○	0%
Soto, Juan	664	27 ●	24.6 ●	5.6 ●	4.36 ●	0.0 ○	0%
Seager, Corey	663	27 ●	24.6 ●	5.6 ●	4.39 ●	0.0 ○	0%

Of those 16, only Marcus Semien and Freddie Freeman had delivered a playing time trifecta in 2021 as well. The takeaway for fantasy managers is that players can be elite in one category, great in another, and maybe only good or borderline in the others, and that this is the exact type of insight that will help us quickly make sense of player's demonstrated playing time strengths and weaknesses, as well as opportunities and risks in the context of their respective teams.

To that end, here are a few examples of players with mixed playing time signals according to our new metrics heading into 2023:

Name	PA	AW	PAAW	SAW	PAS	EAW	GPA%
Kirk, Alejandro	541	27 ●	20.0 ◑	4.6 ◑	4.25 ◕	0.7 ◔	0%
Mullins II, Cedric	672	27 ●	24.9 ●	5.3 ◕	4.57 ●	0.5 ◔	0%
Pasquantino, Vinnie	298	13 ○	22.0 ◕	5.3 ◕	4.14 ◑	0.0 ○	4%
Reynolds, Bryan	614	25 ◕	24.5 ●	5.8 ◕	4.25 ◕	0.1 ○	0%
Tucker, Kyle	609	27 ●	22.6 ◕	5.5 ◕	4.10 ◑	0.1 ○	0%

- *Alejandro Kirk:* What would 625 PA of .300 BA from a C be worth? If Kirk can earn his way to 5.3-5.5 SAW between C and DH, we may find out! Players with similar playing time profiles include Steven Kwan, Luis Arraez, and Will Smith.

- *Cedric Mullins:* With an improving Orioles lineup and increased expectations of winning, both Mullins' PAS and SAW could be at some risk. Even with a SAW of ~5.0 and PAS of ~4.25 (both still "great"), he could lose 100 PAs. Players with similar playing time profiles include Christian Yelich, Amed Rosario, Jake Cronenworth, and Tommy Edman.

- *Vinnie Pasquantino:* Great SAW and good PAS as a rookie; only AW held him back. This is a PA total that is easy to double. Players with similar playing time profiles include Riley Greene, Oneil Cruz, and Luis García.

- *Bryan Reynolds:* Ultra-elite SAW means he rarely gets a day off when he's active. If he can avoid injury to stay active all 27 weeks and boost his PAS to 4.40 through either a trade or an improved Pirates offense, he could make the leap to triple-elite 675+ PA territory in 2023. Players with similar playing time profiles include Alex Bregman, Nolan Arenado, and Anthony Santander.

- *Kyle Tucker:* Can't seem to make his way up Houston's stacked lineup, but if he ever does, his PAS could jump and boost him into 650+ PA territory. Players with similar playing time profiles include Andrés Giménez, Jeff McNeil, and Jorge Mateo.

These kinds of insights make it plain to see just how blindly we've been playing this game for so many years. We believe that these new metrics will eventually become ubiquitous for fantasy managers everywhere, and now that we know what we know, we'll never look at playing time "the old way" ever again.

NOTE: Find full charts of 2022 players, complete with the above metrics and grouped by position, beginning on page 275 in our Draft Guides section.

The Value of volume

By Steve Weimer

Quality or quantity? Many fantasy baseball decisions boil down to this choice. How should we value "compilers," whose value largely derives from playing time volume? When and to what extent should we forego volume by prioritizing "skills over roles"? In-season, should we start the better hitter with a five-game week or the less-skilled hitter with seven games? The marginal two-start pitcher or a highly-skilled middle reliever?

There is no universal answer to the "quality or quantity?" question. How that dilemma should be resolved in a given case will depend upon details of the situation—how much of each is at stake, a particular team's strengths and needs, etc. Nevertheless, because we face variations of that question so many times over the course of a season, it's useful to have a general sense of the value of volume.

To that end, an examination was made of the importance of at-bats (AB) and innings pitched (IP) in three of the largest rotisserie competitions hosted by the National Fantasy Baseball Championship (NFBC): the 15-team Draft & Hold "Draft Champions" contest, the 15-team mixed "Main Event," and the 12-team mixed "Online Championship."

Hitting

To assess the value of volume, the correlation between each team's total AB and its total hitting points (i.e. overall points in the five standard roto hitting categories) was calculated. For sake of comparison, the correlation between total hitting points and totals in each of the five hitting categories was also determined. The same method is applied to pitching below.

Correlation with Total Hitting Points:

Format: Season	Teams	AB	R	HR	RBI	SB	BA
Draft & Hold: 2021	4545	0.80	0.91	0.80	0.86	0.52	0.59
Draft & Hold: 2022	4815	0.74	0.89	0.74	0.86	0.49	0.56
15-team mixed: 2021	645	0.74	0.89	0.80	0.86	0.57	0.59
15-team mixed: 2022	705	0.72	0.88	0.73	0.86	0.52	0.61
12-team mixed: 2021	2388	0.75	0.89	0.79	0.85	0.53	0.56
12-team mixed: 2022	2388	0.73	0.88	0.75	0.87	0.56	0.56

The correlation between AB and total hitting points is quite strong—on par with one of the five stats that directly contribute to hitting points (HR), and significantly stronger than two others (SB and BA). That AB have a stronger correlation with total hitting points than BA is particularly notable, as this is the only pure "quality" hitting category in standard roto scoring.

If we look at the relationship between AB and the five hitting categories, we see that the correlation is positive for all five, even BA:

Correlation with AB:

Format: Season	R	HR	RBI	SB	BA
Draft & Hold: 2021	0.89	0.63	0.82	0.43	0.33
Draft & Hold: 2022	0.85	0.53	0.80	0.33	0.28
15-team mixed: 2021	0.85	0.57	0.77	0.44	0.30
15-team mixed: 2022	0.79	0.46	0.74	0.34	0.33
12-team mixed: 2021	0.86	0.61	0.78	0.41	0.25
12-team mixed: 2022	0.82	0.53	0.77	0.41	0.28

As shown in the first table, the categories most strongly correlated with total hitting points are R and RBI. Here we see that R and RBI are strongly correlated with AB. Teams that maximize AB tend to do well in R and RBI, and teams that do well in R and RBI tend to do well with respect to total hitting points. With correlation coefficients of 0.74-0.91, the relationships between these statistics are about as reliable as one can hope to find in fantasy baseball. Taking advantage of that fact by maximizing AB should be a core part of one's hitting strategy.

Pitching

While quantity is king for hitting, quality rules for pitching.

Correlation with Total Pitching Points:

Format: Season	IP	K	W	Sv	ERA	WHIP
Draft & Hold: 2021	0.50	0.70	0.69	0.36	-0.82	-0.82
Draft & Hold: 2022	0.51	0.66	0.70	0.33	-0.80	-0.82
15-team mixed: 2021	0.47	0.69	0.65	0.44	-0.83	-0.82
15-team mixed: 2022	0.41	0.67	0.70	0.35	-0.85	-0.87
12-team mixed: 2021	0.47	0.70	0.67	0.44	-0.82	-0.80
12-team mixed: 2022	0.47	0.69	0.68	0.41	-0.84	-0.85

An unsuccessful at-bat directly hurts you in just one category: BA; a poor inning drags you down in two: ERA and WHIP. While we would therefore expect to see a weaker correlation between IP and pitching points than we did between AB and hitting points, it is surprising just how poorly pitching volume correlates with pitching points. IP are more weakly correlated to total pitching points than all but one category: saves (Sv). And in the formats that allow participants to chase saves with in-season pickups, IP trump Sv by only the smallest of margins. The strongest predictors of total pitching points are easily the pure "quality" ratio categories: ERA and WHIP. The prudent approach to pitching would seem to be "quality over quantity."

If by following that approach you establish a strong base in ratios and find yourself behind in strikeouts and wins, then it may make sense to prioritize volume. For although IP aren't strongly correlated with total pitching points, they have a predictably strong connection to K and W, specifically.

Correlation with Innings:

Format: Season	K	W	Sv	ERA	WHIP
Draft & Hold: 2021	0.86	0.78	-0.24	-0.16	-0.23
Draft & Hold: 2022	0.85	0.76	-0.19	-0.16	-0.20
15-team mixed: 2021	0.81	0.67	-0.19	-0.20	-0.23
15-team mixed: 2022	0.77	0.65	-0.28	-0.19	-0.20
12-team mixed: 2021	0.85	0.74	-0.11	-0.14	-0.15
12-team mixed: 2022	0.82	0.72	-0.15	-0.22	-0.24

Teams with more innings tend to do better in K and W, but worse in the other three pitching categories. Exercise caution in streaming starting pitchers.

Conclusion

As the season progresses, team-specific variables may necessitate departures from this mantra, but as a general plan of attack: quantity over quality for hitting, quality over quantity for pitching. Teams that successfully pile up AB and protect pitching ratios will tend to find themselves toward the top of the standings, and in a strong position from which to pursue specific categories as necessary down the stretch.

Reliability of ratio-protecting relievers

by Steve Weimer

Starting highly-skilled relievers can be an effective strategy for protecting pitching ratios. However, because reliever statistics are notoriously volatile, that strategy can be difficult to effectively put into practice. It is therefore useful to determine which first-half reliever statistics best predict second-half ratios and the "hit rate"

of those statistics – i.e. how reliably they lead to valuable second-half contributions to ERA and WHIP. ("First half" and "second half" refers to before and after the All-Star break).

Method

The rotisserie value of reliever statistics from the second half of 2019, 2021, and 2022 was calculated using Standings Gain Points (SGP) formulas for each season's NFBC Main Event. (Those formulas can be found in *The Process*, by Tanner Bell and Jeff Zimmerman). Those three seasons had very different scoring environments, but this is accounted for by the SGP formulas for each season. To contribute positively to ERA in 2022, a pitcher needed be under 3.65 (the average across all Main Event leagues). In 2021, that number was 3.92 and in the even livelier scoring environment of 2019, any ERA under 4.11 contributed positively to the category. For WHIP, the threshold for positive contributions was 1.25 in 2019, 1.21 in 2021, and 1.20 in 2022.

The sample includes pitchers who both (A) pitched at least 20 relief innings in each half of a given season and (B) threw more innings as a reliever than as a starter in each half of that season. Across the three years in question, 371 pitcher-seasons met these criteria.

For that sample, correlations were calculated between second-half value provided in the five standard pitching categories and a range of potential first-half indicator statistics. A summary of the most relevant findings is below.

Results

Correlation between first-half statistics and second-half categorical value:

1st-half stat	2nd-half SGP				
	ERA+WHIP	K	W	Sv	Total SGP
K-BB%	0.26	0.43	0.04	0.35	0.40
Ball%	-0.23	-0.07	-0.02	-0.23	-0.25
SwK	0.23	0.39	0.01	0.26	0.32
FpK	0.13	0.01	0.00	0.15	0.15
ERA	-0.21	-0.26	-0.16	-0.32	-0.38
WHIP	-0.20	-0.24	-0.09	-0.24	-0.30

Taking the first cell as an example, first-half K-BB% had a 0.26 correlation with second-half SGP in the two ratio categories combined. While the focus here is on protecting ratios, I included correlations with the other categories for reference.

The first-half statistic most strongly correlated with second-half reliever value, both in general and with respect to the ratio categories specifically, was K-BB%. Note, though, that two of the command sub-indicators (Ball% and SwK) had a similarly strong relation to second-half ratios. Given the unavoidably small samples we're working with, it helps that the denominator for those sub-indicators is pitches rather than plate appearances. More surprisingly, the surface-level ratios ERA and WHIP also fared relatively well.

In attempting to identify ratio-protecting relievers, it seems the focus should be on K-BB%, Ball%, and SwK.

None of the correlations listed above are overwhelming, though, suggesting that there is a good bit of variance in reliever production from first half to second. It is thus reasonable to wonder: How confident can we be that a reliever who displays good skills in the first half will effectively protect ratios in the second half? And how much can they be expected to contribute to the ratio categories? The following table addresses those questions:

1st Half Skill(s)	K-BB%>20	K-BB%>20 & GB%>40	Ball%<34 & SwK>13
Number of pitcher seasons	122	61	55
>1 ERA+WHIP SGP	41 (33%)	27 (44%)	21 (38%)
>0 ERA+WHIP SGP	84 (69%)	44 (72%)	40 (73%)
Avg ERA+WHIP SGP	0.47	0.59	0.68
Avg ERA+WHIP+K SGP	2.19	2.30	2.35
Avg Total SGP	4.83	4.95	5.15

Of the 122 relievers who posted a K-BB%>20 in the first half of 2019, 2021, or 2022 (while also meeting criteria (A) and (B) above), a little over two-thirds contributed positively to the ratio categories in the second half of that same season, with an average contribution of 0.47 SGP in ERA+WHIP. Those relievers typically didn't move teams up much in the standings for ERA and WHIP, but they didn't hurt them in those categories, which is often enough (by comparison, relievers with a first-half K-BB%<20 were worth negative 0.16 SGP in ERA+WHIP in the second half on average). When we factor in their contribution to K as well as ERA and WHIP, relievers with a first-half K-BB%>20 were worth more than two standings points in the second half on average. That's not counting any contribution they might make to W or Sv, which are included in the last row.

Since a couple of ill-timed home runs can significantly skew a reliever's ERA, it might be thought that groundball pitchers who are less susceptible to the longball would be a safer bet for protecting ratios. As the third column shows, that may be true to some extent. While relievers with a first-half K-BB%>20 and GB%>40 were only slightly more likely to contribute positively to ratios in the second half than those who met only the K-BB% threshold (72% vs. 69%), their average contribution to ERA and WHIP was noticeably higher (0.59 vs. 0.47).

Finally, it is interesting that the command sub-indicators thresholds yield even better results than K-BB%. A K-BB% of 20 would be roughly 14% better than the average across the 371-pitcher season sample. The Ball% and SwK thresholds used above—under 34% and over 13%, respectively—are each about 2.5% better than the average across that sample. Yet a pitcher hitting both of those marks in the first half is more likely to contribute positively to the ratio categories in the second half than one who posts a first-half K-BB% over 20. And the pitchers who hit the (relatively) lower Ball% and SwK thresholds were more valuable in the second half, on average.

Although the skills surveyed above are relatively strong predictors of second-half ratios in the aggregate, contextual factors must also be considered, most notably park factors and strength of opposing offenses. By taking advantage of the schedule and bypassing relievers who meet the relevant first-half thresholds but whose skills have clearly declined in the second half (i.e. loss of velocity, precipitous drop in strikeout rate), fantasy players should be able to do even better than the hit rates of the thresholds described above.

Draft and Hold strategy

by Brian Rudd

One format that has gained popularity over the past several seasons is Draft and Hold leagues. These contests typically consist of 12 or 15 teams and run for 50 rounds with 23 starting spots (14 hitters, nine pitchers) and 27 bench spots. The players you draft stick on your roster all year, and there are no in-season pickups. In most cases, you compete against teams in your league for league prizes, and against many others for an overall prize.

Roster construction

With no free agent pickups, it's essential to acquire quality depth because injuries are inevitable. You should roster at least four hitters each at each infield position: first base, second base, shortstop, and third base.

Selecting four catchers (two starters, two bench) is the most popular strategy, but if you draft two strong catchers, using just one bench spot is a viable alternative. If you wait to take one or both of your starting catchers, you should select two backups.

You need more depth on the bench to back up your five starting outfield spots. You'll want no less than four additional outfielders, but preferably five or more.

Multi-positional players provide extra value in these formats, as you never know where or when injuries or poor performance will leave you short-handed. These players can slide into a variety of spots and give you an edge.

Don't be afraid to take a utility-only player—their draft cost would be higher if they were eligible at any position. Just be careful not to take an additional UT-only player, as you can't start more than one. An exception can be made for someone in the mid to late rounds with a chance of qualifying at a position early in the season. But even someone like this is better suited for teams that haven't already locked up their utility spot.

Go into the draft with a good idea of what your hitter/pitcher splits will look like. There's no single right answer to how many of each you should end up with, as everyone has different strengths and weaknesses. Your roster construction also depends on whether you load up on hitting or pitching early, as you may want to make up for it with more depth on the other side. In most cases, you'll want to draft anywhere between 20 and 25 pitchers.

The NFBC Draft Champions contest is a popular option for the Draft and Hold format. Looking back at recent overall Draft Champions winners, Michael Maier and Thomas Olownia rostered 22 pitchers on their 2022 and 2021 winning teams, respectively, while Rob DiPietro drafted 21 in 2020. Steve Weimer finished second overall twice (2018 and 2021) with 26 hitters and 24 pitchers, respectively. These examples show there are multiple paths to success if you balance your roster effectively.

Strive for balance

It's important to have a balanced team if you have hopes of competing for the overall prize. History shows that in the Draft Champions contest, you need at least 90 percent of all possible points to win the overall title.

Therefore, it's helpful to have category goals and an idea of how you're tracking in each one throughout the draft. Previous-season results give us a good baseline to use, and taking multiple seasons into account is helpful.

Below are 80th and 90th percentile results in each category for the past two seasons. The targets changed quite a bit from one year to the next, but they still give us a decent sense of what to strive for. You'll have little chance of placing high in the overall standings if you finish way behind in any category:

Draft Champions Percentiles	2022 90th / 80th		2021 90th / 80th	
Runs	1,000	971	1,099	1,062
HR	280	266	329	312
RBI	981	948	1,057	1,019
SB	137	125	132	119
BA	.2587	.2553	.2652	.2620
K	1,378	1,325	1,425	1,369
W	95	89	92	87
Sv	73	63	78	67
ERA	3.273	3.386	3.484	3.625
WHIP	1.119	1.141	1.140	1.163

Closer conundrum

The closing landscape has changed dramatically in recent seasons. Top closers are being pushed up in Draft and Hold formats with fewer teams using one reliever to handle the ninth inning. In stand-alone leagues, punting saves is a viable strategy, and in overall contests with free agent pickups, targeting saves late in drafts and via free agency can work. In Draft and Holds, however, all saves must be accumulated during the draft.

When selecting top closers, you are paying a premium and passing on high-end options at other positions. Locking down a big chunk of your saves early can pay huge dividends, as only a few of these relievers have a stranglehold on the job with little risk of losing it.

If you wait on saves, you'll have to throw several late darts at relievers. While a few late picks will emerge with 20+ saves and others will provide strong ratios, many will be unusable with ugly ratios in a low-leverage role. There are multiple ways to attack saves but be sure to know where the closers typically get taken. Have a plan going into the draft and be ready to adapt to closer runs.

Limit the risk

A common mistake in Draft and Hold leagues is taking on too much risk. If you chase the upside of an injury-prone player with one of your first few picks, avoid injury risks with your other early picks and take safer options when filling out your roster at that same position.

Chasing prospects can also be fool's gold. The upside is enticing, and some will pay off, but even top prospects often struggle in their first taste of the majors, and some won't even reach the majors this season. The boring option is often the wiser choice because accumulating plate appearances and innings in your lineup is key to success.

The Benefits of structured drafting in rotisserie leagues
by Daniel Marcus

Introduction
Pocket aces. Early catcher. Drafting speed early. Drafting closers early. These are a few examples of draft strategies you'll hear fantasy analysts talk about all offseason. We sought to determine whether there's an advantage to any of these structured forms of drafting, or if drafting the best players and the right mix of stats is enough to win fantasy championships.

Methodology
We gathered data from the National Fantasy Baseball Championship (NFBC) because its league information is publicly available and easy to navigate. In addition, most of its leagues are traditional 5x5 formats, which was the targeted league type for this study. Finally, these leagues are growing in popularity, and many readers of both this book and BaseballHQ are likely to participate in them. The data collected was from the first five rounds of every league winner in the NFBC Main Event (15 teams) and Online Championship (12 teams) competitions from 2018-2022 (2020 short-season data omitted).

While perhaps more appropriate for the "conclusions" portion of the abstract, it's important to note what this data does and does not tell us. The data will tell us which type of roster builds appeared most frequently among league winners. It should also shed light on draft trends. This data does not tell us the "win rate" for each type of build, which would require data of every team that was drafted rather than just league winners. This is something we hope to expand to in the future, but it is a long-term project.

Analysis/Findings
Starting simply, we can identify the most common combination of hitters (H), starting pitchers (SP) and relief pitchers (RP) selected by league-winners in the first five rounds. Percentages refer to how often the combinations appeared:

12-team leagues	2018	2019	2021	2022
Most Common	3H/2SP (42%)	3H/2SP (44%)	3H/2SP (41%)	4H/1SP (29%)
Second-Most Common	4H/1SP (30%)	4H/1SP (29%)	4H/1SP (24%)	3H/1SP/1RP (23%)
Third-Most Common	2H/3SP (9%)	2H/3SP (12%)	3H/1SP/1RP (11%)	3H/2SP (15%)

15-team leagues	2018	2019	2021	2022
Most Common	3H/2SP (47%)	3H/2SP (47%)	3H/2SP (28%)	3H/2SP (30%)
Second-Most Common	4H/1SP (29%)	4H/1SP (39%)	4H/1SP (26%)	2H/2SP/1RP (28%)
Third-Most Common	3H/1SP/1RP (12%)	3H/1SP/1RP (5%)	3H/1SP/1RP (23%)	3H/1SP/1RP (17%)

Hitter-heavy approaches were the most common approach on league-winning teams. We saw starting pitchers picked at an increased rate in 12-team leagues. The trend of taking closers early in recent seasons is also clear from looking at this data, and once again particularly in 12-team leagues.

Starting Pitchers

The number of starting pitchers selected in the first five rounds followed the same trend among 12- and 15-team leagues. The most common league-winning build was two starting pitchers in the first five rounds among both league sizes.

Taking a pitcher in the first round or first two rounds (pocket aces) are also strategies that have grown in popularity and have at least some degree of effectiveness for league-winners:

12-team	R1 SP	Pocket Aces
2018	32%	9%
2019	21%	6%
2021	34%	14%
2022	24%	4%

15-team	R1 SP	Pocket Aces
2018	38%	9%
2019	42%	21%
2021	50%	21%
2022	36%	6%

Closers

Closers have shot up draft boards as saves have become less concentrated, a topic that was heavily featured in last year's edition of the *Baseball Forecaster*. This trend has become much more common in 15-team leagues. Selecting one closer early appears to be effective, while two closers is unpopular and perhaps ineffective in a team's first five rounds:

12-team	0 RP	1 RP	2 RP
2018	84%	14%	2%
2019	95%	5%	0%
2021	78%	20%	2%
2022	57%	40%	3%

15-team	0 RP	1 RP	2 RP
2018	79%	21%	0%
2019	87%	13%	0%
2021	53%	40%	5%
2022	45%	51%	4%

Stolen Bases

Pivoting to hitters, it's vital to get speed early, regardless of league size. Typically, 75% of league-winning teams drafted at least one hitter with 20+ stolen bases in the first five rounds, however, those numbers dropped in 2022:

20+ SB player, R1-5	12-tm	15-tm
2018	80%	85%
2019	68%	76%
2021	77%	75%
2022	64%	55%

Catchers

Drafting elite catchers early has also become a touted strategy, though it's still uncommon enough that it is difficult to draw conclusions with the current data:

Drafted CA, R1-5	12-tm	15-tm
2018	14%	15%
2019	22%	13%
2021	10%	11%
2022	26%	15%

Can you hack the waiver wire?

by Cary James

Is there a method or criteria that can help you preempt your league mates and hack the waiver wire? What method of filtering gives us the best opportunity to do so? When you peruse the contents of your league's waiver wire, you only have a few in-house methods to narrow down possible candidates.

Previous Production

The usefulness of a single game as a sign of future production is the worst indicator when picking up hitters. While a one-week sample is useful, your league is usually monitoring the same player using the same information, and most importantly, you are not acquiring their past production.

Pitchers are a totally different animal. In competitive leagues, you can't wait for consecutive starts before nabbing starters who have made changes like tweaking a pitch mix; one game must be enough. Treat starters like potential closer candidates on the wire and strike quickly to avoid bidding wars.

Does it hack? For hitters, past production helps you form a decision, but it does not guarantee an outcome. This is a better hack for pitchers, especially when determining the legitimacy of a breakout start.

Rostership Percentage

This isn't a useful filter in most leagues. Rostership percentage doesn't provide much information besides creating enough noise that upon losing a hitter to injury, outcome bias convinces us that an otherwise mediocre corner infielder rostered in 36% of leagues might be able to produce your third-round first baseman's weekly output. 36% of all leagues can't be wrong!

Does it hack? For both hitters and pitchers, rostership percentage serves to weaken your decision-making process. Ignore this filter as much as one ignores those little stop signs at the exits of Walgreens or CVS.

Transaction Trends

Most sites have a tool that allows you to see the Top 50-100 popular pickups over the last 24 hours. Once we exclude daily streamers, we can use this in tandem with a watch list to see if your window for cheap acquisition is closing. Getting ahead of the curve is the name of the game, and this tool delivers.

Does it hack? Once you exclude the streaming pitchers, this option hacks. Remember, our goal is to find the season-changing pick-ups for $1 rather than to lose your FAB or waiver priority later.

Rest-of-Season Projections

What began as friendly guesses have become a cottage industry of machine-learning servers attempting to account for every possible bit of baseball-related outcomes. To ignore this resource is folly. Combine them with season-to-date production and weigh them against category totals to analyze weaknesses as the season goes on. However, they are admittedly imperfect systems vulnerable to outcome bias.

Does it hack? This approach absolutely hacks.

In sum, rest-of-season projections and transaction trends are your best in-house tools when attempting to resist both recency and outcome bias.

The following section contains player boxes for every batter who had significant playing time in 2022 and/or is expected to get fantasy roster-worthy plate appearances in 2023. You will find some prospects here, specifically the most impactful names who we project to play in 2023. For more complete prospect coverage, see our Prospects section.

Snapshot Section

The top band of each player box contains the following information:

Age as of July 1, 2023.

Bats shows which side of the plate he bats from—(L)eft, (R)ight or (B)oth.

Positions: Up to three defensive positions are listed and represent those for which he appeared a minimum of 20 games in 2022. Note that an additional multiposition chart (with 20-, 10- and 5-game eligibility minimums) can be found on page 274.

Ht/Wt: Each batter's height and weight.

Reliability Grades analyze each batter's forecast risk, on an A-F scale. High grades go to those who have accumulated few disabled list days (Health), have a history of substantial and regular major league playing time (PT/Exp) and have displayed consistent performance over the past three years, using RC/G (Consist).

LIMA Plan Grade evaluates how well a batter would fit into a team using the LIMA Plan draft strategy. Best grades go to batters who have excellent base skills, are expected to see regular playing time, and are in the $10-$30 Rotisserie dollar range. Lowest grades will go to poor skills, few AB and values less than $5 or more than $30.

Random Variance Score (Rand Var) measures the impact random variance had on the batter's 2022 stats and the probability that his 2023 performance will exceed or fall short of 2022. The variables tracked are those prone to regression—h%, HR/F and xBA to BA variance. Players are rated on a scale of –5 to +5 with positive scores indicating rebounds and negative scores indicating corrections. Note that this score is computer-generated and the projections will override it on occasion.

Mayberry Method (MM) acknowledges the imprecision of the forecasting process by projecting player performance in broad strokes. The four digits of MM each represent a fantasy-relevant skill—power, speed, batting average and playing time (PA)—and are all on a scale of 0 to 5.

Commentaries provide a brief analysis of his skills and the potential impact on 2023 performance. MLB statistics are listed first for those who played only a portion of 2022 at the major league level. Note that these commentaries generally look at

performance related issues only. Role and playing time expectations may impact these analyses, so you will have to adjust accordingly. Upside (UP) and downside (DN) statistical potential appears for some players; these are less grounded in hard data and more speculative of skills potential.

Player Stat Section

The past five years' statistics represent the total accumulated in the majors as well as in Triple-A, Double-A ball and various foreign leagues during each year. All non-major league stats have been converted to a major league equivalent (MLE) performance level. Minor league levels below Double-A are not included.

Nearly all baseball publications separate a player's statistical experiences in the major leagues from the minor leagues and outside leagues. While this may be appropriate for official record-keeping purposes, it is not an easy-to-analyze snapshot of a player's complete performance for a given year.

Bill James has proven that minor league statistics (converted to MLEs), at Double-A level or above, provide as accurate a record of a player's performance as major league statistics. Other researchers have also devised conversion factors for foreign leagues. Since these are adequate barometers, we include them in the pool of historical data for each year.

Team designations: An asterisk (*) appearing with a team name means that Triple-A and/or Double-A numbers are included in that year's stat line. Any stints of less than 20 AB are not included (to screen out most rehab appearances). A designation of "a/a" means the stats were accumulated at both AA and AAA levels that year. "for" represents a foreign or independent league. The designation "2TM" appears whenever a player was on more than one major league team, crossing leagues, in a season. "2AL" and "2NL" represent more than one team in the same league. Players who were cut during the season and finished 2022 as a free agent are designated as FAA (Free agent, AL) and FAN (Free agent, NL).

Stats: Descriptions of all the categories appear in the Encyclopedia.

- The leading decimal point has been suppressed on some categories to conserve space.
- Data for platoons (vL+, vR+), xHR and xHR/F, balls-in-play (G/L/F) and batted ball characteristics (HctX, QBaB, Brl%) are for major league performance only.
- Formulas that use BIP data, like xBA and xPX, only appear for years in which G/L/F data is available.

After the traditional five rotisserie stat categories, expected HR, expected SB, and expected BA are presented for comparison. On base average and slugging average appear next, and then OPS+, which is adjusted to league average, for both OPS itself, and OPS splits vs. left-handed and right-handed pitchers.

Batting eye and contact skill are measured with walk rate (bb%), contact rate (ct%). Eye is the ratio of walks to strikeouts.

Once the ball leaves the bat, it will either be a (G)round ball, (L)ine drive or (F)ly ball. Hit rate (h%), also referred to as batting average on balls-in-play (BABIP), measures how often a ball put into play results in a base hit. Hard contact index (HctX) measures the frequency of hard contact, compared to overall league levels. QBaB is a quality-of-contact metric that encapsulates average exit velocity, average launch angle, and launch angle variability, and Brl% is a percentage of batted balls hit with the optimal exit velocity and launch angle combination.

Linear weighted power index (PX) measures a batter's skill at hitting extra base hits as compared to overall league levels. xPX measures power by assessing how hard the ball is being hit (rather than the outcomes of those hits). And the ratio of home runs to fly balls shows the results of those hits. Expected home runs to fly balls give a sense of whether the player over or underperformed in the power department.

To assess speed, first look at on-base average (does he get on base?), then Spd (is he fast enough to steal bases?), then SBA (how often is he attempting to steal bases?) and finally, SB% (when he attempts, what is his rate of success?).

The final section includes two overall performance measures: runs above replacement (RAR) and base performance index (BPX, which is BPV indexed to each year's league average) and the Rotisserie value (R$).

2023 Projections

Forecasts are computed from a player's trends over the past five years. Adjustments were made for leading indicators and variances between skill and statistical output. After reviewing the leading indicators, you might opt to make further adjustments.

Although each year's numbers include all playing time at the Double-A level or above, the 2023 forecast only represents potential playing time at the major league level, and again is highly preliminary.

Note that the projected Rotisserie values in this book will not necessarily align with each player's historical actuals. Since we currently have no idea who is going to play shortstop for the Dodgers, or whether Anthony Volpe is going to break camp with the Yankees, it is impossible to create a finite pool of playing time, something which is required for valuation. So the projections are roughly based on a 12-team AL/NL league, and include an inflated number of plate appearances, league-wide. This serves to flatten the spread of values and depress individual player dollar projections. In truth, a $25 player in this book might actually be worth $21, or $28. This level of precision is irrelevant in a process that is driven by market forces anyway. So, don't obsess over it.

Be aware of other sources that publish perfectly calibrated Rotisserie values over the winter. They are likely making arbitrary decisions as to where free agents are going to sign and who is going to land jobs in the spring. We do not make those leaps of faith here.

Bottom line… It is far too early to be making definitive projections for 2023, especially on playing time. Focus on the skill levels and trends, then consult BaseballHQ.com for playing time revisions as players change teams and roles become more defined. A free projections update will be available online in March.

Do-it-yourself analysis

Here are some data points you can look at in doing your own player analysis:

- Variance between vL+ and vR+ OPS+
- Growth or decline in walk rate (bb%)
- Growth or decline in contact rate (ct%)
- Growth or decline in G/L/F individually, or concurrent shifts
- Variance in 2022 hit rate (h%) to 2019-2021 three-year average
- Variance between BA and xBA each year
- Variance between 2022 HR and 2022 xHR
- Growth or decline in HctX level
- Growth or decline in QBaB scores
- Growth or decline in Brl%
- Growth or decline in power index (PX) rate
- Variance between PX and xPX each year
- Variance in 2022 HR/F rate to 2019-2021 three-year average
- Variance in 2022 HR/F rate to 2022 xHR/F rate
- Growth or decline in statistically scouted speed (Spd) score
- Concurrent growth/decline of gauges like ct%, FB, PX, xPX, HR/F
- Concurrent growth/decline of gauges like OB, Spd, SBA, SB%

Abrams,CJ

Age: 22	Pos: SS	Health	A	LIMA Plan	C+
Bats: L	Ht: 6' 2" Wt: 185	PT/Exp	C	Rand Var	-1
		Consist	B	MM	1515

2-21-.246 with 7 SB in 302 PA at SD/WAS. Top MI prospect—and key return in huge Juan Soto trade—ended year on a high note (.303 BA, 91% ct% in Sept/Oct.). Sure, there's currently no pop in the bat, he's not walking at all, and lefties give him fits. But there's time for all that. For now, his value lies in still-developing running game.

Yr	Tm	PA	R	HR	RBI	SB	BA	xHR	xSB	xBA	OBP	SLG	OPS+	vL+	vR+	bb%	ct%	Eye	G	L	F	h%	HctX	QBaB	Brl%	PX	xPX	HR/F	xHR/F	Spd	SBA%	SB%	RAR	BPX	R$
18																																			
19																																			
20																																			
21	aa	174	20	1	18	10	259		2		311	364	93			7	76	0.31				34				78				87	30%	82%		27	$6
22	2 NL *	480	63	7	42	17	255	3	20	243	274	351	89	54	100	2	81	0.14	51	18	31	30	88	DDf	2%	61	65	3%	4%	134	23%	67%	-16.1	69	$16
1st Half		258	38	6	28	8	246	1	10	226	275	360	90	34	90	4	79	0.19	45	16	39	29	72	FDf	4%	69	86	3%	3%	109	23%	65%	-7.2	45	$16
2nd Half		222	25	1	14	9	264	1	9	252	272	342	87	62	106	1	83	0.07	54	19	28	31	97	DFf	1%	52	55	2%	2%	148	23%	68%	-7.0	83	$8
23	Proj	**560**	**70**	**4**	**52**	**26**	**258**	**4**	**19**	**234**	**308**	**344**	**91**	**63**	**102**	**4**	**79**	**0.21**	**50**	**17**	**32**	**32**	**87**		**2%**	**65**	**67**	**3%**	**3%**	**129**	**18%**	**75%**	**-7.5**	**51**	**$21**

Abreu,José

Age: 36	Pos: 1B DH	Health	A	LIMA Plan	B
Bats: R	Ht: 6' 3" Wt: 235	PT/Exp	A	Rand Var	-2
		Consist	C	MM	3245

Let's flip the usual order... CON: Another GB increase led to big power dip; 2nd-half hit rate buoyed BA. PRO: Many plate skills (see Eye, HctX) as good/better than ever; vintage exit velocity; xHR suggests power rebound. Even at 36, this is still a skill set to own. Just use .275, 20 HR as your baseline, and figure at least one of those will be higher.

Yr	Tm	PA	R	HR	RBI	SB	BA	xHR	xSB	xBA	OBP	SLG	OPS+	vL+	vR+	bb%	ct%	Eye	G	L	F	h%	HctX	QBaB	Brl%	PX	xPX	HR/F	xHR/F	Spd	SBA%	SB%	RAR	BPX	R$
18	CHW	553	68	22	78	2	265	24	7	276	325	473	107	121	102	7	78	0.34	44	21	35	30	109	ACc	9%	127	103	16%	18%	79	2%	100%	11.1	177	$16
19	CHW	693	85	33	123	2	284	37	3	272	330	503	115	140	106	5	76	0.24	46	22	32	33	107	ACb	13%	117	104	21%	24%	82	3%	50%	14.3	130	$24
20	CHW	262	43	19	60	0	317	17	1	295	370	617	131	114	136	7	75	0.31	45	24	32	35	122	ACb	14%	163	127	33%	29%	74	0%	0%	19.3	280	$38
21	CHW	659	86	30	117	1	261	28	2	261	351	481	114	132	109	9	75	0.43	46	19	35	30	114	ACc	10%	126	99	20%	19%	73	1%	100%	15.9	162	$22
22	CHW	679	85	15	75	0	304	24	4	261	378	446	117	120	116	9	82	0.56	48	20	32	35	133	ADc	9%	93	105	10%	15%	86	0%	0%	31.8	162	$26
1st Half		338	46	10	37	0	289	16	2	260	379	459	119	126	117	12	83	0.78	47	17	36	32	142	ACb	11%	107	118	11%	18%	88	0%	0%	14.7	234	$21
2nd Half		341	39	5	38	0	319	8	2	263	378	433	115	115	115	7	81	0.37	49	24	27	38	124	ADc	8%	80	92	7%	12%	84	0%	0%	12.7	97	$22
23	Proj	**630**	**84**	**23**	**96**	**1**	**286**	**26**	**2**	**267**	**359**	**469**	**115**	**122**	**113**	**9**	**78**	**0.43**	**47**	**21**	**32**	**33**	**123**		**10%**	**118**	**104**	**16%**	**18%**	**74**	**1%**	**85%**	**27.7**	**168**	**$28**

Acuña Jr.,Ronald

Age: 25	Pos: RF DH	Health	D	LIMA Plan	D+
Bats: R	Ht: 6' 0" Wt: 205	PT/Exp	A	Rand Var	0
		Consist	C	MM	4335

Struggled somewhat after late April return from 2021 ACL tear, and he admitted the knee hurt all season—a lot. That almost certainly explains startling decline in previously elite launch angle, which doused both power and BA. Still pre-peak, yet already has a solid track record to rely on. Together, that points to a big rebound with full health.

Yr	Tm	PA	R	HR	RBI	SB	BA	xHR	xSB	xBA	OBP	SLG	OPS+	vL+	vR+	bb%	ct%	Eye	G	L	F	h%	HctX	QBaB	Brl%	PX	xPX	HR/F	xHR/F	Spd	SBA%	SB%	RAR	BPX	R$
18	ATL *	586	86	27	67	20	276	29	8	252	344	499	113	132	117	9	71	0.36	42	18	39	34	117	ACc	13%	139	140	21%	24%	129	18%	77%	24.3	187	$27
19	ATL	712	127	41	101	37	280	50	22	254	365	518	122	125	120	11	70	0.40	38	24	38	34	111	BBb	15%	128	139	25%	30%	129	24%	80%	21.5	163	$42
20	ATL	202	46	14	29	8	250	15	7	263	406	581	131	111	136	19	63	0.63	35	22	43	30	129	AAc	16%	217	186	33%	35%	89	16%	89%	13.3	360	$29
21	ATL	360	72	24	52	17	283	26	9	277	394	596	136	145	134	14	71	0.58	31	23	46	32	113	AAc	20%	185	139	24%	26%	102	23%	74%	27.6	358	$23
22	ATL	533	71	15	50	29	266	25	19	241	351	413	108	100	111	10	73	0.42	48	18	34	33	110	ACf	13%	102	109	13%	21%	97	27%	73%	8.7	86	$27
1st Half		220	33	7	19	17	285	11	9	242	382	446	117	130	113	11	72	0.44	46	19	35	36	106	ACf	17%	110	131	15%	23%	116	27%	81%	9.4	121	$22
2nd Half		313	38	8	31	12	253	14	10	239	329	391	102	78	109	10	74	0.41	49	18	33	32	114	ACf	11%	97	94	12%	20%	86	27%	63%	-0.2	66	$22
23	Proj	**630**	**108**	**29**	**77**	**32**	**270**	**38**	**26**	**255**	**369**	**489**	**119**	**116**	**120**	**12**	**71**	**0.48**	**41**	**20**	**39**	**33**	**114**		**16%**	**148**	**129**	**19%**	**25%**	**92**	**19%**	**75%**	**34.7**	**205**	**$41**

Adames,Willy

Age: 27	Pos: SS	Health	B	LIMA Plan	B
Bats: R	Ht: 6' 0" Wt: 210	PT/Exp	A	Rand Var	+4
		Consist	A	MM	4225

Further launch-angle gains propelled still more power growth. He's probably just about maxed that out, but xBA says the average should bounce back, at least a little. So, given peaking skills and stabilizing numbers, let's go out on a limb and just duplicate this projection for two or three more seasons.

Yr	Tm	PA	R	HR	RBI	SB	BA	xHR	xSB	xBA	OBP	SLG	OPS+	vL+	vR+	bb%	ct%	Eye	G	L	F	h%	HctX	QBaB	Brl%	PX	xPX	HR/F	xHR/F	Spd	SBA%	SB%	RAR	BPX	R$
18	TAM *	591	74	13	63	9	268	10	9	212	335	386	97	89	104	9	68	0.32	52	18	30	37	87	CDc	7%	77	89	17%	17%	161	10%	51%	7.9	3	$17
19	TAM	584	69	20	52	4	254	22	9	246	317	418	102	80	112	8	71	0.30	47	23	30	32	104	CCb	8%	94	91	18%	19%	105	4%	67%	-4.6	33	$11
20	TAM	205	29	8	23	2	259	7	2	240	332	481	108	129	100	10	60	0.27	43	25	32	39	90	CCf	10%	165	111	23%	20%	122	7%	67%	5.0	120	$16
21	2 TM	555	77	25	73	5	262	25	7	248	337	481	112	105	116	10	69	0.37	37	23	41	33	106	BBc	11%	142	131	18%	18%	105	7%	56%	13.8	162	$18
22	MIL	617	83	31	98	8	238	30	5	248	298	458	107	98	110	8	71	0.30	34	20	46	28	108	CAc	13%	149	170	17%	16%	88	9%	73%	3.3	159	$22
1st Half		262	41	16	45	2	207	15	2	252	282	456	104	111	102	9	69	0.33	35	19	46	22	109	BAc	16%	165	176	21%	20%	88	9%	67%	-1.1	193	$19
2nd Half		355	42	15	53	6	261	15	3	245	310	460	109	89	117	7	71	0.27	34	21	46	32	108	CAd	11%	137	166	14%	14%	91	9%	75%	7.0	134	$31
23	Proj	**595**	**81**	**27**	**84**	**7**	**250**	**27**	**8**	**246**	**316**	**464**	**108**	**101**	**111**	**9**	**69**	**0.31**	**37**	**21**	**41**	**31**	**105**		**12%**	**151**	**144**	**18%**	**17%**	**99**	**8%**	**66%**	**16.7**	**141**	**$24**

Adams,Riley

Age: 27	Pos: CA	Health	A	LIMA Plan	D
Bats: R	Ht: 6' 4" Wt: 246	PT/Exp	F	Rand Var	+5
		Consist	B	MM	3001

5-10-.176 in 155 PA at WAS. 2017 3rd-rounder again posted cringe-worthy MLB hitting numbers, threw out only 5 of 37 base stealers (14%; MLB average ~25%), and isn't a young pup anymore. On the plus side, his Wiki page says he was a Science Fair whiz in middle school, and he once grabbed 31 rebounds in a HS basketball game. So that's cool.

Yr	Tm	PA	R	HR	RBI	SB	BA	xHR	xSB	xBA	OBP	SLG	OPS+	vL+	vR+	bb%	ct%	Eye	G	L	F	h%	HctX	QBaB	Brl%	PX	xPX	HR/F	xHR/F	Spd	SBA%	SB%	RAR	BPX	R$
18																																			
19	aa	317	44	11	37	3	252		4		323	431	104			10	61	0.27				38				122				109	5%	73%		-19	$6
20																																			
21	2 TM *	253	28	7	22	0	211	4	3	212	301	390	95	96	106	11	58	0.31	46	20	34	33	80	CCb	14%	140	105	10%	20%	105	0%	0%	-0.3	0	$0
22	WAS *	269	21	8	21	0	176	5	0	187	234	310	77	56	97	7	62	0.20	45	15	41	25	88	BCd	10%	107	105	13%	13%	72	2%	0%	-11.4	-93	-$4
1st Half		92	9	4	6	0	203	4	0	192	282	361	91	65	105	10	67	0.33	44	12	44	25	90	BBc	10%	105	139	13%	17%	95	2%	0%	-1.3	3	-$7
2nd Half		177	12	4	15	0	163	2	0	190	210	286	70	42	88	6	60	0.15	45	18	36	24	89	BCf	10%	108	65	13%	13%	67	2%	0%	-9.6	-141	-$6
23	Proj	**175**	**17**	**4**	**15**	**0**	**199**	**6**	**1**	**198**	**291**	**337**	**87**	**71**	**99**	**9**	**61**	**0.26**	**45**	**17**	**37**	**30**	**86**		**11%**	**116**	**100**	**12%**	**17%**	**86**	**3%**	**27%**	**-2.4**	**-44**	**$1**

Adell,Jo

Age: 24	Pos: LF	Health	A	LIMA Plan	D+
Bats: R	Ht: 6' 3" Wt: 215	PT/Exp	B	Rand Var	0
		Consist	C	MM	4303

8-27-.224 in 285 PA at LAA. And the big-league struggles continue for former top prospect. He's still young-ish, he's been SO good in the minors, and he shows just enough flashes to keep us interested long-term. But awful plate skills simply must improve in the majors before he can tap into those gaudy tools.

Yr	Tm	PA	R	HR	RBI	SB	BA	xHR	xSB	xBA	OBP	SLG	OPS+	vL+	vR+	bb%	ct%	Eye	G	L	F	h%	HctX	QBaB	Brl%	PX	xPX	HR/F	xHR/F	Spd	SBA%	SB%	RAR	BPX	R$
18	aa	68	13	2	6	2	225		1		285	402	92			8	63	0.23				32				146				104	18%	100%		60	-$1
19	a/a	303	40	7	25	6	257		7		315	415	101			8	67	0.25				36				110				97	9%	100%		11	$5
20	LAA	132	9	3	7	0	161	3	1	167	212	266	63	74	58	5	56	0.13	43	19	38	26	72	BCf	4%	82	60	12%	12%	115	5%	0%	-15.8	-256	-$4
21	LAA *	465	53	18	70	7	234	4	4	235	271	419	95	104	92	5	67	0.15	47	20	33	31	88	DCd	9%	118	83	13%	13%	127	12%	68%	-7.9	42	$11
22	LAA *	451	42	16	46	6	208	6	6	213	249	385	90	79	97	5	59	0.13	39	21	41	31	64	CBd	10%	146	85	12%	9%	112	14%	57%	-14.6	0	$6
1st Half		228	19	9	25	2	193	3	2	231	243	385	89	78	106	6	59	0.16	43	25	32	28	67	CCb	13%	162	103	18%	18%	85	14%	39%	-8.8	21	$2
2nd Half		223	22	7	21	4	225	3	3	199	256	388	91	79	91	4	60	0.10	36	19	45	34	63	DAf	9%	130	76	10%	6%	141	14%	78%	-5.0	-17	$7
23	Proj	**385**	**39**	**11**	**42**	**5**	**218**	**10**	**6**	**210**	**265**	**367**	**88**	**85**	**89**	**5**	**62**	**0.14**	**43**	**21**	**37**	**32**	**75**		**9%**	**121**	**83**	**13%**	**11%**	**108**	**11%**	**67%**	**-8.8**	**-13**	**$8**

Aguilar,Jesús

Age: 33	Pos: 1B DH	Health	B	LIMA Plan	D
Bats: R	Ht: 6' 3" Wt: 277	PT/Exp	A	Rand Var	0
		Consist	B	MM	3021

Several signs of decline here, as exit velocity was a career worst for a full season, contact rate looks to have crested the hill, and walk rate fell yet again. It all led to a DFA in August, and he didn't exactly sparkle after BAL picked him up (.484 Sept OPS). As this projection suggests, he may have trouble getting a job in 2023. DN: 0 AB in MLB

Yr	Tm	PA	R	HR	RBI	SB	BA	xHR	xSB	xBA	OBP	SLG	OPS+	vL+	vR+	bb%	ct%	Eye	G	L	F	h%	HctX	QBaB	Brl%	PX	xPX	HR/F	xHR/F	Spd	SBA%	SB%	RAR	BPX	R$
18	MIL	566	80	35	108	0	274	31	8	269	352	539	119	123	116	10	71	0.41	35	24	41	32	115	BBc	11%	163	158	24%	21%	33	0%	0%	31.1	157	$23
19	2 TM	366	39	12	50	0	236	15	0	230	325	389	99	97	100	12	74	0.53	42	20	38	28	107	BCc	8%	83	106	13%	16%	59	0%	0%	-6.2	22	$4
20	MIA	216	31	8	34	0	277	8	0	265	352	457	107	125	100	11	79	0.58	36	26	38	31	113	BBb	7%	99	121	14%	14%	60	2%	0%	1.3	140	$18
21	MIA	505	49	22	93	0	261	18	1	253	329	459	108	109	108	9	79	0.49	33	20	47	28	116	BAc	7%	109	132	13%	11%	46	0%	0%	8.3	146	$14
22	2 TM	501	39	16	51	1	235	16	0	235	281	379	94	78	99	6	74	0.24	31	24	45	28	97	CAc	7%	94	120	10%	10%	45	1%	100%	-7.8	0	$7
1st Half		297	26	10	35	1	248	8	0	245	293	405	99	84	103	6	74	0.26	31	25	44	30	98	CBc	7%	104	117	11%	9%	47	1%	100%	-2.4	31	$11
2nd Half		204	13	6	16	0	216	8	0	222	265	342	86	71	92	5	74	0.20	30	23	47	26	98	CAc	6%	81	123	9%	12%	52	1%	0%	-9.0	-38	-$1
23	Proj	**245**	**23**	**9**	**34**	**0**	**246**	**9**	**0**	**243**	**305**	**412**	**100**	**95**	**101**	**8**	**76**	**0.34**	**33**	**23**	**45**	**28**	**106**		**8%**	**106**	**125**	**12%**	**12%**	**49**	**0%**	**58%**	**0.8**	**62**	**$7**

ROD TRUESDELL

Ahmed,Nick

Age: 33	Pos: SS	Health	F	LIMA Plan	D+
Bats: R	Ht: 6' 2" Wt: 201	PT/Exp	D	Rand Var	0
		Consist	B	MM	2221

Felled by chronic shoulder woes, which have made his 2019 power seem like a distant memory. Eroding plate skills, consecutive years of subpar batted-ball quality add further risk to an underwhelming profile. It's time to recalibrate expectations; he's nothing more than end-game fodder now.

Yr Tm	PA	R	HR	RBI	SB	BA	xHR	xSB	xBA	OBP	SLG	OPS+	vL+	vR+	bb%	ct%	Eye	G	L	F	h%	HctX	QBaB	Brl%	PX	xPX	HR/F	xHR/F	Spd	SBA%	SB%	RAR	BPX	R$
18 ARI	564	61	16	70	5	234	12	6	270	290	411	94	102	88	7	79	0.37	41	24	35	27	113	CCc	5%	107	124	11%	8%	94	8%	56%	0.9	153	$11
19 ARI	625	79	19	82	8	254	20	9	272	316	437	104	130	95	8	80	0.46	48	20	32	29	104	CDd	7%	95	99	13%	14%	121	7%	80%	0.0	185	$16
20 ARI	217	29	5	29	4	266	5	3	249	327	402	97	100	95	8	77	0.39	52	19	29	32	92	CDd	5%	79	66	11%	11%	107	7%	100%	1.0	84	$18
21 ARI	473	46	5	38	7	221	5	6	238	280	339	85	106	75	7	76	0.33	48	18	34	28	80	DCf	2%	80	67	5%	5%	117	10%	78%	-19.2	77	$4
22 ARI	54	7	3	7	0	231	1	1	246	259	442	99	44	124	4	71	0.13	58	11	31	26	92	DDf	5%	136	131	27%	9%	98	11%	0%	-1.4	110	-$2
1st Half	54	7	3	7	0	231	1	1	246	259	442	99	44	123	4	71	0.13	58	11	31	26	92	DDf	5%	136	131	27%	9%	98	11%	0%	-1.2	110	-$8
2nd Half																																		
23 Proj	245	30	5	30	3	242	5	3	240	293	375	93	85	96	7	75	0.29	51	17	31	30	93		5%	92	95	10%	9%	98	9%	60%	-1.7	107	$4

Albies,Ozzie

Age: 26	Pos: 2B	Health	F	LIMA Plan	B+
Bats: B	Ht: 5' 8" Wt: 165	PT/Exp	B	Rand Var	+1
		Consist	B	MM	3335

8-35-.247 in 269 PA at ATL. Couldn't catch a break...unless you count those to foot, pinkie. Prior to lost season, surging launch angle helped inch Brl% to impact level, which puts return to 30 HR in play. Pair that with track record of Spd + acumen on basepaths, and you've got a premium profit play heading into his age-26 season. UP: 35 HR, 30 SB

Yr Tm	PA	R	HR	RBI	SB	BA	xHR	xSB	xBA	OBP	SLG	OPS+	vL+	vR+	bb%	ct%	Eye	G	L	F	h%	HctX	QBaB	Brl%	PX	xPX	HR/F	xHR/F	Spd	SBA%	SB%	RAR	BPX	R$
18 ATL	684	105	24	72	14	261	19	8	268	305	452	101	120	92	5	82	0.31	39	21	40	29	104	CBc	5%	109	100	12%	9%	123	12%	82%	8.4	213	$24
19 ATL	702	102	24	86	15	295	27	15	284	352	500	118	153	107	8	83	0.48	38	25	37	33	121	CBb	7%	103	114	12%	14%	133	11%	79%	32.0	259	$28
20 ATL	124	21	6	19	3	271	5	2	231	306	466	103	64	114	4	75	0.17	41	14	45	32	82	DBd	9%	108	82	15%	13%	132	15%	75%	-0.4	136	$14
21 ATL	686	103	30	106	20	259	29	13	259	310	488	110	128	103	7	80	0.37	31	20	49	28	113	BAc	9%	126	129	12%	12%	116	18%	83%	14.9	269	$31
22 ATL *	296	39	9	40	3	251	8	6	247	292	411	100	100	99	5	80	0.30	38	18	44	28	114	CBd	5%	101	125	9%	9%	97	13%	38%	-2.6	152	$8
1st Half	263	34	8	33	3	244	8	5	251	289	405	98	103	95	6	81	0.33	38	19	44	27	117	CBd	6%	102	128	9%	9%	90	13%	38%	-2.1	159	$13
2nd Half	33	5	1	7	0	307	0	1	192	328	459	111	0	355	3	75	0.12	50	0	50	39	0	CAf		90	-14	0%	0%	135	13%	0%	1.4	69	-$7
23 Proj	630	95	25	88	13	262	23	11	254	306	455	106	105	106	6	79	0.29	38	18	44	29	105		7%	120	110	12%	11%	123	12%	67%	16.5	190	$30

Alcantara,Sergio

Age: 26	Pos: 3B SS 2B	Health	A	LIMA Plan	D
Bats: B	Ht: 5' 9" Wt: 151	PT/Exp	D	Rand Var	0
		Consist	B	MM	2301

When a batter's stats don't impress, focus on metrics like QBaB, xPX, and Spd to find latent reasons for optimism. Here... well, the first two offer no reason for hope. Okay... legs are his path to value, as shown by sexy Spd! But... big holes in swing and zero trust from managers render that skill useless. Yeah... sometimes it's a painful exercise.

Yr Tm	PA	R	HR	RBI	SB	BA	xHR	xSB	xBA	OBP	SLG	OPS+	vL+	vR+	bb%	ct%	Eye	G	L	F	h%	HctX	QBaB	Brl%	PX	xPX	HR/F	xHR/F	Spd	SBA%	SB%	RAR	BPX	R$
18 aa	476	45	1	31	7	252		7		307	310	83			7	78	0.36				32				41				115	10%	56%		-13	$6
19 aa	369	44	2	26	7	237		7		329	285	85			12	77	0.61				30				31				102	12%	51%		-30	$4
20 DET	23	2	1	1	0	143	0	0	227	217	381	79	217	56	9	81	0.50	35	12	53	13	96	DAb		99	106	11%	0%	156	0%	0%	-1.4	276	-$3
21 CHC *	352	43	7	23	5	217	3	4	207	318	334	90	59	99	13	67	0.44	46	20	34	30	97	CCd	3%	75	99	10%	6%	154	5%	100%	-9.1	0	$3
22 2 NL	224	26	6	29	1	220	3	2	227	261	356	87	87	87	5	72	0.21	43	20	37	27	84	DCc	1%	91	75	11%	5%	125	7%	33%	-9.0	41	$1
1st Half	95	9	1	10	0	159	1	1	203	183	239	60	61	59	3	72	0.12	41	22	38	21	61	FDf	3%	52	67	4%	4%	123	7%	0%	-9.1	-93	-$10
2nd Half	129	17	5	19	1	265	1	2	244	318	444	108	107	108	7	73	0.28	45	18	37	33	102	CBb	0%	120	80	16%	3%	131	7%	100%	2.5	145	$3
23 Proj	175	21	4	18	2	225	2	3	222	291	353	89	77	94	8	72	0.33	44	20	36	29	90		2%	87	84	11%	4%	139	9%	60%	-2.3	21	$4

Alfaro,Jorge

Age: 30	Pos: CA	Health	D	LIMA Plan	D
Bats: R	Ht: 6' 3" Wt: 230	PT/Exp	C	Rand Var	-2
		Consist	A	MM	2203

Early batted-ball returns had us hoping for long-awaited breakthrough with bat, but regression is a powerful force. PRO: xHR/Brl% keep hinting at more power; groundball rate lowest of career. CON: Horrible plate skills show no hope; steep GB lean returned in 2nd half. If knee injury was cause of late fade, there's some one-category impact here, but that's it.

Yr Tm	PA	R	HR	RBI	SB	BA	xHR	xSB	xBA	OBP	SLG	OPS+	vL+	vR+	bb%	ct%	Eye	G	L	F	h%	HctX	QBaB	Brl%	PX	xPX	HR/F	xHR/F	Spd	SBA%	SB%	RAR	BPX	R$
18 PHI	377	35	10	37	3	262	15	5	213	324	407	98	96	97	5	60	0.13	48	23	29	41	83	ADb	11%	113	102	17%	25%	131	3%	100%	7.2	-60	$7
19 MIA	465	44	18	57	4	262	23	3	227	312	425	102	113	97	5	64	0.14	53	22	25	37	97	BFb	12%	98	102	25%	32%	88	7%	50%	-1.3	-96	$10
20 MIA	100	12	3	16	2	226	4	1	198	280	344	83	83	82	4	61	0.11	49	21	30	33	113	CFf	7%	78	140	18%	24%	87	9%	100%	-2.8	-220	$6
21 MIA	311	22	4	30	8	244	8	4	222	283	342	86	100	80	4	66	0.11	57	20	22	35	98	AFd	8%	74	81	9%	18%	92	13%	89%	-5.6	-142	$5
22 SD	274	25	7	40	1	246	10	4	219	285	383	95	108	90	4	62	0.11	47	24	29	37	84	BDc	11%	115	106	15%	21%	81	2%	100%	0.0	-90	$4
1st Half	169	18	6	24	1	272	8	3	239	308	456	108	136	99	5	63	0.14	42	26	33	40	95	ACb	14%	150	131	18%	24%	86	2%	100%	6.1	28	$5
2nd Half	105	7	1	16	0	204	2	2	181	248	265	73	71	73	3	60	0.08	55	22	23	33	66	CFd	8%	56	65	7%	14%	83	2%	0%	-5.0	-283	-$6
23 Proj	315	27	7	42	3	238	10	1	212	280	358	89	98	85	4	63	0.11	51	22	27	35	89		9%	98	94	14%	20%	81	3%	86%	-1.3	-152	$8

Allen,Greg

Age: 30	Pos: LF	Health	D	LIMA Plan	D
Bats: B	Ht: 6' 0" Wt: 185	PT/Exp	F	Rand Var	0
		Consist	D	MM	1501

Hurt left hamstring in April, then right hamstring just as he was about to be activated in June, and didn't see a pitch until July 22. Given that speed is the only thing that keeps him relevant, consider 2022 a washout. Even still, his one-category appeal is stymied by holes in swing, and speed history tells us his legs are more good than great anyway.

Yr Tm	PA	R	HR	RBI	SB	BA	xHR	xSB	xBA	OBP	SLG	OPS+	vL+	vR+	bb%	ct%	Eye	G	L	F	h%	HctX	QBaB	Brl%	PX	xPX	HR/F	xHR/F	Spd	SBA%	SB%	RAR	BPX	R$
18 CLE *	477	60	4	31	30	260	3	7	241	306	352	88	64	91	6	75	0.27	47	24	29	34	101	CDb	1%	66	84	3%	5%	122	34%	73%	-9.5	13	$18
19 CLE *	470	59	8	40	16	231	5	22	237	276	350	87	59	100	6	76	0.26	49	19	32	29	82	CDc	3%	65	54	7%	9%	159	23%	67%	-30.2	59	$10
20 2 TM	32	4	1	4	2	154	1	1	186	281	308	78	0	104	9	62	0.30	24	24	53	20	29	FAf	6%	105	18	11%	11%	103	29%	100%	-2.2	-68	$0
21 NYY *	282	44	4	22	24	259	0	12	194	324	371	95	186	88	9	72	0.34	21	25	54	35	94	FAb	8%	77	145	0%	0%	115	36%	90%	-1.6	12	$15
22 PIT	134	17	2	8	8	186	1	6	189	260	271	75	69	80	7	64	0.24	53	14	34	27	84	FFf	3%	68	110	8%	4%	105	36%	80%	-7.4	-131	$0
1st Half																																		
2nd Half	134	17	2	8	8	186	1	6	189	260	271	0	69	80	8	64	0.24	53	14	34	27	84	FFf	3%	68	110	8%	4%	105	36%	80%	-7.5	-134	$0
23 Proj	210	29	3	16	10	236	2	11	220	305	332	88	69	97	7	72	0.26	50	19	31	32	90		2%	71	86	6%	5%	122	27%	74%	-3.6	-13	$8

Allen,Nick

Age: 24	Pos: SS 2B	Health	A	LIMA Plan	D+
Bats: R	Ht: 5' 8" Wt: 166	PT/Exp	B	Rand Var	+1
		Consist	A	MM	1205

4-19-.207 with 3 SB in 326 PA at OAK. Glove-first prospect a clear work-in-progress with bat. Among AL batters with 300+ PA, his average exit velocity was the worst. The hope here is that his glove helps him to qualify all over diamond, letting him use ct% + Spd combo to reach double-digit steals. That's a best-case scenario for now.

Yr Tm	PA	R	HR	RBI	SB	BA	xHR	xSB	xBA	OBP	SLG	OPS+	vL+	vR+	bb%	ct%	Eye	G	L	F	h%	HctX	QBaB	Brl%	PX	xPX	HR/F	xHR/F	Spd	SBA%	SB%	RAR	BPX	R$
18																																		
19																																		
20																																		
21 a/a	359	34	4	29	8	241		4		284	331	85			6	74	0.23				31				60				100	18%	55%		-38	$6
22 OAK *	513	48	5	28	8	202	1	11	224	255	277	75	107	65	7	78	0.32	52	17	32	25	67	FFf	1%	55	56	5%	1%	110	12%	66%	-27.4	10	$1
1st Half	264	26	2	14	6	204	0	6	220	269	276	77	113	78	8	77	0.39	49	17	34	26	62	FDf	2%	56	61	6%	0%	120	12%	59%	-14.9	31	$1
2nd Half	249	22	3	14	2	200	1	5	224	239	278	73	104	62	5	78	0.24	52	17	31	24	70	FFf	1%	55	54	5%	2%	108	12%	100%	-14.8	3	-$1
23 Proj	525	47	7	31	9	228	1	9	220	277	314	82	111	69	6	76	0.27	51	17	32	28	67		2%	63	57	5%	1%	106	10%	60%	-17.0	-6	$9

Alonso,Pete

Age: 28	Pos: 1B DH	Health	A	LIMA Plan	D+
Bats: R	Ht: 6' 3" Wt: 245	PT/Exp	A	Rand Var	0
		Consist	A	MM	4145

Since 2019, no batter has amassed more HR or RBI than this one. That consistency makes him a low-risk target among the top bats. And if you look hard enough, you'll see multi-year gains in contact that give his batting average a path to value, as validated by xBA trend. Don't assume he has peaked yet... UP: .285 BA, 50+ HR again

Yr Tm	PA	R	HR	RBI	SB	BA	xHR	xSB	xBA	OBP	SLG	OPS+	vL+	vR+	bb%	ct%	Eye	G	L	F	h%	HctX	QBaB	Brl%	PX	xPX	HR/F	xHR/F	Spd	SBA%	SB%	RAR	BPX	R$
18 a/a	534	66	25	85	0	229		7		311	443	101			11	68	0.37				28				142				82	3%	0%		110	$12
19 NYM	693	103	53	120	1	260	49	4	271	358	583	130	131	129	10	69	0.39	41	18	41	28	101	BBc	16%	176	153	31%	28%	91	1%	100%	24.5	252	$26
20 NYM	239	31	16	35	1	231	15	1	243	326	490	108	93	115	10	71	0.39	39	17	44	24	91	BBd	13%	142	100	25%	23%	73	2%	100%	-5.2	160	$18
21 NYM	637	81	37	94	3	262	39	4	269	344	519	118	123	117	9	77	0.47	39	18	43	28	120	ABd	15%	138	129	20%	21%	87	2%	100%	18.0	258	$22
22 NYM	685	95	40	131	5	271	35	2	274	352	518	123	117	125	10	79	0.52	36	20	44	28	116	BAc	12%	143	112	19%	17%	63	3%	83%	27.7	238	$34
1st Half	341	46	22	69	2	272	19	1	279	352	537	126	106	132	10	77	0.49	35	21	44	28	120	BAc	14%	155	126	22%	19%	72	3%	67%	17.6	259	$36
2nd Half	344	49	18	62	3	271	16	1	270	352	498	120	128	118	10	80	0.57	38	18	44	28	113	BBc	11%	133	100	17%	15%	63	3%	100%	14.7	234	$36
23 Proj	665	92	41	116	4	270	38	4	270	352	526	122	120	123	10	77	0.47	38	19	43	29	113		13%	153	119	21%	19%	66	3%	87%	38.0	234	$33

STEPHEN NICKRAND

Altuve,Jose

Age: 33	Pos: 2B	Health	C	LIMA Plan	A
Bats: R	Ht: 5' 6" Wt: 166	PT/Exp	A	Rand Var	-2
		Consist	D	MM	4355

Another terrific season, and considering league context, one of his best (see BPX). Low launch angle again belied HR output, but they weren't just Crawford Box shots; he hit more on the road than at home. After all these years of him overachieving the power metrics, we can toss the model or just call him a freak.

Yr Tm	PA	R	HR	RBI	SB	BA	xHR	xSB	xBA	OBP	SLG	OPS+	vL+	vR+	bb%	ct%	Eye	G	L	F	h%	HctX	QBaB	Brl%	PX	xPX	HR/F	xHR/F	Spd	SBA%	SB%	RAR	BPX	R$
18 HOU	599	84	13	61	17	316	16	11	278	386	451	112	102	114	9	85	0.70	46	24	30	35	105	CCc	6%	78	95	10%	12%	122	11%	81%	34.5	200	$27
19 HOU *	570	91	31	74	6	291	26	11	291	345	535	122	147	116	7	83	0.46	50	18	33	30	116	CCd	8%	115	85	23%	20%	125	8%	55%	24.8	281	$23
20 HOU	210	32	5	18	2	219	5	3	252	286	344	84	66	89	8	80	0.44	49	21	30	25	99	DDf	5%	71	68	11%	11%	103	11%	40%	-9.7	100	$9
21 HOU	678	117	31	83	5	278	20	11	284	350	489	115	107	119	10	85	0.73	39	22	39	28	107	CBf	6%	108	90	16%	10%	97	5%	63%	29.3	292	$27
22 HOU	604	103	28	57	18	300	20	7	297	387	533	130	152	122	11	83	0.76	41	20	39	32	110	DBc	8%	139	99	17%	12%	111	11%	95%	56.0	352	$35
1st Half	286	43	16	29	6	278	9	3	292	364	528	126	150	119	10	82	0.63	40	20	40	28	113	DBc	9%	145	102	20%	11%	99	11%	86%	19.5	328	$25
2nd Half	318	60	12	28	12	320	11	4	300	409	538	134	153	126	12	85	0.90	41	21	38	34	108	DBc	7%	133	97	14%	13%	114	11%	100%	33.3	369	$37
23 Proj	595	102	26	63	13	287	20	12	287	365	499	120	126	117	10	84	0.69	42	21	37	30	108		7%	125	92	16%	12%	105	10%	83%	41.3	298	$29

Alvarez,Yordan

Age: 26	Pos: DH LF	Health	C	LIMA Plan	C
Bats: L	Ht: 6' 5" Wt: 225	PT/Exp	A	Rand Var	0
		Consist	D	MM	5155

Arguably the second-best offensive season in baseball, all at the tender age of 25. He made them pitch to him, then simply destroyed the ball when they did—that HctX was higher than Aaron Judge's. You don't want to mess with a good thing, but he's just a launch-angle tweak (and a full season of health) away from... UP: 50+ HR

Yr Tm	PA	R	HR	RBI	SB	BA	xHR	xSB	xBA	OBP	SLG	OPS+	vL+	vR+	bb%	ct%	Eye	G	L	F	h%	HctX	QBaB	Brl%	PX	xPX	HR/F	xHR/F	Spd	SBA%	SB%	RAR	BPX	R$
18 a/a	369	51	17	60	5	261		5		328	469	107			9	70	0.33				32				136				83	8%	69%		110	$13
19 HOU *	610	95	44	130	1	305	27	7	295	396	632	142	144	148	13	71	0.53	38	25	37	35	126	ACa	17%	183	155	33%	33%	71	1%	56%	55.8	300	$30
20 HOU	9	2	1	4	0	250	0	0	338	333	625	127	183	33	0	88	0.00	57	14	29	17	202	ADf		153	116	50%	0%	108	0%	0%	0.1	428	-$1
21 HOU	598	92	33	104	1	277	41	2	272	346	531	120	120	121	8	73	0.34	38	23	39	32	118	ACc	16%	151	153	21%	27%	88	1%	100%	19.4	223	$25
22 HOU	561	95	37	97	1	306	43	2	304	406	613	144	140	146	14	77	0.74	39	22	39	33	150	ACb	21%	182	170	25%	29%	79	1%	50%	56.9	376	$33
1st Half	298	53	25	58	0	313	23	1	322	413	663	152	117	169	14	80	0.80	38	24	38	31	153	ACc	18%	189	163	32%	30%	97	1%	0%	36.4	445	$38
2nd Half	263	42	12	39	1	298	20	1	283	399	555	135	164	118	15	75	0.67	40	19	41	35	146	ACb	24%	174	180	17%	29%	77	1%	100%	21.0	317	$23
23 Proj	595	97	39	105	1	292	44	3	293	380	587	134	135	133	12	74	0.53	39	22	39	32	134		20%	188	163	26%	29%	83	2%	52%	53.9	292	$34

Alvarez,Francisco

Age: 21	Pos: CA	Health	A	LIMA Plan	D
Bats: R	Ht: 5' 10" Wt: 233	PT/Exp	D	Rand Var	0
		Consist	F	MM	4003

1-1-.167 in 14 PA with NYM. Exciting talent debuted as the youngest player in the majors in the season's final week. Already boasts solid plate patience paired with outstanding power, and consistently gaudy MiLB numbers are impressive given that he's been among the youngest at each stop. A terrific all-around hitting prospect at a scarce position.

Yr Tm	PA	R	HR	RBI	SB	BA	xHR	xSB	xBA	OBP	SLG	OPS+	vL+	vR+	bb%	ct%	Eye	G	L	F	h%	HctX	QBaB	Brl%	PX	xPX	HR/F	xHR/F	Spd	SBA%	SB%	RAR	BPX	R$
18																																		
19																																		
20																																		
21																																		
22 NYM *	469	53	20	54	0	210	1	3	211	293	395	97	0	163	10	65	0.33	50	13	38	27	142	CBa	20%	135	204	33%	33%	56	0%	0%	1.5	28	$6
1st Half	279	30	13	33	0	230		2	238	301	433	104	0	0	9	67	0.31	44	20	36	29	0			144	-14	0%		63	0%	0%	5.6	79	$11
2nd Half	191	23	7	22	0	183	1	1	196	286	347	90	0	163	13	62	0.38	50	13	38	24	135	CBa	20%	124	204	33%	33%	67	0%	0%	-2.6	-24	$2
23 Proj	280	32	10	33	0	235	10	0	215	322	398	100	99	100	11	64	0.36	45	20	35	33	94		9%	123		18%	18%	65	1%	0%	6.8	17	$7

Anderson,Brian

Age: 30	Pos: 3B RF	Health	D	LIMA Plan	D+
Bats: R	Ht: 6' 3" Wt: 208	PT/Exp	C	Rand Var	+2
		Consist	B	MM	2303

8-28-.222 in 383 PA at MIA. Again missed time to injuries (bulging disc, shoulder strain). Judging by 2nd-half collapse, it seems likely the back problem was a nagging one (though peripherals weren't great before that, either). Still owns 2019-20 power skills, but as mediocre QBaB ratings suggest, that's likely the best case even if healthy.

Yr Tm	PA	R	HR	RBI	SB	BA	xHR	xSB	xBA	OBP	SLG	OPS+	vL+	vR+	bb%	ct%	Eye	G	L	F	h%	HctX	QBaB	Brl%	PX	xPX	HR/F	xHR/F	Spd	SBA%	SB%	RAR	BPX	R$
18 MIA	670	87	11	65	2	273	17	11	252	357	400	101	100	100	9	78	0.48	52	20	29	33	110	BDc	6%	82	78	8%	13%	114	3%	33%	0.3	110	$16
19 MIA	520	57	20	66	5	261	21	3	263	342	468	112	103	114	8	75	0.39	45	19	35	31	115	BCc	9%	117	108	16%	17%	87	5%	83%	-1.7	144	$13
20 MIA	229	27	11	38	0	255	11	3	239	345	465	108	103	109	10	67	0.33	49	21	30	33	96	CCc	10%	125	120	27%	27%	115	0%	0%	-0.3	96	$17
21 MIA	264	24	7	28	5	249	8	1	214	337	378	98	58	111	10	72	0.40	49	15	36	32	86	CCc	8%	80	93	11%	13%	97	7%	100%	-0.5	12	$5
22 MIA *	410	45	9	29	1	218	11	5	223	292	347	90	104	90	9	69	0.34	50	18	31	29	92	CDd	10%	95	82	11%	15%	103	1%	100%	-11.7	7	$2
1st Half	161	24	3	9	1	255	4	2	225	342	384	103	134	102	12	65	0.38	47	23	30	37	91	CDf	11%	109	83	12%	15%	103	1%	100%	1.5	10	$0
2nd Half	250	22	6	20	0	195	7	3	218	260	324	83	83	82	8	71	0.30	52	16	32	24	93	CDc	9%	88	81	10%	15%	106	1%	0%	-10.7	17	$1
23 Proj	385	42	10	37	3	237	12	2	226	324	376	97	90	99	10	70	0.36	50	18	33	31	93		9%	99	90	13%	16%	98	3%	95%	1.6	33	$9

Anderson,Tim

Age: 30	Pos: SS	Health	C	LIMA Plan	B
Bats: R	Ht: 6' 1" Wt: 185	PT/Exp	A	Rand Var	+1
		Consist	B	MM	1545

Finger surgery ended season in early August, following groin strain that cost him most of June. Around those, it was mostly his typical campaign. Note, though, how the gap between BA and xBA is steadily declining. That's a trend worth watching, as a player who's relied on speed to consistently post inflated hit rates and is now on the wrong side of 30.

Yr Tm	PA	R	HR	RBI	SB	BA	xHR	xSB	xBA	OBP	SLG	OPS+	vL+	vR+	bb%	ct%	Eye	G	L	F	h%	HctX	QBaB	Brl%	PX	xPX	HR/F	xHR/F	Spd	SBA%	SB%	RAR	BPX	R$
18 CHW	606	77	20	64	26	240	16	7	248	281	406	92	104	86	5	74	0.20	47	20	33	29	82	DCc	5%	104	83	14%	11%	123	29%	76%	-5.9	90	$21
19 CHW *	541	83	19	59	17	333	17	23	279	352	505	119	117	120	3	79	0.13	49	24	28	40	88	CDa	5%	94	84	17%	16%	115	16%	77%	22.2	119	$28
20 CHW	221	45	10	21	5	322	11	7	274	357	529	118	197	92	5	76	0.20	55	19	26	39	101	CDa	10%	114	101	24%	26%	155	12%	71%	12.8	212	$31
21 CHW	551	94	17	61	18	309	17	12	278	338	469	111	113	110	4	77	0.18	55	23	22	37	107	BFa	8%	94	85	19%	19%	136	18%	72%	20.9	138	$31
22 CHW	351	50	6	25	13	301	7	11	276	339	395	104	135	97	4	83	0.25	55	24	21	35	104	CFa	6%	59	73	10%	12%	120	13%	100%	8.5	93	$17
1st Half	235	32	5	20	10	320	5	8	279	357	432	112	152	104	4	85	0.26	54	22	23	36	102	CFa	8%	69	86	11%	11%	116	13%	100%	10.2	131	$19
2nd Half	116	18	1	5	3	264	2	3	269	302	318	88	108	82	4	81	0.24	56	28	16	32	107	CFa	3%	37	44	7%	14%	124	13%	100%	-2.6	3	-$1
23 Proj	525	85	12	44	17	297	14	13	271	330	418	104	126	97	4	80	0.21	55	24	22	35	103		6%	78	74	14%	16%	128	12%	85%	15.8	100	$29

Andrus,Elvis

Age: 34	Pos: SS	Health	C	LIMA Plan	C
Bats: R	Ht: 6' 0" Wt: 210	PT/Exp	A	Rand Var	0
		Consist	A	MM	2233

Career rebirth began during late June trip to NYY... a spiritual interaction with Derek Jeter's monument, perhaps? Regardless, was it enough to keep him employed full time? Body of work since age 30 says no. But even MLB GMs can suffer from recency bias, and he's not exactly ancient. So while this projection is very reasonable... UP: 2022 redux

Yr Tm	PA	R	HR	RBI	SB	BA	xHR	xSB	xBA	OBP	SLG	OPS+	vL+	vR+	bb%	ct%	Eye	G	L	F	h%	HctX	QBaB	Brl%	PX	xPX	HR/F	xHR/F	Spd	SBA%	SB%	RAR	BPX	R$
18 TEX *	454	54	6	33	5	243	7	6	252	294	348	86	96	86	7	83	0.43	50	19	31	28	104	CDc	4%	63	59	6%	7%	127	8%	54%	-9.4	123	$6
19 TEX	648	81	12	72	31	275	15	10	271	313	393	98	102	95	5	84	0.35	51	21	28	31	112	CDc	4%	60	72	8%	11%	115	24%	79%	-13.0	115	$26
20 TEX	111	11	3	7	3	194	4	3	249	252	330	77	76	77	7	85	0.53	49	15	36	20	118	CDf	6%	71	120	10%	13%	81	20%	75%	-6.5	156	$3
21 OAK	541	60	3	37	12	243	7	14	257	294	320	84	65	94	6	84	0.38	46	24	30	29	93	CDf	2%	49	71	2%	6%	101	11%	86%	-16.4	69	$10
22 2 AL	577	66	17	58	18	249	11	7	264	303	404	100	116	94	7	83	0.42	46	17	36	27	107	CCd	4%	97	71	11%	7%	68	17%	82%	1.3	155	$20
1st Half	277	28	5	20	4	225	4	3	254	292	356	92	91	92	8	84	0.58	43	17	39	25	92	CCd	4%	87	64	6%	5%	73	17%	67%	-6.7	162	$6
2nd Half	300	38	12	38	14	270	7	4	270	313	447	108	147	96	5	82	0.31	49	17	33	29	121	DCf	5%	105	78	16%	9%	69	17%	88%	6.0	152	$30
23 Proj	315	36	7	28	9	244	6	7	258	294	371	92	94	92	6	83	0.39	47	19	33	27	105		4%	81	76	8%	8%	82	12%	82%	-1.7	126	$11

Andujar,Miguel

Age: 28	Pos: LF	Health	F	LIMA Plan	D+
Bats: R	Ht: 6' 0" Wt: 211	PT/Exp	C	Rand Var	+2
		Consist	B	MM	1223

1-17-.235 in 140 PA at NYY/PIT. Maybe the change of scenery will turn out to be exactly what the doctor ordered. As usual, his MiLB numbers were solid, but he's too old to ride the AAA shuttle any longer. So it's put up or shut up time. And yes, that 2018 stat line will be gone from his box next year. DN: Doesn't even GET a box next year

Yr Tm	PA	R	HR	RBI	SB	BA	xHR	xSB	xBA	OBP	SLG	OPS+	vL+	vR+	bb%	ct%	Eye	G	L	F	h%	HctX	QBaB	Brl%	PX	xPX	HR/F	xHR/F	Spd	SBA%	SB%	RAR	BPX	R$
18 NYY	606	83	27	92	2	297	19	7	295	328	527	115	109	115	4	83	0.26	44	20	36	32	110	CCc	6%	133	99	16%	11%	97	2%	67%	25.3	260	$25
19 NYY	49	1	0	1	0	128	1	0	114	143	128	37	0	48	2	77	0.09	49	8	43	17	86	FCf	0%	0	65	0%	6%	94	0%	0%	-7.4	-215	-$5
20 NYY	65	5	1	5	0	242	1	0	222	277	355	84	104	68	5	85	0.33	45	13	42	27	85	DCf	4%	55	68	5%	5%	133	0%	0%	-3.5	148	$0
21 NYY *	221	29	10	22	0	260	5	1	247	302	417	99	80	99	6	83	0.35	53	17	31	27	93	CDf	6%	74	69	15%	13%	96	2%	0%	-2.0	127	$4
22 2 TM *	429	41	10	51	7	223	2	2	253	263	344	85	82	79	4	82	0.23	42	22	36	25	80	DDf	4%	74	69	3%	5%	92	10%	88%	-13.4	90	$7
1st Half	231	24	5	22	5	243	1	1	224	277	346	88	67	89	4	82	0.27	40	17	43	28	77	DDf	6%	63	81	0%	6%	81	10%	100%	-4.5	52	$7
2nd Half	197	17	5	29	2	199	1	1	274	226	342	80	97	75	3	83	0.19	42	26	32	22	82	DCf	3%	86	61	5%	5%	105	10%	70%	-9.6	134	$3
23 Proj	315	36	8	37	2	242	8	4	245	272	360	88	85	89	4	83	0.26	46	19	35	27	87		5%	70	72	9%	9%	89	8%	69%	-4.5	127	$8

ROD TRUESDELL

Aquino,Aristides

Age: 29	Pos: RF	Health	D	LIMA Plan	D
Bats: R	Ht: 6' 4" Wt: 220	PT/Exp	D	Rand Var	0
		Consist	A	MM	4201

10-30-.197 in 276 PA at CIN. Man, does that power outburst from 2019 look like a blip now. Current version features bottom-feeder exit velocity when he does make contact, which has become little more than a coin flip. It's hard even to recommend him as a short-term injury fill-in anymore.

Yr	Tm	PA	R	HR	RBI	SB	BA	xHR	xSB	xBA	OBP	SLG	OPS+	vL+	vR+	bb%	ct%	Eye	G	L	F	h%	HctX	QBaB	Brl%	PX	xPX	HR/F	xHR/F	Spd	SBA%	SB%	RAR	BPX	R$
18	CIN *	435	41	18	46	3	216		5	234	270	403	90	0	0	7	68	0.23	44	20	36	27	0			123	-27	0%		100	11%	37%	-13.3	53	$5
19	CIN *	539	77	44	91	11	264	14	7	262	313	574	123	126	122	7	68	0.23	35	20	45	29	92	CAf	14%	169	110	29%	21%	90	11%	91%	13.2	189	$24
20	CIN	56	7	2	8	1	170	2	1	218	304	319	83	85	80	11	62	0.33	52	24	24	22	52	FCd	7%	95	34	29%	29%	99	7%	100%	-3.7	-92	$0
21	CIN	204	25	10	23	2	190	10	3	197	299	408	97	104	91	13	57	0.36	29	18	53	26	85	CAf	15%	157	151	19%	19%	132	9%	50%	-5.7	81	$1
22	CIN *	359	36	16	43	3	210	9	3	211	261	408	95	69	97	6	57	0.16	38	18	44	31	65	DBf	8%	166	74	14%	13%	82	12%	44%	-9.5	7	$5
1st Half		128	13	6	14	3	197	3	1	202	233	399	89	56	95	4	51	0.10	43	17	39	32	68	DBf	11%	191	99	17%	17%	79	12%	77%	-4.8	-34	-$2
2nd Half		231	23	10	29	0	218	6	2	216	277	413	98	80	97	8	61	0.21	36	19	46	30	65	DAf	7%	154	64	14%	12%	92	12%	0%	-4.7	45	$8
23	**Proj**	**210**	**23**	**8**	**26**	**2**	**200**	**9**	**3**	**201**	**269**	**381**	**90**	**84**	**94**	**9**	**59**	**0.23**	**34**	**18**	**47**	**28**	**76**		**12%**	**146**	**110**	**16%**	**16%**	**102**	**10%**	**51%**	**-4.9**	**55**	**$1**

Aranda,Jonathan

Age: 25	Pos: 2B	Health	A	LIMA Plan	D
Bats: L	Ht: 5' 10" Wt: 173	PT/Exp	B	Rand Var	-1
		Consist	B	MM	3303

2-6-.192 in 87 PA at TAM. Solid prospect looked overmatched in debut, but production potential was evident in high exit velocity. That's consistent with upside scouts saw in him: a hitter who can work counts and hit the ball hard. Biggest roadblock for him will be with the glove, not bat, as he's a below-average defender.

Yr	Tm	PA	R	HR	RBI	SB	BA	xHR	xSB	xBA	OBP	SLG	OPS+	vL+	vR+	bb%	ct%	Eye	G	L	F	h%	HctX	QBaB	Brl%	PX	xPX	HR/F	xHR/F	Spd	SBA%	SB%	RAR	BPX	R$
18																																			
19																																			
20																																			
21	aa	299	41	8	44	3	280		4		341	452	109			8	73	0.34				36				106				114	7%	57%		112	$10
22	TAM *	522	60	14	66	4	247	2	5	223	305	389	98	40	89	8	70	0.28	55	13	33	33	116	ADd	8%	105	113	11%	11%	93	3%	100%	5.3	24	$13
1st Half		289	34	8	36	4	265	0	3	256	322	413	104	0	189	8	72	0.30	100	0	0	34	210	AFa		101	-14	0%	#DIV/0!	108	3%	100%	6.1	69	$17
2nd Half		233	26	5	30	0	223	2	2	206	284	359	91	40	85	8	66	0.25	52	13	35	31	106	BDd	9%	110	120	11%	11%	87	3%	0%	-3.7	-10	$6
23	**Proj**	**280**	**35**	**6**	**38**	**2**	**257**	**4**	**3**	**224**	**326**	**401**	**101**	**68**	**104**	**8**	**70**	**0.30**	**52**	**13**	**35**	**34**	**95**		**8%**	**105**	**108**	**10%**	**6%**	**103**	**5%**	**74%**	**4.9**	**59**	**$9**

Arenado,Nolan

Age: 32	Pos: 3B	Health	A	LIMA Plan	C
Bats: R	Ht: 6' 2" Wt: 215	PT/Exp	A	Rand Var	0
		Consist	B	MM	4155

The best stat in this book? He has put up *seven* straight 30+ HR, 100+ RBI full seasons (ignoring 2020, obviously). The second-longest active streak? Two (Olson). And he's still not drafted as a top-50 player. As a high-contact bat with an uppercut swing, there's no reason to expect BA/HR package to erode anytime soon. This is a $30 lock.

Yr	Tm	PA	R	HR	RBI	SB	BA	xHR	xSB	xBA	OBP	SLG	OPS+	vL+	vR+	bb%	ct%	Eye	G	L	F	h%	HctX	QBaB	Brl%	PX	xPX	HR/F	xHR/F	Spd	SBA%	SB%	RAR	BPX	R$
18	COL	673	104	38	110	2	297	28	10	291	374	561	125	159	109	11	79	0.60	40	21	39	32	126	BBc	7%	150	138	21%	15%	85	2%	50%	46.8	290	$31
19	COL	662	102	41	118	3	315	29	6	287	379	583	133	143	129	9	84	0.67	36	19	45	32	123	BAd	8%	124	139	18%	13%	111	3%	60%	43.7	333	$32
20	COL	201	23	8	26	0	253	6	1	251	303	434	98	89	101	7	89	0.75	37	16	47	25	126	CAf	5%	87	103	10%	8%	79	0%	0%	-3.8	264	$12
21	STL	653	81	34	105	2	255	22	2	271	312	494	111	127	107	8	84	0.52	31	19	50	25	116	CAf	7%	123	127	14%	9%	88	2%	100%	16.2	296	$21
22	STL	620	73	30	103	5	293	21	2	292	358	533	126	131	125	8	87	0.72	30	20	50	29	121	CAd	8%	136	116	12%	9%	71	5%	63%	36.3	334	$31
1st Half		333	38	17	55	0	296	9	1	288	357	538	127	149	122	9	85	0.62	30	21	50	30	114	CAd	7%	137	112	13%	7%	93	5%	0%	20.9	334	$28
2nd Half		287	35	13	48	5	289	12	1	297	359	527	125	116	128	9	89	0.89	29	20	50	28	130	CAd	8%	135	121	11%	10%	55	5%	100%	18.4	352	$27
23	**Proj**	**630**	**79**	**32**	**103**	**4**	**280**	**23**	**4**	**283**	**344**	**516**	**119**	**126**	**117**	**9**	**86**	**0.67**	**32**	**19**	**49**	**28**	**122**		**8%**	**134**	**121**	**13%**	**9%**	**68**	**4%**	**76%**	**39.8**	**319**	**$31**

Arozarena,Randy

Age: 28	Pos: LF DH RF	Health	A	LIMA Plan	D+
Bats: R	Ht: 5' 11" Wt: 185	PT/Exp	A	Rand Var	+2
		Consist	C	MM	4435

A sneaky-good season; just one of two players (Witt Jr.) with 20+ HR and 30+ SB. That power threshold is both his baseline and ceiling, as shown by supporting xHR and tempering GB%. Uptick from good to great speed fueled by super-strong green light more than skill, so best to side with regression there. Still, he's a legit $30 bat now.

Yr	Tm	PA	R	HR	RBI	SB	BA	xHR	xSB	xBA	OBP	SLG	OPS+	vL+	vR+	bb%	ct%	Eye	G	L	F	h%	HctX	QBaB	Brl%	PX	xPX	HR/F	xHR/F	Spd	SBA%	SB%	RAR	BPX	R$
18	a/a	384	49	9	38	20	237		5		288	361	87			7	74	0.28				30				83				92	35%	69%		20	$12
19	STL *	395	56	13	45	16	299	1	20	259	354	481	116	162	115	8	77	0.37	56	13	31	36	100	BFf	6%	100	42	20%	20%	129	30%	51%	3.2	163	$17
20	TAM	76	15	7	11	4	281	4	3	280	382	641	136	193	109	8	66	0.27	47	19	35	31	99	BDf	14%	208	113	47%	27%	113	20%	100%	5.0	324	$12
21	TAM	604	94	20	69	20	274	18	22	240	356	459	112	125	103	9	68	0.33	49	18	33	37	89	BDf	8%	123	89	17%	15%	146	19%	67%	16.2	131	$27
22	TAM	645	72	20	89	32	263	19	16	259	327	445	109	129	104	7	73	0.29	51	16	33	33	101	BDf	8%	127	88	14%	13%	110	30%	73%	11.7	152	$33
1st Half		327	37	8	36	18	256	7	8	254	312	409	102	88	106	6	72	0.21	52	20	28	33	97	BDf	7%	109	68	13%	11%	123	30%	72%	0.1	90	$28
2nd Half		318	35	12	53	14	270	12	8	266	343	484	117	177	103	9	75	0.39	49	13	38	32	105	BCf	9%	146	109	15%	15%	100	30%	74%	12.8	228	$33
23	**Proj**	**630**	**83**	**22**	**80**	**26**	**268**	**20**	**27**	**257**	**342**	**460**	**111**	**135**	**102**	**8**	**72**	**0.32**	**50**	**17**	**33**	**34**	**96**		**9%**	**134**	**93**	**16%**	**15%**	**116**	**23%**	**67%**	**20.8**	**144**	**$34**

Arraez,Luis

Age: 26	Pos: 1B 2B DH	Health	C	LIMA Plan	B
Bats: L	Ht: 5' 10" Wt: 175	PT/Exp	A	Rand Var	-2
		Consist	B	MM	1255

Can breakout stick? PRO: Plate skills don't get any better; BA surge wasn't fueled by out-of-line h%, and it has consistently outpaced xBA. CON: QBaB is meh at best; both Spd and SB% limit upside on basepaths. That leaves him as an elite one-category producer, which now is worth a Jackson from your pocket in these BA-starved days.

Yr	Tm	PA	R	HR	RBI	SB	BA	xHR	xSB	xBA	OBP	SLG	OPS+	vL+	vR+	bb%	ct%	Eye	G	L	F	h%	HctX	QBaB	Brl%	PX	xPX	HR/F	xHR/F	Spd	SBA%	SB%	RAR	BPX	R$
18	aa	189	21	2	13	2	277		3		317	337	88			6	91	0.63				30				35				100	4%	100%		113	$2
19	MIN *	600	77	4	48	6	333	5	9	297	398	418	113	97	122	10	92	1.29	41	29	29	36	110	CCa	3%	46	73	5%	6%	110	5%	52%	20.6	215	$19
20	MIN	121	16	0	13	0	321	3	2	293	364	402	102	74	110	7	90	0.73	41	29	29	36	104	CCa	3%	55	88	0%	10%	101	0%	0%	2.7	200	$8
21	MIN	479	58	2	42	2	294	6	5	275	357	376	101	89	104	9	89	0.90	46	26	28	33	102	CCa	2%	44	63	2%	6%	136	3%	50%	6.7	196	$12
22	MIN	603	88	8	49	4	316	9	6	287	375	420	113	96	117	8	92	1.16	41	26	33	33	112	CCb	4%	63	75	5%	5%	106	4%	50%	30.6	238	$25
1st Half		308	46	4	28	2	346	5	4	288	419	449	123	86	132	11	91	1.32	46	25	29	37	115	CCb	4%	62	86	6%	7%	112	4%	50%	22.9	241	$22
2nd Half		295	42	4	21	2	287	4	3	287	329	393	102	105	101	6	93	0.94	37	26	37	30	109	CBb	4%	65	64	4%	4%	101	4%	50%	4.8	241	$15
23	**Proj**	**525**	**71**	**5**	**45**	**3**	**306**	**8**	**7**	**281**	**362**	**398**	**106**	**91**	**110**	**8**	**91**	**0.98**	**42**	**27**	**31**	**33**	**108**		**3%**	**58**	**71**	**3%**	**6%**	**111**	**6%**	**53%**	**15.1**	**216**	**$21**

Arroyo,Christian

Age: 28	Pos: 2B	Health	F	LIMA Plan	C+
Bats: R	Ht: 6' 1" Wt: 210	PT/Exp	D	Rand Var	0
		Consist	B	MM	2333

Mini-breakout fueled entirely by batting average jump, most of which was validated by contact spike that boosted xBA gains. Any hope he can contribute in multiple categories dashed by absence of barreled ball quality, plus fact that speed never has been his thing. A good fit in your MI slot, especially if you need BA padding.

Yr	Tm	PA	R	HR	RBI	SB	BA	xHR	xSB	xBA	OBP	SLG	OPS+	vL+	vR+	bb%	ct%	Eye	G	L	F	h%	HctX	QBaB	Brl%	PX	xPX	HR/F	xHR/F	Spd	SBA%	SB%	RAR	BPX	R$
18	TAM *	236	21	3	23	2	220	1	3	245	263	321	78	97	98	5	76	0.24	70	14	16	28	144	AFa	8%	70	81	17%	17%	100	11%	34%	-10.2	10	$0
19	TAM *	188	25	8	31	1	255	2	3	268	316	467	108	84	105	8	71	0.30	47	25	28	31	67	DFf	6%	120	65	22%	22%	111	2%	100%	1.5	119	$3
20	2 AL	54	7	3	8	0	240	2	0	209	296	440	98	62	118	7	78	0.36	56	5	38	25	113	BDc	8%	98	121	20%	13%	100	0%	0%	-0.3	148	$2
21	BOS *	214	25	6	26	2	231	6	1	242	266	388	90	120	94	4	71	0.16	49	20	31	30	86	DDd	7%	107	84	16%	16%	85	5%	100%	-4.6	15	$2
22	BOS	300	32	6	36	5	286	7	3	275	322	414	104	109	102	4	83	0.27	45	25	29	33	114	CDc	7%	82	79	9%	10%	98	8%	83%	8.3	124	$10
1st Half		120	14	4	13	3	229	5	1	256	286	376	94	76	105	5	83	0.33	45	18	37	24	86	CCf	12%	84	86	12%	15%	83	8%	100%	-1.4	134	-$1
2nd Half		180	18	2	23	2	322	2	2	288	346	439	111	139	100	4	82	0.23	46	30	24	38	131	CDb	3%	82	74	6%	6%	112	8%	67%	8.1	128	$7
23	**Proj**	**420**	**48**	**11**	**53**	**5**	**270**	**12**	**5**	**258**	**317**	**418**	**102**	**104**	**100**	**5**	**77**	**0.22**	**49**	**21**	**30**	**33**	**104**		**7%**	**100**	**84**	**12%**	**13%**	**92**	**7%**	**81%**	**8.7**	**83**	**$16**

Azocar,Jose

Age: 27	Pos: RF CF LF	Health	A	LIMA Plan	D
Bats: R	Ht: 5' 11" Wt: 185	PT/Exp	C	Rand Var	0
		Consist	A	MM	1311

0-10-.257 with 5 SB in 216 PA at SD. Signed as a 16-year-old, made major-league debut 10 years later and showed us why there was such a long wait. QBaB, xPX, and xHR all temper hope with bat. Possible path to value will come with legs, but middling plate skills don't get him on base enough to use them.

Yr	Tm	PA	R	HR	RBI	SB	BA	xHR	xSB	xBA	OBP	SLG	OPS+	vL+	vR+	bb%	ct%	Eye	G	L	F	h%	HctX	QBaB	Brl%	PX	xPX	HR/F	xHR/F	Spd	SBA%	SB%	RAR	BPX	R$
18																																			
19	aa	524	62	10	55	10	276		7		303	389	96			4	73	0.14				36				66				114	10%	75%		-41	$14
20																																			
21	a/a	519	47	5	46	21	219		7		262	323	80			5	72	0.20				29				64				137	36%	55%		-27	$10
22	SD *	318	30	3	18	7	243	2	15	233	281	332	87	86	92	5	75	0.21	49	21	29	32	76	DCc	3%	64	55	0%	4%	153	20%	47%	-11.8	31	$4
1st Half		122	11	0	7	3	257	1	6	235	303	363	94	94	93	7	74	0.28	46	22	32	35	76	DCf	3%	74	59	0%	4%	169	20%	38%	-3.3	76	-$5
2nd Half		196	19	3	11	4	234	1	9	231	265	314	82	73	91	4	75	0.17	53	21	26	30	74	CCa	3%	58	50	0%	5%	115	20%	61%	-8.4	-28	$1
23	**Proj**	**210**	**20**	**2**	**16**	**6**	**237**	**2**	**6**	**228**	**276**	**329**	**84**	**80**	**88**	**5**	**74**	**0.20**	**50**	**21**	**28**	**32**	**75**		**3%**	**64**	**54**	**4%**	**5%**	**140**	**17%**	**54%**	**-6.9**	**-8**	**$5**

STEPHEN NICKRAND

Baddoo,Akil

Age: 24	Pos: LF	Health: A	LIMA Plan: D
Bats: L	Ht: 6' 1" Wt: 214	PT/Exp: C	Rand Var: -1
		Consist: D	MM: 2503

2-9-.204 with 9 SB in 225 PA at DET. Awful in two different stints with Tigers. Plate control skills unchanged from promising rookie year, but he apparently tried to control it with a wet noodle, judging by total disappearance of power. Speed to burn, and plenty young enough for the 2021 version to return. But, of course, we now have more doubts.

Yr Tm	PA	R	HR	RBI	SB	BA	xHR	xSB	xBA	OBP	SLG	OPS+	vL+	vR+	bb%	ct%	Eye	G	L	F	h%	HctX	QBaB	Brl%	PX	xPX	HR/F	xHR/F	Spd	SBA%	SB%	RAR	BPX	R$
18																																		
19																																		
20																																		
21 DET	461	60	13	55	18	259	17	7	233	330	436	105	71	116	10	70	0.37	40	21	39	34	90	DCd	9%	108	118	11%	15%	134	20%	82%	8.8	115	$18
22 DET *	348	39	4	19	14	221	3	12	200	303	319	88	76	80	11	70	0.40	42	18	40	30	69	DCf	2%	68	63	4%	6%	164	28%	56%	-11.4	24	$6
1st Half	149	11	2	9	5	208	0	4	215	281	335	87	64	61	9	73	0.38	40	17	43	27	55	DCf	3%	84	28	7%	0%	115	28%	53%	-5.6	52	-$4
2nd Half	199	28	2	10	9	230	2	8	187	320	306	89	80	86	12	68	0.41	43	18	39	33	72	DBf	2%	55	75	3%	5%	175	28%	58%	-5.5	-28	$6
23 Proj	280	34	5	23	11	237	5	12	213	315	366	95	79	99	10	70	0.39	41	19	40	32	75		5%	89	80	7%	8%	150	23%	66%	-0.6	49	$7

Bader,Harrison

Age: 29	Pos: CF	Health: F	LIMA Plan: C+
Bats: R	Ht: 6' 0" Wt: 210	PT/Exp: C	Rand Var: 0
		Consist: B	MM: 3415

5-30-.250 with 17 SB in 313 PA with STL/NYY. Struggles with plantar fasciitis eventually tamped down speed, and it (or something) clearly took a bite out of his bat, though he retained the contact gains that had us thinking he could take a step up. If he's healthy and thus power/speed combo returns, here's a low-likelihood, but plausible, UP: 20 HR/30 SB

Yr Tm	PA	R	HR	RBI	SB	BA	xHR	xSB	xBA	OBP	SLG	OPS+	vL+	vR+	bb%	ct%	Eye	G	L	F	h%	HctX	QBaB	Brl%	PX	xPX	HR/F	xHR/F	Spd	SBA%	SB%	RAR	BPX	R$
18 STL	427	61	12	37	15	264	10	6	234	334	422	101	117	92	7	67	0.25	40	27	33	36	93	CCc	7%	111	95	14%	12%	140	17%	83%	7.9	50	$15
19 STL *	475	72	17	50	13	214	15	12	214	302	394	96	89	95	11	67	0.38	38	17	44	27	88	CBd	10%	105	141	12%	15%	133	14%	82%	-4.5	59	$11
20 STL	125	21	4	11	3	226	6	3	219	336	443	103	160	86	10	62	0.33	41	15	44	32	90	DBf	12%	148	147	14%	21%	155	14%	75%	-0.6	148	$8
21 STL	401	45	16	50	9	267	14	8	248	324	460	108	104	109	7	77	0.32	43	16	41	31	96	DCf	7%	112	106	14%	12%	106	14%	69%	6.4	169	$14
22 2 TM *	339	41	6	33	18	245	4	8	218	284	354	90	79	95	5	79	0.26	40	16	44	29	88	FBf	4%	67	77	5%	4%	150	27%	85%	-3.1	93	$12
1st Half	264	35	5	21	15	256	4	7	220	303	370	95	70	101	5	81	0.28	40	17	44	30	90	FBf	4%	65	80	6%	5%	171	27%	88%	-0.3	134	$19
2nd Half	75	6	1	12	3	206	0	1	209	249	298	77	154	64	5	73	0.21	44	16	41	27	80	FCf	0%	76	56	0%	0%	91	27%	73%	-3.5	-24	-$5
23 Proj	490	58	17	60	18	238	17	16	236	294	411	98	120	93	6	74	0.27	42	16	42	29	89		5%	115	91	12%	12%	114	20%	78%	2.5	91	$20

Báez,Javier

Age: 30	Pos: SS	Health: A	LIMA Plan: B
Bats: R	Ht: 6' 0" Wt: 190	PT/Exp: A	Rand Var: +3
		Consist: C	MM: 3415

The 2020 blip was mostly dismissed as sample size; now, it's part of a three-year trend—and it ain't pretty. xBA says forget about those near-.300 BA days. Best hope for value now is a return to 30 HR, double-digit SB levels. Speed skills support the latter, but power metrics are skeptical of the former. Set 20 HR as your baseline and hope for more.

Yr Tm	PA	R	HR	RBI	SB	BA	xHR	xSB	xBA	OBP	SLG	OPS+	vL+	vR+	bb%	ct%	Eye	G	L	F	h%	HctX	QBaB	Brl%	PX	xPX	HR/F	xHR/F	Spd	SBA%	SB%	RAR	BPX	R$
18 CHC	645	101	34	111	21	290	34	7	283	326	554	118	124	114	4	72	0.17	46	22	32	35	96	BCc	13%	163	110	24%	24%	155	24%	70%	36.6	260	$37
19 CHC	561	89	29	85	11	281	31	15	272	316	531	117	134	112	5	71	0.18	50	18	32	35	91	ADa	13%	145	108	24%	26%	125	17%	61%	9.2	178	$24
20 CHC	235	27	8	24	3	203	9	4	222	238	360	79	85	77	3	66	0.09	50	18	32	27	97	CCf	8%	100	87	17%	19%	111	8%	100%	-13.5	-52	$9
21 2 NL	542	79	30	86	18	265	28	9	237	319	490	111	127	106	5	64	0.15	47	19	34	36	95	BCd	13%	145	117	28%	26%	131	19%	78%	12.4	85	$27
22 DET	590	64	17	67	9	238	18	14	242	278	393	95	117	88	4	74	0.18	50	17	34	29	86	CCc	8%	103	94	12%	13%	132	9%	82%	-7.9	93	$15
1st Half	273	22	7	27	3	209	9	5	240	245	357	85	130	70	4	74	0.16	51	17	32	26	82	CDc	9%	99	83	11%	15%	130	9%	75%	-11.6	79	$4
2nd Half	317	42	10	40	6	263	10	8	242	306	424	103	105	103	5	73	0.19	49	16	35	33	89	CCc	7%	106	103	13%	13%	127	9%	86%	1.8	97	$24
23 Proj	560	73	19	75	12	249	20	8	236	293	417	98	114	93	5	70	0.16	49	18	34	32	91		10%	117	102	16%	16%	118	9%	79%	2.2	87	$23

Barnhart,Tucker

Age: 32	Pos: CA	Health: A	LIMA Plan: D
Bats: L	Ht: 5' 11" Wt: 192	PT/Exp: C	Rand Var: -2
		Consist: A	MM: 1003

There's something austerely beautiful about a BPX of exactly -100; it's like a stark desert scene. Even the oasis that was his occasional power has all but dried up. Maybe he's great with a pitching staff, but he's got to hit at least a little, or it'll be a long, hot summer. DN: <200 PA

Yr Tm	PA	R	HR	RBI	SB	BA	xHR	xSB	xBA	OBP	SLG	OPS+	vL+	vR+	bb%	ct%	Eye	G	L	F	h%	HctX	QBaB	Brl%	PX	xPX	HR/F	xHR/F	Spd	SBA%	SB%	RAR	BPX	R$
18 CIN	522	50	10	46	0	248	8	8	254	328	372	94	99	90	10	79	0.56	45	24	31	29	112	CCb	4%	75	81	9%	7%	88	3%	0%	8.2	87	$6
19 CIN	364	32	11	40	1	231	5	1	241	328	380	98	54	104	12	74	0.53	45	22	32	28	86	DCc	3%	83	71	15%	7%	62	1%	100%	4.8	22	$3
20 CIN	110	10	5	13	0	204	4	0	236	291	388	90	37	103	11	71	0.43	33	24	43	23	78	FBf	7%	103	85	17%	14%	71	0%	0%	-1.5	52	$2
21 CIN	388	41	7	48	0	247	7	1	233	317	368	94	91	95	7	71	0.29	40	25	35	33	97	CBb	4%	85	102	8%	8%	71	0%	0%	-1.3	-31	$5
22 DET	308	16	1	16	0	221	2	1	179	287	267	78	78	78	8	74	0.34	53	16	30	30	60	FCd	2%	39	25	2%	3%	86	0%	0%	-9.0	-100	-$3
1st Half	164	7	0	8	0	216	1	1	152	268	255	74	81	72	7	68	0.22	57	13	30	32	63	FDf	1%	40	25	0%	3%	92	0%	0%	-6.4	-183	-$10
2nd Half	144	9	1	8	0	227	1	1	211	308	281	83	74	86	10	80	0.56	50	20	30	27	57	DCd	3%	39	25	3%	3%	86	0%	0%	-3.0	3	-$7
23 Proj	280	22	4	24	0	230	4	1	215	303	319	86	77	89	9	74	0.37	46	21	33	30	77		3%	66	59	6%	6%	74	1%	27%	-1.7	-34	$3

Barrero,Jose

Age: 25	Pos: SS	Health: C	LIMA Plan: D
Bats: R	Ht: 6' 2" Wt: 175	PT/Exp: C	Rand Var: 0
		Consist: F	MM: 2403

2-10-.152 with 4 SB in 174 PA at CIN. Well, this was less than ideal. Fractured a hamate bone in March, then proceeded to live this nightmare upon his return—just a year after torching the high minors with a .919 OPS. One has to think the injury at least contributed, but... wow. Still owns 2021 skills, but this debacle casts a long shadow.

Yr Tm	PA	R	HR	RBI	SB	BA	xHR	xSB	xBA	OBP	SLG	OPS+	vL+	vR+	bb%	ct%	Eye	G	L	F	h%	HctX	QBaB	Brl%	PX	xPX	HR/F	xHR/F	Spd	SBA%	SB%	RAR	BPX	R$
18																																		
19																																		
20 CIN	68	4	0	2	1	194	1	1	185	206	194	53	78	42	1	61	0.04	39	34	27	32	36	CDd	2%	0	10	0%	9%	133	14%	50%	-7.1	-436	-$3
21 CIN *	416	54	17	57	14	264	1	9	217	324	462	108	79	86	8	69	0.29	36	12	52	34	69	BAb	9%	126	61	0%	6%	142	19%	76%	6.7	154	$18
22 CIN *	402	32	10	27	8	169	2	7	160	204	271	67	70	53	4	53	0.10	40	17	43	28	60	CAc	2%	91	85	5%	5%	117	18%	70%	-33.9	-231	-$2
1st Half	147	14	5	11	2	179		3	170	217	313	75	0	0	5	50	0.09	44	20	36	31	0			119	-14	0%		140	18%	66%	-9.7	-183	-$4
2nd Half	255	19	5	16	5	162	2	4	159	197	248	63	70	53	4	56	0.10	40	17	43	27	63	CAc	2%	77	85	5%	5%	107	18%	72%	-22.3	-252	-$1
23 Proj	315	36	6	34	8	234	4	8	180	289	336	87	97	82	6	60	0.15	40	20	41	37	54		4%	87	49	8%	6%	121	15%	74%	-6.9	-72	$9

Bart,Joey

Age: 26	Pos: CA	Health: A	LIMA Plan: D+
Bats: R	Ht: 6' 2" Wt: 238	PT/Exp: D	Rand Var: -2
		Consist: A	MM: 3105

11-25-.215 in 291 PA at SF. Sturdily-built backstop's power—a plus for him in the low minors—seemed to finally rejoin him in 2022, with a hint of 2nd-half growth. He'll need it to have much value, as poor contact rate says it's not coming from BA. But with enough playing time and another year's development... UP: 20 HR

Yr Tm	PA	R	HR	RBI	SB	BA	xHR	xSB	xBA	OBP	SLG	OPS+	vL+	vR+	bb%	ct%	Eye	G	L	F	h%	HctX	QBaB	Brl%	PX	xPX	HR/F	xHR/F	Spd	SBA%	SB%	RAR	BPX	R$
18																																		
19 aa	86	9	3	11	0	302		1		358	505	119			8	72	0.31				39				112				117	9%	0%		111	$0
20 SF	111	15	0	7	0	233	1	2	183	288	320	81	67	85	3	60	0.07	52	16	32	39	98	CCb	5%	69	78	0%	5%	142	0%	0%	-4.1	-212	$1
21 SF *	272	26	6	32	0	233	0	1	263	273	349	85	181	0	5	61	0.14	25	50	25	36	0	CAf	0%	91	-22	0%	0%	78	0%	0%	-5.3	-177	$2
22 SF *	320	37	12	27	2	214	11	1	195	282	355	90	91	94	8	59	0.23	43	21	36	32	86	CBc	10%	107	99	21%	21%	80	4%	67%	-3.4	-124	$3
1st Half	137	15	5	9	1	169	2	0	180	269	293	79	62	91	12	52	0.29	46	24	29	27	72	BCc	8%	101	77	33%	17%	102	4%	50%	-4.7	-186	-$5
2nd Half	183	22	7	18	1	246	9	1	207	295	398	98	100	97	6	63	0.17	42	20	39	35	95	DBc	12%	111	108	17%	22%	76	4%	100%	1.9	-76	$5
23 Proj	455	51	14	44	1	224	9	3	198	294	361	91	88	92	7	60	0.18	47	19	34	34	90		8%	109	88	16%	10%	80	4%	67%	-1.5	-152	$9

Baty,Brett

Age: 23	Pos: 3B	Health: B	LIMA Plan: C
Bats: L	Ht: 6' 3" Wt: 210	PT/Exp: C	Rand Var: -2
		Consist: A	MM: 3023

2-5-.184 in 42 PA at NYM. While a thumb injury ended MLB debut before he could get untracked, 2019 first-rounder has advanced quickly through the NYM system; impressively, he's improved his numbers at each step up. Power continues to develop, with 30-HR potential. Will probably get more AAA seasoning early in 2023, but one to watch.

Yr Tm	PA	R	HR	RBI	SB	BA	xHR	xSB	xBA	OBP	SLG	OPS+	vL+	vR+	bb%	ct%	Eye	G	L	F	h%	HctX	QBaB	Brl%	PX	xPX	HR/F	xHR/F	Spd	SBA%	SB%	RAR	BPX	R$
18																																		
19																																		
20																																		
21 aa	169	12	4	16	1	219		2		293	331	86			9	65	0.30				32				81				86	3%	100%		-112	-$1
22 NYM *	437	55	15	45	1	247	1	2	221	309	403	101	31	99	8	66	0.26	53	17	30	34	87	ACa	7%	114	77	22%	11%	77	6%	22%	-4.0	-3	$10
1st Half	256	34	7	19	1	228		1	205	297	372	94	0	0	9	60	0.24	44	20	36	35	0			124	-14	0%		103	6%	23%	-4.8	-41	$6
2nd Half	181	22	8	27	1	278	1	1	246	330	454	111	31	99	7	76	0.33	53	17	30	32	100	ACa	7%	105	77	22%	11%	78	6%	22%	4.0	97	$10
23 Proj	420	43	17	45	2	253	13	3	240	337	427	106	85	112	9	74	0.40	50	18	32	30	95		6%	112	69	19%	14%	65	4%	48%	9.3	-21	$13

ROD TRUESDELL

Beer,Seth

Age: 26 Pos: DH	Health A	LIMA Plan F
Bats: L Ht: 6' 3" Wt: 213	PT/Exp C	Rand Var +5
	Consist B	MM 3011

1-9-.189 in 126 PA at ARI. Often, the best profit targets are those whose prospect star has dimmed...but not always. His is barely flickering at this point, as raw power is stymied by GB stroke and mid-80s exit velocity. Defensive deficiencies add another obstacle. 1st-round pedigree still provides hope, but don't bid more than a buck for it.

Yr Tm	PA	R	HR	RBI	SB	BA	xHR	xSB	xBA	OBP	SLG	OPS+	vL+	vR+	bb%	ct%	Eye	G	L	F	h%	HctX	QBaB	Brl%	PX	xPX	HR/F	xHR/F	Spd	SBA%	SB%	RAR	BPX	R$
18																																		
19 aa	353	45	16	65	0	258		4		324	450	107			9	72	0.35				31				106				82	1%	0%		67	$8
20																																		
21 ARI *	393	44	9	35	0	215	0	3	290	259	358	85	150	241	6	74	0.23	0	50	50	27	152	CAa	0%	96	269	33%	0%	89	0%	0%	-23.6	50	$1
22 ARI *	479	33	8	41	0	175	1	1	235	232	270	71	89	70	7	74	0.29	47	25	28	22	108	DCc	4%	67	109	4%	4%	75	1%	0%	-38.1	-34	-$6
1st Half	245	18	4	25	0	176	1	0	223	234	267	71	93	79	7	74	0.29	47	22	31	22	116	CCc	4%	66	132	6%	6%	76	1%	0%	-19.4	-48	-$4
2nd Half	234	15	4	16	0	175	0	0	260	231	274	72	0	51	7	75	0.29	48	30	22	21	85	FCf	5%	69	51	0%	0%	93	1%	0%	-19.3	-7	-$5
23 Proj	140	13	4	13	0	237	4	1	234	296	386	95	133	90	7	74	0.27	47	18	34	29	97		4%	102	83	12%	11%	92	3%	0%	-2.1	15	-$1

Bell,Josh

Age: 30 Pos: 1B DH	Health A	LIMA Plan B
Bats: B Ht: 6' 4" Wt: 255	PT/Exp A	Rand Var 0
	Consist B	MM 3035

Deadline deal did him no favors, as his 2nd half was really rough. Backtrack in exit velocity zapped power, but history says it should bounce back. Still, low launch angle is cemented in profile now, so best to use 20 HR as baseline. Upside here is in batting average, given 1st half surge, rising ct%, and prior hard-hit rate. UP: .300 BA

Yr Tm	PA	R	HR	RBI	SB	BA	xHR	xSB	xBA	OBP	SLG	OPS+	vL+	vR+	bb%	ct%	Eye	G	L	F	h%	HctX	QBaB	Brl%	PX	xPX	HR/F	xHR/F	Spd	SBA%	SB%	RAR	BPX	R$
18 PIT	583	74	12	62	2	261	17	9	256	357	411	103	97	103	13	79	0.74	49	19	33	31	99	BCc	7%	93	88	9%	13%	95	4%	29%	-2.3	160	$13
19 PIT	613	94	37	116	0	277	38	3	291	367	569	130	106	137	12	78	0.63	44	19	37	29	122	ACc	13%	150	135	24%	25%	65	1%	0%	28.3	281	$23
20 PIT	223	22	8	22	0	226	8	1	212	305	364	89	77	93	10	70	0.37	56	19	26	28	117	ADd	9%	77	57	22%	22%	83	0%	0%	-13.3	-48	$8
21 WAS	568	75	27	88	0	261	24	1	278	347	476	113	114	112	11	80	0.64	54	20	27	28	122	AFc	9%	115	101	25%	23%	68	0%	0%	11.4	215	$17
22 2 NL	644	78	17	71	0	266	17	3	263	362	422	111	114	109	13	82	0.79	50	19	31	30	105	CDd	7%	95	74	12%	12%	88	1%	0%	9.7	193	$18
1st Half	342	44	12	47	0	315	9	2	289	398	508	128	120	133	11	84	0.83	48	21	31	34	105	BDc	8%	111	72	15%	11%	84	1%	0%	23.8	262	$27
2nd Half	302	34	5	24	0	210	8	1	232	321	323	91	106	85	14	78	0.77	54	16	31	25	106	CDf	7%	75	77	8%	13%	93	1%	0%	-8.0	110	$5
23 Proj	630	83	22	82	0	276	22	2	262	363	450	113	114	112	12	79	0.66	52	19	29	31	112		8%	107	85	17%	17%	80	2%	14%	25.6	167	$24

Bellinger,Cody

Age: 27 Pos: CF	Health B	LIMA Plan B
Bats: L Ht: 6' 4" Wt: 203	PT/Exp A	Rand Var +1
	Consist D	MM 3415

Last season, we gave him an injury mulligan. Now he's at a crossroads. PRO: xPX, Spd still show power/speed potential; young enough to rebound; could benefit from shift restrictions. DN: Eroding Eye will keep him volatile; high whiff rate, xBA confirm you'll need to surround him with BA padding. Still owns 2019, but boy, does it seem long ago.

Yr Tm	PA	R	HR	RBI	SB	BA	xHR	xSB	xBA	OBP	SLG	OPS+	vL+	vR+	bb%	ct%	Eye	G	L	F	h%	HctX	QBaB	Brl%	PX	xPX	HR/F	xHR/F	Spd	SBA%	SB%	RAR	BPX	R$
18 LA	632	84	25	76	14	260	26	9	250	343	470	109	90	116	11	73	0.46	40	20	40	31	108	BBd	9%	128	129	15%	16%	143	10%	93%	23.1	203	$22
19 LA	660	121	47	115	15	305	46	13	306	406	629	143	137	145	14	81	0.88	31	26	42	31	137	AAb	13%	155	165	25%	24%	120	11%	75%	77.1	422	$37
20 LA	243	33	12	30	6	239	11	4	267	333	455	105	87	114	12	80	0.71	38	22	41	25	124	CBd	9%	111	120	17%	16%	94	12%	86%	0.7	260	$22
21 LA	350	39	10	36	3	165	11	5	205	240	302	74	52	83	9	70	0.33	31	22	48	20	88	CAd	7%	82	110	9%	10%	110	6%	75%	-23.3	0	-$2
22 LA	550	70	19	68	14	210	16	5	225	265	389	93	82	97	7	70	0.25	36	17	47	26	107	BAd	8%	124	128	11%	9%	118	18%	82%	-10.6	107	$14
1st Half	298	37	11	31	9	205	9	3	219	265	392	93	76	101	7	67	0.24	35	17	48	26	108	BAd	9%	133	130	12%	10%	126	18%	90%	-4.6	100	$16
2nd Half	252	33	8	37	5	216	7	2	232	266	385	92	89	93	6	74	0.27	37	17	46	26	105	CAd	8%	113	127	10%	9%	108	18%	71%	-4.6	117	$14
23 Proj	455	59	17	57	9	239	16	11	229	302	416	100	86	105	8	72	0.33	35	20	46	29	104		8%	117	124	12%	11%	109	14%	80%	5.8	112	$16

Belt,Brandon

Age: 35 Pos: 1B	Health F	LIMA Plan C+
Bats: L Ht: 6' 3" Wt: 231	PT/Exp B	Rand Var +2
	Consist D	MM 4225

Few batters—if any—have received more UP treatment in this book, but we're still waiting for his first $20 season. Steadily elite xPX confirms power upside remains intact, so that hope still exists. Problem is, now we have to deal with flunking health that is unlikely to reverse course given age. The perpetual profit tease.

Yr Tm	PA	R	HR	RBI	SB	BA	xHR	xSB	xBA	OBP	SLG	OPS+	vL+	vR+	bb%	ct%	Eye	G	L	F	h%	HctX	QBaB	Brl%	PX	xPX	HR/F	xHR/F	Spd	SBA%	SB%	RAR	BPX	R$
18 SF	456	50	14	46	4	253	23	7	235	342	414	101	83	109	11	73	0.46	24	29	47	31	112	CAa	11%	100	146	10%	17%	102	3%	100%	-3.6	90	$10
19 SF	616	76	17	57	4	234	28	5	238	339	403	103	92	105	13	76	0.65	28	23	49	28	107	CAa	9%	95	139	9%	15%	89	4%	57%	-14.6	130	$9
20 SF	179	25	9	30	0	309	12	2	292	425	591	135	72	148	17	76	0.83	31	27	42	36	125	BBc	17%	161	160	19%	26%	77	0%	0%	13.5	364	$18
21 SF	381	65	29	59	3	274	25	2	265	378	597	134	113	139	13	68	0.47	27	23	50	31	108	CAc	17%	190	165	27%	23%	96	5%	60%	25.1	312	$17
22 SF	298	25	8	23	1	213	12	3	207	326	350	96	84	100	12	68	0.46	27	23	50	28	86	CAc	13%	96	140	10%	14%	85	1%	100%	-8.3	7	$0
1st Half	170	17	5	13	1	211	7	2	200	335	352	97	88	100	14	66	0.48	29	23	48	28	85	CAc	14%	94	144	11%	16%	105	1%	100%	-3.0	3	-$2
2nd Half	128	8	3	10	0	214	6	1	222	313	348	94	81	100	11	71	0.42	25	23	52	28	86	DAb	11%	99	135	8%	15%	68	1%	0%	-3.3	21	-$5
23 Proj	455	54	21	52	2	244	26	2	241	350	460	112	90	120	13	70	0.49	27	23	49	30	99		14%	145	149	15%	19%	83	2%	70%	13.8	148	$14

Benintendi,Andrew

Age: 28 Pos: LF	Health F	LIMA Plan C+
Bats: L Ht: 5' 9" Wt: 180	PT/Exp A	Rand Var -5
	Consist D	MM 2235

Trade of power for batting average worked well, as he posted best returns since 2018. But primary driver of that uptick came from inflated hit rate, as QBaB remained marginal. Even contact gains didn't move xBA needle, so the regression there will be steep. Assuming he recovers from late-season wrist injury, 2019 is now our working baseline.

Yr Tm	PA	R	HR	RBI	SB	BA	xHR	xSB	xBA	OBP	SLG	OPS+	vL+	vR+	bb%	ct%	Eye	G	L	F	h%	HctX	QBaB	Brl%	PX	xPX	HR/F	xHR/F	Spd	SBA%	SB%	RAR	BPX	R$
18 BOS	661	103	16	87	21	290	20	10	274	366	465	111	92	116	11	82	0.67	41	24	35	33	84	CCb	6%	104	81	9%	12%	108	13%	88%	27.4	220	$30
19 BOS	615	72	13	68	10	266	23	13	243	343	431	107	111	105	10	74	0.42	38	21	41	34	98	CBa	8%	99	107	8%	14%	113	9%	77%	-0.7	115	$15
20 BOS	52	4	0	1	1	103	1	1	120	314	128	59	47	61	21	56	0.65	57	5	38	18	60	FFf	4%	28	57	0%	13%	111	20%	33%	-6.4	-292	-$4
21 KC	538	63	17	73	8	276	21	14	254	324	442	105	108	104	8	80	0.37	39	21	41	31	115	CBc	9%	94	133	10%	13%	102	13%	47%	6.5	165	$19
22 2 AL	521	54	5	51	8	304	11	14	250	373	399	109	95	115	10	83	0.68	43	22	35	36	114	CCb	5%	63	96	4%	8%	121	7%	73%	17.4	145	$20
1st Half	331	31	3	32	1	313	6	9	244	381	398	110	92	118	10	84	0.72	47	20	33	36	115	CCb	5%	54	93	4%	7%	131	7%	33%	11.9	145	$15
2nd Half	190	23	2	19	7	287	5	5	254	360	401	108	100	110	10	81	0.61	38	25	38	34	113	CBb	5%	79	101	4%	10%	97	7%	88%	6.2	141	$9
23 Proj	525	63	10	61	9	270	16	7	252	336	404	103	96	105	9	81	0.52	40	22	38	32	110		7%	87	108	7%	11%	103	7%	67%	12.0	154	$20

Benson,Will

Age: 25 Pos: OF	Health A	LIMA Plan D
Bats: L Ht: 6' 5" Wt: 225	PT/Exp C	Rand Var 0
	Consist A	MM 3303

0-3-.182 in 61 PA at CLE. It's been a long road for the hulking 14th-overall pick from 2016 draft. Added BA to power/speed combo at second AAA stint, but chronically high rate of whiffs is a bugaboo he can't seem to shake. Has done better when he repeats a level, so keep him on your radar if you play in a deep keeper league.

Yr Tm	PA	R	HR	RBI	SB	BA	xHR	xSB	xBA	OBP	SLG	OPS+	vL+	vR+	bb%	ct%	Eye	G	L	F	h%	HctX	QBaB	Brl%	PX	xPX	HR/F	xHR/F	Spd	SBA%	SB%	RAR	BPX	R$
18																																		
19																																		
20																																		
21 a/a	410	52	13	38	10	177		5		288	352	88			14	54	0.34				28				141				122	19%	65%		-27	$3
22 CLE *	420	51	10	29	9	208	0	11	217	295	343	90	23	68	11	65	0.35	47	19	33	29	46	FDf		102	48	0%	0%	122	15%	66%	-11.0	10	$5
1st Half	273	32	7	19	8	187		7	213	288	322	86	0	0	12	65	0.40	44	20	36	25	0			102	-14	0%		107	15%	77%	-9.4	0	$8
2nd Half	147	19	3	10	1	249	0	4	220	310	384	98	23	68	8	66	0.26	47	19	33	36	47	FDf	0%	104	48	0%	0%	127	15%	33%	-1.6	10	$0
23 Proj	280	35	6	28	6	206	5	7	205	314	342	91	111	89	11	61	0.32	47	19	33	31	42		6%	113	43	12%	10%	125	13%	61%	-5.5	-7	$6

Berti,Jon

Age: 33 Pos: 2B 3B	Health F	LIMA Plan C+
Bats: R Ht: 5' 10" Wt: 190	PT/Exp B	Rand Var +1
	Consist B	MM 1515

Second best stat in book? In the last 30 years, just one other basestealer has topped 40 SB in fewer PA than him (Rajai Davis, 2013). Spd gives him tools to repeat, but confluence of manager letting him run wild and high success rate can't be guaranteed, especially at his age and with that xSB. The regression there will be steep.

Yr Tm	PA	R	HR	RBI	SB	BA	xHR	xSB	xBA	OBP	SLG	OPS+	vL+	vR+	bb%	ct%	Eye	G	L	F	h%	HctX	QBaB	Brl%	PX	xPX	HR/F	xHR/F	Spd	SBA%	SB%	RAR	BPX	R$
18 TOR *	389	53	6	38	23	250	0	5	285	306	375	91	83	113	8	78	0.37	45	36	18	30	183	AFa	9%	73	177	0%	0%	160	38%	66%	-7.9	120	$14
19 MIA *	361	63	9	30	21	264	6	22	264	339	400	102	123	99	10	73	0.41	53	26	21	34	91	CFc	4%	79	59	16%	16%	133	24%	87%	-4.1	56	$15
20 MIA	149	21	2	14	9	258	1	7	219	388	350	98	88	102	15	69	0.62	53	20	27	36	62	DFd	3%	63	40	9%	5%	98	22%	82%	-1.3	-40	$16
21 MIA	271	35	4	19	8	210	3	9	245	311	313	86	75	92	12	74	0.52	59	20	21	27	76	CFc	2%	66	49	11%	8%	107	17%	67%	-12.4	23	$3
22 MIA	404	47	4	28	41	240	9	12	233	324	338	94	97	93	10	75	0.47	53	17	30	31	86	CFd	6%	70	85	5%	11%	144	43%	89%	-1.2	79	$22
1st Half	190	29	2	18	25	268	3	7	244	363	378	105	123	99	12	74	0.55	52	20	28	35	85	CFf	5%	77	77	6%	9%	144	43%	89%	5.8	100	$23
2nd Half	214	18	2	10	16	216	5	6	222	290	304	84	71	88	9	76	0.40	54	14	33	28	88	CFd	7%	64	92	4%	10%	126	43%	89%	-6.4	41	$7
23 Proj	455	58	6	34	26	233	7	30	239	324	339	92	88	93	11	74	0.48	55	19	26	30	82		5%	75	68	8%	9%	117	32%	80%	-0.1	44	$19

STEPHEN NICKRAND

Bethancourt,Christian

Age: 31 Pos: CA 1B
Bats: R Ht: 6' 2" Wt: 213
Health A | PT/Exp C | Consist C
LIMA Plan D+ | Rand Var 0 | MM 3323

Journeyman found his power bat way back in 2018 with 20 longballs in the minors, but then missed two seasons and most forgot about him. Now 31, he's turned into a consistent double-digit HR threat, with ct%, QBaB/Brl% and xPX support. For a number two CA, that's about all you can ask for.

Yr	Tm	PA	R	HR	RBI	SB	BA	xHR	xSB	xBA	OBP	SLG	OPS+	vL+	vR+	bb%	ct%	Eye	G	L	F	h%	HctX	QBaB	Brl%	PX	xPX	HR/F	xHR/F	Spd	SBA%	SB%	RAR	BPX	R$
18	aaa	403	36	14	44	4	227		4		251	374	84			3	75	0.13				27				90				81	7%	75%		20	$6
19																																			
20																																			
21	aaa	349	29	8	38	3	209		3		250	331	80			5	72	0.20				26				78				82	6%	66%		-42	$1
22	2 AL	333	39	11	34	5	252	14	3	247	283	409	98	96	99	4	75	0.15	45	19	35	30	107	BCd	12%	105	111	13%	17%	95	9%	83%	3.4	72	$9
1st Half		178	22	4	19	4	248	8	2	245	299	388	97	103	91	6	76	0.25	48	18	35	31	121	ADc	14%	100	118	9%	19%	90	9%	80%	1.4	79	$4
2nd Half		155	17	7	15	1	255	6	1	249	265	431	99	82	104	1	74	0.05	43	21	36	30	91	CCf	9%	112	104	18%	15%	103	9%	100%	1.6	69	$4
23	Proj	315	32	11	33	3	232	13	4	241	266	392	91	88	92	4	74	0.15	45	20	35	28	103		11%	106	110	14%	16%	98	8%	81%	0.5	22	$5

Betts,Mookie

Age: 30 Pos: RF
Bats: R Ht: 5' 9" Wt: 180
Health B | PT/Exp A | Consist B
LIMA Plan C | Rand Var +2 | MM 4455

No big skills change between this and "down" 2021; mostly just returned to usual health, plus knocked a few more FB with a few more barrels. In short, he's plateaued at a terrific level, is just entering his age-30 season, and shows no real signs of slowing down. Ride this one another few years.

Yr	Tm	PA	R	HR	RBI	SB	BA	xHR	xSB	xBA	OBP	SLG	OPS+	vL+	vR+	bb%	ct%	Eye	G	L	F	h%	HctX	QBaB	Brl%	PX	xPX	HR/F	xHR/F	Spd	SBA%	SB%	RAR	BPX	R$
18	BOS	614	129	32	80	30	346	40	11	302	438	640	145	160	137	13	83	0.89	34	21	45	37	135	AAb	14%	166	151	16%	21%	141	19%	83%	88.6	443	$46
19	BOS	706	135	29	80	16	295	38	25	279	391	524	127	117	130	14	83	0.96	31	25	44	31	124	AAb	10%	113	134	13%	17%	133	9%	84%	35.6	341	$31
20	LA	246	47	16	39	10	292	10	5	277	366	562	123	69	141	10	83	0.63	32	21	46	29	149	BAb	8%	129	179	19%	12%	144	19%	83%	13.5	396	$40
21	LA	550	93	23	58	10	264	19	18	272	367	487	117	117	118	12	82	0.79	35	22	43	28	137	BAc	8%	120	140	14%	11%	137	10%	67%	16.2	346	$21
22	LA	639	117	35	82	12	269	27	10	285	340	533	124	138	118	9	82	0.53	34	19	48	27	137	BAc	10%	154	159	16%	12%	111	10%	86%	34.0	355	$33
1st Half		288	56	18	42	6	277	11	5	285	354	547	127	129	127	10	81	0.59	35	18	47	28	122	BAc	10%	156	140	18%	11%	92	10%	86%	19.4	338	$33
2nd Half		351	61	17	40	6	263	16	5	287	328	522	120	147	112	8	83	0.47	33	19	48	27	149	AAc	10%	153	174	13%	13%	120	10%	86%	14.9	366	$34
23	Proj	630	117	32	79	11	275	27	12	281	357	525	122	124	121	10	82	0.65	34	20	46	29	138		9%	147	154	15%	13%	119	10%	75%	40.4	360	$34

Bichette,Bo

Age: 25 Pos: SS
Bats: R Ht: 6' 0" Wt: 185
Health B | PT/Exp A | Consist A
LIMA Plan D+ | Rand Var -1 | MM 4345

Posted a .303/.348/.498 slash from May 1 on, with 22 of his homers. That included torrid Sept/Oct where he hit over .400; a strong finish from a growth-stage hitter is always a great sign. Launch angle keeping lid on HR totals; a return even to 2019-2020 levels there, with some age-related power growth tossed in, could unlock... UP: 35 HR

Yr	Tm	PA	R	HR	RBI	SB	BA	xHR	xSB	xBA	OBP	SLG	OPS+	vL+	vR+	bb%	ct%	Eye	G	L	F	h%	HctX	QBaB	Brl%	PX	xPX	HR/F	xHR/F	Spd	SBA%	SB%	RAR	BPX	R$
18	aa	582	84	10	66	28	281		8		333	442	104			7	81	0.41				33				104				108	29%	71%		183	$26
19	TOR *	451	62	18	49	17	287	10	16	279	335	508	117	150	119	7	76	0.30	44	23	34	34	86	BCc	9%	125	97	22%	20%	122	27%	65%	7.8	207	$19
20	TOR	128	18	5	23	4	301	6	4	281	328	512	112	112	111	4	78	0.19	41	26	33	35	102	BCc	13%	120	111	16%	19%	119	19%	80%	5.1	216	$16
21	TOR	690	121	29	102	25	298	30	19	272	343	484	114	129	109	6	79	0.29	49	21	30	34	117	ADd	10%	103	91	19%	19%	105	15%	96%	33.8	162	$42
22	TOR	697	91	24	93	13	290	21	14	269	333	469	114	111	114	6	76	0.26	49	20	31	35	116	ADb	10%	120	106	16%	14%	96	13%	62%	25.1	152	$34
1st Half		364	44	12	43	5	257	11	7	254	299	420	102	99	102	6	74	0.24	50	20	31	31	110	ADb	9%	112	112	15%	14%	95	13%	50%	-1.0	97	$24
2nd Half		333	47	12	50	8	327	10	8	284	369	524	127	121	128	6	79	0.30	48	21	31	39	123	ADb	10%	128	100	16%	13%	101	13%	73%	24.8	214	$38
23	Proj	630	94	25	90	18	297	23	12	276	340	493	116	123	113	6	78	0.28	47	21	31	35	113		10%	126	101	17%	16%	100	10%	77%	35.3	173	$39

Biggio,Cavan

Age: 28 Pos: 2B 1B
Bats: L Ht: 6' 2" Wt: 200
Health C | PT/Exp C | Consist B
LIMA Plan D | Rand Var +3 | MM 3301

6-24-.202 with 2 SB in 303 PA at TOR. The only one of the TOR legacy triplets who's not holding up his end. If he's even trying to make adjustments, they aren't taking, because long-term problems aren't getting any better. He's not a developing kid anymore, either. Pedigree and plate patience will only go so far.

Yr	Tm	PA	R	HR	RBI	SB	BA	xHR	xSB	xBA	OBP	SLG	OPS+	vL+	vR+	bb%	ct%	Eye	G	L	F	h%	HctX	QBaB	Brl%	PX	xPX	HR/F	xHR/F	Spd	SBA%	SB%	RAR	BPX	R$
18	aa	533	68	22	84	17	233		8		355	450	108			16	64	0.53				31				150				104	19%	66%		140	$19
19	TOR *	595	85	21	71	18	249	15	18	228	375	439	113	103	112	17	69	0.64	25	28	47	32	94	CAa	9%	112	151	15%	14%	105	11%	94%	15.0	115	$19
20	TOR	264	41	8	28	6	250	6	6	242	375	432	107	118	101	16	72	0.67	38	21	41	31	88	CBd	5%	116	110	13%	9%	107	8%	100%	6.2	188	$23
21	TOR *	379	40	10	36	3	209	6	5	210	307	340	89	73	99	12	67	0.43	38	22	40	28	83	CBc	6%	86	111	10%	9%	96	4%	75%	-9.0	-27	$2
22	TOR *	339	49	6	26	3	204	7	4	220	312	345	93	76	98	13	68	0.48	35	21	44	28	80	CAc	7%	114	97	8%	9%	115	4%	100%	-1.4	86	$2
1st Half		176	24	2	14	2	235	4	2	230	367	379	106	99	112	17	67	0.64	32	26	42	33	98	CAc	11%	123	133	6%	13%	123	4%	100%	3.6	141	$0
2nd Half		163	25	4	12	1	174	3	1	211	264	313	82	54	87	9	68	0.33	38	17	44	22	66	CAb	5%	106	71	9%	7%	103	4%	100%	-6.8	31	-$2
23	Proj	245	34	6	23	3	210	6	2	219	319	358	94	84	97	13	68	0.46	36	22	43	28	83		7%	112	107	10%	9%	101	5%	87%	-0.4	61	$5

Blackmon,Charlie

Age: 37 Pos: DH RF
Bats: L Ht: 6' 3" Wt: 221
Health A | PT/Exp A | Consist A
LIMA Plan B | Rand Var 0 | MM 2335

After a decent start—with Coors Field again on his side—skills eroded further as he battled hamstring and meniscus issues late. After exercising a player option for 2023, he should have one more year with COL, so numbers likely won't fall off a cliff. But at his age, the injury risk grows, with counting stats at similar risk. DN: <400 PA, <$10

Yr	Tm	PA	R	HR	RBI	SB	BA	xHR	xSB	xBA	OBP	SLG	OPS+	vL+	vR+	bb%	ct%	Eye	G	L	F	h%	HctX	QBaB	Brl%	PX	xPX	HR/F	xHR/F	Spd	SBA%	SB%	RAR	BPX	R$
18	COL	696	119	29	70	12	291	23	10	277	358	502	115	108	117	8	79	0.44	43	23	33	33	104	CCb	7%	119	97	18%	14%	121	9%	75%	31.7	217	$30
19	COL	634	112	32	86	2	314	31	10	298	364	576	130	131	129	6	82	0.38	39	23	38	34	114	CBb	8%	129	132	18%	17%	121	5%	29%	34.2	304	$27
20	COL	247	31	6	42	2	303	6	2	265	356	448	107	121	98	8	80	0.43	36	28	35	36	100	DCf	5%	81	92	10%	10%	90	4%	67%	5.9	120	$25
21	COL	582	76	13	78	3	270	16	6	266	351	411	105	105	105	9	82	0.59	47	22	31	31	112	CCd	7%	77	91	10%	12%	100	2%	100%	-2.5	158	$17
22	COL	577	60	16	78	4	264	12	5	260	314	419	104	106	103	6	79	0.29	43	23	34	31	100	DCd	4%	92	100	11%	8%	116	4%	80%	-1.9	134	$18
1st Half		317	42	13	45	2	269	9	3	279	319	466	111	101	115	6	81	0.36	43	22	34	29	100	DCf	6%	114	97	16%	11%	92	4%	67%	4.1	200	$23
2nd Half		260	18	3	33	2	258	3	2	238	308	363	95	111	88	5	78	0.22	43	24	33	32	99	DCc	3%	64	104	5%	5%	137	4%	100%	-6.3	48	$7
23	Proj	525	63	13	73	4	265	13	6	260	325	414	103	107	100	7	80	0.38	44	23	33	31	104		5%	91	99	10%	10%	114	6%	80%	4.5	140	$19

Bleday,J.J.

Age: 25 Pos: CF LF
Bats: L Ht: 6' 3" Wt: 205
Health A | PT/Exp B | Consist A
LIMA Plan D+ | Rand Var +2 | MM 3203

5-16-.167 with 4 SB in 238 PA at MIA. After adding some 20 pounds of muscle before the season, number 4 overall pick in 2019 brought upgraded power bat with him to the big leagues. Unfortunately, that's also the bat with the inconveniently large holes in it. Still a prospect, but until he shows he can put the ball in play reliably, he'll be volatile.

Yr	Tm	PA	R	HR	RBI	SB	BA	xHR	xSB	xBA	OBP	SLG	OPS+	vL+	vR+	bb%	ct%	Eye	G	L	F	h%	HctX	QBaB	Brl%	PX	xPX	HR/F	xHR/F	Spd	SBA%	SB%	RAR	BPX	R$
18																																			
19																																			
20																																			
21	aa	450	43	9	45	4	180		5		277	309	80			12	71	0.46				23				83				101	7%	55%		23	-$2
22	MIA *	580	58	17	51	5	173	5	6	199	274	325	85	62	88	12	64	0.38	24	24	53	23	74	DAd	8%	114	108	7%	7%	93	6%	68%	-21.5	0	$0
1st Half		291	32	10	30	1	173		3	205	272	328	85	0	0	12	61	0.35	44	20	36	23	0			117	-14	0%		96	6%	37%	-10.4	-28	$5
2nd Half		289	26	7	21	4	174	5	3	204	276	322	85	62	88	12	66	0.42	24	24	53	23	77	DAd	8%	111	108	7%	7%	102	6%	80%	-9.6	34	$3
23	Proj	385	38	10	35	4	189	8	4	200	289	330	86	68	90	12	67	0.41	24	24	53	25	69		8%	103	97	8%	7%	96	6%	66%	-8.9	14	$3

Bogaerts,Xander

Age: 30 Pos: SS
Bats: R Ht: 6' 2" Wt: 218
Health A | PT/Exp A | Consist A
LIMA Plan D+ | Rand Var -3 | MM 4345

Most skills holding steady at their typical fine levels. Across-the-board drop in power metrics (G/F, exit velocity, barrels) is concerning; but may be related to injuries from an OF collision in May, which he says altered his swing. Given previous stability of those metrics, and still-prime age, we're inclined to buy the excuse and project a near-full rebound.

Yr	Tm	PA	R	HR	RBI	SB	BA	xHR	xSB	xBA	OBP	SLG	OPS+	vL+	vR+	bb%	ct%	Eye	G	L	F	h%	HctX	QBaB	Brl%	PX	xPX	HR/F	xHR/F	Spd	SBA%	SB%	RAR	BPX	R$
18	BOS	580	72	23	103	8	288	25	8	292	360	522	118	107	119	9	80	0.54	43	21	36	32	112	BCd	10%	141	101	16%	17%	102	7%	80%	37.3	283	$25
19	BOS	698	110	33	117	4	309	29	9	283	384	555	130	127	130	11	80	0.62	41	19	40	34	107	BCc	8%	130	116	17%	15%	88	3%	67%	45.4	278	$30
20	BOS	225	36	11	28	8	300	11	2	261	364	502	115	132	106	9	80	0.51	46	18	36	33	117	CDf	9%	103	116	19%	19%	94	13%	100%	13.2	200	$31
21	BOS	603	90	23	79	5	295	22	13	270	370	493	119	111	122	10	79	0.55	40	23	37	34	113	BCd	10%	114	103	15%	14%	96	4%	83%	33.9	219	$25
22	BOS	631	84	15	73	8	307	14	7	265	377	456	118	145	110	9	79	0.48	46	22	32	37	105	CCd	6%	101	71	11%	10%	101	5%	80%	33.2	159	$29
1st Half		327	48	7	34	3	318	7	4	264	391	465	121	145	115	10	77	0.49	45	23	32	39	107	CCf	7%	104	67	10%	10%	111	5%	100%	19.8	166	$24
2nd Half		304	36	8	39	5	295	7	3	265	362	446	114	145	104	8	80	0.47	48	20	32	34	103	CCd	6%	98	76	11%	10%	90	5%	71%	11.2	159	$23
23	Proj	630	90	24	83	9	301	21	7	275	370	493	120	130	115	9	80	0.51	44	21	35	34	109		10%	122	90	15%	14%	91	5%	83%	43.1	195	$34

ROD TRUESDELL

Bohm,Alec

Age: 26 Pos: 3B	Health A	LIMA Plan B	
Bats: R Ht: 6' 5" Wt: 218	PT/Exp A	Rand Var -1	
	Consist D	MM 2235	

3 reasons a breakout is coming... 1) Holes in swing closed as season went along; 2) xPX, OPS vR heading in right direction, too; 3) Made some headway with swing plane; 4) Spd points to modest SB potential if acumen increases and green light follows. With another increase in launch angle... UP: .300 BA, 20 HR, 10 SB

Yr	Tm	PA	R	HR	RBI	SB	BA	xHR	xSB	xBA	OBP	SLG	OPS+	vL+	vR+	bb%	ct%	Eye	G	L	F	h%	HctX	QBaB	Brl%	PX	xPX	HR/F	xHR/F	Spd	SBA%	SB%	RAR	BPX	R$
18																																			
19	aa	263	34	14	38	2	252		3		323	478	111			10	82	0.57				25				107				100	7%	45%		233	$6
20	PHI	180	24	4	23	1	338	6	3	259	400	481	117	113	118	9	78	0.44	53	21	25	42	87	BFb	10%	89	73	13%	19%	104	4%	50%	8.1	128	$18
21	PHI *	481	52	8	51	6	245	9	3	235	302	342	88	108	79	7	71	0.28	53	25	23	33	110	AFb	7%	66	78	11%	15%	87	6%	84%	-10.9	-81	$9
22	PHI	631	79	13	72	2	280	15	9	258	315	398	101	131	89	5	81	0.28	46	23	30	33	112	BCc	7%	72	86	9%	10%	126	3%	40%	0.0	110	$21
1st Half		314	38	4	30	1	268	7	4	252	303	364	94	122	82	5	78	0.23	45	27	28	33	97	BCb	7%	64	84	6%	11%	145	3%	33%	-3.5	66	$12
2nd Half		317	41	9	42	1	292	9	5	265	328	431	108	142	96	5	84	0.35	47	21	32	32	127	BCd	7%	80	87	11%	11%	103	3%	50%	7.0	155	$23
23	Proj	630	78	15	80	4	279	17	5	255	326	406	102	124	92	7	78	0.32	47	24	29	34	110		7%	82	81	11%	13%	95	4%	62%	14.1	72	$21

Bote,David

Age: 30 Pos: 2B	Health F	LIMA Plan D	
Bats: R Ht: 6' 1" Wt: 205	PT/Exp D	Rand Var -2	
	Consist A	MM 4311	

4-12-.259 in 127 PA at CHC. QBaB shows that he keeps hitting the ball really hard, but that was muted by inability to put bat anywhere near ball. Thump in bat also trumped by chronic swing plane issues. Add poor durability to mix, and the only reason to roster him is as a last resort.

Yr	Tm	PA	R	HR	RBI	SB	BA	xHR	xSB	xBA	OBP	SLG	OPS+	vL+	vR+	bb%	ct%	Eye	G	L	F	h%	HctX	QBaB	Brl%	PX	xPX	HR/F	xHR/F	Spd	SBA%	SB%	RAR	BPX	R$
18	CHC *	465	48	15	63	5	230	10	6	242	295	399	93	115	88	8	68	0.29	57	18	24	30	97	AFa	11%	111	101	19%	32%	122	10%	50%	-11.8	53	$9
19	CHC	356	47	11	41	5	257	8	6	249	362	422	109	95	112	12	69	0.47	50	23	27	34	87	BDa	6%	101	78	19%	14%	99	6%	83%	-2.4	52	$8
20	CHC	145	15	7	29	2	200	5	2	232	303	408	94	69	107	12	68	0.43	50	16	34	23	99	ACf	10%	117	107	24%	17%	108	6%	100%	-5.3	92	$9
21	CHC	327	32	8	35	0	199	11	4	213	276	330	83	96	78	8	75	0.37	48	14	39	24	121	BCf	10%	75	117	9%	13%	125	1%	0%	-14.6	62	-$1
22	CHC *	276	23	6	25	4	214	3	1	217	249	339	83	79	116	4	63	0.12	49	22	29	32	88	ADf	7%	103	107	19%	14%	93	10%	75%	-13.1	-90	$1
1st Half		94	8	0	7	2	200	0	0	214	247	276	74	103	66	6	69	0.20	36	27	36	29	82	ABc		68	99	0%	0%	113	10%	100%	-5.3	-72	-$8
2nd Half		181	15	6	18	2	222	2	1	215	249	371	88	75	128	4	60	0.09	51	21	28	33	86	ADf	8%	125	108	24%	12%	81	10%	63%	-6.3	-97	$2
23	Proj	210	20	8	24	2	212	5	3	237	280	394	94	78	100	7	68	0.24	51	18	31	27	98		9%	127	106	20%	11%	96	8%	76%	-1.9	-10	$4

Brantley,Michael

Age: 36 Pos: DH LF	Health D	LIMA Plan B	
Bats: L Ht: 6' 2" Wt: 209	PT/Exp B	Rand Var 0	
	Consist A	MM 2253	

Torn labrum wiped away 2nd half and puts start of 2023 in question. That's an injury that he might be able to overcome more than most though, since he's turned into an elite one-category producer. Among hitters with 2,500 PA since 2017, his .306 BA trails only one (Freeman). Keep milking that value out of him in these BA-starved times.

Yr	Tm	PA	R	HR	RBI	SB	BA	xHR	xSB	xBA	OBP	SLG	OPS+	vL+	vR+	bb%	ct%	Eye	G	L	F	h%	HctX	QBaB	Brl%	PX	xPX	HR/F	xHR/F	Spd	SBA%	SB%	RAR	BPX	R$
18	CLE	630	89	17	76	12	309	14	10	299	364	468	112	91	117	8	89	0.80	45	25	30	32	122	BCa	4%	87	79	11%	9%	83	9%	80%	26.4	233	$27
19	HOU	637	88	22	90	3	311	20	8	306	372	503	121	103	127	8	89	0.77	45	24	31	32	128	CCa	6%	92	89	14%	13%	75	3%	60%	25.9	252	$24
20	HOU	187	24	5	22	2	300	5	1	284	364	476	112	83	123	9	84	0.61	47	22	31	34	126	CCc	5%	102	104	11%	11%	85	4%	100%	4.4	248	$17
21	HOU	508	68	8	47	1	311	12	7	293	362	437	110	78	127	6	89	0.62	46	26	28	34	125	BCb	6%	70	80	7%	10%	114	1%	100%	18.6	231	$18
22	HOU	277	28	5	26	1	288	6	1	282	370	416	111	103	115	11	88	1.03	44	24	31	31	123	BCa	6%	77	100	7%	9%	78	2%	50%	9.2	207	$6
1st Half		277	28	5	26	1	288	6	1	282	370	416	111	102	115	11	88	1.03	44	24	31	31	123	BCa	6%	77	100	7%	9%	78	2%	50%	9.5	207	$10
2nd Half																																			
23	Proj	385	48	7	42	3	295	10	3	284	360	430	110	89	119	9	87	0.74	46	24	30	32	123		5%	86	94	8%	10%	89	3%	79%	13.1	231	$16

Bregman,Alex

Age: 29 Pos: 3B	Health D	LIMA Plan A	
Bats: R Ht: 6' 0" Wt: 192	PT/Exp A	Rand Var +1	
	Consist A	MM 3145	

Another year removed from his last $30 season. Can he get back to that level? PRO: Best FB%, xPX since 2019; plate skills firmly elite. CON: <50th percentile in both exit velocity and barrels give him meh QBaB; xHR from 2018-19 peak confirms HR output was inflated. Best hope for return to glory is in BA, given bat-to-ball skills.

Yr	Tm	PA	R	HR	RBI	SB	BA	xHR	xSB	xBA	OBP	SLG	OPS+	vL+	vR+	bb%	ct%	Eye	G	L	F	h%	HctX	QBaB	Brl%	PX	xPX	HR/F	xHR/F	Spd	SBA%	SB%	RAR	BPX	R$
18	HOU	705	105	31	103	10	286	24	11	298	394	532	124	129	120	14	86	1.13	35	22	43	29	112	BBc	8%	137	127	14%	11%	97	7%	71%	49.3	370	$30
19	HOU	690	122	41	112	5	296	22	11	303	423	592	141	165	130	17	85	1.43	32	23	46	29	131	BAc	5%	138	135	19%	10%	96	3%	83%	61.5	430	$31
20	HOU	180	19	6	22	0	242	5	1	284	350	451	106	129	96	13	83	0.92	34	25	41	26	123	CBc	4%	113	92	11%	9%	86	0%	0%	1.7	308	$8
21	HOU *	440	58	13	58	1	262	11	2	253	345	411	104	114	103	11	86	0.87	41	18	41	28	110	CBd	6%	80	93	10%	9%	87	1%	100%	8.5	215	$11
22	HOU	656	93	23	93	1	259	17	2	271	366	454	116	99	125	13	86	1.13	33	19	48	27	116	CAd	7%	115	126	10%	7%	69	2%	33%	25.5	293	$22
1st Half		326	43	10	42	0	244	7	1	260	359	417	110	81	124	15	83	1.02	34	20	46	26	120	BAd	7%	106	129	9%	7%	68	2%	0%	6.4	241	$16
2nd Half		330	50	13	51	1	274	10	1	283	373	491	122	114	126	13	88	1.28	32	18	49	27	112	CAc	8%	124	124	10%	8%	80	2%	33%	16.1	362	$28
23	Proj	630	92	23	92	2	272	18	3	271	372	464	116	114	117	13	86	1.05	35	20	45	28	115		7%	113	113	11%	8%	81	3%	55%	33.6	292	$26

Brennan,Will

Age: 25 Pos: OF	Health A	LIMA Plan C+	
Bats: L Ht: 6' 0" Wt: 190	PT/Exp B	Rand Var 0	
	Consist A	MM 1233	

1-8-.357 with 2 SB in 45 PA at CLE. Pop-up prospect became one by unlocking power in swing, after prior calling card was good plate discipline. Missing loft in bat makes modest power his upside for now, so you'll buy him for the potential of average and bags, two scarce categories nowadays. An intriguing end-gamer as your fifth outfielder.

Yr	Tm	PA	R	HR	RBI	SB	BA	xHR	xSB	xBA	OBP	SLG	OPS+	vL+	vR+	bb%	ct%	Eye	G	L	F	h%	HctX	QBaB	Brl%	PX	xPX	HR/F	xHR/F	Spd	SBA%	SB%	RAR	BPX	R$
18																																			
19																																			
20																																			
21	aa	164	22	2	16	2	249		2		314	317	87			9	78	0.44				31				45				96	9%	42%		-12	$1
22	CLE *	605	50	10	77	15	261	1	8	270	302	383	97	47	141	6	85	0.39	53	18	29	29	127	BFa	7%	78	104	9%	9%	96	15%	77%	-2.6	148	$20
1st Half		298	26	5	45	8	277		4	261	333	405	104	0	0	8	83	0.50	44	20	36	32	0			87	-14	0%		86	15%	78%	4.8	159	$19
2nd Half		307	24	5	32	6	246	1	4	269	273	363	90	47	141	4	86	0.26	53	18	29	27	129	CFa	7%	70	104	9%	9%	112	15%	75%	-7.3	148	$12
23	Proj	350	36	7	40	6	267	7	8	258	331	392	100	34	111	7	82	0.41	53	18	29	31	116		6%	79	94	9%	9%	101	11%	67%	4.0	87	$13

Bride,Jonah

Age: 27 Pos: 2B 3B	Health A	LIMA Plan D+	
Bats: R Ht: 5' 10" Wt: 200	PT/Exp D	Rand Var 0	
	Consist A	MM 0303	

1-6-.204 in 187 PA at OAK. Led farm system with lowest chase rate and carried that patience to majors after call-up. Questions remain about how much oomph he has in bat. Just two barrels at MLB level and struggled to hit ball hard, so they are valid. Age isn't on his side either. Unless you're desperate, leave him at the altar.

Yr	Tm	PA	R	HR	RBI	SB	BA	xHR	xSB	xBA	OBP	SLG	OPS+	vL+	vR+	bb%	ct%	Eye	G	L	F	h%	HctX	QBaB	Brl%	PX	xPX	HR/F	xHR/F	Spd	SBA%	SB%	RAR	BPX	R$
18																																			
19	aa																																		
20																																			
21	aa	303	31	6	33	1	211		4		312	326	88			13	74	0.57				26				69				102	1%	100%		38	$1
22	OAK *	334	35	4	24	1	226	1	2	235	302	319	88	63	85	10	79	0.52	45	21	34	27	100	DCc	2%	66	94	2%	2%	88	1%	100%	-6.9	59	$1
1st Half		179	18	3	17	0	243	1	1	225	300	359	93	102	63	8	83	0.47	45	13	42	28	133	DCc	3%	82	150	0%	6%	90	1%	0%	-2.7	138	-$1
2nd Half		156	17	2	7	1	205	1	1	220	305	269	81	53	93	13	75	0.57	45	24	31	26	84	CCc	1%	45	71	3%	3%	100	1%	100%	-6.1	-24	-$4
23	Proj	350	37	2	29	1	234	4	2	210	333	296	87	77	92	12	76	0.56	45	19	36	30	104		2%	49	103	2%	5%	85	3%	100%	-4.7	41	$5

Brosseau,Michael

Age: 29 Pos: 3B	Health B	LIMA Plan D	
Bats: R Ht: 5' 10" Wt: 205	PT/Exp D	Rand Var -4	
	Consist F	MM 3301	

We know he can produce pop in bursts, as shown by flashes of impactful QBaB and xPX. However, inconsistency always seems to bite him and is bred by a contact rate that is showing no signs of improving. His path to value continues to be as a spot-starter against southpaws, which only makes him roster-worthy in the deepest of leagues.

Yr	Tm	PA	R	HR	RBI	SB	BA	xHR	xSB	xBA	OBP	SLG	OPS+	vL+	vR+	bb%	ct%	Eye	G	L	F	h%	HctX	QBaB	Brl%	PX	xPX	HR/F	xHR/F	Spd	SBA%	SB%	RAR	BPX	R$
18	aa	394	44	10	51	9	226		4		273	379	87			6	76	0.27				27				96				98	18%	67%		83	$8
19	TAM *	440	60	18	64	3	261	4	9	240	320	462	108	115	100	8	73	0.32	40	17	43	32	104	DBf	4%	115	149	15%	10%	80	7%	43%	-5.7	89	$11
20	TAM	98	12	5	12	2	302	4	2	244	378	558	124	146	101	8	64	0.26	45	18	38	42	120	ABb	9%	164	143	24%	19%	131	8%	100%	5.3	180	$10
21	TAM *	357	41	11	35	4	183	4	4	198	260	326	81	102	53	9	64	0.29	37	19	43	24	90	BAf	7%	96	104	12%	9%	108	6%	100%	-17.1	-50	$0
22	MIL	160	15	6	23	2	255	4	2	208	344	418	108	107	108	9	66	0.29	41	16	43	34	108	CBb	9%	115	165	15%	10%	89	5%	100%	1.4	7	$3
1st Half		90	8	4	13	1	278	3	1	236	367	468	118	139	88	11	72	0.45	49	16	35	34	116	CCc	8%	122	139	20%	15%	87	5%	100%	4.2	128	-$3
2nd Half		70	7	2	10	1	226	2	1	168	314	355	95	77	157	6	58	0.15	28	17	56	35	99	BAb	11%	106	207	10%	10%	96	5%	100%	-1.7	-138	-$5
23	Proj	245	27	8	32	3	227	7	2	205	308	374	95	97	88	8	66	0.26	40	17	43	31	102		8%	108	150	12%	11%	96	5%	86%	-1.3	-14	$7

STEPHEN NICKRAND

Brown,Seth

Age: 30 Pos: 1B LF RF | Bats: L Ht: 6' 1" Wt: 223

Health A | PT/Exp A | Consist D | LIMA Plan B | Rand Var -3 | MM 4225

Earned a full-time shot—okay, he was one of the few veteran OAK survivors. Regardless, he did... fine. The power he's flashed in smaller samples mostly held up, and hey, how 'bout those steals? Issues vL would limit PA/counting stats on a better club, and he'll never hit for average. But for a cheap power source with a few bags, you can do worse.

Yr	Tm	PA	R	HR	RBI	SB	BA	xHR	xSB	xBA	OBP	SLG	OPS+	vL+	vR+	bb%	ct%	Eye	G	L	F	h%	HctX	QBaB	Brl%	PX	xPX	HR/F	xHR/F	Spd	SBA%	SB%	RAR	BPX	R$
18	aa	536	49	10	67	4	233		6		282	366	87			6	67	0.21				33				102				90	4%	100%		-27	$8
19	OAK *	561	84	25	88	7	245	2	4	246	291	473	106	60	123	6	66	0.19	33	29	38	32	92	CBd	12%	139	93	0%	10%	98	8%	85%	-3.8	70	$16
20	OAK	5	0	0	0	0	0	1	0	0	0	0	0	0	0	0	60	0.00	33	0	67	0	81	CAf	33%	0	223	0%	50%	96	7%	0%	-1.0	-512	-$4
21	OAK	307	43	20	48	4	214	17	2	243	274	480	104	69	107	7	68	0.26	31	19	50	23	95	CAf	14%	161	144	21%	18%	75	10%	80%	-2.7	162	$7
22	OAK	555	55	25	73	11	230	24	6	246	305	444	106	77	113	9	71	0.35	36	20	44	27	108	CBf	13%	142	117	16%	15%	65	11%	85%	5.7	128	$16
1st Half		266	25	10	36	7	217	11	2	251	278	418	98	64	106	7	71	0.27	34	24	41	26	112	BBf	11%	137	122	14%	15%	65	11%	100%	-3.8	107	$13
2nd Half		289	30	15	37	4	242	13	3	241	329	469	113	87	119	11	70	0.42	37	16	47	28	104	CBf	15%	147	112	18%	15%	74	11%	67%	5.4	155	$20
23	Proj	**525**	**61**	**25**	**74**	**8**	**238**	**24**	**7**	**240**	**303**	**458**	**106**	**73**	**111**	**8**	**69**	**0.29**	**34**	**20**	**46**	**29**	**101**		**14%**	**151**	**125**	**16%**	**16%**	**76**	**8%**	**82%**	**7.8**	**121**	**$16**

Bruján,Vidal

Age: 25 Pos: 2B OF | Bats: R Ht: 5' 10" Wt: 180

Health A | PT/Exp C | Consist B | LIMA Plan D | Rand Var +1 | MM 1411

3-16-.163 with 5 SB in 162 PA at TAM. This apparently self-aware player knows steals are his thing, judging by extravagant SBA%. But a 50% MLB success rate is a red light waiting to happen. Yes, he's shown better, and he's been a prospect for... how many years now? So he'll get more chances, but needs to be more than a half-trick pony.

Yr	Tm	PA	R	HR	RBI	SB	BA	xHR	xSB	xBA	OBP	SLG	OPS+	vL+	vR+	bb%	ct%	Eye	G	L	F	h%	HctX	QBaB	Brl%	PX	xPX	HR/F	xHR/F	Spd	SBA%	SB%	RAR	BPX	R$
18																																			
19	aa	227	27	3	24	22	256		4		321	377	97			9	81	0.51				30				61				140	52%	73%		130	$10
20																																			
21	TAM *	458	70	10	51	39	224	0	5	236	297	369	91	16	31	9	79	0.49	56	6	39	26	90	FFf	0%	89	34	0%	0%	93	49%	82%	-8.4	142	$23
22	TAM *	438	52	7	31	23	210	1	26	217	267	312	82	100	52	7	76	0.33	46	15	39	26	83	DBf	2%	69	55	7%	2%	123	46%	55%	-20.1	45	$11
1st Half		214	20	2	16	8	190	1	12	224	259	287	77	106	44	9	75	0.38	48	17	35	24	82	DCf	2%	71	48	6%	3%	118	46%	46%	-13.1	41	$1
2nd Half		224	32	5	14	15	228	0	14	139	274	336	86	0	118	6	77	0.28	25	0	75	27	84	DAf		68	110	11%	0%	128	46%	62%	-8.3	55	$14
23	Proj	**210**	**28**	**3**	**19**	**15**	**222**	**0**	**12**	**232**	**282**	**326**	**84**	**131**	**58**	**8**	**78**	**0.41**	**48**	**17**	**35**	**27**	**74**		**2%**	**73**	**43**	**5%**	**1%**	**112**	**34%**	**69%**	**-4.9**	**95**	**$10**

Bryant,Kris

Age: 31 Pos: LF | Bats: R Ht: 6' 5" Wt: 230

Health F | PT/Exp C | Consist C | LIMA Plan B+ | Rand Var -3 | MM 4235

Good thing THIS wasn't his walk year. Struggled first with lower back woes, then with debilitating plantar fasciitis in his left foot that ended things for good in early August. Terrific when he played, obviously, and is expected to be ready for spring training. So he should be productive once more—given a full season of health.

Yr	Tm	PA	R	HR	RBI	SB	BA	xHR	xSB	xBA	OBP	SLG	OPS+	vL+	vR+	bb%	ct%	Eye	G	L	F	h%	HctX	QBaB	Brl%	PX	xPX	HR/F	xHR/F	Spd	SBA%	SB%	RAR	BPX	R$
18	CHC	457	59	13	52	2	272	18	7	252	374	460	112	151	99	11	72	0.45	34	25	41	35	83	DAb	10%	125	119	11%	16%	121	5%	33%	10.0	163	$12
19	CHC	634	108	31	77	4	282	29	8	259	382	521	125	147	119	12	73	0.51	36	21	43	33	91	CAb	9%	133	105	18%	17%	116	2%	100%	25.6	222	$22
20	CHC	147	20	4	11	0	206	4	2	205	293	351	85	107	78	8	69	0.30	37	18	45	26	87	DAb	5%	87	111	10%	10%	142	0%	0%	-8.8	32	$3
21	2 NL	586	86	25	73	10	265	21	3	261	353	481	115	124	111	11	74	0.46	37	23	39	31	109	CBc	10%	130	133	17%	14%	102	8%	83%	18.0	204	$22
22	COL	181	28	5	14	0	306	5	3	273	376	475	120	137	108	9	83	0.63	40	21	39	34	124	DCd	7%	108	137	10%	10%	106	0%	0%	11.0	248	$5
1st Half		103	16	1	6	0	293	1	2	248	350	380	103	105	102	8	82	0.47	44	23	32	35	116	FCf	3%	62	99	4%	4%	113	0%	0%	2.0	97	-$4
2nd Half		78	12	4	8	0	324	4	1	311	410	603	143	173	118	12	85	0.90	34	19	47	33	135	DBb	10%	167	188	15%	15%	92	0%	0%	9.2	441	-$1
23	Proj	**560**	**86**	**23**	**67**	**3**	**274**	**19**	**3**	**264**	**357**	**485**	**117**	**138**	**106**	**10**	**75**	**0.46**	**38**	**21**	**41**	**32**	**114**		**10%**	**142**	**138**	**15%**	**12%**	**96**	**2%**	**79%**	**30.5**	**235**	**$24**

Burger,Jake

Age: 27 Pos: 3B | Bats: R Ht: 6' 2" Wt: 230

Health C | PT/Exp D | Consist A | LIMA Plan D | Rand Var -1 | MM 3003

8-26-.250 in 183 PA at CHW. PRO: Power stroke coming around, with gaudy barrels, solid exit velocity; contact improving; raked lefties at two levels. CON: Shaky plate skills mean BA/OBP issues; low launch angle; hand injury wrecked 2nd half. He's been slow to develop, but he's opportunity, plus a swing tweak, from... UP: 25 HR

Yr	Tm	PA	R	HR	RBI	SB	BA	xHR	xSB	xBA	OBP	SLG	OPS+	vL+	vR+	bb%	ct%	Eye	G	L	F	h%	HctX	QBaB	Brl%	PX	xPX	HR/F	xHR/F	Spd	SBA%	SB%	RAR	BPX	R$
18																																			
19																																			
20																																			
21	CHW *	369	37	13	41	0	223	2	4	232	267	395	91	44	139	6	64	0.17	43	26	30	31	102	ACc	13%	117	108	14%	29%	124	0%	0%	-7.2	0	$3
22	CHW *	340	33	11	35	0	221	11	2	207	270	371	91	146	94	6	69	0.21	42	15	42	28	98	BCd	15%	99	125	17%	23%	121	1%	0%	-7.3	17	$2
1st Half		235	26	10	31	0	230	11	1	223	282	421	99	145	94	7	68	0.22	42	15	42	29	96	BCd	15%	131	125	17%	23%	102	1%	0%	-1.6	76	$8
2nd Half		105	6	1	5	0	201	0	1	189	243	261	71	0	0	5	71	0.19	44	20	36	27	0	FA		33	-14	0%	#DIV/0!	149	1%	0%	-7.2	-110	-$9
23	Proj	**280**	**25**	**12**	**33**	**0**	**229**	**13**	**1**	**212**	**283**	**408**	**96**	**127**	**84**	**6**	**67**	**0.19**	**42**	**15**	**42**	**29**	**86**		**14%**	**119**	**113**	**16%**	**17%**	**100**	**3%**	**0%**	**-1.4**	**-20**	**$6**

Burleson,Alec

Age: 24 Pos: OF | Bats: L Ht: 6' 2" Wt: 212

Health A | PT/Exp B | Consist B | LIMA Plan D | Rand Var 0 | MM 1321

1-3-.188 in 53 PA at STL. Rough MLB debut, but polished former two-way collegian has moved up quickly, hitting well in two MiLB seasons. That's good, because with few other tools, he definitely needs to hit. Expect more AAA seasoning as he continues work on swing path. But if he keeps improving there, there's BA and power potential... in time.

Yr	Tm	PA	R	HR	RBI	SB	BA	xHR	xSB	xBA	OBP	SLG	OPS+	vL+	vR+	bb%	ct%	Eye	G	L	F	h%	HctX	QBaB	Brl%	PX	xPX	HR/F	xHR/F	Spd	SBA%	SB%	RAR	BPX	R$
18																																			
19																																			
20																																			
21	a/a	437	35	11	44	1	214		4		255	328	80			5	77	0.24				25				66				81	2%	53%		-12	$1
22	STL *	503	48	13	59	4	252	2	3	261	286	377	94	93	75	5	82	0.27	50	21	29	28	110	BFd	9%	76	117	9%	18%	90	4%	100%	-3.7	93	$12
1st Half		287	26	9	37	2	262		2	256	292	406	99	0	0	4	83	0.25	44	20	36	29	0			83	-14	0%		90	4%	100%	0.8	121	$13
2nd Half		216	21	3	22	2	238	2	1	251	278	338	87	93	75	5	81	0.29	50	21	29	28	109	BFd	9%	67	117	9%	18%	94	4%	100%	-5.2	62	$4
23	Proj	**210**	**19**	**4**	**23**	**1**	**245**	**8**	**2**	**241**	**282**	**343**	**87**	**61**	**89**	**5**	**80**	**0.25**	**50**	**21**	**29**	**29**	**98**		**8%**	**65**	**105**	**8%**	**18%**	**95**	**5%**	**87%**	**-3.3**	**47**	**$5**

Buxton,Byron

Age: 29 Pos: CF DH | Bats: R Ht: 6' 2" Wt: 190

Health F | PT/Exp B | Consist F | LIMA Plan B | Rand Var +4 | MM 5543

PRO: Elite power metrics spiking; walk rate growth; bad 1st-half h% luck means a BA rebound. CON: We all know the drill: More injury woes (knee, hip) trashed 2nd-half contact, production. Face it, he'll get hurt again, we just don't know how badly. DN: <300 PA (again). But imagine... what if it's not serious this time? UP: >500 PA, 40 HR

Yr	Tm	PA	R	HR	RBI	SB	BA	xHR	xSB	xBA	OBP	SLG	OPS+	vL+	vR+	bb%	ct%	Eye	G	L	F	h%	HctX	QBaB	Brl%	PX	xPX	HR/F	xHR/F	Spd	SBA%	SB%	RAR	BPX	R$
18	MIN *	238	27	4	16	9	212	0	2	222	248	330	77	29	56	5	67	0.14	43	23	33	30	75	CCd	2%	92	48	0%	0%	123	25%	88%	-9.0	-30	$2
19	MIN	295	48	10	46	14	262	11	7	263	314	513	114	128	109	6	75	0.28	29	22	49	32	92	BAf	8%	148	92	10%	11%	120	35%	82%	8.3	256	$12
20	MIN	135	19	13	27	2	254	11	4	255	267	577	112	100	115	1	72	0.06	36	13	51	25	104	AAf	14%	168	116	27%	22%	122	15%	67%	1.3	260	$16
21	MIN *	277	54	21	38	9	309	19	5	313	346	658	138	136	139	5	74	0.22	40	22	38	34	130	ACd	18%	207	141	29%	29%	122	19%	90%	28.8	431	$18
22	MIN	382	61	28	51	6	224	24	9	254	306	526	118	128	113	9	66	0.29	31	18	51	24	120	AAf	16%	201	165	24%	21%	146	8%	100%	13.7	303	$14
1st Half		261	46	22	40	2	222	17	6	278	299	564	122	134	118	8	69	0.29	33	18	49	22	117	AAf	17%	217	153	28%	21%	134	8%	100%	9.9	369	$24
2nd Half		121	15	6	11	4	226	8	4	201	322	443	108	119	101	11	59	0.30	25	19	56	32	128	AAd	16%	159	195	17%	23%	152	8%	100%	2.6	117	$2
23	Proj	**420**	**68**	**29**	**56**	**9**	**254**	**28**	**6**	**265**	**318**	**551**	**121**	**125**	**118**	**7**	**68**	**0.24**	**33**	**19**	**47**	**29**	**120**		**15%**	**201**	**150**	**23%**	**23%**	**130**	**9%**	**89%**	**23.7**	**276**	**$22**

Cabrera,Miguel

Age: 40 Pos: DH | Bats: R Ht: 6' 4" Wt: 267

Health C | PT/Exp A | Consist A | LIMA Plan D+ | Rand Var -2 | MM 1113

It was all sorts of fun to see him get hit #3000, serve as the AL's token old guy All-Star, and even bat .300 for a while (though xBA shows that was a mirage). But that second half reminded us once again why we didn't draft him. He's got 32 million reasons to play one more year, but would a buyout and graceful exit be all that bad?

Yr	Tm	PA	R	HR	RBI	SB	BA	xHR	xSB	xBA	OBP	SLG	OPS+	vL+	vR+	bb%	ct%	Eye	G	L	F	h%	HctX	QBaB	Brl%	PX	xPX	HR/F	xHR/F	Spd	SBA%	SB%	RAR	BPX	R$
18	DET	157	17	3	22	0	299	3	3	279	395	448	113	100	116	14	80	0.81	55	25	20	36	136	ADa	5%	100	58	14%	14%	46	0%	0%	7.2	143	$2
19	DET	549	41	12	59	0	282	16	0	245	346	398	103	135	94	9	78	0.44	44	24	32	34	119	BCa	6%	64	93	10%	13%	54	0%	0%	-5.2	0	$10
20	DET	231	28	10	35	1	250	11	0	253	329	417	99	146	89	10	75	0.47	42	26	32	29	92	ACb	10%	86	81	20%	22%	51	2%	100%	-1.0	28	$17
21	DET	526	48	15	75	0	256	21	1	224	316	386	96	95	97	8	75	0.34	48	20	32	31	114	ACc	8%	76	107	13%	18%	57	0%	0%	-12.7	-15	$11
22	DET	433	25	5	43	1	254	6	0	217	305	317	88	97	85	6	75	0.28	53	22	25	33	76	BFb	5%	44	56	7%	8%	55	1%	100%	-15.3	-117	$5
1st Half		270	18	3	28	0	308	4	0	225	348	372	102	118	96	6	73	0.22	52	26	21	41	74	BDa	6%	47	54	8%	10%	65	1%	0%	1.0	-131	$8
2nd Half		163	7	2	15	1	163	2	0	198	233	224	65	51	69	8	78	0.39	53	16	31	20	79	BFd	3%	39	59	6%	6%	52	1%	100%	-14.5	-86	-$7
23	Proj	**385**	**30**	**10**	**47**	**1**	**242**	**10**	**0**	**227**	**304**	**352**	**91**	**96**	**89**	**8**	**76**	**0.36**	**50**	**21**	**29**	**29**	**95**		**6%**	**71**	**76**	**12%**	**13%**	**48**	**0%**	**100%**	**-6.7**	**-47**	**$8**

ROD TRUESDELL

Cabrera,Oswaldo

Age: 24	Pos: RF	Health A	LIMA Plan D+
Bats: B	Ht: 5' 10" Wt: 145	PT/Exp C	Rand Var -1
		Consist A	MM 4403

6-19-.247 with 3 SB in 171 PA at NYY. Became legit prospect after adding bulk in 2021. Held his own in major-league debut; key for success will come down to strikeouts. They have been his bugaboo, continued after recall, and warn of the BA risk. Still, power/speed tools seem legit, so he's worthy of speculation. If he finds 450 AB, UP: 15 HR, 15 SB

Yr	Tm	PA	R	HR	RBI	SB	BA	xHR	xSB	xBA	OBP	SLG	OPS+	vL+	vR+	bb%	ct%	Eye	G	L	F	h%	HctX	QBaB	Brl%	PX	xPX	HR/F	xHR/F	Spd	SBA%	SB%	RAR	BPX	R$
18																																			
19																																			
20																																			
21	a/a	501	59	25	73	17	243		4		295	466	104			7	70	0.24				29				139				85	23%	76%		119	$19
22	NYY *	368	42	12	40	10	230	4	10	218	291	406	99	103	105	8	68	0.27	28	22	50	30	87	DAc	7%	125	122	11%	7%	133	20%	66%	-3.8	100	$9
1st Half		92	7	1	4	1	147		2	197	202	259	65	0	0	6	58	0.16	44	20	36	24	0			112	-14	0%		129	20%	56%	-7.8	-79	-$11
2nd Half		276	35	11	36	9	259	4	9	231	322	457	110	103	105	8	71	0.32	28	22	50	32	92	DAc	7%	129	122	11%	7%	136	20%	67%	5.5	166	$23
23	Proj	**315**	**35**	**9**	**36**	**9**	**225**	**7**	**7**	**216**	**278**	**387**	**92**	**93**	**92**	**7**	**67**	**0.23**	**30**	**23**	**47**	**30**	**83**		**6%**	**120**	**110**	**10%**	**7%**	**126**	**16%**	**70%**	**-4.0**	**86**	**$7**

Calhoun,Kole

Age: 35	Pos: RF LF DH	Health F	LIMA Plan D
Bats: L	Ht: 5' 10" Wt: 205	PT/Exp B	Rand Var +2
		Consist C	MM 2103

Man, do those 2019-20 returns look like outliers now. He still can provide power in doses due to high exit velocity, but dwindling OPS vR+ confirms he's no longer even a good long-side platoon option. And his huge dropoff in the 2nd half—when he struck out almost HALF the time he stepped to plate—puts even part-time value at risk.

Yr	Tm	PA	R	HR	RBI	SB	BA	xHR	xSB	xBA	OBP	SLG	OPS+	vL+	vR+	bb%	ct%	Eye	G	L	F	h%	HctX	QBaB	Brl%	PX	xPX	HR/F	xHR/F	Spd	SBA%	SB%	RAR	BPX	R$
18	LAA	551	71	19	57	6	208	23	7	240	283	369	87	80	89	10	73	0.40	43	21	35	24	120	BCb	9%	98	132	15%	18%	76	7%	75%	-17.2	47	$8
19	LAA	631	92	33	74	4	232	31	5	259	325	467	110	102	112	11	71	0.43	41	22	37	27	104	BBc	11%	132	121	23%	22%	68	4%	80%	-5.2	122	$15
20	ARI	228	35	16	40	1	226	12	1	283	338	526	115	107	117	12	74	0.56	38	24	39	22	120	BBc	12%	162	154	29%	21%	61	4%	50%	4.0	276	$20
21	ARI	182	17	5	17	1	235	5	1	234	297	373	92	45	107	8	75	0.37	37	22	41	28	112	CBd	6%	85	145	10%	10%	86	2%	100%	-6.6	54	$1
22	TEX	424	36	12	49	3	196	13	1	214	257	330	83	90	81	6	65	0.20	38	24	38	27	101	ABc	10%	99	121	13%	14%	63	6%	60%	-25.5	-90	$2
1st Half		271	28	10	36	2	232	10	1	243	284	408	98	101	97	6	71	0.22	37	24	39	29	116	ABc	11%	119	133	14%	14%	69	6%	50%	-7.2	45	$11
2nd Half		153	8	2	13	1	130	3	0	162	209	188	56	60	56	7	54	0.17	41	25	34	22	75	BCc	6%	51	91	8%	12%	62	6%	100%	-16.5	-366	-$9
23	Proj	**315**	**30**	**10**	**35**	**2**	**218**	**10**	**2**	**219**	**287**	**356**	**89**	**77**	**93**	**8**	**68**	**0.27**	**39**	**24**	**38**	**29**	**103**		**8%**	**99**	**125**	**13%**	**13%**	**69**	**5%**	**75%**	**-6.0**	**-49**	**$6**

Campusano,Luis

Age: 24	Pos: CA	Health A	LIMA Plan D
Bats: R	Ht: 5' 11" Wt: 232	PT/Exp C	Rand Var 0
		Consist F	MM 1203

1-5-.250 in 50 PA at SD. Top prospect and first catcher picked in 2017 draft now is one of the best backstop prospects in the game. With nearly 700 PA at Triple-A, seems to have enough seasoning in the minors. Power bat not reflected in underlying metrics given small MLB sample sizes over past two years. A strong investment in keeper leagues.

Yr	Tm	PA	R	HR	RBI	SB	BA	xHR	xSB	xBA	OBP	SLG	OPS+	vL+	vR+	bb%	ct%	Eye	G	L	F	h%	HctX	QBaB	Brl%	PX	xPX	HR/F	xHR/F	Spd	SBA%	SB%	RAR	BPX	R$
18																																			
19																																			
20	SD	4	2	1	1	0	333	0	0	471	500	1333	243	348	0	0	33	0.00	0	0	100	0	135	AA		1071	722	100%	0%	97	0%	0%	1.0	2484	-$2
21	SD *	348	29	9	29	1	215	0	1	244	263	357	85	0	41	6	73	0.25	39	26	35	27	104	ABf	0%	90	54	0%	0%	89	2%	100%	-7.9	19	$0
22	SD *	388	38	8	38	0	219	1	1	199	259	323	82	83	84	5	76	0.22	45	13	42	27	113	CBf	6%	68	77	6%	6%	69	0%	0%	-9.9	-28	$2
1st Half		198	21	3	17	0	233	1	1	167	275	329	85	70	0	6	74	0.23	55	0	45	30	59	DDf	9%	70	54	0%	20%	76	0%	0%	-3.2	-34	-$1
2nd Half		190	17	6	21	0	206	1	1	214	243	317	79	87	116	5	77	0.22	41	19	41	24	138	CAf	4%	65	87	9%	9%	78	0%	0%	-6.2	-14	$1
23	Proj	**315**	**29**	**7**	**31**	**0**	**229**	**7**	**1**	**216**	**273**	**347**	**86**	**74**	**93**	**6**	**75**	**0.24**	**41**	**19**	**41**	**28**	**124**		**4%**	**79**	**78**	**8%**	**8%**	**75**	**1%**	**100%**	**-2.0**	**-6**	**$5**

Candelario,Jeimer

Age: 29	Pos: 3B	Health B	LIMA Plan B
Bats: B	Ht: 6' 1" Wt: 216	PT/Exp A	Rand Var +4
		Consist C	MM 3125

Seems to always salvage his season in the 2nd half, but the sum of his parts ends up underwhelming. Just nothing in his player box that sticks out; power and speed are just okay, plate skills are marginal. Some hope in deflated hit rate, regression of which should bring BA north...likely to a still underwhelming level. DN: <300 PA

Yr	Tm	PA	R	HR	RBI	SB	BA	xHR	xSB	xBA	OBP	SLG	OPS+	vL+	vR+	bb%	ct%	Eye	G	L	F	h%	HctX	QBaB	Brl%	PX	xPX	HR/F	xHR/F	Spd	SBA%	SB%	RAR	BPX	R$
18	DET	619	78	19	54	3	224	18	8	228	317	393	95	112	87	11	70	0.41	42	18	41	28	91	CBc	6%	112	88	12%	12%	98	3%	60%	-6.0	80	$9
19	DET *	556	57	15	59	3	227	9	4	236	313	392	97	80	91	11	72	0.44	37	23	40	29	93	CBc	6%	95	86	9%	10%	84	3%	75%	-14.5	44	$6
20	DET	206	30	7	29	1	297	8	2	262	369	503	116	144	107	10	74	0.41	40	26	34	37	107	BCc	10%	118	118	15%	17%	118	4%	50%	8.8	180	$19
21	DET	626	75	16	67	0	271	22	5	267	351	443	109	102	112	10	76	0.48	39	26	34	33	103	CCc	9%	109	108	11%	15%	97	0%	0%	19.7	162	$15
22	DET	467	49	13	50	0	217	14	2	232	272	361	90	95	88	6	75	0.26	42	19	40	26	91	CCd	9%	95	100	10%	11%	100	1%	0%	-11.8	62	$4
1st Half		237	24	5	19	0	188	7	1	215	253	307	79	72	82	6	74	0.26	40	19	41	23	88	CBf	9%	76	97	8%	11%	120	1%	0%	-13.3	24	-$2
2nd Half		230	25	8	31	0	246	8	1	245	291	417	100	116	94	6	75	0.25	43	19	38	29	93	CCd	8%	113	102	13%	13%	84	1%	0%	-0.5	107	$10
23	Proj	**455**	**53**	**13**	**52**	**0**	**245**	**16**	**2**	**247**	**312**	**408**	**100**	**104**	**98**	**8**	**75**	**0.35**	**41**	**22**	**37**	**30**	**96**		**9%**	**111**	**103**	**11%**	**13%**	**98**	**3%**	**39%**	**5.1**	**110**	**$12**

Canha,Mark

Age: 34	Pos: LF	Health B	LIMA Plan B
Bats: R	Ht: 6' 2" Wt: 209	PT/Exp A	Rand Var -1
		Consist A	MM 2325

Even though his results aren't sexy, fourth straight year of value in teens underscores valuable consistency. Has sneakier value in OBP leagues; since 2019, only 12 batters own a higher OBP. While QBaB tempers hope of more production and age is working against him, xSB puts double-digit steals in play again. An underrated commodity.

Yr	Tm	PA	R	HR	RBI	SB	BA	xHR	xSB	xBA	OBP	SLG	OPS+	vL+	vR+	bb%	ct%	Eye	G	L	F	h%	HctX	QBaB	Brl%	PX	xPX	HR/F	xHR/F	Spd	SBA%	SB%	RAR	BPX	R$
18	OAK	411	60	17	52	1	249	17	5	259	328	449	104	125	88	8	76	0.39	38	22	40	28	104	CBd	9%	123	114	15%	15%	99	3%	33%	0.9	167	$10
19	OAK	497	80	26	58	3	273	23	7	256	396	517	126	111	132	13	74	0.63	41	18	41	31	101	CBd	10%	124	100	21%	19%	140	3%	60%	18.2	244	$15
20	OAK	243	32	5	33	4	246	8	3	225	387	408	106	128	99	15	72	0.69	35	20	44	32	108	BAb	8%	102	126	8%	13%	130	5%	100%	-0.1	160	$17
21	OAK	625	93	17	61	12	231	15	12	245	358	387	102	99	104	12	75	0.60	41	23	36	28	97	CCd	7%	90	96	12%	11%	146	8%	86%	-4.0	169	$15
22	NYM	542	71	13	61	3	266	10	8	250	367	403	109	103	112	9	79	0.49	45	20	35	31	98	CCd	5%	89	82	10%	8%	91	2%	75%	9.5	117	$16
1st Half		263	36	6	30	1	271	4	4	237	361	376	104	93	110	9	79	0.49	48	21	31	32	89	CCc	4%	63	53	11%	7%	96	2%	50%	2.5	52	$12
2nd Half		279	35	7	31	2	262	6	4	263	373	429	114	112	114	9	79	0.50	43	19	38	30	107	CCd	6%	113	109	10%	8%	88	2%	100%	6.2	190	$14
23	Proj	**525**	**72**	**13**	**60**	**6**	**253**	**13**	**5**	**246**	**363**	**398**	**106**	**103**	**106**	**11**	**77**	**0.52**	**43**	**21**	**36**	**30**	**100**		**6%**	**96**	**95**	**10%**	**10%**	**105**	**4%**	**84%**	**10.2**	**155**	**$18**

Capel,Conner

Age: 26	Pos: OF	Health A	LIMA Plan D
Bats: L	Ht: 6' 1" Wt: 185	PT/Exp C	Rand Var +3
		Consist A	MM 2331

3-11-.308 in 59 PA at STL/OAK. Small sample-production will put him on some end-game lists, but don't follow suit. Batted ball skills, plate discipline all were mediocre. There's a twinge of potential with his wheels given Spd, assuming he hits enough to get playing time. That's the rub, and mediocre hit tool says he won't.

Yr	Tm	PA	R	HR	RBI	SB	BA	xHR	xSB	xBA	OBP	SLG	OPS+	vL+	vR+	bb%	ct%	Eye	G	L	F	h%	HctX	QBaB	Brl%	PX	xPX	HR/F	xHR/F	Spd	SBA%	SB%	RAR	BPX	R$
18																																			
19	a/a	390	36	9	39	8	222		4		260	337	83			5	74	0.20				28				66				94	16%	65%		-37	$4
20																																			
21	a/a	396	35	8	33	4	201		4		256	320	79			7	75	0.29				25				70				108	12%	45%		15	$0
22	2 TM *	440	37	8	33	12	202	2	7	235	262	308	81	175	120	7	76	0.34	43	23	34	25	84	CDf	8%	69	82	20%	13%	119	27%	50%	-22.8	48	$4
1st Half		251	20	5	16	8	195	0	4	207	249	308	79	140	104	7	78	0.32	50	8	42	23	113	CFa		70	48	20%	0%	118	27%	54%	-14.0	59	$3
2nd Half		189	17	2	17	4	211	2	3	243	278	309	83	163	125	8	75	0.37	41	28	31	27	72	CCf	9%	68	95	20%	20%	119	27%	44%	-8.2	31	$0
23	Proj	**140**	**12**	**4**	**12**	**3**	**227**	**4**	**4**	**255**	**275**	**372**	**90**	**170**	**85**	**7**	**75**	**0.31**	**41**	**28**	**31**	**27**	**65**		**8%**	**92**	**86**	**14%**	**12%**	**119**	**20%**	**49%**	**-2.5**	**23**	**$3**

Caratini,Victor

Age: 29	Pos: CA	Health A	LIMA Plan D+
Bats: B	Ht: 6' 1" Wt: 215	PT/Exp C	Rand Var +5
		Consist A	MM 2113

There's a cadre of catchers who always seem to be available to fill your second slot. This is one. Mendoza-line batting average will keep some away, but if his hit rate comes back to prior steady baseline, he won't be a drag there again. Gaze at that steadily climbing hard hit rate, and UP: 15 HR, .250 BA

Yr	Tm	PA	R	HR	RBI	SB	BA	xHR	xSB	xBA	OBP	SLG	OPS+	vL+	vR+	bb%	ct%	Eye	G	L	F	h%	HctX	QBaB	Brl%	PX	xPX	HR/F	xHR/F	Spd	SBA%	SB%	RAR	BPX	R$
18	CHC *	329	31	5	37	0	243	3	5	236	303	336	86	59	85	8	76	0.36	53	23	24	30	79	CDb	4%	63	62	6%	9%	89	0%	0%	-0.6	-3	$3
19	CHC	279	31	11	34	1	266	10	1	267	348	447	110	108	109	10	76	0.49	49	24	27	31	88	BDb	9%	96	83	22%	20%	78	1%	100%	7.2	96	$5
20	CHC	132	10	1	16	0	241	2	1	212	333	328	88	116	79	9	73	0.39	49	19	32	32	91	CDd	4%	63	73	4%	7%	85	3%	0%	-2.5	-40	$3
21	SD	356	33	7	39	2	227	8	2	215	309	323	87	88	87	10	74	0.43	51	18	31	29	94	BDc	7%	58	74	10%	11%	74	2%	100%	-5.4	-54	$3
22	MIL	314	26	9	34	0	199	6	1	233	300	342	91	79	98	10	75	0.46	50	18	31	23	118	CDf	6%	94	85	14%	9%	62	0%	0%	-4.8	59	$0
1st Half		137	15	7	18	0	246	4	1	253	365	456	116	124	110	13	74	0.57	46	21	33	27	114	CDd	12%	126	138	25%	14%	81	0%	0%	5.8	166	$0
2nd Half		177	11	2	16	0	165	2	0	217	250	259	72	45	89	8	77	0.38	54	17	30	20	121	BDf	3%	72	47	6%	6%	61	0%	0%	-9.0	3	-$7
23	Proj	**350**	**31**	**10**	**40**	**1**	**232**	**7**	**1**	**230**	**321**	**365**	**95**	**88**	**98**	**10**	**75**	**0.43**	**51**	**19**	**31**	**28**	**105**		**6%**	**88**	**78**	**13%**	**10%**	**67**	**1%**	**71%**	**3.3**	**19**	**$7**

STEPHEN NICKRAND

Carlson,Dylan

Age: 24	Pos: CF RF	Health	B	LIMA Plan	B
Bats: B	Ht: 6' 2" Wt: 205	PT/Exp	A	Rand Var	+3
		Consist	C	MM	4235

A tale of three seasons, delineated by injuries: started with contact-heavy approach (84% ct% April/May), but quality was bad. Shelved with a hamstring injury; returned with best stretch in June/July. Thumb injury from August led to IL stint in Sept. Prospect pedigree demands patience, but slipping QBaB, GB%, vR+, Brl% say payoff not imminent.

Yr	Tm	PA	R	HR	RBI	SB	BA	xHR	xSB	xBA	OBP	SLG	OPS+	vL+	vR+	bb%	ct%	Eye	G	L	F	h%	HctX	QBaB	Brl%	PX	xPX	HR/F	xHR/F	Spd	SBA%	SB%	RAR	BPX	R$
18																																			
19	a/a	536	80	21	57	17	265		8		330	470	111			9	75	0.38				32				109				128	21%	66%		163	$20
20	STL	119	11	3	16	1	200	4	2	239	252	364	82	73	83	7	68	0.23	45	24	32	26	98	CCd	9%	108	131	13%	17%	99	11%	50%	-8.3	16	$2
21	STL	619	79	18	65	2	266	18	11	245	343	437	107	126	102	9	72	0.38	38	25	38	34	84	CBc	7%	108	102	12%	12%	111	2%	67%	7.8	108	$16
22	STL	488	56	8	42	5	236	10	3	253	316	380	98	118	90	9	78	0.48	42	21	37	28	95	DCd	5%	98	98	6%	8%	103	6%	71%	-1.0	148	$8
1st Half		249	26	5	23	4	250	5	2	268	313	411	102	134	93	8	80	0.43	44	20	36	29	90	DCf	4%	107	93	8%	8%	100	6%	100%	2.5	190	$8
2nd Half		239	30	3	19	1	221	5	2	238	318	346	94	108	85	11	76	0.52	40	21	39	28	100	DCd	5%	89	103	5%	8%	108	6%	33%	-4.2	110	$3
23	**Proj**	**490**	**61**	**15**	**54**	**5**	**243**	**14**	**6**	**256**	**319**	**424**	**103**	**120**	**97**	**9**	**75**	**0.40**	**40**	**23**	**37**	**29**	**91**		**6%**	**122**	**103**	**12%**	**11%**	**104**	**7%**	**63%**	**8.4**	**121**	**$11**

Carpenter,Kerry

Age: 25	Pos: OF	Health	A	LIMA Plan	C+
Bats: L	Ht: 6' 2" Wt: 220	PT/Exp	B	Rand Var	0
		Consist	B	MM	4023

6-10-.252 in 113 PA at DET. Formerly-unheralded prospect rebooted his swing in offseason, socked 30 HR across AA/AAA by early August, and earned his MLB ticket. The power played in the bigs, but it was as one-dimensional as MLEs advertised: lots of swing-and-miss, little patience, no speed. Profiles as a roster filler when he gets hot.

Yr	Tm	PA	R	HR	RBI	SB	BA	xHR	xSB	xBA	OBP	SLG	OPS+	vL+	vR+	bb%	ct%	Eye	G	L	F	h%	HctX	QBaB	Brl%	PX	xPX	HR/F	xHR/F	Spd	SBA%	SB%	RAR	BPX	R$
18																																			
19																																			
20																																			
21	aa	437	43	11	57	4	227		4		265	363	86			5	76	0.21				27				84				84	13%	36%		27	$6
22	DET *	493	56	25	61	2	250	5	6	246	293	476	109	84	121	6	71	0.21	40	15	44	30	103	CBc	11%	152	159	19%	16%	82	15%	14%	1.9	145	$15
1st Half		276	31	14	36	1	247		3	248	282	466	106	0	0	5	67	0.15	44	20	36	31	0			157	-14	0%		78	15%	18%	-0.2	97	$15
2nd Half		217	25	10	25	1	254	5	3	260	308	489	113	84	121	7	76	0.32	40	15	44	29	110	CBc	11%	146	159	19%	16%	98	15%	10%	2.8	224	$10
23	**Proj**	**350**	**38**	**18**	**44**	**2**	**241**	**17**	**5**	**249**	**298**	**469**	**107**	**78**	**115**	**6**	**74**	**0.23**	**40**	**15**	**44**	**27**	**99**		**10%**	**147**	**143**	**17%**	**16%**	**80**	**11%**	**22%**	**1.9**	**113**	**$11**

Carpenter,Matt

Age: 37	Pos: DH	Health	C	LIMA Plan	D+
Bats: L	Ht: 6' 4" Wt: 210	PT/Exp	D	Rand Var	-2
		Consist	D	MM	5231

15-37-.305 in 154 PA at NYY. Spent offseason retooling swing, recaptured a representative version of his prime form. Copious grains of salt apply to HR/F (thanks, Yankee Stadium short porch), and h% hit a level not seen since 2016. But Eye, G/L/F, HctX, Brl%, xPX are all in line with 2018. Can't assume those PAs at age 37, but part-time power looks legit.

Yr	Tm	PA	R	HR	RBI	SB	BA	xHR	xSB	xBA	OBP	SLG	OPS+	vL+	vR+	bb%	ct%	Eye	G	L	F	h%	HctX	QBaB	Brl%	PX	xPX	HR/F	xHR/F	Spd	SBA%	SB%	RAR	BPX	R$
18	STL	676	111	36	81	4	257	39	10	273	374	523	120	108	123	15	72	0.65	26	27	47	29	130	BAa	14%	170	189	19%	21%	78	3%	80%	35.5	267	$23
19	STL *	523	60	15	48	6	216	19	5	224	320	374	96	95	101	13	69	0.49	32	25	43	28	99	CAb	7%	95	138	12%	15%	105	5%	86%	-18.0	37	$6
20	STL	169	22	4	24	0	186	6	2	206	325	314	85	79	86	14	66	0.48	38	22	40	25	107	CBa	10%	87	146	11%	17%	92	0%	0%	-8.4	-40	$4
21	STL	249	18	3	21	2	169	10	1	187	305	275	80	37	84	14	63	0.45	27	23	49	25	94	CAb	11%	84	161	5%	16%	81	3%	100%	-17.4	-100	-$4
22	NYY *	242	36	18	47	1	259	9	1	285	343	589	132	178	155	11	70	0.43	23	24	53	28	113	CAc	14%	213	189	31%	18%	73	4%	29%	13.1	338	$10
1st Half		144	21	11	28	1	229	4	1	255	314	544	121	189	173	11	66	0.37	17	24	59	25	131	CAb	21%	205	287	47%	24%	96	4%	29%	3.2	283	$7
2nd Half		98	15	7	19	0	305	5	1	325	408	659	151	168	146	12	77	0.58	25	24	51	32	110	CAc	11%	223	144	22%	16%	69	4%	0%	10.6	455	$4
23	**Proj**	**245**	**31**	**15**	**37**	**1**	**249**	**13**	**2**	**263**	**362**	**525**	**123**	**139**	**119**	**13**	**69**	**0.47**	**26**	**24**	**50**	**29**	**110**		**13%**	**189**	**180**	**20%**	**18%**	**76**	**3%**	**76%**	**12.1**	**174**	**$10**

Carroll,Corbin

Age: 22	Pos: LF	Health	A	LIMA Plan	B
Bats: L	Ht: 5' 10" Wt: 165	PT/Exp	D	Rand Var	+1
		Consist	F	MM	4535

4-14-.260 with 2 SB in 115 PA at ARI. Five-tool prospect started year in Double-A, made a summer pit stop in Triple-A, and reached Arizona in late August. Big-league debut flashed both the potential (speed, line drives in bunches) and the to-do list (poor QBaB, PX/xPX gap). But he's likely up for good, and wheels set a nice value foundation on his growth years.

Yr	Tm	PA	R	HR	RBI	SB	BA	xHR	xSB	xBA	OBP	SLG	OPS+	vL+	vR+	bb%	ct%	Eye	G	L	F	h%	HctX	QBaB	Brl%	PX	xPX	HR/F	xHR/F	Spd	SBA%	SB%	RAR	BPX	R$
18																																			
19																																			
20																																			
21																																			
22	ARI *	508	64	17	50	20	247	3	8	260	315	448	108	83	130	9	68	0.31	48	25	27	33	77	DDf	5%	142	71	20%	15%	155	25%	75%	9.4	176	$20
1st Half		252	38	9	24	12	258		4	242	331	472	114	0	0	10	66	0.32	44	20	36	35	0			144	-14	0%		170	25%	78%	9.5	183	$21
2nd Half		258	28	8	27	8	241	3	4	268	306	437	105	83	130	9	69	0.30	48	25	27	32	79	DDf	5%	145	71	20%	15%	129	25%	72%	3.3	176	$14
23	**Proj**	**504**	**65**	**17**	**50**	**21**	**253**	**17**	**20**	**260**	**353**	**462**	**113**	**76**	**126**	**11**	**72**	**0.46**	**42**	**23**	**35**	**31**	**71**		**4%**	**140**	**64**	**15%**	**15%**	**157**	**21%**	**78%**	**20.1**	**179**	**$24**

Casas,Triston

Age: 23	Pos: 1B	Health	A	LIMA Plan	B
Bats: L	Ht: 6' 4" Wt: 252	PT/Exp	C	Rand Var	0
		Consist	A	MM	4125

5-12-.197 in 95 PA at BOS. Fun with micro-samples... first 14 MLB games: 3-for-38, 2 HR, 6 BB/12 K. Last 13 games: 12-for-38, 3 HR, 13 BB/11 K. That patience is his hallmark, along with plus (but not mammoth) power. Strike zone control is key to a smooth MLB transition: he should be an immediate OBP asset, though power may come later.

Yr	Tm	PA	R	HR	RBI	SB	BA	xHR	xSB	xBA	OBP	SLG	OPS+	vL+	vR+	bb%	ct%	Eye	G	L	F	h%	HctX	QBaB	Brl%	PX	xPX	HR/F	xHR/F	Spd	SBA%	SB%	RAR	BPX	R$
18																																			
19																																			
20																																			
21	a/a	355	50	10	47	6	257		5		351	424	106			13	75	0.58				31				99				106	9%	63%		146	$10
22	BOS *	390	42	12	38	1	231	3	5	225	329	403	104	86	116	13	72	0.52	57	8	36	29	100	DFf	6%	122	113	26%	16%	71	1%	100%	3.2	114	$5
1st Half		144	15	4	15	0	217		1	237	301	376	96	0	0	11	71	0.41	44	20	36	28	0			119	-14	0%		76	1%	0%	-2.7	86	-$3
2nd Half		245	27	8	23	1	239	3	3	229	346	419	108	86	116	14	72	0.59	57	8	36	29	101	DFf	6%	123	113	26%	16%	78	1%	100%	3.3	141	$8
23	**Proj**	**490**	**59**	**19**	**58**	**4**	**245**	**18**	**2**	**240**	**341**	**442**	**109**	**90**	**115**	**13**	**73**	**0.54**	**57**	**8**	**36**	**29**	**91**		**6%**	**133**	**102**	**17%**	**16%**	**73**	**2%**	**71%**	**12.5**	**129**	**$16**

Castellanos,Nick

Age: 31	Pos: RF	Health	B	LIMA Plan	B
Bats: R	Ht: 6' 4" Wt: 203	PT/Exp	A	Rand Var	-1
		Consist	F	MM	4345

Had 5 HR by early May, then wife had a baby and he took an HBP off the wrist. Could either of those events explain the ensuing half-season funk (3 more HR through July)? He got right again in August (5 HR, .833 OPS) before turf toe/oblique shelved him for most of Sept. 2021 will stand as career year, but there's still room to rebound to prior baselines.

Yr	Tm	PA	R	HR	RBI	SB	BA	xHR	xSB	xBA	OBP	SLG	OPS+	vL+	vR+	bb%	ct%	Eye	G	L	F	h%	HctX	QBaB	Brl%	PX	xPX	HR/F	xHR/F	Spd	SBA%	SB%	RAR	BPX	R$
18	DET	678	88	23	89	2	298	32	9	276	354	500	114	133	107	7	76	0.32	35	29	36	36	133	BBa	11%	128	139	14%	19%	116	2%	67%	31.3	187	$25
19	2 TM	664	100	27	73	2	289	40	5	280	337	525	119	158	110	6	77	0.29	38	23	40	34	113	CCa	11%	134	131	14%	21%	124	3%	50%	16.7	244	$21
20	CIN	242	37	14	34	0	225	15	2	258	298	486	104	100	105	8	68	0.28	35	26	39	26	101	ABa	16%	154	161	24%	25%	126	4%	0%	-3.0	208	$16
21	CIN	585	95	34	100	3	309	29	4	297	362	576	129	129	129	7	77	0.34	38	27	36	35	127	BCb	11%	152	146	23%	19%	91	3%	75%	36.3	285	$31
22	PHI	558	56	13	62	7	263	16	4	233	305	389	98	99	98	5	75	0.22	42	20	38	33	91	CBc	6%	87	100	9%	11%	93	6%	88%	-7.0	38	$16
1st Half		336	34	8	44	4	251	10	2	241	301	386	97	102	95	6	75	0.27	42	21	37	31	95	CCb	8%	95	110	9%	11%	86	6%	80%	-6.2	59	$17
2nd Half		222	22	5	18	3	282	6	2	220	311	394	100	93	101	4	75	0.15	43	18	39	35	86	CBd	4%	77	84	8%	10%	111	6%	100%	-1.3	17	$8
23	**Proj**	**560**	**78**	**27**	**78**	**5**	**279**	**23**	**6**	**268**	**326**	**494**	**114**	**116**	**113**	**6**	**75**	**0.26**	**39**	**23**	**38**	**33**	**105**		**9%**	**139**	**121**	**18%**	**16%**	**99**	**6%**	**79%**	**25.3**	**145**	**$27**

Castillo,Diego

Age: 25	Pos: SS 2B RF	Health	A	LIMA Plan	D+
Bats: R	Ht: 6' 0" Wt: 170	PT/Exp	C	Rand Var	+1
		Consist	B	MM	3133

11-29-.206 in 283 PA at PIT. Marginal prospect surprised with head-turning batted ball metrics (see HctX, Brl%, xPX), but still earned a demotion in August as ct% problems and ineptitude vR were debilitating. There's work to be done, specifically marrying minors ct% with those batted ball metrics. Worth a cheap look to see what sophomore season holds.

Yr	Tm	PA	R	HR	RBI	SB	BA	xHR	xSB	xBA	OBP	SLG	OPS+	vL+	vR+	bb%	ct%	Eye	G	L	F	h%	HctX	QBaB	Brl%	PX	xPX	HR/F	xHR/F	Spd	SBA%	SB%	RAR	BPX	R$
18																																			
19																																			
20																																			
21	a/a	420	52	13	39	6	234		4		293	389	94			8	84	0.52				25				86				88	13%	58%		185	$8
22	PIT *	426	41	13	37	2	202	10	5	225	246	344	84	110	64	5	71	0.21	40	20	40	25	116	CBc	10%	99	154	14%	13%	98	5%	43%	-18.6	24	$2
1st Half		210	20	8	20	1	194	8	2	225	233	357	83	104	64	4	72	0.16	42	17	42	23	116	BBc	11%	108	162	13%	13%	102	5%	50%	-8.5	52	$1
2nd Half		216	21	5	17	1	209	2	3	240	262	331	84	122	58	7	71	0.24	34	30	36	27	119	CBc	9%	90	129	18%	12%	107	5%	35%	-7.3	10	$1
23	**Proj**	**315**	**34**	**12**	**30**	**3**	**226**	**11**	**3**	**256**	**281**	**399**	**94**	**112**	**61**	**7**	**76**	**0.30**	**37**	**25**	**38**	**26**	**118**		**10%**	**111**	**142**	**14%**	**12%**	**102**	**6%**	**53%**	**-3.1**	**91**	**$7**

RAY MURPHY

Castro,Harold

Age: 29 Pos: 1B 3B | Bats: L Ht: 5' 10" Wt: 195

Health B | PT/Exp B | Consist C | LIMA Plan D+ | Rand Var +1 | MM 1133

More contact with more barrels counts as progress, but we're still a long way from getting excited. QBaB declined from its already-poor baseline; running game (such as it was) has to be considered gone for good. He only plays vR, but he's just scratching average against them. Loss of MI eligibility ruins any swiss-army value.

Yr	Tm	PA	R	HR	RBI	SB	BA	xHR	xSB	xBA	OBP	SLG	OPS+	vL+	vR+	bb%	ct%	Eye	G	L	F	h%	HctX	QBaB	Brl%	PX	xPX	HR/F	xHR/F	Spd	SBA%	SB%	RAR	BPX	R$
18	DET *	368	30	2	24	5	234	0	4	210	249	280	71	0	79	2	79	0.10	63	13	25	29	145	DFa	0%	34	66	0%	0%	85	13%	53%	-24.1	-87	$2
19	DET *	498	46	8	58	5	290	7	11	254	313	394	98	62	102	3	76	0.14	52	25	22	37	104	CDa	4%	55	67	8%	12%	123	9%	47%	-8.8	-22	$12
20	DET	54	6	0	3	0	347	1	1	262	407	429	111	109	111	9	78	0.45	47	29	24	45	66	CCa	3%	64	59	0%	11%	103	0%	0%	1.8	52	$2
21	DET	339	35	3	37	1	283	6	1	262	310	359	92	62	97	4	77	0.19	41	34	26	36	90	CCa	3%	50	77	5%	10%	88	2%	50%	-5.4	-54	$7
22	DET	443	37	7	47	0	271	11	3	262	300	381	96	102	96	4	81	0.22	44	26	30	32	84	DCb	6%	72	80	7%	11%	91	1%	0%	-1.7	66	$9
1st Half		183	19	4	17	0	276	6	1	266	298	414	101	109	99	3	80	0.14	46	24	29	33	89	CDb	8%	85	88	10%	15%	108	1%	0%	-0.3	93	$2
2nd Half		260	18	3	30	0	268	5	2	260	301	358	93	97	93	5	82	0.27	43	27	30	32	81	DCb	5%	63	74	5%	8%	80	1%	0%	-4.8	48	$6
23	Proj	350	32	5	37	1	273	7	2	257	300	365	92	80	94	4	79	0.19	44	29	27	33	89		5%	63	77	6%	9%	93	3%	41%	-3.0	6	$7

Castro,Rodolfo

Age: 24 Pos: 2B 3B | Bats: B Ht: 6' 0" Wt: 205

Health A | PT/Exp B | Consist A | LIMA Plan C | Rand Var +1 | MM 4223

11-27-.233 with 5 SB in 278 PA at PIT. Got 2nd-half look and acquitted himself well. An emerging power/speed MI? Not so fast: GB% tilt remains an obstacle; QBaB and Brl% aren't those of a slugger, nor is SB% that of a speedster. Switch-hitter did more damage vL, raising short-side-platoon downside. Fine end-gamer; just keep expectations modest.

Yr	Tm	PA	R	HR	RBI	SB	BA	xHR	xSB	xBA	OBP	SLG	OPS+	vL+	vR+	bb%	ct%	Eye	G	L	F	h%	HctX	QBaB	Brl%	PX	xPX	HR/F	xHR/F	Spd	SBA%	SB%	RAR	BPX	R$
18																																			
19																																			
20																																			
21	PIT *	430	46	15	49	5	211	3	3	235	253	375	86	117	75	5	72	0.20	53	15	32	26	94	CDf	10%	102	84	26%	16%	83	12%	54%	-18.9	23	$5
22	PIT *	572	49	18	53	9	217	9	9	230	277	379	93	127	91	8	68	0.26	48	19	33	28	72	DCf	7%	111	90	19%	15%	123	13%	58%	-13.5	48	$9
1st Half		267	21	6	24	6	184	1	4	204	250	307	79	69	84	8	66	0.26	44	17	38	25	50	CDf	6%	91	62	5%	5%	109	13%	59%	-12.9	-41	$3
2nd Half		305	28	12	30	3	245	8	5	248	301	442	105	149	94	7	69	0.26	50	19	31	31	83	DCf	8%	128	101	26%	21%	129	13%	57%	4.1	121	$15
23	Proj	350	35	16	38	5	235	11	6	245	293	437	101	125	90	7	69	0.23	49	17	33	29	79		8%	135	84	21%	15%	110	11%	58%	3.2	41	$11

Castro,Willi

Age: 26 Pos: RF LF | Bats: B Ht: 6' 1" Wt: 206

Health A | PT/Exp B | Consist D | LIMA Plan C | Rand Var +3 | MM 2423

8-31-.241 with 9 SB in 392 PA at PIT. After another near-full season devoid of anything resembling an above-average skill (other than the Spd that's rendered useless by those awful OBPs), we can officially declare that gaudy 2020 a mirage. Rest of world: "Man, 2020 was the worst year ever, amirite?" Willi: "Hey, it wasn't all bad... I hit .349".

Yr	Tm	PA	R	HR	RBI	SB	BA	xHR	xSB	xBA	OBP	SLG	OPS+	vL+	vR+	bb%	ct%	Eye	G	L	F	h%	HctX	QBaB	Brl%	PX	xPX	HR/F	xHR/F	Spd	SBA%	SB%	RAR	BPX	R$
18	a/a	527	59	8	48	16	250		6		292	372	89			6	77	0.25				31				80				110	18%	75%		53	$13
19	DET *	607	76	11	63	15	279	2	17	238	324	431	105	107	81	6	74	0.26	36	24	39	36	64	DAb	2%	87	43	4%	8%	137	14%	74%	-3.3	78	$19
20	DET	140	21	6	24	0	349	7	4	253	381	550	124	131	122	5	71	0.18	42	27	31	46	82	DCc	10%	111	78	21%	24%	157	2%	0%	8.5	120	$17
21	DET *	473	62	10	40	11	227	10	4	238	266	361	86	94	82	5	75	0.21	46	21	33	28	67	DCd	5%	78	55	9%	10%	133	15%	73%	-15.6	46	$9
22	DET *	427	48	8	32	11	238	3	8	241	268	358	89	92	92	4	77	0.17	42	23	36	29	73	DCd	3%	81	49	8%	3%	113	18%	68%	-11.4	52	$9
1st Half		225	21	2	15	4	257	1	5	239	285	354	90	90	97	4	78	0.18	44	22	34	32	63	FCd	2%	67	31	4%	2%	118	18%	49%	-5.0	41	$3
2nd Half		202	27	6	17	7	218	2	4	241	269	362	89	94	86	4	74	0.17	40	23	37	26	83	DBc	5%	96	68	12%	4%	104	18%	88%	-5.8	55	$8
23	Proj	350	45	8	33	9	246	7	9	240	292	383	94	98	92	5	75	0.19	42	23	35	31	72		4%	91	55	9%	8%	123	15%	72%	-3.4	57	$12

Celestino,Gilberto

Age: 24 Pos: CF LF | Bats: R Ht: 6' 0" Wt: 170

Health A | PT/Exp C | Consist A | LIMA Plan D | Rand Var 0 | MM 1311

Pressed into a lot more playing time than anticipated; such is the life of Byron Buxton's understudy. Much like when the PA guy says "tonight, the role of Alexander Hamilton will be played by Joe Understudy instead of Lin-Manuel Miranda", the similarities stop with the costume. Extreme GB tendencies, can run a bit, but can't act a lick.

Yr	Tm	PA	R	HR	RBI	SB	BA	xHR	xSB	xBA	OBP	SLG	OPS+	vL+	vR+	bb%	ct%	Eye	G	L	F	h%	HctX	QBaB	Brl%	PX	xPX	HR/F	xHR/F	Spd	SBA%	SB%	RAR	BPX	R$
18																																			
19																																			
20																																			
21	MIN *	357	36	7	27	3	230	1	4	221	297	359	90	52	81	9	73	0.36	47	16	38	29	73	CFf	7%	87	106	12%	6%	90	5%	74%	-8.4	35	$3
22	MIN	347	30	2	24	4	238	3	5	238	313	302	87	81	90	9	75	0.42	60	21	19	31	67	CFf	3%	49	32	5%	7%	135	5%	80%	-6.5	3	$3
1st Half		153	16	0	6	0	283	1	2	248	344	348	98	78	108	7	76	0.33	61	23	16	37	68	DFf	2%	53	26	0%	6%	168	5%	0%	0.3	48	-$4
2nd Half		194	14	2	18	4	202	2	3	226	289	266	79	83	76	11	75	0.48	60	19	21	26	66	CFf	3%	46	38	7%	7%	103	5%	100%	-7.5	-34	-$1
23	Proj	245	23	3	18	3	233	3	3	229	306	328	88	74	98	9	74	0.39	55	19	26	30	69		4%	70	62	7%	6%	105	6%	79%	-3.0	14	$4

Chapman,Matt

Age: 30 Pos: 3B | Bats: R Ht: 6' 0" Wt: 215

Health B | PT/Exp A | Consist A | LIMA Plan B+ | Rand Var 0 | MM 4115

Stat line looks pretty stable, but under the hood there's a ton to like: recovered some contact while spiking HctX and hanging a full-season peak xPX; also reversed weird 2021 dip vR. Has both exit velocity and launch angle dialed in. Still in prime power years and out of OAK, it's not too late for... UP: 2019 redux

Yr	Tm	PA	R	HR	RBI	SB	BA	xHR	xSB	xBA	OBP	SLG	OPS+	vL+	vR+	bb%	ct%	Eye	G	L	F	h%	HctX	QBaB	Brl%	PX	xPX	HR/F	xHR/F	Spd	SBA%	SB%	RAR	BPX	R$
18	OAK	616	100	24	68	1	278	21	8	266	356	508	116	107	117	9	73	0.40	40	20	39	34	117	ABd	9%	148	114	15%	13%	117	2%	33%	28.2	223	$20
19	OAK	670	102	36	91	1	249	37	4	261	342	506	117	118	116	11	75	0.50	41	15	43	27	117	ABf	12%	137	107	19%	20%	101	1%	50%	11.2	233	$18
20	OAK	152	22	10	25	0	232	11	1	244	276	535	108	84	112	5	62	0.15	26	24	51	29	104	AAf	18%	198	150	22%	24%	109	0%	0%	0.0	204	$11
21	OAK	622	75	27	72	3	210	30	5	195	314	403	98	110	92	13	62	0.40	34	15	52	28	76	BAf	14%	126	130	16%	17%	131	3%	60%	-1.6	58	$9
22	TOR	621	83	27	76	2	229	29	5	230	324	433	107	105	108	11	68	0.40	34	17	49	28	120	AAf	13%	142	154	15%	16%	94	3%	50%	7.9	134	$15
1st Half		300	41	12	39	0	220	15	2	226	293	407	99	112	96	9	72	0.35	31	16	52	26	127	AAf	12%	125	153	12%	15%	99	3%	0%	-2.7	134	$14
2nd Half		321	42	15	37	2	237	15	3	233	352	459	115	97	119	13	64	0.44	37	19	44	31	114	ABf	14%	160	156	19%	19%	90	3%	50%	7.6	145	$21
23	Proj	595	81	29	75	2	235	31	4	229	326	455	108	108	108	11	66	0.37	34	17	49	30	105		14%	156	142	17%	18%	94	4%	53%	16.2	131	$19

Chavis,Michael

Age: 27 Pos: 1B | Bats: R Ht: 5' 10" Wt: 210

Health B | PT/Exp B | Consist A | LIMA Plan D | Rand Var 0 | MM 3101

Former prospect reaches Bull Durham years fighting for relevance. PRO: Got longest look vR since 2019 and wasn't awful. CON: Doesn't exactly mash vL either; power isn't far enough above average to obscure the appalling plate skills; now only 1B eligible. Sorry, the CONs have it.

Yr	Tm	PA	R	HR	RBI	SB	BA	xHR	xSB	xBA	OBP	SLG	OPS+	vL+	vR+	bb%	ct%	Eye	G	L	F	h%	HctX	QBaB	Brl%	PX	xPX	HR/F	xHR/F	Spd	SBA%	SB%	RAR	BPX	R$
18	a/a	166	26	6	20	2	279		2		327	468	107			7	68	0.23				37				134				94	8%	69%		73	$4
19	BOS *	458	55	24	67	2	251	16	5	228	312	459	107	103	106	8	64	0.25	45	20	35	33	75	CCc	11%	123	90	23%	21%	92	3%	67%	-6.7	4	$11
20	BOS	158	16	5	19	3	212	5	1	227	259	377	84	80	87	5	66	0.16	46	23	31	29	90	CCb	7%	100	80	17%	17%	122	10%	100%	-12.2	-28	$7
21	2 TM *	326	42	12	36	2	228	3	4	230	254	394	89	109	75	3	66	0.10	50	20	30	31	67	BDc	5%	111	66	13%	13%	113	9%	43%	-16.4	-19	$4
22	PIT	426	39	14	49	1	229	10	5	221	265	389	93	98	88	4	69	0.15	45	17	39	30	92	DCf	8%	110	93	13%	9%	112	3%	50%	-15.3	24	$6
1st Half		228	23	9	27	1	246	6	3	223	289	427	101	122	86	5	70	0.19	42	15	43	31	91	DCf	9%	117	95	14%	9%	124	3%	50%	-1.8	76	$7
2nd Half		198	16	5	22	0	211	4	2	216	237	347	83	74	89	4	67	0.11	48	18	34	28	94	DDf	6%	101	91	11%	9%	96	3%	0%	-10.0	-41	$0
23	Proj	175	19	5	20	1	228	4	1	221	265	379	89	95	85	4	67	0.14	47	19	34	31	83		7%	109	83	14%	12%	95	4%	58%	-4.3	-2	$4

Chisholm,Jazz

Age: 25 Pos: 2B | Bats: L Ht: 5' 11" Wt: 184

Health F | PT/Exp C | Consist C | LIMA Plan C+ | Rand Var -1 | MM 4515

Stress fracture in his back ended his season in late June; eventually had surgery for torn right meniscus as well. Before that, was riding a wave of more hard contact and a better launch angle to fantastic results. We never got to see whether he could keep it up for a full year, but this sizzling half season evokes visions of... UP: 30 HR/30 SB

Yr	Tm	PA	R	HR	RBI	SB	BA	xHR	xSB	xBA	OBP	SLG	OPS+	vL+	vR+	bb%	ct%	Eye	G	L	F	h%	HctX	QBaB	Brl%	PX	xPX	HR/F	xHR/F	Spd	SBA%	SB%	RAR	BPX	R$
18																																			
19	aa	455	63	21	61	18	220		8		320	442	106			13	61	0.38				30				133				152	21%	81%		85	$14
20	MIA	62	8	2	6	2	161	3	1	183	242	321	75	121	59	8	66	0.26	37	11	51	20	72	DBf	11%	91	145	11%	17%	141	36%	50%	-5.8	-8	$1
21	MIA	507	70	18	53	23	248	18	23	241	303	425	100	91	104	7	69	0.23	49	20	31	32	87	BDf	9%	110	88	18%	18%	144	28%	74%	-2.8	85	$21
22	MIA	240	39	14	45	12	254	13	8	267	325	535	122	73	132	9	69	0.32	37	22	41	30	111	BCf	17%	181	159	23%	22%	130	34%	71%	9.5	272	$13
1st Half		240	39	14	45	12	254	13	8	267	325	535	122	73	131	9	69	0.32	37	22	41	30	111	BCf	17%	181	159	23%	22%	130	34%	71%	10.9	276	$28
2nd Half																																			
23	Proj	490	73	22	73	22	250	26	24	234	327	468	110	114	109	9	68	0.32	40	17	42	32	89		12%	145	136	17%	20%	146	27%	75%	17.5	152	$28

RAY MURPHY

Choi,Ji-Man

Age: 32 Pos: 1B | Bats: L Ht: 6' 1" Wt: 260

Health: D | LIMA Plan: D+
PT/Exp: B | Rand Var: -1
Consist: A | MM: 4013

First half looked like it was a nice bounceback from injury-plagued 2021. But rather than being rooted in something sustainable like ct% recovery, instead it was just an outlying h%-fueled hallucination. The inevitable reversal, with accompanying GB% spike, drove the 2nd half line into a ditch. Still draws a walk with the best of 'em, though.

Yr	Tm	PA	R	HR	RBI	SB	BA	xHR	xSB	xBA	OBP	SLG	OPS+	vL+	vR+	bb%	ct%	Eye	G	L	F	h%	HctX	QBaB	Brl%	PX	xPX	HR/F	xHR/F	Spd	SBA%	SB%	RAR	BPX	R$
18	2 TM *	458	46	15	61	3	250	11	7	245	349	434	105	68	120	13	70	0.51	43	21	35	32	113	BCc	12%	125	116	21%	23%	53	2%	100%	9.0	83	$10
19	TAM	487	54	19	63	2	261	23	3	258	363	459	114	88	119	13	74	0.59	42	24	35	31	109	ACb	11%	107	120	18%	21%	73	4%	40%	8.0	111	$11
20	TAM	145	16	3	16	0	230	3	1	242	331	410	98	66	104	14	70	0.56	39	20	40	30	99	CBf	3%	130	100	8%	8%	60	0%	0%	-2.8	136	$4
21	TAM *	330	39	11	47	0	226	11	0	234	338	399	101	72	116	14	66	0.49	40	25	35	30	104	ABc	9%	119	110	19%	19%	52	0%	0%	-1.0	15	$4
22	TAM	419	36	11	52	0	233	15	1	228	341	388	103	101	104	14	65	0.47	45	23	32	32	95	ACc	12%	123	115	15%	20%	68	0%	0%	3.1	34	$5
1st Half		221	23	7	36	0	283	9	0	248	385	471	121	142	117	15	66	0.51	41	25	34	39	87	ACc	12%	147	133	16%	21%	80	0%	0%	11.2	131	$10
2nd Half		198	13	4	16	0	178	7	0	204	293	296	83	46	89	13	64	0.43	50	21	29	25	102	ADc	11%	95	94	13%	22%	55	0%	0%	-9.5	-72	-$5
23	Proj	350	35	10	44	0	227	13	0	233	336	393	101	78	106	14	67	0.48	43	23	34	30	100		10%	129	110	15%	19%	51	0%	63%	2.1	32	$4

Conforto,Michael

Age: 30 Pos: DH | Bats: L Ht: 6' 1" Wt: 215

Health: B | LIMA Plan: C+
PT/Exp: F | Rand Var:
Consist: D | MM: 4135

Was the last major free agent to sign in the accelerated run-up to Opening Day, but once his shoulder injury (and resulting surgery) was revealed, no team would touch him. A year ago, we looked at the power metrics and said "UP: 30 HR." That's still valid, with a decent BA floor, so it's worth watching where he signs and whether he's restricted in spring camp.

Yr	Tm	PA	R	HR	RBI	SB	BA	xHR	xSB	xBA	OBP	SLG	OPS+	vL+	vR+	bb%	ct%	Eye	G	L	F	h%	HctX	QBaB	Brl%	PX	xPX	HR/F	xHR/F	Spd	SBA%	SB%	RAR	BPX	R$
18	NYM	638	78	28	82	3	243	24	10	245	350	448	107	106	105	13	71	0.53	44	20	37	29	93	CCc	10%	128	130	20%	17%	86	4%	43%	10.2	130	$16
19	NYM	648	90	33	92	7	257	34	5	262	363	494	119	98	127	13	73	0.56	36	24	40	29	92	BBc	12%	128	120	20%	21%	87	5%	78%	13.1	178	$20
20	NYM	233	40	9	31	3	322	9	3	270	412	515	123	114	128	10	72	0.42	41	30	28	41	106	CCc	11%	117	108	22%	22%	85	8%	50%	12.4	116	$29
21	NYM	479	52	14	55	1	232	17	6	241	344	384	100	79	109	12	74	0.57	45	21	34	28	112	CCc	9%	93	110	13%	16%	73	1%	100%	-4.3	77	$6
22																																			
1st Half																																			
2nd Half																																			
23	Proj	525	73	22	71	4	261	23	7	259	363	460	114	98	122	12	73	0.52	41	24	36	31	101		11%	132	116	19%	19%	78	6%	64%	17.4	131	$21

Contreras,William

Age: 25 Pos: CA DH | Bats: R Ht: 6' 0" Wt: 180

Health: A | LIMA Plan: C+
PT/Exp: C | Rand Var: -1
Consist: D | MM: 4523

20-45-.278 in 376 PA at ATL. We called him a "future long ball threat" a year ago in this space; that future came quickly. And it wasn't driven by a retooled swing or skills reboot: it's just more playing time, with some more barrels thrown in as sweetener. BA/xBA gap got silly in 2nd half (thanks, h%), so expect some BA pullback. But the power can stick.

Yr	Tm	PA	R	HR	RBI	SB	BA	xHR	xSB	xBA	OBP	SLG	OPS+	vL+	vR+	bb%	ct%	Eye	G	L	F	h%	HctX	QBaB	Brl%	PX	xPX	HR/F	xHR/F	Spd	SBA%	SB%	RAR	BPX	R$
18																																			
19	aa	207	26	3	19	0	253		3		311	351	92			8	79	0.39				31				58				98	0%	0%		30	$0
20	ATL	10	0	0	1	0	400	0	0	391	400	500	119	0	150	0	60	0.00	17	67	17	67	81	DAa	17%	102	140	0%	0%	113	0%	0%	1.0	-164	-$2
21	ATL *	350	40	15	46	0	235	8	2	237	299	419	99	91	98	8	70	0.31	49	19	32	29	94	ADd	11%	110	90	23%	23%	107	0%	0%	3.1	77	$6
22	ATL *	426	53	20	51	2	275	21	3	247	346	481	117	145	111	10	70	0.36	53	15	32	35	113	BDd	14%	137	126	27%	28%	125	2%	100%	24.6	162	$15
1st Half		202	22	10	27	2	263	9	1	260	333	490	116	142	120	10	71	0.36	52	16	32	32	120	BFf	16%	156	146	33%	30%	98	2%	100%	11.3	200	$9
2nd Half		224	31	10	24	0	286	12	2	229	357	472	118	147	105	10	69	0.35	54	14	32	37	108	BDd	13%	119	113	23%	27%	158	2%	0%	13.7	138	$13
23	Proj	350	43	18	42	1	258	19	3	252	328	475	111	128	105	9	71	0.34	51	17	32	31	105		13%	141	112	25%	26%	117	5%	100%	18.2	115	$13

Contreras,Willson

Age: 31 Pos: CA DH | Bats: R Ht: 6' 1" Wt: 225

Health: C | LIMA Plan: B
PT/Exp: A | Rand Var: +4
Consist: A | MM: 4135

Recurring hamstring/ankle ailments cost him some time, including almost all of September. Looked like he was on his way to long-awaited career year in first half, before h% cratered in 2nd half. But skills stayed robust amidst that late fade. BPX column shows the scope of the latent growth, there's still a career year lurking here... UP: 30 HR, .275 BA

Yr	Tm	PA	R	HR	RBI	SB	BA	xHR	xSB	xBA	OBP	SLG	OPS+	vL+	vR+	bb%	ct%	Eye	G	L	F	h%	HctX	QBaB	Brl%	PX	xPX	HR/F	xHR/F	Spd	SBA%	SB%	RAR	BPX	R$
18	CHC	544	50	10	54	4	249	13	8	242	339	390	98	109	93	10	74	0.44	52	17	31	31	79	CDc	7%	92	71	9%	12%	111	4%	80%	11.1	87	$9
19	CHC	409	57	24	64	1	272	21	4	263	355	533	123	143	117	9	72	0.37	50	16	34	32	92	CDc	12%	141	128	27%	24%	89	3%	33%	19.8	185	$13
20	CHC	225	37	7	26	1	243	9	1	234	356	407	101	71	110	9	70	0.35	47	20	33	31	99	BDd	10%	103	125	16%	20%	80	5%	33%	0.7	24	$15
21	CHC	483	61	21	57	5	237	23	4	233	340	438	107	121	101	11	67	0.38	50	16	34	30	106	ACc	11%	131	127	22%	24%	80	7%	56%	9.4	73	$11
22	CHC	487	65	22	55	4	243	21	6	272	349	466	115	120	114	9	75	0.44	51	16	33	27	137	BDd	10%	141	129	21%	20%	94	5%	67%	16.3	214	$14
1st Half		309	46	13	35	3	274	14	4	273	392	498	126	168	112	12	75	0.55	50	16	34	32	147	ADf	10%	145	139	20%	21%	110	5%	60%	19.5	262	$23
2nd Half		178	19	9	20	1	191	7	2	267	275	414	98	42	117	6	75	0.26	53	15	32	19	120	BDc	11%	134	112	24%	18%	78	5%	100%	-2.1	155	$3
23	Proj	525	71	24	64	4	255	24	4	253	350	462	113	107	114	9	72	0.36	51	16	33	31	116		11%	137	122	21%	21%	73	4%	60%	23.6	137	$20

Cooper,Garrett

Age: 32 Pos: 1B DH | Bats: R Ht: 6' 5" Wt: 235

Health: F | LIMA Plan: C+
PT/Exp: B | Rand Var: +2
Consist: A | MM: 3023

His first foundational skill is he hits the ball hard, per Brl% and HctX. Unfortunately, he doesn't hit it frequently enough, and it's on the ground too often. His other foundational skill is getting hurt, (avg 65 IL days/yr for last six years). Oh, and he's landed on the COVID IL three years running, which we hope is a record that never gets broken.

Yr	Tm	PA	R	HR	RBI	SB	BA	xHR	xSB	xBA	OBP	SLG	OPS+	vL+	vR+	bb%	ct%	Eye	G	L	F	h%	HctX	QBaB	Brl%	PX	xPX	HR/F	xHR/F	Spd	SBA%	SB%	RAR	BPX	R$
18	MIA *	70	4	1	6	0	223	0	1	209	293	284	77	114	64	9	71	0.34	67	24	10	30	37	CFc	0%	44	-27	0%	0%	81	0%	0%	-4.5	-120	-$2
19	MIA	421	52	15	50	0	281	18	2	255	344	446	109	89	116	8	71	0.30	52	25	23	36	100	CFb	10%	93	93	24%	29%	97	0%	0%	-0.5	22	$10
20	MIA	133	20	6	20	0	283	6	0	276	353	500	113	153	93	8	74	0.35	46	26	28	34	94	BCa	10%	127	72	24%	24%	73	0%	0%	0.7	156	$11
21	MIA	250	30	9	33	1	284	9	1	244	380	465	116	132	109	12	68	0.44	51	22	27	38	94	ADa	11%	115	101	23%	23%	99	3%	50%	7.2	81	$7
22	MIA	469	37	9	50	0	261	15	2	258	337	415	107	87	112	9	71	0.34	44	26	29	35	106	BDb	11%	119	121	10%	17%	77	0%	0%	0.4	76	$9
1st Half		288	26	6	37	0	315	8	2	271	382	472	121	96	127	9	74	0.36	46	28	27	41	111	ADa	9%	117	112	12%	16%	81	0%	0%	15.1	110	$15
2nd Half		181	11	3	13	0	175	7	1	239	265	325	84	76	86	9	68	0.31	42	24	34	24	97	CCb	13%	123	137	8%	19%	79	0%	0%	-9.6	41	-$6
23	Proj	385	39	10	45	0	269	15	1	249	350	429	108	111	107	10	70	0.36	47	24	29	36	99		11%	119	110	14%	21%	77	1%	50%	9.6	76	$12

Cordero,Franchy

Age: 28 Pos: 1B RF | Bats: L Ht: 6' 3" Wt: 226

Health: F | LIMA Plan: D
PT/Exp: C | Rand Var: -3
Consist: A | MM: 4201

8-29-.219 in 275 PA at BOS. Spent April in minors, then got May-July big-league look with little production, despite some appealing skills (ct% gains, plus HctX, Brl%, QBaB). Spent most of August back in AAA, got hot, and brought it back for a couple of weeks (4 HR in 27 AB) before ankle injury ended his season. Are we still interested? Yes, but barely.

Yr	Tm	PA	R	HR	RBI	SB	BA	xHR	xSB	xBA	OBP	SLG	OPS+	vL+	vR+	bb%	ct%	Eye	G	L	F	h%	HctX	QBaB	Brl%	PX	xPX	HR/F	xHR/F	Spd	SBA%	SB%	RAR	BPX	R$
18	SD *	183	21	8	20	7	234	9	2	227	305	421	97	78	108	9	60	0.25	46	25	29	34	107	ADc	13%	134	144	29%	38%	100	22%	78%	-1.6	-3	$4
19	SD *	69	7	2	6	1	209	0	2	196	287	362	90	0	117	10	52	0.23	25	38	38	36	101	AAa	0%	118	276	0%	0%	117	7%	100%	-3.2	-144	-$2
20	KC	42	7	2	7	1	211	3	0	312	286	447	97	43	107	10	89	1.00	62	12	26	19	117	AFb	12%	117	120	22%	33%	85	14%	100%	-1.3	392	$1
21	BOS *	453	51	10	50	10	233	3	8	224	298	381	93	58	70	8	60	0.23	45	27	28	36	64	CDf	5%	120	38	5%	14%	90	13%	82%	-6.3	-58	$9
22	BOS *	401	50	12	51	6	230	10	6	222	302	408	101	85	101	9	60	0.26	39	23	39	35	100	CCc	12%	154	135	14%	17%	83	12%	65%	-0.8	28	$9
1st Half		260	32	5	35	4	244	7	4	238	317	395	101	82	106	10	67	0.32	40	25	35	35	123	BCb	12%	126	126	8%	18%	87	12%	62%	0.7	52	$12
2nd Half		141	18	7	15	3	206	3	2	195	274	433	100	91	93	9	47	0.18	34	16	50	36	57	FDf	14%	226	163	26%	16%	84	12%	69%	-1.2	52	$3
23	Proj	245	29	7	28	5	231	8	4	209	301	391	96	83	98	9	58	0.23	41	23	36	37	78		10%	144	104	14%	18%	86	9%	77%	-1.3	3	$8

Correa,Carlos

Age: 28 Pos: SS | Bats: R Ht: 6' 4" Wt: 220

Health: C | LIMA Plan: B
PT/Exp: A | Rand Var: -3
Consist: B | MM: 3035

This is as unassailable a skill set as you'll find in these pages. The worst thing you can say about him is that he doesn't run, even though his Spd is just a tick below average. But he's good-to-very-good at literally everything else. Second-half shift from GB to FB, with concurrent ct% uptick, opens a potential path to... UP: 30 HR.

Yr	Tm	PA	R	HR	RBI	SB	BA	xHR	xSB	xBA	OBP	SLG	OPS+	vL+	vR+	bb%	ct%	Eye	G	L	F	h%	HctX	QBaB	Brl%	PX	xPX	HR/F	xHR/F	Spd	SBA%	SB%	RAR	BPX	R$
18	HOU	468	60	15	65	3	239	13	7	241	323	405	98	106	93	11	72	0.48	44	20	36	29	77	CCd	7%	107	83	14%	12%	94	3%	100%	4.7	93	$10
19	HOU *	344	43	21	60	1	277	19	3	274	357	554	126	134	125	11	73	0.46	39	21	40	31	114	CCd	13%	149	132	26%	23%	96	1%	100%	15.9	237	$11
20	HOU	221	22	5	25	0	264	6	1	231	326	383	94	101	91	7	76	0.33	50	21	29	33	110	CCf	6%	71	86	11%	13%	86	0%	0%	-2.3	8	$11
21	HOU	640	104	26	92	0	279	21	3	277	366	485	117	115	118	12	79	0.65	42	24	35	31	118	BCd	9%	116	102	17%	14%	92	0%	0%	30.9	238	$23
22	MIN	590	70	22	64	0	291	26	3	250	366	467	118	132	113	10	77	0.50	43	20	38	34	121	BCd	12%	110	111	14%	17%	95	1%	0%	29.5	159	$22
1st Half		264	35	9	29	0	286	11	1	247	360	453	115	120	113	10	74	0.45	46	20	34	35	126	ACd	12%	110	120	15%	19%	86	1%	0%	10.6	117	$14
2nd Half		326	35	13	35	0	295	15	2	252	371	479	120	142	113	11	79	0.56	40	19	41	34	117	CCd	11%	109	104	14%	16%	107	1%	0%	16.9	200	$22
23	Proj	630	83	24	80	0	277	25	3	258	355	459	113	120	110	11	77	0.52	43	21	36	32	116		10%	116	105	15%	16%	89	2%	34%	29.1	172	$25

RAY MURPHY

Cowser,Colton

Age: 23 Pos: CF | Health A | LIMA Plan D
Bats: L Ht: 6' 3" Wt: 195 | PT/Exp D | Rand Var
Consist F | MM 2001

4th overall pick in 2021 climbed through three levels in 2022, finishing with 124 PA at Triple-A. More of a hard-contact/line drive profile than a slugger, strikeouts did spike a bit at Triple-A, so he'll likely return there for more polish. But he's not far away, and despite lack of speed, this is a future top-of-order skill set in BAL.

Yr	Tm	PA	R	HR	RBI	SB	BA	xHR	xSB	xBA	OBP	SLG	OPS+	vL+	vR+	bb%	ct%	Eye	G	L	F	h%	HctX	QBaB	Brl%	PX	xPX	HR/F	xHR/F	Spd	SBA%	SB%	RAR	BPX	R$
18																																			
19																																			
20																																			
21																																			
22	a/a	313	48	12	29	1	251		4		328	425	107			10	63	0.31				36				135				98	4%	37%		41	$7
1st Half		18	4	1	2	1	337		0		515	589	156			27	57	0.86				54				211				119	4%	100%		307	-$10
2nd Half		295	44	11	27	1	247		3	222	317	418	104			9	63	0.28	44	20	36	35	0			132	-14	0%		108	4%	23%	3.2	41	$17
23	Proj	**210**	**25**	**5**	**19**	**1**	**237**	**5**	**2**	**209**	**299**	**358**	**91**	**90**	**91**	**8**	**68**	**0.27**	**42**	**20**	**38**	**32**	**98**		**9%**	**91**		**10%**	**10%**	**104**	**5%**	**33%**	**-1.6**	**37**	**$1**

Crawford,Brandon

Age: 36 Pos: SS | Health B | LIMA Plan C+
Bats: L Ht: 6' 1" Wt: 223 | PT/Exp A | Rand Var +1
Consist D | MM 2213

Late-career power surge of 2020-21 went "poof." Instead of assigning blame to outside factors like humidors, more GBs and quite a bit less hard contact are less nefarious explanations. Had a handful of leg problems that maybe contributed, but a) struggles were year-long, and b) nagging leg problems are to be expected at his age. Time to lower expectations.

Yr	Tm	PA	R	HR	RBI	SB	BA	xHR	xSB	xBA	OBP	SLG	OPS+	vL+	vR+	bb%	ct%	Eye	G	L	F	h%	HctX	QBaB	Brl%	PX	xPX	HR/F	xHR/F	Spd	SBA%	SB%	RAR	BPX	R$
18	SF	594	63	14	54	4	254	12	8	258	325	394	96	101	91	8	77	0.41	44	25	31	31	103	CCb	4%	88	91	11%	9%	78	6%	44%	5.3	70	$11
19	SF	560	58	11	59	3	228	16	5	252	304	350	90	83	92	9	77	0.45	48	23	28	28	104	CDb	5%	69	106	10%	15%	79	4%	60%	-19.6	22	$5
20	SF	193	26	8	28	1	256	6	1	259	326	465	105	84	110	8	73	0.32	42	23	35	31	102	CCd	9%	127	123	18%	13%	72	7%	33%	1.5	124	$14
21	SF	549	79	24	90	11	298	28	7	266	373	522	123	98	133	10	78	0.53	40	19	41	34	101	CBd	11%	126	137	15%	18%	104	9%	79%	33.4	258	$28
22	SF	458	50	9	52	1	231	10	7	225	308	344	92	93	92	9	76	0.40	47	18	36	28	86	CCd	7%	73	95	8%	9%	95	2%	50%	-12.0	34	$6
1st Half		247	26	5	30	1	225	6	4	227	312	353	94	95	94	9	77	0.42	46	15	39	27	76	DBd	8%	81	84	8%	9%	101	2%	50%	-5.7	79	$5
2nd Half		211	24	4	22	0	238	4	3	220	303	333	90	91	89	9	75	0.38	48	20	32	30	97	CCd	5%	64	108	9%	9%	81	2%	0%	-4.6	-24	$4
23	Proj	**420**	**53**	**10**	**56**	**3**	**248**	**13**	**2**	**237**	**323**	**383**	**98**	**89**	**101**	**9**	**76**	**0.43**	**44**	**20**	**36**	**30**	**95**		**8%**	**90**	**112**	**10%**	**12%**	**90**	**3%**	**66%**	**2.4**	**103**	**$13**

Crawford,J.P.

Age: 28 Pos: SS | Health A | LIMA Plan B+
Bats: L Ht: 6' 2" Wt: 199 | PT/Exp A | Rand Var +2
Consist A | MM 1225

Started with a red-hot April (3 HR, .360 BA), five anemic months followed. A couple of nagging injuries may have contributed. Still makes gobs of contact, but QBaB has barely ever scraped the "gentlemen's C" level; HctX doesn't cut it either. Big PA totals with plus OBP prop up R/RBI totals, but at some point those PAs get called into question.

Yr	Tm	PA	R	HR	RBI	SB	BA	xHR	xSB	xBA	OBP	SLG	OPS+	vL+	vR+	bb%	ct%	Eye	G	L	F	h%	HctX	QBaB	Brl%	PX	xPX	HR/F	xHR/F	Spd	SBA%	SB%	RAR	BPX	R$
18	PHI *	199	22	4	18	3	220	3	2	220	289	374	89	66	99	9	68	0.30	38	23	39	30	64	CBb	5%	102	74	10%	10%	128	7%	100%	-1.0	30	$1
19	SEA *	527	58	9	57	7	236	5	7	242	321	371	96	62	108	11	75	0.51	45	20	35	29	74	DCc	3%	79	69	8%	5%	111	8%	71%	-16.3	81	$8
20	SEA	232	33	2	24	6	255	3	5	240	336	338	90	86	91	10	81	0.59	44	23	33	31	96	DCd	2%	46	83	4%	6%	141	13%	67%	-5.1	96	$18
21	SEA	687	89	9	54	3	273	6	15	256	338	376	98	95	100	8	82	0.51	46	24	31	32	75	DCd	2%	66	42	6%	4%	100	5%	33%	0.0	108	$16
22	SEA	603	57	6	42	3	243	5	8	258	339	336	96	93	97	11	85	0.85	45	23	31	28	82	DDf	2%	59	58	4%	4%	114	3%	60%	-5.2	152	$8
1st Half		316	34	5	23	3	267	3	4	270	348	390	104	88	111	10	83	0.65	41	26	33	31	87	FCf	3%	77	64	7%	4%	123	3%	75%	3.1	186	$11
2nd Half		287	23	1	19	0	216	2	4	239	330	274	86	97	80	14	86	1.12	50	20	30	25	76	DDf	1%	39	51	2%	3%	103	3%	0%	-10.4	121	-$1
23	Proj	**595**	**66**	**7**	**48**	**4**	**256**	**6**	**6**	**250**	**342**	**352**	**96**	**93**	**98**	**11**	**82**	**0.67**	**45**	**23**	**32**	**30**	**79**		**2%**	**64**	**56**	**5%**	**4%**	**109**	**5%**	**55%**	**1.7**	**121**	**$14**

Cron,C.J.

Age: 33 Pos: 1B DH | Health B | LIMA Plan B
Bats: R Ht: 6' 4" Wt: 235 | PT/Exp A | Rand Var -1
Consist B | MM 4135

Second season at altitude saw a little bit of skills pullback, offset by more PA that leveled out the counting stats. But those skill dips (ct%, HctX) really only manifested vL, and those sample sizes can be flaky year-to-year. Second half fade looks equally flaky, as QBaB actually got better while h% and hr/f tanked. Bid confidently on a full-season repeat.

Yr	Tm	PA	R	HR	RBI	SB	BA	xHR	xSB	xBA	OBP	SLG	OPS+	vL+	vR+	bb%	ct%	Eye	G	L	F	h%	HctX	QBaB	Brl%	PX	xPX	HR/F	xHR/F	Spd	SBA%	SB%	RAR	BPX	R$
18	TAM	560	68	30	74	1	253	31	7	260	323	493	109	123	101	7	71	0.26	40	21	39	30	104	CBd	12%	151	115	21%	22%	85	2%	33%	-0.7	153	$16
19	MIN	499	51	25	78	0	253	33	1	262	311	469	108	142	94	6	77	0.27	42	22	36	28	109	ACc	15%	113	114	20%	26%	59	0%	0%	-8.4	104	$11
20	DET	52	9	4	8	0	190	4	0	264	346	548	119	80	133	17	62	0.56	38	15	46	18	106	DAf	19%	235	194	33%	33%	89	0%	0%	-0.1	396	$1
21	COL	547	70	28	92	1	281	27	1	267	375	530	124	133	121	11	75	0.51	39	19	42	32	111	CBd	11%	145	115	19%	18%	71	1%	100%	25.5	238	$21
22	COL	631	79	29	102	0	257	27	3	251	315	468	111	97	117	7	71	0.26	39	20	40	31	98	CCf	11%	138	104	17%	16%	94	0%	0%	5.4	138	$22
1st Half		346	49	20	65	0	297	15	2	268	347	552	127	114	132	6	72	0.23	39	20	41	36	99	CCf	12%	165	107	21%	16%	103	0%	0%	21.3	221	$36
2nd Half		285	30	9	37	0	209	12	1	230	277	364	91	79	97	8	71	0.30	40	20	39	26	96	BBd	9%	104	100	12%	16%	81	0%	0%	-9.4	38	$10
23	Proj	**595**	**74**	**28**	**95**	**0**	**257**	**29**	**1**	**255**	**328**	**473**	**111**	**111**	**111**	**8**	**73**	**0.33**	**40**	**20**	**40**	**30**	**103**		**11%**	**141**	**109**	**18%**	**18%**	**70**	**1%**	**68%**	**16.7**	**153**	**$23**

Cronenworth,Jake

Age: 29 Pos: 2B 1B | Health A | LIMA Plan B+
Bats: L Ht: 6' 0" Wt: 187 | PT/Exp A | Rand Var +1
Consist B | MM 3325

Apparently his was a multi-year adoption of the launch angle revolution, and in the "crawl, walk, run" progression, this year was "run." HR gains are obvious, though average power sets a HR ceiling. But xBA/BA show the associated penalty. Healthy OBP and lack of a platoon split keep him near top of lineup every day, making him a premier accumulator.

Yr	Tm	PA	R	HR	RBI	SB	BA	xHR	xSB	xBA	OBP	SLG	OPS+	vL+	vR+	bb%	ct%	Eye	G	L	F	h%	HctX	QBaB	Brl%	PX	xPX	HR/F	xHR/F	Spd	SBA%	SB%	RAR	BPX	R$
18	a/a	480	66	3	43	18	219		6		279	296	77			8	80	0.42				27				49				115	19%	84%		40	$9
19	aaa	384	60	8	36	10	283		12		358	433	109			10	78	0.53				35				84				121	15%	62%		137	$12
20	SD	192	26	4	20	3	285	8	4	295	354	477	110	72	128	9	83	0.60	45	25	29	33	122	BCb	10%	108	104	10%	19%	107	9%	75%	4.6	276	$16
21	SD	638	94	21	71	4	266	19	11	281	340	460	110	105	112	9	84	0.61	42	22	36	29	102	CCd	7%	102	95	12%	11%	125	5%	57%	12.8	288	$19
22	SD	681	88	17	88	3	239	16	8	229	332	390	102	100	103	10	78	0.53	35	17	48	28	87	CAd	6%	97	97	8%	7%	111	2%	100%	1.2	152	$16
1st Half		361	51	7	43	1	240	7	4	233	335	385	102	106	100	10	77	0.51	35	19	47	29	93	CAc	6%	98	100	6%	6%	99	2%	100%	2.1	138	$18
2nd Half		320	37	10	45	2	236	9	4	225	328	396	103	93	107	11	78	0.57	36	15	49	27	81	CAf	6%	95	94	9%	8%	125	2%	100%	3.1	172	$18
23	Proj	**630**	**88**	**19**	**77**	**6**	**247**	**21**	**6**	**245**	**330**	**421**	**104**	**96**	**108**	**10**	**80**	**0.55**	**35**	**18**	**46**	**28**	**96**		**7%**	**107**	**97**	**9%**	**10%**	**119**	**5%**	**75%**	**14.2**	**202**	**$21**

Cruz,Nelson

Age: 43 Pos: DH | Health B | LIMA Plan C
Bats: R Ht: 6' 2" Wt: 230 | PT/Exp A | Rand Var +4
Consist D | MM 3213

Had post-season surgery on left eye, which he says affected him for last year and a half... i.e., exactly when this decline started. Taking him at his word and projecting an age-43 rebound is a bridge too far, but... the skill decline hasn't been enormous; some FB% and Brl% recovery would get interesting quickly. Worth a buck to see if he really is ageless.

Yr	Tm	PA	R	HR	RBI	SB	BA	xHR	xSB	xBA	OBP	SLG	OPS+	vL+	vR+	bb%	ct%	Eye	G	L	F	h%	HctX	QBaB	Brl%	PX	xPX	HR/F	xHR/F	Spd	SBA%	SB%	RAR	BPX	R$
18	SEA	591	70	37	97	1	256	39	8	266	342	509	114	124	108	9	76	0.45	44	18	39	27	119	ACc	14%	139	123	24%	25%	56	1%	100%	18.4	183	$20
19	MIN	520	81	41	108	0	311	45	2	281	392	639	143	168	133	11	71	0.43	40	20	40	35	129	ACc	20%	177	156	31%	34%	74	1%	0%	46.7	267	$26
20	MIN	214	33	16	33	0	303	13	1	267	397	595	132	190	113	12	69	0.43	46	23	31	36	107	ACc	15%	164	113	41%	33%	78	0%	0%	17.8	220	$25
21	2 AL	580	79	32	86	3	265	34	1	260	334	497	114	124	109	9	75	0.40	43	18	39	29	118	ACf	14%	128	113	21%	22%	72	2%	100%	9.8	173	$21
22	WAS	504	50	10	64	4	234	16	2	228	313	337	92	102	87	10	73	0.41	52	19	28	30	103	ADc	9%	71	88	11%	17%	68	3%	100%	-14.0	-24	$9
1st Half		317	38	8	46	2	241	13	1	241	322	369	98	93	100	10	76	0.48	50	20	30	29	108	BDd	13%	85	104	13%	20%	71	3%	100%	-5.0	48	$16
2nd Half		187	12	2	18	2	223	4	1	200	299	283	83	117	64	9	70	0.32	56	19	25	31	96	ADb	4%	45	60	7%	13%	72	3%	100%	-9.3	-148	-$1
23	Proj	**420**	**49**	**16**	**59**	**3**	**248**	**19**	**2**	**239**	**325**	**413**	**103**	**119**	**94**	**10**	**73**	**0.39**	**48**	**19**	**33**	**30**	**109**		**11%**	**107**	**98**	**18%**	**21%**	**67**	**3%**	**98%**	**3.2**	**62**	**$14**

Cruz,Oneil

Age: 24 Pos: SS | Health A | LIMA Plan B
Bats: L Ht: 6' 7" Wt: 210 | PT/Exp B | Rand Var +4
Consist D | MM 4525

17-54-.233 with 11 SB in 361 PA at PIT. Nice when our metrics match the eye test: that "A" for Exit Velo reflects those "hardest hit ball by a Pirate in the Statcast era" graphics that we saw repeatedly this summer. Concerning ct% level shows a dramatic platoon split (42% vL, 71% vR). PIT may let him play through that, but BA would benefit if they don't.

Yr	Tm	PA	R	HR	RBI	SB	BA	xHR	xSB	xBA	OBP	SLG	OPS+	vL+	vR+	bb%	ct%	Eye	G	L	F	h%	HctX	QBaB	Brl%	PX	xPX	HR/F	xHR/F	Spd	SBA%	SB%	RAR	BPX	R$
18																																			
19	aa	134	14	1	17	3	269		2		349	409	105			11	70	0.42				38				89				125	11%	74%		48	$1
20																																			
21	PIT *	301	48	13	38	14	269	1	4	280	320	482	110	0	248	7	71	0.27	60	20	20	33	234	AFa	40%	128	178	100%	100%	129	26%	80%	7.0	165	$15
22	PIT *	592	71	22	77	17	214	17	19	227	278	395	95	75	119	8	65	0.25	49	17	34	28	109	ADf	16%	126	119	24%	24%	139	24%	61%	-16.5	72	$17
1st Half		291	34	8	36	8	187	1	8	207	249	333	82	88	91	8	69	0.27	38	15	46	24	116	ABf	14%	100	120	17%	6%	125	24%	51%	-16.6	41	$12
2nd Half		301	37	14	41	9	241	16	11	233	309	456	108	71	124	9	61	0.24	51	17	32	34	102	ADf	17%	156	118	26%	30%	148	24%	75%	3.7	110	$25
23	Proj	**560**	**72**	**27**	**72**	**19**	**232**	**26**	**16**	**247**	**295**	**459**	**105**	**83**	**115**	**8**	**68**	**0.28**	**46**	**16**	**38**	**29**	**108**		**16%**	**154**	**119**	**21%**	**20%**	**138**	**19%**	**75%**	**8.8**	**112**	**$24**

RAY MURPHY

d'Arnaud,Travis

Age: 34	Pos: CA	Health	F	LIMA Plan	C+
Bats: R	Ht: 6' 2" Wt: 210	PT/Exp	B	Rand Var	0
		Consist	D	MM	4133

Defied our axiom "chronically injured players don't suddenly get healthy" by staying off the IL all year and racking up his highest PA total since 2014. So many injury-interrupted seasons makes it tough to tease out his true skill levels, but 2022 and 2019 lines (two largest samples in this box) look quite similar. That's the skill baseline; PA is the variable.

Yr Tm	PA	R	HR	RBI	SB	BA	xHR	xSB	xBA	OBP	SLG	OPS+	vL+	vR+	bb%	ct%	Eye	G	L	F	h%	HctX	QBaB	Brl%	PX	xPX	HR/F	xHR/F	Spd	SBA%	SB%	RAR	BPX	R$
18 NYM	16	1	1	3	0	200	1	0	316	250	400	87	66	93	6	67	0.20	10	40	50	22	123	AAa	20%	115	222	20%	20%	91	0%	0%	-0.1	0	-$3
19 3 TM	391	52	16	69	0	251	15	1	248	312	433	103	123	90	8	76	0.38	41	21	39	29	109	BBf	8%	97	100	15%	14%	69	1%	0%	2.2	74	$9
20 ATL	184	19	9	34	1	321	10	1	259	386	533	122	66	136	9	70	0.32	43	27	30	42	129	ADb	11%	126	122	26%	29%	83	2%	100%	15.9	96	$21
21 ATL	229	21	7	26	0	220	7	1	252	284	388	92	113	87	7	75	0.32	46	22	31	26	95	BDd	8%	106	80	14%	14%	65	0%	0%	-2.0	77	$0
22 ATL	426	61	18	60	0	268	15	1	267	319	472	112	133	106	4	77	0.21	45	19	36	31	106	CCf	8%	130	103	16%	14%	88	0%	0%	15.2	172	$15
1st Half	230	33	11	36	0	264	9	1	275	309	481	112	129	107	4	79	0.17	45	19	36	29	117	CCf	10%	135	115	18%	15%	69	0%	0%	7.9	183	$14
2nd Half	196	28	7	24	0	272	5	1	258	332	461	112	136	105	6	76	0.25	46	18	36	33	92	CCd	6%	123	88	14%	10%	110	0%	0%	7.7	162	$9
23 Proj	**406**	**51**	**16**	**57**	**0**	**258**	**14**	**1**	**260**	**317**	**448**	**106**	**120**	**102**	**7**	**75**	**0.28**	**45**	**21**	**34**	**30**	**103**		**8%**	**126**	**96**	**16%**	**15%**	**78**	**2%**	**68%**	**14.8**	**125**	**$11**

Dalbec,Bobby

Age: 28	Pos: 1B 3B	Health	A	LIMA Plan	D
Bats: R	Ht: 6' 4" Wt: 227	PT/Exp	B	Rand Var	+4
		Consist	C	MM	4311

12-39-.215 in 353 AB at BOS. About that "UP: 50 HR" from a year ago: we're sorry; we were wrong. Still a lot of good happening when he makes contact, but that just doesn't happen enough, and in 2022 even less. 2021 is still a baseline in his skill set, and 2nd half power metrics are encouraging, but it's time to step up now.

Yr Tm	PA	R	HR	RBI	SB	BA	xHR	xSB	xBA	OBP	SLG	OPS+	vL+	vR+	bb%	ct%	Eye	G	L	F	h%	HctX	QBaB	Brl%	PX	xPX	HR/F	xHR/F	Spd	SBA%	SB%	RAR	BPX	R$
18 aa	116	11	4	19	0	240		1		269	447	96			4	56	0.09				39				176				95	0%	0%		10	$0
19 a/a	533	59	22	63	5	224		2		313	416	101			11	68	0.41				28				110				99	10%	44%		59	$9
20 BOS	92	13	8	16	0	263	8	1	230	359	600	127	139	120	11	51	0.26	37	20	44	39	86	BBf	22%	254	205	44%	44%	95	0%	0%	4.1	244	$8
21 BOS	453	50	25	78	2	240	34	2	236	298	494	109	119	101	6	63	0.18	37	19	43	32	97	ABb	20%	169	137	22%	30%	114	2%	100%	2.8	131	$12
22 BOS *	403	45	15	44	4	211	13	4	206	273	370	91	106	86	8	63	0.23	39	20	41	29	79	BBf	12%	112	91	14%	16%	136	5%	100%	-8.9	0	$6
1st Half	221	24	5	18	2	208	6	2	200	285	325	86	94	83	9	66	0.29	40	20	41	29	79	BBf	9%	83	68	9%	11%	129	5%	100%	-8.7	-31	$1
2nd Half	182	21	10	26	2	215	7	2	213	266	422	97	124	92	7	59	0.17	37	21	41	29	81	BCf	18%	150	135	24%	24%	133	5%	100%	-3.5	38	$8
23 Proj	**245**	**27**	**12**	**34**	**2**	**225**	**13**	**2**	**226**	**287**	**441**	**101**	**115**	**93**	**7**	**63**	**0.21**	**38**	**20**	**42**	**30**	**88**		**16%**	**156**	**129**	**20%**	**21%**	**102**	**6%**	**85%**	**-0.1**	**51**	**$7**

Davis,J.D.

Age: 30	Pos: DH 3B	Health	C	LIMA Plan	C
Bats: R	Ht: 6' 3" Wt: 218	PT/Exp	B	Rand Var	-1
		Consist	B	MM	4313

Barrels galore, elite exit velocity, xHR says there should be even more power—all undermined by too many strikeouts, mediocre launch angle, and defensive woes. Maybe this is all there is... But universal DH mitigates poor glove, and after trade to SF, launch angle and GLF show a long-awaited swing path adjustment. BA risk remains, but... UP: 25 HR.

Yr Tm	PA	R	HR	RBI	SB	BA	xHR	xSB	xBA	OBP	SLG	OPS+	vL+	vR+	bb%	ct%	Eye	G	L	F	h%	HctX	QBaB	Brl%	PX	xPX	HR/F	xHR/F	Spd	SBA%	SB%	RAR	BPX	R$
18 HOU *	470	48	13	61	2	250	4	6	248	304	396	94	75	55	7	74	0.30	50	22	28	31	88	CDc	8%	94	71	5%	19%	88	2%	100%	-4.9	47	$9
19 NYM	453	65	22	57	3	307	23	4	278	369	527	124	127	122	8	76	0.39	47	23	30	36	110	ACa	11%	115	111	23%	24%	107	2%	100%	21.1	178	$17
20 NYM	229	26	6	19	0	247	8	2	229	371	389	101	101	100	14	71	0.55	56	20	24	32	102	BFc	9%	89	73	19%	25%	106	0%	0%	-1.1	56	$10
21 NYM *	255	23	7	27	1	274	7	1	234	363	445	111	93	121	12	60	0.35	39	31	30	43	76	BCb	12%	135	95	15%	21%	100	1%	100%	3.9	12	$5
22 2 NL	365	46	12	35	1	248	19	4	221	340	418	107	106	107	11	62	0.32	45	21	34	36	98	ACc	17%	134	117	18%	28%	125	2%	50%	0.7	52	$7
1st Half	177	22	2	14	1	240	6	2	215	328	338	94	88	99	10	64	0.30	47	26	27	36	100	ACa	12%	81	85	7%	22%	136	2%	50%	-5.0	-62	-$1
2nd Half	188	24	10	21	0	256	13	2	227	351	494	120	122	116	12	60	0.33	43	16	41	36	96	ABf	21%	187	148	25%	33%	104	2%	0%	5.8	155	$8
23 Proj	**420**	**49**	**13**	**44**	**1**	**250**	**17**	**4**	**228**	**346**	**416**	**106**	**102**	**108**	**11**	**63**	**0.35**	**44**	**24**	**32**	**36**	**97**		**14%**	**133**	**106**	**18%**	**22%**	**106**	**4%**	**72%**	**5.4**	**55**	**$12**

Davis,Brennen

Age: 23	Pos: OF	Health	A	LIMA Plan	F
Bats: R	Ht: 6' 4" Wt: 210	PT/Exp	D	Rand Var	0
		Consist	D	MM	2101

Cubs' top prospect missed big chunk of summer due to back surgery, then went to Arizona Fall League to get lost PT, only to get shut down with more back pain. When health cooperates, he projects as a potential top-of-order, power/speed blend of a profile. But first order of business now is to get healthy and bank at least a few hundred more PA in high minors.

Yr Tm	PA	R	HR	RBI	SB	BA	xHR	xSB	xBA	OBP	SLG	OPS+	vL+	vR+	bb%	ct%	Eye	G	L	F	h%	HctX	QBaB	Brl%	PX	xPX	HR/F	xHR/F	Spd	SBA%	SB%	RAR	BPX	R$
18																																		
19																																		
20																																		
21 a/a	358	44	12	35	4	221		3		298	398	96			10	62	0.29				31				132				87	11%	50%		12	$5
22 aaa	156	11	3	9	0	151		2		233	240	67			10	58	0.25				24				78				96	4%	0%		-186	-$6
1st Half	84	5	1	5	0	155		1		221	226	63			8	54	0.19				26				64				111	4%	0%		-279	-$12
2nd Half	72	6	1	4	0	148		1	196	247	258	72			12	63	0.36	44	20	36	21	0			93	-14	0%		109	4%	0%	-4.4	-55	-$10
23 Proj	**140**	**13**	**2**	**10**	**1**	**208**	**2**	**1**	**189**	**288**	**308**	**83**	**82**	**83**	**10**	**64**	**0.31**	**44**	**18**	**38**	**31**	**82**		**6%**	**86**		**7%**	**7%**	**101**	**5%**	**38%**	**-4.2**	**-84**	**$1**

Daza,Yonathan

Age: 29	Pos: CF LF	Health	C	LIMA Plan	C+
Bats: R	Ht: 6' 2" Wt: 207	PT/Exp	B	Rand Var	-2
		Consist	A	MM	1143

A year ago we called his h% "inflated"; boy, he sure showed us. Turns out he can snake softly-hit GBs through the infield with regularity. Legit speed continues to lurk as a potentially foundational skill (that would pair well with this ct% and GB), but he's never shown any inclination to steal. Career .306 BA at Coors makes him best used as a homestand streamer.

Yr Tm	PA	R	HR	RBI	SB	BA	xHR	xSB	xBA	OBP	SLG	OPS+	vL+	vR+	bb%	ct%	Eye	G	L	F	h%	HctX	QBaB	Brl%	PX	xPX	HR/F	xHR/F	Spd	SBA%	SB%	RAR	BPX	R$
18 aa	225	21	3	23	3	289		3		307	435	100			2	89	0.22				31				86				100	19%	36%		200	$4
19 COL *	508	50	8	34	9	294	1	14	275	327	421	103	61	72	5	84	0.30	59	18	23	34	71	DFc	1%	68	28	0%	6%	134	16%	45%	4.7	152	$13
20																																		
21 COL *	357	28	2	31	3	279	3	6	244	323	347	92	99	92	6	80	0.32	54	22	24	34	82	FDc	2%	42	51	3%	5%	123	4%	72%	-4.7	19	$7
22 COL	408	56	2	34	0	301	3	5	274	349	384	104	112	99	6	84	0.45	55	24	21	35	91	DFc	2%	58	55	3%	5%	117	3%	0%	6.7	117	$12
1st Half	229	30	0	17	0	308	2	3	263	362	361	102	121	92	7	87	0.57	52	24	23	36	89	DFc	3%	38	66	0%	5%	124	3%	0%	3.0	103	$5
2nd Half	179	26	2	17	0	293	1	2	287	331	415	106	102	108	6	82	0.33	59	23	18	35	93	FFb	1%	85	40	8%	4%	105	3%	0%	4.7	138	$5
23 Proj	**385**	**44**	**3**	**34**	**2**	**291**	**3**	**3**	**266**	**333**	**381**	**99**	**103**	**96**	**6**	**83**	**0.36**	**56**	**22**	**22**	**34**	**86**		**2%**	**62**	**48**	**4%**	**5%**	**106**	**4%**	**40%**	**6.4**	**103**	**$13**

De La Cruz,Bryan

Age: 26	Pos: CF RF LF	Health	A	LIMA Plan	B+
Bats: R	Ht: 6' 2" Wt: 175	PT/Exp	C	Rand Var	+2
		Consist	A	MM	3235

14-43-.252 in 355 PA at MIA. Made Opening Day roster and underwhelmed in reserve OF role, eventually sent down in early August. Raked in Triple-A for a few weeks to earn Sept callup, stayed hot for rest of year (6 HR, 1.137 OPS). 2nd half HctX, QBaB, Brl% generate some real intrigue, vR+ gains suggest he's ready for everyday work, and... UP: 30 HR

Yr Tm	PA	R	HR	RBI	SB	BA	xHR	xSB	xBA	OBP	SLG	OPS+	vL+	vR+	bb%	ct%	Eye	G	L	F	h%	HctX	QBaB	Brl%	PX	xPX	HR/F	xHR/F	Spd	SBA%	SB%	RAR	BPX	R$
18																																		
19 aa	290	40	4	21	6	256		5		311	366	94			7	75	0.32				33				64				133	17%	53%		26	$4
20																																		
21 MIA *	502	49	14	52	2	274	4	8	240	316	411	100	129	101	6	73	0.23	48	22	30	35	98	CCc	5%	84	75	11%	9%	141	7%	29%	-1.6	65	$13
22 MIA *	407	45	15	50	5	252	16	3	266	292	434	103	71	114	5	72	0.20	42	28	31	31	123	BCa	12%	126	146	17%	21%	88	6%	100%	3.8	97	$11
1st Half	164	19	6	17	2	217	5	1	266	268	375	91	51	109	6	75	0.26	46	27	27	25	100	CDa	7%	100	105	19%	16%	105	6%	100%	-3.0	90	$1
2nd Half	243	26	9	33	3	275	12	2	265	311	473	111	94	118	5	70	0.17	38	28	34	35	143	ACa	15%	144	182	16%	27%	88	6%	100%	8.3	114	$15
23 Proj	**560**	**61**	**18**	**62**	**6**	**261**	**20**	**7**	**252**	**304**	**417**	**100**	**90**	**103**	**6**	**73**	**0.23**	**44**	**25**	**31**	**33**	**114**		**9%**	**107**	**120**	**15%**	**17%**	**109**	**7%**	**59%**	**7.8**	**81**	**$19**

DeJong,Paul

Age: 29	Pos: SS	Health	B	LIMA Plan	D
Bats: R	Ht: 6' 0" Wt: 205	PT/Exp	B	Rand Var	+5
		Consist	B	MM	3103

6-25-.177 in 210 PA at STL. Rough start led to early May demotion. Didn't return until late July, with similarly terrible results. Lost a chunk of contact that he couldn't afford to lose, and high FB rate paired with very average power just yields an awful lot of cans of corn. Needs a change in approach, and quickly.

Yr Tm	PA	R	HR	RBI	SB	BA	xHR	xSB	xBA	OBP	SLG	OPS+	vL+	vR+	bb%	ct%	Eye	G	L	F	h%	HctX	QBaB	Brl%	PX	xPX	HR/F	xHR/F	Spd	SBA%	SB%	RAR	BPX	R$
18 STL	489	68	19	68	1	241	22	6	245	313	433	100	86	103	7	72	0.29	32	24	44	29	102	BAc	9%	125	134	14%	16%	100	2%	50%	6.5	113	$11
19 STL	664	97	30	78	9	233	31	4	245	318	444	105	94	107	9	74	0.42	38	18	44	26	107	CAc	9%	114	123	15%	16%	99	9%	64%	-5.3	144	$17
20 STL	174	17	3	25	1	250	5	3	208	322	349	89	52	96	10	67	0.34	27	28	44	35	105	CAc	8%	68	152	6%	11%	88	2%	100%	-2.7	-112	$9
21 STL	402	44	19	45	4	197	18	2	221	284	390	93	82	96	9	71	0.34	38	16	47	22	100	DBf	11%	111	151	16%	15%	96	6%	80%	-13.4	81	$4
22 STL *	449	39	15	56	4	163	7	2	195	223	309	75	71	76	7	65	0.22	33	17	50	21	85	CAf	10%	108	102	9%	10%	52	10%	52%	-31.5	-72	-$1
1st Half	253	21	7	27	4	141	1	1	184	188	261	64	81	54	5	66	0.17	38	13	49	18	66	CAf	6%	88	42	4%	4%	64	10%	73%	-22.2	-110	-$1
2nd Half	197	19	8	29	0	193	6	1	209	270	376	92	67	91	10	63	0.29	30	19	51	25	96	CAd	14%	138	141	12%	15%	66	10%	0%	-6.5	10	$4
23 Proj	**280**	**29**	**9**	**36**	**2**	**209**	**10**	**3**	**203**	**286**	**358**	**89**	**79**	**92**	**8**	**68**	**0.28**	**34**	**18**	**48**	**27**	**93**		**10%**	**105**	**124**	**11%**	**12%**	**77**	**7%**	**59%**	**-6.0**	**7**	**$5**

RAY MURPHY

Delay,Jason

Age: 28 Pos: CA | Bats: R Ht: 5' 11" Wt: 200
Health A | PT/Exp F | Consist B | LIMA Plan F | Rand Var 0 | MM 1101

1-11-.213 in 167 PA at PIT. Described as a "defense first" catcher, which is good because it's not clear that offense is even his second priority. Plate skills sub-par (always disappointing when a CA can't tell balls and strikes), exit velocity is worse, and expected power metrics are downright bleak. Average speed is wasted. Defense better be Pudge Rodriguez-good.

Yr	Tm	PA	R	HR	RBI	SB	BA	xHR	xSB	xBA	OBP	SLG	OPS+	vL+	vR+	bb%	ct%	Eye	G	L	F	h%	HctX	QBaB	Brl%	PX	xPX	HR/F	xHR/F	Spd	SBA%	SB%	RAR	BPX	R$
18																																			
19	aa	243	20	7	34	1	219		2		258	369	87			5	71	0.18				28				89				92	2%	100%		-19	$0
20																																			
21	a/a	97	5	1	5	0	135		1		160	212	51			3	60	0.07				21				63				93	0%	0%		-281	-$5
22	PIT *	261	23	1	16	1	195	1	1	197	238	257	70	87	67	5	71	0.20	42	20	38	27	87	DBd	2%	53	57	3%	3%	100	6%	23%	-13.6	-107	-$4
1st Half		97	6	0	5	1	159	0	0	163	211	227	62	47	0	6	76	0.28	50	0	50	21	167	FCf		56	360	0%	0%	109	6%	100%	-6.3	-10	-$12
2nd Half		164	17	1	11	0	216	1	1	188	264	275	76	88	67	5	67	0.16	42	20	38	31	82	DBd	2%	52	51	3%	3%	94	6%	0%	-7.0	-169	-$4
23	**Proj**	**175**	**15**	**1**	**16**	**1**	**202**	**1**	**1**	**203**	**253**	**278**	**74**	**85**	**65**	**5**	**71**	**0.19**	**42**	**20**	**38**	**28**	**74**		**2%**	**63**	**46**	**2%**	**1%**	**93**	**6%**	**49%**	**-6.4**	**-69**	**-$3**

Devers,Rafael

Age: 26 Pos: 3B | Bats: L Ht: 6' 0" Wt: 240
Health A | PT/Exp A | Consist A | LIMA Plan D+ | Rand Var 0 | MM 4145

A case where dramatic half-season splits are mostly noise: h% and HR/F regressed hard in second half; full-season output and skills are an accurate accounting of his work. 2021 HR/F now looks like a minor high side outlier, but continued incremental gains in ct% and xBA bring .300 BA back in range. An unimpeachable four-category building block.

Yr	Tm	PA	R	HR	RBI	SB	BA	xHR	xSB	xBA	OBP	SLG	OPS+	vL+	vR+	bb%	ct%	Eye	G	L	F	h%	HctX	QBaB	Brl%	PX	xPX	HR/F	xHR/F	Spd	SBA%	SB%	RAR	BPX	R$
18	BOS *	512	62	22	68	5	244	17	6	242	302	439	99	82	102	8	73	0.31	46	15	39	29	93	ACf	9%	123	95	17%	13%	62	7%	71%	1.4	87	$14
19	BOS	702	129	32	115	8	311	33	7	298	361	555	127	103	137	7	82	0.40	44	21	34	34	107	ACc	9%	126	93	18%	18%	85	10%	50%	36.5	252	$34
20	BOS	248	32	11	43	0	263	12	3	255	310	483	105	80	118	5	71	0.19	45	20	35	32	120	ACc	12%	135	78	19%	21%	75	0%	0%	1.2	112	$20
21	BOS	664	101	38	113	5	279	42	1	278	352	538	122	102	135	9	76	0.43	41	20	38	31	124	ACd	15%	148	124	22%	24%	63	6%	50%	38.9	235	$30
22	BOS	614	84	27	88	3	295	28	5	285	358	521	125	103	132	8	79	0.44	42	20	37	33	124	ACf	12%	142	115	16%	17%	67	3%	75%	41.1	241	$29
1st Half		347	57	17	46	2	327	16	3	306	383	579	136	125	140	7	81	0.39	44	22	34	36	135	ACc	13%	156	111	19%	18%	75	3%	67%	33.5	300	$37
2nd Half		267	27	10	42	1	253	12	2	254	326	443	109	76	122	10	78	0.49	40	18	42	29	109	ACf	10%	122	119	13%	15%	64	3%	100%	5.5	169	$16
23	**Proj**	**630**	**87**	**30**	**100**	**4**	**284**	**33**	**3**	**275**	**349**	**515**	**120**	**97**	**130**	**8**	**77**	**0.40**	**42**	**20**	**38**	**32**	**119**		**12%**	**147**	**112**	**18%**	**19%**	**65**	**2%**	**61%**	**40.1**	**209**	**$31**

Díaz,Aledmys

Age: 32 Pos: LF 2B | Bats: R Ht: 6' 1" Wt: 195
Health F | PT/Exp C | Consist A | LIMA Plan D+ | Rand Var +2 | MM 2133

Missed four weeks in Aug/Sept with a groin strain, which came after a red-hot July (6 HR, .311 BA) where he played nearly every day. That's his gig, though: tread along with part-time work, waiting for periodic bursts of full-time PA when a need arises. Full-season value never amounts to much, but he's very usable during those high-volume stretches.

Yr	Tm	PA	R	HR	RBI	SB	BA	xHR	xSB	xBA	OBP	SLG	OPS+	vL+	vR+	bb%	ct%	Eye	G	L	F	h%	HctX	QBaB	Brl%	PX	xPX	HR/F	xHR/F	Spd	SBA%	SB%	RAR	BPX	R$
18	TOR	452	55	18	55	3	263	16	5	269	303	453	101	94	102	5	85	0.37	41	18	41	27	100	CCc	7%	105	105	12%	11%	95	8%	43%	5.9	220	$12
19	HOU *	270	37	9	40	2	253	8	4	265	334	431	106	105	117	10	84	0.76	46	17	37	27	94	CCf	6%	87	70	13%	11%	110	3%	100%	1.3	230	$5
20	HOU	59	8	3	6	0	241	1	0	287	254	483	98	59	118	2	79	0.08	43	22	35	26	91	CCd	2%	136	77	19%	6%	91	0%	0%	-0.8	236	$1
21	HOU	319	28	8	45	0	259	7	1	258	317	405	99	107	95	5	79	0.26	42	24	34	30	111	CCd	6%	90	89	10%	9%	77	1%	0%	-1.6	88	$5
22	HOU	327	35	12	38	1	243	8	1	265	287	403	98	107	94	6	83	0.34	40	23	37	26	104	DCf	7%	93	78	13%	9%	85	3%	50%	1.3	152	$6
1st Half		156	13	4	16	0	226	2	1	242	276	329	85	112	77	6	79	0.30	41	25	34	26	93	DCd	5%	60	59	10%	5%	87	3%	0%	-4.8	21	-$3
2nd Half		171	22	8	22	1	258	6	1	288	298	472	109	104	112	5	86	0.39	40	20	40	26	114	CCf	8%	122	94	15%	11%	93	3%	100%	4.4	276	$7
23	**Proj**	**315**	**35**	**10**	**41**	**1**	**252**	**8**	**2**	**264**	**302**	**410**	**99**	**100**	**98**	**6**	**82**	**0.34**	**41**	**22**	**36**	**28**	**105**		**6%**	**98**	**83**	**12%**	**9%**	**84**	**3%**	**51%**	**2.2**	**158**	**$10**

Díaz,Elias

Age: 32 Pos: CA | Bats: R Ht: 6' 1" Wt: 223
Health A | PT/Exp B | Consist C | LIMA Plan D+ | Rand Var 0 | MM 3023

All the drivers of 2021's power spike—more ct%, better launch angle, improved HR/F—snapped right back to their prior, less-exciting levels. August wrist sprain likely didn't help, but the regression was baked in long before that. That 2021 looks like an outlier now, but catchers can be weird. Wide range of outcomes here.

Yr	Tm	PA	R	HR	RBI	SB	BA	xHR	xSB	xBA	OBP	SLG	OPS+	vL+	vR+	bb%	ct%	Eye	G	L	F	h%	HctX	QBaB	Brl%	PX	xPX	HR/F	xHR/F	Spd	SBA%	SB%	RAR	BPX	R$
18	PIT	277	33	10	34	0	286	7	4	263	339	452	106	123	96	8	84	0.53	45	20	35	31	112	BCd	7%	92	104	13%	9%	80	1%	0%	13.4	170	$7
19	PIT *	362	35	2	31	0	249	4	1	235	299	317	85	90	80	7	81	0.38	47	21	31	30	88	CDf	2%	43	46	3%	5%	74	0%	0%	-10.9	-7	$1
20	COL	73	4	2	9	0	235	1	0	235	288	353	85	87	83	7	78	0.33	40	25	36	27	125	CCf	11%	64	119	11%	5%	75	0%	0%	-1.3	4	$0
21	COL	371	52	18	44	0	246	12	1	272	310	464	106	104	107	8	82	0.50	41	19	40	25	118	CBf	8%	115	104	16%	11%	74	0%	0%	9.6	238	$8
22	COL	381	29	9	51	0	228	7	1	233	281	368	92	105	83	7	77	0.30	48	16	36	27	105	CCf	6%	92	99	9%	7%	92	1%	0%	-2.8	79	$4
1st Half		201	15	5	20	0	211	3	1	225	264	335	85	121	61	7	77	0.33	49	17	34	25	93	CCf	5%	76	75	10%	6%	97	1%	0%	-4.0	52	-$2
2nd Half		180	14	4	31	0	247	4	1	242	300	404	100	86	107	6	76	0.28	46	16	38	30	118	CCd	7%	110	127	8%	8%	92	1%	0%	1.6	117	$4
23	**Proj**	**385**	**40**	**12**	**50**	**0**	**243**	**9**	**1**	**249**	**299**	**404**	**98**	**102**	**95**	**7**	**79**	**0.37**	**45**	**18**	**37**	**28**	**112**		**7%**	**102**	**104**	**11%**	**8%**	**76**	**2%**	**0%**	**6.8**	**133**	**$10**

Díaz,Jordan

Age: 22 Pos: 2B | Bats: R Ht: 5' 10" Wt: 175
Health A | PT/Exp C | Consist F | LIMA Plan D+ | Rand Var -2 | MM 1013

0-1-.265 in 51 PA at OAK. Prospect hit enough (.326 BA across AA/AAA) to earn a Sept ticket to OAK. Skills built on a foundation of frequent contact, though high GB%/poor launch angle mute the outcomes. Scouts pan his defense at 2B, and doesn't seem like there is enough bat here to stick as a 1B/DH. But OAK can afford to give him a long look.

Yr	Tm	PA	R	HR	RBI	SB	BA	xHR	xSB	xBA	OBP	SLG	OPS+	vL+	vR+	bb%	ct%	Eye	G	L	F	h%	HctX	QBaB	Brl%	PX	xPX	HR/F	xHR/F	Spd	SBA%	SB%	RAR	BPX	R$
18																																			
19																																			
20																																			
21																																			
22	OAK *	559	45	11	53	0	260	0	6	227	285	379	94	85	89	3	82	0.20	67	10	24	30	51	CFd		79	57	0%	0%	101	0%	0%	-5.8	110	$10
1st Half		277	23	7	30	0	241		2	258	274	402	96	0	0	4	79	0.22	44	20	36	28	0			110	-14	0%		88	0%	0%	-5.3	148	$6
2nd Half		283	24	4	26	0	287	0	4	223	308	376	97	85	89	3	86	0.21	67	10	24	32	53	CFd	0%	56	57	0%	0%	115	0%	0%	-1.8	100	$10
23	**Proj**	**280**	**24**	**4**	**28**	**0**	**269**	**4**	**1**	**233**	**294**	**371**	**92**	**92**	**92**	**3**	**83**	**0.21**	**67**	**10**	**24**	**31**	**68**		**4%**	**69**	**51**	**7%**	**7%**	**105**	**3%**	**0%**	**0.6**	**119**	**$7**

Díaz,Lewin

Age: 26 Pos: 1B | Bats: L Ht: 6' 4" Wt: 217
Health A | PT/Exp B | Consist C | LIMA Plan D+ | Rand Var +1 | MM 4303

5-11-.169 in 174 PA at MIA. Got late-season look for second straight year. This time, results were much less interesting. There are components of a "decent power/low-BA" profile: FB tilt/good launch angle, ct% that flirts with adequate. Just didn't hit the ball hard in the majors, and the rest of his skills can't carry that shortcoming. Running out of chances.

Yr	Tm	PA	R	HR	RBI	SB	BA	xHR	xSB	xBA	OBP	SLG	OPS+	vL+	vR+	bb%	ct%	Eye	G	L	F	h%	HctX	QBaB	Brl%	PX	xPX	HR/F	xHR/F	Spd	SBA%	SB%	RAR	BPX	R$
18																																			
19	aa	262	30	14	43	0	240		2		301	506	112			8	77	0.37				26				145				88	2%	0%		252	$4
20	MIA	41	2	0	3	0	154	1	0	152	195	205	53	0	76	5	69	0.17	41	11	48	22	73	DAd	11%	45	38	0%	8%	94	0%	0%	-6.0	-184	-$4
21	MIA *	427	57	23	53	2	204	7	1	228	255	422	93	66	109	6	74	0.26	31	15	54	22	112	CAf	10%	122	149	17%	15%	95	3%	100%	-17.9	142	$6
22	MIA *	520	49	17	54	1	186	3	2	209	237	331	80	39	76	6	70	0.22	37	17	46	23	79	CBf	6%	100	106	10%	6%	84	1%	100%	-33.6	0	$0
1st Half		299	32	9	37	0	198	0	1	181	240	346	83	0	43	5	70	0.19	0	20	80	25	123	AAa	20%	104	185	0%	0%	94	1%	0%	-15.4	17	$7
2nd Half		221	17	7	17	1	170	3	1	205	232	310	77	39	78	7	70	0.27	39	17	45	20	77	CBf	5%	94	102	11%	7%	88	1%	100%	-14.1	-10	-$2
23	**Proj**	**350**	**38**	**15**	**40**	**1**	**211**	**10**	**1**	**224**	**263**	**397**	**92**	**64**	**98**	**6**	**72**	**0.25**	**36**	**16**	**48**	**24**	**91**		**7%**	**121**	**121**	**13%**	**9%**	**87**	**3%**	**89%**	**-7.4**	**82**	**$7**

Diaz,Yainer

Age: 24 Pos: CA | Bats: R Ht: 6' 0" Wt: 195
Health A | PT/Exp D | Consist F | LIMA Plan D+ | Rand Var -3 | MM 1433

0-1-.125 in 9 PA at HOU. Young catcher jumped up the prospect charts with strong AA/AAA campaign, maybe even eclipsing org-mate Korey Lee. Free-swinger is line-drive machine, which mitigates lack of patience. Has produced good HR output without a ton of FBs; remains to be seen if he can bring that trick to MLB. He'll get that chance soon.

Yr	Tm	PA	R	HR	RBI	SB	BA	xHR	xSB	xBA	OBP	SLG	OPS+	vL+	vR+	bb%	ct%	Eye	G	L	F	h%	HctX	QBaB	Brl%	PX	xPX	HR/F	xHR/F	Spd	SBA%	SB%	RAR	BPX	R$
18																																			
19																																			
20																																			
21																																			
22	HOU *	476	48	16	62	1	240	0	5	199	276	400	96	0	88	5	78	0.23	50	0	50	27	114	AAf	17%	96	110	0%	0%	113	1%	100%	2.4	124	$10
1st Half		303	28	8	39	1	243		4	251	283	388	95	0	0	5	81	0.29	44	20	36	28	0			85	-14	0%		133	1%	100%	1.3	148	$11
2nd Half		173	20	8	23	0	234	0	2	193	264	419	97	0	88	4	75	0.16	50	0	50	27	109	AAf	17%	117	110	0%	0%	89	1%	0%	0.5	100	$5
23	**Proj**	**315**	**34**	**6**	**41**	**0**	**245**	**6**	**2**	**253**	**278**	**355**	**88**	**87**	**88**	**4**	**78**	**0.21**	**44**	**27**	**29**	**30**	**90**		**6%**	**72**		**9%**	**9%**	**99**	**3%**	**100%**	**-0.2**	**119**	**$8**

RAY MURPHY

Diaz,Yandy

Age: 31 Pos: 3B | Bats: R Ht: 6' 2" Wt: 215

Health C | PT/Exp A | Consist B | LIMA Plan B+ | Rand Var -1 | MM 2145

Elite plate skills and ct% helped propel BA/OBP and set a decent floor for counting stats. As for the power, HctX and QBaB tell the story: lots of hard contact stifled by poor launch angle. Given GB% history, hope for launch angle improvement is faint, but HR/F history does portend possible recovery. If 2nd half GLF profile sticks, 15-20 HR within reach.

Yr Tm	PA	R	HR	RBI	SB	BA	xHR	xSB	xBA	OBP	SLG	OPS+	vL+	vR+	bb%	ct%	Eye	G	L	F	h%	HctX	QBaB	Brl%	PX	xPX	HR/F	xHR/F	Spd	SBA%	SB%	RAR	BPX	R$
18 CLE *	520	54	3	44	1	264	2	9	246	353	353	95	96	112	12	76	0.58	53	23	23	34	125	AFb	4%	65	84	5%	10%	107	3%	29%	-1.6	50	$7
19 TAM	347	53	14	38	2	267	14	3	276	340	476	113	137	101	10	80	0.57	51	17	32	29	118	AFc	10%	108	115	18%	18%	102	5%	50%	4.7	222	$8
20 TAM	138	16	2	11	0	307	1	2	261	428	386	108	100	111	17	85	1.35	66	23	11	35	96	CFf	2%	41	22	18%	9%	105	0%	0%	3.6	160	$8
21 TAM	541	62	13	64	1	256	13	4	242	353	387	102	110	95	13	82	0.81	52	16	32	29	116	BDf	7%	73	79	11%	11%	113	1%	50%	6.8	181	$11
22 TAM	558	71	9	57	3	296	10	4	270	401	423	117	125	114	14	87	1.30	50	19	32	32	135	ADd	5%	82	86	7%	8%	94	3%	50%	26.2	252	$19
1st Half	296	33	3	18	1	290	3	2	256	405	379	111	113	110	15	88	1.50	53	19	28	32	132	ADd	4%	58	74	5%	5%	114	3%	25%	7.5	224	$9
2nd Half	262	38	6	39	2	302	7	2	283	397	471	123	140	117	13	87	1.10	46	18	36	33	139	ADd	6%	108	99	9%	10%	76	3%	100%	16.2	286	$19
23 Proj	**525**	**66**	**12**	**60**	**2**	**283**	**11**	**5**	**266**	**383**	**424**	**112**	**118**	**109**	**14**	**84**	**1.00**	**52**	**18**	**30**	**31**	**125**		**6%**	**88**	**80**	**11%**	**9%**	**92**	**4%**	**54%**	**24.2**	**215**	**$16**

Dickerson,Corey

Age: 34 Pos: LF DH | Bats: L Ht: 6' 1" Wt: 200

Health D | PT/Exp B | Consist A | LIMA Plan D+ | Rand Var 0 | MM 2233

Calf strain sidelined him for most of June. Joys of small samples: combo of low h% and HctX were a drag in 1st half before positive regression saved him in 2nd half. 2021's SB blip vanished, closing off one path to value. Overall, ct% and BA skills are intact, but subpar power, struggles vL, age, and Health grade cement status as part-time filler only.

Yr Tm	PA	R	HR	RBI	SB	BA	xHR	xSB	xBA	OBP	SLG	OPS+	vL+	vR+	bb%	ct%	Eye	G	L	F	h%	HctX	QBaB	Brl%	PX	xPX	HR/F	xHR/F	Spd	SBA%	SB%	RAR	BPX	R$
18 PIT	533	65	13	55	8	300	16	7	284	330	474	108	97	109	4	84	0.26	38	27	35	34	106	CBb	6%	100	101	9%	11%	129	9%	73%	14.0	217	$19
19 2 NL *	314	36	12	62	1	286	12	3	287	327	520	117	111	129	6	78	0.28	36	25	39	33	105	CBd	8%	133	112	15%	15%	95	2%	100%	7.5	219	$9
20 MIA	209	25	7	17	1	258	7	2	237	311	402	95	84	98	7	82	0.43	52	14	34	28	102	DCf	6%	70	71	13%	13%	110	4%	50%	-5.8	132	$12
21 2 TM	365	43	6	29	6	271	7	4	254	326	408	101	87	103	7	80	0.37	49	19	32	32	111	CCf	3%	79	85	7%	8%	135	12%	55%	-1.7	146	$9
22 STL	297	28	6	36	0	267	5	4	262	300	399	99	36	106	4	83	0.25	46	21	33	30	88	CCd	4%	85	64	8%	6%	82	0%	0%	1.1	117	$6
1st Half	106	11	2	11	0	194	2	1	222	245	286	75	53	78	6	80	0.30	43	19	38	22	66	CBd	5%	58	61	7%	7%	84	0%	0%	-5.8	14	-$7
2nd Half	191	17	4	25	0	306	3	3	283	330	459	112	25	120	3	85	0.21	47	22	30	34	100	CDd	3%	98	66	9%	6%	85	0%	0%	7.5	176	$7
23 Proj	**280**	**30**	**6**	**30**	**2**	**267**	**6**	**1**	**258**	**309**	**407**	**99**	**74**	**104**	**5**	**82**	**0.31**	**46**	**20**	**33**	**31**	**97**		**4%**	**89**	**75**	**8%**	**8%**	**103**	**3%**	**56%**	**3.5**	**134**	**$9**

Donaldson,Josh

Age: 37 Pos: 3B DH | Bats: R Ht: 6' 1" Wt: 210

Health D | PT/Exp A | Consist B | LIMA Plan B | Rand Var +1 | MM 4115

Right shoulder inflammation shelved him for a couple weeks in May/June. Perhaps that contributed to drop in skills and production, particularly the 2nd half QBaB slip. Career-worst chase% (29.4%; lifetime: 23.5%) suggests it wasn't all injury-related. At his age and with his injury history, we can't just assume a rebound.

Yr Tm	PA	R	HR	RBI	SB	BA	xHR	xSB	xBA	OBP	SLG	OPS+	vL+	vR+	bb%	ct%	Eye	G	L	F	h%	HctX	QBaB	Brl%	PX	xPX	HR/F	xHR/F	Spd	SBA%	SB%	RAR	BPX	R$
18 2 AL	219	30	8	23	2	246	8	3	252	352	449	107	119	100	14	71	0.57	48	17	35	30	108	BCd	10%	138	113	17%	17%	93	4%	100%	6.1	177	$4
19 ATL	659	96	37	94	4	259	37	5	270	379	521	125	117	126	15	72	0.65	42	21	36	29	118	ACd	16%	145	124	26%	26%	79	3%	67%	25.9	219	$21
20 MIN	102	14	6	11	0	222	4	1	226	373	469	112	82	118	18	70	0.75	55	10	34	24	98	ADf	7%	134	98	30%	20%	85	0%	0%	1.8	208	$4
21 MIN	543	73	26	72	0	247	32	2	253	352	475	114	128	107	14	75	0.65	43	17	40	27	123	ABd	17%	132	120	19%	23%	78	0%	0%	20.4	223	$14
22 NYY	546	59	15	62	2	222	16	1	225	308	374	97	99	96	10	69	0.36	43	18	39	29	101	BCf	10%	114	109	12%	12%	78	3%	50%	-4.8	41	$8
1st Half	259	23	6	23	1	222	8	1	241	313	373	97	94	98	11	70	0.42	36	25	39	29	109	ABd	10%	116	108	10%	13%	74	3%	50%	-3.1	69	$3
2nd Half	287	36	9	39	1	221	9	1	212	303	375	96	103	94	9	68	0.32	50	12	38	29	93	BCf	10%	112	110	13%	13%	84	3%	50%	-4.7	24	$14
23 Proj	**490**	**62**	**17**	**61**	**1**	**232**	**21**	**3**	**233**	**331**	**407**	**102**	**107**	**101**	**12**	**71**	**0.48**	**45**	**17**	**38**	**29**	**108**		**12%**	**122**	**112**	**15%**	**18%**	**78**	**3%**	**57%**	**7.7**	**129**	**$13**

Donovan,Brendan

Age: 26 Pos: 2B 3B RF | Bats: L Ht: 6' 1" Wt: 195

Health A | PT/Exp B | Consist B | LIMA Plan C+ | Rand Var 0 | MM 1133

5-45-.281 BA in 468 PA at STL. Solid rookie campaign, built on top-tier plate skills that carried over from minors. Simultaneous 2nd half gains in ct%, HctX and xPX are intriguing, though near-term upside capped by lack of power and SB. Still, BA/OBP, counting stats, versatility have value; but a higher ceiling dependent on more pop showing up.

Yr Tm	PA	R	HR	RBI	SB	BA	xHR	xSB	xBA	OBP	SLG	OPS+	vL+	vR+	bb%	ct%	Eye	G	L	F	h%	HctX	QBaB	Brl%	PX	xPX	HR/F	xHR/F	Spd	SBA%	SB%	RAR	BPX	R$
18																																		
19 aaa																																		
20																																		
21 a/a	321	38	6	35	8	243		4		303	350	90			8	76	0.35				30				66				93	21%	49%		4	$7
22 STL *	530	71	6	49	2	274	5	19	266	366	368	104	105	110	12	82	0.82	53	24	24	32	95	CFb	3%	64	72	7%	7%	102	3%	40%	8.6	128	$14
1st Half	294	35	3	30	2	278	1	10	270	363	381	105	120	113	12	80	0.66	52	25	23	34	66	DFb	1%	75	31	6%	3%	103	3%	50%	5.4	121	$12
2nd Half	236	36	3	19	0	270	4	9	260	387	352	105	90	108	14	86	1.11	54	22	24	30	126	CDb	5%	50	109	7%	10%	106	3%	0%	2.4	152	$8
23 Proj	**420**	**56**	**5**	**41**	**5**	**261**	**5**	**4**	**254**	**362**	**349**	**99**	**92**	**100**	**11**	**80**	**0.63**	**53**	**23**	**24**	**32**	**102**		**4%**	**60**	**78**	**7%**	**7%**	**101**	**4%**	**47%**	**2.8**	**85**	**$13**

Dozier,Hunter

Age: 31 Pos: 1B RF 3B DH | Bats: R Ht: 6' 4" Wt: 220

Health B | PT/Exp A | Consist A | LIMA Plan D+ | Rand Var +1 | MM 3313

Another disappointing season, as 2019 feels like a long time ago (for all of us, right?). First-half ct% recovery was short-lived, power skills barely a tick above average, and though he's multi-position eligible, these are not metrics of a successful fantasy cornerman. A playing-time squeeze could well be the next chapter.

Yr Tm	PA	R	HR	RBI	SB	BA	xHR	xSB	xBA	OBP	SLG	OPS+	vL+	vR+	bb%	ct%	Eye	G	L	F	h%	HctX	QBaB	Brl%	PX	xPX	HR/F	xHR/F	Spd	SBA%	SB%	RAR	BPX	R$
18 KC *	524	49	12	42	3	225	14	6	221	287	367	88	80	93	8	67	0.26	41	22	37	31	111	BCc	11%	102	132	12%	15%	108	6%	45%	-14.2	0	$5
19 KC	586	75	26	84	2	279	26	9	252	348	522	120	127	117	9	72	0.37	34	22	44	34	112	ABc	10%	132	144	16%	16%	156	3%	50%	19.6	222	$18
20 KC	186	29	6	12	4	228	5	3	221	344	392	98	98	98	15	70	0.56	36	24	40	29	87	DBd	8%	92	80	14%	11%	160	8%	100%	-1.3	124	$12
21 KC	543	55	16	54	5	216	17	7	226	285	394	93	87	96	8	68	0.28	38	19	42	28	102	BBc	9%	116	121	11%	12%	131	8%	56%	-9.8	88	$6
22 KC	500	51	12	41	4	236	14	7	240	292	387	96	104	93	7	73	0.27	42	20	37	30	91	CCf	8%	105	104	10%	11%	133	7%	57%	-4.3	107	$8
1st Half	283	33	8	27	2	259	9	5	247	322	425	106	105	105	8	75	0.32	43	19	38	32	89	BBf	10%	111	99	11%	12%	137	7%	40%	1.8	162	$12
2nd Half	217	18	4	14	2	207	5	3	230	253	340	84	101	77	6	70	0.22	42	22	36	27	92	CCc	5%	97	110	8%	10%	118	7%	100%	-8.5	31	-$1
23 Proj	**350**	**38**	**9**	**30**	**3**	**226**	**10**	**4**	**231**	**293**	**388**	**94**	**97**	**93**	**8**	**71**	**0.30**	**40**	**21**	**39**	**29**	**96**		**8%**	**113**	**111**	**11%**	**12%**	**110**	**7%**	**66%**	**-4.3**	**92**	**$7**

Drury,Brandon

Age: 30 Pos: 3B 1B 2B DH | Bats: R Ht: 6' 2" Wt: 230

Health A | PT/Exp A | Consist D | LIMA Plan B | Rand Var -3 | MM 4025

Should we have seen this coming? Back in 2019, he flashed legit Brl%, xHR/F levels—but QBaB, xPX, OPS+, BPX and R$ all yawned. In 2021, he put up a .783 OPS and 102 HctX—but in less than 100 MLB PA. So the answer is "No". 2022's improved skills and year-long consistency now has us intrigued, but heed pedestrian QBaB and xHR.

Yr Tm	PA	R	HR	RBI	SB	BA	xHR	xSB	xBA	OBP	SLG	OPS+	vL+	vR+	bb%	ct%	Eye	G	L	F	h%	HctX	QBaB	Brl%	PX	xPX	HR/F	xHR/F	Spd	SBA%	SB%	RAR	BPX	R$
18 2 AL *	334	32	7	36	2	226	2	5	212	312	347	88	63	71	11	65	0.36	42	23	35	32	63	CCd	7%	91	91	5%	10%	71	4%	67%	-8.5	-63	$3
19 TOR	447	43	15	41	0	218	19	2	248	262	380	89	86	90	6	73	0.22	42	24	34	26	97	CCd	9%	93	99	14%	18%	73	1%	0%	-26.3	4	$2
20 TOR	49	3	0	1	0	152	1	0	216	184	174	47	74	21	4	80	0.22	34	26	39	19	69	FAd	5%	17	72	0%	7%	91	0%	0%	-5.8	-104	-$5
21 NYM *	313	24	9	33	0	204	2	0	210	240	345	80	120	98	5	70	0.16	52	16	32	26	97	BCf	6%	93	95	20%	10%	66	0%	0%	-22.5	-54	-$1
22 2 NL	568	87	28	87	2	263	19	2	271	320	492	115	134	107	7	76	0.30	41	20	39	30	116	CCd	11%	145	120	18%	12%	85	4%	40%	9.6	203	$23
1st Half	288	49	17	45	1	266	10	1	279	326	525	120	137	114	7	76	0.32	40	19	41	29	126	BBd	12%	158	128	21%	12%	81	4%	33%	7.8	245	$26
2nd Half	280	38	11	42	1	259	8	1	263	314	459	109	131	101	7	75	0.29	42	21	38	30	106	CCc	10%	131	112	15%	11%	90	4%	50%	1.4	166	$20
23 Proj	**490**	**58**	**19**	**64**	**1**	**250**	**14**	**3**	**251**	**307**	**435**	**103**	**112**	**98**	**7**	**74**	**0.27**	**44**	**19**	**36**	**30**	**102**		**9%**	**122**	**107**	**16%**	**11%**	**75**	**4%**	**44%**	**7.7**	**77**	**$16**

Dubon,Mauricio

Age: 28 Pos: CF SS | Bats: R Ht: 6' 0" Wt: 173

Health A | PT/Exp C | Consist B | LIMA Plan D+ | Rand Var +5 | MM 1221

Can this real-life utilityman ever manage to carve out a larger role? PRO: Career-high ct%; above-average Spd; produces vL. CON: Puny exit velocity; subpar xPX; FB% drags down BA; history of poor SB% (53% in MLB career); difficulties vR. Bottom line: The current usage pattern is probably the optimal use of his skills.

Yr Tm	PA	R	HR	RBI	SB	BA	xHR	xSB	xBA	OBP	SLG	OPS+	vL+	vR+	bb%	ct%	Eye	G	L	F	h%	HctX	QBaB	Brl%	PX	xPX	HR/F	xHR/F	Spd	SBA%	SB%	RAR	BPX	R$
18 aaa	109	12	3	12	4	283		1		292	460	101			1	79	0.06				34				109				107	40%	53%		130	$2
19 2 NL *	636	76	17	53	11	260	2	30	287	291	393	95	115	97	4	84	0.28	48	27	26	29	91	DCb	2%	68	74	18%	9%	118	15%	51%	-9.9	133	$15
20 SF	176	21	4	19	2	274	5	6	231	337	389	96	116	88	9	77	0.42	34	26	40	33	96	DBd	4%	61	108	8%	10%	167	10%	40%	-1.8	104	$12
21 SF *	453	47	10	42	8	248	5	7	240	294	368	91	99	84	6	79	0.31	40	22	38	29	90	DCd	4%	71	97	10%	10%	112	13%	62%	-11.1	81	$10
22 2 TM	265	31	5	24	2	214	3	4	231	252	313	80	107	64	5	88	0.43	39	17	45	23	95	FBf	2%	58	78	5%	3%	113	10%	40%	-10.6	148	$1
1st Half	117	15	3	16	1	224	2	2	235	259	346	85	117	65	5	93	0.75	41	12	48	22	110	FBd	4%	65	99	6%	4%	114	10%	25%	-4.4	238	-$3
2nd Half	148	16	2	8	1	206	1	2	228	247	287	75	98	64	5	84	0.32	37	21	42	23	84	FBf	1%	52	59	4%	2%	120	10%	100%	-7.1	86	-$4
23 Proj	**245**	**28**	**6**	**23**	**3**	**236**	**5**	**3**	**244**	**277**	**362**	**89**	**108**	**78**	**5**	**83**	**0.34**	**39**	**20**	**40**	**26**	**93**		**3%**	**75**	**85**	**8%**	**6%**	**114**	**9%**	**50%**	**-4.0**	**121**	**$6**

GREG PYRON

Duran,Ezequiel

Age: 24 Pos: 3B
Bats: R Ht: 5' 11" Wt: 185

Health	A	LIMA Plan	D
PT/Exp	C	Rand Var	0
Consist	F	MM	3221

5-25-.236 BA with 4 SB in 220 PA at TEX. Made MLB debut in June despite having not played above AA, was sent to AAA later that month; returned to TEX in 2nd half. Looked overmatched vs. MLB pitching with subpar ct% and very little hard contact. There are seeds of intriguing HR/SB combo in minors, but needs more AAA seasoning before it translates.

Yr	Tm	PA	R	HR	RBI	SB	BA	xHR	xSB	xBA	OBP	SLG	OPS+	vL+	vR+	bb%	ct%	Eye	G	L	F	h%	HctX	QBaB	Brl%	PX	xPX	HR/F	xHR/F	Spd	SBA%	SB%	RAR	BPX	R$
18																																			
19																																			
20																																			
21																																			
22	TEX *	561	58	15	61	13	238	4	5	246	273	395	95	101	88	5	73	0.18	51	16	33	30	77	DCf	5%	113	63	10%	8%	106	22%	59%	-8.8	86	$15
1st Half		281	34	8	30	8	249	1	2	284	282	431	101	93	103	4	76	0.19	62	16	22	30	88	CFf	2%	129	41	20%	10%	115	22%	58%	-2.5	176	$17
2nd Half		280	24	7	32	5	228	3	3	219	264	360	88	103	81	5	70	0.17	46	17	38	30	70	DCf	6%	97	73	7%	7%	96	22%	60%	-9.5	-3	$11
23	**Proj**	**210**	**21**	**6**	**23**	**5**	**237**	**4**	**5**	**242**	**272**	**391**	**92**	**97**	**90**	**5**	**73**	**0.18**	**52**	**16**	**31**	**30**	**77**		**4%**	**112**	**60**	**12%**	**8%**	**101**	**16%**	**60%**	**-2.5**	**69**	**$3**

Duran,Jarren

Age: 26 Pos: CF
Bats: L Ht: 6' 2" Wt: 212

Health	A	LIMA Plan	D
PT/Exp	C	Rand Var	0
Consist	A	MM	2401

3-17-.221 BA with 7 SB in 223 PA at BOS. Former top prospect tinkered with swing in 2021 and unlocked power in minors, but manifested in MLB as decreased ct% and terrible BA. Speed is a real asset, and also a completely theoretical one if he can't reach base consistently. There's a lot of work to be done here, and time is starting to become a factor.

Yr	Tm	PA	R	HR	RBI	SB	BA	xHR	xSB	xBA	OBP	SLG	OPS+	vL+	vR+	bb%	ct%	Eye	G	L	F	h%	HctX	QBaB	Brl%	PX	xPX	HR/F	xHR/F	Spd	SBA%	SB%	RAR	BPX	R$
18																																			
19	aa	340	37	1	17	25	247		6		291	323	85			6	73	0.23				34				46				149	42%	75%		-48	$10
20																																			
21	BOS *	379	52	13	37	14	221	1	4	234	276	395	92	60	86	7	67	0.23	49	19	31	29	109	CDf	4%	110	105	10%	5%	125	25%	76%	-9.1	35	$10
22	BOS *	518	54	9	41	18	226	6	14	230	271	369	91	63	98	6	69	0.20	51	15	34	31	83	CDd	8%	106	92	7%	13%	119	23%	79%	-8.0	38	$12
1st Half		269	32	5	24	12	272	1	8	251	322	441	108	57	153	7	71	0.26	46	21	33	36	86	BDa	7%	121	108	5%	5%	130	23%	78%	7.4	128	$18
2nd Half		249	21	4	17	6	176	4	6	207	215	292	72	68	71	5	67	0.15	54	11	34	24	80	DDf	8%	89	80	7%	15%	103	23%	83%	-15.0	-66	$1
23	**Proj**	**210**	**24**	**3**	**17**	**8**	**220**	**4**	**6**	**220**	**275**	**345**	**86**	**59**	**94**	**6**	**68**	**0.21**	**50**	**17**	**33**	**30**	**93**		**6%**	**93**	**97**	**8%**	**8%**	**119**	**18%**	**79%**	**-4.3**	**15**	**$6**

Duvall,Adam

Age: 34 Pos: CF LF
Bats: R Ht: 6' 1" Wt: 215

Health	C	LIMA Plan	C+
PT/Exp	B	Rand Var	0
Consist	B	MM	4113

A season in three acts: shook off horrid first two months (.191 BA, 2 HR in 168 AB) with June/July hot streak (.244 BA, 10 HR in 119 AB) before season-ending surgery to repair a torn tendon sheath in left wrist. Power skills remain intact, though streakiness and durability risk are baked into the package. Expected to be healthy for spring.

Yr	Tm	PA	R	HR	RBI	SB	BA	xHR	xSB	xBA	OBP	SLG	OPS+	vL+	vR+	bb%	ct%	Eye	G	L	F	h%	HctX	QBaB	Brl%	PX	xPX	HR/F	xHR/F	Spd	SBA%	SB%	RAR	BPX	R$
18	2 NL	427	48	15	61	2	195	19	5	224	274	365	86	84	84	9	70	0.32	30	22	48	24	94	CAc	10%	114	116	12%	15%	71	5%	50%	-16.7	33	$4
19	ATL *	534	72	33	89	1	223	12	4	221	284	479	106	157	104	8	70	0.29	27	12	60	25	109	AAf	16%	138	182	20%	24%	103	1%	100%	-13.6	148	$12
20	ATL	209	34	16	33	0	237	15	1	251	301	532	111	117	108	7	72	0.28	29	17	54	24	89	CAf	14%	162	136	22%	20%	93	0%	0%	0.0	240	$18
21	2 NL	555	67	38	113	5	228	38	1	231	281	491	106	83	114	6	66	0.20	30	17	53	26	97	BAd	16%	160	148	21%	21%	84	5%	100%	-3.0	123	$18
22	ATL	315	39	12	36	0	213	14	2	215	276	401	96	118	88	7	65	0.21	29	19	52	28	95	CAc	13%	141	132	12%	14%	83	3%	0%	-7.4	41	$3
1st Half		290	36	10	32	0	205	12	2	206	272	376	92	124	81	7	65	0.23	29	19	52	28	94	CAc	12%	128	123	11%	13%	85	3%	0%	-9.1	10	$9
2nd Half		25	3	2	4	0	292	2	0	310	320	667	140	78	176	0	67	0.00	31	19	50	36	109	BAf	20%	281	219	25%	25%	82	3%	0%	1.9	407	-$8
23	**Proj**	**420**	**58**	**24**	**65**	**1**	**220**	**26**	**2**	**232**	**284**	**456**	**103**	**113**	**99**	**7**	**68**	**0.24**	**29**	**18**	**53**	**25**	**95**		**14%**	**160**	**137**	**17%**	**18%**	**85**	**4%**	**49%**	**3.7**	**118**	**$13**

Eaton,Nate

Age: 26 Pos: RF
Bats: R Ht: 5' 11" Wt: 185

Health	A	LIMA Plan	D+
PT/Exp	D	Rand Var	-2
Consist	F	MM	1503

1-12-.264 BA with 11 SB in 122 PA at KC. Exceeded expectations in first MLB opportunity by showing off elite wheels (combined 34 SB across three levels in 2022). However, subpar ct%/poor Eye (combo producing terrible OBP), and lack of power all threaten to relegate him to a reserve/part time role. This is a risky place to chase bags.

Yr	Tm	PA	R	HR	RBI	SB	BA	xHR	xSB	xBA	OBP	SLG	OPS+	vL+	vR+	bb%	ct%	Eye	G	L	F	h%	HctX	QBaB	Brl%	PX	xPX	HR/F	xHR/F	Spd	SBA%	SB%	RAR	BPX	R$
18																																			
19																																			
20																																			
21																																			
22	KC *	479	48	8	41	24	231	2	8	206	276	344	88	124	92	6	74	0.23	35	19	46	30	72	DCf	5%	74	102	3%	6%	177	30%	77%	-9.4	69	$15
1st Half		270	25	5	22	10	228		4	230	261	337	85	0	0	4	76	0.19	44	20	36	28	0			72	-14	0%		128	30%	74%	-8.6	38	$10
2nd Half		209	23	3	19	14	235	2	4	197	296	354	92	124	92	8	70	0.28	35	19	46	32	69	DCf	5%	78	102	3%	6%	199	30%	80%	-2.2	66	$11
23	**Proj**	**280**	**29**	**2**	**25**	**16**	**232**	**5**	**13**	**194**	**286**	**325**	**85**	**105**	**77**	**6**	**72**	**0.25**	**35**	**19**	**46**	**31**	**62**		**5%**	**64**	**92**	**3%**	**6%**	**160**	**25%**	**79%**	**-6.6**	**55**	**$11**

Edman,Tommy

Age: 28 Pos: 2B SS
Bats: B Ht: 5' 10" Wt: 180

Health	A	LIMA Plan	B
PT/Exp	A	Rand Var	0
Consist	A	MM	2435

Follow-up to 2021 breakout was actually a tad better; see incremental gains in bb%, vR, Brl%. That said, counting stat value is fueled by batting leadoff, but bb%/OBP means grip on that spot may be tenuous. Batted ninth in 30 GS vR (21 of last 48 GS), and only attempted 2 steals in 112 PA from bottom of lineup, so... DN: <20 SB.

Yr	Tm	PA	R	HR	RBI	SB	BA	xHR	xSB	xBA	OBP	SLG	OPS+	vL+	vR+	bb%	ct%	Eye	G	L	F	h%	HctX	QBaB	Brl%	PX	xPX	HR/F	xHR/F	Spd	SBA%	SB%	RAR	BPX	R$
18	a/a	550	65	5	32	23	263		8		306	342	87			6	81	0.34				31				50				121	21%	80%		53	$16
19	STL *	557	89	16	59	22	288	10	17	273	323	470	110	134	111	5	81	0.28	41	25	35	33	116	CBb	5%	90	108	12%	11%	140	18%	96%	13.1	189	$24
20	STL	227	29	5	26	2	250	3	6	248	317	368	91	111	85	7	76	0.33	51	23	26	30	92	DDd	4%	66	67	12%	7%	115	10%	33%	-5.9	36	$14
21	STL	691	91	11	56	30	262	15	11	270	308	387	95	108	92	5	85	0.40	46	22	32	29	102	CDd	4%	73	79	6%	9%	116	22%	86%	-6.7	181	$27
22	STL	630	95	13	57	32	265	12	21	263	324	400	103	109	100	7	81	0.41	49	20	31	31	104	CDd	6%	86	90	9%	8%	121	22%	91%	5.2	155	$31
1st Half		354	58	7	32	19	263	5	13	258	331	384	101	107	99	9	80	0.47	53	19	28	31	98	CDd	7%	74	87	10%	7%	142	22%	86%	2.8	141	$34
2nd Half		276	37	6	25	13	268	6	8	270	315	420	104	112	101	6	82	0.34	45	20	34	31	112	CDd	6%	101	93	8%	8%	97	22%	100%	4.8	176	$21
23	**Proj**	**560**	**79**	**12**	**51**	**24**	**264**	**11**	**18**	**264**	**318**	**401**	**100**	**111**	**96**	**6**	**82**	**0.38**	**47**	**21**	**32**	**30**	**105**		**5%**	**88**	**87**	**9%**	**8%**	**113**	**17%**	**87%**	**11.6**	**151**	**$27**

Escobar,Eduardo

Age: 34 Pos: 3B
Bats: B Ht: 5' 10" Wt: 193

Health	A	LIMA Plan	B
PT/Exp	A	Rand Var	0
Consist	C	MM	4125

Suffered headaches and dizziness in late June (ear pressure); missed most of August (oblique). Extreme peaks-and-valleys can be frustrating, but September surge (8 HR, .340 BA/1.042 OPS) salvaged season and quells concern from sluggish start. Plate skills, power, and launch angle are still there, making a health-permitted repeat possible.

Yr	Tm	PA	R	HR	RBI	SB	BA	xHR	xSB	xBA	OBP	SLG	OPS+	vL+	vR+	bb%	ct%	Eye	G	L	F	h%	HctX	QBaB	Brl%	PX	xPX	HR/F	xHR/F	Spd	SBA%	SB%	RAR	BPX	R$
18	2 TM	631	75	23	84	2	272	23	8	275	334	489	110	103	112	8	78	0.41	32	25	43	31	109	DAb	8%	136	133	12%	12%	70	4%	33%	14.7	197	$19
19	ARI	699	94	35	118	5	269	31	6	268	320	511	115	123	111	7	80	0.38	33	23	45	29	114	CAa	7%	116	152	15%	13%	112	4%	83%	5.9	226	$24
20	ARI	222	22	4	20	1	212	5	2	236	270	335	80	74	83	7	80	0.37	36	24	40	25	97	CAd	5%	64	80	6%	8%	117	2%	100%	-15.0	84	$5
21	2 NL	599	77	28	90	1	253	26	5	254	314	472	108	119	104	8	77	0.39	32	21	47	28	110	CAd	9%	119	134	14%	13%	112	1%	100%	11.0	219	$17
22	NYM	542	58	20	69	0	240	20	2	245	295	430	103	114	97	7	74	0.31	30	23	47	29	91	CAb	9%	123	122	11%	11%	94	2%	0%	-2.2	134	$12
1st Half		310	33	9	37	0	225	7	1	234	284	400	97	124	85	8	72	0.31	30	22	48	28	79	CAb	6%	119	110	9%	7%	101	2%	0%	-4.0	110	$10
2nd Half		232	25	11	32	0	260	13	1	259	310	470	110	104	114	7	76	0.31	30	24	47	29	107	CAb	13%	128	137	14%	17%	85	2%	0%	4.8	169	$13
23	**Proj**	**490**	**57**	**20**	**67**	**1**	**252**	**20**	**3**	**250**	**308**	**448**	**105**	**110**	**102**	**8**	**76**	**0.35**	**31**	**23**	**46**	**29**	**102**		**9%**	**123**	**126**	**12%**	**12%**	**99**	**4%**	**39%**	**11.6**	**168**	**$16**

Espinal,Santiago

Age: 28 Pos: 2B
Bats: R Ht: 5' 10" Wt: 181

Health	B	LIMA Plan	C+
PT/Exp	B	Rand Var	0
Consist	C	MM	1233

Quest to prove he's more than a utility infielder hit a snag: h% regressed, playing time waned in 2nd half, and team acquired trade deadline upgrade. Plate skills and line drive stroke provide a solid BA floor, and he owns decent enough speed to chip in a smattering of SB. But lack of power will probably prevent him from being a lineup regular.

Yr	Tm	PA	R	HR	RBI	SB	BA	xHR	xSB	xBA	OBP	SLG	OPS+	vL+	vR+	bb%	ct%	Eye	G	L	F	h%	HctX	QBaB	Brl%	PX	xPX	HR/F	xHR/F	Spd	SBA%	SB%	RAR	BPX	R$
18	aa	159	14	1	17	2	261		2		315	360	91			7	83	0.48				31				64				106	8%	60%		110	$1
19	a/a	507	49	6	62	10	262		6		314	361	93			7	82	0.44				31				57				87	20%	41%		67	$11
20	TOR	66	10	0	6	1	267	1	2	253	308	333	85	96	69	6	73	0.25	30	40	30	36	77	FCc	2%	56	78	0%	8%	112	6%	100%	-1.5	-52	$2
21	TOR	246	32	2	17	6	311	1	5	259	376	405	107	108	106	9	86	0.73	43	22	35	35	86	DCd	2%	58	55	3%	2%	135	9%	86%	8.7	204	$9
22	TOR	491	51	7	51	6	267	5	7	260	322	370	98	116	92	7	85	0.53	43	23	34	30	92	DCc	3%	68	69	5%	4%	92	10%	50%	4.0	131	$13
1st Half		313	30	6	37	3	268	4	4	267	319	401	102	140	90	7	82	0.42	41	24	35	31	105	CBb	5%	90	83	7%	5%	88	10%	60%	4.1	141	$14
2nd Half		178	21	1	14	3	265	1	3	247	328	315	91	82	95	8	91	0.93	46	21	33	29	70	FCd	2%	32	44	2%	2%	109	10%	43%	-3.0	134	$2
23	**Proj**	**350**	**40**	**3**	**32**	**5**	**266**	**2**	**6**	**256**	**326**	**353**	**94**	**99**	**91**	**8**	**86**	**0.62**	**42**	**24**	**34**	**30**	**84**		**2%**	**59**	**60**	**3%**	**3%**	**112**	**9%**	**54%**	**1.2**	**147**	**$11**

GREG PYRON

Estrada,Thairo

Age: 27	Pos: 2B SS	Health	A	LIMA Plan	B
Bats: R	Ht: 5' 10" Wt: 185	PT/Exp	A	Rand Var	+1
		Consist	C	MM	2335

Pleasant surprise in first full MLB season, with plate skills and xBA forming a solid BA floor. However, xHR, xHR/F, and GB% all question the chances of a power redo; while xSB and SB history do the same for the (value-driving) SB output. Capable of sprinkling value across multiple categories again, but don't pay for a full repeat.

Yr Tm	PA	R	HR	RBI	SB	BA	xHR	xSB	xBA	OBP	SLG	OPS+	vL+	vR+	bb%	ct%	Eye	G	L	F	h%	HctX	QBaB	Brl%	PX	xPX	HR/F	xHR/F	Spd	SBA%	SB%	RAR	BPX	R$
18 aaa	33	1	0	3	0	135		0		135	161	40			0	73	0.00				18				23				101	0%	0%		-180	-$4
19 NYY *	322	43	10	38	6	239	2	1	269	274	408	94	58	111	5	77	0.21	53	20	27	28	74	CDb	4%	92	60	23%	15%	108	11%	85%	-6.8	89	$6
20 NYY	52	8	1	3	1	167	1	1	189	231	229	61	93	36	2	60	0.05	59	21	21	25	67	FFf	3%	37	60	17%	17%	109	9%	100%	-5.7	-356	-$1
21 SF *	356	44	12	49	5	268	5	6	256	315	431	102	93	127	6	80	0.35	51	17	32	30	84	DDf	7%	90	108	23%	16%	109	12%	51%	0.6	158	$11
22 SF	541	71	14	62	21	260	9	11	269	322	402	103	117	96	6	82	0.37	51	20	30	29	85	DDf	5%	86	74	12%	8%	121	20%	78%	1.8	159	$23
1st Half	270	40	6	31	11	256	4	5	279	311	386	99	101	98	6	83	0.39	55	20	25	29	79	DFf	3%	79	58	12%	8%	123	20%	85%	1.3	166	$20
2nd Half	271	31	8	31	10	264	5	5	258	333	417	106	129	93	7	80	0.35	45	20	35	30	91	DCd	6%	93	91	12%	7%	116	20%	71%	3.8	155	$20
23 Proj	490	59	14	56	13	262	11	14	260	322	410	102	98	103	6	81	0.35	50	19	31	30	84		6%	92	88	12%	10%	107	15%	69%	7.6	152	$18

Fairchild,Stuart

Age: 27	Pos: LF CF	Health	A	LIMA Plan	D+
Bats: R	Ht: 6' 0" Wt: 205	PT/Exp	D	Rand Var	-1
		Consist	A	MM	3401

5-6-.247 in 110 PA at SEA/SF/CIN. Altered swing in 2021 to add more loft and scouts think he could eventually hit 20+ HR. Good Spd/SBA% hints at double-digit SB upside as well. But struggles against MLB offspeed pitches has led to horrid ct% and BA. Until he improves there (perhaps by consulting Jobu?), he's limited to a reserve role and unrosterable.

Yr Tm	PA	R	HR	RBI	SB	BA	xHR	xSB	xBA	OBP	SLG	OPS+	vL+	vR+	bb%	ct%	Eye	G	L	F	h%	HctX	QBaB	Brl%	PX	xPX	HR/F	xHR/F	Spd	SBA%	SB%	RAR	BPX	R$
18																																		
19 aa	171	22	4	15	3	257		2		334	421	104			10	83	0.67				29				89				108	12%	55%		211	$1
20																																		
21 ARI *	185	18	5	17	4	214	0	3	236	269	367	87	86	0	7	71	0.26	42	25	33	28	72	FCf	0%	91	61	0%	0%	149	14%	76%	-6.7	62	$1
22 3 TM *	314	36	14	22	5	227	4	6	223	282	423	100	116	111	7	63	0.21	43	18	39	31	96	CCd	8%	144	157	21%	17%	138	14%	53%	-2.6	83	$5
1st Half	144	16	8	12	3	205	0	2	205	248	427	95	0	0	5	61	0.15	50	0	50	27	88	DDf		165	235	0%	0%	107	14%	70%	-2.7	69	$0
2nd Half	170	20	6	10	2	247	4	4	222	312	418	104	135	121	9	65	0.27	42	20	38	34	99	CCd	9%	125	149	24%	19%	143	14%	40%	0.7	72	$3
23 Proj	245	27	8	20	4	227	6	6	226	318	393	99	103	96	8	68	0.25	42	20	38	30	89		8%	116	134	13%	9%	135	13%	64%	-1.5	81	$6

Farmer,Kyle

Age: 32	Pos: SS 3B	Health	A	LIMA Plan	B
Bats: R	Ht: 6' 0" Wt: 205	PT/Exp	A	Rand Var	+1
		Consist	A	MM	2125

Followed up on 2021's surprising PT spike with even more 2022 PAs, and a repeat of double-digit R$. That value is rooted more in accumulation of counting stats than any plus skills; gains he flashed vR in '21 vanished and figure to threaten those big PA totals. He's this year's example of "AAA Reliability isn't always a good thing".

Yr Tm	PA	R	HR	RBI	SB	BA	xHR	xSB	xBA	OBP	SLG	OPS+	vL+	vR+	bb%	ct%	Eye	G	L	F	h%	HctX	QBaB	Brl%	PX	xPX	HR/F	xHR/F	Spd	SBA%	SB%	RAR	BPX	R$
18 LA *	376	27	5	34	1	227	0	4	265	261	343	81	83	85	4	78	0.21	43	28	28	28	112	CCc	0%	80	81	0%	0%	96	3%	36%	-19.0	50	$1
19 CIN	197	22	9	27	4	230	7	1	235	279	410	95	114	84	5	68	0.17	40	24	35	29	94	DAb	6%	103	80	20%	16%	72	13%	80%	-9.7	-44	$3
20 CIN	70	4	0	4	1	266	2	1	235	329	313	85	118	64	7	80	0.38	37	27	35	33	114	BAb	6%	36	101	0%	11%	87	5%	100%	-3.1	-36	$1
21 CIN	529	60	16	63	2	263	11	6	259	316	416	101	107	99	4	80	0.23	41	24	35	30	118	CBc	4%	85	109	12%	8%	108	4%	40%	-3.0	115	$13
22 CIN	583	58	14	78	4	255	11	4	263	315	386	99	133	87	6	81	0.33	45	24	32	29	108	DCb	4%	82	91	10%	8%	84	5%	57%	-7.4	100	$15
1st Half	265	27	5	39	4	280	4	2	290	345	411	107	165	84	7	84	0.49	45	28	27	31	114	DCb	5%	86	77	9%	7%	82	5%	67%	3.9	162	$14
2nd Half	318	31	9	39	0	234	6	2	239	290	366	93	103	89	5	79	0.24	45	20	35	27	102	DCc	4%	78	103	11%	7%	95	5%	0%	-8.0	59	$13
23 Proj	455	48	11	59	3	251	9	4	251	307	379	95	115	87	5	79	0.26	43	24	33	29	111		4%	83	97	10%	8%	83	5%	57%	-2.7	85	$13

Fletcher,David

Age: 29	Pos: 2B SS	Health	F	LIMA Plan	B+
Bats: R	Ht: 5' 9" Wt: 185	PT/Exp	B	Rand Var	+4
		Consist	C	MM	0435

2-17-.255 with 1 SB in 228 PA at LAA. Missed a chunk of 2022 after surgery on adductor muscles in both legs. Typical elite ct% and LD% when healthy. Low h% figures to regress some, so figure on BA moving back toward historical xBA range. But those leg injuries are an obstacle to recovering 2021's SBs, rendering him a one-category asset at best.

Yr Tm	PA	R	HR	RBI	SB	BA	xHR	xSB	xBA	OBP	SLG	OPS+	vL+	vR+	bb%	ct%	Eye	G	L	F	h%	HctX	QBaB	Brl%	PX	xPX	HR/F	xHR/F	Spd	SBA%	SB%	RAR	BPX	R$
18 LAA *	571	70	5	49	7	274	1	7	280	306	388	93	89	90	4	89	0.42	39	27	34	30	95	FCc	0%	69	48	1%	1%	110	7%	76%	1.3	183	$13
19 LAA	653	83	6	49	8	290	3	11	284	350	384	102	102	100	8	89	0.86	44	26	30	32	99	FCb	0%	49	56	4%	2%	123	6%	73%	1.0	193	$16
20 LAA	230	31	3	18	2	319	1	4	292	376	425	106	119	99	9	88	0.80	54	25	21	35	81	DFc	1%	61	25	8%	3%	113	4%	67%	7.6	216	$20
21 LAA	665	74	2	47	15	262	0	8	270	297	324	85	106	76	5	90	0.52	48	23	28	29	64	FDd	0%	37	10	1%	0%	127	11%	83%	-15.8	158	$16
22 LAA *	278	22	2	18	2	233	0	4	251	255	300	79	83	90	3	91	0.32	35	25	40	25	51	FCf		41	23	3%	0%	106	3%	100%	-8.7	121	$0
1st Half	59	2	0	2	0	145	0	1	239	197	218	59	31	77	6	87	0.50	39	22	39	17	42	FDf	0%	43	13	0%	0%	128	3%	0%	-4.8	121	-$14
2nd Half	220	19	2	16	2	256	0	4	255	271	321	84	89	94	2	91	0.25	35	25	40	27	53	FBd	0%	40	25	3%	0%	91	3%	100%	-5.4	107	$2
23 Proj	560	56	4	37	7	264	1	6	261	302	340	89	94	87	5	90	0.48	42	24	33	29	61		0%	48	21	2%	0%	117	6%	84%	-2.6	144	$14

Flores,Wilmer

Age: 31	Pos: 2B 1B 3B DH	Health	B	LIMA Plan	B+
Bats: R	Ht: 6' 2" Wt: 213	PT/Exp	A	Rand Var	+3
		Consist	B	MM	3335

Career high PA by over 150, and exposure hurts. Formerly steady performer posted career-low BA, xBA, and ct%. But ct% remains above average, and xBA says BA plunge wasn't all deserved; power metrics fine but not outstanding. Defensive versatility provides many avenues to playing time, but if he'll be out there for every inning, lower the ceiling.

Yr Tm	PA	R	HR	RBI	SB	BA	xHR	xSB	xBA	OBP	SLG	OPS+	vL+	vR+	bb%	ct%	Eye	G	L	F	h%	HctX	QBaB	Brl%	PX	xPX	HR/F	xHR/F	Spd	SBA%	SB%	RAR	BPX	R$
18 NYM	429	43	11	51	0	267	7	6	261	319	417	99	81	106	7	89	0.69	36	19	45	28	108	DBd	3%	85	109	7%	4%	76	0%	0%	3.8	210	$9
19 ARI	285	31	9	37	0	317	8	1	290	361	487	117	137	104	5	88	0.48	37	25	38	33	114	CBc	5%	84	93	10%	9%	76	0%	0%	13.4	207	$7
20 SF	213	30	12	32	1	268	8	1	280	315	515	110	127	102	6	82	0.36	33	23	44	27	118	CAc	6%	125	130	17%	11%	93	2%	100%	3.5	276	$20
21 SF	436	57	18	53	1	262	13	3	270	335	447	107	109	106	9	86	0.73	38	21	41	27	108	CAc	6%	92	107	13%	9%	99	1%	100%	8.0	258	$12
22 SF	602	72	19	71	0	229	15	3	246	316	394	101	99	101	10	80	0.57	34	19	47	25	105	CAc	6%	102	102	10%	8%	97	0%	0%	-2.2	186	$11
1st Half	294	40	9	41	0	243	7	2	249	333	404	104	96	108	11	82	0.65	37	18	44	27	103	CAc	6%	99	95	10%	7%	92	0%	0%	3.7	200	$15
2nd Half	308	32	10	30	0	215	9	2	243	299	385	97	101	94	10	79	0.51	31	20	49	24	106	CAc	7%	106	109	9%	8%	103	0%	0%	-2.2	183	$10
23 Proj	525	66	18	65	1	248	15	2	255	323	416	103	105	101	9	83	0.59	35	21	44	27	108		6%	100	107	10%	9%	87	2%	100%	10.7	221	$15

Fortes,Nick

Age: 26	Pos: CA	Health	A	LIMA Plan	C+
Bats: R	Ht: 5' 11" Wt: 198	PT/Exp	D	Rand Var	0
		Consist	A	MM	3323

9-24-.230 with 5 SB in 240 PA at MIA. Long viewed as a future backup CA, there's reason to believe he could be something more. Plus plate skills (by today's standards) and HctX suggest BA could have some yeast. Above-average xPX, FB% and QBaB hint at high-teens HR ability. Don't miss those handful of SB, either. Sneaky 2nd CA target.

Yr Tm	PA	R	HR	RBI	SB	BA	xHR	xSB	xBA	OBP	SLG	OPS+	vL+	vR+	bb%	ct%	Eye	G	L	F	h%	HctX	QBaB	Brl%	PX	xPX	HR/F	xHR/F	Spd	SBA%	SB%	RAR	BPX	R$
18																																		
19																																		
20																																		
21 MIA *	390	36	9	42	6	212	2	4	196	270	331	83	110	161	7	80	0.41	30	13	57	24	171	AAd	22%	67	217	31%	15%	98	10%	71%	-10.8	81	$4
22 MIA *	352	50	11	33	6	220	6	6	231	277	356	90	92	101	7	80	0.38	40	17	42	24	111	BBf	7%	79	122	12%	8%	127	11%	65%	-4.4	124	$6
1st Half	168	26	5	17	3	223	2	3	251	285	366	92	84	154	8	82	0.48	43	20	38	24	116	ABb	9%	81	92	20%	13%	140	11%	100%	-0.3	179	$3
2nd Half	184	24	6	16	3	218	5	3	219	277	347	88	94	86	7	78	0.32	39	17	44	25	108	CBf	6%	76	131	10%	9%	105	11%	50%	-3.8	62	$4
23 Proj	350	43	15	35	6	239	13	6	247	316	417	102	87	107	7	80	0.39	41	18	41	26	111		7%	102	115	14%	13%	105	10%	68%	6.9	99	$12

Fraley,Jake

Age: 28	Pos: LF	Health	F	LIMA Plan	C
Bats: L	Ht: 6' 0" Wt: 195	PT/Exp	D	Rand Var	-3
		Consist	C	MM	3213

12-28-.259 with 4 SB in 247 PA at CIN. Missed three months (right knee, toe), returned in late July and made the most of his chances. Maintained above-average bb% and increased ct% by taking a more aggressive approach and improving vs. fastballs. Trouble vL and Health grade cap PT ceiling, but there's part-time power/speed value to be mined here.

Yr Tm	PA	R	HR	RBI	SB	BA	xHR	xSB	xBA	OBP	SLG	OPS+	vL+	vR+	bb%	ct%	Eye	G	L	F	h%	HctX	QBaB	Brl%	PX	xPX	HR/F	xHR/F	Spd	SBA%	SB%	RAR	BPX	R$
18																																		
19 SEA *	452	60	16	68	18	251	0	5	207	299	444	103	31	57	6	72	0.24	31	12	58	31	38	FAf	4%	111	2	0%	0%	107	29%	70%	-10.3	81	$17
20 SEA	29	3	0	0	2	154	0	1	182	241	269	68	19	83	7	58	0.18	27	33	40	27	47	FAc	7%	82	40	0%	0%	143	60%	67%	-3.2	-176	-$1
21 SEA *	311	33	11	41	12	218	7	29	224	352	379	100	72	112	17	64	0.58	39	26	34	29	79	DCc	6%	105	111	18%	14%	86	17%	79%	-1.1	12	$8
22 CIN *	293	38	13	31	5	253	9	7	244	333	437	109	67	122	11	72	0.43	43	20	37	30	85	DCc	8%	117	106	20%	15%	94	8%	82%	7.7	117	$9
1st Half	59	7	2	4	1	126	1	1	211	206	264	67	31	76	9	68	0.32	32	23	45	14	77	DAa	3%	98	106	7%	7%	92	8%	100%	-4.3	-3	-$10
2nd Half	234	31	11	27	4	286	8	6	252	365	482	120	97	131	11	73	0.47	46	20	35	34	87	DCc	9%	122	106	24%	17%	99	8%	79%	13.0	155	$18
23 Proj	420	51	16	50	10	240	11	6	232	340	411	104	66	116	12	68	0.45	40	23	37	31	81		6%	117	108	17%	12%	93	7%	77%	8.9	59	$16

GREG PYRON

France,Ty

Age: 28	Pos: 1B	Health	A	LIMA Plan	B+
Bats: R	Ht: 5' 11" Wt: 217	PT/Exp	A	Rand Var	+1
		Consist	A	MM	3045

2022 was essentially a 2021 repeat with touch of h% correction. Flashed 1st half ct%, HctX, and BA/xBA gains before suffering injuries (left elbow, left wrist, right calf) and 2nd half fade, which was mostly regression. GB% and so-so power caps HR output, but there's enough hard contact to sustain as a BA asset. Loss of 2B eligibility hurts value.

Yr Tm	PA	R	HR	RBI	SB	BA	xHR	xSB	xBA	OBP	SLG	OPS+	vL+	vR+	bb%	ct%	Eye	G	L	F	h%	HctX	QBaB	Brl%	PX	xPX	HR/F	xHR/F	Spd	SBA%	SB%	RAR	BPX	R$
18 a/a	543	63	16	72	2	223		6		272	372	86			6	80	0.33				25				88				89	7%	33%		100	$8
19 SD *	518	77	24	85	1	288	7	5	270	330	510	116	107	91	6	77	0.27	43	21	37	33	112	CBc	6%	118	96	14%	14%	99	3%	25%	6.9	167	$18
20 2 TM	155	19	4	23	0	305	6	1	265	368	468	111	82	130	7	74	0.30	38	31	32	39	95	DBc	9%	100	108	12%	18%	92	0%	0%	2.8	76	$13
21 SEA	650	85	18	73	0	291	20	3	268	368	445	112	119	108	7	81	0.43	46	23	31	33	112	CCc	7%	88	84	12%	14%	94	0%	0%	14.7	154	$21
22 SEA	612	65	20	84	0	276	14	2	270	340	437	110	103	113	6	83	0.37	48	21	31	30	110	CCc	6%	95	80	14%	10%	79	0%	0%	12.8	155	$20
1st Half	310	32	10	45	0	316	7	1	278	390	476	123	112	126	7	84	0.47	48	23	29	35	123	CCc	6%	94	86	15%	10%	80	0%	0%	15.3	179	$21
2nd Half	302	33	10	39	0	236	7	1	264	288	399	97	96	98	5	82	0.29	48	20	33	26	96	DCd	5%	97	73	13%	9%	83	0%	0%	-5.9	141	$14
23 Proj	630	77	21	85	0	272	18	2	270	344	441	109	106	110	7	81	0.40	46	23	32	30	108		6%	104	85	14%	12%	77	1%	30%	14.9	145	$20

Franco,Wander

Age: 22	Pos: SS	Health	D	LIMA Plan	A
Bats: B	Ht: 5' 10" Wt: 189	PT/Exp	C	Rand Var	0
		Consist	B	MM	2455

6-33-.277 with 8 SB in 344 PA at TAM. Injuries (quad strain, broken hamate bone right hand) delayed his progress but didn't derail it. Elite ct% and Eye remain impressive for his age and experience. Capable of double-digit HR/SB right now, while year-long emergence of LD stroke opens door to... UP: batting title

Yr Tm	PA	R	HR	RBI	SB	BA	xHR	xSB	xBA	OBP	SLG	OPS+	vL+	vR+	bb%	ct%	Eye	G	L	F	h%	HctX	QBaB	Brl%	PX	xPX	HR/F	xHR/F	Spd	SBA%	SB%	RAR	BPX	R$
18																																		
19																																		
20																																		
21 TAM *	484	81	13	71	7	293	6	8	291	347	496	116	139	96	8	86	0.61	45	20	34	32	102	CCf	5%	103	80	8%	7%	140	10%	56%	21.7	338	$21
22 TAM *	368	48	6	35	8	283	7	6	292	341	420	108	110	104	8	89	0.80	44	25	31	30	111	CDf	4%	82	81	7%	8%	104	10%	87%	10.5	245	$13
1st Half	247	35	5	23	5	262	5	4	294	312	403	101	107	98	7	88	0.63	47	24	29	28	114	CDf	5%	82	70	9%	9%	107	10%	100%	1.8	231	$12
2nd Half	122	14	1	12	3	327	2	2	289	397	456	121	119	117	10	91	1.23	39	25	36	35	103	DCf	4%	83	105	3%	6%	104	10%	72%	7.5	286	$2
23 Proj	595	86	11	70	12	297	12	11	288	354	455	112	130	106	8	88	0.79	43	23	34	32	105		4%	94	86	7%	7%	122	10%	74%	29.5	293	$29

Frazier,Adam

Age: 31	Pos: 2B RF	Health	A	LIMA Plan	B
Bats: L	Ht: 5' 10" Wt: 185	PT/Exp	A	Rand Var	+3
		Consist	D	MM	1335

Career-high .305 BA he boasted in 2021 unsurprisingly proved to be unsustainable. PRO: Owns top-tier ct%; decent Spd. CON: poor contact quality/lack of power; poor SB% could curtail green lights; shakiness vL (lifetime .660 OPS vL) could cost him playing time. 2nd half BA is the correct, and uninspiring, baseline.

Yr Tm	PA	R	HR	RBI	SB	BA	xHR	xSB	xBA	OBP	SLG	OPS+	vL+	vR+	bb%	ct%	Eye	G	L	F	h%	HctX	QBaB	Brl%	PX	xPX	HR/F	xHR/F	Spd	SBA%	SB%	RAR	BPX	R$
18 PIT *	481	59	10	48	2	251	7	6	266	309	397	95	78	113	8	83	0.49	49	20	31	28	106	CCa	4%	87	79	12%	8%	106	8%	21%	-4.4	163	$8
19 PIT	608	80	10	50	5	278	11	9	283	336	417	104	93	107	7	86	0.53	41	26	33	31	89	CCb	2%	70	69	6%	7%	127	7%	50%	-1.3	204	$13
20 PIT	230	22	7	23	1	230	6	2	250	297	364	88	70	92	7	83	0.49	44	21	35	25	85	DCd	4%	68	67	11%	10%	86	7%	25%	-8.7	120	$9
21 2 NL	639	83	5	43	10	305	5	11	288	368	411	107	102	109	8	88	0.70	41	29	30	34	86	DCb	1%	62	53	3%	3%	127	8%	67%	17.1	219	$23
22 SEA	602	61	3	42	11	238	4	9	250	301	311	87	81	89	8	87	0.63	41	24	35	27	79	DCc	2%	46	55	2%	2%	108	11%	65%	-10.1	110	$10
1st Half	329	32	2	21	2	219	2	5	262	287	290	81	83	81	9	87	0.74	41	26	33	25	71	DCc	1%	47	39	2%	2%	85	11%	33%	-12.3	107	$3
2nd Half	273	29	1	21	9	262	2	4	238	319	336	93	78	99	7	86	0.51	41	21	37	30	88	DBb	2%	46	74	1%	3%	131	11%	82%	-1.4	117	$11
23 Proj	490	57	5	38	8	263	5	10	261	326	361	95	87	98	8	86	0.60	42	25	33	30	85		2%	61	60	4%	4%	119	10%	64%	2.7	153	$15

Freeman,Freddie

Age: 33	Pos: 1B	Health	A	LIMA Plan	C
Bats: L	Ht: 6' 5" Wt: 220	PT/Exp	A	Rand Var	-2
		Consist	D	MM	4255

Produced the highest R$ of his career. Strong plate skills, HctX, and LD% have sparked a .300+ BA in six of the past seven seasons with no sign of slowing down. History of underperforming xHR, so don't count on more than a modest HR uptick: just not enough FBs for that. Throw in near double-digit SB, elite skills make him a terrific foundation piece.

Yr Tm	PA	R	HR	RBI	SB	BA	xHR	xSB	xBA	OBP	SLG	OPS+	vL+	vR+	bb%	ct%	Eye	G	L	F	h%	HctX	QBaB	Brl%	PX	xPX	HR/F	xHR/F	Spd	SBA%	SB%	RAR	BPX	R$
18 ATL	707	94	23	98	10	309	33	12	290	388	505	120	122	116	11	79	0.58	36	32	31	36	121	CBa	9%	119	123	15%	21%	83	6%	77%	34.6	193	$31
19 ATL	692	113	38	121	6	295	42	9	296	389	549	130	104	138	11	79	0.69	38	28	34	32	128	BBa	13%	128	133	24%	26%	90	5%	67%	36.0	267	$31
20 ATL	262	51	13	53	2	341	16	3	326	462	640	146	93	163	17	83	1.22	32	31	37	37	146	ABa	15%	162	143	20%	24%	93	2%	100%	30.2	500	$39
21 ATL	695	120	31	83	8	300	39	7	285	393	503	123	103	131	12	82	0.79	43	24	33	32	129	ACb	12%	104	114	19%	24%	103	5%	73%	35.9	265	$33
22 LA	708	117	21	100	13	325	32	9	295	407	511	130	115	136	12	83	0.82	39	27	34	36	135	ACa	10%	116	140	12%	18%	101	7%	81%	53.1	283	$43
1st Half	361	52	10	50	7	302	16	4	284	382	489	123	113	128	11	79	0.62	37	28	35	35	122	ABa	11%	123	138	11%	18%	97	7%	100%	22.3	241	$33
2nd Half	347	65	11	50	6	350	16	5	307	432	535	137	118	143	13	88	1.19	40	27	33	37	148	ACa	9%	110	141	13%	18%	102	7%	67%	35.4	334	$42
23 Proj	665	116	25	102	9	315	34	11	296	404	520	128	108	136	13	83	0.85	39	27	34	34	135		11%	124	131	16%	21%	96	7%	75%	57.4	301	$41

Freeman,Tyler

Age: 24	Pos: 3B	Health	A	LIMA Plan	D+
Bats: R	Ht: 6' 0" Wt: 170	PT/Exp	D	Rand Var	+1
		Consist	D	MM	0321

0-3-.247 with 1 SB in 86 PA at CLE. Made MLB debut in August and displayed the same bat-to-ball ability he did in the minors. Problem is he doesn't draw many walks, has no power, and his SB% has been subpar. OK, that's more than one problem. Maybe there's enough contact here to be a one-category BA asset, but he's going to have to show it first.

Yr Tm	PA	R	HR	RBI	SB	BA	xHR	xSB	xBA	OBP	SLG	OPS+	vL+	vR+	bb%	ct%	Eye	G	L	F	h%	HctX	QBaB	Brl%	PX	xPX	HR/F	xHR/F	Spd	SBA%	SB%	RAR	BPX	R$
18																																		
19																																		
20																																		
21 aa	171	21	2	16	3	295		2		322	423	102			4	86	0.28				34				79				103	13%	60%		181	$4
22 CLE *	398	39	4	29	5	224	0	8	236	260	276	76	88	83	5	87	0.38	52	18	30	25	68	DCf	2%	32	34	0%	0%	116	7%	66%	-15.3	69	$3
1st Half	223	23	2	20	2	208		4	237	243	268	72	0	0	4	88	0.40	44	20	36	23	0			36	-14	0%		112	7%	43%	-12.7	93	-$1
2nd Half	175	16	1	9	3	245	0	4	226	283	286	81	88	83	5	85	0.36	52	18	30	28	67	DCf	2%	26	34	0%	0%	128	7%	100%	-5.2	38	-$2
23 Proj	245	26	1	19	4	249	1	4	243	309	315	87	91	84	4	86	0.33	52	18	30	28	60		1%	46	31	2%	2%	120	8%	69%	-5.6	109	$6

Frelick,Sal

Age: 23	Pos: CF	Health	A	LIMA Plan	D
Bats: L	Ht: 5' 9" Wt: 175	PT/Exp	C	Rand Var	
		Consist	F	MM	1331

Multi-sport high school star was the 15th overall pick in the 2021 amateur draft after three years at Boston College. He appeared at three levels in 2022, rising from Single-A to AAA. Speedy outfielder with good bat-to-ball ability, limited power, and good CF glove. Rapid rise to MIL is encouraging, but he's still developing, so be patient in keeper leagues.

Yr Tm	PA	R	HR	RBI	SB	BA	xHR	xSB	xBA	OBP	SLG	OPS+	vL+	vR+	bb%	ct%	Eye	G	L	F	h%	HctX	QBaB	Brl%	PX	xPX	HR/F	xHR/F	Spd	SBA%	SB%	RAR	BPX	R$
18																																		
19																																		
20																																		
21																																		
22 a/a	442	55	7	35	13	286		7		332	396	103			6	86	0.49				32				66				119	16%	69%		162	$17
1st Half	149	17	1	9	3	244		2		285	345	89			5	80	0.29				30				63				137	16%	71%		86	-$3
2nd Half	293	38	5	26	10	309		5	265	358	424	111			7	89	0.69	44	20	36	33	0			67	-14	0%		113	16%	68%	11.5	207	$23
23 Proj	175	22	2	14	5	282	2	5	259	326	373	97	96	97	6	85	0.45	50	21	29	32	88		6%	58		4%	4%	121	14%	69%	2.3	159	$7

Friedl,T.J.

Age: 27	Pos: LF CF	Health	A	LIMA Plan	C
Bats: L	Ht: 5' 10" Wt: 180	PT/Exp	C	Rand Var	0
		Consist	A	MM	2403

8-25-.240 with 7 SB in 258 PA at CIN. Minor-league speedster surprised with big-league power spike. Extreme FB% is good for HR, but it hurts his BA, which caps upside of his most consistent asset, Spd/SB. <Insert clip of Willie Mays Hayes doing pushups every time he hit a ball in the air.> Still, power/speed blend worth an end-game bid.

Yr Tm	PA	R	HR	RBI	SB	BA	xHR	xSB	xBA	OBP	SLG	OPS+	vL+	vR+	bb%	ct%	Eye	G	L	F	h%	HctX	QBaB	Brl%	PX	xPX	HR/F	xHR/F	Spd	SBA%	SB%	RAR	BPX	R$
18 aa	286	40	2	14	16	251		4		316	326	86			9	76	0.39				33				49				135	28%	75%		3	$8
19 aa	252	33	5	25	11	216		9		298	356	91			10	74	0.45				27				78				133	27%	72%		78	$4
20																																		
21 CIN *	457	55	11	30	10	229	0	7	219	296	360	90	113	106	9	80	0.48	30	20	50	26	87	CAd	7%	70	70	7%	0%	137	17%	55%	-15.8	142	$8
22 CIN *	483	56	14	51	14	233	5	11	227	298	404	99	157	102	8	77	0.40	32	18	50	27	98	FAf	5%	103	116	9%	6%	124	16%	76%	0.2	155	$14
1st Half	225	24	4	20	6	202	1	5	209	268	334	85	87	75	8	73	0.33	34	18	48	26	89	FBf	3%	89	105	0%	3%	117	16%	84%	-7.1	52	$4
2nd Half	257	32	10	31	7	262	4	7	243	325	466	112	206	119	9	80	0.48	31	17	51	28	106	FAd	6%	114	123	14%	7%	130	16%	70%	7.3	245	$19
23 Proj	315	39	10	28	10	236	4	9	223	315	397	99	144	95	9	78	0.43	32	18	50	27	99		5%	97	116	9%	3%	131	14%	69%	1.0	135	$11

GREG PYRON

Gallo,Joey

Age: 29 Pos: LF RF | Bats: L Ht: 6' 5" Wt: 250
Health B | PT/Exp A | Consist C
LIMA Plan D+ | Rand Var +5 | MM 5303

Bronx blunder didn't get much better after Aug trade to LA. Strikeouts went from bad to worst (lowest ct% in majors, min. 250 AB) while xPX, xHR/F hint the power has gone from elite to just "great". HR ceiling no longer high enough to justify the extreme BA drag. However, as the player most affected by the shift, the new rules might buy him some points.

Yr	Tm	PA	R	HR	RBI	SB	BA	xHR	xSB	xBA	OBP	SLG	OPS+	vL+	vR+	bb%	ct%	Eye	G	L	F	h%	HctX	QBaB	Brl%	PX	xPX	HR/F	xHR/F	Spd	SBA%	SB%	RAR	BPX	R$
18	TEX	577	82	40	92	3	206	46	7	238	312	498	109	109	106	13	59	0.36	30	21	50	25	105	AAb	23%	213	180	28%	32%	75	6%	43%	3.1	183	$16
19	TEX	297	54	22	49	4	253	28	3	240	389	598	136	163	124	18	53	0.46	27	26	47	37	95	AAc	26%	251	199	37%	47%	89	8%	67%	18.3	278	$11
20	TEX	226	23	10	26	2	181	11	2	194	301	378	90	82	94	13	59	0.37	27	18	55	24	99	CAf	14%	137	173	17%	18%	89	4%	100%	-11.1	0	$7
21	2 AL	616	90	38	77	6	199	40	5	212	351	458	111	104	115	18	57	0.52	33	17	51	25	88	BAf	19%	179	160	27%	29%	79	4%	100%	8.1	131	$13
22	2 TM	410	48	19	47	3	160	21	3	186	280	357	90	61	98	14	53	0.34	28	19	53	22	77	CAf	17%	160	141	19%	21%	100	3%	100%	-10.8	3	$1
1st Half		224	25	9	18	1	165	13	2	183	277	325	85	57	96	13	54	0.34	29	23	49	24	70	CAf	18%	130	128	18%	25%	83	3%	100%	-8.0	-90	$0
2nd Half		186	23	10	29	2	154	8	1	194	285	397	97	72	100	14	53	0.35	27	15	58	19	86	BAc	16%	198	158	21%	17%	113	3%	100%	-3.6	114	$6
23	**Proj**	**420**	**56**	**24**	**55**	**4**	**213**	**26**	**4**	**205**	**338**	**453**	**110**	**100**	**113**	**15**	**55**	**0.39**	**29**	**18**	**53**	**30**	**86**		**18%**	**191**	**157**	**23%**	**25%**	**94**	**4%**	**93%**	**12.1**	**79**	**$9**

Gamel,Ben

Age: 31 Pos: LF RF DH | Bats: L Ht: 5' 11" Wt: 177
Health C | PT/Exp B | Consist A
LIMA Plan D+ | Rand Var +3 | MM 3223

9-46-.232 in 423 PA at PIT. Highest PA total since 2017; just didn't do much with it. Fewer LDs neutralized ct% gains; streak of "C"s from QBaB says power is mired in mediocrity; hasn't earned playing time vL. There isn't a plus skill on this page, so even if he gets another long look, you're better off chasing higher ceilings elsewhere.

Yr	Tm	PA	R	HR	RBI	SB	BA	xHR	xSB	xBA	OBP	SLG	OPS+	vL+	vR+	bb%	ct%	Eye	G	L	F	h%	HctX	QBaB	Brl%	PX	xPX	HR/F	xHR/F	Spd	SBA%	SB%	RAR	BPX	R$
18	SEA *	384	51	2	31	10	276	3	6	256	349	387	99	88	98	10	78	0.51	47	25	28	35	75	CDb	3%	74	50	2%	5%	134	12%	77%	1.7	107	$10
19	MIL	356	47	7	33	2	248	7	8	231	337	373	98	125	90	11	67	0.38	44	26	29	35	87	CCb	4%	85	89	11%	11%	113	4%	50%	-9.6	-26	$4
20	MIL	127	13	3	10	0	237	3	1	261	315	404	95	87	97	10	66	0.33	37	39	24	33	78	CCc	7%	116	73	17%	17%	104	7%	0%	-4.5	40	$3
21	2 TM	400	43	8	26	3	247	9	6	230	347	388	101	85	107	13	69	0.49	31	29	40	33	96	CBd	8%	94	128	9%	10%	128	8%	33%	-2.9	69	$5
22	PIT *	455	47	10	48	5	226	8	6	239	311	359	95	74	107	11	74	0.47	43	22	35	28	114	CCc	6%	92	107	10%	9%	99	5%	83%	-3.3	76	$7
1st Half		195	25	4	20	3	247	3	3	262	328	369	99	102	108	11	74	0.46	42	32	26	32	120	CDc	6%	86	85	11%	11%	105	5%	75%	0.4	66	$5
2nd Half		260	22	6	28	2	211	6	3	224	304	351	93	62	106	11	74	0.47	44	15	41	26	111	CCc	7%	97	120	9%	9%	97	5%	100%	-4.4	86	$5
23	**Proj**	**350**	**38**	**8**	**31**	**3**	**237**	**8**	**4**	**240**	**327**	**378**	**98**	**81**	**104**	**11**	**71**	**0.45**	**39**	**26**	**35**	**31**	**102**		**7%**	**102**	**106**	**10%**	**10%**	**110**	**6%**	**54%**	**1.7**	**68**	**$8**

Garcia,Adolis

Age: 30 Pos: RF CF DH | Bats: R Ht: 6' 1" Wt: 205
Health A | PT/Exp A | Consist D
LIMA Plan B | Rand Var -5 | MM 4415

Put 2021's 2nd half fade in rearview with monster breakout, and it came with plenty of skill support: xHR was in lockstep with HR; SB prowess kept the light green; upticks in ct%, xBA kept BA out of the gutter. Hard to project 25/25 again—only three others did so in 2022—but Mayberry confirms this is a potent power/speed blend.

Yr	Tm	PA	R	HR	RBI	SB	BA	xHR	xSB	xBA	OBP	SLG	OPS+	vL+	vR+	bb%	ct%	Eye	G	L	F	h%	HctX	QBaB	Brl%	PX	xPX	HR/F	xHR/F	Spd	SBA%	SB%	RAR	BPX	R$
18	STL *	433	49	16	54	7	209	0	3	228	227	384	82	0	60	2	72	0.09	50	10	40	25	53	DBf	0%	113	-2	0%	0%	99	18%	68%	-21.7	43	$7
19	aaa	507	71	23	71	10	205		8		230	396	87			3	62	0.09				28				118				116	31%	47%		-48	$10
20	TEX	7	0	0	0	0	0	0	0	0	143	0	19	0	67	14	33	0.25	50	0	50	0	0	FDf		0	-26	0%	0%	100	0%	0%	-1.1	-820	-$4
21	TEX	622	77	31	90	16	243	31	3	231	286	454	102	95	105	5	67	0.16	43	16	41	31	106	BBd	12%	134	127	20%	20%	112	18%	76%	-1.7	73	$23
22	TEX	657	88	27	101	25	250	28	15	247	300	456	107	104	108	6	70	0.22	41	19	40	31	120	ACf	13%	142	139	16%	16%	140	24%	81%	8.1	169	$32
1st Half		328	47	15	51	12	246	15	7	254	287	466	106	85	114	5	71	0.19	37	23	40	30	118	ABd	12%	145	150	17%	17%	131	24%	86%	3.6	176	$33
2nd Half		329	41	12	50	13	253	13	8	239	313	447	108	118	101	7	69	0.24	45	15	40	33	121	ACf	14%	138	128	14%	16%	139	24%	76%	4.2	148	$31
23	**Proj**	**595**	**78**	**27**	**89**	**19**	**246**	**24**	**16**	**238**	**290**	**451**	**103**	**99**	**104**	**5**	**68**	**0.17**	**42**	**18**	**40**	**31**	**114**		**12%**	**143**	**133**	**17%**	**16%**	**123**	**19%**	**75%**	**6.3**	**101**	**$28**

García,Avisaíl

Age: 32 Pos: RF | Bats: R Ht: 6' 4" Wt: 250
Health C | PT/Exp D | Consist D
LIMA Plan C+ | Rand Var 0 | MM 3215

8-35-.224 in 380 PA at MIA. Complete dud featured back, hand issues in April, June; IL stints in Aug/Sept (hamstring). On the field, GB% spike and softer contact drove HR outage; the latter took BA/xBA down with it. An injury-related pass might work given track record—he still owns 2019, 2021 skills—but only as a speculative dart.

Yr	Tm	PA	R	HR	RBI	SB	BA	xHR	xSB	xBA	OBP	SLG	OPS+	vL+	vR+	bb%	ct%	Eye	G	L	F	h%	HctX	QBaB	Brl%	PX	xPX	HR/F	xHR/F	Spd	SBA%	SB%	RAR	BPX	R$
18	CHW *	412	51	22	56	3	240	20	5	247	282	455	99	107	91	5	70	0.20	48	17	34	28	99	BCc	12%	130	101	21%	22%	108	5%	75%	-3.4	100	$11
19	TAM	530	61	20	72	10	282	26	5	260	332	464	110	108	110	6	74	0.25	46	22	32	34	103	BCc	12%	100	90	17%	22%	98	11%	71%	1.5	78	$18
20	MIL	207	20	2	15	1	238	4	3	232	333	326	88	114	75	10	73	0.41	48	24	27	32	81	CDc	4%	63	68	6%	11%	82	7%	25%	-11.2	-44	$6
21	MIL	515	68	29	86	8	262	28	4	265	330	490	113	127	108	7	74	0.31	47	21	32	30	113	BCc	12%	128	117	26%	25%	70	10%	67%	9.8	135	$21
22	MIA *	411	33	8	36	5	221	10	5	208	259	310	81	81	83	5	68	0.16	56	18	26	30	88	CFd	7%	65	93	12%	15%	83	5%	100%	-15.0	-134	$4
1st Half		263	23	6	25	3	230	8	3	216	266	331	84	65	89	4	70	0.12	56	18	27	30	84	CFf	8%	70	96	13%	17%	84	5%	100%	-8.7	-100	$6
2nd Half		148	10	2	11	2	205	2	2	190	264	274	76	114	70	7	64	0.22	55	19	26	30	98	CFb	2%	55	87	11%	11%	88	5%	100%	-7.0	-197	-$5
23	**Proj**	**490**	**50**	**18**	**56**	**6**	**236**	**18**	**4**	**234**	**295**	**389**	**95**	**112**	**90**	**7**	**70**	**0.24**	**49**	**21**	**30**	**30**	**98**		**10%**	**103**	**97**	**19%**	**18%**	**78**	**5%**	**74%**	**-3.0**	**-34**	**$14**

Garcia,Dermis

Age: 25 Pos: 1B | Bats: R Ht: 6' 3" Wt: 200
Health A | PT/Exp C | Consist B
LIMA Plan D | Rand Var 0 | MM 4303

5-20-.207 in 125 PA at OAK. Received everyday 1B audition in Sept, which didn't go too well. Calling-card power carried over despite underlying skepticism from QBaB, xPX; and MLB plate skills (53% ct%, 0.15 Eye) say he was overmatched. Tack on minimal prospect pedigree and he's safe to cross off your end game sleeper list.

Yr	Tm	PA	R	HR	RBI	SB	BA	xHR	xSB	xBA	OBP	SLG	OPS+	vL+	vR+	bb%	ct%	Eye	G	L	F	h%	HctX	QBaB	Brl%	PX	xPX	HR/F	xHR/F	Spd	SBA%	SB%	RAR	BPX	R$
18																																			
19																																			
20																																			
21	aa	427	46	26	53	8	185		4		266	415	94			10	51	0.22				27				178				92	13%	78%		-12	$6
22	OAK *	381	41	11	44	2	195	5	6	197	248	343	84	73	101	7	57	0.16	46	18	36	31	85	DCf	14%	130	108	23%	23%	114	4%	64%	-14.5	-66	$1
1st Half		187	20	4	16	2	189		3	197	243	308	78	0	0	7	60	0.17	44	20	36	29	0			106	-14	0%		101	4%	64%	-10.4	-107	-$2
2nd Half		194	21	7	28	0	201	5	3	197	254	377	89	73	101	7	53	0.15	46	18	36	32	80	DCf	14%	157	108	23%	23%	120	4%	0%	-6.3	-31	$4
23	**Proj**	**280**	**30**	**10**	**34**	**3**	**203**	**13**	**3**	**186**	**273**	**356**	**87**	**68**	**96**	**8**	**54**	**0.19**	**40**	**20**	**40**	**33**	**72**		**12%**	**136**	**97**	**17%**	**23%**	**115**	**6%**	**76%**	**-8.5**	**-42**	**$5**

García,Leury

Age: 32 Pos: 2B OF | Bats: B Ht: 5' 8" Wt: 190
Health F | PT/Exp B | Consist C
LIMA Plan D | Rand Var +5 | MM 1311

Question: Why did CHW give him 315 plate appearances? Hmm... on-base skills? Nope; had the lowest OBP in baseball (min. 300 PA) as bb% collapsed. Power? QBaB shuts that down pretty quick. Speed? Maybe, but he didn't use it (SBA%). Another question: How many PA should he have on your roster? Answer: Zero.

Yr	Tm	PA	R	HR	RBI	SB	BA	xHR	xSB	xBA	OBP	SLG	OPS+	vL+	vR+	bb%	ct%	Eye	G	L	F	h%	HctX	QBaB	Brl%	PX	xPX	HR/F	xHR/F	Spd	SBA%	SB%	RAR	BPX	R$
18	CHW	275	23	4	32	12	271	4	4	248	303	376	91	105	83	3	73	0.13	49	29	23	36	81	CDa	3%	63	63	10%	10%	131	19%	92%	0.0	-27	$8
19	CHW	618	93	8	40	15	279	11	19	252	310	378	95	109	88	3	76	0.15	55	22	24	36	75	CDb	4%	59	45	8%	11%	142	13%	75%	-11.7	7	$18
20	CHW	63	6	3	8	0	271	3	1	244	317	441	101	179	88	6	85	0.44	50	18	32	28	96	CDd	6%	77	78	19%	19%	83	0%	0%	0.4	160	$2
21	CHW	474	60	5	54	6	267	6	4	251	335	376	98	95	99	9	77	0.42	56	20	24	34	83	FFd	3%	69	59	6%	8%	120	6%	75%	1.3	65	$12
22	CHW	315	38	3	20	2	210	5	3	225	233	267	71	60	74	2	78	0.11	50	20	29	26	71	DFf	4%	39	54	4%	7%	92	3%	100%	-15.6	-69	-$1
1st Half		209	22	2	14	1	202	4	2	228	226	268	70	73	69	3	78	0.14	49	21	30	25	69	DFf	6%	47	60	4%	9%	86	3%	100%	-12.2	-62	-$3
2nd Half		106	16	1	6	1	225	1	1	217	248	265	73	42	83	1	79	0.05	53	19	29	28	76	DFd	2%	24	42	4%	4%	102	3%	100%	-5.7	-100	-$5
23	**Proj**	**210**	**28**	**2**	**18**	**2**	**238**	**3**	**2**	**233**	**276**	**319**	**83**	**80**	**83**	**4**	**77**	**0.19**	**52**	**20**	**27**	**30**	**79**		**4%**	**54**	**56**	**6%**	**7%**	**109**	**5%**	**80%**	**-5.0**	**-25**	**$5**

García,Luis

Age: 23 Pos: SS 2B | Bats: L Ht: 6' 2" Wt: 224
Health A | PT/Exp B | Consist A
LIMA Plan B | Rand Var -1 | MM 2145

7-45-.275 in 377 PA at WAS. Called up in June and hit .327 in 104 AB, but cooled once Ks picked up and h% regressed in 2nd half. Dismal bb% and struggles vL put everyday playing time at risk, and while xHR/F says he deserved a few more bombs, GB tilt puts a lid on the HR ceiling. Still just a pup; just don't bank on sudden growth.

Yr	Tm	PA	R	HR	RBI	SB	BA	xHR	xSB	xBA	OBP	SLG	OPS+	vL+	vR+	bb%	ct%	Eye	G	L	F	h%	HctX	QBaB	Brl%	PX	xPX	HR/F	xHR/F	Spd	SBA%	SB%	RAR	BPX	R$
18																																			
19	aa	542	68	4	31	11	268		8		292	350	89			3	84	0.20				31				46				128	13%	69%		67	$11
20	WAS	139	18	2	16	1	276	2	2	259	302	366	89	37	106	4	78	0.17	61	23	16	34	82	FFf	5%	55	41	12%	12%	82	6%	50%	-4.6	-32	$9
21	WAS *	401	50	17	42	1	257	6	3	288	300	458	104	105	90	6	81	0.32	56	20	24	28	105	CFd	5%	109	68	13%	13%	87	5%	21%	1.2	200	$9
22	WAS *	574	57	13	68	5	272	12	5	264	302	413	101	81	107	4	77	0.19	51	22	27	33	103	CFc	8%	93	112	9%	16%	93	7%	56%	2.3	76	$18
1st Half		311	40	8	35	2	292	4	3	270	320	444	108	72	131	4	80	0.20	52	21	27	35	122	CFc	8%	93	130	7%	15%	117	7%	46%	9.0	131	$20
2nd Half		263	17	5	33	3	249	7	2	253	282	377	93	87	96	4	75	0.18	51	23	26	32	92	DFc	7%	92	101	11%	15%	74	7%	63%	-2.7	17	$9
23	**Proj**	**455**	**49**	**11**	**50**	**2**	**265**	**12**	**4**	**266**	**297**	**406**	**98**	**85**	**102**	**4**	**79**	**0.22**	**54**	**21**	**24**	**31**	**102**		**7%**	**92**	**88**	**13%**	**14%**	**86**	**6%**	**55%**	**3.4**	**95**	**$14**

RYAN BLOOMFIELD

Garcia,Maikel

Age: 23	Pos: SS	Health	A	LIMA Plan	D
Bats: R	Ht: 6' 0" Wt: 145	PT/Exp	C	Rand Var	0
		Consist	F	MM	1421

0-2-.318 in 23 PA at KC. Spent most of year stealing bases at AA and AAA (37, to be exact) save for two brief cups of coffee. A 47% GB% in upper minors fits his speed like a glove, but there's little power to speak of while bb%/ct% MLEs question the on-base ability. Likely to see time in 2023, but this has strong "one-trick pony" vibes.

Yr	Tm	PA	R	HR	RBI	SB	BA	xHR	xSB	xBA	OBP	SLG	OPS+	vL+	vR+	bb%	ct%	Eye	G	L	F	h%	HctX	QBaB	Brl%	PX	xPX	HR/F	xHR/F	Spd	SBA%	SB%	RAR	BPX	R$
18																																			
19																																			
20																																			
21																																			
22	KC *	544	66	6	40	24	246	0	8	248	295	351	91	158	68	6	78	0.32	53	18	29	31	40	DFd		78	30	0%	0%	144	28%	73%	-9.1	114	$18
1st Half		309	33	2	19	15	250		5	242	304	346	92	0	0	7	80	0.38	44	20	36	31	0			75	-14	0%		130	28%	81%	-4.8	117	$16
2nd Half		235	33	4	21	10	244	0	3	244	287	360	92	158	68	6	76	0.25	53	18	29	30	39	DFd		83	30	0%	0%	141	28%	64%	-6.2	90	$13
23	Proj	175	22	2	14	8	246	2	6	246	295	350	89	88	90	6	78	0.31	47	22	31	31	88		3%	78		5%	5%	126	22%	70%	-2.3	101	$4

Garlick,Kyle

Age: 31	Pos: LF RF	Health	F	LIMA Plan	D
Bats: R	Ht: 6' 1" Wt: 210	PT/Exp	F	Rand Var	-1
		Consist	D	MM	4021

.233-9-18 in 162 PA at MIN. Another injury-marred year; this one featured IL stints in four separate months (calf, hamstring, ribs, wrist). More of the same when on the field, as shaky plate skills drove another sub-.300 OBP despite decent power stroke. With short-side platoon likely entrenched, an easy name to cross off your list.

Yr	Tm	PA	R	HR	RBI	SB	BA	xHR	xSB	xBA	OBP	SLG	OPS+	vL+	vR+	bb%	ct%	Eye	G	L	F	h%	HctX	QBaB	Brl%	PX	xPX	HR/F	xHR/F	Spd	SBA%	SB%	RAR	BPX	R$
18	a/a	416	43	16	43	1	209		4		235	379	82			3	58	0.08				31				133				94	2%	100%		-77	$3
19	LA *	340	45	19	46	1	247	4	1	225	294	508	111	139	79	6	60	0.17	21	21	59	34	108	AAb	21%	178	213	18%	24%	93	4%	52%	-3.6	100	$7
20	PHI	23	0	0	3	0	136	0	0	162	174	182	47	33	55	0	68	0.00	47	20	33	20	110	CBa		41	7	0%	0%	96	0%	0%	-3.0	-252	-$4
21	MIN	107	17	5	10	1	232	7	0	253	280	465	102	119	76	6	68	0.19	37	22	41	29	81	CAb	13%	158	107	18%	25%	89	6%	100%	-0.1	142	$0
22	MIN *	205	26	11	22	0	221	7	2	224	265	413	96	113	90	6	64	0.16	40	22	38	28	89	BBd	10%	130	97	23%	18%	125	0%	0%	-3.3	31	$2
1st Half		121	15	8	19	0	257	6	2	248	312	489	113	159	82	7	67	0.25	38	24	38	31	112	ABc	14%	145	123	27%	27%	136	0%	0%	3.4	148	$1
2nd Half		85	11	3	3	0	171	1	1	192	196	308	72	56	96	3	59	0.08	42	20	38	24	63	CCf	4%	107	63	18%	6%	104	0%	0%	-6.0	-141	-$7
23	Proj	210	29	11	20	0	219	10	1	240	267	429	97	108	83	5	67	0.16	39	22	39	27	82		10%	149	96	20%	19%	90	2%	0%	-1.4	32	$5

Garrett,Stone

Age: 27	Pos: LF	Health	A	LIMA Plan	D+
Bats: R	Ht: 6' 2" Wt: 195	PT/Exp	B	Rand Var	+1
		Consist	A	MM	3303

.276-4-10 with 3 SB in 84 PA at ARI. Called up in Aug after back-to-back 25/15 seasons in minors. Tiny-sample contact quality gets QBaB approval and had green light in majors, but awful batting Eye questions his long-term ability to stick. Flyer-worthy based on counting stats alone; just don't give him too long of a leash.

Yr	Tm	PA	R	HR	RBI	SB	BA	xHR	xSB	xBA	OBP	SLG	OPS+	vL+	vR+	bb%	ct%	Eye	G	L	F	h%	HctX	QBaB	Brl%	PX	xPX	HR/F	xHR/F	Spd	SBA%	SB%	RAR	BPX	R$
18																																			
19	aa	431	58	13	67	16	228		5		263	390	90			4	66	0.14				31				99				112	31%	67%		-44	$12
20																																			
21	a/a	424	38	14	47	10	206		3		229	347	79			3	65	0.08				28				94				87	24%	62%		-123	$6
22	ARI *	486	50	17	58	11	206	3	10	205	237	379	87	123	114	4	66	0.12	34	14	52	27	92	AAc	10%	128	135	15%	12%	128	21%	75%	-17.3	48	$9
1st Half		274	25	9	32	7	204		6	228	240	373	87	0	0	5	66	0.14	44	20	36	27	0			123	-14	0%		130	21%	74%	-9.3	41	$10
2nd Half		212	25	8	26	3	208	3	4	210	234	386	88	123	114	3	66	0.10	34	14	52	27	92	AAc	10%	135	135	15%	12%	110	21%	78%	-6.7	45	$7
23	Proj	350	36	12	42	6	220	10	8	217	253	380	88	89	85	4	65	0.10	39	21	40	30	83		9%	120	122	14%	12%	120	16%	67%	-8.4	-32	$9

Garver,Mitch

Age: 32	Pos: DH	Health	F	LIMA Plan	B
Bats: R	Ht: 6' 1" Wt: 220	PT/Exp	D	Rand Var	+5
		Consist	D	MM	4123

Injury bug bit again with elbow issue in May, season-ending forearm surgery in July. Small-sample caveats aside, he rediscovered pre-2020 ct%, though h% (and thus BA) dip wasn't all bad luck given extreme FB%. Now has IL stints in four years straight, but power baseline makes him a decent rebound target if healthy in the spring.

Yr	Tm	PA	R	HR	RBI	SB	BA	xHR	xSB	xBA	OBP	SLG	OPS+	vL+	vR+	bb%	ct%	Eye	G	L	F	h%	HctX	QBaB	Brl%	PX	xPX	HR/F	xHR/F	Spd	SBA%	SB%	RAR	BPX	R$
18	MIN	335	38	7	45	0	268	9	5	246	335	414	100	83	106	9	76	0.40	40	23	38	33	114	CCd	6%	95	122	8%	10%	107	0%	0%	12.3	107	$7
19	MIN	359	70	31	67	0	273	27	1	278	365	630	138	163	124	11	72	0.47	39	14	47	28	118	ABd	16%	186	159	29%	25%	91	0%	0%	38.2	330	$15
20	MIN	81	8	2	5	0	167	2	0	150	247	264	68	107	49	9	49	0.19	39	22	39	30	82	AAf	8%	79	77	14%	14%	101	0%	0%	-5.1	-368	-$2
21	MIN *	271	32	13	35	1	247	15	0	242	341	479	113	100	136	12	65	0.41	31	23	46	32	122	AAc	17%	157	183	21%	24%	60	3%	50%	10.6	119	$6
22	TEX	215	23	10	24	1	207	8	1	229	298	404	99	144	82	11	72	0.43	34	17	49	23	105	CAd	9%	126	133	15%	12%	88	4%	50%	1.3	131	$1
1st Half		198	22	10	22	1	217	7	1	232	298	429	103	150	83	10	71	0.39	33	17	50	25	106	CAd	8%	137	132	16%	11%	95	4%	50%	2.7	152	$5
2nd Half		17	1	0	2	0	77	1	0	187	294	77	53	35	58	19	85	1.50	45	18	36	9	101	CDd	13%	0	144	0%	25%	83	4%	0%	-1.4	10	-$11
23	Proj	350	52	16	53	1	245	19	3	244	330	459	110	132	98	11	71	0.42	36	20	44	29	104		10%	144	127	17%	19%	84	4%	50%	7.4	212	$13

Giménez,Andrés

Age: 24	Pos: 2B	Health	A	LIMA Plan	B
Bats: L	Ht: 5' 11" Wt: 161	PT/Exp	A	Rand Var	-5
		Consist	C	MM	2525

A five-category breakout, though repeat odds are a mixed bag. PRO: ct% growth a big step forward, held it all year; SB prowess should keep the light green. CON: xBA, massive h% spike still hint at BA pullback; xPX, QBaB say the power is still subpar. VERDICT: A legit age-24 growth season, but could very well be his career year.

Yr	Tm	PA	R	HR	RBI	SB	BA	xHR	xSB	xBA	OBP	SLG	OPS+	vL+	vR+	bb%	ct%	Eye	G	L	F	h%	HctX	QBaB	Brl%	PX	xPX	HR/F	xHR/F	Spd	SBA%	SB%	RAR	BPX	R$
18	aa	145	16	0	14	9	250		2		291	321	82			5	82	0.33				30				52				101	36%	73%		47	$3
19	aa	456	54	9	37	28	235		19		276	363	88			5	74	0.21				30				74				124	47%	64%		11	$15
20	NYM	132	22	3	12	8	263	2	10	237	333	398	97	96	98	5	76	0.25	45	21	34	32	64	DCf	3%	70	35	10%	7%	178	25%	89%	-0.7	108	$16
21	CLE *	428	45	12	38	17	232	4	12	222	269	382	89	78	89	5	70	0.17	50	13	38	30	83	DDf	4%	99	85	10%	8%	112	26%	79%	-10.0	23	$12
22	CLE	557	66	17	69	20	297	15	25	263	371	466	119	124	117	6	77	0.30	46	21	33	36	87	DCd	6%	107	79	14%	12%	141	14%	87%	30.7	176	$30
1st Half		249	27	9	38	6	298	9	10	273	350	484	118	98	124	5	78	0.24	45	23	32	35	96	CCc	8%	114	89	16%	16%	137	14%	75%	12.0	193	$19
2nd Half		308	39	8	31	14	297	6	15	255	388	451	119	148	110	8	77	0.35	47	19	34	36	78	FCf	5%	102	69	12%	9%	142	14%	93%	15.5	166	$28
23	Proj	560	63	15	59	21	269	14	16	241	337	417	105	107	104	6	75	0.25	48	18	35	33	82		5%	99	76	11%	10%	137	13%	79%	12.7	109	$27

Goldschmidt,Paul

Age: 35	Pos: 1B DH	Health	A	LIMA Plan	C
Bats: R	Ht: 6' 3" Wt: 220	PT/Exp	A	Rand Var	-5
		Consist	B	MM	4445

Almost reached last year's "UP: 40 HR", stuffed the rest of the stat sheet along the way. Tough to bank on a $40 encore, but skills say he can come close: h% baseline, xBA say he can flirt with .300; consistent barrage of barrels sets high HR floor; hasn't been caught stealing since 2019. Tack on "AAB" reliability and he's a fine early building block.

Yr	Tm	PA	R	HR	RBI	SB	BA	xHR	xSB	xBA	OBP	SLG	OPS+	vL+	vR+	bb%	ct%	Eye	G	L	F	h%	HctX	QBaB	Brl%	PX	xPX	HR/F	xHR/F	Spd	SBA%	SB%	RAR	BPX	R$
18	ARI	689	95	33	83	7	290	40	11	267	389	533	124	128	119	13	71	0.52	39	25	36	36	121	BBc	14%	153	139	22%	26%	121	6%	64%	35.7	233	$28
19	STL	680	97	34	97	3	260	39	8	251	346	476	114	134	108	11	72	0.47	38	22	39	30	119	BBb	11%	116	140	20%	23%	102	2%	75%	4.2	137	$20
20	STL	230	31	6	21	1	304	10	2	264	417	466	117	134	114	16	77	0.86	35	28	38	37	88	CCc	11%	97	114	11%	18%	100	1%	100%	6.5	208	$18
21	STL	679	102	31	99	12	294	43	5	269	365	514	121	145	115	10	77	0.49	36	24	40	33	131	ABc	14%	125	141	16%	23%	102	7%	100%	33.4	238	$34
22	STL	649	106	35	115	7	317	32	9	282	404	578	139	186	127	12	75	0.56	40	19	41	37	110	BBc	12%	169	131	20%	18%	97	4%	100%	62.0	310	$42
1st Half		345	61	19	65	3	340	17	5	292	423	617	147	198	136	12	77	0.60	37	20	43	39	116	BBc	12%	178	149	19%	17%	84	4%	100%	44.7	348	$45
2nd Half		304	45	16	50	4	291	15	4	268	382	533	129	175	116	12	73	0.52	45	18	38	34	104	ABc	11%	157	111	22%	21%	109	4%	100%	21.8	262	$32
23	Proj	630	98	31	98	6	301	34	7	271	385	533	128	161	119	12	75	0.54	39	21	40	35	115		12%	150	131	18%	21%	101	5%	100%	52.6	259	$36

Gomes,Yan

Age: 35	Pos: CA	Health	B	LIMA Plan	D+
Bats: R	Ht: 6' 2" Wt: 212	PT/Exp	C	Rand Var	+3
		Consist	B	MM	2333

Scant production in backup role, as more contact wasn't necessarily a good thing. Sure, h% dip and xBA say he deserved a better fate, but power skills vanished, uptick in GBs didn't help, and plate patience sunk to new lows. Perhaps May oblique injury played a role, but even with some BA recovery, he's a two-catcher end gamer with little ceiling.

Yr	Tm	PA	R	HR	RBI	SB	BA	xHR	xSB	xBA	OBP	SLG	OPS+	vL+	vR+	bb%	ct%	Eye	G	L	F	h%	HctX	QBaB	Brl%	PX	xPX	HR/F	xHR/F	Spd	SBA%	SB%	RAR	BPX	R$
18	CLE	435	52	16	48	0	266	18	5	251	313	449	102	111	97	5	70	0.18	32	27	41	34	112	CAb	8%	125	142	14%	15%	98	0%	0%	13.8	77	$10
19	WAS	358	36	12	43	2	223	13	1	230	316	389	97	122	89	11	73	0.45	39	19	42	27	83	CAc	7%	94	91	12%	13%	85	2%	100%	-3.8	63	$3
20	WAS	119	14	4	13	1	284	4	1	262	319	468	105	126	97	5	80	0.27	36	24	40	33	101	BAc	6%	99	93	11%	11%	121	4%	100%	4.2	188	$8
21	2 TM	375	49	14	52	0	252	14	3	260	301	421	99	121	88	5	78	0.24	39	25	36	29	111	BCc	9%	95	118	14%	14%	90	0%	0%	3.2	100	$8
22	CHC	293	23	8	31	2	235	7	0	260	260	365	89	94	86	3	83	0.10	45	22	33	26	91	DDf	3%	78	91	10%	9%	60	4%	100%	-3.8	69	$3
1st Half		147	11	3	9	0	222	2	0	255	238	326	80	65	88	1	83	0.08	47	23	30	25	88	DDf	3%	65	90	8%	6%	67	4%	0%	-4.8	34	-$6
2nd Half		146	12	5	22	2	248	4	0	262	283	406	98	143	84	4	83	0.26	44	20	36	27	94	DCd	4%	93	93	12%	10%	72	4%	100%	1.4	128	$3
23	Proj	280	29	9	35	2	247	8	2	257	285	400	95	112	88	4	80	0.22	41	23	36	28	99		6%	94	102	12%	11%	80	4%	100%	3.5	101	$8

RYAN BLOOMFIELD

González,Luis

Age: 27 Pos: RF LF		Health	A	LIMA Plan	D+
Bats: L Ht: 6' 1" Wt: 185		PT/Exp	D	Rand Var	-5
		Consist	C	MM	1303

4-36-.254 with 10 SB in 350 PA at SF. Older prospect bounced between AAA and majors, as hot start quickly fizzled. SB total buoyed R$, but iffy success rate says those chances might dry up, xBA tanked in 2nd half, and there's no power to fall back on. History vL caps playing time too, so best to speculate elsewhere.

Yr	Tm	PA	R	HR	RBI	SB	BA	xHR	xSB	xBA	OBP	SLG	OPS+	vL+	vR+	bb%	ct%	Eye	G	L	F	h%	HctX	QBaB	Brl%	PX	xPX	HR/F	xHR/F	Spd	SBA%	SB%	RAR	BPX	R$
18																																			
19	aa	518	61	9	57	16	231		8		298	340	88			9	79	0.44				28				57				117	21%	62%		52	$11
20	CHW	2	1	0	0	0	0		0	0	500	0	66	130	0	0	0	0.00	0	0	0	0	0			0	-26	0%		123	0%	0%	-0.1	-1440	-$3
21	CHW *	163	18	5	14	6	190	0	1	183	280	322	83	68	140	11	64	0.34	33	17	50	26	130	CBc	0%	91	145	0%	0%	105	22%	72%	-7.6	-62	$1
22	SF *	435	39	7	43	12	245	5	15	220	314	357	95	75	106	9	73	0.38	46	17	37	32	80	DDf	3%	79	85	5%	6%	121	15%	73%	-3.0	45	$11
1st Half		234	25	5	29	9	280	3	8	245	344	424	109	76	126	9	74	0.38	44	21	35	36	85	DDf	3%	102	97	7%	7%	118	15%	67%	6.3	117	$15
2nd Half		201	15	2	15	3	206	1	7	188	280	279	79	75	80	9	72	0.37	48	13	39	27	74	FDf	3%	51	73	2%	2%	127	15%	100%	-7.6	-38	-$2
23	**Proj**	**350**	**35**	**4**	**33**	**11**	**218**	**5**	**9**	**193**	**299**	**297**	**83**	**68**	**90**	**10**	**70**	**0.36**	**46**	**16**	**38**	**30**	**78**		**3%**	**61**	**83**	**4%**	**6%**	**116**	**13%**	**73%**	**-10.5**	**-8**	**$5**

Gonzalez,Oscar

Age: 25 Pos: RF		Health	B	LIMA Plan	B
Bats: R Ht: 6' 2" Wt: 180		PT/Exp	A	Rand Var	-2
		Consist	A	MM	2135

11-43-.296 in 382 PA at CLE. Called up in May, hit stride after July IL stint (intercostal strain). PRO: ct% growth a great sign; it held strong amid 2nd half power recovery. CON: GB% tilt caps HR ceiling, over his BA skis in majors (35% h%), bb% puts OBP on thin ice. Still young, but more of a late-OF filler than potential breakout target.

Yr	Tm	PA	R	HR	RBI	SB	BA	xHR	xSB	xBA	OBP	SLG	OPS+	vL+	vR+	bb%	ct%	Eye	G	L	F	h%	HctX	QBaB	Brl%	PX	xPX	HR/F	xHR/F	Spd	SBA%	SB%	RAR	BPX	R$
18																																			
19	aa	99	7	1	9	0	187		1		211	272	67			3	81	0.16				22				52				95	0%	0%		15	-$4
20																																			
21	a/a	495	53	24	63	1	255		4		280	452	101			3	73	0.13				30				115				83	2%	40%		69	$13
22	CLE *	576	54	17	65	1	268	10	4	268	294	426	102	104	115	3	80	0.18	51	21	28	31	117	CFd	7%	102	89	13%	12%	113	3%	33%	-5.3	152	$16
1st Half		307	24	7	33	0	244	2	2	267	265	386	92	99	109	3	80	0.14	55	21	24	28	146	BFd	5%	94	74	9%	9%	108	3%	0%	-10.2	121	$8
2nd Half		268	29	9	30	1	290	8	2	268	320	458	110	107	118	4	80	0.22	49	21	31	33	103	CDd	8%	108	97	15%	14%	114	3%	33%	3.5	172	$16
23	**Proj**	**490**	**49**	**14**	**58**	**1**	**266**	**13**	**4**	**253**	**295**	**412**	**98**	**94**	**100**	**4**	**77**	**0.16**	**49**	**21**	**30**	**32**	**120**		**7%**	**98**	**88**	**13%**	**12%**	**114**	**5%**	**38%**	**2.4**	**118**	**$15**

Gordon,Nick

Age: 27 Pos: LF CF 2B		Health	A	LIMA Plan	C+
Bats: L Ht: 6' 0" Wt: 160		PT/Exp	B	Rand Var	-2
		Consist	B	MM	3433

A step forward as injuries led to everyday role in August. Surface HR total may not show it, but xHR and xPX say there was legit power growth; xBA uptick shows he didn't sell out for it. There are warts—low bb% puts OBP on shaky ground, platoon risk given issues vL—but a regular gig could make him... UP: 20/20 candidate.

Yr	Tm	PA	R	HR	RBI	SB	BA	xHR	xSB	xBA	OBP	SLG	OPS+	vL+	vR+	bb%	ct%	Eye	G	L	F	h%	HctX	QBaB	Brl%	PX	xPX	HR/F	xHR/F	Spd	SBA%	SB%	RAR	BPX	R$
18	a/a	572	53	6	42	17	230		7		268	325	80			5	79	0.25				28				58				122	18%	76%		33	$9
19	aaa	307	41	3	33	12	271		6		307	417	100			5	76	0.21				35				94				104	26%	72%		74	$9
20																																			
21	MIN *	292	27	6	30	15	240	6	4	244	284	355	88	71	94	6	74	0.24	52	22	26	30	133	ACa	7%	68	88	11%	16%	133	26%	82%	-6.7	23	$9
22	MIN	443	45	9	50	6	272	19	16	253	316	427	105	76	113	4	74	0.18	41	24	35	35	122	BCb	9%	110	135	8%	18%	130	10%	60%	4.3	117	$13
1st Half		183	20	4	12	3	275	7	7	250	315	421	104	79	109	4	74	0.16	43	25	31	35	126	BCb	11%	93	135	10%	18%	161	10%	50%	0.1	103	$3
2nd Half		260	25	5	38	3	269	11	9	257	317	432	106	75	116	5	74	0.20	39	23	38	35	118	BCb	8%	123	135	7%	16%	114	10%	75%	2.4	138	$13
23	**Proj**	**385**	**40**	**11**	**42**	**11**	**258**	**14**	**7**	**257**	**305**	**421**	**101**	**74**	**108**	**5**	**75**	**0.21**	**45**	**23**	**32**	**32**	**126**		**8%**	**110**	**116**	**12%**	**16%**	**132**	**10%**	**75%**	**4.5**	**80**	**$16**

Gorman,Nolan

Age: 23 Pos: 2B		Health	A	LIMA Plan	C+
Bats: L Ht: 6' 1" Wt: 210		PT/Exp	B	Rand Var	0
		Consist	A	MM	4205

14-35-.226 in 313 PA at STL. Arrived in May with plenty of prospect hype; results were a mixed bag. Power came as advertised per Brl% and xPX, but plethora of whiffs hints at growing pains and had just 19 PA against lefties in majors. Long-term outlook is bright, but low-BA platoon power bats are a dime-a-dozen in redraft leagues.

Yr	Tm	PA	R	HR	RBI	SB	BA	xHR	xSB	xBA	OBP	SLG	OPS+	vL+	vR+	bb%	ct%	Eye	G	L	F	h%	HctX	QBaB	Brl%	PX	xPX	HR/F	xHR/F	Spd	SBA%	SB%	RAR	BPX	R$
18																																			
19																																			
20																																			
21	a/a	505	48	16	51	5	230		5		269	368	87			5	74	0.20				28				81				88	6%	81%		-4	$8
22	STL *	493	67	24	52	3	223	17	4	215	282	417	99	93	103	8	61	0.21	27	25	48	31	93	BAb	14%	147	170	16%	20%	92	3%	100%	-3.3	17	$11
1st Half		286	43	16	34	2	251	7	3	232	305	466	109	97	112	7	62	0.21	22	31	47	34	92	BAb	13%	154	151	18%	18%	106	3%	100%	7.5	72	$21
2nd Half		207	25	8	18	1	187	10	2	195	250	352	85	89	95	8	59	0.21	31	19	50	27	93	CAc	16%	136	187	15%	21%	86	3%	100%	-6.9	-45	$3
23	**Proj**	**455**	**54**	**22**	**46**	**3**	**233**	**27**	**2**	**222**	**287**	**425**	**99**	**87**	**100**	**7**	**66**	**0.20**	**27**	**24**	**49**	**30**	**93**		**15%**	**136**	**173**	**16%**	**20%**	**82**	**3%**	**90%**	**4.0**	**1**	**$13**

Grandal,Yasmani

Age: 34 Pos: CA DH		Health	D	LIMA Plan	C+
Bats: B Ht: 6' 2" Wt: 225		PT/Exp	B	Rand Var	+4
		Consist	D	MM	3113

5-27-.202 in 376 PA at CHW. Dearth of on-field production bookended six summer weeks on IL (knee, back). Power outage was the headliner, as hard contact vanished and BA/HR drops were in sync with their "x" counterparts. Can't fully bank on injury rebound given age, but R$ baseline at least stands out in the second-catcher pool.

Yr	Tm	PA	R	HR	RBI	SB	BA	xHR	xSB	xBA	OBP	SLG	OPS+	vL+	vR+	bb%	ct%	Eye	G	L	F	h%	HctX	QBaB	Brl%	PX	xPX	HR/F	xHR/F	Spd	SBA%	SB%	RAR	BPX	R$
18	LA	518	65	24	68	2	241	24	7	248	349	466	109	96	111	14	72	0.58	41	17	42	28	108	CBd	12%	139	140	18%	18%	66	2%	67%	26.9	160	$13
19	MIL	632	79	28	77	5	246	29	4	259	380	468	117	129	112	17	73	0.78	39	23	38	28	114	BBc	11%	120	133	20%	20%	81	3%	83%	36.4	178	$15
20	CHW	194	27	8	27	0	230	7	1	222	351	422	103	118	99	15	64	0.52	36	23	41	31	109	BBc	8%	125	161	19%	16%	69	0%	0%	3.7	36	$11
21	CHW *	410	64	24	64	0	239	18	1	247	408	498	124	142	125	22	69	0.92	41	19	40	27	119	ACd	13%	150	153	28%	22%	62	0%	0%	26.7	231	$11
22	CHW *	421	19	7	32	1	210	5	1	212	312	289	85	108	72	13	77	0.64	43	21	36	25	83	BCf	5%	50	59	6%	6%	73	1%	100%	-6.8	-7	-$1
1st Half		201	6	2	15	1	185	3	0	180	294	237	75	117	63	14	74	0.60	43	18	40	24	75	BCf	6%	35	65	4%	6%	80	1%	100%	-7.5	-79	-$8
2nd Half		220	13	5	17	0	232	2	1	238	328	336	94	100	82	12	79	0.68	43	25	32	27	92	BCd	3%	62	54	8%	5%	77	1%	0%	0.5	59	$0
23	**Proj**	**385**	**39**	**15**	**45**	**1**	**241**	**13**	**1**	**236**	**364**	**416**	**108**	**126**	**103**	**16**	**73**	**0.71**	**41**	**21**	**38**	**28**	**100**		**8%**	**110**	**105**	**17%**	**15%**	**66**	**1%**	**90%**	**16.5**	**92**	**$10**

Greene,Riley

Age: 22 Pos: CF		Health	A	LIMA Plan	B
Bats: L Ht: 6' 3" Wt: 200		PT/Exp	B	Rand Var	-1
		Consist	D	MM	3415

5-42-.243 with 1 SB in 418 PA at DET. Broken foot pushed MLB debut to June. Lofty HR/SB ceiling as a prospect didn't materialize, but the power skills did (Brl%, xHR/F) and running game gets an injury-related pass. Contact remains a concern, but heed the "A-Rod 10-Step Path to Stardom," as age/pedigree makes him a lucrative dart throw.

Yr	Tm	PA	R	HR	RBI	SB	BA	xHR	xSB	xBA	OBP	SLG	OPS+	vL+	vR+	bb%	ct%	Eye	G	L	F	h%	HctX	QBaB	Brl%	PX	xPX	HR/F	xHR/F	Spd	SBA%	SB%	RAR	BPX	R$
18																																			
19																																			
20																																			
21	a/a	536	79	20	70	13	284		9		352	489	116			10	68	0.33				38				128				129	10%	93%		131	$24
22	DET *	484	53	6	46	3	250	13	10	230	313	356	95	105	93	8	69	0.30	56	20	24	35	98	BFd	10%	81	89	8%	21%	134	6%	44%	-2.3	0	$8
1st Half		139	19	2	12	3	253	0	3	259	335	361	98	95	122	11	79	0.58	53	22	25	31	122	DFf	3%	73	113	8%	0%	126	6%	76%	0.7	124	$0
2nd Half		345	34	4	34	0	248	12	7	217	307	354	94	108	88	7	65	0.23	57	20	24	37	91	BFd	11%	84	83	8%	24%	133	6%	0%	-4.3	-52	$11
23	**Proj**	**560**	**72**	**13**	**61**	**9**	**253**	**20**	**8**	**239**	**323**	**401**	**100**	**97**	**102**	**9**	**70**	**0.33**	**46**	**23**	**30**	**34**	**103**		**8%**	**104**	**95**	**12%**	**18%**	**144**	**8%**	**73%**	**9.1**	**65**	**$19**

Grichuk,Randal

Age: 31 Pos: RF CF		Health	A	LIMA Plan	B
Bats: R Ht: 6' 2" Wt: 216		PT/Exp	A	Rand Var	-2
		Consist	B	MM	4225

Potential boon from March trade to Coors was mostly for naught. Major GB% spike drove career-low HR total (min. 400 PA) while xBA repeat says BA gains were more a product of h% jump than underlying skill growth. 2nd half ct%/xPX combo keeps us interested; just needs launch angle (re)adjustment to capitalize.

Yr	Tm	PA	R	HR	RBI	SB	BA	xHR	xSB	xBA	OBP	SLG	OPS+	vL+	vR+	bb%	ct%	Eye	G	L	F	h%	HctX	QBaB	Brl%	PX	xPX	HR/F	xHR/F	Spd	SBA%	SB%	RAR	BPX	R$
18	TOR	462	60	25	61	3	245	26	5	260	301	502	108	107	106	6	71	0.22	35	18	47	29	95	BAf	14%	167	136	18%	18%	90	6%	60%	5.8	197	$13
19	TOR	628	75	31	80	2	232	28	6	247	280	457	102	109	98	6	72	0.21	39	19	42	27	93	BBf	9%	122	93	17%	16%	119	3%	67%	-21.6	130	$12
20	TOR	231	38	12	35	1	273	10	2	262	312	481	105	124	97	6	77	0.27	41	22	37	30	109	CCf	11%	110	95	19%	16%	95	4%	50%	0.3	156	$23
21	TOR	545	59	22	81	0	241	20	3	239	281	423	97	100	96	5	78	0.24	40	17	43	27	107	BBf	8%	103	98	13%	11%	87	3%	0%	-13.7	119	$11
22	COL	538	60	19	73	4	259	15	5	239	299	425	103	130	88	4	75	0.19	51	13	36	31	119	BDf	7%	105	114	14%	11%	126	3%	100%	2.1	110	$17
1st Half		256	28	8	35	2	251	5	2	222	293	389	96	121	85	5	72	0.18	53	14	33	32	103	CDf	4%	93	88	14%	9%	99	3%	100%	-2.3	7	$11
2nd Half		282	32	11	38	2	266	10	2	249	305	457	108	136	91	4	80	0.21	50	12	38	30	134	ACd	9%	114	135	14%	12%	138	3%	100%	4.6	190	$19
23	**Proj**	**525**	**63**	**23**	**75**	**2**	**259**	**18**	**4**	**247**	**300**	**452**	**104**	**123**	**96**	**5**	**76**	**0.21**	**45**	**15**	**39**	**30**	**113**		**8%**	**121**	**108**	**15%**	**12%**	**97**	**4%**	**66%**	**9.2**	**126**	**$20**

RYAN BLOOMFIELD

Grisham,Trent

Age: 26	Pos: CF	Health	A	LIMA Plan	C+
Bats: L	Ht: 5' 11" Wt: 224	PT/Exp	A	Rand Var	+5
		Consist	B	MM	4215

These are supposed to be his peak years. Instead, R$ took another dive thanks to lowest BA of any qualified hitter. Fluky h% only partly to blame, as xBA and 2nd half ct% cratered, and didn't run when he did get on base. He'll bounce back some, and as long as 2019/2020 are still on this chart, there is hope for more. (Once you display a skill...)

Yr	Tm	PA	R	HR	RBI	SB	BA	xHR	xSB	xBA	OBP	SLG	OPS+	vL+	vR+	bb%	ct%	Eye	G	L	F	h%	HctX	QBaB	Brl%	PX	xPX	HR/F	xHR/F	Spd	SBA%	SB%	RAR	BPX	R$
18	aa	394	42	7	29	10	225		7		341	330	90			15	72	0.62				29				67				116	11%	76%		27	$6
19	MIL *	613	87	31	87	12	267	4	10	262	364	520	122	99	101	13	75	0.62	38	19	43	30	94	CBc	5%	129	90	13%	8%	86	11%	68%	33.8	219	$23
20	SD	251	42	10	26	10	251	12	5	247	352	456	107	98	110	12	70	0.48	41	25	34	31	95	DCf	11%	116	111	20%	24%	112	16%	91%	3.2	136	$28
21	SD	527	61	15	62	13	242	11	11	249	327	413	102	112	98	10	74	0.45	41	22	37	30	90	CCf	5%	106	95	12%	9%	73	14%	72%	-0.3	100	$15
22	SD	524	58	17	53	7	184	17	8	208	284	341	89	89	88	11	67	0.38	43	13	43	23	88	DCf	8%	110	110	14%	14%	80	7%	88%	-15.3	10	$4
1st Half		308	31	8	32	2	186	7	5	209	285	331	87	82	89	11	70	0.43	47	12	42	23	70	FCf	6%	98	84	11%	9%	85	7%	100%	-8.6	31	$6
2nd Half		216	27	9	21	5	181	10	3	204	284	356	91	102	88	11	62	0.32	38	16	46	23	115	CBf	11%	129	152	18%	20%	80	7%	83%	-5.5	0	$7
23	**Proj**	**455**	**57**	**16**	**50**	**10**	**226**	**16**	**5**	**227**	**321**	**403**	**101**	**104**	**99**	**11**	**69**	**0.41**	**41**	**18**	**41**	**28**	**94**		**8%**	**121**	**111**	**14%**	**14%**	**83**	**6%**	**80%**	**5.2**	**62**	**$11**

Grissom,Vaughn

Age: 22	Pos: 2B	Health	A	LIMA Plan	C+
Bats: R	Ht: 6' 3" Wt: 180	PT/Exp	F	Rand Var	-3
		Consist	F	MM	2533

5-18-.291 with 5 SB in 156 PA at ATL. Played just 22 games at AA before getting the call in August. Held his own as the power/speed blend came as advertised, and while he's not a .300 threat, xBA says he's not a liability either. Expect some growing pains—he's 22 after all—but seems like a 20/20 candidate with regular playing time.

Yr	Tm	PA	R	HR	RBI	SB	BA	xHR	xSB	xBA	OBP	SLG	OPS+	vL+	vR+	bb%	ct%	Eye	G	L	F	h%	HctX	QBaB	Brl%	PX	xPX	HR/F	xHR/F	Spd	SBA%	SB%	RAR	BPX	R$
18																																			
19																																			
20																																			
21																																			
22	ATL *	250	32	7	27	11	307	4	5	262	347	447	112	132	103	6	79	0.29	44	25	31	36	89	DDc	8%	86	113	15%	12%	138	20%	77%	10.0	131	$13
1st Half																																			
2nd Half		250	32	7	27	11	307	4	5	262	347	447	0	132	103	6	79	0.29	44	25	31	36	89	DDc	8%	86	113	15%	12%	138	20%	77%	11.5	131	$22
23	**Proj**	**385**	**45**	**14**	**38**	**16**	**270**	**13**	**12**	**254**	**320**	**431**	**104**	**123**	**96**	**5**	**79**	**0.27**	**40**	**23**	**37**	**31**	**89**		**7%**	**95**	**102**	**14%**	**12%**	**135**	**17%**	**79%**	**10.0**	**118**	**$20**

Groshans,Jordan

Age: 23	Pos: 3B	Health	A	LIMA Plan	D
Bats: R	Ht: 6' 3" Wt: 205	PT/Exp	C	Rand Var	0
		Consist	C	MM	1313

1-2-.262 in 65 PA at MIA. Disappointing year for former first-round pick, though he got September cup of coffee anyway. Lack of power is the chief concern as PX tanked and he slugged just .331 in 412 PA at AAA. Plate skills are a decent building block, but without any speed, he needs a ton more "oomph" to be fantasy relevant. Track from afar.

Yr	Tm	PA	R	HR	RBI	SB	BA	xHR	xSB	xBA	OBP	SLG	OPS+	vL+	vR+	bb%	ct%	Eye	G	L	F	h%	HctX	QBaB	Brl%	PX	xPX	HR/F	xHR/F	Spd	SBA%	SB%	RAR	BPX	R$
18																																			
19																																			
20																																			
21	aa	303	35	6	30	0	255		3		317	390	97			8	76	0.37				32				92				85	0%	0%		77	$4
22	MIA *	456	40	3	26	2	227	1	2	225	298	279	82	93	87	9	79	0.48	46	23	31	28	93	CFd	2%	38	53	7%	7%	101	2%	100%	-19.9	-7	$1
1st Half		189	18	1	14	1	220		1	207	298	261	79	0	0	10	78	0.52	44	20	36	28	0			32	-14	0%		105	2%	100%	-8.2	-24	-$4
2nd Half		267	23	2	13	1	232	1	1	227	298	292	84	93	87	9	79	0.45	46	23	31	28	94	CFd	2%	42	53	7%	7%	106	2%	100%	-9.3	3	$0
23	**Proj**	**315**	**31**	**4**	**24**	**1**	**245**	**5**	**2**	**237**	**313**	**338**	**90**	**111**	**86**	**9**	**78**	**0.44**	**46**	**23**	**31**	**30**	**85**		**2%**	**67**	**48**	**6%**	**7%**	**96**	**3%**	**100%**	**-1.7**	**26**	**$6**

Grossman,Robbie

Age: 33	Pos: LF RF	Health	A	LIMA Plan	D+
Bats: B	Ht: 6' 0" Wt: 209	PT/Exp	A	Rand Var	0
		Consist	B	MM	2203

Last year, we said "regression will most likely drag counting stats downward," and did it ever. Nothing went right: power vanished as HR/F was cut in half, turning all those flyballs from HR to outs; ct% continued its spiral; running game went stagnant; issues vR cut into playing time. At this stage of his career, think more 2022 repeat than 2021 redux.

Yr	Tm	PA	R	HR	RBI	SB	BA	xHR	xSB	xBA	OBP	SLG	OPS+	vL+	vR+	bb%	ct%	Eye	G	L	F	h%	HctX	QBaB	Brl%	PX	xPX	HR/F	xHR/F	Spd	SBA%	SB%	RAR	BPX	R$
18	MIN	465	50	5	48	0	273	6	8	247	367	384	101	117	91	13	79	0.72	39	24	37	33	92	CBb	2%	77	58	4%	5%	106	1%	0%	5.8	123	$8
19	OAK	482	57	6	38	9	240	8	3	250	334	348	94	76	96	12	80	0.69	41	25	34	29	95	CCc	2%	60	81	5%	7%	107	10%	69%	-19.0	93	$7
20	OAK	192	23	8	23	8	241	6	3	275	344	482	110	59	117	11	77	0.55	39	23	38	27	88	CBc	5%	134	98	16%	12%	99	20%	89%	1.2	276	$19
21	DET	671	88	23	67	20	239	20	23	229	357	415	106	117	101	15	72	0.63	29	24	46	29	81	CAb	8%	104	105	12%	11%	114	13%	80%	3.6	142	$21
22	2 TM	477	40	7	45	6	209	6	9	206	310	311	88	123	72	12	69	0.43	31	24	45	29	84	DAb	4%	79	105	6%	5%	81	7%	75%	-14.1	-41	$3
1st Half		251	19	2	18	3	207	3	5	186	315	277	84	132	63	13	64	0.41	32	24	44	31	80	DAb	5%	63	90	3%	5%	87	7%	75%	-9.4	-134	-$2
2nd Half		226	21	5	27	3	212	3	4	227	305	348	93	114	82	11	73	0.47	31	24	45	26	88	DAc	3%	94	121	8%	5%	79	7%	75%	-4.8	55	$5
23	**Proj**	**315**	**34**	**8**	**33**	**7**	**226**	**6**	**4**	**226**	**330**	**367**	**97**	**115**	**89**	**13**	**72**	**0.52**	**32**	**24**	**44**	**29**	**85**		**5%**	**99**	**103**	**9%**	**7%**	**91**	**6%**	**79%**	**1.2**	**71**	**$8**

Guerrero Jr.,Vladimir

Age: 24	Pos: 1B DH	Health	A	LIMA Plan	C
Bats: R	Ht: 6' 2" Wt: 250	PT/Exp	A	Rand Var	+1
		Consist	F	MM	4155

Somewhat disappointing encore given BA/HR pullback, though late SB surge was unexpected boon. Extreme GB% returned and xHR says HR dip could've been worse, but stable ct% with gobs of hard contact bode well for BA recovery. 2021 may have been an early peak, but think of his career as a mountain range. Many peaks, different elevations.

Yr	Tm	PA	R	HR	RBI	SB	BA	xHR	xSB	xBA	OBP	SLG	OPS+	vL+	vR+	bb%	ct%	Eye	G	L	F	h%	HctX	QBaB	Brl%	PX	xPX	HR/F	xHR/F	Spd	SBA%	SB%	RAR	BPX	R$
18	a/a	378	59	19	71	3	383		7		438	634	144			9	89	0.89				39				133				86	5%	48%		360	$25
19	TOR *	548	58	18	76	1	277	18	5	259	343	448	109	89	113	9	81	0.53	50	17	33	31	98	BDd	8%	88	89	12%	15%	80	1%	48%	6.4	144	$13
20	TOR	243	34	9	33	1	262	8	1	283	329	462	105	116	101	8	83	0.53	55	17	28	28	130	AFc	9%	103	72	18%	16%	96	2%	100%	-1.1	244	$19
21	TOR	698	123	48	111	4	311	44	4	299	401	601	138	129	141	12	82	0.78	45	19	36	31	139	ACd	15%	146	128	27%	24%	84	2%	80%	69.8	369	$40
22	TOR	706	90	32	97	8	274	25	3	284	339	480	116	100	119	8	82	0.50	52	17	31	29	137	AFf	11%	121	107	20%	16%	66	6%	73%	27.6	214	$31
1st Half		349	45	19	53	0	265	14	2	270	350	493	119	128	118	11	79	0.58	50	17	32	28	133	AFd	12%	132	122	24%	18%	72	6%	0%	12.8	231	$28
2nd Half		357	45	13	44	8	283	11	1	289	328	467	113	77	121	6	84	0.40	54	17	29	30	140	AFf	11%	111	93	16%	13%	67	6%	80%	9.9	207	$32
23	**Proj**	**665**	**97**	**34**	**100**	**5**	**291**	**29**	**6**	**290**	**361**	**521**	**122**	**111**	**125**	**9**	**82**	**0.59**	**50**	**18**	**32**	**30**	**133**		**12%**	**133**	**107**	**21%**	**18%**	**70**	**5%**	**71%**	**43.1**	**269**	**$35**

Guillorme,Luis

Age: 28	Pos: 2B 3B	Health	C	LIMA Plan	D+
Bats: L	Ht: 5' 10" Wt: 190	PT/Exp	C	Rand Var	+1
		Consist	D	MM	0033

Started hot with .443 OBP through first 99 PA, but an otherwise listless season in utility role. BA gains did come with xBA support, but it's nowhere near enough to cover for lack of HR/SB, which seems entrenched given hollow contact and lack of running game. Issues vL a final reason to steer clear—just in case you needed one.

Yr	Tm	PA	R	HR	RBI	SB	BA	xHR	xSB	xBA	OBP	SLG	OPS+	vL+	vR+	bb%	ct%	Eye	G	L	F	h%	HctX	QBaB	Brl%	PX	xPX	HR/F	xHR/F	Spd	SBA%	SB%	RAR	BPX	R$
18	NYM *	341	31	2	27	2	230	0	5	239	292	299	79	66	70	8	84	0.54	53	18	29	27	82	CDc	0%	46	57	0%	0%	100	4%	66%	-13.2	67	$1
19	NYM *	330	35	7	29	3	252	2	3	228	341	368	98	93	94	12	77	0.59	41	20	39	31	76	CBb	6%	66	61	6%	11%	88	9%	41%	-3.9	48	$4
20	NYM	68	6	0	9	2	333	1	1	263	426	439	115	55	125	15	70	0.59	49	32	20	48	111	BCa	2%	92	89	0%	13%	92	9%	100%	3.8	52	$5
21	NYM *	181	16	1	6	0	259	1	4	220	361	298	91	80	99	14	83	0.97	52	20	28	30	87	DFb	1%	23	64	3%	3%	116	3%	0%	-4.1	62	$0
22	NYM	335	33	2	17	1	273	3	4	272	351	340	98	80	105	10	85	0.74	55	26	19	32	80	DFb	2%	46	54	4%	6%	111	1%	100%	0.2	107	$4
1st Half		184	22	1	7	1	293	2	2	270	363	348	100	77	110	10	85	0.72	55	27	19	34	100	DFb	3%	39	65	4%	8%	119	1%	100%	3.1	97	$0
2nd Half		151	11	1	10	0	248	1	1	269	338	331	95	85	98	11	84	0.76	56	24	20	29	56	DFb	2%	54	40	5%	5%	100	1%	0%	-0.9	117	-$5
23	**Proj**	**315**	**29**	**3**	**20**	**1**	**259**	**3**	**2**	**253**	**345**	**331**	**94**	**75**	**100**	**11**	**83**	**0.77**	**53**	**24**	**23**	**30**	**82**		**2%**	**48**	**59**	**5%**	**5%**	**101**	**3%**	**33%**	**1.0**	**85**	**$6**

Gurriel Jr.,Lourdes

Age: 29	Pos: LF	Health	B	LIMA Plan	C+
Bats: R	Ht: 6' 4" Wt: 215	PT/Exp	A	Rand Var	-1
		Consist	B	MM	3145

October news that he underwent wrist surgery was an "Aha!" moment for those of us who had spent all year wondering where his power had gone. Didn't muster a single HR after July 1. Another reminder that we never know the whole truth, and when in doubt, blame a hidden injury. Should be healed by spring and bounce back.

Yr	Tm	PA	R	HR	RBI	SB	BA	xHR	xSB	xBA	OBP	SLG	OPS+	vL+	vR+	bb%	ct%	Eye	G	L	F	h%	HctX	QBaB	Brl%	PX	xPX	HR/F	xHR/F	Spd	SBA%	SB%	RAR	BPX	R$
18	TOR *	475	52	17	71	4	276	10	6	253	299	432	98	109	96	3	77	0.14	43	24	33	33	86	ACb	8%	92	92	17%	16%	107	8%	44%	-3.0	67	$15
19	TOR *	468	66	23	71	6	268	21	5	260	303	508	112	138	110	5	74	0.20	39	18	43	31	112	BBf	11%	133	145	20%	21%	117	14%	49%	-0.2	185	$16
20	TOR	224	28	11	33	3	308	9	4	282	348	534	117	108	120	6	77	0.29	41	26	33	36	94	ACd	12%	127	91	20%	17%	101	8%	75%	8.1	216	$26
21	TOR	541	62	21	84	1	276	21	7	267	319	466	108	101	111	6	80	0.31	45	21	34	31	106	BCc	10%	106	93	15%	15%	108	3%	25%	11.5	188	$18
22	TOR	492	52	5	52	3	291	9	5	262	343	400	105	95	108	6	82	0.37	45	24	32	35	118	BCc	4%	78	79	4%	8%	108	5%	43%	7.9	124	$15
1st Half		286	33	5	34	2	295	6	3	262	350	433	111	88	116	6	81	0.36	41	22	37	35	129	BCd	4%	98	105	6%	8%	109	5%	67%	9.2	169	$15
2nd Half		206	19	0	18	1	286	3	2	263	335	354	98	103	96	6	83	0.39	50	26	25	35	102	BDb	3%	52	44	0%	8%	111	5%	25%	-0.4	72	$3
23	**Proj**	**525**	**59**	**19**	**67**	**3**	**286**	**15**	**5**	**276**	**330**	**469**	**111**	**108**	**111**	**6**	**80**	**0.31**	**45**	**23**	**32**	**32**	**108**		**7%**	**115**	**83**	**15%**	**12%**	**98**	**6%**	**41%**	**20.8**	**146**	**$22**

RYAN BLOOMFIELD

Gurriel,Yuli

Age: 39 Pos: 1B | Bats: R Ht: 6' 0" Wt: 215
Health A | PT/Exp A | Consist D
LIMA Plan D+ | Rand Var +2 | MM 2233

Career-best SB total helped salvage some value in disappointing season, but at his age, safe to say that won't happen again. The 2021 spike in bb% and h% proved unsustainable and power disappeared in 2nd half. Contact rate still elite so expect some sort of BA rebound, but it won't come with much help from the other categories.

Yr	Tm	PA	R	HR	RBI	SB	BA	xHR	xSB	xBA	OBP	SLG	OPS+	vL+	vR+	bb%	ct%	Eye	G	L	F	h%	HctX	QBaB	Brl%	PX	xPX	HR/F	xHR/F	Spd	SBA%	SB%	RAR	BPX	R$
18	HOU *	594	72	13	87	5	292	7	8	271	320	431	101	118	91	4	88	0.34	44	20	36	31	99	BCd	2%	80	87	8%	4%	107	4%	83%	8.8	190	$21
19	HOU	612	85	31	104	5	298	13	4	306	343	541	122	112	126	6	88	0.57	38	22	39	29	118	BBf	4%	113	79	16%	7%	80	6%	63%	26.5	304	$25
20	HOU	230	27	6	22	0	232	5	2	258	274	384	87	115	75	5	87	0.44	38	20	42	24	127	BCd	3%	78	123	8%	6%	96	2%	0%	-12.5	208	$9
21	HOU	605	83	15	81	1	319	10	3	263	383	462	116	126	111	10	87	0.87	41	20	39	34	120	BCf	3%	78	83	8%	5%	75	1%	50%	29.8	212	$25
22	HOU	584	53	8	53	8	242	4	2	255	288	360	92	104	86	5	87	0.41	41	19	41	27	103	CBf	2%	79	80	4%	2%	77	7%	100%	-9.8	155	$11
1st Half		291	29	7	24	3	227	3	1	266	282	390	95	100	93	6	86	0.47	38	17	44	24	97	CBf	3%	106	84	7%	3%	74	7%	100%	-6.3	224	$7
2nd Half		293	24	1	29	5	257	2	1	245	294	330	88	107	79	4	87	0.34	43	20	37	29	108	CCd	1%	54	76	1%	2%	83	7%	100%	-8.1	97	$9
23	**Proj**	**280**	**32**	**5**	**32**	**2**	**271**	**4**	**3**	**259**	**319**	**401**	**100**	**113**	**94**	**6**	**87**	**0.52**	**41**	**20**	**40**	**29**	**111**		**3%**	**83**	**85**	**6%**	**4%**	**80**	**5%**	**87%**	**2.8**	**183**	**$6**

Haase,Eric

Age: 30 Pos: CA | Bats: R Ht: 5' 10" Wt: 210
Health A | PT/Exp C | Consist C
LIMA Plan C | Rand Var -2 | MM 4213

Power metrics were still decent for a catcher, though not quite up to 2021 standards. Don't be fooled by BA spike, as ct% bump was offset by lower contact quality and xBA barely budged. Certainly offers enough pop to be a viable second catcher in mixed leagues, but prepare to take a hit in BA/OBP.

Yr	Tm	PA	R	HR	RBI	SB	BA	xHR	xSB	xBA	OBP	SLG	OPS+	vL+	vR+	bb%	ct%	Eye	G	L	F	h%	HctX	QBaB	Brl%	PX	xPX	HR/F	xHR/F	Spd	SBA%	SB%	RAR	BPX	R$
18	CLE *	473	40	15	54	2	200	0	4	206	240	359	80	52	29	5	62	0.14	60	10	30	29	45	FCf	0%	121	73	0%	0%	83	4%	66%	-9.0	-63	$3
19	CLE *	400	52	23	49	1	185	1	3	178	254	413	92	81	0	8	52	0.19	50	0	50	27	67	CCb	13%	163	151	25%	25%	103	3%	39%	-4.2	-44	$3
20	DET	19	1	0	2	0	176	1	0	135	211	176	51	0	52	5	65	0.17	42	17	42	27	65	FAf	8%	0	36	0%	20%	93	0%	0%	-1.5	-400	-$3
21	DET *	408	50	23	65	3	234	21	1	233	290	460	103	123	91	7	65	0.23	38	20	41	29	96	ABd	14%	144	105	23%	22%	83	4%	100%	6.1	65	$10
22	DET	351	41	14	44	0	254	12	3	238	305	443	106	109	104	7	70	0.25	39	20	41	32	89	CBd	9%	130	90	15%	13%	92	0%	0%	10.2	93	$8
1st Half		143	20	7	20	0	227	5	1	250	280	439	102	102	101	7	72	0.27	36	22	42	26	85	DBd	8%	133	97	18%	13%	101	0%	0%	2.0	141	$1
2nd Half		208	21	7	24	0	272	7	2	226	322	445	109	115	105	7	69	0.23	41	18	41	36	92	CBd	9%	128	85	13%	13%	88	0%	0%	7.9	66	$8
23	**Proj**	**350**	**41**	**16**	**47**	**1**	**236**	**14**	**1**	**229**	**290**	**434**	**100**	**110**	**95**	**7**	**66**	**0.22**	**39**	**20**	**41**	**31**	**92**		**11%**	**143**	**96**	**18%**	**15%**	**89**	**2%**	**86%**	**8.1**	**57**	**$10**

Haggerty,Sam

Age: 29 Pos: RF LF | Bats: B Ht: 5' 11" Wt: 175
Health F | PT/Exp D | Consist C
LIMA Plan D+ | Rand Var 0 | MM 3501

5-23-.256 with 13 SB in 201 PA at SEA. Late bloomer took advantage of first extended opportunity and ran wild on bases. Dealt with shoulder/finger issues in late August then went cold down stretch (.531 OPS over final 74 PA). Unless we see gains in ct% or HctX/xPX, looks like a one-trick pony.

Yr	Tm	PA	R	HR	RBI	SB	BA	xHR	xSB	xBA	OBP	SLG	OPS+	vL+	vR+	bb%	ct%	Eye	G	L	F	h%	HctX	QBaB	Brl%	PX	xPX	HR/F	xHR/F	Spd	SBA%	SB%	RAR	BPX	R$
18	a/a	345	37	3	31	21	219		5		327	343	90			14	69	0.52				31				95				108	34%	73%		47	$9
19	NYM *	332	44	3	19	20	223	0	18	68	313	313	87	0	0	12	62	0.35	0	0	100	35	0	FA	0%	60	-36	0%	0%	162	29%	81%	-16.5	-104	$8
20	SEA	54	7	1	6	4	260	1	2	245	315	400	95	132	73	7	68	0.25	41	29	29	36	97	BCb	3%	104	98	10%	10%	107	33%	100%	-0.8	16	$5
21	SEA	94	15	2	5	5	186	3	4	210	247	291	74	60	81	6	67	0.21	51	18	32	25	75	DDd	5%	71	79	11%	17%	124	33%	83%	-5.6	-81	$0
22	SEA *	363	45	8	37	22	227	3	15	237	288	365	93	154	73	8	70	0.28	45	23	32	30	75	FCc	4%	100	40	13%	8%	104	30%	90%	-3.9	28	$13
1st Half		197	22	4	18	12	213	0	7	253	254	350	85	210	88	5	72	0.19	44	28	28	27	93	DAf	0%	99	26	14%	0%	98	30%	90%	-5.6	31	$8
2nd Half		166	23	4	19	10	245	3	8	226	333	385	102	147	69	11	67	0.38	45	22	33	34	68	FCc	5%	101	43	13%	10%	114	30%	91%	2.3	28	$10
23	**Proj**	**245**	**33**	**6**	**22**	**15**	**226**	**1**	**10**	**225**	**300**	**365**	**92**	**123**	**76**	**8**	**66**	**0.25**	**47**	**22**	**31**	**31**	**79**		**4%**	**103**	**60**	**12%**	**3%**	**133**	**23%**	**84%**	**-2.4**	**-22**	**$11**

Hall,Darick

Age: 27 Pos: DH | Bats: L Ht: 6' 4" Wt: 236
Health A | PT/Exp B | Consist A
LIMA Plan D | Rand Var +3 | MM 4121

9-16-.250 in 142 PA at PHI. Held his own in MLB debut, but roster crunch sent him back to AAA in late August. Even in small sample, xPX and Brl% suggest the power is legit, but so is low ct%, and .591 OPS vL in AAA says platoon role was justified. That weakness caps the ceiling, but he's still a good bet to provide plenty of pop vR.

Yr	Tm	PA	R	HR	RBI	SB	BA	xHR	xSB	xBA	OBP	SLG	OPS+	vL+	vR+	bb%	ct%	Eye	G	L	F	h%	HctX	QBaB	Brl%	PX	xPX	HR/F	xHR/F	Spd	SBA%	SB%	RAR	BPX	R$
18	aa	309	31	13	40	1	194		3		231	357	79			5	69	0.15				23				102				94	2%	100%		-10	$2
19	aa	509	61	20	59	4	213		2		294	420	99			10	65	0.33				28				135				90	5%	80%		70	$7
20																																			
21	aaa	437	31	11	40	0	193		3		262	323	80			9	69	0.31				25				89				77	2%	0%		-31	-$2
22	PHI *	557	55	27	70	4	207	8	2	239	251	415	94	23	123	6	69	0.19	34	21	46	24	108	AAc	18%	142	159	21%	19%	73	6%	75%	-21.3	83	$9
1st Half		321	35	16	46	3	210	1	1	254	256	417	95	0	148	6	72	0.22	35	24	41	24	111	DCa	29%	134	147	43%	14%	74	6%	71%	-8.9	110	$18
2nd Half		236	20	11	24	1	202	7	1	228	243	412	93	23	117	5	64	0.16	33	20	47	26	101	AAc	17%	154	162	17%	20%	86	6%	100%	-8.1	66	$6
23	**Proj**	**245**	**25**	**13**	**30**	**1**	**223**	**13**	**2**	**241**	**281**	**452**	**102**	**43**	**109**	**7**	**68**	**0.23**	**33**	**20**	**47**	**27**	**91**		**15%**	**158**	**146**	**18%**	**18%**	**77**	**5%**	**66%**	**-1.2**	**39**	**$6**

Hampson,Garrett

Age: 28 Pos: CF SS | Bats: R Ht: 5' 11" Wt: 196
Health A | PT/Exp C | Consist A
LIMA Plan D+ | Rand Var 0 | MM 2503

Third straight sub-.290 OBP despite playing half his games in Coors, as ct% slipped and he couldn't hold recent xPX gains. Bottom-barrel QBaB, futility vR offer little hope for rebound. Still has the wheels and green light, but it's hard to tap into SB potential (or lock down starting gig) when getting to first base is such a struggle.

Yr	Tm	PA	R	HR	RBI	SB	BA	xHR	xSB	xBA	OBP	SLG	OPS+	vL+	vR+	bb%	ct%	Eye	G	L	F	h%	HctX	QBaB	Brl%	PX	xPX	HR/F	xHR/F	Spd	SBA%	SB%	RAR	BPX	R$
18	COL *	528	60	8	32	27	281	1	8	249	341	411	101	136	97	8	81	0.48	44	20	36	33	85	DCd	4%	77	113	0%	11%	147	24%	83%	11.8	163	$20
19	COL *	439	50	9	33	19	243	6	15	224	290	378	92	100	92	6	72	0.24	43	19	37	32	75	DCd	4%	77	73	11%	8%	152	25%	79%	-6.8	33	$11
20	COL	184	25	5	11	6	234	6	7	204	287	383	89	71	100	7	64	0.22	36	25	39	33	68	FCd	8%	90	141	13%	16%	179	18%	86%	-6.4	-4	$13
21	COL	494	69	11	33	17	234	12	14	234	289	380	92	111	83	7	74	0.28	39	23	38	29	107	FCd	5%	87	139	9%	10%	175	23%	71%	-12.7	127	$13
22	COL	226	29	2	15	12	211	3	8	203	287	307	84	117	65	9	68	0.33	48	16	35	30	70	FDf	4%	69	89	4%	7%	165	27%	86%	-6.4	0	$4
1st Half		101	15	2	9	2	227	1	4	210	313	364	96	129	75	11	70	0.42	50	12	38	30	43	FDd	2%	84	76	9%	5%	179	27%	67%	-0.7	93	-$4
2nd Half		125	14	0	6	10	198	2	4	196	266	261	75	107	56	8	67	0.27	47	19	33	30	91	DDf	7%	56	100	0%	8%	127	27%	91%	-5.1	-110	-$1
23	**Proj**	**315**	**42**	**5**	**21**	**15**	**225**	**7**	**12**	**216**	**288**	**346**	**88**	**108**	**76**	**8**	**70**	**0.29**	**44**	**19**	**37**	**30**	**82**		**5%**	**84**	**108**	**7%**	**9%**	**142**	**22%**	**82%**	**-3.8**	**33**	**$11**

Haniger,Mitch

Age: 32 Pos: RF | Bats: R Ht: 6' 2" Wt: 213
Health F | PT/Exp C | Consist B
LIMA Plan B | Rand Var 0 | MM 4225

11-34-.246 in 247 PA at SEA. Injury bug got him again, as high-ankle sprain in April cost him over three months. Power was a notch below typical levels upon return, while xBA says BA dip was well deserved. Sketchy health history needs to be factored in, but should make another run at 30+ HR if he stays in one piece.

Yr	Tm	PA	R	HR	RBI	SB	BA	xHR	xSB	xBA	OBP	SLG	OPS+	vL+	vR+	bb%	ct%	Eye	G	L	F	h%	HctX	QBaB	Brl%	PX	xPX	HR/F	xHR/F	Spd	SBA%	SB%	RAR	BPX	R$
18	SEA	683	90	26	93	8	285	32	10	265	366	493	115	118	112	10	75	0.47	42	21	36	34	103	BCb	10%	128	109	16%	19%	107	5%	80%	30.9	193	$26
19	SEA	283	46	15	32	4	220	14	3	240	314	463	108	128	101	11	67	0.37	35	20	45	26	82	CAc	11%	143	116	20%	19%	100	7%	100%	-2.4	133	$5
20																																			
21	SEA	691	110	39	100	1	253	37	9	248	318	485	110	125	103	8	73	0.32	43	16	41	29	111	BBd	13%	131	133	21%	20%	114	1%	100%	14.7	185	$23
22	SEA *	273	34	12	37	0	238	11	1	233	309	418	103	107	103	9	72	0.37	37	20	43	28	113	AAc	11%	115	113	16%	16%	87	0%	0%	1.3	90	$5
1st Half		36	3	3	7	0	200	3	0	264	222	486	100	20	117	3	74	0.11	31	19	50	17	87	AAb	19%	166	81	23%	23%	90	0%	0%	-0.8	221	-$9
2nd Half		237	31	9	30	0	244	8	1	227	323	407	103	117	100	10	71	0.40	39	20	41	30	118	ABc	9%	106	119	14%	14%	92	0%	0%	1.7	72	$11
23	**Proj**	**490**	**76**	**26**	**64**	**2**	**244**	**24**	**2**	**248**	**313**	**467**	**108**	**110**	**107**	**9**	**72**	**0.33**	**38**	**19**	**43**	**28**	**105**		**13%**	**145**	**114**	**19%**	**18%**	**100**	**3%**	**59%**	**12.2**	**131**	**$18**

Happ,Ian

Age: 28 Pos: LF | Bats: B Ht: 6' 0" Wt: 205
Health A | PT/Exp A | Consist B
LIMA Plan B | Rand Var 0 | MM 4225

Huge step forward in ct% led to sizable BA jump, but it came with a cost. HR production took a hit, as Brl%, HR/F, and xHR/F each fell well below previous marks. Still, R$ likes this version better. Combination of power, speed, and health give him a high floor, but unless he can combine 2022 ct% with previous power skills, ceiling will be limited.

Yr	Tm	PA	R	HR	RBI	SB	BA	xHR	xSB	xBA	OBP	SLG	OPS+	vL+	vR+	bb%	ct%	Eye	G	L	F	h%	HctX	QBaB	Brl%	PX	xPX	HR/F	xHR/F	Spd	SBA%	SB%	RAR	BPX	R$
18	CHC	462	56	15	44	8	233	18	7	206	353	408	102	81	108	15	57	0.42	40	23	38	37	80	BCb	12%	141	126	18%	21%	105	9%	67%	1.0	13	$10
19	CHC *	569	77	23	72	9	225	10	8	222	319	420	102	107	128	12	66	0.41	43	16	42	29	79	BBd	14%	117	102	26%	24%	103	8%	80%	-11.7	56	$13
20	CHC	231	27	12	28	1	258	10	3	259	361	505	115	93	122	13	68	0.48	45	22	33	32	99	BDc	10%	150	121	27%	23%	95	7%	25%	3.5	196	$17
21	CHC	535	63	25	66	9	226	20	5	242	323	434	104	89	109	12	66	0.40	46	21	33	28	93	CCf	11%	133	115	24%	19%	89	9%	82%	-0.1	92	$13
22	CHC	641	72	17	72	9	271	16	9	257	342	440	111	110	111	9	74	0.39	46	20	33	34	100	BCd	7%	120	105	12%	11%	98	8%	69%	19.2	141	$22
1st Half		325	37	8	38	6	283	9	5	268	382	460	119	139	113	13	76	0.61	49	20	32	35	111	BCd	9%	123	101	12%	13%	110	8%	75%	16.4	214	$21
2nd Half		316	35	9	34	3	259	7	4	247	301	421	102	82	108	5	72	0.21	44	20	35	33	89	BCc	5%	118	110	12%	9%	86	8%	60%	2.0	76	$18
23	**Proj**	**630**	**74**	**24**	**74**	**9**	**256**	**21**	**8**	**250**	**336**	**451**	**109**	**98**	**112**	**10**	**70**	**0.38**	**45**	**20**	**34**	**33**	**95**		**9%**	**139**	**111**	**18%**	**16%**	**89**	**7%**	**69%**	**21.2**	**116**	**$24**

BRIAN RUDD

Harper,Bryce

Age: 30	Pos: DH	Health	C	LIMA Plan	C
Bats: L	Ht: 6' 3" Wt: 210	PT/Exp	A	Rand Var	0
		Consist	D	MM	5255

Early elbow injury limited him to DH duties, costing him OF eligibility to open 2023. Looked as strong as ever prior to June broken thumb but struggled upon return, as ct% slipped, GB% soared, and fly balls weren't leaving the park. Until October, anyway. Offseason should give him time to heal further and reclaim his status as an early-round stud.

Yr	Tm	PA	R	HR	RBI	SB	BA	xHR	xSB	xBA	OBP	SLG	OPS+	vL+	vR+	bb%	ct%	Eye	G	L	F	h%	HctX	QBaB	Brl%	PX	xPX	HR/F	xHR/F	Spd	SBA%	SB%	RAR	BPX	R$
18	WAS	695	103	34	100	13	249	35	12	262	393	496	119	114	119	19	69	0.77	40	22	38	30	108	ABb	12%	161	148	23%	24%	87	8%	81%	37.0	240	$26
19	PHI	682	98	35	114	15	260	40	9	261	372	510	122	132	116	15	69	0.56	38	24	38	32	115	ACc	15%	145	152	23%	27%	88	10%	83%	19.2	181	$27
20	PHI	244	41	13	33	8	268	19	6	266	420	542	128	126	128	20	77	1.14	36	18	46	28	125	BCc	17%	141	148	20%	29%	121	13%	80%	15.3	404	$31
21	PHI	599	101	35	84	13	309	40	14	293	429	615	143	109	159	17	73	0.75	41	22	37	36	128	ACc	18%	186	152	27%	31%	107	9%	81%	66.2	412	$35
22	PHI	426	63	18	65	11	286	22	6	287	364	514	124	109	131	11	76	0.53	41	24	34	33	118	ACc	13%	148	124	18%	22%	84	14%	73%	25.8	252	$22
1st Half		275	49	15	48	9	318	18	4	313	385	599	139	127	145	10	79	0.50	35	29	35	35	124	ACc	15%	176	131	22%	26%	81	14%	82%	29.2	345	$36
2nd Half		151	14	3	17	2	227	4	2	220	325	352	96	71	106	14	73	0.57	54	14	33	29	106	BDc	10%	91	109	10%	13%	93	14%	50%	-1.9	69	$0
23	**Proj**	**630**	**94**	**33**	**95**	**12**	**284**	**39**	**14**	**280**	**390**	**544**	**130**	**108**	**139**	**15**	**74**	**0.67**	**41**	**21**	**38**	**33**	**119**		**14%**	**171**	**134**	**22%**	**26%**	**96**	**11%**	**70%**	**49.6**	**275**	**$32**

Harris II,Michael

Age: 22	Pos: CF	Health	A	LIMA Plan	D+
Bats: L	Ht: 6' 0" Wt: 195	PT/Exp	C	Rand Var	0
		Consist	F	MM	4545

19-64-.297 with 20 SB in 441 PA at ATL. Skipped AAA and hit the ground running with exciting power/speed combo, highlighted by a solid BA/xBA. High GB% casts some doubt on HR pace, though xHR/F says 2022 HR total was legit. SB% (20-for-22) suggests green light should stick, and across-the-board production could yield first-round value.

Yr	Tm	PA	R	HR	RBI	SB	BA	xHR	xSB	xBA	OBP	SLG	OPS+	vL+	vR+	bb%	ct%	Eye	G	L	F	h%	HctX	QBaB	Brl%	PX	xPX	HR/F	xHR/F	Spd	SBA%	SB%	RAR	BPX	R$
18																																			
19																																			
20																																			
21																																			
22	ATL *	628	101	23	90	29	291	19	8	281	330	495	117	91	134	5	75	0.23	56	17	27	36	111	CFd	10%	137	109	23%	23%	118	24%	84%	31.8	193	$41
1st Half		324	50	9	45	15	287	4	4	282	328	471	113	106	123	6	76	0.25	55	20	25	35	107	CDc	9%	124	94	20%	16%	122	24%	82%	13.9	179	$35
2nd Half		304	51	14	45	14	296	15	4	282	340	521	122	84	139	5	73	0.21	57	15	28	36	112	BFd	11%	151	117	24%	26%	109	24%	88%	19.5	203	$39
23	**Proj**	**595**	**92**	**22**	**81**	**25**	**274**	**23**	**18**	**275**	**321**	**479**	**111**	**87**	**122**	**5**	**74**	**0.22**	**53**	**18**	**29**	**33**	**110**		**10%**	**139**	**108**	**18%**	**19%**	**117**	**19%**	**87%**	**26.1**	**193**	**$36**

Harrison,Josh

Age: 35	Pos: 2B 3B	Health	B	LIMA Plan	C+
Bats: R	Ht: 5' 8" Wt: 190	PT/Exp	A	Rand Var	-2
		Consist	A	MM	1223

Couldn't repeat 2021 numbers, as xBA cratered and power flatlined. Most years, he could be counted on for "stats that won't hurt you" rosterability, but that's fading as he crests his mid-30s. Positional versatility may make him useful in a pinch if he falls into regular at-bats, but these skills scream part-timer.

Yr	Tm	PA	R	HR	RBI	SB	BA	xHR	xSB	xBA	OBP	SLG	OPS+	vL+	vR+	bb%	ct%	Eye	G	L	F	h%	HctX	QBaB	Brl%	PX	xPX	HR/F	xHR/F	Spd	SBA%	SB%	RAR	BPX	R$
18	PIT	374	41	8	37	3	250	8	5	245	293	363	88	90	86	5	80	0.26	38	25	37	29	97	DBc	4%	67	114	8%	8%	98	3%	100%	-4.8	53	$6
19	DET *	174	11	1	10	4	170	5	1	212	220	250	65	70	66	6	80	0.33	36	18	45	21	77	DAc	5%	48	54	2%	10%	101	21%	67%	-16.3	11	-$4
20	WAS	91	11	3	14	1	278	3	3	264	352	418	102	105	98	7	85	0.50	41	25	35	30	80	FBa	4%	66	60	13%	13%	83	11%	33%	-0.4	128	$6
21	2 TM	557	58	8	60	9	279	12	9	264	341	400	102	105	101	6	85	0.41	39	24	37	32	98	CBb	4%	72	90	5%	8%	91	10%	64%	2.8	150	$17
22	CHW	425	50	7	27	2	256	6	7	237	317	370	97	93	98	5	82	0.30	44	17	39	30	91	CBb	4%	73	85	6%	5%	114	3%	67%	0.6	107	$7
1st Half		186	27	2	13	1	242	3	3	241	319	358	96	96	96	6	81	0.32	44	18	38	29	76	CBc	5%	75	78	4%	6%	128	3%	100%	-2.2	128	$0
2nd Half		239	23	5	14	1	267	3	4	232	315	380	98	92	100	5	82	0.28	43	17	40	31	102	DBb	3%	72	90	7%	4%	88	3%	50%	0.2	79	$5
23	**Proj**	**385**	**43**	**7**	**32**	**4**	**254**	**7**	**3**	**246**	**315**	**374**	**96**	**97**	**95**	**5**	**82**	**0.33**	**41**	**20**	**38**	**29**	**92**		**4%**	**77**	**84**	**6%**	**6%**	**94**	**4%**	**80%**	**0.7**	**101**	**$10**

Hayes,Ke'Bryan

Age: 26	Pos: 3B	Health	C	LIMA Plan	B
Bats: R	Ht: 5' 10" Wt: 205	PT/Exp	A	Rand Var	+3
		Consist	F	MM	2325

Back strain led to brief IL stint in August, then posted .584 OPS the rest of way. But he wasn't exactly crushing it pre-injury; weak PX/xPX say he's no lock for double-digit HR. Speed from a corner infielder is a plus and did run more late (9 SB in last 151 PA), but SB history, xSB cast doubt on repeat on the bases. Don't pay for a step forward.

Yr	Tm	PA	R	HR	RBI	SB	BA	xHR	xSB	xBA	OBP	SLG	OPS+	vL+	vR+	bb%	ct%	Eye	G	L	F	h%	HctX	QBaB	Brl%	PX	xPX	HR/F	xHR/F	Spd	SBA%	SB%	RAR	BPX	R$
18	aa	486	56	6	41	10	275		7		349	410	102			10	80	0.57				33				86				117	12%	66%		153	$13
19	aaa	464	54	8	45	10	245		7		304	376	94			8	78	0.39				30				78				99	11%	90%		78	$9
20	PIT	95	17	5	11	1	376	4	2	305	442	682	149	175	140	9	76	0.45	48	22	31	45	138	ADd	9%	167	112	25%	20%	142	4%	100%	14.5	412	$13
21	PIT *	421	53	7	40	9	254	8	4	251	312	378	95	101	92	8	75	0.34	57	18	25	32	110	BFd	5%	80	76	9%	11%	103	10%	90%	-2.8	54	$10
22	PIT	560	55	7	41	20	244	9	10	242	314	345	93	106	88	9	76	0.39	49	22	29	31	102	AFf	4%	71	74	6%	8%	119	18%	80%	-10.7	52	$15
1st Half		306	35	3	25	9	252	7	6	239	327	354	96	122	85	10	75	0.42	48	22	31	33	111	ADc	6%	75	87	5%	11%	121	18%	75%	-2.1	59	$14
2nd Half		254	20	4	16	11	234	2	5	246	299	333	90	88	90	8	77	0.36	51	22	27	29	90	BFf	2%	66	58	8%	4%	110	18%	85%	-5.7	38	$9
23	**Proj**	**560**	**61**	**9**	**46**	**14**	**253**	**9**	**14**	**249**	**320**	**371**	**96**	**104**	**92**	**9**	**77**	**0.40**	**52**	**20**	**27**	**31**	**107**		**5%**	**82**	**76**	**8%**	**9%**	**102**	**13%**	**79%**	**3.7**	**63**	**$18**

Hays,Austin

Age: 27	Pos: LF RF	Health	C	LIMA Plan	B
Bats: R	Ht: 6' 0" Wt: 205	PT/Exp	A	Rand Var	+1
		Consist	A	MM	3135

Strong 2021 finish carried over into 1st half, but things quickly went south as July wrist injury, August oblique issue likely played parts in sudden slippage. He doesn't stand out in any one area given low SBA%/SB% and average power, but give him a pass for late fade and look for a return to 2021 level of production.

Yr	Tm	PA	R	HR	RBI	SB	BA	xHR	xSB	xBA	OBP	SLG	OPS+	vL+	vR+	bb%	ct%	Eye	G	L	F	h%	HctX	QBaB	Brl%	PX	xPX	HR/F	xHR/F	Spd	SBA%	SB%	RAR	BPX	R$
18	aa	282	25	10	32	4	209		3		234	363	80			3	77	0.14				24				89				99	16%	57%		53	$2
19	BAL *	384	55	15	45	10	242	2	6	260	282	438	100	48	177	5	75	0.22	41	22	37	28	80	ACa	6%	111	107	20%	10%	112	24%	63%	-12.4	126	$10
20	BAL	134	20	4	9	2	279	2	5	236	328	393	96	95	96	6	80	0.32	49	19	32	32	62	DCf	4%	57	42	13%	6%	141	13%	40%	-4.6	80	$10
21	BAL	529	73	22	71	4	256	22	9	261	308	461	106	122	94	5	78	0.26	43	18	38	29	98	CCf	9%	114	92	15%	15%	119	6%	57%	4.0	200	$16
22	BAL	582	66	16	60	2	250	14	7	256	306	413	102	98	103	6	79	0.30	43	19	38	29	105	CCf	5%	107	103	10%	9%	117	5%	33%	-0.8	169	$13
1st Half		318	40	11	45	1	271	9	4	271	327	459	111	107	113	6	80	0.33	39	21	40	30	122	CCf	8%	119	126	12%	10%	117	5%	25%	6.9	231	$21
2nd Half		264	26	5	15	1	226	5	3	239	280	358	90	88	91	6	77	0.26	48	17	35	28	84	DCf	3%	92	74	8%	8%	118	5%	50%	-6.5	100	$3
23	**Proj**	**560**	**70**	**22**	**69**	**3**	**259**	**16**	**5**	**260**	**309**	**448**	**105**	**101**	**106**	**6**	**78**	**0.27**	**44**	**19**	**37**	**29**	**100**		**6%**	**118**	**90**	**14%**	**10%**	**105**	**6%**	**41%**	**10.2**	**153**	**$20**

Hedges,Austin

Age: 30	Pos: CA	Health	A	LIMA Plan	D
Bats: R	Ht: 6' 1" Wt: 223	PT/Exp	C	Rand Var	+3
		Consist	A	MM	1203

Defense is his calling card as the combination of well below average power and consistent sub-.180 BA isn't cutting it offensively. Career-best ct% didn't change his fortunes and 23% career h% shows positive regression isn't coming anytime soon. Look elsewhere for a second catcher, as the BA damage he'll incur is tough to overcome.

Yr	Tm	PA	R	HR	RBI	SB	BA	xHR	xSB	xBA	OBP	SLG	OPS+	vL+	vR+	bb%	ct%	Eye	G	L	F	h%	HctX	QBaB	Brl%	PX	xPX	HR/F	xHR/F	Spd	SBA%	SB%	RAR	BPX	R$
18	SD *	355	34	16	44	3	239	10	4	235	288	445	98	90	96	6	69	0.23	38	18	44	30	94	DBf	7%	133	116	15%	11%	85	4%	100%	8.2	80	$7
19	SD	347	28	11	36	1	176	10	1	200	252	311	78	67	80	8	65	0.25	32	22	46	23	71	CAd	8%	81	89	12%	11%	53	1%	100%	-12.7	-148	-$2
20	2 TM	83	7	3	6	1	145	2	0	192	231	290	69	53	77	7	67	0.26	43	15	43	16	99	FCf	8%	83	143	15%	10%	81	14%	50%	-5.5	-100	-$2
21	CLE	312	32	10	31	1	178	5	3	203	220	308	72	77	70	5	70	0.17	34	20	45	22	64	FBf	4%	78	77	11%	6%	68	2%	100%	-16.8	-100	-$2
22	CLE	338	26	7	30	2	163	4	1	193	241	248	69	71	69	7	73	0.32	38	18	44	20	70	FBf	3%	52	65	7%	4%	67	3%	100%	-17.1	-93	-$4
1st Half		160	13	5	15	1	160	2	0	195	223	271	70	71	69	6	72	0.25	37	17	46	18	70	FAf	4%	65	68	11%	4%	79	3%	100%	-8.5	-72	-$6
2nd Half		178	13	2	15	1	167	1	1	190	257	227	69	71	68	9	75	0.39	39	18	42	21	70	FCf	3%	40	62	4%	2%	70	3%	100%	-9.2	-97	-$6
23	**Proj**	**315**	**28**	**9**	**32**	**1**	**177**	**5**	**1**	**199**	**241**	**291**	**74**	**74**	**74**	**7**	**71**	**0.25**	**37**	**19**	**44**	**22**	**72**		**4%**	**74**	**80**	**10%**	**5%**	**66**	**3%**	**100%**	**-12.0**	**-80**	**$1**

Heim,Jonah

Age: 28	Pos: CA	Health	A	LIMA Plan	D+
Bats: B	Ht: 6' 4" Wt: 220	PT/Exp	B	Rand Var	0
		Consist	B	MM	2113

Emerged as viable backstop with early power barrage, but it didn't come with full support from underlying numbers (see 1st half xHR/F). Things unraveled in 2nd half, the second straight year in which he suffered late collapse. The flashes of power and solid ct% hint at .250 BA, 20 HR ceiling, but more likely outcome is something close to a repeat.

Yr	Tm	PA	R	HR	RBI	SB	BA	xHR	xSB	xBA	OBP	SLG	OPS+	vL+	vR+	bb%	ct%	Eye	G	L	F	h%	HctX	QBaB	Brl%	PX	xPX	HR/F	xHR/F	Spd	SBA%	SB%	RAR	BPX	R$
18	aa	145	12	1	9	0	157		1		202	199	54			5	83	0.32				18				28				101	0%	0%		-10	-$4
19	a/a	315	34	7	43	0	270		1		335	408	103			9	82	0.55				31				78				83	1%	0%		130	$5
20	OAK	41	5	0	5	0	211	1	0	202	268	211	64	87	56	7	92	1.00	43	17	40	23	117	DBf	6%	0	66	0%	7%	115	0%	0%	-2.6	80	-$2
21	TEX	285	22	10	32	3	196	8	0	239	239	358	82	99	75	5	78	0.26	40	18	42	21	116	CBf	6%	93	117	11%	9%	56	9%	75%	-10.2	62	$0
22	TEX	450	51	16	48	2	227	10	5	245	298	399	99	117	91	9	79	0.47	39	18	43	25	111	CBf	6%	106	106	12%	7%	83	2%	100%	4.9	152	$8
1st Half		217	28	12	31	2	258	5	2	257	313	485	113	150	99	8	79	0.40	41	14	45	27	118	BBf	8%	133	114	17%	7%	87	2%	100%	10.1	224	$13
2nd Half		233	23	4	17	0	197	5	3	235	283	317	85	90	83	10	78	0.53	37	21	42	23	105	CBf	5%	81	99	6%	7%	87	2%	0%	-5.0	93	-$1
23	**Proj**	**420**	**42**	**12**	**44**	**2**	**226**	**10**	**1**	**234**	**285**	**367**	**90**	**107**	**83**	**8**	**79**	**0.39**	**39**	**18**	**43**	**26**	**113**		**6%**	**91**	**110**	**9%**	**8%**	**65**	**2%**	**79%**	**0.9**	**103**	**$8**

BRIAN RUDD

Henderson,Gunnar

Age: 22	Pos: 3B	Health A	LIMA Plan C+
Bats: L	Ht: 6' 3" Wt: 195	PT/Exp C	Rand Var 0
		Consist F	MM 4535

4-18-.259 with 1 SB in 132 PA at BAL. Exciting prospect earned late call-up, held his own with patient approach and some hard contact. Though he didn't put wheels in motion, he did in minors (22-for-25), and Spd says the SB will come. Marginal ct% puts BA at risk, but power/speed blend put 20/20 within reach in first full season.

Yr	Tm	PA	R	HR	RBI	SB	BA	xHR	xSB	xBA	OBP	SLG	OPS+	vL+	vR+	bb%	ct%	Eye	G	L	F	h%	HctX	QBaB	Brl%	PX	xPX	HR/F	xHR/F	Spd	SBA%	SB%	RAR	BPX	R$
18																																			
19																																			
20																																			
21																																			
22	BAL *	591	79	19	69	16	256	5	10	256	342	437	110	63	124	12	69	0.43	60	16	24	33	104	AFd	10%	125	92	20%	25%	137	13%	78%	16.5	152	$23
1st Half		281	43	10	34	10	262		5	255	363	460	116	0	0	14	72	0.57	44	20	36	32	0			130	-14	0%		127	13%	82%	11.7	207	$24
2nd Half		310	36	9	35	6	251	5	5	243	323	416	105	63	124	10	67	0.32	60	16	24	34	100	AFd	10%	120	92	20%	25%	134	13%	73%	2.8	86	$19
23	**Proj**	**560**	**73**	**23**	**65**	**15**	**251**	**24**	**13**	**258**	**338**	**462**	**111**	**82**	**118**	**12**	**71**	**0.45**	**48**	**20**	**32**	**31**	**98**		**10%**	**142**	**83**	**20%**	**21%**	**137**	**13%**	**79%**	**22.7**	**134**	**$21**

Hernández,César

Age: 33	Pos: 2B	Health A	LIMA Plan D+
Bats: B	Ht: 5' 10" Wt: 195	PT/Exp A	Rand Var +1
		Consist B	MM 1223

Power completely vanished, with lone late-season HR coming over a full year after his last one. Salvaged some value by putting above-average speed to use again, but SB repeat is unlikely at his age, and strong BA may be gone for good. Without much else to fall back on, lofty PA total may be next shoe to drop.

Yr	Tm	PA	R	HR	RBI	SB	BA	xHR	xSB	xBA	OBP	SLG	OPS+	vL+	vR+	bb%	ct%	Eye	G	L	F	h%	HctX	QBaB	Brl%	PX	xPX	HR/F	xHR/F	Spd	SBA%	SB%	RAR	BPX	R$
18	PHI	708	91	15	60	19	253	12	12	225	356	362	96	93	96	13	74	0.61	46	21	34	32	66	DCc	4%	65	63	10%	8%	128	11%	76%	2.6	57	$20
19	PHI	667	77	14	71	9	279	11	13	274	333	408	103	89	107	7	84	0.45	49	23	29	32	95	DCc	3%	67	55	10%	7%	105	6%	82%	4.2	130	$18
20	CLE	260	35	3	20	0	283	4	3	253	355	408	101	89	105	9	76	0.42	49	23	27	36	95	CFc	4%	88	93	6%	9%	95	0%	0%	0.4	88	$15
21	2 AL	637	84	21	62	1	232	17	3	239	308	386	95	104	91	9	76	0.44	47	18	35	27	88	DCc	7%	87	91	14%	11%	105	1%	50%	-9.9	104	$10
22	WAS	617	64	1	34	10	248	5	5	240	311	318	89	97	85	7	80	0.39	46	23	31	31	90	FDf	2%	52	59	1%	4%	115	9%	71%	-14.3	38	$10
1st Half		361	41	0	19	3	252	3	3	249	311	315	89	102	82	7	81	0.41	46	25	28	31	88	FDf	3%	49	59	0%	4%	120	9%	60%	-6.4	48	$8
2nd Half		256	23	1	15	7	243	2	2	228	311	322	90	89	90	8	78	0.38	47	19	34	31	93	FDf	1%	57	58	2%	3%	99	9%	78%	-4.2	21	$5
23	**Proj**	**385**	**45**	**6**	**30**	**4**	**248**	**6**	**6**	**239**	**312**	**354**	**92**	**95**	**91**	**8**	**78**	**0.38**	**47**	**21**	**32**	**30**	**89**		**4%**	**73**	**72**	**6%**	**7%**	**103**	**8%**	**69%**	**-0.7**	**65**	**$9**

Hernández,Kiké

Age: 31	Pos: CF	Health D	LIMA Plan B
Bats: R	Ht: 5' 11" Wt: 190	PT/Exp A	Rand Var +2
		Consist C	MM 2125

Hip strain cost him more than two months, but pre-injury power was already lacking, then subpar OBP and futility vR eventually pushed him down the order. Given history of low h% and SBA%, power is his only clear path to double-digit R$. Track record suggests he'll rebound to some extent, but not all the way to 2021 levels.

Yr	Tm	PA	R	HR	RBI	SB	BA	xHR	xSB	xBA	OBP	SLG	OPS+	vL+	vR+	bb%	ct%	Eye	G	L	F	h%	HctX	QBaB	Brl%	PX	xPX	HR/F	xHR/F	Spd	SBA%	SB%	RAR	BPX	R$
18	LA	462	67	21	52	3	256	16	6	260	336	470	108	103	110	11	81	0.64	38	19	44	27	105	CBd	7%	115	105	15%	11%	111	3%	100%	17.2	237	$13
19	LA	460	57	17	64	4	237	16	3	242	304	411	99	105	94	8	77	0.37	36	21	43	27	107	CAc	6%	92	107	12%	12%	88	4%	100%	-4.3	89	$9
20	LA	148	20	5	20	0	230	6	1	251	270	410	90	88	91	4	78	0.19	40	20	39	26	107	CBf	6%	101	104	12%	14%	122	4%	0%	-5.5	152	$7
21	BOS	585	84	20	60	1	250	23	6	256	337	449	108	116	103	10	78	0.55	33	21	46	28	114	BAd	8%	116	123	11%	12%	123	1%	100%	9.9	254	$13
22	BOS	402	48	6	45	0	222	7	2	233	291	338	89	109	83	8	80	0.48	39	18	43	26	103	CBf	5%	82	78	5%	6%	97	2%	0%	-8.1	121	$3
1st Half		238	27	4	24	0	209	5	1	231	273	340	87	116	77	8	82	0.47	34	16	50	24	98	CAf	7%	90	80	4%	6%	91	2%	0%	-7.1	159	$1
2nd Half		164	21	2	21	0	240	2	1	240	317	336	92	97	91	10	77	0.48	47	22	31	30	110	CCc	2%	70	75	6%	6%	105	2%	0%	-2.2	66	$1
23	**Proj**	**490**	**66**	**12**	**58**	**1**	**236**	**13**	**3**	**245**	**310**	**386**	**97**	**107**	**92**	**9**	**79**	**0.47**	**39**	**20**	**41**	**28**	**108**		**6%**	**100**	**96**	**8%**	**9%**	**105**	**4%**	**50%**	**2.0**	**159**	**$12**

Hernández,Teoscar

Age: 30	Pos: RF	Health B	LIMA Plan D+
Bats: R	Ht: 6' 2" Wt: 205	PT/Exp A	Rand Var 0
		Consist B	MM 5235

Took some time to get going after oblique injury in April, but rounded into form and didn't look back. Made a ton of loud contact in 2nd half, as LDs returned and BA/xBA made healthy recoveries. 2021's SB total might be an outlier, but with all these barrels, fly balls should keep leaving the park at a lofty rate... UP: 40 HR.

Yr	Tm	PA	R	HR	RBI	SB	BA	xHR	xSB	xBA	OBP	SLG	OPS+	vL+	vR+	bb%	ct%	Eye	G	L	F	h%	HctX	QBaB	Brl%	PX	xPX	HR/F	xHR/F	Spd	SBA%	SB%	RAR	BPX	R$
18	TOR	523	67	22	57	5	239	33	6	238	302	468	103	99	103	8	66	0.25	36	20	44	32	90	ABc	16%	157	149	16%	24%	147	10%	50%	0.6	170	$12
19	TOR *	544	67	30	74	8	228	25	8	226	299	461	105	116	103	9	64	0.28	39	18	43	29	97	ABf	12%	138	144	23%	22%	118	10%	74%	-11.1	78	$14
20	TOR	206	33	16	34	6	289	17	3	262	340	579	122	122	121	7	67	0.22	36	26	38	35	133	ABb	18%	169	165	33%	35%	102	15%	86%	11.8	196	$31
21	TOR	595	92	32	116	12	296	32	13	268	346	524	119	157	108	6	73	0.24	38	25	36	35	109	ACc	14%	134	109	22%	22%	100	11%	75%	20.0	169	$34
22	TOR	535	71	25	77	6	267	30	7	265	316	491	114	137	109	6	70	0.22	44	22	34	34	133	ACc	15%	159	143	21%	25%	96	8%	67%	9.3	169	$22
1st Half		237	27	9	32	3	258	11	3	251	308	452	108	130	103	6	70	0.21	48	18	34	33	125	ACc	13%	137	140	17%	21%	113	8%	60%	-0.2	131	$12
2nd Half		298	44	16	45	3	273	19	4	276	322	522	120	142	114	7	69	0.23	41	24	34	34	140	ACc	16%	177	145	24%	29%	82	8%	75%	10.1	200	$29
23	**Proj**	**595**	**85**	**31**	**96**	**7**	**275**	**35**	**7**	**263**	**327**	**509**	**116**	**138**	**110**	**7**	**70**	**0.24**	**41**	**23**	**36**	**34**	**122**		**15%**	**161**	**135**	**22%**	**25%**	**96**	**7%**	**68%**	**28.2**	**169**	**$31**

Herrera,Iván

Age: 23	Pos: CA	Health A	LIMA Plan D
Bats: R	Ht: 6' 0" Wt: 180	PT/Exp D	Rand Var -1
		Consist A	MM 1301

0-1-.111 in 22 PA at STL. Heralded prospect cut down on Ks in first real taste at AAA; perhaps at the expense of power. Still a work in progress behind the plate and offensive skills show he's not a finished product with the bat, either. Has plenty of appeal in dynasty leagues, but it will take some time, so don't bank on 2023 impact.

Yr	Tm	PA	R	HR	RBI	SB	BA	xHR	xSB	xBA	OBP	SLG	OPS+	vL+	vR+	bb%	ct%	Eye	G	L	F	h%	HctX	QBaB	Brl%	PX	xPX	HR/F	xHR/F	Spd	SBA%	SB%	RAR	BPX	R$
18	aa																																		
19																																			
20																																			
21	a/a	406	34	11	42	1	186		4		265	303	78			10	72	0.38				23				71				82	5%	29%		-35	-$2
22	STL *	281	27	4	23	3	211	0	3	193	286	291	82	0	54	9	75	0.41	55	9	36	27	109	FFf		55	122	0%	0%	112	6%	74%	-7.2	-10	$0
1st Half		142	12	2	12	1	218	0	1	198	286	301	83	0	54	9	78	0.43	55	9	36	27	113	FFf		54	122	0%	0%	122	6%	37%	-3.4	34	-$5
2nd Half		139	15	2	12	3	205	0	1	204	285	280	80	0	0	10	71	0.39	44	20	36	27	0	AAf		55	-14	0%	#DIV/0!	111	6%	100%	-3.6	-52	-$2
23	**Proj**	**140**	**13**	**2**	**13**	**1**	**202**	**2**	**2**	**212**	**278**	**293**	**79**	**78**	**79**	**10**	**73**	**0.39**	**50**	**18**	**32**	**26**	**88**		**6%**	**63**		**8%**	**7%**	**111**	**7%**	**69%**	**-3.1**	**-24**	**$1**

Hicks,Aaron

Age: 33	Pos: CF LF	Health F	LIMA Plan D
Bats: B	Ht: 6' 1" Wt: 205	PT/Exp B	Rand Var 0
		Consist B	MM 2303

Avoided the IL for just the second time in 10 seasons, but power skills and xBA were ailing all year, eventually costing him everyday role. Good health can't be expected to stick given age and track record, nor can the SB spike. High bb% helps hold some real-life value, but PA and R$ are more likely to go down than up in 2023.

Yr	Tm	PA	R	HR	RBI	SB	BA	xHR	xSB	xBA	OBP	SLG	OPS+	vL+	vR+	bb%	ct%	Eye	G	L	F	h%	HctX	QBaB	Brl%	PX	xPX	HR/F	xHR/F	Spd	SBA%	SB%	RAR	BPX	R$
18	NYY	581	90	27	79	11	248	23	9	264	366	467	112	106	112	15	77	0.81	40	22	38	27	112	BCd	9%	122	131	19%	16%	111	8%	85%	18.3	237	$21
19	NYY	255	41	12	36	1	235	9	3	227	325	443	106	94	112	12	67	0.43	43	16	41	29	89	BCf	9%	122	98	19%	15%	92	5%	33%	-2.6	78	$4
20	NYY	211	28	6	21	4	225	7	3	261	379	414	105	103	106	19	78	1.08	45	20	35	26	93	CCf	7%	105	75	13%	16%	115	8%	80%	-1.3	276	$13
21	NYY	126	13	4	14	0	194	4	2	213	294	333	86	112	74	11	72	0.47	35	20	45	23	89	BAd	10%	81	109	11%	11%	87	0%	0%	-4.3	15	-$2
22	NYY	453	54	8	40	10	216	9	4	201	330	313	91	89	91	14	72	0.57	44	16	39	28	90	CCf	6%	63	70	7%	8%	134	10%	77%	-8.7	21	$7
1st Half		248	26	3	20	7	221	4	3	195	340	288	89	94	87	14	73	0.60	44	19	38	29	83	CCf	3%	42	53	5%	7%	128	10%	70%	-5.8	-24	$6
2nd Half		205	28	5	20	3	210	6	2	208	317	341	93	82	97	14	70	0.54	45	14	41	27	99	CCf	8%	88	90	10%	12%	126	10%	100%	-2.4	69	$5
23	**Proj**	**280**	**35**	**8**	**29**	**3**	**221**	**8**	**5**	**215**	**330**	**354**	**95**	**101**	**92**	**14**	**72**	**0.57**	**41**	**18**	**41**	**27**	**92**		**8%**	**87**	**89**	**11%**	**11%**	**109**	**9%**	**73%**	**0.1**	**64**	**$6**

Higgins,P.J.

Age: 30	Pos: 1B CA	Health D	LIMA Plan D
Bats: R	Ht: 5' 10" Wt: 195	PT/Exp F	Rand Var -2
		Consist C	MM 2121

6-30-.229 in 229 PA at CHC. Called up in May and got off to surprisingly hot start, but crashed down the stretch with .480 OPS in final 110 PA. PX history is pretty uninspiring while xPX and xHR/F question 2022's power gains. Just enough ct% to not kill your BA, but even as second catcher in deep leagues, that may not be enough.

Yr	Tm	PA	R	HR	RBI	SB	BA	xHR	xSB	xBA	OBP	SLG	OPS+	vL+	vR+	bb%	ct%	Eye	G	L	F	h%	HctX	QBaB	Brl%	PX	xPX	HR/F	xHR/F	Spd	SBA%	SB%	RAR	BPX	R$
18	aa	155	11	1	12	1	204		2		256	263	70			7	79	0.33				25				38				108	3%	100%		-20	-$2
19	a/a	421	40	8	47	4	244		4		308	357	92			8	76	0.38				30				64				101	9%	47%		11	$5
20																																			
21	CHC *	69	5	1	4	0	180	0	1	158	265	259	72	34	20	10	65	0.33	53	7	40	27	53	FCf	0%	53	-22	0%	0%	124	0%	0%	-5.4	-142	-$3
22	CHC *	308	28	7	40	1	249	2	1	241	322	391	101	84	105	9	71	0.37	43	24	33	33	57	FDf	3%	105	56	13%	4%	85	1%	100%	-2.8	48	$5
1st Half		151	14	4	21	1	304	0	1	254	370	464	118	101	140	10	73	0.40	37	26	37	39	77	FCf	2%	113	56	18%	0%	104	1%	100%	7.2	124	$3
2nd Half		157	14	3	19	0	196	2	0	226	277	319	84	77	88	10	68	0.34	45	23	32	26	46	DFd	4%	98	56	10%	7%	73	1%	0%	-6.9	-21	-$3
23	**Proj**	**175**	**16**	**4**	**21**	**1**	**238**	**2**	**1**	**240**	**312**	**371**	**95**	**82**	**101**	**9**	**73**	**0.37**	**42**	**24**	**34**	**30**	**58**		**4%**	**93**	**56**	**10%**	**6%**	**84**	**3%**	**55%**	**-1.6**	**21**	**$4**

BRIAN RUDD

Hilliard,Sam

Age: 29 Pos: LF	Health A	LIMA Plan D
Bats: L Ht: 6' 5" Wt: 236	PT/Exp C	Rand Var +4
	Consist A	MM 4401

2-14-.184 with 5 SB in 200 PA at COL. Another down year, as .238 OBP through 41 games sent him to AAA by June. Early h% swoon hid some modest ct% growth, though xBA barely budged thanks to steep drop in power skills. HR/SB ceiling still makes him flyer-worthy with regular gig; but there's A LOT that would have to go right.

Yr	Tm	PA	R	HR	RBI	SB	BA	xHR	xSB	xBA	OBP	SLG	OPS+	vL+	vR+	bb%	ct%	Eye	G	L	F	h%	HctX	QBaB	Brl%	PX	xPX	HR/F	xHR/F	Spd	SBA%	SB%	RAR	BPX	R$
18	aa	468	45	8	31	18	247		6		300	364	89			7	64	0.21				37				89				112	30%	54%		-73	$11
19	COL *	622	83	32	77	16	233	5	18	241	287	478	106	155	133	7	65	0.22	43	19	39	30	83	ADc	13%	146	167	33%	24%	117	20%	74%	3.7	104	$19
20	COL	114	13	6	10	3	210	4	3	217	272	438	94	63	107	8	60	0.21	50	15	35	28	89	CCf	10%	141	98	27%	18%	137	14%	100%	-3.4	48	$6
21	COL *	439	50	23	55	8	205	13	7	228	271	436	97	115	101	8	61	0.23	44	18	38	27	82	BCf	15%	157	123	29%	27%	118	12%	87%	-7.9	88	$8
22	COL *	343	40	9	30	7	204	5	6	211	281	341	88	53	82	10	66	0.32	45	18	37	28	100	ACf	9%	96	107	5%	11%	122	12%	76%	-9.2	0	$4
1st Half		176	18	4	17	3	173	4	3	204	244	289	75	57	75	9	68	0.29	45	16	39	23	108	ACf	11%	82	110	6%	13%	103	12%	57%	-9.8	-41	-$2
2nd Half		167	22	5	14	4	237	1	4	222	321	397	102	44	93	11	64	0.35	44	23	33	33	87	ACc	5%	111	101	0%	8%	133	12%	100%	2.1	34	$4
23	**Proj**	**210**	**25**	**7**	**21**	**5**	**223**	**7**	**4**	**216**	**297**	**393**	**96**	**87**	**98**	**9**	**64**	**0.27**	**44**	**19**	**37**	**31**	**90**		**11%**	**123**	**116**	**16%**	**17%**	**123**	**11%**	**81%**	**0.0**	**35**	**$3**

Hiura,Keston

Age: 26 Pos: 1B DH	Health A	LIMA Plan D+
Bats: R Ht: 6' 0" Wt: 202	PT/Exp C	Rand Var -3
	Consist B	MM 5103

14-32-.226 with 5 SB in 266 PA at MIL. Couldn't dig out of 2021's ct% rut, as barrage of strikeouts led to AAA demotions in May and July. Power skills re-entered the stratosphere, but BA "rebound" was mostly h%-driven, SB success was futile, and issues vL persisted. Always a threat to return to 35+ HR, but hasn't yet earned the PA to get there.

Yr	Tm	PA	R	HR	RBI	SB	BA	xHR	xSB	xBA	OBP	SLG	OPS+	vL+	vR+	bb%	ct%	Eye	G	L	F	h%	HctX	QBaB	Brl%	PX	xPX	HR/F	xHR/F	Spd	SBA%	SB%	RAR	BPX	R$
18	aa	300	34	6	19	10	264		4		315	408	97			7	78	0.34				32				92				112	22%	66%		120	$8
19	MIL *	579	85	35	85	14	298	21	16	262	351	577	128	94	140	7	66	0.24	38	24	38	39	100	ABb	14%	170	140	24%	27%	108	14%	73%	29.3	178	$28
20	MIL	246	30	13	32	3	212	14	5	211	297	410	94	89	95	7	61	0.19	43	20	37	28	72	CBc	13%	124	111	26%	28%	97	9%	60%	-9.6	-52	$16
21	MIL *	388	30	9	35	4	185	7	4	183	256	327	80	55	86	9	53	0.20	37	22	41	31	81	BBf	15%	125	133	10%	18%	88	7%	78%	-27.2	-158	-$1
22	MIL *	319	39	18	43	5	230	14	4	217	302	460	108	87	123	9	54	0.22	37	25	38	35	91	ABb	16%	189	155	30%	30%	102	15%	47%	-2.3	59	$9
1st Half		148	21	9	22	4	239	5	2	205	321	468	112	65	155	11	49	0.24	37	27	35	40	76	ABa	16%	198	132	39%	28%	95	15%	53%	0.2	21	$7
2nd Half		171	18	9	22	1	223	8	2	228	286	454	105	115	101	8	58	0.21	37	23	40	32	103	ABc	15%	183	170	24%	28%	108	15%	31%	-2.8	93	$5
23	**Proj**	**315**	**35**	**15**	**39**	**4**	**236**	**15**	**6**	**212**	**322**	**436**	**105**	**85**	**115**	**9**	**56**	**0.21**	**38**	**23**	**39**	**36**	**88**		**15%**	**166**	**142**	**23%**	**24%**	**92**	**11%**	**49%**	**0.9**	**-6**	**$10**

Hoerner,Nico

Age: 26 Pos: SS	Health D	LIMA Plan B
Bats: R Ht: 6' 1" Wt: 200	PT/Exp A	Rand Var 0
	Consist B	MM 1445

May ankle sprain, Sept triceps soreness held back PA total, but a nice step forward in first full season. Couldn't hold 2021's h% spike, but ct% gains softened the blow and Spd translated to bags on basepaths. This isn't a complete package—Brl%, xHR question HR repeat and bb% waned—but BA/SB combo looks here to stay.

Yr	Tm	PA	R	HR	RBI	SB	BA	xHR	xSB	xBA	OBP	SLG	OPS+	vL+	vR+	bb%	ct%	Eye	G	L	F	h%	HctX	QBaB	Brl%	PX	xPX	HR/F	xHR/F	Spd	SBA%	SB%	RAR	BPX	R$
18																																			
19	CHC *	370	48	6	38	7	277	1	6	298	322	399	100	111	100	6	87	0.53	53	25	22	30	80	DFa	2%	60	48	20%	7%	135	12%	64%	-3.2	193	$9
20	CHC	125	19	0	13	3	222	1	3	230	312	259	76	81	73	10	78	0.50	55	21	24	29	92	CFf	1%	29	59	0%	5%	114	14%	60%	-6.7	-36	$6
21	CHC *	196	15	0	17	5	290	1	5	246	353	352	97	87	110	9	82	0.53	48	23	29	35	80	CDc	2%	48	41	0%	3%	110	13%	63%	-0.8	69	$4
22	CHC	517	60	10	55	20	281	6	13	274	327	410	104	106	104	5	88	0.49	46	21	33	30	92	CCc	2%	73	66	7%	4%	146	17%	91%	6.3	234	$24
1st Half		246	24	4	24	7	307	3	7	276	346	420	108	106	109	5	89	0.44	48	22	30	33	96	CDc	4%	61	67	6%	5%	170	17%	88%	7.1	234	$14
2nd Half		271	36	6	31	13	256	3	6	272	310	400	101	106	99	6	87	0.53	45	19	36	27	89	DCd	1%	84	65	8%	4%	117	17%	93%	1.2	228	$21
23	**Proj**	**560**	**63**	**7**	**57**	**20**	**276**	**6**	**16**	**265**	**333**	**382**	**99**	**95**	**101**	**7**	**86**	**0.53**	**48**	**22**	**30**	**31**	**90**		**2%**	**67**	**56**	**6%**	**4%**	**115**	**14%**	**79%**	**8.4**	**152**	**$25**

Hoskins,Rhys

Age: 30 Pos: 1B	Health C	LIMA Plan B+
Bats: R Ht: 6' 4" Wt: 245	PT/Exp A	Rand Var 0
	Consist A	MM 4135

A near copy of 2021's surface stats; just needed 200+ more PA to get there. More grounders, FB% plunge knocked HR rate and did nothing for xBA. Easy BA projection given baseline (Khris Davis, anyone?), and while PX/xPX baseline hints at a 40-HR ceiling, the fly balls must return to make it happen.

Yr	Tm	PA	R	HR	RBI	SB	BA	xHR	xSB	xBA	OBP	SLG	OPS+	vL+	vR+	bb%	ct%	Eye	G	L	F	h%	HctX	QBaB	Brl%	PX	xPX	HR/F	xHR/F	Spd	SBA%	SB%	RAR	BPX	R$
18	PHI	659	89	34	96	5	246	30	9	256	354	496	114	88	119	13	73	0.58	29	19	52	28	93	CAc	11%	157	145	16%	14%	66	5%	63%	10.9	220	$21
19	PHI	703	86	29	85	2	226	30	8	236	364	454	113	136	105	17	70	0.67	29	21	50	27	111	BAc	10%	131	143	14%	15%	106	2%	50%	-1.8	185	$12
20	PHI	185	35	10	26	1	245	11	1	247	384	503	118	162	100	16	72	0.67	29	19	52	28	94	BAc	15%	150	161	18%	20%	93	2%	100%	1.6	268	$16
21	PHI	443	64	27	71	3	247	33	2	267	334	530	119	127	115	11	72	0.44	29	20	51	27	101	AAc	17%	172	152	19%	23%	72	5%	60%	10.5	273	$15
22	PHI	671	81	30	79	2	246	30	6	255	332	462	112	132	106	11	71	0.43	36	23	42	29	101	BAc	11%	144	124	17%	17%	81	2%	67%	8.3	166	$19
1st Half		342	44	17	42	0	253	15	3	258	345	492	118	140	110	12	71	0.48	36	21	44	30	103	BBd	11%	156	132	18%	16%	104	2%	0%	12.1	234	$22
2nd Half		329	37	13	37	2	240	15	3	253	319	432	106	123	101	10	71	0.37	36	25	40	29	98	BAc	11%	132	115	16%	18%	59	2%	67%	1.1	103	$19
23	**Proj**	**630**	**87**	**31**	**86**	**3**	**245**	**34**	**3**	**257**	**339**	**478**	**113**	**130**	**107**	**12**	**72**	**0.46**	**33**	**21**	**45**	**29**	**100**		**13%**	**158**	**137**	**17%**	**19%**	**72**	**2%**	**65%**	**20.5**	**207**	**$23**

Hosmer,Eric

Age: 33 Pos: 1B	Health C	LIMA Plan D+
Bats: L Ht: 6' 4" Wt: 226	PT/Exp A	Rand Var 0
	Consist B	MM 2131

Not good when your top headline was exercising a no-trade option to temporarily block the Juan Soto deal. Sent to BOS at the deadline instead, where he spent more time on IL (back) than in lineup. On the field, xHR/F and xBA hit new lows while GBs continued to stifle power. Some BA/OBP utility, but consider exercising your no-draft clause.

Yr	Tm	PA	R	HR	RBI	SB	BA	xHR	xSB	xBA	OBP	SLG	OPS+	vL+	vR+	bb%	ct%	Eye	G	L	F	h%	HctX	QBaB	Brl%	PX	xPX	HR/F	xHR/F	Spd	SBA%	SB%	RAR	BPX	R$
18	SD	677	72	18	69	7	253	18	9	266	322	398	97	70	110	9	77	0.44	60	20	20	30	98	CFd	6%	90	68	19%	19%	86	7%	64%	-1.8	87	$15
19	SD	667	72	22	99	0	265	23	7	252	310	425	102	83	107	6	74	0.25	56	21	23	33	102	BFc	7%	89	77	21%	22%	86	2%	0%	-8.1	22	$15
20	SD	156	23	9	36	4	287	8	1	277	333	517	113	80	130	6	80	0.32	46	20	34	30	136	BDc	10%	116	159	23%	20%	70	11%	100%	3.5	196	$22
21	SD	565	53	12	65	5	269	14	9	255	337	395	101	92	104	8	81	0.48	55	19	26	31	107	BFf	6%	76	70	11%	13%	82	6%	56%	-1.1	104	$14
22	2 TM	419	38	8	44	0	268	9	4	244	334	382	101	108	98	9	83	0.58	57	18	25	31	100	CFf	6%	72	71	10%	11%	86	0%	0%	3.6	124	$9
1st Half		304	28	6	33	0	272	5	3	248	329	387	101	115	95	8	82	0.47	58	19	23	32	95	CFd	6%	74	67	11%	9%	87	0%	0%	0.9	103	$11
2nd Half		115	10	2	11	0	257	4	1	235	348	366	101	89	106	11	87	1.00	55	15	31	28	113	CFf	6%	67	79	7%	15%	89	0%	0%	-0.2	186	-$4
23	**Proj**	**245**	**24**	**6**	**30**	**1**	**267**	**7**	**1**	**253**	**335**	**399**	**102**	**92**	**106**	**9**	**82**	**0.54**	**55**	**18**	**27**	**30**	**109**		**6%**	**83**	**81**	**12%**	**14%**	**82**	**2%**	**68%**	**3.2**	**133**	**$8**

Huff,Sam

Age: 25 Pos: CA	Health C	LIMA Plan D
Bats: R Ht: 6' 5" Wt: 240	PT/Exp D	Rand Var +5
	Consist F	MM 2303

4-10-.240 in 132 PA at TEX. Recalled from AAA four times over four separate months in hole-plugging role. Plus power to all fields as a prospect showed through per xPX and xHR/F, but so did massive holes in swing that put firm cap on BA ceiling. The bar for two-catcher relevance is low—there's not enough here (yet) to clear it.

Yr	Tm	PA	R	HR	RBI	SB	BA	xHR	xSB	xBA	OBP	SLG	OPS+	vL+	vR+	bb%	ct%	Eye	G	L	F	h%	HctX	QBaB	Brl%	PX	xPX	HR/F	xHR/F	Spd	SBA%	SB%	RAR	BPX	R$
18																																			
19																																			
20	TEX	33	5	3	4	0	355	2	0	336	394	742	151	149	151	6	65	0.18	25	45	30	47	157	ACa	25%	253	223	50%	33%	92	0%	0%	5.8	408	$3
21	a/a	209	22	10	23	0	210		1		264	394	90			7	51	0.15				35				147				90	0%	0%		-135	$0
22	TEX *	393	37	16	40	1	212	4	1	211	264	363	89	102	91	7	62	0.19	43	24	33	29	89	CCd	9%	108	137	15%	15%	91	1%	100%	-4.7	-83	$4
1st Half		189	16	7	17	1	229	1	1	238	277	364	91	84	102	6	66	0.20	52	28	20	30	64	DFd	4%	91	65	10%	10%	94	1%	100%	-1.2	-66	$1
2nd Half		204	21	9	23	0	196	3	1	179	252	362	87	126	74	7	57	0.17	28	17	55	28	129	AAb	19%	127	261	19%	19%	99	1%	0%	-4.1	-86	$4
23	**Proj**	**280**	**28**	**8**	**30**	**0**	**222**	**8**	**1**	**181**	**273**	**341**	**85**	**96**	**77**	**7**	**57**	**0.17**	**41**	**22**	**37**	**35**	**103**		**13%**	**98**	**183**	**15%**	**15%**	**92**	**3%**	**100%**	**-2.4**	**-101**	**$5**

Iglesias,José

Age: 33 Pos: SS	Health C	LIMA Plan C+
Bats: R Ht: 5' 11" Wt: 195	PT/Exp A	Rand Var 0
	Consist D	MM 1143

Didn't get the memo that you're supposed to hit better in Coors (.264 home BA; .315 away). Elite ct% and h% baseline should lock in another strong BA, but it's completely empty with zero power and shaky track record on basepaths. A decent in-season rental if you need hits, but not someone to target on draft day.

Yr	Tm	PA	R	HR	RBI	SB	BA	xHR	xSB	xBA	OBP	SLG	OPS+	vL+	vR+	bb%	ct%	Eye	G	L	F	h%	HctX	QBaB	Brl%	PX	xPX	HR/F	xHR/F	Spd	SBA%	SB%	RAR	BPX	R$
18	DET	464	43	5	48	15	269	4	6	279	310	389	94	115	87	4	89	0.40	44	23	34	29	88	DCd	1%	73	45	4%	3%	105	20%	71%	2.2	190	$13
19	CIN	530	62	11	59	6	288	9	16	284	318	407	100	96	101	4	86	0.29	52	24	24	32	91	DDc	3%	58	53	10%	9%	114	9%	50%	-4.8	130	$14
20	BAL	150	16	3	24	0	373	3	2	350	400	556	127	117	130	2	88	0.18	43	36	21	41	102	DDc	3%	109	53	11%	11%	71	0%	0%	14.7	268	$17
21	2 AL	511	65	9	48	5	271	6	3	263	309	391	96	107	92	4	84	0.28	42	23	34	31	85	DCd	3%	69	63	6%	4%	107	6%	71%	-5.9	135	$13
22	COL	467	48	3	47	2	292	1	5	273	328	380	100	105	97	4	87	0.30	52	22	26	33	84	FDc	1%	64	35	3%	1%	92	4%	40%	-1.2	128	$13
1st Half		262	24	2	23	2	293	1	3	282	336	386	102	124	91	4	89	0.39	50	24	26	32	80	DDc	1%	65	27	4%	2%	97	4%	50%	1.2	159	$8
2nd Half		205	24	1	24	0	290	1	2	260	317	373	98	83	106	3	85	0.21	55	20	25	34	89	FFd	1%	62	45	2%	2%	86	4%	0%	-0.7	86	$6
23	**Proj**	**385**	**40**	**4**	**38**	**2**	**281**	**4**	**3**	**273**	**316**	**384**	**97**	**98**	**96**	**4**	**86**	**0.27**	**48**	**24**	**28**	**32**	**87**		**2%**	**71**	**48**	**4%**	**4%**	**87**	**4%**	**43%**	**2.2**	**141**	**$12**

RYAN BLOOMFIELD

India,Jonathan

Age: 26 Pos: 2B	Health B	LIMA Plan B+	
Bats: R Ht: 6' 0" Wt: 200	PT/Exp A	Rand Var 0	
	Consist C	MM 3225	

Hamstring was never right (IL stints in April, May; recurrence in Sept); also missed time after various HBP (leg, hand). Injuries likely drove HR/SB to the ground, as every non-ct% skill was down across the board. Short track record cautions against full rebound, but given age, pedigree, and healthy offseason, he can come close.

Yr	Tm	PA	R	HR	RBI	SB	BA	xHR	xSB	xBA	OBP	SLG	OPS+	vL+	vR+	bb%	ct%	Eye	G	L	F	h%	HctX	QBaB	Brl%	PX	xPX	HR/F	xHR/F	Spd	SBA%	SB%	RAR	BPX	R$
18																																			
19	aa	132	22	3	13	4	252		3		369	358	101			16	73	0.68				32				58				110	9%	100%		15	$1
20																																			
21	CIN	631	98	21	69	12	269	22	9	260	376	459	115	112	116	11	73	0.50	44	23	33	33	102	CCc	10%	118	96	16%	17%	102	8%	80%	19.3	165	$23
22	CIN	431	48	10	41	3	249	9	8	239	327	378	100	99	100	7	76	0.33	41	23	36	30	85	DBd	5%	84	81	10%	9%	124	6%	43%	-4.1	79	$9
1st Half		122	8	2	9	1	204	2	2	208	262	283	77	50	86	3	73	0.13	48	20	33	26	77	DBd	4%	55	59	7%	7%	107	6%	25%	-7.6	-86	-$8
2nd Half		309	40	8	32	2	267	7	6	251	353	418	109	116	107	9	77	0.43	39	24	37	32	88	DBd	5%	96	89	10%	9%	127	6%	67%	7.2	148	$17
23	**Proj**	**560**	**82**	**17**	**63**	**10**	**262**	**16**	**7**	**245**	**353**	**416**	**107**	**102**	**108**	**9**	**74**	**0.40**	**43**	**22**	**35**	**32**	**91**		**7%**	**103**	**84**	**13%**	**12%**	**100**	**6%**	**70%**	**14.7**	**95**	**$20**

Isbel,Kyle

Age: 26 Pos: RF CF LF	Health A	LIMA Plan D	
Bats: L Ht: 5' 11" Wt: 190	PT/Exp C	Rand Var 0	
	Consist B	MM 2403	

Minimal yield in part-time role, save for 7-SB spurt in July/Aug. Raw wheels and green light are the most intriguing data points in this box, but hasn't been able to capitalize per sub-par SB%. Middling QBaB, xBA paint a dreary BA/HR picture, while issues vL and shaky OBP are barriers to full-time role. Speculate only if desperate for speed.

Yr	Tm	PA	R	HR	RBI	SB	BA	xHR	xSB	xBA	OBP	SLG	OPS+	vL+	vR+	bb%	ct%	Eye	G	L	F	h%	HctX	QBaB	Brl%	PX	xPX	HR/F	xHR/F	Spd	SBA%	SB%	RAR	BPX	R$
18																																			
19																																			
20																																			
21	KC *	509	60	11	46	18	233	1	7	211	292	366	90	120	104	8	74	0.32	35	18	47	29	80	DAf	4%	81	52	4%	4%	132	21%	75%	-11.9	69	$14
22	KC	278	32	5	28	9	211	4	7	220	264	340	85	70	89	6	71	0.21	43	19	38	28	101	CCf	5%	87	96	7%	6%	132	28%	60%	-12.2	21	$4
1st Half		117	11	2	10	3	223	3	3	239	248	348	84	45	93	3	75	0.11	46	21	32	28	131	BFd	6%	78	125	7%	11%	127	28%	75%	-4.8	28	-$4
2nd Half		161	21	3	18	6	201	1	4	205	275	333	86	88	86	8	67	0.28	40	18	42	28	77	CCf	4%	95	70	7%	2%	129	28%	55%	-7.5	10	$3
23	**Proj**	**315**	**37**	**5**	**31**	**11**	**223**	**5**	**11**	**211**	**278**	**345**	**86**	**81**	**88**	**7**	**72**	**0.25**	**40**	**19**	**42**	**29**	**92**		**5%**	**83**	**77**	**6%**	**5%**	**133**	**22%**	**65%**	**-8.6**	**38**	**$9**

Jansen,Danny

Age: 28 Pos: CA	Health F	LIMA Plan C+	
Bats: R Ht: 6' 2" Wt: 225	PT/Exp D	Rand Var -1	
	Consist B	MM 4033	

Pair of 1st half IL stints (oblique in April, hand in June) cost him two-plus months; had a career (half) year anyway. Full support from the skills too, as ct% continued its upward climb and power growth (xPX, Brl%) mixed with flyball tilt to drive HR spike. If he swats the injury bug, we could see BA repeat along with... UP: 25 HR

Yr	Tm	PA	R	HR	RBI	SB	BA	xHR	xSB	xBA	OBP	SLG	OPS+	vL+	vR+	bb%	ct%	Eye	G	L	F	h%	HctX	QBaB	Brl%	PX	xPX	HR/F	xHR/F	Spd	SBA%	SB%	RAR	BPX	R$
18	TOR *	432	52	14	59	4	257	4	6	256	340	441	105	94	106	11	82	0.68	32	20	48	28	60	DAf	9%	111	69	10%	13%	103	4%	100%	20.4	233	$11
19	TOR	384	41	13	43	0	207	13	3	237	279	360	89	101	82	8	77	0.39	39	20	41	23	114	CBd	6%	78	97	12%	12%	87	1%	0%	-5.2	59	$1
20	TOR	147	18	6	20	0	183	6	1	243	313	358	89	55	105	14	74	0.68	36	25	39	19	65	FBf	9%	93	74	17%	17%	93	0%	0%	-2.7	120	$4
21	TOR *	229	36	12	31	0	221	9	0	272	292	459	103	79	119	9	77	0.43	31	24	45	23	105	BAf	9%	136	117	17%	14%	78	0%	0%	2.8	227	$3
22	TOR	248	34	15	44	1	260	14	1	267	339	516	121	116	123	10	80	0.57	34	16	51	26	144	BAf	13%	147	160	17%	16%	77	2%	100%	15.6	279	$9
1st Half		62	9	7	13	0	232	6	0	288	290	625	129	87	142	5	82	0.30	36	6	57	15	153	CAf	22%	199	214	26%	22%	97	2%	0%	3.5	445	-$3
2nd Half		186	25	8	31	1	270	8	1	257	355	478	118	125	115	12	79	0.65	33	19	48	30	141	AAd	10%	127	140	13%	13%	76	2%	100%	11.2	224	$11
23	**Proj**	**315**	**45**	**18**	**51**	**0**	**256**	**17**	**1**	**264**	**335**	**496**	**115**	**95**	**123**	**10**	**78**	**0.50**	**33**	**19**	**48**	**27**	**120**		**12%**	**142**	**136**	**17%**	**16%**	**73**	**2%**	**0%**	**18.3**	**251**	**$13**

Jeffers,Ryan

Age: 26 Pos: CA	Health C	LIMA Plan D+	
Bats: R Ht: 6' 4" Wt: 235	PT/Exp D	Rand Var +5	
	Consist B	MM 4123	

7-27-.208 in 236 PA at MIN. Missed most of 2nd half with fractured thumb in another "bleh" season on the surface. Skills hint at some upside, though, as he cut down on Ks, produced barrels with ease, and hit with more loft. Major breakout unlikely, but there's enough here to take a flyer when filling that second catcher slot.

Yr	Tm	PA	R	HR	RBI	SB	BA	xHR	xSB	xBA	OBP	SLG	OPS+	vL+	vR+	bb%	ct%	Eye	G	L	F	h%	HctX	QBaB	Brl%	PX	xPX	HR/F	xHR/F	Spd	SBA%	SB%	RAR	BPX	R$
18																																			
19	aa	95	12	4	8	0	279		1		343	467	112			9	77	0.42				32				101				102	0%	0%		148	-$1
20	MIN	62	5	3	7	0	273	3	0	182	355	436	105	93	110	8	65	0.26	53	17	31	36	110	ACf	14%	89	112	27%	27%	110	0%	0%	1.5	-60	$2
21	MIN *	389	38	18	47	0	196	15	1	217	269	394	91	99	88	9	61	0.25	42	21	37	26	98	BCc	14%	136	157	24%	25%	96	1%	0%	-6.8	4	$2
22	MIN *	273	28	9	31	1	203	10	1	225	277	360	90	127	77	9	73	0.38	35	19	46	24	99	CBd	14%	104	115	10%	15%	75	2%	100%	-2.5	62	$1
1st Half		193	19	5	20	0	192	9	1	214	276	331	86	117	72	10	69	0.38	32	20	47	25	93	CAd	17%	103	121	9%	16%	57	2%	0%	-3.8	-3	-$2
2nd Half		80	9	4	11	1	227	1	0	255	280	427	100	173	95	7	82	0.40	47	13	40	23	115	DCf	3%	106	94	17%	8%	128	2%	100%	0.9	224	-$3
23	**Proj**	**315**	**33**	**15**	**39**	**0**	**224**	**14**	**2**	**240**	**296**	**431**	**101**	**121**	**91**	**9**	**70**	**0.31**	**43**	**18**	**39**	**26**	**103**		**11%**	**136**	**126**	**19%**	**17%**	**98**	**4%**	**51%**	**6.3**	**79**	**$7**

Jiménez,Eloy

Age: 26 Pos: DH LF	Health F	LIMA Plan B	
Bats: R Ht: 6' 4" Wt: 240	PT/Exp C	Rand Var -2	
	Consist C	MM 4025	

16-54-.295 in 327 PA at CHW. Yet another partial season; this time an April hamstring strain that shelved him for three months. Good signs aplenty upon return with fewer Ks driving xBA uptick, raw power (xHR/F) snapping right back, and more loft. Likely won't hold 2nd half BA gains, but if he stays upright... UP: 40 HR.

Yr	Tm	PA	R	HR	RBI	SB	BA	xHR	xSB	xBA	OBP	SLG	OPS+	vL+	vR+	bb%	ct%	Eye	G	L	F	h%	HctX	QBaB	Brl%	PX	xPX	HR/F	xHR/F	Spd	SBA%	SB%	RAR	BPX	R$
18	a/a	446	58	21	68	0	315		6		361	544	121			7	81	0.39				35				128				95	1%	0%		240	$19
19	CHW *	526	71	32	80	0	268	31	3	255	310	509	113	109	116	6	71	0.21	48	18	34	31	94	ACc	13%	128	102	27%	27%	107	0%	0%	5.3	126	$16
20	CHW	226	26	14	41	0	296	14	1	268	332	559	118	112	120	5	74	0.21	52	20	28	34	132	AFd	16%	150	125	31%	31%	84	0%	0%	7.6	212	$24
21	CHW *	270	25	11	38	0	243	10	0	239	292	416	97	78	110	6	70	0.24	48	22	29	30	114	BDc	11%	108	104	22%	22%	66	0%	0%	-1.6	12	$4
22	CHW *	388	45	17	58	0	276	18	1	239	336	460	113	118	123	8	75	0.36	50	17	33	32	144	ADc	15%	112	143	22%	24%	85	0%	0%	13.4	117	$13
1st Half		96	6	2	10	0	189	1	0	161	238	280	73	200	63	6	72	0.23	67	7	26	23	129	AFc	7%	55	59	14%	14%	98	0%	0%	-5.5	-83	-$9
2nd Half		292	39	15	47	0	306	17	1	258	369	521	126	111	132	9	76	0.42	48	18	34	35	147	ADc	16%	130	154	22%	25%	86	0%	0%	21.5	190	$28
23	**Proj**	**525**	**56**	**26**	**77**	**0**	**262**	**25**	**1**	**247**	**314**	**463**	**108**	**111**	**107**	**7**	**73**	**0.28**	**50**	**18**	**31**	**31**	**127**		**12%**	**128**	**112**	**23%**	**23%**	**75**	**1%**	**0%**	**11.0**	**84**	**$20**

Joe,Connor

Age: 30 Pos: LF DH 1B	Health B	LIMA Plan D+	
Bats: R Ht: 6' 0" Wt: 205	PT/Exp B	Rand Var 0	
	Consist D	MM 2223	

Hot-ish start in April (.272, 4 HR, 1 SB), but couldn't muster more than 3 HR+SB in any other month. Sparse counting stats sure look entrenched given PX/xPX crash and running game that stayed mostly stagnant. With little else to fall back on—xBA quells much hope for BA growth—it's best to throw your late darts elsewhere.

Yr	Tm	PA	R	HR	RBI	SB	BA	xHR	xSB	xBA	OBP	SLG	OPS+	vL+	vR+	bb%	ct%	Eye	G	L	F	h%	HctX	QBaB	Brl%	PX	xPX	HR/F	xHR/F	Spd	SBA%	SB%	RAR	BPX	R$
18	a/a	405	50	12	40	2	243		5		320	415	99			10	70	0.38				31				116				101	4%	48%		90	$7
19	SF *	422	57	10	46	1	228	0	3	229	315	370	95	31	0	11	71	0.44	70	10	20	29	25	FFc	0%	87	-36	0%	0%	83	3%	22%	-16.4	19	$4
20																																			
21	COL *	311	34	14	49	1	273	7	4	272	355	477	114	128	112	11	75	0.51	33	28	38	32	119	CBc	10%	119	138	15%	13%	80	1%	100%	10.7	165	$9
22	COL	467	56	7	28	6	238	6	6	242	338	359	99	104	95	12	76	0.57	46	21	33	30	86	DCd	5%	82	78	7%	6%	148	6%	75%	-0.1	134	$7
1st Half		335	40	5	19	5	270	4	5	244	370	391	108	122	100	13	76	0.60	44	24	32	34	79	DCc	5%	78	79	7%	6%	168	6%	71%	7.6	148	$14
2nd Half		132	16	2	9	1	157	2	1	235	258	278	76	70	80	10	77	0.48	52	13	35	31	105	CDd	4%	91	75	6%	6%	92	6%	100%	-7.5	100	-$6
23	**Proj**	**350**	**42**	**7**	**36**	**2**	**249**	**6**	**4**	**241**	**340**	**384**	**101**	**101**	**100**	**11**	**75**	**0.49**	**42**	**22**	**36**	**31**	**104**		**7%**	**96**	**101**	**9%**	**8%**	**94**	**6%**	**76%**	**4.8**	**120**	**$9**

Jones,Nolan

Age: 25 Pos: RF	Health A	LIMA Plan D	
Bats: L Ht: 6' 4" Wt: 185	PT/Exp D	Rand Var 0	
	Consist A	MM 4301	

2-13-.244 in 94 PA at CLE. Rehab from ankle surgery pushed AAA start to June, got the call in July, sent back down in August. Brl%, xPX a nod to the plus raw power, but poor ct% and xBA with platoon issues (just 5 PA vL in majors) remain obstacles. First forays can be tough, so worthy of a shot in the end game given pedigree.

Yr	Tm	PA	R	HR	RBI	SB	BA	xHR	xSB	xBA	OBP	SLG	OPS+	vL+	vR+	bb%	ct%	Eye	G	L	F	h%	HctX	QBaB	Brl%	PX	xPX	HR/F	xHR/F	Spd	SBA%	SB%	RAR	BPX	R$
18																																			
19	aa	208	31	8	21	2	252		3		360	460	113			14	63	0.46				35				134				118	4%	100%		93	$3
20																																			
21	aaa	383	43	9	34	7	201		4		290	352	88			11	59	0.30				31				122				91	11%	76%		-50	$3
22	CLE *	326	35	7	38	2	220	3	5	219	282	342	88	0	102	8	64	0.24	35	30	35	32	102	CBc	15%	97	147	11%	16%	102	4%	66%	-9.4	-59	$3
1st Half		96	12	2	15	2	242		2	203	320	372	98	0	0	10	60	0.29	44	20	36	38	0			112	-14	0%		117	4%	66%	-0.6	-38	-$3
2nd Half		230	23	6	23	0	211	3	3	225	266	330	84	0	102	7	65	0.21	35	30	35	30	104	CBc	15%	92	147	11%	16%	100	4%	0%	-8.8	-66	$3
23	**Proj**	**245**	**28**	**6**	**28**	**2**	**236**	**8**	**2**	**213**	**312**	**389**	**97**	**11**	**103**	**10**	**62**	**0.29**	**44**	**21**	**35**	**35**	**94**		**13%**	**126**	**132**	**13%**	**16%**	**110**	**6%**	**67%**	**0.7**	**-38**	**$6**

RYAN BLOOMFIELD

Judge,Aaron

Age: 31 Pos: CF RF DH	Health D	LIMA Plan C	
Bats: R Ht: 6' 7" Wt: 282	PT/Exp A	Rand Var -2	
	Consist D	MM 5155	

A historic season as health, volume, and skills stars all aligned. Ridiculous power (67 xHR!) and FB% uptick got him there, yet barely sacrificed ct% as xBA reached new heights, and career-high SB was icing on the cake. Have to bake in some pullback, but a mixture of 2021 and 2022 still plants him firmly among the top few picks.

Yr Tm	PA	R	HR	RBI	SB	BA	xHR	xSB	xBA	OBP	SLG	OPS+	vL+	vR+	bb%	ct%	Eye	G	L	F	h%	HctX	QBaB	Brl%	PX	xPX	HR/F	xHR/F	Spd	SBA%	SB%	RAR	BPX	R$
18 NYY	498	77	27	67	6	278	29	8	251	392	528	123	128	119	15	63	0.50	42	23	35	38	112	ACa	16%	175	126	29%	31%	77	6%	67%	37.4	160	$20
19 NYY	446	75	27	55	3	272	29	5	256	381	540	127	156	116	14	63	0.45	40	27	32	36	117	ACa	20%	163	150	35%	38%	89	4%	60%	28.0	141	$15
20 NYY	113	23	9	22	0	257	8	1	259	336	554	118	120	117	9	68	0.31	39	20	41	28	116	ABa	12%	166	111	32%	29%	73	4%	0%	3.5	192	$12
21 NYY	633	89	39	98	6	287	40	3	268	373	544	126	135	122	12	71	0.47	41	23	36	34	136	ACa	18%	149	141	28%	28%	54	4%	86%	44.6	177	$30
22 NYY	692	133	62	131	16	311	67	5	302	425	686	157	141	162	12	70	0.63	37	19	44	35	145	ABa	27%	239	200	36%	39%	61	9%	84%	107.4	417	$55
1st Half	342	64	29	60	6	281	30	2	289	360	612	137	119	145	12	71	0.45	41	17	41	30	138	ACa	25%	204	181	32%	33%	62	9%	100%	34.4	317	$47
2nd Half	350	69	33	71	10	343	37	3	316	489	768	178	184	177	21	67	0.81	32	22	46	40	154	ABa	30%	281	223	39%	44%	68	9%	77%	72.8	545	$65
23 Proj	**630**	**113**	**49**	**113**	**10**	**299**	**52**	**8**	**283**	**404**	**619**	**142**	**140**	**143**	**15**	**69**	**0.55**	**38**	**21**	**40**	**35**	**138**		**22%**	**209**	**170**	**33%**	**35%**	**61**	**6%**	**78%**	**78.0**	**314**	**$41**

Jung,Josh

Age: 25 Pos: 3B	Health A	LIMA Plan B	
Bats: R Ht: 6' 2" Wt: 215	PT/Exp F	Rand Var +2	
	Consist F	MM 4115	

5-14-.204 in 102 PA at TEX. Season was in jeopardy after Feb shoulder surgery, but returned by Aug and made MLB debut in Sept. Flashed the raw power we saw as a prospect with elite xPX, but it came with dismal plate skills that aligned with poor BA. Plenty of pedigree and power plays now; just expect some bumps in the road.

Yr Tm	PA	R	HR	RBI	SB	BA	xHR	xSB	xBA	OBP	SLG	OPS+	vL+	vR+	bb%	ct%	Eye	G	L	F	h%	HctX	QBaB	Brl%	PX	xPX	HR/F	xHR/F	Spd	SBA%	SB%	RAR	BPX	R$
18																																		
19																																		
20																																		
21 a/a	329	43	15	48	2	288		3		341	506	116			7	72	0.29				36				136				85	5%	41%		150	$12
22 TEX *	203	18	8	28	3	206	4	1	233	231	393	88	120	75	3	62	0.09	41	25	34	28	102	DBc	10%	142	155	25%	20%	88	10%	100%	-6.1	-3	$1
1st Half																																		
2nd Half	203	18	8	28	3	206	4	1	233	231	393	0	120	75	3	62	0.09	41	25	34	28	102	DBc	10%	142	155	25%	20%	88	10%	100%	-7.4	-7	$6
23 Proj	**560**	**59**	**21**	**79**	**6**	**241**	**22**	**6**	**238**	**277**	**421**	**97**	**126**	**79**	**5**	**66**	**0.15**	**43**	**23**	**34**	**32**	**98**		**9%**	**134**	**140**	**18%**	**18%**	**66**	**7%**	**82%**	**2.1**	**56**	**$18**

Kelenic,Jarred

Age: 23 Pos: CF RF	Health A	LIMA Plan D+	
Bats: L Ht: 6' 1" Wt: 190	PT/Exp B	Rand Var 0	
	Consist A	MM 4213	

7-17-.141 with 5 SB in 181 PA at SEA. Former top prospect fell hard (again) with dreadful BA, but did flash some power and speed. Most power metrics took a step forward, and contact rate showed nice 2nd half improvement. HR/SB combo could buoy his value, but needs to boost career .251 OBP in majors to get the PA to capitalize.

Yr Tm	PA	R	HR	RBI	SB	BA	xHR	xSB	xBA	OBP	SLG	OPS+	vL+	vR+	bb%	ct%	Eye	G	L	F	h%	HctX	QBaB	Brl%	PX	xPX	HR/F	xHR/F	Spd	SBA%	SB%	RAR	BPX	R$
18																																		
19 aa	91	12	6	18	3	255		1		324	556	122			9	78	0.46				25				145				111	17%	100%		300	$1
20																																		
21 SEA *	514	63	21	64	11	206	16	4	230	280	393	92	67	96	9	71	0.36	43	16	42	24	85	CBd	10%	112	111	15%	17%	79	16%	67%	-13.3	73	$10
22 SEA *	555	57	18	58	11	199	8	8	208	254	372	89	60	83	7	69	0.24	37	11	52	25	93	DAf	14%	124	138	13%	15%	85	19%	62%	-20.4	52	$8
1st Half	258	25	8	26	5	192	4	3	197	238	355	84	53	78	6	62	0.16	37	14	49	27	74	DBf	10%	131	123	12%	16%	95	19%	72%	-11.9	-24	$6
2nd Half	297	32	10	32	5	206	4	4	217	269	387	93	64	92	8	75	0.35	37	8	56	24	114	CAf	20%	120	153	14%	14%	90	19%	54%	-8.7	145	$13
23 Proj	**350**	**39**	**15**	**40**	**7**	**214**	**17**	**7**	**231**	**281**	**418**	**97**	**79**	**107**	**8**	**72**	**0.31**	**39**	**12**	**48**	**25**	**92**		**13%**	**137**	**129**	**14%**	**15%**	**87**	**14%**	**62%**	**-1.4**	**74**	**$10**

Kelly,Carson

Age: 28 Pos: CA	Health C	LIMA Plan D+	
Bats: R Ht: 6' 2" Wt: 212	PT/Exp B	Rand Var +4	
	Consist C	MM 2313	

Yo-yo like production in past years continued with down season, possibly due to May oblique strain that shelved him for a month. Contact skills and xBA remain steady, but poor h% history hasn't resulted in a usable BA. Post-injury gains were encouraging and has enough pop to be a decent two-catcher option, but don't expect a big step forward.

Yr Tm	PA	R	HR	RBI	SB	BA	xHR	xSB	xBA	OBP	SLG	OPS+	vL+	vR+	bb%	ct%	Eye	G	L	F	h%	HctX	QBaB	Brl%	PX	xPX	HR/F	xHR/F	Spd	SBA%	SB%	RAR	BPX	R$
18 STL *	372	30	5	34	0	217	1	5	186	300	304	81	24	50	10	82	0.64	54	7	39	25	87	DCd	7%	53	98	0%	9%	87	0%	0%	-5.5	60	$0
19 ARI	365	46	18	47	0	245	16	1	263	348	478	114	157	97	13	75	0.61	37	22	41	27	126	CBc	9%	126	168	19%	16%	79	0%	0%	11.4	193	$7
20 ARI	129	11	5	19	0	221	4	0	232	264	385	86	61	101	5	76	0.21	42	19	39	25	109	DBc	4%	91	100	14%	11%	84	0%	0%	-2.9	56	$4
21 ARI	359	41	13	46	0	240	12	2	245	343	411	104	138	83	12	76	0.59	31	25	44	28	101	CAc	9%	96	115	13%	12%	93	0%	0%	7.1	131	$6
22 ARI	354	40	7	35	2	211	7	1	236	282	334	87	84	89	8	78	0.41	41	20	40	25	100	CBf	5%	85	108	7%	7%	83	3%	100%	-5.7	76	$2
1st Half	115	11	2	9	0	142	2	0	185	191	236	60	66	56	5	75	0.19	43	10	47	17	101	CBf	4%	66	109	5%	5%	92	3%	0%	-8.3	-34	-$10
2nd Half	239	29	5	26	2	246	6	1	259	326	384	101	93	105	10	79	0.55	39	24	36	29	100	CBd	6%	94	107	8%	10%	86	3%	100%	4.2	138	$9
23 Proj	**420**	**47**	**13**	**49**	**1**	**233**	**12**	**2**	**238**	**310**	**383**	**96**	**105**	**90**	**9**	**77**	**0.44**	**38**	**21**	**41**	**27**	**104**		**6%**	**97**	**115**	**11%**	**10%**	**80**	**3%**	**100%**	**5.9**	**92**	**$10**

Kemp,Tony

Age: 31 Pos: 2B LF	Health A	LIMA Plan B+	
Bats: L Ht: 5' 6" Wt: 160	PT/Exp A	Rand Var +1	
	Consist D	MM 1325	

Second straight double-digit R$ season, but more due to PA accumulation than anything else. Solid ct% took step up in 2nd half, so maybe some BA growth if h% corrects, but didn't take advantage of SB% and there's essentially no power. Mediocre per-game production with no guarantee of PA repeat makes for a dicey combo.

Yr Tm	PA	R	HR	RBI	SB	BA	xHR	xSB	xBA	OBP	SLG	OPS+	vL+	vR+	bb%	ct%	Eye	G	L	F	h%	HctX	QBaB	Brl%	PX	xPX	HR/F	xHR/F	Spd	SBA%	SB%	RAR	BPX	R$
18 HOU *	467	59	6	43	18	259	2	7	261	331	363	93	89	102	9	85	0.70	45	23	32	29	94	FCb	1%	61	79	9%	3%	111	19%	76%	1.0	140	$14
19 2 TM	279	31	8	29	4	212	3	7	241	291	380	93	103	90	8	81	0.49	41	16	43	23	99	DBc	2%	80	110	10%	4%	123	13%	50%	-11.5	159	$2
20 OAK	114	15	0	4	3	247	1	3	253	363	301	88	16	94	13	85	1.07	35	29	35	29	92	FAb	1%	39	97	0%	4%	99	11%	75%	-2.6	116	$4
21 OAK	397	54	8	37	8	279	4	10	254	382	418	110	100	113	13	85	1.02	35	23	42	31	90	DBc	1%	75	98	7%	3%	124	8%	80%	12.8	246	$13
22 OAK	558	61	7	46	11	235	3	8	247	307	334	91	84	92	8	86	0.65	41	20	39	26	73	FCf	2%	62	79	4%	2%	98	9%	92%	-3.8	145	$11
1st Half	290	27	2	13	6	213	1	4	222	296	273	80	68	84	9	84	0.61	42	19	39	25	62	FCf	1%	41	58	3%	1%	99	9%	86%	-10.4	62	$2
2nd Half	268	34	5	33	5	258	2	3	272	320	398	102	117	100	8	89	0.71	40	22	39	27	83	FBd	2%	83	99	6%	2%	98	9%	100%	3.6	231	$15
23 Proj	**455**	**58**	**7**	**41**	**10**	**252**	**4**	**8**	**251**	**337**	**368**	**98**	**91**	**99**	**10**	**85**	**0.79**	**39**	**22**	**39**	**28**	**83**		**1%**	**72**	**90**	**5%**	**3%**	**106**	**8%**	**82%**	**5.8**	**182**	**$15**

Kepler,Max

Age: 30 Pos: RF	Health C	LIMA Plan B	
Bats: L Ht: 6' 4" Wt: 225	PT/Exp A	Rand Var +2	
	Consist A	MM 2235	

Battled lower-body injuries in May and July before wrist issue ended season in Sept. Outage in power metrics was likely injury-related but HR should rebound with health. Plate skills held strong, which is good news because shift limitations could close the gap between underperforming BA and xBA - he was shifted against in >90% of PA.

Yr Tm	PA	R	HR	RBI	SB	BA	xHR	xSB	xBA	OBP	SLG	OPS+	vL+	vR+	bb%	ct%	Eye	G	L	F	h%	HctX	QBaB	Brl%	PX	xPX	HR/F	xHR/F	Spd	SBA%	SB%	RAR	BPX	R$
18 MIN	611	80	20	58	4	224	18	8	249	319	408	97	99	95	12	82	0.74	38	16	46	24	112	BBd	7%	104	120	10%	9%	97	6%	44%	-6.6	217	$10
19 MIN	596	98	36	90	1	252	23	4	275	336	519	118	122	116	10	81	0.61	36	17	47	25	119	BAd	9%	131	113	18%	12%	69	5%	17%	9.0	267	$18
20 MIN	196	27	9	23	3	228	7	1	257	321	439	101	49	120	11	79	0.61	32	22	46	24	103	CAd	5%	112	95	15%	11%	80	7%	100%	-1.2	216	$14
21 MIN	490	61	19	54	10	211	19	6	249	306	413	99	69	110	11	77	0.56	37	19	44	23	113	BBd	11%	112	134	13%	13%	109	9%	100%	-3.3	215	$9
22 MIN	446	54	9	43	3	227	11	7	254	318	348	94	95	94	11	83	0.74	46	20	34	25	108	CCf	7%	75	77	8%	10%	93	4%	60%	-7.0	152	$6
1st Half	293	37	9	36	2	235	9	5	258	345	397	105	100	106	14	82	0.87	43	19	38	25	117	BCd	8%	95	90	12%	12%	88	4%	67%	2.2	203	$13
2nd Half	153	17	0	7	1	213	2	2	246	268	262	75	85	71	7	85	0.48	50	21	29	25	92	CDf	5%	40	56	0%	6%	103	4%	50%	-8.6	66	-$5
23 Proj	**525**	**67**	**17**	**52**	**4**	**242**	**15**	**5**	**255**	**326**	**406**	**102**	**88**	**106**	**10**	**81**	**0.62**	**41**	**20**	**40**	**27**	**107**		**8%**	**100**	**96**	**11%**	**10%**	**99**	**5%**	**69%**	**6.1**	**171**	**$15**

Kieboom,Carter

Age: 25 Pos: 3B	Health F	LIMA Plan D+	
Bats: R Ht: 6' 2" Wt: 215	PT/Exp F	Rand Var	
	Consist B	MM 1113	

Spring training elbow/forearm injury turned into season-ending Tommy John surgery by May. Several concerns for former top prospect, including stagnant xBA, lack of barrels, and too many GBs. Needs to make massive leaps in several skills (and stay healthy) to make him an intriguing draft target, so probably best to avoid.

Yr Tm	PA	R	HR	RBI	SB	BA	xHR	xSB	xBA	OBP	SLG	OPS+	vL+	vR+	bb%	ct%	Eye	G	L	F	h%	HctX	QBaB	Brl%	PX	xPX	HR/F	xHR/F	Spd	SBA%	SB%	RAR	BPX	R$
18 aa	267	31	4	20	3	247		3		300	366	89			7	75	0.30				31				83				101	7%	70%		40	$3
19 WAS *	507	65	15	63	4	262	2	6	221	344	418	105	55	70	11	72	0.45	48	13	39	33	109	ACc	9%	90	137	22%	22%	95	4%	64%	-6.6	48	$12
20 WAS	122	15	0	9	0	202	0	2	196	344	212	74	103	58	14	67	0.52	41	30	29	30	56	DCc	0%	9	27	0%	0%	108	2%	0%	-10.0	-252	$0
21 WAS *	416	45	10	37	1	208	5	3	229	294	324	85	84	85	11	74	0.46	49	21	30	25	90	DDd	4%	71	69	13%	11%	95	2%	40%	-15.0	12	$1
22																																		
1st Half																																		
2nd Half																																		
23 Proj	**350**	**43**	**7**	**35**	**2**	**232**	**9**	**5**	**231**	**335**	**342**	**94**	**107**	**86**	**11**	**72**	**0.44**	**46**	**25**	**29**	**30**	**76**		**2%**	**77**	**52**	**11%**	**13%**	**97**	**7%**	**53%**	**-2.2**	**-24**	**$7**

CORBIN YOUNG

Kiermaier,Kevin

Age: 33 Pos: CF	Health F	LIMA Plan D	
Bats: L Ht: 6' 1" Wt: 210	PT/Exp C	Rand Var 0	
	Consist A	MM 2423	

Plagued with more injuries; this time a hip that required season-ending surgery in August. Above-average SB% shows he still has double-digit SB potential, but plate discipline concerns limit BA/OBP, ditto for a heavy GB% and power potential. Worth a flyer for the bags, but bake in the missed time and non-SB production that comes with it.

Yr	Tm	PA	R	HR	RBI	SB	BA	xHR	xSB	xBA	OBP	SLG	OPS+	vL+	vR+	bb%	ct%	Eye	G	L	F	h%	HctX	QBaB	Brl%	PX	xPX	HR/F	xHR/F	Spd	SBA%	SB%	RAR	BPX	R$
18	TAM	367	44	7	29	10	217	6	4	240	282	370	88	73	92	7	73	0.27	50	19	31	28	84	DDf	5%	91	70	10%	8%	152	20%	67%	-8.7	80	$5
19	TAM	480	60	14	55	19	228	15	12	261	278	398	94	109	87	5	77	0.25	54	17	29	27	88	CDd	6%	88	59	14%	15%	136	26%	79%	-12.5	115	$13
20	TAM	159	16	3	22	8	217	4	6	250	321	362	91	59	96	13	70	0.48	56	24	20	29	88	CFf	6%	85	75	16%	21%	131	23%	89%	-3.3	52	$13
21	TAM	390	54	4	37	9	259	4	15	243	328	388	98	92	101	8	72	0.33	57	18	25	35	82	DFf	4%	84	69	6%	6%	152	14%	64%	-1.8	69	$10
22	TAM	221	28	7	22	6	228	6	4	239	281	369	92	88	93	6	70	0.23	52	20	28	29	83	CFd	7%	97	97	18%	15%	92	15%	86%	-2.5	3	$4
1st Half		208	28	7	21	5	231	6	4	236	279	374	92	90	93	6	70	0.20	51	20	29	29	83	CDd	8%	98	99	18%	15%	97	15%	83%	-2.9	0	$8
2nd Half		13	0	0	1	1	182	0	0	281	308	273	82	0	90	15	82	1.00	67	22	11	22	79	DFf		77	69	0%	0%	81	15%	100%	-0.3	159	-$11
23	**Proj**	**280**	**35**	**6**	**31**	**10**	**231**	**7**	**6**	**245**	**301**	**376**	**94**	**85**	**96**	**8**	**71**	**0.32**	**54**	**20**	**26**	**30**	**85**		**6%**	**97**	**79**	**14%**	**15%**	**128**	**13%**	**80%**	**-0.3**	**49**	**$7**

Kim,Ha-Seong

Age: 27 Pos: SS 3B	Health A	LIMA Plan B	
Bats: R Ht: 5' 9" Wt: 168	PT/Exp A	Rand Var 0	
	Consist C	MM 2325	

A step forward in second MLB season with improved bb% and ct%, as xBA supported the BA gains. Low Brl%, identical HR/F and xHR/F mean there's little room for a power boost, yet was plenty successful on basepaths. Running more would be a potential path for growth, but best to expect more of the same modest all-around production.

Yr	Tm	PA	R	HR	RBI	SB	BA	xHR	xSB	xBA	OBP	SLG	OPS+	vL+	vR+	bb%	ct%	Eye	G	L	F	h%	HctX	QBaB	Brl%	PX	xPX	HR/F	xHR/F	Spd	SBA%	SB%	RAR	BPX	R$
18	for	554	93	12	82	7	268		8		325	415	99			8	85	0.57				30	0			82				116	7%	76%	7.9	193	$19
19	for	596	109	11	101	30	287		8		354	431	109			9	86	0.74				32	0			76				100	21%	87%	15.1	207	$36
20	for	528	98	16	97	1	283		18		356	434	105			10	88	0.98				29	0			73				98	1%	45%	8.5	256	$32
21	SD	298	27	8	34	6	202	5	2	224	270	352	85	91	83	7	73	0.31	41	17	41	24	87	DCf	4%	90	74	10%	6%	117	12%	86%	-12.0	65	$2
22	SD	582	58	11	59	12	251	10	12	248	325	383	100	107	97	9	81	0.51	40	21	39	29	96	DBf	4%	85	97	7%	6%	114	10%	86%	1.3	152	$16
1st Half		289	31	5	27	4	233	5	6	233	322	356	96	118	84	10	78	0.53	40	19	41	28	86	FAd	5%	80	95	6%	6%	129	10%	67%	-1.9	131	$9
2nd Half		293	27	6	32	8	269	5	6	264	328	409	104	95	108	8	83	0.49	39	23	38	31	107	CCf	4%	90	98	7%	6%	103	10%	100%	7.0	179	$17
23	**Proj**	**525**	**60**	**12**	**64**	**11**	**254**	**9**	**9**	**244**	**324**	**396**	**100**	**105**	**97**	**9**	**80**	**0.46**	**40**	**20**	**40**	**30**	**94**		**4%**	**90**	**88**	**8%**	**6%**	**103**	**9%**	**87%**	**6.9**	**145**	**$19**

Kiner-Falefa,Isiah

Age: 28 Pos: SS	Health A	LIMA Plan C+	
Bats: R Ht: 5' 11" Wt: 190	PT/Exp A	Rand Var 0	
	Consist A	MM 1435	

New home, similar results with third straight SB-driven $20 season. Stable ct% baseline with SB effectiveness and green light mean BA/SB combo should stick around, though too will handful of HR given meager Brl%, xHR/F. Has "AAA" reliability and should be a quality option for steals; just plan accordingly for the power outage.

Yr	Tm	PA	R	HR	RBI	SB	BA	xHR	xSB	xBA	OBP	SLG	OPS+	vL+	vR+	bb%	ct%	Eye	G	L	F	h%	HctX	QBaB	Brl%	PX	xPX	HR/F	xHR/F	Spd	SBA%	SB%	RAR	BPX	R$
18	TEX	396	43	4	34	7	261	2	6	271	325	357	91	106	82	7	83	0.45	51	25	24	31	89	DDc	1%	60	34	6%	3%	114	12%	58%	-3.5	97	$8
19	TEX *	324	31	3	31	5	230	2	5	235	283	327	84	75	91	7	78	0.33	50	17	33	29	98	CDc	1%	62	85	2%	4%	105	7%	100%	-17.7	33	$2
20	TEX	228	28	3	10	8	280	3	6	259	329	370	93	119	82	6	85	0.44	62	16	22	32	101	CFd	2%	42	33	8%	8%	199	20%	62%	-3.5	188	$20
21	TEX	677	74	8	53	20	271	5	21	263	312	357	92	79	98	4	86	0.31	54	20	26	31	95	DFc	2%	49	49	6%	3%	130	14%	80%	-8.6	123	$22
22	NYY	531	66	4	48	22	261	3	12	260	314	327	91	96	89	7	85	0.49	55	21	24	30	75	DFc	1%	45	34	4%	3%	96	18%	85%	-6.0	69	$20
1st Half		263	37	0	19	12	267	1	6	257	317	317	90	88	90	6	84	0.42	53	23	25	32	70	DDc	1%	41	21	0%	2%	103	18%	80%	-4.7	52	$15
2nd Half		268	29	4	29	10	255	2	6	263	312	337	92	104	89	7	86	0.56	57	19	24	28	79	DFd	2%	50	46	8%	4%	97	18%	91%	-3.4	103	$15
23	**Proj**	**504**	**60**	**5**	**43**	**21**	**264**	**4**	**15**	**259**	**313**	**343**	**91**	**92**	**90**	**6**	**85**	**0.41**	**55**	**20**	**25**	**30**	**86**		**2%**	**51**	**42**	**5%**	**4%**	**111**	**14%**	**80%**	**-2.5**	**104**	**$21**

Kirilloff,Alex

Age: 25 Pos: LF	Health F	LIMA Plan D	
Bats: L Ht: 6' 2" Wt: 195	PT/Exp D	Rand Var -2	
	Consist A	MM 3123	

3-21-.250 in 155 PA at MIN. Wrist surgery in August cut short second straight season, likely impacted his production with GB% spike, xBA dip, and lack of hard contact. Near-elite power skills in 2021 remind us of his potential as a prospect, so it's too early to give up, but health is becoming a major obstacle. Have a backup plan.

Yr	Tm	PA	R	HR	RBI	SB	BA	xHR	xSB	xBA	OBP	SLG	OPS+	vL+	vR+	bb%	ct%	Eye	G	L	F	h%	HctX	QBaB	Brl%	PX	xPX	HR/F	xHR/F	Spd	SBA%	SB%	RAR	BPX	R$
18																																			
19	aa	402	44	8	40	7	276		6		324	402	101			7	79	0.34				33				69				105	13%	51%		67	$9
20																																			
21	MIN	231	23	8	34	1	251	13	2	260	299	423	99	106	96	6	76	0.27	49	22	29	30	108	ADb	13%	101	136	17%	27%	95	4%	50%	-0.6	104	$4
22	MIN *	300	35	9	41	1	265	4	3	234	312	409	102	70	97	6	75	0.28	55	15	30	32	102	BDd	6%	95	97	9%	12%	101	1%	100%	2.8	76	$8
1st Half		243	32	9	37	1	274	2	2	239	326	448	109	40	115	7	74	0.30	49	15	37	33	115	BCf	4%	115	129	12%	8%	103	1%	100%	7.0	128	$15
2nd Half		57	3	0	4	0	226	2	1	185	281	245	75	117	64	4	79	0.18	67	14	19	29	82	CFb	9%	16	45	0%	25%	113	1%	0%	-3.2	-93	-$10
23	**Proj**	**280**	**26**	**10**	**34**	**1**	**251**	**14**	**2**	**247**	**305**	**412**	**99**	**107**	**97**	**6**	**77**	**0.26**	**50**	**18**	**32**	**29**	**101**		**9%**	**101**	**102**	**16%**	**22%**	**99**	**3%**	**57%**	**2.0**	**46**	**$8**

Kirk,Alejandro

Age: 24 Pos: CA DH	Health C	LIMA Plan B	
Bats: R Ht: 5' 8" Wt: 265	PT/Exp A	Rand Var 0	
	Consist D	MM 2035	

Looked to be on breakout path in first full season, but fell off in 2nd half due to major GB% spike and absent power. Elite ct% and batting Eye stuck all year, which bolsters one of the sturdier BA floors at his position. Best to split the 1st/2nd half difference, which given high PA total—he DH'd in 50 games—makes him a solid early catcher choice.

Yr	Tm	PA	R	HR	RBI	SB	BA	xHR	xSB	xBA	OBP	SLG	OPS+	vL+	vR+	bb%	ct%	Eye	G	L	F	h%	HctX	QBaB	Brl%	PX	xPX	HR/F	xHR/F	Spd	SBA%	SB%	RAR	BPX	R$
18																																			
19																																			
20	TOR	25	4	1	3	0	375	1	0	291	400	583	131	37	168	4	83	0.25	55	20	25	42	135	ADb	5%	115	61	20%	20%	57	0%	0%	3.2	212	$1
21	TOR *	242	25	10	36	0	262	8	0	268	335	452	108	134	91	10	85	0.74	41	20	39	27	113	ABc	11%	98	97	14%	14%	23	0%	0%	8.0	181	$5
22	TOR	541	59	14	63	0	285	14	0	259	372	415	111	105	113	12	88	1.09	50	19	31	30	144	BDc	7%	73	102	11%	11%	50	0%	0%	25.4	169	$17
1st Half		263	40	10	33	0	314	10	0	294	403	500	128	115	131	12	89	1.24	44	22	34	32	144	ACd	11%	102	126	14%	14%	73	0%	0%	23.1	293	$19
2nd Half		278	19	4	30	0	258	4	0	217	342	336	96	92	97	12	86	0.97	56	16	28	29	144	BDc	4%	46	80	7%	7%	37	0%	0%	2.8	66	$6
23	**Proj**	**560**	**59**	**18**	**73**	**0**	**274**	**17**	**0**	**260**	**358**	**428**	**109**	**121**	**105**	**11**	**87**	**0.92**	**47**	**19**	**34**	**29**	**132**		**8%**	**88**	**98**	**13%**	**12%**	**23**	**0%**	**0%**	**27.8**	**169**	**$20**

Knizner,Andrew

Age: 28 Pos: CA	Health A	LIMA Plan D+	
Bats: R Ht: 6' 1" Wt: 225	PT/Exp D	Rand Var 0	
	Consist A	MM 1003	

Flashed decent plate skills and swapped groundballs for flyballs in backup role, yet below-average raw power says the loft didn't translate to homers. Some h% regression aligned BA more closely with xBA, which has been flat for years. Without any standout skills, an easy name to cross off your two-catcher end game list.

Yr	Tm	PA	R	HR	RBI	SB	BA	xHR	xSB	xBA	OBP	SLG	OPS+	vL+	vR+	bb%	ct%	Eye	G	L	F	h%	HctX	QBaB	Brl%	PX	xPX	HR/F	xHR/F	Spd	SBA%	SB%	RAR	BPX	R$
18	a/a	355	32	5	35	0	273		5		315	366	91			6	84	0.39				31				58				86	0%	0%		73	$5
19	STL *	322	39	11	33	4	234	1	1	219	286	378	92	56	100	7	81	0.40	62	3	36	25	101	CDf	3%	71	85	14%	7%	83	6%	100%	-6.0	85	$4
20	STL	17	1	0	4	0	250	0	0	228	235	313	73	78	70	0	69	0.00	67	25	8	36	116	AFc	0%	56	57	0%	0%	83	0%	0%	-0.6	-208	-$2
21	STL	185	18	1	9	0	174	2	0	210	281	236	71	37	84	11	76	0.51	52	18	30	22	84	CDf	4%	45	58	3%	5%	76	0%	0%	-10.0	-50	-$4
22	STL	293	28	4	25	0	215	4	0	207	301	300	85	71	89	9	76	0.42	45	17	38	27	89	DBf	4%	59	64	5%	5%	66	1%	0%	-6.9	-28	-$1
1st Half		145	10	1	12	0	183	2	0	199	285	238	74	76	74	11	75	0.48	38	21	41	23	65	DAf	3%	42	51	3%	5%	68	1%	0%	-6.4	-72	-$9
2nd Half		148	18	3	13	0	246	2	0	219	318	358	96	67	105	8	77	0.35	51	14	35	30	111	DCf	4%	76	75	8%	6%	79	1%	0%	-0.1	31	-$1
23	**Proj**	**350**	**36**	**5**	**27**	**0**	**213**	**5**	**1**	**211**	**300**	**299**	**83**	**55**	**92**	**9**	**77**	**0.44**	**50**	**16**	**34**	**26**	**90**		**4%**	**60**	**64**	**6%**	**6%**	**66**	**2%**	**37%**	**-6.1**	**-4**	**$3**

Kreidler,Ryan

Age: 25 Pos: 3B	Health A	LIMA Plan D	
Bats: R Ht: 6' 4" Wt: 208	PT/Exp C	Rand Var +1	
	Consist C	MM 1501	

1-6-.178 in 84 PA at DET. Called up in Sept after spending most of season in AAA. Dreadful ct% all but cements a low BA floor, and while SB baseline seems intriguing, it's mostly minor-league driven with one attempt in the majors. Excellent defense makes him viable, but more a watchlist player for fantasy rather than a draft target in 2023.

Yr	Tm	PA	R	HR	RBI	SB	BA	xHR	xSB	xBA	OBP	SLG	OPS+	vL+	vR+	bb%	ct%	Eye	G	L	F	h%	HctX	QBaB	Brl%	PX	xPX	HR/F	xHR/F	Spd	SBA%	SB%	RAR	BPX	R$
18																																			
19																																			
20																																			
21	a/a	525	75	17	46	12	237		6		300	388	94			8	65	0.25				33				103				96	16%	64%		-38	$14
22	DET *	310	27	6	20	10	172	2	6	184	252	289	77	98	52	10	62	0.29	38	17	45	25	64	CCf	6%	92	99	4%	8%	148	20%	82%	-15.8	-34	$0
1st Half		113	7	4	10	5	176		2	206	238	338	81	0	0	8	59	0.20	44	20	36	26	0			129	-14	0%		133	20%	80%	-5.8	-21	-$4
2nd Half		197	20	2	10	5	170	2	4	179	260	259	74	98	52	11	65	0.35	38	17	45	25	67	CCf	6%	72	99	4%	8%	146	20%	84%	-11.6	-55	-$3
23	**Proj**	**210**	**23**	**2**	**16**	**8**	**197**	**5**	**6**	**172**	**273**	**279**	**77**	**113**	**57**	**9**	**63**	**0.27**	**38**	**17**	**45**	**30**	**60**		**6%**	**70**	**89**	**4%**	**8%**	**124**	**16%**	**81%**	**-8.0**	**-40**	**$4**

CORBIN YOUNG

Kwan,Steven

Age: 25 Pos: LF RF | Bats: L Ht: 5' 9" Wt: 175

Health A | LIMA Plan B+
PT/Exp A | Rand Var -2
Consist A | MM 1535

While heralded hit tool translated brilliantly in MLB debut, surprising SB acumen really boosted this breakout. Near total absence of power puts extra pressure on line drive and hit rates to help overachieve xBA. Plus contact, patience, speed can carry this profile, sterling defense should help sustain PT volume—just budget for dongs elsewhere.

Yr	Tm	PA	R	HR	RBI	SB	BA	xHR	xSB	xBA	OBP	SLG	OPS+	vL+	vR+	bb%	ct%	Eye	G	L	F	h%	HctX	QBaB	Brl%	PX	xPX	HR/F	xHR/F	Spd	SBA%	SB%	RAR	BPX	R$
18																																			
19																																			
20																																			
21	a/a	323	49	9	33	4	281		5		341	435	107			8	88	0.74				30				77				117	7%	66%		254	$10
22	CLE	638	89	6	52	19	298	3	14	265	373	400	109	90	115	10	89	1.03	42	23	35	33	74	DCd	1%	59	40	3%	2%	151	12%	79%	20.6	245	$29
1st Half		266	32	1	20	5	270	1	6	247	357	343	99	90	102	11	90	1.26	48	18	35	30	81	DDf	2%	43	41	1%	1%	147	12%	71%	1.2	217	$9
2nd Half		372	57	5	32	14	318	2	8	276	384	438	116	89	124	9	89	0.89	39	26	35	35	69	DCc	1%	70	39	5%	2%	146	12%	82%	20.7	262	$35
23	Proj	**595**	**87**	**6**	**54**	**14**	**291**	**3**	**17**	**260**	**361**	**390**	**104**	**85**	**110**	**9**	**89**	**0.90**	**42**	**23**	**35**	**32**	**74**		**1%**	**59**	**40**	**3%**	**2%**	**148**	**12%**	**76%**	**18.2**	**248**	**$23**

Langeliers,Shea

Age: 25 Pos: CA | Bats: R Ht: 6' 0" Wt: 190

Health A | LIMA Plan D+
PT/Exp B | Rand Var +1
Consist B | MM 4215

6-22-.218 in 153 PA at OAK. Top prospect matched MiLB track record with plus power and lots of swing-and-miss. Superior Brl% and FB tendency are good omens for future HR output, plus defensive skills will get him plenty of looks. Problem is, won't start 2023 with catcher eligibility in many leagues (17 G), so scoop up late to maximize profit.

Yr	Tm	PA	R	HR	RBI	SB	BA	xHR	xSB	xBA	OBP	SLG	OPS+	vL+	vR+	bb%	ct%	Eye	G	L	F	h%	HctX	QBaB	Brl%	PX	xPX	HR/F	xHR/F	Spd	SBA%	SB%	RAR	BPX	R$
18																																			
19																																			
20																																			
21	a/a	372	49	18	44	1	227		3		293	424	99			9	66	0.28				29				126				86	1%	100%		42	$6
22	OAK *	529	47	15	52	3	206	5	2	223	254	355	86	112	94	6	67	0.20	38	22	40	27	91	CBf	11%	109	95	17%	14%	97	4%	68%	-10.2	0	$4
1st Half		267	24	7	20	2	193		1	213	247	318	80	0	0	7	68	0.22	44	20	36	26	0			89	-14	0%		119	4%	100%	-8.4	-24	$1
2nd Half		262	23	8	32	1	219	5	1	235	261	392	92	112	94	5	67	0.17	38	22	40	29	91	CBf	11%	130	95	17%	14%	92	4%	30%	-2.4	48	$8
23	Proj	**455**	**48**	**17**	**50**	**2**	**220**	**16**	**3**	**227**	**271**	**391**	**92**	**109**	**87**	**7**	**67**	**0.23**	**38**	**22**	**40**	**29**	**82**		**10%**	**124**	**86**	**15%**	**14%**	**85**	**4%**	**76%**	**1.9**	**28**	**$9**

Larnach,Trevor

Age: 26 Pos: LF | Bats: L Ht: 6' 4" Wt: 223

Health F | LIMA Plan D+
PT/Exp F | Rand Var +1
Consist A | MM 3303

5-18-.231 in 180 PA at MIN. Strained groin and core muscle injury that required surgical repair scuttled most of his season. In between, strong exit velocity and just enough fly balls fueled top-shelf xPX while poor contact led to rotgut xBA. Power's nice, but unless he tames the whiffs, you'll need a stiff drink to stomach that average.

Yr	Tm	PA	R	HR	RBI	SB	BA	xHR	xSB	xBA	OBP	SLG	OPS+	vL+	vR+	bb%	ct%	Eye	G	L	F	h%	HctX	QBaB	Brl%	PX	xPX	HR/F	xHR/F	Spd	SBA%	SB%	RAR	BPX	R$
18																																			
19	aa	177	24	7	21	0	286		3		369	439	112			12	67	0.39				39				88				101	0%	0%		-26	$3
20																																			
21	MIN *	357	39	9	33	1	212	11	4	190	293	343	87	71	102	10	59	0.28	46	18	35	32	81	BCb	9%	101	84	13%	20%	83	1%	100%	-17.5	-135	$1
22	MIN *	227	23	6	21	0	215	9	1	212	288	360	92	100	101	9	64	0.29	42	19	39	31	104	BCb	11%	121	147	12%	22%	82	0%	0%	-7.9	-3	$0
1st Half		209	23	6	21	0	210	9	1	215	285	368	93	100	101	10	63	0.28	42	19	39	30	102	BCb	11%	134	147	12%	22%	82	0%	0%	-7.1	14	$1
2nd Half		18	0	0	0	0	277		0	158	328	277	86	0	0	7	78	0.35	44	20	36	35	0			0	-14	0%		109	0%	0%	-0.7	-128	-$11
23	Proj	**350**	**40**	**9**	**34**	**0**	**225**	**16**	**1**	**201**	**313**	**358**	**93**	**84**	**97**	**11**	**63**	**0.32**	**44**	**19**	**38**	**33**	**94**		**11%**	**106**	**122**	**12%**	**21%**	**83**	**2%**	**100%**	**-1.7**	**-39**	**$6**

Laureano,Ramón

Age: 28 Pos: RF CF | Bats: R Ht: 5' 11" Wt: 203

Health C | LIMA Plan C+
PT/Exp B | Rand Var +5
Consist B | MM 4215

13-34-.211 with 11 SB in 383 PA at OAK. Start of 2022 delayed by tail end of PED suspension; oblique, hamstring, hip injuries hastened its ending. Note persistent contact issues and realize that 2019 BA was a high-h% mirage. Moderate power leans heavily on repeating good launch angles; poor SB% undercuts SB potential. Don't overbid.

Yr	Tm	PA	R	HR	RBI	SB	BA	xHR	xSB	xBA	OBP	SLG	OPS+	vL+	vR+	bb%	ct%	Eye	G	L	F	h%	HctX	QBaB	Brl%	PX	xPX	HR/F	xHR/F	Spd	SBA%	SB%	RAR	BPX	R$
18	OAK *	446	62	15	47	16	269	8	6	247	335	449	105	105	112	9	68	0.31	44	25	31	36	100	BCc	11%	124	86	15%	24%	112	17%	83%	9.4	83	$17
19	OAK	481	79	24	67	13	288	23	11	263	340	521	119	117	119	6	72	0.22	36	25	39	35	99	BBc	10%	134	108	19%	18%	101	14%	87%	14.5	137	$21
20	OAK	222	27	6	25	2	213	8	5	225	338	366	93	85	96	11	68	0.41	43	22	35	28	91	CCf	9%	96	100	13%	18%	87	5%	67%	-7.5	0	$10
21	OAK	378	43	14	39	12	246	18	3	253	317	443	104	117	98	7	71	0.28	43	22	35	31	94	CCc	11%	124	108	16%	21%	97	20%	71%	0.3	112	$12
22	OAK *	422	54	13	35	12	199	16	9	225	252	351	85	97	93	6	69	0.23	43	18	39	25	101	CBd	12%	110	101	14%	17%	98	22%	67%	-17.4	31	$7
1st Half		249	31	5	15	9	218	7	7	237	290	346	90	131	92	9	72	0.36	50	18	32	28	113	BCc	10%	96	85	12%	16%	99	22%	69%	-6.6	52	$9
2nd Half		173	23	8	20	3	173	9	3	212	225	358	83	36	94	3	65	0.09	34	17	49	20	86	CAf	14%	131	122	15%	17%	102	22%	60%	-11.2	17	$4
23	Proj	**525**	**71**	**19**	**57**	**14**	**231**	**24**	**14**	**235**	**303**	**407**	**99**	**100**	**98**	**7**	**69**	**0.23**	**41**	**20**	**39**	**29**	**96**		**11%**	**125**	**106**	**15%**	**19%**	**90**	**15%**	**69%**	**-3.2**	**60**	**$19**

Leblanc,Charles

Age: 27 Pos: 2B | Bats: R Ht: 6' 3" Wt: 195

Health A | LIMA Plan F
PT/Exp B | Rand Var -4
Consist B | MM 3301

4-11-.263 with 4 SB in 169 PA at MIA. Improved contact at Triple-A, injuries created an opportunity; decent power, speed, friendly hit rate allowed him to capitalize. Defensive flexibility (he's played every infield position in MiLB plus LF) suggests he could carve out a role as a utility player. But without further ct% gains, that's likely his ceiling.

Yr	Tm	PA	R	HR	RBI	SB	BA	xHR	xSB	xBA	OBP	SLG	OPS+	vL+	vR+	bb%	ct%	Eye	G	L	F	h%	HctX	QBaB	Brl%	PX	xPX	HR/F	xHR/F	Spd	SBA%	SB%	RAR	BPX	R$
18																																			
19	aa	523	67	7	49	3	263		9		324	352	94			8	76	0.37				33				49				125	4%	46%		-4	$9
20																																			
21	aaa	360	35	12	40	4	187		3		251	351	83			8	54	0.19				30				130				105	11%	50%		-112	$1
22	MIA *	510	50	13	41	8	245	5	8	212	297	383	96	94	106	7	63	0.20	36	24	40	36	94	CBc	9%	113	125	10%	12%	116	9%	80%	-3.8	-17	$11
1st Half		278	25	7	27	1	226		4	208	278	367	91	0	0	7	62	0.19	44	20	36	34	0			115	-14	0%		109	9%	100%	-4.1	-45	$5
2nd Half		233	25	5	14	7	268	5	4	218	321	403	103	94	106	7	66	0.23	36	24	40	39	97	CBc	9%	110	125	10%	12%	117	9%	77%	3.8	7	$10
23	Proj	**210**	**21**	**4**	**19**	**3**	**212**	**6**	**3**	**197**	**275**	**334**	**85**	**79**	**87**	**7**	**61**	**0.21**	**36**	**24**	**40**	**32**	**87**		**8%**	**103**	**113**	**9%**	**12%**	**121**	**9%**	**69%**	**-4.9**	**-52**	**$3**

LeMahieu,DJ

Age: 34 Pos: 3B 2B 1B | Bats: R Ht: 6' 4" Wt: 220

Health C | LIMA Plan B+
PT/Exp A | Rand Var +3
Consist D | MM 1235

Tried playing through nagging toe fracture that ended up costing him most of September. Superior plate discipline holding together while exit velocity continues to wane. There's still enough on-base skill to keep the party going another couple tracks, but the lasers and smoke machine are offline and the cops are on their way. DN: part-time role

Yr	Tm	PA	R	HR	RBI	SB	BA	xHR	xSB	xBA	OBP	SLG	OPS+	vL+	vR+	bb%	ct%	Eye	G	L	F	h%	HctX	QBaB	Brl%	PX	xPX	HR/F	xHR/F	Spd	SBA%	SB%	RAR	BPX	R$
18	COL	581	90	15	62	6	276	14	8	280	321	428	100	119	89	6	85	0.45	50	21	29	30	109	ADb	5%	88	97	11%	10%	102	8%	55%	6.1	180	$18
19	NYY	655	109	26	102	5	327	26	10	302	375	518	124	148	114	7	85	0.51	50	24	26	35	119	ADb	8%	92	90	19%	19%	108	4%	71%	36.8	230	$31
20	NYY	216	41	10	27	3	364	5	3	327	421	590	134	131	135	8	89	0.86	57	22	21	37	128	AFb	3%	104	76	27%	14%	134	4%	100%	25.1	396	$33
21	NYY	679	84	10	57	4	268	10	8	262	349	362	98	92	100	11	84	0.78	52	22	26	30	94	BFc	4%	53	62	8%	8%	100	3%	67%	3.8	127	$15
22	NYY	541	74	12	46	4	261	9	5	259	357	377	104	112	101	12	85	0.94	53	18	28	29	85	CFd	5%	68	68	11%	8%	96	4%	57%	7.8	169	$14
1st Half		303	44	8	32	3	262	6	3	271	363	404	108	123	101	13	85	1.03	52	18	29	28	87	CFd	6%	84	75	12%	9%	94	4%	75%	6.2	224	$17
2nd Half		238	30	4	14	1	261	4	2	242	350	343	98	89	100	12	85	0.85	54	19	27	29	81	CFd	4%	48	60	9%	9%	101	4%	33%	-1.0	107	$6
23	Proj	**490**	**69**	**9**	**44**	**3**	**278**	**9**	**6**	**263**	**359**	**386**	**103**	**105**	**103**	**11**	**85**	**0.82**	**53**	**20**	**27**	**31**	**94**		**5%**	**66**	**69**	**10%**	**10%**	**99**	**5%**	**67%**	**13.0**	**175**	**$17**

Lewis,Kyle

Age: 27 Pos: DH | Bats: R Ht: 6' 4" Wt: 205

Health F | LIMA Plan C
PT/Exp D | Rand Var +5
Consist C | MM 3403

3-5-.143 in 62 PA at SEA. More right knee issues cost him the first six weeks, then a concussion shelved him for two months. Although he recovered, his performance didn't (.367 OPS in 46 PA) and finished the year in Triple-A. Age, power, speed keep us interested; health, whiffs keep us grounded. Let's see a full season before buying in.

Yr	Tm	PA	R	HR	RBI	SB	BA	xHR	xSB	xBA	OBP	SLG	OPS+	vL+	vR+	bb%	ct%	Eye	G	L	F	h%	HctX	QBaB	Brl%	PX	xPX	HR/F	xHR/F	Spd	SBA%	SB%	RAR	BPX	R$
18	aa	146	15	3	16	1	190		2		268	318	79			10	72	0.38				24				88				91	3%	100%		20	-$2
19	SEA *	587	70	17	74	3	248	6	6	202	323	404	101	72	140	10	61	0.28	51	14	35	37	69	BCa	23%	108	144	40%	40%	115	4%	57%	-13.6	-44	$11
20	SEA	242	37	11	28	5	262	10	3	215	364	437	106	105	106	14	66	0.48	43	20	36	35	87	CCd	11%	101	97	22%	20%	126	8%	83%	4.4	44	$24
21	SEA	147	15	5	11	2	246	7	3	224	333	392	100	88	103	11	72	0.43	33	24	43	31	101	BBd	14%	87	118	13%	18%	115	5%	100%	-2.3	54	$1
22	SEA *	224	23	10	24	0	164	3	2	194	238	322	79	56	82	9	62	0.25	46	16	38	20	73	BBf	11%	110	93	21%	21%	95	0%	0%	-15.3	-55	-$3
1st Half		55	7	4	10	0	232	2	0	272	281	478	107	140	139	6	82	0.39	57	14	29	21	103	BCf	14%	130	92	50%	50%	104	0%	0%	-0.2	276	-$6
2nd Half		168	16	6	15	0	141	1	1	165	224	269	70	43	55	10	55	0.24	39	17	43	20	63	BAf	9%	99	94	10%	10%	101	0%	0%	-14.4	-172	-$4
23	Proj	**350**	**39**	**15**	**38**	**2**	**242**	**20**	**2**	**217**	**316**	**412**	**101**	**90**	**105**	**10**	**68**	**0.34**	**41**	**20**	**40**	**31**	**81**		**12%**	**112**	**105**	**18%**	**23%**	**106**	**3%**	**92%**	**1.8**	**23**	**$11**

ALAIN DE LEONARDIS

Lewis,Royce

Age: 24	Pos: SS	Health	F	LIMA Plan	D
Bats: R	Ht: 6' 2" Wt: 200	PT/Exp	F	Rand Var	-2
		Consist	F	MM	4421

2-5-.300 in 40 AB at MIN. Knee surgery will keep him out until late 2023, which follows a torn ACL that kept him out of all of 2021, which followed the 2020 pandemic year, so he hasn't been on an actual baseball field much. Too bad, because MIN's top prospect is a future 30/30 stud. Still roster-worthy in dynasty leagues, but only for the excruciatingly patient.

Yr	Tm	PA	R	HR	RBI	SB	BA	xHR	xSB	xBA	OBP	SLG	OPS+	vL+	vR+	bb%	ct%	Eye	G	L	F	h%	HctX	QBaB	Brl%	PX	xPX	HR/F	xHR/F	Spd	SBA%	SB%	RAR	BPX	R$
18																																			
19	aa	145	17	2	13	6	233		2		289	360	90			7	75	0.32				30				80				108	27%	74%		52	$1
20																																			
21																																			
22	MIN *	184	24	5	14	8	265	1	2	245	317	445	108	150	115	7	75	0.31	31	20	49	33	113	BAf	6%	128	142	12%	6%	108	26%	77%	4.0	179	$6
1st Half		184	24	5	14	8	265	1	2	245	317	445	108	150	115	7	75	0.31	31	20	49	33	113	BAf	6%	128	142	12%	6%	108	26%	77%	3.3	179	$9
2nd Half																																			
23	Proj	**175**	**22**	**6**	**14**	**7**	**250**	**4**	**5**	**250**	**304**	**456**	**105**	**143**	**93**	**7**	**75**	**0.31**	**31**	**20**	**49**	**30**	**102**		**5%**	**139**	**128**	**11%**	**6%**	**112**	**20%**	**78%**	**3.9**	**128**	**$5**

Lindor,Francisco

Age: 29	Pos: SS	Health	B	LIMA Plan	D+
Bats: B	Ht: 5' 11" Wt: 190	PT/Exp	A	Rand Var	-2
		Consist	A	MM	3335

After a Big Apple acclimation year, he finally showed off his Cleveland skills... almost. Pedestrian xBA, HctX and xPX are part park effect and part exit velocity issues. Compare those to 2018 and you can see how this is not the same profile. Still, he's plenty productive and $30-worthy. Just not Cleveland-level-pushing-$40-worthy.

Yr	Tm	PA	R	HR	RBI	SB	BA	xHR	xSB	xBA	OBP	SLG	OPS+	vL+	vR+	bb%	ct%	Eye	G	L	F	h%	HctX	QBaB	Brl%	PX	xPX	HR/F	xHR/F	Spd	SBA%	SB%	RAR	BPX	R$
18	CLE	745	129	38	92	25	277	32	10	292	352	519	117	133	108	9	84	0.65	39	22	40	28	128	BBc	9%	131	135	17%	15%	93	20%	71%	45.5	297	$38
19	CLE	654	101	32	74	22	284	25	16	292	335	518	118	108	122	7	84	0.47	44	20	37	29	122	ACd	8%	115	104	17%	14%	106	19%	81%	24.7	274	$30
20	CLE	266	30	8	27	6	258	8	7	270	335	415	100	97	100	9	83	0.59	38	26	36	28	102	BCc	6%	85	82	11%	11%	97	12%	75%	1.0	192	$21
21	NYM	524	73	20	63	10	230	20	10	245	322	412	101	97	102	11	79	0.60	39	19	42	25	104	BCf	8%	96	114	13%	13%	108	11%	71%	-3.2	185	$14
22	NYM	706	98	26	107	16	270	26	15	254	339	449	112	110	112	8	79	0.44	43	18	39	31	107	CCf	8%	105	110	13%	13%	127	12%	73%	14.8	193	$33
1st Half		351	48	13	57	9	244	11	7	246	325	420	105	94	110	9	77	0.46	44	17	39	28	99	CCf	7%	104	95	14%	12%	119	12%	82%	2.8	166	$31
2nd Half		355	50	13	50	7	294	15	8	261	352	477	117	124	114	8	80	0.43	43	19	39	33	115	BCf	9%	106	124	13%	15%	130	12%	64%	14.9	217	$35
23	Proj	**700**	**100**	**25**	**95**	**16**	**265**	**27**	**15**	**253**	**338**	**438**	**108**	**107**	**108**	**9**	**80**	**0.51**	**41**	**19**	**39**	**30**	**108**		**8%**	**103**	**111**	**13%**	**13%**	**112**	**10%**	**72%**	**21.0**	**202**	**$33**

Longoria,Evan

Age: 37	Pos: 3B	Health	F	LIMA Plan	C+
Bats: R	Ht: 6' 1" Wt: 213	PT/Exp	C	Rand Var	-1
		Consist	B	MM	4123

14-42-.244 in 266 AB at SF. He lost more than two months to thumb, oblique and hamstring injuries, and has now lost 223 games to the IL since 2018. These ailments may have affected his ct%, but QBaB, Brl% and xPX all look vintage. There is something still very draftable here, but staying healthy is also a skill, and is the one thing holding him back.

Yr	Tm	PA	R	HR	RBI	SB	BA	xHR	xSB	xBA	OBP	SLG	OPS+	vL+	vR+	bb%	ct%	Eye	G	L	F	h%	HctX	QBaB	Brl%	PX	xPX	HR/F	xHR/F	Spd	SBA%	SB%	RAR	BPX	R$
18	SF	512	51	16	54	3	244	18	6	250	281	413	93	99	88	4	79	0.22	42	18	39	28	120	CCc	8%	99	114	11%	12%	105	4%	75%	-11.7	123	$9
19	SF	508	59	20	69	3	254	25	6	250	325	437	105	118	99	8	75	0.38	41	22	37	30	115	BCa	8%	96	123	16%	19%	119	3%	75%	-8.9	122	$11
20	SF	209	26	7	28	0	254	12	1	258	297	425	96	112	89	5	80	0.28	50	18	32	29	125	ACb	11%	92	115	14%	24%	97	2%	0%	-6.4	136	$13
21	SF	291	45	13	46	1	261	14	1	255	351	482	114	148	102	12	73	0.51	41	19	40	31	129	ABb	13%	136	150	17%	19%	79	3%	50%	10.3	196	$8
22	SF *	323	33	14	42	0	244	14	2	238	309	439	106	114	104	9	68	0.29	37	22	41	31	95	AAd	12%	138	132	18%	18%	90	0%	0%	1.8	93	$7
1st Half		169	19	8	18	0	236	8	1	219	318	430	106	116	109	11	67	0.36	39	17	44	30	91	AAf	15%	131	146	20%	20%	95	0%	0%	1.7	86	$2
2nd Half		154	14	6	24	0	252	6	1	257	300	449	106	112	98	6	68	0.22	34	27	39	33	99	AAd	10%	145	117	17%	17%	86	0%	0%	1.7	103	$3
23	Proj	**420**	**51**	**18**	**60**	**1**	**250**	**20**	**1**	**250**	**318**	**453**	**107**	**119**	**100**	**9**	**72**	**0.34**	**40**	**21**	**39**	**30**	**111**		**12%**	**139**	**133**	**17%**	**18%**	**84**	**2%**	**49%**	**11.8**	**133**	**$14**

Lopez,Alejo

Age: 27	Pos: 2B	Health	A	LIMA Plan	D
Bats: B	Ht: 5' 10" Wt: 170	PT/Exp	D	Rand Var	+2
		Consist	B	MM	1341

1-10-.262 in 145 AB at CIN. His position is listed here as "2B" but really it should read, "Injury replacement at any position." All-contact spray hitter with unrosterable power and barely rosterable speed. xBA levels are the only things here to get a little excited about, but odds are he won't see enough playing time for it to matter.

Yr	Tm	PA	R	HR	RBI	SB	BA	xHR	xSB	xBA	OBP	SLG	OPS+	vL+	vR+	bb%	ct%	Eye	G	L	F	h%	HctX	QBaB	Brl%	PX	xPX	HR/F	xHR/F	Spd	SBA%	SB%	RAR	BPX	R$
18																																			
19																																			
20																																			
21	CIN *	416	60	5	35	7	275	0	6	319	339	378	98	78	61	9	88	0.83	61	28	11	30	80	DFa	0%	62	6	0%	0%	113	9%	67%	0.1	215	$12
22	CIN *	328	25	3	25	4	236	1	5	269	286	315	85	91	91	6	85	0.45	46	27	27	27	66	FCb	1%	50	48	3%	3%	107	6%	81%	-10.1	90	$2
1st Half		168	11	1	10	3	220	0	3	269	288	277	80	94	81	9	82	0.54	45	31	24	26	84	DCa	0%	43	59	0%	0%	97	6%	73%	-6.0	38	-$5
2nd Half		161	14	3	15	2	252	1	2	272	283	352	90	85	97	4	87	0.34	47	25	29	27	52	FDb	1%	57	40	5%	5%	120	6%	100%	-2.1	141	$1
23	Proj	**210**	**22**	**1**	**17**	**3**	**253**	**1**	**3**	**271**	**315**	**326**	**89**	**91**	**88**	**7**	**86**	**0.57**	**46**	**27**	**27**	**29**	**65**		**1%**	**51**	**48**	**3%**	**2%**	**109**	**7%**	**78%**	**-1.6**	**145**	**$5**

Lopez,Nicky

Age: 28	Pos: 2B SS 3B	Health	A	LIMA Plan	C
Bats: L	Ht: 5' 11" Wt: 180	PT/Exp	A	Rand Var	+3
		Consist	D	MM	0533

This was never a .300 hitter; despite sharp drop, xBA shows a gentler decline. He did lose a touch of exit velocity and plate patience, but retains excellent contact (ct%). However, that contact goes nowhere (QBaB). His only fantasy asset is speed, which is minimized with an OBP south of .300. This is essentially a .250 hitter with 10-15 bags. Pay for no more.

Yr	Tm	PA	R	HR	RBI	SB	BA	xHR	xSB	xBA	OBP	SLG	OPS+	vL+	vR+	bb%	ct%	Eye	G	L	F	h%	HctX	QBaB	Brl%	PX	xPX	HR/F	xHR/F	Spd	SBA%	SB%	RAR	BPX	R$
18	a/a	553	61	7	43	12	281		9		345	376	97			9	89	0.87				31				48				140	12%	65%		187	$15
19	KC *	533	65	4	40	8	257	2	10	277	304	349	90	90	80	6	89	0.59	62	16	22	28	78	DFb	1%	50	5	3%	3%	122	10%	64%	-17.2	167	$8
20	KC	192	15	1	13	0	201	1	3	242	286	266	73	58	79	9	76	0.44	55	26	19	26	73	FFf	2%	47	51	4%	4%	86	11%	0%	-14.0	-48	-$1
21	KC	565	78	2	43	22	300	3	14	269	365	378	102	96	104	9	85	0.66	55	21	23	35	87	DFf	1%	46	48	2%	3%	151	13%	96%	13.9	162	$25
22	KC	480	51	0	20	13	227	3	12	252	281	273	78	69	82	6	86	0.46	54	21	25	27	82	FFf	2%	30	46	0%	3%	149	14%	81%	-15.1	86	$6
1st Half		257	24	0	8	5	228	1	6	250	290	276	80	67	84	7	86	0.52	52	21	27	27	75	FFf	1%	35	54	0%	2%	125	14%	83%	-9.1	83	$0
2nd Half		223	27	0	12	8	225	1	5	254	271	270	76	70	79	6	85	0.40	57	21	22	26	89	FFc	2%	24	36	0%	3%	163	14%	80%	-9.1	76	$4
23	Proj	**315**	**38**	**1**	**19**	**11**	**250**	**2**	**8**	**256**	**311**	**312**	**86**	**79**	**89**	**7**	**85**	**0.53**	**56**	**21**	**23**	**29**	**83**		**1%**	**40**	**42**	**1%**	**3%**	**138**	**13%**	**82%**	**-3.3**	**101**	**$10**

Lowe,Brandon

Age: 28	Pos: 2B	Health	D	LIMA Plan	C+
Bats: L	Ht: 5' 10" Wt: 185	PT/Exp	B	Rand Var	+5
		Consist	C	MM	4335

Got off to a slow start and was shut down with a back injury in May. After several setbacks, returned in July and began sitting vs LHPs (despite vL+). August HBP shelved him with an elbow contusion and then he saw only 13 AB in Sept with more back woes. Let's not put too much weight on 2022 as a valid data point. With health, he should bounce back.

Yr	Tm	PA	R	HR	RBI	SB	BA	xHR	xSB	xBA	OBP	SLG	OPS+	vL+	vR+	bb%	ct%	Eye	G	L	F	h%	HctX	QBaB	Brl%	PX	xPX	HR/F	xHR/F	Spd	SBA%	SB%	RAR	BPX	R$
18	TAM *	576	78	24	89	9	251	7	8	254	335	467	108	93	105	11	69	0.40	43	22	35	32	88	BBc	11%	146	100	19%	22%	96	10%	66%	17.8	147	$19
19	TAM	327	42	17	51	5	270	21	5	235	336	514	118	94	123	8	62	0.22	30	27	43	38	92	AAb	16%	156	130	22%	27%	117	7%	100%	10.2	93	$10
20	TAM	224	36	14	37	3	269	15	3	261	362	554	122	148	112	11	70	0.43	33	24	43	31	122	BAc	18%	161	154	24%	25%	121	5%	100%	12.8	276	$25
21	TAM	615	97	39	99	7	247	35	6	261	340	523	119	90	132	11	69	0.41	34	22	44	28	99	CBd	14%	171	137	24%	22%	89	6%	88%	26.2	242	$23
22	TAM	266	31	8	25	1	221	9	3	236	308	383	98	111	95	10	74	0.44	38	21	41	27	92	CBf	10%	103	97	11%	13%	105	2%	100%	0.9	114	$2
1st Half		133	20	5	12	1	212	6	1	242	293	415	100	116	93	9	71	0.35	36	21	42	25	102	BBd	11%	130	132	14%	17%	120	2%	100%	-0.2	155	-$2
2nd Half		133	11	3	13	0	231	3	2	225	323	350	95	97	95	11	77	0.56	39	20	40	28	82	CBf	10%	79	64	8%	8%	89	2%	0%	-0.8	76	-$3
23	Proj	**525**	**75**	**28**	**76**	**4**	**249**	**27**	**4**	**258**	**335**	**488**	**114**	**113**	**114**	**10**	**71**	**0.41**	**36**	**22**	**42**	**29**	**96**		**13%**	**155**	**114**	**20%**	**19%**	**102**	**4%**	**90%**	**24.2**	**166**	**$21**

Lowe,Josh

Age: 25	Pos: RF	Health	A	LIMA Plan	D+
Bats: L	Ht: 6' 4" Wt: 205	PT/Exp	B	Rand Var	-5
		Consist	C	MM	4501

2-13-.221 with 3 SB in 181 AB at TAM. Five-tool prospect provides both power and speed, and could be a 30/30 star if the planets align. There are core skills to build on but big issues with mega-strikeouts. This is not a new problem, but it's not getting any better. Struck out 690 times in parts of six minor league seasons. There is work to be done.

Yr	Tm	PA	R	HR	RBI	SB	BA	xHR	xSB	xBA	OBP	SLG	OPS+	vL+	vR+	bb%	ct%	Eye	G	L	F	h%	HctX	QBaB	Brl%	PX	xPX	HR/F	xHR/F	Spd	SBA%	SB%	RAR	BPX	R$
18																																			
19	aa	507	68	17	61	29	241		8		329	419	104			12	67	0.40				32				107				117	31%	75%		52	$20
20																																			
21	TAM *	457	66	19	68	24	264	0	6	280	351	475	113	0	276	12	65	0.38	100	0	0	36	0	FF	0%	145	-22	0%		109	21%	100%	20.5	127	$25
22	TAM *	532	60	11	60	21	242	4	15	206	309	397	100	38	104	9	57	0.22	36	25	39	40	67	CCc	5%	145	111	4%	9%	125	20%	90%	1.8	3	$19
1st Half		271	27	5	32	6	209	3	6	201	271	355	88	35	82	8	59	0.20	39	19	42	34	66	CDc	7%	134	116	3%	10%	122	20%	84%	-8.0	-17	$8
2nd Half		261	33	6	29	14	278	2	9	214	349	442	112	42	139	10	55	0.25	30	35	35	48	68	CCc	3%	157	105	6%	13%	119	20%	92%	10.6	14	$22
23	Proj	**245**	**32**	**4**	**32**	**12**	**254**	**4**	**8**	**203**	**338**	**392**	**101**	**42**	**119**	**10**	**61**	**0.30**	**37**	**22**	**41**	**40**	**67**		**5%**	**123**	**109**	**8%**	**6%**	**114**	**16%**	**92%**	**5.0**	**57**	**$12**

RON SHANDLER

Lowe,Nate

Age: 27 Pos: 1B	Health A	LIMA Plan B
Bats: L Ht: 6' 4" Wt: 220	PT/Exp A	Rand Var -3
	Consist B	MM 3335

Slightly reversed his declining launch angle trend just enough to recapture the power skills that are the core of his value. Also became more aggressive at the plate (ct% up, bb% down), rediscovering his successful minor league approach and put together this breakout. xPX and xBA say to expect some pullback, but enjoy these peak years.

Yr Tm	PA	R	HR	RBI	SB	BA	xHR	xSB	xBA	OBP	SLG	OPS+	vL+	vR+	bb%	ct%	Eye	G	L	F	h%	HctX	QBaB	Brl%	PX	xPX	HR/F	xHR/F	Spd	SBA%	SB%	RAR	BPX	R$
18 a/a	325	47	14	50	1	278		5		360	483	113			11	77	0.55				32				121				93	2%	43%		187	$10
19 TAM *	558	76	20	71	1	252	7	3	244	350	432	108	136	101	13	69	0.49	40	24	36	32	99	ACc	11%	110	93	19%	19%	79	1%	100%	3.5	59	$12
20 TAM	76	10	4	11	1	224	3	0	229	316	433	99	48	114	12	58	0.32	46	28	26	31	60	CDa	15%	141	82	40%	30%	96	6%	100%	-1.5	0	$4
21 TEX	642	75	18	72	8	264	21	10	239	357	415	106	103	108	12	71	0.49	55	18	27	34	103	AFc	10%	94	87	17%	19%	114	4%	100%	10.4	77	$19
22 TEX	645	74	27	76	2	302	24	8	263	358	492	120	129	116	7	75	0.33	48	21	31	36	116	BDc	10%	118	98	20%	18%	107	2%	50%	36.0	152	$29
1st Half	299	34	12	37	1	282	8	3	259	334	455	112	137	102	7	74	0.31	45	24	31	34	96	BDd	8%	108	80	19%	13%	98	2%	33%	7.0	103	$19
2nd Half	346	40	15	39	1	320	17	4	269	379	525	128	124	130	8	76	0.34	51	19	31	38	133	BDc	11%	128	113	21%	23%	116	2%	100%	25.0	200	$30
23 Proj	**630**	**77**	**23**	**81**	**4**	**284**	**24**	**5**	**256**	**358**	**463**	**114**	**115**	**113**	**10**	**74**	**0.42**	**49**	**21**	**30**	**35**	**106**		**10%**	**117**	**94**	**19%**	**19%**	**104**	**4%**	**78%**	**28.3**	**128**	**$24**

Lux,Gavin

Age: 25 Pos: 2B LF	Health B	LIMA Plan B
Bats: L Ht: 6' 2" Wt: 190	PT/Exp A	Rand Var -2
	Consist B	MM 2425

We're still waiting for this former top prospect to show up. Periodic flashes of brilliance (.331 BA in June/July, .367 last Sept) continue to tease, but skill metrics are showing only sloth-like growth. Still, it's growth nonetheless. We fantasy leaguers are an impatient lot, but this one could break out at any time. UP: 2019 is still in view

Yr Tm	PA	R	HR	RBI	SB	BA	xHR	xSB	xBA	OBP	SLG	OPS+	vL+	vR+	bb%	ct%	Eye	G	L	F	h%	HctX	QBaB	Brl%	PX	xPX	HR/F	xHR/F	Spd	SBA%	SB%	RAR	BPX	R$
18 aa	115	17	3	7	2	287		2		352	424	104			9	79	0.47				34				79				120	13%	42%		113	$1
19 LA *	588	94	24	72	10	304	2	14	268	369	513	122	58	104	9	74	0.40	39	27	33	37	135	CCa	6%	112	164	12%	12%	132	10%	65%	33.3	170	$25
20 LA	69	8	3	8	1	175	2	1	216	246	349	79	37	87	9	70	0.32	48	14	39	20	109	CCa	7%	101	110	18%	12%	101	8%	100%	-4.6	40	$0
21 LA *	453	61	8	53	4	239	8	9	236	315	354	92	72	103	10	75	0.45	47	21	31	30	93	BCc	4%	69	79	9%	10%	143	4%	80%	-8.2	77	$8
22 LA	471	66	6	42	7	276	11	8	252	346	399	106	96	109	10	77	0.49	49	22	29	34	97	CDd	6%	80	86	6%	11%	155	7%	78%	9.3	145	$15
1st Half	259	40	2	17	5	290	5	5	250	359	394	107	99	109	10	79	0.54	45	23	31	36	105	CCd	6%	70	96	3%	9%	163	7%	83%	8.3	152	$12
2nd Half	212	26	4	25	2	258	5	3	254	330	405	104	92	108	10	75	0.45	53	19	27	32	87	CFd	6%	92	72	10%	13%	139	7%	67%	3.8	131	$8
23 Proj	**490**	**68**	**12**	**50**	**6**	**266**	**11**	**9**	**251**	**338**	**417**	**105**	**85**	**110**	**10**	**76**	**0.46**	**48**	**21**	**31**	**33**	**99**		**6%**	**95**	**92**	**11%**	**11%**	**140**	**9%**	**70%**	**14.7**	**121**	**$18**

Machado,Manny

Age: 30 Pos: 3B	Health A	LIMA Plan C
Bats: R Ht: 6' 3" Wt: 218	PT/Exp A	Rand Var -3
	Consist C	MM 4245

The only blemish in this elite skill was a drop in ct%, which helped suppress his xHR. But the same thing happened in 2019 and he recovered just fine. What your investment buys is a level of extreme consistency (bb%, xPX, HctX, GLF) that returns a $30 floor. Would you pay $35+ with a guarantee he won't go completely belly up? I would.

Yr Tm	PA	R	HR	RBI	SB	BA	xHR	xSB	xBA	OBP	SLG	OPS+	vL+	vR+	bb%	ct%	Eye	G	L	F	h%	HctX	QBaB	Brl%	PX	xPX	HR/F	xHR/F	Spd	SBA%	SB%	RAR	BPX	R$
18 2 TM	709	84	37	107	14	297	33	11	281	367	538	121	122	119	10	84	0.67	40	18	42	31	119	ABc	11%	128	115	16%	15%	95	9%	88%	45.1	290	$34
19 SD	661	81	32	85	5	256	27	10	251	334	462	110	151	98	10	78	0.51	42	17	41	28	118	ACf	8%	101	121	17%	14%	99	5%	63%	-4.6	167	$18
20 SD	254	44	16	47	6	304	13	3	294	370	580	126	123	127	10	83	0.70	37	22	41	30	131	BBd	11%	134	108	21%	17%	106	14%	67%	15.4	384	$38
21 SD	640	92	28	106	12	278	32	13	271	347	489	115	109	117	10	82	0.62	39	20	41	30	137	ACf	13%	112	123	15%	17%	97	9%	80%	27.5	262	$29
22 SD	644	100	32	102	9	298	22	10	274	366	531	127	120	130	10	77	0.47	38	21	42	34	128	ABc	10%	146	127	17%	12%	92	6%	90%	44.1	255	$37
1st Half	306	49	12	46	7	316	8	5	271	389	526	129	132	128	11	79	0.56	43	17	40	36	126	BBc	7%	132	100	14%	9%	105	6%	88%	25.9	262	$33
2nd Half	338	51	20	56	2	281	13	5	279	346	536	125	110	131	9	75	0.41	33	24	43	31	129	ABc	13%	160	152	20%	13%	80	6%	100%	21.3	252	$36
23 Proj	**630**	**95**	**31**	**103**	**10**	**289**	**26**	**7**	**275**	**357**	**519**	**122**	**117**	**123**	**10**	**79**	**0.53**	**38**	**21**	**41**	**32**	**130**		**11%**	**139**	**125**	**17%**	**14%**	**87**	**5%**	**81%**	**46.3**	**268**	**$36**

Machin,Vimael

Age: 29 Pos: 3B	Health A	LIMA Plan D
Bats: L Ht: 5' 11" Wt: 185	PT/Exp B	Rand Var +2
	Consist A	MM 0213

1-13-.220 in 223 AB at OAK. Extreme platooner who faced southpaws only 13 times last year and still couldn't crack a .600 OPS against RHers. My rule of thumb when I see an unfamiliar name: Check his writeup in the Minor League Baseball Analyst. If he can't crack the top 1000 prospects, I don't need to write insightful commentary here.

Yr Tm	PA	R	HR	RBI	SB	BA	xHR	xSB	xBA	OBP	SLG	OPS+	vL+	vR+	bb%	ct%	Eye	G	L	F	h%	HctX	QBaB	Brl%	PX	xPX	HR/F	xHR/F	Spd	SBA%	SB%	RAR	BPX	R$
18 aa	283	24	4	23	2	190		4		285	281	76			12	75	0.54				24				59				101	4%	59%		13	-$2
19 a/a	506	44	6	53	7	257		5		343	357	97			12	84	0.81				30				56				95	6%	74%		122	$8
20 OAK	71	11	0	0	0	206	1	1	266	296	238	71	103	65	11	84	0.80	43	32	25	25	90	BDb	0%	23	77	0%	8%	115	0%	0%	-4.5	56	-$2
21 OAK *	403	40	7	36	1	210	0	2	205	275	321	82	80	29	8	72	0.32	48	14	38	27	49	FFf	4%	68	38	0%	0%	112	2%	49%	-16.8	-15	$0
22 OAK *	525	46	3	37	1	217	3	4	241	279	288	80	57	85	8	82	0.47	43	23	34	26	96	BCb	4%	52	86	2%	5%	103	2%	50%	-21.5	59	$0
1st Half	280	20	2	24	0	213	0	2	202	261	286	77	0	56	6	84	0.40	80	0	20	25	146	FF		49	135	0%	0%	98	2%	0%	-14.6	62	-$2
2nd Half	245	26	1	13	1	222	3	2	237	302	292	84	57	86	10	79	0.53	42	24	34	28	91	BCb	4%	56	84	2%	5%	106	2%	50%	-9.1	52	-$1
23 Proj	**280**	**26**	**1**	**22**	**1**	**217**	**1**	**2**	**238**	**288**	**278**	**79**	**91**	**77**	**9**	**78**	**0.45**	**43**	**27**	**30**	**28**	**91**		**2%**	**48**	**81**	**1%**	**2%**	**103**	**4%**	**60%**	**-9.5**	**37**	**$2**

Madrigal,Nick

Age: 26 Pos: 2B	Health F	LIMA Plan C+
Bats: R Ht: 5' 8" Wt: 175	PT/Exp D	Rand Var +2
	Consist B	MM 0353

0-7-.249 in 209 AB at CHC. Lost 100 games to groin and back woes, which continued his streak of injury-shortened campaigns. It also ended his streak of .300 seasons, which was the only skill that made him rosterable. Power metrics deem him completely punchless; speed could yield SBs if ever given a green light. Maybe an end-game consideration.

Yr Tm	PA	R	HR	RBI	SB	BA	xHR	xSB	xBA	OBP	SLG	OPS+	vL+	vR+	bb%	ct%	Eye	G	L	F	h%	HctX	QBaB	Brl%	PX	xPX	HR/F	xHR/F	Spd	SBA%	SB%	RAR	BPX	R$
18																																		
19 a/a	306	51	2	25	16	314		6		369	408	108			8	96	2.17				32				46				125	28%	63%		281	$13
20 CHW	109	8	0	11	2	340	0	6	283	376	369	99	59	109	4	93	0.57	55	26	19	36	83	FFc	0%	19	10	0%	0%	118	8%	67%	0.3	132	$9
21 CHW	215	30	2	21	1	305	1	5	302	349	425	106	135	94	5	92	0.65	60	20	20	33	81	DFc	1%	61	14	6%	3%	164	5%	33%	3.8	292	$6
22 CHC *	270	24	0	10	3	250	0	3	255	295	281	82	76	87	6	87	0.48	61	21	18	29	68	DFc		25	30	0%	0%	102	5%	75%	-9.5	38	$1
1st Half	122	8	0	3	1	215	0	1	240	248	241	69	70	74	4	85	0.29	62	20	19	25	73	DFd	0%	21	35	0%	0%	96	5%	100%	-6.8	-10	-$10
2nd Half	148	16	0	7	2	280	0	2	265	334	316	92	83	100	8	88	0.68	60	22	18	32	63	DFc	0%	28	24	0%	0%	113	5%	67%	-0.7	86	-$2
23 Proj	**385**	**44**	**1**	**26**	**6**	**286**	**1**	**6**	**278**	**337**	**351**	**95**	**97**	**94**	**6**	**90**	**0.62**	**60**	**21**	**19**	**32**	**74**		**0%**	**42**	**21**	**2%**	**1%**	**128**	**7%**	**61%**	**3.2**	**153**	**$13**

Madris,Bligh

Age: 27 Pos: OF	Health A	LIMA Plan D
Bats: L Ht: 6' 0" Wt: 208	PT/Exp C	Rand Var 0
	Consist A	MM 2001

1-7-.177 in 113 AB at PIT. Bull Durham prospect's potential was rated a "5C"—50% odds of becoming an MLB reserve—with the comment, "scouts raved about his makeup." (So did Cover FX.) Minor signs of above average power skill, which we might get more excited about if he was 22, but Crash Davis' job is probably still safe.

Yr Tm	PA	R	HR	RBI	SB	BA	xHR	xSB	xBA	OBP	SLG	OPS+	vL+	vR+	bb%	ct%	Eye	G	L	F	h%	HctX	QBaB	Brl%	PX	xPX	HR/F	xHR/F	Spd	SBA%	SB%	RAR	BPX	R$
18																																		
19 aa	498	47	7	52	3	250		6		312	362	93			8	77	0.40				31				67				96	6%	40%		37	$6
20																																		
21 a/a	394	31	6	39	1	220		4		287	334	85			9	76	0.39				27				76				82	7%	23%		35	$1
22 PIT *	442	40	8	40	5	216	2	4	226	274	347	88	67	73	7	69	0.26	52	16	32	29	107	CCc	5%	100	109	4%	8%	87	9%	58%	-14.6	0	$3
1st Half	223	21	4	19	3	247	1	2	259	297	401	99	117	100	7	70	0.24	62	18	21	33	117	BFa	10%	121	118	14%	14%	93	9%	73%	-1.0	69	$3
2nd Half	219	19	4	20	1	184	1	2	196	251	290	77	0	55	8	68	0.28	45	15	40	25	100	CBd	2%	78	102	0%	5%	91	9%	38%	-13.0	-62	-$1
23 Proj	**175**	**15**	**2**	**17**	**1**	**217**	**3**	**2**	**219**	**280**	**324**	**84**	**77**	**85**	**8**	**73**	**0.32**	**52**	**16**	**32**	**29**	**107**		**5%**	**83**	**108**	**6%**	**9%**	**82**	**7%**	**37%**	**-5.0**	**13**	**$2**

Mancini,Trey

Age: 31 Pos: DH 1B LF	Health D	LIMA Plan B
Bats: R Ht: 6' 3" Wt: 230	PT/Exp A	Rand Var +2
	Consist A	MM 3025

.363 May BA obscured the fact that he failed to crack .240 in any other month. Was at .268 when HOU acquired him, then hit .175 the rest of the way, losing PT. Aside from BA, support metrics were flat or better than 2021, which bodes well for a rebound if he earns back AB. But forget 30+ HR—HctX and xPX said that was never real anyway.

Yr Tm	PA	R	HR	RBI	SB	BA	xHR	xSB	xBA	OBP	SLG	OPS+	vL+	vR+	bb%	ct%	Eye	G	L	F	h%	HctX	QBaB	Brl%	PX	xPX	HR/F	xHR/F	Spd	SBA%	SB%	RAR	BPX	R$
18 BAL	636	69	24	58	0	242	26	8	249	299	416	96	86	98	7	74	0.29	55	19	26	29	91	BFb	12%	104	95	21%	23%	99	1%	0%	-5.5	80	$11
19 BAL	679	106	35	97	1	291	31	4	283	364	535	124	127	123	9	76	0.44	46	22	32	33	98	BDc	10%	129	118	24%	21%	101	1%	100%	33.1	219	$25
20																																		
21 BAL	616	77	21	71	0	255	22	6	252	326	432	104	122	94	8	74	0.36	48	20	31	31	103	CCc	10%	108	94	16%	17%	80	0%	0%	2.1	100	$14
22 2 AL	587	56	18	63	0	239	17	2	236	319	391	101	91	105	9	74	0.39	40	21	39	29	107	BCc	10%	100	125	12%	11%	91	0%	0%	-0.6	79	$10
1st Half	314	32	8	32	0	281	11	1	252	357	428	111	103	115	9	78	0.42	37	24	39	34	115	BCc	12%	96	138	9%	13%	119	0%	0%	6.4	145	$14
2nd Half	273	24	10	31	0	191	7	1	215	275	349	88	78	93	10	70	0.37	43	18	39	23	98	BCd	8%	105	110	15%	10%	59	0%	0%	-10.5	10	$6
23 Proj	**525**	**59**	**20**	**60**	**0**	**252**	**19**	**1**	**246**	**325**	**429**	**105**	**105**	**104**	**9**	**74**	**0.37**	**44**	**20**	**36**	**30**	**102**		**10%**	**117**	**110**	**16%**	**15%**	**72**	**1%**	**49%**	**5.8**	**92**	**$15**

RON SHANDLER

Marcano,Tucupita

Age: 23 Pos: LF 2B | Bats: L Ht: 6' 0" Wt: 170
Health A | PT/Exp C | Consist A
LIMA Plan F | Rand Var 0 | MM 1301

2-13-.206 in 160 AB at PIT. Although these numbers don't reflect it, his minor league profile was bat control and a little speed. Whether that will ever convert to something fantasy-worthy remains to be seen, but he's still young and there's no rush to find a spot for him in 2023. Even with growth, his ceiling is probably as a $10 middle infielder.

Yr	Tm	PA	R	HR	RBI	SB	BA	xHR	xSB	xBA	OBP	SLG	OPS+	vL+	vR+	bb%	ct%	Eye	G	L	F	h%	HctX	QBaB	Brl%	PX	xPX	HR/F	xHR/F	Spd	SBA%	SB%	RAR	BPX	R$
18																																			
19																																			
20																																			
21	SD *	445	51	5	32	9	214	0	7	241	296	289	80	80	63	10	82	0.65	63	14	23	25	86	DFb	0%	42	42	0%	0%	119	13%	58%	-21.9	77	$4
22	PIT *	400	43	5	28	5	228	1	9	222	293	336	89	88	76	8	75	0.37	45	18	38	29	70	FCf	2%	75	82	5%	2%	147	15%	37%	-13.1	79	$4
1st Half		191	24	3	14	4	243	1	5	229	319	373	98	106	84	10	72	0.39	43	20	37	32	53	FFf	4%	94	72	11%	6%	132	15%	62%	0.0	79	$3
2nd Half		209	20	2	14	2	214	0	4	215	268	303	81	75	70	7	78	0.33	46	15	38	27	85	FCf	0%	59	89	0%	0%	151	15%	20%	-10.2	69	-$1
23	Proj	175	20	2	12	3	221	1	4	218	295	314	84	94	80	9	78	0.46	45	17	38	27	72		2%	62	82	4%	1%	141	14%	46%	-5.1	75	$0

Margot,Manuel

Age: 28 Pos: RF | Bats: R Ht: 5' 11" Wt: 180
Health D | PT/Exp B | Consist A
LIMA Plan B | Rand Var -3 | MM 1325

After promising signs in 2021, lost nearly half the season with knee and hamstring woes, ailments you don't want for a player whose value is driven by speed. Disappointing, too, because he got off to such a great start. Support metrics were mostly flat, but at this stage of his career, a healthy season could still produce nice upside. UP: 2019 + 40 pts of BA

Yr	Tm	PA	R	HR	RBI	SB	BA	xHR	xSB	xBA	OBP	SLG	OPS+	vL+	vR+	bb%	ct%	Eye	G	L	F	h%	HctX	QBaB	Brl%	PX	xPX	HR/F	xHR/F	Spd	SBA%	SB%	RAR	BPX	R$
18	SD	519	50	8	51	11	245	9	6	251	292	384	91	87	90	6	82	0.36	43	20	37	29	118	BCf	3%	81	106	6%	6%	150	19%	52%	-13.8	167	$10
19	SD	441	59	12	37	20	234	7	12	238	304	387	96	123	85	9	78	0.43	43	16	40	27	90	CBf	4%	81	82	10%	6%	153	24%	83%	-12.8	156	$12
20	TAM	159	19	1	11	12	269	3	6	251	327	352	90	83	92	8	83	0.52	45	23	32	32	97	DDf	4%	55	86	3%	8%	127	38%	75%	-3.7	124	$19
21	TAM	464	55	10	57	13	254	10	25	250	313	382	96	102	90	8	83	0.53	46	18	36	28	101	CCf	5%	69	80	8%	8%	136	18%	62%	-5.4	185	$15
22	TAM	363	36	4	47	7	274	4	10	250	325	375	99	123	92	7	80	0.35	45	23	32	33	91	CDf	3%	70	62	5%	5%	123	11%	70%	0.5	93	$11
1st Half		200	21	3	27	5	302	3	6	261	365	423	111	126	106	9	81	0.49	42	25	33	36	98	CCf	5%	81	72	6%	6%	132	11%	83%	7.5	162	$10
2nd Half		163	15	1	20	2	240	1	4	235	276	318	84	117	74	4	79	0.21	48	21	31	30	82	CDf	2%	56	50	3%	3%	111	11%	50%	-6.4	10	$0
23	Proj	490	53	7	58	14	260	7	9	245	312	367	94	108	88	7	81	0.39	46	21	34	31	95		4%	71	71	6%	6%	111	10%	67%	-1.1	119	$19

Marsh,Brandon

Age: 25 Pos: LF CF | Bats: L Ht: 6' 4" Wt: 215
Health A | PT/Exp B | Consist A
LIMA Plan C+ | Rand Var -2 | MM 3405

His surface stats seem to reflect some growth, but there are potholes throughout support metrics. Contact and batting eye remain awful, keeping his OBP below .300. xBA has no faith in his BA. xPX bump not supported by declines in HctX and exit velocity. Has speed but SB success rate dropped. Still upside, but lack of growth caps interest, for now.

Yr	Tm	PA	R	HR	RBI	SB	BA	xHR	xSB	xBA	OBP	SLG	OPS+	vL+	vR+	bb%	ct%	Eye	G	L	F	h%	HctX	QBaB	Brl%	PX	xPX	HR/F	xHR/F	Spd	SBA%	SB%	RAR	BPX	R$
18																																			
19	aa	405	45	7	40	17	281		6		361	404	106			11	72	0.44				37				77				99	19%	76%		11	$14
20																																			
21	LAA *	364	43	4	24	7	237	6	5	220	300	346	89	76	100	8	62	0.24	44	31	25	37	100	ADa	11%	84	122	6%	17%	129	9%	88%	-9.1	-104	$5
22	2 TM	461	49	11	52	10	245	13	8	216	295	384	96	68	104	6	63	0.18	43	25	33	36	91	CCc	7%	107	130	13%	15%	133	14%	71%	-3.6	-28	$12
1st Half		261	27	6	31	4	227	8	4	202	278	345	88	72	94	6	62	0.18	43	23	34	34	92	CCc	8%	92	118	12%	16%	124	14%	67%	-6.3	-97	$9
2nd Half		200	22	5	21	6	269	5	3	234	317	435	107	61	117	6	64	0.18	42	27	31	39	89	CCb	7%	127	145	14%	14%	132	14%	75%	4.1	38	$10
23	Proj	490	56	12	45	12	249	14	11	223	307	398	98	72	107	7	63	0.22	43	26	31	37	94		9%	116	129	13%	16%	128	12%	78%	4.1	-49	$17

Marte,Ketel

Age: 29 Pos: 2B DH | Bats: B Ht: 6' 1" Wt: 210
Health D | PT/Exp A | Consist D
LIMA Plan B+ | Rand Var +5 | MM 3355

Hamstring issues explain some of this disappointment. But still a tough player to project. Is he a 30-HR hitter? (Not likely.) A .300 hitter? (Possibly.) Exit velocity grades are exasperating (C,B,C,A,B). Plate approach (bb% up, ct% down) isn't working, though 2nd half h% didn't help (batted .193 from Aug 1 on). For safety, bid like it's 2018.

Yr	Tm	PA	R	HR	RBI	SB	BA	xHR	xSB	xBA	OBP	SLG	OPS+	vL+	vR+	bb%	ct%	Eye	G	L	F	h%	HctX	QBaB	Brl%	PX	xPX	HR/F	xHR/F	Spd	SBA%	SB%	RAR	BPX	R$
18	ARI	580	68	14	59	6	260	13	8	285	332	437	103	129	86	9	85	0.68	51	20	29	28	113	CDd	5%	93	84	11%	10%	128	5%	86%	10.8	243	$14
19	ARI	628	97	32	92	10	329	29	8	307	389	592	136	139	133	8	85	0.62	43	22	35	34	123	BCc	9%	122	107	19%	17%	116	7%	83%	62.7	337	$32
20	ARI	195	19	2	17	1	287	3	3	274	323	409	97	143	78	4	88	0.33	46	21	33	32	114	CDd	4%	71	80	4%	6%	107	2%	100%	-1.9	208	$11
21	ARI	374	52	14	50	2	318	12	3	295	377	532	125	159	109	8	82	0.52	46	22	32	35	134	ACd	9%	123	116	16%	13%	91	2%	100%	27.7	285	$17
22	ARI	558	68	12	52	5	240	11	3	263	321	407	103	114	99	10	79	0.54	42	19	39	28	120	BCd	6%	115	108	8%	7%	92	5%	83%	2.9	203	$11
1st Half		294	38	5	25	4	260	4	2	263	347	419	108	114	106	11	79	0.59	46	17	37	31	113	BCd	4%	115	91	7%	5%	104	5%	100%	8.3	221	$13
2nd Half		264	30	7	27	1	218	7	1	264	292	393	97	114	90	9	80	0.49	39	20	41	24	128	BBd	8%	116	127	9%	9%	79	5%	50%	-1.9	193	$8
23	Proj	560	71	16	62	4	271	15	5	278	338	455	110	134	100	9	82	0.52	44	20	36	30	124		7%	120	109	11%	10%	91	5%	84%	23.6	237	$20

Marte,Starling

Age: 34 Pos: RF | Bats: R Ht: 6' 1" Wt: 195
Health C | PT/Exp A | Consist C
LIMA Plan D+ | Rand Var -1 | MM 3445

2021 was a SB/BA unicorn season in an otherwise normal age-related decline. Note, however, that speed skill has been improving, but a career-low 67% success rate won't cut it going forward. On a team that doesn't run much, 20 bags may be the ceiling (pending the impact of larger bases). Otherwise, expect some HR pullback, but still a solid investment.

Yr	Tm	PA	R	HR	RBI	SB	BA	xHR	xSB	xBA	OBP	SLG	OPS+	vL+	vR+	bb%	ct%	Eye	G	L	F	h%	HctX	QBaB	Brl%	PX	xPX	HR/F	xHR/F	Spd	SBA%	SB%	RAR	BPX	R$
18	PIT	606	81	20	72	33	277	25	8	272	327	460	106	96	107	6	81	0.32	51	17	32	31	99	CDc	8%	105	106	14%	17%	137	33%	70%	9.4	203	$31
19	PIT	586	97	23	82	25	295	25	27	297	342	503	117	108	119	6	83	0.27	50	21	28	32	108	CDc	8%	102	88	19%	20%	135	22%	81%	8.3	233	$30
20	2 NL	250	36	6	27	10	281	8	9	272	340	430	102	92	106	5	82	0.29	53	19	28	32	97	DFd	6%	83	74	12%	16%	123	19%	83%	-1.8	172	$29
21	2 TM	526	89	12	55	47	308	16	20	276	381	456	115	104	120	8	79	0.43	55	21	24	37	106	CFd	8%	88	69	14%	18%	140	33%	90%	24.1	177	$42
22	NYM	505	76	16	63	18	292	14	26	278	347	468	115	123	112	5	79	0.27	49	22	29	34	88	CDc	7%	107	75	15%	13%	146	21%	67%	15.3	200	$28
1st Half		305	50	9	39	10	287	7	15	281	341	461	113	132	105	5	81	0.30	50	21	30	33	79	DDc	6%	105	68	13%	10%	139	21%	63%	7.5	217	$30
2nd Half		200	26	7	24	8	299	7	11	273	355	478	118	107	122	5	76	0.23	48	24	27	36	102	CDb	8%	110	86	18%	18%	141	21%	73%	7.9	162	$16
23	Proj	525	83	15	63	20	288	18	18	273	348	450	111	106	112	6	79	0.30	51	22	27	34	98		7%	102	77	14%	16%	128	17%	70%	17.8	184	$31

Martinez,J.D.

Age: 35 Pos: DH | Bats: R Ht: 6' 3" Wt: 230
Health A | PT/Exp A | Consist C
LIMA Plan B | Rand Var -2 | MM 4235

Was batting .363 on May 31, then spun out for the next three months (.219) before finishing with a flourish. But where did the power go? xPX, HctX not that far off history, except for exit velocity which did tank. Blame intermittent back spasms that cost him occasional games. xHR/F bodes well for some rebound, but at 35, the risk is elevated.

Yr	Tm	PA	R	HR	RBI	SB	BA	xHR	xSB	xBA	OBP	SLG	OPS+	vL+	vR+	bb%	ct%	Eye	G	L	F	h%	HctX	QBaB	Brl%	PX	xPX	HR/F	xHR/F	Spd	SBA%	SB%	RAR	BPX	R$
18	BOS	649	111	43	130	6	330	45	10	298	402	629	138	128	139	11	74	0.47	43	23	34	38	123	ACa	16%	178	148	29%	31%	106	4%	86%	77.4	317	$41
19	BOS	656	98	36	105	2	304	38	6	280	383	557	130	192	109	11	76	0.52	43	22	35	35	121	ACa	12%	131	127	23%	25%	91	1%	100%	40.1	222	$27
20	BOS	237	22	7	27	1	213	10	0	238	291	389	90	89	91	9	72	0.37	35	21	44	26	104	BBc	11%	114	150	10%	15%	61	2%	100%	-7.9	72	$8
21	BOS	633	92	28	99	0	286	33	4	267	349	518	119	112	122	9	74	0.37	34	24	42	34	117	ABb	12%	142	140	16%	19%	92	0%	0%	21.7	212	$25
22	BOS	595	76	16	62	0	274	26	2	253	341	448	112	140	104	9	73	0.36	38	22	40	35	110	CBb	12%	129	132	10%	17%	83	0%	0%	10.5	134	$18
1st Half		311	46	8	33	0	312	13	1	271	379	493	123	160	114	9	73	0.38	39	26	35	40	114	BCb	12%	137	121	11%	18%	82	0%	0%	16.7	162	$21
2nd Half		284	30	8	29	0	233	13	1	232	299	401	99	122	91	9	72	0.34	38	18	45	29	106	CBb	12%	119	145	10%	15%	87	0%	0%	-4.8	103	$9
23	Proj	595	79	22	77	1	271	29	2	257	339	473	113	124	108	9	73	0.37	37	22	41	33	112		12%	141	138	13%	18%	78	2%	93%	21.0	161	$23

Massey,Michael

Age: 25 Pos: 2B | Bats: L Ht: 6' 0" Wt: 190
Health A | PT/Exp C | Consist F
LIMA Plan C+ | Rand Var -1 | MM 3205

4-17-.243 with 3 SB in 173 AB at KC. Soared through minors in 2022, granted first MLB opportunity upon Whit Merrifield's trade to TOR and acquitted himself well. Aggressive hitter and efficient base-stealer, he profiles to provide double-digit power and speed as he matures, though without much BA help. In other words, what his 2022 line looks like.

Yr	Tm	PA	R	HR	RBI	SB	BA	xHR	xSB	xBA	OBP	SLG	OPS+	vL+	vR+	bb%	ct%	Eye	G	L	F	h%	HctX	QBaB	Brl%	PX	xPX	HR/F	xHR/F	Spd	SBA%	SB%	RAR	BPX	R$
18																																			
19																																			
20																																			
21																																			
22	KC *	559	50	13	63	11	251	9	5	228	290	395	97	91	98	5	72	0.20	35	20	44	32	109	CBc	14%	107	159	7%	16%	73	11%	82%	3.8	31	$15
1st Half		305	30	7	42	7	251		2	238	290	396	97	0	0	5	71	0.19	44	20	36	33	0			109	-14	0%		83	11%	74%	-0.2	34	$17
2nd Half		254	21	5	22	4	251	9	2	230	290	393	97	91	98	5	73	0.20	35	20	44	32	111	CBc	14%	104	159	7%	16%	84	11%	100%	0.5	48	$8
23	Proj	455	42	9	50	9	251	23	7	223	313	385	97	86	100	5	73	0.19	35	20	44	33	100		13%	101	143	7%	16%	73	8%	88%	1.5	42	$14

RON SHANDLER

Mateo,Jorge

Age: 28	Pos: SS	Health	A	LIMA Plan	C+
Bats: R	Ht: 6' 0" Wt: 182	PT/Exp	A	Rand Var	0
		Consist	B	MM	3515

Volatile hitter outran his flaws; speed enhances his entire game. 4th-worst Eye (min. 500 PA) puts a heavy burden on premium glove to maintain PT after a career-high PA. 2nd half offers a glint of hope as xPX and xBA supported the surge, but could also raise the 2023 price. Don't pin ALL of your SB to a profile like this, especially with a premium attached.

Yr	Tm	PA	R	HR	RBI	SB	BA	xHR	xSB	xBA	OBP	SLG	OPS+	vL+	vR+	bb%	ct%	Eye	G	L	F	h%	HctX	QBaB	Brl%	PX	xPX	HR/F	xHR/F	Spd	SBA%	SB%	RAR	BPX	R$
18	aaa	493	40	2	36	20	209		5		245	320	76			5	68	0.15				30				70				162	35%	64%		-33	$6
19	aaa	554	72	13	60	18	249		21		279	418	96			4	69	0.13				34				98				145	30%	59%		26	$16
20	SD	28	4	0	2	1	154	0	0	207	185	269	60	67	44	4	58	0.09	13	47	40	27	102	CAd		122	107	0%	0%	109	50%	100%	-2.5	-116	-$2
21	2 TM	209	19	4	14	10	247	4	13	227	293	376	92	90	93	4	72	0.16	39	23	38	33	71	DCf	6%	86	61	8%	8%	120	29%	77%	-4.1	8	$5
22	BAL	531	63	13	50	35	221	12	18	225	267	379	91	87	93	5	70	0.18	38	20	41	29	80	DBf	6%	109	95	9%	8%	167	46%	80%	-12.5	107	$21
1st Half		268	28	6	22	20	195	6	9	207	252	325	82	80	82	6	65	0.17	38	23	39	27	66	DCf	7%	98	81	10%	10%	134	46%	87%	-12.3	-31	$17
2nd Half		263	35	7	28	15	246	6	9	245	282	431	101	94	104	5	76	0.20	39	18	44	30	94	DBf	5%	119	106	9%	7%	182	46%	71%	-2.2	221	$21
23	**Proj**	**490**	**54**	**11**	**43**	**27**	**233**	**11**	**26**	**226**	**278**	**386**	**92**	**89**	**93**	**5**	**71**	**0.17**	**39**	**21**	**40**	**30**	**78**		**6%**	**107**	**82**	**8%**	**8%**	**145**	**36%**	**75%**	**-6.8**	**62**	**$17**

Maton,Nick

Age: 26	Pos: OF	Health	F	LIMA Plan	D
Bats: L	Ht: 6' 2" Wt: 178	PT/Exp	D	Rand Var	0
		Consist	A	MM	4221

5-17-.250 in 85 PA at PHI. xPX gives his small sample power surge a touch of credence, but ugly ct% and an unsustainable spike in HR/F mitigate any real excitement. HctX, bb% and Brl% provide a bit of hope and keeps him watchable, especially if he is able to stick in the majors. As such, he's deep league roster filler for now.

Yr	Tm	PA	R	HR	RBI	SB	BA	xHR	xSB	xBA	OBP	SLG	OPS+	vL+	vR+	bb%	ct%	Eye	G	L	F	h%	HctX	QBaB	Brl%	PX	xPX	HR/F	xHR/F	Spd	SBA%	SB%	RAR	BPX	R$
18																																			
19	aa	70	5	2	5	1	197		1		291	341	88			12	74	0.52				23				80				102	13%	46%		67	-$3
20																																			
21	PHI *	365	36	6	33	4	203	2	5	219	285	321	83	120	85	10	66	0.33	33	30	37	29	71	CBd	6%	84	83	7%	7%	117	7%	65%	-16.7	-38	$1
22	PHI *	318	34	8	40	2	215	3	3	227	295	377	95	112	125	10	67	0.34	32	25	43	29	91	DBf	7%	124	144	26%	16%	98	4%	62%	-6.7	59	$3
1st Half		168	18	4	23	1	200	0	2	234	281	385	94	245	307	10	69	0.36	25	25	50	26	0	FDf		138	-14	50%	0%	116	4%	100%	-3.5	148	-$1
2nd Half		150	16	4	16	1	233	3	2	211	311	368	96	79	117	10	64	0.32	33	25	43	33	98	CAf	8%	105	160	24%	18%	95	4%	52%	-2.0	-28	$0
23	**Proj**	**175**	**18**	**7**	**19**	**1**	**213**	**4**	**2**	**241**	**297**	**414**	**99**	**94**	**100**	**10**	**66**	**0.33**	**33**	**27**	**40**	**27**	**87**		**7%**	**146**	**129**	**17%**	**9%**	**106**	**6%**	**64%**	**0.2**	**12**	**$4**

McCann,James

Age: 33	Pos: CA	Health	D	LIMA Plan	D
Bats: R	Ht: 6' 3" Wt: 220	PT/Exp	D	Rand Var	+5
		Consist	C	MM	2203

3-18-.195 in 191 PA at NYM. Wrist and oblique injuries ate up 60 games. Recaptured his flyball lean, but couldn't buy a hit as a career-worst h% smothered his output, though 11% h% vL is more sample size than cause for concern. xPX, HctX, and xHR/F give some hope for a rebound if the body cooperates, though it's hard to see more than C2 viability.

Yr	Tm	PA	R	HR	RBI	SB	BA	xHR	xSB	xBA	OBP	SLG	OPS+	vL+	vR+	bb%	ct%	Eye	G	L	F	h%	HctX	QBaB	Brl%	PX	xPX	HR/F	xHR/F	Spd	SBA%	SB%	RAR	BPX	R$
18	DET	457	31	8	39	0	220	11	6	211	267	314	78	68	79	6	73	0.22	38	22	39	28	98	CBc	5%	63	90	7%	9%	68	3%	0%	-11.7	-80	$1
19	CHW	476	62	18	60	4	273	19	3	248	328	460	109	120	104	6	69	0.22	44	24	32	36	95	BCb	9%	113	89	19%	20%	85	5%	80%	10.3	22	$13
20	CHW	111	20	7	15	1	289	5	1	254	360	536	119	162	99	7	69	0.27	38	25	38	35	101	BBb	9%	139	125	27%	19%	95	7%	50%	6.4	128	$12
21	NYM	412	29	10	46	1	232	10	5	216	294	349	88	101	83	8	69	0.28	52	20	29	31	84	CDc	6%	74	79	13%	13%	98	3%	33%	-6.0	-62	$3
22	NYM *	231	22	4	20	3	193	6	1	198	239	279	73	45	95	6	67	0.18	36	23	40	27	93	BBc	6%	66	107	6%	12%	83	6%	100%	-9.7	-134	-$1
1st Half		108	8	1	8	1	177	3	1	191	219	253	67	38	92	5	68	0.17	42	18	40	25	102	BBd	9%	64	114	4%	13%	86	6%	100%	-5.7	-131	-$9
2nd Half		123	14	3	12	2	207	4	1	202	256	300	79	52	96	6	66	0.20	32	28	41	29	84	BBb	4%	68	101	7%	14%	85	6%	100%	-3.7	-138	-$2
23	**Proj**	**385**	**39**	**10**	**40**	**3**	**221**	**13**	**4**	**213**	**280**	**337**	**86**	**76**	**90**	**6**	**68**	**0.22**	**41**	**23**	**36**	**30**	**91**		**6%**	**84**	**98**	**11%**	**14%**	**85**	**6%**	**76%**	**-4.1**	**-76**	**$7**

McCarthy,Jake

Age: 25	Pos: RF LF	Health	A	LIMA Plan	C+
Bats: L	Ht: 6' 2" Wt: 215	PT/Exp	C	Rand Var	-1
		Consist	C	MM	3515

8-43-.283 with 23 SB in 354 PA at ARI. Plus Spd, good ct% and Eye are a nice foundation. Swing change and recent MiLB work hint at some power upside (.238 ISO at AAA) despite QBaB and xPX pessimism. Production against southpaws begat more PT as he started in 17 of 22 gms vL in 2nd half. Pay for the SB and BA, don't bank on the HR output.

Yr	Tm	PA	R	HR	RBI	SB	BA	xHR	xSB	xBA	OBP	SLG	OPS+	vL+	vR+	bb%	ct%	Eye	G	L	F	h%	HctX	QBaB	Brl%	PX	xPX	HR/F	xHR/F	Spd	SBA%	SB%	RAR	BPX	R$
18																																			
19																																			
20																																			
21	ARI *	420	49	11	36	20	207	1	6	205	264	374	88	92	100	7	66	0.23	58	3	39	29	44	FFf	3%	104	82	14%	7%	161	35%	76%	-16.1	42	$10
22	ARI *	505	71	11	58	29	282	6	26	264	330	425	107	107	109	7	78	0.32	49	22	29	34	90	DFf	5%	93	80	12%	9%	138	29%	78%	12.8	145	$29
1st Half		220	33	6	22	6	261	2	10	246	310	425	104	104	94	7	73	0.27	40	23	36	33	109	CCf	10%	109	97	18%	12%	140	29%	56%	1.7	128	$12
2nd Half		286	38	5	35	23	299	4	16	272	346	426	109	108	114	7	81	0.38	51	22	27	35	87	DFf	4%	81	76	10%	8%	125	29%	88%	12.5	148	$33
23	**Proj**	**490**	**65**	**12**	**51**	**30**	**252**	**10**	**21**	**238**	**320**	**409**	**101**	**96**	**103**	**7**	**73**	**0.28**	**52**	**15**	**34**	**32**	**75**		**5%**	**104**	**84**	**11%**	**9%**	**147**	**24%**	**79%**	**4.8**	**101**	**$26**

McCormick,Chas

Age: 28	Pos: LF CF	Health	A	LIMA Plan	C
Bats: R	Ht: 6' 0" Wt: 208	PT/Exp	B	Rand Var	0
		Consist	A	MM	3213

Traded power for patience as Eye surge softened the blow of xPX crash. Heavy platoon split due more to h% (40% vL, 27% vR) than skill dip. Must improve SB% to maximize that Spd. Solid approach and enough pop have yielded 23 HR/7 SB per 600 PA, so finding a full season role has $20 compiler upside.

Yr	Tm	PA	R	HR	RBI	SB	BA	xHR	xSB	xBA	OBP	SLG	OPS+	vL+	vR+	bb%	ct%	Eye	G	L	F	h%	HctX	QBaB	Brl%	PX	xPX	HR/F	xHR/F	Spd	SBA%	SB%	RAR	BPX	R$
18	aa	271	30	2	25	11	253		4		312	318	84			8	86	0.59				29				40				101	21%	71%		77	$6
19	a/a	420	50	11	51	12	228		16		323	354	94			12	80	0.72				26				56				150	15%	73%		141	$9
20																																			
21	HOU	320	47	14	50	4	257	15	4	219	319	447	105	112	102	8	63	0.24	36	22	42	36	93	BAc	10%	128	144	18%	19%	89	8%	67%	3.5	0	$10
22	HOU	407	47	14	44	4	245	15	7	236	332	407	105	136	92	11	70	0.43	43	22	35	31	92	CCc	10%	105	110	16%	17%	124	7%	57%	6.5	97	$10
1st Half		188	20	8	19	1	232	7	3	243	309	429	104	131	93	10	73	0.39	46	15	38	27	98	CCd	10%	125	123	17%	15%	109	7%	33%	1.1	152	$3
2nd Half		219	27	6	25	3	257	9	4	231	352	387	105	140	90	13	69	0.47	40	28	32	34	87	DCc	10%	87	97	15%	23%	133	7%	75%	4.1	41	$10
23	**Proj**	**350**	**44**	**14**	**44**	**6**	**249**	**16**	**5**	**236**	**327**	**424**	**104**	**126**	**95**	**10**	**71**	**0.39**	**40**	**22**	**38**	**31**	**92**		**10%**	**114**	**122**	**17%**	**19%**	**108**	**7%**	**66%**	**7.5**	**65**	**$13**

McCutchen,Andrew

Age: 36	Pos: DH LF	Health	C	LIMA Plan	B
Bats: R	Ht: 5' 11" Wt: 195	PT/Exp	A	Rand Var	+1
		Consist	A	MM	3125

Is Father Time lurking? It's a firm... maybe. PRO: Good Eye, firm HctX and Brl%, h% rebound, 4-year high in SB, beat his '21 R$. CON: Severe PX/xPX drops, 6-year low in h% vL, xSB didn't back SB jump. Age could start eating into PT, but luckily this profile type is often very affordable. Could be a deep league gem with vL rebound.

Yr	Tm	PA	R	HR	RBI	SB	BA	xHR	xSB	xBA	OBP	SLG	OPS+	vL+	vR+	bb%	ct%	Eye	G	L	F	h%	HctX	QBaB	Brl%	PX	xPX	HR/F	xHR/F	Spd	SBA%	SB%	RAR	BPX	R$
18	2 TM	682	83	20	65	14	255	23	11	250	368	424	106	109	103	14	75	0.66	41	23	36	31	119	BCb	8%	105	125	13%	15%	102	12%	61%	10.0	140	$19
19	PHI	262	45	10	29	2	256	10	5	255	378	457	115	117	114	16	75	0.78	45	18	37	30	95	BCb	7%	109	101	17%	17%	100	4%	67%	4.0	189	$5
20	PHI	241	32	10	34	4	253	10	2	245	324	433	100	123	91	9	78	0.46	35	22	44	28	126	BAc	8%	96	151	14%	14%	92	7%	100%	0.1	144	$21
21	PHI	574	78	27	80	6	222	23	6	252	334	444	107	140	90	14	73	0.61	40	19	40	25	108	CBd	9%	131	126	19%	16%	79	5%	86%	-2.8	188	$14
22	MIL	580	66	17	69	8	237	16	5	243	316	384	99	103	97	10	76	0.46	42	21	37	28	104	CCd	9%	97	104	11%	11%	77	10%	57%	-10.3	90	$15
1st Half		298	33	7	32	5	249	8	2	242	315	372	97	97	97	8	80	0.44	46	19	35	29	108	CCc	8%	78	99	9%	11%	85	10%	56%	-6.7	83	$14
2nd Half		282	33	10	37	3	224	8	2	244	316	398	101	109	98	12	72	0.48	36	23	41	27	100	BBf	10%	119	110	14%	11%	73	10%	60%	-4.2	107	$15
23	**Proj**	**560**	**72**	**21**	**72**	**7**	**234**	**19**	**7**	**246**	**327**	**413**	**103**	**119**	**95**	**12**	**75**	**0.53**	**40**	**21**	**39**	**27**	**107**		**9%**	**116**	**117**	**14%**	**13%**	**76**	**7%**	**67%**	**2.9**	**136**	**$18**

McGuire,Reese

Age: 28	Pos: CA	Health	A	LIMA Plan	D
Bats: L	Ht: 6' 0" Wt: 215	PT/Exp	D	Rand Var	-5
		Consist	C	MM	2321

Defense-first (only?) backup threw out runners at an American League-best 33% clip and sits at 36% since 2020 (4th in MLB). A total lack of punch at the dish undercut the value of useful ct% and LD% rates. There is nothing in his profile to suggest it's coming anytime soon. Don't get baited by the late bounce in Boston (3 HR, .337 BA)

Yr	Tm	PA	R	HR	RBI	SB	BA	xHR	xSB	xBA	OBP	SLG	OPS+	vL+	vR+	bb%	ct%	Eye	G	L	F	h%	HctX	QBaB	Brl%	PX	xPX	HR/F	xHR/F	Spd	SBA%	SB%	RAR	BPX	R$
18	TOR *	384	32	8	37	4	224	1	5	233	287	338	84	83	133	8	74	0.34	36	27	36	28	99	FCa	9%	71	166	25%	13%	92	7%	63%	-2.3	-3	$3
19	TOR *	368	39	9	35	3	246	2	4	273	303	387	96	95	127	8	80	0.41	40	28	32	28	88	DCc	4%	77	85	20%	8%	95	4%	100%	4.2	104	$4
20	TOR	45	2	1	1	0	73	0	0	191	73	146	29	0	50	0	73	0.00	66	10	24	7	35	FFf	3%	36	8	14%	0%	89	0%	0%	-5.6	-196	-$6
21	TOR	217	22	1	10	0	253	2	1	239	310	343	90	63	97	7	78	0.34	40	24	36	32	71	DCc	3%	69	59	2%	4%	90	0%	0%	-2.0	35	$0
22	2 AL	273	25	3	22	1	269	3	1	234	307	369	96	85	98	4	78	0.21	39	23	39	34	59	DCf	3%	73	55	4%	4%	93	2%	100%	2.7	24	$4
1st Half		146	12	0	10	0	235	2	1	204	275	288	80	36	89	4	80	0.23	37	18	45	29	41	FCf	3%	46	47	0%	4%	91	2%	0%	-4.0	-14	-$7
2nd Half		127	13	3	12	1	308	1	1	262	344	462	114	144	108	5	74	0.20	41	28	31	39	79	CCc	2%	105	64	11%	4%	94	2%	100%	7.3	72	$1
23	**Proj**	**210**	**21**	**3**	**16**	**1**	**262**	**3**	**1**	**244**	**310**	**380**	**96**	**80**	**99**	**6**	**77**	**0.28**	**40**	**24**	**36**	**33**	**69**		**3%**	**84**	**61**	**6%**	**5%**	**88**	**3%**	**89%**	**3.8**	**39**	**$5**

PAUL SPORER

McKenna,Ryan

Age: 26	Pos: LF RF CF	Health	A	LIMA Plan	D
Bats: R	Ht: 5' 11" Wt: 195	PT/Exp	F	Rand Var	-4
		Consist	B	MM	1201

2-11-.237 with 2 SB in 172 PA at BAL. Second straight year that he spent enough time in the majors to get at least 15 AB in every month... but only once more than 34. That's a lot of bench time. But he doesn't make contact or hit the ball hard enough to make better use of moderate power/speed skill. Slight growth here, but not enough to bid on.

Yr	Tm	PA	R	HR	RBI	SB	BA	xHR	xSB	xBA	OBP	SLG	OPS+	vL+	vR+	bb%	ct%	Eye	G	L	F	h%	HctX	QBaB	Brl%	PX	xPX	HR/F	xHR/F	Spd	SBA%	SB%	RAR	BPX	R$
18	aa	235	27	3	12	3	213		3		287	293	78			9	72	0.38				28				54				123	7%	74%		-27	$0
19	aa	544	74	9	50	23	218		8		298	341	88			10	74	0.44				28				71				124	28%	66%		48	$13
20																																			
21	BAL *	314	39	11	32	6	216	3	5	216	317	384	96	64	88	13	59	0.36	45	25	29	32	62	DCc	7%	118	60	7%	11%	129	12%	65%	-4.1	-4	$5
22	BAL *	207	26	4	15	2	234	3	3	207	285	352	90	111	75	6	62	0.19	39	24	37	35	81	DBb	10%	101	120	5%	8%	110	11%	37%	-5.9	-72	$1
1st Half		126	18	3	9	2	243	1	2	202	288	375	94	106	89	6	57	0.15	47	22	31	40	59	FCa	7%	120	82	7%	7%	121	11%	46%	-2.7	-93	-$2
2nd Half		81	8	1	6	0	219	3	1	218	278	315	84	114	50	8	71	0.29	31	25	43	29	110	DAb	12%	77	157	5%	14%	96	11%	0%	-3.4	-28	-$8
23	**Proj**	**245**	**30**	**3**	**20**	**4**	**222**	**5**	**4**	**205**	**301**	**315**	**85**	**93**	**79**	**9**	**65**	**0.30**	**41**	**25**	**34**	**33**	**78**		**9%**	**78**	**99**	**6%**	**11%**	**104**	**9%**	**54%**	**-6.0**	**-26**	**$1**

McKinstry,Zach

Age: 28	Pos: 3B 2B	Health	B	LIMA Plan	D+
Bats: L	Ht: 6' 0" Wt: 180	PT/Exp	D	Rand Var	+3
		Consist	A	MM	2313

5-14-.199 with 7 SB in 171 PA at CHC. Journeyman infielder makes decent contact, has shown some power and speed, but it hasn't coalesced into a firm role due to poor quality of that contact. Might get a shot to land a full-time job in the spring, but will more likely end up as the second man listed on the depth chart... but at half a dozen positions.

Yr	Tm	PA	R	HR	RBI	SB	BA	xHR	xSB	xBA	OBP	SLG	OPS+	vL+	vR+	bb%	ct%	Eye	G	L	F	h%	HctX	QBaB	Brl%	PX	xPX	HR/F	xHR/F	Spd	SBA%	SB%	RAR	BPX	R$
18	aa	86	5	2	6	0	162		1		189	251	59			3	71	0.12				21				55				112	0%	0%		-90	-$4
19	a/a	462	55	15	62	6	259		2		311	432	103			7	75	0.30				31				94				107	15%	38%		85	$11
20	LA	7	1	0	0	0	286	0	0	275	286	429	95	0	95	0	57	0.00	50	50	0	50	173	DFf		153	99	0%	#DIV/0!	114	0%	0%	0.0	-48	-$2
21	LA *	331	42	12	43	4	213	6	1	239	267	388	90	88	93	7	73	0.27	43	18	39	25	110	CCa	8%	106	143	17%	14%	104	12%	51%	-12.4	92	$5
22	2 NL *	390	40	7	27	7	221	3	7	228	282	344	89	65	93	8	73	0.32	37	25	38	28	80	DCf	4%	79	100	12%	7%	133	13%	64%	-13.7	48	$4
1st Half		204	20	3	14	0	231	1	4	208	284	323	86	0	101	7	76	0.30	25	25	50	29	83	CCc	25%	59	173	50%	50%	128	13%	0%	-8.5	17	-$2
2nd Half		186	21	5	14	7	210	3	3	234	279	370	92	65	92	9	71	0.33	38	25	38	27	77	DCf	3%	105	98	10%	7%	135	13%	100%	-3.5	93	$5
23	**Proj**	**350**	**41**	**9**	**36**	**6**	**220**	**10**	**6**	**234**	**282**	**370**	**90**	**83**	**92**	**7**	**73**	**0.30**	**40**	**22**	**38**	**27**	**90**		**5%**	**99**	**116**	**11%**	**11%**	**114**	**11%**	**65%**	**-4.9**	**77**	**$8**

McMahon,Ryan

Age: 28	Pos: 3B	Health	A	LIMA Plan	B+
Bats: L	Ht: 6' 2" Wt: 219	PT/Exp	A	Rand Var	0
		Consist	B	MM	4225

Long, long ago (2017), he went .355/.403/.583 in Triple-A, and we imagined what type of damage he would do in Coors. Reality hasn't come close, and while he has shown occasional flashes, we may have to be content with a 20-25 HR, .250 hitter. xPX still outpaces PX and HctX trend teases us, but launch angle has kept his hits below fence-clearing height.

Yr	Tm	PA	R	HR	RBI	SB	BA	xHR	xSB	xBA	OBP	SLG	OPS+	vL+	vR+	bb%	ct%	Eye	G	L	F	h%	HctX	QBaB	Brl%	PX	xPX	HR/F	xHR/F	Spd	SBA%	SB%	RAR	BPX	R$
18	COL *	436	42	13	49	3	243	4	5	242	292	410	94	128	82	6	68	0.21	46	24	30	33	85	BDc	5%	114	99	14%	11%	83	6%	56%	-8.5	10	$8
19	COL	539	70	24	83	5	250	21	5	246	329	450	108	109	106	10	67	0.35	51	21	28	32	102	ADb	9%	119	112	27%	24%	79	5%	83%	-5.4	30	$15
20	COL	193	23	9	26	0	215	9	2	214	295	419	95	97	93	9	62	0.27	50	15	35	29	100	BCc	11%	131	158	24%	24%	107	2%	0%	-7.8	16	$9
21	COL	596	80	23	86	6	254	21	3	254	331	449	107	90	114	10	72	0.40	39	24	38	31	114	BBc	7%	122	139	16%	15%	87	6%	75%	10.3	131	$18
22	COL	597	67	20	67	7	246	21	6	244	327	414	105	90	111	10	70	0.38	45	23	33	31	121	ACb	11%	114	133	17%	17%	87	7%	70%	1.9	69	$17
1st Half		314	33	7	38	2	245	8	3	234	338	383	102	90	107	12	70	0.44	41	24	35	32	108	ACc	9%	98	121	10%	12%	89	7%	50%	0.3	41	$13
2nd Half		283	34	13	29	5	247	12	3	255	314	447	108	89	115	9	70	0.31	48	21	30	30	136	ACa	12%	131	147	24%	22%	90	7%	83%	4.4	103	$19
23	**Proj**	**560**	**68**	**22**	**71**	**6**	**245**	**21**	**6**	**246**	**323**	**433**	**105**	**94**	**109**	**10**	**70**	**0.36**	**44**	**22**	**34**	**31**	**116**		**9%**	**129**	**136**	**19%**	**18%**	**89**	**6%**	**71%**	**12.9**	**82**	**$19**

McNeil,Jeff

Age: 31	Pos: 2B LF	Health	B	LIMA Plan	B+
Bats: L	Ht: 6' 1" Wt: 195	PT/Exp	A	Rand Var	-4
		Consist	D	MM	1345

Is this the recipe for a batting champion? Elite contact rate is a good start and above average speed helps leg out hits, but this is truly the profile of a flying squirrel. Punchless bat and red light on the bases eliminate useful counting stats; only his surrounding cast gave him the runs/RBI to create a $20-plus earner. But these days, you can't toss away .300 hitters.

Yr	Tm	PA	R	HR	RBI	SB	BA	xHR	xSB	xBA	OBP	SLG	OPS+	vL+	vR+	bb%	ct%	Eye	G	L	F	h%	HctX	QBaB	Brl%	PX	xPX	HR/F	xHR/F	Spd	SBA%	SB%	RAR	BPX	R$
18	NYM *	613	85	16	68	11	292	5	9	270	339	464	108	108	114	7	86	0.52	39	22	40	32	96	CBd	2%	92	103	4%	6%	142	8%	92%	23.4	253	$23
19	NYM	567	83	23	75	5	318	19	9	297	384	531	127	115	130	6	85	0.47	43	22	35	34	111	CCa	5%	107	94	15%	13%	107	7%	45%	32.9	270	$23
20	NYM	209	19	4	23	0	311	4	3	280	383	454	111	97	118	10	87	0.83	44	24	32	34	109	CCc	2%	81	81	8%	8%	110	3%	0%	5.5	268	$15
21	NYM	426	48	7	35	3	249	9	4	256	317	358	93	86	95	7	85	0.50	47	20	33	28	100	CCc	4%	62	70	6%	8%	111	3%	100%	-8.4	150	$6
22	NYM	589	73	9	62	4	326	9	7	282	382	454	118	106	123	7	89	0.66	41	24	35	36	96	CCb	3%	82	68	5%	5%	118	2%	100%	32.9	245	$27
1st Half		273	36	4	34	2	319	4	3	273	377	448	117	100	124	8	85	0.58	44	22	34	36	103	CCb	2%	85	68	6%	6%	120	2%	100%	15.8	221	$17
2nd Half		316	37	5	28	2	333	5	4	291	386	460	120	111	122	6	91	0.76	39	25	36	35	89	DCb	3%	79	68	5%	5%	112	2%	100%	20.4	262	$21
23	**Proj**	**560**	**68**	**8**	**57**	**4**	**300**	**9**	**6**	**270**	**361**	**419**	**108**	**100**	**111**	**7**	**87**	**0.59**	**43**	**23**	**34**	**33**	**99**		**3%**	**77**	**73**	**5%**	**6%**	**111**	**5%**	**81%**	**23.3**	**221**	**$23**

Meadows,Austin

Age: 28	Pos: OF	Health	F	LIMA Plan	B
Bats: L	Ht: 6' 3" Wt: 225	PT/Exp	C	Rand Var	+3
		Consist	C	MM	4125

0-11-.250 in 147 PA at DET. After batting .328 in April, the bottom fell out. Vertigo, COVID, strained Achilles tendons, concussion and mental health issues (obviously) destroyed his season. But even this small sample showed career high ct% and no erosion of HctX or plate patience. Track spring health, but there is a good chance he outearns his draft spot.

Yr	Tm	PA	R	HR	RBI	SB	BA	xHR	xSB	xBA	OBP	SLG	OPS+	vL+	vR+	bb%	ct%	Eye	G	L	F	h%	HctX	QBaB	Brl%	PX	xPX	HR/F	xHR/F	Spd	SBA%	SB%	RAR	BPX	R$
18	2 TM *	467	59	16	54	15	276	6	6	272	314	463	104	122	93	5	81	0.30	41	21	37	31	111	CCb	6%	111	139	12%	12%	116	18%	83%	8.3	200	$18
19	TAM	591	83	33	89	12	291	34	16	270	364	558	128	116	132	9	75	0.41	34	23	43	33	118	BBc	13%	137	139	19%	20%	108	13%	63%	25.1	233	$26
20	TAM	152	19	4	13	2	205	4	2	194	296	371	89	51	102	11	62	0.34	26	20	54	29	93	BAd	7%	119	122	9%	9%	96	9%	67%	-5.7	-8	$5
21	TAM	591	79	27	106	4	234	21	6	245	315	458	106	77	120	10	76	0.48	29	19	53	25	110	BAd	9%	127	130	13%	10%	74	6%	57%	-6.4	200	$16
22	DET *	183	11	1	13	0	220	3	2	219	300	292	84	79	102	10	84	0.73	37	19	44	26	110	CBc	6%	46	80	0%	6%	119	2%	0%	-9.1	110	-$3
1st Half		161	10	1	12	0	237	3	2	226	320	320	91	79	102	11	85	0.84	37	19	44	27	111	CBc	6%	52	80	0%	6%	119	2%	0%	-5.5	148	-$7
2nd Half		22	1	0	1	0	106		0	181	156	106	37	0	0	6	78	0.26	44	20	36	14	0			0	-14	0%		101	2%	0%	-3.0	-159	-$12
23	**Proj**	**490**	**55**	**19**	**55**	**5**	**235**	**15**	**3**	**246**	**318**	**441**	**105**	**83**	**114**	**10**	**75**	**0.45**	**32**	**20**	**48**	**27**	**106**		**8%**	**131**	**114**	**12%**	**10%**	**93**	**3%**	**61%**	**8.9**	**125**	**$14**

Mejía,Francisco

Age: 27	Pos: CA	Health	D	LIMA Plan	D+
Bats: B	Ht: 5' 8" Wt: 188	PT/Exp	C	Rand Var	-1
		Consist	D	MM	3133

Posted an .833 OPS with 90% contact rate versus LHPs. Yes, it was only 86 AB, but you gotta try to find growth somewhere. (Better power vs RHPs, however.) Lost 25 games to COVID and a shoulder impingement. Likely to be in job-share as long as he's on TAM, so ceiling might be limited. And if it ends up in a short-side platoon, even worse.

Yr	Tm	PA	R	HR	RBI	SB	BA	xHR	xSB	xBA	OBP	SLG	OPS+	vL+	vR+	bb%	ct%	Eye	G	L	F	h%	HctX	QBaB	Brl%	PX	xPX	HR/F	xHR/F	Spd	SBA%	SB%	RAR	BPX	R$
18	2 TM *	507	44	12	56	0	234	2	6	234	269	373	86	68	100	4	76	0.19	54	16	30	28	98	CDf	8%	90	74	27%	18%	79	0%	0%	-2.5	37	$5
19	SD *	311	37	11	30	1	273	8	2	248	312	467	108	97	106	5	77	0.24	36	20	44	32	94	CAd	5%	105	94	11%	11%	127	3%	50%	5.9	152	$6
20	SD	42	5	1	2	0	77	0	0	196	143	179	43	33	47	2	77	0.11	40	13	47	7	114	FAf		56	115	7%	0%	94	0%	0%	-5.0	-48	-$5
21	TAM	277	31	6	35	0	260	5	2	241	322	416	101	102	101	6	80	0.35	41	16	42	30	79	DBf	4%	90	71	7%	6%	113	0%	0%	3.4	162	$4
22	TAM	299	32	6	31	0	242	3	0	256	264	381	91	117	80	2	78	0.11	37	24	39	29	78	CBd	3%	100	66	7%	3%	72	0%	0%	-1.7	62	$3
1st Half		146	17	5	17	0	229	1	0	258	233	396	89	109	80	1	74	0.03	44	23	32	27	72	DCd	3%	115	55	14%	3%	67	0%	0%	-2.2	45	-$1
2nd Half		153	15	1	14	0	255	2	0	254	294	366	93	124	80	4	81	0.21	30	26	44	31	84	CAc	3%	87	77	2%	4%	90	0%	0%	-0.1	100	-$2
23	**Proj**	**350**	**38**	**10**	**39**	**0**	**251**	**7**	**1**	**255**	**292**	**418**	**99**	**107**	**94**	**4**	**78**	**0.20**	**39**	**21**	**40**	**29**	**83**		**4%**	**112**	**72**	**9%**	**6%**	**98**	**3%**	**50%**	**6.4**	**107**	**$9**

Melendez,MJ

Age: 24	Pos: CA LF DH	Health	A	LIMA Plan	B+
Bats: L	Ht: 6' 1" Wt: 185	PT/Exp	A	Rand Var	+2
		Consist	C	MM	3115

18-62-.217 in 534 PA at KC. Top prospect hit the ground running after May callup, batting .259 with 4 HR in first month. Then the hits were tougher to come by (.208 the rest of the way). Expect an adjustment period, especially as a CA, where defense comes first (or, at least should). But the pieces are here for a perennial Top 5 CA, and... UP: 30 HR.

Yr	Tm	PA	R	HR	RBI	SB	BA	xHR	xSB	xBA	OBP	SLG	OPS+	vL+	vR+	bb%	ct%	Eye	G	L	F	h%	HctX	QBaB	Brl%	PX	xPX	HR/F	xHR/F	Spd	SBA%	SB%	RAR	BPX	R$
18																																			
19																																			
20																																			
21	a/a	505	73	29	79	2	251		6		336	500	115			11	73	0.47				28				143				98	8%	25%		227	$16
22	KC *	619	61	19	65	4	205	20	7	232	300	368	95	118	94	12	71	0.47	39	20	41	25	110	BBd	11%	110	122	13%	15%	103	5%	55%	-0.7	103	$7
1st Half		293	23	10	24	2	197	6	3	235	285	365	92	130	96	11	73	0.45	40	19	41	23	108	BCf	8%	111	117	16%	11%	100	5%	63%	-2.4	114	$4
2nd Half		326	38	9	41	2	212	14	4	228	310	371	96	107	93	13	70	0.49	38	21	41	27	111	ABc	12%	109	126	11%	17%	111	5%	50%	1.0	100	$14
23	**Proj**	**595**	**71**	**20**	**76**	**3**	**231**	**22**	**6**	**235**	**319**	**405**	**101**	**119**	**94**	**12**	**72**	**0.48**	**39**	**20**	**41**	**28**	**110**		**11%**	**117**	**122**	**13%**	**15%**	**107**	**6%**	**39%**	**13.3**	**154**	**$16**

RON SHANDLER

Meneses,Joey

Age: 31	Pos: 1B RF	Health A	LIMA Plan B
Bats: R	Ht: 6' 3" Wt: 190	PT/Exp B	Rand Var 0
		Consist A	MM 4245

13-34-.324 in 240 PA at WAS. Feel-good story in Aug and Sep for a team that needed positivity. A 38% h% in MLB confirms that he's not a future batting champ threat, but 77% MLB ct% and promising power/platoon metrics point to utility, even in a COR IF spot. With enough draft-day skeptics in the room, there could be a minor profit opportunity.

Yr Tm	PA	R	HR	RBI	SB	BA	xHR	xSB	xBA	OBP	SLG	OPS+	vL+	vR+	bb%	ct%	Eye	G	L	F	h%	HctX	QBaB	Brl%	PX	xPX	HR/F	xHR/F	Spd	SBA%	SB%	RAR	BPX	R$
18 aaa	524	59	20	65	0	263		7		308	434	100			6	72	0.23				33				108				88	0%	0%		53	$13
19																																		
20																																		
21 a/a	351	30	9	47	0	227		2		264	407	92			5	72	0.18				29				121				84	2%	0%		85	$3
22 WAS *	633	64	25	72	2	252	10	3	256	292	423	101	152	122	5	72	0.20	45	26	30	31	113	ACa	10%	112	110	25%	20%	97	1%	100%	-6.9	66	$17
1st Half	306	25	10	29	0	206		1	212	244	342	83	0	0	5	68	0.16	44	20	36	27	0			95	-14	0%		95	1%	0%	-15.2	-41	$5
2nd Half	327	38	15	44	2	296	10	2	278	338	501	119	152	122	6	76	0.26	45	26	30	35	119	ACa	10%	127	110	25%	20%	103	1%	100%	15.1	169	$28
23 Proj	525	51	24	66	1	247	21	3	272	288	461	104	121	96	5	72	0.20	45	26	30	29	107		9%	143	99	23%	20%	98	3%	62%	5.4	82	$13

Merrifield,Whit

Age: 34	Pos: 2B RF	Health A	LIMA Plan C+
Bats: R	Ht: 6' 1" Wt: 195	PT/Exp A	Rand Var +2
		Consist A	MM 2335

His middling Aug (62) and Sept (52) PA totals AFTER the trade remain one of 2022's mysteries. Maybe it was buyer's remorse, as many skills are in slow decline. There's enough of a base that he could reclaim his accumulator status (minus the SB impact), butcha can't accumulate from the bench. Now merely useful, rather than foundational.

Yr Tm	PA	R	HR	RBI	SB	BA	xHR	xSB	xBA	OBP	SLG	OPS+	vL+	vR+	bb%	ct%	Eye	G	L	F	h%	HctX	QBaB	Brl%	PX	xPX	HR/F	xHR/F	Spd	SBA%	SB%	RAR	BPX	R$
18 KC	707	88	12	60	45	304	18	11	269	367	438	108	125	99	9	82	0.54	35	30	35	36	111	CBb	5%	85	100	7%	10%	110	27%	82%	26.1	160	$38
19 KC	735	105	16	74	20	302	18	33	276	348	463	112	113	111	6	81	0.36	38	29	33	35	108	CBa	4%	83	95	9%	10%	163	16%	67%	12.5	207	$29
20 KC	265	38	9	30	12	282	6	6	275	325	440	101	101	101	5	87	0.36	37	26	37	30	83	DBb	5%	79	78	11%	8%	95	23%	80%	0.1	196	$34
21 KC	720	97	10	74	40	277	12	24	263	317	395	98	98	98	6	84	0.39	41	24	35	32	90	DCb	3%	70	85	5%	6%	123	25%	91%	5.4	169	$37
22 2 AL	550	70	11	58	16	250	9	18	250	298	375	95	100	94	7	83	0.45	41	20	39	28	91	DBc	4%	80	103	7%	5%	100	17%	76%	-4.4	145	$18
1st Half	355	43	3	33	14	240	6	12	245	293	330	88	88	88	8	84	0.54	39	22	39	28	100	CBb	4%	62	108	3%	6%	106	17%	88%	-6.9	128	$21
2nd Half	195	27	8	25	2	268	4	6	255	308	454	108	123	102	6	81	0.31	45	14	41	29	76	DBf	5%	112	96	14%	7%	89	17%	40%	2.3	183	$11
23 Proj	455	62	11	50	17	270	9	11	259	315	409	100	105	98	6	83	0.40	41	22	38	30	89		4%	88	93	8%	7%	103	13%	79%	10.1	169	$22

Meyers,Jake

Age: 27	Pos: CF	Health C	LIMA Plan D
Bats: R	Ht: 6' 0" Wt: 200	PT/Exp D	Rand Var 0
		Consist C	MM 2213

1-15-.227 with 2 SB in 160 PA at HOU. Slowed by shoulder injury from 2021 postseason, didn't appear until late June and didn't look the same. BA and power skills both backed up; batted ball profile and quality disintegrated. Easy to write off and give another shot, but no longer a youngster. Make him show the HR/SB combo before buying in.

Yr Tm	PA	R	HR	RBI	SB	BA	xHR	xSB	xBA	OBP	SLG	OPS+	vL+	vR+	bb%	ct%	Eye	G	L	F	h%	HctX	QBaB	Brl%	PX	xPX	HR/F	xHR/F	Spd	SBA%	SB%	RAR	BPX	R$
18																																		
19 aa	99	8	1	5	3	193		2		273	241	71			10	75	0.44				25				21				139	24%	45%		-70	-$3
20																																		
21 HOU *	451	57	17	62	10	270	6	5	248	313	451	105	122	93	6	71	0.22	43	24	33	34	96	CDb	10%	113	117	19%	19%	95	13%	73%	5.9	58	$17
22 HOU *	319	29	5	26	3	229	2	7	226	283	337	88	80	83	7	69	0.24	54	21	25	31	77	DDc	4%	77	64	4%	8%	130	5%	76%	-6.1	-28	$2
1st Half	93	10	3	10	0	224	0	2	239	254	363	87	80	106	4	68	0.13	56	24	20	30	102	BFa	8%	90	125	20%	0%	146	5%	0%	-2.5	-14	-$6
2nd Half	227	19	3	16	3	231	2	5	221	295	326	88	80	74	8	69	0.29	53	20	27	32	68	DDd	4%	72	43	0%	11%	114	5%	76%	-4.7	-45	$2
23 Proj	280	30	6	30	4	246	6	3	231	301	373	94	98	91	6	69	0.21	50	23	28	33	88		7%	91	93	13%	11%	101	6%	73%	-0.8	4	$8

Miller,Owen

Age: 26	Pos: 1B 2B DH	Health A	LIMA Plan D
Bats: R	Ht: 6' 0" Wt: 185	PT/Exp B	Rand Var 0
		Consist A	MM 1313

An amazing April (.400 BA) opened eyes and gained him a near full-time role. But the bill for that first-month's 50% h% came due in May/June, when he slashed .201/.254/.291. Predictably, PA dried up and counting stats shriveled with it. Makes contact and hits line drives, but until the Damage-on-Impact meter improves, look for roster depth elsewhere.

Yr Tm	PA	R	HR	RBI	SB	BA	xHR	xSB	xBA	OBP	SLG	OPS+	vL+	vR+	bb%	ct%	Eye	G	L	F	h%	HctX	QBaB	Brl%	PX	xPX	HR/F	xHR/F	Spd	SBA%	SB%	RAR	BPX	R$
18																																		
19 aa	547	65	10	58	4	261		7		315	380	96			7	81	0.42				30				65				98	7%	44%		89	$10
20																																		
21 CLE *	399	34	9	33	2	223	4	4	228	270	347	85	72	78	6	69	0.20	54	20	25	30	81	DDc	6%	85	80	11%	11%	99	3%	100%	-16.6	-46	$2
22 CLE	472	53	6	51	2	243	6	4	246	301	351	92	87	95	7	78	0.34	43	23	34	30	85	DCf	3%	78	66	5%	5%	100	2%	100%	-7.1	69	$8
1st Half	276	33	4	36	1	244	3	2	256	297	370	94	90	96	7	78	0.35	44	23	33	30	95	CCd	3%	94	71	6%	5%	96	2%	100%	-4.6	107	$9
2nd Half	196	20	2	15	1	242	3	2	233	306	326	90	82	93	7	79	0.34	43	23	35	30	71	FDf	3%	57	58	4%	6%	118	2%	100%	-6.0	38	$0
23 Proj	315	32	5	30	2	236	5	2	236	292	346	89	82	92	7	75	0.28	48	22	31	30	81		4%	79	70	8%	8%	97	4%	82%	-6.8	23	$6

Miranda,Jose

Age: 25	Pos: 1B 3B DH	Health A	LIMA Plan B
Bats: R	Ht: 6' 2" Wt: 210	PT/Exp A	Rand Var 0
		Consist C	MM 3035

15-66-.268 in 483 PA at MIN. Struggled in his 19-game MLB debut; a .484 OPS got him banished to Triple-A. Upon his return on 5/30, looked the part of a big-league COR IF: excellent HctX, hit pitching from both sides, quality QBaB and HR/F. Perfect world includes more barrels and patience, but at his age, there's time. Solid growth stock.

Yr Tm	PA	R	HR	RBI	SB	BA	xHR	xSB	xBA	OBP	SLG	OPS+	vL+	vR+	bb%	ct%	Eye	G	L	F	h%	HctX	QBaB	Brl%	PX	xPX	HR/F	xHR/F	Spd	SBA%	SB%	RAR	BPX	R$
18																																		
19																																		
20																																		
21 a/a	569	75	23	72	2	306		6		347	490	115			6	84	0.40				33				98				81	5%	25%		208	$24
22 MIN *	572	51	16	73	1	257	14	3	255	299	412	101	115	102	5	80	0.29	42	20	38	30	121	BCf	6%	101	101	11%	11%	71	2%	50%	3.3	117	$14
1st Half	258	18	7	31	0	224	4	1	244	255	389	91	100	96	4	80	0.21	45	15	40	25	128	BCf	5%	112	102	12%	8%	65	2%	0%	-7.4	134	$3
2nd Half	314	33	9	42	1	286	10	2	257	354	431	111	123	106	7	80	0.36	40	23	36	33	117	CBd	6%	92	100	11%	12%	85	2%	100%	8.0	114	$20
23 Proj	595	65	19	77	2	278	18	3	258	333	442	108	116	104	6	82	0.34	42	20	38	31	121		6%	103	101	11%	10%	81	3%	37%	13.1	157	$23

Mitchell,Calvin

Age: 24	Pos: RF	Health A	LIMA Plan D+
Bats: L	Ht: 6' 0" Wt: 209	PT/Exp B	Rand Var 0
		Consist B	MM 2133

5-17-.226 with 3 SB in 232 PA at PIT. Does a little bit of everything, but is it enough? PRO: Line-drive hitter with above-average exit velocity; can hit same-side pitching; throws in a few SB. CON: Lacks traditional COR OF power; xBA doesn't point to difference-making BA; speed/on-base metrics uninspiring. A bench bat until further notice.

Yr Tm	PA	R	HR	RBI	SB	BA	xHR	xSB	xBA	OBP	SLG	OPS+	vL+	vR+	bb%	ct%	Eye	G	L	F	h%	HctX	QBaB	Brl%	PX	xPX	HR/F	xHR/F	Spd	SBA%	SB%	RAR	BPX	R$
18																																		
19																																		
20																																		
21 a/a	420	33	8	46	4	244		4		277	357	87			4	80	0.23				29				67				83	14%	37%		35	$6
22 PIT *	480	43	11	50	8	257	4	7	263	303	395	99	96	88	6	79	0.32	47	22	30	31	102	BDb	5%	93	99	10%	8%	79	10%	80%	-0.5	97	$13
1st Half	236	16	5	27	5	243	1	3	272	278	378	93	78	78	5	79	0.24	44	26	30	29	108	BDb	3%	94	104	11%	6%	58	10%	100%	-3.4	72	$6
2nd Half	244	27	5	24	3	271	3	4	286	328	412	105	132	92	8	78	0.39	49	20	31	32	98	CDb	6%	93	95	10%	10%	106	10%	61%	3.0	128	$11
23 Proj	315	28	7	34	4	253	6	4	258	295	388	95	105	91	6	79	0.30	47	23	30	30	102		5%	90	99	10%	8%	89	8%	56%	-1.1	77	$9

Mitchell,Garrett

Age: 24	Pos: CF	Health B	LIMA Plan F
Bats: L	Ht: 6' 3" Wt: 215	PT/Exp D	Rand Var -4
		Consist D	MM 1501

2-9-.311 with 8 SB in 68 PA at MIL. Fun with teeny samples: The rare player whose MLB h% (55%) actually outpaced his ct% (54%). Both figures will correct. xBA, ct% and OBP tamp down any real hopes for potential SBs despite the above average skill, and he's shown meager power so far. With less than 100 Triple-A PA, expect more seasoning.

Yr Tm	PA	R	HR	RBI	SB	BA	xHR	xSB	xBA	OBP	SLG	OPS+	vL+	vR+	bb%	ct%	Eye	G	L	F	h%	HctX	QBaB	Brl%	PX	xPX	HR/F	xHR/F	Spd	SBA%	SB%	RAR	BPX	R$
18																																		
19																																		
20																																		
21 aa	143	12	2	8	4	161		2		244	224	64			10	64	0.30				23				40				108	16%	78%		-227	-$3
22 MIL *	325	38	5	32	19	253	2	8	196	308	365	95	140	117	7	62	0.21	39	21	39	39	120	ADa	10%	95	152	15%	15%	120	25%	94%	0.8	-72	$13
1st Half	116	13	1	7	4	179		2	166	242	263	71	0	0	8	55	0.19	44	20	36	31	0			70	-14	0%		136	25%	78%	-6.8	-224	-$6
2nd Half	209	25	4	25	15	295	2	5	216	347	424	109	140	117	7	66	0.23	39	21	39	43	128	ADa	10%	107	152	15%	15%	106	25%	100%	10.1	-3	$19
23 Proj	210	22	3	17	9	213	3	7	190	279	289	79	99	78	8	62	0.24	55	17	27	33	87		8%	64	137	8%	9%	120	20%	90%	-5.9	-148	$6

BRENT HERSHEY

Molina,Yadier

Age: 40	Pos: CA	Health	D	LIMA Plan	F
Bats: R	Ht: 5' 11" Wt: 225	PT/Exp	B	Rand Var	+4
		Consist	A	MM	0000

An example of how he played the game embodied his real life/fantasy crossover: He ends his career with 11 consecutive successful SB attempts, all after he turned 36 AND with sub-60 Spd score. Never a roto superstar, but lots of PAs produced opportunities for middling pop and counting stats to fill our second CA position. Thanks, Yadi. Enjoy Cooperstown

Yr	Tm	PA	R	HR	RBI	SB	BA	xHR	xSB	xBA	OBP	SLG	OPS+	vL+	vR+	bb%	ct%	Eye	G	L	F	h%	HctX	QBaB	Brl%	PX	xPX	HR/F	xHR/F	Spd	SBA%	SB%	RAR	BPX	R$
18	STL	503	55	20	74	4	261	16	7	279	314	436	101	106	97	6	86	0.44	39	24	37	27	140	CBb	6%	92	130	14%	11%	56	6%	57%	13.3	153	$15
19	STL	452	45	10	57	6	270	13	3	281	312	399	98	120	93	5	86	0.40	39	27	34	29	125	CCb	4%	67	108	8%	11%	57	6%	100%	0.2	100	$10
20	STL	156	12	4	16	0	262	4	1	231	303	359	88	99	85	4	86	0.29	42	21	37	28	88	DCd	2%	44	83	9%	9%	61	0%	0%	-1.8	20	$6
21	STL	472	45	11	66	3	252	13	0	238	297	370	92	116	87	5	82	0.30	42	19	39	29	110	CBc	5%	67	111	8%	9%	58	3%	100%	-1.8	42	$10
22	STL	270	19	5	24	2	214	5	1	234	233	302	76	85	73	2	85	0.13	38	21	41	24	81	DBd	3%	52	77	5%	5%	52	4%	100%	-10.8	7	-$1
1st Half		138	10	2	10	1	213	3	0	219	225	294	73	62	77	1	83	0.09	40	18	42	24	84	CBf	4%	52	89	4%	6%	63	4%	100%	-5.9	-7	-$7
2nd Half		132	9	3	14	1	214	2	0	250	242	310	78	106	68	2	87	0.18	36	25	39	23	79	FAc	3%	52	65	7%	5%	53	4%	100%	-4.7	34	-$4
23	Proj																																		

Moncada,Yoán

Age: 28	Pos: 3B	Health	C	LIMA Plan	B
Bats: B	Ht: 6' 2" Wt: 225	PT/Exp	A	Rand Var	+4
		Consist	C	MM	3215

12-51-.212 in 433 PA at CHW. Missed time from (takes breath) oblique, quad, R hamstring, L hamstring and bone bruise injuries, yet a 2nd half power binge somehow resulted in positive value. Would like to trust pre-2022 LD% history and solid QBaB/Brl%, but track record says that's a risky move. The good news: Won't cost ya much.

Yr	Tm	PA	R	HR	RBI	SB	BA	xHR	xSB	xBA	OBP	SLG	OPS+	vL+	vR+	bb%	ct%	Eye	G	L	F	h%	HctX	QBaB	Brl%	PX	xPX	HR/F	xHR/F	Spd	SBA%	SB%	RAR	BPX	R$
18	CHW	650	73	17	61	12	235	22	8	213	315	400	96	78	100	10	62	0.31	37	23	40	35	84	ABc	10%	123	113	12%	15%	120	12%	67%	-3.5	23	$14
19	CHW *	581	88	27	84	10	317	29	12	264	365	551	127	118	130	7	70	0.25	42	23	35	41	96	ACa	12%	135	103	20%	23%	126	9%	77%	35.2	159	$27
20	CHW	231	28	6	24	0	225	6	4	213	320	385	94	92	94	12	64	0.39	40	22	37	32	86	CCf	6%	103	101	13%	13%	145	0%	0%	-4.8	32	$8
21	CHW	616	74	14	61	3	263	17	3	247	375	412	108	95	113	14	70	0.54	44	27	30	35	116	BCc	8%	102	96	13%	16%	87	3%	60%	15.5	62	$14
22	CHW *	456	44	13	54	2	213	13	2	216	271	358	89	110	83	7	71	0.27	39	17	43	27	95	CBc	10%	101	102	10%	11%	66	3%	61%	-11.1	0	$5
1st Half		166	12	4	20	0	192	4	1	194	228	312	76	78	72	4	68	0.14	50	14	36	25	76	DCc	8%	87	70	9%	12%	58	3%	0%	-10.2	-110	-$5
2nd Half		290	32	9	34	2	225	9	1	225	294	385	96	125	88	9	73	0.36	34	19	47	28	106	CBc	11%	108	117	10%	10%	83	3%	100%	-3.1	76	$12
23	Proj	**560**	**62**	**15**	**63**	**3**	**241**	**18**	**4**	**227**	**319**	**391**	**99**	**103**	**97**	**10**	**69**	**0.35**	**41**	**21**	**38**	**32**	**99**		**9%**	**109**	**99**	**12%**	**13%**	**92**	**4%**	**65%**	**4.7**	**32**	**$14**

Mondesi,Adalberto

Age: 27	Pos: SS	Health	F	LIMA Plan	D+
Bats: B	Ht: 6' 1" Wt: 200	PT/Exp	F	Rand Var	+5
		Consist	B	MM	2503

April ACL tear wiped out the season and should send him plummeting down draft boards this spring due to extreme health risk and post-hype fatigue. But dreaming on that SBA%/SB% combo will set an ADP/bid floor—plate skills, OBP and xBA be damned—and you can't deny there's juice in his bat. But there are (again) multiple paths to disappointment here.

Yr	Tm	PA	R	HR	RBI	SB	BA	xHR	xSB	xBA	OBP	SLG	OPS+	vL+	vR+	bb%	ct%	Eye	G	L	F	h%	HctX	QBaB	Brl%	PX	xPX	HR/F	xHR/F	Spd	SBA%	SB%	RAR	BPX	R$
18	KC *	417	62	18	54	40	262	15	4	254	293	479	104	111	104	4	72	0.16	41	21	38	32	115	BBf	10%	132	130	20%	21%	130	61%	85%	10.3	150	$27
19	KC *	488	62	10	64	45	258	15	36	226	293	418	98	88	103	5	67	0.15	47	19	34	37	88	CCd	9%	95	82	9%	15%	153	55%	85%	-10.2	4	$27
20	KC	233	33	6	22	24	256	7	16	216	294	416	94	136	80	5	68	0.16	49	13	39	35	100	DCf	7%	101	102	11%	13%	161	67%	75%	-4.2	52	$40
21	KC *	201	25	8	21	19	209	8	12	218	241	392	87	113	93	4	67	0.13	43	14	43	27	105	CBf	13%	118	146	18%	24%	117	70%	89%	-6.0	31	$9
22	KC	54	3	0	3	5	140	1	5	132	204	140	49	14	57	7	60	0.20	52	12	36	23	79	FFf	3%	0	115	0%	11%	104	45%	100%	-4.8	-383	-$3
1st Half		54	3	0	3	5	140	1	5	132	204	140	49	14	56	7	60	0.20	52	12	36	23	79	FFf	3%	0	115	0%	11%	104	45%	100%	-5.1	-386	-$9
2nd Half																																			
23	Proj	**315**	**36**	**7**	**29**	**29**	**229**	**12**	**18**	**201**	**271**	**356**	**87**	**99**	**83**	**5**	**66**	**0.16**	**47**	**14**	**38**	**32**	**95**		**8%**	**93**	**116**	**10%**	**16%**	**138**	**35%**	**85%**	**-4.9**	**-79**	**$18**

Moniak,Mickey

Age: 25	Pos: CF	Health	D	LIMA Plan	D
Bats: L	Ht: 6' 2" Wt: 195	PT/Exp	D	Rand Var	+1
		Consist	A	MM	3401

3-8-.170 in 112 PA at PHI/LAA. Three HBP resulted in a broken hand/finger and limited his MLB PA—exactly what he needs to rid himself of the Underperforming #1 Draft Pick stigma. Everything here is somewhere on the work-in-progress scale; more and harder contact the most critical. Young enough to improve, but raw enough to pass over.

Yr	Tm	PA	R	HR	RBI	SB	BA	xHR	xSB	xBA	OBP	SLG	OPS+	vL+	vR+	bb%	ct%	Eye	G	L	F	h%	HctX	QBaB	Brl%	PX	xPX	HR/F	xHR/F	Spd	SBA%	SB%	RAR	BPX	R$
18																																			
19	aa	495	58	11	62	14	241		7		288	421	98			6	73	0.24				31				99				140	18%	81%		104	$12
20	PHI	18	3	0	0	0	214	0	1	169	389	214	80	0	98	22	57	0.67	63	25	13	38	58	CFf		0	-26	0%	0%	120	0%	0%	-0.8	-352	-$2
21	PHI *	425	33	13	49	4	208	1	2	203	255	364	85	0	63	6	67	0.19	59	6	35	27	76	CFc	6%	96	154	17%	17%	129	8%	62%	-18.8	-4	$3
22	2 TM *	232	25	8	19	4	205	3	2	201	237	366	86	33	78	4	65	0.12	38	15	48	27	63	FBf	8%	116	80	10%	10%	120	22%	53%	-8.6	0	$1
1st Half		117	11	3	8	1	214	0	1	212	251	345	84	0	56	5	67	0.15	48	16	36	30	22	FFf	0%	100	-4	0%	0%	112	22%	20%	-5.0	-28	-$6
2nd Half		115	15	5	11	3	195	3	1	195	224	389	87	63	91	4	63	0.10	31	14	56	25	89	DAf	11%	134	138	15%	15%	129	22%	74%	-4.4	21	-$1
23	Proj	**245**	**25**	**7**	**25**	**4**	**208**	**9**	**6**	**196**	**255**	**356**	**85**	**36**	**91**	**5**	**66**	**0.16**	**38**	**15**	**48**	**28**	**62**		**7%**	**105**	**81**	**9%**	**12%**	**130**	**18%**	**65%**	**-7.1**	**10**	**$4**

Montero,Elehuris

Age: 24	Pos: 3B	Health	A	LIMA Plan	B
Bats: R	Ht: 6' 3" Wt: 215	PT/Exp	B	Rand Var	-2
		Consist	A	MM	3215

6-20-.233 in 185 PA at COL. Cornerman part of the Arenado return showed promise in first big-league exposure: solid QBaB/Brl rates, league-average hard contact, and enough FB%/xPX combo to make a dent. MiLB record includes a .276 career BA with plate skills to support it. Still young, but if things come together ... UP: .260, 20 HR

Yr	Tm	PA	R	HR	RBI	SB	BA	xHR	xSB	xBA	OBP	SLG	OPS+	vL+	vR+	bb%	ct%	Eye	G	L	F	h%	HctX	QBaB	Brl%	PX	xPX	HR/F	xHR/F	Spd	SBA%	SB%	RAR	BPX	R$
18																																			
19	aa	236	20	6	15	0	170		2		210	278	68			5	65	0.15				23				69				98	3%	0%		-152	-$4
20																																			
21	a/a	467	45	20	57	0	248		5		306	443	103			8	73	0.31				29				113				94	0%	0%		108	$9
22	COL *	454	45	15	50	2	244	4	2	235	281	414	98	113	90	5	70	0.17	37	22	41	31	103	BCd	9%	119	127	13%	8%	110	5%	49%	-6.7	69	$9
1st Half		246	22	8	24	2	256	1	1	218	289	395	97	36	80	4	72	0.16	25	25	50	33	137	AAd	21%	91	157	0%	13%	108	5%	59%	-2.2	7	$8
2nd Half		208	23	7	26	1	229	3	1	252	271	437	100	128	92	5	68	0.18	39	21	40	30	96	BCd	7%	155	123	15%	8%	112	5%	32%	-2.1	152	$6
23	Proj	**490**	**47**	**15**	**53**	**2**	**247**	**14**	**4**	**239**	**317**	**410**	**101**	**105**	**98**	**9**	**75**	**0.39**	**33**	**23**	**44**	**30**	**112**		**13%**	**108**	**137**	**10%**	**10%**	**99**	**5%**	**66%**	**7.3**	**75**	**$13**

Moore,Dylan

Age: 30	Pos: RF SS	Health	D	LIMA Plan	D+
Bats: R	Ht: 6' 0" Wt: 185	PT/Exp	C	Rand Var	-3
		Consist	C	MM	4403

Missed time with back, oblique injuries but logged another 20-SB season; is a three-peat in the cards? PRO: Finds PA due to versatility; bb% on the rise; no visible cracks in speed skills. CON: Contact rate in free-fall; swings like a slugger (FB%, launch angle); age now starts with a "3." Cheap bags from a non-traditional profile.

Yr	Tm	PA	R	HR	RBI	SB	BA	xHR	xSB	xBA	OBP	SLG	OPS+	vL+	vR+	bb%	ct%	Eye	G	L	F	h%	HctX	QBaB	Brl%	PX	xPX	HR/F	xHR/F	Spd	SBA%	SB%	RAR	BPX	R$
18	a/a	433	51	11	42	17	250		5		294	429	97			6	80	0.31				29				106				118	30%	67%		177	$13
19	SEA *	313	33	9	33	12	199	8	11	201	270	362	87	104	91	9	65	0.28	37	16	47	27	75	CAd	7%	104	100	13%	11%	124	33%	55%	-20.4	0	$5
20	SEA	159	26	8	17	12	255	7	7	254	358	496	113	99	120	9	69	0.33	35	25	40	31	100	BAc	14%	150	137	22%	19%	109	43%	71%	1.1	188	$24
21	SEA	377	42	12	43	21	181	11	19	194	276	334	84	93	77	11	67	0.36	32	18	50	23	65	DAf	9%	97	89	11%	10%	115	33%	81%	-16.3	4	$9
22	SEA	254	41	6	24	21	224	7	14	199	368	385	107	111	101	13	63	0.45	32	18	50	32	88	DAd	13%	125	147	9%	11%	137	39%	72%	0.0	83	$11
1st Half		145	22	4	14	10	184	6	8	192	347	351	99	111	84	16	66	0.56	31	16	53	24	101	DAd	14%	111	155	10%	15%	163	39%	67%	-3.3	121	$5
2nd Half		109	19	2	10	11	275	1	6	209	394	429	117	111	120	12	60	0.33	35	20	45	43	72	DAd	12%	145	135	8%	4%	107	39%	79%	3.6	52	$6
23	Proj	**280**	**42**	**9**	**30**	**21**	**221**	**8**	**16**	**210**	**337**	**393**	**101**	**105**	**98**	**12**	**65**	**0.38**	**33**	**19**	**48**	**30**	**79**		**11%**	**130**	**122**	**11%**	**10%**	**115**	**29%**	**74%**	**0.3**	**69**	**$15**

Morel,Christopher

Age: 24	Pos: CF 2B	Health	A	LIMA Plan	C+
Bats: R	Ht: 6' 0" Wt: 140	PT/Exp	B	Rand Var	0
		Consist	B	MM	4405

16-37-.235 with 10 SB in 425 PA at CHC. Hit the ground running in mid-May, aided by a 38% h%, but reality struck in the 2nd half. Still, impressive power metrics carried him throughout (xHR/F, for one) even as swing-and-miss persisted. Shoddy SB% likely to keep Spd under wraps for now; this is a HR-only play until he adjusts.

Yr	Tm	PA	R	HR	RBI	SB	BA	xHR	xSB	xBA	OBP	SLG	OPS+	vL+	vR+	bb%	ct%	Eye	G	L	F	h%	HctX	QBaB	Brl%	PX	xPX	HR/F	xHR/F	Spd	SBA%	SB%	RAR	BPX	R$
18																																			
19																																			
20																																			
21	a/a	438	48	14	49	13	197		5		259	359	85			8	64	0.23				27				107				116	20%	80%		-15	$7
22	CHC *	539	69	20	60	12	237	20	16	236	300	429	103	88	111	8	65	0.26	50	18	33	32	104	CDd	14%	139	110	21%	26%	168	19%	53%	-5.0	131	$17
1st Half		318	45	12	36	9	260	7	10	247	320	456	110	98	122	8	66	0.25	51	20	29	35	105	BDd	14%	140	93	24%	21%	169	19%	54%	4.2	148	$26
2nd Half		221	24	8	24	3	202	12	6	224	279	389	94	80	100	9	63	0.26	49	15	36	27	102	CCf	14%	139	127	18%	27%	160	19%	50%	-6.1	107	$6
23	Proj	**525**	**62**	**18**	**59**	**9**	**225**	**23**	**14**	**225**	**293**	**400**	**96**	**81**	**102**	**8**	**64**	**0.25**	**50**	**17**	**33**	**31**	**103**		**14%**	**129**	**113**	**17%**	**22%**	**145**	**17%**	**55%**	**-1.9**	**68**	**$14**

BRENT HERSHEY

Moreno,Gabriel

Age: 23 Pos: CA
Bats: R Ht: 5' 11" Wt: 160

Health	A	LIMA Plan	D+
PT/Exp	D	Rand Var	-3
Consist	F	MM	1221

1-7-.319 in 73 PA at TOR. Elite prospect's 2021 power didn't show at either AAA or TOR, putting some of his HR upside into question. But he still owns wondrous bat-to-ball skills and an All-Star defensive ceiling. Athleticism, young legs earned cameo infield/OF appearances at season-end. Work-in-progress is now a worthy #2 catcher selection.

Yr Tm	PA	R	HR	RBI	SB	BA	xHR	xSB	xBA	OBP	SLG	OPS+	vL+	vR+	bb%	ct%	Eye	G	L	F	h%	HctX	QBaB	Brl%	PX	xPX	HR/F	xHR/F	Spd	SBA%	SB%	RAR	BPX	R$
18																																		
19																																		
20																																		
21 a/a	147	24	7	38	1	332		2		385	567	131			8	81	0.44				37				128				92	8%	28%		273	$8
22 TOR *	329	38	4	38	6	289	1	6	250	336	374	101	101	105	7	81	0.38	57	18	25	35	64	BDd	2%	61	26	7%	7%	129	8%	83%	8.8	97	$11
1st Half	197	17	1	22	2	285	0	3	225	325	344	95	104	77	6	82	0.33	56	16	29	34	64	CCf	3%	45	19	0%	0%	130	8%	100%	2.6	55	$3
2nd Half	132	20	3	16	3	294	0	2	295	352	421	110	93	174	8	80	0.46	63	25	13	35	66	BFa		86	48	50%	0%	123	8%	74%	6.0	159	$5
23 Proj	245	34	3	43	3	291	3	4	252	344	398	103	126	91	7	81	0.42	50	21	30	35	74		2%	74	17	6%	6%	108	8%	62%	9.4	179	$8

Mountcastle,Ryan

Age: 26 Pos: 1B DH
Bats: R Ht: 6' 4" Wt: 230

Health	A	LIMA Plan	B
PT/Exp	A	Rand Var	+1
Consist	B	MM	4225

Pull hitter mashed 11 fewer HR following Camden Yards wall retraction—all while xPX, xHR reaffirmed plus power. 2nd-half downturn came with chase tendencies, unfortunate h% and HR/F before more patience helped right the ship in September. This profile remains in good shape; just realize you aren't buying BA or batting eye here.

Yr Tm	PA	R	HR	RBI	SB	BA	xHR	xSB	xBA	OBP	SLG	OPS+	vL+	vR+	bb%	ct%	Eye	G	L	F	h%	HctX	QBaB	Brl%	PX	xPX	HR/F	xHR/F	Spd	SBA%	SB%	RAR	BPX	R$
18 aa	414	49	11	46	2	267		5		302	406	95			5	79	0.24				31				81				108	2%	100%		80	$9
19 aaa	540	66	22	68	2	281		3		307	466	107			4	73	0.14				35				105				89	3%	60%		48	$15
20 BAL	140	12	5	23	0	333	5	2	230	386	492	117	86	126	8	76	0.37	44	19	37	41	107	CCf	7%	88	91	14%	14%	117	2%	0%	5.6	112	$13
21 BAL	586	77	33	89	4	255	30	3	248	309	487	109	115	106	7	70	0.25	35	22	43	30	97	CBd	12%	139	125	20%	19%	92	6%	57%	7.5	131	$20
22 BAL	609	62	22	85	4	250	32	5	242	305	423	103	97	105	7	72	0.28	37	22	41	31	111	ABb	15%	117	138	13%	19%	80	4%	80%	4.7	79	$18
1st Half	293	35	14	40	3	276	14	2	273	314	495	114	116	114	5	73	0.20	38	26	36	33	126	ABa	17%	146	129	19%	19%	76	4%	75%	8.4	152	$22
2nd Half	316	27	8	45	1	225	17	3	210	297	354	92	78	97	9	71	0.35	37	19	45	29	97	BBb	14%	87	146	9%	18%	95	4%	100%	-7.8	14	$12
23 Proj	595	66	26	87	3	260	30	4	244	313	453	106	103	107	7	72	0.27	37	21	41	31	104		13%	127	129	16%	18%	88	4%	64%	11.8	92	$23

Mullins,Cedric

Age: 28 Pos: CF
Bats: L Ht: 5' 8" Wt: 175

Health	A	LIMA Plan	D+
PT/Exp	A	Rand Var	-1
Consist	D	MM	2525

Another BAL hitter unable to replicate 2021 home-field numbers following off-season dimension changes, but 2021 power skills were soft to begin with. BA plunge resulting from FB% lean, less HctX, h% downtick seems less permanent. Elite running game and plus ct% now drive value. With average power, it's still nearly 1st round worthy.

Yr Tm	PA	R	HR	RBI	SB	BA	xHR	xSB	xBA	OBP	SLG	OPS+	vL+	vR+	bb%	ct%	Eye	G	L	F	h%	HctX	QBaB	Brl%	PX	xPX	HR/F	xHR/F	Spd	SBA%	SB%	RAR	BPX	R$
18 BAL *	663	83	14	48	18	247	3	8	246	300	389	92	60	99	7	82	0.41	51	12	37	28	80	CCd	3%	84	65	9%	7%	136	15%	82%	-0.6	170	$17
19 BAL *	580	68	9	38	28	188	1	11	211	249	279	73	34	50	7	80	0.41	53	8	39	22	52	DBf	2%	47	18	0%	5%	120	31%	78%	-38.8	41	$9
20 BAL	153	16	3	12	7	271	2	7	229	315	407	96	65	106	5	74	0.22	43	22	35	35	64	FCf	3%	73	44	9%	6%	153	24%	78%	-1.2	44	$14
21 BAL	674	91	30	59	30	291	24	25	270	360	518	121	107	128	9	79	0.47	39	20	41	32	107	CCd	8%	125	109	15%	12%	137	22%	79%	37.4	300	$37
22 BAL	670	89	16	64	34	258	13	21	237	318	403	102	81	111	7	79	0.37	39	18	44	30	93	CBf	5%	92	92	8%	6%	120	27%	77%	8.3	148	$32
1st Half	351	43	7	35	16	266	7	11	243	326	408	104	90	111	7	81	0.39	36	19	45	31	91	CBf	6%	95	86	6%	6%	104	27%	80%	5.6	162	$29
2nd Half	319	46	9	29	18	249	6	10	233	310	398	100	67	111	7	78	0.35	42	17	42	29	96	CBf	4%	89	100	10%	7%	139	27%	75%	1.0	138	$28
23 Proj	595	80	16	54	29	270	14	25	242	330	427	105	87	113	7	79	0.37	41	18	41	32	92		5%	98	88	9%	8%	131	22%	78%	16.9	179	$32

Muncy,Max

Age: 32 Pos: 3B 2B DH
Bats: L Ht: 6' 0" Wt: 215

Health	C	LIMA Plan	B+
PT/Exp	A	Rand Var	+5
Consist	D	MM	4225

Opted for rest, rehab over surgery for torn left UCL suffered in Sept 2021. It showed in poor 1st-half that included May IL stint (elbow inflammation). Power returned in July, but he was still hitting well below .200 in early August when HctX and h% both finally kicked in. Shifting ban could buy him a few more hits and he's still an OBP force. UP: 2021.

Yr Tm	PA	R	HR	RBI	SB	BA	xHR	xSB	xBA	OBP	SLG	OPS+	vL+	vR+	bb%	ct%	Eye	G	L	F	h%	HctX	QBaB	Brl%	PX	xPX	HR/F	xHR/F	Spd	SBA%	SB%	RAR	BPX	R$
18 LA *	517	80	36	82	3	262	30	8	267	382	571	128	118	132	16	68	0.60	34	21	45	30	118	BAa	17%	192	176	29%	25%	79	2%	100%	38.0	277	$21
19 LA	589	101	35	98	4	251	31	4	262	374	515	123	124	122	15	69	0.60	38	23	39	29	110	BBb	12%	146	150	27%	23%	82	3%	80%	17.1	193	$20
20 LA	248	36	12	27	1	192	14	2	217	331	389	96	104	91	16	70	0.65	44	14	42	21	118	CBd	12%	107	168	20%	23%	87	2%	100%	-5.6	108	$11
21 LA	592	95	36	94	2	249	41	2	279	368	527	123	131	120	14	76	0.69	38	21	41	26	122	ABc	16%	153	154	23%	26%	67	2%	67%	18.8	292	$20
22 LA	565	69	21	69	2	196	24	3	226	329	384	101	95	103	16	70	0.64	31	19	50	23	125	BAc	13%	128	184	13%	15%	75	1%	100%	-8.4	128	$7
1st Half	261	32	8	25	1	171	8	1	208	326	327	92	83	96	19	72	0.81	36	14	50	19	107	CAc	12%	100	164	11%	11%	92	1%	100%	-9.1	121	$3
2nd Half	304	37	13	44	1	217	16	1	242	332	431	108	107	108	14	68	0.51	28	23	49	27	139	AAc	14%	153	201	15%	19%	69	1%	100%	0.2	152	$18
23 Proj	525	78	26	77	2	242	29	2	248	364	472	116	117	115	15	71	0.63	35	20	46	28	123		14%	150	172	18%	20%	73	2%	87%	25.1	192	$19

Murphy,Sean

Age: 28 Pos: CA DH
Bats: R Ht: 6' 3" Wt: 228

Health	A	LIMA Plan	B+
PT/Exp	A	Rand Var	+2
Consist	B	MM	4235

2nd-half BA surge fueled by soaring 2nd-half plate skills, HctX bump, while concurrent h% bump turned GB uptick into a plus. May give some of this back with launch angle rebound, but HR count will welcome that. More projected DH AB a plus; superior road numbers offer something to dream on for obvious trade candidate. UP: .275 BA, 25 HR.

Yr Tm	PA	R	HR	RBI	SB	BA	xHR	xSB	xBA	OBP	SLG	OPS+	vL+	vR+	bb%	ct%	Eye	G	L	F	h%	HctX	QBaB	Brl%	PX	xPX	HR/F	xHR/F	Spd	SBA%	SB%	RAR	BPX	R$
18 a/a	285	42	6	34	2	248		3		301	416	96			7	79	0.36				29				110				99	4%	100%		170	$5
19 OAK *	191	33	11	31	0	253	3	1	281	320	512	115	103	135	9	70	0.33	46	27	27	30	85	BDb	8%	147	99	40%	30%	90	3%	0%	9.4	159	$4
20 OAK	140	21	7	14	0	233	7	1	233	364	457	109	99	113	17	68	0.65	43	18	39	28	94	ABc	13%	134	109	23%	23%	103	0%	0%	4.9	188	$7
21 OAK	448	47	17	59	0	216	20	1	237	306	405	98	86	103	9	71	0.35	39	20	41	26	99	CBc	11%	120	115	15%	17%	64	0%	0%	-1.6	73	$5
22 OAK	611	67	18	66	1	250	22	2	260	332	426	107	119	103	9	77	0.45	42	20	38	29	108	CCd	11%	118	104	11%	14%	83	1%	100%	17.6	162	$14
1st Half	299	30	9	34	1	225	12	1	248	294	397	98	106	94	7	75	0.31	37	21	41	27	103	CBc	10%	117	105	11%	14%	87	1%	100%	0.9	117	$9
2nd Half	312	37	9	32	0	274	11	1	269	369	456	117	135	112	11	79	0.63	47	20	34	32	113	CDd	11%	119	104	12%	15%	85	1%	0%	16.4	217	$17
23 Proj	560	68	20	67	1	240	24	2	255	328	430	105	103	106	10	74	0.43	42	21	37	29	102		11%	129	108	15%	17%	75	2%	80%	18.0	146	$15

Myers,Wil

Age: 32 Pos: RF 1B
Bats: R Ht: 6' 3" Wt: 207

Health	D	LIMA Plan	C
PT/Exp	B	Rand Var	0
Consist	C	MM	4213

7-41-.261 in 286 PA at SD. Thumb injury slowed him early, knee inflammation shelved him in June and July. Apart from fewer PA, some overaggressiveness and absent running game, skills look comparable to 2021. Consistency, health have been issues; production vR nothing special. Still owns age, athleticism; watch where free agent lands.

Yr Tm	PA	R	HR	RBI	SB	BA	xHR	xSB	xBA	OBP	SLG	OPS+	vL+	vR+	bb%	ct%	Eye	G	L	F	h%	HctX	QBaB	Brl%	PX	xPX	HR/F	xHR/F	Spd	SBA%	SB%	RAR	BPX	R$
18 SD	343	39	11	39	13	253	10	4	266	318	446	102	107	97	9	70	0.32	44	28	29	33	120	BCc	7%	137	121	17%	16%	94	19%	93%	5.8	123	$11
19 SD	490	58	18	53	16	239	21	14	220	321	418	102	122	97	10	61	0.30	43	22	35	35	100	BCf	11%	119	121	20%	23%	114	20%	70%	-13.2	-4	$14
20 SD	218	34	15	40	2	288	16	5	287	353	606	127	136	122	8	72	0.32	38	23	38	33	139	BCc	15%	182	175	28%	30%	118	7%	67%	12.6	344	$27
21 SD	500	56	17	63	8	256	16	7	230	334	434	106	113	103	11	68	0.38	45	18	37	34	83	CCf	8%	117	104	15%	14%	116	10%	62%	1.9	92	$15
22 SD *	322	30	8	42	2	247	9	5	217	300	380	96	114	94	7	67	0.23	40	22	38	34	100	CCc	6%	103	120	10%	13%	97	4%	67%	-3.0	-17	$6
1st Half	134	13	1	19	0	234	3	2	200	276	306	82	76	85	6	69	0.21	43	21	37	33	96	CCd	5%	62	106	3%	9%	105	4%	0%	-4.9	-93	-$4
2nd Half	188	17	7	23	2	256	6	3	229	313	432	106	142	102	8	65	0.24	38	22	39	35	104	CCb	6%	135	134	17%	17%	91	4%	67%	2.1	41	$6
23 Proj	420	46	15	56	5	254	16	4	234	318	429	104	115	98	9	68	0.29	42	21	37	34	100		8%	130	122	15%	16%	97	5%	68%	7.7	62	$15

Naquin,Tyler

Age: 32 Pos: RF
Bats: L Ht: 6' 2" Wt: 195

Health	F	LIMA Plan	C+
PT/Exp	A	Rand Var	+2
Consist	C	MM	4223

Banner May ended with a quad injury that sidelined him for 5 weeks. Wasn't the same afterward; trade to contender didn't help, as recent plate skill gains disappeared and h% dragged him down further. Power metrics held up nicely; strong-side platoon still projects as a double-digit HR source with BA inconsistency. An end-game OF selection.

Yr Tm	PA	R	HR	RBI	SB	BA	xHR	xSB	xBA	OBP	SLG	OPS+	vL+	vR+	bb%	ct%	Eye	G	L	F	h%	HctX	QBaB	Brl%	PX	xPX	HR/F	xHR/F	Spd	SBA%	SB%	RAR	BPX	R$
18 CLE	183	22	3	23	1	264	4	2	242	295	356	87	75	87	3	76	0.14	54	23	23	33	107	CDa	5%	61	63	10%	13%	89	5%	50%	-4.4	-37	$2
19 CLE *	317	37	12	39	4	286	13	3	263	318	486	111	116	107	4	76	0.19	44	21	36	34	106	BCd	9%	112	84	13%	17%	99	9%	67%	0.4	122	$9
20 CLE	141	15	4	20	0	218	6	1	240	248	383	84	6	98	4	70	0.13	43	23	34	28	107	ACc	9%	105	107	13%	19%	104	5%	0%	-9.1	16	$4
21 CIN	454	52	19	70	5	270	19	4	264	333	477	111	77	118	8	74	0.33	47	21	32	32	109	CDd	10%	123	105	19%	19%	96	8%	63%	7.3	158	$16
22 2 NL	334	47	11	46	4	229	14	3	245	282	423	100	75	106	6	70	0.20	39	21	40	29	105	CCc	10%	135	138	13%	16%	110	10%	67%	-3.8	117	$7
1st Half	154	22	5	22	3	257	6	2	262	320	457	110	75	121	7	72	0.28	36	26	39	32	99	CCc	10%	142	131	13%	16%	93	10%	75%	2.8	162	$5
2nd Half	180	25	6	24	1	206	7	2	231	250	394	91	74	94	4	68	0.15	42	17	41	26	111	BCd	10%	128	144	13%	15%	127	10%	50%	-6.3	83	$4
23 Proj	350	45	13	51	4	244	14	5	251	293	435	101	72	107	6	72	0.21	43	21	36	30	107		10%	131	119	15%	17%	107	9%	61%	1.8	111	$12

JOCK THOMPSON

Narváez,Omar

Age: 31 Pos: CA
Bats: B Ht: 5' 11" Wt: 220

Health B | LIMA Plan D+
PT/Exp B | Rand Var +3
Consist D | MM 1003

Owned .773 OPS into mid-June before absurdly awful h%-fueled collapse that followed. But it wasn't all bad luck; EV bottomed out, power vacillated along with swing path—something we've seen before in smaller samples. BA should rebound; plate skills still give him #2 catcher consideration vR. But it's limited upside with elite inconsistency.

Yr	Tm	PA	R	HR	RBI	SB	BA	xHR	xSB	xBA	OBP	SLG	OPS+	vL+	vR+	bb%	ct%	Eye	G	L	F	h%	HctX	QBaB	Brl%	PX	xPX	HR/F	xHR/F	Spd	SBA%	SB%	RAR	BPX	R$
18	CHW	322	30	9	30	0	275	5	5	270	366	429	106	75	111	12	77	0.58	42	29	29	33	81	DCa	3%	94	84	15%	8%	77	2%	0%	14.4	103	$6
19	SEA	482	63	22	55	0	278	16	3	263	353	460	113	97	115	10	79	0.51	33	26	41	31	81	DAa	5%	88	94	16%	12%	82	0%	0%	16.1	111	$12
20	MIL	126	8	2	10	0	176	3	0	197	294	269	75	67	76	13	64	0.41	39	25	36	25	52	FAb	7%	67	64	8%	12%	65	0%	0%	-5.9	-172	-$3
21	MIL	445	54	11	49	0	266	10	1	251	342	402	102	59	111	9	79	0.49	33	26	41	31	82	DAc	5%	81	98	9%	8%	68	0%	0%	9.3	77	$10
22	MIL	296	21	4	23	0	206	3	0	218	292	305	85	81	85	10	78	0.51	36	20	45	25	83	FBb	2%	68	81	4%	3%	57	0%	0%	-6.6	21	-$2
1st Half		176	15	3	16	0	258	2	0	242	347	394	105	101	105	10	77	0.50	32	24	44	32	79	FBb	4%	95	89	6%	4%	66	0%	0%	4.3	90	-$2
2nd Half		120	6	1	7	0	131	1	0	173	210	178	55	36	57	9	80	0.52	41	14	45	15	88	FAc	1%	30	70	3%	3%	60	0%	0%	-9.0	-55	-$11
23	**Proj**	**350**	**34**	**7**	**34**	**0**	**244**	**6**	**0**	**225**	**324**	**355**	**94**	**73**	**98**	**10**	**77**	**0.48**	**36**	**22**	**42**	**30**	**80**		**4%**	**74**	**84**	**7%**	**6%**	**61**	**1%**	**0%**	**4.2**	**18**	**$4**

Naylor,Josh

Age: 26 Pos: 1B DH
Bats: L Ht: 5' 11" Wt: 250

Health C | LIMA Plan B
PT/Exp A | Rand Var +1
Consist A | MM 3045

Breakout began fast with improved launch angle, FB% bump and power spike in the 1st half. But problematic GLF returned in July and fueled late dropoff, though HctX soared through Aug/Sept h% woes. Improved health a huge factor; age, contact skills vR keep him relevant even as lofty GB% torments. But with a lasting fix ... UP: .280 BA, 25 HR.

Yr	Tm	PA	R	HR	RBI	SB	BA	xHR	xSB	xBA	OBP	SLG	OPS+	vL+	vR+	bb%	ct%	Eye	G	L	F	h%	HctX	QBaB	Brl%	PX	xPX	HR/F	xHR/F	Spd	SBA%	SB%	RAR	BPX	R$
18	aa	557	63	14	65	4	274		9		347	404	101			10	85	0.73				30				72				90	6%	45%		153	$15
19	SD *	522	65	15	62	2	257	7	3	261	321	420	103	94	100	9	80	0.46	53	17	30	30	114	BFf	6%	91	89	14%	12%	49	3%	63%	-11.1	93	$10
20	2 TM	103	13	1	6	1	247	1	1	269	291	330	82	156	76	5	88	0.42	53	22	25	27	100	CDd	4%	41	44	5%	5%	93	4%	100%	-6.0	92	$3
21	CLE	249	28	7	21	1	253	7	1	254	301	399	96	70	111	6	81	0.31	49	19	32	29	93	BDf	7%	85	84	12%	12%	60	2%	100%	-3.4	85	$3
22	CLE	498	47	20	79	6	256	17	1	277	319	452	109	72	122	8	82	0.48	49	17	34	27	126	BCf	9%	118	89	16%	13%	45	6%	86%	10.5	186	$17
1st Half		217	24	11	43	1	276	7	0	289	332	510	119	81	135	8	83	0.47	44	19	37	28	105	BCd	9%	138	99	18%	11%	57	6%	100%	8.9	259	$15
2nd Half		281	23	9	36	5	241	10	0	267	310	407	102	61	112	8	82	0.48	53	16	31	26	142	CDf	8%	103	81	14%	15%	43	6%	83%	-1.5	141	$14
23	**Proj**	**490**	**52**	**21**	**75**	**4**	**255**	**16**	**3**	**276**	**313**	**452**	**106**	**77**	**116**	**7**	**82**	**0.43**	**49**	**18**	**33**	**27**	**113**		**8%**	**118**	**83**	**17%**	**13%**	**43**	**3%**	**85%**	**9.1**	**141**	**$19**

Naylor,Bo

Age: 23 Pos: CA
Bats: L Ht: 6' 0" Wt: 195

Health A | LIMA Plan D
PT/Exp C | Rand Var -1
Consist C | MM 3301

0-0-.000 in 8 PA at CLE. Youngster earned October glimpse by resurrecting his professional career, fueled by 20/20 season and new willingness to take a walk (82 BB between AA/AAA). BA / contact skills, defense still need polishing; less than 300 PA at Triple-A says he'll begin there in 2023. Age, handedness help; he's watch-worthy.

Yr	Tm	PA	R	HR	RBI	SB	BA	xHR	xSB	xBA	OBP	SLG	OPS+	vL+	vR+	bb%	ct%	Eye	G	L	F	h%	HctX	QBaB	Brl%	PX	xPX	HR/F	xHR/F	Spd	SBA%	SB%	RAR	BPX	R$
18																																			
19																																			
20																																			
21	aa	343	33	8	36	8	171		3		243	292	74			9	61	0.25				25				90				92	13%	100%		-138	$0
22	CLE *	477	48	14	45	13	214	0	9	198	302	378	96	0	0	11	66	0.38	0	33	67	29	97	AAa		122	69	0%	0%	104	16%	75%	2.3	62	$10
1st Half		245	25	5	20	8	230		5	236	339	384	102	0	0	14	70	0.54	44	20	36	30	0			116	-14	0%		105	16%	70%	4.5	114	$8
2nd Half		232	23	9	25	5	198	0	3	194	264	373	90	0	0	8	63	0.24	0	33	67	27	92	AAa		129	69	0%	0%	106	16%	83%	-2.8	17	$8
23	**Proj**	**245**	**28**	**7**	**29**	**6**	**239**	**6**	**5**	**225**	**314**	**390**	**98**	**97**	**98**	**10**	**71**	**0.37**	**38**	**21**	**41**	**31**	**90**		**6%**	**106**		**11%**	**9%**	**102**	**12%**	**84%**	**5.3**	**-21**	**$9**

Neuse,Sheldon

Age: 28 Pos: 3B 2B
Bats: R Ht: 6' 0" Wt: 232

Health A | LIMA Plan F
PT/Exp C | Rand Var 0
Consist A | MM 2201

4-33-.22 in 271 PA at OAK. Another budding journeyman with career-high PA on an offense-challenged rebuilder. But big Cactus League numbers and fast April (.863 OPS, 43% h% over 71 PA) dissipated quickly and it was all downhill from there. Potential once teased is gone; poor plate skills, QBaB, age say it's not returning. Next.

Yr	Tm	PA	R	HR	RBI	SB	BA	xHR	xSB	xBA	OBP	SLG	OPS+	vL+	vR+	bb%	ct%	Eye	G	L	F	h%	HctX	QBaB	Brl%	PX	xPX	HR/F	xHR/F	Spd	SBA%	SB%	RAR	BPX	R$
18	aaa	524	38	4	43	3	228		6		264	307	77			5	62	0.13				36				69				98	4%	74%		-187	$2
19	OAK *	601	78	19	84	2	263	1	3	259	319	428	103	73	97	8	68	0.26	42	32	26	35	100	ADa	5%	102	102	0%	10%	72	4%	39%	-6.4	-19	$15
20																																			
21	LA *	397	42	12	40	5	214	3	4	181	251	343	82	33	132	5	65	0.14	44	10	46	29	75	CCf	13%	84	119	17%	17%	111	8%	83%	-18.2	-100	$4
22	OAK *	403	32	6	36	7	232	3	6	228	273	317	84	60	91	5	71	0.20	64	18	18	31	86	CFb	3%	57	52	11%	9%	120	8%	88%	-12.0	-72	$5
1st Half		282	24	4	27	6	249	2	5	233	294	336	89	73	93	6	71	0.22	63	19	17	34	89	BFb	3%	57	40	8%	8%	139	8%	86%	-5.9	-52	$9
2nd Half		121	8	2	9	1	192	1	1	198	225	274	71	24	81	4	71	0.15	66	12	22	25	75	CFd	4%	55	95	22%	11%	69	8%	100%	-8.1	-145	-$7
23	**Proj**	**210**	**19**	**6**	**20**	**2**	**220**	**5**	**2**	**210**	**260**	**350**	**85**	**50**	**122**	**5**	**68**	**0.17**	**54**	**15**	**31**	**29**	**80**		**8%**	**89**	**94**	**15%**	**12%**	**78**	**6%**	**83%**	**-4.9**	**-105**	**$4**

Newman,Kevin

Age: 29 Pos: 2B SS
Bats: R Ht: 6' 0" Wt: 185

Health D | LIMA Plan D+
PT/Exp B | Rand Var -3
Consist B | MM 1333

2-24-.274, 8 SB in 309 PA at PIT. Groin injury shelved him for 74 days beginning in late April; running game, LD upticks delivered modest value afterward. Still owns fine ct%, the dismal quality of which is evident in QBaB history and power metrics. Still dependent on h% and SB for limited success; age, mediocrity vR are pointing to bench utility role.

Yr	Tm	PA	R	HR	RBI	SB	BA	xHR	xSB	xBA	OBP	SLG	OPS+	vL+	vR+	bb%	ct%	Eye	G	L	F	h%	HctX	QBaB	Brl%	PX	xPX	HR/F	xHR/F	Spd	SBA%	SB%	RAR	BPX	R$
18	PIT *	558	64	3	33	22	250	1	7	263	288	326	82	115	53	5	85	0.35	55	20	25	29	59	FFa	1%	51	45	0%	6%	111	28%	61%	-13.0	87	$14
19	PIT *	565	65	12	65	16	302	7	27	281	342	435	108	101	113	6	87	0.46	49	22	28	33	80	DDb	2%	63	50	10%	6%	157	16%	64%	7.2	211	$21
20	PIT	172	12	1	10	0	224	1	4	236	281	276	74	100	67	7	87	0.57	49	21	30	25	96	DDf	1%	31	74	2%	2%	121	2%	0%	-9.8	92	$0
21	PIT	554	50	5	39	6	226	4	4	258	265	309	79	82	77	5	92	0.66	44	20	36	24	83	FDf	2%	45	50	3%	2%	125	6%	86%	-28.4	204	$4
22	PIT *	359	35	2	28	8	277	2	5	263	314	368	97	117	87	5	83	0.32	43	26	31	33	75	DCc	2%	64	45	3%	3%	116	11%	80%	-2.3	110	$9
1st Half		92	7	0	10	1	266	0	1	238	308	363	95	118	87	6	86	0.43	39	17	44	31	73	DAf	0%	69	52	0%	0%	110	11%	50%	-1.2	155	-$7
2nd Half		267	28	2	17	7	281	2	4	266	316	369	97	117	87	5	82	0.29	43	28	29	33	75	DCc	2%	62	44	4%	4%	120	11%	88%	0.1	93	$11
23	**Proj**	**315**	**29**	**2**	**24**	**5**	**255**	**2**	**6**	**254**	**297**	**342**	**89**	**105**	**81**	**5**	**87**	**0.43**	**44**	**22**	**34**	**29**	**79**		**1%**	**57**	**51**	**3%**	**3%**	**115**	**10%**	**72%**	**-2.4**	**144**	**$8**

Nido,Tomás

Age: 29 Pos: CA
Bats: R Ht: 6' 0" Wt: 211

Health B | LIMA Plan D
PT/Exp D | Rand Var 0
Consist D | MM 1311

Another player who found career-high PA due to injuries, team depth issues and couldn't take advantage. Overaggressive plate approach, poor launch angle were exposed as exit velocity collapsed and GB% soared once again. 2nd half rebound vL salvaged some value; xPX history tempts us a bit—but you can still find better #2 catcher flyers.

Yr	Tm	PA	R	HR	RBI	SB	BA	xHR	xSB	xBA	OBP	SLG	OPS+	vL+	vR+	bb%	ct%	Eye	G	L	F	h%	HctX	QBaB	Brl%	PX	xPX	HR/F	xHR/F	Spd	SBA%	SB%	RAR	BPX	R$
18	NYM *	329	28	4	31	0	204	1	3	252	230	312	73	83	52	3	77	0.15	51	24	25	25	91	DDc	2%	75	74	7%	7%	92	0%	0%	-11.9	13	-$1
19	NYM *	183	11	4	17	0	202	4	0	189	236	304	75	90	70	4	70	0.15	55	15	30	27	79	CDd	5%	62	66	14%	14%	68	0%	0%	-11.1	-148	-$3
20	NYM	26	4	2	6	0	292	1	0	266	346	583	123	203	81	8	75	0.33	67	11	22	31	101	CFb	11%	153	98	50%	25%	88	0%	0%	2.1	264	$1
21	NYM	161	16	3	13	1	222	4	1	230	261	327	81	73	83	3	71	0.11	41	28	31	29	109	CCb	6%	65	132	9%	12%	121	3%	100%	-5.4	-69	-$1
22	NYM	313	31	3	28	0	239	8	2	223	276	324	85	94	79	4	73	0.18	50	21	29	32	91	FDc	6%	67	116	5%	13%	80	0%	0%	-5.2	-59	$2
1st Half		154	11	0	13	0	213	2	1	182	253	234	69	66	70	5	69	0.16	55	20	25	31	77	FFc	3%	21	101	0%	8%	94	0%	0%	-7.3	-234	-$8
2nd Half		159	20	3	15	0	266	6	1	262	298	413	101	124	86	5	78	0.22	46	22	32	32	105	FDc	8%	108	129	8%	17%	78	0%	0%	3.0	110	$1
23	**Proj**	**245**	**24**	**4**	**22**	**0**	**230**	**6**	**1**	**230**	**265**	**330**	**83**	**91**	**78**	**4**	**73**	**0.16**	**48**	**23**	**30**	**30**	**97**		**6%**	**75**	**113**	**7%**	**12%**	**84**	**2%**	**100%**	**-3.5**	**-48**	**$4**

Nimmo,Brandon

Age: 30 Pos: CF
Bats: L Ht: 6' 3" Wt: 206

Health D | LIMA Plan B+
PT/Exp A | Rand Var 0
Consist A | MM 3335

IL avoidance the primary reason behind career PA and counting stats that sparked breakout. GB%, launch angle woes cap HR; running game now almost non-existent despite Spd. But contact skills were solid throughout vs. pitchers from both sides. And plate patience atop the lineup keeps him profitable in OBP leagues. More health will bring a repeat.

Yr	Tm	PA	R	HR	RBI	SB	BA	xHR	xSB	xBA	OBP	SLG	OPS+	vL+	vR+	bb%	ct%	Eye	G	L	F	h%	HctX	QBaB	Brl%	PX	xPX	HR/F	xHR/F	Spd	SBA%	SB%	RAR	BPX	R$
18	NYM	535	77	17	47	9	263	14	9	254	404	483	119	98	125	15	68	0.57	45	22	33	35	93	BCd	7%	148	114	18%	14%	146	9%	60%	24.4	217	$16
19	NYM *	295	42	9	34	5	212	6	5	226	356	386	103	166	93	18	65	0.65	39	23	38	28	81	BCc	7%	110	103	16%	12%	96	6%	100%	2.2	59	$4
20	NYM	225	33	8	18	1	280	7	5	263	404	484	118	85	130	15	77	0.77	47	20	32	33	67	CDd	8%	107	70	17%	15%	154	4%	33%	7.3	284	$17
21	NYM *	418	54	8	28	5	278	6	7	251	378	413	109	112	117	14	77	0.69	47	22	30	34	106	CDd	4%	81	72	11%	8%	138	7%	56%	9.3	162	$11
22	NYM	673	102	16	64	3	274	18	13	263	367	433	113	110	115	11	80	0.61	51	18	32	32	105	CDd	7%	97	93	11%	12%	152	3%	60%	21.3	228	$22
1st Half		318	44	6	27	0	272	8	6	266	354	424	110	114	107	10	81	0.55	50	19	30	32	108	CFc	8%	92	97	9%	12%	160	3%	0%	7.6	228	$14
2nd Half		355	58	10	37	3	276	11	7	260	379	441	116	106	121	12	79	0.67	51	16	33	32	102	CDf	6%	102	89	13%	14%	134	3%	100%	15.3	224	$27
23	**Proj**	**630**	**94**	**17**	**56**	**5**	**272**	**16**	**9**	**258**	**378**	**436**	**113**	**107**	**115**	**13**	**77**	**0.64**	**48**	**20**	**32**	**33**	**99**		**6%**	**104**	**86**	**12%**	**12%**	**144**	**7%**	**60%**	**27.4**	**204**	**$23**

JOCK THOMPSON

Nola,Austin

Age: 33 Pos: CA			
Bats: R Ht: 6' 0" Wt: 197			
Health	C	LIMA Plan	D+
PT/Exp	B	Rand Var	0
Consist	B	MM	1123

Slew of injuries seemed at least partly to blame for 2021 power collapse. In 2022, he repeated good exit velocity and hard contact paired with plus plate skills—and neither HR/F or Brl% budged. All that's left is near-empty batting average as he approaches his mid-30s. And another marginal #2 fantasy catcher.

Yr Tm	PA	R	HR	RBI	SB	BA	xHR	xSB	xBA	OBP	SLG	OPS+	vL+	vR+	bb%	ct%	Eye	G	L	F	h%	HctX	QBaB	Brl%	PX	xPX	HR/F	xHR/F	Spd	SBA%	SB%	RAR	BPX	R$
18 aaa	246	19	1	23	1	212		3		276	283	75			8	75	0.36				28				56				82	2%	100%		-33	-$2
19 SEA *	482	60	15	55	4	256	6	4	232	322	417	102	124	103	9	73	0.36	40	19	41	32	85	CBc	3%	93	90	14%	8%	114	4%	73%	3.1	70	$10
20 2 TM	184	24	7	28	0	273	6	2	267	353	472	110	79	124	10	79	0.53	40	23	37	31	119	BCc	8%	107	105	15%	13%	89	0%	0%	7.7	196	$14
21 SD *	230	17	3	31	0	261	2	1	260	317	362	93	112	89	7	86	0.59	40	24	36	29	111	BBf	1%	63	93	4%	4%	74	2%	0%	0.1	131	$2
22 SD	397	40	4	40	2	251	4	2	233	321	329	92	103	85	9	83	0.57	43	21	37	29	114	BCd	2%	53	89	4%	4%	87	3%	67%	-0.7	66	$6
1st Half	216	23	2	23	1	233	2	1	230	301	302	85	84	85	8	83	0.48	44	20	36	27	116	BCc	3%	47	84	3%	3%	85	3%	50%	-3.9	38	$1
2nd Half	181	17	2	17	1	272	2	1	238	344	361	100	130	85	10	83	0.67	41	21	38	32	113	CCf	2%	61	95	4%	4%	93	3%	100%	3.8	107	$2
23 Proj	**315**	**31**	**5**	**38**	**1**	**258**	**4**	**2**	**245**	**328**	**365**	**96**	**106**	**90**	**9**	**83**	**0.54**	**41**	**22**	**37**	**30**	**111**		**2%**	**71**	**93**	**6%**	**5%**	**84**	**3%**	**58%**	**5.4**	**100**	**$5**

Nootbaar,Lars

Age: 25 Pos: RF			
Bats: L Ht: 6' 3" Wt: 210			
Health	A	LIMA Plan	C+
PT/Exp	D	Rand Var	+5
Consist	A	MM	3223

14-40-.228 in 347 PA at STL. Struggles in limited playing time earned several 1st-half demotions, but light went on in big way afterward. Fixed swing, exit velocity and GB% tilt in unison, hammered lefties and righties alike as patience, contact skills soared. Small samples leave more questions than answers, but with consistency ... UP: .260 BA, 25 HR.

Yr Tm	PA	R	HR	RBI	SB	BA	xHR	xSB	xBA	OBP	SLG	OPS+	vL+	vR+	bb%	ct%	Eye	G	L	F	h%	HctX	QBaB	Brl%	PX	xPX	HR/F	xHR/F	Spd	SBA%	SB%	RAR	BPX	R$
18																																		
19 aa	106	10	0	3	1	245		2		339	281	86			12	75	0.56				33				22				134	6%	44%		-56	-$2
20																																		
21 STL *	252	29	9	28	3	244	3	3	221	317	396	98	118	98	10	75	0.43	46	15	39	29	88	CDf	5%	81	67	16%	10%	107	13%	37%	-5.4	69	$5
22 STL *	416	61	16	49	5	216	12	7	256	325	425	106	118	110	14	74	0.61	44	17	39	25	114	BCf	12%	134	131	16%	14%	113	6%	84%	3.8	224	$9
1st Half	151	17	4	17	2	157	0	2	228	235	287	74	45	73	9	66	0.30	51	23	26	20	70	CFf	4%	96	71	17%	0%	91	6%	100%	-9.3	-45	-$4
2nd Half	265	44	12	32	3	253	11	5	282	374	512	125	131	124	17	79	0.93	42	16	42	27	132	ACf	14%	154	148	16%	15%	124	6%	75%	15.4	383	$20
23 Proj	**420**	**55**	**17**	**45**	**5**	**240**	**11**	**6**	**246**	**328**	**430**	**105**	**116**	**103**	**12**	**74**	**0.53**	**46**	**17**	**37**	**28**	**99**		**10%**	**118**	**96**	**16%**	**11%**	**115**	**7%**	**54%**	**7.9**	**128**	**$14**

O Neill,Tyler

Age: 28 Pos: LF CF			
Bats: R Ht: 5' 11" Wt: 200			
Health	D	LIMA Plan	C+
PT/Exp	A	Rand Var	0
Consist	F	MM	4315

Failure to launch fueled by injuries (shoulder impingement, balky left hamstring) that knocked him out three different times for 66 days. GB% spiked; 2021 launch angle improvement evaporated, though Aug/Sept power metrics say he's fine. 2nd-half h% obscured contact, bb% improvements. Primed for a rebound, health is everything.

Yr Tm	PA	R	HR	RBI	SB	BA	xHR	xSB	xBA	OBP	SLG	OPS+	vL+	vR+	bb%	ct%	Eye	G	L	F	h%	HctX	QBaB	Brl%	PX	xPX	HR/F	xHR/F	Spd	SBA%	SB%	RAR	BPX	R$
18 STL *	402	77	28	73	4	265	9	5	240	319	539	115	106	106	7	64	0.22	29	23	48	33	107	AAb	23%	179	169	25%	25%	123	6%	79%	16.6	177	$18
19 STL *	337	42	15	38	3	236	5	3	213	283	413	96	91	101	6	62	0.17	38	23	40	33	100	CAd	7%	111	108	14%	14%	97	4%	100%	-13.5	-67	$6
20 STL	157	20	7	19	3	173	6	1	221	261	360	82	60	88	10	69	0.35	43	15	41	19	92	CBf	8%	110	115	18%	15%	96	14%	75%	-10.8	56	$6
21 STL	537	89	34	80	15	286	39	12	254	352	560	125	140	122	7	65	0.23	36	23	41	37	114	AAc	18%	176	153	26%	30%	121	15%	79%	27.2	208	$30
22 STL	383	56	14	58	14	228	14	8	229	308	392	99	110	96	10	69	0.37	42	20	38	29	97	BCd	11%	109	119	16%	16%	109	20%	78%	-1.8	62	$14
1st Half	185	22	4	28	6	241	4	4	219	292	361	92	96	92	8	67	0.26	42	24	34	33	83	CCc	9%	87	96	10%	10%	117	20%	67%	-3.2	-28	$8
2nd Half	198	34	10	30	8	214	10	4	240	323	423	106	119	100	13	71	0.49	42	17	41	24	110	BBd	13%	131	140	20%	20%	98	20%	89%	1.4	155	$16
23 Proj	**525**	**83**	**25**	**79**	**16**	**241**	**26**	**14**	**235**	**318**	**444**	**106**	**112**	**104**	**9**	**68**	**0.31**	**40**	**20**	**40**	**30**	**103**		**14%**	**139**	**132**	**20%**	**20%**	**101**	**15%**	**80%**	**12.0**	**114**	**$26**

Odor,Rougned

Age: 29 Pos: 2B			
Bats: L Ht: 5' 11" Wt: 200			
Health	B	LIMA Plan	D
PT/Exp	A	Rand Var	+1
Consist	A	MM	3203

Has seemingly grown older faster than he's aged. Launch angle, FB% have never been healthier but once-plus power, HR/F, Brl% continued their steep descent. Anomalous 2nd half ct%, LD% upticks should have been better news, but historically poor h% didn't budge as exit velocity cratered. Now hurtling toward a part-time role at very best.

Yr Tm	PA	R	HR	RBI	SB	BA	xHR	xSB	xBA	OBP	SLG	OPS+	vL+	vR+	bb%	ct%	Eye	G	L	F	h%	HctX	QBaB	Brl%	PX	xPX	HR/F	xHR/F	Spd	SBA%	SB%	RAR	BPX	R$
18 TEX	535	76	18	63	12	253	17	7	238	326	424	101	94	102	8	73	0.34	41	20	39	31	122	BBd	7%	107	121	14%	13%	99	18%	50%	2.1	87	$17
19 TEX	581	77	30	93	11	205	33	10	230	283	439	100	113	93	9	66	0.29	35	17	48	25	104	AAd	14%	142	157	19%	21%	83	19%	55%	-17.8	81	$14
20 TEX	148	15	10	30	0	167	8	2	223	209	413	83	53	98	5	66	0.15	33	17	50	16	83	DAf	12%	145	112	22%	18%	64	6%	0%	-9.6	40	$5
21 NYY	361	42	15	39	0	202	13	2	210	286	379	91	103	86	7	69	0.27	37	15	47	24	93	CAf	9%	109	111	15%	13%	73	1%	0%	-11.2	8	$2
22 BAL	472	49	13	53	6	207	12	2	221	275	357	90	81	92	7	74	0.29	32	19	49	25	97	CAf	7%	98	109	8%	8%	99	7%	86%	-8.5	72	$6
1st Half	248	29	9	31	0	206	7	1	229	262	408	95	117	90	6	71	0.22	30	17	53	25	93	CAf	8%	135	110	10%	8%	110	7%	0%	-4.3	138	$6
2nd Half	224	20	4	22	6	207	6	1	216	290	298	83	48	93	8	78	0.41	33	23	44	25	102	DAf	6%	58	108	6%	9%	81	7%	86%	-7.5	0	$5
23 Proj	**280**	**31**	**11**	**35**	**3**	**211**	**10**	**3**	**221**	**283**	**382**	**92**	**87**	**94**	**7**	**72**	**0.27**	**34**	**18**	**48**	**25**	**97**		**8%**	**112**	**113**	**12%**	**12%**	**82**	**6%**	**68%**	**-3.6**	**42**	**$6**

Ohtani,Shohei

Age: 28 Pos: DH			
Bats: L Ht: 6' 4" Wt: 210			
Health	A	LIMA Plan	C
PT/Exp	A	Rand Var	0
Consist	D	MM	5345

Lost some launch angle, gave back some HR as wondrously inflated HR/F fell back towards earth. And running game doesn't look as healthy as in prior years. But these are quibbles. Hard contact was as peak as ever, and together with improved ct% fueled BA bump that kept him near 2021 R$. Still the only DH worthy of a 1st round pick.

Yr Tm	PA	R	HR	RBI	SB	BA	xHR	xSB	xBA	OBP	SLG	OPS+	vL+	vR+	bb%	ct%	Eye	G	L	F	h%	HctX	QBaB	Brl%	PX	xPX	HR/F	xHR/F	Spd	SBA%	SB%	RAR	BPX	R$
18 LAA	366	59	22	61	10	285	23	5	279	361	564	124	87	138	10	69	0.36	44	24	33	35	109	ACb	16%	181	129	30%	31%	113	16%	71%	23.9	253	$19
19 LAA	423	51	18	62	12	286	19	11	276	343	505	117	110	119	8	71	0.30	50	26	24	36	123	ADa	12%	121	111	26%	28%	141	15%	80%	10.2	156	$17
20 LAA	175	23	7	24	7	190	8	3	228	291	366	87	82	89	13	67	0.44	50	17	33	23	93	CDd	11%	108	109	21%	24%	87	21%	88%	-6.7	36	$13
21 LAA	639	103	46	100	26	257	54	22	270	372	592	133	133	132	15	65	0.51	38	21	41	30	120	ABc	22%	208	162	33%	39%	147	23%	72%	36.0	392	$36
22 LAA	666	90	34	95	11	273	45	22	269	356	519	124	110	131	11	73	0.45	42	20	38	32	121	ACc	17%	156	142	21%	28%	109	12%	55%	25.9	245	$32
1st Half	338	47	18	51	9	259	25	11	267	343	498	119	97	130	11	73	0.44	41	20	39	30	117	ACc	19%	152	143	21%	30%	95	12%	64%	8.9	224	$34
2nd Half	328	43	16	44	2	287	20	11	270	369	540	129	123	131	11	72	0.45	43	19	38	35	126	ACd	15%	159	141	21%	26%	119	12%	33%	17.6	262	$29
23 Proj	**630**	**91**	**36**	**94**	**14**	**263**	**44**	**12**	**268**	**355**	**531**	**123**	**116**	**126**	**12**	**69**	**0.45**	**42**	**20**	**37**	**31**	**118**		**27%**	**176**	**142**	**25%**	**31%**	**121**	**11%**	**66%**	**33.8**	**265**	**$33**

Olivares,Edward

Age: 27 Pos: RF			
Bats: R Ht: 6' 2" Wt: 190			
Health	D	LIMA Plan	C+
PT/Exp	D	Rand Var	0
Consist	B	MM	3233

4-15-.286 in 174 PA at KC. Quad injuries intervened twice as bench player's PA ramped up, in May and again in July, sidelining him for 104 days. Unsurprisingly, his swing path bounced around all season in small samples. Still owns ct%, speed, average power, along with big chase rate that keeps GB% tilt intact. Projection relies on improved health.

Yr Tm	PA	R	HR	RBI	SB	BA	xHR	xSB	xBA	OBP	SLG	OPS+	vL+	vR+	bb%	ct%	Eye	G	L	F	h%	HctX	QBaB	Brl%	PX	xPX	HR/F	xHR/F	Spd	SBA%	SB%	RAR	BPX	R$
18																																		
19 aa	525	73	14	66	30	254		7		307	397	97			7	78	0.35				30				77				99	34%	73%		70	$22
20 2 TM	101	9	3	10	0	240	2	4	237	267	375	85	69	94	4	74	0.16	48	23	30	29	79	FDf	6%	71	65	14%	10%	139	10%	0%	-4.9	16	$2
21 KC *	387	52	15	37	10	254	4	6	253	303	425	100	74	112	7	80	0.36	47	17	36	28	105	CDf	6%	90	117	17%	13%	142	19%	61%	-2.0	196	$13
22 KC *	256	31	4	21	3	261	5	7	258	303	377	96	127	96	6	78	0.27	46	25	29	32	111	BDd	6%	81	91	11%	14%	111	12%	43%	-1.0	86	$4
1st Half	103	13	3	9	2	243	2	2	290	289	412	99	168	78	6	81	0.34	50	25	25	27	133	AFc	10%	106	121	25%	17%	119	12%	67%	-0.1	200	-$4
2nd Half	153	18	1	12	1	274	3	4	237	312	353	94	73	105	5	77	0.24	44	24	32	35	99	CCd	4%	64	72	4%	12%	106	12%	26%	-1.7	7	$0
23 Proj	**385**	**48**	**13**	**36**	**8**	**256**	**12**	**7**	**260**	**308**	**417**	**101**	**96**	**103**	**6**	**78**	**0.28**	**47**	**21**	**32**	**29**	**106**		**6%**	**101**	**99**	**14%**	**13%**	**110**	**10%**	**53%**	**0.9**	**110**	**$14**

Olson,Matt

Age: 29 Pos: 1B			
Bats: L Ht: 6' 5" Wt: 225			
Health	A	LIMA Plan	B+
PT/Exp	A	Rand Var	+1
Consist	D	MM	4135

Gave back a bunch of BA, as last year's ct% looks like an outlier. But everything else seems rock-solid, notably exit velocity, launch angle and PX. HctX, xBA hints that BA could even retrace some; he hits pretty much everything hard. Buy him for the 30+ HR power; anything else is a bonus. And... players often step up in year #2 on new team.

Yr Tm	PA	R	HR	RBI	SB	BA	xHR	xSB	xBA	OBP	SLG	OPS+	vL+	vR+	bb%	ct%	Eye	G	L	F	h%	HctX	QBaB	Brl%	PX	xPX	HR/F	xHR/F	Spd	SBA%	SB%	RAR	BPX	R$
18 OAK	660	85	29	84	2	247	35	9	247	335	453	106	93	110	11	72	0.43	36	21	43	29	125	AAd	12%	132	140	16%	19%	84	2%	67%	-1.5	140	$17
19 OAK *	570	75	37	92	0	262	38	2	269	330	531	119	107	131	9	72	0.37	31	24	45	29	125	AAc	15%	145	161	24%	25%	77	0%	0%	9.5	174	$18
20 OAK	245	28	14	42	1	195	13	1	220	310	424	97	91	99	14	63	0.44	35	21	44	23	110	AAd	13%	136	143	24%	22%	88	2%	100%	-11.5	72	$14
21 OAK	673	101	39	111	4	271	36	3	279	371	540	125	131	121	13	80	0.78	40	16	44	28	119	ABf	13%	145	128	19%	18%	76	3%	80%	33.5	335	$28
22 ATL	699	86	34	103	0	240	33	2	262	325	477	114	105	117	11	72	0.44	39	19	42	28	124	ABf	13%	161	132	18%	17%	59	0%	0%	9.7	207	$21
1st Half	361	35	12	47	0	256	12	1	270	349	473	116	103	122	13	74	0.56	40	20	40	31	126	ABf	13%	158	121	13%	13%	61	0%	0%	11.7	241	$18
2nd Half	338	51	22	56	0	224	20	1	253	299	482	111	107	112	9	70	0.33	38	17	45	24	123	ABf	13%	164	143	23%	21%	70	0%	0%	2.7	183	$30
23 Proj	**665**	**91**	**37**	**106**	**2**	**253**	**35**	**1**	**262**	**343**	**500**	**117**	**115**	**118**	**12**	**74**	**0.50**	**38**	**18**	**43**	**28**	**121**		**13%**	**160**	**135**	**20%**	**19%**	**69**	**1%**	**82%**	**29.3**	**227**	**$27**

JOCK THOMPSON

Ortega,Rafael

Age: 32 Pos: CF DH | Bats: L Ht: 5' 11" Wt: 180

Health B | PT/Exp C | Consist B | LIMA Plan D+ | Rand Var 0 | MM 2313

Delivered "meh" strong-side platoon PA, down predictably from 2021 performance. Improved bb%, stable ct% didn't compensate for LD% regression. SBA-fueled running game propped up value, but Spd+SB% combo looks shaky. Glove, handedness should keep him in MLB opportunities. But minus authoritative contact, they'll come off the bench.

Yr	Tm	PA	R	HR	RBI	SB	BA	xHR	xSB	xBA	OBP	SLG	OPS+	vL+	vR+	bb%	ct%	Eye	G	L	F	h%	HctX	QBaB	Brl%	PX	xPX	HR/F	xHR/F	Spd	SBA%	SB%	RAR	BPX	R$
18	MIA *	457	49	1	28	14	225	1	7	245	300	302	81	94	69	10	85	0.72	46	22	32	26	88	DCc	0%	40	37	0%	3%	167	15%	81%	-14.8	147	$6
19	ATL *	572	71	17	55	14	229	2	11	245	300	398	97	23	88	9	74	0.39	41	21	38	28	81	CCd	5%	98	85	8%	8%	113	19%	62%	-7.4	104	$12
20																																			
21	CHC *	399	51	13	40	13	271	7	7	245	336	439	106	57	124	9	76	0.40	34	25	41	32	86	CBc	6%	96	86	12%	8%	134	19%	63%	5.1	154	$16
22	CHC	370	35	7	35	12	241	6	10	223	331	358	97	74	99	12	77	0.59	34	21	45	29	84	CBd	5%	78	89	6%	5%	79	19%	63%	-1.6	62	$9
1st Half		227	24	4	21	7	267	3	6	232	363	403	108	77	112	14	75	0.64	32	22	46	34	84	DBf	5%	96	87	6%	4%	87	19%	64%	5.8	117	$9
2nd Half		143	11	3	14	5	200	3	3	209	280	288	80	47	81	10	78	0.52	36	20	44	23	85	CBc	5%	51	90	7%	7%	80	19%	63%	-5.9	0	-$1
23	Proj	**315**	**33**	**7**	**30**	**10**	**241**	**6**	**9**	**228**	**326**	**366**	**96**	**64**	**100**	**11**	**77**	**0.56**	**35**	**22**	**43**	**29**	**85**		**5%**	**80**	**82**	**8%**	**6%**	**107**	**15%**	**65%**	**1.0**	**95**	**$7**

Ozuna,Marcell

Age: 32 Pos: DH LF | Bats: R Ht: 6' 1" Wt: 225

Health C | PT/Exp A | Consist F | LIMA Plan D+ | Rand Var +3 | MM 3123

HR rebounded with health, but the good news ends there. More bb% decline, as soaring 33% chase rate helped keep BA down. LHPs (oddly) had their way with him again, and his second arrest in as many years cut into 2nd half PA. He's running out of goodwill and that plate approach needs a big offseason reset. Power for a fantasy risk portfolio only.

Yr	Tm	PA	R	HR	RBI	SB	BA	xHR	xSB	xBA	OBP	SLG	OPS+	vL+	vR+	bb%	ct%	Eye	G	L	F	h%	HctX	QBaB	Brl%	PX	xPX	HR/F	xHR/F	Spd	SBA%	SB%	RAR	BPX	R$
18	STL	627	69	23	88	3	280	30	9	248	325	433	102	119	95	6	81	0.35	47	18	35	31	135	ACc	10%	81	112	14%	18%	96	2%	100%	8.1	107	$21
19	STL	549	80	29	89	12	243	30	3	275	330	474	111	105	112	11	76	0.54	41	23	35	26	127	ACc	12%	118	119	22%	23%	78	11%	86%	0.9	178	$19
20	ATL	267	38	18	56	0	338	19	5	283	431	636	142	173	133	14	74	0.63	37	23	40	39	138	ABd	15%	166	146	26%	28%	70	0%	0%	33.8	316	$38
21	ATL	208	21	7	26	0	213	8	0	233	288	356	89	82	91	9	76	0.41	37	23	41	24	87	BBd	10%	81	80	12%	14%	50	0%	0%	-10.3	8	$0
22	ATL	507	56	23	56	2	226	28	0	240	274	413	97	70	108	6	74	0.25	38	19	43	26	108	BBf	13%	118	121	15%	18%	51	3%	67%	-12.5	69	$10
1st Half		329	40	16	34	2	228	18	0	241	280	419	99	70	110	6	76	0.29	40	17	43	25	118	BBf	14%	114	125	16%	18%	57	3%	67%	-7.3	93	$18
2nd Half		178	16	7	22	0	222	9	0	241	264	401	94	69	105	6	71	0.20	34	23	44	27	91	BAd	11%	125	113	13%	17%	62	3%	0%	-5.7	48	$2
23	Proj	**350**	**38**	**15**	**47**	**1**	**236**	**18**	**1**	**244**	**298**	**420**	**100**	**85**	**105**	**8**	**74**	**0.34**	**37**	**21**	**42**	**27**	**104**		**12%**	**118**	**109**	**15%**	**18%**	**55**	**2%**	**76%**	**-0.6**	**81**	**$10**

Pache,Cristian

Age: 24 Pos: CF | Bats: R Ht: 6' 2" Wt: 215

Health A | PT/Exp C | Consist B | LIMA Plan D | Rand Var +5 | MM 1103

3-18-.166 with 2 SB in 260 PA at OAK. Traded to rebuilder and plus glove gave once-touted prospect 1st half opportunity. But the results speak for themselves, and even rebuilders have limits. Still has age, pedigree and legs, now along with upticks in ct% and exit velocity. But running game is non-existent, and the clock is ticking. Currently unrosterable.

Yr	Tm	PA	R	HR	RBI	SB	BA	xHR	xSB	xBA	OBP	SLG	OPS+	vL+	vR+	bb%	ct%	Eye	G	L	F	h%	HctX	QBaB	Brl%	PX	xPX	HR/F	xHR/F	Spd	SBA%	SB%	RAR	BPX	R$
18	aa	108	9	1	7	0	256		1		287	329	83			4	72	0.16				35				49				116	8%	0%		-83	-$1
19	a/a	528	62	11	60	8	273		6		330	448	108			8	74	0.33				35				103				117	17%	41%		119	$13
20	ATL	4	0	0	0	0	250	0	0	0	250	250	66	261	0	0	50	0.00	100	0	0	50	0	FFa		0	-26	0%		118	0%	0%	-0.2	-648	-$3
21	ATL *	413	47	10	40	7	217	1	1	191	267	338	83	73	42	6	66	0.20	50	11	39	30	40	FFf	5%	85	82	7%	7%	74	18%	49%	-20.7	-119	$5
22	OAK *	423	26	5	29	3	171	2	8	212	212	248	65	84	55	5	71	0.18	57	18	25	23	78	CFf	4%	55	49	7%	5%	120	8%	44%	-29.8	-83	-$6
1st Half		226	16	2	14	1	165	2	4	212	210	234	63	77	52	5	72	0.20	58	17	25	22	83	CFf	4%	50	55	6%	6%	111	8%	33%	-17.7	-90	-$8
2nd Half		197	10	3	15	2	178	0	4	212	215	265	68	115	70	5	70	0.15	54	19	27	24	56	DFf	0%	60	14	14%	0%	128	8%	56%	-13.4	-86	-$5
23	Proj	**280**	**24**	**5**	**23**	**3**	**204**	**2**	**3**	**210**	**260**	**313**	**79**	**114**	**64**	**6**	**70**	**0.20**	**53**	**16**	**31**	**27**	**56**		**3%**	**79**	**51**	**9%**	**4%**	**95**	**7%**	**44%**	**-11.8**	**-76**	**$3**

Palacios,Richard

Age: 26 Pos: LF | Bats: L Ht: 5' 11" Wt: 180

Health A | PT/Exp D | Consist C | LIMA Plan D | Rand Var 0 | MM 1411

0-10-.232 with 2 SB in 123 PA at CLE. Career .308/.400/.484 hitter (824 minor league PA) struggled in inconsistent playing time at the MLB level. Plate skills and running game (39/6 SB/CS in the minors) hint at something better. But it's gap power at best, and quality contact still needs to show at the highest level. Watchable from a distance.

Yr	Tm	PA	R	HR	RBI	SB	BA	xHR	xSB	xBA	OBP	SLG	OPS+	vL+	vR+	bb%	ct%	Eye	G	L	F	h%	HctX	QBaB	Brl%	PX	xPX	HR/F	xHR/F	Spd	SBA%	SB%	RAR	BPX	R$
18																																			
19																																			
20																																			
21	a/a	400	54	5	36	15	254		5		335	394	100			11	77	0.53				32				94				103	19%	81%		146	$13
22	CLE *	315	26	2	30	9	218	1	7	225	274	306	82	93	80	7	75	0.31	46	21	34	28	60	DCf	1%	64	26	0%	3%	105	16%	78%	-11.8	0	$3
1st Half		179	16	1	22	4	225	1	4	238	285	317	85	93	87	8	77	0.37	48	20	32	29	77	DCf	2%	70	40	0%	5%	96	16%	100%	-4.6	34	$0
2nd Half		137	11	1	8	5	209	0	3	206	259	292	78	0	63	6	72	0.24	39	22	39	28	14	DAf	0%	57	-14	0%	0%	128	16%	67%	-6.7	-41	-$3
23	Proj	**175**	**18**	**1**	**15**	**6**	**233**	**1**	**4**	**227**	**299**	**328**	**87**	**354**	**84**	**8**	**76**	**0.38**	**43**	**21**	**36**	**30**	**39**		**1%**	**73**	**8**	**2%**	**2%**	**115**	**13%**	**81%**	**-2.5**	**53**	**$5**

Paredes,Isaac

Age: 24 Pos: 3B 2B 1B | Bats: R Ht: 5' 11" Wt: 213

Health A | PT/Exp B | Consist B | LIMA Plan B+ | Rand Var +4 | MM 3025

20-45-.2005 in 381 PA at TAM. Torrid 1st half, inflated HR/F crumbled afterward, though youth and excellent plate skills point to something better. Exit velocity bump fed HR total, even with average power and volatile swing path. Zero speed, LD-deficient GLF kept BA suppressed, but better h% luck seems imminent. Versatility keeps him a speculative depth piece.

Yr	Tm	PA	R	HR	RBI	SB	BA	xHR	xSB	xBA	OBP	SLG	OPS+	vL+	vR+	bb%	ct%	Eye	G	L	F	h%	HctX	QBaB	Brl%	PX	xPX	HR/F	xHR/F	Spd	SBA%	SB%	RAR	BPX	R$
18	aa	148	18	3	20	1	311		3		389	441	111			11	83	0.77				36				82				89	2%	100%		167	$3
19	aa	534	64	13	67	5	286		4		360	424	109			10	87	0.93				30				68				94	5%	62%		204	$15
20	DET	108	7	1	6	0	220	0	1	212	278	290	75	118	67	7	76	0.33	47	21	32	28	57	DDf	0%	46	36	4%	0%	91	0%	0%	-6.7	-56	-$1
21	DET *	385	41	10	41	0	240	1	4	245	353	394	103	96	79	15	82	0.96	37	21	43	26	106	DAf	2%	80	93	4%	4%	130	0%	0%	5.0	238	$5
22	TAM *	485	59	23	58	0	208	10	1	247	296	422	102	118	100	11	79	0.60	42	12	45	21	97	CBf	7%	128	96	17%	8%	71	2%	0%	-0.5	221	$7
1st Half		251	34	16	41	0	238	5	0	269	300	501	113	123	129	8	79	0.43	42	12	46	23	101	CBf	9%	153	115	25%	10%	81	2%	0%	4.6	283	$17
2nd Half		234	25	7	17	0	173	5	0	224	299	330	89	112	81	14	79	0.79	42	13	45	18	95	CBf	5%	99	83	10%	7%	76	2%	0%	-7.8	162	$0
23	Proj	**455**	**55**	**17**	**53**	**0**	**244**	**8**	**2**	**246**	**338**	**422**	**105**	**121**	**98**	**12**	**80**	**0.69**	**40**	**17**	**43**	**27**	**97**		**6%**	**107**	**89**	**12%**	**6%**	**81**	**3%**	**31%**	**11.2**	**190**	**$13**

Pasquantino,Vinnie

Age: 25 Pos: 1B DH | Bats: L Ht: 6' 4" Wt: 245

Health A | PT/Exp B | Consist B | LIMA Plan B+ | Rand Var 0 | MM 3245

10-26-.295 in 298 PA at KC. Rookie sailed through MLB debut leaving lots to be excited about. Excellent plate skills, batting eye translated upward. HR didn't jump off the charts, but 135 xPX says they're coming; exit velocity is already near-elite, 138 HctX unassailable. Handled pitchers from both sides like a veteran. If it comes together... UP: 30 HR.

Yr	Tm	PA	R	HR	RBI	SB	BA	xHR	xSB	xBA	OBP	SLG	OPS+	vL+	vR+	bb%	ct%	Eye	G	L	F	h%	HctX	QBaB	Brl%	PX	xPX	HR/F	xHR/F	Spd	SBA%	SB%	RAR	BPX	R$
18																																			
19																																			
20																																			
21	aa	224	28	8	33	2	273		2		352	472	113			11	86	0.87				29				110				80	4%	100%		308	$6
22	KC *	584	55	19	66	3	255	10	4	263	328	419	106	120	117	10	85	0.73	41	19	40	27	138	ACc	9%	94	135	11%	11%	81	3%	70%	9.0	214	$15
1st Half		299	31	10	40	2	213	0	2	281	283	388	95	35	104	9	84	0.61	44	22	33	22	143	ACc		102	166	17%	0%	74	3%	59%	-7.1	207	$11
2nd Half		285	24	9	27	1	300	10	3	255	376	451	117	125	118	11	86	0.89	41	19	41	32	140	ACc	10%	85	133	11%	12%	83	3%	100%	12.7	214	$15
23	Proj	**595**	**63**	**23**	**75**	**4**	**272**	**18**	**4**	**275**	**348**	**466**	**113**	**115**	**112**	**10**	**86**	**0.82**	**41**	**19**	**41**	**28**	**126**		**9%**	**113**	**120**	**13%**	**10%**	**80**	**3%**	**89%**	**24.5**	**250**	**$23**

Pederson,Joc

Age: 31 Pos: LF | Bats: L Ht: 6' 1" Wt: 220

Health A | PT/Exp A | Consist C | LIMA Plan B | Rand Var -3 | MM 4223

Huge 1st half fueled by anomalous Brl%, soaring HR/F before regression and nagging injuries (groin, hand, concussion) brought him back to earth. Lofty career-high BA hung around thanks to 2nd half LD%, h%. Despite holding his own again vL, just 57 PA say he's still best valued as a low-BA HR source vR, while hoping for more.

Yr	Tm	PA	R	HR	RBI	SB	BA	xHR	xSB	xBA	OBP	SLG	OPS+	vL+	vR+	bb%	ct%	Eye	G	L	F	h%	HctX	QBaB	Brl%	PX	xPX	HR/F	xHR/F	Spd	SBA%	SB%	RAR	BPX	R$
18	LA	443	65	25	56	1	248	19	5	281	321	522	113	67	118	9	78	0.47	39	17	44	26	122	ABc	8%	156	134	18%	14%	90	7%	17%	8.6	287	$13
19	LA	514	83	36	74	1	249	26	6	271	339	538	121	70	126	10	75	0.45	42	17	41	25	118	ABd	10%	141	124	26%	19%	109	2%	50%	9.1	252	$16
20	LA	137	21	7	16	1	190	6	1	238	285	397	90	96	90	8	72	0.32	48	15	36	20	107	ACc	10%	114	126	23%	19%	88	4%	100%	-7.6	92	$6
21	2 NL	481	55	18	61	2	238	21	4	235	310	422	101	99	101	8	73	0.33	39	19	42	29	101	BCf	10%	108	118	14%	16%	101	5%	40%	-5.5	100	$9
22	SF	433	57	23	70	3	274	23	5	262	353	521	124	104	127	10	74	0.42	36	19	45	32	129	ABf	15%	154	157	18%	18%	119	5%	60%	24.7	259	$18
1st Half		234	34	17	41	2	274	16	2	280	342	567	129	100	133	8	75	0.37	40	16	44	29	140	ACd	19%	175	152	24%	23%	89	5%	50%	14.6	303	$22
2nd Half		199	23	6	29	1	273	8	2	239	367	465	118	106	119	12	72	0.47	31	23	46	35	116	BBf	11%	127	165	11%	14%	136	5%	100%	9.1	186	$9
23	Proj	**420**	**56**	**20**	**61**	**2**	**247**	**21**	**4**	**251**	**327**	**468**	**110**	**97**	**113**	**9**	**73**	**0.39**	**38**	**19**	**43**	**29**	**116**		**12%**	**140**	**141**	**17%**	**17%**	**108**	**6%**	**56%**	**12.9**	**183**	**$15**

JOCK THOMPSON

Pena,Jeremy

Age: 25	Pos: SS	Health	A	LIMA Plan	B+
Bats: R	Ht: 6' 0" Wt: 179	PT/Exp	B	Rand Var	0
		Consist	A	MM	3425

Fine rookie season deteriorated over 2nd half, as warts became apparent. Abysmal bb% points to overaggressive approach; huge chase tendencies sank BA as GB% soared and HR dropped off. Healthy running game looks growable; glove and age add to promising skill set. But plate approach needs fixing before he can move to the next level.

Yr	Tm	PA	R	HR	RBI	SB	BA	xHR	xSB	xBA	OBP	SLG	OPS+	vL+	vR+	bb%	ct%	Eye	G	L	F	h%	HctX	QBaB	Brl%	PX	xPX	HR/F	xHR/F	Spd	SBA%	SB%	RAR	BPX	R$
18																																			
19																																			
20																																			
21	aaa	126	15	7	13	3	234		1		258	454	98			3	66	0.10				29				132				121	19%	74%		54	$2
22	HOU	555	72	22	63	11	253	16	14	253	289	426	101	114	96	4	74	0.16	46	21	33	30	93	CDf	10%	109	92	17%	13%	131	11%	85%	1.4	114	$20
1st Half		248	36	12	31	6	276	8	7	260	327	482	114	127	110	5	74	0.22	40	23	37	32	91	CCf	9%	127	91	19%	13%	142	11%	86%	7.8	186	$20
2nd Half		307	36	10	32	5	235	8	7	246	258	382	91	105	85	3	74	0.12	51	19	30	29	94	CDd	10%	94	92	15%	12%	120	11%	83%	-7.9	52	$17
23	**Proj**	**595**	**76**	**23**	**66**	**13**	**243**	**17**	**10**	**239**	**275**	**406**	**95**	**106**	**90**	**4**	**72**	**0.13**	**47**	**21**	**33**	**30**	**93**		**10%**	**105**	**92**	**17%**	**13%**	**122**	**11%**	**80%**	**-3.0**	**86**	**$19**

Peralta,David

Age: 35	Pos: LF	Health	B	LIMA Plan	D+
Bats: L	Ht: 6' 1" Wt: 210	PT/Exp	A	Rand Var	+1
		Consist	A	MM	3133

Reminder that decline isn't always linear. Put on a FB%-fueled 1st half HR show following years of dwindling power, but it vanished afterward. Despite poorly-trending BA, bb% and exit velocity are intact; handedness keeps him playable vR. But age is increasingly a factor, with 2nd half suggesting more volatility. PT is at risk; heed R$ history.

Yr	Tm	PA	R	HR	RBI	SB	BA	xHR	xSB	xBA	OBP	SLG	OPS+	vL+	vR+	bb%	ct%	Eye	G	L	F	h%	HctX	QBaB	Brl%	PX	xPX	HR/F	xHR/F	Spd	SBA%	SB%	RAR	BPX	R$
18	ARI	614	75	30	87	4	293	24	9	280	352	516	116	92	125	8	78	0.39	51	20	29	33	139	ADc	8%	124	120	23%	19%	108	3%	100%	30.3	203	$25
19	ARI	423	48	12	57	0	275	10	3	274	343	461	111	98	116	8	77	0.40	51	21	28	33	116	BDd	5%	105	89	15%	12%	105	0%	0%	3.5	159	$9
20	ARI	218	19	5	34	1	300	4	1	251	339	433	103	82	109	6	78	0.29	49	22	29	37	106	CDf	5%	77	67	11%	9%	104	2%	100%	0.0	72	$18
21	ARI	538	57	8	63	2	259	8	5	269	325	402	100	100	100	9	81	0.50	55	19	26	30	107	BFd	5%	83	56	8%	8%	118	2%	67%	1.9	173	$10
22	2 TM	490	39	12	59	1	251	13	3	248	316	415	104	65	110	8	74	0.36	36	23	41	31	108	BBd	9%	115	127	9%	10%	86	4%	25%	3.0	114	$9
1st Half		254	24	11	35	1	250	8	1	261	319	474	112	66	120	9	74	0.38	31	22	47	29	121	ABd	12%	149	160	14%	10%	68	4%	33%	6.4	190	$11
2nd Half		236	15	1	24	0	251	5	1	233	314	351	94	64	100	8	74	0.33	42	23	35	33	95	BCd	5%	78	92	2%	9%	102	4%	0%	-2.5	28	$1
23	**Proj**	**350**	**32**	**7**	**44**	**1**	**261**	**8**	**3**	**253**	**324**	**411**	**102**	**82**	**106**	**8**	**77**	**0.39**	**45**	**21**	**33**	**32**	**108**		**7%**	**102**	**94**	**9%**	**9%**	**104**	**5%**	**44%**	**6.5**	**124**	**$10**

Peraza,Oswald

Age: 23	Pos: SS	Health	A	LIMA Plan	D+
Bats: R	Ht: 6' 0" Wt: 176	PT/Exp	C	Rand Var	0
		Consist	A	MM	1403

1-2-.306, 2 SB in 57 PA at NYY. Aided by legs and h%, promising rookie wasn't overmatched in Sept / Oct small sample, though bb% and ct% aren't ready yet. Previously non-existent power has taken a big step forward over past two minor league seasons (37 HR) and running game speaks for itself. Plus glove completes watchable profile.

Yr	Tm	PA	R	HR	RBI	SB	BA	xHR	xSB	xBA	OBP	SLG	OPS+	vL+	vR+	bb%	ct%	Eye	G	L	F	h%	HctX	QBaB	Brl%	PX	xPX	HR/F	xHR/F	Spd	SBA%	SB%	RAR	BPX	R$
18																																			
19																																			
20																																			
21	a/a	375	46	11	35	18	266		5		308	409	98			6	73	0.22				34				86				105	31%	65%		15	$16
22	NYY *	469	50	16	39	27	229	1	17	239	281	373	93	96	122	7	72	0.26	58	15	28	28	94	FFf	3%	96	42	9%	9%	110	33%	83%	-6.8	41	$18
1st Half		241	20	8	19	12	203		8	227	251	340	84	0	0	6	71	0.22	44	20	36	25	0			91	-14	0%		105	33%	78%	-10.6	14	$9
2nd Half		227	30	8	21	15	256	1	10	243	314	408	102	96	122	8	72	0.30	58	15	28	32	94	FFf	3%	101	42	9%	9%	117	33%	87%	2.3	72	$19
23	**Proj**	**280**	**33**	**6**	**25**	**15**	**246**	**7**	**14**	**216**	**319**	**355**	**93**	**73**	**98**	**7**	**72**	**0.25**	**40**	**22**	**39**	**32**	**85**		**3%**	**76**	**38**	**8%**	**9%**	**114**	**24%**	**77%**	**-2.5**	**35**	**$13**

Perdomo,Geraldo

Age: 23	Pos: SS	Health	A	LIMA Plan	D+
Bats: B	Ht: 6' 2" Wt: 203	PT/Exp	B	Rand Var	+2
		Consist	A	MM	1303

Continued to control the strike zone in first extended opportunity, and running game ticked up nicely in the 2nd half. But contact quality here looks totally anemic, with nothing hinting at budding power or anything more authoritative any time soon. Pedigree, legs, age and defense keep him relevant, but productive MLB years seem far away.

Yr	Tm	PA	R	HR	RBI	SB	BA	xHR	xSB	xBA	OBP	SLG	OPS+	vL+	vR+	bb%	ct%	Eye	G	L	F	h%	HctX	QBaB	Brl%	PX	xPX	HR/F	xHR/F	Spd	SBA%	SB%	RAR	BPX	R$
18																																			
19																																			
20																																			
21	ARI *	366	38	4	23	5	202	1	6	168	282	297	80	111	109	10	71	0.38	33	13	54	28	46	DBf	4%	58	51	0%	8%	144	13%	47%	-20.8	-19	$0
22	ARI	500	58	5	40	9	195	4	9	220	285	262	77	79	77	10	76	0.49	47	21	32	24	75	FDf	2%	44	63	5%	4%	108	9%	82%	-27.2	-17	$3
1st Half		247	23	2	15	2	207	2	5	223	307	282	83	88	82	12	75	0.54	47	22	30	27	79	FCf	3%	50	59	4%	4%	118	9%	67%	-9.9	0	-$2
2nd Half		253	35	3	25	7	183	2	4	217	262	243	72	72	71	9	78	0.43	46	21	33	22	72	FDf	2%	38	67	5%	4%	93	9%	88%	-15.3	-41	$7
23	**Proj**	**420**	**49**	**4**	**32**	**7**	**213**	**5**	**8**	**215**	**299**	**290**	**82**	**83**	**81**	**10**	**74**	**0.44**	**47**	**21**	**32**	**28**	**75**		**2%**	**51**	**64**	**5%**	**5%**	**126**	**9%**	**66%**	**-13.5**	**-22**	**$7**

Perez,Salvador

Age: 33	Pos: CA DH	Health	D	LIMA Plan	B
Bats: R	Ht: 6' 3" Wt: 255	PT/Exp	A	Rand Var	+3
		Consist	C	MM	4145

Thumb injury, mid-season surgery shelved him for 5+ weeks. Almost 200 fewer AB and overdue HR/F regression predictably tanked his overall production from 2021. But 2nd half rebound says he's still a force, with power metrics all still buying in (see ct% over that span). Only health could prevent 30 HR; more DH AB should help. Bid confidently.

Yr	Tm	PA	R	HR	RBI	SB	BA	xHR	xSB	xBA	OBP	SLG	OPS+	vL+	vR+	bb%	ct%	Eye	G	L	F	h%	HctX	QBaB	Brl%	PX	xPX	HR/F	xHR/F	Spd	SBA%	SB%	RAR	BPX	R$
18	KC *	568	55	28	84	1	238	26	6	258	262	444	95	93	95	3	79	0.15	35	20	45	25	134	AAb	11%	116	149	15%	14%	41	2%	50%	7.9	100	$13
19																																			
20	KC	156	22	11	32	1	333	12	1	302	353	633	131	117	135	2	76	0.08	36	27	37	38	131	ABb	14%	168	175	26%	28%	63	3%	100%	16.9	252	$23
21	KC	665	88	48	121	1	273	49	2	270	316	544	118	134	112	4	73	0.16	37	23	40	30	130	ABd	16%	152	153	26%	27%	54	1%	100%	32.9	150	$29
22	KC	473	48	23	76	0	254	26	1	250	292	465	107	118	103	4	76	0.17	36	18	46	29	113	AAc	11%	132	131	15%	17%	70	0%	0%	12.5	131	$15
1st Half		236	25	11	34	0	211	11	0	234	254	426	96	124	84	4	71	0.14	38	13	49	24	98	ABc	11%	146	124	14%	14%	76	0%	0%	-1.8	114	$7
2nd Half		237	23	12	42	0	297	15	1	270	329	505	118	110	120	4	80	0.20	34	23	43	33	128	AAc	12%	121	137	15%	19%	65	0%	0%	14.5	162	$19
23	**Proj**	**525**	**61**	**32**	**88**	**1**	**264**	**34**	**0**	**266**	**302**	**505**	**112**	**119**	**109**	**4**	**76**	**0.16**	**36**	**21**	**43**	**29**	**124**		**13%**	**149**	**144**	**19%**	**21%**	**60**	**1%**	**88%**	**25.4**	**152**	**$23**

Peterson,Jace

Age: 33	Pos: 3B	Health	C	LIMA Plan	D
Bats: L	Ht: 6' 0" Wt: 215	PT/Exp	C	Rand Var	0
		Consist	A	MM	2313

Injuries and versatility created 1st half opportunity that he made the most of, with early running game success and power surge. Sprained elbow shelved him for almost 6 weeks beginning in late July; the same traction and playing time were elusive following his return. Full season a mirror image of 2022 and his upside. Age, R$ are instructive.

Yr	Tm	PA	R	HR	RBI	SB	BA	xHR	xSB	xBA	OBP	SLG	OPS+	vL+	vR+	bb%	ct%	Eye	G	L	F	h%	HctX	QBaB	Brl%	PX	xPX	HR/F	xHR/F	Spd	SBA%	SB%	RAR	BPX	R$
18	2 AL	246	21	3	28	13	200	4	3	232	310	324	85	52	90	13	72	0.53	48	19	34	26	74	CCd	3%	88	65	6%	8%	80	28%	81%	-9.4	37	$4
19	BAL *	467	55	9	44	13	236	2	16	257	300	373	93	99	77	8	78	0.41	43	25	32	28	95	CCb	4%	74	97	8%	8%	95	17%	73%	-22.1	67	$9
20	MIL	61	6	2	5	1	200	2	2	181	393	356	99	52	102	25	56	0.75	54	15	31	30	86	BDa	8%	110	117	25%	25%	103	5%	100%	-0.8	-28	$0
21	MIL *	362	43	9	42	11	233	7	4	228	326	371	96	85	101	12	70	0.46	41	23	35	30	71	CCd	5%	88	77	9%	10%	91	13%	91%	-1.8	15	$9
22	MIL	328	44	8	34	12	236	8	6	240	316	382	99	101	99	10	70	0.39	45	23	32	31	96	CDd	7%	102	119	12%	12%	95	16%	92%	-1.4	48	$10
1st Half		215	30	7	27	10	251	6	4	257	322	445	108	112	108	9	72	0.35	45	20	35	32	105	CDf	8%	133	144	15%	13%	99	16%	100%	5.5	148	$15
2nd Half		113	14	1	7	2	206	1	2	213	304	258	79	76	80	13	68	0.45	46	28	25	29	79	CCb	5%	39	68	6%	6%	82	16%	67%	-5.0	-155	-$5
23	**Proj**	**315**	**39**	**6**	**32**	**10**	**226**	**6**	**7**	**230**	**316**	**345**	**92**	**85**	**93**	**11**	**71**	**0.44**	**44**	**24**	**32**	**30**	**83**		**6%**	**86**	**89**	**10%**	**9%**	**88**	**12%**	**85%**	**-1.1**	**-2**	**$10**

Pham,Tommy

Age: 35	Pos: LF	Health	C	LIMA Plan	C+
Bats: R	Ht: 6' 1" Wt: 223	PT/Exp	A	Rand Var	-1
		Consist	A	MM	2215

More signs of age. HR barely upticked along with PA, as poor HR/F trend and lofty GB% remain entrenched. 2nd half running game disappeared, with opportunity, back issues among the culprits. HctX, exit velocity are in good shape, double-digit HR/SB again within reach ... barely. But another 2nd half drop-off is now a warning. DN: 350 PA.

Yr	Tm	PA	R	HR	RBI	SB	BA	xHR	xSB	xBA	OBP	SLG	OPS+	vL+	vR+	bb%	ct%	Eye	G	L	F	h%	HctX	QBaB	Brl%	PX	xPX	HR/F	xHR/F	Spd	SBA%	SB%	RAR	BPX	R$
18	2 TM	570	102	21	63	15	275	25	9	258	367	464	111	116	108	12	72	0.48	48	24	28	35	128	ADb	10%	113	123	21%	25%	145	13%	68%	17.2	153	$24
19	TAM	654	77	21	68	25	273	24	15	281	369	450	113	131	105	12	78	0.66	53	22	25	32	118	AFc	8%	95	95	19%	22%	106	16%	86%	12.7	178	$25
20	SD	125	13	3	12	6	211	5	3	223	312	312	83	126	66	12	75	0.56	62	13	24	25	145	AFd	7%	54	101	15%	25%	101	18%	100%	-6.8	0	$8
21	SD	561	74	15	49	14	229	18	16	244	340	383	99	94	101	14	73	0.61	48	20	32	28	111	ADd	10%	95	116	14%	16%	104	13%	70%	-0.8	112	$13
22	2 TM	622	89	17	63	8	236	17	12	227	312	374	97	110	93	9	70	0.34	48	18	34	31	117	ADd	8%	96	99	13%	13%	95	7%	73%	-4.5	17	$16
1st Half		301	48	11	34	7	253	10	6	233	342	418	107	118	103	12	72	0.49	46	17	37	31	125	ACc	10%	108	122	15%	14%	92	7%	100%	7.9	93	$23
2nd Half		321	41	6	29	1	222	7	5	220	283	334	88	100	84	6	68	0.22	50	20	30	30	109	ADf	7%	85	78	10%	11%	95	7%	25%	-10.7	-55	$10
23	**Proj**	**490**	**68**	**13**	**48**	**11**	**235**	**16**	**6**	**235**	**322**	**374**	**97**	**107**	**93**	**11**	**72**	**0.43**	**50**	**19**	**31**	**30**	**118**		**9%**	**96**	**104**	**14%**	**16%**	**94**	**7%**	**76%**	**1.9**	**52**	**$16**

JOCK THOMPSON

Pinder,Chad

Age: 31 Pos: LF RF	Health D	LIMA Plan D	
Bats: R Ht: 6' 2" Wt: 210	PT/Exp C	Rand Var -2	
	Consist A	MM 3213	

Bench player with career-high PA on a rebuilder and in MLB's worst offensive lineup. Decaying plate skills, BA took another step down; exit velocity, HctX cratered despite relatively good health. 2nd-half vL still hints at limited utility, good for double-digit HR with enough AB, but that ceiling isn't a lock. Still just fantasy waiver fodder.

Yr	Tm	PA	R	HR	RBI	SB	BA	xHR	xSB	xBA	OBP	SLG	OPS+	vL+	vR+	bb%	ct%	Eye	G	L	F	h%	HctX	QBaB	Brl%	PX	xPX	HR/F	xHR/F	Spd	SBA%	SB%	RAR	BPX	R$
18	OAK	333	43	13	27	0	258	18	5	233	332	436	103	111	94	8	70	0.31	44	19	37	32	120	ACb	14%	112	136	17%	23%	115	2%	0%	0.7	80	$6
19	OAK	370	45	13	47	0	240	14	1	258	290	416	98	104	92	5	74	0.23	49	22	29	29	105	ADc	8%	101	91	17%	19%	76	1%	0%	-12.4	48	$5
20	OAK	61	8	2	8	0	232	3	0	229	295	393	91	77	101	8	77	0.38	49	14	37	27	116	ACc	9%	93	90	13%	19%	105	0%	0%	-2.6	124	$1
21	OAK *	262	34	7	33	1	239	12	1	248	289	408	96	120	76	7	70	0.24	48	21	31	31	109	ADc	16%	116	136	13%	26%	103	2%	100%	-2.4	73	$4
22	OAK	378	38	12	42	2	235	11	1	230	263	385	92	102	84	4	67	0.12	49	20	31	32	83	CCd	7%	111	84	16%	15%	71	3%	100%	-7.2	-34	$6
1st Half		207	16	5	17	2	234	6	1	222	262	360	88	82	92	4	65	0.12	52	21	27	33	81	CDd	7%	101	78	14%	17%	81	3%	100%	-4.9	-79	$1
2nd Half		171	22	7	25	0	238	5	1	237	263	415	96	124	74	4	70	0.12	46	19	35	30	85	DCd	7%	123	92	18%	13%	71	3%	0%	-1.8	24	$6
23	Proj	**280**	**33**	**9**	**34**	**1**	**240**	**11**	**2**	**237**	**282**	**400**	**95**	**108**	**83**	**5**	**69**	**0.18**	**48**	**20**	**32**	**31**	**97**		**10%**	**118**	**104**	**15%**	**19%**	**84**	**4%**	**77%**	**-0.5**	**26**	**$4**

Polanco,Jorge

Age: 29 Pos: 2B	Health B	LIMA Plan B	
Bats: B Ht: 5' 11" Wt: 208	PT/Exp A	Rand Var +1	
	Consist B	MM 4135	

Poor April, June back woes, 2nd-half knee injury impeded lift-off, the latter finishing him in late August. BA, ct% will bounce back with health, but LD%, h% trends temper expectations. Soaring bb%, FB tilt, stable power metrics say power is still most likely profit path. Durability now in question, but age says buy the projected rebound.

Yr	Tm	PA	R	HR	RBI	SB	BA	xHR	xSB	xBA	OBP	SLG	OPS+	vL+	vR+	bb%	ct%	Eye	G	L	F	h%	HctX	QBaB	Brl%	PX	xPX	HR/F	xHR/F	Spd	SBA%	SB%	RAR	BPX	R$
18	MIN	333	38	6	42	7	288	5	5	255	345	427	104	83	112	8	79	0.40	36	26	38	35	94	DAc	4%	86	76	7%	6%	106	16%	50%	7.2	117	$10
19	MIN	704	107	22	79	4	295	26	18	267	356	485	116	101	122	9	82	0.52	29	26	44	33	112	CAb	7%	97	132	10%	11%	122	4%	57%	24.6	222	$23
20	MIN	226	22	4	19	4	258	4	2	243	304	354	87	105	81	6	83	0.37	36	25	39	29	82	DBc	3%	53	75	6%	6%	89	11%	67%	-6.1	64	$14
21	MIN	644	97	33	98	11	269	31	8	273	323	503	114	109	116	7	80	0.38	32	23	45	29	109	CAd	10%	128	117	16%	15%	78	12%	65%	21.2	235	$28
22	MIN	445	54	16	56	3	235	19	8	236	346	405	106	84	118	14	75	0.67	30	22	48	27	108	CAc	10%	109	120	12%	14%	73	5%	50%	10.3	134	$10
1st Half		281	32	10	41	3	240	11	5	241	335	405	105	90	111	13	74	0.57	32	24	44	28	99	CAc	11%	106	105	13%	14%	75	5%	60%	4.5	107	$15
2nd Half		164	22	6	15	0	226	8	3	229	366	406	109	77	132	17	76	0.88	26	18	56	25	124	CAa	10%	113	148	11%	14%	83	5%	0%	3.2	193	$2
23	Proj	**560**	**75**	**23**	**70**	**6**	**251**	**25**	**5**	**252**	**337**	**447**	**109**	**93**	**117**	**11**	**78**	**0.57**	**31**	**22**	**47**	**28**	**108**		**10%**	**120**	**118**	**13%**	**14%**	**80**	**4%**	**55%**	**18.6**	**173**	**$21**

Pollock,A.J.

Age: 35 Pos: LF CF	Health D	LIMA Plan B+	
Bats: R Ht: 6' 1" Wt: 210	PT/Exp A	Rand Var +3	
	Consist C	MM 3235	

More hamstring woes shelved him for 11 days in April, factored into SBA% as running game vanished. Atypical struggles vR (.593 OPS, 3 HR) persisted throughout, as did dominance vL. Exit velocity drooped, age is now relevant. But healthy HR, contact skills during Aug/Sept rebound say he's not done yet. There's profit potential in an underbid.

Yr	Tm	PA	R	HR	RBI	SB	BA	xHR	xSB	xBA	OBP	SLG	OPS+	vL+	vR+	bb%	ct%	Eye	G	L	F	h%	HctX	QBaB	Brl%	PX	xPX	HR/F	xHR/F	Spd	SBA%	SB%	RAR	BPX	R$
18	ARI	460	61	21	65	13	257	21	6	265	316	484	107	98	110	7	76	0.31	42	19	38	29	124	CCc	10%	132	146	17%	17%	118	15%	87%	7.4	200	$18
19	LA	342	49	15	47	5	266	15	7	258	327	468	110	126	102	7	76	0.31	43	20	37	31	115	BCd	8%	106	94	17%	17%	99	7%	83%	0.5	126	$10
20	LA	210	30	16	34	2	276	11	2	281	314	566	117	155	101	6	77	0.27	40	20	40	28	130	BCc	10%	150	158	26%	18%	87	10%	50%	3.7	272	$24
21	LA	422	53	21	69	9	297	19	6	283	355	536	123	119	124	7	79	0.38	40	22	39	33	122	BCf	11%	135	127	18%	16%	95	10%	90%	27.0	265	$21
22	CHW	527	61	14	56	3	245	16	7	252	292	389	96	131	84	6	80	0.33	45	19	36	28	117	CCf	9%	91	104	10%	11%	84	4%	75%	-3.7	110	$12
1st Half		237	28	4	24	1	242	7	3	232	278	359	90	133	77	5	77	0.21	43	19	38	30	101	CCf	10%	81	99	6%	11%	98	4%	100%	-4.4	41	$5
2nd Half		290	33	10	32	2	248	9	4	267	303	414	102	129	90	7	83	0.46	47	19	34	27	130	CCf	9%	99	107	13%	12%	73	4%	67%	1.5	169	$15
23	Proj	**490**	**62**	**19**	**66**	**4**	**266**	**19**	**3**	**263**	**316**	**450**	**106**	**124**	**99**	**6**	**79**	**0.33**	**43**	**20**	**37**	**30**	**121**		**10%**	**116**	**118**	**14%**	**14%**	**85**	**4%**	**73%**	**14.1**	**182**	**$20**

Pratto,Nick

Age: 24 Pos: 1B	Health A	LIMA Plan D+	
Bats: L Ht: 6' 1" Wt: 195	PT/Exp B	Rand Var 0	
	Consist D	MM 4203	

7-20-.184 in 182 PA at KC. Rough MLB debut followed 2nd half promotion; optioned out again after 2-for-27 / 13K stretch in mid-Sept. PX/xPX, FB% bb% look healthy enough, but poor contact skills, BA fell apart at the highest level. Power, age, handedness offer hope for more near-term opportunity, but more minor league time is as good a bet.

Yr	Tm	PA	R	HR	RBI	SB	BA	xHR	xSB	xBA	OBP	SLG	OPS+	vL+	vR+	bb%	ct%	Eye	G	L	F	h%	HctX	QBaB	Brl%	PX	xPX	HR/F	xHR/F	Spd	SBA%	SB%	RAR	BPX	R$
18																																			
19																																			
20																																			
21	a/a	508	74	25	74	9	232		6		328	487	112			12	63	0.38				31				173				113	14%	62%		192	$15
22	KC *	518	51	16	47	5	180	6	8	180	263	335	85	93	93	10	59	0.27	33	14	53	26	78	DAf	13%	124	139	14%	12%	95	7%	67%	-20.5	-48	$1
1st Half		275	28	7	25	5	179		4	194	250	311	79	0	0	9	58	0.23	44	20	36	28	0			108	-14	0%		120	7%	80%	-15.7	-90	$5
2nd Half		243	23	9	22	0	182	6	4	193	278	364	91	93	93	12	60	0.33	33	14	53	25	79	DAf	13%	143	139	14%	12%	90	7%	0%	-8.8	21	$2
23	Proj	**350**	**41**	**11**	**40**	**4**	**201**	**11**	**4**	**202**	**291**	**376**	**93**	**94**	**92**	**11**	**61**	**0.33**	**36**	**17**	**47**	**28**	**71**		**11%**	**137**	**125**	**13%**	**12%**	**95**	**7%**	**62%**	**-6.4**	**62**	**$6**

Profar,Jurickson

Age: 30 Pos: LF	Health A	LIMA Plan B+	
Bats: B Ht: 6' 0" Wt: 184	PT/Exp A	Rand Var +2	
	Consist B	MM 2335	

Exit velocity, HctX returned along with productivity vL, all big contributors to career-high PA and counting stats that fueled value. Apart from rock-solid plate skills, nothing else shines. HR look inflated; running game still hints at more with cooperation from SBA. R$ history is all over the map, which should inform your bidding. DN: 400 AB.

Yr	Tm	PA	R	HR	RBI	SB	BA	xHR	xSB	xBA	OBP	SLG	OPS+	vL+	vR+	bb%	ct%	Eye	G	L	F	h%	HctX	QBaB	Brl%	PX	xPX	HR/F	xHR/F	Spd	SBA%	SB%	RAR	BPX	R$
18	TEX	594	82	20	77	10	254	14	8	288	335	458	106	105	105	9	83	0.61	44	22	34	27	114	CCc	5%	115	98	13%	9%	114	7%	100%	8.8	263	$19
19	OAK	518	65	20	67	9	218	18	5	277	301	410	98	116	92	9	84	0.64	41	22	37	22	109	CCd	7%	93	98	14%	13%	82	9%	90%	-17.2	200	$10
20	SD	202	28	7	25	7	278	5	3	276	343	428	102	100	103	7	84	0.54	44	25	31	30	99	CCf	3%	74	58	15%	11%	101	14%	88%	-0.4	176	$23
21	SD	411	47	4	33	10	227	4	10	239	329	320	89	65	96	12	82	0.75	42	21	37	27	78	DBf	3%	57	53	4%	4%	117	13%	67%	-13.3	127	$6
22	SD	658	82	15	58	5	243	10	14	268	331	391	102	103	102	11	82	0.71	44	22	34	27	106	CCd	4%	94	86	9%	6%	110	4%	83%	6.5	210	$14
1st Half		359	50	8	38	4	244	5	8	276	345	399	105	98	109	13	83	0.88	43	23	34	27	94	CCc	5%	97	80	9%	6%	109	4%	80%	5.4	245	$20
2nd Half		299	32	7	20	1	243	5	6	256	314	382	99	110	94	9	81	0.53	45	20	35	28	119	CCf	3%	91	92	9%	7%	110	4%	100%	0.1	172	$9
23	Proj	**525**	**65**	**12**	**49**	**8**	**241**	**9**	**6**	**259**	**327**	**377**	**98**	**95**	**99**	**11**	**82**	**0.66**	**43**	**22**	**35**	**27**	**99**		**4%**	**86**	**75**	**9%**	**6%**	**110**	**5%**	**76%**	**3.7**	**179**	**$15**

Pujols,Albert

Age: 43 Pos: DH 1B	Health A	LIMA Plan F	
Bats: R Ht: 6' 3" Wt: 235	PT/Exp B	Rand Var 0	
	Consist B	MM 0000	

Past-prime HOFer-to-be entered 2022 unrosterable even in deep leagues; inked final 1yr deal in glory-days setting. Poor 1st half confirmed sentimental farewell tour ... until somehow it wasn't anymore. Paired enduring contact skills with 2H power callback, winning fantasy leagues and giving everyone one last thrill in the process. King Albert indeed.

Yr	Tm	PA	R	HR	RBI	SB	BA	xHR	xSB	xBA	OBP	SLG	OPS+	vL+	vR+	bb%	ct%	Eye	G	L	F	h%	HctX	QBaB	Brl%	PX	xPX	HR/F	xHR/F	Spd	SBA%	SB%	RAR	BPX	R$
18	LAA	498	50	19	64	1	245	17	6	272	289	411	94	89	94	6	86	0.43	40	22	37	25	134	BCd	6%	88	122	13%	11%	59	1%	100%	-6.8	150	$10
19	LAA	545	55	23	93	3	244	20	1	261	305	430	102	115	94	8	86	0.63	46	15	39	24	116	CCd	6%	86	90	14%	12%	60	2%	100%	-11.5	181	$12
20	LAA	163	15	6	25	0	224	4	0	253	270	395	88	82	92	6	84	0.36	40	20	41	23	103	CBf	5%	89	94	12%	8%	56	0%	0%	-6.4	140	$6
21	2 TM	296	29	17	50	2	236	13	0	252	284	433	98	128	69	5	84	0.31	46	16	38	23	130	BCf	9%	90	105	19%	15%	64	3%	100%	-9.0	142	$7
22	STL	351	42	24	68	1	270	18	2	285	345	550	127	161	106	8	82	0.51	38	17	45	26	145	ABf	12%	154	156	21%	15%	63	4%	33%	14.6	307	$15
1st Half		142	11	4	17	1	189	4	1	226	282	320	85	103	72	10	78	0.48	43	17	40	21	122	BBf	7%	80	105	10%	10%	71	4%	50%	-7.8	62	-$5
2nd Half		209	31	20	51	0	324	14	1	326	388	703	154	204	126	8	85	0.54	35	16	49	29	160	AAf	14%	199	187	26%	18%	66	4%	0%	25.3	466	$29
23	Proj																																		

Raleigh,Cal

Age: 26 Pos: CA	Health A	LIMA Plan C+	
Bats: R Ht: 6' 3" Wt: 215	PT/Exp C	Rand Var +5	
	Consist B	MM 5123	

27-63-.211 in 415 PA at SEA. Briefly demoted in April, just one HR thru mid-May. Subsequent HR show had legs even through Sept injuries (broken thumb, torn ligaments), turning Big Dumper into SEA folk hero. BA, ct% issues look enduring, though xBA, h% regression suggest a tad better. Power metrics look unassailable. UP: .250 BA, 30+ HR.

Yr	Tm	PA	R	HR	RBI	SB	BA	xHR	xSB	xBA	OBP	SLG	OPS+	vL+	vR+	bb%	ct%	Eye	G	L	F	h%	HctX	QBaB	Brl%	PX	xPX	HR/F	xHR/F	Spd	SBA%	SB%	RAR	BPX	R$
18																																			
19	aa	159	16	7	16	0	217		2		287	403	95			9	63	0.26				29				115				96	0%	0%		-22	-$1
20																																			
21	SEA *	334	31	8	39	2	224	3	2	239	265	399	91	79	72	5	73	0.21	36	18	45	28	65	CBf	7%	120	78	5%	8%	78	8%	47%	-5.4	96	$3
22	SEA *	444	48	28	65	1	210	25	4	243	281	477	107	103	112	9	67	0.30	28	16	56	23	108	AAc	15%	183	157	19%	18%	91	1%	100%	9.9	214	$9
1st Half		213	19	11	29	1	197	9	2	235	266	432	99	125	94	9	67	0.28	30	17	53	23	118	AAc	15%	167	165	17%	15%	112	1%	100%	0.6	183	$5
2nd Half		231	29	17	36	0	223	15	2	252	294	519	115	80	125	9	67	0.31	27	15	58	24	100	BAc	15%	198	151	21%	18%	77	1%	0%	9.1	248	$16
23	Proj	**420**	**50**	**24**	**62**	**1**	**234**	**23**	**1**	**251**	**292**	**494**	**109**	**104**	**110**	**7**	**69**	**0.26**	**32**	**17**	**52**	**27**	**91**		**12%**	**181**	**125**	**17%**	**17%**	**77**	**2%**	**59%**	**16.3**	**147**	**$14**

JOCK THOMPSON

Ramirez,Harold

Age: 28 Pos: DH 1B RF	Health F	LIMA Plan B
Bats: R Ht: 5' 10" Wt: 232	PT/Exp B	Rand Var -5
	Consist C	MM 2133

HctX, exit velocity down from elite levels, but plus ct% is entrenched, and it's better to be lucky than good. GB-hitter mauled LHP, as line-to-line approach and inflated h% fueled career-best PA and BA excellence in a season where this was scarce. Near-repeat is possible; so is an empty .270 average. Consistency grade speaks volumes.

Yr Tm	PA	R	HR	RBI	SB	BA	xHR	xSB	xBA	OBP	SLG	OPS+	vL+	vR+	bb%	ct%	Eye	G	L	F	h%	HctX	QBaB	Brl%	PX	xPX	HR/F	xHR/F	Spd	SBA%	SB%	RAR	BPX	R$
18 aa	485	50	9	58	13	292		6		324	429	101			5	79	0.23				35				94				81	13%	86%		87	$18
19 MIA *	560	71	14	62	3	282	11	11	271	312	433	103	92	103	4	79	0.21	57	20	23	34	95	CFb	6%	82	63	14%	14%	103	4%	57%	-7.8	78	$14
20 MIA	11	2	0	1	0	200	0	0	176	273	200	63	65	60	9	80	0.50	50	13	38	25	81	FCf		0	161	0%	0%	91	33%	0%	-1.3	-124	-$2
21 CLE	361	33	7	41	3	268	8	12	260	305	398	97	105	92	4	83	0.25	53	17	30	30	120	ADd	6%	77	92	8%	9%	74	5%	75%	-9.3	104	$8
22 TAM	435	46	6	58	3	300	6	4	253	343	404	106	122	99	4	82	0.26	53	19	28	35	104	CFd	5%	72	76	6%	6%	87	7%	38%	0.4	79	$16
1st Half	227	28	4	29	3	314	3	2	271	361	430	112	128	104	6	84	0.42	52	21	27	36	104	CFd	6%	76	79	9%	6%	89	7%	50%	5.0	131	$13
2nd Half	208	18	2	29	0	286	3	2	232	322	378	99	113	95	2	80	0.13	53	17	30	35	104	CFd	3%	68	72	4%	6%	86	7%	0%	-3.9	28	$6
23 Proj	**420**	**44**	**7**	**54**	**4**	**286**	**8**	**4**	**254**	**324**	**405**	**101**	**111**	**97**	**4**	**82**	**0.22**	**53**	**18**	**28**	**34**	**110**		**5%**	**81**	**81**	**8%**	**8%**	**75**	**5%**	**54%**	**2.5**	**82**	**$13**

Ramírez,José

Age: 30 Pos: 3B DH	Health B	LIMA Plan C
Bats: B Ht: 5' 9" Wt: 190	PT/Exp A	Rand Var 0
	Consist B	MM 4355

More elite fantasy value at a scarce position. Not as much hard contact as in 2021, but plate approach, ct% and healthy FB% were more than enough to spike BA. All while playing through 2nd-half wrist injury that required offseason surgery. One has to squint to see running game slippage, but ... nah, no need to go there. Still first 3B off the board.

Yr Tm	PA	R	HR	RBI	SB	BA	xHR	xSB	xBA	OBP	SLG	OPS+	vL+	vR+	bb%	ct%	Eye	G	L	F	h%	HctX	QBaB	Brl%	PX	xPX	HR/F	xHR/F	Spd	SBA%	SB%	RAR	BPX	R$
18 CLE	698	110	39	105	34	270	26	11	299	387	552	126	107	131	15	86	1.33	33	21	46	25	115	CAc	8%	146	119	17%	11%	89	21%	85%	53.6	403	$40
19 CLE	542	68	23	83	24	255	21	14	273	327	479	112	110	112	10	85	0.70	33	21	46	26	118	CAc	6%	109	114	12%	11%	94	24%	86%	6.6	278	$23
20 CLE	254	45	17	46	10	292	14	9	285	386	607	132	184	113	12	80	0.72	30	19	51	30	108	CAc	10%	163	134	19%	16%	101	20%	77%	20.9	436	$42
21 CLE	636	111	36	103	27	266	30	18	287	355	538	123	120	124	11	84	0.83	36	19	45	26	137	BAf	11%	136	125	17%	14%	102	20%	87%	40.9	388	$37
22 CLE	685	90	29	126	20	280	19	19	279	355	514	123	102	130	10	86	0.84	32	17	51	28	110	CAf	7%	133	100	11%	7%	102	16%	74%	41.2	362	$39
1st Half	329	47	16	63	12	289	8	9	301	374	578	135	106	147	12	89	1.19	31	15	54	28	119	CAf	7%	160	113	12%	6%	96	16%	80%	28.8	472	$40
2nd Half	356	43	13	63	8	271	10	10	259	337	455	112	97	117	9	84	0.62	34	19	47	29	102	CAf	6%	107	89	10%	8%	103	16%	67%	9.7	252	$34
23 Proj	**665**	**101**	**33**	**118**	**21**	**283**	**25**	**16**	**282**	**364**	**534**	**125**	**119**	**127**	**11**	**85**	**0.81**	**33**	**18**	**48**	**29**	**118**		**8%**	**142**	**112**	**14%**	**10%**	**102**	**13%**	**77%**	**51.3**	**364**	**$42**

Ramos,Heliot

Age: 23 Pos: OF	Health A	LIMA Plan F
Bats: R Ht: 6' 1" Wt: 188	PT/Exp B	Rand Var +4
	Consist B	MM 1201

0-0-.100 in 20 AB at SF. Once-shiny prospect with a brief, inconsequential look in his MLB debut. Still owns youth and speed, but power and running game haven't materialized at higher levels; plate skills and GB% look distressed. Has time to catch his breath with more development at Triple-A. But this looks like a fourth OF profile at best.

Yr Tm	PA	R	HR	RBI	SB	BA	xHR	xSB	xBA	OBP	SLG	OPS+	vL+	vR+	bb%	ct%	Eye	G	L	F	h%	HctX	QBaB	Brl%	PX	xPX	HR/F	xHR/F	Spd	SBA%	SB%	RAR	BPX	R$
18																																		
19 aa	105	13	3	15	2	244		1		318	416	102			10	65	0.31				35				113				111	22%	40%		19	$0
20																																		
21 a/a	481	50	9	43	11	218		5		270	341	84			7	66	0.21				31				88				102	15%	78%		-69	$7
22 SF *	475	41	6	27	4	176	1	8	189	224	253	68	49	0	6	70	0.21	64	7	29	24	87	CFf	7%	58	39	0%	25%	106	13%	35%	-35.3	-93	-$5
1st Half	279	24	3	14	1	173	1	5	186	223	243	66	60	0	6	70	0.21	60	10	30	23	122	ADa	10%	51	60	0%	33%	123	13%	21%	-21.0	-103	-$6
2nd Half	196	17	3	13	2	180	0	3	188	226	267	70	23	0	6	70	0.20	75	0	25	24	0	FFf		67	-14	0%	0%	99	13%	52%	-13.0	-76	-$4
23 Proj	**175**	**17**	**3**	**14**	**3**	**224**	**3**	**3**	**212**	**275**	**324**	**83**	**82**	**83**	**7**	**68**	**0.22**	**48**	**21**	**29**	**31**	**91**		**6%**	**78**		**8%**	**8%**	**113**	**11%**	**55%**	**-5.1**	**-69**	**$3**

Realmuto,J.T.

Age: 32 Pos: CA	Health A	LIMA Plan D+
Bats: R Ht: 6' 1" Wt: 212	PT/Exp A	Rand Var 0
	Consist A	MM 4435

Doesn't get more consistent behind the plate. But this was a tale of two halves, with 1st half stalled by swing, launch angle issues. Once adjusted, he crushed the rest of the way, with EV, Brl%, xHR leaving us wondering if there's another level. Running game spike a huge, unexpected bonus; health still an elite skill. Still first catcher off the board.

Yr Tm	PA	R	HR	RBI	SB	BA	xHR	xSB	xBA	OBP	SLG	OPS+	vL+	vR+	bb%	ct%	Eye	G	L	F	h%	HctX	QBaB	Brl%	PX	xPX	HR/F	xHR/F	Spd	SBA%	SB%	RAR	BPX	R$
18 MIA	529	74	21	74	3	277	22	7	272	340	484	111	86	116	7	78	0.37	40	23	37	32	111	CBc	9%	123	110	15%	16%	108	4%	60%	28.0	200	$18
19 PHI	592	92	25	83	9	275	22	5	272	328	493	114	118	111	7	77	0.33	39	23	38	32	122	BBb	9%	117	118	16%	14%	111	8%	90%	21.0	189	$21
20 PHI	195	33	11	32	4	266	12	3	244	349	491	112	142	100	8	72	0.33	48	14	38	31	110	BCd	14%	124	121	23%	26%	93	10%	80%	7.8	136	$23
21 PHI	537	64	17	73	13	263	17	11	249	343	439	107	99	111	9	73	0.37	46	20	33	33	107	BCc	9%	107	98	15%	15%	132	12%	81%	16.5	142	$19
22 PHI	562	75	22	84	21	276	22	11	266	342	478	116	113	117	7	76	0.34	44	20	36	32	115	BCc	11%	125	112	16%	16%	122	16%	95%	31.0	203	$31
1st Half	291	39	7	34	11	244	6	6	237	320	384	99	98	100	8	76	0.37	46	17	37	30	100	CCc	6%	89	76	10%	8%	134	16%	100%	4.8	117	$20
2nd Half	271	36	15	50	10	309	16	5	295	365	577	134	132	134	7	77	0.32	42	23	35	35	130	ACb	17%	162	149	22%	24%	104	16%	91%	28.0	290	$35
23 Proj	**560**	**77**	**23**	**86**	**17**	**274**	**24**	**14**	**262**	**344**	**478**	**114**	**112**	**115**	**8**	**75**	**0.34**	**45**	**20**	**35**	**33**	**114**		**11%**	**130**	**113**	**17%**	**17%**	**103**	**12%**	**89%**	**34.3**	**186**	**$31**

Rendon,Anthony

Age: 33 Pos: 3B	Health F	LIMA Plan B
Bats: R Ht: 6' 1" Wt: 200	PT/Exp D	Rand Var +4
	Consist C	MM 3245

A second consecutive poor start followed by season-ending surgery (wrist this time) that finished him before the All-Star break. Firm plate skills, HctX point to BA, OBP rebounds with health. Stagnant power should also get a boost, but these metrics showed slippage before the injuries. Durability is everything; age+brittleness = risk/reward play.

Yr Tm	PA	R	HR	RBI	SB	BA	xHR	xSB	xBA	OBP	SLG	OPS+	vL+	vR+	bb%	ct%	Eye	G	L	F	h%	HctX	QBaB	Brl%	PX	xPX	HR/F	xHR/F	Spd	SBA%	SB%	RAR	BPX	R$
18 WAS	597	88	24	92	2	308	27	9	292	374	535	122	123	119	9	84	0.67	33	24	44	33	118	BAc	10%	130	122	12%	14%	95	2%	67%	43.1	303	$26
19 WAS	646	117	34	126	5	319	38	5	296	412	598	140	146	137	12	84	0.93	33	21	46	33	130	BAb	12%	136	160	16%	18%	97	3%	83%	59.7	374	$33
20 LAA	232	29	9	31	0	286	7	3	270	418	497	122	131	117	16	84	1.23	35	21	44	30	146	BAb	6%	108	119	13%	10%	106	0%	0%	12.4	348	$18
21 LAA	249	24	6	34	0	240	5	0	245	329	382	98	87	103	12	81	0.71	31	22	47	27	99	CAb	6%	84	97	7%	6%	69	0%	0%	0.5	146	$2
22 LAA	193	15	5	24	2	229	5	0	252	326	380	100	122	91	12	79	0.66	35	23	42	26	114	BAc	8%	99	106	9%	9%	73	4%	100%	0.7	148	$1
1st Half	188	15	5	24	2	228	5	0	255	324	383	100	120	92	12	80	0.72	36	22	42	26	117	BAc	8%	100	107	9%	9%	73	4%	100%	0.0	172	$1
2nd Half	5	0	0	0	0	250	0	0	224	400	250	92	163	0	0	25	0.00	0	100	0	100	0							96	4%	0%	-0.2	-928	-$11
23 Proj	**455**	**53**	**16**	**66**	**2**	**265**	**14**	**4**	**266**	**365**	**452**	**113**	**120**	**110**	**13**	**82**	**0.84**	**34**	**22**	**44**	**29**	**124**		**8%**	**115**	**115**	**11%**	**10%**	**82**	**4%**	**93%**	**21.5**	**253**	**$17**

Renfroe,Hunter

Age: 31 Pos: RF	Health B	LIMA Plan B
Bats: R Ht: 6' 1" Wt: 230	PT/Exp A	Rand Var -1
	Consist B	MM 4135

Consistently plus HR source with more good production and rock-solid power metrics. But the real news here is a BA repeat that may have staying power. Contact skills, xBA remained firm; in-line xBA says none of this was a fluke. 2nd half featured more improvement vR. Could give some back, but Mendoza Line downside is no longer a concern.

Yr Tm	PA	R	HR	RBI	SB	BA	xHR	xSB	xBA	OBP	SLG	OPS+	vL+	vR+	bb%	ct%	Eye	G	L	F	h%	HctX	QBaB	Brl%	PX	xPX	HR/F	xHR/F	Spd	SBA%	SB%	RAR	BPX	R$
18 SD *	483	57	27	71	2	241	23	5	259	291	483	104	107	106	6	73	0.26	37	20	43	27	126	BAd	12%	148	136	20%	18%	78	3%	67%	3.8	160	$13
19 SD	494	64	33	64	5	216	28	2	236	289	489	108	126	101	9	65	0.30	36	16	48	25	106	BAd	12%	159	144	24%	20%	76	6%	100%	-9.6	115	$11
20 TAM	139	18	8	22	2	156	7	1	227	252	393	86	105	75	10	70	0.38	42	10	48	14	98	BBf	9%	137	124	20%	17%	71	9%	100%	-8.9	128	$5
21 BOS	572	89	31	96	1	259	33	6	260	315	501	112	120	107	8	75	0.34	39	18	43	29	110	BBf	14%	141	114	18%	19%	66	3%	33%	9.7	192	$20
22 MIL	522	62	29	72	1	255	24	3	256	315	492	114	118	113	7	74	0.32	36	17	46	28	115	BBf	11%	147	131	18%	15%	85	2%	50%	14.4	200	$18
1st Half	217	27	13	27	0	247	12	1	251	300	490	112	121	108	7	73	0.28	37	16	47	27	112	BBf	14%	153	138	19%	17%	82	2%	0%	4.2	186	$10
2nd Half	305	35	16	45	1	261	12	2	259	327	493	116	115	116	8	76	0.36	36	18	46	29	116	BAf	9%	142	126	17%	13%	88	2%	100%	10.3	210	$24
23 Proj	**525**	**70**	**30**	**80**	**2**	**246**	**27**	**2**	**254**	**308**	**485**	**110**	**117**	**107**	**8**	**74**	**0.33**	**38**	**17**	**46**	**27**	**112**		**12%**	**153**	**126**	**18%**	**17%**	**70**	**2%**	**64%**	**15.1**	**184**	**$20**

Rengifo,Luis

Age: 26 Pos: 2B 3B	Health A	LIMA Plan B+
Bats: R Ht: 5' 10" Wt: 195	PT/Exp A	Rand Var -1
	Consist B	MM 2225

17-52-.264 with 6 SB in 511 PA at LAA. Unexpected breakout has limited support. Saw first AB a month into the season; 2nd-half power, uptick vR were encouraging. But season built on lefty-crushing (.909 OPS, 11 HR, 172 PA) doesn't seem sustainable. Owns ct% and legs, but this looks like regression waiting to happen. DN: 400 AB, 10 HR.

Yr Tm	PA	R	HR	RBI	SB	BA	xHR	xSB	xBA	OBP	SLG	OPS+	vL+	vR+	bb%	ct%	Eye	G	L	F	h%	HctX	QBaB	Brl%	PX	xPX	HR/F	xHR/F	Spd	SBA%	SB%	RAR	BPX	R$
18 a/a	376	55	4	36	14	246		5		317	364	91			9	82	0.59				29				68				135	25%	62%		153	$10
19 LAA *	523	54	11	42	4	234	9	18	241	304	362	92	85	99	9	74	0.39	48	22	30	29	83	CCc	6%	73	50	9%	11%	132	10%	32%	-19.1	56	$5
20 LAA	106	12	1	3	3	156	1	2	190	269	200	62	46	71	13	71	0.54	59	14	27	21	83	DFf	2%	26	55	6%	6%	114	15%	75%	-8.8	-124	-$1
21 LAA *	408	50	11	38	9	229	7	8	240	267	361	86	72	78	5	80	0.25	48	17	35	26	95	DCf	6%	72	77	13%	15%	114	18%	60%	-14.1	85	$8
22 LAA *	617	55	19	60	7	259	14	15	259	288	418	100	127	89	4	82	0.22	47	18	35	29	86	CCf	5%	93	67	12%	10%	130	8%	61%	6.5	169	$17
1st Half	278	25	7	20	3	239	4	7	248	280	384	94	125	83	5	77	0.25	43	22	35	28	84	CCf	5%	88	63	11%	9%	132	8%	47%	-3.7	110	$6
2nd Half	339	30	12	40	4	274	10	8	268	298	445	105	128	93	3	85	0.18	49	16	35	29	88	CCd	5%	97	69	12%	10%	120	8%	80%	6.5	207	$23
23 Proj	**560**	**60**	**16**	**50**	**6**	**238**	**16**	**8**	**247**	**286**	**381**	**92**	**100**	**88**	**6**	**80**	**0.29**	**48**	**18**	**34**	**27**	**88**		**5%**	**86**	**67**	**11%**	**11%**	**116**	**8%**	**60%**	**-3.4**	**108**	**$14**

JOCK THOMPSON

Reyes,Franmil

Age: 27	Pos: DH		Health	B	LIMA Plan	D+
Bats: R	Ht: 6' 5"	Wt: 265	PT/Exp	A	Rand Var	+1
			Consist	C	MM	4113

14-47-.221 in 473 PA at CLE/CHC. Slugger has walked a fine line despite elite EV that hints at more. Poor ct%, lofty GB% are also entrenched; together with the collapse of his patience, and more chasing, this outcome was foreseeable. Both BA, HR should rebound some; how much depends on his approach. DH-only adds to limitations.

Yr	Tm	PA	R	HR	RBI	SB	BA	xHR	xSB	xBA	OBP	SLG	OPS+	vL+	vR+	bb%	ct%	Eye	G	L	F	h%	HctX	QBaB	Brl%	PX	xPX	HR/F	xHR/F	Spd	SBA%	SB%	RAR	BPX	R$
18	SD *	521	71	27	68	0	275	13	8	246	345	487	112	136	99	10	68	0.34	49	21	30	35	111	ADd	12%	135	115	30%	24%	81	0%	0%	18.7	90	$17
19	2 TM	548	69	37	81	0	249	37	0	255	310	512	114	123	110	9	68	0.30	44	21	34	29	112	ACd	15%	145	140	31%	31%	51	0%	0%	3.0	89	$15
20	CLE	241	27	9	34	0	275	11	1	214	344	450	105	86	111	10	67	0.35	50	16	33	37	100	ACb	11%	111	104	18%	22%	87	0%	0%	3.9	24	$18
21	CLE	466	57	30	85	4	254	31	2	250	324	522	116	119	115	9	64	0.29	46	18	36	32	115	ACd	17%	171	153	31%	32%	88	5%	80%	8.2	158	$17
22	2 TM *	506	46	15	51	2	222	16	4	212	270	366	90	89	91	6	65	0.19	48	18	35	31	103	ACf	11%	107	116	14%	16%	96	6%	36%	-20.7	-41	$6
1st Half		221	18	7	24	0	222	6	2	194	265	364	89	71	92	6	59	0.14	43	20	37	34	99	ACd	14%	115	149	15%	15%	74	6%	0%	-9.8	-124	$2
2nd Half		285	28	8	27	2	222	10	2	226	275	369	91	112	90	7	69	0.23	50	17	33	29	107	ACf	10%	102	97	14%	17%	111	6%	48%	-11.2	21	$9
23	**Proj**	**420**	**45**	**19**	**57**	**2**	**234**	**20**	**3**	**230**	**295**	**427**	**100**	**103**	**99**	**8**	**65**	**0.25**	**47**	**18**	**35**	**31**	**108**		**13%**	**139**	**128**	**21%**	**23%**	**80**	**5%**	**56%**	**-1.0**	**40**	**$9**

Reyes,Victor

Age: 28	Pos: RF		Health	C	LIMA Plan	C+
Bats: B	Ht: 6' 5"	Wt: 194	PT/Exp	C	Rand Var	+1
			Consist	B	MM	2433

3-34-.254 in 336 PA at DET. Seized regular playing time on a rebuilder following June promotion. Career-high PA fueled by inflated LD%, h% that endured until Sept/Oct collapse (21% h%, .190 BA). Elite wheels helped, but haven't yet translated into a running game. Sub-par power, contact skills say stretches like this are his upside. Waiver fodder.

Yr	Tm	PA	R	HR	RBI	SB	BA	xHR	xSB	xBA	OBP	SLG	OPS+	vL+	vR+	bb%	ct%	Eye	G	L	F	h%	HctX	QBaB	Brl%	PX	xPX	HR/F	xHR/F	Spd	SBA%	SB%	RAR	BPX	R$
18	DET	219	35	1	12	9	222	3	2	246	239	288	71	64	71	2	78	0.11	50	26	24	28	100	DDc	3%	39	63	3%	8%	153	23%	90%	-13.8	-7	$3
19	DET *	592	71	12	73	17	287	4	19	278	318	428	103	99	108	4	79	0.21	45	29	26	35	110	CCa	2%	78	70	5%	7%	120	20%	64%	-5.7	93	$21
20	DET	213	30	4	14	8	277	5	7	251	315	391	94	103	91	4	78	0.20	46	26	28	34	86	BCa	4%	62	77	9%	11%	158	19%	80%	-3.6	72	$21
21	DET *	306	36	6	30	9	278	6	9	258	315	436	103	117	87	5	74	0.21	49	23	28	36	91	CDc	8%	95	65	12%	14%	149	18%	72%	3.3	112	$11
22	DET *	366	33	5	37	3	253	6	9	251	286	370	93	85	95	4	77	0.20	44	24	31	32	89	CCc	4%	82	65	4%	8%	121	8%	44%	-6.6	69	$6
1st Half		124	15	3	14	1	305	2	4	281	336	433	109	87	114	5	84	0.30	44	28	28	34	113	BCc	5%	74	89	5%	10%	125	8%	16%	1.9	155	$0
2nd Half		242	18	2	23	2	227	4	5	237	269	338	86	84	87	4	73	0.16	45	23	33	30	78	DCc	4%	87	54	4%	7%	120	8%	100%	-8.4	28	$2
23	**Proj**	**315**	**35**	**5**	**31**	**6**	**266**	**7**	**5**	**253**	**301**	**391**	**96**	**100**	**95**	**4**	**77**	**0.20**	**46**	**25**	**29**	**33**	**92**		**5%**	**85**	**68**	**7%**	**10%**	**135**	**9%**	**67%**	**0.6**	**85**	**$11**

Reynolds,Bryan

Age: 28	Pos: CF		Health	A	LIMA Plan	B+
Bats: B	Ht: 6' 3"	Wt: 210	PT/Exp	A	Rand Var	0
			Consist	D	MM	4335

Early ct%, bb% declines had staying power; 2021 plate skills now look like high-water marks. BA recovered some in 2nd half along with EV, HctX rebounds. Through it all, power held up nicely as he still beat up on pitchers from both sides. Age, Health add to appealing profile with some odds of a return to .300. But better to bid on .275 and be surprised.

Yr	Tm	PA	R	HR	RBI	SB	BA	xHR	xSB	xBA	OBP	SLG	OPS+	vL+	vR+	bb%	ct%	Eye	G	L	F	h%	HctX	QBaB	Brl%	PX	xPX	HR/F	xHR/F	Spd	SBA%	SB%	RAR	BPX	R$
18	aa	367	47	6	39	3	275		6		347	392	99			10	76	0.46				35				76				108	7%	43%		67	$8
19	PIT *	601	91	20	77	5	315	20	10	275	375	513	123	105	128	9	75	0.39	46	24	30	39	111	BCa	7%	111	108	14%	18%	127	5%	56%	25.8	174	$23
20	PIT	207	24	7	19	1	189	8	2	230	275	357	84	82	84	10	69	0.37	44	22	34	23	105	CCc	10%	97	116	16%	18%	126	5%	50%	-11.0	60	$5
21	PIT	646	93	24	90	5	302	30	9	281	390	522	125	125	126	12	79	0.63	39	26	36	35	111	BCc	10%	122	109	15%	19%	128	4%	71%	34.3	292	$28
22	PIT	614	74	27	62	7	262	22	8	258	345	461	114	110	116	9	74	0.40	43	22	35	31	96	BCc	8%	121	106	19%	16%	125	6%	70%	10.4	172	$22
1st Half		324	38	15	32	3	256	11	4	261	330	464	112	103	116	10	74	0.41	44	22	34	30	88	CCc	7%	124	114	21%	15%	131	6%	50%	3.8	193	$20
2nd Half		290	36	12	30	4	269	11	4	256	362	458	116	121	115	9	74	0.38	42	22	36	32	105	ACc	8%	119	96	18%	16%	114	6%	100%	6.1	155	$20
23	**Proj**	**630**	**83**	**25**	**73**	**6**	**271**	**25**	**10**	**263**	**356**	**469**	**115**	**112**	**115**	**10**	**75**	**0.45**	**42**	**23**	**35**	**32**	**104**		**9%**	**124**	**107**	**17%**	**17%**	**126**	**8%**	**70%**	**30.2**	**191**	**$26**

Riley,Austin

Age: 26	Pos: 3B		Health	A	LIMA Plan	D+
Bats: R	Ht: 6' 3"	Wt: 240	PT/Exp	A	Rand Var	0
			Consist	C	MM	4145

Postseason struggles the only blemish on more top-shelf production. BA drop was fueled by expected h% regression—but it was fine, and xBA says it could even rebound some. Soaring EV, HctX, Brl% fueled another power uptick, as he mashed lefties wire-to-wire and put 40 HR in the crosshairs. Age, Health cement elite profile.

Yr	Tm	PA	R	HR	RBI	SB	BA	xHR	xSB	xBA	OBP	SLG	OPS+	vL+	vR+	bb%	ct%	Eye	G	L	F	h%	HctX	QBaB	Brl%	PX	xPX	HR/F	xHR/F	Spd	SBA%	SB%	RAR	BPX	R$
18	a/a	419	51	16	59	1	280		5		329	484	109			7	67	0.22				38				144				94	1%	100%		87	$13
19	ATL *	488	75	30	85	0	244	17	1	248	296	505	111	137	93	7	67	0.22	26	25	49	29	97	BAd	14%	152	160	22%	21%	75	2%	0%	-6.4	96	$14
20	ATL	206	24	8	27	0	239	9	1	247	301	415	95	103	92	8	74	0.33	42	24	35	28	101	ACd	10%	97	90	17%	19%	106	0%	0%	-6.4	92	$11
21	ATL	662	91	33	107	0	303	33	3	264	367	531	123	102	130	8	72	0.31	38	25	37	38	103	BBd	13%	138	111	21%	21%	94	1%	0%	41.5	162	$30
22	ATL	693	90	38	93	2	273	43	2	279	349	528	124	152	115	8	73	0.34	38	24	38	32	125	ACd	16%	167	150	22%	25%	78	1%	100%	32.6	228	$29
1st Half		347	45	21	51	2	269	21	1	277	337	538	124	146	116	8	71	0.29	38	23	39	32	137	ACd	15%	178	161	24%	24%	86	1%	100%	17.7	238	$31
2nd Half		346	45	17	42	0	277	21	1	281	361	518	125	159	115	9	75	0.40	38	24	38	32	113	ACd	16%	156	140	20%	24%	76	1%	0%	18.2	228	$28
23	**Proj**	**665**	**90**	**35**	**98**	**1**	**278**	**38**	**3**	**269**	**348**	**517**	**120**	**133**	**116**	**8**	**72**	**0.32**	**37**	**24**	**39**	**33**	**112**		**14%**	**158**	**133**	**21%**	**22%**	**79**	**2%**	**66%**	**40.5**	**183**	**$30**

Rios,Edwin

Age: 29	Pos: DH		Health	F	LIMA Plan	D
Bats: L	Ht: 6' 3"	Wt: 220	PT/Exp	F	Rand Var	-3
			Consist	F	MM	5001

7-17-.244 in 92 PA at LA. Health-and-contact challenged slugger found extended strong-side platoon PA in May. Took advantage of it (6 HR, .892 OPS) until torn hamstring and surgery shelved him in early June. 2nd half is all AAA rehab. Elite LH power still jumps, as does almost 300 IL days over last three seasons. Fragility, age are instructive.

Yr	Tm	PA	R	HR	RBI	SB	BA	xHR	xSB	xBA	OBP	SLG	OPS+	vL+	vR+	bb%	ct%	Eye	G	L	F	h%	HctX	QBaB	Brl%	PX	xPX	HR/F	xHR/F	Spd	SBA%	SB%	RAR	BPX	R$
18	aaa	326	35	8	42	0	260		4		298	407	94			5	58	0.13				42				130				82	1%	0%		-83	$6
19	LA *	474	61	26	72	1	226	4	2	227	281	464	103	112	143	7	54	0.17	46	27	27	35	107	AFa	27%	173	184	57%	57%	100	4%	37%	-14.1	0	$9
20	LA	83	13	8	17	0	250	8	0	311	301	645	126	170	113	5	76	0.22	34	19	47	22	157	ABc	14%	211	236	29%	29%	75	0%	0%	3.2	432	$8
21	LA	60	4	1	1	0	78	2	0	132	217	137	49	0	62	12	65	0.39	42	9	48	9	88	BCf	12%	34	152	6%	13%	97	0%	0%	-8.0	-223	-$5
22	LA *	291	28	12	37	0	200	6	0	217	241	379	88	129	109	5	56	0.12	38	28	34	30	78	CCb	14%	154	165	41%	35%	65	4%	0%	-15.5	-72	$1
1st Half		92	12	7	17	0	244	6	0	240	293	500	112	129	109	5	58	0.14	38	28	34	33	81	CCb	14%	184	165	41%	35%	78	4%	0%	-0.1	55	-$1
2nd Half		199	16	5	20	0	180			194	220	324	77	0	0	5	55	0.12	44	20	36	29	0			139	-14	0%		80	4%	0%	-15.2	-117	-$2
23	**Proj**	**175**	**20**	**11**	**25**	**0**	**225**	**20**	**1**	**222**	**285**	**471**	**105**	**113**	**103**	**6**	**55**	**0.14**	**37**	**20**	**43**	**33**	**113**		**13%**	**207**	**190**	**27%**	**50%**	**74**	**4%**	**13%**	**-0.8**	**-32**	**$5**

Rivas III,Alfonso

Age: 26	Pos: 1B		Health	A	LIMA Plan	F
Bats: L	Ht: 5' 11"	Wt: 190	PT/Exp	D	Rand Var	0
			Consist	A	MM	1301

3-25-.235, 6 SB in 287 PA at CHC. Reminder of how awful some rebuilders were. Decent bb%, speed sans running game (despite atypical SB%) and not being gawd-awful vR shouldn't have been enough to amass career-high PA at an offensive position, but here we are. Won't play this much again and you shouldn't care even if he does.

Yr	Tm	PA	R	HR	RBI	SB	BA	xHR	xSB	xBA	OBP	SLG	OPS+	vL+	vR+	bb%	ct%	Eye	G	L	F	h%	HctX	QBaB	Brl%	PX	xPX	HR/F	xHR/F	Spd	SBA%	SB%	RAR	BPX	R$
18																																			
19	aaa	34	2	1	4	0	362		1		392	544	130			5	75	0.20				47				98				121	0%	0%		96	-$2
20																																			
21	CHC *	270	22	4	25	0	247	1	4	200	326	342	92	88	117	10	70	0.39	50	18	32	34	61	CCa	4%	69	41	11%	11%	113	1%	0%	-8.4	-31	$2
22	CHC *	387	36	4	31	6	233	4	3	211	304	309	87	27	97	9	65	0.29	49	26	25	35	69	DFd	4%	58	50	8%	10%	123	7%	86%	-15.1	-124	$5
1st Half		189	17	4	25	3	233	2	2	217	306	332	90	24	101	10	64	0.29	51	26	23	34	72	DFc	4%	71	60	14%	10%	116	7%	100%	-4.5	-107	$3
2nd Half		199	19	0	7	3	234	1	2	204	303	287	84	35	92	9	65	0.29	47	26	26	36	66	DFf	4%	46	38	0%	5%	130	7%	75%	-7.8	-148	-$2
23	**Proj**	**175**	**16**	**2**	**15**	**2**	**241**	**2**	**3**	**216**	**324**	**318**	**89**	**28**	**96**	**10**	**67**	**0.33**	**49**	**26**	**25**	**35**	**68**		**4%**	**63**	**47**	**6%**	**9%**	**105**	**7%**	**74%**	**-3.4**	**-91**	**$3**

Rivera,Emmanuel

Age: 27	Pos: 3B		Health	B	LIMA Plan	D+
Bats: R	Ht: 6' 2"	Wt: 225	PT/Exp	C	Rand Var	+1
			Consist	A	MM	2221

6-18-.227 in 148 PA at KC and ARI. Rookie has tapped into thump as he enters Bull Durham years. HctX, EV, xPX look bullish; bumped 2nd-half BA into respectability via gains vR, h% spike. Impatience, inconsistent swing path, GB tilt keep a lid on for now. But more launch angle tweak, opportunity would make this interesting. UP: 400 PA, .260 BA, 20 HR.

Yr	Tm	PA	R	HR	RBI	SB	BA	xHR	xSB	xBA	OBP	SLG	OPS+	vL+	vR+	bb%	ct%	Eye	G	L	F	h%	HctX	QBaB	Brl%	PX	xPX	HR/F	xHR/F	Spd	SBA%	SB%	RAR	BPX	R$
18																																			
19	aa	519	53	6	52	5	245		7		278	325	83			4	84	0.28				28				43				105	6%	71%		41	$6
20																																			
21	KC *	386	49	14	47	4	244	1	4	280	294	421	98	86	91	7	75	0.28	48	29	23	29	129	ADd	1%	105	105	6%	6%	96	5%	100%	-1.4	108	$9
22	2 TM *	439	53	14	43	2	234	13	5	246	285	403	97	110	94	6	75	0.28	49	16	35	28	119	BCd	9%	105	119	14%	15%	117	4%	44%	-7.5	128	$8
1st Half		226	23	6	21	1	212	6	2	249	259	383	91	117	75	6	76	0.27	46	17	36	25	124	ACd	10%	105	128	13%	15%	133	4%	100%	-6.2	148	$2
2nd Half		213	30	7	22	1	259	6	3	240	312	424	104	102	107	7	73	0.29	51	15	34	32	114	BCd	9%	113	112	15%	13%	90	4%	33%	1.1	93	$9
23	**Proj**	**245**	**31**	**6**	**27**	**2**	**242**	**5**	**2**	**248**	**296**	**380**	**94**	**99**	**91**	**6**	**76**	**0.28**	**48**	**21**	**30**	**30**	**123**		**6%**	**93**	**113**	**11%**	**10%**	**99**	**5%**	**69%**	**-0.7**	**105**	**$6**

JOCK THOMPSON

Rizzo,Anthony

Age: 33 Pos: 1B	Health B	LIMA Plan B+	
Bats: L Ht: 6' 3" Wt: 240	PT/Exp A	Rand Var +5	
	Consist A	MM 4145	

Stayed in Bronx, sold out for power, got results (19 home HR). Back pain in 2nd half sent him to IL and likely cause of HR/SB downturn. Even with more fly balls and Ks, xBA and h% say BA bump is due. As one who was among most shifted against, grant him a few extra points there too. But barrels would need to stick for another run at 30+ HR.

Yr Tm	PA	R	HR	RBI	SB	BA	xHR	xSB	xBA	OBP	SLG	OPS+	vL+	vR+	bb%	ct%	Eye	G	L	F	h%	HctX	QBaB	Brl%	PX	xPX	HR/F	xHR/F	Spd	SBA%	SB%	RAR	BPX	R$
18 CHC	665	74	25	101	6	283	20	11	286	376	470	113	91	119	11	86	0.88	38	25	37	29	108	BBc	7%	100	93	14%	11%	77	5%	60%	24.6	233	$24
19 CHC	613	89	27	94	5	293	21	6	300	405	520	128	112	132	12	83	0.83	43	25	32	31	107	CCb	7%	109	95	20%	15%	78	4%	71%	30.7	252	$23
20 CHC	243	26	11	24	3	222	6	1	267	342	414	100	80	106	12	81	0.74	38	24	38	22	116	CBd	7%	94	99	18%	10%	65	6%	75%	-6.7	180	$14
21 2 TM	576	73	22	61	6	248	19	6	264	344	440	108	123	101	9	82	0.60	41	19	40	26	108	BBd	8%	100	88	13%	12%	84	5%	75%	2.7	212	$15
22 NYY	548	77	32	75	6	224	25	4	267	338	480	116	125	112	11	78	0.57	33	18	49	22	111	BAf	11%	148	139	18%	14%	71	8%	55%	9.1	262	$17
1st Half	324	47	22	52	6	223	16	2	275	336	507	119	109	124	12	79	0.64	35	16	49	20	119	BAd	12%	159	152	21%	15%	71	8%	86%	7.7	310	$30
2nd Half	224	30	10	23	0	225	9	2	258	339	440	110	163	99	10	77	0.49	30	20	49	24	101	CAf	10%	133	120	14%	12%	79	8%	0%	-2.3	214	$9
23 Proj	490	67	24	62	5	260	19	6	266	363	478	117	128	113	10	80	0.59	36	20	44	27	109		9%	127	112	16%	12%	76	6%	53%	17.0	232	$17

Robert,Luis

Age: 25 Pos: CF	Health D	LIMA Plan D+	
Bats: R Ht: 6' 2" Wt: 220	PT/Exp B	Rand Var 0	
	Consist D	MM 4335	

Maladies not as dire as 2021, but with 35 IL days, it was another disjointed season. No SB after June 12, as 2019 elite sprint speed remained AWOL. Before wrist injury ended season, power was surging and plate skills showed growth, so while breakout may not match initial vision (fewer SB, more BA), it's likely still coming. If others feel jilted, pounce.

Yr Tm	PA	R	HR	RBI	SB	BA	xHR	xSB	xBA	OBP	SLG	OPS+	vL+	vR+	bb%	ct%	Eye	G	L	F	h%	HctX	QBaB	Brl%	PX	xPX	HR/F	xHR/F	Spd	SBA%	SB%	RAR	BPX	R$
18																																		
19 a/a	449	79	23	61	25	288		6		322	535	119			5	72	0.18				35				135				132	38%	75%		170	$26
20 CHW	225	33	11	31	9	233	14	10	218	302	436	98	105	96	9	64	0.27	37	20	43	31	77	CBd	13%	129	120	20%	25%	105	22%	82%	-1.9	40	$24
21 CHW *	329	45	14	45	7	327	16	11	277	364	544	125	168	119	5	76	0.25	37	26	37	39	111	ACc	13%	130	116	16%	20%	107	9%	88%	25.8	208	$18
22 CHW	401	54	12	56	11	284	16	6	260	319	426	106	127	100	4	80	0.22	45	22	33	33	107	BCc	9%	89	97	12%	16%	92	14%	79%	10.0	97	$19
1st Half	282	38	8	40	11	286	11	4	257	316	413	103	116	100	3	80	0.17	49	21	30	33	97	BDc	10%	77	83	12%	17%	98	14%	85%	5.3	72	$26
2nd Half	119	16	4	16	0	279	5	2	269	328	459	111	148	99	7	78	0.33	36	24	40	33	130	CCd	7%	119	132	11%	14%	86	14%	0%	3.7	172	$1
23 Proj	588	84	22	82	12	292	28	12	263	337	480	113	143	104	6	76	0.25	39	24	37	35	111		10%	124	115	14%	18%	97	11%	72%	29.6	149	$32

Robles,Victor

Age: 26 Pos: CF	Health A	LIMA Plan C	
Bats: R Ht: 6' 0" Wt: 205	PT/Exp B	Rand Var -1	
	Consist A	MM 1403	

What's it mean when you're 25, playing for a non-contender, and still get benched? Wields utterly punchless bat and strikes out a ton, so you'd think he'd realize walks are best path to tap SB potential; instead, he gets less patient. Young enough to get more chances, but for now, he's like a room full of size-17 roller skates: plenty of wheels, limited utility.

Yr Tm	PA	R	HR	RBI	SB	BA	xHR	xSB	xBA	OBP	SLG	OPS+	vL+	vR+	bb%	ct%	Eye	G	L	F	h%	HctX	QBaB	Brl%	PX	xPX	HR/F	xHR/F	Spd	SBA%	SB%	RAR	BPX	R$
18 WAS *	240	30	5	19	16	271	2	3	237	332	411	100	129	106	8	82	0.51	27	24	49	31	107	DAc	6%	84	106	14%	9%	124	39%	65%	1.3	167	$9
19 WAS	617	86	17	65	28	255	15	32	248	326	419	103	103	102	6	74	0.25	41	23	37	31	64	FBc	5%	95	57	12%	10%	125	25%	76%	-0.3	89	$23
20 WAS	189	20	3	15	4	220	2	7	216	293	315	81	107	70	5	68	0.17	35	30	35	30	63	FAc	2%	60	62	8%	5%	116	11%	80%	-12.1	-124	$8
21 WAS *	461	48	5	25	13	218	5	7	230	289	339	86	78	86	9	71	0.35	36	25	39	29	70	FBf	3%	89	80	2%	6%	102	19%	65%	-17.1	27	$6
22 WAS	407	42	6	33	15	224	4	11	204	273	311	83	105	71	4	72	0.16	40	21	39	30	67	FCf	3%	59	53	6%	4%	143	21%	79%	-15.3	-41	$8
1st Half	207	24	1	20	8	235	2	6	210	310	302	87	121	68	7	70	0.25	42	24	34	33	64	FDf	4%	54	49	3%	5%	123	21%	100%	-4.5	-79	$6
2nd Half	200	18	5	13	7	214	3	4	200	235	321	79	90	73	2	73	0.08	39	18	44	27	69	FBf	3%	65	56	9%	5%	152	21%	64%	-10.0	-17	$4
23 Proj	385	43	6	29	14	225	6	11	215	291	329	86	99	80	6	72	0.22	38	23	39	30	69		3%	76	65	6%	6%	113	16%	72%	-10.0	-12	$11

Rodgers,Brendan

Age: 26 Pos: 2B	Health C	LIMA Plan B+	
Bats: R Ht: 6' 0" Wt: 204	PT/Exp A	Rand Var -2	
	Consist D	MM 2235	

Spring back tightness ruined April (.270 OPS); after that, .286/.342/.441 line was comparable to previous year. Still, power faded sharply in 2nd half, and high GB% suggests no HR leap is imminent. And unlike 2021, Coors saved him, too (.875 OPS home, .588 road). At his age, time to wonder: is this all there is? Maybe not, but each year adds to that case.

Yr Tm	PA	R	HR	RBI	SB	BA	xHR	xSB	xBA	OBP	SLG	OPS+	vL+	vR+	bb%	ct%	Eye	G	L	F	h%	HctX	QBaB	Brl%	PX	xPX	HR/F	xHR/F	Spd	SBA%	SB%	RAR	BPX	R$
18 a/a	449	39	14	49	9	250		5		289	416	94			5	78	0.25				29				102				92	14%	73%		113	$11
19 COL *	234	31	7	21	0	284	1	5	254	325	436	105	66	74	6	75	0.24	49	22	29	35	79	CDf	4%	87	66	0%	7%	128	0%	0%	3.1	74	$3
20 COL	21	1	0	2	0	95	0	0	165	95	143	32	43	22	0	71	0.00	73	0	27	13	39	FFf		41	23	0%	0%	95	0%	0%	-3.4	-200	-$4
21 COL	415	49	15	51	0	284	14	2	267	328	470	110	134	101	5	78	0.23	51	20	29	33	122	CDd	6%	105	97	17%	16%	97	0%	0%	9.5	142	$13
22 COL	581	72	13	63	0	266	14	4	269	325	408	104	126	92	8	81	0.46	52	21	27	31	124	BFc	7%	91	93	11%	12%	121	0%	0%	7.0	172	$15
1st Half	300	38	8	40	0	258	8	2	270	313	425	105	140	89	7	81	0.41	50	18	32	29	121	BFd	9%	105	115	11%	11%	119	0%	0%	5.1	214	$15
2nd Half	281	34	5	23	0	274	7	2	269	338	389	103	115	95	9	80	0.50	55	24	21	32	126	BFb	5%	75	68	12%	16%	121	0%	0%	5.2	128	$11
23 Proj	560	68	14	61	1	272	16	3	265	325	420	103	121	95	7	79	0.34	52	21	27	32	119		6%	95	89	12%	14%	96	3%	75%	14.8	143	$19

Rodríguez,Julio

Age: 22 Pos: CF	Health A	LIMA Plan D+	
Bats: R Ht: 6' 3" Wt: 180	PT/Exp A	Rand Var -1	
	Consist C	MM 4545	

In April, looked like another high-profile SEA rookie OF bust, then: WOW. By Aug, team threw $200M at him, for good reason—he's already showcasing elite exit velocity, sprint speed... at 21. If he can smooth out SB%, build on 2nd half ct% and power gains, and avoid short IL stints (HBP on elbow, back), now where's the ceiling? It'll be fun to find out.

Yr Tm	PA	R	HR	RBI	SB	BA	xHR	xSB	xBA	OBP	SLG	OPS+	vL+	vR+	bb%	ct%	Eye	G	L	F	h%	HctX	QBaB	Brl%	PX	xPX	HR/F	xHR/F	Spd	SBA%	SB%	RAR	BPX	R$
18																																		
19																																		
20																																		
21 aa	198	29	6	22	13	325		3		408	479	122			12	75	0.56				41				95				92	26%	75%		115	$13
22 SEA	560	84	28	75	25	284	25	23	262	345	509	121	116	122	7	72	0.28	46	18	36	35	108	ACd	13%	146	121	21%	19%	159	23%	78%	32.0	231	$35
1st Half	339	48	15	43	21	277	12	14	255	336	487	116	128	113	7	70	0.24	48	18	34	35	107	ACf	14%	142	111	20%	16%	162	23%	84%	15.9	197	$42
2nd Half	221	36	13	32	4	294	13	9	273	357	542	127	97	137	8	75	0.33	43	19	38	34	111	ACd	13%	151	135	23%	23%	145	23%	57%	14.7	276	$22
23 Proj	595	91	31	76	29	290	29	23	267	366	524	123	112	127	9	74	0.40	45	18	36	34	109		13%	149	125	22%	20%	131	19%	75%	43.8	192	$42

Rojas,Josh

Age: 29 Pos: 3B 2B	Health C	LIMA Plan C+	
Bats: L Ht: 6' 1" Wt: 207	PT/Exp A	Rand Var -3	
	Consist C	MM 2325	

PRO: Career-best ct%, bb% in breakout 2nd half; full-season xPX suggests room for more power. CON: Lackluster QBaB, Brl%; Spd slipped, and if SB% regresses, SBA% could dip, too (and note xSB); ended year in defensive doghouse, so enjoy 2B/3B eligibility while you can. He'll have suitors, but between lack of firm role, skills... DN: 400 PA, <10 SB

Yr Tm	PA	R	HR	RBI	SB	BA	xHR	xSB	xBA	OBP	SLG	OPS+	vL+	vR+	bb%	ct%	Eye	G	L	F	h%	HctX	QBaB	Brl%	PX	xPX	HR/F	xHR/F	Spd	SBA%	SB%	RAR	BPX	R$
18 aa	436	56	6	40	23	222		6		304	339	86			11	78	0.53				27				75				111	38%	59%		93	$12
19 ARI *	616	82	18	76	28	265	5	30	270	338	450	109	108	79	10	78	0.50	44	23	33	31	111	CCc	6%	99	139	6%	16%	105	28%	67%	-6.0	163	$25
20 ARI	70	9	0	2	1	180	1	3	185	257	180	58	65	52	10	74	0.44	50	20	30	24	89	DFf	0%	0	98	0%	7%	113	11%	50%	-7.6	-192	-$2
21 ARI	546	69	11	44	9	264	10	10	251	341	411	103	105	103	11	72	0.42	49	23	28	35	86	CDb	5%	99	90	11%	10%	114	9%	69%	6.8	88	$15
22 ARI	510	66	9	56	23	269	10	8	248	349	391	105	93	108	11	78	0.56	42	23	35	33	102	CCd	4%	84	110	7%	8%	92	18%	88%	7.7	103	$23
1st Half	202	31	4	19	5	272	3	3	235	333	400	104	95	107	9	76	0.40	39	22	39	34	123	DCd	2%	86	129	7%	6%	110	18%	100%	3.6	90	$9
2nd Half	308	35	5	37	18	266	7	5	257	359	384	105	92	109	13	79	0.69	43	24	32	32	87	CCd	5%	82	98	7%	10%	82	18%	86%	6.6	117	$26
23 Proj	525	68	10	54	18	262	11	15	250	342	396	102	98	104	11	76	0.51	45	23	32	33	97		4%	94	106	9%	10%	102	14%	79%	13.1	105	$23

Rojas,Miguel

Age: 34 Pos: SS	Health B	LIMA Plan B	
Bats: R Ht: 6' 0" Wt: 188	PT/Exp A	Rand Var +4	
	Consist D	MM 1335	

No thrill-a-minute on his best day, he was fantasy Unisom in 2nd half. If injuries from two different collisions or sore wrist were to blame, he could squeeze out another double-digit SB season, despite 29th-percentile sprint speed. But this may have been his last 500-PA year. Even as deep league third MI, you can do better.

Yr Tm	PA	R	HR	RBI	SB	BA	xHR	xSB	xBA	OBP	SLG	OPS+	vL+	vR+	bb%	ct%	Eye	G	L	F	h%	HctX	QBaB	Brl%	PX	xPX	HR/F	xHR/F	Spd	SBA%	SB%	RAR	BPX	R$
18 MIA	527	44	11	53	6	252	6	7	260	297	346	86	84	85	5	86	0.35	47	24	29	27	85	DCc	1%	51	45	9%	5%	78	7%	67%	-6.6	63	$10
19 MIA	526	52	5	46	9	284	7	7	275	331	379	98	105	95	6	87	0.52	47	24	30	32	107	CDb	3%	54	65	4%	6%	104	10%	64%	-5.6	137	$12
20 MIA	143	20	4	20	5	304	2	3	292	392	496	118	186	90	11	86	0.89	41	25	35	33	107	CCc	1%	103	91	11%	5%	105	15%	83%	8.7	324	$17
21 MIA	539	66	9	48	13	265	6	13	265	322	392	98	120	89	7	85	0.50	45	21	34	30	86	DCc	3%	73	59	6%	4%	122	12%	81%	-2.9	196	$16
22 MIA	507	34	6	36	9	236	4	9	255	283	323	86	79	88	5	87	0.43	47	21	32	26	79	DCc	2%	53	41	5%	3%	108	10%	75%	-19.6	121	$7
1st Half	256	24	6	21	5	250	3	5	271	301	377	96	100	95	6	88	0.54	49	20	32	26	83	DDd	3%	72	40	9%	4%	114	10%	83%	-2.7	200	$8
2nd Half	251	10	0	15	4	221	1	4	240	264	268	75	60	81	4	86	0.33	45	22	33	26	75	DCb	1%	34	41	0%	2%	99	10%	67%	-14.4	41	-$3
23 Proj	525	49	8	45	9	253	5	8	260	305	359	92	104	88	6	86	0.47	46	22	33	28	85		2%	67	53	5%	4%	99	9%	73%	-3.4	154	$15

KRIS OLSON

Rosario,Amed

Age: 27 Pos: SS | Bats: R Ht: 6' 2" Wt: 190
Health A | PT/Exp A | Consist B | LIMA Plan B | Rand Var 0 | MM 1535

Was one of only seven hitters in Top 25 for both BA and SB in 2022. And while Spd hasn't led to as many SB as we'd like, it IS helping BA outperform xBA, as he tied for 2nd in infield hits. "Amed's Lament"—aka "Why don't you run more?"—might finally be put to bed with the larger bases—who knows?—so hope for a greener light and bid $1 more.

Yr	Tm	PA	R	HR	RBI	SB	BA	xHR	xSB	xBA	OBP	SLG	OPS+	vL+	vR+	bb%	ct%	Eye	G	L	F	h%	HctX	QBaB	Brl%	PX	xPX	HR/F	xHR/F	Spd	SBA%	SB%	RAR	BPX	R$
18	NYM	592	76	9	51	24	256	10	7	253	295	381	91	99	86	5	79	0.24	50	21	30	31	80	CDc	4%	75	71	7%	8%	163	27%	69%	-6.4	117	$19
19	NYM	655	75	15	72	19	287	14	26	266	323	432	104	123	98	5	80	0.25	48	22	29	34	92	BDb	4%	75	65	10%	10%	149	18%	66%	-5.8	133	$23
20	NYM	147	20	4	15	0	252	3	4	231	272	371	85	101	73	3	76	0.12	58	16	27	30	68	DFc	4%	62	40	14%	10%	151	3%	0%	-5.4	28	$7
21	CLE	588	77	11	57	13	282	9	7	255	321	409	100	114	94	5	78	0.26	51	21	28	34	92	CFd	3%	74	58	9%	7%	157	9%	100%	7.9	119	$22
22	CLE	670	86	11	71	18	283	13	16	266	312	403	101	112	98	4	83	0.23	52	20	27	33	95	CFd	4%	71	71	8%	9%	187	13%	82%	7.5	183	$29
1st Half		315	43	3	24	9	278	5	8	266	317	383	99	114	94	5	85	0.39	55	19	27	32	96	CFd	3%	61	74	4%	7%	201	13%	75%	0.6	214	$19
2nd Half		355	43	8	47	9	287	8	8	266	307	421	103	109	102	2	80	0.12	51	22	28	34	95	CDc	5%	81	68	10%	10%	161	13%	90%	4.2	141	$30
23	Proj	**630**	**82**	**12**	**66**	**20**	**278**	**12**	**15**	**258**	**309**	**403**	**99**	**111**	**94**	**4**	**80**	**0.21**	**52**	**20**	**28**	**33**	**91**		**4%**	**77**	**63**	**9%**	**9%**	**145**	**13%**	**79%**	**8.9**	**136**	**$27**

Rosario,Eddie

Age: 31 Pos: LF | Bats: L Ht: 6' 1" Wt: 180
Health F | PT/Exp C | Consist B | LIMA Plan B | Rand Var 0 | MM 2313

5-24-.250 with 3 SB in 270 PA at ATL. Dreadful start attributable to blurred vision in right eye, but all was not well upon July return post-surgery. Strikeouts soared past career norms, and quality of contact didn't compensate. Already long relegated to platoon duty, next stop is as 4th OFer, and even that may be hard to come by without improved skills.

Yr	Tm	PA	R	HR	RBI	SB	BA	xHR	xSB	xBA	OBP	SLG	OPS+	vL+	vR+	bb%	ct%	Eye	G	L	F	h%	HctX	QBaB	Brl%	PX	xPX	HR/F	xHR/F	Spd	SBA%	SB%	RAR	BPX	R$
18	MIN	592	87	24	77	8	288	22	8	259	323	479	108	96	111	5	81	0.29	36	20	44	32	109	CAd	8%	108	126	12%	11%	106	7%	80%	15.1	187	$24
19	MIN	590	91	32	109	3	276	32	6	278	300	500	111	107	111	4	85	0.26	37	20	42	28	114	CBd	9%	104	120	16%	16%	87	3%	75%	2.1	211	$22
20	MIN	231	31	13	42	3	257	10	2	258	316	476	105	70	117	8	84	0.56	35	18	47	25	103	CBf	6%	103	135	16%	12%	100	8%	75%	-0.3	264	$24
21	2 TM *	464	47	17	73	11	246	14	5	268	291	425	98	89	107	6	84	0.40	37	23	40	26	108	CBf	6%	93	110	11%	11%	99	15%	79%	-5.1	208	$15
22	ATL *	306	30	5	27	3	212	5	5	212	263	320	83	68	85	6	71	0.24	39	20	41	28	82	CBd	5%	81	91	7%	7%	100	5%	100%	-10.4	-21	$1
1st Half		93	7	0	3	0	141	0	2	162	213	172	54	28	43	8	69	0.30	53	13	35	20	68	DDf	0%	31	23	0%	0%	105	5%	0%	-8.4	-166	-$13
2nd Half		213	23	5	24	3	242	5	4	227	282	384	94	85	95	6	72	0.21	36	22	43	31	86	CBd	7%	101	109	8%	8%	102	5%	100%	-1.5	41	$7
23	Proj	**434**	**47**	**11**	**53**	**6**	**241**	**11**	**4**	**234**	**288**	**378**	**92**	**83**	**95**	**6**	**77**	**0.30**	**39**	**20**	**41**	**29**	**93**		**5%**	**89**	**96**	**9%**	**8%**	**98**	**5%**	**84%**	**-1.3**	**88**	**$13**

Ruiz,Esteury

Age: 24 Pos: OF | Bats: R Ht: 6' 0" Wt: 169
Health A | PT/Exp B | Consist C | LIMA Plan D+ | Rand Var -1 | MM 2511

0-2-.171 with 1 SB in 35 PA at SD/MIL. An estuary is an area where a river meets the ocean; this Esteury is where game-changing speed meets developing raw power. MLB cup of coffee was unremarkable, but as you sip yours, be careful not to do a spit take when looking at 1st half R$. Even in part-time role, has potential to deliver outsized value.

Yr	Tm	PA	R	HR	RBI	SB	BA	xHR	xSB	xBA	OBP	SLG	OPS+	vL+	vR+	bb%	ct%	Eye	G	L	F	h%	HctX	QBaB	Brl%	PX	xPX	HR/F	xHR/F	Spd	SBA%	SB%	RAR	BPX	R$
18																																			
19																																			
20																																			
21	aa	332	40	7	32	28	214		3		267	338	83			7	74	0.28				27				78				102	54%	78%		15	$14
22	2 NL *	520	82	11	47	60	266	0	41	246	334	407	105	65	61	9	75	0.40	48	19	33	34	35	FAf	4%	98	13	0%	0%	121	59%	77%	9.3	114	$40
1st Half		307	55	9	32	39	286		26	257	366	467	118	0	0	11	74	0.48	44	20	36	36	0			125	-14	0%		132	59%	81%	18.2	203	$52
2nd Half		214	26	2	15	21	239	0	15	226	288	326	87	65	61	6	76	0.28	48	19	33	31	35	FAf	4%	63	13	0%	0%	122	59%	70%	-6.1	14	$16
23	Proj	**210**	**29**	**5**	**19**	**21**	**241**	**4**	**16**	**237**	**299**	**372**	**93**	**106**	**71**	**8**	**75**	**0.32**	**43**	**22**	**35**	**30**	**32**		**3%**	**91**	**12**	**9%**	**7%**	**107**	**44%**	**76%**	**-0.9**	**62**	**$14**

Ruiz,Keibert

Age: 24 Pos: CA | Bats: R Ht: 6' 0" Wt: 225
Health B | PT/Exp B | Consist C | LIMA Plan B | Rand Var +2 | MM 2143

Bat-first catcher has yet to really put his bat first in majors, though 2nd half gains in HctX, xPX suggest he might be ready to pair more power with elite bat-to-ball skills. Higher PX should be missing ingredient for BA, as ct%, LD% rates are solid start to recipe for .300 hitter. Small step forward seems more likely than breakout, but don't rule out the latter.

Yr	Tm	PA	R	HR	RBI	SB	BA	xHR	xSB	xBA	OBP	SLG	OPS+	vL+	vR+	bb%	ct%	Eye	G	L	F	h%	HctX	QBaB	Brl%	PX	xPX	HR/F	xHR/F	Spd	SBA%	SB%	RAR	BPX	R$
18	aa	397	35	10	37	0	240		5		278	351	84			5	90	0.55				24				58				87	1%	0%		153	$4
19	a/a	338	32	5	28	0	236		2		289	312	83			7	92	0.97				24				35				95	0%	0%		156	$0
20	LA	8	1	1	1	0	250	1	0	264	250	625	116	0	116	0	63	0.00	20	20	60	25	51	CAf	20%	214	123	33%	33%	100	0%	0%	0.3	212	-$2
21	2 NL *	403	48	20	60	0	280	2	1	274	332	513	116	103	102	7	88	0.64	42	15	43	27	105	DAc	3%	118	64	9%	6%	77	0%	0%	22.9	327	$14
22	WAS	433	33	7	36	6	251	8	1	264	313	360	95	82	99	7	87	0.60	40	23	37	27	106	CBb	4%	69	92	5%	6%	63	7%	86%	1.8	134	$8
1st Half		254	20	3	19	4	257	4	0	279	320	357	96	88	98	8	89	0.76	37	28	35	28	92	CBb	3%	65	84	4%	5%	62	7%	100%	2.4	155	$4
2nd Half		179	13	4	17	2	244	4	0	239	302	366	95	72	101	6	85	0.44	45	16	39	27	124	CBb	5%	75	105	7%	7%	78	7%	67%	-0.1	128	$1
23	Proj	**420**	**39**	**12**	**46**	**3**	**266**	**8**	**4**	**271**	**326**	**413**	**103**	**93**	**106**	**7**	**88**	**0.60**	**39**	**22**	**39**	**28**	**108**		**3%**	**86**	**83**	**9%**	**6%**	**72**	**5%**	**77%**	**13.2**	**198**	**$14**

Rutschman,Adley

Age: 25 Pos: CA DH | Bats: B Ht: 6' 2" Wt: 220
Health A | PT/Exp B | Consist A | LIMA Plan B+ | Rand Var +2 | MM 3245

13-42-.254 in 470 PA at BAL. Lessons in Prospect Patience, Case File #37219: Hit .176 with .513 OPS in first 82 PA, then came 1st HR on June 15, by 2nd half he was already a difference-maker at CA. Outstanding plate discipline gives him strong base to further develop plus power and BA potential, with .300+, 30 HR as future upside. He's a keeper.

Yr	Tm	PA	R	HR	RBI	SB	BA	xHR	xSB	xBA	OBP	SLG	OPS+	vL+	vR+	bb%	ct%	Eye	G	L	F	h%	HctX	QBaB	Brl%	PX	xPX	HR/F	xHR/F	Spd	SBA%	SB%	RAR	BPX	R$
18																																			
19																																			
20																																			
21	a/a	511	65	19	56	2	249		6		336	428	105			12	79	0.61				28				100				95	4%	40%		185	$12
22	BAL *	531	76	15	48	4	250	13	4	275	351	436	111	77	126	13	79	0.75	38	23	38	29	107	CBc	8%	124	114	11%	11%	90	3%	100%	22.9	248	$14
1st Half		208	23	5	16	1	213	4	1	271	276	378	93	67	101	8	81	0.46	37	25	39	24	117	BBc	7%	107	113	7%	10%	98	3%	100%	-1.0	197	$0
2nd Half		323	53	10	32	3	277	9	3	278	399	477	124	82	139	17	78	0.93	39	22	38	32	101	CBc	8%	136	114	13%	11%	87	3%	100%	24.2	286	$24
23	Proj	**595**	**81**	**19**	**66**	**4**	**267**	**16**	**5**	**271**	**370**	**450**	**114**	**77**	**126**	**14**	**80**	**0.77**	**39**	**23**	**37**	**30**	**107**		**8%**	**118**	**114**	**12%**	**11%**	**83**	**3%**	**73%**	**35.2**	**223**	**$22**

Sánchez,Gary

Age: 30 Pos: CA DH | Bats: R Ht: 6' 2" Wt: 230
Health B | PT/Exp A | Consist B | LIMA Plan D+ | Rand Var 0 | MM 4103

At this point, probably best to go Eternal Sunshine of the Spotless Mind on your memories of 2017/2019, so you can see him for what he is now: solid source of CA HR who will hurt you everywhere else. Even then, still subject to frustrating bouts of inconsistency, like 2nd half disappearing act. Set your sights low enough, and you won't be disappointed.

Yr	Tm	PA	R	HR	RBI	SB	BA	xHR	xSB	xBA	OBP	SLG	OPS+	vL+	vR+	bb%	ct%	Eye	G	L	F	h%	HctX	QBaB	Brl%	PX	xPX	HR/F	xHR/F	Spd	SBA%	SB%	RAR	BPX	R$
18	NYY *	402	54	22	56	1	184	21	4	241	279	417	93	116	84	11	70	0.44	43	14	43	19	91	BBf	14%	147	115	18%	21%	49	1%	100%	3.0	123	$5
19	NYY	446	62	34	77	0	232	36	2	252	316	525	116	106	119	9	68	0.32	32	20	48	24	100	AAd	19%	156	140	26%	28%	75	1%	0%	19.3	152	$12
20	NYY	178	19	10	24	0	147	10	0	200	253	365	82	79	82	10	59	0.28	38	16	46	16	99	AAd	17%	143	147	24%	24%	60	0%	0%	-8.1	-32	$2
21	NYY	440	54	23	54	0	204	21	1	228	307	423	100	114	95	12	68	0.43	36	18	46	23	86	BAc	14%	131	103	19%	17%	79	0%	0%	1.3	108	$5
22	MIN	471	42	16	61	2	205	24	0	220	282	377	93	78	99	8	68	0.29	44	15	42	26	122	BCf	13%	127	136	13%	20%	53	2%	100%	-2.5	24	$5
1st Half		259	26	9	34	1	219	16	0	232	278	409	97	65	108	6	70	0.22	38	15	47	28	128	BBf	17%	142	163	12%	21%	68	2%	100%	0.2	93	$8
2nd Half		212	16	7	27	1	187	8	0	200	288	335	88	92	87	12	65	0.38	51	14	35	24	115	BCd	8%	107	99	17%	19%	51	2%	100%	-3.4	-48	$2
23	Proj	**385**	**41**	**17**	**51**	**1**	**211**	**19**	**1**	**221**	**301**	**405**	**98**	**98**	**98**	**10**	**67**	**0.35**	**42**	**16**	**43**	**26**	**105**		**13%**	**137**	**121**	**18%**	**20%**	**54**	**1%**	**95%**	**5.1**	**47**	**$8**

Sánchez,Jesús

Age: 25 Pos: CF | Bats: L Ht: 6' 3" Wt: 222
Health B | PT/Exp B | Consist F | LIMA Plan D+ | Rand Var -1 | MM 4223

13-36-.214 in 343 PA at MIA. Alarming slides in power skills got him demoted for most of Aug/Sept, and leaves 2023 contributions in doubt. Things were especially bad vL (56% ct%, 23 PX), so even if he does get another shot, it'll likely be in platoon role. Too young to give up on, and stable exit velocity offers hope all is not lost, but he's flyer-only for now.

Yr	Tm	PA	R	HR	RBI	SB	BA	xHR	xSB	xBA	OBP	SLG	OPS+	vL+	vR+	bb%	ct%	Eye	G	L	F	h%	HctX	QBaB	Brl%	PX	xPX	HR/F	xHR/F	Spd	SBA%	SB%	RAR	BPX	R$
18	aa	108	12	1	10	1	191		1		263	290	74			9	76	0.40				24				76				95	10%	45%		40	-$2
19	a/a	454	49	12	63	5	245		7		310	369	94			9	74	0.36				31				67				103	8%	54%		0	$8
20	MIA	29	1	0	2	0	40	0	0	138	172	80	34	0	45	14	56	0.36	57	14	29	7	97	ADf	7%	44	80	0%	0%	96	0%	0%	-4.3	-324	-$5
21	MIA *	402	46	22	61	1	271	14	3	255	326	510	115	109	112	7	70	0.27	45	21	34	33	108	BDc	13%	137	141	27%	27%	133	2%	45%	13.6	173	$13
22	MIA *	516	59	17	55	4	225	13	3	230	286	386	95	43	108	8	71	0.29	47	17	37	28	90	BCf	9%	108	94	16%	16%	101	5%	76%	-5.9	59	$9
1st Half		254	31	11	29	1	220	10	1	241	272	424	98	40	112	6	69	0.21	47	17	37	27	88	CDf	11%	133	88	18%	17%	119	5%	100%	-1.7	110	$9
2nd Half		262	28	6	26	3	230	2	2	218	304	348	92	62	95	10	72	0.38	47	17	36	29	92	BBd	5%	85	110	10%	10%	84	5%	70%	-3.3	10	$8
23	Proj	**280**	**32**	**12**	**34**	**2**	**238**	**12**	**3**	**246**	**307**	**437**	**103**	**89**	**107**	**8**	**71**	**0.31**	**46**	**18**	**35**	**29**	**97**		**10%**	**130**	**117**	**19%**	**18%**	**107**	**6%**	**65%**	**4.6**	**81**	**$8**

KRIS OLSON/BRANDON KRUSE

Sanó,Miguel

Age: 30	Pos: 1B	Health F	LIMA Plan D
Bats: R	Ht: 6' 4" Wt: 272	PT/Exp D	Rand Var +5
		Consist C	MM 5201

1-3-.083 in 71 PA at MIN. Spring "best shape of his life" reports didn't exactly translate to big year. Instead, strikeouts piled up, he recorded just one extra base hit, and late April knee injury effectively knocked him out the rest of the way. Has enough power history to bet on rebound, but it will come with the same old BA damage.

Yr	Tm	PA	R	HR	RBI	SB	BA	xHR	xSB	xBA	OBP	SLG	OPS+	vL+	vR+	bb%	ct%	Eye	G	L	F	h%	HctX	QBaB	Brl%	PX	xPX	HR/F	xHR/F	Spd	SBA%	SB%	RAR	BPX	R$
18	MIN *	334	34	15	45	0	204	13	4	201	290	404	93	85	91	11	58	0.29	44	15	41	29	91	BCd	11%	156	121	21%	21%	70	0%	0%	-6.0	7	$3
19	MIN *	474	78	35	84	0	245	34	2	246	336	562	124	140	122	12	58	0.32	37	21	42	33	105	ABd	21%	210	175	37%	37%	90	1%	0%	17.1	189	$15
20	MIN	205	31	13	25	0	204	15	0	224	278	478	100	72	109	9	52	0.20	36	24	40	30	100	AAb	23%	222	148	34%	39%	74	0%	0%	-6.7	104	$11
21	MIN	532	68	30	75	2	223	28	0	229	312	466	107	96	112	11	61	0.32	39	18	43	29	113	AAf	18%	169	138	24%	23%	47	3%	67%	2.2	69	$12
22	MIN *	96	4	3	7	1	129	3	0	159	229	243	67	39	55	11	54	0.28	17	22	61	19	65	AAc	14%	95	131	5%	14%	61	6%	100%	-6.8	-224	-$5
1st Half		65	1	1	3	1	93	3	0	152	231	148	54	47	57	14	61	0.43	15	24	62	13	71	AAc	15%	37	118	5%	14%	69	6%	100%	-6.5	-259	-$13
2nd Half		31	3	2	4	0	197	0	0	162	243	418	94	0	0	6	40	0.10	50	0	50	41	88	ADf		261	360	0%	0%	70	6%	0%	-1.0	14	-$9
23	Proj	**245**	**25**	**13**	**27**	**1**	**225**	**16**	**2**	**216**	**316**	**448**	**106**	**90**	**112**	**11**	**58**	**0.30**	**31**	**22**	**47**	**32**	**94**		**18%**	**178**	**137**	**22%**	**26%**	**65**	**4%**	**91%**	**3.5**	**-13**	**$3**

Santana,Carlos

Age: 37	Pos: 1B DH	Health A	LIMA Plan D+
Bats: B	Ht: 5' 11" Wt: 215	PT/Exp A	Rand Var +4
		Consist A	MM 2013

Just when it looked like the end was near, traded to SEA in June and went on HR binge. When batting left-handed, he was shifted on in 356 of his 362 PA, the highest rate in the majors (98.3%), which may bode well for some BA juice. Floor is low for both production and PA, but consistently high bb% keeps OBP respectable.

Yr	Tm	PA	R	HR	RBI	SB	BA	xHR	xSB	xBA	OBP	SLG	OPS+	vL+	vR+	bb%	ct%	Eye	G	L	F	h%	HctX	QBaB	Brl%	PX	xPX	HR/F	xHR/F	Spd	SBA%	SB%	RAR	BPX	R$
18	PHI	679	82	24	86	2	229	21	11	253	352	414	103	108	99	16	83	1.18	40	16	44	23	101	CBf	7%	101	112	12%	10%	80	2%	67%	7.3	243	$13
19	CLE	686	110	34	93	4	281	29	3	276	397	515	126	136	121	16	81	1.00	45	17	38	29	121	ACd	10%	114	112	19%	16%	74	2%	100%	37.9	267	$24
20	CLE	255	34	8	30	0	199	10	1	231	349	350	93	99	89	18	79	1.09	43	18	40	21	109	CCf	7%	79	106	12%	15%	70	0%	0%	-9.7	160	$9
21	KC	659	66	19	69	2	214	23	1	235	319	342	91	98	88	13	82	0.84	46	18	37	23	113	BCf	7%	66	97	11%	13%	59	1%	100%	-17.8	100	$6
22	2 AL	506	52	19	60	0	202	18	1	239	316	376	98	111	93	14	80	0.81	39	17	44	21	122	BBf	10%	103	122	13%	12%	54	0%	0%	-4.2	162	$5
1st Half		243	20	4	21	0	219	6	0	220	354	328	96	125	86	17	83	1.24	41	16	43	25	120	BCf	8%	70	102	6%	8%	68	0%	0%	-3.5	155	-$1
2nd Half		263	32	15	39	0	187	12	0	254	281	417	99	99	99	11	77	0.54	37	18	45	17	124	ABd	11%	135	141	19%	15%	49	0%	0%	-5.4	183	$13
23	Proj	**385**	**43**	**14**	**46**	**0**	**240**	**14**	**0**	**237**	**347**	**404**	**104**	**116**	**100**	**14**	**80**	**0.83**	**42**	**17**	**41**	**26**	**117**		**8%**	**97**	**114**	**13%**	**13%**	**58**	**0%**	**0%**	**5.8**	**157**	**$10**

Santander,Anthony

Age: 28	Pos: RF LF DH	Health C	LIMA Plan B+
Bats: B	Ht: 6' 2" Wt: 235	PT/Exp A	Rand Var +2
		Consist B	MM 4045

Plus power was on full display as FB% went up and 2nd half Brl%, xPX, and xHR/F all reached new heights. Uptick in ct% even led to usable BA prior to some tough luck late (.150 BA, 13% h% over final 111 PA). As long as health cooperates, no reason he can't follow up with a similar encore plus a potential BA bump.

Yr	Tm	PA	R	HR	RBI	SB	BA	xHR	xSB	xBA	OBP	SLG	OPS+	vL+	vR+	bb%	ct%	Eye	G	L	F	h%	HctX	QBaB	Brl%	PX	xPX	HR/F	xHR/F	Spd	SBA%	SB%	RAR	BPX	R$
18	BAL *	370	31	7	29	4	209	3	4	236	242	327	76	75	71	4	81	0.23	39	20	41	24	94	CBf	5%	69	77	3%	9%	93	8%	78%	-21.5	63	$1
19	BAL *	608	69	24	80	3	246	17	6	245	282	431	99	113	103	5	78	0.23	39	18	43	28	102	BBd	8%	99	110	16%	11%	85	6%	43%	-17.7	96	$13
20	BAL	165	24	11	32	0	261	7	1	308	315	575	118	85	126	6	84	0.40	24	27	50	25	124	CAc	10%	159	129	17%	11%	70	4%	0%	4.4	388	$16
21	BAL	438	54	18	50	1	241	15	1	251	286	433	99	95	101	5	75	0.23	34	23	43	28	110	BAd	8%	115	109	13%	11%	59	2%	50%	-3.7	88	$8
22	BAL	647	78	33	89	0	240	30	2	254	318	455	110	128	102	9	79	0.45	31	19	50	25	120	BAf	12%	125	139	15%	13%	67	1%	0%	7.8	186	$19
1st Half		317	35	15	41	0	238	11	1	238	325	426	106	107	106	10	78	0.50	33	19	48	26	104	BAf	9%	107	117	14%	10%	70	1%	0%	1.6	134	$17
2nd Half		330	43	18	48	0	242	19	1	269	312	481	112	152	99	7	80	0.40	30	19	51	25	134	BAf	13%	142	160	15%	16%	73	1%	0%	6.0	248	$25
23	Proj	**630**	**82**	**35**	**95**	**1**	**259**	**25**	**1**	**267**	**317**	**492**	**112**	**118**	**109**	**7**	**78**	**0.33**	**32**	**21**	**47**	**28**	**116**		**11%**	**141**	**126**	**16%**	**11%**	**63**	**1%**	**32%**	**20.9**	**174**	**$26**

Schoop,Jonathan

Age: 31	Pos: 2B	Health B	LIMA Plan D+
Bats: R	Ht: 6' 1" Wt: 247	PT/Exp A	Rand Var +5
		Consist B	MM 2223

Previously consistent production nosedived, as .561 OPS ranked last among qualified hitters. Career-low h% says tough luck played a role, so expect some minor BA recovery since ct%, xBA barely slipped. But it appears he may no longer be able to outperform free-falling xHR/F, so just getting back to 20 HR may be a tall order.

Yr	Tm	PA	R	HR	RBI	SB	BA	xHR	xSB	xBA	OBP	SLG	OPS+	vL+	vR+	bb%	ct%	Eye	G	L	F	h%	HctX	QBaB	Brl%	PX	xPX	HR/F	xHR/F	Spd	SBA%	SB%	RAR	BPX	R$
18	2 TM	501	61	21	61	1	233	13	5	249	266	416	91	86	92	4	76	0.17	45	18	37	26	78	DCf	5%	110	79	16%	10%	62	2%	50%	-6.7	63	$10
19	MIN	464	61	23	59	1	256	19	2	256	304	473	108	128	100	4	73	0.17	43	20	37	30	98	CCd	9%	119	103	20%	16%	68	2%	50%	-1.3	70	$11
20	DET	176	26	8	23	0	278	5	2	255	324	475	106	96	108	5	76	0.21	51	18	30	32	74	CDf	6%	100	49	21%	13%	137	0%	0%	2.8	144	$14
21	DET	674	85	22	84	2	278	20	2	253	320	435	104	126	95	5	79	0.28	48	19	33	32	98	CCf	7%	90	66	13%	12%	75	1%	100%	11.4	85	$21
22	DET	510	48	11	38	5	202	10	1	240	239	322	80	71	82	4	78	0.18	46	19	35	24	86	CCf	5%	80	81	8%	8%	74	6%	100%	-18.7	24	$2
1st Half		303	26	6	22	3	208	6	1	242	244	323	80	73	82	4	78	0.18	48	19	33	25	100	CCf	6%	75	80	8%	8%	75	6%	100%	-12.5	21	$4
2nd Half		207	22	5	16	2	192	4	1	237	232	321	78	67	82	4	77	0.18	44	19	38	22	67	DDf	4%	88	81	9%	7%	75	6%	100%	-9.8	34	$0
23	Proj	**420**	**49**	**13**	**43**	**2**	**235**	**11**	**3**	**246**	**276**	**384**	**92**	**95**	**90**	**5**	**77**	**0.21**	**47**	**19**	**34**	**27**	**86**		**6%**	**96**	**74**	**12%**	**10%**	**76**	**5%**	**95%**	**-3.2**	**61**	**$10**

Schwarber,Kyle

Age: 30	Pos: LF	Health B	LIMA Plan B+
Bats: L	Ht: 6' 0" Wt: 229	PT/Exp A	Rand Var +3
		Consist D	MM 5125

Fly ball surge fueled massive power outburst, while elite HR/F once again came with full support from xHR/F. Also nearly doubled career SB total for good measure, and xBA shows BA crash was somewhat h% induced. A decent bet for 40+ HR and improved BA, but don't bank on anything close to repeat on the basepaths.

Yr	Tm	PA	R	HR	RBI	SB	BA	xHR	xSB	xBA	OBP	SLG	OPS+	vL+	vR+	bb%	ct%	Eye	G	L	F	h%	HctX	QBaB	Brl%	PX	xPX	HR/F	xHR/F	Spd	SBA%	SB%	RAR	BPX	R$
18	CHC	510	64	26	61	4	238	24	8	243	356	467	110	87	113	15	67	0.56	44	19	37	29	100	ACc	13%	143	119	25%	23%	98	5%	57%	11.3	150	$13
19	CHC	610	82	38	92	2	250	41	4	263	339	531	120	105	123	11	71	0.45	38	20	42	28	102	ABc	15%	154	140	24%	26%	75	4%	40%	12.3	196	$18
20	CHC	224	30	11	24	1	188	11	1	220	308	393	93	78	99	13	65	0.45	51	15	35	22	108	ADd	11%	124	128	26%	26%	85	2%	100%	-9.3	60	$9
21	2 TM	471	76	32	71	1	266	34	2	263	374	554	127	107	137	14	68	0.50	38	21	41	31	109	ABc	18%	174	136	29%	30%	68	2%	50%	28.1	235	$18
22	PHI	669	100	46	94	10	218	48	2	246	323	504	117	96	128	13	65	0.43	33	16	51	24	110	AAd	20%	192	181	24%	25%	75	8%	91%	23.8	224	$25
1st Half		345	57	25	53	4	219	27	1	251	336	517	121	107	129	15	65	0.50	35	13	52	23	106	AAf	21%	202	193	25%	27%	61	8%	100%	15.0	252	$33
2nd Half		324	43	21	41	6	218	21	1	242	309	491	113	82	127	11	65	0.36	32	18	50	25	114	AAd	18%	182	168	23%	23%	93	8%	86%	7.9	203	$27
23	Proj	**630**	**94**	**41**	**90**	**5**	**238**	**43**	**7**	**250**	**342**	**509**	**118**	**97**	**127**	**13**	**67**	**0.45**	**35**	**19**	**46**	**28**	**109**		**17%**	**183**	**156**	**24%**	**25%**	**76**	**6%**	**68%**	**31.0**	**205**	**$26**

Seager,Corey

Age: 29	Pos: SS	Health C	LIMA Plan A
Bats: L	Ht: 6' 4" Wt: 215	PT/Exp A	Rand Var +5
		Consist C	MM 4255

Celebrated first season in TEX with good health while blowing past career-high in HR. While BA took a hit, xBA shows that should not have been the case, and shift restrictions could help push back towards .300. Tough to poke many holes in these skills, so if he can keep injuries at bay, don't be surprised if he combines 2020-21 BA with 2022 power display.

Yr	Tm	PA	R	HR	RBI	SB	BA	xHR	xSB	xBA	OBP	SLG	OPS+	vL+	vR+	bb%	ct%	Eye	G	L	F	h%	HctX	QBaB	Brl%	PX	xPX	HR/F	xHR/F	Spd	SBA%	SB%	RAR	BPX	R$
18	LA	115	13	2	13	0	267	4	2	280	348	396	100	88	104	10	83	0.65	45	28	27	30	108	ACa	8%	74	79	9%	17%	108	0%	0%	1.7	150	$0
19	LA	541	82	19	87	1	272	22	2	278	335	483	113	98	120	8	80	0.45	39	22	39	31	117	CCc	7%	117	130	12%	14%	87	1%	100%	6.8	215	$16
20	LA	232	38	15	41	1	307	17	1	297	358	585	125	108	133	7	83	0.46	38	23	39	31	174	ACb	16%	137	171	22%	25%	99	2%	100%	17.9	344	$30
21	LA	409	54	16	57	1	306	19	4	283	394	521	126	125	126	12	81	0.73	46	21	33	34	136	ACc	12%	117	125	16%	20%	108	2%	50%	29.9	296	$16
22	TEX	663	91	33	83	3	245	33	3	278	317	455	109	107	110	9	83	0.56	40	21	39	25	134	ACc	10%	117	143	17%	17%	78	2%	100%	13.2	231	$21
1st Half		339	40	16	39	3	236	17	1	268	307	426	104	110	101	9	81	0.51	36	24	40	24	128	ABc	10%	106	131	16%	17%	74	2%	100%	1.3	179	$21
2nd Half		324	51	17	44	0	253	16	1	287	327	486	115	104	122	9	84	0.63	44	18	38	25	141	ACb	10%	128	155	18%	17%	88	2%	0%	9.5	293	$27
23	Proj	**595**	**85**	**27**	**83**	**2**	**286**	**30**	**4**	**282**	**359**	**500**	**119**	**113**	**122**	**10**	**82**	**0.60**	**42**	**21**	**37**	**30**	**137**		**11%**	**124**	**138**	**17%**	**18%**	**95**	**4%**	**80%**	**36.9**	**265**	**$28**

Segura,Jean

Age: 33	Pos: 2B	Health D	LIMA Plan C+
Bats: R	Ht: 5' 10" Wt: 220	PT/Exp B	Rand Var -1
		Consist B	MM 1335

10-33-.277 with 13 SB in 387 PA at PHI. Broken finger in May knocked him out for two months and may have played role in power, xBA cratering in 2nd half. Not at an age where SBA% spike is likely to stick, but he'll still run and ct% should help him maintain strong BA. Upside is limited, but seems safe to lock in double-digit HR/SB.

Yr	Tm	PA	R	HR	RBI	SB	BA	xHR	xSB	xBA	OBP	SLG	OPS+	vL+	vR+	bb%	ct%	Eye	G	L	F	h%	HctX	QBaB	Brl%	PX	xPX	HR/F	xHR/F	Spd	SBA%	SB%	RAR	BPX	R$
18	SEA	632	91	10	63	20	304	12	10	272	341	415	101	106	97	5	88	0.46	51	19	29	33	84	CDc	4%	63	59	7%	8%	116	18%	65%	11.6	167	$27
19	PHI	618	79	12	60	10	280	14	15	291	323	420	103	126	95	5	87	0.41	52	21	27	30	100	CDc	3%	72	61	9%	10%	105	8%	83%	2.9	185	$17
20	PHI	217	28	7	25	2	266	6	5	240	347	422	102	108	99	11	77	0.51	48	18	34	31	96	CCf	6%	80	64	14%	12%	146	7%	50%	-0.6	148	$16
21	PHI	567	76	14	58	9	290	12	8	275	348	436	108	120	102	7	85	0.50	52	19	29	32	100	CDd	6%	79	68	11%	10%	106	8%	75%	12.4	192	$21
22	PHI *	420	47	10	35	14	266	7	6	248	317	368	97	120	95	7	83	0.43	57	16	27	30	96	CFf	4%	58	57	13%	9%	91	17%	70%	-1.6	72	$15
1st Half		179	22	6	19	8	275	4	2	259	324	407	103	96	107	6	84	0.38	54	16	30	30	113	BDf	6%	71	70	14%	10%	78	17%	89%	3.8	107	$10
2nd Half		241	25	4	16	6	259	3	4	238	317	337	93	142	85	8	82	0.46	59	17	24	30	82	DFf	3%	47	45	11%	8%	100	17%	55%	-2.8	41	$8
23	Proj	**525**	**66**	**12**	**50**	**11**	**269**	**11**	**14**	**256**	**331**	**385**	**99**	**115**	**93**	**7**	**83**	**0.46**	**54**	**18**	**28**	**30**	**96**		**5%**	**69**	**60**	**11%**	**9%**	**103**	**13%**	**65%**	**7.4**	**124**	**$21**

BRIAN RUDD

Semien,Marcus

Age: 32 Pos: 2B	Health A	LIMA Plan B+
Bats: R Ht: 6' 0" Wt: 195	PT/Exp A	Rand Var +1
	Consist D	MM 3435

Three straight years with D or F in Consistency underlines five-category volatility, and warns to prepare for more swings. Struggled in new home park (.210 BA, 10 HR), though TEX did give greener light that led to career-high SB. xHR suggests 30-ish HR is true ceiling, career .254 xBA sets BA guideline, but he's less dependable than you want in an early pick.

Yr	Tm	PA	R	HR	RBI	SB	BA	xHR	xSB	xBA	OBP	SLG	OPS+	vL+	vR+	bb%	ct%	Eye	G	L	F	h%	HctX	QBaB	Brl%	PX	xPX	HR/F	xHR/F	Spd	SBA%	SB%	RAR	BPX	R$
18	OAK	703	89	15	70	14	255	17	10	248	318	388	95	100	90	9	79	0.47	39	23	38	30	95	CBc	5%	83	90	8%	9%	108	12%	70%	2.5	117	$19
19	OAK	747	123	33	92	10	285	33	17	290	369	522	123	129	120	12	84	0.85	41	20	39	30	122	CBc	9%	114	105	15%	15%	136	9%	56%	35.2	352	$29
20	OAK	236	28	7	23	4	223	7	4	225	305	374	90	103	86	11	76	0.50	33	20	47	26	86	DAf	5%	85	111	9%	9%	125	7%	100%	-4.9	136	$13
21	TOR	724	115	45	102	15	265	32	8	272	334	538	120	106	125	9	78	0.45	31	21	48	28	114	BAc	10%	150	144	18%	13%	98	10%	94%	38.9	308	$34
22	TEX	724	101	26	83	25	248	21	13	249	304	429	104	106	103	7	82	0.44	34	19	47	27	106	CAc	7%	105	116	10%	8%	141	21%	76%	14.2	241	$31
1st Half		348	44	10	35	14	241	6	7	230	296	383	96	109	91	7	81	0.42	36	17	47	27	95	DAc	5%	85	112	8%	5%	119	21%	88%	0.3	152	$26
2nd Half		376	57	16	48	11	255	15	7	266	311	472	111	104	114	8	82	0.47	32	21	47	27	116	CAc	8%	123	119	12%	11%	148	21%	65%	9.5	310	$37
23	Proj	**700**	**103**	**28**	**86**	**19**	**253**	**25**	**19**	**253**	**318**	**450**	**107**	**105**	**107**	**9**	**80**	**0.47**	**33**	**20**	**47**	**28**	**107**		**8%**	**118**	**122**	**12%**	**10%**	**112**	**16%**	**78%**	**22.1**	**253**	**$29**

Senzel,Nick

Age: 28 Pos: CF	Health F	LIMA Plan D+
Bats: R Ht: 6' 1" Wt: 205	PT/Exp C	Rand Var 0
	Consist A	MM 1223

Another year of missed time (two COVID IL trips, recurring back, hammy issues, broken toe) and unfulfilled expectations. Even when in the lineup, he's showing no signs of growth, with QBaB and xHR/F especially flat. Tempting to think, "This time, it'll be different," but isn't that how Charlie Brown winds up on his back every time he goes to kick the football?

Yr	Tm	PA	R	HR	RBI	SB	BA	xHR	xSB	xBA	OBP	SLG	OPS+	vL+	vR+	bb%	ct%	Eye	G	L	F	h%	HctX	QBaB	Brl%	PX	xPX	HR/F	xHR/F	Spd	SBA%	SB%	RAR	BPX	R$
18	aaa	187	19	5	21	7	280		3		342	457	107			9	74	0.36				35				114				102	19%	75%		123	$5
19	CIN *	447	61	13	44	14	254	14	13	243	309	419	101	126	94	7	72	0.28	48	19	33	32	100	CCc	8%	95	77	13%	16%	147	19%	74%	1.2	85	$13
20	CIN	77	8	2	8	2	186	2	1	252	247	357	80	46	101	8	79	0.40	38	20	43	21	119	CBc	4%	106	143	8%	8%	87	27%	67%	-5.2	172	$1
21	CIN *	161	22	1	10	2	250	2	6	263	314	326	88	101	85	8	87	0.74	46	24	30	28	100	CCc	4%	45	59	3%	7%	125	17%	29%	-6.2	162	$1
22	CIN	411	45	5	25	8	231	6	10	237	296	306	85	83	86	7	80	0.39	46	23	31	28	88	CCc	3%	51	74	5%	6%	106	13%	62%	-13.7	28	$5
1st Half		204	25	2	14	5	245	3	5	219	299	303	85	69	91	6	78	0.31	45	22	33	31	97	CCc	4%	40	84	4%	6%	114	13%	71%	-5.4	-28	$4
2nd Half		207	20	3	11	3	216	3	5	253	293	308	85	95	80	8	82	0.50	47	23	29	25	79	DCc	2%	61	64	7%	7%	102	13%	50%	-7.3	86	$0
23	Proj	**385**	**46**	**6**	**27**	**8**	**236**	**7**	**7**	**243**	**298**	**334**	**88**	**88**	**87**	**8**	**80**	**0.42**	**45**	**22**	**32**	**28**	**95**		**4%**	**66**	**76**	**6%**	**8%**	**109**	**11%**	**53%**	**-7.3**	**90**	**$9**

Serven,Brian

Age: 28 Pos: CA	Health A	LIMA Plan D
Bats: R Ht: 6' 0" Wt: 195	PT/Exp D	Rand Var +2
	Consist A	MM 1203

6-16-.203 in 205 PA at COL. Hit all six MLB HR at Coors, where he posted .810 OPS, but subpar power skills across the board warn against a repeat. Strong throwing arm is main asset, and projects out as career backup CA with limited fantasy appeal. Hey, they can't all be Buster Poseys; the baseball world needs Henry Blancos and Sal Fasanos, too.

Yr	Tm	PA	R	HR	RBI	SB	BA	xHR	xSB	xBA	OBP	SLG	OPS+	vL+	vR+	bb%	ct%	Eye	G	L	F	h%	HctX	QBaB	Brl%	PX	xPX	HR/F	xHR/F	Spd	SBA%	SB%	RAR	BPX	R$
18																																			
19	aa	264	34	10	29	1	210		3		275	384	91			8	74	0.35				24				98				92	6%	31%		81	$1
20																																			
21	aaa	262	21	10	22	1	205		2		234	384	85			4	73	0.14				24				104				105	3%	100%		58	$0
22	COL *	290	28	9	22	0	203	2	2	233	262	335	84	89	82	7	77	0.34	45	20	35	23	80	FCf	3%	77	71	12%	4%	110	0%	0%	-6.6	62	-$1
1st Half		160	18	6	15	0	246	1	1	241	316	402	102	133	113	9	78	0.46	45	19	36	28	96	DCd	4%	89	66	16%	5%	130	0%	0%	3.1	141	$0
2nd Half		130	10	3	7	0	151	1	1	222	203	252	64	63	65	5	76	0.21	44	21	34	17	71	FCf	2%	63	74	10%	3%	90	0%	0%	-8.4	-31	-$8
23	Proj	**280**	**26**	**5**	**23**	**1**	**210**	**3**	**1**	**219**	**260**	**308**	**79**	**88**	**76**	**6**	**75**	**0.23**	**45**	**20**	**35**	**26**	**81**		**3%**	**66**	**71**	**7%**	**4%**	**91**	**2%**	**71%**	**-6.9**	**50**	**$2**

Sheets,Gavin

Age: 27 Pos: RF	Health A	LIMA Plan C+
Bats: L Ht: 6' 5" Wt: 230	PT/Exp C	Rand Var 0
	Consist A	MM 4013

15-53-.241 in 410 PA at CHW. He's got some pop, but xHR/F continues to say it's not as strong as it appears (career 18 xHR to 26 actual). Rise in FB% had no impact on xPX due to loss of exit velocity, HctX—all it did was drive xBA further south. Best use is platoon vR (career .785 OPS, 132 PX), so value is likely to stay modest.

Yr	Tm	PA	R	HR	RBI	SB	BA	xHR	xSB	xBA	OBP	SLG	OPS+	vL+	vR+	bb%	ct%	Eye	G	L	F	h%	HctX	QBaB	Brl%	PX	xPX	HR/F	xHR/F	Spd	SBA%	SB%	RAR	BPX	R$
18																																			
19	aa	517	55	17	82	3	256		7		332	404	102			10	76	0.48				30				78				89	3%	73%		59	$12
20																																			
21	CHW *	424	48	19	66	1	241	8	3	236	302	437	102	37	124	8	72	0.31	45	17	38	29	117	BCd	10%	118	110	24%	17%	54	2%	37%	-8.0	69	$9
22	CHW *	448	38	16	57	0	238	10	2	228	286	409	98	65	105	6	77	0.30	40	15	45	27	98	CBd	7%	109	103	11%	8%	83	0%	0%	-8.9	124	$8
1st Half		231	16	6	21	0	219	4	1	226	274	369	91	55	99	7	77	0.33	36	17	46	26	88	CBf	8%	102	101	8%	7%	97	0%	0%	-8.5	117	-$1
2nd Half		217	22	10	36	0	257	7	1	233	295	450	106	74	109	6	78	0.27	43	13	43	28	106	CCc	6%	116	105	14%	10%	78	0%	0%	0.1	145	$12
23	Proj	**420**	**42**	**18**	**62**	**1**	**242**	**16**	**1**	**237**	**302**	**435**	**102**	**53**	**109**	**7**	**75**	**0.33**	**42**	**16**	**43**	**28**	**106**		**8%**	**123**	**106**	**15%**	**13%**	**67**	**1%**	**57%**	**4.9**	**100**	**$13**

Siri,Jose

Age: 27 Pos: CF	Health A	LIMA Plan D
Bats: R Ht: 6' 2" Wt: 175	PT/Exp C	Rand Var +3
	Consist B	MM 3501

7-24-.213 with 14 SB in 325 PA at HOU/TAM. Intriguing HR/SB combo remains perpetually undermined by atrocious plate discipline. Larger MLB sample yielded lackluster power skills, with 20 HR looking further out of reach than it did a year ago. But speed skills are legit and his ticket to profit; worth a flyer in case injuries thrust him into larger role.

Yr	Tm	PA	R	HR	RBI	SB	BA	xHR	xSB	xBA	OBP	SLG	OPS+	vL+	vR+	bb%	ct%	Eye	G	L	F	h%	HctX	QBaB	Brl%	PX	xPX	HR/F	xHR/F	Spd	SBA%	SB%	RAR	BPX	R$
18	aa	274	36	11	29	12	211		3		271	426	93			8	59	0.20				30				147				155	35%	69%		63	$7
19	a/a	506	48	10	46	22	214		21		273	326	83			7	58	0.19				34				80				103	28%	71%		-200	$10
20																																			
21	HOU *	428	56	15	56	19	253	5	6	189	284	433	99	147	123	4	58	0.11	34	14	52	39	82	BBa	17%	137	150	27%	33%	138	29%	80%	-2.1	-15	$18
22	2 AL *	400	63	12	37	15	214	7	14	218	261	373	90	66	93	6	64	0.18	43	21	36	30	66	DBd	6%	117	72	10%	10%	163	22%	88%	-6.8	41	$11
1st Half		166	22	5	14	7	196	3	6	220	249	365	87	42	92	7	65	0.20	44	18	38	26	71	CBc	7%	118	78	9%	9%	157	22%	87%	-4.8	66	$3
2nd Half		234	41	7	23	9	227	3	8	218	270	379	92	83	93	6	63	0.16	42	24	35	33	63	DBf	6%	116	68	11%	8%	155	22%	90%	-3.1	14	$16
23	Proj	**245**	**35**	**5**	**26**	**10**	**226**	**9**	**7**	**200**	**278**	**355**	**88**	**67**	**95**	**6**	**61**	**0.16**	**43**	**21**	**36**	**34**	**66**		**6%**	**105**	**72**	**10%**	**18%**	**144**	**19%**	**81%**	**-3.8**	**-1**	**$9**

Slater,Austin

Age: 30 Pos: CF	Health B	LIMA Plan C
Bats: R Ht: 6' 1" Wt: 204	PT/Exp C	Rand Var -1
	Consist C	MM 3423

Unexpected outbursts—a little BA here, a few extra steals there—have kept him fantasy-relevant even in part-time role, but even his strongest skills (bb%, Spd, SB%) have been subject to troubling inconsistency. xHR, xHR/F suggest power should rebound a bit, while falling xBA matches recent ct%, LD% slide. Streaming him vL remains the way to go.

Yr	Tm	PA	R	HR	RBI	SB	BA	xHR	xSB	xBA	OBP	SLG	OPS+	vL+	vR+	bb%	ct%	Eye	G	L	F	h%	HctX	QBaB	Brl%	PX	xPX	HR/F	xHR/F	Spd	SBA%	SB%	RAR	BPX	R$
18	SF *	435	43	4	45	13	263	2	6	251	323	371	93	87	83	8	70	0.30	63	21	16	37	97	CFa	2%	83	31	5%	10%	102	14%	84%	0.0	-7	$11
19	SF *	467	55	13	55	5	245	9	10	246	337	410	103	117	92	12	65	0.40	52	25	23	34	102	CFb	10%	107	113	20%	36%	111	6%	69%	4.4	22	$9
20	SF	104	18	5	7	8	282	5	2	266	408	506	121	147	98	15	74	0.73	40	29	32	33	94	CCb	14%	114	120	25%	25%	150	26%	89%	6.0	264	$16
21	SF	306	39	12	32	15	241	12	11	255	320	423	102	122	69	9	69	0.33	51	24	26	30	82	DDb	9%	113	88	25%	25%	96	23%	88%	1.0	65	$12
22	SF	325	49	7	34	12	264	10	13	243	366	408	110	115	101	12	68	0.45	52	22	26	36	92	CFa	10%	108	92	15%	21%	125	14%	92%	9.7	76	$12
1st Half		143	22	5	17	4	252	5	6	226	371	420	112	112	111	16	63	0.50	55	20	25	36	91	CFc	12%	109	109	26%	26%	187	14%	100%	5.4	100	$4
2nd Half		182	27	2	17	8	272	5	7	254	363	399	108	119	95	10	72	0.40	51	23	26	37	93	CDa	10%	107	81	7%	17%	91	14%	89%	5.0	72	$9
23	Proj	**280**	**41**	**8**	**29**	**12**	**258**	**10**	**7**	**249**	**353**	**420**	**107**	**120**	**91**	**11**	**69**	**0.42**	**51**	**23**	**26**	**34**	**90**		**10%**	**116**	**92**	**19%**	**23%**	**104**	**11%**	**90%**	**10.1**	**88**	**$14**

Smith,Josh

Age: 25 Pos: 3B LF	Health A	LIMA Plan D
Bats: L Ht: 5' 10" Wt: 172	PT/Exp C	Rand Var 0
	Consist C	MM 1301

2-16-.197 with 4 SB in 253 PA at TEX. Not great that he couldn't hold down role on 94-loss team, with extreme power outage being main driver of poor showing. The fact that plate skills held up well in AAA/MLB is encouraging; drops in SBA%, SB% are not. Too talented and young to write off, but probably best to spend 2023 observing from a distance.

Yr	Tm	PA	R	HR	RBI	SB	BA	xHR	xSB	xBA	OBP	SLG	OPS+	vL+	vR+	bb%	ct%	Eye	G	L	F	h%	HctX	QBaB	Brl%	PX	xPX	HR/F	xHR/F	Spd	SBA%	SB%	RAR	BPX	R$
18																																			
19																																			
20																																			
21	aa	117	10	2	8	6	260		2		353	376	100			13	78	0.65				31				70				94	24%	72%		85	$2
22	TEX *	494	50	5	43	9	208	3	17	208	287	290	82	66	81	10	74	0.42	34	24	42	27	75	DAf	2%	57	82	3%	4%	120	14%	54%	-20.6	-7	$4
1st Half		257	25	2	19	7	207	0	9	238	285	277	79	40	102	10	73	0.41	30	38	33	27	70	DAa	0%	50	92	0%	0%	111	14%	54%	-13.3	-41	$3
2nd Half		237	24	3	24	3	210	3	8	204	289	305	84	74	75	10	74	0.43	35	20	46	27	76	DAf	2%	66	79	4%	5%	124	14%	57%	-9.3	28	$3
23	Proj	**210**	**20**	**2**	**17**	**7**	**227**	**2**	**5**	**217**	**330**	**302**	**88**	**64**	**93**	**11**	**75**	**0.50**	**33**	**27**	**40**	**29**	**74**		**1%**	**56**	**84**	**3%**	**3%**	**117**	**12%**	**67%**	**-4.2**	**34**	**$5**

BRANDON KRUSE

Smith,Kevin

Age: 26 Pos: 3B
Bats: R Ht: 6' 0" Wt: 190

Health	A	LIMA Plan	D
PT/Exp	C	Rand Var	0
Consist	F	MM	2301

2-13-.180 with 4 SB in 151 PA at OAK. There's ct%/BA issues, and then there's ct%/BA issues so bad they get you demoted by a last-place team. Demotion didn't light a fire either, as he continued to struggle in AAA. Hidden behind holes in his swing are some promising power and speed skills, but after 2022, feels like he's light years away from MLB.

Yr	Tm	PA	R	HR	RBI	SB	BA	xHR	xSB	xBA	OBP	SLG	OPS+	vL+	vR+	bb%	ct%	Eye	G	L	F	h%	HctX	QBaB	Brl%	PX	xPX	HR/F	xHR/F	Spd	SBA%	SB%	RAR	BPX	R$
18																																			
19	aa	457	47	18	58	11	205		4		252	395	90			6	62	0.17				28				125				95	24%	62%		-26	$7
20																																			
21	TOR *	430	58	20	61	16	245	2	5	185	319	485	110	75	18	10	69	0.35	19	0	81	30	107	CAb	14%	152	192	6%	12%	124	21%	82%	12.9	212	$18
22	OAK *	498	32	8	38	7	184	4	9	174	220	287	72	106	55	4	61	0.12	41	13	46	28	66	DCf	8%	88	105	4%	9%	102	10%	85%	-29.8	-145	-$2
1st Half		220	13	2	17	5	171	4	4	180	206	257	65	106	54	4	67	0.13	41	13	46	24	72	DCf	8%	71	105	4%	9%	104	10%	100%	-16.5	-114	-$4
2nd Half		278	19	6	22	3	194		6	187	231	312	77	0	0	5	57	0.11	44	20	36	31	0			104	-14	0%		109	10%	67%	-16.1	-155	$2
23	**Proj**	**175**	**17**	**2**	**19**	**4**	**210**	**5**	**2**	**180**	**261**	**310**	**79**	**113**	**60**	**7**	**64**	**0.20**	**41**	**13**	**46**	**32**	**65**		**7%**	**87**	**95**	**4%**	**11%**	**105**	**9%**	**83%**	**-5.6**	**13**	**$0**

Smith,Pavin

Age: 27 Pos: RF DH
Bats: L Ht: 6' 2" Wt: 208

Health	A	LIMA Plan	D
PT/Exp	C	Rand Var	+1
Consist	A	MM	2411

Fractured right wrist four days after being demoted for poor performance; not a good year. Rising FB%, more free-swinging approach has briefly yielded only league average power while coming at steep cost to BA/xBA. Improved plate patience and rising launch angle early on are positive signs to build on, but not necessarily to bid on.

Yr	Tm	PA	R	HR	RBI	SB	BA	xHR	xSB	xBA	OBP	SLG	OPS+	vL+	vR+	bb%	ct%	Eye	G	L	F	h%	HctX	QBaB	Brl%	PX	xPX	HR/F	xHR/F	Spd	SBA%	SB%	RAR	BPX	R$
18																																			
19	aa	497	58	11	63	2	282		9		364	457	114			11	85	0.87				31				86				127	2%	63%		270	$12
20	ARI	44	7	1	4	1	270	1	1	269	341	405	99	112	96	11	78	0.63	45	32	23	32	92	CDf	6%	58	46	14%	14%	148	8%	100%	0.1	116	$2
21	ARI	545	68	11	49	1	267	14	9	253	328	404	101	83	107	8	79	0.40	47	21	32	32	111	CDf	5%	81	94	9%	11%	126	1%	100%	-2.6	135	$12
22	ARI	277	24	9	33	1	220	11	1	210	300	367	94	81	99	10	73	0.42	43	14	43	27	82	CBf	10%	96	92	12%	14%	95	2%	100%	-4.0	62	$2
1st Half		241	20	9	31	1	207	11	1	201	290	362	92	70	99	11	70	0.40	43	13	45	25	81	CBf	12%	100	100	13%	16%	97	2%	100%	-5.2	48	$5
2nd Half		36	4	0	2	0	313	0	0	263	361	406	109	158	93	9	88	0.75	45	21	34	36	92	FCc	0%	74	46	0%	0%	103	2%	0%	1.2	203	-$9
23	**Proj**	**175**	**19**	**3**	**21**	**1**	**252**	**6**	**2**	**238**	**328**	**378**	**98**	**99**	**97**	**10**	**78**	**0.54**	**45**	**19**	**36**	**30**	**97**		**5%**	**82**	**79**	**7%**	**14%**	**117**	**5%**	**81%**	**1.5**	**159**	**$4**

Smith,Will

Age: 28 Pos: CA DH
Bats: R Ht: 5' 10" Wt: 195

Health	B	LIMA Plan	B
PT/Exp	A	Rand Var	+1
Consist	C	MM	4335

Career-high PA, RBI while just missing out on new highs in R, HR helped solidify his status as one of the best backstops in the game. Last two seasons have given us power skills so stable you could set your watch to them, and BA/xBA have stayed in tight range as well. That and good health make him a top-tier CA option you can target with confidence.

Yr	Tm	PA	R	HR	RBI	SB	BA	xHR	xSB	xBA	OBP	SLG	OPS+	vL+	vR+	bb%	ct%	Eye	G	L	F	h%	HctX	QBaB	Brl%	PX	xPX	HR/F	xHR/F	Spd	SBA%	SB%	RAR	BPX	R$
18	a/a	383	44	15	45	4	200		4		265	376	86			8	64	0.25				26				126				86	6%	100%		0	$4
19	LA *	447	65	30	81	3	236	10	4	248	315	515	115	95	140	10	72	0.41	29	17	54	25	111	BAb	11%	147	168	23%	15%	94	3%	100%	12.9	211	$13
20	LA	137	23	8	25	0	289	6	1	301	401	579	130	110	138	15	81	0.91	24	27	49	30	133	BAb	13%	153	161	17%	13%	88	0%	0%	13.2	412	$14
21	LA	501	71	25	76	3	258	23	3	258	365	495	118	100	126	12	76	0.57	31	22	46	28	115	BAc	11%	131	140	17%	15%	104	2%	100%	25.8	246	$17
22	LA	578	68	24	87	1	260	26	4	264	343	465	114	127	110	10	81	0.58	32	21	47	28	116	BAc	11%	119	144	12%	13%	98	1%	100%	25.5	241	$19
1st Half		277	32	13	38	0	253	13	2	272	343	456	113	129	108	11	83	0.78	30	23	48	26	117	BAb	12%	113	145	13%	13%	71	1%	0%	11.9	241	$15
2nd Half		301	36	11	49	1	266	14	2	260	342	472	115	125	112	9	79	0.45	34	20	46	30	115	BAc	10%	126	144	11%	14%	119	1%	100%	14.1	248	$22
23	**Proj**	**525**	**72**	**26**	**84**	**2**	**265**	**25**	**3**	**263**	**356**	**495**	**118**	**112**	**120**	**11**	**78**	**0.55**	**31**	**22**	**48**	**29**	**117**		**11%**	**139**	**147**	**15%**	**14%**	**91**	**3%**	**100%**	**34.8**	**248**	**$23**

Solano,Donovan

Age: 35 Pos: 1B DH
Bats: R Ht: 5' 8" Wt: 210

Health	F	LIMA Plan	D+
PT/Exp	C	Rand Var	0
Consist	B	MM	2143

4-24-.284 in 304 PA at CIN. Spring hamstring injury kept him out of action til June, adding up to 130 IL days last two years. Penchant for roping line drives seems to continually boost BA above skills, while xBA keeps warning what'll happen if those extra hits ever find gloves instead of grass. With most of value tied to BA, that makes him a risky investment.

Yr	Tm	PA	R	HR	RBI	SB	BA	xHR	xSB	xBA	OBP	SLG	OPS+	vL+	vR+	bb%	ct%	Eye	G	L	F	h%	HctX	QBaB	Brl%	PX	xPX	HR/F	xHR/F	Spd	SBA%	SB%	RAR	BPX	R$
18	aaa	324	26	3	29	3	241		4		265	323	79			3	83	0.20				28				55				85	6%	68%		33	$2
19	SF *	321	35	5	34	0	307	5	4	280	343	419	105	117	107	5	79	0.26	37	34	29	37	104	CBb	4%	64	77	8%	10%	104	1%	0%	-0.4	41	$7
20	SF	203	22	3	29	0	326	4	1	265	365	463	110	113	108	5	79	0.26	36	28	36	40	110	CBc	5%	86	90	5%	7%	98	0%	0%	7.2	112	$18
21	SF	344	35	7	31	2	280	9	1	261	344	404	103	112	97	7	81	0.43	40	26	34	33	98	CCb	7%	74	98	8%	10%	71	2%	100%	-2.2	81	$8
22	CIN *	334	23	5	26	0	283	5	1	261	327	391	102	108	100	6	78	0.31	45	27	28	35	113	CCb	6%	79	87	7%	8%	51	0%	0%	-0.1	21	$6
1st Half		71	4	1	5	0	254	1	0	318	290	412	99	114	89	5	78	0.23	39	36	25	31	86	BCa	11%	127	84	0%	14%	64	0%	0%	-1.0	159	-$10
2nd Half		263	19	4	21	0	290	5	1	249	342	386	103	107	102	7	78	0.33	46	26	28	36	117	CCb	5%	66	87	7%	9%	54	0%	0%	0.4	-7	$7
23	**Proj**	**350**	**30**	**5**	**32**	**1**	**274**	**8**	**1**	**267**	**331**	**387**	**100**	**107**	**95**	**6**	**80**	**0.32**	**41**	**29**	**30**	**33**	**103**		**7%**	**82**	**89**	**6%**	**11%**	**65**	**1%**	**88%**	**2.2**	**69**	**$9**

Soler,Jorge

Age: 31 Pos: LF
Bats: R Ht: 6' 4" Wt: 235

Health	F	LIMA Plan	C+
PT/Exp	B	Rand Var	+3
Consist	A	MM	4023

Lower back issues first surfaced in mid-May and were eventually diagnosed as bilateral pelvis inflammation, which ended season in July. Will reportedly be addressed with core-strengthening work, which could be a positive, given his history of oblique injuries. Good sign that power skills held up anyway, but health risk looms large at this point in career.

Yr	Tm	PA	R	HR	RBI	SB	BA	xHR	xSB	xBA	OBP	SLG	OPS+	vL+	vR+	bb%	ct%	Eye	G	L	F	h%	HctX	QBaB	Brl%	PX	xPX	HR/F	xHR/F	Spd	SBA%	SB%	RAR	BPX	R$
18	KC	257	27	9	28	3	265	12	4	251	354	466	110	141	98	11	69	0.41	47	19	34	34	109	BCb	10%	144	110	17%	23%	91	6%	75%	7.0	143	$5
19	KC	676	95	48	117	3	265	52	6	270	354	569	128	121	129	11	70	0.41	39	20	41	30	113	ABc	17%	168	140	28%	30%	71	3%	75%	26.4	215	$25
20	KC	172	17	8	24	0	228	9	1	222	326	443	102	94	103	11	60	0.32	38	23	39	32	102	ABd	19%	151	159	23%	26%	69	0%	0%	-1.0	16	$8
21	2 TM	594	74	27	70	0	223	34	1	234	316	432	103	115	98	11	72	0.47	42	15	43	25	110	ABd	13%	126	122	17%	21%	75	0%	0%	-10.3	146	$10
22	MIA	305	32	13	34	0	207	14	0	227	295	400	98	115	94	10	67	0.34	42	18	40	26	116	ACf	12%	138	133	18%	19%	58	3%	0%	-8.2	59	$2
1st Half		288	31	13	34	0	217	14	0	234	306	421	103	118	98	11	68	0.37	41	18	41	26	115	ACf	12%	144	138	18%	20%	58	3%	0%	-5.1	93	$11
2nd Half		17	1	0	0	0	63	0	0	116	118	63	25	0	29	6	50	0.13	63	13	25	13	137	ACa	13%	0	17	0%	0%	97	3%	0%	-2.6	-541	-$12
23	**Proj**	**420**	**48**	**20**	**55**	**1**	**231**	**23**	**2**	**239**	**323**	**449**	**107**	**117**	**104**	**11**	**67**	**0.37**	**41**	**19**	**40**	**29**	**109**		**15%**	**157**	**139**	**20%**	**23%**	**67**	**3%**	**38%**	**9.4**	**98**	**$12**

Sosa,Edmundo

Age: 27 Pos: SS 3B
Bats: R Ht: 6' 0" Wt: 210

Health	B	LIMA Plan	C
PT/Exp	D	Rand Var	+1
Consist	B	MM	2423

Couldn't crack lineup on deep STL, PHI teams, but did post league average HctX, xPX. That suggests potential for double-digit HR in addition to SB if he ever does find more PA. Career .244 xBA gives him less downside than you might expect. Poor Eye seems to be holding him back, and with no signs of growth there, he's no more than an end-gamer.

Yr	Tm	PA	R	HR	RBI	SB	BA	xHR	xSB	xBA	OBP	SLG	OPS+	vL+	vR+	bb%	ct%	Eye	G	L	F	h%	HctX	QBaB	Brl%	PX	xPX	HR/F	xHR/F	Spd	SBA%	SB%	RAR	BPX	R$
18	STL *	472	52	9	46	5	237	0	5	114	266	358	84	0	66	4	77	0.18	0	0	100	29	0	DA	0%	80	-27	0%	0%	90	10%	52%	-10.1	33	$7
19	STL *	476	58	13	49	3	254	0	7	288	276	387	92	0	100	3	77	0.13	50	33	17	31	88	FFd	0%	69	5	0%	0%	123	6%	43%	-16.2	26	$8
20																																			
21	STL	325	39	6	27	4	271	7	8	248	346	389	101	93	104	5	78	0.27	52	21	27	33	78	DFf	4%	63	66	10%	11%	183	9%	50%	-3.9	115	$7
22	2 NL	190	26	2	21	6	227	3	3	241	275	369	91	100	83	3	72	0.10	46	21	33	31	98	DCd	5%	102	99	5%	7%	159	20%	86%	-6.7	79	$3
1st Half		103	16	0	5	2	196	1	2	196	243	278	74	61	81	2	72	0.07	49	14	37	27	99	CCc	4%	49	89	0%	4%	210	20%	67%	-7.4	-10	-$7
2nd Half		87	10	2	16	4	266	2	1	287	314	481	113	133	85	4	71	0.13	42	30	28	35	96	FCf	7%	167	113	13%	13%	105	20%	100%	2.2	200	$0
23	**Proj**	**280**	**37**	**5**	**32**	**7**	**249**	**5**	**8**	**250**	**308**	**391**	**97**	**103**	**93**	**4**	**75**	**0.16**	**48**	**22**	**30**	**32**	**90**		**5%**	**97**	**88**	**8%**	**8%**	**128**	**16%**	**76%**	**-1.6**	**98**	**$10**

Soto,Juan

Age: 24 Pos: RF
Bats: L Ht: 6' 2" Wt: 224

Health	B	LIMA Plan	C
PT/Exp	A	Rand Var	+5
Consist	F	MM	4255

Slight 2nd half slide in power seemed to be less about move to PETCO and more about late Aug back stiffness, which led to .210 BA, .713 OPS, and 18-HR pace over final 147 PA. BA drop was just bad luck on worst h% of career, which impacted RBI (hit .204 w/RISP). If all of that leaves him a little undervalued this spring, count your blessings and pounce.

Yr	Tm	PA	R	HR	RBI	SB	BA	xHR	xSB	xBA	OBP	SLG	OPS+	vL+	vR+	bb%	ct%	Eye	G	L	F	h%	HctX	QBaB	Brl%	PX	xPX	HR/F	xHR/F	Spd	SBA%	SB%	RAR	BPX	R$
18	WAS *	528	80	24	79	6	293	22	9	277	404	519	124	112	125	16	76	0.78	54	17	29	34	98	BDc	10%	135	105	25%	25%	96	5%	75%	39.0	247	$23
19	WAS	659	110	34	110	12	282	40	8	280	401	548	131	118	137	16	76	0.82	42	21	37	32	108	ACc	12%	138	139	22%	26%	103	7%	92%	39.0	293	$29
20	WAS	196	39	13	37	6	351	14	3	335	490	695	157	158	155	21	82	1.46	52	20	29	36	139	AFd	18%	179	140	36%	39%	83	12%	75%	31.8	556	$36
21	WAS	654	111	29	95	9	313	31	18	285	465	534	137	119	148	22	81	1.56	53	19	29	34	130	ADd	13%	113	99	24%	26%	101	6%	56%	58.9	358	$34
22	2 NL	663	93	27	62	6	242	30	9	273	401	452	121	98	134	20	82	1.41	47	16	37	25	105	ADf	13%	120	107	17%	19%	94	4%	75%	29.4	324	$19
1st Half		344	46	15	33	5	226	17	4	274	384	449	118	97	130	20	81	1.31	51	13	36	23	100	BDf	12%	132	116	19%	21%	77	4%	71%	12.1	328	$21
2nd Half		319	47	12	29	1	260	13	5	271	420	456	124	100	137	21	82	1.52	43	20	37	27	110	ACf	13%	108	97	16%	17%	117	4%	100%	17.4	328	$20
23	**Proj**	**665**	**106**	**31**	**94**	**8**	**281**	**34**	**8**	**286**	**431**	**514**	**131**	**112**	**141**	**21**	**81**	**1.38**	**49**	**18**	**33**	**30**	**116**		**13%**	**134**	**108**	**22%**	**24%**	**94**	**5%**	**69%**	**57.8**	**354**	**$33**

BRANDON KRUSE

Springer,George

Age: 33	Pos: CF DH RF	Health	D	LIMA Plan	A
Bats: R	Ht: 6' 3" Wt: 221	PT/Exp	A	Rand Var	+1
		Consist	A	MM	4355

Looked like prime self in April (.947 OPS, 132 xPX, .292 xBA), then nagging injuries seemed to take a toll on power skills, including lowest Brl%, xPX of career. On plus side, revived long-dormant running game, though likely regression from career-best SB% may prevent double-digit SB repeat. Power should rebound, but health has raised risk level in his 30s.

Yr	Tm	PA	R	HR	RBI	SB	BA	xHR	xSB	xBA	OBP	SLG	OPS+	vL+	vR+	bb%	ct%	Eye	G	L	F	h%	HctX	QBaB	Brl%	PX	xPX	HR/F	xHR/F	Spd	SBA%	SB%	RAR	BPX	R$
18	HOU	616	102	22	71	6	265	27	9	249	346	434	105	111	100	10	78	0.52	49	16	35	31	95	CCc	9%	101	100	15%	18%	109	6%	60%	16.3	157	$20
19	HOU	556	96	39	96	6	292	37	8	289	383	591	135	126	137	12	76	0.59	45	20	36	31	119	BCd	14%	146	127	30%	28%	113	5%	75%	47.5	304	$26
20	HOU	220	37	14	32	1	265	13	4	276	359	540	119	106	124	11	80	0.63	36	21	43	26	118	CAd	12%	132	112	21%	20%	148	5%	33%	8.4	372	$22
21	TOR	341	59	22	50	4	264	20	3	273	352	555	125	128	123	11	74	0.47	33	21	47	29	103	BAc	15%	168	137	21%	19%	100	6%	80%	19.5	315	$14
22	TOR	579	89	25	76	14	267	20	9	270	342	472	115	110	117	9	81	0.54	44	18	38	29	113	CCd	8%	117	89	16%	13%	125	11%	88%	26.0	255	$27
1st Half		312	47	15	38	8	250	10	4	270	333	474	114	100	118	10	78	0.49	43	19	38	27	106	BBd	8%	132	93	18%	12%	111	11%	89%	11.1	245	$27
2nd Half		267	42	10	38	6	286	10	4	270	352	469	116	120	115	9	84	0.62	46	17	37	31	121	CCd	9%	101	85	13%	13%	132	11%	86%	13.5	262	$25
23	Proj	**560**	**93**	**33**	**89**	**9**	**269**	**28**	**10**	**279**	**349**	**525**	**121**	**120**	**122**	**10**	**78**	**0.52**	**40**	**19**	**41**	**28**	**111**		**11%**	**150**	**108**	**20%**	**18%**	**109**	**10%**	**79%**	**36.5**	**282**	**$27**

Stallings,Jacob

Age: 33	Pos: CA	Health	A	LIMA Plan	D+
Bats: R	Ht: 6' 5" Wt: 225	PT/Exp	B	Rand Var	0
		Consist	A	MM	1003

Handful of promising skills from 2021 (vR+, bb%, HctX) went away, leaving behind #2 catcher so lacking in fantasy value you might question whether he even existed. Defense is enough to keep PT coming for now, but lackluster skills suggest existential dilemma over negligible offensive impact will continue. Let this tree fall in someone else's forest.

Yr	Tm	PA	R	HR	RBI	SB	BA	xHR	xSB	xBA	OBP	SLG	OPS+	vL+	vR+	bb%	ct%	Eye	G	L	F	h%	HctX	QBaB	Brl%	PX	xPX	HR/F	xHR/F	Spd	SBA%	SB%	RAR	BPX	R$
18	PIT *	308	28	2	33	1	222	0	3	245	256	307	75	37	74	4	75	0.19	52	24	24	29	96	BCa	0%	65	33	0%	0%	92	7%	22%	-9.3	-23	$0
19	PIT *	264	34	7	18	0	252	7	3	244	306	395	97	134	86	7	79	0.37	48	19	34	29	95	CCb	6%	77	74	12%	14%	101	0%	0%	-1.5	89	$2
20	PIT	143	13	3	18	0	248	3	1	210	326	376	93	126	80	10	68	0.38	40	21	40	34	84	CCb	5%	88	110	9%	9%	96	0%	0%	0.5	-20	$5
21	PIT	427	38	8	53	0	246	8	2	245	335	369	97	81	105	11	77	0.58	44	23	33	30	106	CCc	4%	77	100	8%	8%	88	0%	0%	3.3	85	$5
22	MIA	384	25	4	34	0	223	5	1	202	292	292	83	78	84	8	76	0.35	42	19	39	28	75	DCd	3%	50	81	4%	5%	78	1%	0%	-9.9	-48	$0
1st Half		207	18	2	21	0	196	2	1	200	261	249	72	63	74	8	74	0.33	45	21	34	25	71	DDf	3%	37	78	4%	4%	81	1%	0%	-9.6	-110	-$4
2nd Half		177	7	2	13	0	255	3	1	199	330	344	95	94	96	8	78	0.38	39	18	44	31	79	CBd	4%	65	84	4%	6%	83	1%	0%	0.4	28	-$4
23	Proj	**350**	**25**	**6**	**34**	**0**	**232**	**6**	**1**	**222**	**308**	**335**	**89**	**91**	**89**	**9**	**76**	**0.42**	**43**	**20**	**37**	**29**	**88**		**4%**	**73**	**89**	**7%**	**7%**	**85**	**2%**	**10%**	**-0.3**	**13**	**$5**

Stanton,Giancarlo

Age: 33	Pos: DH RF	Health	F	LIMA Plan	B
Bats: R	Ht: 6' 6" Wt: 245	PT/Exp	A	Rand Var	+5
		Consist	B	MM	4215

Story remains the same: elite power subject to whims of fragile body. Amusingly enough, this time it was Achilles tendinitis that proved to be his Achilles heel, sapping 2nd half power skills and tanking ct%, BA. 1st half shows that when healthy, he's still a $20 hitter, but that's only happened two-and-a-half times in last five years. Not good odds.

Yr	Tm	PA	R	HR	RBI	SB	BA	xHR	xSB	xBA	OBP	SLG	OPS+	vL+	vR+	bb%	ct%	Eye	G	L	F	h%	HctX	QBaB	Brl%	PX	xPX	HR/F	xHR/F	Spd	SBA%	SB%	RAR	BPX	R$
18	NYY	705	102	38	100	5	266	39	10	250	343	509	114	137	105	10	66	0.33	45	19	37	34	103	ACd	15%	164	113	25%	26%	106	3%	100%	27.8	160	$26
19	NYY	72	8	3	13	0	288	4	1	218	403	492	124	147	116	17	59	0.50	44	22	33	44	86	ADf	25%	138	116	25%	33%	74	0%	0%	3.2	19	-$1
20	NYY	93	12	4	11	1	250	5	0	268	387	500	118	97	124	16	64	0.56	47	27	27	33	123	ADc	18%	175	86	31%	38%	67	8%	50%	2.9	208	$5
21	NYY	579	64	35	97	0	273	31	6	241	354	516	119	121	119	11	69	0.40	45	19	37	33	118	ACf	16%	144	113	27%	24%	65	0%	0%	18.7	135	$21
22	NYY	451	53	31	78	0	211	28	1	230	297	462	108	91	113	11	66	0.36	47	15	39	23	112	ACd	19%	163	125	30%	27%	69	0%	0%	-2.0	131	$11
1st Half		275	31	20	53	0	241	20	0	247	324	510	118	110	121	11	70	0.42	45	17	38	26	125	ACd	24%	165	143	31%	31%	73	0%	0%	7.2	200	$21
2nd Half		176	22	11	25	0	166	8	0	203	256	389	91	48	102	11	59	0.30	49	11	40	18	92	ACf	11%	158	93	30%	22%	75	0%	0%	-8.1	31	$4
23	Proj	**490**	**59**	**30**	**80**	**0**	**243**	**26**	**1**	**235**	**326**	**480**	**112**	**102**	**115**	**11**	**66**	**0.36**	**46**	**17**	**37**	**29**	**110**		**17%**	**159**	**110**	**29%**	**25%**	**63**	**1%**	**100%**	**13.2**	**119**	**$18**

Stassi,Max

Age: 32	Pos: CA	Health	D	LIMA Plan	D+
Bats: R	Ht: 5' 10" Wt: 200	PT/Exp	B	Rand Var	+3
		Consist	C	MM	3003

The further we get from 2020, the more his results that season looks like a small sample fluke, especially ct% and QBaB. A normalization of that ultra-low LD% should help BA, xPX bounce back a bit, making him a palatable second catcher option again. But 2022 reminds us that his skill foundation here is very shaky and won't take much for it to collapse.

Yr	Tm	PA	R	HR	RBI	SB	BA	xHR	xSB	xBA	OBP	SLG	OPS+	vL+	vR+	bb%	ct%	Eye	G	L	F	h%	HctX	QBaB	Brl%	PX	xPX	HR/F	xHR/F	Spd	SBA%	SB%	RAR	BPX	R$
18	HOU	250	28	8	27	0	226	9	3	224	316	394	95	90	96	9	67	0.31	52	18	31	30	88	BDf	9%	121	112	18%	20%	82	0%	0%	3.4	27	$2
19	2 AL	147	7	1	5	0	136	2	0	164	211	167	52	27	61	8	63	0.24	46	21	33	21	100	BCd	4%	19	55	4%	7%	85	0%	0%	-11.5	-326	-$6
20	LAA	105	12	7	20	0	278	8	0	265	352	533	118	134	100	10	77	0.52	40	22	38	29	103	ABd	11%	126	98	26%	30%	71	0%	0%	6.6	208	$9
21	LAA	319	45	13	35	0	241	13	2	229	326	426	103	87	108	9	64	0.28	44	23	33	33	79	BCf	11%	121	107	22%	22%	100	0%	0%	4.1	12	$5
22	LAA	375	32	9	30	0	180	12	2	186	267	303	81	64	90	10	66	0.34	52	10	38	24	87	CCf	10%	90	87	11%	14%	98	0%	0%	-11.1	-34	-$3
1st Half		186	14	4	14	0	204	6	1	173	306	315	88	74	95	13	64	0.41	60	12	29	29	84	BFd	11%	87	79	13%	20%	82	0%	0%	-2.5	-72	-$5
2nd Half		189	18	5	16	0	158	5	1	189	229	292	74	55	84	8	68	0.26	46	8	46	20	90	CBf	9%	93	93	9%	9%	112	0%	0%	-9.1	-3	-$4
23	Proj	**350**	**38**	**12**	**36**	**0**	**206**	**14**	**1**	**212**	**290**	**361**	**90**	**80**	**95**	**10**	**67**	**0.32**	**48**	**16**	**36**	**27**	**87**		**10%**	**109**	**94**	**16%**	**18%**	**86**	**2%**	**0%**	**-0.9**	**-6**	**$5**

Steer,Spencer

Age: 25	Pos: 3B	Health	A	LIMA Plan	D+
Bats: R	Ht: 5' 11" Wt: 185	PT/Exp	B	Rand Var	+1
		Consist	A	MM	3213

2-8-.211 in 108 PA at CIN. Hit double, HR in first MLB game, then had only five extra-base hits in 104 PA after that. Still, he's shown power growth in upper minors, and added improved plate discipline in 2022, raising prospect stock in the process. But these initial struggles suggest it might take a couple tries before he can stick the landing in the majors.

Yr	Tm	PA	R	HR	RBI	SB	BA	xHR	xSB	xBA	OBP	SLG	OPS+	vL+	vR+	bb%	ct%	Eye	G	L	F	h%	HctX	QBaB	Brl%	PX	xPX	HR/F	xHR/F	Spd	SBA%	SB%	RAR	BPX	R$
18																																			
19																																			
20																																			
21	aa	264	32	10	30	3	204		2		249	374	85			6	67	0.18				26				109				105	7%	100%		-4	$2
22	CIN *	571	66	20	59	3	226	2	6	249	289	403	98	142	76	8	75	0.35	43	19	38	27	71	DCf	5%	118	83	8%	8%	93	6%	38%	-14.6	134	$10
1st Half		302	38	15	39	1	232		3	279	284	464	106	0	0	7	77	0.31	44	20	36	25	0			146	-14	0%		102	6%	28%	-1.9	238	$17
2nd Half		268	28	5	20	1	218	2	3	218	296	332	89	142	76	10	72	0.39	43	19	38	28	69	DCf	5%	83	83	8%	8%	94	6%	58%	-8.9	17	$4
23	Proj	**420**	**49**	**11**	**43**	**3**	**216**	**8**	**4**	**227**	**287**	**362**	**90**	**148**	**75**	**7**	**71**	**0.28**	**43**	**19**	**38**	**27**	**62**		**4%**	**103**	**75**	**11%**	**8%**	**98**	**6%**	**64%**	**-7.0**	**64**	**$8**

Stephenson,Tyler

Age: 26	Pos: CA	Health	F	LIMA Plan	C+
Bats: R	Ht: 6' 4" Wt: 225	PT/Exp	D	Rand Var	-2
		Consist	C	MM	3343

The painful life of a catcher: concussion in April, near-concussion in May, fractured thumb in June, collarbone fracture ended season in late July. So it's pretty remarkable that skills held up when he did play, though BA continues to be at odds with career .268 xBA, and high GB% still caps HR output. Not as close to a breakout as he might appear.

Yr	Tm	PA	R	HR	RBI	SB	BA	xHR	xSB	xBA	OBP	SLG	OPS+	vL+	vR+	bb%	ct%	Eye	G	L	F	h%	HctX	QBaB	Brl%	PX	xPX	HR/F	xHR/F	Spd	SBA%	SB%	RAR	BPX	R$
18																																			
19	aa	347	42	6	40	0	266		5		339	387	100			10	78	0.50				33				71				96	0%	0%		67	$5
20	CIN	20	4	2	6	0	294	1	0	225	400	647	139	84	196	10	47	0.22	38	25	38	50	71	BBa	13%	268	161	67%	33%	112	0%	0%	2.1	232	$1
21	CIN	402	56	10	45	0	286	9	2	271	366	431	109	111	109	10	79	0.55	50	25	25	34	96	CDc	5%	89	67	14%	13%	96	0%	0%	16.6	142	$11
22	CIN	183	24	6	35	1	319	4	1	261	372	482	121	119	121	7	72	0.26	41	29	30	42	101	CCa	7%	113	97	17%	11%	95	2%	100%	13.4	72	$8
1st Half		155	21	5	31	1	305	3	1	252	361	468	117	110	120	7	71	0.27	42	26	33	40	89	DCa	7%	116	94	15%	9%	96	2%	100%	9.9	76	$8
2nd Half		28	3	1	4	0	400	1	0	328	429	560	140	163	126	4	76	0.17	40	45	15	50	166	ADa	5%	100	110	33%	33%	104	2%	0%	3.8	86	-$8
23	Proj	**420**	**52**	**12**	**56**	**1**	**271**	**8**	**3**	**269**	**345**	**428**	**107**	**113**	**104**	**9**	**75**	**0.40**	**46**	**27**	**26**	**33**	**134**		**6%**	**107**	**89**	**16%**	**11%**	**92**	**3%**	**100%**	**18.6**	**89**	**$15**

Story,Trevor

Age: 30	Pos: 2B	Health	C	LIMA Plan	B
Bats: R	Ht: 6' 2" Wt: 213	PT/Exp	A	Rand Var	0
		Consist	B	MM	4325

Hairline fracture in left wrist, heel contusion ruined 2nd half, closing out disappointing first year post-Coors. Even in 1st half, skills were far cry from typical levels, with career lows in xBA, ct%, HctX, exit velocity, xPX. That he still put up 20/20 pace, $20+ R$ tells us there's profit to be had with return to health, provided you can roster him at a discount.

Yr	Tm	PA	R	HR	RBI	SB	BA	xHR	xSB	xBA	OBP	SLG	OPS+	vL+	vR+	bb%	ct%	Eye	G	L	F	h%	HctX	QBaB	Brl%	PX	xPX	HR/F	xHR/F	Spd	SBA%	SB%	RAR	BPX	R$
18	COL	656	88	37	108	27	291	36	8	271	348	567	123	142	112	7	72	0.28	34	23	43	35	118	ABc	13%	172	155	20%	19%	119	23%	82%	49.2	257	$38
19	COL	656	111	35	85	23	294	27	23	259	363	554	127	130	125	9	70	0.33	33	24	42	36	107	ABb	9%	147	132	20%	15%	139	19%	74%	37.8	226	$34
20	COL	259	41	11	28	15	289	10	9	242	355	519	116	136	107	9	73	0.38	30	23	48	35	121	BAc	9%	129	146	13%	12%	169	28%	83%	13.9	268	$40
21	COL	595	88	24	75	20	251	25	22	250	329	471	110	133	101	9	74	0.38	37	19	44	30	115	BBd	10%	132	135	14%	14%	131	20%	77%	13.2	227	$24
22	BOS	396	53	16	66	13	238	16	9	229	303	434	104	119	100	8	66	0.26	36	19	45	32	95	CAf	11%	147	121	15%	15%	99	16%	100%	9.5	100	$16
1st Half		316	45	14	54	10	224	12	7	222	297	427	103	122	96	9	65	0.28	35	16	48	29	88	CAd	12%	150	118	16%	13%	106	16%	100%	3.5	107	$28
2nd Half		80	8	2	12	3	289	4	2	263	325	461	111	109	112	5	70	0.17	36	30	34	39	121	CCf	10%	137	131	11%	22%	79	16%	100%	3.6	83	-$1
23	Proj	**560**	**77**	**21**	**81**	**21**	**255**	**26**	**11**	**248**	**317**	**461**	**108**	**121**	**103**	**8**	**70**	**0.28**	**35**	**23**	**42**	**32**	**112**		**10%**	**147**	**132**	**14%**	**17%**	**97**	**12%**	**87%**	**20.2**	**165**	**$29**

BRANDON KRUSE

Stott,Bryson

Age: 25	Pos: SS 2B	Health A	LIMA Plan B
Bats: L	Ht: 6' 3" Wt: 200	PT/Exp B	Rand Var 0
		Consist A	MM 2415

10-49-.234 with 12 SB in 466 PA at PHI. Persevered through rough 1st half and blossomed in 2nd as he began making more hard contact. Post-June improvement vL was inflated by 44% h%, though it did also include 128 PX. Low xBA, xPX suggest he's not a breakout candidate, but looks ready to deliver double-digit HR, SB as a follow-up.

Yr	Tm	PA	R	HR	RBI	SB	BA	xHR	xSB	xBA	OBP	SLG	OPS+	vL+	vR+	bb%	ct%	Eye	G	L	F	h%	HctX	QBaB	Brl%	PX	xPX	HR/F	xHR/F	Spd	SBA%	SB%	RAR	BPX	R$
18																																			
19																																			
20																																			
21	a/a	375	36	8	27	4	265		5		323	396	99			8	71	0.29				35				87				100	6%	64%		0	$7
22	PHI *	504	65	11	54	13	237	7	6	241	295	367	94	105	89	8	78	0.38	46	18	36	28	93	CCf	4%	83	72	8%	6%	120	15%	77%	-10.2	110	$14
1st Half		221	30	5	27	4	201	2	3	217	270	316	83	79	76	9	75	0.38	40	19	41	24	77	DAf	3%	71	62	8%	4%	113	15%	81%	-9.3	38	$6
2nd Half		283	35	6	27	9	264	5	4	258	316	406	102	123	96	7	80	0.37	50	17	33	31	104	CCf	5%	91	77	9%	7%	124	15%	75%	1.4	162	$18
23	Proj	595	72	17	55	12	258	9	14	238	317	407	101	113	96	8	75	0.34	46	18	36	32	93		4%	99	71	11%	6%	122	13%	74%	8.5	66	$18

Stowers,Kyle

Age: 25	Pos: OF	Health A	LIMA Plan D+
Bats: L	Ht: 6' 3" Wt: 200	PT/Exp C	Rand Var +1
		Consist B	MM 4203

3-11-.253 in 98 PA at BAL. Power-first prospect followed up 2021 minor league breakout with some impressive MLB skills, including elite QBaB. (However, ignore vL+; it was only 4 PA.) Contact rate is still a work in progress, though tapping into minor league bb% could give Eye, OBP much-needed boost. Take a flyer on HR upside, as 20+ could be within reach.

Yr	Tm	PA	R	HR	RBI	SB	BA	xHR	xSB	xBA	OBP	SLG	OPS+	vL+	vR+	bb%	ct%	Eye	G	L	F	h%	HctX	QBaB	Brl%	PX	xPX	HR/F	xHR/F	Spd	SBA%	SB%	RAR	BPX	R$
18																																			
19																																			
20																																			
21	a/a	352	36	16	40	4	245		4		318	446	105			10	61	0.27				35				142				82	6%	77%		12	$8
22	BAL *	474	44	17	59	2	220	3	4	244	274	407	96	385	95	7	67	0.22	37	26	37	29	98	ABa	11%	139	106	13%	13%	96	5%	44%	-6.9	76	$7
1st Half		252	25	11	29	2	209	0	2	323	268	420	97	140	61	8	69	0.26	0	67	33	25	0	AAa		154	-14	0%	0%	90	5%	44%	-3.9	148	$7
2nd Half		223	20	6	30	0	233	3	2	221	280	392	95	373	98	6	64	0.18	39	24	37	33	99	ABb	11%	120	112	14%	14%	115	5%	0%	-2.5	0	$5
23	Proj	350	34	11	43	2	231	9	3	220	299	395	96	337	90	8	64	0.24	38	23	39	33	89		10%	128	101	13%	11%	96	5%	68%	-0.4	42	$8

Straw,Myles

Age: 28	Pos: CF	Health A	LIMA Plan B
Bats: R	Ht: 5' 10" Wt: 178	PT/Exp A	Rand Var +3
		Consist C	MM 0515

As expected, 2021 BA regressed, which led to less of counting stats that made that season so valuable, including precious, precious steals. Contact gains were nice, but consistent lack of power has prevented xBA from moving higher than .240, and leaves him vulnerable to being replaced by better hitter. Don't let those SB blind you to risk of... DN: 300 PA

Yr	Tm	PA	R	HR	RBI	SB	BA	xHR	xSB	xBA	OBP	SLG	OPS+	vL+	vR+	bb%	ct%	Eye	G	L	F	h%	HctX	QBaB	Brl%	PX	xPX	HR/F	xHR/F	Spd	SBA%	SB%	RAR	BPX	R$
18	HOU *	581	78	2	25	57	246	0	9	181	318	298	83	0	141	10	77	0.47	44	11	44	31	95	DCa	11%	34	139	25%	0%	169	41%	84%	-7.9	30	$27
19	HOU *	427	59	1	30	21	259	1	31	234	330	317	90	109	95	10	78	0.48	48	23	29	33	86	DDa	1%	34	60	0%	4%	169	22%	78%	-8.9	37	$12
20	HOU	86	8	0	8	6	207	1	2	195	244	256	66	9	99	5	73	0.18	36	22	42	28	79	CBb	2%	41	83	0%	4%	115	47%	75%	-7.0	-112	$5
21	2 AL	638	86	4	48	30	271	4	52	239	349	348	96	81	103	11	79	0.55	41	26	34	34	70	DCa	1%	53	52	3%	3%	140	19%	83%	0.3	81	$26
22	CLE	596	72	0	32	21	221	2	19	232	291	273	80	91	76	9	84	0.62	47	19	34	26	90	CCb	1%	39	57	0%	1%	146	15%	95%	-17.4	103	$10
1st Half		320	44	0	10	13	194	1	10	223	291	244	76	81	73	12	81	0.72	49	18	34	24	84	DDc	0%	40	53	0%	1%	145	15%	93%	-13.5	86	$9
2nd Half		276	28	0	22	8	250	1	9	241	292	305	85	106	79	6	87	0.47	46	21	34	29	97	CCb	1%	37	62	0%	1%	144	15%	100%	-5.5	117	$9
23	Proj	490	62	1	32	23	246	2	14	229	315	305	86	80	88	9	81	0.55	44	22	34	30	83		1%	44	59	1%	2%	140	14%	84%	-4.8	83	$18

Suarez,Eugenio

Age: 31	Pos: 3B	Health A	LIMA Plan B+
Bats: R	Ht: 5' 11" Wt: 213	PT/Exp A	Rand Var -1
		Consist B	MM 5115

Didn't miss a beat in transition from homer-happy GAB to less-friendly T-Mobile Park, as h% finally rebounded (especially vL) and he restored QBaB to 2018-19 peak. Three years of FB%, xBA data say we're stuck with this lower-BA version, but if he maintains 2nd half exit velocity, xPX gains, 40 HR could be back in play.

Yr	Tm	PA	R	HR	RBI	SB	BA	xHR	xSB	xBA	OBP	SLG	OPS+	vL+	vR+	bb%	ct%	Eye	G	L	F	h%	HctX	QBaB	Brl%	PX	xPX	HR/F	xHR/F	Spd	SBA%	SB%	RAR	BPX	R$
18	CIN	606	79	34	104	1	283	31	9	269	366	526	120	135	111	11	73	0.45	38	25	37	33	131	ABa	10%	143	150	23%	21%	95	1%	50%	35.1	193	$25
19	CIN	662	87	49	103	3	271	40	4	260	358	572	129	138	125	11	67	0.37	36	22	42	32	108	BAb	14%	166	145	30%	24%	97	3%	60%	31.8	196	$25
20	CIN	231	29	15	38	2	202	14	1	238	312	470	104	98	105	13	66	0.45	35	18	47	22	93	CAc	14%	160	147	24%	23%	62	4%	100%	-1.1	156	$16
21	CIN	574	71	31	79	0	198	33	2	228	286	428	98	84	103	10	66	0.33	36	17	47	23	94	CAc	15%	146	132	20%	21%	56	1%	0%	-6.3	77	$7
22	SEA	629	76	31	87	0	236	35	3	232	332	459	112	128	107	12	64	0.37	34	20	46	31	100	BAb	15%	160	149	19%	22%	100	0%	0%	16.5	134	$17
1st Half		350	37	13	38	0	236	18	2	223	329	426	107	115	104	11	63	0.35	37	20	43	33	92	CAa	14%	146	131	16%	22%	88	0%	0%	3.8	72	$15
2nd Half		279	39	18	49	0	235	17	1	242	337	500	119	143	110	13	65	0.40	30	20	50	28	110	AAb	16%	178	171	23%	22%	115	0%	0%	9.6	217	$24
23	Proj	595	77	33	90	1	235	35	2	236	328	471	111	116	109	11	66	0.37	35	19	46	29	101		15%	165	147	21%	22%	77	1%	61%	19.7	138	$20

Suwinski,Jack

Age: 24	Pos: LF RF	Health A	LIMA Plan D+
Bats: L	Ht: 6' 2" Wt: 206	PT/Exp B	Rand Var +1
		Consist A	MM 4103

19-38-.202 in 372 PA at PIT. Carried plus power skill, patience over to the majors, with high FB% approach that helps HR output but, along with poor ct%, hurts BA. Struggles vL were largely due to fluky 12% h%; 10% bb%, 63% ct%, 110 PX vs. LHP makes platoon splits look less stark. Lots of hurdles to clear on way to 20 HR.

Yr	Tm	PA	R	HR	RBI	SB	BA	xHR	xSB	xBA	OBP	SLG	OPS+	vL+	vR+	bb%	ct%	Eye	G	L	F	h%	HctX	QBaB	Brl%	PX	xPX	HR/F	xHR/F	Spd	SBA%	SB%	RAR	BPX	R$
18																																			
19																																			
20																																			
21	aa	420	50	13	42	8	223		6		321	387	97			13	63	0.39				32				113				109	17%	47%		8	$8
22	PIT *	551	66	24	58	5	204	16	9	217	279	397	96	72	113	9	62	0.28	42	15	42	27	100	CBf	12%	146	145	21%	18%	82	6%	73%	-9.9	41	$9
1st Half		272	41	16	34	3	241	10	5	257	307	501	114	94	123	9	66	0.28	40	17	43	30	100	CCf	13%	188	151	26%	19%	94	6%	100%	7.7	214	$20
2nd Half		278	25	9	25	3	168	6	5	176	253	296	78	20	100	10	59	0.28	45	13	42	24	102	CBf	12%	101	136	14%	17%	80	6%	57%	-15.8	-128	$4
23	Proj	385	45	17	40	5	212	16	4	214	300	408	98	59	113	11	62	0.32	43	15	42	28	101		12%	147	142	19%	17%	89	6%	56%	-0.4	12	$9

Suzuki,Seiya

Age: 28	Pos: RF	Health B	LIMA Plan B
Bats: R	Ht: 5' 11" Wt: 182	PT/Exp A	Rand Var -2
		Consist C	MM 3325

After career-high 38 HR, 2021 batting title in Japan, MLB debut was bit of a letdown, though MLEs indicate power was comparable to NPB output. 2nd half ct% rebound was encouraging, and SB helped prop up R$—just don't expect SB% improvement (NPB career rate = 61%). Sprained finger cost him a month; increased PA alone should boost 2023 value.

Yr	Tm	PA	R	HR	RBI	SB	BA	xHR	xSB	xBA	OBP	SLG	OPS+	vL+	vR+	bb%	ct%	Eye	G	L	F	h%	HctX	QBaB	Brl%	PX	xPX	HR/F	xHR/F	Spd	SBA%	SB%	RAR	BPX	R$
18	for	493	84	18	92	4	298		8		399	516	123			14	74	0.65				37	0			140				96	6%	45%	33.2	227	$22
19	for	582	109	17	85	23	312		7		410	474	122			14	85	1.08				34	0			83				91	21%	56%	20.7	233	$31
20	for	488	83	15	73	5	280		16		365	459	109			12	84	0.84				30	0			93				106	7%	55%	9.0	272	$51
21	for	505	75	23	86	8	296		6		393	513	124			14	81	0.84				32	0			118				78	8%	65%	31.7	273	$25
22	CHC	446	54	14	46	9	262	15	8	241	336	433	109	119	105	9	72	0.38	40	20	40	33	101	BCf	11%	117	121	12%	13%	136	13%	64%	8.0	152	$15
1st Half		172	22	6	25	3	257	6	3	238	349	473	116	124	113	12	67	0.43	32	19	50	34	96	BBf	13%	164	129	12%	12%	112	13%	60%	5.9	203	$6
2nd Half		274	32	8	21	6	265	9	5	243	328	410	105	115	101	8	76	0.34	44	21	35	32	105	BDd	11%	92	116	12%	14%	147	13%	67%	2.3	128	$15
23	Proj	560	79	19	77	10	278	20	13	250	365	457	114	123	110	12	77	0.56	39	20	41	33	101		12%	116	121	12%	13%	123	11%	63%	25.3	211	$27

Swanson,Dansby

Age: 29	Pos: SS	Health A	LIMA Plan B
Bats: R	Ht: 6' 1" Wt: 190	PT/Exp A	Rand Var -4
		Consist A	MM 4325

Built on 2021 HR breakout to reach five-category awesomeness and career year, but only one of 2022 gains looks sustainable. Spd has long been there, just needed greener light to ramp up SB total; BA, on the other hand, was lifted by lucky h%, similar to 2020. Even with BA regression and slight fade across the board, should still rank among elite at SS.

Yr	Tm	PA	R	HR	RBI	SB	BA	xHR	xSB	xBA	OBP	SLG	OPS+	vL+	vR+	bb%	ct%	Eye	G	L	F	h%	HctX	QBaB	Brl%	PX	xPX	HR/F	xHR/F	Spd	SBA%	SB%	RAR	BPX	R$
18	ATL	533	51	14	59	10	238	12	7	240	304	395	94	85	94	8	74	0.36	42	20	38	29	98	CCd	4%	99	89	10%	9%	122	12%	71%	2.2	107	$11
19	ATL	545	77	17	65	10	251	23	11	252	325	422	103	112	101	9	74	0.41	37	26	37	30	109	BBb	10%	96	106	13%	17%	120	11%	67%	-2.9	115	$14
20	ATL	264	49	10	35	5	274	11	5	243	345	464	107	67	116	8	70	0.31	37	24	39	35	110	CBc	11%	120	134	16%	17%	97	8%	100%	7.4	96	$29
21	ATL	653	78	27	88	9	248	28	8	245	311	449	104	104	105	8	72	0.31	40	20	40	30	98	CCc	11%	124	123	16%	16%	109	9%	75%	2.7	138	$20
22	ATL	696	99	25	96	18	277	31	10	239	329	447	110	118	107	7	72	0.27	39	21	40	35	106	BBc	11%	116	127	14%	17%	108	15%	72%	13.7	97	$35
1st Half		340	52	14	49	12	302	17	5	249	359	502	122	134	117	7	70	0.27	35	25	41	39	113	BBb	13%	138	145	16%	19%	121	15%	80%	19.8	155	$39
2nd Half		356	47	11	47	6	252	15	5	227	301	395	99	101	98	7	73	0.27	43	18	39	32	100	BBc	9%	96	110	12%	16%	96	15%	60%	-2.4	41	$27
23	Proj	665	92	24	90	12	263	29	14	240	320	440	106	106	105	8	72	0.29	39	21	40	33	103		11%	122	122	14%	16%	100	11%	72%	16.4	105	$29

BRANDON KRUSE

Tapia,Raimel

Age: 29 Pos: LF CF RF	Health A	LIMA Plan D+	
Bats: L Ht: 6' 3" Wt: 175	PT/Exp A	Rand Var 0	
	Consist B	MM 1443	

The shimmering oasis of 2021's bb%, ct% gains now look like a mirage, leaving us to stagger parched through desert of subpar batting skills. GB%, poor QBaB continue to limit HR, while slide in vL+ (including 66% ct%) makes him questionable as full-timer. Empty BA and SB subject to whims of PA/green light ain't gonna quench your thirst.

Yr	Tm	PA	R	HR	RBI	SB	BA	xHR	xSB	xBA	OBP	SLG	OPS+	vL+	vR+	bb%	ct%	Eye	G	L	F	h%	HctX	QBaB	Brl%	PX	xPX	HR/F	xHR/F	Spd	SBA%	SB%	RAR	BPX	R$
18	COL *	482	57	9	45	13	261	1	5	229	296	424	96	52	115	5	79	0.23	24	24	53	32	64	DAa	6%	100	120	11%	11%	136	17%	80%	-0.8	157	$13
19	COL	447	54	9	44	9	275	9	12	263	309	415	100	97	101	5	77	0.21	52	22	26	34	80	CDb	4%	78	64	11%	11%	140	12%	75%	-6.5	81	$11
20	COL	204	26	1	17	8	321	2	6	257	369	402	102	113	98	7	79	0.37	56	23	21	40	103	DFd	2%	49	57	3%	6%	165	16%	80%	3.6	88	$23
21	COL	533	69	6	50	20	273	4	14	282	327	372	96	91	98	8	86	0.57	67	16	16	31	86	DFd	2%	58	38	9%	6%	125	19%	77%	-1.0	165	$21
22	TOR	431	47	7	52	8	265	8	11	261	292	380	95	89	96	4	80	0.20	55	20	26	32	98	CFd	5%	74	53	8%	9%	122	11%	80%	-3.3	90	$13
1st Half		235	24	3	21	4	261	5	6	264	289	365	93	89	93	4	81	0.21	50	23	27	31	110	CFd	6%	74	68	6%	10%	95	11%	80%	-3.2	76	$6
2nd Half		196	23	4	31	4	270	4	5	257	296	397	98	88	100	4	79	0.18	61	15	24	32	83	CFd	4%	74	34	11%	11%	157	11%	80%	-0.3	114	$10
23	**Proj**	**280**	**34**	**4**	**31**	**7**	**274**	**4**	**6**	**265**	**313**	**386**	**97**	**94**	**98**	**5**	**81**	**0.31**	**59**	**19**	**22**	**32**	**91**		**4%**	**72**	**47**	**9%**	**9%**	**137**	**11%**	**76%**	**3.3**	**120**	**$8**

Tatis Jr.,Fernando

Age: 24 Pos: DH	Health F	LIMA Plan D+	
Bats: R Ht: 6' 3" Wt: 217	PT/Exp D	Rand Var 0	
	Consist B	MM 5435	

Normally when we say "What a year," it's with exuberance, not as a sad lament muttered while shaking our head. Surgery on fractured left wrist, PED suspension (which carries over to start of 2023), labrum surgery, follow-up wrist surgery. Youth, elite skills should win out, but health risk, reduced PA make it much tougher to return first-round value.

Yr	Tm	PA	R	HR	RBI	SB	BA	xHR	xSB	xBA	OBP	SLG	OPS+	vL+	vR+	bb%	ct%	Eye	G	L	F	h%	HctX	QBaB	Brl%	PX	xPX	HR/F	xHR/F	Spd	SBA%	SB%	RAR	BPX	R$
18	aa	383	70	14	39	14	274		5		331	472	108			8	67	0.26				37				136				122	21%	74%		107	$17
19	SD	372	61	22	53	16	317	20	15	265	379	590	134	176	122	8	67	0.27	47	22	31	42	97	BDd	13%	150	126	32%	29%	177	22%	73%	29.8	222	$22
20	SD	257	50	17	45	11	277	19	8	279	366	571	124	105	132	11	73	0.44	48	16	35	31	162	ADb	19%	161	176	29%	33%	115	22%	79%	16.7	308	$42
21	SD	546	99	42	97	25	282	45	16	281	364	611	134	132	135	11	68	0.41	40	20	40	33	133	ACd	21%	203	172	32%	34%	114	23%	86%	47.5	358	$38
22	aa																																		
1st Half																																			
2nd Half																																			
23	**Proj**	**455**	**82**	**25**	**72**	**20**	**278**	**27**	**7**	**264**	**351**	**531**	**123**	**129**	**120**	**10**	**69**	**0.33**	**45**	**20**	**35**	**35**	**126**		**17%**	**171**	**155**	**25%**	**28%**	**128**	**9%**	**78%**	**26.4**	**269**	**$32**

Taveras,Leody

Age: 24 Pos: CF	Health A	LIMA Plan C+	
Bats: B Ht: 6' 2" Wt: 195	PT/Exp A	Rand Var -2	
	Consist B	MM 2405	

4-32-.257 with 10 SB in 330 PA at TEX. "Be patient, he's still young" is a good mantra, but at some point, it'd be nice if he'd throw us a bone and show more signs of growth. While 2nd half R$ is enough to maintain intrigue, xBA puts damper on success, and xPX, xHR/F suggest power skill is moving backwards. Repeat that mantra as you pay for his steals.

Yr	Tm	PA	R	HR	RBI	SB	BA	xHR	xSB	xBA	OBP	SLG	OPS+	vL+	vR+	bb%	ct%	Eye	G	L	F	h%	HctX	QBaB	Brl%	PX	xPX	HR/F	xHR/F	Spd	SBA%	SB%	RAR	BPX	R$
18																																			
19	aa	286	30	3	29	10	273		5		330	391	100			8	77	0.38				34				64				134	24%	56%		70	$7
20	TEX	134	20	4	6	8	227	4	5	227	308	395	93	106	86	10	64	0.33	38	29	33	32	91	DCf	6%	113	110	17%	17%	153	27%	100%	-1.2	60	$12
21	TEX *	543	56	16	50	20	192	3	15	223	260	346	83	68	64	8	66	0.27	52	16	32	25	92	DFf	6%	102	95	9%	9%	111	27%	75%	-24.8	0	$9
22	TEX *	554	60	9	52	15	248	5	20	224	288	359	92	90	98	5	72	0.20	42	22	36	33	95	CCf	4%	79	84	6%	6%	136	20%	61%	-7.8	17	$15
1st Half		265	27	6	22	5	233	0	8	203	264	359	88	109	94	4	72	0.15	29	20	51	30	79	CAf	3%	85	107	11%	0%	122	20%	48%	-8.3	14	$8
2nd Half		289	33	3	30	10	261	5	12	225	313	360	95	87	98	7	72	0.26	45	22	33	35	97	CCf	4%	74	80	5%	8%	136	20%	71%	-1.0	10	$17
23	**Proj**	**455**	**51**	**8**	**41**	**16**	**232**	**8**	**13**	**219**	**290**	**355**	**89**	**92**	**88**	**7**	**70**	**0.26**	**44**	**20**	**36**	**31**	**91**		**5%**	**89**	**94**	**8%**	**7%**	**133**	**17%**	**70%**	**-5.8**	**19**	**$15**

Taylor,Chris

Age: 32 Pos: LF 2B	Health B	LIMA Plan C	
Bats: R Ht: 6' 1" Wt: 196	PT/Exp A	Rand Var 0	
	Consist B	MM 4403	

Fractured left foot likely played role in 2nd half collapse, but seeds of 2022 downturn were already there in shaky ct%, fading xBA, and subpar HctX, QBaB. 1st half shows he's still a serviceable fantasy option, and xHR suggests there's a little more pop left than we might think. An easy rebound candidate, just don't expect return to 2020-21 peak.

Yr	Tm	PA	R	HR	RBI	SB	BA	xHR	xSB	xBA	OBP	SLG	OPS+	vL+	vR+	bb%	ct%	Eye	G	L	F	h%	HctX	QBaB	Brl%	PX	xPX	HR/F	xHR/F	Spd	SBA%	SB%	RAR	BPX	R$
18	LA	604	85	17	63	9	254	20	8	238	331	444	104	100	104	9	67	0.31	34	28	39	35	94	CBa	8%	134	117	12%	14%	153	11%	60%	2.7	133	$16
19	LA	414	52	12	52	8	262	11	7	254	333	462	110	120	103	9	69	0.32	38	27	35	35	90	DCa	6%	126	106	14%	13%	118	9%	100%	2.3	111	$11
20	LA	214	30	8	32	3	270	10	4	263	366	476	112	90	119	12	70	0.47	46	27	28	34	104	DDb	11%	122	142	23%	29%	136	9%	60%	3.2	184	$20
21	LA	582	92	20	73	13	254	22	11	226	344	438	107	122	101	11	67	0.38	36	22	42	34	86	CBc	10%	119	111	14%	16%	141	9%	93%	8.7	112	$21
22	LA	454	45	10	43	10	221	13	7	208	304	373	96	85	100	10	60	0.28	31	26	43	34	87	CAc	10%	130	119	10%	13%	116	11%	91%	-2.9	3	$8
1st Half		285	32	6	27	6	238	8	4	220	319	409	103	105	102	10	60	0.29	34	27	39	37	92	CAc	11%	149	113	10%	14%	120	11%	86%	2.8	62	$12
2nd Half		169	13	4	16	4	193	5	3	190	278	313	84	55	97	9	61	0.25	26	25	48	29	78	DAb	9%	99	128	9%	11%	96	11%	100%	-6.0	-100	-$1
23	**Proj**	**420**	**52**	**13**	**48**	**9**	**243**	**15**	**8**	**220**	**326**	**411**	**102**	**96**	**105**	**10**	**64**	**0.31**	**34**	**25**	**41**	**34**	**87**		**10%**	**131**	**120**	**13%**	**15%**	**117**	**10%**	**89%**	**7.7**	**47**	**$15**

Taylor,Michael A.

Age: 32 Pos: CF	Health A	LIMA Plan C	
Bats: R Ht: 6' 4" Wt: 215	PT/Exp A	Rand Var -4	
	Consist A	MM 2303	

The most frustratingly inscrutable hitter in baseball? For every positive in his skill set (career-best ct% and Spd, above-average PX), there's a negative to cancel it out (career lows in xBA, exit velocity, PX, SBA%). With growing evidence that poor recent SB% rates have killed running game, might be time to let others bang their head against this wall.

Yr	Tm	PA	R	HR	RBI	SB	BA	xHR	xSB	xBA	OBP	SLG	OPS+	vL+	vR+	bb%	ct%	Eye	G	L	F	h%	HctX	QBaB	Brl%	PX	xPX	HR/F	xHR/F	Spd	SBA%	SB%	RAR	BPX	R$
18	WAS	385	46	6	28	24	227	9	4	227	287	357	86	82	87	8	67	0.25	51	18	31	32	80	CDc	6%	99	83	9%	13%	126	38%	80%	-6.5	7	$11
19	WAS *	336	41	9	33	15	226	3	14	224	292	393	95	108	81	8	62	0.24	46	21	33	33	103	ADf	7%	119	141	6%	18%	103	33%	67%	-6.2	-26	$8
20	WAS	99	11	5	16	0	196	7	2	244	253	424	90	91	89	6	71	0.22	43	17	40	22	75	CCf	15%	139	100	20%	28%	76	0%	0%	-4.1	124	$3
21	KC	528	58	12	54	14	244	14	3	218	297	356	90	105	84	6	70	0.23	44	22	34	32	94	CCc	7%	71	89	10%	12%	116	17%	67%	-13.8	-46	$14
22	KC	456	49	9	43	4	254	13	15	205	313	357	95	95	95	8	74	0.32	41	18	42	32	101	DCf	7%	65	114	7%	10%	172	5%	67%	-0.8	55	$10
1st Half		220	25	5	23	1	271	7	8	213	352	396	106	96	110	11	73	0.47	36	20	44	35	98	DBf	8%	77	119	8%	11%	163	5%	50%	4.7	97	$6
2nd Half		236	24	4	20	3	239	6	7	199	277	324	85	93	82	5	74	0.19	45	16	40	31	103	FCf	6%	55	110	6%	9%	151	5%	75%	-6.5	-14	$5
23	**Proj**	**385**	**43**	**9**	**37**	**8**	**236**	**11**	**5**	**213**	**293**	**357**	**90**	**96**	**88**	**7**	**71**	**0.26**	**43**	**19**	**38**	**31**	**95**		**8%**	**83**	**105**	**9%**	**12%**	**122**	**7%**	**68%**	**-3.9**	**0**	**$11**

Taylor,Tyrone

Age: 29 Pos: CF RF LF	Health B	LIMA Plan C+	
Bats: R Ht: 6' 0" Wt: 194	PT/Exp B	Rand Var 0	
	Consist B	MM 4323	

Largest MLB sample yet yielded impressive PX, xPX—especially in 2nd half, as Brl% turned elite. And while ct% drop suggests he sold out to get there, xBA offers reassurance that negative impact of Ks was minimal. He's a little old for a breakout, and has struggled to shed 4th OF label, but if you're feeling speculative, with 500+ PA... UP: 25 HR

Yr	Tm	PA	R	HR	RBI	SB	BA	xHR	xSB	xBA	OBP	SLG	OPS+	vL+	vR+	bb%	ct%	Eye	G	L	F	h%	HctX	QBaB	Brl%	PX	xPX	HR/F	xHR/F	Spd	SBA%	SB%	RAR	BPX	R$
18	aaa	464	48	14	52	8	228		5		257	394	87			4	80	0.20				25				92				117	16%	65%		133	$9
19	MIL *	367	33	11	44	4	232	0	7	264	277	387	92	0	166	6	70	0.21	89	11	0	30	54	FFa	0%	95	-36	0%	#DIV/0!	100	6%	100%	-6.7	0	$4
20	MIL	41	6	2	6	0	237	2	0	266	293	500	105	92	113	5	79	0.25	43	10	47	25	138	CBf	13%	153	165	14%	14%	92	0%	0%	-0.4	312	$0
21	MIL *	302	40	14	50	6	263	9	3	251	321	486	111	114	103	8	76	0.36	41	16	43	30	106	CBd	8%	122	90	15%	11%	143	10%	86%	7.7	242	$11
22	MIL	405	49	17	51	3	233	15	5	248	286	442	103	101	104	5	73	0.22	38	18	44	28	108	CBc	10%	137	145	14%	13%	99	7%	60%	-0.5	148	$9
1st Half		231	23	9	32	1	228	7	3	253	277	423	99	83	105	5	76	0.23	34	21	45	26	103	CAc	8%	126	134	12%	9%	81	7%	50%	-1.7	141	$7
2nd Half		174	26	8	19	2	241	8	2	245	299	468	109	118	102	6	68	0.20	45	14	42	30	114	CBc	14%	154	162	17%	17%	129	7%	67%	2.2	169	$7
23	**Proj**	**350**	**45**	**16**	**48**	**5**	**242**	**12**	**4**	**247**	**302**	**457**	**105**	**109**	**103**	**6**	**74**	**0.25**	**40**	**16**	**43**	**28**	**108**		**10%**	**137**	**126**	**15%**	**12%**	**109**	**7%**	**74%**	**6.3**	**165**	**$13**

Tellez,Rowdy

Age: 28 Pos: 1B	Health B	LIMA Plan B+	
Bats: L Ht: 6' 4" Wt: 255	PT/Exp A	Rand Var +5	
	Consist B	MM 4045	

Finally delivered on our UP: 30 HR prediction from 2021 Forecaster! (That still counts, right??) Unfortunately, low BA, RBI total made this one of the least valuable breakouts ever. Good news is that xBA, h% indicate that was mostly bad luck. Even with xHR suggesting he'll give a few dingers back, 2023 could be year he passes $20 threshold.

Yr	Tm	PA	R	HR	RBI	SB	BA	xHR	xSB	xBA	OBP	SLG	OPS+	vL+	vR+	bb%	ct%	Eye	G	L	F	h%	HctX	QBaB	Brl%	PX	xPX	HR/F	xHR/F	Spd	SBA%	SB%	RAR	BPX	R$
18	TOR *	501	48	15	58	6	263	4	6	268	318	431	100	43	158	7	78	0.37	38	26	36	31	115	CCd	12%	106	138	22%	22%	69	9%	59%	-6.5	117	$13
19	TOR *	514	66	27	72	1	249	21	4	257	310	484	110	116	96	8	69	0.28	39	24	38	30	99	BCc	13%	138	114	22%	22%	55	2%	50%	-4.8	74	$12
20	TOR	127	20	8	23	0	283	6	1	288	346	540	118	106	121	9	82	0.55	46	20	34	28	123	BCc	8%	125	97	25%	19%	83	3%	0%	1.7	292	$13
21	2 TM *	383	40	14	45	0	242	14	2	252	299	425	99	99	99	7	77	0.35	41	21	38	27	112	ACf	12%	104	111	12%	16%	82	0%	0%	-6.6	131	$6
22	MIL	599	67	35	89	2	219	30	0	259	306	461	109	90	114	10	77	0.51	39	16	45	22	136	ABf	13%	143	150	19%	16%	43	2%	67%	-1.8	203	$15
1st Half		303	33	17	55	0	240	16	0	265	317	491	114	94	120	9	77	0.44	40	16	44	25	128	BCf	13%	154	144	18%	17%	47	2%	0%	5.8	231	$21
2nd Half		296	34	18	34	2	198	14	0	248	294	430	103	86	107	12	77	0.58	38	16	47	18	144	ABd	13%	131	156	19%	15%	58	2%	67%	-3.1	190	$17
23	**Proj**	**560**	**68**	**32**	**81**	**2**	**244**	**27**	**2**	**266**	**318**	**482**	**111**	**96**	**115**	**9**	**77**	**0.45**	**40**	**18**	**41**	**25**	**125**		**12%**	**142**	**131**	**20%**	**17%**	**64**	**2%**	**54%**	**14.6**	**181**	**$20**

BRANDON KRUSE

Thomas,Alek

Age: 23	Pos: CF	Health	A	LIMA Plan	C
Bats: L	Ht: 5' 11" Wt: 175	PT/Exp	B	Rand Var	+2
		Consist	B	MM	2235

8-39-.231 with 4 SB in 411 PA at ARI. Promising start gave way to 2nd half where HR, SB disappeared, and .302 Sept OPS led to demotion in final week. History of extreme GB%, lousy SB% are obstacles he'll need to overcome, but prospect pedigree suggests he can get back on track, and 1st half xBA shows further upside. Worth a flyer in deep leagues.

Yr	Tm	PA	R	HR	RBI	SB	BA	xHR	xSB	xBA	OBP	SLG	OPS+	vL+	vR+	bb%	ct%	Eye	G	L	F	h%	HctX	QBaB	Brl%	PX	xPX	HR/F	xHR/F	Spd	SBA%	SB%	RAR	BPX	R$
18																																			
19																																			
20																																			
21	a/a	468	55	11	38	8	266		7		318	448	105			7	75	0.30				33				106				145	19%	40%		165	$13
22	ARI *	534	59	10	50	7	236	6	12	261	280	357	90	66	94	6	81	0.31	58	17	25	27	92	CFd	4%	78	69	10%	8%	108	11%	56%	-12.2	110	$10
1st Half		299	38	9	27	6	235	5	7	270	287	395	96	77	114	7	81	0.38	60	14	26	26	98	CFd	7%	96	95	19%	14%	125	11%	71%	-1.8	183	$15
2nd Half		235	22	1	23	1	240	1	5	245	272	312	83	48	81	4	81	0.23	57	19	24	29	87	CFd	2%	56	47	2%	2%	93	11%	30%	-8.4	28	$2
23	**Proj**	**455**	**51**	**10**	**41**	**6**	**250**	**6**	**8**	**263**	**296**	**395**	**96**	**69**	**104**	**6**	**78**	**0.29**	**55**	**19**	**26**	**30**	**91**		**4%**	**94**	**66**	**11%**	**7%**	**126**	**10%**	**45%**	**-0.6**	**122**	**$10**

Thomas,Lane

Age: 27	Pos: LF CF RF	Health	A	LIMA Plan	B
Bats: R	Ht: 6' 0" Wt: 185	PT/Exp	A	Rand Var	0
		Consist	C	MM	3315

Best season of career still only left him at league average OPS+. Traded previously elite exit velocity for contact, which is not a recipe for growth. Signs that mediocre SB% is gradually killing SBA%. He's at right age for peak performance, but there's nothing in these skills that screams additional breakout, so mashing lefties might be as good as it gets.

Yr	Tm	PA	R	HR	RBI	SB	BA	xHR	xSB	xBA	OBP	SLG	OPS+	vL+	vR+	bb%	ct%	Eye	G	L	F	h%	HctX	QBaB	Brl%	PX	xPX	HR/F	xHR/F	Spd	SBA%	SB%	RAR	BPX	R$
18	a/a	553	65	20	68	13	228		6		280	398	91			7	71	0.26				28				105				110	22%	54%		60	$14
19	STL *	333	39	11	46	10	239	2	10	251	303	415	99	164	145	8	68	0.29	47	27	27	31	102	ADc	13%	105	113	50%	25%	136	24%	55%	-11.8	56	$8
20	STL	40	5	1	2	0	111	0	1	187	200	250	60	33	67	10	64	0.31	39	13	48	14	67	ABf	4%	100	93	9%	0%	102	0%	0%	-4.7	-44	-$4
21	2 NL *	399	49	11	45	8	235	7	3	232	323	404	100	150	84	11	70	0.43	42	19	39	31	122	ACd	7%	110	124	11%	11%	132	14%	60%	-3.8	123	$9
22	WAS	548	62	17	52	8	241	15	11	239	301	404	100	104	97	7	73	0.31	45	17	38	30	88	DCf	7%	109	97	12%	11%	131	10%	67%	0.2	128	$14
1st Half		254	28	8	30	1	221	6	5	234	280	381	93	93	94	8	74	0.31	44	17	39	27	86	CCf	7%	106	101	12%	9%	125	10%	100%	-3.7	117	$7
2nd Half		294	34	9	22	7	258	9	6	244	320	423	105	115	99	8	73	0.31	46	18	36	32	91	DCf	6%	112	94	13%	13%	135	10%	64%	3.2	141	$17
23	**Proj**	**455**	**54**	**13**	**49**	**7**	**239**	**14**	**8**	**233**	**308**	**399**	**98**	**117**	**88**	**9**	**72**	**0.35**	**44**	**18**	**38**	**30**	**102**		**7%**	**111**	**108**	**12%**	**13%**	**121**	**10%**	**60%**	**2.3**	**114**	**$13**

Thompson,Bubba

Age: 25	Pos: LF	Health	A	LIMA Plan	D+
Bats: R	Ht: 6' 2" Wt: 180	PT/Exp	B	Rand Var	-3
		Consist	A	MM	1503

1-9-.265 with 18 SB in 181 PA at TEX. Tempting to think he could deliver 50 SB, but xBA highlights serious downside, which, along with low bb%, would reduce opportunities. And while 2021 AA power would help, flatline QBaB shows he's a long way from that in majors. Elite speed skills make him worth watching while we wait for growth.

Yr	Tm	PA	R	HR	RBI	SB	BA	xHR	xSB	xBA	OBP	SLG	OPS+	vL+	vR+	bb%	ct%	Eye	G	L	F	h%	HctX	QBaB	Brl%	PX	xPX	HR/F	xHR/F	Spd	SBA%	SB%	RAR	BPX	R$
18																																			
19																																			
20																																			
21	aa	453	61	13	43	21	248		6		288	422	98			5	69	0.18				33				110				131	34%	70%		58	$17
22	TEX *	540	65	9	38	48	245	2	27	197	274	331	86	73	93	4	67	0.12	55	12	33	35	66	FFf	2%	63	80	3%	6%	189	45%	88%	-12.0	-41	$29
1st Half		271	31	6	22	22	233		12	200	258	336	84	0	0	3	66	0.10	44	20	36	33	0			72	-14	0%		154	45%	90%	-7.2	-76	$22
2nd Half		270	34	3	16	25	257	2	15	194	290	325	87	73	93	4	69	0.15	55	12	33	36	67	FFf	2%	54	80	3%	6%	174	45%	86%	-4.1	-66	$23
23	**Proj**	**280**	**36**	**3**	**22**	**18**	**235**	**4**	**18**	**203**	**275**	**323**	**83**	**78**	**85**	**4**	**68**	**0.14**	**50**	**17**	**33**	**34**	**60**		**2%**	**66**	**72**	**5%**	**6%**	**183**	**37%**	**81%**	**-6.9**	**-19**	**$12**

Toglia,Michael

Age: 24	Pos: 1B RF	Health	A	LIMA Plan	D+
Bats: B	Ht: 6' 5" Wt: 226	PT/Exp	C	Rand Var	+1
		Consist	A	MM	2303

2-12-.216 in 120 PA at COL. Big dude (6-5, 226) has big power, big holes in swing, and big-time glove at 1B. 2nd half ct% improvement was encouraging, though most of it came in minors; 60% mark in MLB suggests he might need more time in AAA. HR should eventually come, but wait for signs of life in QBaB, Brl%, HR/F before buying in.

Yr	Tm	PA	R	HR	RBI	SB	BA	xHR	xSB	xBA	OBP	SLG	OPS+	vL+	vR+	bb%	ct%	Eye	G	L	F	h%	HctX	QBaB	Brl%	PX	xPX	HR/F	xHR/F	Spd	SBA%	SB%	RAR	BPX	R$
18																																			
19																																			
20																																			
21	aa	159	11	4	12	2	199		2		280	360	88			10	63	0.30				29				121				99	7%	100%		4	-$2
22	COL *	582	53	21	60	6	206	2	6	220	263	377	91	83	96	7	62	0.21	37	24	39	29	106	CBc	6%	131	112	8%	8%	105	9%	63%	-25.4	7	$7
1st Half		286	25	9	27	3	177		3	201	243	323	80	0	0	8	59	0.21	44	20	36	26	0			117	-14	0%		100	9%	100%	-16.0	-76	$4
2nd Half		297	29	12	34	3	238	2	3	241	289	439	103	83	96	7	66	0.21	37	24	39	32	111	CBc	6%	147	112	8%	8%	108	9%	45%	-2.5	97	$16
23	**Proj**	**350**	**29**	**5**	**33**	**4**	**206**	**6**	**4**	**203**	**274**	**324**	**83**	**76**	**86**	**9**	**63**	**0.25**	**37**	**24**	**39**	**31**	**100**		**6%**	**100**	**101**	**7%**	**8%**	**107**	**8%**	**76%**	**-12.4**	**17**	**$4**

Torkelson,Spencer

Age: 23	Pos: 1B	Health	A	LIMA Plan	C
Bats: R	Ht: 6' 1" Wt: 220	PT/Exp	B	Rand Var	0
		Consist	D	MM	2005

8-28-.203 in 404 PA at DET. Latest example that even the best prospects (former #1 pick, consensus Top 10 for 2022) can struggle in the majors. Steady plate discipline shows he wasn't completely overmatched; 1st half issues were mainly too many grounders, too little power. But 2nd half FB%, QBaB, xPX say it's coming, and maybe soon... UP: 25 HR

Yr	Tm	PA	R	HR	RBI	SB	BA	xHR	xSB	xBA	OBP	SLG	OPS+	vL+	vR+	bb%	ct%	Eye	G	L	F	h%	HctX	QBaB	Brl%	PX	xPX	HR/F	xHR/F	Spd	SBA%	SB%	RAR	BPX	R$
18																																			
19																																			
20																																			
21	a/a	364	56	21	52	2	230		4		320	479	110			12	73	0.48				25				145				94	4%	60%		231	$9
22	DET *	551	50	11	40	1	198	11	4	210	276	313	84	91	83	10	71	0.37	40	19	41	26	98	BBd	8%	83	93	7%	10%	97	2%	24%	-21.5	0	$0
1st Half		261	21	5	19	0	192	5	2	200	284	297	82	75	84	11	71	0.40	46	16	37	25	90	CCc	7%	76	66	8%	8%	84	2%	0%	-13.3	-28	-$3
2nd Half		290	29	6	21	1	204	6	2	215	275	328	85	121	81	9	71	0.34	30	23	46	26	109	AAd	9%	89	137	7%	13%	113	2%	38%	-12.5	28	$4
23	**Proj**	**525**	**62**	**13**	**56**	**1**	**224**	**16**	**4**	**219**	**313**	**360**	**93**	**106**	**89**	**11**	**71**	**0.41**	**37**	**21**	**43**	**28**	**101**		**8%**	**96**	**109**	**9%**	**11%**	**95**	**4%**	**32%**	**-7.7**	**95**	**$9**

Toro,Abraham

Age: 26	Pos: 2B 3B DH	Health	A	LIMA Plan	D+
Bats: B	Ht: 6' 0" Wt: 206	PT/Exp	C	Rand Var	+5
		Consist	D	MM	2211

10-35-.185 in 352 PA at SEA. To paraphrase the chorus of a popular Adam Ant song from the '80s, "Don't hit, don't steal, what do you do?" The modest value he offered a year ago faded as ct%, HctX both regressed, and BA/xBA bottomed out. Age, positional flexibility will get him another shot, just don't go looking for him on the Billboard Hot 100 chart.

Yr	Tm	PA	R	HR	RBI	SB	BA	xHR	xSB	xBA	OBP	SLG	OPS+	vL+	vR+	bb%	ct%	Eye	G	L	F	h%	HctX	QBaB	Brl%	PX	xPX	HR/F	xHR/F	Spd	SBA%	SB%	RAR	BPX	R$
18	aa	193	15	2	20	3	211		2		273	337	82			8	72	0.30				28				96				97	17%	46%		37	$0
19	HOU *	577	78	16	73	4	271	2	14	259	341	437	108	39	118	10	78	0.49	50	18	32	32	90	CDc	5%	89	64	11%	11%	109	5%	56%	1.5	141	$15
20	HOU	97	13	3	9	1	149	2	1	233	237	276	68	81	63	3	74	0.13	50	20	30	16	84	DDf	3%	69	52	16%	11%	92	11%	50%	-10.1	-56	-$1
21	2 AL *	436	52	12	53	7	245	13	7	234	312	384	96	86	98	9	84	0.60	42	15	43	26	103	CCf	7%	74	99	9%	11%	98	10%	64%	-2.0	162	$10
22	SEA *	416	40	11	42	4	183	10	4	222	238	318	79	74	82	7	79	0.35	40	14	46	20	80	CBf	7%	83	83	8%	8%	83	5%	100%	-19.2	76	$0
1st Half		241	25	7	22	1	185	8	2	233	237	333	81	83	79	6	82	0.38	38	15	47	19	83	CBf	8%	88	85	8%	9%	89	5%	100%	-12.0	145	$1
2nd Half		175	15	4	20	3	181	3	2	206	241	296	76	56	89	7	74	0.31	43	14	43	22	76	DBf	4%	75	80	9%	9%	87	5%	100%	-9.7	0	-$1
23	**Proj**	**245**	**26**	**7**	**28**	**3**	**226**	**7**	**2**	**232**	**296**	**373**	**93**	**79**	**99**	**8**	**79**	**0.39**	**43**	**16**	**42**	**26**	**88**		**6%**	**91**	**82**	**10%**	**10%**	**91**	**5%**	**73%**	**-1.5**	**95**	**$6**

Torres,Gleyber

Age: 26	Pos: 2B	Health	B	LIMA Plan	B
Bats: R	Ht: 6' 1" Wt: 205	PT/Exp	A	Rand Var	0
		Consist	A	MM	4235

Continues to live in shadow of awesome 2019 season, but here's the thing: HctX, exit velocity, and xPX were all better in 2022, and they came with double-digit SB. Late June wrist inflammation likely caused slight 2nd half decline; finished with .962 OPS after 9/1. Health has been X factor between >$20 and <$20, so aim for price under that dividing line.

Yr	Tm	PA	R	HR	RBI	SB	BA	xHR	xSB	xBA	OBP	SLG	OPS+	vL+	vR+	bb%	ct%	Eye	G	L	F	h%	HctX	QBaB	Brl%	PX	xPX	HR/F	xHR/F	Spd	SBA%	SB%	RAR	BPX	R$
18	NYY *	537	59	25	87	7	276	22	8	247	340	479	110	121	104	9	72	0.35	33	25	43	33	102	CAb	9%	122	115	18%	16%	104	7%	69%	22.0	123	$21
19	NYY	604	96	38	90	5	278	32	6	270	337	535	121	125	118	8	76	0.37	37	21	42	30	105	CAb	10%	130	116	21%	18%	87	5%	71%	24.2	200	$24
20	NYY	160	17	3	16	1	243	3	2	235	356	368	96	96	96	14	79	0.79	42	19	39	29	98	CBb	4%	75	64	7%	7%	88	2%	100%	-1.0	136	$6
21	NYY	516	50	9	51	14	259	15	3	235	331	366	96	109	90	10	77	0.48	42	22	36	32	81	CBd	8%	67	80	7%	12%	86	14%	70%	-1.4	38	$15
22	NYY	572	73	24	76	10	257	24	11	246	310	451	108	116	105	7	75	0.30	36	19	46	30	114	BBc	11%	124	134	13%	13%	107	12%	67%	15.4	169	$22
1st Half		269	35	13	35	4	257	13	5	260	313	482	112	137	101	7	80	0.38	32	18	50	27	119	AAd	11%	134	143	13%	13%	114	12%	67%	8.2	262	$19
2nd Half		303	38	11	41	6	256	11	6	234	307	423	103	88	107	7	72	0.25	39	19	42	32	110	BBc	11%	114	124	13%	13%	99	12%	67%	3.7	83	$23
23	**Proj**	**595**	**70**	**26**	**83**	**11**	**258**	**21**	**10**	**254**	**324**	**456**	**108**	**118**	**104**	**9**	**76**	**0.39**	**38**	**20**	**42**	**29**	**101**		**9%**	**125**	**108**	**15%**	**12%**	**88**	**9%**	**69%**	**20.1**	**118**	**$26**

BRANDON KRUSE

Tovar,Ezequiel

Age: 21 Pos: SS | Bats: R Ht: 6' 0" Wt: 162
Health A | PT/Exp F | Consist F
LIMA Plan B | Rand Var -2 | MM 1315

1-2-.212 in 35 PA at COL. Prospect has grown into defensive wizard with plus speed and growing power, and while he didn't do much during brief call-up, it was on display in AA in 1st half. Even MLB stint wasn't all bad, as indicated by Brl%, xPX, Spd. Likely to be Opening Day starter at SS, and could deliver double-digit HR, SB right out of gate.

Yr	Tm	PA	R	HR	RBI	SB	BA	xHR	xSB	xBA	OBP	SLG	OPS+	vL+	vR+	bb%	ct%	Eye	G	L	F	h%	HctX	QBaB	Brl%	PX	xPX	HR/F	xHR/F	Spd	SBA%	SB%	RAR	BPX	R$
18																																			
19																																			
20																																			
21																																			
22	COL *	336	28	10	32	10	272	1	5	248	311	432	105	153	49	5	76	0.23	50	17	33	33	83	CDd	10%	101	110	13%	13%	130	17%	76%	2.9	124	$12
1st Half		279	25	9	30	11	285		4	254	324	462	111	0	0	5	75	0.24	44	20	36	35	0			113	-14	0%		147	17%	77%	8.2	169	$21
2nd Half		57	4	2	3	0	242	1	1	207	284	353	90	153	49	6	79	0.29	50	17	33	28	87	CDd	10%	63	110	13%	13%	115	17%	0%	-1.3	55	-$8
23	**Proj**	**490**	**52**	**13**	**36**	**11**	**258**	**18**	**11**	**232**	**300**	**385**	**95**	**172**	**57**	**6**	**78**	**0.27**	**39**	**22**	**39**	**31**	**78**		**9%**	**78**	**99**	**9%**	**13%**	**97**	**13%**	**84%**	**1.7**	**101**	**$13**

Trammell,Taylor

Age: 25 Pos: RF | Bats: L Ht: 6' 2" Wt: 213
Health B | PT/Exp D | Consist B
LIMA Plan C | Rand Var +1 | MM 4313

4-10-.196 with 2 SB in 117 PA at SEA. A year of riding AAA shuttle and missing month with July hamstring injury seems to have dimmed former first-rounder's star even further. But there are still small positives in skills: vR+, ct% rebound, HctX/QBaB growth, SB% improvement. Some prospects require excruciating patience; he looks like one of them.

Yr	Tm	PA	R	HR	RBI	SB	BA	xHR	xSB	xBA	OBP	SLG	OPS+	vL+	vR+	bb%	ct%	Eye	G	L	F	h%	HctX	QBaB	Brl%	PX	xPX	HR/F	xHR/F	Spd	SBA%	SB%	RAR	BPX	R$
18																																			
19	aa	495	53	8	37	17	214		9		308	310	86			12	70	0.45				29				55				130	20%	67%		-37	$7
20																																			
21	SEA *	481	54	17	54	8	194	4	4	200	273	356	86	55	99	10	61	0.28	42	16	42	27	82	DCf	7%	116	111	24%	12%	88	14%	60%	-19.3	-50	$5
22	SEA *	211	26	7	17	7	221	3	3	239	294	403	99	45	110	9	71	0.36	36	19	45	27	101	CAf	10%	133	98	13%	10%	86	21%	76%	-1.6	128	$4
1st Half		107	15	4	11	3	228	2	1	264	313	448	108	72	117	11	69	0.40	37	23	40	29	107	DBd	10%	173	108	13%	9%	87	21%	76%	1.3	221	-$2
2nd Half		104	11	3	6	4	214	1	2	167	275	359	90	0	72	8	73	0.32	33	0	67	26	53	BAf	11%	96	48	13%	13%	97	21%	75%	-2.9	55	-$3
23	**Proj**	**350**	**41**	**15**	**32**	**8**	**235**	**10**	**9**	**236**	**311**	**435**	**104**	**63**	**115**	**10**	**67**	**0.33**	**39**	**20**	**41**	**30**	**97**		**9%**	**144**	**109**	**17%**	**11%**	**94**	**16%**	**73%**	**4.8**	**37**	**$12**

Trejo,Alan

Age: 27 Pos: SS | Bats: R Ht: 6' 2" Wt: 205
Health A | PT/Exp C | Consist A
LIMA Plan D | Rand Var 0 | MM 3021

4-17-.271 in 125 PA at COL. Don't get visions of sleeper value based on that small MLB sample. Poor Eye is huge red flag, and lackluster HctX, QBaB, Spd, and SB% add to feeling there's not much to see here. Already being put on utility INF track, and doesn't own skills to argue against that.

Yr	Tm	PA	R	HR	RBI	SB	BA	xHR	xSB	xBA	OBP	SLG	OPS+	vL+	vR+	bb%	ct%	Eye	G	L	F	h%	HctX	QBaB	Brl%	PX	xPX	HR/F	xHR/F	Spd	SBA%	SB%	RAR	BPX	R$
18																																			
19	aa	462	45	16	49	5	255		5		295	419	99			5	76	0.24				30				90				85	9%	54%		56	$9
20																																			
21	COL *	398	40	12	46	1	236	1	4	257	268	444	98	72	85	4	73	0.17	47	16	38	29	84	CCa	3%	133	72	8%	8%	134	7%	26%	-7.2	196	$5
22	COL *	404	39	13	45	2	241	3	3	250	260	401	94	83	110	2	74	0.10	39	24	37	30	70	DCc	5%	110	95	13%	9%	80	8%	32%	-9.5	45	$8
1st Half		160	16	4	18	1	210	1	1	242	224	339	80	80	83	2	76	0.08	40	23	37	25	89	CCc	7%	85	119	9%	9%	105	8%	46%	-7.5	38	-$2
2nd Half		244	23	9	27	1	262	1	2	254	284	443	103	85	121	3	72	0.11	39	25	37	33	60	DCc	4%	127	82	14%	5%	75	8%	24%	1.3	66	$11
23	**Proj**	**175**	**17**	**4**	**20**	**1**	**241**	**3**	**2**	**248**	**279**	**398**	**94**	**80**	**98**	**4**	**74**	**0.14**	**39**	**24**	**37**	**30**	**72**		**5%**	**112**	**97**	**9%**	**7%**	**94**	**7%**	**34%**	**-2.2**	**111**	**$4**

Trevino,Jose

Age: 30 Pos: CA | Bats: R Ht: 5' 11" Wt: 210
Health B | PT/Exp C | Consist A
LIMA Plan D+ | Rand Var 0 | MM 1123

Stable ct%, LD tendencies give him sturdier BA floor (career .250 xBA) than many #2 CA options. On the other hand, xHR says double-digit HR output was a bit over his ability, even with career-high FB%. Overall, it's a pretty bland skill set; he's never going to win anyone a fantasy title, but sometimes he'll deliver more value than you'd expect.

Yr	Tm	PA	R	HR	RBI	SB	BA	xHR	xSB	xBA	OBP	SLG	OPS+	vL+	vR+	bb%	ct%	Eye	G	L	F	h%	HctX	QBaB	Brl%	PX	xPX	HR/F	xHR/F	Spd	SBA%	SB%	RAR	BPX	R$
18	TEX *	202	14	2	15	0	203	0	2	167	243	280	70	66	66	5	84	0.32	57	0	43	23	44	FCf	0%	45	-27	0%	0%	92	3%	0%	-7.5	33	-$3
19	TEX *	278	28	3	28	1	219	2	1	250	243	323	78	122	75	3	78	0.15	46	23	31	27	104	CDd	2%	66	77	7%	7%	90	2%	100%	-8.2	0	-$1
20	TEX	83	10	2	9	0	250	4	0	280	280	434	95	104	89	4	80	0.20	41	24	35	29	122	CCf	13%	115	128	9%	18%	81	0%	0%	0.0	188	$2
21	TEX *	324	27	6	33	1	238	7	0	253	270	345	84	65	92	4	80	0.22	44	25	31	28	98	CDf	4%	67	77	7%	10%	64	3%	50%	-7.8	8	$2
22	NYY	353	39	11	43	2	248	8	2	241	283	388	95	123	87	4	81	0.24	40	19	41	27	96	CCf	5%	82	88	10%	7%	96	4%	67%	1.2	107	$8
1st Half		156	20	7	25	1	248	4	1	257	295	428	102	122	97	6	83	0.38	45	16	39	25	96	CCf	5%	93	86	15%	9%	118	4%	100%	3.0	197	$4
2nd Half		197	19	4	18	1	247	4	1	230	274	358	90	124	80	3	80	0.16	36	21	44	29	97	CBf	5%	73	90	6%	6%	82	4%	50%	-2.0	38	$3
23	**Proj**	**385**	**38**	**9**	**42**	**2**	**243**	**8**	**2**	**244**	**275**	**366**	**89**	**98**	**85**	**4**	**81**	**0.23**	**42**	**22**	**37**	**28**	**100**		**5%**	**77**	**88**	**8%**	**7%**	**78**	**4%**	**58%**	**-0.2**	**57**	**$9**

Trout,Mike

Age: 31 Pos: CF | Bats: R Ht: 6' 2" Wt: 235
Health F | PT/Exp A | Consist D
LIMA Plan D+ | Rand Var +1 | MM 5355

Rare back condition cost him five weeks and has closed door on running game. Former five-category goodness now centers on amazing trio of QBaB/Brl%/HRF, which have held strong as FB tilt has gotten more pronounced. Health questions will linger, but enough PAs seem like the biggest obstacle to... UP: 50 HR

Yr	Tm	PA	R	HR	RBI	SB	BA	xHR	xSB	xBA	OBP	SLG	OPS+	vL+	vR+	bb%	ct%	Eye	G	L	F	h%	HctX	QBaB	Brl%	PX	xPX	HR/F	xHR/F	Spd	SBA%	SB%	RAR	BPX	R$
18	LAA	607	101	39	79	24	312	37	12	281	460	628	146	132	148	20	74	0.98	31	23	45	35	121	AAa	17%	182	156	25%	23%	121	12%	92%	87.6	397	$38
19	LAA	600	110	45	104	11	291	48	14	290	438	645	150	138	154	18	74	0.92	24	27	49	30	113	AAa	19%	180	172	26%	28%	90	7%	85%	71.6	396	$31
20	LAA	241	41	17	46	1	281	18	4	269	390	603	132	102	142	15	72	0.63	25	24	50	31	123	AAb	14%	174	157	23%	24%	130	3%	50%	19.5	388	$29
21	LAA	146	23	8	18	2	333	8	2	270	466	624	150	104	169	18	65	0.66	42	24	34	46	101	ACb	18%	191	123	31%	31%	117	4%	100%	20.5	335	$6
22	LAA	499	85	40	80	1	283	40	4	280	369	630	141	148	139	11	68	0.39	25	19	57	32	115	AAb	20%	232	160	24%	24%	102	1%	100%	52.5	390	$27
1st Half		302	53	23	47	0	277	24	3	274	377	623	142	156	136	13	65	0.42	24	19	57	33	109	AAa	22%	241	160	24%	25%	114	1%	0%	30.6	400	$32
2nd Half		197	32	17	33	1	292	15	2	290	355	640	141	137	142	8	72	0.33	26	18	56	31	124	AAb	18%	219	160	23%	21%	79	1%	100%	20.6	369	$21
23	**Proj**	**525**	**89**	**40**	**92**	**2**	**290**	**40**	**3**	**283**	**396**	**632**	**143**	**125**	**149**	**14**	**69**	**0.52**	**29**	**20**	**50**	**34**	**113**		**18%**	**227**	**149**	**26%**	**25%**	**100**	**3%**	**83%**	**63.8**	**370**	**$32**

Tucker,Kyle

Age: 26 Pos: RF | Bats: L Ht: 6' 4" Wt: 199
Health A | PT/Exp A | Consist C
LIMA Plan C | Rand Var +2 | MM 4345

Even if 5-category upside didn't pan out, this was still his best season. 2021 BA/xBA may look like outliers now, but shift restrictions may put those back in play. xSB, Spd suggest steals might take a step backward. As for HR, with solid vL+ (2022 dip was 21% hit rate) and elite HctX, xPX, not a stretch to think he can still make run at... UP: 40 HR

Yr	Tm	PA	R	HR	RBI	SB	BA	xHR	xSB	xBA	OBP	SLG	OPS+	vL+	vR+	bb%	ct%	Eye	G	L	F	h%	HctX	QBaB	Brl%	PX	xPX	HR/F	xHR/F	Spd	SBA%	SB%	RAR	BPX	R$
18	HOU *	514	73	19	73	16	264	1	7	256	323	447	103	131	41	8	77	0.38	49	16	35	31	95	BBf	4%	109	76	0%	6%	110	17%	74%	6.2	153	$21
19	HOU *	578	81	29	81	27	229	4	11	238	292	452	103	117	119	8	71	0.31	34	19	47	26	116	ABa	13%	124	176	18%	18%	95	30%	83%	-9.9	115	$23
20	HOU	228	33	9	42	8	268	8	9	266	325	512	111	91	120	8	78	0.39	38	20	42	31	119	BBd	9%	127	125	13%	12%	151	19%	89%	6.1	308	$29
21	HOU	565	83	30	92	14	294	33	15	289	359	557	126	124	127	9	82	0.59	34	22	44	31	132	ABb	12%	141	139	16%	18%	107	12%	88%	41.8	365	$31
22	HOU	606	71	30	107	25	257	29	9	269	330	478	114	103	121	10	83	0.62	34	19	47	26	128	BAc	10%	126	158	14%	14%	75	21%	86%	22.0	259	$33
1st Half		303	36	16	56	14	259	16	5	271	350	487	118	122	116	13	82	0.79	30	22	48	26	125	BAb	12%	129	156	15%	15%	81	21%	88%	14.7	283	$34
2nd Half		303	35	14	51	11	256	13	4	267	310	470	110	89	126	7	83	0.45	38	16	46	26	131	BBc	9%	123	161	13%	12%	81	21%	85%	7.1	248	$30
23	**Proj**	**630**	**83**	**32**	**104**	**20**	**277**	**31**	**17**	**274**	**344**	**518**	**120**	**113**	**123**	**9**	**81**	**0.53**	**34**	**20**	**46**	**29**	**126**		**10%**	**141**	**146**	**15%**	**14%**	**97**	**15%**	**85%**	**39.3**	**285**	**$38**

Turner,Justin

Age: 38 Pos: 3B DH | Bats: R Ht: 5' 11" Wt: 202
Health C | PT/Exp A | Consist A
LIMA Plan B+ | Rand Var 0 | MM 2335

Continues to hit better in his 30s than he ever did in his 20s. Steady declines in HctX, xPX show power isn't what it used to be, and 2nd half BA tear was largely driven by high h% (of course, it's also not the first time he's done that). But other than that, skills are still thriving in twilight of career; he can do this again. We should all be so lucky.

Yr	Tm	PA	R	HR	RBI	SB	BA	xHR	xSB	xBA	OBP	SLG	OPS+	vL+	vR+	bb%	ct%	Eye	G	L	F	h%	HctX	QBaB	Brl%	PX	xPX	HR/F	xHR/F	Spd	SBA%	SB%	RAR	BPX	R$
18	LA	426	62	14	52	2	312	16	7	290	406	518	124	136	115	11	85	0.87	29	26	44	34	141	CAa	8%	120	154	10%	12%	81	2%	67%	27.7	283	$16
19	LA	549	80	27	67	2	290	26	4	283	372	509	122	131	117	9	82	0.58	34	26	40	31	142	BAa	8%	107	151	17%	16%	91	1%	100%	15.5	222	$18
20	LA	175	26	4	23	1	307	9	2	251	400	460	114	97	122	10	83	0.69	34	22	44	35	163	BBa	11%	84	191	7%	16%	117	2%	100%	4.8	224	$16
21	LA	612	87	27	87	3	278	24	4	260	361	471	114	111	115	10	82	0.62	35	21	44	30	135	AAb	8%	101	143	14%	12%	86	2%	100%	22.9	212	$23
22	LA	532	61	13	81	3	278	16	2	265	350	438	112	103	115	9	81	0.56	32	25	43	32	113	BAb	8%	107	116	8%	10%	65	2%	100%	13.9	172	$19
1st Half		309	36	7	44	1	242	9	1	257	311	392	99	87	104	10	80	0.54	33	23	44	28	111	CAb	9%	102	115	7%	9%	58	2%	100%	-0.1	141	$14
2nd Half		223	25	6	37	2	328	7	1	280	404	503	128	129	128	10	82	0.60	31	27	43	38	117	BAc	8%	115	116	9%	10%	83	2%	100%	17.5	228	$17
23	**Proj**	**490**	**65**	**13**	**74**	**3**	**273**	**15**	**3**	**257**	**355**	**427**	**109**	**104**	**110**	**10**	**82**	**0.61**	**33**	**24**	**43**	**31**	**128**		**8%**	**100**	**135**	**8%**	**10%**	**86**	**3%**	**98%**	**17.9**	**208**	**$19**

BRANDON KRUSE

Turner,Trea

Age: 30	Pos: SS		Health	A	LIMA Plan	D+
Bats: R	Ht: 6' 2"	Wt: 185	PT/Exp	A	Rand Var	-1
			Consist	B	MM	3545

Continues to deliver on high expectations, providing solid five-category production that's backed by multiple plus skills. Recent drops in xBA, SBA% are minor concerns as he heads into age-30 season, though that can start to chip away at elite R$. But there are few players that offer such a safe floor—his run of first-round value should continue.

Yr	Tm	PA	R	HR	RBI	SB	BA	xHR	xSB	xBA	OBP	SLG	OPS+	vL+	vR+	bb%	ct%	Eye	G	L	F	h%	HctX	QBaB	Brl%	PX	xPX	HR/F	xHR/F	Spd	SBA%	SB%	RAR	BPX	R$
18	WAS	740	103	19	73	43	271	16	11	253	344	416	102	105	99	9	80	0.52	49	18	33	31	93	CCc	6%	82	79	11%	9%	159	26%	83%	24.2	180	$36
19	WAS	569	96	19	57	35	298	20	23	276	353	497	118	113	118	8	78	0.38	47	20	33	35	102	BCc	7%	108	87	14%	15%	158	29%	88%	26.0	237	$32
20	WAS	259	46	12	41	12	335	11	13	300	394	588	130	155	122	8	85	0.61	45	21	35	36	126	BCd	10%	124	115	17%	16%	169	23%	75%	25.9	428	$47
21	2 NL	646	107	28	77	32	328	23	25	283	375	536	125	156	114	6	82	0.37	45	21	34	37	116	BCc	7%	112	91	17%	14%	146	21%	86%	50.1	285	$47
22	LA	706	101	21	100	27	298	22	24	267	343	466	115	124	111	6	80	0.34	43	21	36	35	110	CCf	8%	106	114	11%	12%	145	17%	90%	29.1	217	$43
1st Half		352	43	11	59	16	307	10	13	271	355	484	119	114	120	7	78	0.33	43	24	33	37	112	BDd	9%	114	121	13%	12%	138	17%	89%	20.4	203	$41
2nd Half		354	58	10	41	11	288	12	12	262	331	448	110	135	102	6	82	0.36	42	19	38	33	108	CCf	7%	98	108	10%	12%	147	17%	92%	11.5	224	$35
23	Proj	**700**	**111**	**25**	**92**	**32**	**293**	**24**	**20**	**274**	**343**	**481**	**114**	**132**	**108**	**7**	**81**	**0.38**	**44**	**21**	**35**	**33**	**112**		**7%**	**115**	**104**	**14%**	**13%**	**137**	**15%**	**84%**	**39.1**	**257**	**$43**

Urías,Luis

Age: 26	Pos: 3B 2B SS		Health	A	LIMA Plan	B
Bats: R	Ht: 5' 9"	Wt: 186	PT/Exp	A	Rand Var	+1
			Consist	C	MM	3125

16-47-.239 in 472 PA at MIL. Fell flat after 2021 breakout, as increased FB%, launch angle didn't lead to increased power. As a result, BA and other surface stats dipped across the board, and he lost status as everyday player for lengthy stretches. Despite the step back, above-average plate discipline, xPX could provide a path back to 2021 production.

Yr	Tm	PA	R	HR	RBI	SB	BA	xHR	xSB	xBA	OBP	SLG	OPS+	vL+	vR+	bb%	ct%	Eye	G	L	F	h%	HctX	QBaB	Brl%	PX	xPX	HR/F	xHR/F	Spd	SBA%	SB%	RAR	BPX	R$
18	SD *	551	65	8	37	2	248	1	8	243	318	366	92	163	53	9	73	0.38	63	16	21	33	83	CFf	3%	81	78	25%	13%	120	2%	69%	-10.5	47	$7
19	SD *	570	71	17	60	5	248	6	6	254	317	408	100	124	78	9	75	0.41	49	20	31	30	95	CCb	4%	87	89	8%	13%	131	6%	60%	-16.7	111	$11
20	MIL	120	11	0	11	2	239	1	2	218	308	294	80	92	74	8	71	0.31	63	18	18	34	71	CFf	1%	40	23	0%	7%	127	13%	50%	-8.1	-112	$3
21	MIL	567	77	23	75	5	249	20	10	257	345	445	108	109	108	11	76	0.54	41	21	38	28	109	CCf	9%	112	125	16%	14%	93	4%	83%	10.2	181	$16
22	MIL *	501	57	16	48	1	231	15	5	234	313	387	99	105	104	10	75	0.48	37	20	43	27	105	CAc	8%	99	115	12%	11%	95	2%	33%	-5.2	107	$8
1st Half		259	32	9	27	1	215	6	2	225	295	367	94	116	96	10	74	0.44	38	18	44	25	106	CBd	8%	97	117	13%	9%	87	2%	50%	-4.9	76	$7
2nd Half		242	25	7	21	0	249	8	2	245	351	410	108	97	113	11	77	0.54	36	22	43	29	105	CAc	7%	103	113	10%	12%	107	2%	0%	2.3	155	$6
23	Proj	**490**	**59**	**17**	**56**	**3**	**241**	**16**	**4**	**244**	**333**	**409**	**103**	**106**	**102**	**10**	**75**	**0.47**	**42**	**20**	**38**	**28**	**102**		**7%**	**108**	**106**	**13%**	**12%**	**97**	**4%**	**56%**	**7.2**	**113**	**$14**

Urías,Ramón

Age: 29	Pos: 3B 2B		Health	B	LIMA Plan	C+
Bats: R	Ht: 6' 0"	Wt: 190	PT/Exp	B	Rand Var	+3
			Consist	D	MM	3223

Improved quality of contact allowed him to reach power production that was lacking in 2021. 2nd half HR surge was backed by jump in FB%, but stability of his GB% calls sustainability of that growth into question. Skills look unlikely to coalesce into elite production at this stage of his career, but he can continue to offer serviceable power without killing BA.

Yr	Tm	PA	R	HR	RBI	SB	BA	xHR	xSB	xBA	OBP	SLG	OPS+	vL+	vR+	bb%	ct%	Eye	G	L	F	h%	HctX	QBaB	Brl%	PX	xPX	HR/F	xHR/F	Spd	SBA%	SB%	RAR	BPX	R$
18	a/a	329	36	9	33	1	254		4		294	421	96			5	79	0.27				29				108				86	5%	25%		137	$5
19	a/a	357	41	7	41	3	223		3		295	348	89			9	74	0.40				28				78				86	5%	73%		22	$3
20	BAL	27	3	1	3	0	360	1	0	298	407	560	128	140	123	7	76	0.33	47	32	21	44	178	ADa	5%	121	144	25%	25%	104	0%	0%	2.8	196	$1
21	BAL *	391	43	10	47	2	261	8	2	244	327	405	101	97	113	9	70	0.33	50	24	26	35	102	BFf	10%	96	89	15%	17%	107	5%	35%	1.4	35	$9
22	BAL	445	50	16	51	1	248	16	4	246	305	414	102	93	105	7	76	0.31	47	18	35	29	112	CCf	10%	104	114	15%	15%	110	1%	100%	1.9	117	$10
1st Half		195	23	6	20	0	229	6	2	254	278	385	94	80	99	6	73	0.25	47	24	29	28	112	BCd	9%	108	109	15%	15%	95	1%	0%	-3.7	76	$2
2nd Half		250	27	10	31	1	263	10	3	238	327	438	108	104	110	7	78	0.36	48	14	39	30	113	CCf	10%	101	117	15%	15%	127	1%	100%	4.1	162	$14
23	Proj	**385**	**44**	**12**	**45**	**2**	**251**	**13**	**3**	**248**	**315**	**409**	**101**	**93**	**105**	**7**	**74**	**0.31**	**48**	**20**	**31**	**31**	**108**		**10%**	**106**	**104**	**15%**	**16%**	**105**	**4%**	**55%**	**4.6**	**90**	**$11**

Urshela,Giovanny

Age: 31	Pos: 3B		Health	C	LIMA Plan	B
Bats: R	Ht: 6' 0"	Wt: 215	PT/Exp	A	Rand Var	0
			Consist	C	MM	2335

Career-high PA improved counting stats, but skills remained mostly static. Owns a high BA floor thanks to above-average ct% and balanced batted-ball profile; on the other hand, 2019 power production probably isn't coming back, given three straight seasons of below-average xPX. Useful in multiple categories, but narrow range of outcomes.

Yr	Tm	PA	R	HR	RBI	SB	BA	xHR	xSB	xBA	OBP	SLG	OPS+	vL+	vR+	bb%	ct%	Eye	G	L	F	h%	HctX	QBaB	Brl%	PX	xPX	HR/F	xHR/F	Spd	SBA%	SB%	RAR	BPX	R$
18	TOR *	280	28	3	22	0	234	1	3	195	267	320	79	136	67	4	82	0.25	45	9	45	28	64	DAf	6%	55	41	7%	7%	122	0%	0%	-11.9	63	$0
19	NYY	476	73	21	74	1	314	21	1	293	355	534	123	122	123	5	80	0.29	41	25	33	35	122	BCb	7%	117	122	18%	18%	79	2%	50%	22.6	189	$19
20	NYY	174	24	6	30	1	298	6	1	294	368	490	114	89	120	10	83	0.72	41	27	32	33	107	ACb	7%	104	64	14%	14%	77	2%	100%	7.6	252	$17
21	NYY	442	42	14	49	1	267	14	4	248	301	419	99	106	95	5	74	0.18	48	22	30	33	85	CDc	8%	91	82	15%	15%	114	1%	100%	2.8	54	$10
22	MIN	551	61	13	64	1	285	14	4	262	338	429	109	108	108	7	81	0.43	42	23	35	33	117	CCb	7%	90	97	9%	10%	113	1%	100%	17.3	159	$18
1st Half		282	30	7	33	0	260	9	2	251	309	399	100	97	101	7	81	0.42	45	19	36	30	123	CCc	8%	87	108	9%	12%	103	1%	0%	1.0	145	$10
2nd Half		269	31	6	31	1	313	5	2	271	368	461	117	120	116	8	80	0.44	40	27	33	37	112	CCa	5%	94	85	9%	8%	117	1%	100%	14.0	169	$16
23	Proj	**490**	**55**	**13**	**60**	**1**	**276**	**13**	**3**	**262**	**324**	**424**	**104**	**105**	**103**	**7**	**79**	**0.34**	**44**	**24**	**32**	**33**	**107**		**7%**	**95**	**90**	**11%**	**12%**	**97**	**3%**	**96%**	**13.9**	**134**	**$17**

Vargas,Ildemaro

Age: 31	Pos: 3B		Health	A	LIMA Plan	D
Bats: B	Ht: 6' 0"	Wt: 180	PT/Exp	B	Rand Var	+3
			Consist	A	MM	1331

4-23-.263 in 222 PA at WAS/CHC. Leveraged extreme contact profile into one of his better seasons, as measured by OPS+ and BPX. While that may help him extend his career another season or two, his skills suggest his 2022 sample is as good as it will get. Viable fill-in in deepest of leagues, but nothing else.

Yr	Tm	PA	R	HR	RBI	SB	BA	xHR	xSB	xBA	OBP	SLG	OPS+	vL+	vR+	bb%	ct%	Eye	G	L	F	h%	HctX	QBaB	Brl%	PX	xPX	HR/F	xHR/F	Spd	SBA%	SB%	RAR	BPX	R$
18	ARI *	575	48	5	36	7	229	0	6	293	254	320	77	52	99	3	89	0.30	40	33	27	25	87	CDb	7%	51	56	25%	0%	141	11%	57%	-34.7	157	$4
19	ARI *	342	37	7	38	2	283	4	6	299	316	419	102	143	82	5	91	0.51	53	23	25	29	107	CFf	3%	63	60	14%	9%	124	4%	55%	-7.1	226	$7
20	3 TM	54	6	1	3	0	196	1	0	233	222	314	71	50	97	4	80	0.20	60	12	29	23	93	DFf	2%	56	74	8%	8%	143	0%	0%	-4.8	76	-$2
21	3 NL *	340	32	5	26	2	196	0	1	263	229	298	72	44	72	4	84	0.26	55	20	25	22	114	DFf	2%	61	53	0%	0%	98	5%	65%	-22.9	85	-$2
22	2 NL *	516	41	6	38	5	214	2	5	256	251	312	80	100	96	5	86	0.34	48	20	32	24	80	DDf	2%	61	46	7%	3%	125	9%	57%	-28.4	134	$2
1st Half		246	22	2	14	1	167	1	2	243	219	255	67	87	77	6	84	0.42	57	14	29	19	140	BFd		52	93	17%	17%	144	9%	48%	-19.0	124	-$6
2nd Half		270	19	4	24	4	257	2	3	265	281	362	91	101	99	3	87	0.25	47	21	32	28	73	DDf	3%	70	39	6%	4%	103	9%	61%	-5.7	145	$8
23	Proj	**175**	**15**	**3**	**14**	**2**	**221**	**2**	**2**	**259**	**254**	**330**	**81**	**69**	**90**	**4**	**86**	**0.30**	**54**	**17**	**29**	**24**	**93**		**2%**	**67**	**58**	**6%**	**5%**	**113**	**9%**	**63%**	**-5.7**	**132**	**$2**

Vargas,Miguel

Age: 23	Pos: 1B		Health	A	LIMA Plan	C+
Bats: R	Ht: 6' 3"	Wt: 205	PT/Exp	B	Rand Var	-1
			Consist	C	MM	1303

1-8-.170 with 1 SB in 50 PA at LA. High-end prospect proved everything he needed to at AAA, posting .915 OPS. Higher ct% from minors didn't show up in tiny MLB sample, and PX disappointed, but HctX, QBaB, xPX preach patience. Even if there are continued struggles in short term, track record and scouting reports say buy/hold in keeper leagues.

Yr	Tm	PA	R	HR	RBI	SB	BA	xHR	xSB	xBA	OBP	SLG	OPS+	vL+	vR+	bb%	ct%	Eye	G	L	F	h%	HctX	QBaB	Brl%	PX	xPX	HR/F	xHR/F	Spd	SBA%	SB%	RAR	BPX	R$
18																																			
19																																			
20																																			
21	aa	351	48	12	43	5	275		4		325	432	104			7	80	0.38				31				86				92	7%	82%		127	$12
22	LA *	528	62	12	56	10	230	1	6	216	291	365	93	66	62	8	79	0.40	34	14	51	27	148	BAc	9%	88	142	6%	6%	113	14%	64%	-13.7	128	$12
1st Half		324	38	9	34	5	230		4	248	285	372	93	0	0	7	78	0.36	44	20	36	27	0			89	-14	0%		122	14%	57%	-7.1	131	$15
2nd Half		203	24	4	22	6	230	1	2	217	300	354	93	66	62	9	79	0.48	34	14	51	27	149	BAc	9%	87	142	6%	6%	100	14%	71%	-3.9	128	$7
23	Proj	**420**	**53**	**8**	**48**	**8**	**247**	**9**	**8**	**209**	**300**	**366**	**92**	**86**	**97**	**8**	**79**	**0.40**	**34**	**14**	**51**	**29**	**134**		**8%**	**79**	**128**	**5%**	**6%**	**108**	**11%**	**72%**	**-3.8**	**128**	**$14**

Varsho,Daulton

Age: 26	Pos: RF CF CA		Health	A	LIMA Plan	C+
Bats: L	Ht: 5' 10"	Wt: 207	PT/Exp	A	Rand Var	0
			Consist	B	MM	4325

Flew up draft boards due to power-speed potential as a catcher and delivered as hoped. Power doesn't look like a fluke, as above average FB% covers QBaB shortcomings without cratering BA. However, below-average Spd and mediocre SB% are concerns, as are lost PA vs. LHP. Star will dim once CA eligibility is gone, but that's not an issue for 2023.

Yr	Tm	PA	R	HR	RBI	SB	BA	xHR	xSB	xBA	OBP	SLG	OPS+	vL+	vR+	bb%	ct%	Eye	G	L	F	h%	HctX	QBaB	Brl%	PX	xPX	HR/F	xHR/F	Spd	SBA%	SB%	RAR	BPX	R$
18																																			
19	aa	437	80	16	55	20	289		7		355	502	119			9	83	0.60				31				103				130	23%	78%		274	$21
20	ARI	115	16	3	9	3	188	3	3	218	287	366	87	44	108	10	67	0.36	39	19	42	25	76	FBf	4%	110	87	11%	11%	136	17%	75%	-6.1	84	$4
21	ARI *	399	51	16	52	7	243	12	8	254	307	447	104	111	101	8	76	0.39	36	22	43	28	106	DBf	7%	118	119	12%	13%	96	9%	100%	2.9	181	$11
22	ARI	591	79	27	74	16	235	22	7	241	302	443	105	77	114	8	73	0.32	40	15	44	27	108	DCf	10%	131	158	16%	13%	90	18%	73%	4.3	138	$22
1st Half		299	38	12	41	5	247	11	4	244	305	435	105	71	116	7	74	0.27	39	18	43	29	114	DCf	9%	124	175	14%	13%	81	18%	63%	2.5	121	$20
2nd Half		292	41	15	33	11	223	11	3	239	299	450	106	86	111	9	71	0.36	42	13	45	25	101	CCf	12%	139	140	18%	13%	105	18%	79%	3.4	166	$25
23	Proj	**525**	**74**	**22**	**64**	**14**	**243**	**20**	**12**	**245**	**312**	**448**	**105**	**92**	**110**	**9**	**74**	**0.36**	**39**	**18**	**44**	**28**	**103**		**9%**	**131**	**133**	**14%**	**13%**	**100**	**13%**	**79%**	**10.5**	**164**	**$22**

DANIEL MARCUS

Vaughn,Andrew

		Health	A	LIMA Plan	B+
Age: 25	Pos: RF LF DH 1B	PT/Exp	A	Rand Var	-1
Bats: R	Ht: 6' 0" Wt: 215	Consist	A	MM	3125

Improved results reflected by gains in R$ and BPX, which came primarily through jump in ct%. However, quality of contact stayed mostly stable, and GB%, launch angle show that he still doesn't lift the ball enough. HctX, exit velocity remain above average, but without change to batted-ball profile, he's maxed out power output. Few signs of a next step.

Yr	Tm	PA	R	HR	RBI	SB	BA	xHR	xSB	xBA	OBP	SLG	OPS+	vL+	vR+	bb%	ct%	Eye	G	L	F	h%	HctX	QBaB	Brl%	PX	xPX	HR/F	xHR/F	Spd	SBA%	SB%	RAR	BPX	R$
18																																			
19																																			
20																																			
21	CHW	469	56	15	48	1	235	19	5	244	309	396	97	128	84	9	76	0.41	44	20	36	28	110	ACd	11%	97	117	13%	16%	88	2%	50%	-4.2	104	$7
22	CHW	555	60	17	76	0	271	16	3	257	321	429	106	104	107	6	81	0.32	48	18	34	30	111	BDd	8%	98	108	12%	11%	86	0%	0%	8.7	145	$17
1st Half		261	27	7	36	0	295	7	1	259	345	443	111	126	108	7	81	0.39	46	21	33	34	110	ADd	7%	94	88	11%	11%	90	0%	0%	9.5	148	$13
2nd Half		294	33	10	40	0	249	9	1	255	299	418	102	87	106	5	81	0.27	49	16	35	27	112	BDc	9%	102	125	13%	12%	89	0%	0%	0.1	152	$16
23	**Proj**	**560**	**65**	**18**	**70**	**0**	**255**	**19**	**2**	**251**	**315**	**414**	**101**	**113**	**97**	**7**	**79**	**0.36**	**46**	**19**	**35**	**29**	**111**		**9%**	**102**	**113**	**12%**	**13%**	**79**	**2%**	**50%**	**6.2**	**132**	**$14**

Vavra,Terrin

		Health	A	LIMA Plan	D
Age: 26	Pos: 2B	PT/Exp	D	Rand Var	0
Bats: L	Ht: 6' 1" Wt: 185	Consist	A	MM	1411

1-12-.258 in 103 PA at BAL. The report card is still incomplete, but doesn't appear to have a carrying skill. Scouting reports suggest hit tool is above-average, but initial samples of ct%, HctX, and xBA show he still has work to do. With very little power and SB drying up in upper levels of minors, he's nothing more than a bench bat in majors.

Yr	Tm	PA	R	HR	RBI	SB	BA	xHR	xSB	xBA	OBP	SLG	OPS+	vL+	vR+	bb%	ct%	Eye	G	L	F	h%	HctX	QBaB	Brl%	PX	xPX	HR/F	xHR/F	Spd	SBA%	SB%	RAR	BPX	R$
18																																			
19																																			
20																																			
21	aa	169	20	4	14	4	207		2		302	349	89			12	69	0.44				27				96				101	13%	79%		35	$1
22	BAL *	293	35	2	23	3	256	1	7	246	330	345	96	82	98	10	76	0.47	40	29	31	33	79	DDc		65	78	5%	5%	135	6%	58%	1.2	69	$4
1st Half		141	18	1	7	2	257		3	231	318	353	95	0	0	8	77	0.39	44	20	36	32	0			70	-14	0%		123	6%	67%	-0.4	66	-$3
2nd Half		152	16	1	16	1	255	1	4	241	342	337	96	82	98	12	76	0.55	40	29	31	33	78	DDc	0%	59	78	5%	5%	134	6%	38%	-0.2	55	-$1
23	**Proj**	**245**	**28**	**2**	**20**	**4**	**237**	**2**	**4**	**231**	**315**	**330**	**90**	**74**	**91**	**11**	**73**	**0.46**	**44**	**25**	**31**	**31**	**70**		**0%**	**71**	**70**	**4%**	**5%**	**138**	**8%**	**70%**	**-1.2**	**50**	**$5**

Vázquez,Christian

		Health	A	LIMA Plan	C+
Age: 32	Pos: CA	PT/Exp	A	Rand Var	0
Bats: R	Ht: 5' 9" Wt: 205	Consist	B	MM	1023

Got off to promising start in 1st half, but slipped after mid-season trade to HOU. Rise in FB%, drop in Brl%, PX were primary culprits, and provided more evidence that 2019 power isn't returning. Still likely a starter thanks to strong defense. Contact% can keep BA afloat, which ain't nothing in a thin CA pool, but little fantasy appeal otherwise.

Yr	Tm	PA	R	HR	RBI	SB	BA	xHR	xSB	xBA	OBP	SLG	OPS+	vL+	vR+	bb%	ct%	Eye	G	L	F	h%	HctX	QBaB	Brl%	PX	xPX	HR/F	xHR/F	Spd	SBA%	SB%	RAR	BPX	R$
18	BOS	269	24	3	16	4	207	4	3	237	257	283	72	80	68	5	84	0.32	42	21	36	24	85	CCb	2%	48	51	4%	5%	73	9%	80%	-8.6	23	-$1
19	BOS	521	66	23	72	4	276	19	6	270	320	477	110	124	103	6	79	0.33	39	23	38	31	92	BCb	6%	103	100	16%	13%	82	5%	67%	24.3	141	$16
20	BOS	189	22	7	23	4	283	5	2	242	344	457	106	102	108	8	75	0.37	42	20	38	34	94	CBf	5%	100	96	14%	10%	90	14%	57%	6.0	104	$18
21	BOS	498	51	6	49	8	258	7	9	238	308	352	91	75	98	7	82	0.39	41	22	38	30	76	DCd	3%	58	67	4%	5%	75	10%	67%	-3.5	42	$11
22	2 AL	426	41	9	52	1	274	8	4	262	315	399	101	115	96	5	83	0.32	45	23	32	31	94	CCd	5%	82	73	8%	7%	54	5%	20%	7.6	86	$11
1st Half		235	23	4	31	1	290	4	3	277	340	416	107	117	104	7	82	0.39	46	26	28	34	90	CCc	7%	87	69	8%	8%	54	5%	33%	7.7	103	$9
2nd Half		191	18	5	21	0	255	4	2	244	283	380	94	113	87	4	83	0.23	44	19	37	28	97	CCf	3%	76	77	9%	7%	65	5%	0%	-0.5	76	$4
23	**Proj**	**420**	**43**	**9**	**47**	**4**	**264**	**8**	**3**	**249**	**310**	**387**	**97**	**99**	**95**	**6**	**82**	**0.35**	**43**	**22**	**36**	**30**	**88**		**4%**	**80**	**74**	**8%**	**7%**	**66**	**4%**	**50%**	**7.4**	**75**	**$13**

Velazquez,Andrew

		Health	A	LIMA Plan	F
Age: 28	Pos: SS	PT/Exp	C	Rand Var	-1
Bats: B	Ht: 5' 9" Wt: 170	Consist	B	MM	2401

Set new career high for PA, and would have collected more if not for season-ending knee surgery. But seems unlikely to earn significant playing time again, as QBaB, ct%, and Eye were all well below average and led to disastrous BA. Steals provide reason to pay attention if he stumbles into another role, but they'll come at a steep price.

Yr	Tm	PA	R	HR	RBI	SB	BA	xHR	xSB	xBA	OBP	SLG	OPS+	vL+	vR+	bb%	ct%	Eye	G	L	F	h%	HctX	QBaB	Brl%	PX	xPX	HR/F	xHR/F	Spd	SBA%	SB%	RAR	BPX	R$
18	TAM *	499	60	11	38	27	224	0	6	193	271	355	84	133	96	6	65	0.19	43	14	43	32	0	CBc	0%	90	-27	0%	0%	155	29%	89%	-11.1	-20	$14
19	2 AL *	206	23	3	17	3	218	0	6	225	252	353	84	75	26	4	71	0.16	40	20	40	29	122	AAc	0%	89	138	0%	0%	111	26%	37%	-16.1	0	$0
20	BAL	77	11	0	3	4	159	1	3	169	274	206	64	87	52	13	63	0.43	49	16	35	25	47	FFf	5%	31	88	0%	8%	148	33%	67%	-6.1	-192	$1
21	NYY *	360	40	6	40	25	219	1	13	209	281	352	87	67	90	8	60	0.22	48	20	32	34	78	BCa	14%	106	126	7%	7%	113	41%	84%	-9.2	-81	$13
22	LAA	349	37	9	28	17	196	7	15	198	236	304	77	77	76	4	63	0.13	47	19	34	28	75	FFf	7%	81	107	14%	11%	105	28%	94%	-16.9	-138	$7
1st Half		228	22	5	20	10	165	5	8	195	208	264	67	71	65	4	64	0.12	41	22	37	23	80	CCf	6%	76	110	10%	10%	103	28%	100%	-17.0	-148	$4
2nd Half		121	15	4	8	7	255	2	6	203	291	382	95	90	97	5	62	0.14	59	14	27	38	67	FFf	8%	92	100	24%	12%	114	28%	88%	-0.7	-110	$3
23	**Proj**	**210**	**24**	**5**	**19**	**12**	**219**	**3**	**7**	**205**	**265**	**339**	**84**	**78**	**86**	**6**	**63**	**0.16**	**50**	**19**	**32**	**32**	**72**		**10%**	**95**	**111**	**12%**	**8%**	**112**	**21%**	**84%**	**-5.3**	**-89**	**$8**

Velazquez,Nelson

		Health	A	LIMA Plan	D+
Age: 24	Pos: CF RF	PT/Exp	D	Rand Var	0
Bats: R	Ht: 6' 0" Wt: 190	Consist	D	MM	4403

6-26-.205 with 5 SB in 206 PA at CHC. Called up in late May to play rotational role, which kept compelling power skills (xHR, Brl%, xPX) somewhat hidden. Add in Spd, SBA%, and there's some HR/SB upside potential here. Troublesome ct%, though, will keep BA at the "How much risk can you handle?" level, both for his MLB club and yours.

Yr	Tm	PA	R	HR	RBI	SB	BA	xHR	xSB	xBA	OBP	SLG	OPS+	vL+	vR+	bb%	ct%	Eye	G	L	F	h%	HctX	QBaB	Brl%	PX	xPX	HR/F	xHR/F	Spd	SBA%	SB%	RAR	BPX	R$
18																																			
19																																			
20																																			
21	aa	132	14	6	20	4	253		1		296	480	107			6	69	0.20				32				149				94	17%	100%		138	$3
22	CHC *	426	43	15	46	13	196	8	10	203	264	373	90	106	85	8	58	0.22	43	17	41	29	85	CCf	14%	141	144	12%	16%	151	25%	65%	-14.5	31	$7
1st Half		261	30	10	25	9	204	0	6	204	268	391	93	171	89	8	55	0.19	42	19	38	32	74	CCf	0%	159	120	10%	0%	147	25%	65%	-7.4	28	$12
2nd Half		165	13	5	21	4	182	8	4	206	267	345	87	90	84	9	64	0.28	43	16	41	25	94	BCf	16%	116	150	13%	21%	151	25%	67%	-7.1	41	$1
23	**Proj**	**280**	**28**	**8**	**36**	**8**	**215**	**8**	**8**	**211**	**279**	**376**	**91**	**109**	**79**	**7**	**63**	**0.22**	**42**	**17**	**40**	**31**	**86**		**10%**	**125**	**138**	**12%**	**12%**	**115**	**19%**	**76%**	**-3.6**	**77**	**$8**

Verdugo,Alex

		Health	A	LIMA Plan	B+
Age: 27	Pos: LF RF	PT/Exp	A	Rand Var	+1
Bats: L	Ht: 6' 0" Wt: 192	Consist	B	MM	2245

Continues to leave fantasy managers wishing for more. Underperformance of xHR, xHR/F lingered despite shifting GB%/FB% balance for second straight season. Rebound vL staves off platoon concerns, QBaB and Brl% stable, so expect more of the same... including those hopes for a power breakout still going unanswered.

Yr	Tm	PA	R	HR	RBI	SB	BA	xHR	xSB	xBA	OBP	SLG	OPS+	vL+	vR+	bb%	ct%	Eye	G	L	F	h%	HctX	QBaB	Brl%	PX	xPX	HR/F	xHR/F	Spd	SBA%	SB%	RAR	BPX	R$
18	LA *	455	47	9	40	6	287	1	7	265	341	409	100	74	99	7	84	0.52	62	16	22	32	121	CFb	5%	73	68	7%	7%	104	7%	74%	6.8	147	$12
19	LA	377	43	12	44	4	294	10	4	297	342	475	113	117	111	7	86	0.53	49	23	29	32	129	BDc	6%	90	91	14%	12%	95	5%	80%	8.5	219	$10
20	BOS	221	36	6	15	4	308	5	3	271	367	478	112	103	117	8	78	0.38	52	20	27	37	102	CDd	6%	104	82	14%	12%	128	7%	100%	8.7	196	$22
21	BOS	604	88	13	63	6	289	17	9	271	351	426	107	75	123	8	82	0.53	50	22	29	33	103	BDc	7%	80	71	10%	13%	110	5%	75%	14.5	173	$21
22	BOS	644	75	11	74	1	280	16	6	268	328	405	104	97	106	7	85	0.49	46	21	33	31	114	CDc	6%	81	90	7%	9%	85	3%	25%	7.5	162	$20
1st Half		313	34	6	43	0	264	9	3	268	310	385	98	100	98	6	89	0.63	48	20	32	28	121	BDd	7%	74	93	7%	11%	74	3%	0%	-0.6	179	$14
2nd Half		331	41	5	31	1	295	6	3	267	344	423	109	94	114	7	82	0.41	43	23	34	35	108	CDc	5%	88	86	6%	7%	103	3%	33%	8.1	159	$18
23	**Proj**	**595**	**78**	**12**	**63**	**4**	**288**	**14**	**5**	**270**	**341**	**424**	**106**	**91**	**113**	**7**	**83**	**0.48**	**48**	**21**	**30**	**33**	**110**		**6%**	**89**	**82**	**9%**	**10%**	**102**	**4%**	**65%**	**20.2**	**173**	**$24**

Vientos,Mark

		Health	A	LIMA Plan	D
Age: 23	Pos: DH	PT/Exp	C	Rand Var	-3
Bats: R	Ht: 6' 4" Wt: 185	Consist	A	MM	3003

1-3-.167 in 41 PA at NYM. Spent most of season at AAA and posted .885 OPS to earn cup of coffee with big-league club, where exit velocity was elite. Should compete for roster spot out of spring training, and both PX track record and scouting reports suggests power will play. Just don't expect much BA, given terrible ct% history.

Yr	Tm	PA	R	HR	RBI	SB	BA	xHR	xSB	xBA	OBP	SLG	OPS+	vL+	vR+	bb%	ct%	Eye	G	L	F	h%	HctX	QBaB	Brl%	PX	xPX	HR/F	xHR/F	Spd	SBA%	SB%	RAR	BPX	R$
18																																			
19																																			
20																																			
21	a/a	336	37	17	45	0	227		3		281	440	99			7	62	0.20				31				147				80	3%	0%		15	$5
22	NYM *	448	46	17	50	0	218	1	3	171	278	376	93	113	38	8	61	0.21	50	4	46	31	78	ACf	11%	119	79	9%	9%	107	2%	0%	-16.8	-31	$5
1st Half		226	24	9	25	0	198		1	203	264	367	89	0	0	8	58	0.21	44	20	36	29	0			133	-14	0%		123	2%	0%	-9.6	-28	$3
2nd Half		223	22	8	25	0	238	1	2	168	292	385	96	113	38	7	65	0.22	50	4	46	33	83	ACf	11%	107	79	9%	9%	103	2%	0%	-3.7	-21	$7
23	**Proj**	**280**	**30**	**10**	**34**	**0**	**223**	**7**	**2**	**198**	**280**	**371**	**90**	**133**	**45**	**7**	**62**	**0.20**	**46**	**17**	**37**	**32**	**83**		**9%**	**115**	**71**	**16%**	**12%**	**99**	**4%**	**0%**	**-7.2**	**-8**	**$5**

DANIEL MARCUS

Vierling,Matt

Age: 26 Pos: CF RF LF | Bats: R Ht: 6' 3" Wt: 205
Health: A | PT/Exp: C | Consist: B
LIMA Plan: D+ | Rand Var: 0 | MM: 2423

6-32-.246 with 7 SB in 357 PA at PHI. First true opportunity in majors and flashed potential, but can he be a productive everyday player? PRO: Exit velocity, HctX, and Spd all show path to above-average HR and SB production. CON: Struggles vR threaten playing time and low BA/OBP, SB% could cut into SB opportunities. Worth using a late-round pick to find out.

Yr	Tm	PA	R	HR	RBI	SB	BA	xHR	xSB	xBA	OBP	SLG	OPS+	vL+	vR+	bb%	ct%	Eye	G	L	F	h%	HctX	QBaB	Brl%	PX	xPX	HR/F	xHR/F	Spd	SBA%	SB%	RAR	BPX	R$
18																																			
19																																			
20																																			
21	PHI *	395	38	10	37	9	255	2	7	255	308	385	95	107	127	7	73	0.29	54	25	21	32	115	ADb	4%	77	46	18%	18%	140	11%	79%	-4.1	46	$10
22	PHI *	448	50	7	38	12	239	8	9	239	289	349	90	106	82	7	78	0.33	41	23	36	29	117	ACc	5%	70	91	6%	9%	134	17%	65%	-9.4	86	$10
1st Half		210	26	4	17	7	230	4	4	237	306	360	94	109	93	10	78	0.49	37	22	41	27	88	ABf	8%	83	87	9%	12%	130	17%	61%	-2.7	131	$6
2nd Half		238	24	3	21	5	246	4	4	237	277	339	87	104	78	4	79	0.19	43	23	34	30	130	BCc	4%	60	93	5%	7%	135	17%	71%	-5.6	48	$7
23	Proj	350	37	9	31	9	246	10	9	247	299	374	93	96	91	7	76	0.31	46	24	31	30	114		5%	82	73	11%	13%	118	14%	72%	-0.5	68	$8

Villar,David

Age: 26 Pos: 3B | Bats: R Ht: 6' 1" Wt: 215
Health: A | PT/Exp: B | Consist: A
LIMA Plan: D | Rand Var: 0 | MM: 5111

9-24-.231 in 181 PA at SF. Solid PX got even better in AAA and MLB debut, though HctX, exit velocity were only average, and xHR/F warns of HR pullback. More concerning is poor ct% that will continue to cause BA to suffer and potentially prohibit him from sticking in a big-league lineup. Empty power may be best-case scenario.

Yr	Tm	PA	R	HR	RBI	SB	BA	xHR	xSB	xBA	OBP	SLG	OPS+	vL+	vR+	bb%	ct%	Eye	G	L	F	h%	HctX	QBaB	Brl%	PX	xPX	HR/F	xHR/F	Spd	SBA%	SB%	RAR	BPX	R$
18																																			
19																																			
20																																			
21	aa	422	56	14	46	4	233		4		300	408	97			9	67	0.29				31				124				85	6%	78%		42	$8
22	SF *	513	60	24	72	1	217	6	5	224	297	429	103	137	92	10	62	0.30	37	18	44	29	99	CAa	9%	159	192	20%	14%	94	3%	21%	-0.9	93	$10
1st Half		263	31	11	37	0	220		2	245	303	430	104	245	0	11	59	0.29	33	33	33	31	87			170	235	0%		88	3%	0%	1.9	79	$10
2nd Half		250	29	12	35	1	214	6	2	228	290	429	102	131	95	10	66	0.31	38	18	45	26	104	CAa	9%	148	191	21%	14%	105	3%	37%	0.4	114	$12
23	Proj	210	26	10	27	1	224	8	1	233	320	447	106	125	93	10	65	0.30	38	18	45	29	94		8%	165	172	19%	14%	89	4%	61%	3.3	76	$6

Villar,Jonathan

Age: 32 Pos: 2B 3B | Bats: B Ht: 6' 0" Wt: 233
Health: B | PT/Exp: B | Consist: C
LIMA Plan: D | Rand Var: +5 | MM: 2311

3-18-.232 with 7 SB in 220 PA at CHC/LAA. One-time fantasy first-rounder fell further out of relevance as metrics slipped across the board. SBA% shows willingness to run hasn't left, but that's not enough to keep value afloat when paired with abysmal ct% and inconsistent power. It's fair to question his role on any big-league club in 2023.

Yr	Tm	PA	R	HR	RBI	SB	BA	xHR	xSB	xBA	OBP	SLG	OPS+	vL+	vR+	bb%	ct%	Eye	G	L	F	h%	HctX	QBaB	Brl%	PX	xPX	HR/F	xHR/F	Spd	SBA%	SB%	RAR	BPX	R$
18	2 TM	515	54	14	46	35	260	14	8	235	325	384	95	97	93	8	70	0.30	56	20	24	34	80	CFd	5%	79	71	18%	18%	100	29%	88%	1.8	-20	$23
19	BAL	713	111	24	73	40	274	24	30	253	339	453	110	103	112	9	73	0.35	49	20	31	34	73	CDd	7%	100	70	17%	17%	111	27%	82%	7.8	85	$35
20	2 TM	207	13	2	15	16	232	2	8	215	301	292	79	77	79	9	71	0.35	60	19	21	32	75	DFf	1%	40	23	7%	7%	87	38%	76%	-10.4	-148	$20
21	NYM	505	63	18	42	14	249	15	26	243	322	416	101	98	103	9	71	0.35	49	21	31	31	84	CDf	7%	101	84	18%	15%	103	17%	67%	3.2	62	$16
22	2 TM *	370	36	6	31	12	199	2	7	230	244	304	78	83	79	6	69	0.19	60	17	22	27	79	CFf	3%	74	69	9%	6%	103	24%	76%	-17.7	-66	$4
1st Half		174	19	2	15	6	213	2	3	232	264	313	82	76	83	7	71	0.26	57	18	24	29	81	BFd	3%	70	70	7%	7%	112	24%	100%	-6.4	-31	$1
2nd Half		196	17	4	16	6	188	0	3	232	223	296	74	108	60	4	68	0.14	71	14	14	25	79	DFf	3%	77	66	25%	0%	78	24%	62%	-13.6	-117	$1
23	Proj	175	19	4	15	7	223	2	5	236	279	354	88	97	84	7	70	0.25	59	18	23	29	80		4%	90	68	17%	8%	94	17%	74%	-2.6	-34	$6

Vogelbach,Daniel

Age: 30 Pos: DH | Bats: L Ht: 6' 0" Wt: 270
Health: C | PT/Exp: B | Consist: A
LIMA Plan: C+ | Rand Var: 0 | MM: 3013

Split season between PIT and NYM, and saw re-emergence of 2019 All-Star skills, as more fly balls helped unlock additional power. But track record suggests change in batted-ball profile could disappear as quickly as it came, and he'll always be limited due to struggles vL. But he's all about the lumber - bringing it to the plate and running the bases.

Yr	Tm	PA	R	HR	RBI	SB	BA	xHR	xSB	xBA	OBP	SLG	OPS+	vL+	vR+	bb%	ct%	Eye	G	L	F	h%	HctX	QBaB	Brl%	PX	xPX	HR/F	xHR/F	Spd	SBA%	SB%	RAR	BPX	R$
18	SEA *	457	49	19	58	0	229	4	7	246	349	416	102	36	108	15	74	0.71	44	21	34	26	143	ACb	12%	112	161	19%	19%	47	1%	0%	2.6	107	$8
19	SEA	558	73	30	76	0	208	25	0	240	341	439	108	84	116	16	68	0.62	33	22	45	23	90	CBc	11%	130	123	21%	18%	33	0%	0%	-6.5	74	$9
20	3 TM	136	16	6	16	0	209	5	0	233	331	391	96	46	102	15	71	0.61	46	21	33	24	92	BCc	9%	101	77	22%	19%	44	0%	0%	-2.6	44	$4
21	MIL *	316	35	11	29	0	220	7	0	224	351	375	100	50	108	17	72	0.71	44	20	35	27	98	ACc	8%	91	98	16%	13%	50	0%	0%	-6.2	38	$2
22	2 NL	461	47	18	59	0	238	18	0	243	360	433	112	58	125	16	70	0.64	38	21	41	29	102	BBc	11%	131	136	16%	16%	31	0%	0%	7.2	103	$9
1st Half		236	26	11	27	0	235	12	0	236	335	446	110	54	128	13	73	0.55	40	15	45	27	111	ABc	14%	132	143	16%	18%	53	0%	0%	2.4	138	$8
2nd Half		225	21	7	32	0	242	6	0	255	387	418	114	66	121	19	68	0.72	35	29	36	32	91	CBc	8%	130	128	16%	13%	24	0%	0%	4.2	79	$8
23	Proj	385	41	14	46	0	244	13	0	234	370	420	110	59	120	16	71	0.67	42	21	37	30	100		9%	119	118	17%	15%	34	0%	0%	9.3	76	$10

Voit,Luke

Age: 32 Pos: DH 1B | Bats: R Ht: 6' 3" Wt: 255
Health: F | PT/Exp: A | Consist: C
LIMA Plan: C+ | Rand Var: +2 | MM: 4015

Was headed for forgettable season after hitting just .143 in first 54 PA and landing on IL with late April biceps injury. But end result looks familiar, with QBaB, Brl%, and xPX all continuing to point to elite power potential. Inconsistent ct%, injury history keep risk level high, but 2nd half xHR is another indication that a 30-HR season is still in play.

Yr	Tm	PA	R	HR	RBI	SB	BA	xHR	xSB	xBA	OBP	SLG	OPS+	vL+	vR+	bb%	ct%	Eye	G	L	F	h%	HctX	QBaB	Brl%	PX	xPX	HR/F	xHR/F	Spd	SBA%	SB%	RAR	BPX	R$
18	2 TM *	458	60	25	68	0	276	15	7	274	347	512	115	155	134	10	73	0.40	35	28	37	32	126	ABa	20%	141	158	41%	41%	98	1%	0%	12.7	183	$16
19	NYY	510	72	21	62	0	263	26	2	245	378	464	117	110	118	14	67	0.50	40	26	35	35	90	BCb	13%	120	118	21%	26%	82	0%	0%	6.2	67	$12
20	NYY	234	41	22	52	0	277	19	0	283	338	610	126	118	128	7	75	0.31	41	20	39	27	125	CBd	13%	167	134	35%	30%	66	0%	0%	7.3	272	$31
21	NYY *	292	34	15	46	0	249	13	1	233	312	472	108	103	106	8	65	0.26	40	20	40	32	99	BBb	16%	142	143	20%	24%	74	0%	0%	0.7	54	$7
22	2 NL	568	55	22	69	1	226	27	0	230	308	402	101	80	109	10	64	0.31	34	26	40	30	106	BAc	15%	131	146	17%	20%	45	2%	50%	-9.9	-10	$10
1st Half		264	29	10	35	1	229	11	0	235	318	424	105	88	112	11	61	0.34	38	25	37	33	106	BBc	16%	159	150	19%	21%	57	2%	100%	0.8	52	$10
2nd Half		304	26	12	34	0	223	17	0	226	299	383	97	72	107	9	67	0.28	31	26	43	29	105	BAb	14%	108	142	15%	22%	46	2%	0%	-6.6	-52	$11
23	Proj	525	61	26	77	0	242	30	1	238	323	449	107	96	112	9	66	0.30	37	24	40	31	106		15%	145	143	21%	24%	53	1%	41%	6.7	51	$17

Volpe,Anthony

Age: 22 Pos: SS | Bats: R Ht: 5' 11" Wt: 180
Health: A | PT/Exp: B | Consist: F
LIMA Plan: D+ | Rand Var: | MM: 3511

One of the fastest prospect risers of 2021, he continued march toward big leagues, concluding season at AAA. Spent majority of campaign at AA, and flashed elite SB potential paired with solid .220 ISO. Low ct% at highest level of minors could mean he'll have to wait for summer months to make NYY debut, but will be a name to monitor closely.

Yr	Tm	PA	R	HR	RBI	SB	BA	xHR	xSB	xBA	OBP	SLG	OPS+	vL+	vR+	bb%	ct%	Eye	G	L	F	h%	HctX	QBaB	Brl%	PX	xPX	HR/F	xHR/F	Spd	SBA%	SB%	RAR	BPX	R$
18																																			
19																																			
20																																			
21																																			
22	a/a	561	65	16	49	38	210		6		280	374	93			9	74	0.37				25				110				106	41%	85%		121	$21
1st Half		288	36	9	31	24	208		3		274	369	91			8	74	0.35				25				110				107	41%	92%		117	$27
2nd Half		273	29	8	18	14	212		3	248	288	380	95			10	74	0.41	44	20	36	26	0			110	-14	0%		145	41%	76%	-5.3	166	$14
23	Proj	245	28	6	20	12	237	6	13	232	307	389	97	96	97	9	76	0.42	36	20	44	29	92		7%	101		8%	8%	121	31%	80%	1.1	146	$10

Votto,Joey

Age: 39 Pos: 1B | Bats: L Ht: 6' 2" Wt: 220
Health: D | PT/Exp: A | Consist: D
LIMA Plan: B | Rand Var: +3 | MM: 3215

Downturn in skills can be explained by shoulder injury that nagged him all season and ultimately required surgery. However, that can't explain away steady decline in ct%, Eye across several campaigns. While renewed health offers hope that power will return, 2021 remains outlier. Questionable recovery timeline and age furthers considerable concern.

Yr	Tm	PA	R	HR	RBI	SB	BA	xHR	xSB	xBA	OBP	SLG	OPS+	vL+	vR+	bb%	ct%	Eye	G	L	F	h%	HctX	QBaB	Brl%	PX	xPX	HR/F	xHR/F	Spd	SBA%	SB%	RAR	BPX	R$
18	CIN	623	67	12	67	2	284	19	12	276	417	419	112	101	116	17	80	1.07	38	31	31	34	121	CCa	7%	83	129	10%	15%	82	1%	100%	15.0	157	$16
19	CIN	608	79	15	47	5	261	21	3	253	357	411	106	91	112	13	77	0.62	37	25	38	32	110	CBa	7%	86	116	10%	14%	88	3%	100%	-4.7	107	$12
20	CIN	223	32	11	22	0	226	10	2	262	354	446	106	88	112	17	77	0.86	38	22	39	23	113	CBa	9%	117	144	20%	18%	85	0%	0%	-3.9	248	$12
21	CIN *	555	74	36	100	1	260	38	2	278	366	549	126	96	145	14	71	0.58	32	26	42	29	131	AAb	0%	167	173	26%	28%	78	1%	100%	27.6	281	$21
22	CIN	376	31	11	41	0	205	13	1	229	319	370	98	98	97	12	70	0.45	44	18	37	26	103	BBc	11%	118	104	13%	15%	69	0%	0%	-10.7	69	$1
1st Half		253	22	6	25	0	210	8	1	240	332	374	100	97	101	13	70	0.52	39	22	39	27	102	BBc	11%	122	100	10%	14%	67	0%	0%	-3.7	93	$1
2nd Half		123	9	5	16	0	194	5	0	189	293	361	93	100	89	9	69	0.33	55	11	35	23	105	CCb	11%	109	112	19%	19%	78	0%	0%	-4.4	31	-$3
23	Proj	490	49	16	61	1	240	20	2	235	347	405	104	95	108	13	72	0.51	41	21	38	30	114		7%	113	132	14%	17%	79	2%	100%	6.1	150	$12

DANIEL MARCUS

Wade Jr.,LaMonte

Age: 29 Pos: RF 1B	Health D	LIMA Plan D+	
Bats: L Ht: 6' 1" Wt: 205	PT/Exp D	Rand Var +3	
	Consist C	MM 3223	

8-26-.207 in 251 PA at SF. Managed only 32 PA through end of June due to two IL stints for spring knee injury, which might explain drops in HctX and overall production. Many will write him off as one-year wonder, but xHR, QBaB, and Brl% all show there's still 20 HR in his bat. Even with role likely limited by vL+, he shouldn't be dismissed.

Yr	Tm	PA	R	HR	RBI	SB	BA	xHR	xSB	xBA	OBP	SLG	OPS+	vL+	vR+	bb%	ct%	Eye	G	L	F	h%	HctX	QBaB	Brl%	PX	xPX	HR/F	xHR/F	Spd	SBA%	SB%	RAR	BPX	R$
18	a/a	476	45	9	40	8	234		7		318	340	88			11	81	0.65				27				57				122	9%	71%		103	$7
19	MIN *	404	52	6	28	6	217	2	7	249	335	330	92	42	108	15	81	0.92	45	21	34	25	107	CCd	6%	61	96	13%	13%	113	8%	64%	-19.2	137	$3
20	MIN	44	3	0	1	1	231	0	1	203	318	308	83	0	92	9	77	0.44	37	17	47	30	104	DBf		61	107	0%	0%	90	18%	50%	-2.7	16	-$1
21	SF *	435	60	20	61	6	244	18	10	248	319	464	108	53	119	10	72	0.40	33	23	44	29	111	CAd	11%	128	138	16%	16%	108	8%	73%	2.5	177	$13
22	SF *	301	35	9	32	1	203	10	3	225	289	353	91	35	104	11	78	0.54	32	19	50	23	80	CAf	10%	92	117	10%	12%	79	1%	100%	-7.3	103	$1
1st Half		98	11	3	14	0	199	1	1	237	288	342	89	30	114	11	83	0.73	40	17	43	21	83	ACd	4%	83	85	13%	7%	74	1%	0%	-2.8	152	-$6
2nd Half		203	24	6	18	1	205	9	2	219	303	358	94	38	101	11	75	0.48	30	19	52	24	78	DAf	11%	97	125	9%	13%	93	1%	100%	-4.5	100	$2
23	**Proj**	**385**	**48**	**16**	**44**	**3**	**243**	**15**	**3**	**245**	**336**	**431**	**106**	**43**	**117**	**11**	**77**	**0.53**	**34**	**21**	**45**	**27**	**95**		**9%**	**114**	**119**	**13%**	**13%**	**97**	**3%**	**76%**	**8.2**	**138**	**$9**

Walker,Christian

Age: 32 Pos: 1B	Health B	LIMA Plan B	
Bats: R Ht: 6' 0" Wt: 208	PT/Exp A	Rand Var +3	
	Consist B	MM 4135	

After down 2021, reestablished himself as legitimate power producer. Brl%, HctX, and xPX all rebounded nicely, and xHR, xHR/F both indicate HR production wasn't a fluke. Most significant growth may have been rises in ct%, Eye, and xBA, all of which suggest his BA won't be an anchor. Age tempers expectations for more, but still strong pick behind elites.

Yr	Tm	PA	R	HR	RBI	SB	BA	xHR	xSB	xBA	OBP	SLG	OPS+	vL+	vR+	bb%	ct%	Eye	G	L	F	h%	HctX	QBaB	Brl%	PX	xPX	HR/F	xHR/F	Spd	SBA%	SB%	RAR	BPX	R$
18	ARI *	392	46	13	47	2	211	4	3	198	248	383	85	91	61	5	65	0.14	37	11	52	29	53	DAc	15%	123	111	21%	29%	105	3%	100%	-23.2	3	$4
19	ARI	603	86	29	73	8	259	35	5	248	348	476	114	110	115	11	71	0.43	42	20	38	31	113	ABc	13%	122	127	20%	24%	92	6%	89%	4.0	119	$18
20	ARI	243	35	7	34	1	271	8	2	270	333	459	105	99	107	8	77	0.38	43	23	34	32	140	BCf	6%	114	117	12%	14%	95	4%	50%	-4.3	184	$19
21	ARI	445	55	10	46	0	244	10	4	234	315	382	96	90	98	9	74	0.36	39	22	39	31	107	CBd	6%	89	103	9%	9%	98	0%	0%	-10.7	54	$6
22	ARI	667	84	36	94	2	242	34	3	263	327	477	114	118	112	10	78	0.53	38	17	44	25	128	BBd	12%	138	143	18%	17%	93	3%	50%	8.2	245	$22
1st Half		324	41	21	42	0	209	19	1	267	318	484	113	146	103	13	77	0.65	38	14	48	19	130	BAc	15%	158	160	20%	18%	100	3%	0%	3.0	321	$19
2nd Half		343	43	15	52	2	271	15	1	260	335	471	114	92	121	8	78	0.41	39	20	41	30	127	BBd	9%	120	128	15%	15%	88	3%	100%	10.0	179	$29
23	**Proj**	**595**	**81**	**29**	**83**	**2**	**256**	**26**	**4**	**261**	**329**	**476**	**112**	**107**	**113**	**9**	**75**	**0.41**	**39**	**20**	**41**	**29**	**122**		**10%**	**138**	**126**	**17%**	**16%**	**87**	**3%**	**63%**	**18.5**	**159**	**$23**

Walker,Jordan

Age: 21 Pos: RF	Health A	LIMA Plan D	
Bats: R Ht: 6' 5" Wt: 220	PT/Exp C	Rand Var	
	Consist F	MM 3311	

Showed high level of maturity by delivering above-average production at AA in age-20 season. That isn't to say he's a lock for MLB stardom, as plate discipline, power don't yet project well at highest level. However, all the pieces are there for five-category contributions, and 2023 STL debut is in play after getting reps in OF and extra PA in Arizona Fall League.

Yr	Tm	PA	R	HR	RBI	SB	BA	xHR	xSB	xBA	OBP	SLG	OPS+	vL+	vR+	bb%	ct%	Eye	G	L	F	h%	HctX	QBaB	Brl%	PX	xPX	HR/F	xHR/F	Spd	SBA%	SB%	RAR	BPX	R$
18																																			
19																																			
20																																			
21																																			
22	aa	494	58	10	40	13	238		5		288	363	92			7	73	0.26				31				90				102	18%	69%		31	$12
1st Half		266	32	4	18	9	241		3		297	363	93			7	73	0.30				32				91				125	18%	72%		66	$11
2nd Half		228	27	6	22	4	234		2	227	278	363	91			6	72	0.22	44	20	36	30	0			88	-14	0%		99	18%	64%	-5.8	7	$8
23	**Proj**	**210**	**25**	**6**	**18**	**5**	**246**	**6**	**5**	**234**	**294**	**389**	**95**	**94**	**95**	**6**	**73**	**0.25**	**44**	**20**	**36**	**31**	**92**		**6%**	**101**		**11%**	**11%**	**107**	**14%**	**71%**	**-0.6**	**31**	**$7**

Wallner,Matt

Age: 25 Pos: RF	Health A	LIMA Plan D	
Bats: L Ht: 6' 5" Wt: 220	PT/Exp C	Rand Var 0	
	Consist F	MM 4201	

2-10-.228 in 65 PA at MIN. First-round selection in 2019 draft as college bat, allowing him to rise quickly through minors. Power is calling card, but path to reaching it consistently is endangered by low ct%, high GB%, and high IFFB%. Not much to be taken from MLB cup of coffee; should get a larger serving in 2023, and pedigree says give him a chance.

Yr	Tm	PA	R	HR	RBI	SB	BA	xHR	xSB	xBA	OBP	SLG	OPS+	vL+	vR+	bb%	ct%	Eye	G	L	F	h%	HctX	QBaB	Brl%	PX	xPX	HR/F	xHR/F	Spd	SBA%	SB%	RAR	BPX	R$
18																																			
19																																			
20																																			
21																																			
22	MIN *	584	60	18	69	7	216	1	7	213	307	386	98	48	122	12	56	0.29	53	19	28	35	53	CCf	12%	152	48	22%	11%	104	10%	52%	-6.7	0	$10
1st Half		276	33	11	34	5	216		3	196	317	399	101	0	0	13	51	0.30	44	20	36	37	0			171	-14	0%		97	10%	51%	-2.0	-14	$14
2nd Half		309	27	7	35	2	217	1	3	222	298	377	96	48	122	10	60	0.29	53	19	28	33	57	CCf	12%	139	48	22%	11%	106	10%	58%	-4.6	21	$9
23	**Proj**	**210**	**21**	**5**	**25**	**2**	**218**	**5**	**3**	**193**	**324**	**373**	**97**	**51**	**115**	**11**	**56**	**0.29**	**44**	**21**	**35**	**35**	**82**		**11%**	**122**	**73**	**14%**	**14%**	**107**	**9%**	**55%**	**-1.9**	**7**	**$4**

Walls,Taylor

Age: 26 Pos: SS 2B 3B	Health A	LIMA Plan D+	
Bats: B Ht: 5' 10" Wt: 185	PT/Exp B	Rand Var +5	
	Consist B	MM 2303	

Defensive versatility led to near full-time role, but that didn't translate to fantasy relevance. Hints of league-average power, though that come from heavy FB% approach rather than ability make consistent or quality contact. Batted-ball profile and low ct% hurts ability to contribute BA, R, or RBI, leaving SB as primary source of value.

Yr	Tm	PA	R	HR	RBI	SB	BA	xHR	xSB	xBA	OBP	SLG	OPS+	vL+	vR+	bb%	ct%	Eye	G	L	F	h%	HctX	QBaB	Brl%	PX	xPX	HR/F	xHR/F	Spd	SBA%	SB%	RAR	BPX	R$
18																																			
19	aa	236	40	5	19	14	252		4		332	445	108			11	72	0.43				32				111				146	44%	59%		167	$8
20																																			
21	TAM *	387	48	8	39	12	212	2	5	211	326	339	91	83	84	15	64	0.47	47	20	33	31	91	CCb	3%	95	118	3%	6%	91	20%	61%	-8.7	-31	$7
22	TAM	465	53	8	33	10	172	8	11	211	268	285	78	75	80	11	71	0.43	37	21	42	22	79	DBd	6%	82	100	7%	7%	111	14%	77%	-22.7	17	$0
1st Half		231	21	3	13	6	167	4	5	206	242	273	73	67	75	9	71	0.33	40	19	42	22	77	DBd	5%	76	89	5%	6%	119	14%	86%	-14.7	-3	-$2
2nd Half		234	32	5	20	4	177	5	6	217	293	298	84	82	84	14	70	0.54	35	23	42	22	82	DBd	7%	88	112	9%	9%	101	14%	67%	-10.0	38	$4
23	**Proj**	**350**	**44**	**4**	**30**	**10**	**196**	**6**	**7**	**207**	**301**	**301**	**84**	**81**	**84**	**13**	**68**	**0.46**	**41**	**21**	**38**	**27**	**84**		**5%**	**83**	**109**	**5%**	**7%**	**108**	**11%**	**64%**	**-10.6**	**15**	**$7**

Walsh,Jared

Age: 29 Pos: 1B	Health B	LIMA Plan B+	
Bats: L Ht: 6' 0" Wt: 210	PT/Exp A	Rand Var +2	
	Consist D	MM 4225	

Among biggest disappointments at first base, and significant drop in skills vR was primary culprit. Season ended early by surgery to correct thoracic outlet syndrome, an injury that had nagged him for several years, but worsened in 2022. Full recovery plus previously stable xHR/F offers hope of a bounceback to 2021 levels of production.

Yr	Tm	PA	R	HR	RBI	SB	BA	xHR	xSB	xBA	OBP	SLG	OPS+	vL+	vR+	bb%	ct%	Eye	G	L	F	h%	HctX	QBaB	Brl%	PX	xPX	HR/F	xHR/F	Spd	SBA%	SB%	RAR	BPX	R$
18	a/a	352	41	11	44	1	221		4		277	388	89			7	62	0.20				32				131				83	2%	100%		-23	$4
19	LAA *	505	60	25	57	0	239	3	2	241	303	466	106	104	81	8	61	0.23	39	27	34	33	115	ACc	14%	150	134	7%	20%	76	0%	0%	-2.5	19	$9
20	LAA	108	19	9	26	0	293	6	1	317	324	646	129	101	143	5	85	0.33	48	15	37	27	146	CCc	13%	159	111	28%	19%	142	0%	0%	6.2	480	$14
21	LAA	585	70	29	98	2	277	21	1	269	340	509	117	77	137	8	71	0.32	48	22	30	34	105	BDf	11%	144	97	25%	18%	77	2%	67%	22.2	162	$22
22	LAA	454	41	15	44	2	215	13	2	222	269	374	91	83	94	6	67	0.20	45	18	37	28	102	BCd	9%	112	119	15%	13%	92	3%	67%	-12.1	3	$4
1st Half		302	33	13	40	1	249	11	2	242	291	442	104	95	107	5	68	0.16	45	20	35	32	117	ACd	11%	131	133	19%	16%	101	3%	50%	-1.3	69	$17
2nd Half		152	8	2	4	1	145	2	1	177	224	232	65	61	66	9	65	0.27	46	14	40	20	73	DCf	7%	73	89	6%	6%	84	3%	100%	-13.1	-124	-$10
23	**Proj**	**560**	**66**	**23**	**76**	**2**	**248**	**21**	**4**	**243**	**309**	**443**	**104**	**86**	**111**	**7**	**69**	**0.26**	**46**	**19**	**35**	**31**	**103**		**10%**	**135**	**107**	**19%**	**17%**	**87**	**4%**	**77%**	**7.1**	**73**	**$18**

Ward,Taylor

Age: 29 Pos: RF	Health A	LIMA Plan B	
Bats: R Ht: 6' 1" Wt: 200	PT/Exp A	Rand Var -2	
	Consist A	MM 4335	

Slugged .713 through May 20 and was poised to be breakout star. Cooled considerably after collision with outfield wall and subsequent hamstring injury, but arrow is firmly pointed up. Growth vR appears sustainable, backed by increased ct%. HctX, QBaB, and Brl% all say quality of contact is excellent, and if he sustains increased FB%... UP: 30 HR

Yr	Tm	PA	R	HR	RBI	SB	BA	xHR	xSB	xBA	OBP	SLG	OPS+	vL+	vR+	bb%	ct%	Eye	G	L	F	h%	HctX	QBaB	Brl%	PX	xPX	HR/F	xHR/F	Spd	SBA%	SB%	RAR	BPX	R$
18	LAA *	567	62	16	58	15	255	5	8	213	326	396	97	101	65	10	69	0.34	35	21	44	34	76	CBc	8%	97	99	15%	13%	80	13%	80%	-0.6	-7	$17
19	LAA *	518	66	19	45	7	226	1	9	243	309	412	100	63	95	11	68	0.37	37	26	37	29	98	ACc	11%	116	121	14%	14%	95	12%	52%	-14.0	52	$8
20	LAA	102	16	0	5	2	277	3	2	238	333	383	95	83	103	8	70	0.29	44	29	27	39	95	ACb	5%	74	98	0%	17%	157	8%	100%	-0.7	20	$5
21	LAA *	291	42	10	39	2	262	8	4	264	328	466	109	116	101	9	72	0.35	36	26	38	33	98	CBa	10%	135	113	14%	14%	110	5%	68%	6.4	188	$7
22	LAA	564	73	23	65	5	281	23	8	252	360	473	118	106	123	11	76	0.50	35	22	43	33	118	BBb	13%	119	139	14%	14%	126	5%	63%	25.0	203	$23
1st Half		244	42	12	33	2	303	10	4	260	393	540	132	141	129	13	73	0.56	37	21	43	37	126	BBb	14%	148	159	18%	15%	152	5%	50%	20.2	290	$21
2nd Half		320	31	11	32	3	264	13	4	246	334	423	107	84	117	9	78	0.44	34	23	44	30	112	BBc	13%	98	125	11%	13%	95	5%	75%	5.4	131	$18
23	**Proj**	**560**	**80**	**25**	**72**	**6**	**270**	**22**	**7**	**257**	**347**	**484**	**115**	**112**	**117**	**10**	**73**	**0.40**	**35**	**23**	**42**	**32**	**113**		**13%**	**142**	**123**	**16%**	**14%**	**111**	**6%**	**69%**	**26.0**	**158**	**$25**

DANIEL MARCUS

Waters,Drew

Age: 24	Pos: OF		Health	A	LIMA Plan	D+
Bats: R	Ht: 6' 2"	Wt: 185	PT/Exp	C	Rand Var	+2
			Consist	A	MM	4303

5-18-.240 with 0 SB in 109 PA at KC. Got first big-league chance after mid-season trade from ATL. Mustered HR at rate befitting minors track record, though HctX, QBaB warn of soft support. Pedigree says hang onto hope, but significant ct% struggles in upper minors, first taste of MLB cast doubt on him reaching ceiling too soon.

Yr	Tm	PA	R	HR	RBI	SB	BA	xHR	xSB	xBA	OBP	SLG	OPS+	vL+	vR+	bb%	ct%	Eye	G	L	F	h%	HctX	QBaB	Brl%	PX	xPX	HR/F	xHR/F	Spd	SBA%	SB%	RAR	BPX	R$
18																																			
19	a/a	565	79	6	51	16	306		9		352	449	111			7	68	0.22				44				97				123	15%	71%		7	$20
20																																			
21	aaa	442	57	9	30	23	216		5		283	335	85			9	62	0.24				33				93				104	35%	70%		-108	$12
22	KC *	441	46	11	37	11	219	5	19	215	275	363	90	108	116	7	64	0.22	48	18	34	31	90	FCc	11%	108	101	26%	26%	148	13%	90%	-6.4	14	$8
1st Half		176	13	3	9	2	204		6	208	234	305	76	0	0	4	69	0.13	44	20	36	28	0			71	-14	0%		161	13%	60%	-9.1	-31	-$5
2nd Half		265	33	9	28	9	229	5	12	219	303	404	100	108	116	10	60	0.27	48	18	34	34	85	FCc	11%	138	101	26%	26%	137	13%	100%	2.2	52	$16
23	Proj	350	41	12	27	7	226	13	6	224	287	403	96	90	97	8	63	0.23	48	18	34	31	77		10%	134	91	18%	18%	122	12%	70%	-0.9	-33	$6

Wendle,Joe

Age: 33	Pos: 3B SS 2B		Health	D	LIMA Plan	C+
Bats: L	Ht: 6' 1"	Wt: 195	PT/Exp	A	Rand Var	+2
			Consist	A	MM	2343

Season curtailed by hamstring injury that cost him 57 days on IL, yet still managed impressive SB haul despite dip in Spd. Ongoing struggles to make hard contact cut into production vR and could place already limited PA at risk. However, ct% gains offer hope for bounceback to provide late-round SB and BA production, particularly with return to full health.

Yr	Tm	PA	R	HR	RBI	SB	BA	xHR	xSB	xBA	OBP	SLG	OPS+	vL+	vR+	bb%	ct%	Eye	G	L	F	h%	HctX	QBaB	Brl%	PX	xPX	HR/F	xHR/F	Spd	SBA%	SB%	RAR	BPX	R$
18	TAM	545	62	7	61	16	300	9	8	261	354	435	106	107	104	7	80	0.39	46	22	32	36	109	CCc	3%	86	76	5%	7%	104	14%	80%	12.2	123	$21
19	TAM	263	32	3	19	8	231	2	5	254	293	340	88	49	98	5	80	0.30	44	23	32	28	89	CCc	2%	62	56	5%	3%	122	19%	73%	-17.1	74	$3
20	TAM	184	24	4	17	8	286	3	5	268	342	435	103	90	106	5	79	0.29	49	24	28	34	98	CFf	4%	83	91	11%	8%	123	21%	80%	-1.0	132	$20
21	TAM	501	73	11	54	8	265	8	14	259	319	422	102	82	109	6	75	0.25	49	21	30	33	97	CDd	5%	99	79	11%	8%	124	12%	57%	-0.3	119	$15
22	MIA	371	27	3	32	12	259	3	6	265	297	360	93	83	95	4	86	0.30	55	17	28	30	98	CFf	2%	71	58	4%	4%	93	18%	80%	-7.4	128	$9
1st Half		112	13	2	13	5	297	1	2	290	357	426	111	134	106	8	89	0.82	55	19	26	32	98	CFf	1%	81	76	8%	4%	93	18%	100%	4.6	231	$1
2nd Half		259	14	1	19	7	244	2	4	253	271	333	86	67	90	2	84	0.15	55	16	29	29	98	CFf	2%	66	49	2%	3%	95	18%	70%	-9.5	86	$4
23	Proj	420	47	7	42	13	267	5	11	265	314	395	98	85	102	5	82	0.29	52	19	29	31	98		3%	86	69	7%	5%	107	14%	76%	4.4	131	$17

White,Evan

Age: 27	Pos: 1B		Health	F	LIMA Plan	D
Bats: R	Ht: 6' 3"	Wt: 220	PT/Exp	F	Rand Var	
			Consist	B	MM	3001

Previously well-regarded prospect is running out of time, with health and skill in question. Limited by hip, hernia injuries, costing him two prime development years. As a result, these data samples are too small to draw conclusions from, with mostly negative outcomes. Could be watch list player if he gets healthy and stumbles into playing time.

Yr	Tm	PA	R	HR	RBI	SB	BA	xHR	xSB	xBA	OBP	SLG	OPS+	vL+	vR+	bb%	ct%	Eye	G	L	F	h%	HctX	QBaB	Brl%	PX	xPX	HR/F	xHR/F	Spd	SBA%	SB%	RAR	BPX	R$
18	aaa																																		
19	aa	394	61	18	55	2	281		6		334	474	112			7	71	0.28				35				103				111	2%	100%		67	$12
20	SEA	202	19	8	26	1	176	10	1	179	252	346	79	60	88	9	54	0.21	43	15	42	27	75	ACc	13%	131	147	20%	24%	83	8%	33%	-16.7	-136	$4
21	SEA	104	8	2	9	0	144	2	1	184	202	237	60	47	67	6	68	0.19	42	17	41	19	76	DAc	5%	62	58	7%	7%	74	0%	0%	-10.3	-162	-$4
22	aaa	100	8	4	9	0	144		0		207	310	73			7	69	0.26				16				113				93	0%	0%		34	-$5
1st Half		30	1	0	1	0	76		0		163	76	34			9	50	0.21				15				0				109	0%	0%		-507	-$14
2nd Half		71	7	4	9	0	173		0	273	227	409	90			7	77	0.30	44	20	36	16	0			144	-14	0%		93	0%	0%	-3.2	224	-$6
23	Proj	175	17	5	21	0	190	8	0	198	256	329	81	61	90	8	65	0.24	43	16	41	25	76		8%	104	94	12%	19%	70	1%	38%	-8.0	-13	$2

Williams,Luke

Age: 26	Pos: 3B LF		Health	A	LIMA Plan	F
Bats: R	Ht: 6' 1"	Wt: 186	PT/Exp	F	Rand Var	-5
			Consist	A	MM	1501

1-6-.236 with 11 SB in 136 PA at SF/MIA. DFA'd by SF in mid-June after earning roster spot to begin season, and served as bench bat in MIA for remaining months. Spd, SB% have yet to align, hindering his obvious path to value. There's little else appealing about skills profile, as both rate and quality of contact have been abysmal.

Yr	Tm	PA	R	HR	RBI	SB	BA	xHR	xSB	xBA	OBP	SLG	OPS+	vL+	vR+	bb%	ct%	Eye	G	L	F	h%	HctX	QBaB	Brl%	PX	xPX	HR/F	xHR/F	Spd	SBA%	SB%	RAR	BPX	R$
18																																			
19	aa	485	69	11	46	27	219		6		290	368	91			9	70	0.34				29				93				111	37%	73%		33	$15
20																																			
21	PHI *	242	22	1	16	7	240	0	4	220	297	301	82	101	64	8	74	0.32	55	19	26	32	69	FFf	0%	42	40	6%	0%	140	19%	56%	-11.1	-35	$3
22	2 NL *	190	28	2	11	17	242	1	6	187	299	328	89	85	85	8	62	0.22	40	21	39	38	53	FBd	4%	76	54	3%	3%	142	50%	73%	-4.3	-100	$8
1st Half		108	17	2	10	10	261	0	4	199	332	364	98	86	107	10	61	0.27	47	20	33	41	40	FBa	0%	93	19	10%	0%	109	50%	75%	0.6	-97	$4
2nd Half		82	11	0	1	7	218	1	2	175	256	282	76	84	72	5	64	0.14	36	22	42	34	62	DBf	6%	55	75	0%	5%	167	50%	70%	-4.3	-131	-$4
23	Proj	210	26	2	12	13	237	1	15	205	294	324	86	93	79	7	68	0.25	46	20	34	34	59		2%	69	47	5%	2%	135	39%	70%	-4.2	-69	$9

Winker,Jesse

Age: 29	Pos: LF		Health	C	LIMA Plan	B+
Bats: L	Ht: 6' 3"	Wt: 215	PT/Exp	A	Rand Var	+5
			Consist	D	MM	3235

Quality of contact metrics fell for third consecutive season, which dispels temptation to pin disappointing season on change in park and league. In addition to HctX, xPX, and QBaB all falling, FB% spike cratered BA and didn't deliver any extra HR. Investing now will take leap of faith that knee and neck issues were more to blame than deterioration of skills.

Yr	Tm	PA	R	HR	RBI	SB	BA	xHR	xSB	xBA	OBP	SLG	OPS+	vL+	vR+	bb%	ct%	Eye	G	L	F	h%	HctX	QBaB	Brl%	PX	xPX	HR/F	xHR/F	Spd	SBA%	SB%	RAR	BPX	R$
18	CIN	334	38	7	43	0	299	9	6	265	405	431	112	92	115	15	84	1.07	42	24	34	34	135	ACb	6%	79	107	9%	11%	68	0%	0%	13.3	163	$9
19	CIN	384	51	16	38	0	269	10	2	301	357	473	115	62	122	10	82	0.63	49	26	25	29	117	CDb	4%	99	88	23%	14%	102	2%	0%	4.0	222	$8
20	CIN	183	27	12	23	1	255	10	1	275	388	544	124	116	126	15	69	0.61	48	23	29	29	137	ACb	13%	166	137	40%	33%	77	2%	100%	6.7	260	$16
21	CIN	485	77	24	71	1	305	21	3	306	394	556	130	78	148	11	82	0.71	42	25	33	32	124	BCc	11%	136	112	21%	18%	88	1%	100%	40.3	338	$22
22	SEA	547	51	14	53	0	219	16	2	227	344	344	97	111	92	15	77	0.82	39	21	41	25	97	CBf	8%	77	89	10%	11%	75	0%	0%	-3.5	90	$5
1st Half		331	26	6	33	0	226	10	1	237	341	337	96	110	91	15	78	0.82	37	23	40	27	96	CBd	7%	74	88	7%	11%	77	0%	0%	-2.1	97	$6
2nd Half		216	25	8	20	0	209	6	1	214	347	356	100	114	95	17	76	0.81	42	16	41	23	98	CBf	8%	83	91	14%	11%	89	0%	0%	-0.8	107	$4
23	Proj	490	62	18	55	1	253	19	2	259	367	432	111	99	115	14	78	0.76	42	22	36	28	112		9%	110	102	15%	16%	79	2%	82%	18.3	198	$15

Wisdom,Patrick

Age: 31	Pos: 3B		Health	A	LIMA Plan	C+
Bats: R	Ht: 6' 2"	Wt: 220	PT/Exp	A	Rand Var	-3
			Consist	D	MM	5205

Power was as advertised in first season as full-time player, with exit velocity and launch angle perfectly built for mashing HR. Struggles vR and horrific ct% may be enough to overshadow positives in his profile and cast doubt on his ability to maintain both skills and role, especially after 2nd half collapse. We've likely seen his peak.

Yr	Tm	PA	R	HR	RBI	SB	BA	xHR	xSB	xBA	OBP	SLG	OPS+	vL+	vR+	bb%	ct%	Eye	G	L	F	h%	HctX	QBaB	Brl%	PX	xPX	HR/F	xHR/F	Spd	SBA%	SB%	RAR	BPX	R$
18	STL *	459	58	14	54	10	234	3	6	217	295	387	91	107	123	8	64	0.24	35	26	39	33	106	BBf	13%	113	134	33%	25%	94	13%	74%	-16.8	-27	$11
19	TEX *	461	46	22	50	5	191	0	6	239	258	380	88	48	53	8	62	0.23	9	45	45	25	106	AAa	0%	117	123	0%	0%	82	8%	68%	-31.6	-59	$4
20	CHC	2	0	0	0	0	0	0	0	0	0	0	0	0	0	0	100	0.00	0	0	100	0	0	CAa		0	-26	0%	0%	99	7%	0%	-0.4	128	-$3
21	CHC *	403	58	30	68	5	223	23	3	220	292	507	110	113	113	9	54	0.21	31	19	49	31	100	AAc	16%	214	181	31%	25%	80	8%	82%	-0.3	115	$13
22	CHC	534	67	25	66	8	207	23	5	223	298	426	103	125	94	10	61	0.29	34	17	49	28	97	BAf	15%	174	146	18%	16%	81	11%	67%	-11.1	100	$12
1st Half		315	44	17	45	4	234	15	3	233	321	475	112	122	109	10	62	0.30	35	17	48	31	102	AAd	17%	184	156	20%	18%	90	11%	57%	3.7	152	$24
2nd Half		219	23	8	21	4	168	8	2	208	266	356	88	129	74	10	60	0.27	33	17	50	23	90	CAf	12%	158	132	14%	14%	74	11%	80%	-10.2	31	$4
23	Proj	490	62	23	65	7	211	21	6	210	296	414	99	109	94	9	59	0.25	33	19	48	30	98		15%	165	157	18%	17%	74	8%	75%	0.0	66	$14

Witt Jr.,Bobby

Age: 23	Pos: SS 3B		Health	A	LIMA Plan	D+
Bats: R	Ht: 6' 1"	Wt: 200	PT/Exp	A	Rand Var	-1
			Consist	B	MM	4525

Top prospect broke camp with big-league club and found footing after .558 OPS, .199 xBA in April. Spd, SBA%, and SB% all back elite SB output, and while power didn't reach that same threshold, QBaB, HctX, and FB% all hint that more HR are on the way. Eye, xBA offer areas to nitpick, but ... welcome to the first round, Bobby.

Yr	Tm	PA	R	HR	RBI	SB	BA	xHR	xSB	xBA	OBP	SLG	OPS+	vL+	vR+	bb%	ct%	Eye	G	L	F	h%	HctX	QBaB	Brl%	PX	xPX	HR/F	xHR/F	Spd	SBA%	SB%	RAR	BPX	R$
18																																			
19																																			
20																																			
21	a/a	537	78	24	76	23	263		5		318	488	111			7	73	0.30				32				138				97	31%	68%		185	$27
22	KC	632	82	20	80	30	254	22	24	237	294	428	102	100	103	5	77	0.22	36	17	46	30	104	BBd	9%	109	94	9%	10%	155	29%	81%	3.6	186	$31
1st Half		322	43	12	42	12	236	11	11	242	286	444	103	84	111	6	73	0.24	36	17	47	28	109	ABd	10%	133	105	12%	11%	163	29%	80%	-0.3	217	$27
2nd Half		310	39	8	38	18	272	11	13	234	303	412	101	122	96	4	81	0.20	36	18	46	31	99	CBd	8%	87	84	7%	10%	131	29%	82%	1.3	145	$31
23	Proj	630	86	23	84	33	260	23	23	242	307	451	105	108	104	6	76	0.26	36	17	46	31	103		9%	124	92	11%	11%	135	23%	77%	13.9	179	$36

DANIEL MARCUS

Wong,Connor

Age: 27	Pos: CA	Health	A	LIMA Plan	D
Bats: R	Ht: 6' 1" Wt: 181	PT/Exp	D	Rand Var	+3
		Consist	A	MM	3301

1-7-.188 in 56 PA at BOS. PRO: Contact improved in the 1st half, but he couldn't maintain it; faint signs of latent power. CON: Pretty much everything else. Hit-tool metrics just don't agree; zero loft in swing during small MLB sample; extreme platoon splits; some speed skill negated by terrible success rate.

Yr Tm	PA	R	HR	RBI	SB	BA	xHR	xSB	xBA	OBP	SLG	OPS+	vL+	vR+	bb%	ct%	Eye	G	L	F	h%	HctX	QBaB	Brl%	PX	xPX	HR/F	xHR/F	Spd	SBA%	SB%	RAR	BPX	R$
18																																		
19 aa	158	15	8	28	2	323		2		363	555	127			6	62	0.17				47				150				93	8%	62%		37	$5
20																																		
21 BOS *	220	20	6	21	5	229	1	2	217	256	383	88	45	187	4	65	0.11	17	33	50	32	133	CDf	17%	113	269	0%	33%	111	17%	82%	-4.2	-19	$2
22 BOS *	396	37	10	35	4	226	2	8	214	269	365	90	47	102	6	70	0.20	64	6	30	29	63	CFf	9%	103	69	10%	20%	104	11%	55%	-4.4	28	$5
1st Half	223	16	3	12	4	220	0	4	215	262	320	82	0	64	5	74	0.22	83	0	17	28	0	AFd		76	-14	0%	0%	103	11%	65%	-5.9	7	-$1
2nd Half	173	21	7	22	0	234	2	3	218	279	424	100	53	108	6	65	0.18	59	7	33	31	71	CDf	12%	144	87	11%	22%	107	11%	0%	1.1	72	$5
23 Proj	245	24	5	26	3	225	12	3	221	277	359	88	56	107	5	67	0.15	45	20	34	31	64		10%	108	78	10%	22%	110	9%	70%	-2.2	19	$2

Wong,Kolten

Age: 32	Pos: 2B	Health	C	LIMA Plan	B
Bats: L	Ht: 5' 7" Wt: 185	PT/Exp	A	Rand Var	+1
		Consist	A	MM	3335

Remember when his value was like a yo-yo? Neither do we. Third straight full-season near $20 value driven by double-digit returns in homers and steals. Expected rates in those metrics show he's likely capped out in both, but he's set a high floor now. Guys like this who can help you a little in multiple categories are undervalued nowadays.

Yr Tm	PA	R	HR	RBI	SB	BA	xHR	xSB	xBA	OBP	SLG	OPS+	vL+	vR+	bb%	ct%	Eye	G	L	F	h%	HctX	QBaB	Brl%	PX	xPX	HR/F	xHR/F	Spd	SBA%	SB%	RAR	BPX	R$
18 STL	407	41	9	38	6	249	6	6	263	332	388	96	81	99	8	83	0.52	49	20	31	28	86	CDd	3%	80	59	10%	7%	91	11%	55%	-3.5	137	$7
19 STL	549	61	11	59	24	285	8	10	258	361	423	108	103	109	9	83	0.57	44	20	36	33	97	DCd	2%	71	83	8%	6%	100	18%	86%	11.8	137	$21
20 STL	208	26	1	16	5	265	1	8	240	350	326	90	86	90	10	83	0.67	50	21	29	31	83	DDf	1%	31	44	2%	2%	138	11%	71%	-6.2	84	$14
21 MIL	492	70	14	50	12	272	10	7	273	335	447	107	107	107	6	81	0.37	42	22	35	31	113	CCc	5%	102	107	11%	8%	90	15%	71%	6.1	188	$18
22 MIL	497	65	15	47	17	251	10	11	266	339	430	109	62	120	9	80	0.52	42	21	37	28	92	DCf	5%	110	109	12%	8%	100	18%	74%	7.2	197	$18
1st Half	236	32	6	21	8	236	3	5	264	331	409	105	49	121	11	80	0.60	39	23	38	27	91	DBd	3%	104	113	10%	5%	107	18%	67%	1.8	207	$11
2nd Half	261	33	9	26	9	264	7	6	268	347	449	113	79	119	9	79	0.46	44	20	36	30	92	CCf	7%	115	105	14%	11%	89	18%	82%	8.4	186	$19
23 Proj	525	71	14	52	16	261	10	15	264	340	423	106	87	112	9	81	0.49	43	21	35	30	97		5%	101	98	11%	7%	101	14%	74%	14.0	176	$23

Yastrzemski,Mike

Age: 32	Pos: RF CF	Health	B	LIMA Plan	B
Bats: L	Ht: 5' 10" Wt: 178	PT/Exp	A	Rand Var	+4
		Consist	D	MM	4325

On surface, a down season with some ominous trends heading into 2023 (see BA, OPS+, BPX). But most of his batted ball components (in particular, see QBaB, Brl%) were as good as or better than those in more productive years; xBA says there's a little BA upside, too. Together, those are real reasons to speculate on a rebound.

Yr Tm	PA	R	HR	RBI	SB	BA	xHR	xSB	xBA	OBP	SLG	OPS+	vL+	vR+	bb%	ct%	Eye	G	L	F	h%	HctX	QBaB	Brl%	PX	xPX	HR/F	xHR/F	Spd	SBA%	SB%	RAR	BPX	R$
18 a/a	467	44	8	43	6	198		5		265	321	78			8	71	0.31				26				85				105	13%	48%		3	$2
19 SF *	563	91	28	73	3	264	23	10	253	328	508	116	131	113	9	70	0.32	34	23	43	32	103	BAc	11%	139	142	18%	20%	112	8%	34%	1.8	163	$17
20 SF	225	39	10	35	2	297	12	4	263	400	568	128	130	127	13	71	0.55	39	19	42	37	108	CAf	11%	159	152	17%	21%	148	5%	67%	15.0	344	$25
21 SF	532	75	25	71	4	224	24	4	247	311	457	105	70	117	10	72	0.39	34	19	47	26	89	CAd	10%	140	133	16%	15%	88	4%	100%	-2.5	185	$12
22 SF	558	73	17	57	5	214	19	4	233	305	392	99	81	105	11	71	0.43	34	19	46	27	100	BAc	11%	126	123	11%	12%	84	5%	83%	-4.6	117	$9
1st Half	277	37	8	32	1	234	8	2	248	336	409	105	78	114	13	73	0.56	39	20	40	29	109	BBc	11%	125	114	11%	11%	72	5%	50%	2.2	145	$11
2nd Half	281	36	9	25	4	196	11	2	217	275	376	92	83	95	9	69	0.33	29	18	52	25	91	CAd	11%	128	133	10%	12%	104	5%	100%	-6.7	103	$10
23 Proj	525	74	21	63	5	226	22	5	242	312	437	104	88	109	10	71	0.40	34	20	46	27	97		11%	145	132	14%	14%	100	6%	79%	6.8	158	$15

Yelich,Christian

Age: 31	Pos: LF DH	Health	B	LIMA Plan	B
Bats: L	Ht: 6' 3" Wt: 195	PT/Exp	A	Rand Var	0
		Consist	A	MM	3425

Put health issues from 2021 behind him and stepped to plate the most since 2017. That still didn't get him anywhere near prior high point, though. Tiny launch angle remains the primary roadblock, and with that GB% trend, it seems here to stay. There's plenty of value in a 15/15 player... as long as you don't draft him hoping for a return to glory.

Yr Tm	PA	R	HR	RBI	SB	BA	xHR	xSB	xBA	OBP	SLG	OPS+	vL+	vR+	bb%	ct%	Eye	G	L	F	h%	HctX	QBaB	Brl%	PX	xPX	HR/F	xHR/F	Spd	SBA%	SB%	RAR	BPX	R$
18 MIL	651	118	36	110	22	326	35	11	310	402	598	134	130	133	10	76	0.50	52	25	24	37	134	AFb	13%	156	128	35%	34%	135	14%	85%	68.2	313	$44
19 MIL	580	100	44	97	30	329	42	16	306	429	671	152	130	164	14	76	0.68	43	21	36	36	133	ACc	16%	172	146	33%	31%	113	18%	94%	77.5	389	$42
20 MIL	247	39	12	22	4	205	12	8	234	356	430	104	139	89	19	62	0.61	51	19	30	26	103	ADb	12%	143	112	32%	32%	116	9%	67%	-2.6	148	$16
21 MIL	475	70	9	51	9	248	10	9	245	362	373	101	83	108	15	72	0.62	54	22	24	32	102	BFf	8%	81	84	13%	15%	119	8%	75%	0.1	73	$12
22 MIL	671	99	14	57	19	252	17	15	248	355	383	105	97	108	13	72	0.54	59	18	23	33	106	AFc	8%	90	79	15%	18%	144	11%	86%	12.4	107	$23
1st Half	352	54	8	31	13	251	10	8	243	348	386	104	100	105	12	73	0.52	55	17	27	32	108	BFd	10%	88	90	13%	17%	160	11%	100%	6.8	124	$27
2nd Half	319	45	6	26	6	254	8	7	251	364	379	105	95	110	14	71	0.57	62	20	18	34	104	AFb	6%	92	67	17%	23%	120	11%	67%	4.6	83	$17
23 Proj	595	91	16	60	15	254	18	14	251	362	407	107	100	109	14	71	0.57	56	20	24	33	107		9%	105	88	18%	21%	124	11%	80%	18.6	122	$24

Yepez,Juan

Age: 25	Pos: LF	Health	B	LIMA Plan	D+
Bats: R	Ht: 6' 1" Wt: 200	PT/Exp	B	Rand Var	0
		Consist	A	MM	3003

12-30-.253 in 274 PA at STL. Went undrafted in most leagues, but ended up as a contributor, especially in 1st half. Then pitchers carved him up with velocity and his bat dried up late. Was known as a plus fastball hitter in the minors, so hope isn't lost even with late sag in batted ball metrics. If he adjusts, he'll be a profit center. UP: 20 HR

Yr Tm	PA	R	HR	RBI	SB	BA	xHR	xSB	xBA	OBP	SLG	OPS+	vL+	vR+	bb%	ct%	Eye	G	L	F	h%	HctX	QBaB	Brl%	PX	xPX	HR/F	xHR/F	Spd	SBA%	SB%	RAR	BPX	R$
18																																		
19 aa	56	7	2	9	0	210		1		268	339	84			7	72	0.28				26				74				102	0%	0%		-22	-$2
20																																		
21 a/a	400	44	17	51	1	228		3		292	430	99			8	75	0.35				26				122				79	5%	16%		150	$6
22 STL *	472	49	21	64	0	235	11	3	230	279	425	100	97	107	6	74	0.23	38	15	47	27	96	DBf	10%	121	124	13%	12%	84	0%	0%	-8.3	114	$10
1st Half	287	33	16	43	0	257	9	2	247	294	490	111	97	123	5	75	0.21	35	15	49	29	104	CAd	10%	145	142	16%	13%	94	0%	0%	2.7	190	$19
2nd Half	185	16	5	21	0	200	3	1	204	254	324	82	96	62	7	74	0.27	44	15	41	24	77	FCf	10%	82	78	5%	14%	82	0%	0%	-10.7	0	-$1
23 Proj	350	36	13	51	0	228	14	1	225	279	398	94	101	91	7	74	0.29	41	15	44	27	88		10%	113	104	12%	13%	71	1%	25%	-1.6	108	$8

Zavala,Seby

Age: 29	Pos: CA	Health	A	LIMA Plan	D
Bats: R	Ht: 5' 11" Wt: 205	PT/Exp	D	Rand Var	-5
		Consist	D	MM	4003

2-21.270 in 205 PA at CHW. First extended look in majors was filled with ups-and-downs, including wild swings in ct% from month to month that fueled his volatility at the plate. That aside, hidden within his ugly 2nd half were some reasons for optimism, including a salvageable ct% and intriguing xPX. If contact holds... UP: 20 HR

Yr Tm	PA	R	HR	RBI	SB	BA	xHR	xSB	xBA	OBP	SLG	OPS+	vL+	vR+	bb%	ct%	Eye	G	L	F	h%	HctX	QBaB	Brl%	PX	xPX	HR/F	xHR/F	Spd	SBA%	SB%	RAR	BPX	R$
18 a/a	409	42	12	43	0	224		5		279	367	87			7	66	0.22				31				104				85	2%	0%		-33	$4
19 CHW *	328	38	16	34	1	179	0	1	208	227	368	82	0	25	6	51	0.13	33	33	33	27	0	FAb	0%	143	-36	0%	0%	85	4%	39%	-10.5	-144	$0
20																																		
21 CHW *	271	27	10	28	0	145	3	2	157	206	294	69	80	86	7	45	0.14	38	19	42	25	49	FBd	9%	137	137	23%	14%	86	3%	0%	-18.1	-258	-$5
22 CHW *	362	36	7	30	0	237	4	2	193	310	372	97	91	106	9	55	0.24	28	24	47	41	77	CAc	9%	136	127	4%	7%	95	0%	0%	3.0	-72	$3
1st Half	213	20	6	20	0	232	2	1	200	297	400	99	70	136	9	49	0.18	38	26	35	43	74	CCc	15%	180	103	8%	17%	84	0%	0%	2.1	-48	$1
2nd Half	149	16	1	10	0	244	2	1	187	340	331	95	98	94	11	64	0.35	24	23	52	38	86	CAc	8%	83	138	2%	5%	103	0%	0%	0.3	-79	-$3
23 Proj	315	33	8	29	0	214	7	1	184	287	351	89	78	91	8	54	0.20	33	22	44	36	68		10%	129	129	12%	10%	90	2%	14%	-1.8	-128	$4

Zunino,Mike

Age: 32	Pos: CA	Health	F	LIMA Plan	D+
Bats: R	Ht: 6' 2" Wt: 235	PT/Exp	D	Rand Var	+5
		Consist	D	MM	5003

Shoulder inflammation that eventually required surgery made this a lost season. We know his strikeout-induced volatility is embedded in profile. Still, he mashes when he does connect, and he'll come cheap now. He's an intriguing buy-low power play who probably won't stay healthy enough to torpedo your BA anyway.

Yr Tm	PA	R	HR	RBI	SB	BA	xHR	xSB	xBA	OBP	SLG	OPS+	vL+	vR+	bb%	ct%	Eye	G	L	F	h%	HctX	QBaB	Brl%	PX	xPX	HR/F	xHR/F	Spd	SBA%	SB%	RAR	BPX	R$
18 SEA	405	37	20	44	0	201	21	4	212	259	410	90	76	94	6	60	0.16	37	19	44	27	87	BAd	14%	156	131	20%	21%	68	0%	0%	-1.2	-3	$3
19 TAM	289	30	9	32	0	165	13	0	187	232	312	75	65	80	7	63	0.20	40	14	46	22	85	CAf	11%	93	96	12%	17%	67	0%	0%	-12.8	-133	-$3
20 TAM	84	8	4	10	0	147	5	0	184	238	360	79	45	94	7	51	0.16	21	18	61	21	76	CAf	16%	177	197	17%	22%	66	0%	0%	-4.6	-76	-$1
21 TAM	375	64	33	62	0	216	31	1	246	301	559	118	175	88	9	60	0.26	30	16	54	23	100	BAf	24%	223	178	30%	28%	95	0%	0%	13.4	265	$11
22 TAM	123	7	5	16	0	148	5	0	182	195	304	71	70	71	5	60	0.13	29	17	54	19	94	AAd	9%	118	146	13%	13%	61	0%	0%	-6.9	-121	-$4
1st Half	123	7	5	16	0	148	5	0	182	195	304	71	70	71	5	60	0.13	29	17	54	19	94	AAd	9%	118	146	13%	13%	61	0%	0%	-7.1	-121	-$8
2nd Half																																		
23 Proj	350	36	20	45	0	204	20	0	212	271	428	97	97	97	7	61	0.18	29	17	54	26	88		15%	164	161	18%	19%	60	1%	0%	1.7	-37	$7

STEPHEN NICKRAND

The preceding section provided player boxes and analysis for 441 batters. As we know, far more than 441 batters will play in the major leagues in 2023. Many of those additional hitters are covered in the minor league section, but that still leaves a gap: established major leaguers who don't play enough, or well enough, to merit a player box.

This section looks to fill that gap. Here, you will find "The Next Tier" of batters who are mostly past their growth years, but who are likely to see some playing time in 2023. We are including their 2021-22 statline here for reference for you to do your own analysis. (Years that include MLEs are marked by an asterisk.) This way, if Daz Cameron starts creating some early-season havoc on the bases, you can see his speed-related metrics as a mid-20s player have some teeth. Or when Charlie Culberson pops two HRs in one week in June, you can remind yourself that he's 34 years old with two poor power skills years in his recent past, and save your FAB.

Batter	Yr	B	Age	Pos	PA	R	HR	RBI	SB	BA	xBA	OPS+	vL+	vR+	bb%	ct%	Eye	GLF	HctX	PX	xPX	SPD	SBA%	SB%	BPX
Alberto, Hanser	21	R	28	45	255	25	2	24	3	270	273	95	105	85	2	89	0.15	38/22/40	114	78	101	106	8	75	215
	22	R	29		159	13	2	15	0	244	249	88	95	73	2	84	0.12	49/16/35	87	77	101	116	4	0	131
Almora, Albert	21*	R	27	89	214	18	4	11	1	175	221	66	55	36	5	80	0.25	54/14/31	121	53	85	96	20	17	12
	22*	R	28		317	32	5	34	3	226	257	85	93	88	6	81	0.33	50/22/27	83	66	71	111	7	60	83
Arcia, Orlando	21*	R	26	4	399	50	14	42	5	225	258	92	107	67	8	82	0.47	51/16/33	70	88	50	84	11	57	165
	22	R	27		234	25	9	30	0	244	234	104	84	112	9	76	0.41	46/16/38	118	108	116	102	0	0	134
Barnes, Austin	21	R	31	2	225	28	6	23	1	215	213	88	87	89	9	72	0.36	43/17/40	91	81	95	102	2	100	12
	22	R	32		212	31	8	26	2	212	238	100	96	101	13	79	0.73	42/15/43	86	98	70	76	6	67	159
Beer, Seth	21*	L	24	0	393	44	9	35	0	215	290	85	150	241	6	74	0.23	0/50/50	152	96	269	89	0	0	50
	22*	L	25		479	33	8	41	0	175	235	71	89	70	7	74	0.29	47/25/28	108	67	109	75	1	0	-34
Bolt, Skye	21*	B	27	8	243	31	7	22	5	244	223	97	13	49	9	68	0.30	52/14/33	70	100	61	102	9	100	12
	22*	B	28		215	18	6	25	6	209	205	82	74	87	5	70	0.17	49/13/38	103	85	133	91	17	81	-45
Bradley, Jackie	21	L	31	89	428	39	6	29	7	163	206	68	72	68	7	66	0.21	50/19/31	92	68	77	91	10	88	-150
	22	L	32		370	30	4	38	2	203	236	80	75	82	6	78	0.31	51/17/32	93	80	82	65	8	40	31
Camargo, Johan	21*	B	27	6	438	53	14	50	0	255	237	101	0	20	8	77	0.39	60/10/30	94	97	128	97	1	0	119
	22*	B	28		336	21	4	30	0	203	226	76	75	95	8	77	0.38	41/25/33	58	45	45	89	0	0	-34
Cameron, Daz	21*	R	24	o	289	43	9	32	12	240	232	98	76	95	8	70	0.28	38/22/40	88	111	109	138	24	78	104
	22*	R	25		477	43	7	41	14	195	188	78	111	78	6	64	0.18	32/20/48	89	91	122	137	22	76	-48
Casali, Curtis	21	R	32	2	231	20	5	26	0	210	208	91	57	102	11	67	0.39	32/21/47	99	98	136	105	0	0	8
	22	R	33		176	20	5	17	0	203	202	92	118	76	14	66	0.48	28/23/49	67	90	108	79	0	0	-31
Cave, Jake	21*	L	28	7	212	18	4	17	1	205	220	78	33	88	6	61	0.18	50/30/20	59	76	60	102	7	31	-181
	22*	L	29		523	52	12	52	8	199	205	85	93	91	7	65	0.21	36/20/44	109	111	152	136	9	100	14
Chang, Yu	21*	R	25	4	313	38	12	48	2	234	236	97	91	99	5	69	0.16	36/21/43	81	130	82	120	8	41	100
	22*	R	26		216	20	4	17	0	199	184	80	67	102	9	65	0.28	42/17/41	81	77	123	117	2	0	-83
Chirinos, Robinson	21*	R	37	2	154	17	7	19	0	223	197	103	107	107	10	57	0.27	34/13/52	79	160	121	105	0	0	38
	22	R	38		220	10	4	22	1	179	192	78	86	71	9	66	0.28	40/18/42	77	87	103	65	2	100	-97
Culberson, Charlie	21	R	32	5	271	23	5	22	7	243	244	93	127	53	6	74	0.27	47/21/32	79	89	62	118	14	88	69
	22	R	33		124	19	2	12	2	252	232	91	90	90	4	73	0.16	56/17/27	65	78	60	100	19	40	-14
Duffy, Matt	21	R	30	35	322	45	5	30	8	287	256	101	92	105	8	78	0.40	48/26/25	84	58	63	104	9	89	31
	22*	R	31		283	16	3	17	0	232	207	81	93	83	6	77	0.30	47/21/33	79	42	64	108	0	0	-34
Engel, Adam	21*	R	29	89	196	25	8	21	10	223	251	96	87	129	7	70	0.25	42/23/35	90	126	86	83	28	91	88
	22	R	30		260	32	2	17	12	224	204	82	63	90	4	69	0.14	39/21/39	80	72	52	133	30	75	-52
Ford, Mike	21*	L	28	3	363	29	13	34	1	162	172	76	48	83	9	62	0.28	38/11/51	103	98	154	73	2	100	-108
	22*	L	29		274	16	4	14	0	186	216	78	109	81	10	74	0.46	33/23/44	103	66	84	76	0	0	-14
Franco, Maikel	21*	R	28	5	437	34	11	47	0	204	242	80	77	87	5	82	0.32	49/18/33	95	78	64	52	0	0	69
	22	R	29		388	31	9	39	1	229	236	85	85	84	3	80	0.16	44/20/36	99	72	81	63	1	100	14
Garcia, Aramis	21*	R	28	2	211	17	4	16	0	200	193	72	69	79	3	69	0.10	53/15/32	73	67	66	77	0	0	-150
	22*	R	29		137	7	2	7	0	202	199	70	111	59	3	65	0.08	34/28/38	74	55	77	93	4	0	-210
Gregorius, Didi	21	L	31	6	408	35	13	54	3	209	240	88	76	92	6	82	0.37	37/18/45	81	86	66	94	4	100	146
	22	L	32		232	17	1	19	1	210	229	80	60	87	6	83	0.36	40/19/41	73	57	61	126	2	100	100
Hernandez, Yadiel	21*	L	33	7	351	39	13	40	3	264	265	101	117	95	7	77	0.35	54/23/23	104	83	93	99	5	70	85
	22	L	34		327	30	9	41	2	269	252	102	86	106	6	76	0.26	51/21/27	115	95	124	68	4	67	45
Herrera, Jose	21*	B	24	2	337	27	6	35	2	203	207	80	0	0	9	69	0.33	44/20/36	0	67	-22	114	4	68	-54
	22*	B	25		221	18	1	13	0	218	200	75	85	60	7	77	0.33	64/16/20	58	27	22	83	0	0	-97
Herrera, Odubel	21	L	29	8	491	59	13	51	6	260	273	100	93	103	6	83	0.38	48/21/31	102	88	86	104	6	86	181
	22	L	30		197	23	5	21	6	238	249	93	103	90	6	77	0.26	58/13/30	82	91	51	99	15	100	86
Heyward, Jason	21	L	31	89	353	35	8	30	5	214	245	86	84	87	8	79	0.40	51/17/33	99	77	77	99	8	83	92
	22	L	32		151	15	1	10	1	204	207	79	61	82	7	77	0.34	46/16/38	99	51	92	93	3	100	-24
Higashioka, Kyle	21	R	31	2	211	20	10	29	0	181	233	87	108	77	8	69	0.29	28/21/51	107	130	187	60	0	0	69
	22	R	32		248	27	10	31	0	227	243	92	106	87	5	77	0.23	35/22/43	118	96	125	81	2	0	76
Hill, Derek	21*	R	25	8	283	36	6	26	9	270	231	100	108	87	6	68	0.21	41/29/30	74	85	89	222	18	69	77
	22*	R	26		331	30	5	20	8	177	198	69	117	61	5	62	0.15	49/22/29	51	69	54	153	20	75	-124

THE NEXT TIER

Batters

Batter	Yr	B	Age	Pos	PA	R	HR	RBI	SB	BA	xBA	OPS+	vL+	vR+	bb%	ct%	Eye	GLF	HctX	PX	xPX	SPD	SBA%	SB%	BPX
Hummel, Cooper	21*	B	26	7	326	36	6	27	2	223	233	92	0	0	10	73	0.42	44/20/36	0	87	-22	123	4	62	85
	22*	B	27		342	35	6	26	5	192	202	84	71	90	10	62	0.30	47/18/35	84	101	118	109	15	47	-52
Ibanez, Andy	21*	R	28	5	394	45	12	43	1	274	262	105	122	93	6	84	0.40	37/20/43	106	96	102	109	1	100	231
	22*	R	29		425	33	4	26	6	188	196	70	72	81	6	79	0.29	43/12/45	88	52	108	102	11	68	7
La Stella, Tommy	21*	L	32	0	274	31	7	28	0	237	265	93	75	101	8	87	0.68	43/21/36	102	75	84	80	0	0	192
	22*	L	33		238	21	3	18	0	236	257	90	70	92	7	82	0.41	41/24/36	87	81	65	77	0	0	107
Luplow, Jordan	21*	R	27	79	246	29	13	35	1	197	224	103	94	123	15	66	0.51	31/14/54	87	155	135	97	7	24	192
	22*	R	28		280	31	14	35	5	178	227	89	94	84	9	71	0.36	41/14/45	107	121	119	78	11	83	90
Maile, Luke	21*	R	30	2	176	16	1	12	1	185	184	72	245	91	9	53	0.22	70/17/13	66	87	65	87	3	100	-273
	22	R	31		206	19	3	17	0	221	203	89	98	86	9	70	0.35	38/18/44	78	83	83	88	0	0	-17
Maldonado, Martin	21	R	34	2	426	40	12	36	0	172	200	79	91	73	11	66	0.37	37/21/42	75	82	101	73	0	0	-92
	22	R	35		379	40	15	45	0	186	212	85	107	76	6	66	0.19	42/17/41	84	116	103	51	0	0	-41
Mazara, Nomar	21	L	26	9	181	12	3	19	0	212	219	82	37	89	8	73	0.33	48/20/32	88	65	67	119	0	0	-8
	22*	L	27		310	33	6	32	0	260	235	98	109	92	7	72	0.27	36/25/39	72	92	65	92	0	0	21
Mercado, Oscar	21*	R	26	9	424	46	9	34	13	199	239	83	111	78	9	79	0.44	43/18/39	82	82	59	121	18	85	138
	22*	R	27		304	30	7	32	7	201	207	80	70	101	5	77	0.22	32/16/52	83	79	101	135	26	48	83
Miller, Bradley	21	L	31	057	377	53	20	49	3	227	236	106	73	116	12	66	0.40	45/18/37	116	136	132	123	3	100	138
	22	L	32		241	20	7	32	4	212	192	84	72	85	7	68	0.26	42/17/41	90	69	99	108	11	67	-72
Moran, Colin	21*	L	28	3	386	32	11	57	1	250	239	98	75	108	10	72	0.40	50/23/27	91	85	85	63	1	100	-8
	22*	L	29		333	24	10	40	0	198	210	86	106	94	8	67	0.28	50/20/30	106	101	113	68	0	0	-45
Moustakas, Mike	21	L	32	035	206	21	6	22	0	208	232	90	45	101	9	75	0.39	36/19/46	83	104	64	57	0	0	73
	22	L	33		285	30	7	25	2	214	200	91	79	94	8	70	0.32	35/15/50	95	95	87	75	3	100	-3
Murphy, Tom	21	R	30	2	322	35	11	34	0	202	188	90	108	70	12	64	0.40	44/14/41	100	97	116	85	0	0	-46
	22	R	31		41	9	1	1	0	303	225	127	117	130	20	61	0.62	30/35/35	132	130	210	111	0	0	72
Nevin, Tyler	21*	R	24	5	450	37	14	42	1	199	143	83	315	53	8	75	0.34	22/0/78	68	86	61	88	2	40	50
	22*	R	25		362	35	7	38	2	214	217	85	95	68	9	73	0.37	39/23/39	67	68	53	100	2	100	-14
Phillips, Brett	21	L	27	89	292	50	13	44	14	202	202	98	51	117	11	55	0.29	36/21/43	79	157	156	137	28	82	50
	22*	L	28		299	31	9	25	8	160	173	75	8	78	9	53	0.20	32/24/44	56	115	101	107	15	100	-152
Piscotty, Stephen	21	R	30	9	188	14	5	16	1	220	220	87	97	76	7	72	0.27	39/20/41	71	85	84	83	3	100	-4
	22*	R	31		253	18	9	24	2	201	217	83	72	89	6	64	0.17	46/23/31	77	103	85	80	4	100	-76
Plawecki, Kevin	21	R	30	2	173	15	3	15	0	287	231	101	108	95	7	83	0.46	40/20/40	90	59	89	97	0	0	100
	22	R	31		186	15	1	13	0	220	221	81	50	92	8	81	0.44	47/19/34	103	50	60	91	0	0	28
Refsnyder, Rob	21*	R	30	9	232	30	5	22	1	246	235	97	107	80	11	72	0.45	42/23/35	101	88	125	77	2	100	27
	22*	R	31		346	46	10	39	3	274	254	114	141	113	10	67	0.33	37/28/35	110	143	144	86	5	77	103
Reynolds, Matt	21*	R	30	46	342	25	3	22	3	192	179	75	0	0	10	59	0.26	44/20/36	0	71	-22	92	9	45	-215
	22*	R	31		302	32	4	26	5	236	218	89	88	94	9	68	0.33	51/22/27	88	66	90	120	6	100	-55
Romine, Austin	21	R	32	2	62	5	1	5	0	217	167	74	173	24	3	63	0.09	53/13/34	68	62	77	96	0	0	-227
	22*	R	33		194	15	4	14	0	169	180	63	27	72	3	67	0.11	54/14/31	58	59	64	86	0	0	-172
Ruf, Darin	21	R	34	037	312	41	16	43	2	271	263	124	137	114	15	67	0.53	41/16/43	110	155	136	97	2	100	200
	22	R	35		388	52	11	45	2	204	211	91	105	78	12	69	0.43	41/18/41	99	95	117	66	2	100	-14
Schwindel, Frank	21*	R	29	03	494	71	24	73	2	275	272	111	146	126	5	79	0.25	41/20/39	103	125	106	96	3	67	219
	22*	R	30		329	26	9	38	0	219	227	86	85	92	6	78	0.28	47/18/35	104	81	99	71	0	0	38
Simmons, Andrelton	21	R	31	46	451	37	3	31	1	223	230	77	86	71	7	85	0.52	54/18/28	65	31	23	82	1	100	19
	22*	R	32		132	10	1	8	5	142	181	52	20	75	7	75	0.31	65/8/27	46	15	18	118	33	64	-121
Smith, Dominic	21	L	26	3	493	43	11	58	2	244	240	92	107	86	6	75	0.29	38/26/36	107	74	107	61	3	67	-27
	22*	L	27		385	36	6	40	2	202	221	81	78	80	7	75	0.31	47/16/36	83	78	81	69	4	66	0
Thompson, Trayce	21*	R	30	79	387	36	16	47	4	178	182	84	247	67	9	53	0.22	35/18/47	128	142	272	80	7	75	-108
	22*	R	31		417	56	22	63	5	241	243	114	87	144	10	59	0.26	31/30/39	108	201	167	91	8	69	152
Torrens, Luis	21*	R	25	2	458	47	19	60	0	231	240	98	116	89	8	70	0.28	51/18/31	102	118	115	87	0	0	65
	22*	R	26		230	17	5	24	0	218	211	82	86	79	6	65	0.20	47/26/27	81	69	58	65	0	0	-166
Tsutsugo, Yoshi	21*	L	29	3	425	44	14	51	0	205	210	90	97	94	10	70	0.38	41/14/45	105	103	101	85	1	0	38
	22*	L	30		334	24	7	39	0	195	178	82	67	68	11	65	0.36	48/15/37	66	77	70	63	1	0	-117
Upton, Justin	21	R	33	0	361	47	17	41	2	211	217	97	114	90	11	66	0.36	43/14/43	98	125	114	84	6	80	54
	22*	R	34		105	6	2	6	0	127	133	60	68	64	9	49	0.19	28/16/56	43	89	35	76	0	0	-310
VanMeter, Josh	21*	L	26	34	390	39	11	47	4	226	220	98	119	84	12	68	0.41	35/20/45	99	116	120	90	7	64	62
	22*	L	27		227	19	4	16	4	177	204	77	40	87	10	72	0.41	43/19/43	88	71	99	105	9	100	-3
Wade, Tyler	21	L	26	4	144	31	0	5	17	268	220	93	100	90	11	71	0.43	59/18/23	48	42	27	171	51	74	-23
	22*	L	27		326	40	4	18	18	192	206	75	73	78	9	72	0.35	40/22/38	37	55	45	117	34	74	-38
White, Eli	21*	R	27	78	295	39	8	23	6	201	193	83	62	88	9	66	0.29	40/16/44	53	85	82	158	15	59	-4
	22	R	28		117	16	3	10	12	200	171	82	84	80	9	61	0.27	30/21/48	66	78	106	118	48	92	-124
Wynns, Austin	21*	R	30	2	192	19	6	20	1	205	232	82	87	68	7	75	0.28	45/20/34	83	78	77	84	3	100	12
	22*	R	31		298	26	5	33	1	262	230	97	80	104	9	77	0.43	46/22/32	77	65	55	91	1	100	21

The following section contains player boxes for every pitcher who had significant playing time in 2022 and/or is expected to get fantasy roster-worthy innings in 2023. You will find some prospects here, specifically the most impactful names who we project to play in 2023. For more complete prospect coverage, see our Prospects section.

Snapshot Section

The top band of each player box contains the following information:

Age as of July 1, 2023.

Throws right (R) or left (L).

Role: Starters (SP) are those projected to face 20+ batters per game; the rest are relievers (RP).

Ht/Wt: Each batter's height and weight.

Type evaluates the extent to which a pitcher allows the ball to be put into play and his ground ball or fly ball tendency. CON (contact) represents pitchers who allow the ball to be put into play a great deal. PWR (power) represents those with high strikeout and/or walk totals who keep the ball out of play. GB are those who have a ground ball rate more than 50%; xGB are those who have a GB rate more than 55%. FB are those who have a fly ball rate more than 40%; xFB are those who have a FB rate more than 45%.

Reliability Grades analyze each pitcher's forecast risk, on an A-F scale. High grades go to those who have accumulated few injured list days (Health), have a history of substantial and regular major league playing time (PT/Exp) and have displayed consistent performance over the past three years, using xERA (Consist).

LIMA Plan Grade evaluates how well that pitcher would be a good fit for a team using the LIMA Plan draft strategy. Best grades go to pitchers who have excellent base skills and had a 2022 dollar value less than $20. Lowest grades will go to poor skills and values more than $20.

Random Variance Score (Rand Var) measures the impact random variance had on the pitcher's 2022 stats and the probability that his 2023 performance will exceed or fall short of 2022. The variables tracked are those prone to regression—H%, S%, HR/F and xERA to ERA variance. Players are rated on a scale of −5 to +5 with positive scores indicating rebounds and negative scores indicating corrections. Note that this score is computer-generated and the projections will override it on occasion.

Mayberry Method (MM) acknowledges the imprecision of the forecasting process by projecting player performance in broad strokes. The four digits of MM each represent a fantasy-relevant skill—ERA, strikeout rate, saves potential and playing time (IP)—and are all on a scale of 0 to 5.

Commentaries for each pitcher provide a brief analysis of his skills and the potential impact on performance in 2023. MLB statistics are listed first for those who played only a portion of 2022 at the major league level. Note that these commentaries generally look at performance related issues only. Role and playing time expectations may impact these analyses, so you will have to adjust accordingly. Upside (UP) and downside (DN) statistical potential appears for some players; these are less grounded in hard data and more speculative of skills potential.

Player Stat Section

The past five years' statistics represent the total accumulated in the majors as well as in Triple-A, Double-A ball and various foreign leagues during each year. All non-major league stats have been converted to a major league equivalent (MLE) performance level. Minor league levels below Double-A are not included.

Nearly all baseball publications separate a player's statistical experiences in the major leagues from the minor leagues and outside leagues. While this may be appropriate for official record-keeping purposes, it is not an easy-to-analyze snapshot of a player's complete performance for a given year.

Bill James has proven that minor league statistics (converted to MLEs), at Double-A level or above, provide as accurate a record of a player's performance as major league statistics. Other researchers have also devised conversion factors for foreign leagues. Since these are adequate barometers, we include them in the pool of historical data for each year.

Team designations: An asterisk (*) appearing with a team name means that Triple-A and/or Double-A numbers are included in that year's stat line. Any stints of less than 10 IP are not included (to screen out most rehab appearances). A designation of "a/a" means the stats were accumulated at both AA and AAA levels that year. "for" represents a foreign or independent league. The designation "2TM" appears whenever a player was on more than one major league team, crossing leagues, in a season. "2AL" and "2NL" represent more than one team in the same league. Players who were cut during the season and finished 2022 as a free agent are designated as FAA (Free agent, AL) and FAN (Free agent, NL).

Stats: Descriptions of all the categories appear in the Encyclopedia.

- The leading decimal point has been suppressed on some categories to conserve space.
- Data for platoons (vL+, vR+), SwK, balls-in-play (G/L/F), HR/F and xHR/F, consistency (GS, APC, DOM, DIS), xWHIP and velocity (Vel) are for major league performance only.
- Formulas that use BIP data, like xERA and BPV, are used for years in which G/L/F data is available. Where feasible, older versions of these formulas are used otherwise.

Earned run average and WHIP are presented first next to each other, then skills-based xERA and xWHIP for comparison. Next is opponents' OPS splits vs. left-handed and right-handed batters (indexed to league average). Batters faced per game (BF/G) provide a quick view of a pitcher's role—starters will generally have levels over 20.

Basic pitching skills are measured by percentage of batters faced: BB% or walk rate, K% or strikeout rate, and K-BB%. xBB% and Swinging strike rate (SwK) are also presented with these basic skills; compare xBB% to BB% and our research shows that SwK serves as a skills-based indicator of K%. Vel is the pitcher's average fastball velocity.

Once the ball leaves the bat, it will either be a (G)round ball, (L)ine drive or (F)ly ball.

Random variance indicators include hit rate (H%)—often referred to as batting average on balls-in-play (BABIP)—which tends to regress to 30%. Normal strand rates (S%) fall within the tolerances of 65% to 80%. The ratio of home runs to fly balls (HR/F) is another sanity check; levels far from the league average of 12% are prone to regression, as is HR/F vs. xHR/F disparity.

In looking at consistency for starting pitchers, we track games started (GS), average pitch counts (APC) for all outings (for starters and relievers), the percentage of DOMinating starts (PQS 4 or 5) and DISaster starts (PQS 0 or 1). The larger the variance between DOM and DIS, the greater the consistency of good or bad performance.

For relievers, we look at their saves success rate (Sv%) and Leverage Index (LI). A Doug Dennis study showed little correlation between saves success and future opportunity. However, you can increase your odds by prospecting for pitchers who have *both* a high saves percentage (80% or better) *and* high skills. Relievers with LI levels over 1.0 are being used more often by managers to win ballgames.

The final section includes several overall performance measures: runs above replacement (RAR), Base performance index (BPX, which is BPV indexed to each year's league average) and the Rotisserie value (R$).

2023 Projections

Forecasts are computed from a player's trends over the past five years. Adjustments were made for leading indicators and variances between skill and statistical output. After reviewing the leading indicators, you might opt to make further adjustments.

Although each year's numbers include all playing time at the Double-A level or above, the 2023 forecast only represents potential playing time at the major league level, and again is highly preliminary.

Note that the projected Rotisserie values in this book will not necessarily align with each player's historical actuals. Since we currently have no idea who is going to close games for the Phillies, or whether Grayson Rodriguez is going to break camp with the Orioles, it is impossible to create a finite pool of playing time, something which is required for valuation. So the projections are roughly based on a 12-team AL/NL league, and include an inflated number of innings, league-wide. This serves to flatten the spread of values and depress individual player dollar projections. In truth, a $25 player in this book might actually be worth $21, or $28. This level of precision is irrelevant in a process that is driven by market forces anyway. So, don't obsess over it.

Be aware of other sources that publish perfectly calibrated Rotisserie values over the winter. They are likely making arbitrary decisions as to where free agents are going to sign and who is going to land jobs in the spring. We do not make those leaps of faith here.

Bottom line… It is far too early to be making definitive projections for 2023, especially on playing time. Focus on the skill levels and trends, then consult BaseballHQ.com for playing time revisions as players change teams and roles become more defined. A free projections update will be available online in March.

Do-it-yourself analysis

Here are some data points you can look at in doing your own player analysis:

- Variance between vL+ and vR+ (opposition OPS)
- Variance in 2022 HR/F rate from 11-12%
- Variance in HR/F and xHR/F each year
- Variance in 2022 hit rate (H%) from 30%
- Variance in 2022 strand rate (S%) to tolerances (65% - 80%)
- Variance between ERA and xERA each year
- Growth or decline in base performance index (BPX)
- Spikes in innings pitched
- Trends in average pitch counts (APC)
- Trends in DOM/DIS splits
- Trends in saves success rate (Sv%)
- Variance between K% changes and corresponding SwK levels
- Variance between BB% changes and corresponding xBB% levels
- Improvement or decline in velocity

Abreu,Bryan

Age: 26	Th: R	Role RP	Health C	LIMA Plan A
Ht: 6' 1"	Wt: 225	Type Pwr	PT/Exp D	Rand Var -5
			Consist F	MM 5510

Added velocity and posted double-digit SwK on all three pitches (four-seamer, slider, curveball). Still too many walks, but a step in right direction and GB% should continue keeping HR in check. ERA should rise once S% and HR/F normalize, but these skills look good enough to thrive in high-leverage role. An intriguing candidate for saves.

Yr Tm	W	Sv	IP	K	ERA	WHIP	xERA	xWHIP	vL+	vR+	BF/G	BB%	K%	K-BB%	xBB%	SwK	Vel	G	L	F	H%	S%	HR/F	xHR/F	GS	APC	DOM%	DIS%	Sv%	LI	RAR	BPX	R$
18																																	
19 HOU *	6	2	87	102	6.39	1.53	4.23	1.03	19	80	14.0	15%	27%	12%	9%	19.2%	95.1	50	25	25	33%	57%	0%	1%	0	21			67	0.44	-20.2	92	-$7
20 HOU	0	0	3	3	2.70	2.40	14.18		41	160	5.0	35%	15%	-20%		5.3%	92.9	38	25	38	14%	88%	0%	0%	0	19			0	0.49	0.7	-394	-$8
21 HOU *	3	1	52	56	4.49	1.47	4.07	1.42	107	99	4.9	13%	25%	12%	12%	13.5%	95.7	48	20	32	32%	70%	12%	13%	0	22			17	1.32	-1.4	92	-$4
22 HOU	4	2	60	88	1.94	1.18	2.70	1.12	71	90	4.5	10%	35%	25%	9%	18.1%	97.2	48	20	32	34%	84%	5%	10%	0	19			100	0.82	15.1	174	$7
1st Half	4	0	29	42	2.17	1.24	2.73	1.12	85	86	5.1	10%	34%	24%	9%	16.7%	97.7	47	24	29	37%	83%	5%	15%	0	21			0	0.68	6.4	175	$2
2nd Half	0	2	31	46	1.72	1.12	2.67	1.13	59	95	4.0	11%	37%	26%	9%	19.4%	96.7	50	16	34	32%	85%	5%	5%	0	16			100	0.92	8.7	174	$2
Proj	4	5	58	77	3.43	1.17	2.79	1.21	73	96	5.2	11%	33%	22%	10%	17.2%	96.8	49	19	32	30%	72%	11%	9%	0						3.9	145	$4

Acevedo,Domingo

Age: 29	Th: R	Role RP	Health A	LIMA Plan A
Ht: 6' 7"	Wt: 240	Type Con	PT/Exp D	Rand Var -3
			Consist C	MM 3211

Posted sub-3.00 ERA after rocky April and emerged as late-inning arm with four Sept saves. Low H% certainly helped, but solid BB% looks legit and SwK% hints at strong possibility for K% spike. Ratios are more likely to land near xERA/xWHIP than repeat, but that still gives him a shot to settle in as mid-tier closing option.

Yr Tm	W	Sv	IP	K	ERA	WHIP	xERA	xWHIP	vL+	vR+	BF/G	BB%	K%	K-BB%	xBB%	SwK	Vel	G	L	F	H%	S%	HR/F	xHR/F	GS	APC	DOM%	DIS%	Sv%	LI	RAR	BPX	R$
18 aa	3	0	66	44	3.88	1.28	3.59				19.4	8%	16%	8%							29%	70%									2.2	75	-$1
19 a/a	8	0	53	44	5.60	1.27	5.49				6.8	7%	20%	13%							26%	66%									-7.2	34	-$1
20																																	
21 OAK *	2	9	45	50	2.62	0.95	2.70	1.37	78	119	4.3	6%	29%	23%	6%	14.4%	92.9	42	19	39	26%	80%	25%	14%	0	17			82	0.11	9.2	161	$7
22 OAK	4	4	68	58	3.33	0.99	3.78	1.21	105	82	3.8	6%	22%	15%	6%	16.2%	93.0	41	20	40	24%	72%	12%	10%	0	14			50	1.17	5.4	107	$5
1st Half	1	0	37	33	3.19	1.01	3.92	1.21	128	75	3.9	7%	23%	16%	6%	16.2%	92.8	34	22	44	23%	77%	14%	11%	0	15			0	1.26	3.5	101	-$1
2nd Half	3	4	31	25	3.48	0.97	3.60	1.21	69	90	3.7	6%	21%	15%	6%	16.3%	93.3	48	17	34	24%	67%	10%	8%	0	14			80	1.06	1.9	113	$3
Proj	5	7	65	56	3.72	1.17	3.60	1.21	113	101	4.8	6%	22%	16%	6%	16.2%	93.1	43	19	38	29%	75%	14%	11%	0						2.0	114	$4

Adam,Jason

Age: 31	Th: R	Role RP	Health A	LIMA Plan B+
Ht: 6' 3"	Wt: 229	Type Pwr/FB	PT/Exp D	Rand Var -5
			Consist A	MM 5421

Swing-and-miss stuff was already part of profile, but took SwK% up another notch with more sliders and change-ups. Paired it with better BB% that had full support from xBB%, and GB% spiked in 2nd half. Got some help from H%, but this wasn't all luck, as he was as good as anyone at limiting hard contact. The pieces are here for... UP: 25 Sv.

Yr Tm	W	Sv	IP	K	ERA	WHIP	xERA	xWHIP	vL+	vR+	BF/G	BB%	K%	K-BB%	xBB%	SwK	Vel	G	L	F	H%	S%	HR/F	xHR/F	GS	APC	DOM%	DIS%	Sv%	LI	RAR	BPX	R$
18 KC *	3	5	59	61	4.21	1.21	3.60	1.33	117	121	4.9	11%	26%	14%	10%	12.8%	94.1	25	18	56	25%	70%	18%	15%	0	18			63	0.57	-0.4	86	$2
19 TOR	3	0	22	18	2.91	1.15	5.62	1.54	58	95	4.0	11%	20%	9%	12%	11.3%	94.5	25	23	52	25%	75%	3%	6%	0	17			0	1.12	4.3	28	-$1
20 CHC	2	0	14	21	3.29	1.24	3.79	1.28	85	100	4.5	14%	36%	22%	11%	17.7%	94.8	39	14	46	29%	80%	15%	10%	0	20			0	0.41	2.0	140	$0
21 CHC	1	0	11	19	5.91	1.50	3.36	1.15	124	92	4.2	12%	38%	26%	12%	14.2%	93.8	36	14	50	45%	60%	9%	11%	0	18			0	0.46	-2.2	182	-$6
22 TAM	2	8	63	75	1.56	0.76	2.87	1.06	62	69	3.5	7%	32%	25%	6%	18.7%	94.8	46	13	41	20%	86%	9%	7%	0	14			67	1.28	18.8	166	$13
1st Half	1	3	32	37	1.39	0.74	3.06	1.06	75	55	3.4	7%	31%	24%	6%	17.7%	94.7	38	15	46	22%	83%	3%	4%	0	14			100	1.28	10.3	156	$8
2nd Half	1	5	31	38	1.74	0.77	2.65	1.07	50	84	3.7	8%	32%	25%	6%	19.7%	95.1	54	10	36	18%	90%	17%	12%	0	14			56	1.28	8.5	176	$8
Proj	3	12	65	75	2.72	1.01	3.10	1.17	81	89	4.0	9%	30%	21%	6%	17.4%	94.8	43	14	44	25%	78%	10%	10%	0						10.1	136	$11

Adon,Joan

Age: 24	Th: R	Role SP	Health A	LIMA Plan C
Ht: 6' 2"	Wt: 242	Type Pwr	PT/Exp D	Rand Var +2
			Consist B	MM 1200

1-12, 7.10 ERA in 65 IP at WAS. Opened season in MLB rotation despite just two career starts above AA and took his lumps. Couldn't miss bats or throw strikes, had second-highest ERA among pitchers with 60+ IP, and spent most of 2nd half back in minors. Signs point to him needing more time there, so odds of positive 2023 impact are low.

Yr Tm	W	Sv	IP	K	ERA	WHIP	xERA	xWHIP	vL+	vR+	BF/G	BB%	K%	K-BB%	xBB%	SwK	Vel	G	L	F	H%	S%	HR/F	xHR/F	GS	APC	DOM%	DIS%	Sv%	LI	RAR	BPX	R$
18																																	
19																																	
20																																	
21 WAS *	1	0	23	35	5.39	1.57	4.98		204	60	20.5	11%	34%	23%		12.8%	95.1	73	18	9	43%	66%	100%	91%	1	94	0%	0%			-3.2	133	-$7
22 WAS *	3	0	108	90	6.12	1.68	5.57	1.56	125	123	20.2	13%	18%	5%	10%	7.0%	95.0	48	19	33	33%	64%	12%	16%	14	86	7%	57%			-28.7	47	-$17
1st Half	1	0	68	57	6.66	1.73	5.97	1.54	122	121	20.5	12%	18%	6%	10%	6.7%	95.0	48	19	32	34%	62%	13%	17%	13	85	8%	62%			-22.4	41	-$27
2nd Half	2	0	40	34	5.23	1.58	4.88	1.52	161	144	19.6	12%	19%	7%	10%	10.4%	96.0	38	23	38	32%	67%	0%	13%	1	96	0%	0%			-6.2	59	-$11
Proj	2	0	58	49	5.29	1.55	4.33	1.55	116	115	21.2	13%	19%	7%	10%	6.7%	95.0	48	19	32	31%	67%	13%	15%	12						-9.5	30	-$8

Akin,Keegan

Age: 28	Th: L	Role RP	Health A	LIMA Plan A+
Ht: 5' 11"	Wt: 235	Type	PT/Exp B	Rand Var 0
			Consist D	MM 5211

Move to 'pen worked wonders, as improved velocity, SwK, and BB% helped cut ERA in half. Surface stats weren't as shiny in 2nd half but blame inflated H%, as skills were the best he's shown to date. Track record of success is short and ongoing struggles vR make closer gig a long shot, but he's one to at least track in deeper leagues.

Yr Tm	W	Sv	IP	K	ERA	WHIP	xERA	xWHIP	vL+	vR+	BF/G	BB%	K%	K-BB%	xBB%	SwK	Vel	G	L	F	H%	S%	HR/F	xHR/F	GS	APC	DOM%	DIS%	Sv%	LI	RAR	BPX	R$
18 aa	14	0	139	117	3.68	1.32	4.15				23.1	10%	20%	10%							28%	77%									8.1	68	$8
19 aaa	6	0	113	105	5.66	1.68	5.35				20.3	12%	21%	8%							35%	67%									-16.1	61	-$10
20 BAL	1	0	26	35	4.56	1.44	4.09	1.18	80	108	14.5	9%	30%	22%	8%	13.6%	91.9	35	25	41	39%	71%	11%	11%	6	63	33%	33%	0	0.85	-0.3	157	-$4
21 BAL	2	0	95	82	6.63	1.58	5.33	1.41	119	112	17.8	9%	19%	10%	7%	10.2%	92.1	36	21	43	33%	60%	13%	14%	17	74	12%	65%	0	0.68	-27.7	57	-$17
22 BAL	3	2	82	77	3.20	1.09	3.42	1.17	64	110	7.3	6%	23%	17%	4%	12.6%	93.6	49	18	33	28%	76%	14%	11%	1	27	0%	0%	100	0.73	7.8	132	$5
1st Half	1	1	49	39	2.39	0.88	3.75	1.25	43	101	9.0	7%	21%	14%	4%	11.4%	93.3	47	16	37	19%	83%	14%	11%	0	34			100	0.81	9.6	98	$7
2nd Half	2	1	33	38	4.41	1.41	2.93	1.06	88	122	5.9	5%	27%	22%	4%	14.3%	94.0	53	21	26	40%	70%	13%	11%	1	22	0%	0%	100	0.66	-1.8	185	-$5
Proj	3	2	65	62	3.47	1.17	3.18	1.15	78	111	7.0	6%	24%	18%	5%	12.5%	93.4	48	19	33	31%	75%	14%	11%	0						4.0	138	$2

Alcantara,Sandy

Age: 27	Th: R	Role SP	Health A	LIMA Plan C
Ht: 6' 5"	Wt: 200	Type Con/GB	PT/Exp A	Rand Var -5
			Consist A	MM 5205

Another outstanding year from the only pitcher to top 400 IP in the last two seasons combined. His SwK isn't elite but he makes up for it with volume, and also proved 2021 BB% gains weren't a fluke. Though xERA and xWHIP warn against paying for full repeat, combo of strong skills and "AAA" reliability make him a fine rotation anchor.

Yr Tm	W	Sv	IP	K	ERA	WHIP	xERA	xWHIP	vL+	vR+	BF/G	BB%	K%	K-BB%	xBB%	SwK	Vel	G	L	F	H%	S%	HR/F	xHR/F	GS	APC	DOM%	DIS%	Sv%	LI	RAR	BPX	R$
18 MIA *	8	0	151	106	4.13	1.36	3.93	1.67	86	112	25.3	10%	17%	7%	10%	10.6%	95.5	48	16	36	29%	70%	9%	8%	6	95	33%	33%			0.4	65	$1
19 MIA	6	0	197	151	3.88	1.32	5.11	1.49	100	90	26.2	10%	18%	8%	7%	11.4%	95.6	45	19	36	28%	74%	11%	15%	32	97	25%	28%			15.3	51	$7
20 MIA	3	0	42	39	3.00	1.19	4.08	1.32	119	63	24.6	9%	23%	14%	8%	11.3%	96.5	49	22	29	28%	78%	12%	12%	7	95	29%	29%			7.5	102	$8
21 MIA	9	0	206	201	3.19	1.07	3.44	1.17	96	78	25.4	6%	24%	18%	5%	13.9%	97.9	53	19	28	28%	74%	13%	14%	33	94	48%	18%			27.2	143	$23
22 MIA	14	0	229	207	2.28	0.98	3.18	1.15	79	88	27.7	6%	23%	18%	5%	12.6%	97.9	53	16	31	27%	80%	9%	11%	32	102	56%	13%			47.6	137	$36
1st Half	9	0	123	107	1.82	0.91	3.16	1.19	77	76	27.6	6%	23%	16%	6%	12.5%	97.8	56	14	30	24%	82%	6%	9%	17	103	59%	12%			32.6	128	$45
2nd Half	5	0	105	100	2.82	1.06	3.21	1.11	82	101	27.8	5%	24%	19%	4%	12.7%	98.1	50	18	32	29%	77%	11%	13%	15	100	53%	13%			14.9	150	$21
Proj	12	0	203	186	2.93	1.07	3.10	1.18	92	84	25.6	6%	24%	17%	6%	12.6%	97.3	52	18	30	28%	76%	11%	12%	31						26.1	131	$24

Alexander,Jason

Age: 30	Th: R	Role SP	Health A	LIMA Plan C+
Ht: 6' 3"	Wt: 200	Type Con/GB	PT/Exp D	Rand Var 0
			Consist C	MM 2001

2-3, 5.40 ERA in 72 IP at MIL. First crack at majors didn't go so well, as he struggled to miss bats and LHB teed off on him. Did nudge the SwK up in small 2nd half sample while shuffling back and forth between MIL and AAA, but this combination of age and soft skills doesn't offer much optimism. "Struggle," "soft skills" - essentially, the epitome of George Costanza.

Yr Tm	W	Sv	IP	K	ERA	WHIP	xERA	xWHIP	vL+	vR+	BF/G	BB%	K%	K-BB%	xBB%	SwK	Vel	G	L	F	H%	S%	HR/F	xHR/F	GS	APC	DOM%	DIS%	Sv%	LI	RAR	BPX	R$
18 a/a	2	0	71	39	4.56	1.41	4.82				20.2	6%	13%	7%							32%	69%									-3.6	51	-$6
19 a/a	4	0	102	78	7.50	1.89	7.08				20.9	8%	16%	9%							41%	59%									-37.7	43	-$21
20																																	
21 a/a	1	0	19	15	1.90	1.25	3.85				13.0	4%	19%	15%							33%	87%									5.6	133	-$3
22 MIL *	10	0	136	82	4.34	1.50	5.31	1.45	147	109	18.9	9%	14%	6%	9%	7.2%	92.5	51	22	28	32%	74%	18%	16%	11	64	9%	73%	0	0.63	-6.2	36	-$5
1st Half	8	0	85	42	3.67	1.44	4.55	1.46	141	106	21.3	8%	12%	4%	10%	5.1%	92.7	51	22	27	31%	75%	9%	11%	6	71	0%	83%	0	0.73	3.2	42	$0
2nd Half	2	0	53	40	5.23	1.53	6.17	1.35	152	113	16.4	8%	18%	10%	8%	9.3%	92.3	50	21	28	32%	72%	29%	21%	5	59	20%	60%	0	0.55	-8.2	28	-$12
Proj	4	0	87	56	4.82	1.47	4.14	1.39	129	100	20.8	7%	15%	7%	9%	7.7%	92.5	51	22	28	32%	70%	14%	17%	15						-9.1	60	-$7

BRIAN RUDD

Alexander,Tyler

Age: 28 | Th: L | Role: RP
Ht: 6' 2" | Wt: 203 | Type: Con/FB
Health: D | PT/Exp: A | Consist: A
LIMA Plan: B | Rand Var: 0 | MM: 2001

Split time as starter and reliever, but didn't excel in either role. Recorded ugly 5.74 ERA across 17 starts with brutal DOM%/DIS%, while 1.29 ERA in relief wasn't at all supported by skills (11% K%). With his already weak SwK reaching new depths, there's no good reason to have him on your roster. Or radar. Or remotely close to your consciousness.

Yr Tm	W	Sv	IP	K	ERA	WHIP	xERA	xWHIP	vL+	vR+	BF/G	BB%	K%	K-BB%	xBB%	SwK	Vel	G	L	F	H%	S%	HR/F	xHR/F	GS	APC	DOM%	DIS%	Sv%	LI	RAR	BPX	R$
18 a/a	6	0	140	76	5.94	1.78	7.36				24.8	4%	12%	8%							39%	68%									-30.8	48	-$22
19 DET *	6	0	153	131	6.25	1.57	6.68	1.18	89	117	20.3	5%	20%	15%	5%	8.8%	90.7	36	26	38	37%	64%	13%	16%	8	71	0%	50%	0	0.59	-32.8	73	-$14
20 DET	2	0	36	34	3.96	1.32	4.20	1.21	72	130	10.9	6%	22%	16%	8%	9.3%	90.6	45	18	37	31%	80%	21%	17%	2	43	0%	50%	0	0.81	2.2	129	$1
21 DET	2	0	106	87	3.81	1.26	4.82	1.27	77	104	11.0	6%	19%	13%	6%	9.0%	90.4	38	18	44	30%	75%	11%	11%	15	40	13%	67%	0	0.56	6.0	93	$0
22 DET	4	0	101	61	4.81	1.32	4.91	1.33	101	114	15.8	6%	14%	8%	6%	7.9%	90.1	35	22	43	29%	69%	13%	13%	17	59	6%	53%	0	0.80	-10.5	56	-$6
1st Half	2	0	26	16	4.56	1.25	4.78	1.34	86	103	10.7	7%	15%	8%	8%	7.6%	90.1	36	23	41	28%	66%	9%	10%	4	41	0%	75%	0	0.79	-1.9	54	-$8
2nd Half	2	0	75	45	4.90	1.34	4.95	1.32	109	117	18.8	6%	14%	8%	6%	8.0%	90.2	35	22	43	29%	70%	14%	15%	13	70	8%	46%	0	0.81	-8.6	57	-$9
Proj	4	0	87	63	4.67	1.35	4.19	1.29	89	119	13.4	6%	17%	12%	7%	8.5%	90.3	38	21	41	31%	71%	14%	14%	9						-7.5	82	-$5

Alvarado,José

Age: 28 | Th: L | Role: RP
Ht: 6' 2" | Wt: 245 | Type: Pwr/GB
Health: D | PT/Exp: C | Consist: C
LIMA Plan: A+ | Rand Var: +1 | MM: 5510

Finally stayed healthy for full season, as ERA took big step forward with even bigger gains underneath. More cutters led to huge spike in SwK, K%; got BB% to almost respectable level that xBB% says could have been better; put a stop to struggles vR (42% K%). If those gains stick, this could be the year he gets double-digit saves.

Yr Tm	W	Sv	IP	K	ERA	WHIP	xERA	xWHIP	vL+	vR+	BF/G	BB%	K%	K-BB%	xBB%	SwK	Vel	G	L	F	H%	S%	HR/F	xHR/F	GS	APC	DOM%	DIS%	Sv%	LI	RAR	BPX	R$
18 TAM	1	8	64	80	2.39	1.11	3.13	1.26	79	69	3.8	11%	30%	19%	9%	13.2%	97.4	55	17	28	29%	77%	2%	8%	0	15			67	1.48	13.9	144	$8
19 TAM	1	7	30	39	4.80	1.87	5.29	1.70	71	113	4.2	18%	27%	8%	12%	12.8%	98.2	48	22	30	37%	74%	9%	10%	1	17	0%	100%	78	1.17	-1.1	19	-$3
20 TAM	0	0	9	13	6.00	1.67	4.41	1.40	35	140	5.0	13%	29%	16%	11%	10.8%	96.9	42	25	33	36%	69%	25%	28%	0	22			0	0.42	-1.7	104	-$8
21 PHI	7	5	56	68	4.20	1.60	4.21	1.67	65	113	3.9	19%	27%	8%	12%	12.8%	99.4	57	21	22	29%	75%	18%	13%	0	16			63	1.29	0.4	30	$0
22 PHI	4	2	51	81	3.18	1.22	2.35	1.11	90	79	3.6	11%	38%	27%	9%	17.5%	99.6	56	20	24	36%	73%	8%	11%	0	15			50	1.10	5.0	195	$3
1st Half	2	0	22	31	5.40	1.75	3.33	1.44	104	107	3.8	16%	30%	15%	12%	16.2%	99.2	59	20	20	41%	68%	9%	20%	0	15			0	0.98	-3.8	99	-$11
2nd Half	2	2	29	50	1.53	0.82	1.78	0.86	71	59	3.5	7%	45%	38%	7%	18.5%	100.0	53	19	28	31%	83%	7%	5%	0	15			67	1.20	8.8	266	$7
Proj	4	5	58	93	3.14	1.02	1.94	0.99	67	77	3.3	10%	42%	32%	10%	15.1%	99.0	54	20	26	32%	70%	14%	11%	0						5.9	222	$7

Alzolay,Adbert

Age: 28 | Th: R | Role: RP
Ht: 6' 1" | Wt: 208 | Type: Pwr
Health: F | PT/Exp: B | Consist: B
LIMA Plan: B | Rand Var: +2 | MM: 5501

Spring lat strain kept him out until September, then stuff played up in relief role upon return. A glance back at 2021 xERA and K-BB% serves as reminder he can succeed as a starter, too. Worth a look as end-gamer regardless of role, but history of low IP totals says not to count on much of a heavy workload.

Yr Tm	W	Sv	IP	K	ERA	WHIP	xERA	xWHIP	vL+	vR+	BF/G	BB%	K%	K-BB%	xBB%	SwK	Vel	G	L	F	H%	S%	HR/F	xHR/F	GS	APC	DOM%	DIS%	Sv%	LI	RAR	BPX	R$
18 aaa	2	0	41	23	5.06	1.47	4.91				22.1	7%	13%	6%							32%	66%									-4.6	43	-$6
19 CHC *	3	0	78	88	5.84	1.52	5.34	1.67	133	109	17.9	13%	26%	13%	10%	11.1%	94.4	32	24	43	32%	66%	25%	19%	2	56	0%	100%	0	0.54	-12.9	60	-$7
20 CHC	1	0	21	29	2.95	1.17	3.59	1.37	90	66	14.5	15%	33%	18%	9%	11.4%	94.7	43	27	30	26%	75%	8%	10%	4	65	25%	0%	0	0.72	3.9	105	$1
21 CHC	5	1	126	128	4.58	1.16	3.74	1.18	128	74	17.9	7%	25%	18%	6%	12.4%	93.9	45	21	34	28%	68%	22%	21%	21	67	29%	38%	100	0.84	-4.9	134	$3
22 CHC	2	0	13	19	3.38	0.83	2.50	0.86	108	68	8.7	4%	37%	33%	6%	16.1%	94.8	40	20	40	30%	60%	8%	10%	0	32			0	1.21	1.0	234	-$2
1st Half																																	
2nd Half	2	0	13	19	3.38	0.83	2.50	0.86	108	68	8.7	4%	37%	33%	6%	16.1%	94.8	40	20	40	30%	60%	8%	10%	0	32			0	1.21	1.0	234	-$4
Proj	5	0	102	122	3.94	1.19	2.81	1.09	128	82	18.6	7%	30%	23%		12.4%	93.9	45	21	34	33%	70%	15%	13%	19						0.4	167	$4

Anderson,Ian

Age: 25 | Th: R | Role: SP
Ht: 6' 3" | Wt: 170 | Type: Pwr
Health: C | PT/Exp: C | Consist: B
LIMA Plan: A+ | Rand Var: 0 | MM: 3301

10-6, 5.00 ERA in 112 IP at ATL. Declining K% combined with hit rate spike bloated his ERA, leading to AAA demotion in August. Strikeouts should rebound with SwK holding firm and GB% tilt stayed intact, but xWHIP hints ratios were always at risk. When setting expectations, split the difference between 2021 and 2022.

Yr Tm	W	Sv	IP	K	ERA	WHIP	xERA	xWHIP	vL+	vR+	BF/G	BB%	K%	K-BB%	xBB%	SwK	Vel	G	L	F	H%	S%	HR/F	xHR/F	GS	APC	DOM%	DIS%	Sv%	LI	RAR	BPX	R$
18 aa	2	0	20	21	2.87	1.24	2.47				20.4	11%	26%	15%							31%	74%									3.2	136	-$2
19 a/a	8	0	137	147	4.77	1.45	4.37				22.5	12%	25%	13%							32%	69%									-4.4	83	$0
20 ATL	3	0	32	41	1.95	1.08	3.45	1.24	55	80	23.0	10%	30%	20%	10%	12.3%	94.1	53	20	28	28%	82%	5%	3%	6	95	17%	0%			10.0	148	$11
21 ATL *	9	0	145	141	3.64	1.25	3.61	1.35	89	92	21.0	11%	24%	13%	10%	12.4%	94.6	49	20	31	28%	74%	15%	17%	24	91	17%	21%			11.2	88	$9
22 ATL *	11	0	135	116	5.22	1.55	5.01	1.44	87	124	22.7	11%	20%	9%	11%	12.5%	94.0	48	22	30	33%	67%	12%	11%	22	91	9%	36%			-20.9	61	-$8
1st Half	7	0	81	69	5.09	1.54	4.45	1.44	91	124	22.5	11%	19%	9%	10%	12.4%	93.9	46	22	31	32%	69%	13%	9%	16	90	6%	38%			-11.2	53	-$9
2nd Half	4	0	54	47	5.42	1.57	4.85	1.44	80	123	23.5	11%	20%	9%	12%	12.8%	94.4	52	20	27	34%	65%	8%	16%	6	94	17%	33%			-9.6	70	-$10
Proj	8	0	102	102	4.14	1.38	3.62	1.37	80	112	22.1	11%	24%	13%	11%	12.5%	94.2	49	21	30	31%	72%	11%	11%	19						-2.1	85	$0

Anderson,Nick

Age: 32 | Th: R | Role: RP
Ht: 6' 4" | Wt: 205 | Type: Pwr
Health: F | PT/Exp: F | Consist: F
LIMA Plan: B | Rand Var: -1 | MM: 5510

Missed most of season recovering from elbow surgery, then was shut down again in September (plantar fasciitis). With just 6 MLB IP over last two seasons, previous jaw-dropping skills are becoming a distant memory. A case where spring reports and velocity will be worth monitoring, but for now looks like a boom/bust dart throw.

Yr Tm	W	Sv	IP	K	ERA	WHIP	xERA	xWHIP	vL+	vR+	BF/G	BB%	K%	K-BB%	xBB%	SwK	Vel	G	L	F	H%	S%	HR/F	xHR/F	GS	APC	DOM%	DIS%	Sv%	LI	RAR	BPX	R$
18 aaa	8	4	60	65	5.26	1.52	5.86				6.7	9%	25%	16%							35%	71%									-8.3	71	-$2
19 2 TM	5	1	65	110	3.32	1.08	2.80	0.94	102	72	3.9	7%	42%	35%	5%	20.3%	96.1	29	30	42	38%	74%	15%	17%	0	16			20	1.19	9.5	233	$7
20 TAM	2	6	16	26	0.55	0.49	3.05	0.82	63	27	3.1	5%	45%	40%	4%	21.9%	95.2	21	7	72	17%	100%	5%	13%	0	12			100	1.55	7.9	240	$17
21 TAM	0	1	6	1	4.50	1.00	7.55		114	90	4.0	8%	4%	-4%	8%	8.8%	93.0	15	15	70	11%	75%	14%	24%	0	17			100	0.45	-0.2	-67	-$5
22 aaa	1	1	16	9	6.16	1.67	8.04				4.2	0%	0%	0%							35%	71%									-4.3	2	-$7
1st Half																																	
2nd Half	1	1	16	9	6.16	1.67	8.04				4.2	4%	13%	9%							35%	71%									-4.3	2	-$12
Proj	3	1	36	45	3.59	1.39	3.16	1.06	155	108	4.6	6%	30%	24%	5%	15.3%	96.1	29	30	42	39%	81%	16%	15%	0						1.7	165	-$2

Anderson,Tyler

Age: 33 | Th: L | Role: SP
Ht: 6' 2" | Wt: 220 | Type: Con/FB
Health: D | PT/Exp: A | Consist: B
LIMA Plan: C+ | Rand Var: -5 | MM: 2105

The perfect combination of excellent team context paired with H%, S%, and HR/F fortune, especially in 2nd half. Held 2021 BB% gains and the rest of his skills weren't all that different, save for an uptick in GB%. Sub-indicators (xBB%, SwK) say he won't completely fall off, but this feels like a trap. Heed xERA and don't pay for anything close to a repeat.

Yr Tm	W	Sv	IP	K	ERA	WHIP	xERA	xWHIP	vL+	vR+	BF/G	BB%	K%	K-BB%	xBB%	SwK	Vel	G	L	F	H%	S%	HR/F	xHR/F	GS	APC	DOM%	DIS%	Sv%	LI	RAR	BPX	R$
18 COL	7	0	176	164	4.55	1.27	4.30	1.29	113	103	23.0	8%	22%	14%	6%	12.3%	91.8	37	24	39	29%	70%	15%	10%	32	89	25%	34%			-8.7	97	$2
19 COL	0	0	21	23	11.76	2.13	5.45	1.44	154	155	21.2	10%	22%	11%	7%	11.4%	91.3	41	26	33	41%	47%	35%	32%	5	86	0%	40%			-18.5	76	-$12
20 SF	4	0	60	41	4.37	1.39	5.89	1.52	119	92	20.0	10%	16%	6%	7%	10.9%	90.2	28	27	44	29%	69%	6%	8%	11	73	9%	36%	0	0.95	0.6	18	$2
21 2 TM	7	0	167	134	4.53	1.25	4.75	1.25	96	103	22.7	5%	19%	14%	5%	12.0%	90.2	35	22	43	30%	69%	12%	11%	31	84	19%	39%			-5.4	96	$2
22 LA	15	0	179	138	2.57	1.00	3.98	1.19	90	86	23.6	5%	20%	15%	5%	12.2%	90.5	40	18	42	26%	78%	6%	7%	28	86	36%	18%	0	0.78	30.9	107	$26
1st Half	9	0	84	73	3.09	1.06	3.90	1.14	87	97	22.6	4%	22%	17%	5%	13.3%	90.3	37	20	43	29%	74%	8%	8%	13	83	38%	31%	0	0.78	9.1	123	$19
2nd Half	6	0	94	65	2.10	0.95	4.06	1.24	92	77	24.5	5%	18%	13%	5%	11.2%	90.7	43	16	41	24%	81%	5%	6%	15	88	33%	7%			21.8	92	$25
Proj	12	0	174	136	3.74	1.20	3.98	1.27	111	97	23.3	6%	19%	13%	5%	11.8%	90.5	36	21	42	29%	73%	10%	10%	29						5.0	86	$10

Antone,Tejay

Age: 29 | Th: R | Role: RP
Ht: 6' 4" | Wt: 230 | Type: Pwr
Health: F | PT/Exp: D | Consist: F
LIMA Plan: A+ | Rand Var: 0 | MM: 5510

Tommy John surgery in August 2021 kept him out all year, but he's expected to be good to go by spring. Can't bank on H%/S% continuing to cooperate and BB% history is iffy, so he's not a lock for great ratios. But pre-injury stuff was pretty electric, so with health, he could quickly jump back into late-inning mix.

Yr Tm	W	Sv	IP	K	ERA	WHIP	xERA	xWHIP	vL+	vR+	BF/G	BB%	K%	K-BB%	xBB%	SwK	Vel	G	L	F	H%	S%	HR/F	xHR/F	GS	APC	DOM%	DIS%	Sv%	LI	RAR	BPX	R$
18																																	
19 a/a	11	0	149	112	5.47	1.74	6.10				25.2	9%	16%	7%							37%	69%									-17.7	45	-$11
20 CIN	0	0	35	45	2.80	1.02	3.62	1.25	98	59	10.8	11%	32%	21%	9%	13.2%	95.7	49	10	41	23%	78%	13%	12%	4	46	0%	25%	0	0.77	7.2	139	$5
21 CIN	2	3	34	42	2.14	0.89	2.98	1.17	77	59	5.6	10%	33%	23%	6%	13.6%	96.8	47	21	31	21%	81%	14%	18%	0	23			43	1.54	8.8	146	$4
22																																	
1st Half																																	
2nd Half																																	
Proj	2	2	58	70	3.52	1.19	3.05	1.20	117	79	8.8	10%	30%	20%	8%	13.4%	96.4	48	17	35	29%	75%	15%	16%	0						3.2	140	$1

BRIAN RUDD

Archer,Chris

Age: 34	Th: R	Role: SP	Health: F	LIMA Plan: C+
Ht: 6' 2"	Wt: 195	Type:	PT/Exp: D	Rand Var: -2
			Consist: A	MM: 2201

Fifth straight season with time spent on IL; this time a July hip injury and September pectoral issue. He didn't go more than five frames in a single start and 1st half success was a H%/S%-driven fluke, as SwK and K-BB% both nosedived. Looks like a poor bet from both a health and skills perspective, so all signs point to another negative R$.

Yr	Tm	W	Sv	IP	K	ERA	WHIP	xERA	xWHIP	vL+	vR+	BF/G	BB%	K%	K-BB%	xBB%	SwK	Vel	G	L	F	H%	S%	HR/F	xHR/F	GS	APC	DOM%	DIS%	Sv%	LI	RAR	BPX	R$
18	2 TM	6	0	148	162	4.31	1.38	3.71	1.22	110	103	23.6	8%	25%	18%	7%	13.4%	94.7	45	23	32	35%	72%	14%	14%	27	93	26%	33%			-2.9	138	$0
19	PIT	3	0	120	143	5.19	1.41	4.47	1.34	105	106	22.9	10%	27%	17%	8%	13.3%	94.1	36	24	39	31%	69%	20%	19%	23	91	17%	39%			-10.1	104	-$4
20																																		
21	TAM	1	0	19	21	4.66	1.34	4.83	1.31	73	111	13.8	10%	25%	16%	8%	12.8%	92.0	31	17	52	31%	70%	11%	17%	5	55	0%	20%	0	0.82	-0.9	93	-$5
22	MIN	2	0	103	84	4.56	1.31	4.53	1.45	92	105	17.5	11%	19%	8%	10%	9.9%	93.1	44	19	37	27%	67%	11%	10%	25	71	8%	40%			-7.5	45	-$5
1st Half		2	0	61	47	3.08	1.26	4.86	1.50	93	98	17.5	11%	18%	6%	11%	10.1%	93.1	39	19	41	24%	81%	11%	10%	15	71	7%	33%			6.7	25	$1
2nd Half		0	0	41	37	6.75	1.40	4.03	1.38	91	114	17.5	10%	21%	11%	9%	9.7%	93.0	50	19	31	31%	50%	11%	9%	10	72	10%	50%			-14.2	74	-$16
Proj		**4**	**0**	**102**	**87**	**4.72**	**1.38**	**4.09**	**1.43**	**100**	**105**	**21.0**	**11%**	**20%**	**10%**	**9%**	**10.7%**	**93.6**	**44**	**21**	**35**	**29%**	**68%**	**13%**	**12%**	**20**						**-9.4**	**58**	**-$5**

Ashby,Aaron

Age: 25	Th: L	Role: SP	Health: D	LIMA Plan: B
Ht: 6' 2"	Wt: 181	Type: Pwr/GB	PT/Exp: C	Rand Var: +5
			Consist: A	MM: 5403

Some H%, HR/F misfortune masked strong skills and inflated ratios well above xERA/xWHIP. A few yellow flags—SwK and elite GB% dipped in 2nd half; high BB% but xBB% says it's fixable; hit IL twice (forearm, shoulder) and went past 5 IP in just six starts. But this strikeout/ground ball profile can take the next step... UP: 3.25 ERA, 180 K.

Yr	Tm	W	Sv	IP	K	ERA	WHIP	xERA	xWHIP	vL+	vR+	BF/G	BB%	K%	K-BB%	xBB%	SwK	Vel	G	L	F	H%	S%	HR/F	xHR/F	GS	APC	DOM%	DIS%	Sv%	LI	RAR	BPX	R$
18																																		
19																																		
20																																		
21	MIL *	8	1	96	127	4.42	1.30	3.55	1.19	121	76	11.6	11%	32%	22%	6%	13.3%	96.6	61	14	25	34%	66%	20%	20%	4	41	0%	50%	33	0.75	-1.8	134	$3
22	MIL	2	1	107	126	4.44	1.43	3.29	1.26	105	106	17.6	10%	27%	17%	8%	12.7%	95.7	57	17	26	34%	72%	20%	18%	19	70	5%	26%	100	0.73	-6.3	131	-$4
1st Half		1	1	59	73	4.60	1.47	3.02	1.26	135	95	17.3	10%	28%	18%	7%	13.4%	96.0	62	16	22	36%	72%	23%	13%	9	69	0%	33%	100	0.69	-4.6	143	-$7
2nd Half		1	0	49	53	4.25	1.38	3.60	1.27	65	120	17.9	9%	25%	15%	8%	11.9%	95.3	51	18	31	32%	73%	17%	22%	10	71	10%	20%	0	0.79	-1.7	117	-$6
Proj		**7**	**0**	**131**	**145**	**3.63**	**1.30**	**3.06**	**1.28**	**94**	**95**	**20.9**	**10%**	**27%**	**17%**	**8%**	**12.7%**	**95.8**	**57**	**16**	**27**	**31%**	**74%**	**14%**	**15%**	**26**						**5.5**	**123**	**$5**

Ashcraft,Graham

Age: 25	Th: R	Role: SP	Health: C	LIMA Plan: B
Ht: 6' 2"	Wt: 240	Type: Con/GB	PT/Exp: D	Rand Var: 0
			Consist: D	MM: 3103

5-6, 4.89 ERA in 105 IP at CIN. PRO: Brings the heat with cutter and sinker that averaged over 97 mph; kept BB% in check; GB tilt kept homers at bay. CON: Velocity didn't translate to whiffs; DOM%/DIS% split was pretty ugly. A work in progress, but top-tier velocity offers some upside worth gambling on in the end game.

Yr	Tm	W	Sv	IP	K	ERA	WHIP	xERA	xWHIP	vL+	vR+	BF/G	BB%	K%	K-BB%	xBB%	SwK	Vel	G	L	F	H%	S%	HR/F	xHR/F	GS	APC	DOM%	DIS%	Sv%	LI	RAR	BPX	R$
18																																		
19																																		
20																																		
21	aa	7	0	73	66	4.05	1.27	3.51				21.3	8%	22%	14%							31%	68%									1.9	101	$1
22	CIN *	8	0	144	106	4.56	1.52	5.01	1.33	80	126	22.4	6%	15%	9%	8%	8.9%	97.2	55	21	25	35%	70%	13%	10%	19	92	21%	53%			-10.5	67	-$7
1st Half		7	0	78	54	3.38	1.39	4.15	1.39	72	120	21.9	8%	16%	8%	6%	8.9%	97.1	55	21	24	31%	76%	14%	11%	8	88	25%	38%			5.6	69	$3
2nd Half		1	0	69	52	5.80	1.65	5.82	1.33	86	130	23.6	7%	17%	10%	8%	8.9%	97.3	54	20	25	38%	64%	12%	10%	11	96	18%	64%			-15.5	65	-$19
Proj		**8**	**0**	**145**	**106**	**4.11**	**1.41**	**3.75**	**1.35**	**76**	**117**	**23.3**	**7%**	**17%**	**10%**	**8%**	**10.1%**	**97.2**	**55**	**21**	**25**	**33%**	**72%**	**11%**	**10%**	**26**						**-2.5**	**81**	**-$1**

Assad,Javier

Age: 25	Th: R	Role: SP	Health: A	LIMA Plan: C
Ht: 6' 1"	Wt: 200	Type: Con	PT/Exp: D	Rand Var: -5
			Consist: F	MM: 1101

2-2, 3.11 ERA in 38 IP at CHC. Showed improvement at AA/AAA and ERA stayed solid after August call-up. It didn't come with support from skills though (5.08 xERA), as he got plenty of help from S%, and the weak K-BB% is troubling. Without prospect pedigree on his side, odds are against this small-sample success carrying into 2023.

Yr	Tm	W	Sv	IP	K	ERA	WHIP	xERA	xWHIP	vL+	vR+	BF/G	BB%	K%	K-BB%	xBB%	SwK	Vel	G	L	F	H%	S%	HR/F	xHR/F	GS	APC	DOM%	DIS%	Sv%	LI	RAR	BPX	R$
18																																		
19																																		
20																																		
21	aa	4	0	94	62	5.98	1.69	6.39				19.3	8%	15%	7%							36%	66%									-19.8	32	-$16
22	CHC *	7	0	149	121	2.62	1.27	3.69	1.53	124	81	19.1	12%	18%	6%	10%	10.1%	92.6	39	22	40	30%	83%	9%	9%	8	77	0%	50%	0	0.71	24.8	84	$10
1st Half		4	0	73	61	2.25	1.29	3.65				20.1	8%	20%	12%							31%	85%	0%		0	0					15.6	91	$9
2nd Half		3	0	76	60	2.89	1.23	3.60	1.34	124	81	18.1	8%	19%	11%	10%	10.1%	92.6	39	22	40	28%	80%	9%	9%	8	77	0%	50%	0	0.71	10.1	79	$7
Proj		**4**	**0**	**102**	**75**	**4.46**	**1.41**	**4.39**	**1.45**	**137**	**90**	**21.2**	**10%**	**17%**	**8%**		**10.1%**	**92.6**	**39**	**22**	**40**	**30%**	**71%**	**11%**	**10%**	**20**						**-6.2**	**41**	**-$5**

Baker,Bryan

Age: 28	Th: R	Role: RP	Health: A	LIMA Plan: A+
Ht: 6' 6"	Wt: 245	Type: Pwr	PT/Exp: D	Rand Var: -2
			Consist: D	MM: 4311

Had the look of a low-leverage arm who wouldn't make the cut for this book for much of the 1st half. Then came big velocity increase and a jump in change-up usage that fueled SwK and K% surges, while also flashing improved BB%. He now looks like an intriguing reliever to speculate on in deeper leagues... UP: 20 Sv.

Yr	Tm	W	Sv	IP	K	ERA	WHIP	xERA	xWHIP	vL+	vR+	BF/G	BB%	K%	K-BB%	xBB%	SwK	Vel	G	L	F	H%	S%	HR/F	xHR/F	GS	APC	DOM%	DIS%	Sv%	LI	RAR	BPX	R$
18																																		
19	a/a	3	12	54	58	4.58	1.58	4.06				4.8	17%	24%	8%							30%	71%									-0.5	84	$2
20																																		
21	TOR *	6	11	43	38	1.85	1.03	1.65			66	4.1	11%	23%	11%		21.1%	94.9	0	33	67	22%	83%	0%	0%	0	19			85	0.01	12.8	111	$10
22	BAL	4	1	70	76	3.49	1.23	3.60	1.23	90	85	4.4	9%	26%	17%	9%	11.4%	96.3	42	22	35	32%	71%	5%	6%	2	18	0%	50%	33	1.02	4.1	117	$2
1st Half		3	0	33	31	4.59	1.35	4.08	1.32	106	89	4.8	9%	22%	13%	10%	10.6%	95.2	41	25	34	33%	64%	3%	6%	2	19	0%	50%	0	1.24	-2.6	83	-$6
2nd Half		1	1	36	45	2.48	1.13	3.19	1.15	70	83	4.1	9%	30%	22%	8%	12.2%	97.4	44	20	37	31%	79%	6%	6%	0	17			50	0.83	6.7	149	$1
Proj		**4**	**2**	**65**	**70**	**3.56**	**1.16**	**3.30**	**1.23**	**87**	**85**	**4.2**	**9%**	**27%**	**18%**	**8%**	**11.6%**	**96.5**	**43**	**22**	**36**	**29%**	**72%**	**10%**	**9%**	**0**						**3.3**	**119**	**$3**

Bard,Daniel

Age: 38	Th: R	Role: RP	Health: A	LIMA Plan: C+
Ht: 6' 4"	Wt: 215	Type: Pwr	PT/Exp: A	Rand Var: -5
			Consist: B	MM: 4330

Unleashed sinker-heavy approach that led to a jump in GB% and a nudge up in K%. Overall it worked, with xERA improving significantly and ERA/WHIP by much more than that thanks to trifecta of good fortune (H%/S%, HR/F). Certainly can't expect another sub-2.00 ERA, but at 38, at least a 50-50 bet to hold ninth-inning gig for another year.

Yr	Tm	W	Sv	IP	K	ERA	WHIP	xERA	xWHIP	vL+	vR+	BF/G	BB%	K%	K-BB%	xBB%	SwK	Vel	G	L	F	H%	S%	HR/F	xHR/F	GS	APC	DOM%	DIS%	Sv%	LI	RAR	BPX	R$
18																																		
19																																		
20	COL	4	6	25	27	3.65	1.30	4.08	1.30	109	72	4.6	9%	25%	16%	6%	12.9%	97.1	48	17	35	32%	73%	9%	12%	0	18			100	1.42	2.4	118	$12
21	COL	7	20	66	80	5.21	1.60	4.22	1.37	139	77	4.5	12%	26%	14%	8%	13.4%	97.5	42	26	31	37%	69%	14%	10%	0	18			71	1.07	-7.6	92	$3
22	COL	6	34	60	69	1.79	0.99	3.18	1.25	78	63	4.3	10%	28%	18%	8%	11.8%	98.0	52	18	30	24%	84%	7%	9%	0	17			92	1.56	16.2	126	$23
1st Half		3	16	31	38	2.05	1.01	3.10	1.28	81	70	4.3	12%	30%	18%	8%	12.6%	97.9	55	13	32	21%	86%	14%	10%	0	17			89	1.60	7.2	127	$17
2nd Half		3	18	30	31	1.52	0.98	3.26	1.21	75	56	4.3	8%	26%	18%	7%	10.9%	98.1	49	23	28	27%	83%	0%	8%	0	16			95	1.53	9.0	126	$20
Proj		**6**	**32**	**58**	**60**	**3.43**	**1.24**	**3.30**	**1.30**	**109**	**78**	**4.4**	**10%**	**25%**	**15%**	**8%**	**12.0%**	**97.9**	**49**	**21**	**30**	**29%**	**74%**	**12%**	**10%**	**0**						**3.9**	**105**	**$15**

Barlow,Joe

Age: 27	Th: R	Role: RP	Health: D	LIMA Plan: A+
Ht: 6' 2"	Wt: 210	Type: /FB	PT/Exp: D	Rand Var: -4
			Consist: F	MM: 2210

Returned solid value in 1st half with some help (again) from friendly H%, but things quickly unraveled. Lost closer gig in early July, then lingering blister sent him to IL twice. Strong SwK suggests the K% dip was a little fluky, but H% can't stay this low over the long haul. These aren't closer-worthy skills, so take those shots elsewhere.

Yr	Tm	W	Sv	IP	K	ERA	WHIP	xERA	xWHIP	vL+	vR+	BF/G	BB%	K%	K-BB%	xBB%	SwK	Vel	G	L	F	H%	S%	HR/F	xHR/F	GS	APC	DOM%	DIS%	Sv%	LI	RAR	BPX	R$
18																																		
19	a/a	2	0	34	39	6.74	1.93	5.55				5.1	19%	24%	6%							37%	64%									-9.4	75	-$9
20																																		
21	TEX *	0	18	50	50	2.16	0.83	0.93	1.37	51	64	3.8	11%	27%	16%	7%	12.3%	94.5	38	17	46	17%	77%	6%	10%	0	15			95	0.84	13.0	130	$13
22	TEX	3	13	35	28	3.86	1.14	4.52	1.36	91	100	4.2	9%	19%	10%	7%	13.4%	94.6	37	18	45	24%	71%	11%	15%	0	16			76	0.92	0.5	60	$4
1st Half		3	13	28	22	3.18	0.99	4.44	1.28	83	93	4.1	7%	19%	12%	7%	14.6%	94.8	35	16	49	22%	75%	10%	13%	0	15			76	1.09	2.8	77	$10
2nd Half		0	0	7	6	6.75	1.80	4.87	1.70	132	119	4.6	16%	19%	3%	8%	9.2%	93.9	47	26	26	32%	64%	20%	33%	0	19			0	0.28	-2.3	-12	-$13
Proj		**3**	**2**	**51**	**45**	**3.98**	**1.31**	**4.03**	**1.34**	**108**	**122**	**4.5**	**9%**	**21%**	**12%**	**7%**	**14.6%**	**94.8**	**38**	**17**	**45**	**29%**	**74%**	**12%**	**12%**	**0**						**-0.1**	**77**	**-$2**

BRIAN RUDD

Barlow,Scott

Age: 30	Th: R	Role RP	Health A	LIMA Plan C+
Ht: 6' 3"	Wt: 210	Type Pwr	PT/Exp A	Rand Var -5
			Consist A	MM 5431

Though 1st half ERA was right in line with 2021, it included sizable dropoffs in velocity, SwK, and K%. Those mostly returned to form in 2nd half, while H%/S% luck remained on his side. Full repeat unlikely per xERA/xWHIP, but these skills are strong and consistent enough to continue locking down ninth-inning chances.

Yr Tm	W	Sv	IP	K	ERA	WHIP	xERA	xWHIP	vL+	vR+	BF/G	BB%	K%	K-BB%	xBB%	SwK	Vel	G	L	F	H%	S%	HR/F	xHR/F	GS	APC	DOM%	DIS%	Sv%	LI	RAR	BPX	R$
18 KC *	2	1	66	57	6.59	1.70	6.65	1.14	84	101	15.0	9%	19%	10%	5%	11.4%	90.6	38	26	36	37%	64%	12%	17%	0	40			50	1.33	-19.9	42	-$13
19 KC	3	1	70	92	4.22	1.44	4.19	1.35	112	88	5.1	12%	30%	18%	8%	14.8%	94.1	40	23	37	35%	72%	9%	11%	0	21			33	1.13	2.5	111	-$1
20 KC	2	2	30	39	4.20	1.20	3.31	1.10	103	85	3.9	7%	31%	24%	8%	17.2%	94.9	47	19	34	34%	69%	16%	18%	0	16			100	0.95	0.9	184	$4
21 KC	5	16	74	91	2.42	1.20	3.68	1.20	93	78	4.3	9%	30%	21%	8%	16.2%	95.4	39	23	38	32%	81%	6%	12%	0	17			73	1.26	16.9	136	$14
22 KC	7	24	74	77	2.18	1.00	3.31	1.17	86	82	4.2	8%	27%	19%	7%	14.6%	93.7	48	16	37	24%	86%	13%	11%	0	17			86	1.46	16.4	134	$20
1st Half	2	12	37	36	2.45	1.04	3.58	1.20	101	82	4.5	7%	24%	17%	6%	13.0%	93.2	45	16	38	25%	85%	14%	12%	0	18			86	1.58	6.8	121	$12
2nd Half	5	12	38	41	1.91	0.96	3.04	1.14	72	81	4.0	8%	29%	21%	8%	16.3%	94.1	50	14	36	24%	88%	13%	11%	0	17			86	1.35	9.6	147	$20
Proj	**5**	**26**	**73**	**83**	**3.02**	**1.14**	**3.10**	**1.18**	**95**	**85**	**4.3**	**8%**	**29%**	**20%**	**8%**	**15.7%**	**94.3**	**46**	**18**	**36**	**29%**	**78%**	**12%**	**13%**	**0**						**8.5**	**139**	**$16**

Barnes,Matt

Age: 33	Th: R	Role RP	Health F	LIMA Plan B
Ht: 6' 4"	Wt: 208	Type Pwr	PT/Exp B	Rand Var -3
			Consist C	MM 3420

Late 2021 struggles carried over to 1st half, then May shoulder injury knocked him out for two months. Minuscule ERA upon return as BB% was down and he got back into the saves mix, but credit goes to S% and HR/F, as K% was nowhere near previous levels. Looks like a poor bet for helpful ratios or consistent Sv opps.

Yr Tm	W	Sv	IP	K	ERA	WHIP	xERA	xWHIP	vL+	vR+	BF/G	BB%	K%	K-BB%	xBB%	SwK	Vel	G	L	F	H%	S%	HR/F	xHR/F	GS	APC	DOM%	DIS%	Sv%	LI	RAR	BPX	R$
18 BOS	6	0	62	96	3.65	1.26	2.88	1.18	88	85	4.3	12%	36%	25%	11%	14.9%	96.6	53	14	33	35%	73%	11%	15%	0	18			0	1.08	3.8	185	$3
19 BOS	5	4	64	110	3.78	1.38	3.10	1.22	84	91	4.1	13%	39%	25%	10%	15.4%	96.7	47	22	31	38%	77%	20%	15%	0	19			33	1.42	5.8	173	$4
20 BOS	1	9	23	31	4.30	1.39	3.96	1.38	68	115	4.3	14%	30%	17%	9%	11.6%	95.6	45	23	32	29%	75%	24%	27%	0	19			69	1.32	0.4	106	$8
21 BOS	6	24	55	84	3.79	1.12	3.08	1.05	80	89	3.7	9%	38%	29%	6%	15.1%	95.9	42	12	46	32%	72%	15%	14%	0	15			80	1.30	3.2	197	$14
22 BOS	0	8	40	34	4.31	1.44	4.78	1.50	98	94	4.0	12%	19%	7%	10%	11.4%	95.0	45	15	40	30%	69%	4%	10%	0	16			80	1.29	-1.7	37	-$3
1st Half	0	2	17	14	7.94	1.71	5.72	1.68	133	99	4.1	15%	17%	2%	10%	11.0%	94.6	43	15	42	31%	52%	9%	11%	0	15			67	1.57	-8.3	-18	-$15
2nd Half	0	6	23	20	1.59	1.24	4.14	1.35	76	88	4.0	9%	21%	12%	10%	11.7%	95.3	47	14	39	30%	86%	0%	9%	0	16			86	1.06	6.7	79	$0
Proj	**3**	**11**	**58**	**67**	**4.10**	**1.35**	**3.59**	**1.36**	**95**	**95**	**3.8**	**12%**	**28%**	**15%**	**9%**	**13.4%**	**95.7**	**46**	**16**	**38**	**30%**	**73%**	**13%**	**13%**	**0**						**-0.9**	**95**	**$2**

Barria,Jaime

Age: 26	Th: R	Role RP	Health A	LIMA Plan A
Ht: 6' 1"	Wt: 210	Type Con/FB	PT/Exp C	Rand Var -5
			Consist B	MM 2001

Transition to relief role worked wonders for ratios, with plenty of help from H% and S%. While SwK surge hints at potential for higher K%, the dip in velocity says that's far from guaranteed. A consistently low BB% is nice and all, but that's his strongest asset. The rest of these skills don't look ready for high-leverage role.

Yr Tm	W	Sv	IP	K	ERA	WHIP	xERA	xWHIP	vL+	vR+	BF/G	BB%	K%	K-BB%	xBB%	SwK	Vel	G	L	F	H%	S%	HR/F	xHR/F	GS	APC	DOM%	DIS%	Sv%	LI	RAR	BPX	R$
18 LAA *	10	0	147	115	3.37	1.27	4.02	1.40	84	115	19.5	8%	19%	11%	9%	10.8%	91.2	37	20	43	28%	78%	10%	11%	26	84	15%	42%			14.2	70	$9
19 LAA *	7	0	132	113	7.17	1.52	6.90	1.35	96	142	19.7	6%	20%	13%	10%	9.6%	91.7	34	19	46	33%	59%	20%	17%	13	79	0%	62%	0	0.81	-43.3	30	-$14
20 LAA	1	0	32	27	3.62	1.11	4.84	1.30	117	64	18.9	7%	20%	14%	6%	10.8%	92.1	34	21	45	27%	70%	7%	5%	5	73	20%	40%	0	0.73	3.3	90	$2
21 LAA *	5	0	106	63	4.32	1.43	5.48	1.43	116	111	19.5	6%	14%	8%	9%	8.4%	93.1	44	23	33	32%	74%	13%	12%	11	71	9%	55%	0	0.80	-0.7	42	-$5
22 LAA	3	0	79	54	2.61	1.03	4.27	1.28	111	82	9.0	6%	17%	11%	6%	11.3%	91.9	41	18	41	23%	83%	11%	14%	1	32	0%	100%	0	0.75	13.3	78	$5
1st Half	1	0	38	29	3.05	1.04	4.02	1.21	129	81	10.1	5%	19%	14%	6%	12.5%	92.1	38	22	40	24%	82%	16%	19%	0	37			0	0.50	4.3	96	-$1
2nd Half	2	0	41	25	2.20	1.02	4.50	1.35	95	83	8.2	7%	15%	9%	6%	10.2%	91.8	44	14	42	23%	84%	8%	9%	1	29	0%	100%	0	0.93	9.0	61	$2
Proj	**4**	**0**	**87**	**62**	**3.94**	**1.26**	**4.14**	**1.30**	**116**	**99**	**12.3**	**6%**	**18%**	**11%**	**7%**	**10.4%**	**92.1**	**39**	**19**	**41**	**29%**	**74%**	**11%**	**12%**	**3**						**0.3**	**77**	**-$1**

Bass,Anthony

Age: 35	Th: R	Role RP	Health B	LIMA Plan A
Ht: 6' 2"	Wt: 200	Type	PT/Exp C	Rand Var -5
			Consist B	MM 4210

Luck was on his side all year, but BPX and xERA show the skills took real step forward too. More sliders and whiffs than ever before, with SwK and K% really taking off in 2nd half, while he also trimmed the BB%. He won't be this good again, but firmly back on radar as LIMA option with an outside shot at getting back into saves mix.

Yr Tm	W	Sv	IP	K	ERA	WHIP	xERA	xWHIP	vL+	vR+	BF/G	BB%	K%	K-BB%	xBB%	SwK	Vel	G	L	F	H%	S%	HR/F	xHR/F	GS	APC	DOM%	DIS%	Sv%	LI	RAR	BPX	R$
18 CHC *	0	3	47	32	3.86	1.50	5.36	1.15	112	93	4.8	5%	16%	11%	10%	8.2%	94.1	53	27	20	36%	76%	11%	4%	0	15			60	0.69	1.7	83	-$4
19 SEA *	3	14	69	58	3.44	1.05	2.48	1.35	69	79	4.2	9%	22%	13%	9%	11.4%	95.4	52	21	28	23%	70%	14%	17%	0	17			64	1.28	9.1	93	$10
20 TOR	2	7	26	21	3.51	1.01	4.04	1.36	58	85	3.8	9%	21%	12%	10%	11.9%	94.7	62	4	33	23%	67%	9%	7%	0	15			78	1.45	3.0	99	$12
21 MIA	3	0	61	58	3.82	1.29	4.31	1.34	139	72	3.7	9%	22%	13%	7%	12.2%	95.4	44	22	34	28%	78%	18%	16%	1	14	0%	100%	0	1.09	3.4	88	-$1
22 2 TM	4	0	70	73	1.54	1.01	3.44	1.16	105	66	3.8	7%	27%	19%	6%	14.9%	95.3	41	21	38	26%	91%	9%	9%	0	14			0	1.16	21.1	130	$9
1st Half	1	0	34	30	1.60	1.01	3.86	1.15	95	71	3.9	5%	23%	17%	5%	12.7%	95.2	36	21	43	29%	85%	2%	6%	0	13			0	1.35	9.8	119	$2
2nd Half	3	0	37	43	1.47	1.01	3.03	1.17	115	62	3.6	9%	30%	21%	7%	16.9%	95.4	47	21	33	24%	97%	18%	12%	0	14			0	1.00	11.3	142	$7
Proj	**3**	**2**	**58**	**55**	**3.18**	**1.18**	**3.43**	**1.25**	**117**	**78**	**4.0**	**8%**	**24%**	**16%**	**7%**	**13.7%**	**95.4**	**45**	**21**	**34**	**28%**	**78%**	**13%**	**12%**	**0**						**5.6**	**110**	**$2**

Bassitt,Chris

Age: 34	Th: R	Role SP	Health B	LIMA Plan B
Ht: 6' 5"	Wt: 217	Type	PT/Exp A	Rand Var -4
			Consist A	MM 4205

Set career-high in IP as previous injury issues faded further in rearview—only IL stints the last three years have been liner off head and COVID. While K% jumped around, SwK and velocity held steady all year with yet another solid BPX. There's probably not another level, but a good bet to post similar numbers for at least one more year.

Yr Tm	W	Sv	IP	K	ERA	WHIP	xERA	xWHIP	vL+	vR+	BF/G	BB%	K%	K-BB%	xBB%	SwK	Vel	G	L	F	H%	S%	HR/F	xHR/F	GS	APC	DOM%	DIS%	Sv%	LI	RAR	BPX	R$
18 OAK *	7	0	131	101	4.68	1.51	4.89	1.39	79	93	19.6	8%	18%	10%	8%	7.2%	92.0	45	22	34	34%	69%	9%	12%	7	73	14%	43%	0	0.69	-8.6	71	-$6
19 OAK	10	0	144	141	3.81	1.19	4.42	1.30	92	93	21.9	8%	23%	15%	7%	9.3%	93.5	41	21	38	28%	74%	14%	13%	25	87	24%	36%	0	0.71	12.3	107	$11
20 OAK	5	0	63	55	2.29	1.16	4.46	1.27	104	78	23.7	7%	21%	15%	7%	10.4%	92.9	44	18	38	29%	85%	9%	11%	11	86	27%	18%			16.8	111	$20
21 OAK	12	0	157	159	3.15	1.06	3.81	1.16	85	85	23.6	6%	25%	19%	6%	10.8%	93.0	42	20	38	28%	74%	9%	10%	27	88	44%	15%			21.7	135	$21
22 NYM	15	0	182	167	3.42	1.14	3.58	1.20	105	83	24.8	7%	22%	16%	6%	10.4%	92.9	49	17	34	29%	74%	11%	12%	30	96	37%	17%			12.3	122	$17
1st Half	6	0	90	95	4.01	1.15	3.51	1.16	117	78	24.6	7%	26%	19%	7%	10.4%	92.9	46	16	38	29%	70%	14%	13%	15	98	33%	7%			-0.5	138	$10
2nd Half	9	0	92	72	2.84	1.14	3.66	1.25	94	87	25.1	6%	19%	13%	6%	10.3%	93.0	51	18	30	29%	77%	7%	10%	15	95	40%	27%			12.8	105	$20
Proj	**13**	**0**	**174**	**158**	**3.51**	**1.18**	**3.47**	**1.22**	**101**	**87**	**23.0**	**7%**	**23%**	**16%**	**7%**	**10.6%**	**93.0**	**46**	**19**	**35**	**30%**	**73%**	**10%**	**11%**	**30**						**9.9**	**115**	**$14**

Bautista,Félix

Age: 28	Th: R	Role RP	Health A	LIMA Plan B+
Ht: 6' 5"	Wt: 190	Type Pwr	PT/Exp D	Rand Var -5
			Consist C	MM 5531

Impressive 1st half skills turned downright filthy in 2nd half as saves came in bunches. Hit triple-digits with regularity and missed bats at ridiculous clip, all while throwing more strikes (xBB%). Sure, H% was on his side and track record is short, but skills point to more success with chance to emerge as top-tier closer. UP: 40 saves

Yr Tm	W	Sv	IP	K	ERA	WHIP	xERA	xWHIP	vL+	vR+	BF/G	BB%	K%	K-BB%	xBB%	SwK	Vel	G	L	F	H%	S%	HR/F	xHR/F	GS	APC	DOM%	DIS%	Sv%	LI	RAR	BPX	R$
18																																	
19																																	
20																																	
21 a/a	1	9	33	37	1.95	1.08	1.47				4.5	16%	29%	12%							20%	83%									9.5	127	$4
22 BAL	4	15	66	88	2.19	0.93	2.86	1.09	75	76	3.9	9%	35%	26%	7%	15.9%	99.2	43	18	39	24%	83%	13%	10%	0	15			88	1.48	14.4	169	$15
1st Half	3	2	33	41	1.89	1.05	3.30	1.15	98	76	3.7	9%	31%	22%	8%	14.7%	98.7	38	21	41	26%	90%	13%	11%	0	15			67	1.51	8.5	141	$6
2nd Half	1	13	32	47	2.51	0.80	2.41	1.02	44	75	4.2	9%	39%	30%	6%	17.3%	100.0	48	15	37	21%	74%	13%	8%	0	15			93	1.44	5.8	198	$15
Proj	**3**	**25**	**65**	**81**	**2.90**	**1.05**	**2.95**	**1.18**	**77**	**84**	**4.3**	**10%**	**32%**	**22%**	**6%**	**16.2%**	**99.5**	**44**	**17**	**39**	**26%**	**78%**	**13%**	**11%**	**0**						**8.6**	**143**	**$16**

Baz,Shane

Age: 24	Th: R	Role RP	Health F	LIMA Plan B
Ht: 6' 2"	Wt: 190	Type Pwr	PT/Exp D	Rand Var +4
			Consist D	MM 5500

Minor elbow procedure in spring kept him out until June, then briefly put electric stuff on display before going down again. Eventually had Tommy John surgery in September that should keep him out for 2023. No appeal in redraft leagues, but prime target for dynasty rebuild, as he's been one of the top pitching prospects in the game.

Yr Tm	W	Sv	IP	K	ERA	WHIP	xERA	xWHIP	vL+	vR+	BF/G	BB%	K%	K-BB%	xBB%	SwK	Vel	G	L	F	H%	S%	HR/F	xHR/F	GS	APC	DOM%	DIS%	Sv%	LI	RAR	BPX	R$
18																																	
19																																	
20																																	
21 TAM *	7	0	94	119	2.24	0.82	2.11	0.96	115	48	17.0	5%	35%	30%	6%	16.7%	97.0	43	11	46	25%	83%	23%	17%	3	66	33%	33%			23.4	234	$19
22 TAM	1	0	27	30	5.00	1.33	3.62	1.19	88	120	19.5	8%	26%	18%	8%	13.7%	96.0	43	23	34	32%	68%	19%	15%	6	74	33%	33%			-3.4	132	-$5
1st Half	1	0	25	28	2.92	1.14	3.35	1.20	78	90	20.2	9%	28%	19%	9%	13.6%	96.0	44	22	33	29%	77%	10%	14%	5	78	40%	20%			3.2	130	-$4
2nd Half	0	0	2	2	27.00	3.43	6.64		179	257	16.0	0%	13%	13%	4%	15.1%	96.1	36	29	36	52%	20%	60%	20%	1	53	0%	100%			-6.6	168	-$16
Proj	**1**	**0**	**15**	**17**	**2.64**	**1.01**	**2.70**	**1.10**	**81**	**93**	**18.5**	**8%**	**31%**	**24%**	**9%**	**13.6%**	**96.0**	**44**	**22**	**33**	**28%**	**79%**	**14%**	**12%**	**3**						**2.4**	**160**	**-$3**

BRIAN RUDD

Bednar,David

Age: 28	Th: R	Role RP	Health D	LIMA Plan B+
Ht: 6' 1"	Wt: 245	Type Pwr/FB	PT/Exp C	Rand Var -2
			Consist D	MM 5531

Two-month IL stint (back) was all that prevented him from hitting last year's "UP: 30 Sv". Held mostly all of the 2021 gains that led us to that call with plenty of whiffs and primo velocity to back elite K%, an xBB% that hints at even better control, and back-to-back elite BPX. Everything seems in place for a jump to upper-tier closer status.

Yr	Tm	W	Sv	IP	K	ERA	WHIP	xERA	xWHIP	vL+	vR+	BF/G	BB%	K%	K-BB%	xBB%	SwK	Vel	G	L	F	H%	S%	HR/F	xHR/F	GS	APC	DOM%	DIS%	Sv%	LI	RAR	BPX	R$
18																																		
19	SD *	2	14	69	83	4.30	1.37	4.31	1.31	107	129	5.1	9%	29%	20%	8%	14.8%	95.3	30	22	48	36%	71%	23%	16%	0	15			93	0.62	1.8	118	$5
20	SD	0	0	6	5	7.11	2.05	6.20	1.37	135	129	8.0	6%	16%	9%	6%	13.6%	95.8	36	24	40	44%	67%	10%	17%	0	30			0	0.25	-2.1	74	-$10
21	PIT	3	3	61	77	2.23	0.97	3.26	1.10	73	81	3.9	8%	32%	24%	5%	17.0%	96.8	41	20	39	27%	81%	9%	9%	0	15			60	0.82	15.3	163	$9
22	PIT	3	19	52	69	2.61	1.12	3.12	1.06	78	94	4.7	8%	33%	25%	6%	16.0%	96.5	33	27	40	33%	80%	8%	10%	0	19			83	1.32	8.6	168	$11
1st Half		3	13	38	51	2.37	1.00	3.12	1.06	80	81	4.9	8%	34%	26%	6%	16.4%	96.6	32	24	44	29%	80%	8%	10%	0	19			81	1.33	7.5	166	$17
2nd Half		0	6	14	18	3.29	1.46	3.11	1.07	73	126	4.2	7%	31%	24%	5%	15.2%	96.1	36	33	31	42%	79%	9%	6%	0	17			86	1.30	1.1	173	-$4
Proj		**3**	**29**	**65**	**80**	**2.59**	**1.08**	**3.04**	**1.11**	**83**	**88**	**4.7**	**8%**	**31%**	**24%**	**6%**	**16.6%**	**96.7**	**36**	**22**	**42**	**30%**	**79%**	**8%**	**10%**	**0**						**11.1**	**151**	**$17**

Beeks,Jalen

Age: 29	Th: L	Role RP	Health F	LIMA Plan A+
Ht: 5' 11"	Wt: 215	Type Pwr	PT/Exp D	Rand Var -2
			Consist A	MM 5401

Successful return from August 2020 Tommy John surgery, as more zip on heater drove SwK jump (ignoring 19 IP from short season) and change-up produced grounders in bunches (62% GB%). Shaky control returned, however, and xERA/ERA gap questions repeat. He'll be effective, but look for more than "effective" when throwing late closer darts.

Yr	Tm	W	Sv	IP	K	ERA	WHIP	xERA	xWHIP	vL+	vR+	BF/G	BB%	K%	K-BB%	xBB%	SwK	Vel	G	L	F	H%	S%	HR/F	xHR/F	GS	APC	DOM%	DIS%	Sv%	LI	RAR	BPX	R$
18	2 AL *	10	0	139	134	4.73	1.41	4.75	1.48	80	120	19.6	9%	23%	14%	10%	11.9%	91.8	47	21	32	33%	69%	13%	11%	1	63	0%	100%	0	0.88	-9.9	81	-$2
19	TAM	6	1	104	89	4.31	1.49	4.79	1.41	114	102	14.1	9%	19%	11%	8%	10.2%	92.2	46	24	31	33%	73%	12%	14%	3	55	0%	67%	100	0.77	2.5	75	-$1
20	TAM	1	1	19	26	3.26	1.29	3.11	1.01	89	95	6.8	5%	32%	27%	4%	17.6%	93.1	43	27	31	41%	75%	7%	3%	0	27			100	1.16	2.8	213	$0
21																																		
22	TAM	2	2	61	70	2.80	1.16	3.31	1.19	108	90	6.0	9%	28%	19%	8%	14.6%	95.1	46	21	34	29%	81%	13%	15%	7	24	0%	71%	33	0.89	8.8	135	$3
1st Half		1	0	35	43	2.55	1.10	3.20	1.14	108	86	6.8	8%	30%	22%	7%	14.9%	95.0	48	13	40	28%	85%	15%	16%	5	27	0%	60%	0	0.94	6.2	155	$0
2nd Half		1	2	26	27	3.16	1.25	3.47	1.27	108	94	5.1	9%	25%	16%	10%	14.2%	95.2	43	30	26	31%	77%	11%	13%	2	20	0%	100%	50	1.04	2.6	107	-$3
Proj		**3**	**0**	**73**	**84**	**3.45**	**1.25**	**3.12**	**1.21**	**99**	**95**	**7.6**	**9%**	**28%**	**19%**	**9%**	**14.5%**	**93.8**	**46**	**23**	**32**	**32%**	**75%**	**13%**	**13%**	**0**						**4.7**	**132**	**$2**

Bellatti,Andrew

Age: 31	Th: R	Role RP	Health A	LIMA Plan A+
Ht: 6' 1"	Wt: 190	Type Pwr/xFB	PT/Exp D	Rand Var 0
			Consist C	MM 2510

Journeyman's long, winding road finally led to extended MLB stay; even picked up a pair of saves. Some legit swing-and-miss led to excellent K%, but already-dicey control unraveled in 2nd half and those extra runners are a risky mix for an xFBer. A cool story, but next chapter probably doesn't include much fantasy relevance.

Yr	Tm	W	Sv	IP	K	ERA	WHIP	xERA	xWHIP	vL+	vR+	BF/G	BB%	K%	K-BB%	xBB%	SwK	Vel	G	L	F	H%	S%	HR/F	xHR/F	GS	APC	DOM%	DIS%	Sv%	LI	RAR	BPX	R$
18																																		
19	aa	2	0	32	21	7.59	1.70	6.98				6.9	7%	14%	8%							35%	57%									-12.2	16	-$9
20																																		
21	MIA *	1	11	39	35	2.79	1.12	2.51		106	123	4.6	10%	23%	12%		13.3%	94.4	31	38	31	25%	77%	0%	6%	0	28			79	0.14	7.0	102	$4
22	PHI	4	2	54	78	3.31	1.33	3.58	1.17	125	85	3.9	11%	34%	23%	10%	16.6%	94.4	27	23	50	36%	78%	8%	11%	1	16	0%	100%	67	0.87	4.4	139	$1
1st Half		1	1	28	41	3.25	1.19	3.50	1.09	137	76	3.7	10%	36%	26%	9%	15.1%	94.4	25	18	57	31%	82%	14%	15%	0	16			100	0.90	2.4	161	-$3
2nd Half		3	1	27	37	3.38	1.46	3.67	1.25	110	93	4.1	12%	32%	20%	10%	18.2%	94.5	30	27	43	40%	74%	0%	6%	1	17	0%	100%	50	0.84	2.0	116	-$2
Proj		**4**	**2**	**58**	**74**	**4.30**	**1.49**	**3.88**	**1.30**	**133**	**93**	**4.6**	**12%**	**30%**	**18%**	**10%**	**15.0%**	**94.4**	**28**	**23**	**49**	**36%**	**73%**	**8%**	**10%**	**0**						**-2.4**	**98**	**-$2**

Bello,Brayan

Age: 24	Th: R	Role SP	Health B	LIMA Plan A
Ht: 6' 1"	Wt: 170	Type Pwr/GB	PT/Exp D	Rand Var -2
			Consist C	MM 5305

2-8, 4.71 ERA in 57 IP at BOS. Tore through upper minors with 2.33 ERA through 15 starts, but success didn't translate after July call-up. Elite GB% should keep ERA in check, but posted average SwK and K% in majors, iffy control, and far more DISaster than DOMinant starts. Pedigree, age make him a decent late-round flyer, but there's work to do.

Yr	Tm	W	Sv	IP	K	ERA	WHIP	xERA	xWHIP	vL+	vR+	BF/G	BB%	K%	K-BB%	xBB%	SwK	Vel	G	L	F	H%	S%	HR/F	xHR/F	GS	APC	DOM%	DIS%	Sv%	LI	RAR	BPX	R$
18																																		
19																																		
20																																		
21	aa	2	0	65	75	5.09	1.46	4.61				18.6	8%	27%	19%							38%	65%									-6.6	121	-$7
22	BOS *	12	0	156	162	3.25	1.31	3.38	1.39	111	116	20.7	10%	21%	10%	9%	11.8%	96.6	56	21	23	33%	75%	2%	9%	11	77	9%	55%	0	0.70	13.8	118	$10
1st Half		10	0	87	95	2.37	1.03	2.13				22.4	9%	28%	19%							26%	79%	0%		0	0					17.2	135	$28
2nd Half		2	0	71	67	4.22	1.62	4.72	1.35	110	116	19.6	10%	21%	12%	9%	11.8%	96.6	56	21	23	39%	72%	2%	9%	11	77	9%	55%	0	0.70	-2.2	100	-$9
Proj		**9**	**0**	**174**	**171**	**3.78**	**1.26**	**3.09**	**1.28**	**99**	**91**	**20.5**	**9%**	**24%**	**15%**		**11.8%**	**96.6**	**56**	**21**	**23**	**31%**	**70%**	**10%**	**8%**	**35**						**4.1**	**114**	**$8**

Berríos,José

Age: 29	Th: R	Role SP	Health A	LIMA Plan B
Ht: 6' 0"	Wt: 205	Type	PT/Exp A	Rand Var +2
			Consist B	MM 3305

That collective groan you just heard came from anyone who touched him in 2022, as this was an ugly confluence of lesser skills (career-low K-BB%, SwK) and bad luck (H%/S%, ERA/xERA gap). The latter should correct itself, while track record hints at some hope for the former. Still a volume stud, but per-inning productivity is in peril.

Yr	Tm	W	Sv	IP	K	ERA	WHIP	xERA	xWHIP	vL+	vR+	BF/G	BB%	K%	K-BB%	xBB%	SwK	Vel	G	L	F	H%	S%	HR/F	xHR/F	GS	APC	DOM%	DIS%	Sv%	LI	RAR	BPX	R$
18	MIN	12	0	192	202	3.84	1.14	3.79	1.22	93	91	24.9	8%	25%	18%	8%	11.7%	93.2	42	20	38	28%	71%	13%	11%	32	96	38%	25%			7.4	130	$16
19	MIN	14	0	200	195	3.68	1.22	4.30	1.23	93	95	26.3	6%	23%	17%	6%	11.5%	92.8	42	21	37	31%	74%	12%	14%	32	98	25%	25%			20.3	126	$17
20	MIN	5	0	63	68	4.00	1.32	4.34	1.32	98	92	22.6	10%	25%	15%	8%	12.3%	94.3	40	24	36	31%	73%	13%	15%	12	92	17%	42%			3.5	105	$10
21	2 AL	12	0	192	204	3.52	1.06	3.54	1.12	109	72	24.4	6%	26%	20%	6%	10.2%	94.0	43	23	34	29%	71%	13%	16%	32	95	44%	16%			17.8	149	$22
22	TOR	12	0	172	149	5.23	1.42	4.27	1.23	124	104	23.5	6%	20%	14%	6%	9.9%	94.0	40	20	40	34%	67%	13%	14%	32	85	22%	41%			-26.8	104	-$7
1st Half		6	0	83	67	5.72	1.43	4.44	1.26	133	109	22.9	6%	18%	12%	6%	9.3%	93.7	39	22	39	32%	65%	16%	17%	16	82	25%	50%			-18.0	92	-$11
2nd Half		6	0	89	82	4.77	1.41	4.11	1.20	118	96	24.1	6%	21%	15%	6%	10.5%	94.2	42	18	41	35%	69%	11%	10%	16	88	19%	31%			-8.8	117	-$2
Proj		**12**	**0**	**174**	**168**	**4.31**	**1.28**	**3.59**	**1.22**	**109**	**92**	**22.8**	**7%**	**24%**	**16%**	**6%**	**10.7%**	**93.9**	**41**	**21**	**38**	**31%**	**70%**	**13%**	**14%**	**31**						**-7.3**	**115**	**$6**

Bickford,Phil

Age: 27	Th: R	Role RP	Health A	LIMA Plan B
Ht: 6' 4"	Wt: 200	Type /FB	PT/Exp C	Rand Var +3
			Consist A	MM 4301

Remember this name the next time you head out for trivia—he gave up Albert Pujols' 700th home run. Seems stuck in lower-leverage role given mediocre whiff rate and FB% tilt. However, H%/S% correction might lead to slightly better ratios, and xERA, bb% hold some optimism that he won't just be linked with Mike Bacsik and Al Downing.

Yr	Tm	W	Sv	IP	K	ERA	WHIP	xERA	xWHIP	vL+	vR+	BF/G	BB%	K%	K-BB%	xBB%	SwK	Vel	G	L	F	H%	S%	HR/F	xHR/F	GS	APC	DOM%	DIS%	Sv%	LI	RAR	BPX	R$
18																																		
19																																		
20	MIL	0	0	1	2	36.00	4.00	3.75		173	195	9.0	0%	22%	22%		15.2%	89.4	0	80	20	83%	0%	0%	2%	0	33			0	0.10	-3.9	341	-$10
21	2 NL	4	1	51	59	2.81	1.07	3.54	1.22	102	77	3.6	9%	29%	19%	6%	13.9%	93.9	47	18	35	25%	81%	16%	14%	0	14			33	0.72	9.2	133	$4
22	LA	2	0	61	67	4.72	1.10	3.64	1.09	108	101	4.1	6%	27%	21%	5%	11.5%	94.2	37	15	48	28%	64%	16%	15%	0	17			0	0.52	-5.7	151	-$2
1st Half		0	0	27	22	4.73	1.05	3.78	1.08	112	100	3.7	3%	21%	18%	5%	10.6%	93.6	42	13	45	27%	61%	14%	13%	0	15			0	0.49	-2.5	140	-$8
2nd Half		2	0	34	45	4.72	1.14	3.53	1.09	104	100	4.5	8%	31%	24%	5%	12.2%	94.6	33	17	51	29%	66%	17%	16%	0	18			0	0.55	-3.2	160	-$4
Proj		**3**	**0**	**65**	**66**	**3.96**	**1.12**	**3.43**	**1.16**	**111**	**100**	**4.1**	**6%**	**26%**	**19%**	**5%**	**12.0%**	**94.1**	**39**	**16**	**46**	**28%**	**72%**	**15%**	**14%**	**0**						**0.0**	**130**	**$0**

Bieber,Shane

Age: 28	Th: R	Role SP	Health D	LIMA Plan C+
Ht: 6' 3"	Wt: 200	Type	PT/Exp A	Rand Var -1
			Consist A	MM 5305

Put 2021 shoulder problems behind him with strong R$ rebound. Got there via a slightly different path, countering velocity drop with more sliders (23% SwK), more strikes (xBB%), more ground balls, and more innings. Gaudy strikeout rate likely gone as SwK went from "great" to "good", but xERA/xWHIP stability like this is hard to find. Still an anchor.

Yr	Tm	W	Sv	IP	K	ERA	WHIP	xERA	xWHIP	vL+	vR+	BF/G	BB%	K%	K-BB%	xBB%	SwK	Vel	G	L	F	H%	S%	HR/F	xHR/F	GS	APC	DOM%	DIS%	Sv%	LI	RAR	BPX	R$
18	CLE *	17	0	196	183	3.45	1.16	3.64	1.12	124	91	23.6	4%	23%	19%	6%	11.8%	93.1	47	22	31	33%	73%	12%	16%	19	90	42%	21%	0	0.79	16.9	178	$19
19	CLE	15	0	214	259	3.28	1.05	3.34	1.05	90	86	25.3	5%	30%	25%	6%	14.3%	93.1	44	21	35	31%	76%	16%	18%	33	98	48%	9%	0	0.76	32.5	188	$30
20	CLE	8	0	77	122	1.63	0.87	2.34	0.93	58	75	24.8	7%	41%	34%	8%	18.0%	94.2	48	22	30	29%	88%	15%	19%	12	103	67%	0%			26.9	244	$48
21	CLE	7	0	97	134	3.17	1.21	3.11	1.09	105	78	25.3	8%	33%	25%	7%	16.6%	92.8	44	24	32	34%	78%	15%	18%	16	97	38%	6%			13.1	179	$9
22	CLE	13	0	200	198	2.88	1.04	3.15	1.08	85	88	25.5	5%	25%	20%	6%	14.1%	91.3	48	20	31	30%	76%	10%	12%	31	93	48%	10%			26.9	157	$25
1st Half		3	0	91	93	3.16	1.16	3.41	1.13	84	99	24.5	6%	25%	19%	6%	13.9%	90.9	42	24	34	32%	75%	8%	13%	15	91	33%	13%			9.0	140	$11
2nd Half		10	0	109	105	2.64	0.94	2.94	1.04	86	78	26.4	3%	25%	22%	5%	14.3%	91.7	53	17	29	28%	77%	13%	11%	16	94	63%	6%			17.8	172	$35
Proj		**15**	**0**	**189**	**183**	**2.96**	**1.03**	**3.01**	**1.13**	**85**	**83**	**24.5**	**6%**	**25%**	**20%**	**6%**	**15.3%**	**92.4**	**47**	**21**	**31**	**28%**	**75%**	**12%**	**15%**	**30**						**23.3**	**143**	**$26**

RYAN BLOOMFIELD

Blackburn,Paul

Age: 29	Th: R	Role	SP	Health	F	LIMA Plan	A+
Ht: 6' 1"	Wt: 196	Type	Con	PT/Exp	C	Rand Var	0
				Consist	F	MM	3103

Started hot with luck-fueled 1.70 ERA through nine starts, but things unraveled before finger injury ended season in August. Noteworthy gains in Ks and whiffs, but both were still subpar while xBB% remained skeptical of the walk rate. Has deep-league relevance, but low ceiling makes him more of a streamer than a draft target.

Yr	Tm	W	Sv	IP	K	ERA	WHIP	xERA	xWHIP	vL+	vR+	BF/G	BB%	K%	K-BB%	xBB%	SwK	Vel	G	L	F	H%	S%	HR/F	xHR/F	GS	APC	DOM%	DIS%	Sv%	LI	RAR	BPX	R$
18	OAK	2	0	28	19	7.16	1.41	4.36	1.29	112	106	19.8	5%	16%	11%	8%	9.0%	89.7	47	21	32	34%	46%	7%	8%	6	74	17%	33%			-10.3	96	-$7
19	OAK *	11	0	145	81	5.56	1.48	5.52	1.44	165	121	22.3	6%	13%	7%	12%	10.3%	90.6	52	26	21	32%	65%	33%	32%	1	56	0%	100%	0	0.99	-18.9	32	-$6
20	OAK	0	0	2	2	27.00	3.00	8.36		162	133	14.0	14%	14%	0%		4.2%	89.9	50	10	40	52%	0%	0%	0%	1	48	0%	100%			-6.5	-47	-$12
21	OAK *	5	0	129	87	5.33	1.69	6.52	1.33	132	114	22.3	6%	15%	9%	11%	6.3%	91.0	50	21	29	38%	70%	21%	13%	9	76	0%	44%			-16.9	46	-$16
22	OAK	7	0	111	89	4.28	1.26	3.92	1.26	110	104	22.2	6%	19%	13%	9%	9.8%	91.7	47	21	32	30%	70%	14%	12%	21	84	24%	24%			-4.3	98	$0
1st Half		6	0	87	67	2.90	1.16	3.71	1.26	111	82	22.3	6%	19%	13%	8%	9.7%	91.8	49	24	28	29%	78%	10%	9%	16	84	31%	19%			11.5	99	$13
2nd Half		1	0	24	22	9.25	1.60	4.67	1.28	105	180	22.2	7%	20%	13%	11%	10.1%	91.5	43	11	46	33%	45%	22%	16%	5	85	0%	40%			-15.8	97	-$18
Proj		**6**	**0**	**160**	**120**	**4.29**	**1.29**	**3.85**	**1.28**	**100**	**117**	**20.9**	**6%**	**18%**	**12%**	**10%**	**9.2%**	**91.5**	**46**	**17**	**36**	**30%**	**71%**	**14%**	**12%**	**31**						**-6.3**	**91**	**$0**

Boxberger,Brad

Age: 35	Th: R	Role	RP	Health	A	LIMA Plan	A+
Ht: 5' 10"	Wt: 211	Type	Pwr/FB	PT/Exp	C	Rand Var	-4
				Consist	B	MM	3400

Effective run prevention from middle-relief role, but it didn't come with much skill support. Whiffs disappeared, as SwK says K% dip could've been even worse; walks continued to be an issue; fortunate HR/F limited damage from all those fly balls. Use xERA as your guide here and throw your closer darts elsewhere.

Yr	Tm	W	Sv	IP	K	ERA	WHIP	xERA	xWHIP	vL+	vR+	BF/G	BB%	K%	K-BB%	xBB%	SwK	Vel	G	L	F	H%	S%	HR/F	xHR/F	GS	APC	DOM%	DIS%	Sv%	LI	RAR	BPX	R$
18	ARI	3	32	53	71	4.39	1.43	3.89	1.37	115	92	3.9	14%	30%	17%	8%	11.2%	91.4	46	16	38	31%	75%	18%	15%	0	16			80	1.31	-1.6	108	$10
19	KC *	2	2	43	42	5.88	1.73	5.73	1.60	87	114	4.7	14%	21%	8%	9%	12.1%	90.2	39	21	39	34%	68%	10%	10%	0	17			40	0.75	-7.3	50	-$7
20	MIA	1	0	18	18	3.00	1.39	4.59	1.38	86	110	3.4	10%	23%	13%	11%	10.4%	92.5	51	12	37	30%	86%	16%	19%	0	16			0	1.05	3.2	94	-$2
21	MIL	5	4	65	83	3.34	1.07	3.59	1.18	61	103	3.7	9%	31%	22%	8%	13.7%	93.6	37	20	43	27%	74%	13%	12%	0	15			44	1.22	7.4	142	$7
22	MIL	4	1	64	68	2.95	1.23	4.09	1.30	97	88	3.8	10%	25%	15%	8%	10.0%	92.8	34	21	45	29%	79%	8%	11%	0	16			13	1.46	8.0	90	$2
1st Half		3	1	32	29	1.99	1.01	3.98	1.32	66	91	3.9	10%	23%	14%	6%	9.0%	92.8	39	18	44	22%	86%	9%	8%	0	16			20	1.64	7.7	81	$3
2nd Half		1	0	32	39	3.90	1.45	4.18	1.28	130	85	3.8	10%	27%	17%	8%	10.9%	92.7	30	24	45	36%	75%	8%	15%	0	16			0	1.31	0.3	100	-$7
Proj		**3**	**0**	**58**	**65**	**3.97**	**1.28**	**3.62**	**1.27**	**104**	**95**	**3.8**	**10%**	**27%**	**17%**	**8%**	**10.9%**	**92.5**	**37**	**20**	**43**	**30%**	**73%**	**12%**	**13%**	**0**						**0.0**	**108**	**-$1**

Boyd,Matt

Age: 32	Th: L	Role	RP	Health	F	LIMA Plan	B
Ht: 6' 3"	Wt: 223	Type	/FB	PT/Exp	C	Rand Var	-5
				Consist	A	MM	3301

Elbow surgery kept him out until September, when he shined in multi-inning relief role. Tough to glean much from a 13-IP sample, but velocity snapped right back to previous levels, whiffs returned as well, and he threw plenty of strikes (xBB%). Legit questions around role and workload, but a fine late flyer in case those 2019 skills reappear.

Yr	Tm	W	Sv	IP	K	ERA	WHIP	xERA	xWHIP	vL+	vR+	BF/G	BB%	K%	K-BB%	xBB%	SwK	Vel	G	L	F	H%	S%	HR/F	xHR/F	GS	APC	DOM%	DIS%	Sv%	LI	RAR	BPX	R$
18	DET	9	0	170	159	4.39	1.16	4.55	1.26	89	100	22.9	7%	22%	15%	8%	10.7%	90.4	29	21	50	27%	67%	11%	9%	31	92	16%	26%			-5.0	98	$8
19	DET	9	0	185	238	4.56	1.23	3.90	1.12	94	104	24.6	6%	30%	24%	6%	14.8%	92.0	36	20	45	33%	71%	18%	16%	32	97	34%	13%			-1.4	170	$10
20	DET	3	0	60	60	6.71	1.48	4.92	1.32	58	131	22.6	8%	22%	14%	9%	13.2%	91.7	37	21	42	32%	59%	20%	17%	12	91	8%	50%			-16.8	99	-$11
21	DET	3	0	79	67	3.89	1.27	4.64	1.29	98	95	22.5	7%	20%	13%	5%	11.1%	92.0	38	21	41	31%	73%	9%	11%	15	85	27%	33%			3.6	91	-$1
22	SEA	2	0	13	13	1.35	0.98	4.05	1.54	46	63	5.3	15%	25%	9%	6%	13.5%	92.1	41	21	38	17%	85%	0%	7%	0	19			0	0.58	4.3	34	-$2
1st Half																																		
2nd Half		2	0	13	13	1.35	0.98	4.05	1.54	45	63	5.3	15%	25%	9%	6%	13.5%	92.1	41	21	38	17%	85%	0%	7%	0	19			0	0.58	4.3	35	-$3
Proj		**4**	**0**	**87**	**85**	**4.10**	**1.29**	**3.81**	**1.24**	**90**	**109**	**13.6**	**8%**	**24%**	**16%**		**12.1%**	**91.5**	**35**	**21**	**44**	**30%**	**75%**	**14%**	**13%**	**9**						**-1.4**	**105**	**-$1**

Bradish,Kyle

Age: 26	Th: R	Role	SP	Health	C	LIMA Plan	A+
Ht: 6' 4"	Wt: 190	Type		PT/Exp	D	Rand Var	0
				Consist	B	MM	3203

4-7, 4.90 ERA in 118 IP at BAL. Knocked around before June shoulder strain cost him six weeks, then halved his ERA over last 13 starts. Dual 10-point H%/S% swings were the difference, as 1st/2nd half MLB xERA (4.19/3.86), K% (22%/22%), and BB (8%/9%) were near-mirror images. He'll be effective, but late surge just doesn't have breakout vibes.

Yr	Tm	W	Sv	IP	K	ERA	WHIP	xERA	xWHIP	vL+	vR+	BF/G	BB%	K%	K-BB%	xBB%	SwK	Vel	G	L	F	H%	S%	HR/F	xHR/F	GS	APC	DOM%	DIS%	Sv%	LI	RAR	BPX	R$
18																																		
19																																		
20																																		
21	a/a	6	0	103	102	4.19	1.46	4.77				18.5	10%	23%	13%							33%	74%									0.9	80	-$2
22	BAL *	7	0	147	136	4.18	1.25	3.91	1.32	96	113	20.6	9%	22%	13%	10%	10.4%	94.7	46	21	33	29%	70%	15%	13%	23	87	17%	39%			-3.8	88	$3
1st Half		3	0	61	59	5.88	1.53	5.90	1.26	99	162	20.5	8%	22%	14%	10%	11.1%	94.9	42	25	33	35%	65%	23%	21%	10	83	10%	50%			-14.4	65	-$14
2nd Half		4	0	86	77	2.96	1.05	2.47	1.28	94	82	20.7	9%	23%	14%	10%	10.0%	94.6	48	18	34	25%	75%	9%	7%	13	89	23%	31%			10.7	106	$14
Proj		**6**	**0**	**145**	**129**	**3.92**	**1.26**	**3.71**	**1.34**	**83**	**97**	**21.0**	**9%**	**22%**	**13%**	**10%**	**10.4%**	**94.7**	**46**	**21**	**33**	**29%**	**72%**	**12%**	**12%**	**28**						**0.8**	**85**	**$4**

Bradley,Taj

Age: 22	Th: R	Role	SP	Health	A	LIMA Plan	B
Ht: 6' 2"	Wt: 190	Type	Con/FB	PT/Exp	F	Rand Var	-1
				Consist	F	MM	4200

Dominated AA through 16 starts (1.70 ERA, 25% K-BB%), but step up to AAA wasn't as fruitful (3.66 ERA, 15% K-BB%) despite being young for the level. Solid command of three primary pitches, plus four-seamer and slider give him lofty ceiling, but he likely returns to minors for more seasoning. Give this one some time - TAM awaits.

Yr	Tm	W	Sv	IP	K	ERA	WHIP	xERA	xWHIP	vL+	vR+	BF/G	BB%	K%	K-BB%	xBB%	SwK	Vel	G	L	F	H%	S%	HR/F	xHR/F	GS	APC	DOM%	DIS%	Sv%	LI	RAR	BPX	R$
18																																		
19																																		
20																																		
21																																		
22	a/a	7	0	134	129	2.31	0.99	2.44				18.2	5%	24%	19%							27%	80%									27.5	150	$18
1st Half		3	0	66	70	1.45	0.86	1.41				17.4	6%	28%	22%							25%	86%									20.5	179	$20
2nd Half		4	0	68	60	3.11	1.10	3.39				19.1	5%	21%	16%							29%	76%									7.2	125	$8
Proj		**3**	**0**	**58**	**55**	**3.75**	**1.14**	**3.48**	**1.15**			**20.8**	**5%**	**24%**	**19%**				**38**	**20**	**42**	**30%**	**71%**	**10%**	**10%**	**11**						**1.6**	**130**	**$0**

Brash,Matt

Age: 25	Th: R	Role	RP	Health	A	LIMA Plan	A+
Ht: 6' 1"	Wt: 170	Type	Pwr/GB	PT/Exp	D	Rand Var	0
				Consist	D	MM	5511

4-4, 4.44 ERA in 51 IP at SEA. An easy way to kill your preseason hype? Walk 17 batters in your first five starts! Demoted to AAA for two months, then came back as RP with much better skills. Elite slider drove 2nd half SwK/K% surge which paired well with GB% tilt, so if he stays in bullpen and walk rate approaches xBB%... UP: sub-3.00 ERA, 20 Sv

Yr	Tm	W	Sv	IP	K	ERA	WHIP	xERA	xWHIP	vL+	vR+	BF/G	BB%	K%	K-BB%	xBB%	SwK	Vel	G	L	F	H%	S%	HR/F	xHR/F	GS	APC	DOM%	DIS%	Sv%	LI	RAR	BPX	R$
18																																		
19																																		
20																																		
21	aa	3	0	55	72	2.39	1.06	2.06				21.3	11%	34%	23%							28%	79%									12.7	154	$5
22	SEA *	4	3	77	97	3.95	1.43	3.80	1.45	98	98	5.3	15%	28%	13%	9%	13.0%	96.9	52	22	27	33%	73%	9%	12%	5	24	0%	60%	75	0.94	0.2	112	-$1
1st Half		1	2	44	52	5.25	1.63	5.20	1.48	112	137	7.8	15%	27%	12%	12%	11.0%	95.9	57	22	21	34%	70%	25%	28%	5	78	0%	60%			-7.0	74	-$12
2nd Half		3	1	33	46	2.20	1.16	1.90	1.20	88	70	3.6	12%	35%	23%	8%	14.5%	97.9	47	21	32	32%	79%	0%	3%	0	16			100	0.97	7.1	167	$4
Proj		**4**	**4**	**65**	**86**	**3.22**	**1.23**	**2.86**	**1.27**	**79**	**79**	**5.8**	**12%**	**32%**	**20%**	**9%**	**13.0%**	**97.1**	**51**	**22**	**27**	**31%**	**74%**	**8%**	**13%**	**0**						**6.1**	**131**	**$4**

Brieske,Beau

Age: 25	Th: R	Role	SP	Health	D	LIMA Plan	C+
Ht: 6' 3"	Wt: 200	Type	Con	PT/Exp	D	Rand Var	-1
				Consist	C	MM	1000

3-6, 4.19 ERA in 82 IP at DET. Called up from AAA in April and made 15 starts before biceps/forearm injury ended season in July. Low H% and decent control kept ratios in check, but this skill set is built on shaky ground given lack of swing-and-miss, meager K-BB%, and FB% tilt. Tack on low-caliber pedigree and he's a pretty easy pass.

Yr	Tm	W	Sv	IP	K	ERA	WHIP	xERA	xWHIP	vL+	vR+	BF/G	BB%	K%	K-BB%	xBB%	SwK	Vel	G	L	F	H%	S%	HR/F	xHR/F	GS	APC	DOM%	DIS%	Sv%	LI	RAR	BPX	R$
18																																		
19																																		
20																																		
21	aa	3	0	44	32	3.19	1.12	3.05				21.7	5%	18%	14%							30%	71%									5.9	129	$0
22	DET *	3	0	100	69	4.16	1.21	4.22	1.36	85	111	21.2	7%	16%	9%	8%	8.6%	94.3	38	19	44	26%	72%	13%	13%	15	86	13%	60%			-2.3	53	-$1
1st Half		1	0	79	53	4.55	1.28	4.79	1.38	84	120	21.7	8%	16%	8%	8%	8.4%	94.3	38	18	44	26%	72%	14%	14%	13	86	8%	69%			-5.6	34	-$7
2nd Half		2	0	20	16	2.66	0.95	2.00	1.18	88	54	19.3	5%	21%	16%	6%	9.9%	93.9	33	24	42	26%	72%	0%	3%	2	86	50%	0%			3.3	144	-$3
Proj		**3**	**0**	**58**	**37**	**4.14**	**1.31**	**4.34**	**1.35**	**90**	**126**	**22.8**	**7%**	**16%**	**9%**	**8%**	**8.4%**	**94.3**	**38**	**18**	**44**	**29%**	**73%**	**11%**	**13%**	**11**						**-1.2**	**59**	**-$3**

RYAN BLOOMFIELD

Britton,Zack

Age: 35	Th: L	Role	RP	Health	F	LIMA Plan	C+
Ht: 6' 1"	Wt: 200	Type	Pwr/xGB	PT/Exp	D	Rand Var	+5
				Consist	F	MM	4200

Spent most of season rehabbing from elbow surgery, pitched three games in September, then returned to IL (shoulder). Extreme GB% is about all that's left from this rubble, as velocity hasn't been right for years, K-BB% history is brutal, and has less than 40 IP since 2019. An epic run from 2014-16, but that version is well in the rearview.

Yr Tm	W	Sv	IP	K	ERA	WHIP	xERA	xWHIP	vL+	vR+	BF/G	BB%	K%	K-BB%	xBB%	SwK	Vel	G	L	F	H%	S%	HR/F	xHR/F	GS	APC	DOM%	DIS%	Sv%	LI	RAR	BPX	R$
18 2 AL	2	7	41	34	3.10	1.23	3.31	1.52	94	80	4.1	12%	20%	8%	12%	12.8%	94.9	73	16	11	24%	77%	25%	29%	0	16			70	0.86	5.3	70	$2
19 NYY	3	3	61	53	1.91	1.14	3.32	1.53	61	77	3.7	13%	22%	9%	12%	10.9%	94.8	77	13	9	23%	85%	20%	28%	0	14			43	1.02	19.7	74	$7
20 NYY	1	8	19	16	1.89	1.00	3.34	1.35	45	69	3.8	9%	21%	12%	12%	11.8%	94.8	72	13	15	24%	79%	0%	11%	0	14			100	0.97	6.0	109	$12
21 NYY	0	1	18	16	5.89	1.69	4.59	1.76	79	116	3.7	17%	20%	2%	12%	9.8%	92.6	68	12	20	30%	66%	20%	13%	0	15			25	1.23	-3.7	2	-$8
22 NYY	0	0	1	1	13.50	10.50	0.00		86	281	3.0	67%	11%	-56%	12%	5.1%	92.6	50	50	0	53%	86%	0%		0	13			0	1.31	-0.8	-2111	-$7
1st Half																																	
2nd Half	0	0	1	1	13.50	10.50	0.00		86	280	3.0	67%	11%	-56%	12%	5.1%	92.6	50	50	0	53%	86%	0%		0	13			0	1.31	-0.8	-2114	-$13
Proj	1	0	29	25	3.63	1.38	3.32	1.50	93	94	4.0	12%	20%	8%		11.7%	94.8	70	16	14	29%	74%	15%	13%	0						1.2	65	-$4

Brogdon,Connor

Age: 28	Th: R	Role	RP	Health	D	LIMA Plan	B
Ht: 6' 6"	Wt: 205	Type	Pwr/FB	PT/Exp	C	Rand Var	-1
				Consist	B	MM	4411

Some stops and starts (early AAA shuttling, June bout with COVID), but this was a legitimate step forward. More cutters and change-ups pushed SwK to new heights, particularly in 2nd half, while control gains came with full support from xBB%. Fly ball tilt opens up some HR risk, but this profile can absolutely thrive late in games... UP: 25 Sv.

Yr Tm	W	Sv	IP	K	ERA	WHIP	xERA	xWHIP	vL+	vR+	BF/G	BB%	K%	K-BB%	xBB%	SwK	Vel	G	L	F	H%	S%	HR/F	xHR/F	GS	APC	DOM%	DIS%	Sv%	LI	RAR	BPX	R$
18																																	
19 a/a	4	4	58	73	3.49	1.05	3.23				5.5	9%	32%	23%							25%	76%									7.3	122	$6
20 PHI	1	0	11	17	3.97	0.88	3.27	1.14	72	89	4.9	11%	39%	27%	7%	16.8%	95.3	36	18	45	12%	71%	30%	14%	0	20			0	0.73	0.7	169	-$1
21 PHI	5	1	58	50	3.43	1.13	4.30	1.29	86	89	4.2	8%	21%	14%	8%	13.8%	96.0	44	18	38	27%	73%	10%	9%	1	16	0%	100%	20	0.97	5.9	95	$3
22 PHI	2	2	44	50	3.27	1.25	3.79	1.10	90	110	4.0	6%	27%	21%	6%	16.3%	95.2	31	25	44	34%	80%	11%	9%	0	15			50	0.86	3.8	146	$0
1st Half	2	0	18	21	2.04	1.13	3.71	1.11	64	106	3.8	7%	29%	22%	7%	15.1%	95.1	30	20	50	31%	89%	9%	10%	0	15			0	0.66	4.2	145	-$3
2nd Half	0	2	26	29	4.10	1.33	3.84	1.10	111	112	4.1	5%	25%	20%	5%	17.2%	95.2	32	27	41	36%	74%	13%	8%	0	15			50	1.00	-0.4	147	-$7
Proj	4	3	65	73	3.62	1.18	3.30	1.14	88	107	4.2	7%	28%	21%	6%	15.8%	95.4	34	23	43	31%	75%	13%	9%	0						2.8	138	$3

Brown,Hunter

Age: 24	Th: R	Role	RP	Health	A	LIMA Plan	A
Ht: 6' 2"	Wt: 203	Type	Pwr	PT/Exp	D	Rand Var	-5
				Consist	F	MM	4203

2-0, 0.89 ERA in 20 IP at HOU. Pacific Coast League Pitcher of the Year came as advertised in September. PRO: Elite GB% in upper minors (52%) should keep ERA in check; K% looks fantastic. CON: Lack of whiffs (11.7% SwK in AAA) suggests Ks might not translate; iffy control. Rosy long-term outlook, but don't get too carried away on draft day.

Yr Tm	W	Sv	IP	K	ERA	WHIP	xERA	xWHIP	vL+	vR+	BF/G	BB%	K%	K-BB%	xBB%	SwK	Vel	G	L	F	H%	S%	HR/F	xHR/F	GS	APC	DOM%	DIS%	Sv%	LI	RAR	BPX	R$
18																																	
19																																	
20																																	
21 a/a	6	1	101	113	4.20	1.44	4.60				17.9	11%	26%	15%							34%	74%									0.8	91	-$1
22 HOU *	11	1	126	136	2.15	1.07	2.02	1.20	62	108	16.4	9%	28%	19%	6%	10.0%	96.6	68	10	22	27%	80%	0%	11%	2	44	100%	0%	100	0.59	28.4	137	$19
1st Half	5	1	67	79	2.27	1.08	2.06				17.4	10%	29%	19%							28%	80%	0%		0	0					14.0	143	$16
2nd Half	6	0	59	58	2.01	1.05	1.99	1.26	61	108	15.3	9%	25%	16%	6%	10.0%	96.6	68	10	22	27%	81%	0%	11%	2	44	100%	0%	0	0.59	14.3	131	$15
Proj	10	0	131	125	3.44	1.24	3.37	1.30	82	143	17.8	9%	24%	14%		10.0%	96.6	50	19	31	30%	74%	10%	10%	23						8.5	102	$9

Brubaker,Jonathan

Age: 29	Th: R	Role	SP	Health	D	LIMA Plan	B
Ht: 6' 3"	Wt: 180	Type	Pwr	PT/Exp	A	Rand Var	+2
				Consist	A	MM	3303

Frequently appeared on deep-league streamer menus, but ugly ratios and another negative R$ had you sending him back. A shift from four-seamers to sinkers didn't do much, as K%, BB%, and GB% barely budged. Low ceiling isn't worth a late flyer in drafts, and DOM%/DIS% says those streaming odds are against you yet again.

Yr Tm	W	Sv	IP	K	ERA	WHIP	xERA	xWHIP	vL+	vR+	BF/G	BB%	K%	K-BB%	xBB%	SwK	Vel	G	L	F	H%	S%	HR/F	xHR/F	GS	APC	DOM%	DIS%	Sv%	LI	RAR	BPX	R$
18 a/a	10	0	154	103	3.51	1.47	4.58				23.6	7%	16%	9%							34%	76%									12.2	74	$2
19 aaa	2	0	21	15	3.42	1.34	4.57				21.8	5%	17%	13%							33%	78%									2.8	89	-$3
20 PIT	1	0	47	48	4.94	1.37	4.18	1.29	113	91	18.6	8%	23%	15%	8%	11.7%	93.7	47	22	31	33%	66%	14%	17%	9	73	11%	44%	0	0.77	-2.9	115	-$4
21 PIT	5	0	124	129	5.36	1.29	4.03	1.22	115	102	22.4	7%	24%	17%	8%	12.4%	93.2	43	22	35	30%	65%	22%	16%	24	81	17%	25%			-16.7	126	-$4
22 PIT	3	0	144	147	4.69	1.47	3.99	1.27	118	103	23.1	8%	23%	14%	8%	12.3%	93.1	44	23	33	35%	70%	12%	13%	28	85	14%	43%			-12.8	106	-$8
1st Half	2	0	82	82	4.28	1.44	4.30	1.31	108	103	23.3	9%	22%	13%	8%	12.2%	93.2	43	19	38	34%	72%	9%	11%	16	85	13%	44%			-3.2	94	-$6
2nd Half	1	0	62	65	5.23	1.50	3.59	1.22	132	102	22.8	8%	24%	16%	7%	12.5%	93.1	46	27	27	37%	67%	16%	17%	12	85	17%	42%			-9.6	123	-$12
Proj	6	0	152	151	4.81	1.42	3.59	1.27	117	99	21.0	8%	23%	15%	8%	12.2%	93.3	45	23	32	34%	69%	14%	16%	31						-15.9	109	-$5

Bubic,Kris

Age: 25	Th: L	Role	SP	Health	A	LIMA Plan	C+
Ht: 6' 3"	Wt: 225	Type	Pwr	PT/Exp	A	Rand Var	+1
				Consist	B	MM	2203

3-13, 5.58 ERA in 129 IP at KC. Ugly ratios from 2021 turned even worse, and the skills offer little solace. Already-shaky SwK dipped further, walks were plentiful, and xWHIP says likely H% regression will barely move the needle. A case where "AAB" reliability isn't a good thing; it just means you can have a high degree of confidence that he will be bad..

Yr Tm	W	Sv	IP	K	ERA	WHIP	xERA	xWHIP	vL+	vR+	BF/G	BB%	K%	K-BB%	xBB%	SwK	Vel	G	L	F	H%	S%	HR/F	xHR/F	GS	APC	DOM%	DIS%	Sv%	LI	RAR	BPX	R$
18																																	
19																																	
20 KC	1	0	50	49	4.32	1.48	4.61	1.38	123	101	22.2	10%	22%	12%	10%	10.5%	91.5	47	21	32	32%	76%	17%	18%	10	93	10%	30%			0.8	87	-$4
21 KC	6	0	130	114	4.43	1.38	4.52	1.43	117	102	19.2	11%	21%	10%	9%	10.0%	90.9	47	21	32	28%	73%	18%	19%	20	76	15%	45%	0	0.79	-2.7	62	-$2
22 KC *	3	0	144	123	5.59	1.64	5.83	1.45	153	111	20.8	11%	19%	8%	8%	9.5%	91.9	41	26	33	35%	68%	13%	13%	27	81	15%	37%	0	0.77	-28.9	49	-$18
1st Half	1	0	59	50	6.70	1.69	6.07	1.46	182	106	17.6	11%	19%	8%	11%	8.0%	91.6	43	23	34	35%	61%	15%	13%	11	72	9%	55%	0	0.74	-19.7	42	-$24
2nd Half	2	0	86	73	4.83	1.61	4.49	1.40	135	114	23.8	10%	19%	9%	7%	10.5%	92.2	40	27	33	35%	72%	13%	13%	16	88	19%	25%			-9.1	57	-$13
Proj	3	0	131	114	5.13	1.54	4.22	1.44	140	102	20.5	11%	20%	9%	9%	9.7%	91.7	43	24	33	32%	70%	15%	15%	28						-18.6	54	-$11

Buehler,Walker

Age: 28	Th: R	Role	SP	Health	F	LIMA Plan	B
Ht: 6' 2"	Wt: 185	Type		PT/Exp	A	Rand Var	0
				Consist	A	MM	5300

A massive early bust, as elbow/forearm issues in June led to Tommy John surgery (his second) in August. Pre-injury skills were pretty stable save for a dip in strikeouts, but H%/S% correction drove career-worst ERA and WHIP. Cross him off your redraft lists, but throwing him late for a buck in keeper leagues could pay off in 2024.

Yr Tm	W	Sv	IP	K	ERA	WHIP	xERA	xWHIP	vL+	vR+	BF/G	BB%	K%	K-BB%	xBB%	SwK	Vel	G	L	F	H%	S%	HR/F	xHR/F	GS	APC	DOM%	DIS%	Sv%	LI	RAR	BPX	R$
18 LA	8	0	137	151	2.62	0.96	3.14	1.14	78	76	22.5	7%	28%	21%	6%	11.8%	96.2	50	18	32	26%	77%	11%	9%	23	91	39%	9%	0	0.79	25.9	162	$21
19 LA	14	0	182	215	3.26	1.04	3.45	1.08	81	88	24.6	5%	29%	24%	5%	12.8%	96.6	43	23	35	31%	73%	12%	12%	30	95	43%	13%			28.1	177	$26
20 LA	1	0	37	42	3.44	0.95	3.92	1.17	76	88	18.4	7%	29%	21%	8%	12.8%	96.9	35	23	42	22%	75%	18%	15%	8	75	38%	25%			4.6	142	$6
21 LA	16	0	208	212	2.47	0.97	3.56	1.15	82	76	24.7	6%	26%	20%	6%	12.3%	95.4	45	20	35	26%	79%	10%	10%	33	96	45%	12%			46.0	140	$39
22 LA	6	0	65	58	4.02	1.29	3.75	1.21	107	98	22.8	6%	21%	15%	8%	12.0%	95.2	48	20	32	32%	72%	13%	14%	12	87	17%	50%			-0.4	118	-$1
1st Half	6	0	65	58	4.02	1.29	3.75	1.21	107	98	22.8	6%	21%	15%	8%	12.0%	95.2	48	20	32	32%	72%	13%	14%	12	87	17%	50%			-0.4	118	$2
2nd Half																																	
Proj	1	0	15	14	3.29	1.08	3.20	1.16	90	88	21.9	6%	25%	19%		12.3%	95.9	44	21	35	28%	74%	13%	12%	3						1.2	132	-$4

Bumgarner,Madison

Age: 33	Th: L	Role	SP	Health	D	LIMA Plan	C+
Ht: 6' 4"	Wt: 257	Type	Con/FB	PT/Exp	A	Rand Var	0
				Consist	B	MM	2103

This is like watching a bad movie knowing full well how it ends. Latest scene was another dud, as he couldn't hold 2021's SwK "spike" and Ks fell back despite some velocity recovery, 2nd half ratios reached new levels of futility. Likely still too young to be on the Steve Carlton Path to Retirement, but there's little need to keep watching. Go outside or something.

Yr Tm	W	Sv	IP	K	ERA	WHIP	xERA	xWHIP	vL+	vR+	BF/G	BB%	K%	K-BB%	xBB%	SwK	Vel	G	L	F	H%	S%	HR/F	xHR/F	GS	APC	DOM%	DIS%	Sv%	LI	RAR	BPX	R$
18 SF	6	0	130	109	3.26	1.24	4.35	1.33	87	99	26.2	8%	20%	12%	8%	9.4%	90.9	43	22	35	29%	78%	10%	15%	21	98	29%	14%			14.2	88	$7
19 SF	9	0	208	203	3.90	1.13	4.22	1.18	73	102	24.8	5%	24%	19%	6%	12.0%	91.4	36	23	42	30%	71%	13%	16%	34	95	35%	18%			15.5	133	$17
20 ARI	1	0	42	30	6.48	1.44	5.66	1.39	106	131	21.1	7%	16%	9%	6%	8.0%	88.4	32	26	42	28%	64%	22%	23%	9	79	11%	56%			-10.4	57	-$11
21 ARI	7	0	146	124	4.67	1.18	4.70	1.26	92	101	23.6	6%	20%	14%	6%	10.1%	90.4	33	22	45	28%	65%	12%	12%	26	88	23%	42%			-7.4	92	$3
22 ARI	7	0	159	112	4.88	1.44	4.88	1.34	105	120	23.3	7%	16%	9%	7%	8.3%	91.2	37	21	42	31%	70%	11%	14%	30	91	13%	57%			-17.8	60	-$8
1st Half	4	0	84	61	3.74	1.39	4.87	1.37	109	110	21.7	8%	17%	9%	8%	8.0%	91.3	40	18	42	30%	78%	10%	12%	17	87	12%	53%			2.4	57	-$1
2nd Half	3	0	74	51	6.17	1.49	4.89	1.31	99	129	25.3	6%	16%	9%	7%	8.5%	91.1	34	25	42	33%	61%	13%	18%	13	95	15%	62%			-20.2	64	-$16
Proj	6	0	160	121	4.92	1.37	4.26	1.32	99	117	22.4	7%	18%	11%	6%	8.9%	90.5	35	23	42	30%	69%	14%	16%	30						-18.8	73	-$6

RYAN BLOOMFIELD

Bummer,Aaron

Age: 29	Th: L	Role: RP	Health: F	LIMA Plan: B
Ht: 6' 3"	Wt: 215	Type: Pwr/xGB	PT/Exp: C	Rand Var: 0
			Consist: A	MM: 5300

An odd combo of small-sample luck factors, as super-high S% suppressed ERA, yet high H% bloated the WHIP. May knee injury, June shoulder issue likely contributed to SwK decline and drop in velocity, and calling-card GB% stayed mostly intact. Unless the whiffs return, he's more of a watch list type than a draft target.

Yr	Tm	W	Sv	IP	K	ERA	WHIP	xERA	xWHIP	vL+	vR+	BF/G	BB%	K%	K-BB%	xBB%	SwK	Vel	G	L	F	H%	S%	HR/F	xHR/F	GS	APC	DOM%	DIS%	Sv%	LI	RAR	BPX	R$
18	CHW *	2	0	64	60	3.72	1.48	4.16	1.20	82	114	4.0	8%	22%	14%	11%	10.5%	93.1	61	22	16	37%	73%	6%	13%	0	16			0	0.92	3.4	117	-$3
19	CHW	0	1	68	60	2.13	0.99	3.15	1.34	60	75	4.5	9%	23%	14%	8%	11.0%	95.6	72	11	17	23%	81%	14%	10%	0	18			33	1.23	19.8	117	$7
20	CHW	1	0	9	14	0.96	1.07	2.42	1.22	64	51	4.2	13%	37%	24%	8%	12.9%	95.7	68	16	16	29%	90%	0%	32%	0	17			0	0.77	4.0	179	$0
21	CHW	5	2	56	75	3.51	1.26	2.47	1.27	45	90	3.9	12%	31%	19%	9%	13.2%	95.4	76	11	13	32%	72%	18%	19%	0	16			25	1.05	5.2	159	$3
22	CHW	2	2	27	30	2.36	1.50	2.80	1.22	86	115	3.7	9%	26%	17%	11%	10.7%	94.5	64	22	15	38%	87%	18%	14%	0	14			33	1.08	5.3	147	-$2
1st Half		0	1	18	21	3.06	1.58	3.07	1.33	85	114	4.0	11%	26%	15%	12%	11.0%	94.3	58	27	15	38%	81%	14%	17%	0	16			50	1.08	2.0	116	-$9
2nd Half		2	1	9	9	1.00	1.33	2.33	1.03	84	115	3.1	3%	24%	22%	10%	10.0%	94.9	73	12	15	38%	100%	25%	10%	0	12			25	1.07	3.3	205	-$5
Proj		2	0	51	54	3.18	1.29	2.81	1.32	66	92	3.9	11%	26%	15%	10%	11.4%	94.5	66	20	15	31%	75%	12%	15%	0						4.9	117	-$1

Bundy,Dylan

Age: 30	Th: R	Role: SP	Health: D	LIMA Plan: B
Ht: 6' 1"	Wt: 225	Type: Con/FB	PT/Exp: A	Rand Var: 0
			Consist: B	MM: 2103

Ratios improved considerably, yet STILL posted a negative R$. Steep drop in 2021's SwK hung around and velocity fell again, which combined to drive career-worst K%. Low walk rate (with support from xBB%) is about all that's left, so be cautious even using him as a streamer—recent DIS% says you're playing with fire.

Yr	Tm	W	Sv	IP	K	ERA	WHIP	xERA	xWHIP	vL+	vR+	BF/G	BB%	K%	K-BB%	xBB%	SwK	Vel	G	L	F	H%	S%	HR/F	xHR/F	GS	APC	DOM%	DIS%	Sv%	LI	RAR	BPX	R$
18	BAL	8	0	172	184	5.45	1.41	4.37	1.22	128	108	24.2	7%	25%	17%	6%	13.2%	91.6	34	20	46	33%	69%	18%	14%	31	92	35%	32%			-27.6	126	-$7
19	BAL	7	0	162	162	4.79	1.35	4.60	1.33	103	105	23.3	8%	23%	15%	7%	13.3%	91.2	41	21	38	31%	70%	16%	13%	30	93	17%	37%			-5.6	103	$1
20	LAA	6	0	66	72	3.29	1.04	3.72	1.15	95	69	24.3	6%	27%	21%	6%	13.2%	90.2	41	24	36	29%	70%	8%	8%	11	93	45%	27%			9.4	151	$23
21	LAA	2	0	91	84	6.06	1.36	4.64	1.33	104	115	17.3	9%	21%	13%	7%	10.1%	90.8	41	21	39	29%	60%	19%	17%	19	66	16%	42%	0	0.69	-20.0	86	-$10
22	MIN	8	0	140	94	4.89	1.28	4.81	1.25	98	117	20.5	5%	16%	11%	5%	10.3%	89.2	34	20	46	30%	66%	11%	10%	29	75	7%	45%			-15.8	80	-$3
1st Half		4	0	70	53	4.50	1.26	4.45	1.21	112	103	21.1	5%	18%	13%	5%	10.8%	89.4	38	19	43	30%	69%	11%	9%	14	76	14%	36%			-4.6	99	-$3
2nd Half		4	0	70	41	5.27	1.30	5.17	1.29	84	130	19.9	5%	14%	9%	5%	9.8%	88.8	30	21	49	29%	64%	11%	12%	15	75	0%	53%			-11.2	60	-$7
Proj		7	0	138	116	4.80	1.26	3.92	1.25	99	108	20.0	6%	21%	14%	6%	11.2%	89.9	37	21	42	30%	66%	13%	11%	28						-14.1	96	-$1

Burke,Brock

Age: 26	Th: L	Role: RP	Health: D	LIMA Plan: B+
Ht: 6' 4"	Wt: 180	Type: Pwr/FB	PT/Exp: D	Rand Var: -5
			Consist: D	MM: 3301

Transitioned to bullpen and posted near-elite ratios, which combined with heavy volume and win total led to decent R$. Strikeouts picked up, ditto for SwK in 2nd half, though unsustainable H%/S% means xERA and xWHIP are better baselines. An interesting flyer, but unlikely to repeat in pretty much any category.

Yr	Tm	W	Sv	IP	K	ERA	WHIP	xERA	xWHIP	vL+	vR+	BF/G	BB%	K%	K-BB%	xBB%	SwK	Vel	G	L	F	H%	S%	HR/F	xHR/F	GS	APC	DOM%	DIS%	Sv%	LI	RAR	BPX	R$
18	aa	6	0	56	64	2.28	1.03	2.20				24.0	6%	30%	23%							31%	78%									13.0	185	$7
19	TEX *	3	0	81	63	5.83	1.42	4.70	1.60	129	113	20.2	9%	18%	10%	9%	5.3%	91.6	50	18	32	31%	60%	21%	17%	6	79	0%	67%			-13.2	59	-$7
20																																		
21	aaa	1	0	79	79	6.34	1.49	5.52				16.3	9%	23%	14%							34%	59%									-20.3	66	-$13
22	TEX	7	0	82	90	1.97	1.06	3.53	1.15	91	88	6.3	7%	27%	20%	8%	11.4%	95.0	40	17	43	28%	88%	10%	10%	0	26			0	1.06	20.3	137	$11
1st Half		4	0	40	44	1.12	1.02	3.41	1.12	79	83	6.5	7%	28%	21%	8%	10.1%	95.0	38	19	42	29%	92%	5%	9%	0	26			0	1.06	14.2	140	$10
2nd Half		3	0	42	46	2.79	1.10	3.64	1.17	101	93	6.1	8%	27%	19%	7%	12.5%	94.9	41	15	44	26%	85%	15%	11%	0	25			0	1.06	6.1	133	$4
Proj		5	0	73	73	3.69	1.21	3.64	1.23	100	96	9.4	8%	25%	17%	8%	11.6%	95.0	40	17	44	30%	73%	10%	10%	0						2.5	112	$2

Burnes,Corbin

Age: 28	Th: R	Role: SP	Health: B	LIMA Plan: C+
Ht: 6' 3"	Wt: 225	Type: Pwr	PT/Exp: A	Rand Var: 0
			Consist: A	MM: 5505

Squashed any lingering workload concerns en route to third straight elite season. A slight drop in whiffs, but still had four pitches with double-digit SwK, and steady xERA says not to worry about 2nd half ERA spike (which S% blames on the bullpen). Consistently high DOM%, BPX baseline, and "BAA" reliability cement him firmly among the elite.

Yr	Tm	W	Sv	IP	K	ERA	WHIP	xERA	xWHIP	vL+	vR+	BF/G	BB%	K%	K-BB%	xBB%	SwK	Vel	G	L	F	H%	S%	HR/F	xHR/F	GS	APC	DOM%	DIS%	Sv%	LI	RAR	BPX	R$
18	MIL *	10	1	118	103	4.33	1.32	3.99	1.24	70	89	10.0	8%	21%	13%	6%	15.9%	95.3	49	21	30	31%	68%	13%	13%	0	19			33	0.96	-2.6	92	$2
19	MIL *	1	1	72	91	9.06	1.84	8.03	1.20	167	111	8.4	9%	27%	18%	8%	17.7%	95.2	45	24	31	43%	53%	39%	30%	4	28	0%	75%	100	1.05	-40.5	53	-$19
20	MIL	4	0	60	88	2.11	1.02	2.99	1.11	80	57	20.0	10%	37%	27%	10%	15.0%	96.0	46	19	34	30%	80%	5%	15%	9	84	56%	11%	0	0.84	17.2	187	$25
21	MIL	11	0	167	234	2.43	0.94	2.55	0.94	78	63	23.5	5%	36%	30%	6%	17.5%	96.9	49	21	30	33%	75%	6%	6%	28	93	50%	4%			37.9	224	$32
22	MIL	12	0	202	243	2.94	0.97	2.85	1.06	88	83	24.2	6%	30%	24%	8%	15.5%	96.3	47	20	33	27%	75%	14%	12%	33	99	45%	15%			25.6	175	$29
1st Half		7	0	99	124	2.36	0.92	2.90	1.03	76	86	24.4	6%	32%	25%	8%	16.5%	96.2	43	19	38	26%	82%	13%	11%	16	100	50%	6%			19.8	179	$34
2nd Half		5	0	103	119	3.51	1.01	2.81	1.08	96	80	23.9	6%	29%	23%	8%	14.7%	96.3	51	20	29	28%	69%	15%	14%	17	98	41%	24%			5.9	171	$20
Proj		13	0	203	258	2.99	1.06	2.60	1.05	92	79	23.6	7%	33%	26%	8%	15.9%	96.2	47	20	32	31%	76%	13%	14%	33						24.4	181	$28

Cabrera,Edward

Age: 25	Th: R	Role: SP	Health: D	LIMA Plan: A
Ht: 6' 5"	Wt: 217	Type: Pwr	PT/Exp: D	Rand Var: -1
			Consist: F	MM: 3303

6-4, 3.01 ERA in 73 IP at MIA. IL stints in April (biceps) and June (elbow) cost him two months, but posted quality numbers after June call-up. More change-ups led to excellent SwK, but walks and likely regression (3.67 xERA, 21% H% in majors) question ratio repeat. Still a growth stock given age and pedigree; this could come together quickly.

Yr	Tm	W	Sv	IP	K	ERA	WHIP	xERA	xWHIP	vL+	vR+	BF/G	BB%	K%	K-BB%	xBB%	SwK	Vel	G	L	F	H%	S%	HR/F	xHR/F	GS	APC	DOM%	DIS%	Sv%	LI	RAR	BPX	R$
18																																		
19	aa	4	0	40	38	3.78	1.26	4.37				20.5	9%	23%	14%							27%	78%									3.6	67	$0
20																																		
21	MIA *	3	0	82	97	4.50	1.41	4.56	1.62	131	110	19.4	13%	28%	15%	12%	12.7%	96.7	42	25	33	30%	73%	27%	30%	7	69	0%	43%			-2.4	81	-$4
22	MIA *	8	0	108	114	3.08	1.04	2.44	1.34	69	106	18.9	11%	26%	14%	10%	13.7%	96.0	45	16	38	23%	75%	15%	15%	14	87	29%	43%			11.8	110	$11
1st Half		3	0	41	42	4.08	1.27	3.31	1.38	49	131	20.9	12%	25%	13%	12%	13.6%	96.8	50	14	36	28%	69%	13%	12%	3	95	0%	67%			-0.6	95	-$4
2nd Half		5	0	67	73	2.42	0.90	1.87	1.22	75	98	17.8	10%	28%	19%	8%	13.8%	95.8	44	17	39	19%	81%	16%	16%	11	84	36%	36%			12.8	122	$18
Proj		9	0	138	145	3.71	1.28	3.58	1.32	77	126	20.0	10%	26%	15%	10%	13.7%	96.2	46	16	38	29%	76%	14%	15%	28						4.4	99	$7

Cabrera,Génesis

Age: 26	Th: L	Role: RP	Health: A	LIMA Plan: C+
Ht: 6' 2"	Wt: 180	Type: Pwr	PT/Exp: C	Rand Var: -1
			Consist: A	MM: 3210

Ran hot in the 1st half (thanks, H%/S%), but ratios imploded and got demoted to AAA by September. Several concerns: below-average SwK and velocity drop combined to sink K%, too many walks, xERA and xWHIP baselines don't offer much hope. A low-ceiling reliever to ignore on draft day, even if the Ks return.

Yr	Tm	W	Sv	IP	K	ERA	WHIP	xERA	xWHIP	vL+	vR+	BF/G	BB%	K%	K-BB%	xBB%	SwK	Vel	G	L	F	H%	S%	HR/F	xHR/F	GS	APC	DOM%	DIS%	Sv%	LI	RAR	BPX	R$
18	a/a	8	0	141	125	4.41	1.33	3.68				21.7	11%	21%	10%							29%	68%									-4.5	83	$1
19	STL *	5	1	119	107	6.49	1.61	6.11	1.54	157	83	16.0	9%	20%	11%	8%	7.8%	96.3	36	26	38	35%	62%	8%	12%	2	29	0%	100%	50	0.57	-29.2	44	-$13
20	STL	4	1	22	32	2.42	1.16	4.11	1.46	44	100	5.1	17%	33%	17%	12%	14.9%	96.2	34	25	41	18%	87%	17%	19%	0	21			100	0.92	5.6	79	$9
21	STL	4	0	70	77	3.73	1.26	4.24	1.39	105	73	4.2	12%	26%	14%	9%	11.8%	97.7	42	20	38	29%	69%	5%	9%	0	17			0	1.08	4.6	80	$1
22	STL	4	1	45	32	4.63	1.32	4.70	1.48	98	109	5.0	10%	16%	6%	8%	10.2%	96.1	44	21	35	25%	71%	17%	14%	0	19			50	1.04	-3.7	32	-$3
1st Half		3	1	32	26	2.27	1.04	3.94	1.36	84	94	5.2	9%	20%	11%	8%	10.6%	96.4	49	17	34	20%	89%	17%	16%	0	20			100	1.11	6.6	75	$2
2nd Half		1	0	13	6	10.38	2.00	6.75	1.74	124	138	4.6	12%	9%	-3%	7%	9.4%	95.5	36	28	36	33%	48%	17%	11%	0	18			0	0.92	-10.3	-67	-$17
Proj		3	1	44	40	4.01	1.25	3.80	1.39	103	94	6.6	11%	23%	12%	8%	11.1%	96.9	46	18	36	27%	71%	12%	13%	0						-0.2	73	-$2

Canning,Griffin

Age: 27	Th: R	Role: RP	Health: F	LIMA Plan: B
Ht: 6' 2"	Wt: 180	Type: Pwr/FB	PT/Exp: C	Rand Var: 0
			Consist: A	MM: 2301

A stress fracture in lower back from August 2021 lingered and caused him to miss entire season. When healthy, SwK% lures us in, but K-BB% is heading the wrong way, and FB% tilt hints at more HR issues. 2020-21 xERA suggests he's a back-end SP that could blow up your ratios with major questions about his health.

Yr	Tm	W	Sv	IP	K	ERA	WHIP	xERA	xWHIP	vL+	vR+	BF/G	BB%	K%	K-BB%	xBB%	SwK	Vel	G	L	F	H%	S%	HR/F	xHR/F	GS	APC	DOM%	DIS%	Sv%	LI	RAR	BPX	R$
18	a/a	4	0	106	100	4.02	1.29	3.61				19.0	8%	23%	14%							32%	69%									1.7	107	$1
19	LAA *	6	0	106	111	3.97	1.17	3.61	1.27	92	104	20.2	8%	26%	19%	9%	14.0%	93.9	38	18	44	29%	70%	13%	13%	17	86	35%	29%	0	0.86	7.0	111	$6
20	LAA	2	0	56	56	3.99	1.37	4.81	1.36	100	107	21.6	10%	24%	14%	10%	11.8%	92.8	36	20	43	31%	75%	12%	14%	11	88	9%	36%			3.2	86	$2
21	LAA	5	0	63	62	5.60	1.48	4.88	1.38	108	118	19.8	10%	22%	12%	9%	14.1%	93.6	35	24	41	31%	68%	18%	14%	13	77	15%	62%	0	0.79	-10.3	71	-$7
22																																		
1st Half																																		
2nd Half																																		
Proj		5	0	87	86	4.55	1.39	4.00	1.35	106	115	20.0	10%	23%	13%	9%	13.3%	93.4	36	21	43	31%	72%	13%	13%	18						-6.2	78	-$3

CORBIN YOUNG

Carrasco,Carlos

Age: 36	Th: R	Role SP	Health F	LIMA Plan A
Ht: 6' 4"	Wt: 224	Type	PT/Exp B	Rand Var +1
			Consist B	MM 4303

Highest IP total since 2018 with only one IL stint (oblique) sidelining him for two weeks. Improved 2nd half ERA mostly due to S% spike, but season-long recoveries of both K% (supported by SwK) and BB% give this rebound year some legs. Health concerns linger at this age, but he can repeat on a per-inning basis.

Yr Tm	W	Sv	IP	K	ERA	WHIP	xERA	xWHIP	vL+	vR+	BF/G	BB%	K%	K-BB%	xBB%	SwK	Vel	G	L	F	H%	S%	HR/F	xHR/F	GS	APC	DOM%	DIS%	Sv%	LI	RAR	BPX	R$
18 CLE	17	0	192	231	3.38	1.13	3.07	1.06	96	89	24.5	5%	29%	24%	6%	15.7%	93.5	47	21	32	33%	74%	13%	14%	30	93	47%	17%	0	0.80	18.3	191	$23
19 CLE	6	1	80	96	5.29	1.35	3.73	1.09	111	118	14.8	5%	28%	23%	6%	15.3%	93.5	41	23	36	36%	68%	22%	22%	12	55	42%	25%	50	0.70	-7.7	180	-$1
20 CLE	3	0	68	82	2.91	1.21	3.70	1.23	97	83	23.3	10%	29%	20%	8%	15.4%	93.6	44	22	34	30%	81%	14%	14%	12	92	33%	8%			12.9	137	$16
21 NYM	1	0	54	50	6.04	1.43	4.59	1.29	96	126	19.8	8%	21%	14%	6%	12.9%	93.3	42	21	36	32%	63%	20%	17%	12	74	8%	33%			-11.7	98	-$9
22 NYM	15	0	152	152	3.97	1.33	3.55	1.18	104	108	22.2	6%	24%	17%	6%	13.6%	92.9	46	22	32	34%	73%	12%	13%	29	83	28%	34%			0.0	133	$7
1st Half	9	0	87	89	4.64	1.33	3.60	1.15	116	101	23.3	6%	24%	18%	6%	13.7%	93.3	44	21	35	35%	68%	13%	13%	16	85	25%	25%			-7.2	139	$4
2nd Half	6	0	65	63	3.06	1.33	3.49	1.21	83	115	20.9	7%	23%	16%	7%	13.5%	92.4	48	24	28	34%	80%	11%	14%	13	81	31%	46%			7.2	124	$7
Proj	10	0	145	144	3.72	1.28	3.38	1.21	96	103	20.2	7%	24%	17%	6%	13.4%	93.1	45	22	33	32%	75%	14%	15%	29						4.4	122	$7

Castillo,Diego

Age: 29	Th: R	Role RP	Health C	LIMA Plan A
Ht: 6' 3"	Wt: 250	Type Pwr/GB	PT/Exp B	Rand Var -2
			Consist B	MM 5310

A tale of two halves, as H%/S% and HR/F fortune completely flipped. Late-July shoulder inflammation cost him a couple weeks too, and may have contributed to 2nd half skills collapse, which saw K-BB% tumble and go-to slider lose effectiveness. An outside shot at saves given ERA history, but slider (and strikeouts) need to bounce back.

Yr Tm	W	Sv	IP	K	ERA	WHIP	xERA	xWHIP	vL+	vR+	BF/G	BB%	K%	K-BB%	xBB%	SwK	Vel	G	L	F	H%	S%	HR/F	xHR/F	GS	APC	DOM%	DIS%	Sv%	LI	RAR	BPX	R$
18 TAM *	4	4	84	93	2.55	0.94	1.99	1.16	70	81	5.1	8%	29%	22%	8%	13.7%	97.7	45	18	37	25%	77%	12%	13%	11	21	0%	36%	57	1.20	16.5	152	$12
19 TAM	5	8	69	81	3.41	1.24	3.53	1.25	101	85	4.5	9%	28%	19%	8%	14.0%	98.3	57	13	30	31%	77%	15%	15%	6	17	0%	83%	80	1.16	9.3	146	$7
20 TAM	3	4	22	23	1.66	1.06	3.81	1.41	70	81	4.0	12%	26%	13%	9%	15.6%	96.2	60	11	28	19%	95%	20%	9%	0	15			80	1.39	7.5	98	$12
21 2 AL	5	16	58	75	2.78	0.98	3.02	1.07	113	69	3.8	7%	32%	25%	7%	15.6%	94.7	49	15	36	26%	81%	19%	10%	0	15			73	1.34	10.7	180	$14
22 SEA	7	7	54	53	3.64	1.14	3.76	1.32	103	72	3.8	10%	24%	14%	8%	12.5%	95.3	46	19	34	26%	70%	10%	11%	0	14			100	1.21	2.2	92	$5
1st Half	6	4	29	32	4.66	1.21	3.49	1.23	91	81	3.9	9%	27%	18%	7%	13.8%	95.1	39	29	32	31%	61%	8%	11%	0	15			100	1.22	-2.5	115	$2
2nd Half	1	3	25	21	2.49	1.07	4.06	1.42	114	60	3.6	11%	21%	10%	8%	10.9%	95.5	54	9	38	20%	83%	12%	11%	0	14			100	1.19	4.6	67	-$1
Proj	5	2	58	62	3.20	1.11	3.17	1.25	102	74	3.9	10%	27%	18%	8%	13.3%	96.2	50	16	34	26%	75%	13%	12%	0						5.5	121	$4

Castillo,Luis

Age: 30	Th: R	Role SP	Health C	LIMA Plan B
Ht: 6' 2"	Wt: 200	Type Pwr/GB	PT/Exp A	Rand Var -1
			Consist B	MM 5405

Shoulder issue delayed start by a month and was traded to SEA mid-season, but cruised all year long with career-best ERA. Swapped change-ups for more four-seamers, which fueled K% and BB% gains despite fewer GBs, but xERA/xWHIP ultimately approved. No longer a WHIP underachiever, skills and volume open door to... UP: first 200 IP/200 K season

Yr Tm	W	Sv	IP	K	ERA	WHIP	xERA	xWHIP	vL+	vR+	BF/G	BB%	K%	K-BB%	xBB%	SwK	Vel	G	L	F	H%	S%	HR/F	xHR/F	GS	APC	DOM%	DIS%	Sv%	LI	RAR	BPX	R$
18 CIN	10	0	170	165	4.30	1.22	3.77	1.23	120	82	22.8	7%	23%	16%	7%	13.9%	95.8	46	22	32	29%	70%	18%	17%	31	90	26%	32%			-3.1	128	$7
19 CIN	15	0	191	226	3.40	1.14	3.43	1.27	89	78	24.4	10%	29%	19%	10%	16.4%	96.5	55	18	27	27%	74%	18%	15%	32	99	28%	16%			26.0	135	$23
20 CIN	4	0	70	89	3.21	1.23	3.01	1.15	106	74	24.3	8%	30%	22%	7%	16.0%	97.5	58	19	22	34%	75%	13%	12%	12	96	25%	0%			10.7	179	$17
21 CIN	8	0	188	192	3.98	1.36	3.67	1.30	101	98	24.3	9%	24%	15%	8%	13.5%	97.3	57	19	25	32%	73%	15%	13%	33	96	30%	24%			6.6	114	$4
22 2 TM	8	0	150	167	2.99	1.08	3.24	1.15	91	83	24.6	7%	27%	20%	7%	13.0%	97.1	47	20	34	29%	75%	10%	10%	25	100	44%	12%			18.1	146	$16
1st Half	3	0	64	66	3.09	1.14	3.47	1.23	94	81	24.3	8%	25%	16%	8%	11.9%	96.7	48	20	31	29%	75%	9%	9%	11	102	45%	9%			6.9	121	$6
2nd Half	5	0	86	101	2.92	1.04	3.08	1.09	89	83	24.9	7%	29%	22%	6%	13.8%	97.3	46	19	35	29%	76%	11%	11%	14	99	43%	14%			11.2	164	$19
Proj	12	0	181	205	3.09	1.11	2.81	1.14	94	80	23.1	8%	29%	21%	7%	14.1%	97.1	51	19	29	30%	75%	13%	12%	31						19.6	154	$21

Castillo,Max

Age: 24	Th: R	Role RP	Health A	LIMA Plan C+
Ht: 6' 2"	Wt: 256	Type Con	PT/Exp D	Rand Var +2
			Consist C	MM 2101

0-2, 5.95 ERA in 39 IP at TOR/KC. Chaotic season featured deadline trade to KC, numerous recalls from AAA, and stints as both starter and reliever. Brutal ratios through it all, especially as SP (6.92 ERA, 1.50 WHIP in 26 IP) with mediocre strikeout upside and iffy control. Not worth a late flyer given lack of a single standout skill.

Yr Tm	W	Sv	IP	K	ERA	WHIP	xERA	xWHIP	vL+	vR+	BF/G	BB%	K%	K-BB%	xBB%	SwK	Vel	G	L	F	H%	S%	HR/F	xHR/F	GS	APC	DOM%	DIS%	Sv%	LI	RAR	BPX	R$
18																																	
19																																	
20																																	
21 aa	11	0	102	77	5.06	1.41	4.90				20.6	7%	18%	10%							32%	66%									-10.0	64	-$3
22 2 AL *	6	0	119	105	4.25	1.25	3.81	1.31	119	99	15.1	9%	22%	13%	9%	10.0%	93.0	47	17	36	28%	69%	20%	16%	6	50	0%	50%	0	0.43	-4.1	82	$1
1st Half	5	0	65	61	1.82	0.91	1.79	1.26	116	72	16.3	9%	24%	15%	8%	11.6%	93.8	57	10	33	20%	86%	29%	33%	0	37			0	0.21	17.3	116	$19
2nd Half	1	0	53	45	7.24	1.66	6.29	1.36	120	109	14.0	8%	18%	10%	9%	9.6%	92.8	45	18	37	36%	57%	18%	13%	6	55	0%	50%	0	0.52	-21.5	46	-$22
Proj	4	0	73	57	4.82	1.33	4.01	1.38	112	103	16.4	9%	19%	10%	9%	9.6%	92.8	45	18	37	29%	66%	12%	12%	12						-7.6	66	-$4

Cavalli,Cade

Age: 24	Th: R	Role SP	Health C	LIMA Plan A+
Ht: 6' 4"	Wt: 226	Type Pwr	PT/Exp D	Rand Var 0
			Consist D	MM 3201

0-1, 14.54 ERA in 4 IP at WAS. Debuted in late August for one start, then landed on the IL with shoulder issue that ended his season. Three plus pitches led to excellent K% in the minors, but not without command and control issues. Long-term outlook is bright given prospect pedigree, but expect growing pains with those BB% concerns.

Yr Tm	W	Sv	IP	K	ERA	WHIP	xERA	xWHIP	vL+	vR+	BF/G	BB%	K%	K-BB%	xBB%	SwK	Vel	G	L	F	H%	S%	HR/F	xHR/F	GS	APC	DOM%	DIS%	Sv%	LI	RAR	BPX	R$
18																																	
19																																	
20																																	
21 a/a	4	0	84	87	4.86	1.55	4.35				21.7	13%	24%	11%							34%	68%									-6.2	90	-$7
22 WAS *	6	0	101	91	4.23	1.22	2.84	1.22	105	150	19.5	9%	26%	17%	12%	13.1%	95.6	50	8	42	30%	63%	0%	12%	1	99	0%	0%			-3.3	111	$1
1st Half	3	0	61	50	5.09	1.31	3.42				19.4	10%	20%	10%							30%	59%	0%		0	0					-8.4	89	-$8
2nd Half	3	0	43	41	2.77	1.02	1.70	1.21	105	150	20.4	8%	24%	17%	12%	13.1%	95.6	50	8	42	28%	70%	0%	12%	1	99	0%	0%			6.3	147	$4
Proj	5	0	87	83	3.95	1.27	3.74	1.31			21.6	9%	23%	14%				43	18	39	29%	73%	12%	12%	16						0.2	93	$1

Cease,Dylan

Age: 27	Th: R	Role SP	Health A	LIMA Plan C+
Ht: 6' 2"	Wt: 195	Type Pwr/FB	PT/Exp A	Rand Var -5
			Consist C	MM 4405

An ace-like R$ via elite ratios, a ton of Ks, and plenty of volume. Strikeouts should keep piling up given dominant slider (21% SwK), though it's worth noting 2nd half dip in xERA/xWHIP, good fortune in H%/S% and HR/F, and walk rate concerns. Expect regression, somewhere between 2021 and 2022. xERA and xWHIP are useful baselines.

Yr Tm	W	Sv	IP	K	ERA	WHIP	xERA	xWHIP	vL+	vR+	BF/G	BB%	K%	K-BB%	xBB%	SwK	Vel	G	L	F	H%	S%	HR/F	xHR/F	GS	APC	DOM%	DIS%	Sv%	LI	RAR	BPX	R$
18 aa	3	0	53	68	2.33	1.16	2.60				21.1	12%	32%	20%							29%	83%									11.9	141	$4
19 CHW *	9	0	142	143	5.56	1.63	5.65	1.39	120	102	21.8	11%	23%	12%	11%	11.1%	96.5	46	21	34	36%	68%	21%	17%	14	97	14%	36%			-18.4	64	-$8
20 CHW	5	0	58	44	4.01	1.44	5.74	1.66	121	101	21.3	13%	17%	4%	12%	9.9%	97.5	40	22	39	24%	81%	18%	16%	12	90	0%	42%			3.2	-2	$5
21 CHW	13	0	166	226	3.91	1.25	3.78	1.18	94	88	22.1	10%	32%	22%	9%	15.5%	96.7	33	23	44	33%	72%	11%	12%	32	92	22%	16%			7.2	145	$13
22 CHW	14	0	184	227	2.20	1.11	3.54	1.22	92	74	23.3	10%	30%	20%	9%	15.3%	96.8	39	17	44	27%	85%	8%	8%	32	98	34%	19%			40.1	125	$29
1st Half	7	0	86	125	2.51	1.24	3.10	1.17	104	75	22.8	11%	34%	23%	8%	16.7%	96.8	44	18	38	34%	83%	9%	8%	16	96	38%	19%			15.5	159	$20
2nd Half	7	0	98	102	1.93	0.99	3.91	1.27	82	72	23.9	10%	27%	17%	10%	14.0%	96.9	35	17	49	22%	86%	8%	8%	16	99	31%	19%			24.7	96	$31
Proj	14	0	181	214	3.39	1.24	3.50	1.29	102	84	23.2	11%	29%	18%	10%	14.7%	97.0	39	20	42	29%	77%	12%	12%	32						12.9	106	$16

Cessa,Luis

Age: 31	Th: R	Role RP	Health D	LIMA Plan B
Ht: 6' 0"	Wt: 208	Type Con	PT/Exp C	Rand Var 0
			Consist B	MM 3101

Posted scary early ratios as a reliever, then H% ran hot as a starter come mid-August. A decline in SwK, particularly in 2nd half, took its toll on K% and change-up became a non-factor (17.5% SwK in 2021, 8.2% in 2022). One quality pitch (slider) might send him back to 'pen, but not worth targeting in either role.

Yr Tm	W	Sv	IP	K	ERA	WHIP	xERA	xWHIP	vL+	vR+	BF/G	BB%	K%	K-BB%	xBB%	SwK	Vel	G	L	F	H%	S%	HR/F	xHR/F	GS	APC	DOM%	DIS%	Sv%	LI	RAR	BPX	R$
18 NYY *	4	2	82	69	4.54	1.24	3.76	1.28	99	110	13.8	6%	21%	15%	7%	12.4%	94.8	47	23	30	32%	63%	12%	12%	5	44	0%	60%	67	0.39	-4.0	120	$0
19 NYY	2	1	81	75	4.11	1.31	4.46	1.38	102	99	8.0	9%	22%	13%	8%	13.2%	94.5	49	18	33	28%	75%	18%	13%	0	31			100	0.67	3.9	92	$0
20 NYY	0	1	22	17	3.32	1.25	5.10	1.37	94	94	5.8	8%	18%	11%	8%	12.5%	93.7	40	21	40	29%	76%	7%	10%	0	23			100	0.59	3.0	75	-$2
21 2 TM	5	0	65	54	2.51	1.14	3.92	1.28	90	82	4.9	7%	21%	13%	7%	12.0%	93.6	51	20	28	28%	81%	9%	10%	0	18			0	0.76	14.0	102	$5
22 CIN	4	0	81	59	4.57	1.29	4.25	1.37	99	113	7.3	8%	18%	9%	8%	9.6%	93.5	49	17	34	27%	70%	17%	15%	10	27	10%	60%	0	0.67	-6.0	67	-$4
1st Half	3	0	31	25	6.75	1.63	4.24	1.37	100	143	4.6	9%	18%	9%	8%	11.0%	94.1	53	17	30	34%	61%	21%	22%	1	16	0%	100%	0	0.72	-10.5	75	-$14
2nd Half	1	0	50	34	3.24	1.08	4.24	1.37	99	90	12.4	8%	17%	9%	8%	8.7%	93.2	46	17	37	22%	78%	15%	11%	9	47	11%	56%	0	0.57	4.5	62	$0
Proj	4	0	87	70	4.18	1.27	3.77	1.34	98	102	7.1	8%	20%	12%	8%	11.2%	93.9	49	19	32	28%	72%	16%	14%	0						-2.2	83	-$1

CORBIN YOUNG

Chafin,Andrew

Age: 33	Th: L	Role RP	Health D	LIMA Plan A+	
Ht: 6' 2"	Wt: 235	Type Pwr	PT/Exp C	Rand Var -2	
			Consist A	MM 5400	

Another rock-solid year in middle relief. Skills are as good as ever, and that's saying something. Checks all relief boxes: strong K-BB%, copious SwK, GB tilt, effective both vL and vR, keeps ball in yard. It's shocking he's only got 11 saves in his 9 year career. LI column shows he's trusted by his manager wherever he goes. Why not the 9th? UP: 20 Sv

Yr Tm	W	Sv	IP	K	ERA	WHIP	xERA	xWHIP	vL+	vR+	BF/G	BB%	K%	K-BB%	xBB%	SwK	Vel	G	L	F	H%	S%	HR/F	xHR/F	GS	APC	DOM%	DIS%	Sv%	LI	RAR	BPX	R$
18 ARI	1	0	49	53	3.10	1.34	3.71	1.39	91	80	2.7	12%	25%	13%	10%	14.6%	93.5	50	26	24	32%	74%	0%	8%	0	11			0	1.20	6.4	91	-$1
19 ARI	2	0	53	68	3.76	1.33	3.49	1.17	89	95	2.9	8%	30%	22%	7%	15.8%	93.8	43	28	29	36%	75%	15%	17%	0	12			0	1.23	4.8	160	-$1
20 2 NL	1	1	10	13	6.52	1.66	4.26	1.30	109	125	3.0	11%	29%	18%	10%	10.3%	93.6	41	26	33	39%	64%	22%	20%	0	12			33	1.38	-2.5	126	-$5
21 2 TM	2	5	69	64	1.83	0.93	3.84	1.22	65	73	3.7	7%	24%	17%	6%	12.1%	92.0	45	16	39	24%	83%	6%	10%	0	13			63	1.14	20.6	117	$11
22 DET	2	3	57	67	2.83	1.17	3.29	1.16	95	82	3.8	8%	28%	20%	8%	14.0%	91.6	51	14	35	31%	79%	10%	10%	0	14			75	1.25	8.1	152	$3
1st Half	0	1	24	30	2.66	1.01	2.66	1.07	73	79	3.4	7%	32%	24%	6%	15.5%	90.9	56	13	31	30%	74%	6%	11%	0	13			100	1.01	3.8	184	-$3
2nd Half	2	2	34	37	2.94	1.28	3.74	1.22	111	84	4.1	8%	25%	17%	9%	13.1%	92.0	49	15	36	32%	82%	11%	10%	0	15			67	1.44	4.3	131	$0
Proj	2	0	58	67	2.94	1.19	3.03	1.18	91	82	3.3	9%	29%	20%	8%	14.3%	92.4	48	19	33	32%	78%	10%	12%	0						7.4	142	$1

Chapman,Aroldis

Age: 35	Th: L	Role RP	Health D	LIMA Plan A+	
Ht: 6' 4"	Wt: 218	Type Pwr/FB	PT/Exp A	Rand Var -3	
			Consist C	MM 4510	

Catastrophic season on multiple levels. BPX summarizes the skills collapse, and injuries/off field issues raise questions about whether he even gets a chance to reverse the decline. Second half shows that velocity is (mostly) still there, so we can't rule out a return to effectiveness, at least in spurts. But full-season dominance is likely a thing of the past.

Yr Tm	W	Sv	IP	K	ERA	WHIP	xERA	xWHIP	vL+	vR+	BF/G	BB%	K%	K-BB%	xBB%	SwK	Vel	G	L	F	H%	S%	HR/F	xHR/F	GS	APC	DOM%	DIS%	Sv%	LI	RAR	BPX	R$
18 NYY	3	32	51	93	2.45	1.05	2.48	1.13	64	70	3.9	14%	44%	30%	8%	16.2%	98.9	44	19	37	30%	77%	6%	7%	0	17			94	1.10	10.7	200	$19
19 NYY	3	37	57	85	2.21	1.11	3.08	1.16	61	75	3.9	11%	36%	26%	7%	14.7%	98.4	42	28	30	32%	82%	8%	8%	0	16			88	1.05	16.1	169	$22
20 NYY	1	3	12	22	3.09	0.86	2.50	0.87	38	104	3.5	9%	49%	40%	5%	20.1%	98.1	22	22	56	27%	75%	20%	16%	0	15			60	1.29	2.0	251	$4
21 NYY	6	30	56	97	3.36	1.31	3.14	1.27	66	98	4.0	16%	40%	24%	10%	17.0%	98.5	43	19	38	30%	82%	23%	26%	0	16			88	1.39	6.3	149	$16
22 NYY	4	9	36	43	4.46	1.43	4.72	1.60	70	102	3.7	18%	27%	9%	11%	13.3%	97.7	36	18	46	25%	71%	10%	11%	0	16			100	0.97	-2.2	20	$0
1st Half	0	9	15	15	4.80	1.73	5.91	1.76	84	112	3.8	18%	21%	3%	11%	11.6%	97.3	36	20	43	29%	75%	11%	13%	0	15			100	1.13	-1.5	-38	-$5
2nd Half	4	0	21	28	4.22	1.22	3.96	1.47	62	90	3.7	17%	32%	15%	11%	14.5%	98.1	35	16	49	22%	67%	10%	9%	0	16			0	0.84	-0.7	60	-$3
Proj	4	10	51	71	3.53	1.29	3.36	1.39	67	90	3.7	16%	34%	18%	9%	14.5%	98.1	39	21	40	28%	75%	12%	12%	0						2.8	95	$4

Chirinos,Yonny

Age: 29	Th: R	Role RP	Health F	LIMA Plan A+	
Ht: 6' 2"	Wt: 225	Type Con	PT/Exp F	Rand Var -5	
			Consist D	MM 3101	

1-0, 0.00 ERA in 7 IP at TAM. Nearly two-year journey back from late-2020 Tommy John surgery, a trip that also included a second surgery to repair a fractured elbow late in 2021. This cup-o-coffee was good for shaking off rust, flashing velocity and pitch mix consistent with 2019 emergence. Now let's see if he can ramp up the innings again.

Yr Tm	W	Sv	IP	K	ERA	WHIP	xERA	xWHIP	vL+	vR+	BF/G	BB%	K%	K-BB%	xBB%	SwK	Vel	G	L	F	H%	S%	HR/F	xHR/F	GS	APC	DOM%	DIS%	Sv%	LI	RAR	BPX	R$
18 TAM *	5	0	122	101	4.29	1.30	4.36	1.28	93	97	19.3	6%	20%	14%	7%	11.5%	93.7	44	24	32	32%	70%	8%	12%	7	73	29%	43%	0	0.90	-2.1	91	$0
19 TAM	9	0	133	114	3.85	1.05	4.10	1.23	78	101	20.4	5%	22%	16%	7%	10.7%	93.9	43	23	33	25%	71%	18%	18%	18	76	33%	22%	0	0.73	10.8	118	$12
20 TAM	0	0	11	10	2.38	1.59	4.97	1.35	83	152	17.3	8%	19%	12%	10%	14.2%	93.4	31	34	34	35%	94%	17%	15%	3	63	0%	100%			2.9	75	-$6
21																																	
22 TAM *	1	0	23	16	2.12	1.18	3.21	1.12	41	102	13.1	3%	20%	17%	6%	9.0%	93.6	73	9	18	27%	86%	0%	16%	1	50	0%	0%	0	0.81	5.3	79	-$2
1st Half																																	
2nd Half	1	0	23	16	2.12	1.18	3.21	1.34	41	102	13.1	8%	17%	10%	6%	9.0%	93.6	73	9	18	27%	86%	0%	16%	1	50	0%	0%	0	0.81	5.3	79	-$4
Proj	6	0	102	75	3.78	1.15	3.66	1.25	91	104	16.7	6%	19%	13%		11.0%	93.8	43	24	33	28%	72%	14%	16%	16						2.4	95	$4

Cimber,Adam

Age: 32	Th: R	Role RP	Health A	LIMA Plan A	
Ht: 6' 3"	Wt: 195	Type Con	PT/Exp C	Rand Var -3	
			Consist B	MM 3101	

Perhaps his greatest trick yet: continues to survive with 80-something MPH sinker/slider combo that doesn't miss bats, and this year didn't even generate GBs at its usual 50%+ clip. But no matter, still hung a sub-3.00 ERA. How? He simply avoids hard contact, and keeps the ball in the yard. It's unique, and should be appreciated... from a distance.

Yr Tm	W	Sv	IP	K	ERA	WHIP	xERA	xWHIP	vL+	vR+	BF/G	BB%	K%	K-BB%	xBB%	SwK	Vel	G	L	F	H%	S%	HR/F	xHR/F	GS	APC	DOM%	DIS%	Sv%	LI	RAR	BPX	R$
18 2 TM	3	0	68	58	3.42	1.24	3.39	1.24	145	85	4.1	6%	20%	14%	4%	10.4%	86.5	57	21	21	32%	74%	12%	6%	0	14			0	0.88	6.1	129	$1
19 CLE	6	1	57	41	4.45	1.32	4.45	1.41	124	86	3.6	8%	17%	9%	5%	10.2%	85.2	56	20	24	30%	68%	14%	14%	0	12			33	1.32	0.4	76	$0
20 CLE	0	0	11	5	3.97	1.32	5.48	1.37	57	120	3.5	4%	10%	6%	4%	10.7%	85.9	52	12	36	31%	71%	7%	11%	0	13			0	0.75	0.7	66	-$6
21 2 TM	3	1	72	51	2.26	1.07	3.89	1.27	79	82	4.0	6%	18%	12%	6%	10.2%	87.1	54	17	29	28%	79%	3%	7%	0	14			100	0.79	17.7	102	$7
22 TOR	10	4	71	58	2.80	1.12	3.74	1.16	92	96	3.8	4%	20%	15%	5%	9.8%	86.5	42	24	35	30%	78%	8%	7%	0	14			50	1.17	10.2	119	$9
1st Half	7	4	34	26	3.48	1.04	3.75	1.18	78	98	3.6	5%	20%	15%	4%	10.5%	86.7	42	22	36	27%	69%	9%	9%	0	13			57	1.38	2.1	113	$7
2nd Half	3	0	37	32	2.19	1.19	3.73	1.15	100	94	4.0	4%	20%	16%	5%	9.2%	86.4	41	25	33	32%	85%	8%	6%	0	14			0	0.96	8.1	125	$2
Proj	6	0	73	57	3.27	1.15	3.52	1.24	101	88	3.6	6%	20%	14%	5%	9.9%	86.3	47	22	32	29%	74%	9%	9%	0						6.3	104	$4

Civale,Aaron

Age: 28	Th: R	Role SP	Health F	LIMA Plan B	
Ht: 6' 2"	Wt: 215	Type	PT/Exp A	Rand Var +4	
			Consist A	MM 4301	

Arm, wrist, and glute injuries led to three interruptions of this roller-coaster season. Got racked around the yard in first half; then normalization of both skills and luck factors drove a strong finish. Skills gains highlighted by new pitch mix, leaning on cutter/curve combo that yielded SwK% and GB% gains. Need to see this new version again, but we're intrigued.

Yr Tm	W	Sv	IP	K	ERA	WHIP	xERA	xWHIP	vL+	vR+	BF/G	BB%	K%	K-BB%	xBB%	SwK	Vel	G	L	F	H%	S%	HR/F	xHR/F	GS	APC	DOM%	DIS%	Sv%	LI	RAR	BPX	R$
18 aa	5	0	107	66	5.27	1.53	5.91				22.2	5%	14%	9%							35%	68%									-14.8	54	-$10
19 CLE *	10	0	132	104	2.83	1.19	3.59	1.33	91	81	23.0	6%	20%	13%	9%	9.0%	92.6	40	22	37	29%	80%	7%	6%	10	86	40%	40%			27.2	95	$14
20 CLE	4	0	74	69	4.74	1.32	4.07	1.19	91	125	26.0	5%	22%	17%	7%	10.6%	91.8	44	25	31	34%	68%	16%	15%	12	100	17%	42%			-2.6	136	$4
21 CLE	12	0	124	99	3.84	1.12	4.23	1.26	91	107	23.7	6%	20%	14%	8%	9.6%	91.6	45	18	37	25%	74%	17%	16%	21	91	29%	29%			6.6	100	$11
22 CLE	5	0	97	98	4.92	1.19	3.65	1.13	103	102	20.4	5%	24%	19%	8%	10.7%	91.2	41	20	38	31%	61%	13%	11%	20	79	20%	30%			-11.3	141	-$1
1st Half	2	0	46	45	7.04	1.54	4.31	1.24	127	124	20.9	7%	22%	14%	8%	9.9%	90.8	37	23	40	36%	56%	14%	9%	10	85	10%	50%			-17.4	104	-$18
2nd Half	3	0	51	53	3.00	0.86	3.08	1.01	81	77	19.8	4%	27%	23%	8%	11.6%	91.6	46	18	37	25%	71%	12%	12%	10	74	30%	10%			6.1	175	$8
Proj	9	0	116	115	3.76	1.16	3.25	1.13	95	104	21.3	6%	25%	19%	8%	11.2%	91.6	43	21	36	30%	73%	14%	12%	22						3.0	140	$8

Clarke,Taylor

Age: 30	Th: R	Role RP	Health F	LIMA Plan B	
Ht: 6' 4"	Wt: 217	Type Con/FB	PT/Exp C	Rand Var -1	
			Consist B	MM 3211	

Changed teams and did what everyone says you should do: throw your best pitches more and your worst pitches less. Junked his curve, threw fewer fastballs; leaning more on slider and change. BB% plunged, SwK% popped, K-BB% got downright interesting. 2nd half BB% slippage and lingering FB/HR concern keep us from getting too excited, though.

Yr Tm	W	Sv	IP	K	ERA	WHIP	xERA	xWHIP	vL+	vR+	BF/G	BB%	K%	K-BB%	xBB%	SwK	Vel	G	L	F	H%	S%	HR/F	xHR/F	GS	APC	DOM%	DIS%	Sv%	LI	RAR	BPX	R$
18 aaa	13	0	152	101	3.72	1.27	3.68				23.0	6%	16%	10%							31%	71%									8.1	87	$8
19 ARI *	8	1	123	90	5.59	1.43	5.66	1.42	114	120	16.9	9%	17%	8%	9%	10.4%	93.7	40	17	44	28%	67%	20%	19%	15	66	7%	53%	100	0.76	-16.5	21	-$4
20 ARI	3	0	43	40	4.36	1.29	4.91	1.46	89	104	15.3	11%	22%	10%	9%	9.0%	94.4	43	20	38	25%	73%	17%	19%	5	59	0%	60%	0	0.58	0.5	60	$2
21 ARI	1	0	43	39	4.98	1.52	4.85	1.30	107	104	4.5	7%	20%	13%	8%	10.6%	95.6	36	26	38	37%	68%	8%	12%	0	18			0	1.00	-3.8	89	-$7
22 KC	3	3	49	48	4.04	1.18	3.84	1.08	106	99	4.3	4%	24%	20%	8%	12.9%	95.7	37	19	44	33%	69%	9%	9%	0	18			38	1.02	-0.4	148	$0
1st Half	1	1	35	33	4.33	1.25	3.94	1.09	122	96	4.5	3%	22%	19%	6%	12.6%	95.6	38	19	44	34%	69%	11%	10%	0	19			25	1.05	-1.6	147	-$6
2nd Half	2	2	14	15	3.29	1.02	3.59	1.07	65	106	3.9	6%	28%	22%	9%	13.9%	96.0	33	19	47	30%	69%	6%	8%	0	17			50	0.96	1.1	150	-$3
Proj	3	5	65	55	4.03	1.23	3.77	1.21	106	99	6.7	6%	21%	15%	8%	11.0%	94.9	39	20	41	30%	73%	12%	14%	0						-0.5	110	$1

Clase,Emmanuel

Age: 25	Th: R	Role RP	Health A	LIMA Plan C	
Ht: 6' 2"	Wt: 206	Type /xGB	PT/Exp A	Rand Var -5	
			Consist A	MM 5331	

If you grew a closer in a lab, he would pound the strike zone with 100mph sinkers that yield nothing but Ks and GBs. Behold! The biggest "complaint" you can lodge here is that he gets batters to ground out before they strike out, which keeps him from being a 100-K reliever. We're quibbling, of course. The most bankable saves source in the game today.

Yr Tm	W	Sv	IP	K	ERA	WHIP	xERA	xWHIP	vL+	vR+	BF/G	BB%	K%	K-BB%	xBB%	SwK	Vel	G	L	F	H%	S%	HR/F	xHR/F	GS	APC	DOM%	DIS%	Sv%	LI	RAR	BPX	R$
18																																	
19 TEX *	3	12	63	54	3.78	1.24	3.46	1.24	90	90	4.7	6%	21%	15%	6%	11.3%	99.3	61	20	20	32%	69%	15%	17%	1	16	0%	100%	86	1.00	5.6	119	$6
20																																	
21 CLE	4	24	70	74	1.29	0.96	2.71	1.11	61	69	3.9	6%	27%	21%	5%	17.6%	100.3	68	14	18	29%	88%	6%	7%	0	15			83	1.11	25.6	178	$22
22 CLE	3	42	73	77	1.36	0.73	2.25	0.99	63	58	3.5	4%	28%	25%	4%	17.6%	99.6	64	16	20	24%	84%	8%	8%	0	12			91	1.16	23.4	199	$31
1st Half	2	19	34	37	1.31	0.82	2.38	1.03	50	71	3.7	5%	28%	23%	4%	16.3%	99.8	60	22	18	26%	85%	6%	8%	0	12			90	1.23	11.3	187	$23
2nd Half	1	23	38	40	1.41	0.65	2.14	0.96	73	44	3.4	5%	29%	26%	4%	18.8%	99.3	68	11	22	22%	83%	10%	9%	0	12			92	1.11	12.1	209	$29
Proj	3	38	73	73	1.95	0.88	2.26	1.06	75	68	3.7	5%	27%	23%	4%	17.7%	99.7	65	15	20	27%	79%	9%	8%	0						18.1	181	$26

RAY MURPHY

Clevinger,Mike

Age: 32	Th: R	Role SP	Health F	LIMA Plan A+	
Ht: 6' 4"	Wt: 215	Type /FB	PT/Exp D	Rand Var -2	
			Consist A	MM 3203	

Preseason knee injury delayed his return from late-2020 Tommy John, triceps strain cost him a couple more weeks in May. Overall, this was not the same pitcher from pre-TJS days: Velocity and SwK each down multiple ticks, K-BB% was there for first half but didn't last. Not too old to dial back the vintage version, but there are no guarantees either.

Yr Tm	W	Sv	IP	K	ERA	WHIP	xERA	xWHIP	vL+	vR+	BF/G	BB%	K%	K-BB%	xBB%	SwK	Vel	G	L	F	H%	S%	HR/F	xHR/F	GS	APC	DOM%	DIS%	Sv%	LI	RAR	BPX	R$
18 CLE	13	0	200	207	3.02	1.16	3.85	1.24	99	82	25.3	8%	26%	17%	8%	12.4%	93.6	40	20	39	29%	78%	10%	10%	32	102	31%	13%			28.0	120	$22
19 CLE	13	0	126	169	2.71	1.06	3.22	1.09	85	74	23.8	7%	34%	26%	8%	15.7%	95.5	41	24	36	32%	77%	10%	13%	21	100	57%	10%			27.8	180	$21
20 2 TM	3	0	42	40	3.02	1.15	4.19	1.29	102	91	20.3	9%	25%	16%	9%	13.3%	95.2	34	27	39	27%	81%	15%	14%	8	81	25%	25%			7.3	97	$9
21																																	
22 SD	7	0	114	91	4.33	1.20	4.58	1.30	100	103	21.1	7%	19%	12%	8%	11.1%	93.5	35	19	46	26%	70%	13%	12%	22	84	18%	41%	0	0.74	-5.1	74	$1
1st Half	2	0	35	36	3.34	1.17	3.84	1.23	100	72	18.4	8%	24%	16%	8%	11.0%	94.1	43	18	40	29%	76%	11%	7%	7	78	29%	29%	0	0.75	2.7	115	-$2
2nd Half	5	0	79	55	4.76	1.21	4.91	1.33	100	114	22.5	7%	16%	9%	8%	11.1%	93.3	32	20	48	25%	68%	13%	13%	15	87	13%	47%			-7.8	58	$0
Proj	**9**	**0**	**131**	**120**	**4.15**	**1.16**	**3.79**	**1.28**	**98**	**89**	**22.0**	**8%**	**23%**	**15%**	**8%**	**12.7%**	**94.3**	**37**	**20**	**43**	**27%**	**68%**	**11%**	**12%**	**24**						**-3.0**	**92**	**$6**

Cobb,Alex

Age: 35	Th: R	Role SP	Health F	LIMA Plan A+	
Ht: 6' 3"	Wt: 205	Type /xGB	PT/Exp A	Rand Var +1	
			Consist B	MM 5303	

Took his act up the coast and replicated 2021's success, this time with more innings and better skills support. Dialed up the velocity while leaning into sinker/splitter combo that both produced GBs in bunches. Health grade and age are large drags on our optimism, but these skills and better defense (H%) behind him could yield... UP: 3.00 ERA

Yr Tm	W	Sv	IP	K	ERA	WHIP	xERA	xWHIP	vL+	vR+	BF/G	BB%	K%	K-BB%	xBB%	SwK	Vel	G	L	F	H%	S%	HR/F	xHR/F	GS	APC	DOM%	DIS%	Sv%	LI	RAR	BPX	R$
18 BAL	5	0	152	102	4.90	1.41	4.57	1.36	105	120	23.6	7%	15%	9%	8%	7.6%	92.0	50	19	31	31%	69%	15%	15%	28	87	21%	36%			-14.2	78	-$7
19 BAL	0	0	12	8	10.95	1.86	5.49	1.31	130	203	20.0	3%	13%	10%	7%	10.5%	92.3	46	24	30	31%	57%	60%	55%	3	76	0%	67%			-9.8	98	-$9
20 BAL	2	0	52	38	4.30	1.34	4.42	1.39	109	92	22.6	8%	17%	9%	8%	9.8%	92.5	54	24	22	29%	73%	22%	23%	10	81	0%	40%			1.0	75	$0
21 LAA	8	0	93	98	3.76	1.26	3.50	1.25	84	90	21.8	8%	25%	17%	8%	11.3%	92.8	53	23	24	33%	70%	8%	9%	18	88	33%	22%			5.8	126	$4
22 SF	7	0	150	151	3.73	1.30	2.99	1.19	97	92	22.5	7%	24%	17%	8%	10.8%	94.8	62	18	21	35%	72%	10%	10%	28	86	25%	21%			4.4	147	$4
1st Half	3	0	51	56	4.59	1.37	2.89	1.16	119	93	19.9	7%	26%	19%	6%	11.1%	94.6	62	17	21	36%	68%	17%	9%	11	74	18%	27%			-3.9	161	-$5
2nd Half	4	0	99	95	3.28	1.27	3.05	1.20	87	92	24.2	7%	23%	16%	8%	10.7%	95.0	61	18	21	34%	74%	7%	11%	17	94	29%	18%			8.3	139	$10
Proj	**7**	**0**	**145**	**143**	**3.60**	**1.20**	**2.90**	**1.19**	**90**	**85**	**21.2**	**7%**	**24%**	**18%**	**8%**	**10.9%**	**93.7**	**57**	**20**	**22**	**32%**	**71%**	**11%**	**14%**	**28**						**6.6**	**140**	**$8**

Cole,Gerrit

Age: 32	Th: R	Role SP	Health B	LIMA Plan C+	
Ht: 6' 4"	Wt: 220	Type Pwr/FB	PT/Exp A	Rand Var +1	
			Consist A	MM 5505	

For all of the hand-wringing last offseason (What was wrong with him? Was it the hamstring, or the sticky stuff?) he has now answered all questions: three lines worth of NYY work here are incredibly consistent: ERA/xERA bounces in a narrow range, K-BB% is equal parts flat and elite, HR/F issues are baked in and don't hurt much. Safest ace around.

Yr Tm	W	Sv	IP	K	ERA	WHIP	xERA	xWHIP	vL+	vR+	BF/G	BB%	K%	K-BB%	xBB%	SwK	Vel	G	L	F	H%	S%	HR/F	xHR/F	GS	APC	DOM%	DIS%	Sv%	LI	RAR	BPX	R$
18 HOU	15	0	200	276	2.88	1.03	3.13	1.07	71	94	25.0	8%	35%	27%	6%	14.7%	96.6	36	21	43	30%	76%	10%	11%	32	102	50%	0%			31.5	184	$31
19 HOU	20	0	212	326	2.50	0.89	2.71	0.93	77	76	24.8	6%	40%	34%	6%	17.6%	97.2	40	20	39	29%	81%	17%	14%	33	102	42%	12%			52.5	231	$46
20 NYY	7	0	73	94	2.84	0.96	3.43	1.04	106	77	24.0	6%	33%	27%	6%	16.0%	96.7	37	20	43	26%	84%	19%	17%	12	100	50%	8%			14.6	189	$33
21 NYY	16	0	181	243	3.23	1.06	3.14	1.00	92	82	24.2	6%	33%	28%	6%	14.9%	97.7	43	16	41	32%	76%	13%	15%	30	99	37%	7%			23.2	201	$28
22 NYY	13	0	201	257	3.50	1.02	2.99	1.02	90	94	24.0	6%	32%	26%	6%	15.0%	97.8	42	17	41	28%	74%	17%	15%	33	99	48%	6%			11.6	184	$24
1st Half	7	0	93	117	2.99	1.01	3.05	1.06	72	97	23.3	7%	31%	24%	6%	15.0%	97.8	45	16	39	27%	79%	16%	12%	16	95	63%	13%			11.3	174	$25
2nd Half	6	0	107	140	3.94	1.02	2.93	0.99	104	91	24.8	6%	33%	28%	6%	15.1%	97.9	40	18	42	29%	69%	18%	18%	17	103	35%	0%			0.4	193	$21
Proj	**14**	**0**	**174**	**230**	**3.33**	**1.02**	**2.67**	**1.00**	**93**	**88**	**23.6**	**6%**	**34%**	**28%**	**6%**	**15.4%**	**97.5**	**41**	**18**	**41**	**29%**	**76%**	**17%**	**15%**	**28**						**13.7**	**192**	**$24**

Coleman,Dylan

Age: 26	Th: R	Role RP	Health A	LIMA Plan A+	
Ht: 6' 5"	Wt: 230	Type Pwr	PT/Exp D	Rand Var -5	
			Consist D	MM 3311	

Even a pitcher with a two-pitch arsenal can benefit from pitch mix changes: amped up his slider usage as season went on, which helped to both cut his BB% and flip his GB/FB for the better. LI says manager noticed, too. xBB% doesn't totally buy the gains, and RP samples can be flaky, so we'll need confirmation. But he may be figuring it out. If so... UP: 20 Sv

Yr Tm	W	Sv	IP	K	ERA	WHIP	xERA	xWHIP	vL+	vR+	BF/G	BB%	K%	K-BB%	xBB%	SwK	Vel	G	L	F	H%	S%	HR/F	xHR/F	GS	APC	DOM%	DIS%	Sv%	LI	RAR	BPX	R$
18																																	
19																																	
20																																	
21 KC *	5	7	66	79	3.55	1.11	2.55		138	40	5.2	9%	31%	22%	10%	13.8%	98.3	24	24	53	30%	68%	0%	0%	0	22			64	0.81	5.8	145	$7
22 KC	5	0	68	71	2.78	1.24	4.14	1.43	93	84	4.3	13%	25%	12%	11%	13.4%	97.6	41	20	39	26%	80%	7%	9%	0	18			0	1.01	10.0	62	$3
1st Half	2	0	32	35	3.62	1.42	4.91	1.61	85	102	4.4	17%	24%	8%	12%	13.4%	97.5	35	24	42	24%	79%	11%	12%	0	19			0	0.78	1.4	8	-$6
2nd Half	3	0	36	36	2.02	1.07	3.49	1.26	99	63	4.1	9%	25%	16%	11%	13.5%	97.7	48	17	36	27%	81%	3%	7%	0	17			0	1.22	8.6	111	$4
Proj	**5**	**5**	**65**	**67**	**3.40**	**1.25**	**3.72**	**1.36**	**104**	**88**	**4.5**	**11%**	**25%**	**14%**	**11%**	**13.4%**	**97.6**	**42**	**20**	**38**	**28%**	**76%**	**11%**	**9%**	**0**						**4.6**	**82**	**$3**

Contreras,Roansy

Age: 23	Th: R	Role RP	Health A	LIMA Plan A	
Ht: 6' 0"	Wt: 175	Type /FB	PT/Exp D	Rand Var -1	
			Consist D	MM 3203	

5-5, 3.79 ERA in 95 IP at PIT. Started year in majors, took a couple trips on the Triple-A shuttle to manage his workload (also reflected in BF/G). 2021's electric K% and K-BB% didn't carry over, but you wonder whether some of that was a by-product of the tight usage pattern. Should be unrestricted entering 2023, with a decent floor and room to soar.

Yr Tm	W	Sv	IP	K	ERA	WHIP	xERA	xWHIP	vL+	vR+	BF/G	BB%	K%	K-BB%	xBB%	SwK	Vel	G	L	F	H%	S%	HR/F	xHR/F	GS	APC	DOM%	DIS%	Sv%	LI	RAR	BPX	R$
18																																	
19																																	
20																																	
21 PIT *	3	0	63	73	2.48	0.94	2.12		90	95	17.0	5%	31%	25%		13.0%	96.4	57	0	43	28%	76%	0%	16%	1	46	0%	0%			13.9	188	$7
22 PIT *	6	0	130	124	3.57	1.25	3.81	1.36	97	104	17.7	10%	21%	12%	7%	13.0%	95.6	36	20	43	28%	76%	11%	13%	18	76	11%	39%	0	0.74	6.3	85	$4
1st Half	2	0	65	63	3.57	1.35	4.38	1.39	102	128	17.0	11%	23%	12%	8%	12.7%	96.3	38	20	42	28%	80%	15%	13%	8	72	13%	50%	0	0.72	3.2	65	-$1
2nd Half	4	0	65	61	3.58	1.16	3.23	1.24	89	88	18.5	7%	23%	15%	7%	13.3%	94.9	35	21	44	29%	71%	7%	13%	10	79	10%	30%			3.1	110	$5
Proj	**7**	**0**	**160**	**150**	**3.86**	**1.23**	**3.85**	**1.29**	**93**	**99**	**18.9**	**9%**	**23%**	**15%**	**7%**	**13.0%**	**95.5**	**36**	**20**	**43**	**29%**	**72%**	**10%**	**13%**	**30**						**2.2**	**91**	**$7**

Corbin,Patrick

Age: 33	Th: L	Role SP	Health A	LIMA Plan B	
Ht: 6' 4"	Wt: 220	Type	PT/Exp A	Rand Var +5	
			Consist A	MM 2103	

Keeps trying to reinvent his arsenal, to no avail: this year, threw more four-seamers at the expense of sinker/slider. That cut HR rate, but batters hit .346 vs the fastball. Slider remains his big swing-and-miss pitch, but also yields nearly half his HR. Even if he reaches xERA levels, stuff is just not good enough anymore, and changing the mix is shuffling deck chairs.

Yr Tm	W	Sv	IP	K	ERA	WHIP	xERA	xWHIP	vL+	vR+	BF/G	BB%	K%	K-BB%	xBB%	SwK	Vel	G	L	F	H%	S%	HR/F	xHR/F	GS	APC	DOM%	DIS%	Sv%	LI	RAR	BPX	R$
18 ARI	11	0	200	246	3.15	1.05	2.81	1.06	95	81	24.2	6%	31%	25%	8%	16.2%	90.8	48	24	27	32%	72%	11%	14%	33	95	39%	0%			24.7	192	$25
19 WAS	14	0	202	238	3.25	1.18	3.65	1.22	67	94	25.3	8%	29%	20%	9%	14.7%	91.9	50	18	33	30%	77%	14%	20%	33	100	30%	27%			31.2	147	$24
20 WAS	2	0	66	60	4.66	1.57	4.56	1.26	101	116	26.8	6%	20%	14%	7%	11.1%	90.2	44	26	31	37%	74%	15%	16%	11	97	18%	45%			-1.7	117	-$6
21 WAS	9	0	172	143	5.82	1.47	4.51	1.35	85	122	24.2	8%	19%	11%	8%	11.6%	92.5	47	22	31	31%	66%	23%	21%	31	89	19%	48%			-32.9	82	-$13
22 WAS	6	0	153	128	6.31	1.70	4.51	1.30	120	126	23.0	7%	18%	11%	8%	9.5%	92.7	44	23	33	38%	66%	16%	19%	31	85	10%	52%			-44.0	88	-$23
1st Half	4	0	89	79	5.68	1.67	4.44	1.31	129	119	24.4	7%	19%	12%	8%	10.1%	92.2	45	21	33	38%	69%	14%	18%	17	88	12%	41%			-18.8	91	-$20
2nd Half	2	0	64	49	7.17	1.73	4.60	1.29	107	135	21.3	6%	16%	10%	8%	8.8%	93.2	42	25	33	38%	61%	18%	21%	14	80	7%	64%			-25.3	84	-$25
Proj	**6**	**0**	**145**	**122**	**5.27**	**1.60**	**4.12**	**1.34**	**104**	**120**	**23.4**	**8%**	**19%**	**11%**	**8%**	**10.8%**	**92.0**	**44**	**23**	**33**	**35%**	**71%**	**16%**	**19%**	**27**						**-23.2**	**80**	**-$13**

Cortes,Nestor

Age: 28	Th: L	Role SP	Health D	LIMA Plan C+	
Ht: 5' 11"	Wt: 210	Type /xFB	PT/Exp C	Rand Var -5	
			Consist F	MM 4305	

After he flashed breakout performance in late 2021, we said "regression is coming." We're still waiting, as he went out and Xeroxed a repeat, complete with more SwK% and a bit of FB reduction. It's a matter of faith in these parts, though, that the H%/S%/HR/F gods are not to be trifled with. Set your expectations around xERA and you won't be smited.

Yr Tm	W	Sv	IP	K	ERA	WHIP	xERA	xWHIP	vL+	vR+	BF/G	BB%	K%	K-BB%	xBB%	SwK	Vel	G	L	F	H%	S%	HR/F	xHR/F	GS	APC	DOM%	DIS%	Sv%	LI	RAR	BPX	R$
18 BAL *	6	0	122	87	4.91	1.43	5.18		196	183	18.5	9%	17%	8%	8%	10.2%	88.0	47	16	37	30%	70%	29%	16%	0	27			0	0.97	-11.5	39	-$6
19 NYY *	7	0	108	103	5.27	1.39	5.02	1.38	131	103	11.3	9%	23%	14%	8%	10.9%	89.6	34	22	44	31%	67%	18%	14%	1	39	0%	100%	0	0.72	-10.2	64	-$2
20 SEA	0	0	8	8	15.26	2.35	7.09	1.67	208	176	8.8	14%	19%	5%	12%	7.9%	88.1	37	19	44	31%	42%	50%	24%	1	33	0%	100%	0	0.51	-10.2	-7	-$15
21 NYY *	3	1	108	117	2.71	1.03	3.16	1.15	94	87	15.4	6%	28%	22%	7%	11.0%	90.7	27	21	51	27%	82%	11%	10%	14	69	21%	14%	100	0.64	20.7	139	$12
22 NYY	12	0	158	163	2.44	0.92	3.67	1.12	49	83	22.0	6%	27%	20%	5%	11.8%	91.8	34	19	47	25%	79%	8%	7%	28	88	36%	18%			29.8	132	$26
1st Half	7	0	85	91	2.44	0.95	3.62	1.09	49	90	22.1	6%	27%	22%	5%	11.3%	91.3	34	18	48	26%	83%	10%	7%	15	89	47%	20%			16.1	145	$25
2nd Half	5	0	73	72	2.45	0.89	3.74	1.16	48	74	21.8	7%	25%	19%	6%	12.4%	92.3	33	21	46	23%	75%	6%	7%	13	87	23%	15%			13.7	118	$19
Proj	**12**	**0**	**174**	**179**	**3.50**	**1.03**	**3.40**	**1.14**	**91**	**83**	**22.3**	**6%**	**27%**	**20%**	**6%**	**11.5%**	**91.1**	**33**	**20**	**47**	**27%**	**71%**	**11%**	**9%**	**30**						**10.2**	**130**	**$19**

RAY MURPHY

Crawford,Kutter

Age: 27	Th: R	Role: RP	Health: C	LIMA Plan: B
Ht: 6' 1"	Wt: 209	Type: /xFB	PT/Exp: D	Rand Var: +1
			Consist: B	MM: 2201

3-6, 5.47 ERA in 77 IP at BOS. Swingman spent bulk of first half in long relief, before being pushed into rotation for second half. Wasn't effective in either role, though SwK% and K% were playing up a bit more out of the bullpen. Could conceivably stick there if he can combine that swing-and-miss with fewer walks and/or FB. Safe to ignore at this point.

Yr	Tm	W	Sv	IP	K	ERA	WHIP	xERA	xWHIP	vL+	vR+	BF/G	BB%	K%	K-BB%	xBB%	SwK	Vel	G	L	F	H%	S%	HR/F	xHR/F	GS	APC	DOM%	DIS%	Sv%	LI	RAR	BPX	R$
18																																		
19	aa	1	0	20	19	5.83	1.99	6.55				19.4	17%	20%	3%							36%	72%									-3.3	40	-$7
20																																		
21	BOS *	6	0	98	108	5.51	1.27	4.49		35	260	19.1	6%	27%	21%		15.8%	93.9	11	33	56	34%	58%	20%	30%	1	57	0%	100%			-15.1	137	-$3
22	BOS *	4	0	102	95	5.49	1.45	5.37	1.28	139	95	16.2	9%	23%	14%	8%	11.9%	94.6	31	22	47	33%	65%	11%	11%	12	62	0%	33%	0	0.74	-19.2	68	-$9
1st Half		3	0	50	50	5.29	1.51	5.70	1.29	103	103	12.8	8%	22%	14%	12%	12.5%	95.3	32	16	51	35%	69%	11%	15%	2	44	0%	50%	0	0.72	-8.2	65	-$10
2nd Half		1	0	52	45	5.68	1.39	4.47	1.27	164	92	22.1	7%	20%	13%	6%	11.5%	94.1	31	24	45	32%	62%	11%	10%	10	82	0%	30%			-11.0	81	-$12
Proj		**3**	**0**	**65**	**59**	**5.08**	**1.38**	**4.24**	**1.31**	**128**	**92**	**18.2**	**8%**	**22%**	**13%**	**8%**	**12.0%**	**94.6**	**31**	**21**	**48**	**32%**	**66%**	**11%**	**12%**	**12**						**-8.9**	**80**	**-$6**

Crismatt,Nabil

Age: 28	Th: R	Role: RP	Health: A	LIMA Plan: A+
Ht: 6' 1"	Wt: 220	Type:	PT/Exp: C	Rand Var: -2
			Consist: B	MM: 4301

Jumped up the bullpen leverage ladder early in season, as H%/S%/HR/F troika was making him temporarily bulletproof. That predictably didn't last, but full-season incremental gains in K% and xBB, while holding GB tilt, mean he's worthy of more meaningful work. Just think LIMA/holds/vulture wins-type work, rather than saves.

Yr	Tm	W	Sv	IP	K	ERA	WHIP	xERA	xWHIP	vL+	vR+	BF/G	BB%	K%	K-BB%	xBB%	SwK	Vel	G	L	F	H%	S%	HR/F	xHR/F	GS	APC	DOM%	DIS%	Sv%	LI	RAR	BPX	R$
18	a/a	11	0	146	120	5.01	1.51	4.99				23.5	9%	19%	10%							34%	68%									-15.6	70	-$7
19	a/a	4	0	133	134	5.67	1.39	5.37				20.8	6%	24%	18%							34%	63%									-19.2	90	-$6
20	STL	0	0	8	8	3.24	0.84	3.28	1.05	135	58	5.2	3%	26%	23%	5%	14.0%	89.5	50	18	32	21%	80%	29%	17%	0	19			0	0.19	1.2	174	-$4
21	SD	3	0	81	71	3.76	1.36	4.16	1.27	106	101	7.8	7%	20%	13%	8%	12.0%	89.9	51	17	33	33%	76%	13%	12%	0	30			0	0.51	5.0	108	-$2
22	SD	5	0	67	65	2.94	1.17	3.51	1.24	88	94	5.6	8%	23%	15%	6%	11.8%	90.4	51	21	29	29%	77%	9%	9%	1	21	0%	0%	0	0.80	8.5	117	$3
1st Half		4	0	38	33	1.88	0.97	3.29	1.24	82	69	5.5	7%	22%	15%	8%	11.0%	90.4	54	18	27	25%	81%	4%	7%	1	21	0%	0%	0	0.92	9.9	113	$7
2nd Half		1	0	29	32	4.34	1.45	3.78	1.24	98	117	5.7	8%	24%	16%	6%	12.6%	90.4	46	23	31	35%	74%	15%	12%	0	22			0	0.67	-1.3	122	-$8
Proj		**4**	**0**	**73**	**70**	**3.54**	**1.25**	**3.28**	**1.24**	**98**	**106**	**7.7**	**8%**	**24%**	**16%**	**7%**	**12.0%**	**90.3**	**50**	**20**	**30**	**30%**	**76%**	**15%**	**10%**	**0**						**3.8**	**118**	**$1**

Crochet,Garrett

Age: 24	Th: L	Role: RP	Health: F	LIMA Plan: B
Ht: 6' 6"	Wt: 230	Type: Pwr	PT/Exp: D	Rand Var: 0
			Consist: D	MM: 3400

March elbow injury required Tommy John surgery, putting him on track for a summer-2023 return. Pre-injury, we were encouraged by 2nd-half 2021 control gains, and had role questions (SP vs. RP) for the longer term. Seems logical they would bring him back in relief, so re-establishing those BB% gains will be his first yardstick toward being a 2024 asset.

Yr	Tm	W	Sv	IP	K	ERA	WHIP	xERA	xWHIP	vL+	vR+	BF/G	BB%	K%	K-BB%	xBB%	SwK	Vel	G	L	F	H%	S%	HR/F	xHR/F	GS	APC	DOM%	DIS%	Sv%	LI	RAR	BPX	R$
18																																		
19																																		
20	CHW	0	0	6	8	0.00	0.50	2.24		40	46	4.4	0%	36%	36%		16.5%	100.2	62	0	38	25%	100%	0%	10%	0	17			0	0.57	3.3	289	-$2
21	CHW	3	0	54	65	2.82	1.27	4.03	1.33	69	87	4.3	12%	28%	17%	10%	12.7%	96.7	40	22	38	31%	78%	4%	6%	0	17			0	1.00	9.7	100	$1
22																																		
1st Half																																		
2nd Half																																		
Proj		**2**	**0**	**36**	**39**	**3.53**	**1.28**	**3.55**	**1.33**	**79**	**112**	**4.6**	**11%**	**26%**	**15%**	**10%**	**12.7%**	**96.7**	**40**	**22**	**38**	**30%**	**75%**	**10%**	**8%**	**0**						**2.0**	**92**	**-$2**

Crowe,Wil

Age: 28	Th: R	Role: RP	Health: A	LIMA Plan: C
Ht: 6' 2"	Wt: 235	Type:	PT/Exp: B	Rand Var: 0
			Consist: F	MM: 2101

After washing out of rotation in 2021, transitioned to bullpen and tried narrowing his arsenal: focused on a sinker/slider/change mix, which created a pronounced GB tilt, but didn't help paltry K-BB% at all... well, it did help for 1st half, but couldn't hold those gains. Even 1st half was below-average per BPX, confirming he's an easy pass.

Yr	Tm	W	Sv	IP	K	ERA	WHIP	xERA	xWHIP	vL+	vR+	BF/G	BB%	K%	K-BB%	xBB%	SwK	Vel	G	L	F	H%	S%	HR/F	xHR/F	GS	APC	DOM%	DIS%	Sv%	LI	RAR	BPX	R$
18	aa	0	0	27	12	7.53	1.97	7.44				26.0	12%	9%	-3%							33%	63%									-11.3	-18	-$12
19	a/a	7	0	150	106	6.33	1.60	5.74				25.5	8%	16%	8%							35%	61%									-33.8	44	-$15
20	WAS	0	0	8	8	11.88	2.64	8.30	1.88	238	149	15.3	17%	17%	0%	12%	6.2%	91.4	28	24	48	37%	65%	36%	36%	3	65	0%	100%			-7.6	-81	-$15
21	PIT	4	0	117	111	5.48	1.57	4.92	1.43	110	122	20.2	11%	21%	10%	11%	10.8%	93.6	43	19	38	32%	71%	19%	17%	25	84	16%	56%	0	0.76	-17.4	62	-$12
22	PIT	6	4	76	68	4.38	1.39	4.26	1.45	82	107	5.5	11%	20%	9%	11%	12.1%	94.7	50	19	31	29%	70%	12%	9%	1	23	0%	0%	40	1.23	-3.9	57	-$1
1st Half		3	2	47	47	3.28	1.18	3.83	1.37	77	78	6.1	11%	24%	13%	10%	12.6%	94.3	50	16	34	27%	72%	5%	5%	1	27	0%	0%	40	1.11	4.0	85	$3
2nd Half		3	2	29	21	6.14	1.74	5.00	1.57	89	146	4.9	12%	15%	4%	11%	11.4%	95.3	49	23	27	32%	69%	22%	15%	0	19			40	1.36	-7.8	12	-$11
Proj		**4**	**0**	**65**	**54**	**4.55**	**1.48**	**4.14**	**1.47**	**90**	**120**	**7.4**	**11%**	**19%**	**8%**	**11%**	**11.6%**	**94.6**	**48**	**20**	**32**	**31%**	**72%**	**14%**	**11%**	**0**						**-4.7**	**50**	**-$5**

Cuas,Jose

Age: 29	Th: R	Role: RP	Health: A	LIMA Plan: C
Ht: 6' 3"	Wt: 195	Type:	PT/Exp: F	Rand Var: -5
			Consist: A	MM: 2100

4-2, 3.58 ERA in 38 IP at CHC. Former infielder converted to pitching in 2018. Just about everything here is typical of a sidearm-firing righty: generates copious groundballs, keeps ball in yard. But has no answer vL, defaults to walking them far too often (22%, vs 10% vR). That's a tough road with today's rules, and an easy cross-off for our purposes.

Yr	Tm	W	Sv	IP	K	ERA	WHIP	xERA	xWHIP	vL+	vR+	BF/G	BB%	K%	K-BB%	xBB%	SwK	Vel	G	L	F	H%	S%	HR/F	xHR/F	GS	APC	DOM%	DIS%	Sv%	LI	RAR	BPX	R$
18																																		
19																																		
20																																		
21	a/a	4	3	38	27	2.04	1.28	3.59				6.2	6%	17%	12%							33%	84%									10.4	106	$2
22	KC *	4	4	61	49	2.83	1.46	3.92	1.57	153	89	3.8	13%	19%	6%	9%	10.8%	93.1	49	25	26	31%	81%	7%	6%	0	15			80	1.14	8.5	76	$1
1st Half		2	3	36	23	1.78	1.10	2.55	1.40	159	66	3.8	8%	16%	8%	9%	13.4%	92.8	55	11	34	25%	86%	8%	7%	0	13			75	1.13	9.7	81	$4
2nd Half		2	1	27	26	3.97	1.80	5.15	1.61	151	100	3.9	15%	20%	5%	9%	9.6%	93.3	46	32	22	37%	77%	6%	5%	0	16			100	1.15	0.0	77	-$9
Proj		**4**	**0**	**58**	**44**	**3.98**	**1.40**	**3.97**	**1.49**	**137**	**85**	**4.4**	**11%**	**18%**	**7%**	**9%**	**9.6%**	**93.3**	**46**	**32**	**22**	**30%**	**71%**	**9%**	**7%**	**0**						**-0.1**	**39**	**-$3**

Cueto,Johnny

Age: 37	Th: R	Role: SP	Health: F	LIMA Plan: A+
Ht: 5' 11"	Wt: 229	Type: Con	PT/Exp: A	Rand Var: -2
			Consist: A	MM: 2103

Unexpected late-career bounce turns out to be a turn-back-the-clock effect: he resurrected a cutter from mid-last-decade, which helped keep batted balls out of air and in the park. But, pump the brakes: SwK and velocity are diminished from those days; age and Health are red flags. xERA is instructive: guile can get you just so far, regression is coming.

Yr	Tm	W	Sv	IP	K	ERA	WHIP	xERA	xWHIP	vL+	vR+	BF/G	BB%	K%	K-BB%	xBB%	SwK	Vel	G	L	F	H%	S%	HR/F	xHR/F	GS	APC	DOM%	DIS%	Sv%	LI	RAR	BPX	R$
18	SF	3	0	53	38	3.23	1.11	4.21	1.30	96	98	23.8	6%	18%	12%	9%	9.6%	89.4	44	19	37	25%	78%	14%	17%	9	88	33%	56%			6.0	90	$1
19	SF	1	0	16	13	5.06	1.25	4.92	1.62	149	60	16.8	13%	19%	6%	11%	7.9%	91.3	53	16	30	20%	65%	23%	26%	4	66	0%	25%			-1.1	28	-$4
20	SF	2	0	63	56	5.40	1.37	4.88	1.40	110	93	23.1	9%	20%	11%	9%	8.6%	91.3	41	25	34	30%	63%	14%	14%	12	95	17%	50%			-7.4	71	-$5
21	SF	7	0	115	98	4.08	1.37	4.45	1.25	112	105	22.3	6%	20%	14%	7%	10.5%	91.8	38	26	36	33%	74%	12%	14%	21	85	14%	33%	0	0.77	2.6	100	$0
22	CHW *	8	0	176	115	3.50	1.23	4.00	1.27	108	96	24.5	5%	16%	11%	7%	8.2%	91.4	43	19	38	30%	75%	8%	9%	24	95	17%	13%	0	0.77	10.2	82	$7
1st Half		2	0	77	61	3.64	1.22	4.24	1.28	102	103	22.3	7%	20%	13%	7%	8.9%	91.4	41	19	40	28%	77%	13%	11%	9	91	22%	11%	0	0.75	3.1	69	$1
2nd Half		6	0	98	54	3.39	1.23	4.43	1.26	110	91	27.1	4%	13%	10%	6%	7.8%	91.4	43	19	37	31%	73%	5%	9%	15	97	13%	13%			7.1	81	$9
Proj		**7**	**0**	**145**	**108**	**4.33**	**1.29**	**4.01**	**1.31**	**108**	**97**	**23.4**	**7%**	**18%**	**11%**	**8%**	**8.8%**	**91.3**	**42**	**22**	**37**	**30%**	**69%**	**11%**	**12%**	**25**						**-6.5**	**78**	**$0**

Darvish,Yu

Age: 36	Th: R	Role: SP	Health: C	LIMA Plan: C+
Ht: 6' 5"	Wt: 220	Type: Pwr/FB	PT/Exp: A	Rand Var: -3
			Consist: A	MM: 5405

Ended 2021 with health questions, answered them emphatically by carrying biggest workload since 2013. While R$ history in this box paints a portrait of volatility, xERA and BPX across his last three full seasons (2019, 2021-22) are actually quite stable. That's your skills baseline; hedge on IP total due to age and you net this projection.

Yr	Tm	W	Sv	IP	K	ERA	WHIP	xERA	xWHIP	vL+	vR+	BF/G	BB%	K%	K-BB%	xBB%	SwK	Vel	G	L	F	H%	S%	HR/F	xHR/F	GS	APC	DOM%	DIS%	Sv%	LI	RAR	BPX	R$
18	CHC	1	0	40	49	4.95	1.43	4.15	1.35	115	97	22.5	12%	27%	16%	10%	11.2%	93.9	38	23	40	31%	70%	18%	17%	8	93	13%	50%			-3.9	100	-$5
19	CHC	6	0	179	229	3.98	1.10	3.36	1.14	101	83	23.6	8%	31%	24%	6%	14.0%	94.2	45	21	34	28%	72%	23%	19%	31	92	32%	16%			11.6	168	$15
20	CHC	8	0	76	93	2.01	0.96	3.02	1.01	84	70	24.8	5%	31%	27%	5%	15.0%	95.5	43	26	31	31%	82%	9%	10%	12	96	58%	0%			22.9	197	$40
21	SD	8	0	166	199	4.22	1.09	3.74	1.10	99	93	22.7	6%	29%	23%	6%	12.4%	94.5	37	18	45	29%	68%	15%	12%	30	92	33%	20%			0.9	159	$12
22	SD	16	0	195	197	3.10	0.95	3.54	1.08	77	91	25.7	5%	26%	21%	5%	11.8%	95.0	37	19	44	26%	72%	10%	12%	30	99	50%	7%			20.9	146	$28
1st Half		7	0	94	85	3.53	1.01	3.75	1.13	76	93	25.3	5%	22%	18%	6%	11.8%	95.1	39	19	42	27%	67%	8%	10%	15	97	40%	13%			5.1	128	$18
2nd Half		9	0	100	112	2.69	0.90	3.35	1.03	78	87	26.1	5%	29%	24%	5%	11.7%	94.8	35	20	45	25%	78%	11%	14%	15	101	60%	0%			15.8	163	$33
Proj		**13**	**0**	**167**	**186**	**3.46**	**1.10**	**3.12**	**1.09**	**92**	**92**	**24.1**	**6%**	**29%**	**22%**	**6%**	**12.7%**	**94.9**	**39**	**21**	**40**	**30%**	**73%**	**12%**	**13%**	**27**						**10.4**	**153**	**$18**

RAY MURPHY

Davidson,Tucker

Age: 27 Th: L Role SP	Health D	LIMA Plan C+	
Ht: 6' 2" Wt: 215 Type	PT/Exp D	Rand Var +1	
	Consist F	MM 1101	

2-7, 6.75 ERA in 52 IP at ATL/LAA. Sent to Angels in deadline deal, they took a good look and saw the same awful results the Braves saw. More walks than strikeouts is simply disqualifying in today's game. He's shown (marginally) better than this in past, and he's left-handed, so he'll get more chances. But give him a wide berth for now.

Yr Tm	W	Sv	IP	K	ERA	WHIP	xERA	xWHIP	vL+	vR+	BF/G	BB%	K%	K-BB%	xBB%	SwK	Vel	G	L	F	H%	S%	HR/F	xHR/F	GS	APC	DOM%	DIS%	Sv%	LI	RAR	BPX	R$
18																																	
19 a/a	8	0	131	111	3.12	1.50	4.21				22.6	10%	20%	9%							34%	79%									22.4	80	$5
20 ATL	0	0	2	2	10.80	4.20	20.89		55	216	13.0	31%	15%	-15%		3.8%	92.1	29	14	57	43%	83%	25%	25%	1	53	0%	100%			-1.3	-431	-$9
21 ATL *	2	0	43	41	2.49	0.97	2.51	1.37	96	87	20.4	8%	25%	17%	7%	13.2%	93.0	41	21	38	22%	82%	14%	21%	4	76	0%	25%			9.4	108	$2
22 2 TM *	5	0	133	110	6.26	1.63	6.14	1.74	140	110	21.9	14%	14%	-1%	11%	9.6%	93.2	44	19	37	33%	64%	11%	8%	11	76	0%	55%	0	0.76	-37.6	33	-$19
1st Half	3	0	76	73	6.06	1.61	5.88	1.37	58	110	22.6	10%	22%	12%	12%	10.0%	94.0	49	18	33	35%	65%	0%	5%	3	70	0%	33%	0	0.68	-19.7	55	-$19
2nd Half	2	0	57	37	6.52	1.65	6.48	1.53	168	109	21.1	11%	14%	4%	11%	9.5%	92.8	42	19	39	31%	64%	15%	9%	8	79	0%	63%			-17.8	5	-$19
Proj	**3**	**0**	**73**	**60**	**4.95**	**1.53**	**4.33**	**1.43**	**130**	**109**	**21.9**	**10%**	**19%**	**9%**	**11%**	**9.7%**	**93.3**	**45**	**19**	**36**	**32%**	**71%**	**13%**	**9%**	**14**						**-8.7**	**55**	**-$8**

Davies,Zach

Age: 30 Th: R Role SP	Health D	LIMA Plan C+	
Ht: 6' 0" Wt: 180 Type Con	PT/Exp A	Rand Var -2	
	Consist B	MM 2103	

Mostly reversed 2021's collapse, albeit without major skill changes: sure, he shaved a few walks and hard hit balls, but in truth this was just a case of the H%/S% gods finding his sacrificial offering acceptable this year, after they belched it back at him last year. That's life for a sub-90 mph, pitch-to-contact type. Know that 2021 is the roster risk.

Yr Tm	W	Sv	IP	K	ERA	WHIP	xERA	xWHIP	vL+	vR+	BF/G	BB%	K%	K-BB%	xBB%	SwK	Vel	G	L	F	H%	S%	HR/F	xHR/F	GS	APC	DOM%	DIS%	Sv%	LI	RAR	BPX	R$
18 MIL *	3	0	94	70	5.35	1.43	4.46	1.36	107	105	20.0	10%	18%	8%	9%	8.5%	89.9	48	22	30	31%	63%	13%	12%	13	86	8%	38%			-13.9	62	-$8
19 MIL	10	0	160	102	3.55	1.29	5.30	1.46	99	95	21.7	8%	15%	8%	10%	7.4%	88.5	40	24	36	28%	77%	11%	13%	31	86	6%	32%			18.8	48	$9
20 SD	7	0	69	63	2.73	1.07	4.20	1.25	70	99	23.0	7%	23%	16%	10%	10.4%	88.6	41	22	37	26%	82%	13%	19%	12	88	42%	17%			14.8	113	$26
21 CHC	6	0	148	114	5.78	1.60	5.26	1.53	114	116	20.9	11%	17%	6%	11%	9.2%	88.0	42	25	32	31%	67%	17%	16%	32	81	3%	56%			-27.6	24	-$17
22 ARI	2	0	134	102	4.09	1.30	4.60	1.40	98	105	21.1	9%	18%	9%	11%	8.9%	89.6	43	17	40	27%	74%	13%	13%	27	85	15%	41%			-2.0	55	-$2
1st Half	2	0	80	62	3.94	1.19	4.34	1.33	102	91	22.1	8%	19%	11%	9%	9.4%	89.3	43	17	39	27%	71%	11%	12%	15	88	27%	33%			0.3	75	$1
2nd Half	0	0	54	40	4.31	1.45	5.01	1.50	90	121	19.8	11%	17%	6%	12%	8.1%	90.0	42	18	40	27%	78%	17%	16%	12	81	0%	50%			-2.3	26	-$11
Proj	**5**	**0**	**138**	**107**	**4.51**	**1.37**	**4.24**	**1.41**	**97**	**111**	**20.9**	**9%**	**18%**	**9%**	**11%**	**8.9%**	**89.1**	**42**	**20**	**37**	**29%**	**72%**	**14%**	**15%**	**28**						**-9.1**	**56**	**-$4**

De Los Santos,Enyel

Age: 27 Th: R Role RP	Health A	LIMA Plan A+	
Ht: 6' 3" Wt: 235 Type Pwr	PT/Exp D	Rand Var -2	
	Consist C	MM 5400	

Former starter transitioned to bullpen work post-pandemic, where his arsenal is blossoming: fastball has added some hop, slider has achieved wipeout status (37% swing/miss), and change-up is enough to make him effective vL. In-season BB% gains, still-emerging GB tilt suggest he hasn't peaked yet, either. Premium middle reliever for leagues that value them.

Yr Tm	W	Sv	IP	K	ERA	WHIP	xERA	xWHIP	vL+	vR+	BF/G	BB%	K%	K-BB%	xBB%	SwK	Vel	G	L	F	H%	S%	HR/F	xHR/F	GS	APC	DOM%	DIS%	Sv%	LI	RAR	BPX	R$
18 PHI *	11	0	147	113	3.40	1.31	4.08	1.44	70	157	21.0	9%	19%	10%	9%	10.7%	94.7	47	25	27	29%	78%	13%	10%	2	48	50%	50%	0	0.31	13.6	69	$8
19 PHI *	5	0	105	82	5.40	1.39	5.35	1.51	243	105	18.4	9%	19%	9%	6%	12.5%	93.3	39	26	35	28%	68%	36%	28%	1	35	0%	100%	0	0.26	-11.5	30	-$4
20																																	
21 2 NL	2	0	35	48	6.37	1.73	4.37	1.28	128	121	5.2	10%	28%	17%	6%	15.5%	94.9	38	22	40	40%	68%	21%	19%	0	21			0	0.46	-9.2	123	-$9
22 CLE	5	1	53	61	3.04	1.07	3.27	1.15	89	82	4.3	8%	28%	20%	6%	14.6%	95.3	40	26	35	29%	72%	7%	13%	0	17			50	0.96	6.1	139	$4
1st Half	1	1	25	31	3.55	1.18	3.38	1.23	99	88	4.4	10%	29%	19%	6%	14.3%	95.7	39	29	32	30%	71%	10%	14%	0	18			100	0.93	1.3	121	-$4
2nd Half	4	0	28	30	2.57	0.96	3.17	1.07	81	76	4.2	6%	28%	22%	5%	14.9%	94.8	41	23	37	29%	73%	4%	12%	0	16			0	0.98	4.8	155	$3
Proj	**5**	**0**	**58**	**65**	**3.51**	**1.18**	**3.21**	**1.21**	**104**	**93**	**5.8**	**9%**	**28%**	**19%**	**6%**	**14.8%**	**95.1**	**40**	**25**	**36**	**30%**	**74%**	**13%**	**13%**	**0**						**3.3**	**124**	**$2**

deGrom,Jacob

Age: 35 Th: R Role SP	Health F	LIMA Plan A	
Ht: 6' 4" Wt: 180 Type Pwr	PT/Exp B	Rand Var +2	
	Consist A	MM 5503	

Skills remain without peer; you can compare K-BB% or BPX with the game's top relievers. Problem is, the IP column now also compares with top RPs. GLASS HALF FULL: None of 2021-22 injuries have been surgical; he was a workhorse before that. HALF EMPTY: At 35, nagging things get worse, not better. Pay for 120 IP, know you might still be disappointed.

Yr Tm	W	Sv	IP	K	ERA	WHIP	xERA	xWHIP	vL+	vR+	BF/G	BB%	K%	K-BB%	xBB%	SwK	Vel	G	L	F	H%	S%	HR/F	xHR/F	GS	APC	DOM%	DIS%	Sv%	LI	RAR	BPX	R$
18 NYM	10	0	217	269	1.70	0.91	2.75	1.01	79	64	26.1	6%	32%	27%	5%	15.9%	96.0	46	22	32	29%	84%	6%	9%	32	100	75%	0%			65.6	200	$44
19 NYM	11	0	204	255	2.43	0.97	3.18	1.05	82	74	25.1	5%	32%	26%	6%	16.1%	96.9	44	21	35	30%	80%	11%	10%	32	103	66%	13%			52.3	187	$36
20 NYM	4	0	68	104	2.38	0.96	2.77	0.96	85	68	22.3	7%	39%	32%	6%	22.0%	98.6	42	21	37	31%	81%	13%	15%	12	95	50%	8%			17.4	230	$30
21 NYM	7	0	92	146	1.08	0.55	2.00	0.74	61	49	21.6	3%	45%	42%	4%	22.4%	99.3	44	17	39	23%	89%	9%	11%	15	82	80%	0%			36.2	274	$28
22 NYM	5	0	64	102	3.08	0.75	2.13	0.76	73	76	21.7	3%	43%	39%	5%	21.5%	98.9	39	19	42	28%	67%	17%	17%	11	85	45%	9%			7.1	268	$9
1st Half																																	
2nd Half	5	0	64	102	3.08	0.75	2.13	0.76	73	76	21.7	3%	43%	39%	5%	21.5%	98.9	39	19	42	28%	67%	17%	17%	11	85	45%	9%			7.1	269	$21
Proj	**8**	**0**	**123**	**180**	**2.78**	**0.86**	**2.16**	**0.89**	**79**	**71**	**22.4**	**5%**	**40%**	**34%**		**19.7%**	**98.2**	**43**	**20**	**38**	**29%**	**72%**	**13%**	**13%**	**20**						**18.0**	**229**	**$21**

DeSclafani,Anthony

Age: 33 Th: R Role RP	Health F	LIMA Plan B	
Ht: 6' 2" Wt: 195 Type	PT/Exp A	Rand Var +5	
	Consist C	MM 3203	

Right ankle injury from April cost him two months, then he came back for two June starts and had to shut down for the year due to same injury. Best to disregard all this. 2019, 2021 show what he can do when healthy, but aligning health and effectiveness is no easy feat. Fine to scoop out of discount bin, just have an exit strategy.

Yr Tm	W	Sv	IP	K	ERA	WHIP	xERA	xWHIP	vL+	vR+	BF/G	BB%	K%	K-BB%	xBB%	SwK	Vel	G	L	F	H%	S%	HR/F	xHR/F	GS	APC	DOM%	DIS%	Sv%	LI	RAR	BPX	R$
18 CIN *	7	0	135	125	5.15	1.32	5.42	1.22	125	94	22.4	6%	22%	16%	7%	10.2%	93.6	41	22	36	31%	69%	20%	14%	21	85	14%	24%			-16.6	76	-$3
19 CIN	9	0	167	167	3.89	1.20	4.30	1.26	105	85	22.5	7%	24%	17%	8%	10.4%	94.7	43	19	38	29%	75%	16%	13%	31	86	23%	26%			12.7	122	$12
20 CIN	1	0	34	25	7.22	1.69	5.81	1.53	136	106	17.6	10%	16%	6%	12%	9.8%	94.9	39	27	35	33%	60%	18%	18%	7	67	14%	43%	0	0.71	-11.5	25	-$15
21 SF	13	0	168	152	3.17	1.09	4.00	1.21	96	77	21.8	6%	22%	16%	7%	11.5%	94.1	44	19	36	28%	76%	11%	14%	31	83	26%	23%			22.7	118	$21
22 SF	0	0	19	17	6.63	2.00	4.62	1.19	160	148	18.8	4%	18%	14%	8%	10.0%	92.4	44	20	37	45%	71%	15%	14%	5	66	0%	60%			-6.2	128	-$9
1st Half	0	0	19	17	6.63	2.00	4.62	1.19	160	148	18.8	4%	18%	14%	8%	10.0%	92.4	44	20	37	45%	71%	15%	14%	5	66	0%	60%			-6.2	127	-$17
2nd Half																																	
Proj	**5**	**0**	**131**	**118**	**4.36**	**1.37**	**3.74**	**1.24**	**121**	**103**	**18.9**	**7%**	**22%**	**15%**		**10.4%**	**93.8**	**43**	**21**	**37**	**32%**	**76%**	**18%**	**14%**	**26**						**-6.3**	**108**	**-$2**

Detmers,Reid

Age: 23 Th: L Role SP	Health B	LIMA Plan A	
Ht: 6' 2" Wt: 210 Type Pwr/FB	PT/Exp C	Rand Var -2	
	Consist A	MM 3303	

We wrote "He's close" a year ago in this space; he responded with "How about now?" May no-hitter was his signature performance, but season actually turned during brief minor-league stint in late June. While in Triple-A, he reworked his slider into the SwK-inducing beast that unlocked his 2nd half skills surge. Now appears ready for... UP: 3.25 ERA, 200 K.

Yr Tm	W	Sv	IP	K	ERA	WHIP	xERA	xWHIP	vL+	vR+	BF/G	BB%	K%	K-BB%	xBB%	SwK	Vel	G	L	F	H%	S%	HR/F	xHR/F	GS	APC	DOM%	DIS%	Sv%	LI	RAR	BPX	R$
18																																	
19																																	
20																																	
21 LAA *	4	0	83	114	4.14	1.29	4.50	1.49	134	120	17.9	8%	34%	25%	8%	11.6%	92.9	34	21	46	35%	74%	16%	14%	5	76	0%	80%			1.3	132	$1
22 LAA	7	0	129	122	3.77	1.21	4.13	1.28	86	99	21.6	9%	23%	14%	8%	11.6%	93.2	36	22	42	29%	71%	9%	9%	25	87	20%	28%			3.2	89	$5
1st Half	2	0	58	44	4.66	1.10	4.56	1.37	69	109	19.8	9%	19%	10%	8%	9.3%	93.0	36	19	45	21%	64%	15%	14%	12	81	0%	33%			-4.9	54	-$3
2nd Half	5	0	71	78	3.04	1.30	3.79	1.21	100	92	23.2	8%	26%	18%	7%	13.5%	93.4	36	25	39	35%	76%	3%	5%	13	93	38%	23%			8.1	118	$8
Proj	**9**	**0**	**160**	**163**	**3.59**	**1.17**	**3.56**	**1.23**	**84**	**95**	**22.4**	**8%**	**26%**	**17%**	**7%**	**12.9%**	**93.3**	**36**	**23**	**41**	**29%**	**72%**	**9%**	**8%**	**28**						**7.4**	**108**	**$12**

Diaz,Alexis

Age: 26 Th: R Role RP	Health B	LIMA Plan B+	
Ht: 6' 2" Wt: 224 Type Pwr/xFB	PT/Exp D	Rand Var -5	
	Consist A	MM 3521	

Amid the season-long carnage in the CIN bullpen, Edwin's kid brother eventually worked his way into the 9th inning gig and ran with it in 2nd half. Combo of walks and fly balls looks problematic, but xBB% says BB% can get better, and minors pop-up rates suggest he might be able to survive with elevated FB%. Might be rocky at times, but a worthy Saves target.

Yr Tm	W	Sv	IP	K	ERA	WHIP	xERA	xWHIP	vL+	vR+	BF/G	BB%	K%	K-BB%	xBB%	SwK	Vel	G	L	F	H%	S%	HR/F	xHR/F	GS	APC	DOM%	DIS%	Sv%	LI	RAR	BPX	R$
18																																	
19																																	
20																																	
21 aa	3	2	43	60	4.78	1.35	3.40				5.1	12%	33%	21%							35%	63%									-2.7	139	-$3
22 CIN	7	10	64	83	1.84	0.96	3.71	1.28	83	54	4.3	13%	33%	20%	8%	17.1%	95.7	30	15	55	19%	86%	7%	9%	0	18			71	1.26	16.7	103	$14
1st Half	2	2	30	36	2.40	1.00	4.12	1.35	90	56	4.6	13%	29%	16%	9%	16.7%	95.8	29	15	56	18%	81%	8%	11%	0	19			67	0.86	5.8	80	$3
2nd Half	5	8	34	47	1.34	0.92	3.35	1.22	75	51	4.1	13%	36%	23%	8%	17.5%	95.6	31	16	53	20%	90%	6%	6%	0	17			73	1.59	10.9	124	$17
Proj	**5**	**24**	**65**	**83**	**3.11**	**1.20**	**3.62**	**1.27**	**112**	**73**	**4.7**	**12%**	**32%**	**20%**	**8%**	**17.1%**	**95.7**	**31**	**15**	**54**	**28%**	**79%**	**9%**	**10%**	**0**						**6.9**	**108**	**$14**

RAY MURPHY

Díaz,Edwin

Age: 29	Th: R	Role RP	Health	A	LIMA Plan	C+
Ht: 6' 3"	Wt: 165	Type Pwr	PT/Exp	A	Rand Var	-4
			Consist	C	MM	5531

Flipped four-seam fastball/slider mix from 62%/38% usage to relying on the slider 58% of the time. Safe to say it worked. Both pitches induced a GB% of 47% with the slider garnering an amazing 31% SwK. That 2nd half line crosses into Vintage Eck territory. There's bound to be a little pullback, but this is an outstanding collection of skills. Sound the trumpets!

Yr	Tm	W	Sv	IP	K	ERA	WHIP	xERA	xWHIP	vL+	vR+	BF/G	BB%	K%	K-BB%	xBB%	SwK	Vel	G	L	F	H%	S%	HR/F	xHR/F	GS	APC	DOM%	DIS%	Sv%	LI	RAR	BPX	R$
18	SEA	0	57	73	124	1.96	0.79	2.01	0.83	61	68	3.8	6%	44%	38%	6%	19.7%	97.3	44	20	35	30%	79%	11%	8%	0	16			93	1.40	19.8	276	$36
19	NYM	2	26	58	99	5.59	1.38	3.19	1.04	91	124	3.8	9%	39%	30%	6%	18.5%	97.5	37	20	44	40%	68%	27%	14%	0	16			79	1.18	-7.7	217	$8
20	NYM	2	6	26	50	1.75	1.25	2.45	1.06	85	75	4.2	13%	45%	33%	9%	21.5%	97.8	43	23	34	42%	90%	13%	6%	0	19			67	1.22	8.5	230	$15
21	NYM	5	32	63	89	3.45	1.05	3.24	1.09	76	81	4.1	9%	35%	26%	7%	16.7%	98.8	34	23	43	31%	67%	5%	6%	0	16			84	1.35	6.3	168	$19
22	NYM	3	32	62	118	1.31	0.84	1.60	0.79	57	68	3.9	8%	50%	43%	5%	25.5%	99.1	47	20	33	35%	88%	9%	8%	0	15			91	1.15	20.4	290	$25
1st Half		2	18	32	63	1.95	1.14	1.75	0.87	76	90	3.9	9%	48%	39%	6%	22.2%	99.0	43	28	30	44%	88%	19%	8%	0	16			86	1.16	8.1	271	$19
2nd Half		1	14	30	55	0.61	0.51	1.43	0.69	32	42	3.8	6%	52%	47%	4%	30.2%	99.4	52	10	38	24%	87%	0%	8%	0	14			100	1.12	12.3	311	$22
Proj		**3**	**32**	**65**	**114**	**2.41**	**0.96**	**1.91**	**0.86**	**68**	**83**	**3.7**	**8%**	**46%**	**38%**	**5%**	**22.0%**	**98.5**	**43**	**19**	**38**	**34%**	**80%**	**15%**	**9%**	**0**						**12.6**	**253**	**$22**

Domínguez,Seranthony

Age: 28	Th: R	Role RP	Health	F	LIMA Plan	A
Ht: 6' 1"	Wt: 225	Type Pwr	PT/Exp	D	Rand Var	-1
			Consist	F	MM	4421

First full season after Tommy John surgery was a tale of two halves. Started with a career-best BB%/K%, but that soured in 2nd half as past wildness returned, along with 22 days on IL (triceps tendinitis). The overall SwK and GB% lean form solid foundation, and xBB% hints at some control upside. If arm cooperates... UP: 25 Sv

Yr	Tm	W	Sv	IP	K	ERA	WHIP	xERA	xWHIP	vL+	vR+	BF/G	BB%	K%	K-BB%	xBB%	SwK	Vel	G	L	F	H%	S%	HR/F	xHR/F	GS	APC	DOM%	DIS%	Sv%	LI	RAR	BPX	R$
18	PHI *	4	16	76	92	2.67	0.87	1.24	1.17	86	52	4.4	9%	33%	24%	7%	16.0%	98.1	56	15	29	23%	70%	11%	11%	0	18			76	1.48	13.9	174	$17
19	PHI	3	0	25	29	4.01	1.46	4.02	1.36	133	67	4.1	11%	26%	15%	8%	14.0%	97.4	55	17	29	34%	76%	16%	11%	0	17			0	1.11	1.5	115	-$3
20																																		
21	PHI *	1	0	19	16	9.83	1.89	8.40				5.3	12%	18%	6%		14.3%	95.2	50	0	50	33%	51%	0%	1%	0	14			0	0.35	-13.1	-17	-$11
22	PHI	6	9	51	61	3.00	1.14	3.27	1.24	87	83	3.8	11%	29%	19%	9%	15.1%	98.0	48	19	33	28%	76%	10%	11%	0	15			82	1.39	6.1	127	$7
1st Half		4	2	30	39	1.80	0.83	2.47	0.98	96	57	3.6	6%	35%	28%	8%	16.1%	97.4	52	15	33	26%	83%	9%	6%	0	15			67	1.33	8.0	202	$8
2nd Half		2	7	21	22	4.71	1.57	4.64	1.60	74	113	4.1	16%	23%	7%	11%	13.8%	98.7	44	23	33	30%	71%	11%	16%	0	16			88	1.46	-1.9	20	-$2
Proj		**6**	**15**	**65**	**72**	**3.20**	**1.21**	**3.28**	**1.32**	**90**	**91**	**4.1**	**11%**	**27%**	**16%**	**9%**	**14.9%**	**98.2**	**49**	**19**	**32**	**28%**	**76%**	**12%**	**12%**	**0**						**6.2**	**104**	**$10**

Doval,Camilo

Age: 25	Th: R	Role RP	Health	A	LIMA Plan	B
Ht: 6' 2"	Wt: 185	Type Pwr/xGB	PT/Exp	C	Rand Var	-3
			Consist	B	MM	5431

Unveiled new sinker in July and it quickly became primary pitch (57% usage). 2nd half GB spike tracks with that change, but so does BB% jump, which is sub-optimal. 2nd half HR rate of <checks notes> zero won't repeat, so don't fall for "2H x 2" trap. Trio of GB%, premium velocity, and healthy K% form foundation of at least a 2nd-tier closer, maybe more.

Yr	Tm	W	Sv	IP	K	ERA	WHIP	xERA	xWHIP	vL+	vR+	BF/G	BB%	K%	K-BB%	xBB%	SwK	Vel	G	L	F	H%	S%	HR/F	xHR/F	GS	APC	DOM%	DIS%	Sv%	LI	RAR	BPX	R$
18																																		
19																																		
20																																		
21	SF *	8	4	59	73	3.93	1.35	3.79	1.08	104	65	4.3	13%	30%	17%	7%	14.4%	98.7	48	19	32	31%	73%	20%	15%	0	16			50	1.02	2.4	107	$3
22	SF	6	27	68	80	2.53	1.24	3.03	1.26	110	71	4.2	10%	28%	17%	8%	14.1%	99.0	56	22	22	31%	81%	11%	10%	0	16			90	1.52	12.0	130	$16
1st Half		2	12	35	42	3.09	1.17	3.24	1.19	133	64	4.1	9%	29%	20%	7%	14.7%	99.2	49	19	32	30%	78%	14%	8%	0	16			86	1.54	3.8	145	$9
2nd Half		4	15	33	38	1.93	1.32	2.77	1.35	91	79	4.3	12%	27%	15%	10%	13.5%	98.9	65	24	11	32%	84%	0%	18%	0	18			94	1.49	8.2	115	$16
Proj		**4**	**30**	**65**	**74**	**3.00**	**1.21**	**2.84**	**1.30**	**102**	**69**	**4.3**	**11%**	**28%**	**17%**	**8%**	**14.0%**	**99.0**	**58**	**22**	**19**	**30%**	**76%**	**11%**	**14%**	**0**						**7.8**	**121**	**$16**

Dunning,Dane

Age: 28	Th: R	Role SP	Health	D	LIMA Plan	B
Ht: 6' 4"	Wt: 225	Type /GB	PT/Exp	A	Rand Var	+1
			Consist	A	MM	3203

Underwent season-ending surgery on Sept 26 to repair torn labrum in right hip. Added a new "sweeper" this spring, but it garnered fewer swings-and-misses and GB than his previous slider. Overall, GB% continues to be best asset, but it can't overcome subpar K-BB% and bottom rung velocity, as seen in horrid DOM%/DIS%. Hopeful to be ready by spring.

Yr	Tm	W	Sv	IP	K	ERA	WHIP	xERA	xWHIP	vL+	vR+	BF/G	BB%	K%	K-BB%	xBB%	SwK	Vel	G	L	F	H%	S%	HR/F	xHR/F	GS	APC	DOM%	DIS%	Sv%	LI	RAR	BPX	R$
18	aa	5	0	62	59	3.87	1.58	4.32				24.8	10%	22%	12%							38%	73%									2.2	110	-$3
19																																		
20	CHW	2	0	34	35	3.97	1.12	4.11	1.30	103	60	20.3	9%	25%	15%	10%	11.6%	91.9	45	22	33	26%	68%	13%	11%	7	82	29%	29%			2.0	109	$3
21	TEX	5	0	118	114	4.51	1.44	3.89	1.30	108	102	18.9	8%	22%	14%	7%	10.3%	90.4	54	20	26	34%	71%	14%	16%	25	71	12%	36%	0	0.72	-3.6	110	-$4
22	TEX	4	0	153	137	4.46	1.43	3.92	1.35	115	109	23.1	9%	20%	11%	9%	10.4%	89.5	53	18	29	32%	72%	15%	14%	29	88	10%	45%			-9.3	85	-$6
1st Half		1	0	93	82	4.15	1.35	3.81	1.31	128	85	23.8	8%	20%	12%	8%	10.5%	89.1	53	19	29	31%	72%	13%	13%	17	88	12%	29%			-2.0	96	-$4
2nd Half		3	0	60	55	4.95	1.57	4.11	1.42	93	143	22.2	11%	21%	10%	10%	10.2%	90.1	54	16	30	33%	73%	19%	17%	12	88	8%	67%			-7.3	70	-$10
Proj		**6**	**0**	**145**	**129**	**4.38**	**1.39**	**3.74**	**1.37**	**106**	**100**	**21.1**	**10%**	**21%**	**11%**	**9%**	**10.6%**	**90.4**	**52**	**19**	**30**	**31%**	**71%**	**14%**	**14%**	**29**						**-7.3**	**81**	**-$3**

Duran,Jhoan

Age: 25	Th: R	Role RP	Health	A	LIMA Plan	B+
Ht: 6' 5"	Wt: 230	Type Pwr/xGB	PT/Exp	D	Rand Var	-3
			Consist	F	MM	5410

Starter in minors worked exclusively as reliever in rookie season. Electric blend of 101 mph four-seam fastball, a curve and a splinker produced ideal mix of extreme GB%, elite SwK/K%, and good BB%. A weapon in setup role, had manager's trust in big spots (LI), but could also force his way into 9th. Where... UP: 30 Sv

Yr	Tm	W	Sv	IP	K	ERA	WHIP	xERA	xWHIP	vL+	vR+	BF/G	BB%	K%	K-BB%	xBB%	SwK	Vel	G	L	F	H%	S%	HR/F	xHR/F	GS	APC	DOM%	DIS%	Sv%	LI	RAR	BPX	R$
18																																		
19	aa	3	0	37	35	6.68	1.37	4.23				22.1	6%	23%	16%							36%	48%									-9.9	118	-$5
20																																		
21	aaa	0	0	16	19	6.12	2.01	6.12				15.4	18%	25%	6%							40%	68%									-3.7	77	-$9
22	MIN	2	8	68	89	1.86	0.98	2.17	0.99	85	78	4.7	6%	33%	27%	5%	18.5%	100.9	61	17	22	30%	87%	18%	12%	0	18			100	1.34	17.6	214	$11
1st Half		0	5	36	48	2.00	0.86	2.13	0.91	81	79	5.0	4%	35%	30%	4%	18.6%	100.6	58	15	27	28%	85%	18%	12%	0	19			100	1.37	8.7	233	$8
2nd Half		2	3	32	41	1.71	1.11	2.21	1.08	89	76	4.4	8%	32%	24%	5%	18.3%	101.2	64	19	16	32%	88%	17%	12%	0	17			100	1.31	8.8	194	$5
Proj		**3**	**10**	**58**	**68**	**2.37**	**1.03**	**2.29**	**1.06**	**85**	**77**	**5.6**	**6%**	**30%**	**24%**	**5%**	**18.4%**	**100.9**	**62**	**17**	**21**	**30%**	**81%**	**15%**	**12%**	**0**						**11.4**	**187**	**$9**

Effross,Scott

Age: 29	Th: R	Role RP	Health	C	LIMA Plan	A+
Ht: 6' 2"	Wt: 202	Type Con	PT/Exp	D	Rand Var	-3
			Consist	A	MM	2110

Missed most of September due to shoulder strain and underwent Tommy John surgery in October. Exceeded expectations in first full MLB season, with less-than-full skills support. The 1st half K% far outpaced SwK and when it regressed in 2nd half, he was bailed out by H%/S%. 2nd half xERA/xWHIP is probably fair expectation for 2024.

Yr	Tm	W	Sv	IP	K	ERA	WHIP	xERA	xWHIP	vL+	vR+	BF/G	BB%	K%	K-BB%	xBB%	SwK	Vel	G	L	F	H%	S%	HR/F	xHR/F	GS	APC	DOM%	DIS%	Sv%	LI	RAR	BPX	R$
18	aa	2	1	64	49	7.78	1.94	7.64				6.9	7%	16%	9%							41%	60%									-28.7	39	-$18
19	aa	1	0	35	14	8.41	1.77	6.68				9.5	7%	9%	2%							36%	51%									-17.0	3	-$12
20																																		
21	CHC *	9	2	77	68	3.93	1.09	3.53	0.90	82	107	6.7	6%	23%	17%	5%	12.6%	90.7	47	17	36	27%	69%	15%	13%	0	16			67	1.04	3.2	110	$7
22	2 TM	1	4	57	62	2.54	1.06	3.31	1.12	63	88	3.8	7%	27%	21%	5%	11.2%	90.5	45	19	36	30%	77%	6%	7%	1	14	0%	100%	67	1.21	10.0	150	$4
1st Half		1	0	35	44	3.09	1.11	2.97	1.05	84	82	3.9	6%	31%	24%	5%	11.1%	90.1	45	20	34	34%	73%	7%	6%	1	14	0%	100%	0	1.01	3.8	182	-$1
2nd Half		0	4	22	18	1.66	0.97	3.87	1.25	39	102	3.7	7%	21%	14%	5%	11.2%	91.1	43	17	40	25%	85%	4%	8%	0	14			80	1.52	6.2	98	$0
Proj		**0**	**2**	**15**	**12**	**4.59**	**1.32**	**3.89**	**1.28**	**68**	**120**	**5.1**	**7%**	**20%**	**13%**	**5%**	**11.2%**	**90.7**	**44**	**18**	**38**	**32%**	**66%**	**8%**	**8%**	**0**						**-1.1**	**94**	**-$4**

Eflin,Zach

Age: 29	Th: R	Role SP	Health	F	LIMA Plan	A+
Ht: 6' 6"	Wt: 220	Type Con	PT/Exp	A	Rand Var	0
			Consist	A	MM	4201

Sidelined late-June to mid-Sept (patellofemoral pain right knee). That's same knee that required Sept 2021 surgery to repair torn patellar tendon (same surgery on both knees in 2016). Added cutter and threw curveball more, largely at expense of slider, and induced career-best exit velocity. Knee is a concern, but 2021-22 xERA/xWHIP shows ceiling.

Yr	Tm	W	Sv	IP	K	ERA	WHIP	xERA	xWHIP	vL+	vR+	BF/G	BB%	K%	K-BB%	xBB%	SwK	Vel	G	L	F	H%	S%	HR/F	xHR/F	GS	APC	DOM%	DIS%	Sv%	LI	RAR	BPX	R$
18	PHI *	13	0	148	136	4.46	1.32	4.29	1.24	115	93	21.9	7%	22%	15%	6%	11.1%	94.3	41	21	38	33%	68%	11%	11%	24	85	29%	29%			-5.7	103	$4
19	PHI	10	0	163	129	4.13	1.35	4.83	1.36	113	95	22.0	7%	18%	11%	6%	9.4%	93.6	45	21	35	30%	76%	16%	14%	28	80	21%	43%	0	0.74	7.5	87	$6
20	PHI	4	0	59	70	3.97	1.27	3.45	1.11	125	84	22.3	6%	29%	22%	6%	10.7%	93.9	47	21	31	35%	73%	16%	15%	10	83	30%	10%	0	0.74	3.5	176	$9
21	PHI	4	0	106	99	4.17	1.25	3.83	1.11	102	106	24.6	4%	22%	19%	5%	10.9%	92.6	43	24	33	34%	71%	14%	14%	18	90	28%	22%			1.2	149	$1
22	PHI	3	1	76	65	4.04	1.12	3.78	1.16	115	80	15.7	5%	21%	16%	7%	10.2%	92.8	44	19	37	29%	66%	10%	10%	13	60	23%	23%	100	0.77	-0.7	125	$1
1st Half		3	0	68	56	4.37	1.19	4.00	1.20	116	86	21.9	5%	20%	14%	7%	10.2%	92.7	44	19	37	30%	66%	10%	11%	13	84	23%	23%			-3.3	112	-$1
2nd Half		0	1	8	9	1.17	0.52	2.04		72	48	4.0	0%	32%	32%	4%	10.7%	93.8	56	17	28	24%	75%	0%	1%	0	15			100	0.80	2.6	247	-$6
Proj		**6**	**0**	**109**	**98**	**3.97**	**1.18**	**3.39**	**1.16**	**111**	**89**	**21.4**	**5%**	**23%**	**17%**	**6%**	**10.3%**	**93.2**	**44**	**21**	**35**	**30%**	**71%**	**14%**	**13%**	**20**						**0.0**	**129**	**$4**

GREG PYRON

Elder,Bryce

Age: 24	Th: R	Role SP	Health A	LIMA Plan B
Ht: 6' 2"	Wt: 220	Type Con	PT/Exp D	Rand Var 0
			Consist C	MM 3101

2-4, 3.17 ERA in 54 IP with ATL. Tweaked pitch mix in 2H, opting for more sinkers, yielding improved BB% and a 2.31 ERA/3.24 xERA in six MLB outings (five against MIA and WAS). GB% tilt is a good start, but subpar velocity and SwK% caps upside. Ability to sustain 2nd half K-BB% will determine whether he's a backend starter or someone to avoid.

Yr Tm	W	Sv	IP	K	ERA	WHIP	xERA	xWHIP	vL+	vR+	BF/G	BB%	K%	K-BB%	xBB%	SwK	Vel	G	L	F	H%	S%	HR/F	xHR/F	GS	APC	DOM%	DIS%	Sv%	LI	RAR	BPX	R$
18																																	
19																																	
20																																	
21 a/a	9	0	94	86	3.49	1.10	2.74				23.1	10%	23%	13%							24%	71%									9.0	95	$9
22 ATL *	8	0	159	130	4.68	1.31	4.23	1.39	102	82	23.4	10%	21%	11%	9%	10.3%	90.8	49	18	32	29%	67%	8%	13%	9	87	44%	33%	0	0.71	-14.0	70	-$2
1st Half	5	0	83	65	6.27	1.47	5.20	1.43	115	115	23.7	10%	18%	8%	12%	10.9%	91.4	52	14	34	30%	59%	15%	20%	4	85	0%	75%			-23.5	43	-$17
2nd Half	3	0	76	65	2.95	1.13	3.16	1.22	90	67	23.1	7%	22%	15%	8%	9.9%	90.6	48	21	31	28%	77%	3%	8%	5	89	80%	0%	0	0.67	9.5	108	$9
Proj	**4**	**0**	**73**	**58**	**4.30**	**1.30**	**3.78**	**1.33**	**115**	**91**	**25.0**	**8%**	**19%**	**12%**	**9%**	**10.4%**	**90.9**	**49**	**18**	**32**	**30%**	**69%**	**11%**	**13%**	**12**						**-2.9**	**86**	**-$2**

Eovaldi,Nathan

Age: 33	Th: R	Role SP	Health F	LIMA Plan A+
Ht: 6' 2"	Wt: 217	Type	PT/Exp A	Rand Var 0
			Consist A	MM 4303

Usual injury bug returned after skipping him in 2021. Missed significant time due to lower back/hip, plus right shoulder inflammation. First half was terrific, then skills and velocity declined post-injury. 2021's skills are a reasonable baseline for 2023, but "F" Health grade can't be ignored, and he's now at an age where injuries don't just roll off as easily.

Yr Tm	W	Sv	IP	K	ERA	WHIP	xERA	xWHIP	vL+	vR+	BF/G	BB%	K%	K-BB%	xBB%	SwK	Vel	G	L	F	H%	S%	HR/F	xHR/F	GS	APC	DOM%	DIS%	Sv%	LI	RAR	BPX	R$
18 2 AL	6	0	111	101	3.81	1.13	3.75	1.15	101	88	20.7	4%	22%	18%	5%	11.3%	97.2	46	19	35	30%	70%	12%	11%	21	82	24%	19%	0	0.75	4.6	147	$6
19 BOS	2	0	68	70	5.99	1.58	4.89	1.46	126	107	13.1	12%	23%	12%	9%	10.9%	97.5	45	19	36	32%	68%	23%	19%	12	55	8%	58%	0	0.88	-12.3	71	-$8
20 BOS	4	0	48	52	3.72	1.20	3.35	1.05	86	128	22.1	4%	26%	23%	5%	13.8%	97.4	49	21	30	34%	76%	20%	18%	9	83	22%	33%			4.3	188	$9
21 BOS	11	0	182	195	3.75	1.19	3.67	1.09	91	97	23.9	5%	26%	21%	5%	12.9%	96.9	42	23	35	34%	70%	8%	10%	32	91	41%	13%			11.6	161	$14
22 BOS	6	0	109	103	3.87	1.23	3.69	1.12	105	108	23.0	4%	22%	18%	5%	12.7%	95.8	47	16	37	31%	77%	17%	15%	20	87	35%	30%			1.3	147	$3
1st Half	4	0	68	72	3.16	1.10	3.34	1.03	106	100	23.3	4%	26%	22%	5%	13.9%	96.6	45	17	38	29%	86%	22%	17%	12	89	50%	17%			6.8	175	$9
2nd Half	2	0	41	31	5.05	1.46	4.32	1.26	103	119	22.6	6%	17%	12%	6%	10.7%	94.3	50	16	35	35%	67%	10%	14%	8	85	13%	50%			-5.5	100	-$10
Proj	**8**	**0**	**131**	**126**	**3.69**	**1.21**	**3.28**	**1.15**	**96**	**105**	**21.7**	**5%**	**24%**	**18%**	**5%**	**12.3%**	**96.2**	**47**	**19**	**35**	**31%**	**76%**	**16%**	**15%**	**24**						**4.5**	**139**	**$7**

Espino,Paolo

Age: 36	Th: R	Role RP	Health A	LIMA Plan B
Ht: 5' 10"	Wt: 215	Type Con	PT/Exp A	Rand Var +1
			Consist A	MM 2101

Swingman matched career high with 19 GS, yet failed to complete 6 IP in any of them. Again posted better numbers as RP (lifetime SP: 5.20 ERA, 19% K-BB% in 182 IP; RP: 3.41 ERA, 21% K-BB% in 71 IP), but the skills remained rather pedestrian. Poor velocity and age say it's too late for new tricks.

Yr Tm	W	Sv	IP	K	ERA	WHIP	xERA	xWHIP	vL+	vR+	BF/G	BB%	K%	K-BB%	xBB%	SwK	Vel	G	L	F	H%	S%	HR/F	xHR/F	GS	APC	DOM%	DIS%	Sv%	LI	RAR	BPX	R$
18 aaa	4	0	60	43	6.73	1.91	7.52				12.9	10%	15%	6%							38%	67%									-19.1	15	-$14
19 aaa	8	0	93	68	7.41	1.64	6.73				24.4	7%	16%	10%							36%	57%									-33.4	32	-$13
20 WAS	0	0	6	7	4.50	1.67	3.95		117	113	13.5	7%	26%	19%	11%	10.9%	90.3	44	28	28	41%	78%	20%	37%	1	55	0%	100%	0	0.43	0.0	147	-$7
21 WAS	5	1	110	92	4.27	1.21	4.56	1.23	106	99	13.0	5%	20%	15%	7%	8.9%	89.0	36	21	43	29%	71%	14%	14%	19	50	11%	37%	100	0.59	0.0	104	$2
22 WAS	0	0	113	92	4.84	1.37	4.34	1.20	119	113	11.6	5%	19%	14%	8%	9.3%	88.6	39	20	41	32%	72%	16%	14%	19	45	0%	58%	0	0.40	-12.2	107	-$8
1st Half	0	0	49	37	3.33	1.19	4.48	1.23	101	101	8.0	6%	19%	13%	8%	8.3%	88.7	35	19	46	28%	80%	11%	9%	5	31	0%	80%	0	0.22	3.8	90	-$3
2nd Half	0	0	65	55	5.98	1.50	4.23	1.18	131	120	16.9	5%	19%	15%	8%	10.1%	88.5	42	20	38	35%	67%	20%	18%	14	65	0%	50%	0	0.66	-16.1	120	-$18
Proj	**2**	**0**	**65**	**51**	**4.95**	**1.29**	**3.97**	**1.27**	**113**	**106**	**13.2**	**6%**	**19%**	**13%**	**8%**	**9.3%**	**88.7**	**39**	**20**	**42**	**29%**	**67%**	**15%**	**14%**	**6**						**-7.9**	**90**	**-$5**

Estévez,Carlos

Age: 30	Th: R	Role RP	Health D	LIMA Plan A+
Ht: 6' 6"	Wt: 277	Type Pwr/FB	PT/Exp B	Rand Var -3
			Consist A	MM 3211

Rebounded from horrid 1st half with a much better 2nd half, where he reestablished his usual BB% and K%. Fortuitous H%/S% in the 2nd half drove massive ERA/xERA gap. Overall, xERA says he was essentially the same pitcher he was in 2021: high velocity arm with average peripherals. There are better places to speculate.

Yr Tm	W	Sv	IP	K	ERA	WHIP	xERA	xWHIP	vL+	vR+	BF/G	BB%	K%	K-BB%	xBB%	SwK	Vel	G	L	F	H%	S%	HR/F	xHR/F	GS	APC	DOM%	DIS%	Sv%	LI	RAR	BPX	R$
18 aaa	0	1	29	26	7.52	1.92	8.38				4.9	9%	19%	10%							40%	65%									-12.1	15	-$11
19 COL	2	0	72	81	3.75	1.29	4.38	1.24	112	91	4.3	7%	26%	19%	6%	14.4%	97.9	38	20	42	32%	78%	14%	14%	0	17			0	0.93	6.7	131	$1
20 COL	1	1	24	27	7.50	1.75	5.00	1.28	140	132	4.5	8%	23%	16%	6%	11.7%	96.9	31	29	40	40%	61%	19%	17%	0	17			25	1.16	-9.0	113	-$11
21 COL	3	11	62	60	4.38	1.49	4.35	1.28	109	109	4.2	8%	22%	14%	8%	11.7%	97.1	44	21	36	36%	74%	12%	12%	0	16			65	1.32	-0.9	106	$0
22 COL	4	2	57	54	3.47	1.18	4.27	1.33	103	84	3.8	10%	23%	13%	9%	9.9%	97.6	36	19	45	26%	75%	10%	10%	0	16			33	1.01	3.5	76	$2
1st Half	1	0	26	23	5.13	1.44	4.76	1.45	127	97	3.7	11%	20%	9%	10%	8.5%	97.3	36	24	41	29%	68%	13%	11%	0	16			0	0.75	-3.8	39	-$11
2nd Half	3	2	31	31	2.05	0.95	3.88	1.22	81	70	3.9	8%	26%	18%	8%	11.2%	97.9	37	15	48	22%	85%	8%	9%	0	17			40	1.27	7.2	109	$5
Proj	**4**	**6**	**65**	**62**	**4.01**	**1.24**	**3.85**	**1.30**	**105**	**89**	**3.9**	**9%**	**23%**	**14%**	**8%**	**11.3%**	**97.6**	**38**	**19**	**43**	**28%**	**72%**	**11%**	**11%**	**0**						**-0.3**	**89**	**$2**

Faedo,Alex

Age: 27	Th: R	Role SP	Health A	LIMA Plan C+
Ht: 6' 5"	Wt: 230	Type Con/FB	PT/Exp F	Rand Var 0
			Consist F	MM 2100

18th overall pick in 2017 draft essentially missed all of 2020-2021 with elbow injury that ultimately required Jan 2021 Tommy John surgery. Logged 1 QS in 12 GS in his return, backed by below-average BB%, K%, and SwK% before undergoing season-ending hip surgery. Expected ready for spring, but probably best to wait and see.

Yr Tm	W	Sv	IP	K	ERA	WHIP	xERA	xWHIP	vL+	vR+	BF/G	BB%	K%	K-BB%	xBB%	SwK	Vel	G	L	F	H%	S%	HR/F	xHR/F	GS	APC	DOM%	DIS%	Sv%	LI	RAR	BPX	R$
18 aa	3	0	60	48	6.24	1.43	6.23				21.3	9%	19%	10%							28%	65%									-15.5	12	-$8
19 aa	6	0	116	107	5.86	1.41	5.66				22.3	6%	22%	16%							34%	63%									-19.3	78	-$6
20																																	
21																																	
22 DET	1	0	54	44	5.53	1.64	5.25	1.45	123	112	20.3	10%	18%	8%	9%	10.3%	92.8	31	25	44	34%	68%	9%	11%	12	81	8%	50%			-10.4	32	-$10
1st Half	1	0	52	42	5.02	1.54	5.05	1.39	120	110	21.0	9%	18%	9%	8%	10.6%	92.7	32	23	45	33%	70%	9%	11%	11	82	9%	45%			-6.7	47	-$14
2nd Half	0	0	2	2	21.60	4.80	17.59		174	154	13.0	31%	15%	-15%	12%	6.7%	93.3	14	57	29	60%	50%	0%	11%	1	60	0%	100%			-3.6	-438	-$14
Proj	**1**	**0**	**44**	**35**	**4.87**	**1.40**	**4.28**	**1.34**	**129**	**115**	**22.0**	**8%**	**19%**	**11%**	**8%**	**10.6%**	**92.7**	**32**	**23**	**45**	**31%**	**70%**	**14%**	**10%**	**8**						**-4.8**	**66**	**-$6**

Fairbanks,Peter

Age: 29	Th: R	Role RP	Health F	LIMA Plan A+
Ht: 6' 6"	Wt: 225	Type Pwr	PT/Exp C	Rand Var -5
			Consist C	MM 5520

Add a spring torn lat muscle to lengthy history of arm ailments, including two Tommy John surgeries, so the "F" Health grade is well-earned. However, he was truly dominant when on the mound in 2022, boasting elite BB%, K%, SwK% and velocity along with appealing GB%. Some pullback likely and risk is undeniable, but potential payoff could be big.

Yr Tm	W	Sv	IP	K	ERA	WHIP	xERA	xWHIP	vL+	vR+	BF/G	BB%	K%	K-BB%	xBB%	SwK	Vel	G	L	F	H%	S%	HR/F	xHR/F	GS	APC	DOM%	DIS%	Sv%	LI	RAR	BPX	R$
18																																	
19 2 AL *	4	2	53	74	6.87	1.47	5.46	1.29	65	167	4.6	8%	32%	24%	8%	14.0%	97.4	43	27	30	39%	55%	28%	20%	0	18			40	0.80	-15.5	115	-$6
20 TAM	6	0	27	39	2.70	1.39	3.55	1.25	84	89	4.3	12%	33%	21%	9%	16.9%	97.5	47	19	34	37%	83%	10%	9%	2	18	0%	50%	0	1.02	5.8	152	$10
21 TAM	3	5	43	56	3.59	1.43	3.94	1.28	128	62	4.0	11%	30%	19%	8%	13.7%	97.2	43	20	37	37%	75%	5%	8%	0	16			71	1.23	3.6	125	$0
22 TAM	0	8	24	38	1.13	0.67	1.66	0.75	61	51	3.6	3%	44%	41%	4%	18.2%	99.0	53	18	29	29%	87%	8%	5%	0	15			100	1.34	8.4	283	$4
1st Half																																	
2nd Half	0	8	24	38	1.13	0.67	1.66	0.75	61	51	3.6	3%	44%	40%	4%	18.2%	99.0	53	18	29	29%	87%	8%	5%	0	15			100	1.34	8.4	284	$9
Proj	**2**	**11**	**58**	**80**	**2.97**	**1.02**	**2.35**	**1.00**	**97**	**62**	**4.0**	**7%**	**36%**	**29%**		**16.1%**	**98.3**	**49**	**19**	**32**	**32%**	**73%**	**10%**	**6%**	**0**						**7.1**	**203**	**$9**

Falter,Bailey

Age: 26	Th: L	Role SP	Health B	LIMA Plan A+
Ht: 6' 4"	Wt: 175	Type Con/FB	PT/Exp D	Rand Var -1
			Consist A	MM 3201

6-4, 3.86 ERA in 84 IP with PHI. Struggled in MLB in 1st half (4.88 ERA in 24 IP). Returned from AAA in 2nd half and was much better, with pitch mix changes (increased four-seam fastball/curve usage at expense of sinker/slider) that led to more missed bats. But a soft schedule was also partly responsible for those gains, so don't buy in fully.

Yr Tm	W	Sv	IP	K	ERA	WHIP	xERA	xWHIP	vL+	vR+	BF/G	BB%	K%	K-BB%	xBB%	SwK	Vel	G	L	F	H%	S%	HR/F	xHR/F	GS	APC	DOM%	DIS%	Sv%	LI	RAR	BPX	R$
18																																	
19 aa	6	0	78	57	4.94	1.44	5.53				23.8	5%	17%	12%							34%	69%									-4.2	74	-$3
20																																	
21 PHI *	4	0	66	72	3.79	1.12	3.64	1.10	97	98	8.7	5%	28%	22%	6%	10.3%	91.8	36	23	41	31%	70%	13%	9%	1	25	0%	100%	0	0.66	3.8	152	$2
22 PHI *	10	0	131	114	3.18	1.03	3.45	1.16	96	115	17.4	5%	21%	16%	5%	11.2%	91.2	32	24	44	26%	77%	14%	13%	16	65	13%	25%	0	0.68	12.8	131	$14
1st Half	4	0	54	45	3.01	0.96	3.02	1.15	136	126	14.6	5%	22%	17%	5%	9.1%	90.8	31	21	49	24%	77%	16%	14%	4	49	0%	50%	0	0.53	6.4	123	$8
2nd Half	6	0	79	69	3.19	1.04	3.55	1.11	76	110	20.4	4%	22%	18%	5%	12.1%	91.4	32	26	42	27%	77%	14%	13%	12	75	17%	17%			7.6	139	$14
Proj	**7**	**0**	**94**	**81**	**3.87**	**1.19**	**3.71**	**1.16**	**100**	**109**	**21.0**	**5%**	**21%**	**17%**	**5%**	**10.7%**	**91.3**	**33**	**24**	**44**	**30%**	**73%**	**12%**	**12%**	**18**						**1.2**	**115**	**$3**

GREG PYRON

Fedde,Erick

Age: 30	Th: R	Role: SP	Health: D	LIMA Plan: C
Ht: 6' 4"	Wt: 200	Type: Con	PT/Exp: A	Rand Var: +1
			Consist: B	MM: 1003

Brutal DOM%/DIS% highlights his ineffectiveness. Heavy GB% lean had been his best asset, but it and the 2021 K% uptick vanished. That left him with bad control, a puny K%/SwK, and continued HR issues. Even if he regains the GB%, he's a low ceiling streaming option. If he doesn't, you don't want him near your roster.

Yr	Tm	W	Sv	IP	K	ERA	WHIP	xERA	xWHIP	vL+	vR+	BF/G	BB%	K%	K-BB%	xBB%	SwK	Vel	G	L	F	H%	S%	HR/F	xHR/F	GS	APC	DOM%	DIS%	Sv%	LI	RAR	BPX	R$
18	WAS *	5	0	122	105	5.58	1.63	5.61	1.40	120	115	21.8	8%	19%	11%	12%	9.1%	93.7	53	22	24	38%	66%	22%	25%	11	86	9%	64%			-21.6	75	-$13
19	WAS *	7	0	114	70	5.36	1.50	5.55	1.61	121	91	17.6	9%	14%	5%	11%	7.3%	92.3	51	22	27	30%	68%	16%	19%	12	61	0%	67%	0	0.60	-12.1	20	-$6
20	WAS	2	0	50	28	4.29	1.37	5.32	1.57	82	118	20.2	10%	13%	3%	12%	6.1%	93.5	54	20	26	25%	76%	23%	19%	8	77	25%	50%	0	0.64	1.0	18	-$2
21	WAS	7	0	133	128	5.47	1.44	4.22	1.30	116	102	20.3	8%	22%	14%	10%	9.5%	93.9	50	19	31	33%	66%	19%	20%	27	83	11%	41%	0	0.76	-19.8	105	-$8
22	WAS	6	0	127	94	5.81	1.63	5.01	1.47	110	125	21.2	10%	16%	6%	11%	7.7%	92.6	42	22	36	33%	67%	14%	13%	27	90	7%	67%			-28.9	32	-$16
1st Half		5	0	80	65	4.29	1.41	4.60	1.45	98	103	21.4	11%	19%	8%	11%	7.7%	92.7	44	19	37	29%	72%	10%	10%	16	92	13%	56%			-3.2	46	-$3
2nd Half		1	0	47	29	8.37	2.01	5.72	1.50	127	159	21.0	9%	13%	3%	11%	7.7%	92.4	39	27	34	37%	61%	20%	17%	11	86	0%	82%			-25.7	9	-$30
Proj		**6**	**0**	**138**	**97**	**5.21**	**1.60**	**4.49**	**1.47**	**112**	**124**	**20.0**	**10%**	**16%**	**6%**	**11%**	**7.7%**	**93.0**	**47**	**22**	**31**	**32%**	**72%**	**18%**	**17%**	**30**						**-21.1**	**40**	**-$13**

Feltner,Ryan

Age: 26	Th: R	Role: SP	Health: A	LIMA Plan: C+
Ht: 6' 4"	Wt: 190	Type: Con	PT/Exp: D	Rand Var: +1
			Consist: B	MM: 2103

4-9, 5.83 ERA in 97 IP with COL. Labored in most of his 19 GS at MLB level, with just 4 QS. Though S% was a tad unfortunate, this is a shaky collection of skills that worsened in the 2nd half, which was mostly spent in MLB. Could get more chances as a starter, but seems more likely to settle into middle relief... and a long-term home on your waiver wire.

Yr	Tm	W	Sv	IP	K	ERA	WHIP	xERA	xWHIP	vL+	vR+	BF/G	BB%	K%	K-BB%	xBB%	SwK	Vel	G	L	F	H%	S%	HR/F	xHR/F	GS	APC	DOM%	DIS%	Sv%	LI	RAR	BPX	R$
18																																		
19																																		
20																																		
21	COL *	5	0	85	69	4.39	1.45	5.39	1.73	111	191	22.6	8%	19%	11%	12%	12.0%	92.4	10	33	57	32%	75%	25%	13%	2	71	0%	50%			-1.3	52	-$4
22	COL *	9	0	151	128	5.10	1.37	4.72	1.32	110	115	20.4	8%	20%	11%	8%	9.1%	94.2	41	19	39	31%	65%	13%	15%	19	84	16%	58%	0	0.81	-20.9	69	-$5
1st Half		5	0	73	68	4.84	1.26	4.32	1.20	131	99	19.8	6%	22%	16%	7%	10.8%	94.5	43	20	37	32%	64%	16%	19%	7	84	29%	43%			-7.9	102	-$2
2nd Half		4	0	78	60	5.33	1.48	5.10	1.42	98	124	20.9	9%	18%	8%	9%	8.2%	94.1	40	19	41	31%	66%	12%	13%	12	83	8%	67%	0	0.83	-13.1	47	-$10
Proj		**7**	**0**	**131**	**103**	**4.92**	**1.35**	**4.13**	**1.35**	**103**	**105**	**21.7**	**8%**	**19%**	**11%**	**8%**	**9.3%**	**94.2**	**41**	**20**	**39**	**30%**	**66%**	**12%**	**15%**	**25**						**-15.3**	**73**	**-$4**

Festa,Matt

Age: 30	Th: R	Role: RP	Health: B	LIMA Plan: B
Ht: 6' 2"	Wt: 195	Type: Pwr/xFB	PT/Exp: D	Rand Var: +2
			Consist: A	MM: 4400

Underwent Tommy John surgery in early 2020 and missed over a year. Struggled early, landed on IL for a few weeks (elbow), then emerged as a reliable reliever. Combo of four-seamer and revamped slider missed lots of bats despite lackluster velocity. BB% was merely average, but xBB% hints at some upside. Nice end target for Holds leagues.

Yr	Tm	W	Sv	IP	K	ERA	WHIP	xERA	xWHIP	vL+	vR+	BF/G	BB%	K%	K-BB%	xBB%	SwK	Vel	G	L	F	H%	S%	HR/F	xHR/F	GS	APC	DOM%	DIS%	Sv%	LI	RAR	BPX	R$
18	SEA *	5	20	57	61	3.18	1.51	5.44	1.41	133	111	4.8	6%	25%	19%	7%	6.9%	92.8	33	33	33	39%	83%	0%	8%	1	20	0%	0%	91	0.50	6.9	124	$7
19	SEA *	1	5	55	49	3.99	1.33	4.14	1.54	101	124	5.3	11%	22%	10%	9%	10.3%	92.6	38	19	43	27%	75%	19%	17%	0	20			63	0.81	3.5	60	$0
20																																		
21	aaa	4	1	22	25	3.29	1.06	3.99				4.5	3%	29%	26%							30%	79%									2.7	201	$0
22	SEA	2	2	54	64	4.17	1.13	3.50	1.15	117	92	4.1	8%	29%	21%	6%	14.4%	92.6	39	17	45	27%	71%	17%	13%	0	17			67	0.64	-1.3	141	$0
1st Half		0	0	21	31	4.35	1.16	3.24	1.03	104	108	4.1	8%	36%	28%	7%	15.9%	92.7	33	13	54	31%	74%	20%	17%	0	18			0	0.44	-1.0	189	-$8
2nd Half		2	2	33	33	4.05	1.11	3.68	1.23	123	78	4.1	8%	25%	17%	5%	13.3%	92.5	42	19	40	26%	69%	15%	10%	0	16			67	0.78	-0.3	110	-$1
Proj		**3**	**0**	**58**	**65**	**3.42**	**1.17**	**3.39**	**1.16**	**114**	**93**	**4.3**	**8%**	**28%**	**21%**	**6%**	**14.4%**	**92.6**	**38**	**16**	**45**	**29%**	**79%**	**14%**	**13%**	**0**						**3.9**	**137**	**$1**

Finnegan,Kyle

Age: 31	Th: R	Role: RP	Health: B	LIMA Plan: A
Ht: 6' 2"	Wt: 200	Type: Pwr	PT/Exp: B	Rand Var: +1
			Consist: B	MM: 4321

Found himself back in the closer role in 2nd half and fared well. Best full-year BB% of his career and it came with full xBB% support. Maintained GB% and managed to miss a few more bats while throwing his sinker more than ever (79%) and scaling back slider and splitter usage. If these gains hold, he's capable of sticking as a lower-tier closer.

Yr	Tm	W	Sv	IP	K	ERA	WHIP	xERA	xWHIP	vL+	vR+	BF/G	BB%	K%	K-BB%	xBB%	SwK	Vel	G	L	F	H%	S%	HR/F	xHR/F	GS	APC	DOM%	DIS%	Sv%	LI	RAR	BPX	R$
18	a/a	1	14	44	34	5.13	1.54	4.54				5.7	10%	18%	8%							34%	65%									-5.4	75	-$1
19	a/a	3	14	52	55	2.98	1.36	3.72				5.2	10%	25%	16%							33%	79%									9.8	107	$7
20	WAS	1	0	25	27	2.92	1.38	4.17	1.41	82	90	4.3	12%	25%	13%	8%	12.2%	95.1	51	22	28	31%	81%	11%	15%	0	17			0	1.13	4.7	88	-$1
21	WAS	5	11	66	68	3.55	1.48	4.54	1.42	98	104	4.3	12%	23%	12%	8%	11.2%	95.6	48	17	35	32%	81%	14%	12%	0	18			79	1.18	5.9	74	$4
22	WAS	6	11	67	70	3.51	1.14	3.33	1.21	76	108	4.1	8%	26%	18%	7%	13.2%	97.1	48	20	32	28%	75%	16%	15%	0	16			73	1.25	3.8	128	$8
1st Half		2	1	32	37	3.94	1.31	3.09	1.18	101	106	3.9	8%	27%	19%	6%	12.6%	96.5	51	25	25	33%	76%	24%	17%	0	15			33	1.04	0.1	146	-$4
2nd Half		4	10	35	33	3.12	0.98	3.55	1.23	50	109	4.3	8%	25%	17%	7%	13.8%	97.6	46	16	38	23%	73%	12%	14%	0	17			83	1.48	3.6	112	$12
Proj		**5**	**20**	**65**	**66**	**3.50**	**1.27**	**3.43**	**1.29**	**82**	**112**	**4.5**	**9%**	**25%**	**15%**	**7%**	**12.8%**	**96.8**	**48**	**19**	**33**	**30%**	**76%**	**12%**	**14%**	**0**						**3.8**	**106**	**$9**

Flaherty,Jack

Age: 27	Th: R	Role: SP	Health: F	LIMA Plan: A
Ht: 6' 4"	Wt: 225	Type: Pwr	PT/Exp: C	Rand Var: -1
			Consist: A	MM: 4303

2-1, 4.25 ERA in 36 IP with STL. After missing most of 2021 (shoulder/oblique), opened 2022 on IL again (shoulder). Returned in June, but threw just 8 innings before again landing on IL (yup, shoulder). Eventually displayed pre-injury velocity in 2nd half, though SwK/K% and BB% lagged. Open question whether he can "shoulder" a full-season workload.

Yr	Tm	W	Sv	IP	K	ERA	WHIP	xERA	xWHIP	vL+	vR+	BF/G	BB%	K%	K-BB%	xBB%	SwK	Vel	G	L	F	H%	S%	HR/F	xHR/F	GS	APC	DOM%	DIS%	Sv%	LI	RAR	BPX	R$
18	STL *	12	0	184	216	3.17	1.07	2.83	1.22	83	92	21.7	9%	30%	21%	8%	14.1%	92.7	42	21	37	27%	76%	15%	10%	28	92	21%	18%			22.3	132	$23
19	STL	11	0	196	231	2.75	0.97	3.59	1.15	81	76	23.4	7%	30%	23%	8%	14.2%	93.9	40	22	38	25%	79%	14%	13%	33	96	42%	12%			42.5	153	$32
20	STL	4	0	40	49	4.91	1.21	3.53	1.23	106	76	18.9	9%	29%	19%	8%	14.7%	93.6	43	32	26	29%	63%	23%	21%	9	80	22%	22%			-2.3	137	$5
21	STL	9	0	78	85	3.22	1.06	3.86	1.21	82	93	18.9	8%	26%	18%	10%	12.3%	93.3	39	23	38	25%	77%	16%	20%	15	80	33%	27%	0	0.72	10.1	123	$9
22	STL *	3	0	65	58	3.42	1.32	3.72	1.55	121	105	16.9	13%	20%	7%	12%	10.7%	93.1	42	25	33	30%	76%	12%	13%	8	74	13%	38%	0	0.82	4.4	84	-$1
1st Half		0	0	15	13	3.52	1.20	2.87	1.58	124	121	12.1	14%	20%	6%	12%	8.9%	91.8	46	8	46	20%	75%	9%	9%	3	60	0%	67%			0.8	71	-$9
2nd Half		3	0	50	46	3.39	1.36	3.98	1.32	120	98	19.1	9%	22%	13%	11%	11.4%	93.6	41	30	29	32%	76%	13%	15%	5	80	20%	20%	0	0.82	3.6	91	-$1
Proj		**8**	**0**	**131**	**134**	**3.64**	**1.20**	**3.48**	**1.31**	**97**	**86**	**21.2**	**10%**	**26%**	**15%**	**9%**	**13.0%**	**93.5**	**40**	**26**	**33**	**27%**	**74%**	**14%**	**16%**	**25**						**5.3**	**94**	**$8**

Flexen,Chris

Age: 29	Th: R	Role: RP	Health: A	LIMA Plan: A
Ht: 6' 3"	Wt: 250	Type: Con/FB	PT/Exp: A	Rand Var: -3
			Consist: B	MM: 1101

Back-to-back seasons of outpitching his xERA, but can it continue? Puny K% in 2021-22, but small sample 2nd half SwK% uptick is mildly interesting, as it coincided with increased usage of a new slider. That suggests there could be a few more strikeouts in his future. As is, the pathetic K-BB% puts him at the mercy of H%/S% and xERA highlights the downside.

Yr	Tm	W	Sv	IP	K	ERA	WHIP	xERA	xWHIP	vL+	vR+	BF/G	BB%	K%	K-BB%	xBB%	SwK	Vel	G	L	F	H%	S%	HR/F	xHR/F	GS	APC	DOM%	DIS%	Sv%	LI	RAR	BPX	R$
18	NYM *	6	0	98	70	4.59	1.62	5.73	1.95	171	180	19.8	8%	16%	8%	12%	4.0%	92.6	40	23	37	35%	74%	18%	19%	1	38	0%	100%	0	0.77	-5.4	50	-$7
19	NYM *	5	0	94	88	5.53	1.72	6.37	2.05	91	120	12.2	8%	21%	12%	12%	8.0%	94.3	32	21	47	39%	70%	5%	9%	1	30	0%	100%	0	1.09	-11.9	62	-$9
20	for	8	0	117	125	3.73	1.21	3.44				22.4	8%	27%	19%							32%	71%									10.5	127	$29
21	SEA	14	0	180	125	3.61	1.25	4.60	1.28	90	104	23.9	5%	17%	11%	7%	9.1%	92.8	42	21	37	30%	74%	9%	12%	31	91	32%	45%			14.6	86	$12
22	SEA	8	2	138	95	3.73	1.33	5.11	1.41	91	112	17.9	9%	16%	7%	9%	10.1%	91.7	34	20	46	28%	76%	9%	10%	22	67	14%	50%	100	0.63	4.1	37	$3
1st Half		5	0	90	66	4.00	1.40	5.01	1.38	93	116	24.2	8%	17%	9%	10%	9.5%	91.6	33	22	46	31%	75%	8%	11%	16	90	19%	38%			-0.3	47	-$2
2nd Half		3	2	48	29	3.21	1.20	5.31	1.48	88	103	11.9	9%	14%	5%	8%	11.2%	92.0	36	18	46	23%	78%	9%	8%	6	45	0%	83%	100	0.48	4.5	18	$2
Proj		**5**	**0**	**73**	**56**	**4.32**	**1.38**	**4.32**	**1.36**	**101**	**124**	**16.6**	**8%**	**19%**	**10%**	**8%**	**10.2%**	**92.0**	**36**	**20**	**44**	**30%**	**73%**	**11%**	**9%**	**12**						**-3.2**	**63**	**-$3**

Floro,Dylan

Age: 32	Th: R	Role: RP	Health: D	LIMA Plan: A+
Ht: 6' 2"	Wt: 203	Type:	PT/Exp: B	Rand Var: -2
			Consist: A	MM: 4221

Missed first month (rotator cuff tendinitis). Velocity down overall, but rose as season progressed (93.3 mph in Sept). K% increased in 2nd half, just like 2021. Unfortunately, that lacked SwK support and was accompanied by GB% drop. 2nd half BPX was closer-worthy, but historical inability to sustain those skills makes him a high risk target for saves.

Yr	Tm	W	Sv	IP	K	ERA	WHIP	xERA	xWHIP	vL+	vR+	BF/G	BB%	K%	K-BB%	xBB%	SwK	Vel	G	L	F	H%	S%	HR/F	xHR/F	GS	APC	DOM%	DIS%	Sv%	LI	RAR	BPX	R$
18	2 NL	6	0	64	58	2.25	1.25	3.79	1.32	103	78	5.0	8%	21%	13%	7%	11.6%	93.3	55	18	26	31%	83%	6%	7%	0	18			0	1.06	15.0	106	$5
19	LA	5	0	47	42	4.24	1.29	4.21	1.30	123	75	4.0	7%	21%	14%	6%	13.1%	93.9	51	20	28	32%	68%	10%	12%	0	15			0	1.14	1.5	111	$0
20	LA	3	0	24	19	2.59	1.11	3.58	1.19	63	95	3.9	4%	19%	15%	6%	10.2%	93.4	56	24	20	31%	77%	7%	8%	0	15			0	0.79	5.6	136	$5
21	MIA	6	15	64	62	2.81	1.22	4.09	1.32	89	69	4.0	9%	23%	14%	7%	10.5%	93.7	49	20	31	30%	76%	4%	11%	0	16			71	1.20	11.5	98	$11
22	MIA	1	10	54	48	3.02	1.17	3.75	1.23	111	75	3.9	7%	22%	15%	5%	9.8%	92.6	45	21	34	30%	76%	8%	8%	0	15			71	0.94	6.3	110	$4
1st Half		0	2	20	9	4.95	1.30	4.61	1.35	135	76	4.0	5%	11%	6%	6%	7.4%	91.9	49	20	31	30%	63%	9%	6%	0	15			100	0.61	-2.4	56	-$10
2nd Half		1	8	34	39	1.87	1.10	3.29	1.15	93	75	3.9	8%	29%	21%	5%	11.3%	92.9	42	22	35	30%	86%	7%	9%	0	15			67	1.14	8.7	142	$8
Proj		**4**	**16**	**73**	**65**	**3.26**	**1.22**	**3.46**	**1.26**	**110**	**74**	**3.9**	**8%**	**22%**	**15%**	**6%**	**10.9%**	**93.1**	**48**	**21**	**31**	**30%**	**74%**	**8%**	**9%**	**0**						**6.3**	**106**	**$9**

GREG PYRON

Foley,Jason

Age: 27	Th: R	Role	RP	Health	A	LIMA Plan	B
Ht: 6' 4"	Wt: 215	Type	Con/xGB	PT/Exp	D	Rand Var	0
				Consist	F	MM	3000

Undrafted free agent rose thru minors working exclusively out of bullpen, made Opening Day roster. Induces tons of groundballs and does a good job of limiting free passes; but lacks an out pitch, as the slider (24% usage; 12% SwK%) is his only double-digit SwK offering. Middle relief is a good living, just not terribly relevant to us.

Yr Tm	W	Sv	IP	K	ERA	WHIP	xERA	xWHIP	vL+	vR+	BF/G	BB%	K%	K-BB%	xBB%	SwK	Vel	G	L	F	H%	S%	HR/F	xHR/F	GS	APC	DOM%	DIS%	Sv%	LI	RAR	BPX	R$
18																																	
19																																	
20																																	
21 DET *	1	2	47	33	5.20	1.66	5.94	1.60	56	127	4.9	12%	16%	3%	12%	7.1%	95.8	55	19	26	31%	72%	13%	8%	0	18			67	0.44	-5.4	23	-$9
22 DET	1	0	60	43	3.88	1.38	3.67	1.22	121	86	4.3	4%	17%	13%	6%	8.2%	96.3	57	18	25	36%	70%	4%	8%	0	16			0	0.67	0.7	117	-$5
1st Half	0	0	28	18	2.86	1.41	3.98	1.31	118	88	4.8	6%	15%	9%	5%	6.5%	96.0	55	18	26	35%	78%	0%	7%	0	17			0	0.43	3.9	84	-$8
2nd Half	1	0	32	25	4.78	1.34	3.40	1.13	122	84	3.9	3%	19%	16%	7%	9.6%	96.5	58	17	25	36%	63%	8%	10%	0	15			0	0.84	-3.2	146	-$9
Proj	**1**	**0**	**58**	**40**	**4.05**	**1.36**	**3.63**	**1.30**	**117**	**82**	**4.4**	**6%**	**16%**	**11%**	**6%**	**8.4%**	**96.3**	**57**	**18**	**25**	**33%**	**70%**	**7%**	**9%**	**0**						**-0.6**	**96**	**-$5**

Freeland,Kyle

Age: 30	Th: L	Role	SP	Health	D	LIMA Plan	C+
Ht: 6' 4"	Wt: 204	Type	Con	PT/Exp	A	Rand Var	-1
				Consist	A	MM	2105

Avoided IL and posted highest IP total since 2018. Velocity and K% both slipped to well below average. Again performed better away from Coors Field, amassing a 3.08 ERA and 1.30 WHIP in 88 IP (career 3.77 ERA, 1.36 WHIP in 415 IP on road), though weak K-BB% lurks there too. Bad option outside of those favorable road matchups.

Yr Tm	W	Sv	IP	K	ERA	WHIP	xERA	xWHIP	vL+	vR+	BF/G	BB%	K%	K-BB%	xBB%	SwK	Vel	G	L	F	H%	S%	HR/F	xHR/F	GS	APC	DOM%	DIS%	Sv%	LI	RAR	BPX	R$
18 COL	17	0	202	173	2.85	1.25	4.19	1.34	71	98	25.6	8%	20%	12%	8%	9.6%	91.6	46	19	35	29%	80%	8%	11%	33	98	33%	21%			32.5	90	$21
19 COL *	3	0	136	100	7.40	1.68	6.80	1.45	103	126	21.8	9%	16%	7%	8%	9.9%	91.9	47	21	33	34%	59%	22%	19%	22	81	9%	59%			-48.4	13	-$22
20 COL	2	0	71	46	4.33	1.42	4.72	1.42	113	101	23.4	8%	15%	8%	8%	9.4%	91.9	52	23	25	31%	73%	16%	16%	13	86	0%	46%			1.1	64	-$2
21 COL	7	0	121	105	4.33	1.42	4.35	1.30	109	109	22.4	7%	20%	13%	8%	9.2%	91.4	45	21	34	32%	75%	16%	14%	23	82	22%	35%			-0.9	96	-$2
22 COL	9	0	175	131	4.53	1.41	4.44	1.32	134	107	24.7	7%	17%	10%	8%	9.4%	90.0	42	23	36	32%	70%	10%	14%	31	92	13%	39%			-12.2	75	-$4
1st Half	4	0	91	63	4.43	1.37	4.60	1.34	136	102	25.0	7%	16%	9%	8%	10.0%	90.1	40	24	36	31%	70%	9%	11%	16	90	13%	31%			-5.2	64	-$5
2nd Half	5	0	83	68	4.64	1.45	4.26	1.30	130	111	24.4	7%	19%	11%	8%	8.9%	89.9	44	21	35	34%	70%	10%	17%	15	94	13%	47%			-6.9	86	-$4
Proj	**8**	**0**	**167**	**127**	**4.40**	**1.44**	**4.06**	**1.35**	**119**	**108**	**23.2**	**8%**	**18%**	**10%**	**8%**	**9.4%**	**90.9**	**45**	**22**	**33**	**32%**	**73%**	**13%**	**15%**	**31**						**-9.0**	**75**	**-$4**

Fried,Max

Age: 29	Th: L	Role	SP	Health	D	LIMA Plan	C+
Ht: 6' 4"	Wt: 190	Type	Con/GB	PT/Exp	A	Rand Var	-3
				Consist	A	MM	5205

Took another step forward, thanks to a vastly improved change-up (19% SwK/53% GB%; usage 14% after only 2% in 2021). That fueled the career-best SwK, and firm up his strikeouts floor even if there's no new level coming. xBB%, xERA, and xWHIP all point to some mild pullback, but that's one heck of a soft landing.

Yr Tm	W	Sv	IP	K	ERA	WHIP	xERA	xWHIP	vL+	vR+	BF/G	BB%	K%	K-BB%	xBB%	SwK	Vel	G	L	F	H%	S%	HR/F	xHR/F	GS	APC	DOM%	DIS%	Sv%	LI	RAR	BPX	R$
18 ATL *	4	0	113	115	4.40	1.46	4.12	1.37	114	88	16.7	11%	24%	13%	10%	14.4%	93.0	51	28	20	34%	70%	20%	12%	5	41	20%	20%	0	0.64	-3.4	98	-$4
19 ATL	17	0	166	173	4.02	1.33	3.54	1.21	86	103	21.3	7%	25%	18%	7%	11.9%	93.8	54	24	22	34%	74%	20%	16%	30	81	17%	23%	0	0.80	9.9	144	$12
20 ATL	7	0	56	50	2.25	1.09	3.85	1.31	94	81	20.4	8%	22%	14%	8%	11.8%	93.0	53	19	28	27%	80%	5%	9%	11	82	36%	18%			15.2	105	$24
21 ATL	14	0	166	158	3.04	1.09	3.47	1.18	98	81	23.8	6%	24%	18%	6%	11.7%	93.9	52	21	28	29%	75%	12%	14%	28	91	36%	18%			25.0	136	$22
22 ATL	14	0	185	170	2.48	1.01	3.18	1.11	75	84	24.4	4%	23%	19%	7%	12.6%	93.9	51	19	30	29%	78%	8%	8%	30	94	33%	7%			34.1	149	$27
1st Half	8	0	101	96	2.66	1.03	3.01	1.08	70	84	25.1	4%	24%	20%	6%	12.7%	94.2	52	22	26	30%	76%	8%	10%	16	95	38%	6%			16.3	160	$26
2nd Half	6	0	84	74	2.25	1.00	3.39	1.14	80	84	23.6	5%	22%	18%	8%	12.4%	93.6	50	16	33	28%	81%	8%	6%	14	92	29%	7%			17.8	138	$22
Proj	**15**	**0**	**174**	**162**	**2.74**	**1.06**	**2.97**	**1.14**	**86**	**85**	**21.7**	**5%**	**24%**	**19%**	**8%**	**12.3%**	**93.7**	**52**	**20**	**28**	**29%**	**76%**	**9%**	**10%**	**31**						**26.5**	**142**	**$25**

Fulmer,Michael

Age: 30	Th: R	Role	RP	Health	F	LIMA Plan	A+
Ht: 6' 3"	Wt: 224	Type	Pwr	PT/Exp	B	Rand Var	-3
				Consist	C	MM	2210

Second full season as a reliever didn't go as well the first. Leaned even harder on his slider (usage increased from 40% to 63%), mostly at the expense of the sinker (28% to 13% usage), but SwK and K% actually decreased and BB% went up. Velocity also fell a tick. Though he has outpitched xERA for a couple of years running, that downside still applies.

Yr Tm	W	Sv	IP	K	ERA	WHIP	xERA	xWHIP	vL+	vR+	BF/G	BB%	K%	K-BB%	xBB%	SwK	Vel	G	L	F	H%	S%	HR/F	xHR/F	GS	APC	DOM%	DIS%	Sv%	LI	RAR	BPX	R$
18 DET	3	0	132	110	4.69	1.31	4.29	1.35	108	100	23.3	8%	20%	11%	7%	11.1%	95.8	44	22	34	29%	68%	15%	14%	24	90	25%	33%			-8.9	83	-$3
19																																	
20 DET	0	0	28	20	8.78	2.06	6.21	1.50	98	194	13.6	9%	15%	6%	12%	7.8%	93.1	36	28	36	39%	61%	22%	17%	10	53	0%	80%			-14.8	29	-$22
21 DET	5	14	70	73	2.97	1.28	3.87	1.19	77	108	5.7	7%	25%	18%	8%	13.6%	95.7	45	21	34	33%	80%	10%	13%	4	23	0%	50%	78	1.31	11.1	135	$9
22 2 AL	5	3	64	61	3.39	1.37	4.38	1.36	133	76	4.1	10%	22%	12%	10%	12.3%	94.4	35	24	40	32%	76%	5%	7%	0	16			43	1.23	4.5	68	$1
1st Half	2	1	30	30	2.10	1.00	4.03	1.37	111	40	4.0	12%	25%	13%	12%	12.2%	94.0	36	20	43	22%	79%	3%	4%	0	15			33	1.30	6.9	70	$2
2nd Half	3	2	34	31	4.54	1.69	4.70	1.35	151	103	4.2	9%	20%	11%	8%	12.3%	94.6	35	27	38	38%	74%	7%	10%	0	16			50	1.17	-2.4	67	-$7
Proj	**4**	**2**	**58**	**54**	**3.73**	**1.36**	**3.92**	**1.34**	**117**	**87**	**5.3**	**9%**	**22%**	**13%**	**9%**	**12.2%**	**94.9**	**39**	**23**	**38**	**32%**	**75%**	**8%**	**10%**	**0**						**1.7**	**81**	**-$1**

Gallegos,Giovanny

Age: 31	Th: R	Role	RP	Health	B	LIMA Plan	A
Ht: 6' 2"	Wt: 215	Type	Pwr/xFB	PT/Exp	A	Rand Var	-2
				Consist	A	MM	5521

Began year as closer before shifting into setup role. Didn't really earn that demotion, as SwK and K% remained elite, and dominance vR continued. BB% crept back up despite stable xBB%. Extreme FB% is a concern, particularly in light of xHR/F. Shaky Sv% might keep him from full-time closer, but he's a great target in Sv+H leagues.

Yr Tm	W	Sv	IP	K	ERA	WHIP	xERA	xWHIP	vL+	vR+	BF/G	BB%	K%	K-BB%	xBB%	SwK	Vel	G	L	F	H%	S%	HR/F	xHR/F	GS	APC	DOM%	DIS%	Sv%	LI	RAR	BPX	R$
18 2 TM *	2	4	56	55	3.29	1.09	2.69	1.16	138	81	6.1	6%	25%	19%	5%	9.3%	94.4	34	24	41	30%	70%	17%	14%	0	30			80	0.16	6.0	155	$3
19 STL	3	1	74	93	2.31	0.81	3.44	1.04	68	76	4.2	6%	33%	28%	5%	16.7%	93.7	34	19	47	23%	80%	11%	12%	0	17			25	0.94	20.0	178	$12
20 STL	2	4	15	21	3.60	0.87	2.91	1.00	55	69	3.6	7%	37%	30%	4%	21.0%	93.7	42	19	39	27%	58%	8%	13%	0	14			100	1.17	1.6	206	$7
21 STL	6	14	80	95	3.02	0.88	3.51	1.07	75	75	4.2	6%	31%	24%	6%	16.6%	94.5	33	20	47	25%	68%	7%	10%	0	17			64	1.37	12.3	156	$18
22 STL	3	14	59	73	3.05	1.02	3.67	1.10	104	69	4.1	8%	31%	23%	6%	18.0%	94.4	27	18	55	28%	74%	8%	11%	0	17			70	1.38	6.7	145	$10
1st Half	2	9	30	37	3.00	1.07	3.71	1.09	113	67	4.3	8%	31%	24%	6%	17.1%	94.1	26	18	56	30%	76%	7%	9%	0	18			69	1.30	3.6	144	$7
2nd Half	1	5	29	36	3.10	0.97	3.62	1.10	94	71	4.0	8%	31%	23%	6%	19.0%	94.6	29	17	54	26%	72%	8%	12%	0	17			71	1.46	3.1	146	$3
Proj	**4**	**11**	**73**	**88**	**3.39**	**0.95**	**3.12**	**1.07**	**91**	**73**	**4.1**	**7%**	**32%**	**25%**	**6%**	**17.6%**	**94.2**	**30**	**18**	**52**	**26%**	**68%**	**9%**	**11%**	**0**						**5.1**	**152**	**$11**

Gallen,Zac

Age: 27	Th: R	Role	SP	Health	D	LIMA Plan	C+
Ht: 6' 2"	Wt: 189	Type	Pwr	PT/Exp	A	Rand Var	-4
				Consist	B	MM	5403

After 67 days on IL in 2021 and shoulder bursitis in spring 2022, he suddenly found both health and 2019-20's ace form in 2nd half. 44 IP scoreless streak was the headliner. xERA and xWHIP point to some regression, and then there's the Health grade, but his skills floor provides comfort. Still, don't pay for a full repeat.

Yr Tm	W	Sv	IP	K	ERA	WHIP	xERA	xWHIP	vL+	vR+	BF/G	BB%	K%	K-BB%	xBB%	SwK	Vel	G	L	F	H%	S%	HR/F	xHR/F	GS	APC	DOM%	DIS%	Sv%	LI	RAR	BPX	R$
18 aaa	8	0	134	117	4.08	1.59	5.41				23.6	8%	20%	12%							37%	76%									1.1	77	-$4
19 2 NL *	12	0	172	190	2.54	1.01	2.51	1.32	88	87	22.7	8%	29%	21%	7%	13.2%	92.9	39	24	37	26%	81%	11%	12%	15	92	27%	7%			41.8	130	$28
20 ARI	3	0	72	82	2.75	1.11	3.64	1.21	86	82	24.3	9%	28%	20%	8%	12.3%	93.3	46	22	33	28%	82%	15%	15%	12	93	33%	8%			15.1	140	$20
21 ARI	4	0	121	139	4.30	1.29	4.01	1.26	97	100	22.7	9%	27%	17%	9%	9.9%	93.4	44	19	37	30%	72%	16%	13%	23	91	17%	30%			-0.5	120	$1
22 ARI	12	0	184	192	2.54	0.91	3.17	1.12	68	89	23.0	7%	27%	20%	7%	10.5%	94.2	46	18	36	24%	76%	9%	11%	31	95	45%	26%			32.4	144	$30
1st Half	4	0	82	77	3.40	1.05	3.62	1.21	84	93	22.5	7%	23%	16%	8%	10.0%	94.2	46	19	36	26%	71%	11%	12%	15	92	27%	33%			5.7	119	$12
2nd Half	8	0	102	115	1.85	0.80	2.83	1.06	53	86	23.6	6%	31%	24%	6%	10.9%	94.2	46	17	36	23%	80%	7%	10%	16	97	63%	19%			26.6	165	$41
Proj	**10**	**0**	**160**	**172**	**3.34**	**1.11**	**3.13**	**1.17**	**84**	**94**	**22.9**	**8%**	**27%**	**20%**	**8%**	**11.1%**	**93.7**	**45**	**20**	**36**	**29%**	**73%**	**11%**	**12%**	**27**						**12.4**	**136**	**$16**

García,Jarlín

Age: 30	Th: L	Role	RP	Health	A	LIMA Plan	B
Ht: 6' 3"	Wt: 215	Type	Con/FB	PT/Exp	C	Rand Var	-1
				Consist	B	MM	2100

Outpaced xERA and xWHIP by wide margins from 2018-21, but that narrowed in 2022. While 2021 K% was ripe for regression, increased usage of improved change-up led to 2022's uptick in SwK that aligns with a 25% xK%. Career-high FB% makes him more susceptible to HR. LI shows he's not in the bullpen trust tree, which limits even his Holds appeal.

Yr Tm	W	Sv	IP	K	ERA	WHIP	xERA	xWHIP	vL+	vR+	BF/G	BB%	K%	K-BB%	xBB%	SwK	Vel	G	L	F	H%	S%	HR/F	xHR/F	GS	APC	DOM%	DIS%	Sv%	LI	RAR	BPX	R$
18 MIA *	5	0	116	67	5.15	1.44	5.36	1.54	109	110	12.7	9%	14%	5%	9%	8.3%	92.1	43	20	37	29%	69%	21%	20%	7	36	0%	29%	0	0.86	-14.4	18	-$8
19 MIA	4	0	51	39	3.02	1.11	4.60	1.38	79	81	3.9	8%	19%	11%	7%	9.1%	93.3	47	18	35	26%	75%	8%	14%	0	14			0	0.90	9.3	79	$3
20 SF	2	0	18	14	0.49	0.98	4.57	1.43	63	71	3.8	10%	19%	10%	8%	6.3%	93.8	46	18	36	23%	94%	0%	5%	0	15			0	0.80	9.0	62	$6
21 SF	6	1	69	68	2.62	0.96	3.74	1.18	71	97	4.6	7%	25%	19%	6%	9.9%	93.2	40	22	37	24%	81%	14%	10%	0	17			33	1.10	13.9	126	$9
22 SF	1	1	65	56	3.74	1.20	4.29	1.24	87	109	4.7	7%	21%	14%	7%	11.6%	93.9	39	16	45	28%	75%	11%	12%	0	18			33	0.81	1.8	98	-$1
1st Half	1	0	29	21	2.20	1.01	4.30	1.34	85	77	4.5	8%	19%	11%	8%	11.6%	93.6	46	11	43	22%	85%	8%	9%	0	18			0	0.75	6.3	73	-$2
2nd Half	0	1	36	35	4.95	1.35	4.28	1.17	89	136	4.8	6%	22%	17%	6%	11.7%	94.0	34	19	47	33%	69%	14%	15%	0	17			50	0.86	-4.4	119	-$9
Proj	**3**	**0**	**58**	**48**	**4.06**	**1.22**	**3.87**	**1.28**	**89**	**105**	**4.7**	**7%**	**21%**	**13%**	**7%**	**10.4%**	**93.5**	**41**	**18**	**41**	**29%**	**71%**	**11%**	**13%**	**0**						**-0.6**	**92**	**-$2**

GREG PYRON

Garcia,Luis H.

Age: 26	Th: R	Role SP	Health A	LIMA Plan B+
Ht: 6' 1"	Wt: 244	Type /FB	PT/Exp A	Rand Var 0
			Consist A	MM 3203

Nearly carbon copy follow-up to impressive rookie campaign. Four of five pitches had a SwK of 13-19%, including a dazzling cutter (19% SwK, 29% usage). Though he has yet to tap into it, SwK hints at K% upside (29% xK%). FB% led to a few more HR, but low traffic on basepaths limited damage. Solid floor, and a tweak could unlock another level.

Yr Tm	W	Sv	IP	K	ERA	WHIP	xERA	xWHIP	vL+	vR+	BF/G	BB%	K%	K-BB%	xBB%	SwK	Vel	G	L	F	H%	S%	HR/F	xHR/F	GS	APC	DOM%	DIS%	Sv%	LI	RAR	BPX	R$
18																																	
19																																	
20 HOU	0	0	12	9	2.92	0.97	4.87	1.48	142	28	9.8	10%	18%	8%	12%	11.3%	94.0	41	21	38	19%	73%	8%	10%	1	41	0%	0%	0	0.67	2.3	44	-$3
21 HOU	11	0	155	167	3.30	1.17	3.97	1.21	113	73	21.1	8%	26%	18%	8%	13.8%	93.3	38	21	41	29%	77%	11%	12%	28	83	25%	14%	0	0.74	18.4	123	$16
22 HOU	15	0	157	157	3.72	1.13	3.93	1.20	104	90	23.0	7%	24%	17%	7%	13.7%	94.0	38	19	44	27%	73%	12%	10%	28	88	14%	14%			4.9	116	$14
1st Half	7	0	83	87	3.81	1.09	3.75	1.14	104	91	22.5	7%	26%	19%	7%	14.5%	94.3	37	20	43	27%	73%	15%	11%	15	85	13%	13%			1.6	133	$13
2nd Half	8	0	75	70	3.62	1.18	4.13	1.26	103	88	23.5	8%	23%	15%	8%	12.7%	93.8	39	18	44	28%	73%	9%	10%	13	92	15%	15%			3.3	96	$12
Proj	14	0	160	152	3.43	1.15	3.61	1.24	108	88	23.2	8%	24%	16%	8%	13.5%	93.8	38	19	43	28%	75%	11%	10%	27						10.6	105	$15

García,Luis A.

Age: 36	Th: R	Role RP	Health C	LIMA Plan A+
Ht: 6' 2"	Wt: 240	Type Pwr	PT/Exp D	Rand Var 0
			Consist D	MM 5310

Journeyman began 2022 in setup role and wound up earning a few save chances in 2nd half. Predominantly a sinker/slider guy with the slider serving as his primary swing-and-miss offering (22% SwK), but splitter was also effective (17% SwK, 77% GB%, 13% usage). Blend of GB%, K%, and BB% gives him appeal in Sv+H leagues.

Yr Tm	W	Sv	IP	K	ERA	WHIP	xERA	xWHIP	vL+	vR+	BF/G	BB%	K%	K-BB%	xBB%	SwK	Vel	G	L	F	H%	S%	HR/F	xHR/F	GS	APC	DOM%	DIS%	Sv%	LI	RAR	BPX	R$
18 PHI	3	1	46	51	6.07	1.46	3.65	1.27	105	109	3.5	9%	25%	16%	9%	14.8%	97.2	48	24	27	36%	57%	11%	12%	0	13			25	1.29	-10.9	127	-$6
19 LAA	2	1	62	57	4.35	1.52	5.05	1.53	105	108	4.3	12%	21%	9%	11%	13.1%	97.1	47	20	33	29%	79%	22%	18%	2	16	0%	100%	33	0.64	1.2	49	-$3
20 TEX	0	0	8	11	7.56	2.28	6.52	1.81	150	79	4.1	20%	24%	4%	12%	10.3%	96.6	44	24	32	42%	67%	13%	16%	2	17	0%	100%	0	0.59	-3.2	-30	-$11
21 STL *	2	13	51	48	3.75	1.12	3.24	1.15	120	49	3.9	5%	24%	18%	6%	15.4%	98.3	46	22	33	30%	68%	7%	14%	0	15			93	0.88	3.3	133	$6
22 SD	4	3	61	68	3.39	1.21	3.10	1.13	97	80	4.0	7%	26%	20%	8%	14.2%	98.7	53	19	28	34%	72%	6%	6%	0	15			75	1.21	4.3	159	$2
1st Half	4	0	32	34	3.41	1.26	2.93	1.13	101	78	4.2	6%	25%	19%	8%	14.4%	98.2	57	20	23	36%	72%	5%	7%	0	16			0	1.27	2.2	163	-$1
2nd Half	0	3	29	34	3.38	1.16	3.28	1.14	91	83	3.9	7%	27%	20%	8%	14.0%	99.2	49	16	34	32%	72%	7%	5%	0	14			100	1.14	2.1	155	-$2
Proj	3	5	58	61	3.32	1.21	3.19	1.23	100	81	3.8	9%	26%	17%	8%	14.1%	98.1	50	20	31	30%	76%	13%	11%	0						4.6	123	$2

Garcia,Rony

Age: 25	Th: R	Role RP	Health F	LIMA Plan C+
Ht: 6' 3"	Wt: 200	Type Pwr/FB	PT/Exp D	Rand Var 0
			Consist C	MM 2200

Moved from bullpen to starter in late May and made eight starts before shoulder inflammation ended his season in July. Tiny sample, but best work came as a reliever (2.57 ERA, 28% K-BB% in 14 IP). Overall, xBB%/SwK cast doubt on BB%/K% sustainability and 16% Brl%/51% HH% allowed is worrisome. Worth watching in deeper leagues.

Yr Tm	W	Sv	IP	K	ERA	WHIP	xERA	xWHIP	vL+	vR+	BF/G	BB%	K%	K-BB%	xBB%	SwK	Vel	G	L	F	H%	S%	HR/F	xHR/F	GS	APC	DOM%	DIS%	Sv%	LI	RAR	BPX	R$
18																																	
19 aa	4	0	106	91	5.86	1.45	5.30				22.6	9%	20%	11%							31%	63%									-17.7	47	-$7
20 DET	1	0	21	14	8.14	1.62	6.18	1.53	58	181	6.4	9%	15%	5%	11%	8.4%	93.3	33	26	40	28%	56%	24%	20%	2	26	0%	100%	0	0.36	-9.6	17	-$12
21 DET *	0	0	25	21	3.77	1.18	4.16		254	17	16.6	12%	21%	9%		3.6%	92.1	25	13	63	18%	81%	20%	21%	0	28			0	1.17	1.5	36	-$4
22 DET	3	0	51	48	4.41	1.04	4.00	1.18	85	111	12.9	6%	23%	17%	10%	9.0%	92.8	31	22	47	24%	64%	14%	20%	8	55	0%	25%	0	0.59	-2.8	110	-$1
1st Half	3	0	48	48	4.28	1.06	3.93	1.17	84	112	12.8	7%	25%	18%	10%	9.4%	93.0	30	22	48	25%	67%	15%	21%	7	55	0%	29%	0	0.58	-1.9	114	$0
2nd Half	0	0	3	0	6.75	0.75	5.48		89	91	14.0	0%	0%	0%	8%	4.8%	90.0	45	18	36	21%	0%	0%	2%	1	62	0%	0%			-0.9	26	-$11
Proj	3	0	58	54	4.91	1.38	4.17	1.35	106	141	16.1	10%	22%	13%	10%	9.4%	93.0	30	22	48	30%	70%	15%	19%	9						-6.7	69	-$5

Garcia,Yimi

Age: 32	Th: R	Role RP	Health C	LIMA Plan A+
Ht: 6' 2"	Wt: 228	Type /xFB	PT/Exp B	Rand Var -4
			Consist A	MM 3310

On the surface, it would appear that 2022 was a lot better than 2021, but xERA and xWHIP indicate otherwise. The return of FB% tilt is notable as it makes him more vulnerable to HR issues. Dip in K%/SwK was result of reduced slider usage. Not without flaws, but should remain useful in Holds leagues.

Yr Tm	W	Sv	IP	K	ERA	WHIP	xERA	xWHIP	vL+	vR+	BF/G	BB%	K%	K-BB%	xBB%	SwK	Vel	G	L	F	H%	S%	HR/F	xHR/F	GS	APC	DOM%	DIS%	Sv%	LI	RAR	BPX	R$
18 LA *	2	1	39	30	5.26	1.36	6.16	1.19	113	146	4.1	2%	19%	16%	5%	12.4%	94.5	36	21	43	33%	69%	21%	22%	0	16			33	0.56	-5.3	146	-$5
19 LA	1	0	62	66	3.61	0.87	4.37	1.16	91	88	3.9	6%	27%	21%	6%	12.4%	94.2	30	14	56	19%	74%	17%	11%	0	16			0	0.63	6.9	136	$4
20 MIA	3	1	15	19	0.60	0.93	3.40	1.14	87	43	4.3	8%	32%	23%	8%	12.4%	94.5	42	25	33	28%	93%	0%	10%	0	17			50	0.97	7.1	163	$8
21 2 TM	4	15	58	60	4.21	1.16	3.90	1.21	117	78	3.8	8%	25%	18%	6%	13.0%	95.9	40	25	35	29%	68%	15%	20%	0	15			83	1.38	0.4	121	$7
22 TOR	4	1	61	58	3.10	1.05	3.92	1.18	102	79	4.0	6%	23%	17%	8%	10.9%	94.7	40	14	46	27%	74%	8%	8%	0	17			20	1.25	6.6	119	$4
1st Half	1	0	26	26	3.42	0.99	3.55	1.09	90	91	3.8	5%	25%	20%	9%	11.7%	94.3	42	15	43	27%	70%	10%	5%	0	16			0	1.27	1.8	147	-$4
2nd Half	3	1	35	32	2.86	1.10	4.22	1.25	108	68	4.3	8%	23%	15%	6%	10.3%	94.9	38	13	48	27%	77%	6%	10%	0	18			50	1.24	4.8	98	$2
Proj	3	2	51	49	3.61	1.15	3.63	1.17	115	92	3.9	6%	24%	18%	7%	11.6%	94.7	37	16	47	29%	75%	12%	11%	0						2.2	124	$1

Garrett,Braxton

Age: 25	Th: L	Role SP	Health B	LIMA Plan A+
Ht: 6' 2"	Wt: 202	Type	PT/Exp C	Rand Var 0
			Consist B	MM 4201

3-7, 3.58 ERA in 88 IP with MIA. 7th overall pick in the 2016 draft struggled mightily in small-sample 2021 MLB debut, thus opened 2022 in minors. Recalled in June and flashed above-average BB% and K% while inducing lots of groundballs. But velocity was subpar and slider was only pitch with SwK >10%. Don't overpay based on small sample.

Yr Tm	W	Sv	IP	K	ERA	WHIP	xERA	xWHIP	vL+	vR+	BF/G	BB%	K%	K-BB%	xBB%	SwK	Vel	G	L	F	H%	S%	HR/F	xHR/F	GS	APC	DOM%	DIS%	Sv%	LI	RAR	BPX	R$
18																																	
19																																	
20 MIA	1	0	8	8	5.87	1.70	4.54	1.56	124	136	17.0	15%	24%	9%	12%	8.8%	89.7	62	10	29	27%	80%	50%	44%	2	69	0%	50%			-1.3	57	-$6
21 MIA *	6	0	121	104	4.77	1.49	4.89	1.53	134	109	20.1	10%	20%	10%	9%	9.6%	90.0	38	34	27	32%	70%	11%	12%	7	76	14%	43%	0	0.67	-7.5	64	-$6
22 MIA *	5	0	123	114	3.50	1.22	3.69	1.17	69	112	20.7	6%	24%	18%	6%	12.3%	91.2	48	21	31	31%	74%	12%	13%	17	84	18%	24%			7.2	113	$5
1st Half	3	0	56	43	3.82	1.27	3.95	1.26	102	113	20.7	5%	18%	12%	5%	13.2%	91.5	46	26	29	32%	71%	7%	9%	6	82	17%	17%			1.0	96	-$3
2nd Half	2	0	67	71	3.23	1.17	3.47	1.16	48	112	20.7	7%	25%	19%	6%	11.9%	91.1	49	19	32	31%	76%	14%	15%	11	86	18%	27%			6.1	126	$5
Proj	5	0	116	102	3.79	1.24	3.47	1.26	82	106	21.5	7%	22%	14%	6%	11.8%	91.0	46	24	30	30%	72%	12%	12%	22						2.6	103	$3

Gausman,Kevin

Age: 32	Th: R	Role SP	Health C	LIMA Plan B+
Ht: 6' 2"	Wt: 190	Type Pwr	PT/Exp A	Rand Var +1
			Consist A	MM 5505

Surface decline from 2021 career-year due to expected regression and a bloated H% (thanks, Rogers Centre - 4.57 home ERA). Led all 2022 qualified starters in SwK while posting elite BB%. Dynamite splitter continues to drive success (26% SwK, 51% GB%, 36% usage). Skepticism some carried into 2022 was quelled by even better skills. UP: Cy Young

Yr Tm	W	Sv	IP	K	ERA	WHIP	xERA	xWHIP	vL+	vR+	BF/G	BB%	K%	K-BB%	xBB%	SwK	Vel	G	L	F	H%	S%	HR/F	xHR/F	GS	APC	DOM%	DIS%	Sv%	LI	RAR	BPX	R$
18 2 TM	10	0	184	148	3.92	1.30	4.21	1.29	98	110	25.0	6%	19%	13%	7%	11.6%	93.6	46	21	33	31%	75%	14%	14%	31	97	26%	42%			5.2	102	$6
19 2 NL	3	0	102	114	5.72	1.42	4.24	1.24	105	106	14.5	7%	25%	18%	6%	15.5%	94.0	38	27	35	36%	62%	15%	17%	17	54	29%	41%	0	0.79	-15.3	131	-$6
20 SF	3	0	60	79	3.62	1.11	3.34	1.06	94	85	20.4	7%	32%	26%	6%	16.0%	95.1	42	22	36	32%	72%	15%	14%	10	81	20%	0%	0	0.71	6.1	191	$14
21 SF	14	0	192	227	2.81	1.04	3.42	1.10	83	82	23.5	6%	29%	23%	5%	15.8%	94.6	42	22	36	29%	78%	11%	14%	33	91	48%	18%			34.4	163	$31
22 TOR	12	0	175	205	3.35	1.24	3.20	1.00	87	107	23.4	4%	28%	24%	4%	16.0%	95.0	39	25	36	38%	75%	9%	11%	31	90	39%	6%			13.4	185	$14
1st Half	6	0	88	100	2.86	1.27	3.25	1.04	82	102	23.2	4%	27%	23%	4%	16.7%	94.9	43	24	33	39%	76%	2%	10%	16	88	44%	13%			12.0	177	$14
2nd Half	6	0	87	105	3.84	1.20	3.14	0.96	92	112	23.6	3%	30%	26%	4%	15.3%	95.1	36	25	39	36%	74%	14%	12%	15	91	33%	0%			1.4	194	$11
Proj	15	0	189	223	3.26	1.07	2.80	1.02	84	92	20.2	5%	30%	25%	5%	15.6%	94.8	40	24	36	32%	74%	12%	13%	36						16.6	179	$24

Germán,Domingo

Age: 30	Th: R	Role RP	Health F	LIMA Plan A+
Ht: 6' 2"	Wt: 181	Type /FB	PT/Exp B	Rand Var -2
			Consist C	MM 3301

2-5, 3.61 ERA in 72 IP with NYY. Shoulder inflammation cut his 2021 season short and right shoulder impingement syndrome forced him to open 2022 on IL. Finally returned in July and tallied a 4.23 MLB xERA. Fair to attribute K%/SwK tumble to rust. Lifetime 4.20 ERA/1.20 WHIP sets baseline, but only one season of triple-digit IP in this box.

Yr Tm	W	Sv	IP	K	ERA	WHIP	xERA	xWHIP	vL+	vR+	BF/G	BB%	K%	K-BB%	xBB%	SwK	Vel	G	L	F	H%	S%	HR/F	xHR/F	GS	APC	DOM%	DIS%	Sv%	LI	RAR	BPX	R$
18 NYY	2	0	86	102	5.57	1.33	3.98	1.23	114	100	17.9	9%	27%	18%	7%	15.2%	94.7	37	22	40	32%	62%	16%	11%	14	70	14%	36%	0	0.68	-15.0	132	-$6
19 NYY	18	0	143	153	4.03	1.15	4.20	1.21	103	87	22.0	7%	26%	19%	6%	13.4%	93.6	38	21	41	28%	75%	19%	16%	24	83	25%	13%	0	0.90	8.4	134	$16
20																																	
21 NYY	4	0	98	98	4.58	1.18	4.26	1.20	87	104	18.6	7%	24%	17%	6%	14.8%	93.5	42	14	44	29%	67%	14%	14%	18	72	28%	22%	0	0.75	-3.8	126	$1
22 NYY *	3	0	90	66	3.00	1.05	3.16	1.25	100	102	18.4	6%	19%	13%	6%	11.8%	92.7	40	18	42	25%	77%	12%	9%	14	72	7%	14%	0	0.77	10.8	94	$5
1st Half	0	0	8	5	1.32	0.60	0.32				13.9	0%	20%	20%							21%	76%	0%		0	0					2.7	0	-$7
2nd Half	3	0	82	62	3.17	1.09	3.44	1.25	100	102	19.0	6%	19%	13%	6%	11.8%	92.7	40	18	42	26%	77%	12%	9%	14	72	7%	14%	0	0.77	8.1	86	$9
Proj	6	0	116	113	4.25	1.18	3.59	1.21	100	98	18.4	7%	24%	17%	6%	13.7%	93.6	40	19	42	28%	70%	14%	12%	21						-4.0	114	$3

GREG PYRON

Gibson,Kyle

Age: 35	Th: R	Role SP	Health B	LIMA Plan B	
Ht: 6' 6"	Wt: 215	Type	PT/Exp A	Rand Var +2	
			Consist A	MM 3205	

Validated perception that huge turnaround seasons in your mid-30s rarely stick. That said, skills actually improved; it was mostly flipping of hit and strand rate fortune that caused erosion in stats. After this implosion, you should be able to get him at end-rotation prices; as reflected by expected rates of ERA and WHIP, he can still provide mid-rotation value.

Yr Tm	W	Sv	IP	K	ERA	WHIP	xERA	xWHIP	vL+	vR+	BF/G	BB%	K%	K-BB%	xBB%	SwK	Vel	G	L	F	H%	S%	HR/F	xHR/F	GS	APC	DOM%	DIS%	Sv%	LI	RAR	BPX	R$
18 MIN	10	0	197	179	3.62	1.30	3.95	1.36	100	94	25.8	10%	22%	12%	11%	11.7%	93.0	50	22	28	29%	76%	15%	14%	32	101	22%	28%			13.0	90	$10
19 MIN	13	0	160	160	4.84	1.44	4.02	1.30	107	100	20.8	8%	23%	15%	9%	13.4%	93.3	51	25	24	34%	70%	20%	21%	29	81	21%	31%	0	0.88	-6.6	115	$2
20 TEX	2	0	67	58	5.35	1.53	4.47	1.43	118	106	25.1	10%	19%	9%	11%	9.6%	92.3	51	27	22	32%	69%	27%	23%	12	95	17%	58%			-7.4	68	-$9
21 2 TM	10	0	182	155	3.71	1.22	4.07	1.34	102	79	24.3	8%	21%	12%	9%	10.8%	92.5	52	19	29	28%	72%	11%	11%	30	93	23%	17%	0	0.78	12.5	91	$11
22 PHI	10	0	168	144	5.05	1.34	3.98	1.25	109	106	23.2	7%	20%	13%	8%	11.3%	91.8	46	20	34	32%	65%	14%	13%	31	88	19%	48%			-22.3	103	-$4
1st Half	4	0	84	70	4.91	1.30	3.95	1.27	101	110	22.4	7%	19%	13%	8%	11.9%	91.4	47	21	32	30%	66%	16%	12%	16	87	13%	50%			-9.8	96	-$5
2nd Half	6	0	83	74	5.18	1.37	4.01	1.23	116	102	23.9	6%	21%	14%	8%	10.7%	92.2	45	20	35	33%	64%	12%	14%	15	90	27%	47%			-12.5	110	-$3
Proj	**9**	**0**	**167**	**146**	**4.29**	**1.37**	**3.65**	**1.31**	**110**	**101**	**23.0**	**8%**	**21%**	**13%**	**9%**	**11.0%**	**92.3**	**49**	**22**	**30**	**31%**	**73%**	**16%**	**15%**	**30**						**-6.5**	**95**	**$1**

Gilbert,Logan

Age: 26	Th: R	Role SP	Health A	LIMA Plan B	
Ht: 6' 6"	Wt: 225	Type	PT/Exp A	Rand Var -2	
			Consist A	MM 4305	

Sophomore campaign saw him turn into a workhorse, with a shiny ERA to boot. But there's risk here if you expect this to be his new baseline. Command sub-indicators were more good than great, and average exit velocity ranked in game's bottom 3%, leaving him prone to hard contact. Still a keeper gem, but expect regression.

Yr Tm	W	Sv	IP	K	ERA	WHIP	xERA	xWHIP	vL+	vR+	BF/G	BB%	K%	K-BB%	xBB%	SwK	Vel	G	L	F	H%	S%	HR/F	xHR/F	GS	APC	DOM%	DIS%	Sv%	LI	RAR	BPX	R$
18																																	
19 aa	4	0	50	51	4.20	1.19	2.92				22.3	8%	25%	17%							31%	63%									1.9	123	$0
20																																	
21 SEA	6	0	119	128	4.68	1.17	4.21	1.14	92	101	21.0	6%	25%	20%	8%	12.8%	95.3	32	21	46	31%	63%	11%	12%	24	89	25%	17%			-6.0	139	$3
22 SEA	13	0	186	174	3.20	1.18	3.89	1.19	83	108	23.9	6%	23%	16%	7%	11.5%	96.2	37	24	39	30%	77%	9%	10%	32	94	28%	19%			17.6	113	$16
1st Half	10	0	100	93	2.61	1.15	3.93	1.22	72	105	24.1	7%	23%	16%	7%	11.4%	96.0	37	24	39	29%	82%	9%	10%	17	97	29%	18%			16.8	105	$24
2nd Half	3	0	86	81	3.89	1.21	3.84	1.16	96	111	23.7	6%	23%	17%	8%	11.6%	96.4	36	25	39	32%	71%	9%	11%	15	91	27%	20%			0.9	122	$4
Proj	**12**	**0**	**189**	**185**	**3.75**	**1.19**	**3.51**	**1.19**	**89**	**107**	**22.4**	**7%**	**24%**	**18%**	**8%**	**11.8%**	**96.0**	**36**	**24**	**41**	**31%**	**71%**	**9%**	**10%**	**34**						**5.1**	**116**	**$13**

Giolito,Lucas

Age: 28	Th: R	Role SP	Health C	LIMA Plan B	
Ht: 6' 6"	Wt: 245	Type Pwr	PT/Exp A	Rand Var +3	
			Consist A	MM 4405	

Note xERA. Proof that there is a thin margin for error even for established high-end starters. His stats tanked as hit and strand rates turned unfavorable. Dropoff in SwK and vR+ hurt, too, but prior three-year run in both categories suggest they can come back. He's a second-tier rotation anchor that you might be able to get at SP2 or SP3 prices now.

Yr Tm	W	Sv	IP	K	ERA	WHIP	xERA	xWHIP	vL+	vR+	BF/G	BB%	K%	K-BB%	xBB%	SwK	Vel	G	L	F	H%	S%	HR/F	xHR/F	GS	APC	DOM%	DIS%	Sv%	LI	RAR	BPX	R$
18 CHW	10	0	173	125	6.13	1.48	5.29	1.58	114	105	24.2	12%	16%	5%	11%	8.6%	92.4	44	18	37	28%	60%	13%	13%	32	94	16%	41%			-42.3	15	-$14
19 CHW	14	0	177	228	3.41	1.06	3.66	1.15	74	96	24.3	8%	32%	24%	6%	15.5%	94.3	36	21	43	28%	74%	14%	12%	29	97	38%	10%			23.8	158	$24
20 CHW	4	0	72	97	3.48	1.04	3.38	1.16	82	73	24.0	10%	34%	24%	7%	17.9%	94.0	41	21	38	27%	70%	13%	12%	12	101	33%	17%			8.6	161	$22
21 CHW	11	0	179	201	3.53	1.10	3.87	1.16	89	92	23.2	7%	28%	21%	7%	15.6%	93.9	33	25	42	28%	75%	14%	10%	31	96	32%	16%			16.3	134	$19
22 CHW	11	0	162	177	4.90	1.44	3.86	1.24	90	128	23.3	9%	25%	17%	8%	12.7%	92.6	39	25	37	35%	69%	14%	13%	30	92	23%	23%			-18.5	113	-$3
1st Half	5	0	75	89	4.90	1.47	3.94	1.21	87	142	23.3	9%	27%	18%	8%	13.7%	93.1	33	23	43	35%	73%	17%	15%	14	92	21%	29%			-8.6	120	-$5
2nd Half	6	0	86	88	4.90	1.40	3.79	1.27	93	116	23.3	9%	24%	15%	7%	11.8%	92.2	43	26	31	34%	66%	12%	10%	16	92	25%	19%			-9.9	106	-$1
Proj	**12**	**0**	**174**	**199**	**3.70**	**1.25**	**3.35**	**1.21**	**87**	**107**	**22.9**	**9%**	**28%**	**19%**	**8%**	**14.1%**	**93.2**	**39**	**23**	**38**	**31%**	**75%**	**14%**	**12%**	**31**						**5.7**	**124**	**$12**

Givens,Mychal

Age: 33	Th: R	Role RP	Health C	LIMA Plan A+	
Ht: 6' 0"	Wt: 230	Type Pwr	PT/Exp C	Rand Var -1	
			Consist B	MM 4410	

The recipe of a skills turnaround: chop walks, add strikeouts and groundballs, and whisk until blended. If he were 10 years younger, this would be something to work with. As it stands, history of so-so command and only semi-decent SwK for a reliever mean regression is more likely than another step forward.

Yr Tm	W	Sv	IP	K	ERA	WHIP	xERA	xWHIP	vL+	vR+	BF/G	BB%	K%	K-BB%	xBB%	SwK	Vel	G	L	F	H%	S%	HR/F	xHR/F	GS	APC	DOM%	DIS%	Sv%	LI	RAR	BPX	R$
18 BAL	0	9	77	79	3.99	1.19	4.08	1.30	94	81	4.6	9%	25%	15%	6%	12.1%	95.1	36	24	39	29%	66%	5%	7%	0	18			69	1.34	1.5	99	$3
19 BAL	2	11	63	86	4.57	1.19	3.65	1.20	122	79	4.5	10%	33%	23%	7%	16.7%	95.3	38	23	39	28%	69%	23%	19%	0	19			58	1.45	-0.5	149	$5
20 2 TM	1	1	22	25	3.63	1.16	4.98	1.35	103	100	4.2	11%	27%	16%	8%	13.3%	94.7	23	18	59	22%	81%	15%	12%	0	19			33	1.02	2.3	83	$1
21 2 NL	4	8	51	54	3.35	1.37	4.48	1.43	98	103	4.0	13%	25%	13%	10%	11.8%	94.8	36	27	37	29%	81%	14%	12%	0	16			73	1.30	5.7	62	$3
22 2 NL	7	2	61	71	3.38	1.32	3.58	1.24	118	95	4.4	10%	27%	18%	8%	11.8%	93.5	43	21	36	32%	79%	14%	12%	1	17	0%	100%	33	1.05	4.5	121	$3
1st Half	4	1	32	41	3.34	1.30	3.69	1.25	115	86	4.5	11%	29%	19%	8%	11.5%	93.5	40	19	42	30%	81%	15%	16%	0	18			25	1.07	2.5	122	$0
2nd Half	3	1	29	30	3.41	1.34	3.45	1.23	123	104	4.3	8%	25%	17%	8%	12.2%	93.5	46	23	31	33%	78%	13%	7%	1	17	0%	100%	50	1.02	2.0	119	-$2
Proj	**4**	**2**	**58**	**68**	**3.74**	**1.29**	**3.38**	**1.25**	**115**	**91**	**4.3**	**10%**	**28%**	**18%**	**8%**	**13.1%**	**94.3**	**40**	**23**	**37**	**31%**	**76%**	**15%**	**13%**	**0**						**1.7**	**116**	**$1**

Glasnow,Tyler

Age: 29	Th: R	Role SP	Health F	LIMA Plan B	
Ht: 6' 8"	Wt: 225	Type Pwr	PT/Exp B	Rand Var -5	
			Consist A	MM 5503	

Returned from Tommy John surgery at very end of season, giving us hope yet again that he can fulfill rotation-anchor upside. Long history of elite skills says he can, as few starters can generate more space between bat and ball than this one. It really all depends on the price at which you can get him, since we're still waiting for his first 120+ IP season.

Yr Tm	W	Sv	IP	K	ERA	WHIP	xERA	xWHIP	vL+	vR+	BF/G	BB%	K%	K-BB%	xBB%	SwK	Vel	G	L	F	H%	S%	HR/F	xHR/F	GS	APC	DOM%	DIS%	Sv%	LI	RAR	BPX	R$
18 2 TM	2	0	112	136	4.27	1.27	3.44	1.30	93	97	10.4	11%	29%	18%	10%	12.2%	96.6	50	20	30	29%	70%	18%	19%	11	41	27%	9%	0	0.56	-1.7	127	$1
19 TAM	6	0	61	76	1.78	0.89	2.98	1.05	55	78	19.2	6%	33%	27%	7%	12.1%	97.0	50	16	34	27%	84%	9%	11%	12	75	58%	8%			20.4	190	$11
20 TAM	5	0	57	91	4.08	1.13	3.08	1.06	84	98	21.6	9%	38%	29%	8%	14.5%	97.0	39	23	38	31%	72%	23%	20%	11	88	27%	9%			2.6	204	$16
21 TAM	5	0	88	123	2.66	0.93	2.87	1.04	65	84	24.3	8%	36%	28%	6%	17.5%	97.0	45	18	37	26%	78%	14%	14%	14	96	64%	7%			17.4	192	$13
22 TAM	0	0	7	10	1.35	0.90	2.86		61	91	13.0	8%	38%	31%	8%	14.9%	97.4	36	14	50	25%	100%	14%	23%	2	57	50%	0%			2.2	203	-$4
1st Half																																	
2nd Half	0	0	7	10	1.35	0.90	2.86		61	91	13.0	8%	38%	31%	8%	14.9%	97.4	36	14	50	25%	100%	14%	23%	2	57	50%	0%			2.2	203	-$8
Proj	**9**	**0**	**131**	**180**	**3.29**	**1.06**	**2.59**	**1.09**	**78**	**91**	**21.5**	**9%**	**36%**	**26%**		**14.6%**	**96.9**	**46**	**20**	**35**	**28%**	**75%**	**17%**	**16%**	**24**						**11.0**	**176**	**$15**

Gomber,Austin

Age: 29	Th: L	Role RP	Health D	LIMA Plan B	
Ht: 6' 5"	Wt: 220	Type Con	PT/Exp A	Rand Var +3	
			Consist A	MM 2101	

The twinge of roster-worthiness he produced in 2021 all but disappeared. Sure, that strand rate didn't help. His main problem, though, was another year of erosion in OPS vR+. You simply don't want to speculate on a lefty starter who struggles against RHB and has an xERA and K-BB% history like this—no matter what park he's pitching in.

Yr Tm	W	Sv	IP	K	ERA	WHIP	xERA	xWHIP	vL+	vR+	BF/G	BB%	K%	K-BB%	xBB%	SwK	Vel	G	L	F	H%	S%	HR/F	xHR/F	GS	APC	DOM%	DIS%	Sv%	LI	RAR	BPX	R$
18 STL *	13	0	144	127	4.18	1.44	4.73	1.40	102	112	15.0	8%	21%	12%	8%	9.5%	92.5	38	27	35	33%	73%	9%	16%	11	42	18%	27%	0	0.95	-0.5	80	$2
19 a/a	4	0	50	42	3.41	1.40	4.49				19.2	9%	20%	11%							32%	79%									6.8	73	$0
20 STL	1	0	29	27	1.86	1.17	4.50	1.49	98	68	8.5	13%	23%	10%	10%	10.1%	92.5	49	18	34	25%	85%	4%	4%	4	38	0%	0%	0	1.01	9.3	59	$4
21 COL	9	0	115	113	4.53	1.24	4.23	1.29	91	99	21.2	8%	23%	15%	7%	11.7%	91.6	44	19	37	28%	69%	17%	14%	23	80	30%	26%			-3.7	103	$3
22 COL	5	0	125	95	5.56	1.37	4.32	1.28	88	124	16.0	6%	18%	12%	8%	10.3%	91.0	43	20	37	31%	62%	14%	12%	17	62	12%	47%	0	0.67	-24.4	86	-$9
1st Half	4	0	73	54	6.53	1.45	4.42	1.32	87	130	20.9	7%	17%	10%	8%	10.0%	91.2	43	21	36	32%	57%	16%	13%	13	80	15%	54%	0	0.72	-23.1	75	-$18
2nd Half	1	0	52	41	4.18	1.26	4.19	1.23	88	112	12.0	6%	19%	13%	8%	10.9%	90.7	42	19	39	31%	71%	11%	11%	4	48	0%	25%	0	0.63	-1.3	102	-$5
Proj	**6**	**0**	**102**	**84**	**4.51**	**1.35**	**3.93**	**1.30**	**91**	**112**	**16.1**	**7%**	**20%**	**13%**	**8%**	**10.4%**	**91.4**	**42**	**22**	**37**	**31%**	**70%**	**12%**	**13%**	**16**						**-6.8**	**87**	**-$2**

Gonsolin,Tony

Age: 29	Th: R	Role RP	Health F	LIMA Plan C+	
Ht: 6' 3"	Wt: 205	Type /FB	PT/Exp B	Rand Var -5	
			Consist C	MM 3303	

Third best stat in book? Since 2000, no SP had more wins in fewer innings than this one. Doubling of aggregate skills helped fuel career season, as did cutting walk rate in half. xBB% says it can stick, but that minuscule hit rate won't, and xERA confirms that's what really drove his sub-3 ERA. It's best to view him as a mid-rotation target.

Yr Tm	W	Sv	IP	K	ERA	WHIP	xERA	xWHIP	vL+	vR+	BF/G	BB%	K%	K-BB%	xBB%	SwK	Vel	G	L	F	H%	S%	HR/F	xHR/F	GS	APC	DOM%	DIS%	Sv%	LI	RAR	BPX	R$
18 aa	6	0	45	41	2.58	1.10	2.64				19.7	8%	23%	15%							27%	79%									8.8	119	$4
19 LA *	6	1	82	78	3.83	1.30	3.67	1.38	75	79	14.1	10%	23%	13%	10%	12.3%	93.7	42	15	44	29%	73%	9%	9%	6	63	17%	50%	100	0.65	6.8	87	$3
20 LA	2	0	47	46	2.31	0.84	3.75	1.08	74	67	19.6	4%	26%	22%	6%	14.6%	95.1	34	24	42	26%	73%	4%	8%	8	78	25%	0%	0	0.81	12.3	153	$17
21 LA	4	0	56	65	3.23	1.35	4.69	1.46	90	98	15.9	14%	27%	13%	11%	13.0%	93.8	37	18	45	26%	82%	13%	9%	13	66	15%	23%	0	0.73	7.1	60	$0
22 LA	16	0	130	119	2.14	0.87	3.56	1.20	72	81	20.8	7%	24%	17%	6%	12.6%	93.2	43	18	39	21%	81%	8%	8%	24	83	29%	4%			29.4	114	$26
1st Half	10	0	82	77	1.54	0.82	3.57	1.19	75	70	20.6	7%	25%	17%	6%	13.1%	93.1	41	16	42	19%	88%	8%	6%	15	83	33%	0%			24.4	114	$35
2nd Half	6	0	49	42	3.14	0.97	3.55	1.20	66	96	21.0	6%	22%	16%	6%	11.9%	93.3	46	20	34	25%	70%	9%	10%	9	85	22%	11%			5.0	114	$9
Proj	**11**	**0**	**131**	**125**	**3.33**	**1.13**	**3.57**	**1.25**	**87**	**96**	**18.8**	**8%**	**24%**	**16%**	**7%**	**13.0%**	**93.8**	**40**	**20**	**40**	**27%**	**74%**	**9%**	**9%**	**24**						**10.2**	**104**	**$13**

STEPHEN NICKRAND

Gonzales,Marco

Gonzales,Marco						Health	C	LIMA Plan	C+
Age:	31	Th:	L	Role	SP	PT/Exp	A	Rand Var	-1
Ht:	6' 1"	Wt:	197	Type	Con/FB	Consist	B	MM	2003

His hit and strand rate luck from 2021's 2nd half continued into the first three months of 2022, likely suckering in the uninitiated. But luck ran out in 2nd half, and he ultimately was left off SEA's postseason roster. As xERA shows, he's been roughly the same guy for the last three full seasons. Don't bid expecting anything else.

Yr Tm	W	Sv	IP	K	ERA	WHIP	xERA	xWHIP	vL+	vR+	BF/G	BB%	K%	K-BB%	xBB%	SwK	Vel	G	L	F	H%	S%	HR/F	xHR/F	GS	APC	DOM%	DIS%	Sv%	LI	RAR	BPX	R$
18 SEA	13	0	167	145	4.00	1.22	3.71	1.18	95	101	23.7	5%	21%	16%	5%	9.7%	90.1	45	25	30	32%	70%	11%	12%	29	88	28%	14%			3.2	135	$9
19 SEA	16	0	203	147	3.99	1.31	5.12	1.38	108	95	25.5	6%	17%	11%	6%	8.3%	88.9	41	21	38	31%	72%	9%	10%	34	95	26%	32%			12.9	75	$12
20 SEA	7	0	70	64	3.10	0.95	4.02	1.08	97	77	25.2	3%	23%	21%	5%	8.7%	88.2	38	21	41	28%	72%	10%	14%	11	96	55%	18%			11.6	159	$28
21 SEA	10	0	143	108	3.96	1.17	5.00	1.33	83	108	23.4	7%	18%	11%	7%	9.4%	88.4	32	20	48	24%	75%	14%	15%	25	93	16%	36%			5.5	67	$9
22 SEA	10	0	183	103	4.13	1.33	4.91	1.37	116	108	24.5	6%	13%	7%	6%	8.7%	88.5	42	19	39	28%	75%	12%	11%	32	89	13%	53%			-3.7	49	$0
1st Half	4	0	88	49	3.29	1.32	4.94	1.47	132	99	23.5	9%	13%	5%	8%	8.0%	88.1	46	18	36	26%	82%	13%	12%	16	88	19%	50%			7.4	28	$2
2nd Half	6	0	95	54	4.91	1.34	4.87	1.29	105	117	25.4	4%	13%	9%	5%	9.4%	88.9	39	19	43	30%	68%	11%	11%	16	90	6%	56%			-11.1	69	-$4
Proj	8	0	160	101	4.79	1.26	4.18	1.35	105	102	24.0	7%	15%	9%	6%	8.9%	88.6	39	20	41	28%	66%	12%	12%	27						-16.1	60	-$2

Gore,MacKenzie

Gore,MacKenzie						Health	D	LIMA Plan	A
Age:	24	Th:	L	Role	SP	PT/Exp	F	Rand Var	-1
Ht:	6' 2"	Wt:	197	Type	Pwr	Consist	A	MM	3301

4-4, 4.50 ERA in 70 IP at SD. Top prospect got off to a terrific start (1.50 ERA in 48 IP through June 4). But velocity began slowly dropping in June, and he started getting lit up. Then—cue ominous music—he hit the IL in late July with a sore elbow before trade to WAS. Happily, he was rehabbing and healthy by season's end. We'd like to see a full season.

Yr Tm	W	Sv	IP	K	ERA	WHIP	xERA	xWHIP	vL+	vR+	BF/G	BB%	K%	K-BB%	xBB%	SwK	Vel	G	L	F	H%	S%	HR/F	xHR/F	GS	APC	DOM%	DIS%	Sv%	LI	RAR	BPX	R$
18																																	
19 aa	2	0	23	22	4.64	1.31	4.22				19.2	8%	23%	15%							31%	67%									-0.4	84	-$3
20																																	
21 a/a	0	0	29	29	4.57	1.66	5.00				16.2	14%	22%	8%							34%	73%									-1.1	75	-$8
22 SD *	4	0	87	85	4.34	1.44	4.50	1.42	89	105	17.7	12%	23%	11%	9%	10.8%	94.7	38	23	39	32%	72%	9%	13%	13	79	31%	31%	0	0.78	-4.0	78	-$4
1st Half	4	0	70	74	2.96	1.29	3.20	1.33	82	95	20.5	11%	25%	14%	8%	10.9%	94.9	38	23	39	30%	78%	6%	10%	12	86	33%	25%	0	0.82	8.7	110	$6
2nd Half	0	0	17	12	10.04	2.08	9.88	1.54	215	191	11.9	11%	14%	4%	12%	10.3%	93.5	33	24	43	37%	55%	33%	33%	1	45	0%	100%	0	0.61	-12.7	-49	-$21
Proj	7	0	94	95	3.88	1.37	3.74	1.37	89	116	21.0	11%	24%	13%	8%	10.9%	94.9	38	23	39	30%	76%	14%	9%	19						1.1	74	$1

Graterol,Brusdar

Graterol,Brusdar						Health	F	LIMA Plan	A+
Age:	24	Th:	R	Role	RP	PT/Exp	D	Rand Var	0
Ht:	6' 1"	Wt:	265	Type	Con/xGB	Consist	A	MM	5110

PRO: Best skills of career—married improving K/SwK rates with better control, and GB rate again spiked. CON: Durability issues continued—it was the shoulder and elbow that flared up this time, costing him two big chunks of the 2nd half. With his stuff, he's just a healthy season and an opportunity away from... UP: 25 Sv

Yr Tm	W	Sv	IP	K	ERA	WHIP	xERA	xWHIP	vL+	vR+	BF/G	BB%	K%	K-BB%	xBB%	SwK	Vel	G	L	F	H%	S%	HR/F	xHR/F	GS	APC	DOM%	DIS%	Sv%	LI	RAR	BPX	R$
18																																	
19 MIN *	8	1	70	59	2.84	1.12	2.60	1.15	100	91	10.6	9%	21%	12%	4%	9.0%	99.0	48	30	22	26%	76%	17%	14%	0	14			100	1.49	14.4	96	$8
20 LA	1	0	23	13	3.09	0.90	3.57	1.24	125	54	3.8	3%	15%	11%	4%	6.5%	99.3	62	16	22	24%	65%	7%	8%	2	13	0%	0%	0	0.84	3.9	112	$2
21 LA *	5	1	52	44	4.99	1.23	3.30	1.39	134	79	4.1	8%	21%	13%	5%	9.0%	100.0	58	23	18	30%	58%	11%	10%	1	15	0%	100%	20	0.93	-4.6	100	-$2
22 LA	2	4	50	43	3.26	0.99	2.94	1.16	109	66	4.3	5%	22%	17%	4%	11.0%	99.7	63	14	23	27%	67%	9%	8%	1	15	0%	100%	80	1.03	4.3	146	$3
1st Half	2	2	38	34	3.55	1.03	3.21	1.21	104	76	4.4	6%	22%	16%	4%	11.0%	99.8	61	12	27	26%	67%	10%	9%	0	15			67	0.99	2.0	132	$1
2nd Half	0	2	12	9	2.31	0.86	2.10	0.99	126	32	3.9	0%	21%	21%	4%	10.7%	99.3	71	21	9	29%	70%	0%	2%	1	14	0%	100%	100	1.15	2.4	192	-$5
Proj	3	4	44	36	3.06	1.05	3.01	1.27	106	70	4.9	8%	21%	14%	4%	10.2%	99.9	60	17	24	26%	72%	10%	9%	0						4.9	111	$3

Graveman,Kendall

Graveman,Kendall						Health	C	LIMA Plan	A+
Age:	32	Th:	R	Role	RP	PT/Exp	B	Rand Var	-1
Ht:	6' 2"	Wt:	200	Type	Pwr/GB	Consist	C	MM	5311

Several raw skills were actually better than in 2021. But he was less fortunate: hit rate jumped, and strand rate was correspondingly down, the main reason for 2nd-half ERA spike. Overall, though, he's settled into something of a reliable groove out of the bullpen, making for a low-risk, high-LIMA option.

Yr Tm	W	Sv	IP	K	ERA	WHIP	xERA	xWHIP	vL+	vR+	BF/G	BB%	K%	K-BB%	xBB%	SwK	Vel	G	L	F	H%	S%	HR/F	xHR/F	GS	APC	DOM%	DIS%	Sv%	LI	RAR	BPX	R$
18 OAK *	3	0	58	39	6.89	1.87	7.92	1.40	125	126	24.9	8%	14%	7%	11%	7.8%	93.7	55	16	28	38%	66%	27%	27%	7	90	0%	71%			-19.7	5	-$15
19																																	
20 SEA	1	0	19	15	5.79	1.23	4.82	1.46	44	127	7.0	10%	19%	9%	12%	7.3%	94.8	48	17	35	26%	52%	11%	9%	2	30	0%	50%	0	1.15	-3.1	59	-$5
21 2 AL	5	10	56	61	1.77	0.98	3.06	1.22	103	46	4.2	9%	27%	18%	8%	11.3%	96.6	55	22	23	25%	85%	10%	13%	0	16			67	1.38	17.3	135	$13
22 CHW	3	6	65	66	3.18	1.40	3.52	1.30	105	93	4.4	9%	23%	14%	8%	11.8%	96.5	54	22	24	34%	79%	11%	11%	0	16			50	1.23	6.3	109	$1
1st Half	2	5	36	34	2.27	1.32	3.51	1.26	87	101	4.5	8%	22%	14%	6%	9.8%	96.4	55	19	26	33%	84%	7%	11%	0	16			56	1.16	7.5	117	$3
2nd Half	1	1	29	32	4.30	1.50	3.53	1.34	121	80	4.3	11%	24%	14%	9%	14.0%	96.6	52	26	21	35%	73%	17%	11%	0	16			33	1.31	-1.2	101	-$8
Proj	3	5	65	68	3.38	1.32	3.10	1.28	103	84	4.4	10%	25%	16%	8%	11.4%	95.8	54	21	25	31%	78%	17%	15%	0						4.7	116	$2

Gray,Jon

Gray,Jon						Health	F	LIMA Plan	A
Age:	31	Th:	R	Role	SP	PT/Exp	A	Rand Var	0
Ht:	6' 4"	Wt:	225	Type	Pwr	Consist	C	MM	5303

Once again, injuries (blister, knee strain, oblique strain) gnawed into what was otherwise an effective season. Moving to a more pitcher-friendly home park was certainly good for his stats, but skills were also among the best of his career. Appears set for more of the same—and yes, that probably includes more IL time, too.

Yr Tm	W	Sv	IP	K	ERA	WHIP	xERA	xWHIP	vL+	vR+	BF/G	BB%	K%	K-BB%	xBB%	SwK	Vel	G	L	F	H%	S%	HR/F	xHR/F	GS	APC	DOM%	DIS%	Sv%	LI	RAR	BPX	R$
18 COL	12	0	172	183	5.12	1.35	3.63	1.20	113	100	24.0	7%	25%	18%	8%	12.9%	94.8	47	22	30	34%	65%	18%	14%	31	90	29%	29%			-20.6	142	-$1
19 COL	11	0	150	150	3.84	1.35	4.02	1.33	108	96	24.5	9%	24%	15%	8%	12.3%	96.1	50	23	26	32%	76%	17%	18%	25	91	28%	32%	0	1.01	12.3	108	$8
20 COL	2	0	39	22	6.69	1.44	5.82	1.43	119	99	21.8	6%	13%	6%	8%	9.9%	94.0	37	25	38	31%	54%	11%	11%	8	82	13%	50%			-10.8	43	-$10
21 COL	8	0	149	157	4.59	1.33	4.03	1.29	101	100	22.2	9%	24%	15%	8%	11.5%	94.9	48	18	33	31%	69%	15%	12%	29	87	14%	28%			-6.0	112	$1
22 TEX	7	0	127	134	3.96	1.13	3.47	1.18	105	84	21.7	7%	26%	18%	6%	12.2%	96.0	44	21	35	28%	69%	14%	12%	24	86	25%	17%			0.2	130	$6
1st Half	4	0	77	83	3.96	1.16	3.46	1.20	94	90	22.6	8%	26%	18%	6%	12.7%	95.8	44	23	34	29%	68%	12%	13%	14	89	29%	14%			0.1	126	$6
2nd Half	3	0	50	51	3.96	1.08	3.50	1.15	121	75	20.4	6%	25%	19%	5%	11.4%	96.2	45	18	38	26%	71%	18%	12%	10	81	20%	20%			0.1	138	$2
Proj	9	0	145	149	3.78	1.18	3.19	1.21	104	83	20.7	8%	26%	18%	7%	11.5%	95.4	44	21	35	29%	72%	14%	13%	28						3.4	124	$9

Gray,Josiah

Gray,Josiah						Health	A	LIMA Plan	B
Age:	25	Th:	R	Role	SP	PT/Exp	C	Rand Var	+1
Ht:	6' 1"	Wt:	190	Type	Pwr/xFB	Consist	A	MM	2305

As xERA describes, it wasn't all bad in his first full season. But lefties ate him up; when he wasn't walking them (16% BB% vL, 6% vR), they were clobbering him (22 HR in just 280 PA vL). As a result, he led the league in both walks and HR allowed. He's got the raw stuff for better, but he'll remain a flammable play until he can reign in those issues.

Yr Tm	W	Sv	IP	K	ERA	WHIP	xERA	xWHIP	vL+	vR+	BF/G	BB%	K%	K-BB%	xBB%	SwK	Vel	G	L	F	H%	S%	HR/F	xHR/F	GS	APC	DOM%	DIS%	Sv%	LI	RAR	BPX	R$
18																																	
19 aa	3	0	40	36	3.45	1.23	2.90				18.1	7%	22%	15%							33%	69%									5.2	134	$0
20																																	
21 2 NL *	3	0	88	94	4.91	1.21	4.67	1.36	112	113	19.7	10%	27%	17%	8%	14.7%	94.6	31	16	54	24%	69%	19%	15%	13	87	0%	31%	0	0.74	-7.0	64	-$2
22 WAS	7	0	149	154	5.02	1.36	4.53	1.33	141	97	23.2	10%	24%	14%	10%	11.6%	94.5	33	18	49	27%	73%	19%	15%	28	93	4%	43%			-19.4	78	-$4
1st Half	6	0	81	88	4.22	1.27	4.30	1.30	129	88	23.1	10%	25%	15%	10%	12.6%	94.2	27	24	49	27%	75%	15%	13%	15	92	7%	33%			-2.5	84	$4
2nd Half	1	0	68	66	5.99	1.46	4.80	1.37	153	108	23.3	10%	22%	12%	10%	10.5%	94.8	39	12	50	27%	70%	22%	17%	13	93	0%	54%			-16.8	70	-$15
Proj	8	0	167	166	4.46	1.32	3.90	1.32	128	98	22.7	10%	24%	15%	9%	12.0%	94.6	34	16	50	28%	74%	15%	15%	28						-10.1	84	$1

Gray,Sonny

Gray,Sonny						Health	F	LIMA Plan	B+
Age:	33	Th:	R	Role	SP	PT/Exp	A	Rand Var	-2
Ht:	5' 10"	Wt:	195	Type	Pwr	Consist	A	MM	5403

Stats were fine around trips to the IL (hammy, pec, hammy) that are now becoming an annual tradition. But his recent steady skills foundation is showing some cracks, with fastball velocity, SwK, and groundball rate all trending in the wrong direction. None are foreboding enough to warrant panic, but at 33, it's a trend worth monitoring.

Yr Tm	W	Sv	IP	K	ERA	WHIP	xERA	xWHIP	vL+	vR+	BF/G	BB%	K%	K-BB%	xBB%	SwK	Vel	G	L	F	H%	S%	HR/F	xHR/F	GS	APC	DOM%	DIS%	Sv%	LI	RAR	BPX	R$
18 NYY	11	0	130	123	4.90	1.50	4.14	1.39	99	113	19.4	10%	21%	11%	10%	10.4%	93.3	50	23	27	34%	69%	13%	12%	23	75	22%	43%	0	0.72	-12.1	86	-$4
19 CIN	11	0	175	205	2.87	1.08	3.55	1.26	81	80	22.8	10%	29%	19%	10%	11.8%	93.3	51	18	31	27%	77%	13%	15%	31	94	39%	13%			35.3	135	$24
20 CIN	5	0	56	72	3.70	1.21	3.32	1.26	86	78	21.4	11%	31%	20%	10%	11.6%	93.0	51	26	23	31%	70%	13%	15%	11	88	18%	18%			5.2	141	$14
21 CIN	7	0	135	155	4.19	1.22	3.67	1.22	94	93	22.1	9%	27%	18%	8%	11.0%	92.4	47	21	32	30%	70%	17%	9%	26	86	31%	15%			1.3	132	$6
22 MIN	8	0	120	117	3.08	1.13	3.61	1.21	79	100	20.3	7%	24%	17%	8%	9.5%	92.1	45	20	36	29%	76%	9%	9%	24	78	25%	33%			13.1	119	$10
1st Half	4	0	55	54	2.47	1.04	3.54	1.16	83	89	19.9	6%	25%	18%	7%	9.4%	92.0	44	19	38	28%	81%	9%	7%	11	77	27%	36%			10.1	132	$9
2nd Half	4	0	65	63	3.60	1.20	3.68	1.25	76	109	20.7	8%	23%	15%	8%	9.6%	92.3	45	21	34	29%	72%	10%	11%	13	79	23%	31%			3.0	108	$4
Proj	10	0	145	157	3.47	1.18	3.08	1.23	84	94	21.8	9%	27%	18%	8%	10.5%	92.5	47	21	32	29%	73%	12%	11%	27						8.8	124	$12

ROD TRUESDELL

Greene,Hunter

Age: 23	Th: R	Role SP	Health	D	LIMA Plan	A+
Ht: 6' 4"	Wt: 215	Type Pwr/FB	PT/Exp	C	Rand Var	+2
			Consist	B	MM	5503

Light turned on in 2nd half in spite of a shoulder strain that cost him time. Sure, it was only eight starts. But developing change-up stymied LH and gave him third pitch behind high-whiff four-seamer and slider. If he expands it against RHers, his next step up will be a very big one...assuming shoulder stays intact. UP: 3.00 ERA, 220 K

Yr Tm	W	Sv	IP	K	ERA	WHIP	xERA	xWHIP	vL+	vR+	BF/G	BB%	K%	K-BB%	xBB%	SwK	Vel	G	L	F	H%	S%	HR/F	xHR/F	GS	APC	DOM%	DIS%	Sv%	LI	RAR	BPX	R$
18																																	
19																																	
20																																	
21 a/a	10	0	107	127	4.00	1.30	4.30				21.0	9%	29%	19%							32%	74%									3.5	105	$5
22 CIN	5	0	126	164	4.44	1.21	3.65	1.15	99	107	22.1	9%	31%	22%	8%	15.0%	99.0	29	22	49	30%	70%	16%	13%	24	92	33%	17%			-7.3	138	$3
1st Half	3	0	79	98	6.01	1.35	4.21	1.22	109	125	21.7	10%	28%	19%	9%	13.3%	98.4	25	22	53	29%	64%	20%	13%	16	90	19%	19%			-20.0	112	-$10
2nd Half	2	0	46	66	1.75	0.97	2.69	1.03	82	66	23.0	8%	36%	28%	6%	18.0%	99.8	39	23	38	30%	84%	5%	13%	8	96	63%	13%			12.7	187	$10
Proj	**8**	**0**	**152**	**190**	**3.46**	**1.10**	**3.10**	**1.11**	**91**	**92**	**22.1**	**8%**	**32%**	**24%**	**8%**	**16.0%**	**99.3**	**33**	**22**	**44**	**29%**	**74%**	**13%**	**13%**	**27**						**9.6**	**151**	**$14**

Greinke,Zack

Age: 39	Th: R	Role SP	Health	D	LIMA Plan	B
Ht: 6' 2"	Wt: 200	Type Con	PT/Exp	A	Rand Var	-3
			Consist	A	MM	3003

Surface stats can be volatile, but you'd be hard-pressed to find a more consistent 5-year downward skills trend than a scan of his xERA and DOM%/DIS% rates. Three years of K%, K-BB%, and SwK are just as damning. His 2nd half line will lure some unsuspecting drafters, but that 1st half is a more likely baseline now.

Yr Tm	W	Sv	IP	K	ERA	WHIP	xERA	xWHIP	vL+	vR+	BF/G	BB%	K%	K-BB%	xBB%	SwK	Vel	G	L	F	H%	S%	HR/F	xHR/F	GS	APC	DOM%	DIS%	Sv%	LI	RAR	BPX	R$
18 ARI	15	0	208	199	3.21	1.08	3.53	1.15	88	96	25.4	5%	24%	19%	7%	11.3%	89.6	45	23	32	28%	77%	15%	15%	33	97	45%	15%			24.1	147	$25
19 2 TM	18	0	209	187	2.93	0.98	3.74	1.14	80	86	24.5	4%	23%	19%	7%	10.7%	90.0	45	22	33	28%	74%	11%	13%	33	94	45%	18%			40.5	145	$33
20 HOU	3	0	67	67	4.03	1.13	3.75	1.08	73	112	22.8	3%	25%	21%	9%	10.8%	87.1	41	25	34	33%	66%	9%	16%	12	88	25%	17%			3.5	168	$11
21 HOU	11	0	171	120	4.16	1.17	4.33	1.27	78	110	23.2	5%	17%	12%	8%	9.5%	88.9	44	23	32	27%	71%	17%	13%	29	86	24%	48%	0	0.78	2.3	93	$9
22 KC	4	0	137	73	3.68	1.34	4.72	1.31	103	105	22.5	5%	12%	8%	8%	7.5%	89.2	41	23	35	31%	75%	8%	10%	26	87	12%	46%			4.9	63	-$2
1st Half	2	0	69	34	4.85	1.31	4.90	1.32	101	113	22.5	4%	12%	7%	8%	7.4%	89.0	38	24	38	30%	66%	11%	12%	13	87	0%	38%			-7.5	55	-$10
2nd Half	2	0	68	39	2.50	1.38	4.54	1.30	105	98	22.5	5%	13%	9%	8%	7.6%	89.4	45	23	33	33%	83%	5%	8%	13	87	23%	54%			12.4	72	$1
Proj	**5**	**0**	**131**	**93**	**4.29**	**1.23**	**3.75**	**1.23**	**90**	**104**	**22.4**	**5%**	**18%**	**13%**	**8%**	**8.9%**	**88.9**	**43**	**23**	**34**	**31%**	**67%**	**10%**	**12%**	**24**						**-5.2**	**101**	**$0**

Hader,Josh

Age: 29	Th: L	Role RP	Health	A	LIMA Plan	B+
Ht: 6' 3"	Wt: 180	Type Pwr/xFB	PT/Exp	A	Rand Var	+5
			Consist	B	MM	5530

Temporarily fell from top closer perch after surprising mid-season trade. In truth, we can blame that tumble almost entirely on hit and strand rates that torpedoed his stats. While skills did regress as batters made more contact, ability to miss bats didn't really wane much, and results came back in line during nice September run. There's profit here now.

Yr Tm	W	Sv	IP	K	ERA	WHIP	xERA	xWHIP	vL+	vR+	BF/G	BB%	K%	K-BB%	xBB%	SwK	Vel	G	L	F	H%	S%	HR/F	xHR/F	GS	APC	DOM%	DIS%	Sv%	LI	RAR	BPX	R$
18 MIL	6	12	81	143	2.43	0.81	2.37	0.93	48	77	5.6	10%	47%	37%	6%	19.8%	94.5	29	23	48	24%	77%	15%	13%	0	24			71	1.31	17.2	233	$21
19 MIL	3	37	76	138	2.62	0.81	2.57	0.84	82	78	4.7	7%	48%	41%	5%	24.0%	95.6	22	23	55	26%	85%	21%	16%	0	19			84	1.71	17.6	252	$29
20 MIL	1	13	19	31	3.79	0.95	3.54	1.17	96	70	3.7	13%	40%	27%	9%	16.7%	94.6	26	15	59	18%	67%	15%	11%	0	18			87	1.63	1.6	159	$17
21 MIL	4	34	59	102	1.23	0.84	2.54	0.98	52	58	3.7	11%	46%	35%	6%	21.9%	96.4	31	23	46	26%	89%	7%	7%	0	16			97	1.37	22.0	210	$28
22 2 NL	2	36	50	81	5.22	1.28	3.15	1.06	91	103	3.9	10%	37%	27%	8%	16.3%	97.5	29	24	47	37%	63%	15%	15%	0	17			90	1.51	-7.7	184	$11
1st Half	0	25	27	45	1.35	0.79	2.50	0.89	64	69	3.6	8%	44%	36%	7%	17.6%	97.1	33	14	53	25%	94%	12%	9%	0	16			96	1.50	8.6	233	$24
2nd Half	2	11	23	36	9.64	1.84	3.98	1.23	108	138	4.2	11%	31%	20%	9%	15.2%	97.8	27	31	42	46%	47%	19%	20%	0	18			79	1.52	-16.3	131	-$7
Proj	**3**	**33**	**58**	**98**	**3.31**	**1.12**	**2.51**	**0.98**	**82**	**93**	**4.0**	**10%**	**43%**	**33%**	**7%**	**18.9%**	**96.6**	**27**	**24**	**49**	**34%**	**78%**	**17%**	**14%**	**0**						**4.7**	**203**	**$17**

Hall,DL

Age: 24	Th: L	Role SP	Health	A	LIMA Plan	A+
Ht: 6' 2"	Wt: 195	Type Pwr	PT/Exp	D	Rand Var	-1
			Consist	D	MM	4501

1-1, 5.93 ERA in 13 IP at BAL. 2017 first-rounder owns some of best stuff in the minors, including upper-90s fastball and dynamite slider. While that upside might entice, walks have plagued him at every professional stop, and he has battled elbow injuries in the recent past. Those are big risks that make it more likely his eventual home will be in relief.

Yr Tm	W	Sv	IP	K	ERA	WHIP	xERA	xWHIP	vL+	vR+	BF/G	BB%	K%	K-BB%	xBB%	SwK	Vel	G	L	F	H%	S%	HR/F	xHR/F	GS	APC	DOM%	DIS%	Sv%	LI	RAR	BPX	R$
18																																	
19																																	
20																																	
21 aa	2	0	33	46	3.23	0.98	2.19				18.0	12%	36%	25%							21%	73%									4.2	138	$0
22 BAL *	4	1	97	125	4.74	1.42	4.15	1.19	139	88	12.1	9%	30%	20%	6%	14.1%	96.3	46	26	28	34%	68%	0%	1%	1	24	0%	0%	100	0.80	-9.2	108	-$4
1st Half	1	0	48	59	4.48	1.38	3.86				16.9	13%	28%	15%							31%	70%	0%		0	0					-3.1	101	-$7
2nd Half	3	1	49	66	4.99	1.46	4.44	1.24	138	88	9.5	11%	30%	19%	6%	14.1%	96.3	46	26	28	37%	67%	0%	1%	1	24	0%	0%	100	0.80	-6.2	116	-$5
Proj	**5**	**0**	**87**	**106**	**3.92**	**1.26**	**3.31**	**1.30**			**21.1**	**12%**	**30%**	**18%**				**44**	**20**	**36**	**30%**	**71%**	**12%**	**11%**	**17**						**0.5**	**111**	**$2**

Hancock,Emerson

Age: 24	Th: R	Role SP	Health	C	LIMA Plan	B+
Ht: 6' 4"	Wt: 213	Type	PT/Exp	F	Rand Var	-1
			Consist	D	MM	2100

First full-season in high minors of SEA system went well on surface and included a decent helping of strikeouts. Still, delivery has become a high-maintenance one in effort to get more Ks. That approach has opened up him up to walks, as well as shoulder woes that are becoming chronic. He's another young pitcher whose risk outweighs his reward for now.

Yr Tm	W	Sv	IP	K	ERA	WHIP	xERA	xWHIP	vL+	vR+	BF/G	BB%	K%	K-BB%	xBB%	SwK	Vel	G	L	F	H%	S%	HR/F	xHR/F	GS	APC	DOM%	DIS%	Sv%	LI	RAR	BPX	R$
18																																	
19																																	
20																																	
21 aa	1	0	15	12	3.25	0.97	1.58				19.2	7%	21%	14%							26%	63%									1.9	133	-$4
22 aa	7	0	99	81	3.41	1.14	3.46				18.7	8%	20%	12%							25%	76%									6.8	77	$5
1st Half	1	0	36	30	2.28	0.91	2.27				15.0	6%	21%	15%							22%	82%									7.5	114	$2
2nd Half	6	0	63	51	4.06	1.28	4.14				21.5	9%	19%	10%							27%	73%									-0.7	62	$3
Proj	**3**	**0**	**58**	**47**	**4.07**	**1.35**	**4.22**	**1.38**			**21.2**	**9%**	**20%**	**11%**				**37**	**23**	**40**	**30%**	**74%**	**11%**	**10%**	**11**						**-0.7**	**61**	**-$3**

Hand,Brad

Age: 33	Th: L	Role RP	Health	B	LIMA Plan	A+
Ht: 6' 3"	Wt: 224	Type Pwr	PT/Exp	A	Rand Var	-5
			Consist	B	MM	3310

Give a...ahem...hand to owners who drafted him for nothing and got 18 saves + holds, as well as a sub-3.00 ERA. Problem is, plummeting SwK continued its nosedive. His savior was keeping flyballs in the park, which isn't something we can expect to repeat. Let BPX, xERA trends be your guide that tells you to leave him for others.

Yr Tm	W	Sv	IP	K	ERA	WHIP	xERA	xWHIP	vL+	vR+	BF/G	BB%	K%	K-BB%	xBB%	SwK	Vel	G	L	F	H%	S%	HR/F	xHR/F	GS	APC	DOM%	DIS%	Sv%	LI	RAR	BPX	R$
18 2 TM	2	32	72	106	2.75	1.11	2.83	1.10	73	102	4.4	9%	35%	26%	8%	13.7%	93.6	45	21	34	31%	81%	15%	14%	0	18			82	1.36	12.4	192	$19
19 CLE	6	34	57	84	3.30	1.24	3.52	1.08	66	102	4.0	7%	35%	27%	5%	14.0%	92.7	27	31	42	38%	77%	11%	12%	0	16			87	1.31	8.6	181	$19
20 CLE	2	16	22	29	2.05	0.77	3.53	0.96	48	67	3.7	5%	35%	30%	8%	10.7%	91.4	27	16	57	28%	71%	0%	7%	0	16			100	1.10	6.5	197	$27
21 3 TM	6	21	65	61	3.90	1.27	4.58	1.35	92	100	4.1	9%	22%	13%	8%	8.2%	93.0	40	20	40	28%	74%	12%	15%	0	16			72	1.15	2.9	80	$10
22 PHI	3	5	45	38	2.80	1.33	4.62	1.49	100	88	3.6	12%	19%	8%	9%	7.3%	92.6	40	23	36	28%	79%	4%	10%	0	15			71	0.96	6.5	34	$1
1st Half	2	3	25	25	2.16	1.24	4.18	1.43	98	67	3.2	12%	23%	11%	9%	8.4%	92.5	38	25	37	28%	81%	0%	6%	0	14			75	1.07	5.6	57	$0
2nd Half	1	2	20	13	3.60	1.45	5.20	1.56	101	109	4.1	11%	14%	3%	10%	6.0%	92.7	42	22	36	28%	78%	9%	15%	0	16			67	0.79	0.9	4	-$7
Proj	**4**	**2**	**58**	**61**	**4.28**	**1.36**	**3.84**	**1.36**	**92**	**101**	**3.8**	**11%**	**25%**	**14%**	**8%**	**9.5%**	**92.8**	**37**	**24**	**38**	**31%**	**70%**	**9%**	**12%**	**0**						**-2.2**	**79**	**-$1**

Harvey,Hunter

Age: 28	Th: R	Role RP	Health	F	LIMA Plan	A+
Ht: 6' 3"	Wt: 210	Type	PT/Exp	D	Rand Var	-5
			Consist	B	MM	3210

Perennial future closer due to good stuff and better paternity finally got healthy enough to put tools to use. Upper-tier command in 2nd half came with backing of high volume of strikes and decent level of whiffs, so it can stick. Can his health? Track record says no way, but this was a nice step forward. UP: 20 Sv

Yr Tm	W	Sv	IP	K	ERA	WHIP	xERA	xWHIP	vL+	vR+	BF/G	BB%	K%	K-BB%	xBB%	SwK	Vel	G	L	F	H%	S%	HR/F	xHR/F	GS	APC	DOM%	DIS%	Sv%	LI	RAR	BPX	R$
18 aa	1	0	33	24	6.31	1.51	5.32				15.9	6%	17%	10%							35%	58%									-8.8	71	-$8
19 BAL *	4	1	84	76	6.11	1.55	6.44		90	88	11.1	9%	21%	12%	7%	12.4%	98.4	45	27	27	32%	67%	33%	12%	0	20			50	1.49	-16.6	29	-$8
20 BAL	0	0	9	6	4.15	1.15	4.89	1.31	60	115	3.7	5%	16%	11%	6%	11.0%	97.4	39	25	36	25%	75%	20%	17%	0	15			0	1.38	0.3	83	-$6
21 BAL	0	0	9	6	4.15	1.27	4.59	1.41	85	113	4.0	8%	17%	8%	6%	5.8%	97.1	48	22	30	28%	70%	13%	7%	0	15			0	1.14	0.1	59	-$6
22 WAS	2	0	39	45	2.52	1.14	3.52	1.14	78	97	4.1	8%	29%	21%	6%	12.6%	98.3	39	17	44	33%	77%	2%	6%	0	17			0	0.77	7.0	141	$0
1st Half	0	0	3	3	0.00	0.75	2.67		24	93	2.3	11%	33%	22%	12%	11.4%	96.9	60	0	40	18%	100%	0%	3%	0	11			0	0.50	1.3	142	-$10
2nd Half	2	0	37	42	2.70	1.17	3.58	1.13	82	97	4.4	7%	28%	21%	6%	12.6%	98.4	38	18	44	34%	76%	2%	7%	0	18			0	0.81	5.7	142	$0
Proj	**3**	**5**	**58**	**54**	**3.84**	**1.24**	**3.72**	**1.25**	**91**	**128**	**6.9**	**7%**	**23%**	**15%**	**6%**	**12.6%**	**98.4**	**38**	**18**	**44**	**31%**	**72%**	**9%**	**8%**	**0**						**0.9**	**102**	**$1**

STEPHEN NICKRAND

Heaney,Andrew

Age: 32	Th: L	Role: SP	Health: F	LIMA Plan: A
Ht: 6' 2"	Wt: 200	Type: Pwr/FB	PT/Exp: A	Rand Var: -1
			Consist: B	MM: 5501

Bum shoulder cost him most of the first four months. But when he pitched, he was a revelation, thanks to improved fastball and an effective new slider. However, he also allowed lots of hard contact, especially to RH hitters, and it was another low-IP season for a guy who's now squarely on the wrong side of 30. The uncertainty bars here are VERY large.

Yr Tm	W	Sv	IP	K	ERA	WHIP	xERA	xWHIP	vL+	vR+	BF/G	BB%	K%	K-BB%	xBB%	SwK	Vel	G	L	F	H%	S%	HR/F	xHR/F	GS	APC	DOM%	DIS%	Sv%	LI	RAR	BPX	R$
18 LAA	9	0	180	180	4.15	1.20	3.75	1.18	74	107	25.0	6%	24%	18%	6%	12.1%	92.0	41	24	35	31%	70%	15%	14%	30	92	37%	13%			0.0	138	$9
19 LAA	4	0	95	118	4.91	1.29	4.11	1.18	121	98	22.7	7%	29%	22%	7%	14.5%	92.5	34	23	44	33%	69%	18%	16%	18	94	17%	28%			-4.7	148	$0
20 LAA	4	0	67	70	4.46	1.23	4.21	1.20	95	97	23.3	7%	25%	18%	6%	13.0%	91.5	39	22	39	31%	67%	12%	16%	12	90	25%	17%			0.0	133	$8
21 2 AL	8	0	130	150	5.83	1.32	4.19	1.18	107	108	18.6	7%	27%	20%	7%	13.0%	92.0	33	22	45	32%	61%	18%	14%	23	78	30%	30%	0	0.69	-25.0	133	-$5
22 LA	4	0	73	110	3.10	1.09	2.95	0.96	96	102	19.4	6%	35%	29%	6%	17.6%	93.0	35	19	46	33%	83%	18%	15%	14	77	21%	7%	0	0.72	7.8	215	$6
1st Half	1	0	15	23	0.59	0.85	2.70	0.95	49	91	21.0	6%	37%	30%	7%	18.5%	91.5	35	24	41	28%	100%	7%	7%	3	78	67%	0%			6.4	213	-$2
2nd Half	3	0	57	87	3.77	1.15	3.01	0.96	113	104	19.0	6%	35%	29%	6%	17.4%	93.3	34	18	48	34%	79%	20%	16%	11	77	9%	9%	0	0.71	1.4	215	$5
Proj	**7**	**0**	**116**	**152**	**3.71**	**1.15**	**2.94**	**1.05**	**93**	**100**	**21.1**	**7%**	**33%**	**26%**	**6%**	**15.5%**	**92.3**	**36**	**21**	**43**	**32%**	**75%**	**17%**	**14%**	**22**						**3.7**	**174**	**$8**

Hearn,Taylor

Age: 28	Th: L	Role: RP	Health: D	LIMA Plan: B
Ht: 6' 6"	Wt: 230	Type:	PT/Exp: B	Rand Var: +1
			Consist: A	MM: 3301

Starter or reliever? As SP: 6.25 ERA, .877 oOPS, 19% K%, 9% K-BB%. As RP: 3.51 ERA, .595 oOPS, 25% K%, 16% K-BB%. Okay, that was too easy. Apparently it was easy for TEX too, because he finished the year working out of the 'pen and didn't get a sniff at a start after May. Seems pegged for glamorless multi-inning role, but could vulture a few Ws.

Yr Tm	W	Sv	IP	K	ERA	WHIP	xERA	xWHIP	vL+	vR+	BF/G	BB%	K%	K-BB%	xBB%	SwK	Vel	G	L	F	H%	S%	HR/F	xHR/F	GS	APC	DOM%	DIS%	Sv%	LI	RAR	BPX	R$
18 aa	4	0	129	113	4.67	1.40	4.35				22.7	10%	21%	11%							31%	68%									-8.3	76	-$4
19 TEX *	1	0	20	20	6.66	1.69	5.60		66	312	18.4	16%	22%	5%		2.6%	91.6	50	25	25	30%	63%	0%	2%	1	39	0%	100%			-5.4	42	-$7
20 TEX	0	0	17	23	3.63	1.38	4.91	1.44	123	67	5.4	14%	30%	16%	9%	9.9%	95.0	27	20	54	30%	77%	9%	7%	0	25			0	0.51	1.8	74	-$4
21 TEX	6	0	104	92	4.66	1.32	4.77	1.38	87	106	10.5	10%	21%	11%	8%	10.0%	94.8	39	19	42	28%	69%	14%	12%	11	41	9%	45%	0	0.78	-5.1	68	-$2
22 TEX	6	1	100	97	5.13	1.50	4.42	1.35	106	109	14.5	10%	22%	12%	8%	10.3%	94.6	38	26	37	34%	67%	10%	11%	13	58	8%	54%	50	0.79	-14.3	76	-$7
1st Half	4	0	63	55	5.86	1.67	4.90	1.43	114	120	20.9	10%	19%	9%	8%	9.7%	94.2	38	25	37	35%	67%	12%	15%	13	80	8%	54%	0	0.75	-14.7	46	-$17
2nd Half	2	1	37	42	3.89	1.22	3.66	1.20	91	89	9.2	8%	27%	18%	6%	11.4%	95.2	37	28	36	32%	67%	6%	3%	0	39			50	0.81	0.4	125	-$2
Proj	**4**	**0**	**80**	**77**	**3.79**	**1.23**	**3.60**	**1.27**	**92**	**98**	**9.6**	**8%**	**24%**	**15%**	**7%**	**10.5%**	**94.8**	**38**	**25**	**37**	**30%**	**72%**	**11%**	**8%**	**0**						**1.8**	**98**	**$1**

Heasley,Jon

Age: 26	Th: R	Role: SP	Health: B	LIMA Plan: C
Ht: 6' 3"	Wt: 225	Type: Con/xFB	PT/Exp: C	Rand Var: 0
			Consist: A	MM: 1001

4-10, 5.28 ERA in 104 IP at KC. Struggles to throw strikes, then gives up a lot of flyballs when he does get it over. It makes for an unseemly cocktail. His K-BB rate has been better in the minors; that'll have to find its way to MLB for him to have any success. But honestly, you can probably find another guy with more upside to fill out your roster.

Yr Tm	W	Sv	IP	K	ERA	WHIP	xERA	xWHIP	vL+	vR+	BF/G	BB%	K%	K-BB%	xBB%	SwK	Vel	G	L	F	H%	S%	HR/F	xHR/F	GS	APC	DOM%	DIS%	Sv%	LI	RAR	BPX	R$
18																																	
19																																	
20																																	
21 KC *	8	0	121	101	4.16	1.36	5.11	1.40	99	142	20.2	8%	20%	12%	12%	5.6%	93.6	46	15	40	30%	76%	16%	21%	3	83	0%	67%			1.6	59	$1
22 KC *	5	0	144	104	4.95	1.39	4.98	1.50	128	106	20.2	10%	15%	5%	10%	8.1%	93.4	37	18	45	28%	69%	12%	10%	21	86	10%	52%			-17.4	39	-$8
1st Half	2	0	78	61	4.55	1.26	3.97	1.40	135	84	19.9	9%	19%	9%	11%	9.0%	94.0	36	20	44	26%	67%	12%	11%	10	89	10%	50%			-5.6	59	-$4
2nd Half	3	0	66	43	5.42	1.55	6.17	1.42	121	126	20.6	8%	14%	6%	10%	7.3%	92.8	38	16	46	31%	70%	13%	10%	11	82	9%	55%			-11.8	16	-$14
Proj	**4**	**0**	**102**	**71**	**4.64**	**1.34**	**4.55**	**1.41**	**114**	**99**	**21.0**	**8%**	**17%**	**8%**	**10%**	**8.0%**	**93.3**	**37**	**17**	**45**	**28%**	**70%**	**12%**	**10%**	**20**						**-8.4**	**48**	**-$4**

Helsley,Ryan

Age: 28	Th: R	Role: RP	Health: D	LIMA Plan: C+
Ht: 6' 2"	Wt: 230	Type: Pwr/xFB	PT/Exp: C	Rand Var: -5
			Consist: D	MM: 4431

Found his footing in Sept 2021, and has only gotten better since, with newfound control of dominant stuff letting him air it out in spades. He's unlikely to post those hit/strand rate numbers again, but throwing like this, he won't have to. Signs all point to this being his new, true level. UP: 40 Sv

Yr Tm	W	Sv	IP	K	ERA	WHIP	xERA	xWHIP	vL+	vR+	BF/G	BB%	K%	K-BB%	xBB%	SwK	Vel	G	L	F	H%	S%	HR/F	xHR/F	GS	APC	DOM%	DIS%	Sv%	LI	RAR	BPX	R$
18 a/a	5	0	69	63	4.47	1.17	3.08				23.0	10%	23%	13%							26%	63%									-2.7	96	$0
19 STL *	4	1	75	65	4.20	1.34	3.96	1.36	100	95	7.6	10%	21%	11%	6%	10.7%	97.8	34	21	46	29%	71%	10%	10%	0	24			50	0.65	2.8	72	$0
20 STL	1	1	12	10	5.25	1.33	6.20	1.72	108	101	4.3	15%	19%	4%	10%	14.4%	96.9	33	15	52	17%	69%	18%	14%	0	16			33	0.97	-1.2	-18	-$4
21 STL	6	1	47	47	4.56	1.42	4.69	1.50	88	91	4.0	13%	23%	10%	10%	11.8%	97.5	42	26	32	29%	68%	10%	15%	0	16			33	1.03	-1.7	46	-$2
22 STL	9	19	65	94	1.25	0.74	2.77	0.98	64	60	4.4	8%	39%	31%	6%	19.2%	99.7	35	14	52	20%	93%	9%	10%	0	18			83	1.49	21.7	191	$24
1st Half	4	6	33	50	0.83	0.64	2.44	0.97	40	53	4.5	9%	42%	33%	7%	18.5%	99.0	41	11	48	18%	90%	4%	7%	0	20			67	1.45	12.7	204	$18
2nd Half	5	13	32	44	1.69	0.84	3.10	1.00	87	67	4.3	7%	36%	29%	4%	20.0%	100.4	29	16	54	22%	95%	14%	12%	0	16			93	1.53	9.0	179	$21
Proj	**4**	**27**	**65**	**77**	**2.85**	**1.05**	**3.33**	**1.21**	**85**	**77**	**5.2**	**10%**	**30%**	**20%**	**6%**	**15.9%**	**99.0**	**35**	**17**	**47**	**25%**	**77%**	**9%**	**11%**	**0**						**9.0**	**121**	**$17**

Hendricks,Kyle

Age: 33	Th: R	Role: SP	Health: F	LIMA Plan: B
Ht: 6' 3"	Wt: 190	Type: Con	PT/Exp: A	Rand Var: 0
			Consist: A	MM: 2103

Shoulder strain ended things just as they were looking up, as numbers were improving in May/June. But overall, the problems that started in earnest in 2021 (notably, with lefties, walks) continued, and a new issue reared its head, a FB spike that meant a bunch of HR. The May/June recovery gives hope, but it's hard to see pre-2021 version returning.

Yr Tm	W	Sv	IP	K	ERA	WHIP	xERA	xWHIP	vL+	vR+	BF/G	BB%	K%	K-BB%	xBB%	SwK	Vel	G	L	F	H%	S%	HR/F	xHR/F	GS	APC	DOM%	DIS%	Sv%	LI	RAR	BPX	R$
18 CHC	14	0	199	161	3.44	1.15	3.85	1.23	91	98	24.6	5%	20%	14%	6%	9.6%	86.9	47	21	32	29%	74%	12%	12%	33	92	24%	30%			17.5	118	$18
19 CHC	11	0	177	150	3.46	1.13	4.26	1.22	88	94	24.3	4%	21%	16%	5%	10.5%	86.9	41	24	35	30%	73%	10%	11%	30	90	30%	27%			22.9	122	$17
20 CHC	6	0	81	64	2.88	1.00	3.82	1.12	78	93	26.3	3%	20%	18%	5%	12.0%	87.4	47	21	32	28%	77%	13%	12%	12	97	42%	17%			15.8	145	$28
21 CHC	14	0	181	131	4.77	1.35	4.64	1.29	123	99	24.5	6%	17%	11%	6%	9.2%	87.3	43	23	34	31%	69%	16%	14%	32	88	25%	41%			-11.3	87	$1
22 CHC	4	0	84	66	4.80	1.29	4.49	1.28	135	86	22.3	7%	19%	12%	8%	10.5%	86.7	36	21	43	29%	68%	14%	12%	16	84	19%	44%			-8.7	79	-$4
1st Half	4	0	84	66	4.80	1.29	4.49	1.28	135	86	22.3	7%	19%	12%	8%	10.5%	86.7	36	21	43	29%	68%	14%	12%	16	84	19%	44%			-8.7	79	-$4
2nd Half																																	
Proj	**9**	**0**	**145**	**107**	**4.35**	**1.20**	**3.88**	**1.25**	**110**	**94**	**23.2**	**5%**	**18%**	**13%**	**6%**	**10.4%**	**87.0**	**40**	**22**	**38**	**29%**	**68%**	**12%**	**12%**	**25**						**-6.7**	**92**	**$4**

Hendriks,Liam

Age: 34	Th: R	Role: RP	Health: C	LIMA Plan: C+
Ht: 6' 0"	Wt: 235	Type: Pwr/xFB	PT/Exp: A	Rand Var: -2
			Consist: A	MM: 5531

Another terrific year. But you can start to see skills inching down the right side of the bell curve... walks up, strikeouts down, a few more hits by lefties. They're small declines, for sure, and if he was 29 or 30, you'd be confident they're just random fluctuation. But at 34, there's more risk that they're part of a real trend. DN: ERA > 3.50, < 25 saves

Yr Tm	W	Sv	IP	K	ERA	WHIP	xERA	xWHIP	vL+	vR+	BF/G	BB%	K%	K-BB%	xBB%	SwK	Vel	G	L	F	H%	S%	HR/F	xHR/F	GS	APC	DOM%	DIS%	Sv%	LI	RAR	BPX	R$
18 OAK *	4	6	50	53	3.90	1.33	4.07	1.38	89	117	4.3	7%	25%	19%	9%	11.4%	94.4	40	21	39	35%	72%	11%	5%	8	18	0%	63%	86	0.64	1.6	131	$1
19 OAK	4	25	85	124	1.80	0.96	3.27	1.00	93	57	4.4	6%	37%	31%	6%	17.7%	96.5	31	19	49	33%	84%	6%	8%	2	18	0%	100%	78	1.37	28.4	202	$25
20 OAK	3	14	25	37	1.78	0.67	2.48	0.82	77	40	3.8	3%	40%	37%	5%	20.0%	96.1	32	30	38	27%	75%	5%	10%	0	15			93	1.36	8.4	246	$30
21 CHW	8	38	71	113	2.54	0.73	2.55	0.76	60	80	3.9	3%	42%	40%	6%	20.1%	97.7	33	17	51	28%	78%	15%	13%	0	16			86	1.54	15.2	269	$32
22 CHW	4	37	58	85	2.81	1.04	2.94	0.98	91	85	4.1	7%	36%	29%	9%	18.8%	97.6	35	19	47	32%	79%	12%	11%	0	16			90	1.42	8.2	203	$20
1st Half	1	16	27	40	2.70	1.09	2.93	0.99	85	88	4.2	7%	36%	29%	10%	17.0%	97.7	34	21	44	34%	81%	11%	18%	0	17			84	1.40	4.2	201	$12
2nd Half	3	21	31	45	2.90	1.00	2.94	0.96	96	83	3.9	6%	36%	30%	8%	20.5%	97.6	35	16	49	31%	78%	12%	6%	0	15			95	1.44	4.1	205	$21
Proj	**4**	**36**	**65**	**94**	**2.91**	**1.03**	**2.65**	**0.95**	**91**	**81**	**4.0**	**6%**	**38%**	**31%**	**8%**	**18.8%**	**97.4**	**34**	**18**	**48**	**33%**	**77%**	**10%**	**10%**	**0**						**8.5**	**205**	**$21**

Henry,Thomas

Age: 25	Th: L	Role: SP	Health: A	LIMA Plan: C+
Ht: 6' 3"	Wt: 205	Type: Con	PT/Exp: D	Rand Var: 0
			Consist: D	MM: 2101

3-4, 5.36 ERA in 47 IP at ARI. Solid AAA 1st half ultimately earned August call-up, but strike zone command issues really showed up in the bigs. In truth, he's shown a similar mix of somewhat hittable stuff and shaky control throughout his time in the minors, so it wasn't a big surprise. Avoid until or unless he takes a step up in K-BB%.

Yr Tm	W	Sv	IP	K	ERA	WHIP	xERA	xWHIP	vL+	vR+	BF/G	BB%	K%	K-BB%	xBB%	SwK	Vel	G	L	F	H%	S%	HR/F	xHR/F	GS	APC	DOM%	DIS%	Sv%	LI	RAR	BPX	R$
18																																	
19																																	
20																																	
21 aa	4	0	117	112	5.41	1.51	5.66				22.0	10%	22%	12%							32%	69%									-16.6	52	-$10
22 ARI *	7	0	160	119	3.76	1.29	3.95	1.46	151	108	21.9	10%	18%	7%	8%	11.1%	91.6	39	19	42	28%	74%	17%	11%	9	86	11%	44%			4.2	65	$3
1st Half	4	0	81	57	2.65	1.19	2.83				21.7	9%	17%	8%							27%	78%	0%		0	0					13.2	85	$10
2nd Half	3	0	81	62	4.75	1.35	4.87	1.37	150	108	22.5	8%	18%	10%	8%	11.1%	91.6	39	19	42	28%	70%	17%	11%	9	86	11%	44%			-7.9	45	-$6
Proj	**4**	**0**	**102**	**76**	**4.46**	**1.29**	**4.18**	**1.39**	**139**	**100**	**23.1**	**9%**	**18%**	**10%**		**11.1%**	**91.6**	**39**	**19**	**42**	**28%**	**68%**	**12%**	**10%**	**18**						**-6.2**	**58**	**-$3**

ROD TRUESDELL

Hentges,Sam

Age: 26	Th: L	Role RP	Health A	LIMA Plan A	
Ht: 6' 6"	Wt: 245	Type Pwr/xGB	PT/Exp C	Rand Var -3	
			Consist F	MM 5401	

Lefty overcame struggles with RH bats by developing four-seamer, sinker into strikeout pitches. Tripling utilization of said sinker sent groundballs soaring, which turned skills from meh to great. Those sharpened instruments in his toolbox give him goods of an end-game arm, and they got even better late. A LIMA gem with added value in holds leagues.

Yr	Tm		W	Sv	IP	K	ERA	WHIP	xERA	xWHIP	vL+	vR+	BF/G	BB%	K%	K-BB%	xBB%	SwK	Vel	G	L	F	H%	S%	HR/F	xHR/F	GS	APC	DOM%	DIS%	Sv%	LI	RAR	BPX	R$
18																																			
19	aa		2	0	130	107	7.32	1.99	7.13				24.1	11%	17%	6%							40%	63%									-45.2	35	-$28
20																																			
21	CLE		1	0	69	68	6.68	1.78	4.84	1.39	90	125	10.6	10%	21%	11%	11%	10.4%	94.4	46	19	35	39%	63%	13%	19%	12	42	0%	67%	0	0.49	-20.5	78	-$16
22	CLE		3	1	62	72	2.32	0.97	2.57	1.13	53	87	4.3	8%	29%	22%	6%	14.4%	95.8	61	16	23	27%	77%	9%	13%	0	17			100	0.75	12.6	168	$6
1st Half			2	0	30	33	3.34	1.08	2.92	1.22	53	104	4.1	9%	28%	18%	7%	12.9%	95.3	58	18	25	26%	72%	17%	21%	0	16			0	0.45	2.3	139	-$2
2nd Half			1	1	32	39	1.39	0.87	2.25	1.05	53	69	4.5	6%	31%	25%	5%	15.9%	96.1	65	13	21	28%	82%	0%	4%	0	17			100	1.06	10.3	197	$5
Proj			**2**	**0**	**65**	**74**	**2.91**	**1.03**	**2.50**	**1.10**	**58**	**95**	**4.3**	**7%**	**29%**	**22%**	**7%**	**14.1%**	**95.5**	**59**	**16**	**25**	**29%**	**73%**	**10%**	**12%**	**0**						**8.5**	**171**	**$4**

Herget,Jimmy

Age: 29	Th: R	Role RP	Health C	LIMA Plan A	
Ht: 6' 3"	Wt: 170	Type	PT/Exp D	Rand Var -5	
			Consist C	MM 3221	

He'll be viewed as an emerging saves source given sexy stats in 2nd half, but he's far from a safe bet. CON: 2nd-half hit and strand rates don't get friendlier; steadily declining fastball velocity; whiff rate barely closer-worthy. PRO: Multi-year skills growth; righties have no shot against him. Bid, but view him as a better fit as your plan B or C.

Yr	Tm		W	Sv	IP	K	ERA	WHIP	xERA	xWHIP	vL+	vR+	BF/G	BB%	K%	K-BB%	xBB%	SwK	Vel	G	L	F	H%	S%	HR/F	xHR/F	GS	APC	DOM%	DIS%	Sv%	LI	RAR	BPX	R$
18	aaa		1	0	61	54	4.42	1.56	5.27				5.4	9%	20%	12%							36%	73%									-2.1	75	-$6
19	CIN	*	3	2	67	57	3.91	1.57	5.09		174	124	5.5	15%	20%	4%		7.4%	93.3	22	35	43	27%	81%	20%	10%	0	19			40	0.10	4.9	36	-$2
20	TEX		1	0	20	17	3.20	1.37	6.00	1.75	91	88	4.4	16%	20%	3%	11%	11.1%	93.1	36	21	43	22%	80%	9%	9%	1	18	0%	0%	0	0.44	3.0	-21	-$2
21	2 AL	*	4	3	62	61	4.14	1.24	3.79	1.11	85	114	5.1	7%	24%	17%	8%	13.7%	91.0	46	22	32	31%	68%	6%	8%	0	17			43	0.94	1.0	111	$1
22	LAA		2	9	69	63	2.48	0.91	3.44	1.15	99	67	5.4	6%	24%	18%	6%	11.5%	90.6	40	24	36	25%	75%	6%	8%	1	20	0%	0%	75	1.39	12.7	125	$10
1st Half			2	1	36	34	3.72	0.99	3.30	1.09	103	81	5.8	4%	24%	19%	6%	10.1%	91.0	42	27	32	28%	66%	13%	13%	1	22	0%	0%	50	1.14	1.1	145	$0
2nd Half			0	8	33	29	1.10	0.83	3.60	1.21	94	51	5.1	7%	24%	16%	6%	13.4%	89.9	38	20	42	22%	85%	0%	4%	0	18			80	1.65	11.6	103	$10
Proj			**3**	**12**	**65**	**59**	**3.52**	**1.24**	**3.70**	**1.26**	**131**	**86**	**5.4**	**7%**	**22%**	**15%**	**6%**	**12.0%**	**90.3**	**40**	**23**	**38**	**31%**	**74%**	**9%**	**8%**	**0**						**3.6**	**100**	**$5**

Hernandez,Elieser

Age: 28	Th: R	Role RP	Health F	LIMA Plan B	
Ht: 6' 0"	Wt: 214	Type /xFB	PT/Exp D	Rand Var +1	
			Consist B	MM 2301	

3-6, 6.35 ERA in 62 IP at MIA. Lost season makes prior breakout target talk seem foolish now. Gopheritis torpedoed his results, and without a GB pitch, homers will continue to plague him. He did get strikeout rate back to prior lofty levels during a short stint in relief, so maybe that's his best shot at a turnaround. For now, he's just not draftable.

Yr	Tm		W	Sv	IP	K	ERA	WHIP	xERA	xWHIP	vL+	vR+	BF/G	BB%	K%	K-BB%	xBB%	SwK	Vel	G	L	F	H%	S%	HR/F	xHR/F	GS	APC	DOM%	DIS%	Sv%	LI	RAR	BPX	R$
18	MIA		2	0	66	45	5.21	1.45	5.69	1.49	121	102	8.9	10%	16%	6%	10%	8.8%	90.7	28	21	51	29%	68%	10%	11%	6	35	0%	67%	0	0.69	-8.6	20	-$7
19	MIA	*	6	0	130	143	3.72	1.22	4.02	1.28	120	99	17.6	8%	27%	19%	6%	11.7%	90.6	34	17	49	30%	76%	18%	12%	15	69	13%	20%	0	0.67	12.7	106	$8
20	MIA		1	0	26	34	3.16	1.01	3.54	1.00	100	84	17.7	5%	32%	27%	5%	13.9%	91.4	34	22	45	29%	81%	17%	12%	6	76	33%	17%			4.1	202	$3
21	MIA	*	1	0	78	81	3.81	1.10	4.24	1.19	140	87	18.0	6%	26%	21%	4%	11.7%	90.9	38	19	43	27%	76%	20%	16%	11	74	0%	18%			4.4	116	$2
22	MIA	*	7	0	119	113	5.51	1.38	5.53	1.28	144	117	15.7	8%	22%	14%	6%	11.1%	91.7	27	15	58	31%	66%	17%	14%	10	55	0%	50%	0	0.81	-22.6	59	-$7
1st Half			5	0	69	69	5.86	1.42	6.51	1.21	148	121	19.5	7%	23%	16%	6%	11.2%	91.5	30	13	57	31%	69%	21%	17%	9	78	0%	56%	0	0.76	-16.1	44	-$10
2nd Half			2	0	50	44	5.02	1.33	4.19	1.32	118	105	12.3	9%	21%	12%	6%	10.5%	92.3	18	20	63	31%	63%	4%	6%	1	26	0%	0%	0	0.87	-6.5	81	-$8
Proj			**3**	**0**	**65**	**63**	**4.70**	**1.30**	**4.06**	**1.26**	**120**	**92**	**14.5**	**8%**	**23%**	**16%**	**6%**	**10.8%**	**91.0**	**32**	**17**	**51**	**30%**	**70%**	**13%**	**14%**	**8**						**-5.9**	**97**	**-$4**

Hernández,Jonathan

Age: 26	Th: R	Role RP	Health F	LIMA Plan A	
Ht: 6' 3"	Wt: 190	Type Pwr/xGB	PT/Exp F	Rand Var -3	
			Consist A	MM 3211	

2-3, 2.97 ERA in 30 IP at TEX. Long road back from Tommy John surgery ended in saves mix. Tools for a successful end-game option remain intact, including extreme groundball tilt and bunches of swings-and-misses behind triple-digit heat. That combination gives skills more life than they showed. Keep him among your $1 speculations.

Yr	Tm		W	Sv	IP	K	ERA	WHIP	xERA	xWHIP	vL+	vR+	BF/G	BB%	K%	K-BB%	xBB%	SwK	Vel	G	L	F	H%	S%	HR/F	xHR/F	GS	APC	DOM%	DIS%	Sv%	LI	RAR	BPX	R$
18	aa		4	0	64	48	6.33	1.68	5.35				24.0	14%	17%	3%							32%	62%									-17.2	41	-$11
19	TEX	*	7	0	113	96	7.20	1.77	6.56	1.66	113	81	16.7	11%	19%	8%	12%	13.0%	96.9	52	17	30	36%	61%	21%	17%	2	37	0%	50%	0	0.49	-37.5	32	-$17
20	TEX		5	0	31	31	2.90	1.03	3.94	1.19	102	71	4.6	6%	25%	18%	9%	14.5%	97.8	46	14	41	28%	73%	6%	6%	0	18			0	0.89	5.9	139	$12
21																																			
22	TEX	*	2	4	48	41	2.97	1.46	3.71	1.51	105	87	4.5	13%	21%	8%	12%	12.7%	98.0	62	16	21	28%	81%	11%	15%	0	18			50	0.88	5.9	76	-$1
1st Half			0	0	11	9	4.48	1.94	5.63				4.4	19%	17%	-2%							33%	77%	0%		0	0					-0.7	52	-$13
2nd Half			2	4	37	32	2.46	1.31	3.09	1.52	105	87	4.6	13%	21%	8%	12%	12.7%	98.0	62	16	21	27%	83%	11%	15%	0	18			67	0.88	6.8	86	$2
Proj			**5**	**7**	**65**	**57**	**3.83**	**1.40**	**3.85**	**1.46**	**114**	**90**	**6.8**	**11%**	**21%**	**9%**		**13.4%**	**97.9**	**56**	**15**	**29**	**30%**	**74%**	**11%**	**11%**	**0**						**1.1**	**63**	**$1**

Heuer,Codi

Age: 26	Th: R	Role RP	Health F	LIMA Plan C+	
Ht: 6' 5"	Wt: 200	Type Con	PT/Exp C	Rand Var 0	
			Consist B	MM 2100	

CHC arm underwent Tommy John surgery in March. Before elbow woes, mixed-bag skills provided some hidden signs to support role expansion, including bunches of whiffs and control that was headed in right direction. Arm likely won't be near full strength until midseason, so stash him among your very late speculation options if you have a deep bench.

Yr	Tm		W	Sv	IP	K	ERA	WHIP	xERA	xWHIP	vL+	vR+	BF/G	BB%	K%	K-BB%	xBB%	SwK	Vel	G	L	F	H%	S%	HR/F	xHR/F	GS	APC	DOM%	DIS%	Sv%	LI	RAR	BPX	R$
18																																			
19	aa		2	9	30	19	2.67	1.32	3.40				5.7	6%	15%	9%							33%	78%									6.8	94	$2
20	CHW		3	1	24	25	1.52	0.89	3.61	1.28	56	62	4.4	10%	27%	17%	8%	15.0%	97.6	50	21	29	21%	85%	6%	8%	0	18			100	1.02	8.6	121	$11
21	2 TM		7	2	67	56	4.28	1.31	4.44	1.34	125	80	4.3	8%	20%	12%	7%	14.0%	95.9	44	22	35	30%	69%	10%	10%	0	16			40	1.26	-0.1	81	$1
22																																			
1st Half																																			
2nd Half																																			
Proj			**4**	**0**	**44**	**33**	**3.64**	**1.32**	**3.92**	**1.34**	**133**	**90**	**4.7**	**8%**	**18%**	**11%**	**7%**	**14.0%**	**95.9**	**44**	**22**	**35**	**31%**	**73%**	**6%**	**9%**	**0**						**1.8**	**74**	**-$2**

Hicks,Jordan

Age: 26	Th: R	Role RP	Health F	LIMA Plan C+	
Ht: 6' 2"	Wt: 220	Type Pwr/xGB	PT/Exp D	Rand Var +3	
			Consist C	MM 4310	

Starter or reliever? You decide... As SP: 21% K%, 18% BB%, 3.3% K-BB%. As RP: 27% K%, 10% BB%, 17% K-BB%. Early skills collapse product of role, not talent. When he returned home to bullpen late in year, whiffs soared and skills followed. With a tweak against LH bats, this is a premium post-hype place to speculate. UP: 20 Sv

Yr	Tm		W	Sv	IP	K	ERA	WHIP	xERA	xWHIP	vL+	vR+	BF/G	BB%	K%	K-BB%	xBB%	SwK	Vel	G	L	F	H%	S%	HR/F	xHR/F	GS	APC	DOM%	DIS%	Sv%	LI	RAR	BPX	R$
18	STL		3	6	78	70	3.59	1.34	3.95	1.55	98	64	4.6	13%	21%	7%	10%	10.0%	100.5	61	21	19	28%	72%	5%	5%	0	17			46	1.25	5.3	51	$2
19	STL		2	14	29	31	3.14	0.94	2.86	1.27	106	44	3.8	10%	28%	18%	11%	12.1%	101.2	67	16	16	22%	68%	18%	17%	0	16			93	0.94	4.8	138	$6
20																																			
21	STL		0	0	10	10	5.40	1.50	4.77	1.97	72	79	4.4	23%	23%	0%	12%	8.7%	99.3	71	13	17	22%	60%	0%	0%	0	21			0	0.47	-1.4	-35	-$6
22	STL		3	0	61	63	4.84	1.32	3.61	1.46	111	82	7.5	13%	24%	11%	11%	9.7%	99.4	58	18	24	27%	63%	13%	14%	8	30	0%	38%	0	1.13	-6.6	70	-$4
1st Half			1	0	30	29	4.75	1.38	4.04	1.59	92	102	13.3	15%	22%	7%	12%	8.4%	99.0	57	18	25	25%	67%	15%	21%	7	55	0%	43%	0	0.71	-2.9	33	-$9
2nd Half			2	0	31	34	4.94	1.26	3.22	1.34	146	69	5.2	12%	26%	15%	8%	11.1%	99.9	58	19	23	29%	59%	11%	7%	1	20	0%	0%	0	1.30	-3.7	106	-$6
Proj			**3**	**2**	**58**	**56**	**3.90**	**1.25**	**3.40**	**1.47**	**110**	**75**	**6.3**	**13%**	**24%**	**11%**	**10%**	**10.0%**	**99.8**	**58**	**19**	**23**	**26%**	**69%**	**11%**	**10%**	**0**						**0.5**	**69**	**-$1**

Hill,Garrett

Age: 27	Th: R	Role RP	Health A	LIMA Plan C	
Ht: 6' 0"	Wt: 185	Type /FB	PT/Exp D	Rand Var -1	
			Consist A	MM 1101	

3-3, 4.03 ERA in 60 IP at DET. Late-round draftee has overachieved to this point behind plus splitter and deceptive delivery. Strong command in upper minors didn't convert to majors, largely because his pitches didn't miss many bats. Given age and lack of pedigree, his window to make an impact will be smaller than most. For now, let others gamble.

Yr	Tm		W	Sv	IP	K	ERA	WHIP	xERA	xWHIP	vL+	vR+	BF/G	BB%	K%	K-BB%	xBB%	SwK	Vel	G	L	F	H%	S%	HR/F	xHR/F	GS	APC	DOM%	DIS%	Sv%	LI	RAR	BPX	R$
18																																			
19																																			
20																																			
21	aa		3	0	21	22	3.71	1.33	3.35				22.0	11%	25%	14%							31%	72%									1.5	103	-$3
22	DET	*	7	0	132	116	3.67	1.23	3.52	1.54	92	105	16.7	11%	15%	4%	9%	8.3%	91.9	37	17	46	27%	73%	9%	12%	8	60	0%	75%	0	0.70	4.9	81	$5
1st Half			5	0	77	79	3.22	1.08	2.75	1.21	111	13	18.8	8%	26%	18%		6.4%	91.6	25	13	63	27%	73%	10%		1	78	0%	0%			7.1	119	$12
2nd Half			2	0	54	37	4.31	1.45	5.50	1.57	89	112	15.2	12%	15%	4%	9%	8.5%	91.9	38	18	45	27%	74%	9%	14%	7	59	0%	86%	0	0.70	-2.3	1	-$8
Proj			**5**	**0**	**102**	**81**	**4.16**	**1.36**	**4.41**	**1.46**	**90**	**115**	**16.1**	**11%**	**19%**	**8%**		**8.5%**	**91.9**	**38**	**18**	**45**	**28%**	**72%**	**10%**	**12%**	**16**						**-2.3**	**39**	**-$2**

STEPHEN NICKRAND

Hill,Rich

Age: 43 Th: L Role SP	Health F	LIMA Plan A+
Ht: 6' 5" Wt: 221 Type	PT/Exp A	Rand Var -1
	Consist A	MM 3201

Missed a month with a knee sprain; otherwise, picked up where he left off in 2021, skills-wise. For a quadragenarian, that's a real accomplishment. Even gained a few ticks on his "fastball." (Sorry, couldn't resist the quotes.) Seems like he can do this a while longer; just acknowledge the light beer-like DN: Same okay pitching, but half the innings.

Yr Tm	W	Sv	IP	K	ERA	WHIP	xERA	xWHIP	vL+	vR+	BF/G	BB%	K%	K-BB%	xBB%	SwK	Vel	G	L	F	H%	S%	HR/F	xHR/F	GS	APC	DOM%	DIS%	Sv%	LI	RAR	BPX	R$
18 LA	11	0	133	150	3.66	1.12	3.66	1.17	95	96	21.9	7%	27%	20%	5%	11.1%	89.3	39	21	40	28%	74%	15%	15%	24	84	29%	17%	0	0.81	8.0	144	$12
19 LA	4	0	59	72	2.45	1.13	3.36	1.15	70	99	18.6	7%	30%	22%	5%	11.4%	90.3	50	18	32	29%	89%	22%	12%	13	74	15%	23%			14.8	166	$5
20 MIN	2	0	39	31	3.03	1.16	4.86	1.48	71	82	19.5	11%	20%	9%	8%	6.6%	87.7	41	23	37	24%	76%	8%	18%	8	77	13%	13%			6.8	47	$5
21 2 TM	7	0	159	150	3.86	1.21	4.45	1.30	78	102	20.7	8%	23%	14%	6%	10.3%	88.0	35	22	43	28%	73%	11%	12%	31	78	13%	42%	0	0.77	8.0	90	$8
22 BOS	8	0	124	109	4.27	1.30	4.19	1.26	103	105	20.2	7%	21%	14%	5%	9.7%	88.3	40	20	40	31%	70%	10%	13%	26	77	15%	38%			-4.6	97	$1
1st Half	4	0	71	58	4.20	1.29	4.32	1.31	90	108	19.9	8%	19%	12%	6%	9.1%	88.2	40	21	39	30%	70%	10%	14%	15	76	13%	33%			-2.0	79	-$1
2nd Half	4	0	54	51	4.36	1.32	4.04	1.19	120	102	20.7	6%	22%	16%	5%	10.6%	88.4	41	18	42	33%	70%	11%	13%	11	78	18%	45%			-2.6	120	-$2
Proj	7	0	116	108	4.15	1.24	3.72	1.27	90	98	20.4	8%	23%	15%	6%	9.6%	88.4	40	20	39	29%	70%	11%	14%	23						-2.6	98	$3

Hill,Tim

Age: 33 Th: L Role RP	Health B	LIMA Plan B
Ht: 6' 4" Wt: 200 Type Con/xGB	PT/Exp C	Rand Var -3
	Consist A	MM 4000

Lost a smidge off his fastball, and missed far fewer bats. However, thanks to not allowing a single HR until Sept—a HR/F rate far below his established level—ERA was unscathed. But those expected stats show that he dodged a bullet. So watch that whiff rate for signs of life; if it recovers, he should be fine for more middle-relief goodness. Otherwise, avoid.

Yr Tm	W	Sv	IP	K	ERA	WHIP	xERA	xWHIP	vL+	vR+	BF/G	BB%	K%	K-BB%	xBB%	SwK	Vel	G	L	F	H%	S%	HR/F	xHR/F	GS	APC	DOM%	DIS%	Sv%	LI	RAR	BPX	R$
18 KC	1	2	46	42	4.53	1.31	3.38	1.27	78	108	2.8	7%	21%	14%	6%	9.0%	91.0	62	19	19	33%	66%	15%	14%	0	11			50	1.16	-2.2	132	-$3
19 KC *	3	4	71	61	3.21	1.19	3.39	1.28	61	101	3.9	7%	21%	14%	7%	9.6%	90.2	57	17	26	30%	76%	15%	13%	0	14			67	1.39	11.3	101	$5
20 SD	3	0	18	20	4.50	1.28	3.71	1.22	91	112	3.4	8%	25%	18%	7%	10.3%	90.7	53	20	27	31%	70%	21%	10%	0	15			0	0.96	-0.1	147	$1
21 SD	6	1	60	56	3.62	1.24	3.78	1.33	86	106	3.3	9%	22%	13%	6%	11.0%	91.7	61	12	27	27%	77%	20%	18%	0	12			20	1.23	4.7	107	$2
22 SD	3	0	48	25	3.56	1.23	4.02	1.41	77	97	3.6	7%	13%	6%	8%	7.1%	90.2	60	17	23	29%	69%	3%	3%	0	14			0	0.93	2.4	57	-$2
1st Half	2	0	23	10	4.76	1.24	4.13	1.33	74	101	3.6	4%	11%	6%	8%	6.0%	90.1	61	13	27	31%	57%	0%	1%	0	13			0	1.19	-2.2	74	-$9
2nd Half	1	0	25	15	2.49	1.22	3.92	1.49	80	93	3.6	10%	14%	5%	8%	8.1%	90.3	59	21	20	26%	80%	7%	5%	0	14			0	0.70	4.6	41	-$5
Proj	3	0	58	41	3.80	1.23	3.51	1.35	77	101	3.4	8%	18%	10%	7%	8.6%	90.5	60	17	24	29%	69%	9%	9%	0						1.2	85	-$1

Holmes,Clay

Age: 30 Th: R Role RP	Health D	LIMA Plan B
Ht: 6' 5" Wt: 245 Type Pwr/xGB	PT/Exp B	Rand Var 0
	Consist B	MM 5321

Among the best over the first half, continuing 2021's 2nd-half gains. But control vanished in July, then he landed on the IL with back spasms in August—which, one imagines, could be related. True, walks used to plague him. But he appeared to have cemented his new power/xGB/low-walk profile, so we'll bet on that holding form—with health.

Yr Tm	W	Sv	IP	K	ERA	WHIP	xERA	xWHIP	vL+	vR+	BF/G	BB%	K%	K-BB%	xBB%	SwK	Vel	G	L	F	H%	S%	HR/F	xHR/F	GS	APC	DOM%	DIS%	Sv%	LI	RAR	BPX	R$
18 PIT *	9	0	122	100	4.69	1.68	5.03	1.87	105	122	16.7	12%	18%	7%	12%	7.6%	94.3	57	21	22	35%	71%	11%	9%	4	45	25%	75%	0	0.44	-8.2	69	-$8
19 PIT *	4	1	71	68	6.45	1.80	5.28	1.60	107	93	7.0	16%	21%	4%	12%	9.7%	94.3	60	18	22	34%	63%	17%	20%	0	26			20	0.57	-17.1	61	-$11
20 PIT	0	0	1	1	0.00	1.50	3.77		92	89	6.0	0%	17%	17%		18.2%	92.4	60	20	20	42%	100%	0%	0%	0	22			0	1.12	0.7	180	-$6
21 2 TM	8	0	70	78	3.60	1.17	2.96	1.27	112	63	4.2	10%	27%	17%	8%	11.6%	96.1	69	13	18	29%	70%	16%	16%	0	16			0	1.06	5.7	139	$5
22 NYY	7	20	64	65	2.54	1.02	2.33	1.20	99	63	4.2	8%	25%	17%	8%	13.6%	97.1	76	12	12	27%	75%	10%	7%	0	16			80	1.41	11.2	158	$15
1st Half	4	15	37	38	0.49	0.73	1.65	1.00	67	53	3.9	4%	27%	24%	5%	16.0%	96.9	83	10	8	25%	93%	0%	2%	0	15			94	1.28	15.9	214	$26
2nd Half	3	5	27	27	5.40	1.43	3.39	1.46	127	77	4.7	12%	22%	10%	11%	10.8%	97.2	67	15	18	30%	61%	15%	10%	0	18			56	1.59	-4.7	80	-$3
Proj	6	23	65	68	3.10	1.12	2.46	1.19	106	70	4.8	8%	26%	18%	9%	13.5%	96.3	70	14	16	30%	73%	14%	12%	0						7.0	153	$14

Houck,Tanner

Age: 27 Th: R Role RP	Health D	LIMA Plan A
Ht: 6' 5" Wt: 230 Type Pwr	PT/Exp C	Rand Var -2
	Consist A	MM 4311

Missed most of final two months with a spinal disc issue that required Sept surgery. He's cleared for offseason work, so expect a full return to health. Before the injury, was again effective in a swingman role. Watch that role as we head into 2023: There's real upside with a rotation slot, but he's also unheralded. A small draft-day investment could pay off.

Yr Tm	W	Sv	IP	K	ERA	WHIP	xERA	xWHIP	vL+	vR+	BF/G	BB%	K%	K-BB%	xBB%	SwK	Vel	G	L	F	H%	S%	HR/F	xHR/F	GS	APC	DOM%	DIS%	Sv%	LI	RAR	BPX	R$
18																																	
19 a/a	8	1	109	88	5.50	1.63	5.21				14.7	10%	18%	8%							36%	66%									-13.3	61	-$7
20 BOS	3	0	17	21	0.53	0.88	3.38	1.35	61	59	21.0	14%	33%	19%	12%	12.1%	92.1	47	19	34	16%	100%	9%	17%	3	88	0%	0%			8.2	109	$8
21 BOS *	1	1	90	108	4.22	1.20	3.14	1.11	88	77	15.1	8%	30%	22%	8%	13.7%	94.1	48	20	32	34%	64%	7%	11%	13	64	46%	31%	100	1.11	0.5	150	$0
22 BOS	5	8	60	56	3.15	1.18	3.44	1.30	111	70	7.7	9%	23%	14%	8%	13.3%	94.9	51	23	26	29%	74%	7%	12%	4	29	0%	50%	89	1.05	6.1	100	$5
1st Half	4	6	49	51	3.47	1.22	3.33	1.23	108	75	8.5	8%	25%	17%	8%	13.5%	94.8	45	27	28	32%	71%	6%	8%	4	32	0%	50%	100	0.84	3.1	118	$7
2nd Half	2	1	11	5	1.69	1.03	3.95	1.65	128	47	5.4	12%	12%	0%	12%	12.0%	95.4	74	6	19	17%	90%	17%	34%	0	19			67	1.67	3.0	16	-$5
Proj	7	2	102	100	3.57	1.23	3.32	1.25	103	78	11.3	8%	24%	16%	8%	13.6%	94.5	47	24	29	32%	71%	6%	9%	5						5.0	113	$5

Houser,Adrian

Age: 30 Th: R Role SP	Health D	LIMA Plan C
Ht: 6' 3" Wt: 222 Type Con/GB	PT/Exp A	Rand Var -1
	Consist A	MM 2003

Missed about six weeks with an elbow strain. But poor skills suggest he felt it for most of the year, as this was worse than just a stats regression. Elbow injuries are foreboding, so here's hoping he's pain-free going forward. If so, he's established that low-4s xERA baseline as the one to expect, not the low-3s he's teased with at times.

Yr Tm	W	Sv	IP	K	ERA	WHIP	xERA	xWHIP	vL+	vR+	BF/G	BB%	K%	K-BB%	xBB%	SwK	Vel	G	L	F	H%	S%	HR/F	xHR/F	GS	APC	DOM%	DIS%	Sv%	LI	RAR	BPX	R$
18 MIL *	2	0	94	63	5.65	1.70	6.23	1.64	63	131	15.2	8%	15%	7%	9%	10.6%	94.3	40	21	40	37%	68%	0%	4%	0	32			0	0.24	-17.4	41	-$15
19 MIL *	8	0	133	136	3.34	1.18	3.55	1.26	109	83	13.7	8%	25%	18%	8%	10.4%	94.4	53	21	26	29%	76%	18%	14%	18	52	11%	39%	0	1.00	19.1	108	$12
20 MIL	1	0	56	44	5.30	1.50	4.20	1.39	137	78	20.5	9%	18%	9%	8%	10.3%	93.4	59	23	19	33%	67%	24%	19%	11	77	18%	55%	0	0.69	-5.9	83	-$10
21 MIL	10	0	142	105	3.22	1.28	4.19	1.49	105	78	21.4	11%	18%	7%	10%	8.0%	93.7	59	20	21	26%	77%	14%	13%	26	84	8%	46%	0	0.80	18.3	52	$10
22 MIL	6	0	103	69	4.73	1.46	4.81	1.51	124	85	20.7	10%	15%	5%	11%	6.8%	94.0	47	23	30	30%	68%	8%	12%	21	84	5%	29%	0	0.74	-9.7	25	-$6
1st Half	4	0	76	57	4.72	1.48	4.48	1.42	128	89	22.4	9%	17%	8%	10%	7.5%	94.2	47	23	29	32%	70%	11%	13%	15	90	7%	27%			-7.0	53	-$9
2nd Half	2	0	26	12	4.78	1.41	5.84	1.77	112	71	17.0	13%	10%	-3%	12%	4.9%	93.2	45	24	31	25%	62%	0%	10%	6	71	0%	33%	0	0.70	-2.7	-56	-$9
Proj	8	0	145	100	4.54	1.41	4.18	1.51	122	79	20.4	11%	16%	6%	10%	7.7%	93.7	52	23	26	29%	68%	10%	14%	26						-10.3	34	-$4

Howard,Spencer

Age: 26 Th: R Role SP	Health D	LIMA Plan B
Ht: 6' 3" Wt: 210 Type /FB	PT/Exp D	Rand Var +3
	Consist B	MM 2200

2-4, 7.41 ERA in 38 IP at TEX. Finger and shoulder issues cost him two months, and added to the frustration of another season of struggles for the one-time top prospect. Whiff rate and velocity remained up when his shoulder wasn't bothering him, so there's still hope for the arm. But everything else in the package needs a LOT of work.

Yr Tm	W	Sv	IP	K	ERA	WHIP	xERA	xWHIP	vL+	vR+	BF/G	BB%	K%	K-BB%	xBB%	SwK	Vel	G	L	F	H%	S%	HR/F	xHR/F	GS	APC	DOM%	DIS%	Sv%	LI	RAR	BPX	R$
18																																	
19 aa	1	0	32	34	2.96	1.05	2.54				20.8	8%	27%	19%							27%	74%									6.1	134	$0
20 PHI	1	0	24	23	5.92	1.64	5.26	1.38	148	93	18.8	9%	20%	12%	7%	10.7%	94.1	38	24	38	34%	71%	20%	13%	6	73	0%	50%			-4.4	78	-$9
21 2 TM *	1	0	75	77	5.47	1.43	4.41	1.45	100	118	12.2	11%	24%	13%	8%	10.6%	94.2	36	23	40	32%	62%	12%	11%	15	49	0%	47%	0	0.75	-11.2	84	-$9
22 TEX *	5	0	97	89	5.55	1.48	5.47	1.37	122	153	17.3	8%	18%	9%	7%	8.2%	94.4	39	19	42	33%	66%	22%	16%	8	69	13%	75%	0	0.76	-18.8	57	-$9
1st Half	3	0	58	61	4.76	1.35	4.56	1.24	62	210	17.2	9%	25%	16%	7%	10.1%	95.4	38	22	41	32%	68%	46%	28%	2	52	0%	50%	0	0.78	-5.6	90	-$6
2nd Half	2	0	41	28	6.35	1.58	6.26	1.46	138	122	18.1	9%	15%	6%	7%	7.4%	93.9	40	18	42	31%	64%	15%	13%	6	81	17%	83%			-12.1	15	-$15
Proj	2	0	51	47	4.67	1.38	4.05	1.34	105	101	20.5	9%	22%	13%	8%	8.7%	94.0	38	20	41	31%	69%	12%	12%	10						-4.4	79	-$5

Hudson,Dakota

Age: 28 Th: R Role SP	Health F	LIMA Plan C
Ht: 6' 5" Wt: 215 Type Con/GB	PT/Exp D	Rand Var -2
	Consist F	MM 2001

8-7, 4.45 ERA in 140 IP at STL. Stats finally caught up to—or better put, fell down to—his skill level. Sure, the groundballs are nice, but if you pitch to contact, you'd better not also dole out free passes. He's made no strides in that area, so there's not much here to suggest he'll get the ERA back under 4.00. Unless you believe luck is a skill.

Yr Tm	W	Sv	IP	K	ERA	WHIP	xERA	xWHIP	vL+	vR+	BF/G	BB%	K%	K-BB%	xBB%	SwK	Vel	G	L	F	H%	S%	HR/F	xHR/F	GS	APC	DOM%	DIS%	Sv%	LI	RAR	BPX	R$
18 STL *	17	0	141	90	2.75	1.38	3.45	1.74	104	57	13.1	9%	15%	6%	11%	9.9%	96.0	61	20	19	31%	78%	0%	4%	0	17			0	1.35	24.3	81	$12
19 STL	16	1	175	136	3.35	1.41	4.61	1.55	108	90	22.9	11%	18%	7%	11%	10.2%	93.7	57	22	21	28%	81%	20%	21%	32	86	16%	41%	100	0.95	24.9	45	$13
20 STL	3	0	39	31	2.77	1.00	4.13	1.41	66	95	18.9	10%	21%	11%	9%	10.0%	92.9	57	13	31	19%	79%	16%	13%	8	74	25%	38%			8.1	79	$11
21 STL *	2	0	27	13	1.33	0.98	1.50	1.16	82	68	17.0	8%	13%	5%	8%	7.6%	92.1	65	8	27	22%	85%	0%	0%	1	66	0%	0%	0	1.05	9.7	82	$0
22 STL *	9	0	161	92	4.08	1.44	4.15	1.55	103	104	22.8	10%	13%	3%	11%	7.4%	91.8	53	19	28	30%	71%	7%	10%	26	83	12%	54%	0	0.74	-2.3	51	-$3
1st Half	6	0	84	46	4.29	1.43	4.63	1.58	91	115	22.1	11%	13%	2%	12%	7.4%	92.2	54	19	27	28%	70%	9%	11%	16	86	13%	56%			-3.3	9	-$5
2nd Half	3	0	77	46	3.86	1.45	4.18	1.46	122	89	23.4	9%	14%	5%	9%	7.4%	91.2	52	18	30	32%	72%	5%	10%	10	80	10%	50%	0	0.69	1.0	60	-$5
Proj	6	0	87	58	4.17	1.36	4.11	1.50	100	94	20.6	10%	16%	6%	11%	8.5%	92.3	54	19	27	28%	70%	9%	13%	18						-2.1	41	-$2

ROD TRUESDELL

Hudson,Daniel

Age: 36	Th: R	Role RP	Health F	LIMA Plan A+	
Ht: 6' 3"	Wt: 215	Type Pwr	PT/Exp C	Rand Var -2	
			Consist C	MM 5410	

Three reasons to look here for an injury discount: 1) Four straight years of BPX growth before torn ACL; 2) SwK has a firmly elite baseline now; 3) xERA last two seasons confirms he's aging really well. Given age and flunking health, you'll be able to get him cheaply. At minimum, a premium LIMA arm. If he stays healthy and gets another shot... UP: 25 Sv

Yr	Tm	W	Sv	IP	K	ERA	WHIP	xERA	xWHIP	vL+	vR+	BF/G	BB%	K%	K-BB%	xBB%	SwK	Vel	G	L	F	H%	S%	HR/F	xHR/F	GS	APC	DOM%	DIS%	Sv%	LI	RAR	BPX	R$
18	LA	3	0	46	44	4.11	1.22	4.25	1.34	72	102	4.9	9%	22%	13%	7%	13.5%	95.4	37	27	36	27%	70%	13%	8%	1	18	0%	0%	0	0.95	0.2	86	-$1
19	2 TM	9	8	73	71	2.47	1.14	4.81	1.35	85	87	4.4	9%	23%	14%	6%	10.6%	96.1	37	16	47	26%	84%	9%	13%	1	18	0%	100%	67	1.14	18.4	90	$13
20	WAS	3	10	21	28	6.10	1.26	4.75	1.33	94	117	4.4	12%	30%	18%	6%	16.4%	96.5	18	24	57	23%	60%	21%	17%	0	18			67	1.39	-4.2	97	$11
21	2 NL	5	0	52	75	3.31	1.08	3.47	1.04	98	86	3.9	8%	36%	28%	7%	16.6%	97.0	30	19	51	31%	77%	13%	15%	0	16			0	1.05	6.1	184	$4
22	LA	2	5	24	30	2.22	0.90	2.47	1.00	77	67	3.9	5%	31%	26%	8%	16.7%	97.0	53	21	26	29%	76%	7%	9%	0	16			83	1.38	5.3	199	$2
1st Half		2	5	24	30	2.22	0.90	2.47	1.00	77	67	3.9	5%	31%	26%	8%	16.8%	97.0	53	21	26	29%	76%	7%	9%	0	16			83	1.38	5.3	200	$5
2nd Half																																		
Proj		5	9	58	68	3.00	1.06	2.98	1.12	83	85	4.0	8%	30%	23%		15.0%	96.5	41	21	38	29%	76%	11%	11%	0						6.9	150	$8

Hughes,Brandon

Age: 27	Th: L	Role RP	Health A	LIMA Plan B+	
Ht: 6' 2"	Wt: 215	Type Pwr/FB	PT/Exp F	Rand Var -5	
			Consist C	MM 3321	

2-3, 3.12 ERA with 8 Sv in 58 IP at CHC. Rookie ran with closer role behind filthy stuff, which included 13 inches of break on four-seamer and whiffs on half of his sliders. Sure, friendly hit and strand rates kept his ERA and WHIP better than they should have been. But if he can keep his walk rate in single digits, there's a stopper here. UP: 30 Sv

Yr	Tm	W	Sv	IP	K	ERA	WHIP	xERA	xWHIP	vL+	vR+	BF/G	BB%	K%	K-BB%	xBB%	SwK	Vel	G	L	F	H%	S%	HR/F	xHR/F	GS	APC	DOM%	DIS%	Sv%	LI	RAR	BPX	R$
18																																		
19																																		
20																																		
21	aa	0	1	32	34	1.98	1.31	3.78				7.4	11%	26%	15%							31%	90%									9.1	98	-$2
22	CHC *	3	9	76	85	2.37	0.94	2.49	1.18	89	103	4.3	9%	28%	20%	8%	15.4%	93.2	34	22	44	22%	85%	17%	14%	0	17			69	1.17	14.9	127	$12
1st Half		2	1	39	44	2.10	0.92	1.78	1.13	114	92	5.1	8%	30%	22%	6%	15.5%	92.7	33	31	35	24%	81%	17%	15%	0	21			50	0.74	8.9	153	$7
2nd Half		1	8	37	41	2.65	0.96	3.69	1.17	66	107	3.8	8%	27%	19%	8%	15.4%	93.5	34	16	49	20%	89%	18%	14%	0	15			73	1.37	6.1	123	$9
Proj		3	18	65	68	3.04	1.15	3.55	1.21	94	95	5.0	8%	26%	18%	8%	15.4%	93.2	34	22	44	28%	80%	12%	15%	0						7.5	113	$10

Iglesias,Raisel

Age: 33	Th: R	Role RP	Health A	LIMA Plan B+	
Ht: 6' 2"	Wt: 190	Type Pwr/FB	PT/Exp A	Rand Var -3	
			Consist A	MM 5531	

Move at trade deadline dried up save chances, but this is still a legit upper-tier closer. SwK has settled at an elite level, he doesn't walk anyone, and he consistently converts his opps. Those strengths mean the only thing preventing return to prominence is opportunity. If it aligns, this is a pretty low-risk forecast.

Yr	Tm	W	Sv	IP	K	ERA	WHIP	xERA	xWHIP	vL+	vR+	BF/G	BB%	K%	K-BB%	xBB%	SwK	Vel	G	L	F	H%	S%	HR/F	xHR/F	GS	APC	DOM%	DIS%	Sv%	LI	RAR	BPX	R$
18	CIN	2	30	72	80	2.38	1.07	3.59	1.22	91	87	4.4	9%	27%	19%	7%	15.7%	95.2	38	26	35	25%	89%	19%	17%	0	17			88	1.02	15.8	129	$19
19	CIN	3	34	67	89	4.16	1.22	3.83	1.14	105	94	4.1	8%	32%	24%	7%	16.0%	95.5	30	26	44	33%	73%	17%	12%	0	17			85	1.54	2.8	160	$16
20	CIN	4	8	23	31	2.74	0.91	3.02	0.99	74	65	4.1	5%	34%	29%	5%	19.7%	96.2	42	23	36	31%	70%	5%	9%	0	16			80	1.79	4.9	210	$20
21	LAA	7	34	70	103	2.57	0.93	2.67	0.89	89	78	4.2	4%	38%	33%	4%	21.1%	96.4	39	22	39	31%	83%	18%	14%	0	16			87	1.43	14.6	234	$27
22	2 TM	2	17	62	78	2.47	0.97	3.13	1.01	85	78	3.7	6%	32%	26%	5%	17.2%	95.0	34	21	44	30%	78%	8%	12%	0	15			81	1.10	11.5	177	$13
1st Half		2	15	28	42	3.49	0.81	2.54	0.86	96	76	3.5	5%	39%	34%	5%	17.5%	95.1	34	20	46	26%	67%	19%	20%	0	13			88	1.07	1.7	231	$14
2nd Half		0	2	34	36	1.60	1.10	3.69	1.14	76	80	3.8	7%	26%	20%	6%	16.9%	94.9	34	22	43	32%	84%	0%	6%	0	16			50	1.12	9.8	133	$2
Proj		3	28	65	84	2.84	1.04	2.86	1.03	92	83	3.8	7%	33%	27%	6%	17.2%	95.3	34	23	42	30%	79%	12%	13%	0						9.1	174	$17

Irvin,Cole

Age: 29	Th: L	Role SP	Health B	LIMA Plan A	
Ht: 6' 4"	Wt: 217	Type Con	PT/Exp A	Rand Var -1	
			Consist B	MM 2003	

On surface, step forward makes him a high-floor arm worth targeting... or does it? PRO: Pinpoint control cemented in profile; long history of beating xERA. CON: Fourth quartile batted ball metrics hidden only by friendly hit rate; still doesn't have a true strikeout pitch. Put him at the back of your rotation? Yes. Expect another sub-4.00 ERA? Heck no.

Yr	Tm	W	Sv	IP	K	ERA	WHIP	xERA	xWHIP	vL+	vR+	BF/G	BB%	K%	K-BB%	xBB%	SwK	Vel	G	L	F	H%	S%	HR/F	xHR/F	GS	APC	DOM%	DIS%	Sv%	LI	RAR	BPX	R$
18	aaa	14	0	162	114	3.21	1.22	3.71				25.2	6%	17%	12%							30%	76%									18.7	95	$14
19	PHI *	8	1	137	87	5.00	1.50	5.95	1.41	123	98	17.9	5%	15%	10%	6%	10.0%	89.8	34	31	34	34%	71%	16%	17%	3	40	33%	67%	100	0.57	-8.4	52	-$4
20	PHI	0	0	4	4	17.18	3.27	5.77		254	158	7.3	5%	18%	14%		7.3%	92.4	41	29	29	61%	45%	20%	24%	0	27			0	0.46	-5.8	146	-$13
21	OAK	10	0	178	125	4.24	1.33	4.90	1.30	106	98	24.0	5%	16%	11%	5%	9.6%	90.7	38	24	38	31%	71%	10%	10%	32	84	19%	44%			0.6	79	$2
22	OAK	9	0	181	128	3.98	1.16	4.34	1.23	92	102	24.7	5%	17%	12%	5%	9.8%	90.6	38	20	42	28%	70%	11%	13%	30	87	30%	40%			-0.2	91	$7
1st Half		3	0	83	56	3.35	1.15	4.38	1.26	86	101	24.3	5%	16%	11%	6%	9.5%	90.6	39	21	40	27%	76%	10%	14%	14	88	29%	43%			6.4	81	$6
2nd Half		6	0	98	72	4.52	1.17	4.31	1.20	96	103	25.1	4%	18%	13%	5%	10.1%	90.5	36	20	44	29%	65%	11%	11%	16	86	31%	38%			-6.6	98	$5
Proj		9	0	160	110	4.23	1.27	4.09	1.26	110	102	22.0	5%	17%	12%	5%	9.9%	90.4	37	24	40	30%	71%	11%	13%	30						-5.2	84	$2

Jackson,Zach

Age: 28	Th: R	Role RP	Health C	LIMA Plan A	
Ht: 6' 4"	Wt: 230	Type Pwr/xFB	PT/Exp D	Rand Var -4	
			Consist F	MM 1510	

Top-tier strikeout ability put him in saves mix, but he's got more work to do. PRO: SwK confirms closer-worthy stuff; xBB% gives ugly walk rate some hope. CON: Control a chronic issue in minors; extreme FB% hidden by friendly HR/F. Flyball pitchers with bad control are recipes for disasters, so don't bid anything more than a buck or two.

Yr	Tm	W	Sv	IP	K	ERA	WHIP	xERA	xWHIP	vL+	vR+	BF/G	BB%	K%	K-BB%	xBB%	SwK	Vel	G	L	F	H%	S%	HR/F	xHR/F	GS	APC	DOM%	DIS%	Sv%	LI	RAR	BPX	R$
18	aa	2	2	62	62	3.21	1.44	2.66				6.1	20%	23%	3%							22%	77%									7.2	102	$0
19	aaa	9	1	68	55	5.41	1.57	5.54				6.5	12%	18%	6%							30%	70%									-7.6	30	-$3
20																																		
21	a/a	2	6	30	37	2.54	1.10	2.04				4.8	11%	31%	20%							28%	76%									6.5	146	$2
22	OAK	2	3	48	67	3.00	1.27	4.06	1.41	79	77	3.7	16%	33%	17%	12%	13.1%	94.5	27	19	55	28%	75%	2%	9%	0	16			50	1.20	5.7	71	$1
1st Half		2	1	33	45	3.27	1.33	4.08	1.51	74	79	3.9	18%	33%	14%	12%	12.8%	94.8	32	18	49	28%	73%	0%	7%	0	17			50	1.13	2.8	52	-$2
2nd Half		0	2	15	22	2.40	1.13	4.00	1.23	87	71	3.4	13%	34%	22%	11%	13.6%	94.0	16	19	66	28%	81%	5%	12%	0	15			50	1.32	2.9	112	-$5
Proj		4	2	58	72	4.05	1.37	4.29	1.45	90	84	4.9	15%	30%	14%	12%	13.3%	94.3	22	19	59	30%	69%	3%	10%	0						-0.6	51	-$1

Jameson,Drey

Age: 25	Th: R	Role SP	Health A	LIMA Plan B	
Ht: 6' 0"	Wt: 165	Type Con/GB	PT/Exp D	Rand Var 0	
			Consist B	MM 5101	

3-0, 1.48 ERA in 24 IP at ARI. Former 1st rounder combined whiffs and groundballs in tiny MLB sample after posting near-7 ERA at HR-friendly AAA park. K% potential validated by velocity and multiple strikeout pitches. Scouts question whether he'll stick as a starter given diminutive stature, but this could be a sneaky growth stock. UP: 3.75 ERA

Yr	Tm	W	Sv	IP	K	ERA	WHIP	xERA	xWHIP	vL+	vR+	BF/G	BB%	K%	K-BB%	xBB%	SwK	Vel	G	L	F	H%	S%	HR/F	xHR/F	GS	APC	DOM%	DIS%	Sv%	LI	RAR	BPX	R$
18																																		
19																																		
20																																		
21	aa	3	0	47	56	4.22	1.24	3.75				23.9	9%	29%	20%							32%	69%									0.3	121	-$2
22	ARI *	10	0	159	130	4.79	1.37	4.61	1.19	72	104	22.2	7%	24%	17%	7%	12.2%	95.3	56	23	21	33%	67%	14%	20%	4	92	25%	0%			-16.1	81	-$3
1st Half		4	0	71	66	4.91	1.28	3.85				19.5	9%	22%	13%							30%	62%	0%		0	0					-8.3	90	-$4
2nd Half		6	0	90	64	4.57	1.41	5.01	1.27	72	104	25.3	6%	17%	11%	7%	12.2%	95.3	56	23	21	34%	70%	14%	20%	4	92	25%	0%			-6.7	77	-$3
Proj		6	0	102	85	4.40	1.27	3.19	1.27	90	130	23.7	7%	20%	13%		12.2%	95.3	56	23	21	31%	67%	18%	18%	18						-5.4	110	$0

Jansen,Kenley

Age: 35	Th: R	Role RP	Health B	LIMA Plan C+	
Ht: 6' 5"	Wt: 265	Type Pwr/xFB	PT/Exp A	Rand Var -1	
			Consist A	MM 5530	

As steady as they come at the back-end. His 382 saves since 2012 are 35 more than any other arm. Skills rebound bodes well for more of the same, especially given copy-paste K-BB% in three of past four seasons. Only chink here is deterioration in whiffs during 2nd half, but the sample size was small enough not to get worried for now.

Yr	Tm	W	Sv	IP	K	ERA	WHIP	xERA	xWHIP	vL+	vR+	BF/G	BB%	K%	K-BB%	xBB%	SwK	Vel	G	L	F	H%	S%	HR/F	xHR/F	GS	APC	DOM%	DIS%	Sv%	LI	RAR	BPX	R$
18	LA	1	38	72	82	3.01	0.99	3.62	1.10	78	97	4.2	6%	28%	22%	5%	13.9%	92.3	35	21	44	25%	81%	16%	12%	0	17			90	1.15	10.0	162	$21
19	LA	5	33	63	80	3.71	1.06	3.79	1.11	83	91	4.2	6%	30%	24%	5%	16.3%	92.0	32	24	43	30%	71%	13%	11%	0	17			80	1.24	6.1	168	$19
20	LA	3	11	24	33	3.33	1.15	3.93	1.15	72	94	3.8	9%	32%	24%	6%	15.7%	92.4	25	25	50	32%	73%	7%	7%	0	17			85	1.39	3.4	150	$19
21	LA	4	38	69	86	2.22	1.04	3.93	1.33	76	61	4.0	13%	31%	18%	6%	15.8%	93.9	37	19	44	23%	81%	6%	7%	0	16			88	1.53	17.4	99	$25
22	ATL	5	41	64	85	3.38	1.05	3.55	1.10	100	75	4.0	8%	33%	24%	5%	12.9%	93.7	30	15	55	28%	73%	10%	8%	0	15			85	1.26	4.7	154	$22
1st Half		4	20	33	47	3.58	0.95	2.97	0.95	106	55	4.0	6%	36%	30%	5%	13.9%	93.9	32	19	49	31%	64%	8%	10%	0	16			83	1.24	1.6	202	$20
2nd Half		1	21	31	38	3.16	1.15	4.19	1.25	94	97	4.0	11%	29%	18%	5%	11.9%	93.4	28	11	61	25%	81%	11%	6%	0	15			88	1.29	3.1	104	$16
Proj		4	27	58	74	3.23	1.06	3.18	1.13	90	81	3.9	9%	33%	24%	5%	14.2%	93.1	32	18	50	27%	75%	11%	9%	0						5.3	144	$15

STEPHEN NICKRAND

Javier,Cristian

Age: 26	Th: R	Role SP	Health A	LIMA Plan C+	
Ht: 6' 1"	Wt: 213	Type Pwr/xFB	PT/Exp A	Rand Var -5	
			Consist B	MM 4503	

World Series "co-hero" continues to defy hit-rate norms, and high pop-up rate says he may be at least partially earning that. Superb K% offsets some walk issues, too. He's probably not THIS good, and those who only watch the playoffs will bid him up. But with a regular turn, and if 2nd-half xBB% presages a BB% drop... UP: 190 IP, 17 W

Yr Tm	W	Sv	IP	K	ERA	WHIP	xERA	xWHIP	vL+	vR+	BF/G	BB%	K%	K-BB%	xBB%	SwK	Vel	G	L	F	H%	S%	HR/F	xHR/F	GS	APC	DOM%	DIS%	Sv%	LI	RAR	BPX	R$
18																																	
19 a/a	6	3	85	115	2.47	1.00	1.64				17.1	13%	35%	22%							22%	79%									21.3	144	$14
20 HOU	5	0	54	54	3.48	0.99	4.58	1.28	109	61	17.8	8%	25%	17%	10%	8.9%	92.3	29	19	52	20%	77%	15%	10%	10	74	0%	30%	0	0.70	6.5	99	$17
21 HOU	4	2	101	130	3.55	1.18	4.21	1.32	103	78	11.8	13%	31%	18%	11%	13.6%	93.6	28	24	49	25%	77%	14%	15%	9	50	44%	11%	50	1.01	8.9	95	$7
22 HOU	11	0	149	194	2.54	0.95	3.52	1.10	85	72	19.5	9%	33%	24%	8%	14.2%	93.9	26	17	57	24%	80%	9%	8%	25	85	24%	24%	0	0.73	26.2	144	$25
1st Half	6	0	70	95	2.58	0.96	3.46	1.07	92	62	18.5	9%	34%	26%	10%	14.1%	93.8	24	17	59	27%	76%	6%	7%	11	80	27%	36%	0	0.67	11.9	154	$20
2nd Half	5	0	79	99	2.51	0.94	3.57	1.13	79	81	20.5	9%	32%	23%	6%	14.3%	93.9	28	18	55	22%	84%	12%	8%	14	91	21%	14%	0	0.79	14.3	135	$22
Proj	12	0	160	195	3.14	1.00	3.38	1.19	92	70	21.1	10%	32%	22%	8%	12.8%	93.4	27	19	54	23%	76%	12%	10%	29						16.3	120	$22

Jax,Griffin

Age: 28	Th: R	Role RP	Health A	LIMA Plan A	
Ht: 6' 2"	Wt: 195	Type	PT/Exp C	Rand Var -1	
			Consist F	MM 4311	

Stuff really played up in full transition to relief work, as he threw his terrific slider even more often and let the four-seamer fly. Hey, a 50% spike in strikeout rate while cutting walks? Pretty impressive. A solid LIMA/holds roster filler even if he stays in setup role. But this is a profile that could earn more leverage. UP: 20 saves

Yr Tm	W	Sv	IP	K	ERA	WHIP	xERA	xWHIP	vL+	vR+	BF/G	BB%	K%	K-BB%	xBB%	SwK	Vel	G	L	F	H%	S%	HR/F	xHR/F	GS	APC	DOM%	DIS%	Sv%	LI	RAR	BPX	R$
18																																	
19 a/a	5	0	128	75	4.06	1.40	4.49				23.5	6%	14%	8%							33%	71%									7.0	67	$0
20																																	
21 MIN *	8	0	124	93	5.82	1.41	5.48	1.38	117	115	20.2	9%	18%	9%	8%	9.9%	92.7	32	16	52	29%	63%	17%	17%	14	77	0%	57%	0	0.65	-23.9	31	-$9
22 MIN	7	1	72	78	3.36	1.05	3.30	1.14	85	86	4.5	7%	27%	20%	5%	13.7%	95.5	47	16	37	28%	71%	10%	11%	0	18			14	1.05	5.4	146	$6
1st Half	4	1	39	44	2.75	1.02	3.15	1.12	98	85	5.5	7%	29%	21%	6%	15.3%	95.3	48	14	39	27%	78%	11%	10%	0	22			33	0.95	5.9	154	$6
2nd Half	3	0	33	34	4.09	1.09	3.48	1.16	70	87	3.7	7%	25%	18%	5%	11.9%	95.8	47	18	35	29%	64%	9%	13%	0	14			0	1.12	-0.5	138	-$2
Proj	6	2	65	67	3.32	1.20	3.35	1.18	95	98	4.6	7%	25%	18%	6%	12.5%	95.0	44	16	40	31%	76%	10%	12%	0						5.3	131	$4

Jiménez,Dany

Age: 29	Th: R	Role RP	Health D	LIMA Plan A	
Ht: 6' 1"	Wt: 182	Type Pwr	PT/Exp D	Rand Var -5	
			Consist F	MM 3300	

Older rookie spent two stretches on the IL with shoulder woes. When healthy, he was effectively wild... though at times minus the "effectively" part. Solid SwK and xBB% point to a bit of untapped K-BB upside, but expect hit rate to regress, too, so that's a wash. Key is walk rate: If he can cut it down to match xBB%, we're interested.

Yr Tm	W	Sv	IP	K	ERA	WHIP	xERA	xWHIP	vL+	vR+	BF/G	BB%	K%	K-BB%	xBB%	SwK	Vel	G	L	F	H%	S%	HR/F	xHR/F	GS	APC	DOM%	DIS%	Sv%	LI	RAR	BPX	R$
18																																	
19 aa	2	6	35	37	2.82	1.25	4.04				5.7	10%	26%	16%							28%	86%									7.3	81	$2
20 SF	0	0	1	1	6.75	3.00	17.33		92	86	4.0	38%	13%	-25%		8.1%	93.1	50	0	50	27%	75%	0%	11%	0	19			0	0.22	-0.4	-449	-$8
21 aaa	3	3	46	55	3.24	1.49	4.71				5.1	15%	28%	13%							30%	85%									5.8	77	-$1
22 OAK	3	11	34	34	3.41	1.19	4.47	1.43	92	66	4.3	12%	23%	11%	9%	14.5%	94.0	41	15	44	25%	72%	5%	7%	0	16			79	1.45	2.4	57	$3
1st Half	2	11	25	23	4.38	1.26	4.46	1.42	102	67	4.1	11%	22%	10%	10%	13.1%	94.1	46	13	41	28%	63%	3%	7%	0	16			85	1.33	-1.2	63	$2
2nd Half	1	0	10	11	0.93	1.03	4.48	1.47	68	64	4.9	15%	28%	13%	7%	18.9%	93.7	23	23	55	16%	100%	8%	4%	0	16			0	1.85	3.6	38	-$6
Proj	4	0	58	57	4.15	1.26	3.78	1.41	130	72	4.7	12%	24%	12%	10%	13.1%	94.1	46	13	41	27%	69%	10%	7%	0						-1.3	73	-$1

Jiménez,Joe

Age: 28	Th: R	Role RP	Health B	LIMA Plan A+	
Ht: 6' 3"	Wt: 277	Type Pwr/xFB	PT/Exp C	Rand Var 0	
			Consist C	MM 5510	

With all the "closer of the future" talk long gone, this post-post-post-hype prospect quietly turned in his best season, consolidating the skills he's flashed separately over the years. Only bad 2nd-half H% luck kept it from looking even better. Probably best to leave well enough alone and let him keep setting up. But... look at those skills! UP: 20 Sv

Yr Tm	W	Sv	IP	K	ERA	WHIP	xERA	xWHIP	vL+	vR+	BF/G	BB%	K%	K-BB%	xBB%	SwK	Vel	G	L	F	H%	S%	HR/F	xHR/F	GS	APC	DOM%	DIS%	Sv%	LI	RAR	BPX	R$
18 DET	5	3	63	78	4.31	1.20	3.83	1.17	96	83	3.9	8%	29%	21%	8%	14.1%	95.6	36	19	45	33%	64%	7%	10%	0	17			43	1.08	-1.2	150	$2
19 DET	4	9	60	82	4.37	1.32	4.11	1.19	107	104	3.9	9%	32%	23%	6%	15.2%	95.2	29	22	49	33%	76%	18%	16%	0	16			64	1.08	1.0	148	$4
20 DET	1	5	23	22	7.15	1.37	4.69	1.23	143	115	4.0	6%	22%	16%	6%	13.1%	94.3	31	26	43	30%	54%	24%	17%	0	16			83	0.92	-7.5	115	-$2
21 DET	6	1	45	57	5.96	1.52	5.26	1.59	106	99	4.0	17%	27%	10%	10%	14.3%	94.7	34	13	53	28%	62%	10%	11%	0	17			50	0.61	-9.5	31	-$5
22 DET	3	2	57	77	3.49	1.09	3.12	0.98	98	78	3.7	6%	33%	28%	5%	15.0%	95.8	33	22	45	35%	69%	6%	9%	0	15			50	0.72	3.3	193	$3
1st Half	3	1	31	40	3.16	0.99	3.24	1.00	90	77	3.8	6%	32%	26%	5%	14.3%	95.7	34	18	47	30%	71%	8%	9%	0	16			100	0.42	3.1	182	$2
2nd Half	0	1	25	37	3.91	1.22	2.98	0.96	107	79	3.7	6%	35%	29%	4%	16.0%	95.9	32	27	41	41%	67%	4%	10%	0	14			33	1.06	0.2	208	-$6
Proj	4	3	58	78	3.91	1.24	3.17	1.12	104	88	3.7	9%	33%	24%	6%	15.0%	95.5	32	21	47	34%	72%	10%	12%	0						0.4	155	$1

Junis,Jakob

Age: 30	Th: R	Role SP	Health D	LIMA Plan B	
Ht: 6' 3"	Wt: 220	Type	PT/Exp C	Rand Var 0	
			Consist D	MM 3203	

"Quiet quit" his fastball, actually throwing more than 50% sliders. (Aside: Does the catcher put down a 1 for slider now?) And voila, the HR woes vanished. Hit rate torpedoed 2nd half, and that's always a concern for a low-SwK hurler. But xERA shows this new path forward is working. He's back on our radar. UP: 10 wins, sub-4.00 ERA

Yr Tm	W	Sv	IP	K	ERA	WHIP	xERA	xWHIP	vL+	vR+	BF/G	BB%	K%	K-BB%	xBB%	SwK	Vel	G	L	F	H%	S%	HR/F	xHR/F	GS	APC	DOM%	DIS%	Sv%	LI	RAR	BPX	R$
18 KC	9	0	177	164	4.37	1.27	4.06	1.21	107	106	25.3	6%	22%	16%	7%	10.0%	91.1	42	21	37	31%	72%	16%	16%	30	95	23%	30%			-4.9	128	$4
19 KC	9	0	175	164	5.24	1.43	4.65	1.33	110	104	24.9	8%	21%	14%	8%	10.0%	91.5	42	23	35	33%	68%	17%	19%	31	94	23%	29%			-15.8	99	-$3
20 KC	0	0	25	19	6.39	1.62	4.88	1.29	141	114	14.3	5%	17%	11%	6%	9.4%	91.0	45	23	32	35%	68%	25%	21%	6	49	0%	83%	0	0.79	-6.1	98	-$12
21 KC *	2	0	59	54	5.61	1.55	6.16	1.21	117	95	11.6	8%	21%	13%	7%	11.0%	90.9	42	22	37	35%	68%	17%	20%	6	39	33%	33%	0	0.60	-9.7	53	-$9
22 SF	5	0	112	98	4.42	1.29	3.87	1.19	122	94	20.8	5%	21%	15%	6%	9.7%	91.9	43	24	33	33%	68%	11%	13%	17	78	12%	35%	0	0.67	-6.2	120	-$2
1st Half	4	0	48	40	2.63	0.96	3.54	1.18	91	81	20.8	5%	21%	16%	7%	9.7%	91.4	48	18	35	24%	80%	13%	15%	7	79	0%	29%	0	0.68	8.0	122	$7
2nd Half	1	0	64	58	5.77	1.55	4.10	1.19	138	104	20.8	5%	20%	15%	6%	9.6%	92.2	40	27	33	39%	63%	10%	11%	10	78	20%	40%	0	0.65	-14.2	119	-$16
Proj	6	0	131	118	4.35	1.37	3.68	1.23	120	99	20.4	7%	22%	15%	7%	10.0%	91.6	43	23	35	33%	73%	14%	16%	27						-6.1	111	-$2

Kahnle,Tommy

Age: 33	Th: R	Role RP	Health F	LIMA Plan B	
Ht: 6' 1"	Wt: 230	Type Pwr	PT/Exp F	Rand Var -1	
			Consist F	MM 5500	

Between recovering from Tommy John surgery and a subsequent forearm strain, missed most of yet another season. Encouragingly, he looked terrific in Sept/Oct after rehabbing the forearm. Of course, expectations should be kept low given injury history and all that missed time. But also keep in mind that, in "the before times," he was a rising star.

Yr Tm	W	Sv	IP	K	ERA	WHIP	xERA	xWHIP	vL+	vR+	BF/G	BB%	K%	K-BB%	xBB%	SwK	Vel	G	L	F	H%	S%	HR/F	xHR/F	GS	APC	DOM%	DIS%	Sv%	LI	RAR	BPX	R$
18 NYY *	4	2	50	58	6.00	1.66	5.41	1.44	90	133	4.5	13%	26%	14%	9%	15.1%	95.1	35	24	40	37%	65%	12%	13%	0	20			67	0.79	-11.3	84	-$7
19 NYY	3	0	61	88	3.67	1.06	2.83	1.07	89	79	3.4	8%	35%	27%	7%	18.2%	96.5	50	21	28	30%	71%	23%	18%	0	14			0	1.03	6.3	197	$4
20 NYY	0	0	1	3	0.00	2.00	0.00		207	33	6.0	17%	50%	33%		30.0%	97.6	100	0	0	122%	100%	0%		0	20			0	1.86	0.5	363	-$6
21																																	
22 LA	0	1	13	14	2.84	0.63	2.17	1.05	90	44	3.5	7%	30%	24%	5%	17.2%	95.7	68	4	28	12%	67%	29%	17%	0	13			100	0.88	1.8	185	-$3
1st Half	0	0	4	5	6.75	1.25	3.13		172	47	4.0	13%	31%	19%	11%	18.0%	95.4	43	14	43	14%	67%	67%	25%	0	13			0	0.70	-1.4	112	-$11
2nd Half	0	1	9	9	1.04	0.35	1.77	0.93	27	43	3.3	3%	30%	27%	4%	16.9%	96.1	78	0	22	11%	67%	0%	11%	0	14			100	0.95	3.1	216	-$5
Proj	4	0	58	77	3.36	1.11	2.43	1.07	107	91	3.6	8%	34%	26%	7%	18.2%	96.5	50	21	28	30%	76%	23%	16%	0						4.4	183	$3

Kaprielian,James

Age: 29	Th: R	Role SP	Health C	LIMA Plan C+	
Ht: 6' 3"	Wt: 225	Type Con/FB	PT/Exp A	Rand Var -2	
			Consist C	MM 1103	

Missed April with a sore shoulder, then got regular work in depleted OAK rotation. Some will see that shiny 2nd-half ERA and think he's turned a corner. You'll see that he got very lucky in the 2nd-half HR department, that his K-BB% is among the worst in MLB, and that his xERA paints a very different picture. DN: 5.00+ ERA

Yr Tm	W	Sv	IP	K	ERA	WHIP	xERA	xWHIP	vL+	vR+	BF/G	BB%	K%	K-BB%	xBB%	SwK	Vel	G	L	F	H%	S%	HR/F	xHR/F	GS	APC	DOM%	DIS%	Sv%	LI	RAR	BPX	R$
18																																	
19 a/a	2	0	33	26	2.03	1.11	2.86				16.3	6%	20%	14%							28%	85%									10.2	108	$1
20 OAK	0	0	4	4	7.36	1.64	6.11		207	63	8.5	12%	24%	12%		15.5%	95.0	36	0	64	24%	75%	29%	31%	0	36			0	0.44	-1.3	66	-$8
21 OAK	8	0	119	123	4.07	1.22	4.48	1.26	119	80	20.9	8%	25%	16%	8%	11.6%	93.0	35	18	47	29%	72%	12%	14%	21	84	14%	33%	0	0.72	2.8	106	$5
22 OAK	5	0	134	98	4.23	1.34	5.02	1.47	100	109	22.2	10%	17%	7%	8%	9.8%	94.1	38	19	44	27%	71%	9%	10%	26	86	8%	42%			-4.3	30	-$3
1st Half	1	0	58	40	5.43	1.38	5.13	1.51	116	108	20.9	11%	16%	5%	8%	10.0%	93.8	41	17	43	25%	65%	14%	11%	12	81	0%	50%			-10.5	19	-$13
2nd Half	4	0	76	58	3.32	1.32	4.94	1.43	87	109	23.3	10%	18%	8%	8%	9.7%	94.3	36	20	44	29%	76%	5%	9%	14	90	14%	36%			6.1	38	$3
Proj	5	0	145	115	4.47	1.34	4.31	1.39	110	109	21.6	9%	19%	10%	8%	10.2%	93.9	37	19	44	29%	69%	10%	10%	28						-9.0	57	-$3

ROD TRUESDELL

Karinchak,James

Age: 27	Th: R	Role RP	Health F	LIMA Plan A+	
Ht: 6' 3"	Wt: 215	Type Pwr/xFB	PT/Exp C	Rand Var -5	
			Consist B	MM 5511	

Strained shoulder wiped away 1st half. Skills and velocity both returned when healthy, though elite 2nd-half ERA was driven by concurrent aid from both hit and HR/F rates. Talent will keep him in late-game mix if he can stay healthy, so he'll remain a good target in holds leagues and a premium one for those looking for LIMA relievers.

Yr Tm	W	Sv	IP	K	ERA	WHIP	xERA	xWHIP	vL+	vR+	BF/G	BB%	K%	K-BB%	xBB%	SwK	Vel	G	L	F	H%	S%	HR/F	xHR/F	GS	APC	DOM%	DIS%	Sv%	LI	RAR	BPX	R$
18																																	
19 CLE *	1	8	33	63	3.64	1.22	2.69		23	85	4.2	13%	47%	33%		16.0%	97.1	38	31	31	39%	71%	0%	9%	0	19			100	0.09	3.6	185	$3
20 CLE	1	1	27	53	2.67	1.11	2.70	1.09	81	59	4.0	15%	49%	34%	9%	17.9%	95.5	23	31	46	36%	76%	6%	7%	0	17			25	1.01	6.0	198	$7
21 CLE	7	11	55	78	4.07	1.21	3.76	1.31	79	98	3.9	14%	33%	20%	11%	13.5%	95.9	39	20	40	25%	72%	18%	13%	0	17			69	1.43	1.4	115	$7
22 CLE	2	3	39	62	2.08	1.10	3.25	1.17	66	80	4.2	13%	39%	26%	12%	12.9%	95.2	25	24	51	29%	83%	5%	7%	0	19			75	0.85	9.1	143	$3
1st Half	0	0	1	3	9.00	3.00	0.00			280	6.0	17%	50%	33%		14.3%	95.1	50	50	0	110%	67%	0%		0	28			0	1.69	-0.6	299	-$12
2nd Half	2	3	38	59	1.89	1.05	3.29	1.17	69	73	4.2	13%	38%	25%	12%	12.9%	95.2	24	23	53	27%	84%	5%	7%	0	18			75	0.83	9.7	139	$8
Proj	**4**	**6**	**65**	**98**	**2.83**	**1.08**	**2.96**	**1.20**	**71**	**81**	**4.1**	**13%**	**38%**	**25%**		**13.1%**	**95.5**	**30**	**22**	**48**	**26%**	**77%**	**10%**	**9%**	**0**						**9.2**	**138**	**$9**

Keller,Brad

Age: 27	Th: R	Role RP	Health C	LIMA Plan C+	
Ht: 6' 5"	Wt: 255	Type /GB	PT/Exp A	Rand Var 0	
			Consist A	MM 2100	

After another year of flopping as a starter, was moved to the bullpen in August and somehow looked worse. His one good skill is keeping the ball on the ground, but with consistently marginal command and no signs of hope from xBB% or SwK, there's nothing to suggest he'll help you—unless he's on a leaguemate's roster.

Yr Tm	W	Sv	IP	K	ERA	WHIP	xERA	xWHIP	vL+	vR+	BF/G	BB%	K%	K-BB%	xBB%	SwK	Vel	G	L	F	H%	S%	HR/F	xHR/F	GS	APC	DOM%	DIS%	Sv%	LI	RAR	BPX	R$
18 KC	9	0	140	96	3.08	1.30	4.24	1.42	100	82	14.2	9%	16%	8%	9%	9.3%	93.9	54	19	27	30%	77%	6%	9%	20	54	30%	25%	0	0.97	18.5	65	$8
19 KC	7	0	165	122	4.19	1.35	4.92	1.51	95	94	25.3	10%	17%	7%	9%	8.6%	93.4	50	21	29	29%	70%	10%	14%	28	97	21%	36%			6.4	49	$3
20 KC	5	0	55	35	2.47	1.02	4.26	1.41	79	56	23.9	8%	16%	8%	8%	8.6%	92.8	53	23	25	24%	76%	5%	11%	9	95	44%	22%			13.4	67	$19
21 KC	8	0	134	120	5.39	1.66	4.74	1.44	115	110	23.6	10%	20%	9%	10%	9.5%	93.9	48	23	29	35%	70%	15%	22%	26	90	23%	54%			-18.5	60	-$13
22 KC	6	1	140	102	5.09	1.50	4.46	1.43	106	112	17.6	9%	17%	7%	9%	10.1%	94.1	52	18	30	32%	68%	13%	14%	22	65	14%	55%	100	0.63	-19.3	54	-$10
1st Half	3	0	85	56	4.02	1.32	4.34	1.38	107	96	23.9	8%	16%	8%	9%	8.7%	93.6	50	20	30	29%	73%	12%	12%	15	88	13%	47%			-0.6	60	-$3
2nd Half	3	1	55	46	6.75	1.79	4.65	1.49	104	135	12.9	11%	18%	7%	8%	12.1%	94.8	55	16	29	36%	63%	13%	17%	7	48	14%	71%	100	0.53	-18.8	45	-$19
Proj	**3**	**0**	**58**	**44**	**4.70**	**1.46**	**4.06**	**1.44**	**100**	**104**	**13.2**	**10%**	**18%**	**8%**	**9%**	**9.9%**	**93.8**	**52**	**20**	**28**	**31%**	**69%**	**12%**	**15%**	**6**						**-5.3**	**56**	**-$5**

Keller,Mitch

Age: 27	Th: R	Role SP	Health B	LIMA Plan B	
Ht: 6' 2"	Wt: 220	Type Pwr	PT/Exp B	Rand Var -1	
			Consist C	MM 3205	

Finally stuck in majors for first full season and results were a mixed bag. But there's some legit reason for hope if you haven't completely lost patience... 1) Added sinker to profile; 2) Bumped up whiffs in 2nd half; 3) Had four 100+ BPV weeks from late August on. There could be a next step, but it's more likely to be league average than a full breakout.

Yr Tm	W	Sv	IP	K	ERA	WHIP	xERA	xWHIP	vL+	vR+	BF/G	BB%	K%	K-BB%	xBB%	SwK	Vel	G	L	F	H%	S%	HR/F	xHR/F	GS	APC	DOM%	DIS%	Sv%	LI	RAR	BPX	R$
18 a/a	12	0	139	111	4.10	1.38	4.02				24.3	9%	19%	10%							31%	71%									0.8	81	$3
19 PIT *	8	0	153	166	5.24	1.53	5.13	1.17	130	121	22.2	8%	25%	17%	6%	12.4%	95.4	39	29	32	38%	66%	13%	10%	11	85	9%	27%			-13.8	102	-$5
20 PIT	1	0	22	16	2.91	1.25	6.24	2.02	112	61	17.4	21%	18%	-2%	12%	7.8%	94.0	44	8	48	10%	87%	16%	19%	5	77	20%	40%			4.1	-68	-$1
21 PIT *	6	0	129	123	5.59	1.74	5.92	1.45	124	114	18.9	11%	21%	10%	9%	8.9%	93.9	40	26	34	38%	68%	9%	11%	23	81	4%	48%			-21.0	68	-$17
22 PIT	5	0	159	138	3.91	1.40	3.93	1.34	107	100	22.2	9%	20%	11%	8%	9.1%	95.1	49	22	29	32%	74%	10%	11%	29	86	21%	41%	0	0.77	1.2	84	-$1
1st Half	2	0	70	59	5.14	1.53	4.31	1.41	106	110	20.8	10%	19%	9%	10%	8.6%	95.7	51	18	31	34%	66%	9%	11%	13	83	15%	54%	0	0.77	-10.1	64	-$14
2nd Half	3	0	89	79	2.93	1.29	3.64	1.28	108	92	23.4	8%	21%	13%	8%	9.5%	94.6	47	26	27	31%	80%	12%	11%	16	89	25%	31%			11.4	99	$8
Proj	**8**	**0**	**174**	**162**	**4.00**	**1.30**	**3.61**	**1.33**	**98**	**90**	**20.7**	**9%**	**23%**	**13%**	**8%**	**10.0%**	**95.0**	**45**	**25**	**30**	**30%**	**71%**	**11%**	**11%**	**35**						**-0.6**	**89**	**$4**

Kelly,Joe

Age: 35	Th: R	Role RP	Health F	LIMA Plan B	
Ht: 6' 1"	Wt: 174	Type Pwr/xGB	PT/Exp C	Rand Var +5	
			Consist B	MM 5510	

Biceps, hammy, knee all contributed to more time on shelf. When he pitched, most wished he was back on shelf. But very unfavorable hit and strand rates were the drivers. With extreme groundball tilt and elite skills in 2nd half, he's an excellent rebound candidate; xERA trend agrees. If he can somehow stay healthy... UP: 20 Sv

Yr Tm	W	Sv	IP	K	ERA	WHIP	xERA	xWHIP	vL+	vR+	BF/G	BB%	K%	K-BB%	xBB%	SwK	Vel	G	L	F	H%	S%	HR/F	xHR/F	GS	APC	DOM%	DIS%	Sv%	LI	RAR	BPX	R$
18 BOS	4	2	66	68	4.39	1.36	3.96	1.39	83	98	3.9	11%	24%	13%	10%	10.8%	98.1	47	25	28	31%	67%	8%	9%	0	16			29	1.05	-1.9	86	-$1
19 LA	5	1	51	62	4.56	1.38	3.28	1.28	98	91	4.1	10%	27%	18%	8%	10.4%	98.0	61	22	17	34%	69%	25%	24%	0	16			17	0.87	-0.3	142	-$1
20 LA	0	0	10	9	1.80	1.50	4.59	1.69	81	98	3.5	17%	21%	5%	12%	10.5%	97.0	58	23	19	29%	87%	0%	5%	1	14	0%	100%	0	0.53	3.3	13	-$5
21 LA	2	2	44	50	2.86	0.98	3.02	1.19	77	71	3.8	8%	27%	19%	8%	11.7%	97.7	59	20	21	25%	73%	13%	15%	0	15			67	0.95	7.6	152	$3
22 CHW	1	1	37	53	6.08	1.59	2.94	1.33	98	106	4.0	14%	31%	18%	10%	13.5%	97.9	64	13	22	40%	60%	10%	13%	1	16	0%	100%	100	0.94	-9.6	136	-$8
1st Half	0	1	12	17	9.49	2.27	4.08	1.59	135	120	4.6	17%	27%	9%	11%	10.0%	97.7	67	11	22	47%	56%	13%	18%	0	18			100	1.17	-8.4	57	-$17
2nd Half	1	0	25	36	4.38	1.26	2.45	1.18	74	98	3.7	11%	34%	23%	9%	15.5%	98.0	63	15	22	35%	63%	8%	9%	1	16	0%	100%	0	0.83	-1.2	176	-$6
Proj	**3**	**2**	**51**	**63**	**3.32**	**1.23**	**2.72**	**1.24**	**82**	**90**	**3.6**	**11%**	**30%**	**20%**	**8%**	**12.7%**	**97.9**	**58**	**20**	**23**	**31%**	**74%**	**12%**	**13%**	**0**						**4.1**	**141**	**$1**

Kelly,Merrill

Age: 34	Th: R	Role SP	Health D	LIMA Plan B	
Ht: 6' 2"	Wt: 202	Type Con	PT/Exp A	Rand Var -1	
			Consist A	MM 3205	

It's funny how much the ebbs and flows of hit and strand rates can make a marginal pitcher look good. Breakout season was entirely driven by handful of favorable points of H% and S%. If he were 10 years younger, that 2nd half might give us hope for a repeat. As it stands, uninspiring skills tell us to expect his ERA to head back towards 4.00.

Yr Tm	W	Sv	IP	K	ERA	WHIP	xERA	xWHIP	vL+	vR+	BF/G	BB%	K%	K-BB%	xBB%	SwK	Vel	G	L	F	H%	S%	HR/F	xHR/F	GS	APC	DOM%	DIS%	Sv%	LI	RAR	BPX	R$
18 for	12	0	158	161	4.10	1.26	3.95				23.0	7%	25%	18%							32%	70%									0.9	116	$8
19 ARI	13	0	183	158	4.42	1.31	4.69	1.34	101	101	24.3	7%	20%	13%	8%	10.1%	91.9	42	22	36	30%	71%	15%	20%	32	93	22%	41%			2.0	92	$7
20 ARI	3	0	31	29	2.59	0.99	3.91	1.13	73	99	25.0	4%	23%	19%	7%	10.1%	92.1	46	18	37	26%	85%	15%	16%	5	95	40%	40%			7.2	153	$9
21 ARI	7	0	158	130	4.44	1.29	4.36	1.26	90	111	24.7	6%	19%	13%	6%	9.5%	91.8	44	22	34	31%	69%	13%	13%	27	90	22%	26%			-3.5	101	$1
22 ARI	13	0	200	177	3.37	1.14	3.88	1.25	103	85	24.4	8%	22%	14%	7%	10.4%	92.7	43	19	38	27%	74%	10%	11%	33	93	39%	27%			14.8	99	$17
1st Half	7	0	91	74	3.46	1.26	4.09	1.33	98	92	23.6	8%	20%	11%	6%	9.4%	92.7	46	20	34	30%	73%	7%	8%	16	90	25%	38%			5.7	80	$9
2nd Half	6	0	109	103	3.29	1.03	3.71	1.19	107	77	25.1	7%	24%	17%	7%	11.3%	92.6	40	18	42	25%	74%	13%	14%	17	96	53%	18%			9.1	115	$21
Proj	**10**	**0**	**181**	**161**	**3.81**	**1.20**	**3.58**	**1.23**	**98**	**98**	**24.3**	**7%**	**22%**	**15%**	**7%**	**10.2%**	**92.3**	**43**	**20**	**37**	**30%**	**73%**	**12%**	**14%**	**30**						**3.6**	**111**	**$10**

Kennedy,Ian

Age: 38	Th: R	Role RP	Health D	LIMA Plan B	
Ht: 6' 0"	Wt: 210	Type Pwr/xFB	PT/Exp B	Rand Var 0	
			Consist C	MM 2300	

Worst skills since rookie year removed him from high-leverage work as season went along. Plummeting SwK the product of completely ineffective curveball, which resulted in ZERO strikeouts (compared to a 40% K% in 2021). As a flyball pitcher, his risk to you soars if full arsenal isn't working. As he nears 40, we can't expect it to come back.

Yr Tm	W	Sv	IP	K	ERA	WHIP	xERA	xWHIP	vL+	vR+	BF/G	BB%	K%	K-BB%	xBB%	SwK	Vel	G	L	F	H%	S%	HR/F	xHR/F	GS	APC	DOM%	DIS%	Sv%	LI	RAR	BPX	R$
18 KC	3	0	120	105	4.66	1.38	4.82	1.32	103	113	23.5	8%	20%	13%	7%	8.7%	91.9	30	26	44	31%	71%	13%	15%	22	94	14%	45%			-7.6	79	-$4
19 KC	3	30	63	73	3.41	1.28	3.88	1.17	85	95	4.2	6%	27%	21%	6%	11.0%	94.5	44	18	37	35%	76%	9%	13%	0	17			88	0.88	8.6	156	$15
20 KC	0	0	14	15	9.00	1.79	5.44	1.29	146	145	4.6	7%	22%	14%	5%	10.7%	93.6	38	15	47	35%	61%	32%	24%	1	17	0%	0%	0	0.86	-7.9	116	-$13
21 2 TM	3	26	56	62	3.20	1.10	4.36	1.18	106	86	4.1	7%	27%	20%	5%	13.8%	94.1	23	23	54	25%	84%	15%	13%	0	16			87	1.38	7.4	116	$14
22 ARI	4	10	50	44	5.36	1.57	5.33	1.39	115	123	4.1	10%	19%	10%	7%	9.1%	93.4	24	27	48	32%	72%	14%	12%	0	15			63	1.25	-8.7	41	-$3
1st Half	3	4	28	25	3.58	1.52	5.25	1.41	72	131	3.9	10%	20%	10%	6%	10.1%	93.4	21	30	49	32%	82%	10%	10%	0	15			67	1.49	1.3	34	-$3
2nd Half	1	6	23	19	7.54	1.63	5.42	1.37	171	114	4.3	8%	18%	9%	8%	7.9%	93.3	28	24	47	32%	60%	19%	15%	0	16			60	0.95	-10.0	50	-$10
Proj	**2**	**0**	**44**	**42**	**4.78**	**1.42**	**4.12**	**1.29**	**111**	**108**	**4.3**	**8%**	**23%**	**15%**	**6%**	**10.1%**	**93.6**	**30**	**24**	**46**	**32%**	**72%**	**15%**	**13%**	**0**						**-4.3**	**86**	**-$5**

Kershaw,Clayton

Age: 35	Th: L	Role SP	Health F	LIMA Plan C+	
Ht: 6' 4"	Wt: 225	Type	PT/Exp A	Rand Var -3	
			Consist A	MM 5401	

Turn-back-the-clock season reminds us that he's still a rotation anchor, as xERA dipped below 3.00 for first time since 2016. Superb skills foundation supports more of the same, too. Trouble is, chronic back woes aren't likely to go away, which means his former $30+ returns need to come at a ~40% discount in order to get your money back.

Yr Tm	W	Sv	IP	K	ERA	WHIP	xERA	xWHIP	vL+	vR+	BF/G	BB%	K%	K-BB%	xBB%	SwK	Vel	G	L	F	H%	S%	HR/F	xHR/F	GS	APC	DOM%	DIS%	Sv%	LI	RAR	BPX	R$
18 LA	9	0	161	155	2.73	1.04	3.36	1.12	93	86	25.0	4%	24%	19%	5%	11.5%	90.9	48	23	30	29%	79%	13%	12%	26	91	35%	8%			28.2	159	$21
19 LA	16	0	178	189	3.03	1.04	3.55	1.15	84	90	24.3	6%	27%	21%	6%	13.7%	90.4	48	19	33	27%	80%	19%	16%	28	92	50%	14%	0	0.77	32.5	154	$27
20 LA	6	0	58	62	2.16	0.84	3.07	1.02	87	77	22.1	4%	28%	24%	5%	13.0%	91.6	53	16	31	24%	85%	17%	19%	10	89	60%	10%			16.5	192	$30
21 LA	10	0	122	144	3.55	1.02	3.06	1.01	61	95	22.2	4%	30%	25%	6%	17.1%	90.7	49	18	33	31%	70%	15%	16%	22	82	50%	23%			10.7	194	$15
22 LA	12	0	126	137	2.28	0.94	2.99	1.04	88	76	22.4	5%	28%	23%	5%	14.4%	90.8	47	19	33	28%	80%	9%	7%	22	84	27%	9%			26.3	172	$22
1st Half	5	0	56	59	2.57	1.05	3.21	1.09	111	79	22.2	5%	27%	21%	6%	13.7%	90.7	47	17	35	30%	80%	9%	6%	10	82	30%	20%			9.7	159	$11
2nd Half	7	0	70	78	2.05	0.85	2.81	1.00	66	74	22.6	4%	29%	25%	5%	15.0%	90.9	47	21	32	27%	80%	9%	7%	12	86	25%	0%			16.7	184	$25
Proj	**11**	**0**	**116**	**126**	**2.92**	**1.03**	**2.75**	**1.04**	**88**	**87**	**22.3**	**5%**	**28%**	**24%**	**5%**	**14.3%**	**90.9**	**49**	**19**	**33**	**30%**	**76%**	**13%**	**12%**	**20**						**15.0**	**176**	**$15**

STEPHEN NICKRAND

Kikuchi,Yusei

Age: 32	Th: L	Role SP	Health C	LIMA Plan B
Ht: 6' 0"	Wt: 200	Type Pwr	PT/Exp A	Rand Var +5
			Consist A	MM 4401

PRO: Spike in K's and SwK; consistent xERAs/xBB% say he should be better. CON: Again allowed a ton of HR and BB, which conspired to balloon ERA; righties smacked him around; sent to the bullpen for most of the last two months. The stronger the skills/stats disconnect remains, the deeper into the draft you can go with a reserve round speculation.

Yr Tm	W	Sv	IP	K	ERA	WHIP	xERA	xWHIP	vL+	vR+	BF/G	BB%	K%	K-BB%	xBB%	SwK	Vel	G	L	F	H%	S%	HR/F	xHR/F	GS	APC	DOM%	DIS%	Sv%	LI	RAR	BPX	R$
18																																	
19 SEA	6	0	162	116	5.46	1.52	5.30	1.41	108	121	22.5	7%	16%	9%	8%	8.9%	92.5	44	21	35	32%	70%	19%	16%	32	85	16%	50%			-18.9	69	-$9
20 SEA	2	0	47	47	5.17	1.30	3.93	1.35	91	92	21.6	10%	24%	14%	9%	12.8%	95.0	52	23	25	31%	59%	9%	8%	9	88	11%	22%			-4.2	100	-$2
21 SEA	7	0	157	163	4.41	1.32	3.92	1.30	66	110	23.0	9%	24%	15%	7%	12.7%	95.2	48	21	30	30%	72%	21%	21%	29	88	24%	28%			-2.9	108	$2
22 TOR	6	1	101	124	5.19	1.50	3.96	1.37	91	127	14.2	13%	27%	15%	9%	13.8%	95.0	44	19	37	30%	73%	24%	21%	20	58	5%	35%	100	0.66	-15.1	90	-$6
1st Half	3	0	65	74	5.12	1.57	4.29	1.47	84	129	18.4	14%	25%	11%	9%	12.7%	94.9	45	18	37	30%	74%	22%	22%	16	76	0%	31%			-9.3	60	-$11
2nd Half	3	1	36	50	5.30	1.37	3.40	1.21	100	122	9.9	11%	31%	21%	9%	16.0%	95.1	42	21	37	31%	70%	27%	20%	4	40	25%	50%	100	0.55	-5.9	144	-$5
Proj	**6**	**0**	**116**	**131**	**4.49**	**1.40**	**3.50**	**1.32**	**91**	**115**	**21.9**	**11%**	**27%**	**16%**	**8%**	**13.4%**	**94.8**	**46**	**21**	**33**	**31%**	**74%**	**21%**	**17%**	**22**						**-7.5**	**103**	**-$2**

Kimbrel,Craig

Age: 35	Th: R	Role RP	Health B	LIMA Plan A
Ht: 6' 0"	Wt: 215	Type Pwr/xFB	PT/Exp A	Rand Var -2
			Consist B	MM 4520

Two odd halves, thanks to whims of hit rate. Actually was pretty good early, despite ERA. But then K and SwK rate tanked, he threw his curve less, and both it and his fastball were less effective, all of which hints at a hidden 2nd-half injury. Watch that K rate: If it stays around 2nd-half levels, we're looking at... DN: 4.00+ ERA, < 10 Sv

Yr Tm	W	Sv	IP	K	ERA	WHIP	xERA	xWHIP	vL+	vR+	BF/G	BB%	K%	K-BB%	xBB%	SwK	Vel	G	L	F	H%	S%	HR/F	xHR/F	GS	APC	DOM%	DIS%	Sv%	LI	RAR	BPX	R$
18 BOS	5	42	62	96	2.74	0.99	3.16	1.17	86	71	3.9	13%	39%	26%	9%	17.6%	97.1	28	25	47	23%	78%	13%	10%	0	18			89	1.39	10.8	155	$25
19 CHC	0	13	21	30	6.53	1.60	4.62	1.35	114	159	4.2	13%	31%	19%	10%	14.8%	96.2	30	20	50	30%	75%	36%	26%	0	17			81	1.29	-5.2	111	-$1
20 CHC	0	2	15	28	5.28	1.43	3.60	1.34	121	65	3.8	17%	41%	23%	11%	13.3%	96.9	33	22	44	34%	65%	17%	21%	0	17			67	0.65	-1.6	132	-$3
21 2 TM	4	24	60	100	2.26	0.91	2.80	0.99	70	69	3.7	10%	43%	33%	8%	19.0%	96.5	30	22	48	27%	81%	12%	8%	0	16			83	1.53	14.7	204	$20
22 LA	6	22	60	72	3.75	1.32	3.91	1.28	112	81	4.1	11%	28%	17%	9%	12.6%	95.8	40	15	45	33%	72%	6%	10%	0	17			81	0.84	1.6	109	$10
1st Half	1	14	26	41	4.78	1.52	3.27	1.13	137	66	4.3	10%	34%	24%	8%	13.9%	96.1	43	15	42	45%	67%	4%	8%	0	18			82	0.76	-2.7	179	$3
2nd Half	5	8	34	31	2.94	1.16	4.43	1.42	85	92	4.0	11%	22%	11%	9%	11.6%	95.6	37	15	48	24%	78%	7%	12%	0	17			80	0.90	4.3	54	$10
Proj	**5**	**24**	**58**	**70**	**3.56**	**1.17**	**3.48**	**1.28**	**101**	**77**	**3.8**	**12%**	**30%**	**19%**	**9%**	**14.8%**	**96.3**	**35**	**19**	**46**	**27%**	**72%**	**9%**	**10%**	**0**						**2.9**	**107**	**$13**

King,John

Age: 28	Th: L	Role RP	Health D	LIMA Plan B
Ht: 6' 2"	Wt: 215	Type Con/xGB	PT/Exp D	Rand Var 0
			Consist D	MM 5100

1-4, 4.03 ERA in 51 IP at TEX. Obscured here is that he started and finished the season rather well; in between, not so much. That slump was likely due to a sore shoulder that finally sent him to the IL in July. When he's right, and thus missing at least a few bats, the groundball tilt is effective. A Magic Wall behind his infielders wouldn't hurt, either.

Yr Tm	W	Sv	IP	K	ERA	WHIP	xERA	xWHIP	vL+	vR+	BF/G	BB%	K%	K-BB%	xBB%	SwK	Vel	G	L	F	H%	S%	HR/F	xHR/F	GS	APC	DOM%	DIS%	Sv%	LI	RAR	BPX	R$
18																																	
19																																	
20 TEX	1	0	10	9	6.10	1.65	4.75	1.37	108	115	8.5	8%	18%	10%	8%	8.6%	93.1	56	19	25	35%	67%	22%	16%	0	31			0	0.66	-2.1	92	-$7
21 TEX	7	0	46	40	3.52	1.15	3.45	1.23	56	98	7.1	6%	21%	15%	6%	12.4%	92.3	57	24	19	30%	70%	12%	13%	0	26			0	1.02	4.2	123	$2
22 TEX *	3	0	69	44	4.73	1.49	5.44	1.36	90	113	5.6	6%	14%	7%	6%	9.3%	92.4	65	19	17	33%	71%	17%	16%	0	19			0	0.82	-6.5	42	-$8
1st Half	1	0	31	22	4.60	1.63	4.25	1.44	84	123	5.0	9%	15%	6%	8%	10.7%	92.4	61	17	22	34%	74%	17%	15%	0	17			0	0.86	-2.4	58	-$13
2nd Half	2	0	38	22	4.84	1.38	5.14	1.30	102	94	6.7	5%	14%	9%	5%	6.6%	92.4	70	22	9	31%	68%	17%	17%	0	24			0	0.73	-4.1	53	-$9
Proj	**3**	**0**	**51**	**38**	**4.31**	**1.34**	**3.15**	**1.29**	**92**	**109**	**6.1**	**7%**	**18%**	**11%**	**6%**	**9.4%**	**92.4**	**64**	**21**	**15**	**32%**	**70%**	**25%**	**15%**	**0**						**-2.2**	**106**	**-$4**

King,Michael

Age: 28	Th: R	Role RP	Health F	LIMA Plan A
Ht: 6' 3"	Wt: 210	Type Pwr	PT/Exp C	Rand Var -3
			Consist C	MM 5410

Fractured his elbow in July while throwing a pitch (ouch). Before that, big step up in whiff rate had propelled him into a prominent bullpen role. Fortunately, there was no ligament damage to the elbow, and he's expected to be ready for spring training. If he keeps those 2022 gains, he could very well work his way into an even bigger role. UP: 20 Sv

Yr Tm	W	Sv	IP	K	ERA	WHIP	xERA	xWHIP	vL+	vR+	BF/G	BB%	K%	K-BB%	xBB%	SwK	Vel	G	L	F	H%	S%	HR/F	xHR/F	GS	APC	DOM%	DIS%	Sv%	LI	RAR	BPX	R$
18 a/a	10	0	121	92	2.33	1.01	2.70				25.7	4%	20%	16%							27%	81%									27.2	144	$18
19 NYY *	3	0	41	31	7.04	1.42	5.21		66	54	22.0	5%	18%	13%		2.4%	91.5	38	13	50	34%	50%	0%	0%	0	41			0	0.00	-13.0	82	-$7
20 NYY	1	0	27	26	7.76	1.54	5.05	1.37	125	106	13.4	9%	21%	12%	8%	9.4%	93.1	40	20	40	34%	50%	15%	13%	4	52	0%	25%	0	0.70	-10.9	86	-$12
21 NYY	2	0	63	62	3.55	1.28	4.12	1.31	113	80	12.5	9%	23%	14%	7%	10.8%	94.1	45	24	31	30%	75%	11%	14%	6	46	0%	67%	0	0.69	5.6	98	-$1
22 NYY	6	1	51	66	2.29	1.00	2.66	1.08	79	76	5.9	8%	33%	25%	6%	15.1%	95.9	47	25	28	29%	79%	9%	12%	0	23			33	1.72	10.5	175	$6
1st Half	5	1	44	59	2.27	1.01	2.61	1.06	81	76	6.3	8%	35%	26%	6%	15.8%	95.8	47	23	30	30%	80%	10%	13%	0	25			33	1.68	9.2	183	$11
2nd Half	1	0	7	7	2.45	0.95	2.97		65	75	4.0	7%	25%	18%	6%	13.4%	96.6	47	32	21	27%	71%	0%	5%	0	16			0	1.86	1.4	125	-$7
Proj	**5**	**2**	**58**	**63**	**3.30**	**1.14**	**2.97**	**1.15**	**99**	**82**	**6.3**	**7%**	**28%**	**20%**	**6%**	**13.5%**	**95.1**	**46**	**24**	**30**	**31%**	**73%**	**11%**	**13%**	**0**						**4.8**	**146**	**$3**

Kinley,Tyler

Age: 32	Th: R	Role RP	Health F	LIMA Plan B
Ht: 6' 4"	Wt: 220	Type Pwr	PT/Exp C	Rand Var -5
			Consist B	MM 4310

Shelved in June with a flexor tear in his elbow. Didn't need a second Tommy John surgery, but his less extensive repair still requires an 8-12 month rehab time, so he may not be ready for Opening Day. Before the injury, a big drop in walks had fueled a solid half-season, though xERA shows true level, not ERA. Monitor spring health reports for outlook.

Yr Tm	W	Sv	IP	K	ERA	WHIP	xERA	xWHIP	vL+	vR+	BF/G	BB%	K%	K-BB%	xBB%	SwK	Vel	G	L	F	H%	S%	HR/F	xHR/F	GS	APC	DOM%	DIS%	Sv%	LI	RAR	BPX	R$
18 2 TM *	2	8	51	57	5.46	1.68	4.99	1.54	98	167	4.3	14%	25%	11%	8%	13.0%	96.6	54	11	34	37%	67%	17%	15%	0	18			80	0.33	-8.3	89	-$5
19 MIA *	3	3	67	61	3.28	1.39	3.44	1.75	101	93	4.2	16%	22%	6%	9%	13.5%	95.0	38	23	40	25%	79%	9%	9%	0	17			60	0.84	10.0	73	$2
20 COL	0	0	24	26	5.32	1.06	4.10	1.40	55	103	4.0	13%	27%	15%	8%	17.0%	95.9	46	15	39	21%	48%	10%	11%	0	15			0	0.68	-2.5	89	-$4
21 COL	3	0	70	68	4.73	1.21	4.49	1.31	96	99	4.2	9%	23%	14%	7%	13.9%	96.0	39	19	42	27%	66%	14%	11%	0	16			0	0.92	-4.1	92	-$2
22 COL	1	0	24	27	0.75	1.13	3.36	1.10	46	106	4.0	6%	27%	21%	6%	16.7%	95.4	39	26	35	34%	93%	0%	4%	0	15			0	1.17	9.5	153	$0
1st Half	1	0	24	27	0.75	1.13	3.36	1.10	46	106	4.0	6%	27%	21%	6%	16.7%	95.4	39	26	35	34%	93%	0%	4%	0	15			0	1.17	9.5	153	-$1
2nd Half																																	
Proj	**3**	**2**	**44**	**46**	**3.30**	**1.26**	**3.50**	**1.26**	**78**	**108**	**4.0**	**9%**	**26%**	**17%**		**15.1%**	**95.5**	**39**	**23**	**38**	**32%**	**75%**	**8%**	**7%**	**0**						**3.6**	**108**	**$0**

Kirby,George

Age: 25	Th: R	Role SP	Health A	LIMA Plan B
Ht: 6' 4"	Wt: 201	Type	PT/Exp D	Rand Var 0
			Consist A	MM 5305

8-5, 3.39 ERA in 130 IP at SEA. Superb debut for the former Elon Phoenix star. While SwK casts some doubt on whether he'll maintain that sparkling K rate, his polished, strike-throwing approach was effective, especially as he increased his groundball rate in 2nd half. It makes this a high-floor profile, and there's plenty of room for growth, too. UP: sub-3.00 ERA

Yr Tm	W	Sv	IP	K	ERA	WHIP	xERA	xWHIP	vL+	vR+	BF/G	BB%	K%	K-BB%	xBB%	SwK	Vel	G	L	F	H%	S%	HR/F	xHR/F	GS	APC	DOM%	DIS%	Sv%	LI	RAR	BPX	R$
18																																	
19																																	
20																																	
21 aa	1	0	26	25	3.11	1.33	3.52				18.0	6%	23%	17%							37%	74%									3.7	141	-$4
22 SEA *	10	0	158	162	3.25	1.17	3.69	1.07	79	119	20.3	4%	25%	20%	5%	10.4%	95.2	46	16	38	33%	75%	9%	10%	25	84	32%	24%			14.1	173	$13
1st Half	4	0	86	86	3.10	1.05	3.79	1.04	83	129	20.9	3%	25%	22%	5%	11.3%	95.6	42	17	41	29%	80%	16%	13%	11	91	36%	27%			9.3	175	$15
2nd Half	6	0	72	77	3.45	1.30	3.60	1.09	76	109	19.8	5%	25%	20%	5%	9.5%	94.9	49	16	36	38%	71%	1%	6%	14	78	29%	21%			4.6	178	$7
Proj	**12**	**0**	**181**	**189**	**3.35**	**1.20**	**3.15**	**1.08**	**76**	**111**	**20.2**	**4%**	**26%**	**21%**	**5%**	**10.3%**	**95.2**	**46**	**16**	**38**	**35%**	**74%**	**7%**	**9%**	**36**						**13.8**	**163**	**$16**

Kluber,Corey

Age: 37	Th: R	Role SP	Health F	LIMA Plan A+
Ht: 6' 4"	Wt: 215	Type	PT/Exp B	Rand Var 0
			Consist B	MM 3203

PRO: First healthy year since Cy Young-winning 2018; tiny walk rate was best of career. CON: Missing fewer bats, with clear downtick in velocity on all offerings; groundball rate declining; DOM% still subpar. Certainly doesn't have Cy Young stuff anymore, and you can't count on IP, but at least he won't kill your ratios. Not the most ringing endorsement.

Yr Tm	W	Sv	IP	K	ERA	WHIP	xERA	xWHIP	vL+	vR+	BF/G	BB%	K%	K-BB%	xBB%	SwK	Vel	G	L	F	H%	S%	HR/F	xHR/F	GS	APC	DOM%	DIS%	Sv%	LI	RAR	BPX	R$
18 CLE	20	0	215	222	2.89	0.99	3.22	1.06	92	80	25.5	4%	26%	22%	6%	12.4%	92.0	44	22	33	29%	77%	13%	12%	33	96	58%	9%			33.4	174	$35
19 CLE	2	0	36	38	5.80	1.65	4.95	1.36	119	102	24.0	9%	23%	14%	8%	13.3%	91.6	40	23	37	39%	65%	10%	17%	7	87	29%	29%			-5.7	96	-$6
20 TEX	0	0	1	1	0.00	1.00	5.41			133	3.0	33%	33%	0%		5.6%	91.7	0	0	100	0%	0%	0%	0%	1	18	0%	0%			0.5	-116	-$6
21 NYY	5	0	80	82	3.83	1.34	4.29	1.32	74	108	21.3	10%	24%	14%	8%	12.9%	90.6	42	20	38	31%	74%	10%	9%	16	84	19%	31%			4.3	94	$0
22 TAM	10	0	164	139	4.34	1.21	4.02	1.11	108	100	22.2	3%	20%	17%	4%	11.8%	88.9	36	22	42	33%	67%	9%	10%	31	79	19%	32%			-7.4	132	$4
1st Half	3	0	76	67	3.91	1.16	3.93	1.13	97	103	20.9	4%	21%	17%	5%	11.5%	88.9	38	20	42	31%	70%	9%	10%	15	76	20%	27%			0.6	129	$3
2nd Half	7	0	88	72	4.70	1.26	4.10	1.09	116	97	23.4	2%	19%	17%	4%	12.0%	89.0	35	23	42	34%	65%	9%	10%	16	82	19%	38%			-8.0	136	$3
Proj	**8**	**0**	**131**	**123**	**4.51**	**1.30**	**3.64**	**1.18**	**105**	**98**	**21.9**	**6%**	**23%**	**17%**	**6%**	**12.4%**	**90.2**	**39**	**22**	**39**	**33%**	**68%**	**10%**	**12%**	**25**						**-8.7**	**121**	**$1**

ROD TRUESDELL

Knebel,Corey

Age: 31	Th: R	Role	RP	Health	F	LIMA Plan	A+
Ht: 6' 3"	Wt: 224	Type	Pwr	PT/Exp	D	Rand Var	-5
				Consist	D	MM	3410

Before straining lat, he excelled in closer role...or did he? Skills say otherwise and were torpedoed by shoddy control. xBB% does offer some hope, but you still don't want a high-leverage arm with a double-digit walk rate. Add in long, long history of ailments, and you've got an unattractive speculation—unless you can get him for nothing.

Yr Tm	W	Sv	IP	K	ERA	WHIP	xERA	xWHIP	vL+	vR+	BF/G	BB%	K%	K-BB%	xBB%	SwK	Vel	G	L	F	H%	S%	HR/F	xHR/F	GS	APC	DOM%	DIS%	Sv%	LI	RAR	BPX	R$
18 MIL	4	16	55	88	3.58	1.08	2.44	1.05	84	99	3.9	10%	39%	30%	8%	13.8%	96.9	48	21	31	31%	72%	21%	20%	0	17			84	1.21	3.9	215	$10
19																																	
20 MIL	0	0	13	15	6.08	1.73	5.86	1.49	132	118	4.1	13%	24%	11%	11%	7.6%	94.4	31	15	54	33%	74%	19%	12%	0	18			0	0.56	-2.7	51	-$9
21 LA	4	3	26	30	2.45	0.97	3.33	1.18	66	75	3.7	9%	30%	21%	6%	13.0%	96.4	46	21	33	25%	78%	10%	10%	4	15	0%	75%	60	1.16	5.7	141	$2
22 PHI	3	12	45	41	3.43	1.37	4.79	1.58	78	108	4.2	14%	21%	7%	11%	11.6%	95.7	39	22	39	25%	77%	9%	9%	0	17			75	1.04	3.0	15	$3
1st Half	2	11	33	30	3.27	1.36	4.94	1.59	85	102	4.2	15%	21%	6%	12%	11.3%	95.6	37	20	43	25%	79%	8%	9%	0	17			73	1.18	2.8	9	$4
2nd Half	1	1	12	11	3.86	1.37	4.34	1.53	55	122	4.3	13%	21%	8%	8%	12.3%	96.0	45	27	27	27%	73%	11%	10%	0	18			100	0.65	0.2	34	-$8
Proj	**3**	**6**	**44**	**51**	**4.02**	**1.32**	**3.61**	**1.37**	**89**	**104**	**4.0**	**13%**	**29%**	**15%**	**10%**	**12.3%**	**96.1**	**41**	**21**	**38**	**29%**	**72%**	**11%**	**13%**	**0**						**-0.3**	**87**	**$0**

Kopech,Michael

Age: 27	Th: R	Role	RP	Health	F	LIMA Plan	A+
Ht: 6' 3"	Wt: 210	Type	Pwr/FB	PT/Exp	D	Rand Var	-5
				Consist	C	MM	2303

Sparkling relief work in 2021 had him on breakout lists, but transition to starter wasn't as rosy as it appeared, as near-5 xERA showed. xBB% does pave path for better control, and elite raw stuff converted to whiffs as RP, so those aren't a lost cause either. But there will be a wait, and you can't draft him as a sub-4 ERA arm in a single-year league.

Yr Tm	W	Sv	IP	K	ERA	WHIP	xERA	xWHIP	vL+	vR+	BF/G	BB%	K%	K-BB%	xBB%	SwK	Vel	G	L	F	H%	S%	HR/F	xHR/F	GS	APC	DOM%	DIS%	Sv%	LI	RAR	BPX	R$
18 CHW *	8	0	141	166	4.45	1.40	4.18	1.10	102	177	21.3	11%	28%	17%	5%	10.5%	95.4	28	26	46	34%	70%	19%	20%	4	64	0%	0%			-5.3	109	$0
19																																	
20																																	
21 CHW	4	0	69	103	3.50	1.13	3.21	1.06	82	92	6.5	8%	36%	28%	7%	14.7%	97.4	38	19	44	33%	74%	13%	12%	4	26	0%	0%	0	0.95	6.5	189	$4
22 CHW	5	0	119	105	3.54	1.19	4.70	1.44	100	84	19.8	12%	21%	10%	9%	10.1%	94.9	36	16	48	23%	75%	9%	11%	25	80	20%	36%			6.2	45	$5
1st Half	2	0	73	68	3.34	1.13	4.66	1.42	111	69	19.9	12%	23%	11%	10%	10.0%	95.1	31	17	52	22%	75%	9%	9%	15	82	27%	20%			5.6	48	$5
2nd Half	3	0	47	37	3.86	1.29	4.77	1.47	84	107	19.6	11%	19%	8%	8%	10.2%	94.7	42	15	43	25%	74%	10%	14%	10	79	10%	60%			0.6	37	-$3
Proj	**8**	**0**	**145**	**149**	**4.01**	**1.27**	**3.89**	**1.36**	**99**	**99**	**15.1**	**11%**	**25%**	**14%**	**8%**	**11.1%**	**95.4**	**38**	**16**	**46**	**28%**	**72%**	**11%**	**11%**	**20**						**-0.8**	**80**	**$5**

Kremer,Dean

Age: 27	Th: R	Role	SP	Health	D	LIMA Plan	B+
Ht: 6' 2"	Wt: 200	Type	Con/FB	PT/Exp	C	Rand Var	-3
				Consist	D	MM	2103

Five good reasons he'll be overvalued... 1) Bad K-BB%; 2) Bad SwK offers little hope for command growth; 3) Bad xERA a run higher than ERA; 4) History of bad numbers; 5) Regression is just around the corner, and it will be bad. Triple-digit skills in August had us momentarily interested, but they were a mirage. Pass.

Yr Tm	W	Sv	IP	K	ERA	WHIP	xERA	xWHIP	vL+	vR+	BF/G	BB%	K%	K-BB%	xBB%	SwK	Vel	G	L	F	H%	S%	HR/F	xHR/F	GS	APC	DOM%	DIS%	Sv%	LI	RAR	BPX	R$
18 aa	5	0	53	54	2.46	1.21	3.05				23.8	9%	25%	16%							30%	82%									11.1	121	$4
19 a/a	9	0	106	89	5.06	1.49	5.22				24.1	8%	19%	12%							34%	68%									-7.3	67	-$3
20 BAL	1	0	19	22	4.82	1.45	5.28	1.51	77	113	20.8	14%	27%	12%	12%	10.4%	93.0	31	22	47	33%	63%	0%	14%	4	87	0%	25%			-0.8	49	-$5
21 BAL *	1	0	117	101	6.68	1.55	6.49	1.45	120	134	17.0	9%	20%	11%	10%	8.8%	92.6	30	19	51	32%	62%	20%	16%	13	76	0%	77%			-34.8	28	-$20
22 BAL	8	0	125	87	3.23	1.25	4.37	1.31	102	99	23.3	7%	17%	10%	6%	10.4%	93.2	39	21	39	30%	77%	7%	10%	21	89	24%	38%	0	0.78	11.4	70	$6
1st Half	2	0	33	23	2.48	1.29	4.71	1.31	91	97	22.5	7%	17%	10%	8%	10.4%	93.6	34	20	46	31%	83%	4%	9%	6	85	33%	33%			6.0	66	-$3
2nd Half	6	0	93	64	3.50	1.24	4.25	1.31	108	99	23.6	7%	17%	10%	6%	10.5%	93.0	41	22	37	29%	75%	9%	10%	15	90	20%	40%	0	0.78	5.4	72	$8
Proj	**9**	**0**	**145**	**114**	**4.31**	**1.36**	**4.19**	**1.33**	**107**	**109**	**22.1**	**7%**	**19%**	**11%**	**8%**	**10.0%**	**93.1**	**37**	**20**	**43**	**31%**	**71%**	**9%**	**11%**	**27**						**-6.0**	**73**	**$0**

Kuhl,Chad

Age: 30	Th: R	Role	RP	Health	F	LIMA Plan	C
Ht: 6' 3"	Wt: 205	Type	Pwr	PT/Exp	B	Rand Var	+1
				Consist	A	MM	1201

Why would COL want a non-dominant FB pitcher? Some guys like this are able to hang on by pitching on bad teams. Skills—or rather lack thereof—tell the true story. Gradual step-downs in velocity give no hope for any upticks in marginal command sub-indicators. He was bad as a reliever, now he's bad as a starter. Drafting him wouldn't be Kuhl.

Yr Tm	W	Sv	IP	K	ERA	WHIP	xERA	xWHIP	vL+	vR+	BF/G	BB%	K%	K-BB%	xBB%	SwK	Vel	G	L	F	H%	S%	HR/F	xHR/F	GS	APC	DOM%	DIS%	Sv%	LI	RAR	BPX	R$
18 PIT	5	0	85	81	4.55	1.44	4.45	1.34	118	104	23.3	9%	22%	13%	10%	10.1%	95.4	36	26	37	32%	73%	15%	19%	16	90	6%	38%			-4.2	85	-$3
19																																	
20 PIT	2	0	46	44	4.27	1.36	4.95	1.58	97	101	17.9	14%	22%	8%	12%	10.3%	93.9	43	22	35	24%	75%	19%	24%	9	72	11%	44%	0	0.79	1.0	32	$0
21 PIT	5	0	80	75	4.82	1.43	4.66	1.48	119	100	12.5	12%	21%	9%	12%	11.1%	94.2	44	21	35	28%	71%	17%	14%	14	51	0%	29%	0	0.81	-5.5	51	-$5
22 COL	6	0	137	110	5.72	1.55	4.94	1.41	122	121	22.9	9%	18%	8%	9%	10.4%	92.8	37	24	40	32%	67%	14%	13%	27	88	4%	52%			-29.5	46	-$15
1st Half	5	0	82	59	3.83	1.32	4.80	1.40	112	88	23.3	9%	17%	8%	9%	10.6%	92.5	37	22	41	29%	73%	8%	8%	15	89	7%	40%			1.5	47	$1
2nd Half	1	0	55	51	8.56	1.90	5.14	1.44	134	165	22.3	10%	19%	9%	10%	10.1%	93.2	36	25	39	36%	60%	24%	21%	12	87	0%	67%			-31.0	45	-$30
Proj	**4**	**0**	**102**	**91**	**5.58**	**1.53**	**4.38**	**1.46**	**116**	**119**	**18.7**	**11%**	**21%**	**9%**	**11%**	**10.4%**	**93.6**	**39**	**23**	**38**	**30%**	**68%**	**18%**	**18%**	**21**						**-20.2**	**46**	**-$10**

Kuhnel,Joel

Age: 28	Th: R	Role	RP	Health	A	LIMA Plan	B
Ht: 6' 4"	Wt: 280	Type	Con/GB	PT/Exp	D	Rand Var	+5
				Consist	D	MM	4210

Based on latest surface results, he will likely be relegated to free agent wasteland on draft day. But lost in his bad stats were some building blocks: groundball tilt, control, and velocity. Hit and strand rates torpedoed him, but if those regress, he could emerge as a bullpen weapon. An intriguing $1 play in deep leagues.

Yr Tm	W	Sv	IP	K	ERA	WHIP	xERA	xWHIP	vL+	vR+	BF/G	BB%	K%	K-BB%	xBB%	SwK	Vel	G	L	F	H%	S%	HR/F	xHR/F	GS	APC	DOM%	DIS%	Sv%	LI	RAR	BPX	R$
18																																	
19 CIN *	6	14	65	53	3.11	1.21	3.77	1.51	117	62	5.0	9%	20%	11%	9%	14.5%	96.1	54	14	32	26%	81%	11%	9%	0	15			78	0.58	11.2	69	$10
20 CIN	1	0	3	3	6.00	1.33	5.42		121	186	4.3	0%	23%	23%		3.5%	95.4	30	0	70	27%	100%	29%	26%	0	19			0	0.27	-0.6	192	-$5
21																																	
22 CIN	2	1	58	56	6.36	1.40	3.55	1.17	107	118	4.8	5%	22%	16%	6%	11.6%	96.1	52	18	30	35%	55%	15%	14%	0	18			33	0.63	-17.1	141	-$9
1st Half	0	1	22	24	6.85	1.39	3.55	1.15	104	118	5.1	6%	25%	19%	6%	12.1%	95.4	48	17	35	36%	50%	13%	11%	0	17			50	0.59	-7.9	148	-$13
2nd Half	2	0	36	32	6.06	1.40	3.55	1.18	109	118	4.6	5%	20%	15%	7%	11.3%	96.5	55	19	27	35%	58%	17%	17%	0	18			0	0.65	-9.2	136	-$11
Proj	**3**	**2**	**58**	**52**	**3.84**	**1.17**	**3.26**	**1.21**	**86**	**97**	**4.7**	**6%**	**22%**	**16%**	**6%**	**11.6%**	**96.0**	**52**	**18**	**30**	**29%**	**70%**	**13%**	**14%**	**0**						**0.9**	**124**	**$0**

Lamet,Dinelson

Age: 30	Th: R	Role	RP	Health	F	LIMA Plan	A+
Ht: 6' 3"	Wt: 228	Type	Pwr	PT/Exp	C	Rand Var	+1
				Consist	B	MM	5511

1-2, 6.12 ERA in 32 IP at SD/MIL/COL. Slider remains unhittable, but batters smoked his four-seamers, which caused his real managers not to trust him. You already don't due to long injury history, and that needs to baked into your bid. Still, there's a twinge of optimism in his 2nd half. If that command sticks, he still has goods for high-LI work. UP: 20 Sv

Yr Tm	W	Sv	IP	K	ERA	WHIP	xERA	xWHIP	vL+	vR+	BF/G	BB%	K%	K-BB%	xBB%	SwK	Vel	G	L	F	H%	S%	HR/F	xHR/F	GS	APC	DOM%	DIS%	Sv%	LI	RAR	BPX	R$
18																																	
19 SD *	4	0	88	120	4.26	1.22	3.91	1.18	98	93	20.9	10%	34%	24%	8%	14.4%	96.1	36	27	36	31%	71%	20%	17%	14	88	14%	7%			2.7	121	$3
20 SD	3	0	69	93	2.09	0.86	3.23	1.05	60	76	22.3	7%	35%	27%	6%	14.8%	97.1	37	21	42	25%	80%	8%	11%	12	87	42%	8%			20.1	184	$31
21 SD	2	0	47	57	4.40	1.49	4.28	1.30	117	90	9.5	11%	27%	17%	7%	15.7%	95.5	39	21	40	36%	73%	12%	11%	9	38	11%	44%	0	0.60	-0.8	109	-$5
22 2 NL *	1	0	53	65	4.44	1.43	4.36	1.32	120	101	4.6	13%	30%	17%	11%	16.6%	95.4	34	25	41	35%	71%	13%	13%	0	18			0	0.74	-3.1	107	-$5
1st Half	0	0	26	27	4.56	1.65	5.78	1.39	188	123	4.8	12%	24%	12%	12%	16.6%	95.3	26	22	52	36%	76%	17%	19%	0	17			0	0.76	-1.9	63	-$12
2nd Half	1	0	27	39	4.33	1.23	3.02	1.15	99	92	4.4	10%	33%	23%	10%	16.7%	95.5	38	27	36	34%	65%	10%	10%	0	19			0	0.74	-1.2	151	-$6
Proj	**2**	**5**	**65**	**85**	**3.83**	**1.25**	**3.14**	**1.19**	**97**	**89**	**6.8**	**10%**	**32%**	**22%**	**8%**	**15.6%**	**95.9**	**37**	**25**	**38**	**32%**	**72%**	**12%**	**12%**	**0**						**1.1**	**137**	**$2**

Lange,Alex

Age: 27	Th: R	Role	RP	Health	B	LIMA Plan	A+
Ht: 6' 3"	Wt: 202	Type	Pwr/GB	PT/Exp	D	Rand Var	0
				Consist	F	MM	5511

One of game's biggest bullpen surprises rode overhauled change-up to big season. To put SwK into perspective, only two other relievers (Díaz, Muñoz) induced more whiffs. When bats did make contact, they pounded ball into ground. xERA in 2nd half confirms late drop-off wasn't skills induced. If bb% improves and opportunity arises... UP: 30 Sv

Yr Tm	W	Sv	IP	K	ERA	WHIP	xERA	xWHIP	vL+	vR+	BF/G	BB%	K%	K-BB%	xBB%	SwK	Vel	G	L	F	H%	S%	HR/F	xHR/F	GS	APC	DOM%	DIS%	Sv%	LI	RAR	BPX	R$
18																																	
19 aa	4	0	56	34	5.56	1.67	5.37				15.8	12%	13%	2%							32%	67%									-7.3	30	-$7
20																																	
21 DET *	3	2	59	59	4.81	1.69	5.34	1.33	98	108	4.8	13%	22%	9%	8%	15.5%	96.4	44	26	30	36%	72%	16%	23%	0	18			50	0.84	-4.0	73	-$7
22 DET	7	0	63	82	3.69	1.25	3.06	1.26	91	88	3.8	11%	30%	19%	11%	19.3%	96.2	56	16	28	31%	72%	12%	11%	0	15			0	1.17	2.1	138	$2
1st Half	4	0	30	39	2.08	1.15	3.02	1.27	81	76	3.7	12%	31%	19%	12%	17.6%	96.1	56	16	29	29%	82%	5%	7%	0	15			0	1.03	7.1	134	$3
2nd Half	3	0	33	43	5.18	1.33	3.10	1.25	98	98	3.9	11%	30%	19%	11%	20.8%	96.3	56	16	28	32%	63%	17%	14%	0	15			0	1.30	-4.9	140	-$5
Proj	**6**	**9**	**65**	**78**	**3.48**	**1.26**	**3.02**	**1.29**	**92**	**92**	**4.6**	**12%**	**29%**	**18%**	**11%**	**18.7%**	**96.3**	**53**	**18**	**29**	**30%**	**75%**	**14%**	**13%**	**0**						**3.9**	**123**	**$6**

STEPHEN NICKRAND

Lauer,Eric

Age: 28	Th: L	Role: SP	Health: B	LIMA Plan: A
Ht: 6' 3"	Wt: 228	Type: Pwr/FB	PT/Exp: A	Rand Var: -1
			Consist: D	MM: 2203

Another velocity boost couldn't strengthen the core skills. More HR yielded major DOM/DIS flip and pushed the ERA up, and persistent FB lean says they aren't going anywhere, either. September elbow inflammation kept him from 30 GS, but he returned to post 11 scoreless 1-hit IP, alleviating carryover concerns. Ks and volume will drive the value.

Yr	Tm	W	Sv	IP	K	ERA	WHIP	xERA	xWHIP	vL+	vR+	BF/G	BB%	K%	K-BB%	xBB%	SwK	Vel	G	L	F	H%	S%	HR/F	xHR/F	GS	APC	DOM%	DIS%	Sv%	LI	RAR	BPX	R$
18	SD *	8	0	134	119	4.01	1.45	4.73	1.39	115	110	21.2	9%	21%	11%	8%	9.0%	91.2	38	28	35	32%	75%	13%	11%	23	88	13%	43%			2.2	73	$0
19	SD	8	0	150	138	4.45	1.40	4.83	1.35	120	95	21.7	8%	21%	13%	7%	9.2%	91.9	40	22	38	33%	71%	12%	12%	29	84	10%	34%	0	0.82	1.0	92	$2
20	MIL	0	0	11	12	13.09	2.36	7.29	1.69	117	145	15.3	15%	20%	5%	12%	11.1%	91.6	21	34	45	44%	42%	12%	14%	2	61	0%	100%	0	0.59	-11.7	-26	-$17
21	MIL	7	0	119	117	3.19	1.14	4.32	1.28	88	85	20.4	8%	24%	16%	8%	11.1%	92.6	36	23	41	26%	78%	12%	12%	20	82	35%	20%	0	0.76	15.8	98	$11
22	MIL	11	0	159	157	3.69	1.22	4.16	1.28	90	102	22.8	9%	24%	15%	8%	10.4%	93.4	34	22	44	27%	77%	14%	11%	29	92	21%	31%			5.5	90	$9
1st Half		6	0	84	89	3.84	1.19	3.94	1.20	109	103	23.3	8%	25%	18%	7%	11.8%	93.5	33	22	46	27%	77%	17%	12%	15	93	27%	27%			1.3	115	$9
2nd Half		5	0	74	68	3.51	1.26	4.43	1.37	75	99	22.2	10%	22%	12%	8%	8.9%	93.2	35	23	43	27%	77%	11%	9%	14	91	14%	36%			4.2	62	$6
Proj		**10**	**0**	**160**	**152**	**3.93**	**1.28**	**3.88**	**1.31**	**102**	**97**	**21.3**	**9%**	**23%**	**14%**	**8%**	**9.9%**	**92.7**	**36**	**23**	**41**	**29%**	**74%**	**13%**	**11%**	**31**						**0.8**	**86**	**$6**

Leclerc,José

Age: 29	Th: R	Role: RP	Health: F	LIMA Plan: A+
Ht: 6' 0"	Wt: 195	Type: Pwr/xFB	PT/Exp: D	Rand Var: -5
			Consist: D	MM: 4520

Returned from Tommy John in mid-June with velocity intact and command no worse than normal. SwK says he was shorted on K%. Flyball spike didn't cause HR jump—infield fly rate soared, which also aided the h% suppression. Has the raw stuff to be a premium closer, but must improve his control to reach those heights.

Yr	Tm	W	Sv	IP	K	ERA	WHIP	xERA	xWHIP	vL+	vR+	BF/G	BB%	K%	K-BB%	xBB%	SwK	Vel	G	L	F	H%	S%	HR/F	xHR/F	GS	APC	DOM%	DIS%	Sv%	LI	RAR	BPX	R$
18	TEX	2	12	58	85	1.56	0.85	3.04	1.12	61	59	3.8	11%	38%	27%	9%	18.1%	95.3	32	21	47	23%	81%	2%	4%	0	16			75	1.30	18.4	165	$14
19	TEX	2	14	69	100	4.33	1.33	4.05	1.32	112	77	4.3	13%	33%	20%	10%	14.1%	96.8	35	20	45	32%	69%	10%	9%	3	18	0%	67%	78	0.90	1.5	121	$6
20	TEX	0	1	2	3	4.50	2.00	5.92		121		5.0	20%	30%	10%		12.8%	94.5	0	60	40	43%	75%	0%	0%	0	24			100	0.97	0.0	-25	-$6
21																																		
22	TEX	0	7	48	54	2.83	1.13	4.22	1.28	96	82	5.1	11%	27%	17%	11%	17.6%	96.5	29	17	54	26%	80%	8%	9%	0	20			78	0.92	6.7	92	$3
1st Half		0	0	5	4	9.00	1.60	5.68		148	148	6.0	4%	17%	13%	5%	14.9%	96.1	17	22	61	37%	43%	9%	8%	0	22			0	0.07	-3.1	83	-$13
2nd Half		0	7	43	50	2.11	1.08	4.04	1.29	87	74	5.0	11%	29%	17%	11%	18.0%	96.5	31	16	53	24%	86%	7%	9%	0	20			78	1.02	9.8	94	$8
Proj		**1**	**23**	**58**	**73**	**3.33**	**1.14**	**3.40**	**1.26**	**105**	**81**	**4.5**	**12%**	**32%**	**20%**	**10%**	**16.7%**	**96.4**	**33**	**18**	**49**	**26%**	**75%**	**11%**	**8%**	**0**						**4.5**	**111**	**$10**

Lee,Dylan

Age: 28	Th: L	Role: RP	Health: A	LIMA Plan: A+
Ht: 6' 3"	Wt: 214	Type: Pwr/xFB	PT/Exp: D	Rand Var: -5
			Consist: A	MM: 5510

5-1, 2.13 ERA in 51 IP at ATL. Might've been a LOOGY before 3-batter minimum, but holds his own vR enough to be a weapon. If he can continue to improve that split, he could flex that elite SwK and premium control in higher leveraged spots, including perhaps the 9th inning. For now, he's a deep league stopgap for some ratio and K help.

Yr	Tm	W	Sv	IP	K	ERA	WHIP	xERA	xWHIP	vL+	vR+	BF/G	BB%	K%	K-BB%	xBB%	SwK	Vel	G	L	F	H%	S%	HR/F	xHR/F	GS	APC	DOM%	DIS%	Sv%	LI	RAR	BPX	R$
18	a/a	2	4	31	32	2.04	1.03	1.66				5.4	8%	27%	18%							28%	78%									8.1	158	$3
19	a/a	1	13	60	46	4.19	1.50	5.18				5.8	9%	18%	8%							32%	76%									2.4	46	$2
20																																		
21	ATL *	5	1	50	45	2.30	0.93	2.71		231	133	5.1	4%	24%	20%		17.2%	93.4	33	33	33	26%	83%	50%	47%	0	15			50	0.22	12.2	185	$6
22	ATL *	6	2	68	77	2.31	1.04	3.08	1.03	56	96	4.4	5%	29%	24%	5%	19.5%	92.2	35	19	45	31%	84%	8%	8%	0	16			40	1.10	13.9	188	$9
1st Half		2	2	34	32	1.96	1.03	3.43	1.03	69	85	4.9	3%	25%	22%	4%	20.9%	91.9	43	14	43	29%	91%	10%	9%	0	18			67	1.12	8.5	194	$4
2nd Half		4	0	34	45	2.67	1.04	3.18	0.99	49	102	4.1	6%	33%	27%	5%	18.8%	92.3	31	22	47	32%	78%	8%	8%	0	16			0	1.09	5.4	185	$5
Proj		**4**	**2**	**58**	**71**	**2.77**	**1.13**	**3.09**	**1.06**	**63**	**104**	**4.8**	**6%**	**31%**	**25%**	**5%**	**19.6%**	**92.1**	**36**	**19**	**45**	**33%**	**80%**	**10%**	**8%**	**0**						**8.6**	**167**	**$5**

Leiter,Jack

Age: 23	Th: R	Role: SP	Health: A	LIMA Plan: C+
Ht: 6' 1"	Wt: 205	Type: Pwr	PT/Exp: F	Rand Var: +1
			Consist: F	MM: 2300

Modest pro debut for 2021's #2 pick for TEX. He missed plenty of bats, but also consistently missed the strike zone. Half of his outings were 4 IP or less thanks to persistent control issues (3+ BB in 12 of 22 GS). Change-up development was a focus to round out his 4-pitch mix. Surface results could lower dynasty/keeper prices despite his high upside.

Yr	Tm	W	Sv	IP	K	ERA	WHIP	xERA	xWHIP	vL+	vR+	BF/G	BB%	K%	K-BB%	xBB%	SwK	Vel	G	L	F	H%	S%	HR/F	xHR/F	GS	APC	DOM%	DIS%	Sv%	LI	RAR	BPX	R$
18																																		
19																																		
20																																		
21																																		
22	aa	3	0	94	93	4.93	1.44	4.18				17.5	11%	22%	11%							31%	66%									-11.2	82	-$7
1st Half		2	0	50	51	4.71	1.35	3.53				16.1	11%	23%	12%							31%	64%									-4.6	99	-$7
2nd Half		1	0	44	42	5.19	1.54	4.93				19.2	12%	21%	9%							32%	68%									-6.6	62	-$12
Proj		**1**	**0**	**44**	**43**	**4.93**	**1.45**	**4.19**	**1.45**			**22.0**	**12%**	**23%**	**11%**				**36**	**26**	**38**	**31%**	**67%**	**10%**	**10%**	**8**						**-5.2**	**51**	**-$6**

Liberatore,Matthew

Age: 23	Th: L	Role: SP	Health: A	LIMA Plan: C+
Ht: 6' 5"	Wt: 200	Type: Con/FB	PT/Exp: D	Rand Var: 0
			Consist: B	MM: 2101

2-2, 5.97 ERA in 35 IP at STL. Never found his footing across six call-ups with an ugly 6% MLB K-BB (16% at AAA). His 1.3 HR/9 in 351 Triple-A innings is concerning especially with the weak fastball (14.6% Brl% against). Young enough to improve vR issues; possesses the frame and depth of arsenal to take 30 turns in a rotation. But not yet.

Yr	Tm	W	Sv	IP	K	ERA	WHIP	xERA	xWHIP	vL+	vR+	BF/G	BB%	K%	K-BB%	xBB%	SwK	Vel	G	L	F	H%	S%	HR/F	xHR/F	GS	APC	DOM%	DIS%	Sv%	LI	RAR	BPX	R$
18																																		
19																																		
20																																		
21	aaa	9	0	126	104	3.75	1.20	4.02				23.1	6%	20%	15%							30%	73%									8.0	102	$7
22	STL *	9	0	150	122	4.87	1.41	4.63	1.50	88	142	20.4	11%	17%	6%	11%	8.9%	93.4	38	24	38	32%	67%	12%	12%	7	72	0%	43%	0	0.67	-16.7	70	-$5
1st Half		6	0	79	68	4.10	1.35	4.46	1.28	106	142	21.9	7%	20%	13%	11%	8.9%	92.7	29	24	47	32%	72%	13%	12%	5	81	0%	40%			-1.3	80	$1
2nd Half		3	0	71	55	5.72	1.47	4.83	1.38	57	141	19.0	8%	17%	9%	11%	9.0%	94.7	52	25	23	32%	61%	10%	14%	2	61	0%	50%	0	0.62	-15.4	60	-$13
Proj		**5**	**0**	**87**	**67**	**4.56**	**1.30**	**4.27**	**1.33**	**90**	**115**	**21.3**	**8%**	**19%**	**11%**	**11%**	**8.9%**	**92.7**	**29**	**24**	**47**	**30%**	**67%**	**8%**	**11%**	**15**						**-6.3**	**63**	**-$3**

Loáisiga,Jonathan

Age: 28	Th: R	Role: RP	Health: F	LIMA Plan: B
Ht: 5' 11"	Wt: 165	Type: /GB	PT/Exp: C	Rand Var: 0
			Consist: B	MM: 5210

Shoulder that prematurely ended '21 breakout flared up again and ate 2 months. Blowups inflicted ratio damage as 11 of 22 ER came in three outings. S% and K% crumbled, the latter due in part to increased efficiency (50% of PA ended in 1-2 pitches). Health remains elusive, but core elements to close (velocity, SwK, xBB%) are still there if opportunity arises.

Yr	Tm	W	Sv	IP	K	ERA	WHIP	xERA	xWHIP	vL+	vR+	BF/G	BB%	K%	K-BB%	xBB%	SwK	Vel	G	L	F	H%	S%	HR/F	xHR/F	GS	APC	DOM%	DIS%	Sv%	LI	RAR	BPX	R$
18	NYY *	5	0	60	67	5.18	1.51	5.96	1.26	108	110	14.4	7%	26%	19%	8%	13.8%	96.0	49	27	24	37%	71%	20%	20%	4	55	25%	50%	0	0.44	-7.6	91	-$5
19	NYY *	2	0	51	55	5.41	1.40	5.05	1.39	110	108	10.2	10%	26%	15%	9%	14.4%	96.9	40	24	36	31%	66%	19%	14%	4	39	0%	75%	0	0.67	-5.7	67	-$5
20	NYY	3	0	23	22	3.52	1.22	3.84	1.25	96	103	8.3	7%	22%	15%	6%	10.2%	96.7	51	23	26	30%	76%	18%	20%	3	33	0%	0%	0	1.00	2.6	124	$3
21	NYY	9	5	71	69	2.17	1.02	3.10	1.15	86	66	5.0	6%	24%	19%	5%	13.8%	98.4	61	16	23	29%	80%	7%	6%	0	19			56	1.61	18.3	156	$14
22	NYY	2	2	48	37	4.13	1.29	3.81	1.40	90	82	4.1	9%	18%	9%	6%	12.0%	98.1	60	18	23	29%	68%	9%	8%	0	15			67	1.24	-0.9	73	-$3
1st Half		1	0	17	18	7.02	1.56	3.99	1.47	98	110	4.1	14%	25%	11%	8%	14.0%	97.6	51	20	29	31%	57%	23%	16%	0	16			0	1.46	-6.3	64	-$13
2nd Half		1	2	31	19	2.59	1.15	3.73	1.37	86	65	4.1	7%	15%	8%	6%	10.8%	98.4	63	17	20	28%	75%	0%	2%	0	15			100	1.13	5.3	77	-$2
Proj		**3**	**5**	**58**	**54**	**3.46**	**1.19**	**3.17**	**1.23**	**93**	**83**	**5.2**	**7%**	**23%**	**16%**	**7%**	**13.0%**	**97.8**	**54**	**19**	**27**	**30%**	**74%**	**13%**	**10%**	**0**						**3.7**	**122**	**$2**

Lodolo,Nick

Age: 25	Th: L	Role: SP	Health: D	LIMA Plan: A+
Ht: 6' 6"	Wt: 202	Type: Pwr	PT/Exp: D	Rand Var: +1
			Consist: A	MM: 5503

Early back injury sidelined him for 2+ months. Showed no ill effects upon return with excellent swing-and-miss stuff and 6+ IP in 8 of last 16. BB% undersells command issues: 19 HBP (1 per GS) led MLB, just 1 start with 0 BB or HBP. Ace potential when he's on: 1.97 ERA, 0.75 WHIP, 36% K-BB in 32 IP in starts with <1 BB+HBP. Must improve vR, but upside is rich.

Yr	Tm	W	Sv	IP	K	ERA	WHIP	xERA	xWHIP	vL+	vR+	BF/G	BB%	K%	K-BB%	xBB%	SwK	Vel	G	L	F	H%	S%	HR/F	xHR/F	GS	APC	DOM%	DIS%	Sv%	LI	RAR	BPX	R$
18																																		
19																																		
20																																		
21	a/a	2	0	52	70	2.79	1.08	2.82				15.7	6%	34%	29%							35%	76%									9.5	205	$3
22	CIN	4	0	103	131	3.66	1.25	3.13	1.16	51	109	23.2	9%	30%	21%	8%	12.8%	94.2	46	20	34	32%	75%	15%	14%	19	94	42%	16%			4.0	152	$3
1st Half		1	0	19	27	4.19	1.50	3.06	1.15	55	119	22.3	9%	30%	21%	6%	13.4%	94.3	47	25	27	40%	77%	21%	7%	4	84	25%	25%			-0.5	166	-$9
2nd Half		3	0	84	104	3.54	1.19	3.14	1.16	50	106	23.5	9%	30%	21%	9%	12.7%	94.2	46	18	36	31%	74%	14%	15%	15	96	47%	13%			4.5	149	$9
Proj		**6**	**0**	**145**	**180**	**3.46**	**1.25**	**2.98**	**1.18**	**49**	**102**	**22.8**	**9%**	**31%**	**21%**	**8%**	**13.0%**	**94.3**	**46**	**21**	**32**	**32%**	**76%**	**15%**	**12%**	**26**						**9.1**	**146**	**$8**

PAUL SPORER

Logue,Zach

Age: 27	Th: L	Role RP	Health A	LIMA Plan C
Ht: 6' 0"	Wt: 165	Type Con/xFB	PT/Exp D	Rand Var 0
			Consist F	MM 0001

3-8, 6.79 ERA in 57 IP at OAK. Kitchen sink-type southpaw can eat some innings at the backend of a rotation, but that's it. Hard to find an upside path with modest velocity, weak SwK, average BB%, a major HR issue, and terrible DIS%. Also debuted late so he's not exactly young despite entering his 2nd season. Pass.

Yr Tm	W	Sv	IP	K	ERA	WHIP	xERA	xWHIP	vL+	vR+	BF/G	BB%	K%	K-BB%	xBB%	SwK	Vel	G	L	F	H%	S%	HR/F	xHR/F	GS	APC	DOM%	DIS%	Sv%	LI	RAR	BPX	R$
18																																	
19 a/a	4	0	105	70	5.71	1.54	5.86				22.9	9%	15%	7%							32%	67%									-15.6	23	-$9
20																																	
21 a/a	12	0	127	117	4.49	1.27	4.56				20.8	5%	22%	17%							32%	68%									-3.5	111	$4
22 OAK *	6	0	137	89	6.40	1.69	7.01	1.37	105	136	20.0	8%	16%	9%	9%	9.1%	90.2	30	19	51	34%	66%	13%	14%	10	73	10%	60%	0	0.67	-41.2	7	-$23
1st Half	5	0	75	55	4.50	1.60	6.61	1.39	145	129	20.6	8%	16%	8%	11%	10.2%	89.9	25	20	55	33%	80%	16%	18%	5	75	20%	80%	0	0.81	-4.9	17	-$10
2nd Half	1	0	63	34	8.68	1.80	7.49	1.47	73	141	19.3	8%	11%	4%	8%	8.2%	90.3	33	19	48	35%	52%	11%	11%	5	72	0%	40%	0	0.56	-36.3	-6	-$34
Proj	**3**	**0**	**73**	**49**	**5.00**	**1.46**	**4.96**	**1.43**	**92**	**122**	**19.9**	**8%**	**16%**	**7%**	**9%**	**9.0%**	**90.2**	**30**	**19**	**51**	**30%**	**71%**	**11%**	**14%**	**15**						**-9.2**	**33**	**-$7**

López,Jorge

Age: 30	Th: R	Role RP	Health B	LIMA Plan B+
Ht: 6' 3"	Wt: 200	Type /GB	PT/Exp A	Rand Var -4
			Consist B	MM 3230

Added 2+ MPH to sinker and rode a gaudy H%/S% combo to an All-Star bid. SwK and GB surged in tandem until trade. Regression and bad luck (hit rate swing) converged in MIN and yielded ugly early-Sept stretch (8 ER, 21 runners in 6 2/3 IP). xBB% softens control concerns, but the 2nd half numbers and metrics scream "Modest CL2!" Don't overpay.

Yr Tm	W	Sv	IP	K	ERA	WHIP	xERA	xWHIP	vL+	vR+	BF/G	BB%	K%	K-BB%	xBB%	SwK	Vel	G	L	F	H%	S%	HR/F	xHR/F	GS	APC	DOM%	DIS%	Sv%	LI	RAR	BPX	R$
18 2 TM *	6	5	93	65	5.64	1.51	5.21	1.47	99	114	9.4	8%	16%	8%	8%	9.0%	93.7	45	23	32	33%	64%	11%	12%	7	52	29%	71%	71	0.57	-17.1	49	-$7
19 KC	4	1	124	109	6.33	1.47	4.75	1.36	129	100	14.1	8%	20%	12%	9%	9.2%	94.2	46	20	34	32%	61%	21%	23%	18	53	11%	39%	50	0.78	-27.9	92	-$10
20 2 AL	2	0	39	28	6.69	1.49	4.93	1.37	121	101	17.4	7%	16%	9%	11%	8.8%	93.8	49	20	31	32%	57%	18%	21%	6	64	0%	17%	0	0.76	-10.8	77	-$10
21 BAL	3	0	122	112	6.07	1.63	4.51	1.41	129	107	16.8	10%	20%	10%	9%	8.7%	95.2	50	22	28	34%	66%	20%	18%	25	66	12%	56%	0	0.88	-27.0	72	-$18
22 2 AL	4	23	71	72	2.54	1.18	3.36	1.33	98	78	4.4	10%	24%	14%	6%	11.0%	97.7	58	17	26	28%	80%	8%	13%	0	17			79	1.32	12.6	104	$14
1st Half	3	13	38	42	1.88	0.99	3.05	1.25	94	65	4.5	10%	27%	17%	6%	11.9%	97.8	60	13	27	23%	86%	12%	7%	0	18			76	1.61	9.9	133	$17
2nd Half	1	10	33	30	3.31	1.41	3.75	1.43	102	94	4.4	11%	21%	10%	6%	10.0%	97.5	56	20	24	32%	76%	5%	20%	0	17			83	1.00	2.7	70	$3
Proj	**3**	**25**	**58**	**52**	**3.44**	**1.26**	**3.54**	**1.37**	**100**	**82**	**6.6**	**10%**	**22%**	**12%**	**8%**	**9.8%**	**96.0**	**53**	**19**	**28**	**29%**	**74%**	**10%**	**17%**	**0**						**3.8**	**85**	**$10**

López,Pablo

Age: 27	Th: R	Role SP	Health D	LIMA Plan B+
Ht: 6' 4"	Wt: 225	Type	PT/Exp A	Rand Var 0
			Consist A	MM 4303

Chronic shoulder issue stayed at bay for career-high 32 starts. Suffered 3 of his 4 duds (6+ ER) in 2nd half when lefties did a lot of the damage (35% H%). Couldn't hold 2021 K% gains despite SwK boost, giving him a tinge of strikeout upside. Talent has never been the issue (29th FIP since 2018, min. 500 IP); he'll go as far as the shoulder allows.

Yr Tm	W	Sv	IP	K	ERA	WHIP	xERA	xWHIP	vL+	vR+	BF/G	BB%	K%	K-BB%	xBB%	SwK	Vel	G	L	F	H%	S%	HR/F	xHR/F	GS	APC	DOM%	DIS%	Sv%	LI	RAR	BPX	R$
18 MIA *	4	0	124	104	2.77	1.10	3.24	1.33	93	113	22.1	6%	21%	15%	7%	11.3%	92.4	50	21	29	27%	80%	16%	17%	10	95	10%	40%			21.1	112	$11
19 MIA *	5	0	126	109	5.89	1.38	4.92	1.27	116	84	20.4	7%	21%	14%	8%	10.6%	93.6	48	21	31	33%	59%	15%	17%	21	86	33%	29%			-21.7	78	-$7
20 MIA	6	0	57	59	3.61	1.19	3.78	1.23	99	73	21.8	8%	25%	17%	7%	12.6%	93.7	52	19	29	31%	70%	9%	12%	11	82	45%	27%			6.0	136	$15
21 MIA	5	0	103	115	3.07	1.12	3.32	1.12	92	92	20.9	6%	28%	21%	6%	12.6%	94.0	47	22	31	31%	77%	13%	14%	20	83	35%	20%			15.2	159	$9
22 MIA	10	0	180	174	3.75	1.17	3.56	1.21	107	91	23.0	7%	24%	16%	7%	13.2%	93.6	46	21	33	29%	71%	13%	11%	32	91	38%	19%			4.9	120	$11
1st Half	5	0	94	93	2.97	1.07	3.42	1.19	96	90	23.6	7%	25%	17%	7%	14.0%	92.9	46	21	33	27%	77%	12%	12%	16	92	50%	13%			11.6	126	$18
2nd Half	5	0	86	81	4.60	1.27	3.71	1.23	118	91	22.4	7%	23%	15%	7%	12.4%	94.3	46	21	33	31%	66%	13%	11%	16	90	25%	25%			-6.7	114	$2
Proj	**10**	**0**	**160**	**157**	**3.89**	**1.19**	**3.25**	**1.20**	**105**	**88**	**21.5**	**7%**	**24%**	**17%**	**7%**	**12.6%**	**93.7**	**48**	**21**	**32**	**30%**	**70%**	**13%**	**13%**	**30**						**1.6**	**126**	**$9**

López,Reynaldo

Age: 29	Th: R	Role RP	Health B	LIMA Plan A
Ht: 6' 1"	Wt: 225	Type Pwr/FB	PT/Exp C	Rand Var -4
			Consist C	MM 4400

His '21 RP stint called this breakout and the lowest HR/F among qualified RP took it to another level. Heed xERA before rushing to buy the superstar-looking 2nd half. Built upon control gains (6% MLB BB% in '21). All four pitches had 13% SwK or better suggesting major K% upside. If the HR suppression wasn't all good luck, there's 9th inning potential here.

Yr Tm	W	Sv	IP	K	ERA	WHIP	xERA	xWHIP	vL+	vR+	BF/G	BB%	K%	K-BB%	xBB%	SwK	Vel	G	L	F	H%	S%	HR/F	xHR/F	GS	APC	DOM%	DIS%	Sv%	LI	RAR	BPX	R$
18 CHW	7	0	189	151	3.91	1.27	5.05	1.42	96	101	25.0	9%	19%	10%	8%	9.6%	95.5	33	20	47	27%	73%	9%	11%	32	96	31%	28%			5.5	51	$6
19 CHW	10	0	184	169	5.38	1.46	5.21	1.37	114	107	24.5	8%	21%	13%	8%	11.7%	95.5	35	21	44	32%	68%	14%	15%	33	96	24%	55%			-19.9	83	-$4
20 CHW	1	0	26	24	6.49	1.63	6.15	1.56	102	154	15.1	12%	20%	7%	9%	9.3%	94.2	35	13	53	27%	71%	22%	17%	8	63	0%	63%			-6.6	25	-$10
21 CHW *	5	0	97	95	5.57	1.44	5.30	1.16	96	85	13.7	9%	23%	15%	8%	11.9%	95.8	39	22	39	33%	64%	17%	13%	9	47	0%	33%	0	0.66	-15.5	72	-$8
22 CHW	6	0	65	63	2.76	0.95	3.40	1.08	93	71	4.2	4%	25%	21%	6%	14.4%	97.1	39	22	39	29%	69%	1%	7%	1	16	0%	0%	0	1.02	9.8	146	$7
1st Half	4	0	36	37	3.25	1.11	3.30	1.11	103	83	4.8	6%	26%	20%	7%	14.8%	96.7	43	22	35	33%	68%	0%	8%	1	19	0%	0%	0	0.85	3.2	147	$1
2nd Half	2	0	29	26	2.15	0.75	3.50	1.04	83	53	3.5	3%	24%	21%	6%	13.8%	97.6	34	22	44	24%	71%	3%	6%	0	14			0	1.19	6.6	144	$3
Proj	**3**	**0**	**44**	**47**	**3.66**	**1.15**	**3.30**	**1.13**	**105**	**86**	**6.7**	**6%**	**27%**	**21%**	**7%**	**12.7%**	**96.4**	**37**	**21**	**42**	**32%**	**71%**	**9%**	**10%**	**0**						**1.6**	**141**	**-$1**

Lorenzen,Michael

Age: 31	Th: R	Role SP	Health F	LIMA Plan A+
Ht: 6' 3"	Wt: 217	Type Pwr	PT/Exp C	Rand Var -1
			Consist B	MM 3201

Shift to SP wasn't a total flop with glimpses of quality, stifled by a return of the chronic shoulder injury that sidelined him for two months. Closed well (see: 2nd half) and has the depth of arsenal and SwK to continue starting. xBB% has consistently suggested he can fix his control issue and push beyond deep league viability. Role will determine interest.

Yr Tm	W	Sv	IP	K	ERA	WHIP	xERA	xWHIP	vL+	vR+	BF/G	BB%	K%	K-BB%	xBB%	SwK	Vel	G	L	F	H%	S%	HR/F	xHR/F	GS	APC	DOM%	DIS%	Sv%	LI	RAR	BPX	R$
18 CIN	4	1	81	54	3.11	1.38	4.50	1.50	109	89	7.6	10%	16%	6%	8%	7.3%	95.1	50	25	25	29%	79%	10%	11%	3	29	0%	33%	50	0.84	10.4	39	$1
19 CIN	1	7	83	85	2.92	1.15	4.04	1.28	83	88	4.7	8%	25%	17%	8%	14.6%	96.9	44	23	32	28%	79%	13%	10%	0	18			64	1.20	16.3	115	$8
20 CIN	3	0	34	35	4.28	1.40	4.57	1.42	82	106	8.2	12%	24%	12%	11%	15.0%	96.7	48	17	34	31%	70%	9%	10%	2	34	100%	0%	0	1.14	0.7	81	$1
21 CIN	1	4	29	21	5.59	1.38	5.02	1.54	95	87	4.6	11%	17%	6%	8%	12.7%	96.5	45	24	31	28%	58%	7%	4%	0	18			100	1.31	-4.7	25	-$5
22 LAA	8	0	98	85	4.24	1.28	4.08	1.41	109	86	22.8	11%	21%	10%	9%	11.7%	94.3	50	18	32	27%	69%	12%	10%	18	92	17%	22%			-3.3	66	$1
1st Half	6	0	71	55	4.94	1.35	4.27	1.43	127	83	23.4	10%	18%	8%	9%	11.4%	94.3	52	16	32	29%	65%	12%	9%	13	91	15%	23%			-8.5	58	-$5
2nd Half	2	0	27	30	2.36	1.09	3.59	1.37	58	97	21.4	13%	28%	15%	10%	12.6%	94.2	44	22	33	21%	85%	14%	11%	5	94	20%	20%			5.3	85	-$1
Proj	**7**	**0**	**109**	**101**	**3.79**	**1.29**	**3.73**	**1.39**	**91**	**96**	**20.6**	**11%**	**23%**	**12%**	**9%**	**12.7%**	**95.4**	**47**	**21**	**32**	**28%**	**73%**	**12%**	**10%**	**17**						**2.4**	**75**	**$3**

Loup,Aaron

Age: 35	Th: L	Role RP	Health D	LIMA Plan B
Ht: 5' 11"	Wt: 210	Type /GB	PT/Exp C	Rand Var -1
			Consist B	MM 4200

Reliever volatility strikes again! Lost 1 mph and regressed everywhere but his control. The major pullback on his S% and H% drove the drop, but xERA says it wasn't just bad luck. He has 1 Sv since 2015—and it came last year—so even returning to 2020-21 levels would only make him deep league worthy. Will give you 15-20 holds too.

Yr Tm	W	Sv	IP	K	ERA	WHIP	xERA	xWHIP	vL+	vR+	BF/G	BB%	K%	K-BB%	xBB%	SwK	Vel	G	L	F	H%	S%	HR/F	xHR/F	GS	APC	DOM%	DIS%	Sv%	LI	RAR	BPX	R$
18 2 TM	0	0	40	44	4.54	1.56	3.78	1.24	93	131	3.1	8%	24%	16%	6%	11.6%	92.0	49	23	28	39%	72%	12%	11%	0	12			0	0.51	-1.9	139	-$6
19 SD	0	0	3	5	0.00	0.90	2.11		165	17	3.5	7%	36%	29%		15.1%	91.7	57	29	14	31%	100%	0%	0%	0	13			0	0.88	1.9	223	-$4
20 TAM	3	0	25	22	2.52	0.84	3.54	1.13	80	89	4.0	4%	23%	19%	5%	8.5%	92.1	40	29	32	22%	78%	15%	15%	0	14			0	0.78	6.0	137	$9
21 NYM	6	0	57	57	0.95	0.94	3.20	1.18	61	73	3.4	7%	26%	19%	6%	12.1%	92.4	50	23	27	26%	90%	3%	5%	2	13	0%	50%	0	1.53	23.2	134	$11
22 LAA	0	1	59	52	3.84	1.30	3.90	1.33	91	97	4.0	8%	20%	12%	7%	11.6%	91.2	50	22	28	31%	71%	8%	11%	0	15			17	1.22	1.0	89	-$3
1st Half	0	0	29	33	4.66	1.38	3.80	1.23	93	111	3.9	8%	25%	17%	7%	12.6%	91.6	43	23	35	34%	69%	14%	14%	0	15			0	1.14	-2.5	125	-$10
2nd Half	0	1	30	19	3.03	1.21	4.00	1.44	90	77	4.1	9%	15%	6%	6%	10.4%	90.7	56	22	22	28%	72%	0%	8%	0	14			33	1.31	3.4	53	-$6
Proj	**3**	**0**	**58**	**54**	**3.50**	**1.27**	**3.39**	**1.29**	**85**	**95**	**3.4**	**9%**	**23%**	**14%**	**6%**	**11.6%**	**91.5**	**50**	**22**	**27**	**31%**	**73%**	**8%**	**10%**	**0**						**3.3**	**103**	**-$1**

Lugo,Seth

Age: 33	Th: R	Role RP	Health D	LIMA Plan A+
Ht: 6' 4"	Wt: 225	Type Pwr	PT/Exp C	Rand Var 0
			Consist A	MM 5411

Stayed healthy for the first full season since 2018. Control rebounded as predicted by xBB%. SwK tumble hurt K%, but his 2nd half surge salvaged it. Platoon vL is driven by 21% H%. Ratios haven't really been mixed-league worthy since 2019, but will give you 15-20 holds, which is where he'll find his best value.

Yr Tm	W	Sv	IP	K	ERA	WHIP	xERA	xWHIP	vL+	vR+	BF/G	BB%	K%	K-BB%	xBB%	SwK	Vel	G	L	F	H%	S%	HR/F	xHR/F	GS	APC	DOM%	DIS%	Sv%	LI	RAR	BPX	R$
18 NYM	3	3	101	103	2.66	1.08	3.54	1.19	75	88	7.6	7%	25%	18%	6%	10.5%	93.9	46	20	33	28%	79%	10%	11%	5	30	20%	40%	75	0.93	18.6	140	$11
19 NYM	7	6	80	104	2.70	0.90	3.17	1.01	71	77	5.1	5%	33%	28%	6%	11.8%	94.4	43	18	39	28%	75%	11%	11%	0	21			55	1.34	17.8	199	$15
20 NYM	3	3	37	47	5.15	1.36	3.30	1.09	114	110	10.0	6%	29%	23%	7%	14.3%	93.4	49	25	27	36%	69%	30%	24%	7	38	29%	29%	60	1.08	-3.2	190	$4
21 NYM	4	1	46	55	3.50	1.29	3.77	1.25	106	88	4.2	10%	28%	18%	6%	13.8%	93.8	42	25	34	32%	78%	15%	14%	0	16			25	1.25	4.4	124	$0
22 NYM	3	3	65	69	3.60	1.17	3.56	1.15	74	109	4.4	7%	25%	19%	8%	9.5%	94.5	46	17	38	30%	75%	13%	11%	0	17			50	0.97	3.0	142	$2
1st Half	1	3	32	30	3.69	1.20	3.91	1.21	79	108	4.3	7%	23%	16%	9%	8.5%	94.2	43	17	39	30%	74%	11%	9%	0	17			50	1.16	1.1	117	-$3
2nd Half	2	0	33	39	3.51	1.14	3.23	1.10	67	109	4.5	6%	28%	21%	8%	10.3%	94.7	48	16	36	30%	76%	16%	14%	0	18			0	0.79	1.9	165	-$2
Proj	**4**	**2**	**65**	**70**	**3.75**	**1.19**	**3.16**	**1.16**	**88**	**102**	**4.9**	**7%**	**27%**	**20%**	**8%**	**11.4%**	**94.1**	**46**	**20**	**35**	**30%**	**74%**	**16%**	**15%**	**0**						**1.8**	**141**	**$2**

PAUL SPORER

Luzardo,Jesús

Age: 25	Th: L	Role	SP	Health	F	LIMA Plan	A
Ht: 6' 0"	Wt: 218	Type	Pwr	PT/Exp	C	Rand Var	-1
				Consist	F	MM	4403

May forearm strain knocked him out for almost three months, but returned with swing-and-miss stuff and better control. There will likely be some H% pullback, but this was a solid rebound that makes 2021 xERA look like clear outlier. Injury history says we can't count on huge step forward in IP, but even so... UP: 2nd half x2

Yr	Tm	W	Sv	IP	K	ERA	WHIP	xERA	xWHIP	vL+	vR+	BF/G	BB%	K%	K-BB%	xBB%	SwK	Vel	G	L	F	H%	S%	HR/F	xHR/F	GS	APC	DOM%	DIS%	Sv%	LI	RAR	BPX	R$
18	a/a	8	0	96	89	3.47	1.19	3.34				19.3	6%	23%	17%							32%	72%									8.1	133	$6
19	OAK *	1	2	43	45	2.96	1.10	2.98	1.04	27	73	13.0	7%	27%	20%	10%	15.2%	96.4	42	15	42	30%	76%	9%	14%	0	29			100	0.85	8.2	144	$2
20	OAK	3	0	59	59	4.12	1.27	3.96	1.22	97	101	20.7	7%	24%	17%	8%	13.0%	95.5	45	24	31	31%	73%	18%	15%	9	78	33%	11%	0	0.70	2.4	130	$6
21	2 TM *	8	0	124	120	6.52	1.62	6.07	1.41	105	123	16.7	11%	22%	10%	10%	13.5%	95.5	38	21	40	34%	62%	18%	17%	18	69	11%	50%	0	0.69	-34.6	46	-$17
22	MIA	4	0	100	120	3.32	1.04	3.22	1.16	84	85	22.2	9%	30%	21%	8%	14.3%	96.1	40	24	36	27%	71%	11%	12%	18	91	39%	17%			8.0	140	$8
1st Half		2	0	29	41	4.03	1.17	3.29	1.26	32	111	19.8	13%	34%	21%	8%	14.3%	97.0	39	23	39	26%	70%	17%	19%	6	86	17%	17%			-0.2	123	-$3
2nd Half		2	0	71	79	3.03	0.98	3.19	1.11	110	75	23.4	7%	28%	21%	8%	14.3%	95.7	41	24	35	27%	72%	10%	9%	12	94	50%	17%			8.3	147	$11
Proj		7	0	145	161	3.73	1.21	3.35	1.23	86	97	21.0	9%	28%	18%	8%	13.9%	96.0	40	23	37	29%	73%	13%	14%	28						4.2	118	$8

Lyles,Jordan

Age: 32	Th: R	Role	SP	Health	B	LIMA Plan	C+
Ht: 6' 5"	Wt: 230	Type	Con/FB	PT/Exp	A	Rand Var	0
				Consist	B	MM	2105

Took a liking to new pitcher-friendly home park, where he put up 3.47 ERA, but looked like recent version of himself everywhere else (5.25 ERA). With velocity dip came a step back in already below-average SwK, and DIS% remained too high. Now has 30+ starts in back-to-back seasons, but volume isn't what you want with these types of ratios.

Yr	Tm	W	Sv	IP	K	ERA	WHIP	xERA	xWHIP	vL+	vR+	BF/G	BB%	K%	K-BB%	xBB%	SwK	Vel	G	L	F	H%	S%	HR/F	xHR/F	GS	APC	DOM%	DIS%	Sv%	LI	RAR	BPX	R$
18	2 NL	3	0	88	84	4.11	1.27	4.07	1.26	78	117	10.6	8%	23%	15%	7%	10.6%	93.6	46	17	37	30%	72%	13%	14%	8	40	38%	50%	0	0.65	0.5	117	$0
19	2 NL	12	0	141	146	4.15	1.32	4.63	1.34	121	88	21.4	9%	24%	15%	8%	10.7%	92.6	40	18	41	30%	75%	16%	15%	28	88	11%	29%			6.2	99	$8
20	TEX	1	0	58	36	7.02	1.56	6.13	1.51	112	116	22.2	9%	14%	5%	9%	6.9%	92.2	40	21	39	30%	58%	15%	14%	9	83	0%	67%	0	0.69	-18.3	25	-$19
21	TEX	10	0	180	146	5.15	1.39	4.79	1.32	112	113	24.0	7%	19%	12%	8%	10.6%	92.8	38	23	40	30%	69%	17%	15%	30	93	20%	40%	0	0.76	-19.6	79	-$5
22	BAL	12	0	179	144	4.42	1.39	4.45	1.28	122	103	24.2	7%	19%	12%	8%	9.4%	91.5	40	20	40	32%	72%	11%	13%	32	93	22%	38%			-10.1	86	-$1
1st Half		4	0	92	77	4.70	1.41	4.34	1.29	128	99	25.2	7%	19%	12%	8%	9.9%	91.6	42	21	37	33%	69%	11%	12%	16	96	25%	38%			-8.2	87	-$7
2nd Half		8	0	87	67	4.14	1.36	4.57	1.27	115	108	23.2	6%	18%	12%	8%	8.9%	91.3	38	18	44	31%	75%	12%	14%	16	91	19%	38%			-1.8	85	$5
Proj		10	0	167	131	4.82	1.42	4.27	1.35	115	107	23.5	8%	19%	11%	8%	9.2%	92.0	40	20	40	31%	71%	14%	14%	30						-17.4	70	-$5

Lynch,Daniel

Age: 26	Th: L	Role	SP	Health	C	LIMA Plan	C+
Ht: 6' 6"	Wt: 200	Type		PT/Exp	C	Rand Var	+2
				Consist	F	MM	2103

First full MLB season was a mixed bag. PRO: High SwK before blisters sent him to IL twice; cut down on walks in 2nd half. CON: DOM starts were few and far between; K% fell off late; slider was hit hard and missed fewer bats. Should take small step forward with H% normalization, but doesn't look ready to put it all together yet.

Yr	Tm	W	Sv	IP	K	ERA	WHIP	xERA	xWHIP	vL+	vR+	BF/G	BB%	K%	K-BB%	xBB%	SwK	Vel	G	L	F	H%	S%	HR/F	xHR/F	GS	APC	DOM%	DIS%	Sv%	LI	RAR	BPX	R$
18																																		
19																																		
20																																		
21	KC *	8	0	125	103	6.09	1.70	6.50	1.47	58	118	20.9	9%	18%	10%	10%	11.6%	93.7	39	24	37	37%	66%	11%	16%	15	84	13%	47%			-28.1	45	-$18
22	KC	4	0	132	122	5.13	1.57	4.49	1.33	124	113	22.2	9%	20%	12%	8%	11.9%	94.0	41	21	37	35%	71%	14%	13%	27	90	7%	30%			-18.8	81	-$12
1st Half		3	0	64	65	4.95	1.54	4.64	1.36	92	111	22.3	10%	22%	12%	8%	13.1%	94.1	38	18	44	34%	71%	11%	9%	13	91	15%	23%			-7.7	74	-$10
2nd Half		1	0	68	57	5.29	1.60	4.36	1.30	138	114	22.1	7%	18%	11%	8%	10.7%	94.0	44	24	32	36%	71%	17%	17%	14	89	0%	36%			-11.1	88	-$16
Proj		6	0	145	121	4.84	1.45	4.16	1.37	108	109	22.5	9%	20%	11%	8%	11.7%	94.0	40	22	38	32%	70%	14%	14%	28						-15.6	67	-$7

Lynn,Lance

Age: 36	Th: R	Role	SP	Health	F	LIMA Plan	A
Ht: 6' 5"	Wt: 270	Type		PT/Exp	A	Rand Var	0
				Consist	A	MM	4303

Spring knee surgery kept him out until June, then a few early blowups led to 7.50 ERA after seven starts. But quickly righted the ship and when all was said and done, it was his best work yet in terms of SwK, BB%, and xERA. The 200 IP seasons are likely gone and velocity dip is a minor concern, but enough left in this tank to go an extra buck.

Yr	Tm	W	Sv	IP	K	ERA	WHIP	xERA	xWHIP	vL+	vR+	BF/G	BB%	K%	K-BB%	xBB%	SwK	Vel	G	L	F	H%	S%	HR/F	xHR/F	GS	APC	DOM%	DIS%	Sv%	LI	RAR	BPX	R$
18	2 AL	10	0	157	161	4.77	1.53	4.08	1.39	115	94	22.6	11%	23%	12%	11%	10.7%	93.2	50	23	27	35%	69%	11%	12%	29	95	17%	34%	0	0.79	-12.0	88	-$5
19	TEX	16	0	208	246	3.67	1.22	3.90	1.17	94	88	26.5	7%	28%	21%	8%	12.9%	94.2	40	21	38	34%	73%	10%	12%	33	108	45%	12%			21.4	153	$21
20	TEX	6	0	84	89	3.32	1.06	4.18	1.21	76	103	26.5	7%	26%	19%	7%	11.6%	93.5	36	22	42	26%	76%	14%	10%	13	108	31%	8%			11.7	128	$27
21	CHW	11	0	157	176	2.69	1.07	3.89	1.16	94	71	22.9	7%	28%	21%	8%	12.5%	93.5	38	19	43	28%	81%	10%	8%	28	93	25%	14%			30.4	140	$23
22	CHW	8	0	122	124	3.99	1.13	3.51	1.06	102	95	24.4	4%	24%	21%	6%	13.7%	92.7	42	20	38	31%	71%	14%	11%	21	96	38%	24%			-0.4	162	$6
1st Half		1	0	22	22	4.50	1.27	3.75	1.14	122	84	24.0	5%	23%	18%	9%	12.8%	92.3	42	21	36	33%	68%	13%	7%	4	100	25%	25%			-1.4	140	-$8
2nd Half		7	0	100	102	3.88	1.10	3.46	1.04	98	99	24.5	3%	25%	21%	6%	14.0%	92.8	42	19	38	31%	71%	14%	12%	17	95	41%	24%			1.1	168	$16
Proj		10	0	160	167	3.63	1.17	3.33	1.14	98	91	23.3	6%	26%	20%	8%	12.8%	93.1	40	20	40	30%	74%	13%	10%	27						6.7	137	$12

Maeda,Kenta

Age: 35	Th: R	Role	SP	Health	F	LIMA Plan	A
Ht: 6' 1"	Wt: 185	Type		PT/Exp	B	Rand Var	0
				Consist	C	MM	4303

Recovery from Sept 2021 Tommy John surgery reportedly went well, and should be good to go for 2023. The last time we saw him, velocity and K% had taken a step back from prior levels but skills were still pretty strong. Age, a lost season, and 2021 ERA should keep price down, so there's plenty of profit potential, even if workload is fairly light.

Yr	Tm	W	Sv	IP	K	ERA	WHIP	xERA	xWHIP	vL+	vR+	BF/G	BB%	K%	K-BB%	xBB%	SwK	Vel	G	L	F	H%	S%	HR/F	xHR/F	GS	APC	DOM%	DIS%	Sv%	LI	RAR	BPX	R$
18	LA	8	2	125	153	3.81	1.26	3.52	1.17	112	85	13.6	8%	29%	21%	6%	14.8%	91.9	40	24	35	34%	72%	11%	11%	20	53	35%	45%	100	1.04	5.3	152	$7
19	LA	10	3	154	169	4.04	1.07	4.01	1.24	99	72	16.9	8%	27%	19%	6%	15.1%	92.1	41	21	38	26%	67%	15%	10%	26	66	27%	19%	100	0.91	8.8	127	$16
20	MIN	6	0	67	80	2.70	0.75	2.80	0.97	73	64	22.5	4%	32%	28%	5%	18.1%	91.4	49	20	31	22%	73%	19%	19%	11	90	36%	0%			14.4	209	$34
21	MIN	6	0	106	113	4.66	1.30	4.02	1.20	107	97	21.6	7%	25%	18%	8%	14.3%	90.5	38	24	37	33%	68%	14%	12%	21	85	24%	24%			-5.1	126	$0
22																																		
1st Half																																		
2nd Half																																		
Proj		9	0	145	146	3.92	1.17	3.33	1.20	103	87	21.8	7%	25%	18%	6%	15.4%	91.3	42	23	35	29%	71%	14%	13%	27						0.8	123	$8

Mahle,Tyler

Age: 28	Th: R	Role	SP	Health	D	LIMA Plan	A+
Ht: 6' 3"	Wt: 210	Type	Pwr/FB	PT/Exp	A	Rand Var	0
				Consist	A	MM	3303

Shoulder issue sent him to IL three times, finally putting an end to season in September. The 2nd half drops in velocity and SwK can probably be chalked up to injury, and stand a strong chance of snapping back after offseason of rest. Should get back to being solid strikeout source with health, but don't count on full ERA rebound.

Yr	Tm	W	Sv	IP	K	ERA	WHIP	xERA	xWHIP	vL+	vR+	BF/G	BB%	K%	K-BB%	xBB%	SwK	Vel	G	L	F	H%	S%	HR/F	xHR/F	GS	APC	DOM%	DIS%	Sv%	LI	RAR	BPX	R$
18	CIN *	9	0	143	127	4.62	1.51	5.53	1.41	135	98	22.1	10%	20%	10%	7%	10.5%	92.4	39	25	36	31%	75%	18%	13%	23	90	9%	39%			-8.3	44	-$5
19	CIN	3	0	130	129	5.14	1.31	4.08	1.23	115	92	22.2	6%	23%	17%	6%	10.0%	93.3	47	22	31	32%	66%	21%	18%	25	88	24%	32%			-10.1	133	-$2
20	CIN	2	0	48	60	3.59	1.15	4.36	1.27	88	92	20.1	10%	30%	19%	8%	14.7%	93.9	29	21	50	27%	73%	10%	12%	9	85	44%	33%	0	0.79	5.1	117	$8
21	CIN	13	0	180	210	3.75	1.23	3.76	1.20	79	111	23.0	8%	28%	19%	8%	12.0%	94.1	42	21	37	31%	74%	14%	12%	33	97	30%	24%			11.4	134	$15
22	2 TM	6	0	121	126	4.40	1.22	4.10	1.24	86	110	21.9	9%	25%	17%	8%	11.8%	93.3	36	18	47	29%	67%	10%	10%	23	91	26%	30%			-6.4	106	$2
1st Half		3	0	92	102	4.48	1.30	4.14	1.25	97	104	23.2	9%	26%	17%	9%	12.2%	93.5	35	19	47	32%	67%	8%	8%	17	98	24%	35%			-5.9	107	$0
2nd Half		3	0	28	24	4.13	0.95	3.95	1.21	34	126	18.0	6%	22%	16%	6%	10.1%	92.4	39	14	47	20%	67%	17%	16%	6	71	33%	17%			-0.6	104	-$2
Proj		8	0	145	152	4.04	1.24	3.68	1.26	85	111	22.0	9%	26%	17%	8%	11.5%	93.3	37	19	44	29%	73%	13%	13%	27						-1.2	106	$6

Manaea,Sean

Age: 31	Th: L	Role	SP	Health	D	LIMA Plan	B
Ht: 6' 5"	Wt: 245	Type		PT/Exp	A	Rand Var	+1
				Consist	A	MM	3203

Avoided IL for third straight year and was on track for near-repeat until 11-game stretch late (7.61 ERA, 2.9 HR/9). His xERA says not all that much changed amid struggles, and he even reversed course on 1st half slippage in BB%, velocity. While 2021 is probably as good as it gets, it seems safe to use 4.00 ERA as your baseline.

Yr	Tm	W	Sv	IP	K	ERA	WHIP	xERA	xWHIP	vL+	vR+	BF/G	BB%	K%	K-BB%	xBB%	SwK	Vel	G	L	F	H%	S%	HR/F	xHR/F	GS	APC	DOM%	DIS%	Sv%	LI	RAR	BPX	R$
18	OAK	12	0	161	108	3.59	1.08	4.24	1.27	86	94	24.2	5%	17%	12%	5%	10.2%	90.5	44	21	35	26%	72%	12%	15%	27	88	26%	41%			11.2	95	$14
19	OAK *	7	0	58	63	2.54	0.84	2.14	1.17	74	64	21.1	6%	30%	24%	7%	12.2%	89.8	41	18	41	22%	80%	11%	12%	5	89	60%	20%			14.0	153	$9
20	OAK	4	0	54	45	4.50	1.20	3.93	1.16	106	94	20.2	4%	20%	17%	6%	10.2%	90.4	50	20	29	32%	66%	14%	12%	11	74	27%	27%			-0.3	143	$6
21	OAK	11	0	179	194	3.91	1.23	3.74	1.12	82	101	23.6	5%	26%	20%	5%	13.2%	92.2	42	22	36	33%	73%	14%	15%	32	93	41%	22%			7.8	153	$12
22	SD	8	0	158	156	4.96	1.30	4.10	1.23	86	114	22.4	7%	23%	16%	6%	12.5%	91.2	38	19	43	30%	67%	15%	12%	28	83	25%	29%	0	0.74	-19.2	109	-$2
1st Half		3	0	88	92	4.18	1.23	4.01	1.28	79	103	24.5	10%	25%	16%	6%	12.8%	91.0	39	19	42	28%	70%	12%	9%	15	93	33%	13%			-2.3	98	$3
2nd Half		5	0	70	64	5.94	1.38	4.22	1.16	98	127	20.3	5%	21%	16%	6%	12.1%	91.5	38	20	43	33%	63%	18%	14%	13	73	15%	46%	0	0.72	-17.0	124	-$8
Proj		10	0	160	150	4.14	1.30	3.73	1.24	93	107	23.0	7%	23%	16%	6%	11.8%	91.1	40	20	39	31%	74%	15%	13%	29						-3.4	107	$4

BRIAN RUDD

Manning,Matt

Age: 25	Th: R	Role	SP	Health	F	LIMA Plan	A
Ht: 6' 6"	Wt: 195	Type	Con	PT/Exp	D	Rand Var	-2
				Consist	F	MM	2103

2-3, 3.43 ERA in 63 IP at DET. Shoulder, biceps, forearm strains took big bites out of otherwise promising sophomore campaign. Although trading sinkers for four-seamers and sliders bumped up SwK%, K% remained underwhelming. Inducing tons of popups (14.1%) is nice but needs more oomph to excel. Let others gamble on the next step for now.

Yr Tm	W	Sv	IP	K	ERA	WHIP	xERA	xWHIP	vL+	vR+	BF/G	BB%	K%	K-BB%	xBB%	SwK	Vel	G	L	F	H%	S%	HR/F	xHR/F	GS	APC	DOM%	DIS%	Sv%	LI	RAR	BPX	R$
18																																	
19 aa	11	0	135	124	3.63	1.15	2.96				22.4	7%	23%	16%							29%	69%									14.6	114	$13
20																																	
21 DET *	5	0	118	86	7.09	1.58	6.36	1.46	105	108	20.9	8%	16%	8%	7%	7.5%	93.7	44	22	34	33%	57%	10%	13%	18	79	6%	50%			-41.3	25	-$20
22 DET *	3	0	84	66	3.22	1.23	3.38	1.31	94	82	18.9	7%	18%	11%	7%	10.4%	93.2	41	19	40	29%	75%	8%	8%	12	83	42%	50%			7.8	88	$1
1st Half	0	0	19	14	1.90	1.05	2.21	1.39	61	84	12.3	9%	19%	9%	4%	9.4%	93.5	52	20	28	24%	84%	14%	21%	2	53	0%	100%			4.9	97	-$5
2nd Half	3	0	65	52	3.61	1.29	3.73	1.33	98	82	22.2	8%	19%	11%	7%	10.5%	93.2	39	19	42	30%	73%	7%	7%	10	80	50%	40%			2.9	85	$0
Proj	**6**	**0**	**131**	**105**	**4.05**	**1.28**	**4.06**	**1.34**	**98**	**90**	**21.7**	**8%**	**20%**	**11%**	**7%**	**9.3%**	**93.4**	**40**	**20**	**40**	**29%**	**71%**	**9%**	**10%**	**25**						**-1.3**	**73**	**$1**

Manoah,Alek

Age: 25	Th: R	Role	SP	Health	A	LIMA Plan	C
Ht: 6' 6"	Wt: 260	Type		PT/Exp	B	Rand Var	-5
				Consist	C	MM	3205

More like Man...whoah! Followed up exciting debut with outstanding breakout. But before you go all gangbusters, note huge discrepancy between actual and expected ERA and WHIP. Leaned heavily on control, hit and strand rates, homer suppression to hulk out. Buy the innings, command, and efficiency, just don't expect full redux of ace numbers just yet.

Yr Tm	W	Sv	IP	K	ERA	WHIP	xERA	xWHIP	vL+	vR+	BF/G	BB%	K%	K-BB%	xBB%	SwK	Vel	G	L	F	H%	S%	HR/F	xHR/F	GS	APC	DOM%	DIS%	Sv%	LI	RAR	BPX	R$
18																																	
19																																	
20																																	
21 TOR *	12	0	130	150	2.87	0.99	2.37	1.21	98	66	21.5	9%	30%	22%	8%	13.4%	93.4	39	21	41	25%	76%	11%	10%	20	92	50%	20%			22.3	137	$21
22 TOR	16	0	197	180	2.24	0.99	3.81	1.19	98	65	25.4	6%	23%	16%	6%	11.6%	93.6	37	21	42	25%	82%	7%	8%	31	95	35%	10%			41.9	110	$32
1st Half	9	0	100	90	2.33	0.99	3.72	1.15	102	67	25.0	5%	23%	17%	6%	11.9%	93.7	38	21	41	26%	81%	8%	6%	16	93	31%	13%			20.3	122	$30
2nd Half	7	0	96	90	2.15	1.00	3.90	1.24	94	61	25.7	8%	23%	16%	7%	11.3%	93.6	37	20	43	25%	82%	6%	10%	15	97	40%	7%			21.6	100	$28
Proj	**14**	**0**	**196**	**180**	**3.39**	**1.15**	**3.59**	**1.21**	**119**	**78**	**25.9**	**7%**	**23%**	**16%**	**7%**	**12.0%**	**93.6**	**38**	**21**	**42**	**29%**	**75%**	**10%**	**9%**	**30**						**14.1**	**109**	**$19**

Mantiply,Joe

Age: 32	Th: L	Role	RP	Health	B	LIMA Plan	A+
Ht: 6' 4"	Wt: 219	Type	Con	PT/Exp	D	Rand Var	0
				Consist	F	MM	5210

Achieved Olympian results in first half by refining command to god-tier level before reverting to merely heroic skills. That massive improvement in walk rate is unsustainable; still, xBB% shows consistency over last two seasons. Not a fireballer, but if this lefty killer could coax more Ks from fancy SwK%, BPX and second half LI support... UP: 15 Sv

Yr Tm	W	Sv	IP	K	ERA	WHIP	xERA	xWHIP	vL+	vR+	BF/G	BB%	K%	K-BB%	xBB%	SwK	Vel	G	L	F	H%	S%	HR/F	xHR/F	GS	APC	DOM%	DIS%	Sv%	LI	RAR	BPX	R$
18																																	
19 NYY *	2	1	44	27	6.08	1.47	5.97		33	245	7.3	5%	14%	9%		7.7%	89.3	60	10	30	33%	62%	33%	29%	0	52			100	0.16	-8.6	41	-$6
20 ARI	0	0	2	2	15.43	3.00	12.96		109	120	3.8	27%	13%	-13%		10.5%	91.1	44	22	33	40%	43%	0%	1%	0	14			0	0.28	-3.2	-289	-$10
21 ARI	0	0	40	38	3.40	1.56	4.33	1.37	98	118	3.1	10%	21%	12%	5%	13.4%	91.2	46	27	27	37%	77%	3%	9%	0	11			0	1.09	4.2	82	-$6
22 ARI	2	2	60	61	2.85	1.08	2.74	1.00	83	95	3.5	2%	25%	23%	4%	14.9%	90.5	54	23	24	33%	78%	15%	15%	0	12			25	1.34	8.3	190	$3
1st Half	1	2	32	33	1.13	0.84	2.35	0.91	80	63	3.7	1%	27%	26%	4%	14.6%	90.5	57	19	24	30%	88%	5%	2%	0	14			67	0.98	11.2	215	$6
2nd Half	1	0	28	28	4.82	1.36	3.20	1.10	87	122	3.4	4%	23%	19%	4%	15.2%	90.6	50	27	23	35%	70%	25%	27%	0	11			0	1.66	-2.9	162	-$9
Proj	**2**	**4**	**58**	**52**	**3.70**	**1.20**	**3.03**	**1.14**	**89**	**109**	**3.8**	**5%**	**22%**	**18%**	**4%**	**14.6%**	**90.7**	**50**	**24**	**25**	**32%**	**73%**	**17%**	**15%**	**0**						**2.0**	**143**	**$1**

Marinaccio,Ron

Age: 28	Th: R	Role	RP	Health	B	LIMA Plan	A+
Ht: 6' 2"	Wt: 205	Type	Pwr/xFB	PT/Exp	D	Rand Var	-5
				Consist	D	MM	4501

Robust MiLB strikeout rate translated beautifully to rookie campaign, supported by equally chonky SwK%. Expected stats pull back the curtain on hard-to-replicate H%, S%, HR/F. A walk rate closer to his xBB% could help offset some expected regression, and paired with minimal splits could lead to... UP: 15 Sv

Yr Tm	W	Sv	IP	K	ERA	WHIP	xERA	xWHIP	vL+	vR+	BF/G	BB%	K%	K-BB%	xBB%	SwK	Vel	G	L	F	H%	S%	HR/F	xHR/F	GS	APC	DOM%	DIS%	Sv%	LI	RAR	BPX	R$
18																																	
19																																	
20																																	
21 a/a	2	5	69	85	2.43	1.03	2.02				6.7	11%	32%	21%							25%	79%									15.7	141	$9
22 NYY	1	0	44	56	2.05	1.05	3.56	1.32	69	81	4.5	13%	31%	18%	9%	14.5%	94.7	41	13	46	23%	82%	5%	5%	0	19			0	0.79	10.4	102	$2
1st Half	1	0	19	23	2.33	0.88	3.73	1.33	51	74	4.8	12%	28%	16%	10%	14.0%	94.3	40	10	50	18%	71%	0%	4%	0	20			0	0.59	3.9	94	-$3
2nd Half	0	0	25	33	1.82	1.18	3.43	1.32	78	88	4.3	14%	33%	19%	8%	15.0%	95.0	42	15	42	26%	89%	9%	7%	0	18			0	0.95	6.5	109	-$3
Proj	**1**	**0**	**65**	**79**	**3.39**	**1.18**	**3.35**	**1.22**	**93**	**104**	**5.0**	**10%**	**30%**	**20%**	**9%**	**14.6%**	**94.7**	**42**	**13**	**45**	**29%**	**75%**	**10%**	**8%**	**0**						**4.7**	**128**	**$1**

Márquez,Germán

Age: 28	Th: R	Role	SP	Health	B	LIMA Plan	B
Ht: 6' 1"	Wt: 230	Type		PT/Exp	A	Rand Var	+2
				Consist	A	MM	4205

Plummeting stock followed from erosion of SwK%, K%, GB%, ending impressive five-year run of positive value from an SP at COL. If you're looking for silver linings, swinging strike rate rebounded in second half along with velocity, racked up IP (6th in MLB since 2017), and road ERA (3.43) and WHIP (1.18) were plus once again. Hey, a boy can dream...

Yr Tm	W	Sv	IP	K	ERA	WHIP	xERA	xWHIP	vL+	vR+	BF/G	BB%	K%	K-BB%	xBB%	SwK	Vel	G	L	F	H%	S%	HR/F	xHR/F	GS	APC	DOM%	DIS%	Sv%	LI	RAR	BPX	R$
18 COL	14	0	196	230	3.77	1.20	3.22	1.14	109	83	24.8	7%	28%	21%	6%	13.0%	95.2	47	23	30	32%	73%	16%	12%	33	95	36%	18%			9.3	166	$16
19 COL	12	0	174	175	4.76	1.20	3.69	1.16	104	93	25.8	5%	24%	19%	6%	13.0%	95.5	49	22	29	31%	65%	20%	20%	28	93	29%	18%			-5.4	154	$9
20 COL	4	0	82	73	3.75	1.26	4.09	1.28	95	87	26.5	7%	21%	14%	6%	12.6%	95.7	51	23	26	31%	71%	9%	12%	13	94	38%	23%			7.1	112	$12
21 COL	12	0	180	176	4.40	1.27	3.76	1.28	103	86	23.6	8%	23%	15%	8%	12.3%	94.8	52	22	26	30%	68%	16%	14%	32	87	25%	31%			-3.0	112	$7
22 COL	9	0	182	150	5.00	1.37	4.12	1.33	121	103	25.1	8%	19%	11%	7%	10.6%	95.4	48	21	32	30%	67%	17%	14%	31	92	13%	35%			-23.2	83	-$6
1st Half	4	0	90	77	5.90	1.53	4.24	1.36	119	125	25.0	9%	19%	11%	7%	9.6%	95.1	49	20	31	33%	65%	19%	15%	16	90	13%	44%			-21.4	78	-$17
2nd Half	5	0	92	73	4.12	1.20	4.00	1.30	122	79	25.3	7%	19%	12%	6%	11.7%	95.7	46	21	33	27%	70%	14%	13%	15	93	13%	27%			-1.7	87	$5
Proj	**10**	**0**	**174**	**156**	**4.49**	**1.29**	**3.50**	**1.28**	**111**	**93**	**24.5**	**8%**	**22%**	**14%**	**6%**	**11.7%**	**95.4**	**49**	**22**	**30**	**30%**	**69%**	**16%**	**14%**	**29**						**-11.2**	**104**	**$2**

Martin,Brett

Age: 28	Th: L	Role	RP	Health	C	LIMA Plan	B
Ht: 6' 4"	Wt: 200	Type	Con/GB	PT/Exp	C	Rand Var	0
				Consist	C	MM	3110

Season ended a week early due to shoulder strain. Second half collapse in SwK%, soaring vR+ while facing more righties really underlined the danger of straying outside his lane as a lefty specialist. Look up "fungible" in the dictionary and you'll see a handsome illustration of this guy—although it could just as easily be someone else.

Yr Tm	W	Sv	IP	K	ERA	WHIP	xERA	xWHIP	vL+	vR+	BF/G	BB%	K%	K-BB%	xBB%	SwK	Vel	G	L	F	H%	S%	HR/F	xHR/F	GS	APC	DOM%	DIS%	Sv%	LI	RAR	BPX	R$
18 aa	2	0	89	79	9.55	2.22	8.79				15.5	7%	18%	10%							48%	55%									-59.3	56	-$35
19 TEX	2	0	62	62	4.76	1.44	3.97	1.25	92	104	5.5	6%	22%	16%	6%	13.7%	93.9	54	23	23	36%	69%	15%	19%	2	20	0%	100%	0	0.65	-2.0	134	-$4
20 TEX	1	0	15	8	1.84	1.16	6.26	1.81	99	74	4.1	15%	13%	-2%	10%	8.1%	94.0	51	5	44	15%	93%	11%	3%	0	15			0	1.04	4.7	-36	-$1
21 TEX	4	0	62	42	3.18	1.30	4.13	1.29	82	99	4.0	5%	16%	11%	5%	11.4%	93.4	57	18	25	32%	78%	10%	9%	0	14			0	0.87	8.4	98	$0
22 TEX	1	3	50	40	4.14	1.36	3.97	1.35	76	113	3.9	8%	19%	10%	6%	11.6%	93.6	51	22	27	31%	70%	10%	12%	1	14	0%	100%	50	1.18	-1.1	78	-$4
1st Half	0	0	25	21	3.24	1.24	3.52	1.33	74	98	3.4	9%	20%	12%	6%	14.8%	93.9	57	21	22	30%	73%	6%	12%	1	12	0%	100%	0	1.18	2.2	92	-$7
2nd Half	1	3	25	19	5.04	1.48	4.41	1.37	80	124	4.4	8%	17%	9%	6%	8.5%	93.3	45	24	31	33%	68%	12%	11%	0	15			60	1.17	-3.3	65	-$8
Proj	**2**	**2**	**58**	**45**	**4.00**	**1.30**	**3.61**	**1.33**	**79**	**103**	**4.4**	**8%**	**19%**	**11%**	**6%**	**11.8%**	**93.6**	**52**	**22**	**26**	**30%**	**71%**	**12%**	**13%**	**0**						**-0.2**	**86**	**-$2**

Martin,Christopher

Age: 37	Th: R	Role	RP	Health	D	LIMA Plan	A
Ht: 6' 8"	Wt: 225	Type		PT/Exp	C	Rand Var	+2
				Consist	C	MM	5410

Career-best skills led to another excellent showing, with sparkling rate stats fully supported by their expected counterparts. He even found another gear in the second half, throwing almost a tick harder while walking one measly batter and striking out 46 over his last 31 IP. Doesn't have a history of closing games, but he totally could. Just sayin'.

Yr Tm	W	Sv	IP	K	ERA	WHIP	xERA	xWHIP	vL+	vR+	BF/G	BB%	K%	K-BB%	xBB%	SwK	Vel	G	L	F	H%	S%	HR/F	xHR/F	GS	APC	DOM%	DIS%	Sv%	LI	RAR	BPX	R$
18 TEX	1	0	42	37	4.54	1.22	3.77	1.11	108	96	3.8	3%	21%	18%	6%	10.0%	95.2	40	27	32	34%	65%	12%	14%	0	15			0	0.90	-2.0	153	-$3
19 2 TM	1	4	56	65	3.40	1.02	2.96	0.97	77	102	3.7	2%	30%	28%	4%	13.2%	95.7	50	20	30	32%	75%	20%	21%	0	15			67	0.95	7.6	213	$4
20 ATL	1	1	18	20	1.00	0.61	3.14	1.02	47	54	3.5	5%	30%	26%	6%	12.1%	94.1	39	24	37	19%	90%	7%	18%	0	15			100	0.98	7.7	177	$7
21 ATL	2	1	43	33	3.95	1.27	3.99	1.17	108	90	3.9	3%	18%	15%	4%	10.1%	94.8	49	20	31	34%	71%	10%	11%	0	14			20	0.94	1.7	128	-$3
22 2 NL	4	2	56	74	3.05	0.98	2.49	0.87	93	84	3.8	2%	33%	31%	4%	13.4%	95.2	49	19	32	34%	73%	13%	14%	0	14			50	1.06	6.3	242	$5
1st Half	1	0	25	28	3.55	1.22	2.68	1.02	84	121	3.7	4%	27%	23%	7%	12.3%	94.8	59	17	24	36%	75%	18%	17%	0	14			0	0.99	1.3	196	-$6
2nd Half	3	2	31	46	2.64	0.78	2.36	0.75	101	56	3.8	1%	38%	37%	4%	14.4%	95.5	40	21	40	33%	71%	10%	12%	0	15			67	1.12	5.0	279	$7
Proj	**4**	**3**	**58**	**68**	**3.40**	**1.05**	**2.53**	**0.93**	**94**	**88**	**3.6**	**2%**	**30%**	**28%**	**4%**	**12.5%**	**95.3**	**48**	**20**	**32**	**33%**	**72%**	**14%**	**15%**	**0**						**4.1**	**210**	**$4**

ALAIN DE LEONARDIS

Martin,Davis

Age: 26	Th: R	Role	RP	Health	A	LIMA Plan	B
Ht: 6' 2"	Wt: 200	Type		PT/Exp	D	Rand Var	-1
				Consist	A	MM	2200

3-6, 4.83 ERA in 63 IP at CHW. Average skills place him very much in the middle of the rat pack. Team sent him on a zany cannonball run between Charlotte and Chicago nine (!) times. Still oceans away from matching exciting K% exhibited in high minors. Sammy and Dino say: come back when the kid starts missing some bats.

Yr Tm	W	Sv	IP	K	ERA	WHIP	xERA	xWHIP	vL+	vR+	BF/G	BB%	K%	K-BB%	xBB%	SwK	Vel	G	L	F	H%	S%	HR/F	xHR/F	GS	APC	DOM%	DIS%	Sv%	LI	RAR	BPX	R$
18																																	
19																																	
20																																	
21 aa	1	0	21	17	4.65	1.53	5.21				15.3	10%	19%	9%							33%	72%									-1.0	57	-$6
22 CHW *	8	0	140	129	4.90	1.38	5.09	1.31	110	102	18.4	7%	18%	11%	6%	11.6%	94.1	37	24	39	32%	69%	11%	11%	9	75	11%	56%	0	0.80	-16.1	75	-$4
1st Half	6	0	76	71	3.57	1.10	3.82	1.16	61	138	18.7	6%	23%	17%	6%	12.8%	93.9	42	23	34	27%	76%	14%	14%	2	71	0%	50%	0	0.98	3.7	102	$11
2nd Half	2	0	66	58	6.25	1.65	6.25	1.32	132	83	18.6	8%	19%	11%	6%	11.0%	94.1	34	25	41	37%	64%	9%	10%	7	77	14%	57%	0	0.69	-18.7	53	-$19
Proj	3	0	58	52	4.85	1.39	3.92	1.27	112	113	19.9	7%	21%	14%	6%	11.7%	94.0	37	24	38	32%	69%	14%	11%	12						-6.3	93	-$5

Martinez,Adrian

Age: 26	Th: R	Role	SP	Health	A	LIMA Plan	B
Ht: 6' 2"	Wt: 215	Type	Con	PT/Exp	D	Rand Var	+1
				Consist	D	MM	2100

4-6, 6.24 ERA in 57 IP at OAK. Good command but little margin for error due to lack of dominance. Pitching to contact only works when your fielders can actually get to the ball; will have to tame HR issue before he can be a dependable back end SP option. Otherwise, he may get slapped with the dreaded quad-A label.

Yr Tm	W	Sv	IP	K	ERA	WHIP	xERA	xWHIP	vL+	vR+	BF/G	BB%	K%	K-BB%	xBB%	SwK	Vel	G	L	F	H%	S%	HR/F	xHR/F	GS	APC	DOM%	DIS%	Sv%	LI	RAR	BPX	R$
18																																	
19																																	
20																																	
21 a/a	8	0	127	99	3.25	1.26	3.59				20.0	8%	19%	11%							30%	75%									15.9	89	$8
22 OAK *	9	0	149	132	5.07	1.37	5.25	1.27	123	120	20.8	7%	20%	13%	8%	10.7%	93.9	41	23	36	31%	68%	20%	18%	12	85	8%	33%			-20.2	63	-$5
1st Half	6	0	79	69	4.65	1.31	4.74	1.23	102	140	20.4	6%	20%	14%	6%	9.8%	93.7	35	22	43	31%	69%	18%	10%	3	81	0%	33%			-6.6	83	-$1
2nd Half	3	0	70	63	5.55	1.44	5.83	1.31	129	112	21.3	8%	21%	12%	8%	11.0%	93.9	44	23	33	31%	68%	20%	23%	9	86	11%	33%			-13.6	44	-$10
Proj	2	0	44	36	4.54	1.30	3.91	1.30	96	99	21.5	7%	20%	13%	8%	10.6%	93.8	40	23	37	29%	70%	15%	18%	8						-3.1	86	-$4

Martinez,Nick

Age: 32	Th: R	Role	RP	Health	A	LIMA Plan	B+
Ht: 6' 1"	Wt: 200	Type		PT/Exp	A	Rand Var	-1
				Consist	F	MM	2213

Returned to MLB after multi-year sojourn in Japan. Started season as an SP then found his niche in relief (2.67 ERA, 1.04 WHIP), even closing out a few games. Ground ball lean, history as a starter make him especially suitable for swingman role. Despite token saves, LI, BPX suggest he won't rack up too many more.

Yr Tm	W	Sv	IP	K	ERA	WHIP	xERA	xWHIP	vL+	vR+	BF/G	BB%	K%	K-BB%	xBB%	SwK	Vel	G	L	F	H%	S%	HR/F	xHR/F	GS	APC	DOM%	DIS%	Sv%	LI	RAR	BPX	R$
18 for	10	0	162	88	4.35	1.42	5.26				27.5	7%	13%	6%							29%	75%									-3.9	24	-$2
19																																	
20 for	2	0	76	63	5.74	1.73	6.15				20.3	14%	18%	4%							31%	70%									-12.0	27	-$18
21 for	9	0	141	131	1.98	1.16	2.99				26.7	8%	23%	15%							28%	86%									39.7	109	$20
22 SD	4	8	106	95	3.47	1.29	4.01	1.33	103	99	9.5	9%	21%	12%	7%	12.1%	93.4	47	19	34	28%	79%	14%	12%	10	37	20%	40%	89	0.80	6.5	84	$5
1st Half	3	2	69	62	3.63	1.37	4.13	1.37	100	112	19.8	10%	21%	11%	7%	11.9%	93.1	48	19	33	29%	80%	16%	14%	10	76	20%	40%	100	0.73	2.9	76	$0
2nd Half	1	6	37	33	3.16	1.14	3.79	1.27	107	74	4.7	8%	22%	14%	8%	12.4%	94.2	46	19	35	27%	76%	11%	8%	0	18			86	0.83	3.7	99	$3
Proj	5	2	131	111	3.83	1.36	4.01	1.41	110	94	10.6	10%	20%	10%	8%	12.2%	93.8	47	19	35	29%	76%	13%	11%	3						2.3	64	$1

Martinez,Seth

Age: 28	Th: R	Role	RP	Health	A	LIMA Plan	B
Ht: 6' 2"	Wt: 200	Type	Pwr	PT/Exp	D	Rand Var	-5
				Consist	A	MM	3300

1-2, 2.09 ERA in 38 IP at HOU. Frequent member of the team's taxi squad excelled when called upon. Slider absolutely devastated RHB (.159 BA, .244 SLG) but vL+ shows he ain't fooling many from the other side. Lopsided platoon splits, low-octane fastball limit his upside to that of a middle-inning short man, although he could be a damn fine one.

Yr Tm	W	Sv	IP	K	ERA	WHIP	xERA	xWHIP	vL+	vR+	BF/G	BB%	K%	K-BB%	xBB%	SwK	Vel	G	L	F	H%	S%	HR/F	xHR/F	GS	APC	DOM%	DIS%	Sv%	LI	RAR	BPX	R$
18																																	
19 aa	4	0	30	27	1.58	1.18	2.46				7.6	8%	22%	14%							31%	85%									10.9	125	$2
20																																	
21 HOU *	5	0	62	65	3.49	1.08	2.58		128	150	6.2	9%	27%	17%		9.5%	90.4	30	30	40	26%	69%	0%	3%	0	21			0	0.02	5.9	119	$4
22 HOU *	3	0	54	50	2.54	1.06	2.55	1.27	111	55	4.8	9%	25%	15%	6%	11.8%	91.6	42	17	42	24%	80%	7%	6%	0	20			0	0.83	9.5	103	$3
1st Half	0	0	22	19	0.83	0.78	4.03	1.32	58	56	5.9	10%	23%	13%	6%	11.8%	91.6	38	13	49	16%	94%	4%	4%	0	22			0	0.49	8.4	75	-$1
2nd Half	1	0	17	19	3.71	1.35	3.59	1.21	175	54	4.9	8%	26%	18%	7%	11.8%	91.5	46	21	33	34%	76%	13%	10%	0	19			0	1.14	0.6	131	-$8
Proj	3	0	44	43	3.64	1.22	3.61	1.27	144	59	5.8	9%	24%	16%	7%	11.8%	91.6	43	18	40	29%	74%	10%	9%	0						1.8	104	-$1

Maton,Phil

Age: 30	Th: R	Role	RP	Health	A	LIMA Plan	B
Ht: 6' 2"	Wt: 206	Type	Pwr	PT/Exp	C	Rand Var	0
				Consist	B	MM	4400

Middle reliever maximizes fastball effectiveness with high spin rates despite declining velocity. Swinging strike and K% trend heading in wrong direction, although xBB% suggests walk rate upside. Established track record of inducing weak contact (career 30.6% HardHit%) helps soften dominance slide. Skills, history suggest he's capable of more.

Yr Tm	W	Sv	IP	K	ERA	WHIP	xERA	xWHIP	vL+	vR+	BF/G	BB%	K%	K-BB%	xBB%	SwK	Vel	G	L	F	H%	S%	HR/F	xHR/F	GS	APC	DOM%	DIS%	Sv%	LI	RAR	BPX	R$
18 SD	0	0	47	55	4.37	1.54	4.42	1.34	99	109	4.8	11%	26%	15%	10%	14.7%	91.1	36	23	41	37%	71%	6%	6%	0	19			0	0.85	-1.3	97	-$6
19 2 TM *	2	5	67	70	5.04	1.34	4.61	1.34	104	109	5.3	8%	25%	17%	6%	11.8%	91.0	45	25	31	32%	66%	20%	14%	0	20			83	0.43	-4.4	87	-$1
20 CLE	3	0	22	32	4.57	1.34	2.97	1.02	96	98	4.2	6%	33%	27%	6%	17.9%	93.6	44	26	30	43%	64%	6%	4%	0	16			0	1.11	-0.3	219	$1
21 2 AL	6	0	67	85	4.73	1.44	4.10	1.28	100	106	4.6	11%	29%	18%	7%	16.5%	91.7	39	21	40	36%	68%	9%	10%	1	18	0%	0%	0	0.82	-3.8	117	-$3
22 HOU	0	0	66	73	3.84	1.25	3.67	1.22	109	99	4.2	9%	26%	17%	7%	14.3%	90.9	38	24	38	30%	75%	15%	12%	0	16			0	0.78	1.1	118	-$2
1st Half	0	0	34	33	3.74	1.25	4.00	1.24	89	133	4.3	8%	23%	15%	8%	13.4%	90.9	33	28	39	28%	80%	19%	13%	0	17			0	0.88	0.9	100	-$7
2nd Half	0	0	32	40	3.94	1.25	3.32	1.20	129	60	4.1	10%	30%	20%	6%	15.4%	91.0	44	20	35	32%	70%	11%	10%	0	16			0	0.67	0.1	139	-$6
Proj	2	0	58	66	4.01	1.33	3.42	1.24	107	99	4.4	9%	27%	18%	7%	14.2%	91.1	41	23	36	32%	74%	14%	11%	0						-0.3	118	-$2

Matz,Steven

Age: 32	Th: L	Role	SP	Health	F	LIMA Plan	A
Ht: 6' 2"	Wt: 201	Type		PT/Exp	A	Rand Var	+1
				Consist	A	MM	4303

5-3, 5.25 ERA in 48 IP at STL. Shoulder, knee injuries cost him 112 G on IL, returned as RP in Sept with velocity intact. Career best BB% supported by xBB%, but don't read too much into second half SwK% inflated by relief work and one great game. Skills still strong enough for mid-rotation success. If health, GB% cooperate... UP: 3.50 ERA, 1.15 WHIP

Yr Tm	W	Sv	IP	K	ERA	WHIP	xERA	xWHIP	vL+	vR+	BF/G	BB%	K%	K-BB%	xBB%	SwK	Vel	G	L	F	H%	S%	HR/F	xHR/F	GS	APC	DOM%	DIS%	Sv%	LI	RAR	BPX	R$
18 NYM	5	0	154	152	3.97	1.25	3.98	1.31	92	104	21.8	9%	23%	14%	8%	9.7%	93.4	49	15	36	28%	74%	17%	12%	30	90	30%	27%			3.3	110	$5
19 NYM	11	0	160	153	4.21	1.34	4.37	1.31	106	103	21.6	8%	22%	15%	8%	10.1%	93.4	47	20	33	31%	74%	17%	19%	30	84	10%	33%	0	0.80	5.8	110	$7
20 NYM	0	0	31	36	9.68	1.70	4.61	1.21	132	146	15.8	7%	25%	18%	8%	10.7%	94.5	33	28	39	36%	50%	38%	24%	6	70	0%	67%	0	0.67	-19.8	138	-$20
21 TOR	14	0	151	144	3.82	1.33	4.08	1.23	100	97	22.3	7%	22%	16%	7%	9.9%	94.5	45	22	32	33%	75%	12%	11%	29	88	17%	31%			8.2	119	$8
22 STL *	5	0	67	70	4.36	1.18	3.85	1.07	109	101	11.7	5%	26%	21%	5%	12.8%	94.6	38	26	35	31%	66%	16%	8%	10	57	20%	20%	0	0.89	-3.2	126	$0
1st Half	3	0	42	48	5.53	1.36	5.50	1.06	118	112	16.1	4%	26%	22%	5%	11.7%	94.4	37	29	34	37%	64%	21%	9%	9	75	11%	22%			-8.2	147	-$8
2nd Half	2	0	25	21	2.41	0.88	1.11	1.29	68	59	7.7	9%	22%	14%	5%	17.4%	95.0	43	17	40	21%	72%	0%	3%	1	29	100%	0%	0	1.00	4.8	125	-$1
Proj	9	0	145	145	4.12	1.24	3.46	1.20	98	95	21.5	7%	25%	17%	7%	10.6%	94.1	40	24	36	30%	72%	16%	15%	27						-2.7	120	$5

Matzek,Tyler

Age: 32	Th: L	Role	RP	Health	D	LIMA Plan	D+
Ht: 6' 3"	Wt: 230	Type	#DIV/0!	PT/Exp	C	Rand Var	-5
				Consist	C	MM	#DIV/0!

Magical 2020 season now looking more like a mirage as skills, velocity plummeted. That said, shoulder injury in May that shelved him for 52 days could have hampered him all year. Elbow discomfort kept him off the NLDS and eventually led to Tommy John surgery in Oct, so you can safely disregard for 2023.

Yr Tm	W	Sv	IP	K	ERA	WHIP	xERA	xWHIP	vL+	vR+	BF/G	BB%	K%	K-BB%	xBB%	SwK	Vel	G	L	F	H%	S%	HR/F	xHR/F	GS	APC	DOM%	DIS%	Sv%	LI	RAR	BPX	R$
18																																	
19 a/a	0	0	15	15	12.05	1.99	6.18				8.0	17%	21%	4%							37%	34%									-14.0	56	-$10
20 ATL	4	0	29	43	2.79	1.14	3.08	1.07	71	81	5.8	8%	36%	27%	5%	13.5%	94.4	43	22	35	36%	75%	4%	9%	0	23			0	0.76	5.9	200	$10
21 ATL	0	0	63	77	2.57	1.22	4.03	1.41	92	70	3.8	14%	29%	15%	10%	13.4%	96.1	40	24	36	27%	80%	6%	6%	0	15			0	1.14	13.2	80	$2
22 ATL	4	1	44	36	3.50	1.26	5.37	1.68	100	75	4.4	16%	20%	4%	10%	12.3%	94.1	33	16	51	21%	73%	5%	8%	0	17			100	0.89	2.5	-19	-$1
1st Half	0	0	12	10	4.63	1.37	5.74	1.90	82	85	3.6	20%	20%	0%	9%	13.4%	94.6	38	10	52	18%	67%	7%	9%	0	16			0	0.87	-0.9	-59	-$11
2nd Half	4	1	32	26	3.09	1.22	5.25	1.60	102	70	4.8	14%	20%	5%	10%	11.9%	93.9	31	17	51	22%	76%	5%	8%	0	17			100	0.90	3.5	-4	$1
Proj																																	

ALAIN DE LEONARDIS

May,Dustin

Age: 25	Th: R	Role	SP	Health	F	LIMA Plan	B+
Ht: 6' 6"	Wt: 180	Type	Pwr	PT/Exp	D	Rand Var	0
				Consist	C	MM	5303

2-3, 4.50 ERA in 30 IP at LA. The Tommy John comeback trail went about as well as one could expect. K% and BB% were not fully recovered in the 6-start sample, but velocity, SwK and GB% were all reasonably close to pre-injury levels. The question will be 2023 workload, but it looks like one of the game's young stars is on his way back.

Yr Tm	W	Sv	IP	K	ERA	WHIP	xERA	xWHIP	vL+	vR+	BF/G	BB%	K%	K-BB%	xBB%	SwK	Vel	G	L	F	H%	S%	HR/F	xHR/F	GS	APC	DOM%	DIS%	Sv%	LI	RAR	BPX	R$
18 aa	2	0	35	25	3.67	1.10	2.14				22.9	7%	18%	11%							28%	63%									2.1	114	-$1
19 LA *	8	0	143	129	3.76	1.17	3.12	1.14	116	64	16.8	6%	23%	17%	6%	9.2%	96.0	44	28	27	32%	67%	7%	14%	4	40	25%	0%	0	0.94	13.1	136	$10
20 LA	3	0	56	44	2.57	1.09	3.98	1.31	108	69	18.7	7%	20%	13%	6%	9.0%	98.1	55	19	26	24%	87%	21%	19%	10	72	0%	40%	0	0.86	13.0	103	$15
21 LA	1	0	23	35	2.74	0.96	2.13	0.95	79	81	18.6	6%	38%	31%	6%	14.7%	98.0	56	24	20	29%	83%	40%	31%	5	74	20%	0%			4.3	238	-$1
22 LA *	3	0	49	56	3.36	1.09	2.68	1.38	75	98	17.4	11%	23%	12%	8%	13.5%	97.7	51	19	29	27%	72%	13%	8%	6	79	17%	33%			3.7	125	$1
1st Half																																	
2nd Half	3	0	49	56	3.36	1.09	2.68	1.22	75	98	17.4	9%	27%	18%	8%	13.5%	97.7	51	19	29	27%	72%	13%	8%	6	79	17%	33%			3.7	125	$4
Proj	10	0	145	146	3.26	1.10	3.01	1.21	93	81	21.4	8%	26%	18%		13.1%	97.5	51	21	28	28%	72%	11%	12%	27						12.6	128	$15

Mayza,Tim

Age: 31	Th: L	Role	RP	Health	C	LIMA Plan	A+
Ht: 6' 3"	Wt: 220	Type	Pwr/xGB	PT/Exp	C	Rand Var	+3
				Consist	A	MM	5300

Perfectly serviceable reliever who throws strikes, gets a ton of ground balls, and keeps your ratios in check. Found a bit of another gear in 2nd half, but xBB% and H% says WHIP will regress. Home-run numbers look scary until you realize how few balls are put in the air. Little chance of saves, so best for -Only leagues or ones that count holds.

Yr Tm	W	Sv	IP	K	ERA	WHIP	xERA	xWHIP	vL+	vR+	BF/G	BB%	K%	K-BB%	xBB%	SwK	Vel	G	L	F	H%	S%	HR/F	xHR/F	GS	APC	DOM%	DIS%	Sv%	LI	RAR	BPX	R$
18 TOR *	8	1	63	68	4.50	1.48	4.56	1.26	79	110	4.7	10%	25%	16%	8%	14.1%	93.9	45	16	39	36%	70%	8%	10%	0	16			25	0.81	-2.7	103	-$1
19 TOR	1	0	51	55	4.91	1.40	4.25	1.44	95	102	3.3	12%	24%	12%	11%	14.4%	94.2	53	21	26	29%	69%	22%	23%	0	14			0	1.04	-2.6	84	-$4
20																																	
21 TOR	5	1	53	57	3.40	0.98	2.87	1.10	62	87	3.4	6%	27%	21%	8%	11.4%	94.1	59	18	23	27%	68%	16%	10%	0	14			25	1.00	5.7	171	$4
22 TOR	8	2	49	44	3.14	1.11	2.97	1.18	72	115	3.1	6%	23%	17%	8%	10.1%	93.7	58	22	20	27%	79%	26%	24%	0	12			33	1.25	5.0	135	$4
1st Half	2	0	22	20	2.86	1.45	3.08	1.30	105	110	3.4	9%	22%	13%	8%	9.7%	93.8	56	35	10	34%	83%	33%	30%	0	12			0	0.89	3.0	102	-$6
2nd Half	6	2	27	24	3.38	0.83	2.89	1.08	48	119	2.8	4%	24%	20%	8%	10.5%	93.6	60	10	30	20%	71%	24%	22%	0	11			50	1.52	2.0	163	$6
Proj	6	0	51	50	3.59	1.18	3.02	1.23	79	107	3.2	8%	25%	17%	8%	12.0%	93.9	56	20	25	28%	75%	21%	21%	0						2.4	127	$1

McClanahan,Shane

Age: 26	Th: L	Role	SP	Health	B	LIMA Plan	C+
Ht: 6' 1"	Wt: 200	Type		PT/Exp	A	Rand Var	-2
				Consist	B	MM	5303

Perhaps 2022's biggest pitching breakout star, he comes with lots of 2nd half red flags: command, SwK/K% and surface stats all took an in-season step back. Easy to tag his late-Aug shoulder impingement as the reason, but will offseason rest assuage those concerns, or does it cloud his 2023 outlook? Return on a high-level pick or bid hangs in the balance.

Yr Tm	W	Sv	IP	K	ERA	WHIP	xERA	xWHIP	vL+	vR+	BF/G	BB%	K%	K-BB%	xBB%	SwK	Vel	G	L	F	H%	S%	HR/F	xHR/F	GS	APC	DOM%	DIS%	Sv%	LI	RAR	BPX	R$
18																																	
19 aa	1	0	19	19	10.87	2.24	9.63				24.2	6%	20%	13%							48%	50%									-15.0	44	-$11
20																																	
21 TAM	10	0	123	141	3.43	1.27	3.49	1.16	98	92	20.7	7%	27%	20%	6%	15.1%	96.5	45	25	30	34%	77%	14%	17%	25	78	16%	16%			12.7	148	$9
22 TAM	12	0	166	194	2.54	0.93	2.72	1.04	86	78	22.9	6%	30%	24%	6%	16.0%	96.8	50	20	30	26%	79%	16%	13%	28	88	46%	18%			29.3	178	$28
1st Half	9	0	98	133	1.74	0.81	2.26	0.91	82	70	23.1	5%	36%	31%	5%	17.2%	96.9	51	18	31	26%	88%	16%	15%	16	90	50%	0%			27.0	228	$44
2nd Half	3	0	68	61	3.71	1.09	3.47	1.25	91	89	22.6	8%	23%	15%	7%	14.2%	96.7	49	22	29	26%	70%	15%	11%	12	79	42%	42%			2.2	108	$5
Proj	11	0	160	168	3.16	1.03	2.83	1.13	93	86	22.8	7%	27%	21%	6%	15.3%	96.7	49	21	30	28%	74%	15%	13%	27						16.0	150	$20

McCullers Jr.,Lance

Age: 29	Th: R	Role	SP	Health	F	LIMA Plan	A+
Ht: 6' 1"	Wt: 202	Type	Pwr/GB	PT/Exp	A	Rand Var	-5
				Consist	A	MM	4303

Terrific outcome after he missed four months with a flexor tendon strain, extending his IL streak to seven seasons. But xERA, BPX and Consistency grade tell a familiar story: GB% and Ks are the highlight, but his outings can be flush with baserunners. Which makes keeping H%, S% and HR/F in check a priority. Well, that and staying on the mound.

Yr Tm	W	Sv	IP	K	ERA	WHIP	xERA	xWHIP	vL+	vR+	BF/G	BB%	K%	K-BB%	xBB%	SwK	Vel	G	L	F	H%	S%	HR/F	xHR/F	GS	APC	DOM%	DIS%	Sv%	LI	RAR	BPX	R$
18 HOU	10	0	128	142	3.86	1.17	3.28	1.26	78	102	21.1	9%	27%	17%	8%	13.9%	94.3	55	18	27	29%	69%	13%	15%	22	84	36%	27%	0	0.91	4.6	135	$9
19																																	
20 HOU	3	0	55	56	3.93	1.16	3.46	1.28	91	102	20.6	9%	25%	16%	10%	11.8%	93.8	60	17	23	28%	68%	15%	23%	11	80	36%	36%			3.6	129	$9
21 HOU	13	0	162	185	3.16	1.22	3.53	1.32	95	76	24.4	11%	27%	16%	10%	11.9%	94.0	56	17	27	29%	76%	12%	12%	28	100	21%	21%			22.1	115	$18
22 HOU	4	0	48	50	2.27	1.24	3.59	1.34	80	100	24.4	11%	26%	14%	10%	11.5%	93.1	50	19	31	28%	85%	11%	12%	8	95	25%	13%			10.0	95	$2
1st Half																																	
2nd Half	4	0	48	50	2.27	1.24	3.59	1.34	80	100	24.4	11%	26%	14%	10%	11.5%	93.1	50	19	31	28%	85%	11%	12%	8	95	25%	13%			10.0	95	$6
Proj	10	0	138	144	3.53	1.23	3.30	1.32	87	96	23.4	11%	26%	15%		11.2%	93.7	52	18	30	29%	73%	11%	14%	24						7.5	104	$9

McHugh,Collin

Age: 36	Th: R	Role	RP	Health	D	LIMA Plan	A
Ht: 6' 2"	Wt: 191	Type	Pwr	PT/Exp	C	Rand Var	-2
				Consist	A	MM	5401

Second year in a row putting up elite reliever numbers driven by legit strikezone control and swing-and-miss stuff. Only has low-90s velocity, but small in-season bump was a positive, especially at his age. Not a saves threat, but deep-league end-gamer and holds league staple for whom a repeat season seems reasonable.

Yr Tm	W	Sv	IP	K	ERA	WHIP	xERA	xWHIP	vL+	vR+	BF/G	BB%	K%	K-BB%	xBB%	SwK	Vel	G	L	F	H%	S%	HR/F	xHR/F	GS	APC	DOM%	DIS%	Sv%	LI	RAR	BPX	R$
18 HOU	6	0	72	94	1.99	0.91	3.18	1.07	95	58	4.9	7%	33%	26%	7%	13.8%	92.1	35	22	44	26%	83%	8%	11%	0	21			0	0.87	19.3	176	$12
19 HOU	4	0	75	82	4.70	1.23	4.35	1.32	85	108	9.1	9%	26%	16%	8%	11.9%	90.8	38	25	38	28%	66%	16%	15%	8	37	13%	38%	0	0.55	-1.8	105	$0
20																																	
21 TAM	6	1	64	74	1.55	0.94	3.13	1.03	61	79	6.7	5%	30%	25%	5%	14.4%	90.6	44	20	36	30%	86%	5%	5%	7	26	14%	43%	33	0.90	21.5	180	$12
22 ATL	3	0	69	75	2.60	0.94	3.20	1.06	72	84	4.7	5%	28%	22%	6%	13.0%	91.3	40	21	39	28%	75%	7%	8%	0	19			0	1.12	11.7	159	$7
1st Half	1	0	35	42	3.60	1.11	3.32	1.02	86	92	5.1	5%	29%	24%	6%	13.2%	91.1	33	25	42	34%	69%	8%	8%	0	21			0	1.34	1.6	173	-$3
2nd Half	2	0	34	33	1.57	0.76	3.07	1.10	55	74	4.3	5%	26%	20%	6%	12.8%	93.0	48	17	35	21%	83%	7%	9%	0	17			0	0.93	10.1	145	$6
Proj	5	0	65	70	3.07	1.02	3.08	1.12	78	88	5.4	7%	28%	21%	6%	13.0%	91.6	40	21	38	28%	73%	9%	10%	0						7.2	143	$5

McKenzie,Triston

Age: 25	Th: R	Role	SP	Health	A	LIMA Plan	C+
Ht: 6' 5"	Wt: 165	Type	Pwr/xFB	PT/Exp	B	Rand Var	-4
				Consist	A	MM	4305

A huge step forward, but is there even another level? PRO: Control gains backed by xBB%; 2nd half K% blitz lines up with SwK; rare-air DOM%/DIS% figures. CON: Massive IP jump for a string-bean frame; all those FB pose HR risk; xERA says "Cool your jets." Even with H% regression baked in, age and skills point to staying power.

Yr Tm	W	Sv	IP	K	ERA	WHIP	xERA	xWHIP	vL+	vR+	BF/G	BB%	K%	K-BB%	xBB%	SwK	Vel	G	L	F	H%	S%	HR/F	xHR/F	GS	APC	DOM%	DIS%	Sv%	LI	RAR	BPX	R$
18 aa	7	0	92	76	3.49	1.13	3.17				22.8	8%	21%	13%							26%	73%									7.5	92	$6
19																																	
20 CLE	2	0	33	42	3.24	0.90	3.45	1.07	100	68	15.9	7%	33%	26%	8%	13.1%	92.8	40	13	47	22%	75%	17%	19%	6	69	17%	33%	0	0.71	5.0	177	$9
21 CLE *	6	0	142	155	4.66	1.22	3.90	1.35	94	89	19.1	12%	27%	15%	8%	13.1%	92.1	30	22	48	24%	68%	15%	12%	24	79	29%	38%	0	0.74	-7.0	77	$2
22 CLE	11	0	191	190	2.96	0.95	3.74	1.12	85	88	23.9	6%	26%	20%	6%	13.3%	92.5	33	18	49	24%	76%	10%	11%	30	91	40%	3%	0	0.80	23.7	128	$26
1st Half	5	0	87	80	3.71	0.98	4.14	1.18	79	105	23.0	6%	23%	17%	7%	12.1%	92.4	30	17	53	22%	71%	13%	12%	14	87	36%	0%	0	0.78	2.8	105	$14
2nd Half	6	0	104	110	2.34	0.92	3.41	1.07	89	71	24.8	6%	28%	22%	5%	14.4%	92.7	35	20	45	26%	79%	8%	10%	16	94	44%	6%			20.9	147	$31
Proj	12	0	189	200	3.31	1.05	3.44	1.16	95	87	23.0	7%	27%	20%	6%	13.3%	92.6	34	18	48	26%	75%	12%	13%	32						15.4	126	$22

Means,John

Age: 30	Th: L	Role	SP	Health	F	LIMA Plan	B
Ht: 6' 3"	Wt: 235	Type	Con/FB	PT/Exp	A	Rand Var	-3
				Consist	A	MM	3101

Tommy John surgery in April undercut his chance to experience the new dimensions in Baltimore. On track to return in mid-2023, expect some of the usual TJS command rust on top of his overperforming xBB% in recent seasons. Pre-injury improvements in velocity and K% keep him interesting, but aiming for 2024 impact is the prudent course of action.

Yr Tm	W	Sv	IP	K	ERA	WHIP	xERA	xWHIP	vL+	vR+	BF/G	BB%	K%	K-BB%	xBB%	SwK	Vel	G	L	F	H%	S%	HR/F	xHR/F	GS	APC	DOM%	DIS%	Sv%	LI	RAR	BPX	R$
18 BAL *	7	0	161	106	4.88	1.49	5.53		137	171	24.0	5%	15%	10%		12.1%	90.1	25	42	33	35%	69%	25%	22%	0	66			0	0.52	-14.6	70	-$9
19 BAL	12	0	155	121	3.60	1.14	5.23	1.33	73	100	20.5	6%	19%	13%	8%	10.2%	91.8	31	19	50	27%	75%	10%	11%	27	86	30%	44%	0	0.88	17.3	83	$15
20 BAL	2	0	44	42	4.53	0.98	4.09	1.11	106	93	17.6	4%	24%	20%	6%	12.8%	93.8	44	11	45	23%	68%	22%	16%	10	75	0%	50%			-0.4	157	$5
21 BAL	6	0	147	134	3.62	1.03	4.32	1.14	87	94	22.7	4%	23%	18%	7%	12.4%	92.8	33	20	47	25%	76%	15%	13%	26	90	31%	31%			11.7	127	$13
22 BAL	0	0	8	7	3.38	1.25	4.06	1.21	73	86	17.0	6%	21%	15%	7%	11.1%	91.8	40	24	36	34%	70%	0%	8%	2	68	0%	0%			0.6	109	-$5
1st Half	0	0	8	7	3.38	1.25	4.06	1.21	73	86	17.0	6%	21%	15%	7%	11.1%	91.8	40	24	36	34%	70%	0%	8%	2	68	0%	0%			0.6	109	-$10
2nd Half																																	
Proj	3	0	73	61	4.17	1.15	3.76	1.17	104	107	20.4	5%	21%	16%		12.0%	92.9	36	17	47	28%	72%	15%	13%	14						-1.8	114	$0

BRENT HERSHEY

Megill,Trevor

Age: 29 Th: R Role RP | Health D | LIMA Plan B
Ht: 6' 8" Wt: 250 Type Pwr | PT/Exp D | Rand Var +3
Consist B | MM 4300

Missed time with shoulder and late-season oblique injuries. For second year in a row, nasty H%/S% combo torpedoed above-average skills profile. Throws hard, has a slight GB lean along with some ERA/WHIP upside, but it's another example of the trickiness in evaluating small-sample relievers. Tuck the name away and poke us if his LI improves.

Yr	Tm	W	Sv	IP	K	ERA	WHIP	xERA	xWHIP	vL+	vR+	BF/G	BB%	K%	K-BB%	xBB%	SwK	Vel	G	L	F	H%	S%	HR/F	xHR/F	GS	APC	DOM%	DIS%	Sv%	LI	RAR	BPX	R$
18	aa	1	0	17	7	3.98	1.56	5.38				6.8	9%	9%	0%							30%	78%									0.3	9	-$5
19	a/a	2	6	58	62	4.74	1.61	5.33				7.2	9%	24%	16%							40%	71%									-1.7	96	-$3
20																																		
21	CHC	1	0	24	30	8.37	1.86	4.33	1.18	98	164	4.1	7%	26%	19%	8%	11.1%	96.4	40	21	39	44%	59%	24%	16%	0	16			0	0.69	-12.0	155	-$11
22	MIN	4	0	45	49	4.80	1.49	3.72	1.24	93	115	5.0	9%	25%	16%	6%	11.9%	98.1	45	22	33	37%	68%	10%	15%	0	20			0	0.70	-4.6	119	-$5
1st Half		2	0	13	15	2.03	1.05	3.31	1.21	89	63	5.8	10%	29%	19%	6%	12.2%	97.1	53	6	41	26%	85%	8%	15%	0	21			0	0.80	3.2	135	-$4
2nd Half		2	0	32	34	5.97	1.67	3.88	1.26	95	134	4.8	8%	24%	15%	7%	11.8%	98.4	42	28	30	41%	64%	10%	14%	0	19			0	0.67	-7.8	113	-$12
Proj		**3**	**0**	**51**	**52**	**4.08**	**1.28**	**3.37**	**1.30**	**76**	**111**	**5.0**	**10%**	**25%**	**15%**	**7%**	**11.8%**	**98.4**	**42**	**28**	**30**	**31%**	**69%**	**13%**	**13%**	**0**						**-0.7**	**99**	**-$2**

Megill,Tylor

Age: 27 Th: R Role SP | Health F | LIMA Plan B
Ht: 6' 7" Wt: 230 Type Pwr | PT/Exp C | Rand Var +5
Consist B | MM 4301

So maybe the early-season Baby deGrom talk was a bit out of place... but then again, he couldn't stay healthy, either. Missed a month with biceps tendinitis, then three months with a strained shoulder. Skills shone as control, K-BB% and velocity point to bigger things, but until he can steer clear of IL and figure out LHH, deRisk is real.

Yr	Tm	W	Sv	IP	K	ERA	WHIP	xERA	xWHIP	vL+	vR+	BF/G	BB%	K%	K-BB%	xBB%	SwK	Vel	G	L	F	H%	S%	HR/F	xHR/F	GS	APC	DOM%	DIS%	Sv%	LI	RAR	BPX	R$
18																																		
19																																		
20																																		
21	NYM *	6	0	131	148	4.11	1.23	4.32	1.18	138	77	20.4	7%	28%	21%	7%	12.6%	94.7	42	16	41	31%	73%	19%	16%	18	86	22%	28%			2.5	113	$5
22	NYM	4	0	47	51	5.13	1.25	3.59	1.15	120	81	13.3	7%	26%	19%	7%	12.9%	95.8	41	23	36	32%	62%	15%	16%	9	53	44%	33%	0	0.54	-6.8	140	-$3
1st Half		4	0	41	47	5.01	1.21	3.31	1.11	117	76	19.3	6%	27%	21%	7%	13.4%	95.8	43	24	33	32%	61%	16%	19%	9	77	44%	33%			-5.3	155	-$3
2nd Half		0	0	6	4	6.00	1.50	5.55		140	118	4.3	8%	15%	8%	7%	9.4%	95.6	30	15	55	32%	63%	9%	6%	0	16			0	0.18	-1.5	39	-$12
Proj		**7**	**0**	**87**	**93**	**4.14**	**1.19**	**3.23**	**1.16**	**116**	**71**	**21.4**	**7%**	**27%**	**20%**	**7%**	**12.8%**	**95.3**	**43**	**21**	**36**	**31%**	**70%**	**15%**	**16%**	**16**						**-1.8**	**139**	**$3**

Melancon,Mark

Age: 38 Th: R Role RP | Health C | LIMA Plan A
Ht: 6' 1" Wt: 215 Type Con | PT/Exp A | Rand Var -1
Consist C | MM 2110

Not always a straight line, but important skills are slowly eroding away over the past three seasons: strikeout rate, velocity, ground balls, BPX among them. Things got really ugly in the 2nd half, when he logged just 2 saves after mid-August. And if those dry up completely, there's no reason to have him near your roster.

Yr	Tm	W	Sv	IP	K	ERA	WHIP	xERA	xWHIP	vL+	vR+	BF/G	BB%	K%	K-BB%	xBB%	SwK	Vel	G	L	F	H%	S%	HR/F	xHR/F	GS	APC	DOM%	DIS%	Sv%	LI	RAR	BPX	R$
18	SF	1	3	39	31	3.23	1.59	4.17	1.37	105	108	4.2	8%	18%	10%	8%	10.4%	91.5	52	26	22	37%	80%	7%	18%	0	16			43	1.24	4.4	82	-$3
19	2 NL	5	12	67	68	3.61	1.32	3.25	1.21	89	91	4.3	6%	24%	18%	8%	10.9%	92.2	62	21	17	35%	73%	12%	12%	0	16			100	0.86	7.4	151	$7
20	ATL	2	11	23	14	2.78	1.28	4.31	1.41	104	74	4.1	7%	15%	7%	7%	9.3%	91.7	59	19	22	30%	79%	7%	7%	0	14			85	1.21	4.7	70	$14
21	SD	4	39	65	59	2.23	1.22	3.56	1.34	57	102	4.1	9%	22%	13%	8%	9.2%	92.2	56	25	18	29%	84%	12%	13%	0	16			87	1.30	16.3	96	$22
22	ARI	3	18	56	35	4.66	1.50	4.83	1.44	114	98	4.0	9%	14%	6%	8%	9.9%	91.2	44	24	32	32%	70%	8%	9%	0	14			86	1.07	-4.8	35	$1
1st Half		3	11	28	17	5.08	1.45	4.53	1.33	108	94	3.9	6%	14%	8%	7%	9.6%	91.4	47	21	31	34%	64%	6%	7%	0	14			85	1.23	-3.9	69	$0
2nd Half		0	7	28	18	4.23	1.55	5.17	1.57	120	101	4.1	11%	15%	3%	10%	10.3%	91.1	40	27	33	30%	75%	10%	11%	0	15			88	0.91	-0.9	1	-$5
Proj		**3**	**10**	**58**	**45**	**4.31**	**1.43**	**3.92**	**1.37**	**100**	**97**	**4.0**	**9%**	**18%**	**10%**	**8%**	**10.1%**	**91.6**	**48**	**24**	**28**	**33%**	**70%**	**9%**	**12%**	**0**						**-2.4**	**71**	**$0**

Mikolas,Miles

Age: 34 Th: R Role SP | Health C | LIMA Plan C+
Ht: 6' 4" Wt: 230 Type Con | PT/Exp C | Rand Var -2
Consist B | MM 3103

Reached 200 IP for the second time in five years, all the while thumbing his nose at the third time through the order penalty (see BF/G). That's how a 109 BPX returns $20, as the volume anchors ERA/WHIP. But 2019 and 2021 show the volatility in the pitch-to-contact approach, and makes paying for a full repeat in 2023 a low-percentage play.

Yr	Tm	W	Sv	IP	K	ERA	WHIP	xERA	xWHIP	vL+	vR+	BF/G	BB%	K%	K-BB%	xBB%	SwK	Vel	G	L	F	H%	S%	HR/F	xHR/F	GS	APC	DOM%	DIS%	Sv%	LI	RAR	BPX	R$
18	STL	18	0	201	146	2.83	1.07	3.71	1.19	99	70	25.3	4%	18%	14%	5%	10.1%	93.9	49	22	28	29%	76%	9%	12%	32	94	38%	22%			32.8	126	$27
19	STL	9	0	184	144	4.16	1.22	4.18	1.23	103	99	23.9	4%	19%	15%	6%	10.2%	93.6	47	23	30	31%	71%	16%	16%	32	90	19%	44%			7.9	119	$9
20																																		
21	STL *	4	0	76	45	4.11	1.28	4.59	1.30	102	90	19.4	5%	14%	9%	5%	7.9%	93.1	49	21	29	29%	72%	15%	16%	9	79	0%	33%			1.5	57	-$2
22	STL	12	0	202	153	3.29	1.03	3.79	1.20	87	94	24.4	5%	19%	14%	6%	8.6%	93.3	45	20	35	26%	73%	12%	12%	32	96	44%	25%	0	0.78	16.9	109	$20
1st Half		5	0	100	79	2.61	0.99	3.77	1.20	90	78	24.9	5%	20%	15%	6%	8.7%	92.9	44	21	36	25%	78%	9%	7%	16	98	50%	25%			16.8	109	$22
2nd Half		7	0	102	74	3.96	1.07	3.81	1.20	83	108	23.9	4%	18%	14%	6%	8.5%	93.6	46	20	34	26%	69%	15%	16%	16	93	38%	25%	0	0.79	0.1	109	$13
Proj		**10**	**0**	**160**	**117**	**3.65**	**1.13**	**3.52**	**1.21**	**97**	**95**	**22.8**	**5%**	**19%**	**14%**	**6%**	**9.0%**	**93.4**	**47**	**21**	**32**	**28%**	**72%**	**13%**	**14%**	**28**						**6.2**	**108**	**$11**

Miley,Wade

Age: 36 Th: L Role SP | Health F | LIMA Plan A
Ht: 6' 2" Wt: 220 Type Con/GB | PT/Exp A | Rand Var -2
Consist B | MM 2103

2-2, 3.16 in 37 IP at CHC. Infirmary report: Bum elbow held him out until May 10, then shoulder started barking. Off for three weeks, pitched three innings, then missed three months. Via a broader view, K% and GB% have been consistent as he's aged, but velocity has consistently dropped. 2021 was his late-career peak.

Yr	Tm	W	Sv	IP	K	ERA	WHIP	xERA	xWHIP	vL+	vR+	BF/G	BB%	K%	K-BB%	xBB%	SwK	Vel	G	L	F	H%	S%	HR/F	xHR/F	GS	APC	DOM%	DIS%	Sv%	LI	RAR	BPX	R$
18	MIL *	6	0	107	71	3.33	1.33	4.02	1.43	83	90	19.3	7%	16%	9%	10%	9.4%	90.8	53	24	24	31%	76%	5%	8%	16	81	19%	44%			10.8	73	$3
19	HOU	14	0	167	140	3.98	1.34	4.60	1.40	86	100	21.8	8%	19%	11%	10%	9.6%	90.5	50	21	30	30%	75%	15%	12%	33	90	12%	48%			10.8	82	$9
20	CIN	0	0	14	12	5.65	1.67	5.05	1.62	34	133	11.2	13%	18%	4%	12%	11.6%	90.2	50	32	18	33%	65%	13%	14%	4	48	0%	75%	0	0.56	-2.1	12	-$9
21	CIN	12	0	163	125	3.37	1.33	4.26	1.33	80	102	24.6	7%	18%	11%	8%	10.5%	89.8	49	23	27	31%	78%	13%	14%	28	93	32%	29%			18.0	84	$10
22	CHC *	2	0	53	37	3.14	1.21	3.32	1.39	49	100	16.5	9%	18%	9%	8%	10.8%	89.0	53	14	33	27%	76%	8%	10%	8	63	25%	50%	0	0.79	5.4	75	-$1
1st Half		1	0	23	14	2.35	1.10	2.04	1.43	53	92	18.0	9%	15%	7%	9%	10.0%	89.5	53	19	28	26%	76%	0%	4%	4	68	25%	75%			4.6	92	-$4
2nd Half		1	0	30	23	3.74	1.30	4.30	1.34	24	104	15.5	8%	18%	10%	8%	11.5%	88.3	52	9	39	29%	76%	14%	14%	4	59	25%	25%	0	0.82	0.9	62	-$7
Proj		**7**	**0**	**123**	**92**	**4.12**	**1.32**	**3.89**	**1.37**	**72**	**106**	**21.2**	**8%**	**18%**	**10%**	**9%**	**10.4%**	**89.6**	**51**	**17**	**31**	**30%**	**72%**	**12%**	**12%**	**24**						**-2.3**	**75**	**$0**

Miller,Bobby

Age: 24 Th: R Role SP | Health A | LIMA Plan A
Ht: 6' 5" Wt: 220 Type Pwr | PT/Exp F | Rand Var +1
Consist F | MM 5400

Prototypical RH power pitcher with four-pitch mix led by high-90s fastball and power slider. Was inconsistent in 2022, though ended up in Triple-A by season's end and logged a 14-K outing. Once he hits majors in LA in 2023, expect some growing pains along with a bunch of strikeouts. Great keeper-league asset.

Yr	Tm	W	Sv	IP	K	ERA	WHIP	xERA	xWHIP	vL+	vR+	BF/G	BB%	K%	K-BB%	xBB%	SwK	Vel	G	L	F	H%	S%	HR/F	xHR/F	GS	APC	DOM%	DIS%	Sv%	LI	RAR	BPX	R$
18																																		
19																																		
20																																		
21																																		
22	a/a	7	0	113	124	3.62	1.08	2.95				18.4	6%	26%	20%							30%	69%									4.8	143	$8
1st Half		3	0	64	62	4.06	1.16	2.90				18.2	8%	23%	16%							30%	64%									-0.7	121	$1
2nd Half		4	0	51	62	3.32	1.00	3.06				19.6	5%	30%	25%							29%	73%									4.1	177	$7
Proj		**4**	**0**	**58**	**65**	**3.63**	**1.10**	**2.91**	**1.11**			**23.1**	**6%**	**28%**	**22%**				**45**	**23**	**32**	**30%**	**70%**	**13%**	**12%**	**10**						**2.4**	**156**	**$2**

Mills,Alec

Age: 31 Th: R Role SP | Health F | LIMA Plan B
Ht: 6' 4" Wt: 205 Type Con | PT/Exp B | Rand Var +5
Consist B | MM 2001

Spring-training back injury plagued him all season and resulted in September surgery. Chronic strand rates, lack of swing-and-miss stuff and huge platoon splits have also persisted through his MLB career. Does have a no-hitter to his credit, but 19 of his 33 GS in last three seasons were PQS disasters. Can only hurt you at this point.

Yr	Tm	W	Sv	IP	K	ERA	WHIP	xERA	xWHIP	vL+	vR+	BF/G	BB%	K%	K-BB%	xBB%	SwK	Vel	G	L	F	H%	S%	HR/F	xHR/F	GS	APC	DOM%	DIS%	Sv%	LI	RAR	BPX	R$
18	CHC *	5	0	144	107	5.53	1.44	4.52	1.18	73	78	20.5	8%	17%	9%	8%	12.0%	90.6	51	12	37	32%	61%	7%	12%	2	42	50%	50%	0	0.38	-24.5	70	-$11
19	CHC *	7	1	140	115	6.00	1.64	6.49	1.19	127	71	22.3	8%	18%	11%	8%	12.7%	89.7	49	20	32	36%	67%	17%	23%	4	61	25%	0%	100	0.54	-25.7	41	-$12
20	CHC	5	0	62	46	4.48	1.16	4.53	1.36	123	69	22.9	8%	18%	11%	8%	7.7%	90.0	47	20	33	24%	69%	21%	19%	11	86	9%	45%			-0.2	80	$9
21	CHC	6	1	119	87	5.07	1.44	4.40	1.33	132	88	16.2	7%	17%	10%	8%	8.2%	89.0	51	21	28	33%	67%	15%	13%	20	61	5%	50%	100	0.79	-11.8	86	-$7
22	CHC	0	0	18	11	9.68	1.75	5.36	1.25	166	167	12.0	4%	13%	10%	6%	7.9%	88.6	34	19	46	35%	50%	23%	20%	2	43	0%	100%	0	0.65	-12.4	79	-$11
1st Half		0	0	18	11	9.68	1.75	5.36	1.25	165	167	12.0	4%	13%	10%	6%	8.0%	88.6	34	19	46	35%	50%	23%	20%	2	43	0%	100%	0	0.65	-12.4	79	-$20
2nd Half																																		
Proj		**3**	**0**	**73**	**52**	**5.40**	**1.46**	**4.17**	**1.31**	**142**	**105**	**21.3**	**6%**	**17%**	**11%**		**8.0%**	**89.2**	**44**	**20**	**36**	**32%**	**68%**	**17%**	**19%**	**15**						**-12.8**	**80**	**-$8**

BRENT HERSHEY

Milner,Hoby

Age: 32	Th: L	Role RP	Health B	LIMA Plan A+
Ht: 6' 3"	Wt: 175	Type	PT/Exp D	Rand Var 0
			Consist B	MM 5300

How is he tip-toeing through the 3-batter minimum rule with a vR like this? Could be his new sinker, which replaced his four-seamer and drove his GB spike. Or could be his exit-velocity and Brl% suppression (both in the 97th percentile for 2022). Throw strikes, induce grounders, limit hard contact. As a southpaw, you can hang around.

Yr Tm	W	Sv	IP	K	ERA	WHIP	xERA	xWHIP	vL+	vR+	BF/G	BB%	K%	K-BB%	xBB%	SwK	Vel	G	L	F	H%	S%	HR/F	xHR/F	GS	APC	DOM%	DIS%	Sv%	LI	RAR	BPX	R$
18 2 TM *	1	2	50	48	4.25	1.56	5.20	1.55	123	158	4.0	11%	22%	11%	10%	6.7%	89.3	33	17	50	34%	76%	25%	17%	0	11			67	0.85	-0.6	68	-$5
19 TAM *	3	12	67	74	4.15	1.19	3.78		106	112	5.0	6%	28%	22%		4.3%	87.6	25	42	33	33%	68%	0%	0%	0	18			80	0.75	2.9	142	$6
20 LAA	0	0	13	13	8.10	1.43	5.21	1.41	123	121	3.1	10%	22%	12%	8%	6.9%	87.9	38	15	46	25%	50%	28%	23%	0	13			0	1.04	-6.0	73	-$10
21 MIL *	1	5	54	67	3.34	1.08	4.29	0.96	77	158	4.3	2%	32%	30%	5%	10.4%	89.2	25	35	40	34%	80%	32%	25%	0	21			83	0.22	6.1	319	$3
22 MIL	3	0	65	64	3.76	1.18	3.29	1.14	94	99	4.1	6%	24%	18%	8%	9.7%	89.0	49	22	29	32%	69%	9%	9%	0	16			0	1.01	1.7	144	$0
1st Half	3	0	31	26	2.32	1.16	3.59	1.26	88	85	3.9	7%	20%	13%	10%	9.8%	88.7	54	18	28	30%	80%	4%	4%	0	15			0	0.73	6.3	107	$0
2nd Half	0	0	34	38	5.08	1.19	3.04	1.03	98	112	4.2	4%	26%	22%	8%	9.5%	89.2	44	26	30	35%	58%	14%	13%	0	17			0	1.29	-4.6	178	-$8
Proj	**2**	**0**	**58**	**61**	**3.95**	**1.22**	**3.11**	**1.14**	**96**	**104**	**4.2**	**6%**	**26%**	**20%**	**8%**	**9.6%**	**89.0**	**45**	**24**	**31**	**33%**	**71%**	**13%**	**9%**	**0**						**0.1**	**145**	**-$1**

Minter,A.J.

Age: 29	Th: L	Role RP	Health A	LIMA Plan B+
Ht: 6' 0"	Wt: 215	Type Pwr/FB	PT/Exp C	Rand Var -4
			Consist B	MM 5510

Succeeded in several-year quest to get BB% to match xBB%. Conveniently, SwK rose during that time and culminated with an elite K-BB%. Even with some ERA regression, this mostly looks repeatable, given his effectiveness vR, mid-90s velocity from the left side, and newly-actualized control. He's a Sv% adjustment away from UP: 25 Sv

Yr Tm	W	Sv	IP	K	ERA	WHIP	xERA	xWHIP	vL+	vR+	BF/G	BB%	K%	K-BB%	xBB%	SwK	Vel	G	L	F	H%	S%	HR/F	xHR/F	GS	APC	DOM%	DIS%	Sv%	LI	RAR	BPX	R$
18 ATL	4	15	61	69	3.23	1.29	3.78	1.23	72	98	4.0	8%	27%	18%	8%	15.3%	96.6	37	28	35	34%	75%	5%	6%	0	16			88	1.08	7.0	127	$8
19 ATL *	5	10	54	58	5.97	1.73	6.18	1.64	95	127	4.4	11%	24%	13%	8%	14.3%	96.0	37	29	34	39%	67%	10%	15%	0	16			83	1.14	-9.6	66	-$2
20 ATL	1	0	22	24	0.83	1.11	3.71	1.29	89	78	3.9	11%	28%	18%	8%	13.9%	95.6	49	18	33	27%	96%	6%	7%	0	18			0	0.92	9.7	119	$4
21 ATL	3	0	52	57	3.78	1.22	3.91	1.26	76	96	3.6	9%	26%	17%	6%	14.8%	96.1	45	21	34	32%	68%	4%	7%	0	14			0	1.23	3.1	117	-$1
22 ATL	5	5	70	94	2.06	0.91	2.83	0.95	60	85	3.6	6%	35%	29%	6%	16.6%	96.7	38	17	45	30%	81%	7%	9%	0	15			56	1.16	16.5	200	$12
1st Half	4	1	34	45	1.85	0.85	2.79	0.92	33	89	3.5	5%	35%	30%	6%	16.3%	96.8	37	16	47	30%	79%	3%	8%	0	14			33	1.18	8.9	206	$9
2nd Half	1	4	36	49	2.25	0.97	2.88	0.99	84	82	3.7	6%	35%	28%	6%	16.8%	96.6	40	17	43	30%	84%	11%	10%	0	15			67	1.14	7.6	196	$6
Proj	**4**	**5**	**58**	**71**	**3.25**	**1.12**	**3.02**	**1.10**	**73**	**95**	**3.7**	**7%**	**31%**	**24%**	**6%**	**16.0%**	**96.6**	**39**	**20**	**41**	**32%**	**74%**	**9%**	**8%**	**0**						**5.1**	**159**	**$5**

Mize,Casey

Age: 26	Th: R	Role SP	Health F	LIMA Plan B
Ht: 6' 3"	Wt: 212	Type Con	PT/Exp A	Rand Var 0
			Consist C	MM 3100

More waiting for former prospect to fulfill first-player-drafted expectations, as Tommy John surgery will sideline him until late in the year. Professional K% has been underwhelming, and lack of pristine control or reliable GB% has left him without a signature skill so far. 2024 seems like his earliest return to relevance.

Yr Tm	W	Sv	IP	K	ERA	WHIP	xERA	xWHIP	vL+	vR+	BF/G	BB%	K%	K-BB%	xBB%	SwK	Vel	G	L	F	H%	S%	HR/F	xHR/F	GS	APC	DOM%	DIS%	Sv%	LI	RAR	BPX	R$
18																																	
19 aa	6	0	80	63	4.56	1.31	4.14				22.1	6%	19%	13%							33%	66%									-0.5	97	$0
20 DET	0	0	28	26	6.99	1.48	5.20	1.44	145	78	19.0	10%	20%	10%	10%	10.1%	93.7	39	26	35	29%	57%	23%	22%	7	78	0%	71%			-8.9	61	-$12
21 DET	7	0	150	118	3.71	1.14	4.17	1.29	117	80	20.4	7%	19%	13%	8%	9.8%	93.6	48	18	34	26%	74%	16%	19%	30	79	10%	33%			10.3	95	$10
22 DET	0	0	10	4	5.40	1.50	5.84	1.37	82	145	22.5	4%	9%	4%	9%	5.3%	93.5	37	16	47	33%	64%	6%	16%	2	85	0%	100%			-1.8	34	-$6
1st Half	0	0	10	4	5.40	1.50	5.84	1.37	81	145	22.5	4%	9%	4%	9%	5.3%	93.5	37	16	47	33%	64%	6%	16%	2	85	0%	100%			-1.8	34	-$12
2nd Half																																	
Proj	**2**	**0**	**29**	**23**	**4.07**	**1.21**	**3.57**	**1.27**	**131**	**94**	**20.7**	**6%**	**20%**	**13%**		**9.8%**	**93.6**	**48**	**18**	**34**	**29%**	**70%**	**14%**	**17%**	**6**						**-0.4**	**99**	**-$3**

Montas,Frankie

Age: 30	Th: R	Role SP	Health B	LIMA Plan A+
Ht: 6' 2"	Wt: 255	Type Pwr	PT/Exp A	Rand Var 0
			Consist A	MM 3305

Despite our season-long wishes to get him out of OAK, he pitched much better by the Bay (3.35 ERA/1.14 WHIP) than in the Big Apple (4.93/1.54). Rather than "West Coast bias", multiple bouts of shoulder inflammation (July, Sept IL stints) are a more likely explanation. If shoulder quiets down, 2019/2021 ceiling still very attainable. A high-variance wild card.

Yr Tm	W	Sv	IP	K	ERA	WHIP	xERA	xWHIP	vL+	vR+	BF/G	BB%	K%	K-BB%	xBB%	SwK	Vel	G	L	F	H%	S%	HR/F	xHR/F	GS	APC	DOM%	DIS%	Sv%	LI	RAR	BPX	R$
18 OAK *	9	0	138	92	4.77	1.47	4.76	1.40	121	99	21.2	8%	16%	8%	8%	9.2%	95.8	44	25	31	32%	68%	7%	13%	11	77	27%	36%	0	0.64	-10.5	58	-$5
19 OAK	9	0	96	103	2.63	1.11	3.54	1.16	85	87	24.6	6%	26%	20%	7%	11.7%	96.6	49	22	29	31%	80%	11%	11%	16	93	31%	13%			22.3	155	$13
20 OAK	3	0	53	60	5.60	1.51	4.60	1.32	147	76	21.5	10%	25%	16%	6%	12.1%	95.8	37	26	38	34%	67%	18%	16%	11	83	27%	55%			-7.5	105	-$5
21 OAK	13	0	187	207	3.37	1.18	3.73	1.18	92	89	24.3	7%	27%	19%	6%	14.3%	96.3	43	22	35	31%	75%	11%	15%	32	95	31%	16%			20.7	139	$19
22 2 AL	5	0	144	142	4.05	1.25	3.67	1.21	108	94	22.5	7%	23%	16%	8%	13.3%	95.9	46	20	34	31%	71%	13%	14%	27	86	22%	41%			-1.5	122	$2
1st Half	3	0	97	100	3.26	1.09	3.27	1.13	91	89	22.8	6%	26%	20%	6%	13.7%	96.0	47	20	33	29%	74%	13%	14%	17	88	29%	29%			8.5	146	$14
2nd Half	2	0	48	42	5.66	1.57	4.53	1.35	149	100	22.1	9%	19%	10%	9%	12.6%	95.9	43	21	36	35%	66%	13%	14%	10	83	10%	60%			-10.0	74	-$13
Proj	**10**	**0**	**167**	**167**	**3.61**	**1.35**	**3.57**	**1.25**	**119**	**90**	**22.4**	**8%**	**24%**	**16%**	**7%**	**12.7%**	**96.0**	**43**	**22**	**35**	**33%**	**78%**	**14%**	**14%**	**31**						**7.3**	**111**	**$7**

Montero,Rafael

Age: 32	Th: R	Role RP	Health F	LIMA Plan B+
Ht: 6' 0"	Wt: 190	Type /GB	PT/Exp B	Rand Var -5
			Consist B	MM 5311

Didn't get to camp until late March, but earned double digits for the first time by stepping in as temporary backup closer. Skills were a full-season best also, with improved velocity, a K% rebound, and a doubling-down of his extreme GB profile. Role versatility is an asset; elements in place for a ratio repeat with saves upside.

Yr Tm	W	Sv	IP	K	ERA	WHIP	xERA	xWHIP	vL+	vR+	BF/G	BB%	K%	K-BB%	xBB%	SwK	Vel	G	L	F	H%	S%	HR/F	xHR/F	GS	APC	DOM%	DIS%	Sv%	LI	RAR	BPX	R$
18																																	
19 TEX	2	0	29	34	2.48	0.97	3.34	1.04	48	131	5.1	4%	30%	26%	8%	13.1%	95.8	40	22	38	27%	87%	19%	24%	0	21			0	0.88	7.2	181	$1
20 TEX	0	8	18	19	4.08	1.02	4.57	1.25	73	103	4.2	8%	27%	18%	6%	11.1%	95.5	25	20	55	24%	63%	8%	15%	0	17			100	0.77	0.8	107	$7
21 2 AL	5	7	49	42	6.39	1.54	4.36	1.33	117	99	5.1	8%	19%	11%	7%	11.1%	95.5	55	16	28	36%	57%	9%	8%	0	20			54	1.03	-12.9	96	-$5
22 HOU	5	14	68	73	2.37	1.02	3.14	1.20	72	79	3.8	9%	27%	19%	8%	12.0%	96.3	53	16	31	27%	78%	6%	6%	0	15			88	1.12	13.5	135	$13
1st Half	3	6	33	35	1.93	1.01	3.05	1.20	70	75	3.8	9%	27%	19%	7%	10.0%	96.3	56	14	30	27%	81%	4%	7%	0	15			100	1.06	8.2	139	$9
2nd Half	2	8	36	38	2.78	1.04	3.22	1.20	74	83	3.8	8%	27%	18%	9%	13.7%	96.3	50	18	32	27%	74%	7%	6%	0	16			80	1.18	5.2	131	$8
Proj	**5**	**9**	**73**	**70**	**3.10**	**1.08**	**3.10**	**1.24**	**80**	**84**	**4.1**	**8%**	**25%**	**17%**	**8%**	**12.0%**	**96.1**	**53**	**16**	**31**	**28%**	**71%**	**7%**	**6%**	**0**						**7.7**	**121**	**$9**

Montgomery,Jordan

Age: 30	Th: L	Role SP	Health B	LIMA Plan B+
Ht: 6' 6"	Wt: 228	Type	PT/Exp A	Rand Var 0
			Consist A	MM 5305

Incremental improvements paid off with best fantasy season yet: GB% rose due to increased sinker usage; added a half-tick of velocity, continued to clamp down on walks; frustrated LHH. Ks returned in the 2nd half and allayed fears of a pitch-to-contact-only stage. While there are no obvious signs of a Next Big Step, reliable mid-rotation SP have their place.

Yr Tm	W	Sv	IP	K	ERA	WHIP	xERA	xWHIP	vL+	vR+	BF/G	BB%	K%	K-BB%	xBB%	SwK	Vel	G	L	F	H%	S%	HR/F	xHR/F	GS	APC	DOM%	DIS%	Sv%	LI	RAR	BPX	R$
18 NYY	2	0	27	23	3.62	1.35	4.67	1.44		105	19.3	10%	20%	10%	8%	10.4%	90.3	46	16	38	29%	76%	10%	9%	6	76	0%	17%			1.8	62	-$3
19 NYY	0	0	4	5	6.75	1.75	4.05		66	195	9.5	0%	26%	26%		12.2%	91.7	29	36	36	49%	67%	20%	24%	1	41	0%	0%	0	0.75	-1.1	228	-$6
20 NYY	2	0	44	47	5.11	1.30	3.91	1.13	85	106	19.3	5%	24%	20%	6%	13.5%	92.5	43	26	32	35%	64%	17%	15%	10	75	10%	30%			-3.6	163	-$1
21 NYY	6	0	157	162	3.83	1.28	4.06	1.23	83	95	22.0	8%	25%	17%	7%	14.1%	92.5	43	21	36	32%	74%	12%	12%	30	86	23%	30%			8.4	120	$6
22 2 TM	9	0	178	158	3.48	1.09	3.47	1.15	68	98	22.6	5%	22%	17%	6%	13.4%	93.1	48	21	32	29%	72%	13%	12%	32	85	25%	25%			10.7	133	$14
1st Half	3	0	90	72	3.19	1.03	3.53	1.18	59	94	22.8	5%	20%	15%	6%	14.4%	92.6	48	21	31	27%	73%	12%	10%	16	82	19%	19%			8.7	121	$13
2nd Half	6	0	88	86	3.78	1.16	3.40	1.13	77	102	22.5	5%	24%	19%	6%	12.5%	93.4	47	21	32	31%	71%	14%	14%	16	88	31%	31%			2.0	144	$11
Proj	**10**	**0**	**174**	**168**	**3.51**	**1.12**	**3.15**	**1.14**	**74**	**95**	**21.7**	**6%**	**24%**	**19%**	**6%**	**13.4%**	**92.9**	**46**	**22**	**32**	**29%**	**74%**	**14%**	**13%**	**32**						**9.9**	**138**	**$14**

Moore,Matt

Age: 34	Th: L	Role RP	Health F	LIMA Plan A
Ht: 6' 3"	Wt: 210	Type Pwr/FB	PT/Exp C	Rand Var -5
			Consist F	MM 3311

Reinvented himself as a RP in his mid-30s; does it have staying power? PRO: Bumps in velocity, SwK led to hefty strikeout rate; xBB% points to control upside; successful in a few Sv opps. CON: H%/S%/HR/F trifecta throws some shade on smashing surface stats; dubious health grade still lingers. Depending where he lands, could be a sneaky bullpen play.

Yr Tm	W	Sv	IP	K	ERA	WHIP	xERA	xWHIP	vL+	vR+	BF/G	BB%	K%	K-BB%	xBB%	SwK	Vel	G	L	F	H%	S%	HR/F	xHR/F	GS	APC	DOM%	DIS%	Sv%	LI	RAR	BPX	R$
18 TEX	3	0	102	86	6.79	1.66	5.18	1.40	119	129	12.1	9%	18%	10%	7%	9.9%	92.4	38	21	41	35%	61%	14%	13%	12	46	8%	67%	0	0.68	-33.3	63	-$18
19 DET	0	0	10	9	0.00	0.40	2.79	1.04		30	16.5	3%	27%	24%	5%	15.4%	93.0	59	9	32	14%	100%	0%	10%	2	59	50%	0%			5.6	173	-$2
20 for	6	0	85	93	3.29	1.25	3.96				23.1	9%	27%	18%							30%	79%									12.2	102	$21
21 PHI *	2	0	93	80	6.16	1.65	6.55	1.51	106	122	14.4	12%	19%	7%	8%	9.5%	92.5	39	21	41	31%	68%	17%	13%	13	52	8%	69%	0	0.86	-21.8	17	-$16
22 TEX	5	5	74	83	1.95	1.18	3.82	1.36	91	75	4.8	13%	27%	15%	7%	15.1%	94.0	44	17	39	27%	85%	4%	7%	0	20			83	1.15	18.5	87	$9
1st Half	3	1	36	41	1.98	1.29	3.66	1.42	97	73	5.8	14%	27%	13%	8%	14.1%	94.3	53	15	32	30%	83%	0%	7%	0	24			100	0.87	8.9	81	$2
2nd Half	2	4	38	42	1.91	1.06	3.94	1.30	84	77	4.1	11%	28%	16%	6%	16.2%	93.7	35	18	46	24%	86%	7%	8%	0	17			80	1.35	9.6	93	$7
Proj	**4**	**7**	**65**	**68**	**3.40**	**1.30**	**3.80**	**1.36**	**96**	**95**	**5.2**	**11%**	**25%**	**14%**	**7%**	**13.0%**	**93.3**	**41**	**19**	**41**	**29%**	**78%**	**11%**	**10%**	**0**						**4.6**	**83**	**$3**

BRENT HERSHEY

Moran,Jovani

Age: 26	Th: L	Role: RP	Health	A	LIMA Plan	A+
Ht: 6' 1"	Wt: 167	Type: Pwr	PT/Exp	D	Rand Var	-1
			Consist	B	MM	5510

0-1, 2.21 ERA in 41 IP at MIN. Lefty with filthy stuff has the makings of a dominant bullpen arm. Gets whiffs half the time when he uses change-up, a pitch that has helped him dominate RH bats. Next step is doing the same in higher-leverage innings. Given stuff and ability to avoid barrels, he could come quickly. One of the better sneaky bullpen plays.

Yr Tm	W	Sv	IP	K	ERA	WHIP	xERA	xWHIP	vL+	vR+	BF/G	BB%	K%	K-BB%	xBB%	SwK	Vel	G	L	F	H%	S%	HR/F	xHR/F	GS	APC	DOM%	DIS%	Sv%	LI	RAR	BPX	R$
18																																	
19 aa	2	0	35	42	6.75	1.64	4.79				7.8	16%	27%	11%							34%	58%									-9.7	84	-$7
20																																	
21 MIN *	4	3	78	100	3.23	1.04	1.90	1.66	90	103	7.6	13%	33%	20%	12%	17.3%	92.6	50	30	20	22%	71%	0%	3%	0	32			50	0.72	10.1	135	$9
22 MIN *	1	1	65	89	3.48	1.27	2.72	1.19	79	64	5.2	11%	33%	22%	9%	17.3%	93.4	49	18	33	35%	71%	0%	7%	0	22			25	0.50	3.9	153	$0
1st Half	0	1	30	41	3.17	1.41	2.93	1.40	44	64	5.2	15%	31%	16%	12%	18.0%	93.1	50	14	36	33%	76%	0%	10%	0	23			50	0.58	2.9	136	-$5
2nd Half	1	0	35	48	3.75	1.15	2.53	1.06	94	64	5.1	8%	33%	26%	7%	16.8%	93.7	48	20	31	36%	65%	0%	5%	0	21			0	0.46	1.0	188	-$3
Proj	4	2	58	76	3.64	1.24	2.96	1.30	110	79	5.9	13%	32%	19%	7%	16.8%	93.7	48	20	31	30%	71%	9%	8%	0						2.4	121	$2

Morejon,Adrian

Age: 24	Th: L	Role: RP	Health	F	LIMA Plan	B
Ht: 5' 11"	Wt: 224	Type: Pwr/xFB	PT/Exp	D	Rand Var	-2
			Consist	B	MM	2301

Returned from April 2021 Tommy John surgery and flashed the swing-and-miss stuff that made him a premium international prospect five years ago. Given long history of arm injuries, bullpen seems to be his destiny. Success there will hinge on finding an out-pitch against RH bats, who have been his bugaboo. Still young, so keep monitoring.

Yr Tm	W	Sv	IP	K	ERA	WHIP	xERA	xWHIP	vL+	vR+	BF/G	BB%	K%	K-BB%	xBB%	SwK	Vel	G	L	F	H%	S%	HR/F	xHR/F	GS	APC	DOM%	DIS%	Sv%	LI	RAR	BPX	R$
18																																	
19 SD *	0	0	44	48	6.01	1.49	4.64	1.31	139	138	9.0	9%	25%	16%	6%	8.4%	96.4	37	30	33	36%	59%	10%	17%	2	31	0%	100%	0	0.37	-8.1	97	-$7
20 SD	2	0	19	25	4.66	1.24	3.28	1.02	126	113	8.8	5%	32%	27%	6%	13.4%	96.6	46	18	36	31%	82%	39%	31%	4	36	0%	75%	0	0.57	-0.5	207	-$1
21 SD	0	0	5	3	3.86	1.50	4.61		46	138	10.0	10%	15%	5%		15.0%	96.3	53	27	20	23%	100%	67%	46%	2	40	0%	50%			0.2	34	-$6
22 SD	5	0	34	28	4.24	1.18	4.56	1.25	73	102	5.4	6%	20%	13%	6%	12.8%	96.9	32	18	50	28%	67%	8%	10%	0	21			0	0.91	-1.1	87	-$2
1st Half	1	0	5	1	3.86	0.86	5.46		41	99	6.3	5%	5%	0%	6%	9.7%	96.4	47	12	41	14%	67%	14%	7%	0	24			0	0.08	0.1	8	-$9
2nd Half	4	0	29	27	4.30	1.23	4.42	1.21	79	102	5.3	7%	22%	16%	6%	13.3%	97.0	29	19	52	31%	67%	7%	11%	0	20			0	1.01	-1.2	100	-$3
Proj	7	0	87	86	4.33	1.28	3.91	1.25	86	114	6.2	8%	24%	16%	6%	13.2%	97.0	29	19	52	31%	69%	9%	10%	0						-3.9	97	$1

Morgan,Elijah

Age: 27	Th: R	Role: RP	Health	A	LIMA Plan	A
Ht: 5' 10"	Wt: 190	Type: /xFB	PT/Exp	C	Rand Var	-3
			Consist	C	MM	3201

Bidders stayed away after his 5.00+ ERA, but solid MLB skills said there was something good here, and move to bullpen brought it out. Arsenal includes three strikeout pitches, all of which he commands well. That suggests another rotation shot could be in cards. Either way, carries nice value as a LIMA target because he'll be cheap and has good skills.

Yr Tm	W	Sv	IP	K	ERA	WHIP	xERA	xWHIP	vL+	vR+	BF/G	BB%	K%	K-BB%	xBB%	SwK	Vel	G	L	F	H%	S%	HR/F	xHR/F	GS	APC	DOM%	DIS%	Sv%	LI	RAR	BPX	R$
18																																	
19 a/a	6	0	107	90	5.28	1.56	5.63				23.4	8%	19%	11%							35%	69%									-10.3	55	-$6
20																																	
21 CLE *	5	0	112	98	5.13	1.29	4.90	1.22	114	106	20.1	7%	21%	14%	6%	11.1%	90.4	29	20	51	30%	65%	15%	15%	18	79	17%	39%			-12.0	68	-$4
22 CLE	5	0	67	72	3.38	0.89	3.55	1.05	89	87	5.1	5%	28%	23%	5%	12.6%	92.2	30	18	51	24%	69%	12%	9%	1	20	0%	0%	0	1.05	4.9	149	$6
1st Half	4	0	37	47	2.68	0.68	2.86	0.91	84	67	5.7	4%	35%	30%	5%	14.2%	92.0	31	19	50	20%	70%	13%	10%	1	23	0%	0%	0	1.24	5.9	194	$9
2nd Half	1	0	30	25	4.25	1.15	4.48	1.21	93	112	4.6	6%	21%	15%	6%	10.7%	92.4	30	18	52	27%	69%	11%	9%	0	18			0	0.87	-1.0	96	-$6
Proj	5	0	87	83	3.73	1.15	3.77	1.19	104	106	7.3	6%	24%	18%	6%	11.8%	91.8	30	19	51	28%	74%	12%	10%	0						2.6	110	$3

Morris,Cody

Age: 26	Th: R	Role: RP	Health	F	LIMA Plan	A+
Ht: 6' 5"	Wt: 222	Type: Pwr	PT/Exp	F	Rand Var	-5
			Consist	A	MM	5401

1-2, 2.28 ERA in 24 IP at CLE. Unheralded prospect consistently has shown ability to miss bats and keep the ball over the plate in minors. Problem is, he's another pitcher whose development has been stalled due to injuries. That spotty durability means you can't count on him, but there's enough here to bid a buck or two and cross your fingers.

Yr Tm	W	Sv	IP	K	ERA	WHIP	xERA	xWHIP	vL+	vR+	BF/G	BB%	K%	K-BB%	xBB%	SwK	Vel	G	L	F	H%	S%	HR/F	xHR/F	GS	APC	DOM%	DIS%	Sv%	LI	RAR	BPX	R$
18																																	
19																																	
20																																	
21 a/a	2	0	58	67	1.82	1.11	2.42				16.3	8%	29%	21%							31%	85%									17.6	150	$5
22 CLE *	1	1	40	47	2.16	1.09	2.71	1.42	123	82	12.0	12%	23%	11%	8%	13.9%	94.7	35	28	37	25%	87%	13%	16%	5	58	0%	40%	100	0.78	8.9	118	$1
1st Half																																	
2nd Half	1	1	40	47	2.16	1.09	2.71	1.24	123	82	12.0	11%	30%	19%	8%	13.9%	94.7	35	28	37	25%	87%	13%	16%	5	58	0%	40%	100	0.78	8.9	119	$3
Proj	4	0	73	85	3.34	1.16	3.22	1.22	113	76	15.9	10%	29%	20%		13.9%	94.7	40	19	41	29%	75%	11%	14%	11						5.6	124	$3

Morton,Charlie

Age: 39	Th: R	Role: SP	Health	C	LIMA Plan	A
Ht: 6' 5"	Wt: 215	Type: Pwr	PT/Exp	A	Rand Var	+2
			Consist	B	MM	5405

Given jump in ERA and age, many will use those as reasons to believe the end is near. But skills remained largely intact, and stuff actually ticked up a couple of notches in 2nd half. Jump in HR/F is correctable, and return of prior groundball lean also will help keep ball in park. This is a 3.50 ERA arm that you might be able to get at a 4.00 ERA price.

Yr Tm	W	Sv	IP	K	ERA	WHIP	xERA	xWHIP	vL+	vR+	BF/G	BB%	K%	K-BB%	xBB%	SwK	Vel	G	L	F	H%	S%	HR/F	xHR/F	GS	APC	DOM%	DIS%	Sv%	LI	RAR	BPX	R$
18 HOU	15	0	167	201	3.13	1.16	3.26	1.21	95	88	23.2	9%	29%	20%	8%	12.2%	95.7	47	22	30	29%	77%	15%	12%	30	90	27%	17%			21.1	146	$20
19 TAM	16	0	195	240	3.05	1.08	3.26	1.13	90	75	23.9	7%	30%	23%	6%	13.4%	94.4	48	22	30	31%	74%	10%	12%	33	95	48%	15%			34.9	168	$29
20 TAM	2	0	38	42	4.74	1.39	4.07	1.17	109	100	18.9	6%	25%	19%	6%	12.4%	93.3	42	25	34	37%	67%	11%	12%	9	73	0%	33%			-1.3	153	-$2
21 ATL	14	0	186	216	3.34	1.04	3.22	1.15	79	81	22.9	8%	29%	21%	7%	13.0%	95.3	48	23	29	28%	70%	12%	12%	33	91	33%	18%			21.1	152	$26
22 ATL	9	0	172	205	4.34	1.23	3.50	1.18	111	96	23.5	9%	28%	20%	8%	12.8%	94.9	40	22	39	30%	70%	16%	14%	31	94	32%	29%			-7.9	135	$6
1st Half	4	0	87	101	4.34	1.24	3.54	1.19	119	85	23.1	8%	27%	19%	8%	11.9%	95.1	37	26	37	31%	68%	13%	12%	16	92	31%	38%			-4.0	129	$3
2nd Half	5	0	85	104	4.34	1.22	3.45	1.18	103	108	23.9	9%	29%	20%	8%	13.7%	94.7	43	17	40	29%	72%	20%	16%	15	96	33%	20%			-3.9	141	$6
Proj	10	0	167	196	3.65	1.22	3.10	1.16	102	93	23.5	8%	29%	21%	7%	12.9%	94.6	43	22	35	31%	75%	15%	13%	29						6.6	144	$12

Muller,Kyle

Age: 25	Th: L	Role: SP	Health	A	LIMA Plan	C+
Ht: 6' 7"	Wt: 250	Type: Pwr	PT/Exp	C	Rand Var	+2
			Consist	B	MM	2200

1-1, 8.03 ERA in 12 IP at ATL. Hulking size gives this pitching prospect big strikeout upside due to near-elite fastball. However, those long levers have left him prone to chronic control issues. He made headway with command at AAA, and if it sticks, he's got upper-rotation potential. A high risk/reward play only worth taking if you have a bench.

Yr Tm	W	Sv	IP	K	ERA	WHIP	xERA	xWHIP	vL+	vR+	BF/G	BB%	K%	K-BB%	xBB%	SwK	Vel	G	L	F	H%	S%	HR/F	xHR/F	GS	APC	DOM%	DIS%	Sv%	LI	RAR	BPX	R$
18 aa	4	0	29	23	4.06	1.10	3.47				22.7	5%	20%	15%							28%	67%									0.3	115	-$1
19 aa	7	0	113	102	5.11	1.64	4.45				23.0	15%	20%	5%							32%	68%									-8.4	69	-$6
20																																	
21 ATL *	7	0	118	113	4.21	1.43	4.19	1.47	77	83	19.3	13%	23%	10%	10%	13.4%	93.4	38	19	43	30%	72%	5%	7%	8	75	25%	13%	0	0.77	0.8	75	-$1
22 ATL *	7	0	149	142	4.62	1.40	4.73	1.55	48	118	24.1	14%	20%	7%	8%	12.0%	94.3	39	32	29	33%	70%	18%	15%	3	78	0%	67%			-11.8	85	-$4
1st Half	4	0	85	87	4.41	1.35	4.29	1.29	107	121	23.5	10%	25%	15%	12%	10.8%	95.0	44	44	11	31%	70%	0%	0%	1	74	0%	100%			-4.6	88	-$2
2nd Half	3	0	64	56	4.89	1.47	5.33	1.22		116	24.9	7%	22%	15%	5%	12.6%	94.0	38	28	34	36%	69%	20%	17%	2	80	0%	50%			-7.3	86	-$8
Proj	2	0	44	41	4.75	1.48	4.19	1.39	124	121	23.1	10%	22%	11%	10%	13.4%	93.4	38	19	43	33%	69%	9%	7%	8						-4.2	64	-$6

Muñoz,Andrés

Age: 24	Th: R	Role: RP	Health	F	LIMA Plan	A
Ht: 6' 2"	Wt: 243	Type: Pwr/GB	PT/Exp	D	Rand Var	0
			Consist	F	MM	5521

The anatomy of a bullpen stud... 1) Filthy K% with full SwK backing; 2) good control turned great in 2nd half; 3) groundball tilt became extreme late in season. Increasing leverage during year came concurrent with xGB approach, which put early gopheritis to bed. If opportunity aligns, his next step forward will be a big one. UP: 40 Sv

Yr Tm	W	Sv	IP	K	ERA	WHIP	xERA	xWHIP	vL+	vR+	BF/G	BB%	K%	K-BB%	xBB%	SwK	Vel	G	L	F	H%	S%	HR/F	xHR/F	GS	APC	DOM%	DIS%	Sv%	LI	RAR	BPX	R$
18 aa	2	7	19	18	1.06	1.17	1.79				3.8	13%	24%	11%							25%	90%									7.2	120	$2
19 SD *	4	7	60	81	3.38	1.16	2.76	1.30	88	74	4.2	12%	34%	22%	7%	15.6%	99.9	40	24	36	29%	74%	10%	17%	0	19			64	0.95	8.3	135	$7
20																																	
21 SEA	0	0	1	1	0.00	3.00	0.00		138	44	4.0	50%	25%	-25%		5.9%	99.8	100	0	0	0%	100%	0%		0	17			0	0.16	0.4	-448	-$6
22 SEA	2	4	65	96	2.49	0.89	2.16	0.91	63	85	3.9	6%	39%	33%	5%	22.2%	100.2	53	14	33	30%	75%	11%	9%	0	16			50	1.30	11.8	236	$9
1st Half	1	1	32	48	3.41	1.11	2.36	0.95	91	97	4.0	7%	38%	31%	6%	20.7%	99.9	47	18	35	34%	77%	22%	14%	0	17			33	1.17	2.2	222	-$1
2nd Half	1	3	33	48	1.62	0.69	1.97	0.86	41	70	3.7	5%	39%	34%	4%	23.9%	100.7	58	10	31	27%	74%	0%	9%	0	15			60	1.43	9.7	249	$9
Proj	2	14	65	90	2.30	0.94	2.25	0.98	62	86	4.0	7%	37%	30%	5%	22.4%	100.4	54	14	33	30%	78%	10%	8%	0						13.4	210	$13

STEPHEN NICKRAND

Murfee,Penn

Age: 29	Th: R	Role RP	Health A	LIMA Plan A
Ht: 6' 2"	Wt: 195	Type /xFB	PT/Exp D	Rand Var -4
			Consist D	MM 3300

Nowadays, it's hard to find a 3.00 ERA reliever who can't top 90 mph with fastball. This is one, and it's the result of his ability to avoid nearly all hard contact using slider-heavy approach. Still, it seems likely that batters will figure out how to square up soft-tossing four-seamer, and as a flyball pitcher, that could bring ugly Rand Var to fruition.

Yr Tm	W	Sv	IP	K	ERA	WHIP	xERA	xWHIP	vL+	vR+	BF/G	BB%	K%	K-BB%	xBB%	SwK	Vel	G	L	F	H%	S%	HR/F	xHR/F	GS	APC	DOM%	DIS%	Sv%	LI	RAR	BPX	R$
18																																	
19																																	
20																																	
21 a/a	7	0	80	80	4.88	1.52	5.28				13.4	11%	23%	12%							34%	71%									-6.0	67	-$5
22 SEA	4	0	69	76	2.99	0.95	3.60	1.11	85	78	4.3	7%	28%	21%	5%	12.0%	89.0	34	17	49	26%	73%	8%	7%	1	16	0%	0%	0	0.63	8.4	139	$6
1st Half	1	0	32	38	1.99	0.79	3.28	1.04	82	57	4.1	7%	32%	25%	4%	11.2%	89.1	31	18	51	23%	78%	5%	3%	1	15	0%	0%	0	0.46	7.7	156	$4
2nd Half	3	0	38	38	3.82	1.09	3.89	1.16	87	95	4.4	7%	25%	18%	5%	12.6%	88.9	37	17	47	28%	69%	10%	9%	0	16			0	0.77	0.7	126	$0
Proj	**4**	**0**	**58**	**59**	**3.90**	**1.15**	**3.66**	**1.19**	**98**	**92**	**5.2**	**7%**	**26%**	**18%**	**5%**	**12.0%**	**89.0**	**34**	**17**	**49**	**29%**	**70%**	**10%**	**9%**	**0**						**0.5**	**117**	**$0**

Musgrove,Joe

Age: 30	Th: R	Role SP	Health C	LIMA Plan B
Ht: 6' 5"	Wt: 230	Type Pwr	PT/Exp A	Rand Var -2
			Consist A	MM 5405

After first back-to-back 180+ IP seasons of career, prior durability concerns are firmly behind him now. Steadily elite skills suggest we can expect more of the same, as xBB% confirms control gains should stick. The only wart here is a pretty substantial dropoff in whiffs, particularly in 2nd half. Keep riding him, but monitor SwK to manage risk.

Yr Tm	W	Sv	IP	K	ERA	WHIP	xERA	xWHIP	vL+	vR+	BF/G	BB%	K%	K-BB%	xBB%	SwK	Vel	G	L	F	H%	S%	HR/F	xHR/F	GS	APC	DOM%	DIS%	Sv%	LI	RAR	BPX	R$
18 PIT *	7	0	132	112	4.17	1.16	3.61	1.19	106	86	23.8	5%	21%	17%	4%	12.2%	93.0	46	20	34	31%	66%	10%	10%	19	86	26%	11%			-0.3	133	$5
19 PIT	11	0	170	157	4.44	1.22	4.27	1.23	106	91	22.4	5%	22%	16%	5%	12.2%	92.4	44	20	35	31%	66%	12%	14%	31	83	35%	26%	0	0.80	1.4	126	$9
20 PIT	1	0	40	55	3.86	1.24	3.24	1.16	92	103	20.8	10%	33%	23%	6%	15.0%	92.5	48	20	31	33%	73%	17%	14%	8	84	25%	13%			2.9	172	$3
21 SD	11	0	181	203	3.18	1.08	3.53	1.16	100	76	23.4	7%	27%	20%	6%	13.5%	93.3	44	23	33	28%	76%	14%	14%	31	92	29%	29%	0	0.74	24.4	143	$23
22 SD	10	0	181	184	2.93	1.08	3.41	1.12	89	101	24.7	6%	25%	19%	6%	11.4%	92.9	45	19	36	29%	79%	12%	10%	30	95	40%	17%			23.1	145	$20
1st Half	8	0	92	92	2.25	0.95	3.10	1.10	84	83	25.6	5%	26%	20%	6%	12.1%	92.5	48	21	32	26%	82%	12%	9%	14	97	57%	7%			19.5	152	$29
2nd Half	2	0	89	92	3.64	1.22	3.73	1.15	94	118	23.8	6%	24%	18%	6%	10.9%	93.1	42	18	40	31%	76%	13%	10%	16	93	25%	25%			3.6	137	$5
Proj	**11**	**0**	**181**	**198**	**3.24**	**1.09**	**3.00**	**1.11**	**91**	**94**	**23.4**	**7%**	**28%**	**21%**	**6%**	**12.5%**	**92.8**	**45**	**20**	**35**	**29%**	**76%**	**14%**	**12%**	**30**						**16.2**	**151**	**$20**

Nelson,Ryne

Age: 25	Th: R	Role SP	Health B	LIMA Plan A+
Ht: 6' 3"	Wt: 184	Type Con/FB	PT/Exp D	Rand Var -1
			Consist A	MM 2101

1-1, 1.47 ERA in 18 IP at ARI. Former two-way player focused on pitching in 2019 and has risen the prospect ranks ever since, in large part due to improved strike-throwing. Scouts think he has mid-rotation potential now, and if he proves xFB approach was a small sample-size fluke, he could provide value as soon as 2023.

Yr Tm	W	Sv	IP	K	ERA	WHIP	xERA	xWHIP	vL+	vR+	BF/G	BB%	K%	K-BB%	xBB%	SwK	Vel	G	L	F	H%	S%	HR/F	xHR/F	GS	APC	DOM%	DIS%	Sv%	LI	RAR	BPX	R$
18																																	
19																																	
20																																	
21 aa	3	0	77	88	3.61	1.23	4.13				22.3	8%	28%	21%							31%	77%									6.2	113	$2
22 ARI *	11	0	154	121	4.04	1.22	3.94	1.28	74	74	21.5	9%	23%	14%	8%	9.1%	94.9	23	15	62	28%	70%	7%	5%	3	84	67%	33%			-1.3	79	$6
1st Half	6	0	80	73	4.62	1.25	3.83				20.4	7%	21%	14%							30%	64%	0%		0	0					-6.5	96	$1
2nd Half	5	0	76	48	3.30	1.15	3.84	1.32	74	74	23.4	6%	15%	9%	8%	9.1%	94.9	23	15	62	26%	78%	7%	5%	3	84	67%	33%			6.3	60	$8
Proj	**6**	**0**	**102**	**85**	**4.03**	**1.30**	**4.13**	**1.31**	**129**	**119**	**23.9**	**8%**	**20%**	**13%**		**9.1%**	**94.9**	**32**	**20**	**47**	**30%**	**73%**	**10%**	**9%**	**18**						**-0.8**	**75**	**$0**

Neris,Hector

Age: 34	Th: R	Role RP	Health A	LIMA Plan A
Ht: 6' 2"	Wt: 227	Type Pwr	PT/Exp B	Rand Var 0
			Consist B	MM 5511

As high-leverage use continues to wane, it might be easy to look elsewhere to fill out your bullpen. But skills clearly are back-of-bullpen worthy even with eroding SwK, as he still gets plenty of whiffs and has made up for that decline by throwing more strikes. That's a mixture that will net you profit on your modest bid, especially in holds leagues.

Yr Tm	W	Sv	IP	K	ERA	WHIP	xERA	xWHIP	vL+	vR+	BF/G	BB%	K%	K-BB%	xBB%	SwK	Vel	G	L	F	H%	S%	HR/F	xHR/F	GS	APC	DOM%	DIS%	Sv%	LI	RAR	BPX	R$
18 PHI *	3	12	68	100	4.14	1.21	3.90	1.01	122	100	3.8	9%	37%	28%	7%	19.7%	94.6	31	24	45	34%	72%	23%	19%	0	15			75	0.81	0.1	151	$6
19 PHI	3	28	68	89	2.93	1.02	3.35	1.16	78	84	4.0	9%	32%	24%	8%	18.0%	94.6	45	19	36	26%	80%	18%	14%	0	17			82	1.54	13.2	163	$19
20 PHI	2	5	22	27	4.57	1.71	4.61	1.42	99	82	4.3	13%	26%	14%	9%	17.8%	94.0	42	29	29	41%	70%	0%	8%	0	17			63	1.19	-0.3	86	$2
21 PHI	4	12	74	98	3.63	1.17	3.53	1.21	109	77	4.2	10%	32%	21%	7%	16.7%	94.4	47	13	40	28%	76%	17%	12%	0	17			63	1.11	5.8	147	$9
22 HOU	6	3	65	79	3.72	1.01	3.25	1.06	77	86	3.8	6%	30%	24%	6%	14.6%	94.4	35	23	43	30%	62%	4%	9%	0	14			43	1.00	2.0	161	$6
1st Half	1	0	34	36	3.44	0.82	3.67	1.12	42	101	3.6	7%	27%	20%	6%	15.0%	94.4	29	19	52	22%	58%	5%	11%	0	14			0	1.04	2.2	126	$0
2nd Half	5	3	31	43	4.02	1.21	2.79	1.00	113	72	4.0	6%	33%	27%	6%	14.3%	94.5	41	26	33	39%	65%	4%	7%	0	15			50	0.94	-0.2	198	$4
Proj	**6**	**5**	**73**	**94**	**3.58**	**1.08**	**2.85**	**1.08**	**91**	**82**	**3.7**	**8%**	**33%**	**25%**	**7%**	**16.3%**	**94.5**	**40**	**21**	**40**	**30%**	**69%**	**11%**	**11%**	**0**						**3.5**	**165**	**$7**

Nola,Aaron

Age: 30	Th: R	Role SP	Health A	LIMA Plan C+
Ht: 6' 2"	Wt: 200	Type Pwr	PT/Exp A	Rand Var 0
			Consist B	MM 5505

Those who dismissed that 4.00+ ERA as a fluke were rewarded with true rotation-anchor results, and there's more of that to come. Top-tier command cemented by tons of strikes thrown and bats missed, especially late in season. Sure, hit and strand rate swings could cause another ERA blip, but that's no reason to downgrade him.

Yr Tm	W	Sv	IP	K	ERA	WHIP	xERA	xWHIP	vL+	vR+	BF/G	BB%	K%	K-BB%	xBB%	SwK	Vel	G	L	F	H%	S%	HR/F	xHR/F	GS	APC	DOM%	DIS%	Sv%	LI	RAR	BPX	R$
18 PHI	17	0	212	224	2.37	0.97	3.17	1.16	76	81	25.2	7%	27%	20%	6%	12.9%	92.4	51	19	30	26%	79%	11%	11%	33	97	52%	15%			46.5	154	$38
19 PHI	12	0	202	229	3.87	1.27	3.79	1.29	96	93	25.1	9%	27%	17%	7%	11.5%	92.9	50	21	30	30%	74%	17%	17%	34	98	32%	26%			15.9	126	$15
20 PHI	5	0	71	96	3.28	1.08	2.97	1.09	92	79	24.1	8%	33%	25%	6%	14.1%	92.4	50	23	28	30%	75%	20%	17%	12	96	42%	8%			10.3	189	$23
21 PHI	9	0	181	223	4.63	1.13	3.48	1.04	93	94	23.4	5%	30%	25%	5%	13.3%	92.7	41	19	41	33%	62%	14%	12%	32	93	34%	22%			-8.2	183	$10
22 PHI	11	0	205	235	3.25	0.96	2.94	0.98	80	91	25.2	4%	29%	26%	5%	13.0%	92.6	44	20	37	30%	69%	10%	11%	32	95	44%	6%			18.2	191	$26
1st Half	5	0	104	117	3.13	0.92	2.93	0.97	76	96	25.1	3%	29%	26%	5%	11.9%	92.4	44	18	38	28%	71%	12%	12%	16	97	50%	6%			10.8	190	$26
2nd Half	6	0	101	118	3.38	1.01	2.95	0.98	84	85	25.3	4%	29%	25%	4%	14.2%	92.7	43	22	35	32%	67%	8%	9%	16	93	38%	6%			7.4	191	$22
Proj	**12**	**0**	**196**	**234**	**3.26**	**1.02**	**2.68**	**1.03**	**85**	**86**	**24.3**	**6%**	**31%**	**25%**	**5%**	**13.2%**	**92.6**	**45**	**21**	**34**	**30%**	**72%**	**13%**	**13%**	**31**						**17.0**	**179**	**$25**

Ober,Bailey

Age: 27	Th: R	Role SP	Health F	LIMA Plan A+
Ht: 6' 9"	Wt: 260	Type Con/xFB	PT/Exp D	Rand Var -4
			Consist A	MM 3201

Nasty groin strain was the ailment that sidetracked him this time. When he pitched, there were plenty of positives, including jump in missed bats while maintaining good control. Those components give his skills good life and are reasons to bid again, especially if you're going the LIMA route. Just don't expect more than 120 innings until he proves otherwise.

Yr Tm	W	Sv	IP	K	ERA	WHIP	xERA	xWHIP	vL+	vR+	BF/G	BB%	K%	K-BB%	xBB%	SwK	Vel	G	L	F	H%	S%	HR/F	xHR/F	GS	APC	DOM%	DIS%	Sv%	LI	RAR	BPX	R$
18																																	
19 aa	3	0	24	28	1.08	0.62	0.59				20.7	2%	34%	31%							22%	89%									10.1	360	$3
20																																	
21 MIN *	4	0	108	113	4.11	1.22	4.66	1.12	116	98	18.3	6%	26%	20%	6%	11.8%	92.4	33	21	46	31%	74%	17%	16%	20	74	10%	35%			2.1	116	$2
22 MIN	2	0	56	51	3.21	1.05	4.20	1.14	101	78	20.6	5%	22%	18%	6%	13.9%	91.6	28	21	51	29%	71%	5%	11%	11	78	18%	27%			5.2	117	$1
1st Half	1	0	34	29	4.01	1.28	4.55	1.18	116	86	20.3	5%	20%	15%	6%	14.1%	91.7	25	26	50	34%	68%	4%	12%	7	75	0%	29%			-0.2	101	-$7
2nd Half	1	0	22	22	2.01	0.72	3.69	1.07	70	66	21.3	5%	26%	21%	6%	13.7%	91.4	33	12	54	20%	79%	6%	10%	4	82	50%	25%			5.4	141	-$1
Proj	**4**	**0**	**116**	**106**	**3.78**	**1.18**	**3.85**	**1.19**	**117**	**97**	**21.4**	**6%**	**23%**	**17%**	**6%**	**13.4%**	**91.7**	**31**	**18**	**51**	**30%**	**73%**	**10%**	**11%**	**22**						**2.7**	**109**	**$4**

Odorizzi,Jake

Age: 33	Th: R	Role SP	Health F	LIMA Plan C+
Ht: 6' 2"	Wt: 190	Type Con/xFB	PT/Exp B	Rand Var -1
			Consist A	MM 1101

Holding on to end-rotation value by a thread, and MLB clubs seem to agree, as he was traded twice in same season. There's just nothing here that sticks out anymore, except maybe steadily declining BPX. So-so command sub-indicators say he has neither stuff nor approach to turn around that slide. Flunking health adds even more risk. DN: 5.00 ERA

Yr Tm	W	Sv	IP	K	ERA	WHIP	xERA	xWHIP	vL+	vR+	BF/G	BB%	K%	K-BB%	xBB%	SwK	Vel	G	L	F	H%	S%	HR/F	xHR/F	GS	APC	DOM%	DIS%	Sv%	LI	RAR	BPX	R$
18 MIN	7	0	164	162	4.49	1.34	4.81	1.36	104	101	22.2	10%	23%	13%	10%	10.8%	91.1	28	23	49	30%	69%	9%	11%	32	96	28%	31%			-6.9	72	$0
19 MIN	15	0	159	178	3.51	1.21	4.30	1.25	100	78	21.9	8%	27%	19%	8%	13.1%	92.9	35	21	44	31%	74%	9%	12%	30	93	33%	23%			19.5	123	$17
20 MIN	0	0	14	12	6.59	1.39	4.70	1.23	62	157	15.0	5%	20%	15%	8%	8.8%	93.0	36	24	40	31%	60%	24%	25%	4	71	0%	50%			-3.6	116	-$9
21 HOU	6	0	105	91	4.21	1.25	4.80	1.31	108	93	18.4	8%	21%	13%	8%	10.3%	92.2	35	20	45	28%	71%	12%	12%	23	77	13%	30%	0	0.76	0.7	82	$2
22 2 TM	6	0	106	86	4.40	1.33	4.75	1.32	103	101	20.6	8%	19%	11%	8%	10.7%	92.1	32	22	47	30%	70%	9%	8%	22	82	18%	50%			-5.7	67	-$2
1st Half	3	0	36	24	4.04	1.32	4.94	1.42	96	92	18.8	9%	16%	7%	9%	8.7%	92.2	34	23	43	29%	69%	4%	5%	8	73	13%	50%			-0.3	36	-$3
2nd Half	3	0	71	62	4.58	1.33	4.66	1.27	106	106	21.6	7%	20%	13%	8%	11.7%	92.1	30	21	48	30%	71%	11%	10%	14	87	21%	50%			-5.4	83	-$4
Proj	**7**	**0**	**102**	**84**	**4.67**	**1.34**	**4.29**	**1.34**	**109**	**98**	**20.2**	**8%**	**20%**	**12%**	**8%**	**11.2%**	**92.2**	**33**	**21**	**46**	**30%**	**68%**	**10%**	**10%**	**21**						**-8.8**	**68**	**-$2**

STEPHEN NICKRAND

Ohtani,Shohei

Age:	28	Th:	R	Role	SP	Health	B	LIMA Plan	C+
Ht:	6' 4"	Wt:	210	Type	Pwr	PT/Exp	A	Rand Var	-4
						Consist	F	MM	5505

Was good before this, but vaulted into otherworldly and CY contention with creativity and broad repertoire. Turned slider-forward from the outset; introduced new sinker in August. Across-the-board gains included SwK, velocity, control, fewer HR allowed. Some pullback seems likely, but confirmation that he's on another level to stay for a while.

Yr Tm	W	Sv	IP	K	ERA	WHIP	xERA	xWHIP	vL+	vR+	BF/G	BB%	K%	K-BB%	xBB%	SwK	Vel	G	L	F	H%	S%	HR/F	xHR/F	GS	APC	DOM%	DIS%	Sv%	LI	RAR	BPX	R$
18 LAA	4	0	52	63	3.31	1.16	3.58	1.25	73	95	21.1	10%	30%	19%	9%	15.5%	96.7	39	24	37	28%	76%	13%	11%	10	85	30%	40%			5.4	128	$2
19																																	
20 LAA	0	0	2	3	37.80	6.60	65.84		180	129	8.0	50%	19%	-31%		6.3%	93.8	50	25	25	64%	36%	0%	17%	2	40	0%	50%			-6.9	-957	-$14
21 LAA	9	0	130	156	3.18	1.09	3.45	1.16	101	71	23.2	8%	29%	21%	8%	13.4%	95.7	45	20	36	28%	76%	13%	12%	23	88	35%	13%			17.5	148	$16
22 LAA	15	0	166	219	2.33	1.01	2.90	1.02	91	73	23.6	7%	33%	27%	6%	15.4%	97.3	42	20	38	31%	81%	9%	8%	28	94	54%	14%			33.5	187	$29
1st Half	7	0	74	101	2.68	1.01	2.85	0.97	88	81	22.8	6%	34%	28%	6%	15.4%	97.1	40	21	40	32%	79%	11%	10%	13	91	54%	23%			11.8	202	$21
2nd Half	8	0	92	118	2.05	1.01	2.94	1.06	94	66	24.3	7%	32%	25%	7%	15.4%	97.4	44	19	37	30%	83%	7%	7%	15	97	53%	7%			21.7	175	$31
Proj	14	0	167	213	2.69	1.06	2.71	1.09	88	77	22.1	8%	33%	25%	8%	14.6%	96.9	42	21	37	30%	79%	11%	10%	29						26.3	164	$26

Okert,Steven

Age:	31	Th:	L	Role	RP	Health	B	LIMA Plan	A+
Ht:	6' 2"	Wt:	202	Type	Pwr/FB	PT/Exp	D	Rand Var	-5
						Consist	C	MM	3410

Dominant, flyball-leaning lefty posted another credible season, earning 19 holds while moving up the pen pecking order. Things don't look as good under the hood. Reverse splits helped; track record gives little assurance that they'll last. Already shaky BB% ballooned in 2nd half, minimized by a couple less HR. This seems like his peak.

Yr Tm	W	Sv	IP	K	ERA	WHIP	xERA	xWHIP	vL+	vR+	BF/G	BB%	K%	K-BB%	xBB%	SwK	Vel	G	L	F	H%	S%	HR/F	xHR/F	GS	APC	DOM%	DIS%	Sv%	LI	RAR	BPX	R$
18 SF *	2	1	41	41	4.14	1.35	4.44		46	74	3.9	5%	24%	20%		16.1%	91.6	37	11	53	37%	70%	10%	7%	0	9			25	0.47	0.0	158	-$3
19 aaa	8	0	59	56	6.98	1.74	7.44				5.4	7%	21%	13%							38%	64%									-18.0	35	-$8
20																																	
21 MIA *	5	4	56	62	2.65	1.05	2.71	1.29	64	104	4.4	9%	29%	19%	8%	14.0%	92.2	32	17	51	26%	80%	12%	12%	0	18			100	1.06	11.1	121	$7
22 MIA	5	0	51	63	2.98	1.17	3.85	1.31	110	81	3.7	12%	29%	17%	8%	13.2%	93.7	35	20	45	25%	81%	13%	8%	0	16			0	1.24	6.3	98	$3
1st Half	5	0	27	34	2.36	0.98	3.51	1.22	74	84	3.3	11%	31%	20%	8%	14.5%	93.5	34	19	47	20%	86%	14%	4%	0	15			0	1.02	5.3	120	$4
2nd Half	0	0	25	29	3.65	1.38	4.24	1.39	149	77	4.1	13%	26%	13%	8%	11.9%	93.9	36	21	43	30%	77%	12%	11%	0	17			0	1.51	1.0	73	-$8
Proj	5	1	58	64	4.15	1.33	3.62	1.28	133	102	4.1	10%	27%	17%	8%	13.1%	93.4	34	20	46	31%	74%	13%	9%	0						-1.3	100	-$1

Oller,Adam

Age:	28	Th:	R	Role	RP	Health	B	LIMA Plan	D+
Ht:	6' 4"	Wt:	225	Type	Con/xFB	PT/Exp	D	Rand Var	0
						Consist	F	MM	0000

2-8, 6.30 ERA in 74 IP at OAK. Swingman with career 4.02 ERA in the minors made 14 starts in MLB debut for SP-challenged rebuilder. Walks have become an issue at higher levels, SwK speaks to lack of dominance, FB% lean fueled 2.1 HR/9. Velocity is nothing special and age doesn't help him. Seemingly no upside to chase here.

Yr Tm	W	Sv	IP	K	ERA	WHIP	xERA	xWHIP	vL+	vR+	BF/G	BB%	K%	K-BB%	xBB%	SwK	Vel	G	L	F	H%	S%	HR/F	xHR/F	GS	APC	DOM%	DIS%	Sv%	LI	RAR	BPX	R$
18																																	
19																																	
20																																	
21 a/a	9	0	120	113	3.46	1.22	3.20				21.1	9%	23%	14%							29%	72%									12.0	104	$9
22 OAK *	5	0	108	70	5.23	1.53	5.32	1.60	129	130	18.0	12%	14%	2%	10%	9.5%	93.4	32	17	51	29%	69%	13%	12%	14	68	7%	79%	0	0.66	-16.7	24	-$11
1st Half	3	0	46	32	6.07	1.76	5.81	1.70	144	147	15.0	14%	14%	0%	12%	9.4%	93.8	40	17	43	33%	66%	17%	15%	4	52	0%	100%	0	0.49	-11.9	27	-$18
2nd Half	2	0	62	38	4.59	1.36	4.95	1.46	121	122	21.4	9%	15%	6%	8%	9.6%	93.2	28	17	55	27%	72%	12%	11%	10	83	10%	70%			-4.7	25	-$8
Proj	2	0	44	29	4.55	1.39	4.85	1.52	102	105	19.4	11%	16%	5%	10%	9.5%	93.5	32	17	51	27%	70%	9%	13%	9						-3.1	13	-$5

Ortiz,Luis

Age:	24	Th:	R	Role	SP	Health	A	LIMA Plan	A+
Ht:	6' 2"	Wt:	163	Type		PT/Exp	F	Rand Var	0
						Consist	F	MM	4201

0-2, 4.50 ERA in 16 IP at PIT. Late bloomer leapfrogged A+ to begin 2022. Finished up making four MLB starts, allowing just two runs in the first three. Command, consistency and change-up all works-in-progress. But devastating FB/slider combo with big velocity points to high-leverage reliever floor if he can't cut it in the rotation. Speculation worthy now.

Yr Tm	W	Sv	IP	K	ERA	WHIP	xERA	xWHIP	vL+	vR+	BF/G	BB%	K%	K-BB%	xBB%	SwK	Vel	G	L	F	H%	S%	HR/F	xHR/F	GS	APC	DOM%	DIS%	Sv%	LI	RAR	BPX	R$
18																																	
19																																	
20																																	
21																																	
22 PIT *	5	0	141	131	4.42	1.14	3.37	1.50	106	51	18.6	14%	25%	10%	8%	13.1%	98.5	44	15	41	27%	64%	6%	7%	4	69	25%	25%			-7.9	97	$3
1st Half	3	0	68	61	4.90	1.20	3.69				18.2	9%	22%	13%							27%	61%	0%		0	0					-7.8	83	-$4
2nd Half	2	0	73	71	3.98	1.09	3.08	1.21	106	51	19.1	7%	24%	16%	8%	13.1%	98.5	44	15	41	27%	66%	6%	7%	4	69	25%	25%			-0.1	110	$4
Proj	5	0	87	82	3.81	1.14	3.39	1.26	155	71	21.0	8%	24%	16%		13.1%	98.5	44	15	41	27%	70%	12%	6%	16						1.8	106	$3

Ottavino,Adam

Age:	37	Th:	R	Role	RP	Health	B	LIMA Plan	B+
Ht:	6' 5"	Wt:	246	Type	Pwr	PT/Exp	B	Rand Var	-4
						Consist	C	MM	5411

Turned back the clock courtesy of career-best BB%, K% rebound, and soaring GB% that found wings in 2nd half. Everything went right; H%, S% cooperated for the first time in a while, past dominance vR reappeared. Consistency grade is a tell, seems unlikely to repeat all this at his age. But he's suddenly relevant again in Holds leagues.

Yr Tm	W	Sv	IP	K	ERA	WHIP	xERA	xWHIP	vL+	vR+	BF/G	BB%	K%	K-BB%	xBB%	SwK	Vel	G	L	F	H%	S%	HR/F	xHR/F	GS	APC	DOM%	DIS%	Sv%	LI	RAR	BPX	R$
18 COL	6	6	78	112	2.43	0.99	2.95	1.17	77	65	4.1	12%	36%	25%	8%	12.7%	93.9	43	19	38	25%	78%	9%	8%	0	17			55	1.21	16.4	163	$14
19 NYY	6	2	66	88	1.90	1.31	4.26	1.41	99	75	3.9	14%	31%	17%	10%	11.4%	93.9	40	19	41	30%	89%	8%	9%	0	16			22	1.13	21.3	94	$8
20 NYY	2	0	18	25	5.89	1.58	3.93	1.27	112	100	3.5	11%	29%	19%	8%	9.7%	93.5	48	20	32	40%	63%	13%	15%	0	14			0	0.66	-3.3	144	-$5
21 BOS	7	11	62	71	4.21	1.45	4.50	1.42	106	94	4.0	13%	26%	13%	9%	10.8%	95.0	40	21	39	33%	72%	8%	8%	0	17			65	1.39	0.4	73	$4
22 NYM	6	3	66	79	2.06	0.97	2.72	1.04	120	67	3.9	6%	31%	24%	8%	12.8%	94.4	52	16	32	28%	84%	12%	8%	0	16			50	1.03	15.5	183	$10
1st Half	2	0	30	35	2.67	1.05	3.23	1.16	121	69	3.7	8%	28%	20%	8%	12.5%	94.3	46	18	36	27%	79%	11%	9%	0	15			0	1.26	4.9	144	$0
2nd Half	4	3	35	44	1.53	0.91	2.30	0.95	119	65	4.1	4%	33%	28%	7%	13.0%	94.5	57	15	28	29%	90%	13%	7%	0	17			75	0.81	10.6	216	$11
Proj	6	2	65	77	3.03	1.16	2.95	1.18	114	76	3.8	9%	30%	21%	8%	12.1%	94.3	47	18	36	31%	76%	9%	8%	0						7.5	142	$6

Otto Jr.,Glenn

Age:	27	Th:	R	Role	SP	Health	B	LIMA Plan	C+
Ht:	6' 3"	Wt:	240	Type		PT/Exp	C	Rand Var	-1
						Consist	B	MM	2101

Awful in 10 1st-half starts; improved notably afterward with help from BB% retrace and S% regression, but warts remained evident throughout. Dominance collapsed and stayed sub-par; SwK and velocity are nothing special, xBB% says control is suspect at very best. Struggles vR look enduring. Needs fast start to be even worth a dart throw.

Yr Tm	W	Sv	IP	K	ERA	WHIP	xERA	xWHIP	vL+	vR+	BF/G	BB%	K%	K-BB%	xBB%	SwK	Vel	G	L	F	H%	S%	HR/F	xHR/F	GS	APC	DOM%	DIS%	Sv%	LI	RAR	BPX	R$
18																																	
19																																	
20																																	
21 TEX *	9	0	121	137	4.87	1.25	3.67	1.20	158	100	21.3	7%	28%	21%	5%	9.6%	92.7	44	29	26	35%	60%	11%	19%	6	75	17%	33%			-8.9	146	$2
22 TEX	7	0	136	107	4.64	1.33	4.59	1.46	90	116	21.7	11%	18%	8%	10%	9.9%	92.2	43	20	37	26%	69%	14%	14%	27	83	7%	33%			-11.3	42	-$3
1st Half	4	0	46	35	5.63	1.53	5.06	1.65	97	124	20.5	14%	17%	3%	12%	10.0%	92.5	42	23	35	27%	65%	13%	19%	10	84	20%	60%			-9.5	-11	-$12
2nd Half	3	0	89	72	4.13	1.23	4.37	1.36	86	112	22.5	9%	19%	10%	9%	9.8%	92.0	44	18	39	26%	73%	15%	11%	17	82	0%	18%			-1.8	69	$1
Proj	6	0	116	95	4.52	1.26	3.94	1.41	84	108	21.7	10%	20%	10%	10%	9.9%	92.2	43	20	37	27%	67%	12%	14%	22						-7.9	59	$0

Oviedo,Johan

Age:	25	Th:	R	Role	RP	Health	A	LIMA Plan	C+
Ht:	6' 5"	Wt:	245	Type	Pwr	PT/Exp	C	Rand Var	-1
						Consist	B	MM	3200

4-3, 3.21 ERA in 56 IP at STL/PIT. Big-armed prospect offered rotation glimmers following trade deadline move. GB%, K%, velocity all looked rotation worthy in small sample, and he minimized HR damage all year. SwK decline is less optimistic—and walks continue to be his biggest obstacle. A step forward, but he's still only watchable from afar.

Yr Tm	W	Sv	IP	K	ERA	WHIP	xERA	xWHIP	vL+	vR+	BF/G	BB%	K%	K-BB%	xBB%	SwK	Vel	G	L	F	H%	S%	HR/F	xHR/F	GS	APC	DOM%	DIS%	Sv%	LI	RAR	BPX	R$
18																																	
19 aa	7	0	113	109	6.73	1.74	5.53				22.4	12%	21%	9%							38%	60%									-30.9	69	-$14
20 STL	0	0	25	16	5.47	1.38	5.53	1.51	89	124	22.4	9%	14%	5%	10%	9.2%	94.9	40	27	33	28%	61%	11%	17%	5	89	0%	40%			-3.1	28	-$8
21 STL *	1	0	117	100	5.32	1.53	4.90	1.59	115	94	19.7	12%	20%	7%	10%	11.4%	94.9	48	22	30	31%	66%	14%	17%	13	78	15%	54%	0	0.81	-15.3	56	-$13
22 2 NL *	8	0	118	106	3.95	1.28	4.03	1.33	80	100	13.4	10%	22%	13%	7%	11.4%	96.1	49	14	36	28%	74%	8%	8%	8	47	13%	38%	0	0.70	0.3	72	$3
1st Half	5	0	69	59	4.93	1.34	5.04	1.36	42	154	15.1	9%	20%	11%	6%	13.6%	95.5	42	16	42	27%	70%	13%	6%	1	37	0%	100%	0	0.87	-8.2	45	-$5
2nd Half	3	0	49	47	2.56	1.19	2.62	1.35	98	70	11.6	10%	23%	13%	8%	10.3%	96.4	53	13	33	28%	79%	6%	9%	7	54	14%	29%	0	0.58	8.5	110	$4
Proj	3	0	51	47	4.60	1.41	3.82	1.41	93	110	15.4	11%	22%	11%	8%	11.6%	95.8	49	16	35	31%	69%	11%	10%	8						-4.0	69	-$5

JOCK THOMPSON

Paddack,Chris

Age: 27	Th: R	Role: RP	Health: F	LIMA Plan: B	
Ht: 6' 5"	Wt: 217	Type: Con	PT/Exp: B	Rand Var: 0	
			Consist: A	MM: 5200	

More elbow woes shelved him after five starts; Tommy John surgery finished him in mid-May, out until at least mid-2023. History of fine control / command, xERA, age say he still has time to be productive, even as terrific rookie season fades. But near-term looks uncertain; long-term health after second TJS even more so. Check back next March.

Yr	Tm	W	Sv	IP	K	ERA	WHIP	xERA	xWHIP	vL+	vR+	BF/G	BB%	K%	K-BB%	xBB%	SwK	Vel	G	L	F	H%	S%	HR/F	xHR/F	GS	APC	DOM%	DIS%	Sv%	LI	RAR	BPX	R$
18	aa	3	0	39	33	2.16	0.76	1.09				20.1	3%	23%	21%							24%	71%									9.6	263	$4
19	SD	9	0	141	153	3.33	0.98	3.94	1.14	88	81	21.8	5%	27%	21%	4%	12.3%	93.9	40	18	42	26%	75%	15%	13%	26	88	42%	19%			20.4	153	$18
20	SD	4	0	59	58	4.73	1.22	3.87	1.15	117	105	20.4	5%	24%	19%	7%	11.7%	94.2	47	20	33	30%	71%	25%	22%	12	80	8%	17%			-2.0	152	$6
21	SD	7	0	108	99	5.07	1.26	4.12	1.17	83	120	20.0	5%	22%	17%	6%	11.7%	94.9	43	22	35	33%	62%	13%	15%	22	81	14%	36%	0	0.79	-10.7	131	-$2
22	MIN	1	0	22	20	4.03	1.21	3.44	1.05	117	85	18.6	2%	22%	19%	5%	11.7%	93.0	44	24	32	37%	63%	0%	7%	5	73	20%	0%			-0.2	160	-$4
1st Half		1	0	22	20	4.03	1.21	3.44	1.05	117	85	18.6	2%	22%	19%	5%	11.7%	93.0	44	24	32	37%	63%	0%	7%	5	73	20%	0%			-0.2	160	-$7
2nd Half																																		
Proj		**2**	**0**	**29**	**28**	**3.97**	**1.12**	**3.18**	**1.09**	**98**	**92**	**19.3**	**4%**	**24%**	**20%**		**11.9%**	**93.9**	**43**	**21**	**36**	**31%**	**67%**	**11%**	**13%**	**6**						**0.0**	**150**	**-$3**

Pagán,Emilio

Age: 32	Th: R	Role: RP	Health: B	LIMA Plan: A+	
Ht: 6' 2"	Wt: 208	Type: Pwr/xFB	PT/Exp: C	Rand Var: +4	
			Consist: B	MM: 5511	

Fast start and save opps obliterated by awful June (11 runs allowed over 9 IP), a reminder of how fast things can go south despite the plusses. Velocity, SwK, elite K% are all intact; poor H% didn't help. But control continues to wobble, and HR issues look entrenched even with GB spike. Will get more late inning work, and likely be shaky. Again.

Yr	Tm	W	Sv	IP	K	ERA	WHIP	xERA	xWHIP	vL+	vR+	BF/G	BB%	K%	K-BB%	xBB%	SwK	Vel	G	L	F	H%	S%	HR/F	xHR/F	GS	APC	DOM%	DIS%	Sv%	LI	RAR	BPX	R$
18	OAK	3	0	62	63	4.35	1.19	4.63	1.23	141	88	4.8	7%	24%	17%	7%	14.5%	93.8	27	18	55	27%	72%	14%	13%	0	19			0	0.56	-1.6	110	-$1
19	TAM	4	20	70	96	2.31	0.83	3.20	0.97	94	70	4.0	5%	36%	31%	4%	18.5%	95.5	34	19	47	25%	87%	16%	10%	0	16			71	1.47	18.9	206	$20
20	SD	0	2	22	23	4.50	1.05	4.70	1.33	98	76	4.0	10%	26%	16%	8%	12.3%	94.5	29	18	53	20%	63%	14%	15%	0	17			29	1.02	-0.1	87	$0
21	SD	4	0	63	69	4.83	1.17	4.74	1.18	107	109	3.9	7%	26%	19%	7%	14.6%	95.0	22	17	61	27%	69%	15%	15%	0	16			0	0.89	-4.4	118	-$1
22	MIN	4	9	63	84	4.43	1.37	3.50	1.17	88	127	4.6	9%	31%	21%	6%	14.7%	95.7	40	19	40	34%	74%	18%	16%	0	19			56	0.96	-3.6	147	$2
1st Half		3	9	28	36	4.88	1.37	3.63	1.34	78	127	4.2	13%	30%	17%	9%	12.6%	95.2	49	16	35	28%	72%	25%	20%	0	18			64	1.32	-3.1	107	$1
2nd Half		1	0	35	48	4.08	1.36	3.41	1.05	94	126	5.1	7%	31%	25%	5%	16.5%	96.0	34	22	44	38%	76%	15%	13%	0	20			0	0.60	-0.5	181	-$6
Proj		**4**	**2**	**65**	**83**	**3.94**	**1.18**	**3.18**	**1.11**	**98**	**104**	**4.2**	**8%**	**32%**	**24%**	**6%**	**15.6%**	**95.4**	**35**	**19**	**47**	**30%**	**76%**	**17%**	**14%**	**0**						**0.3**	**155**	**$2**

Pallante,Andre

Age: 24	Th: R	Role: RP	Health: A	LIMA Plan: A	
Ht: 6' 0"	Wt: 203	Type: Con/xGB	PT/Exp: C	Rand Var: -1	
			Consist: B	MM: 3000	

Rookie swingman with fine ERA in MLB debut. But control needs work, both SwK, K% are decidedly sub-par and he was helped some by favorable S%. Elite GB% jumps out and can hide a lot of deficiencies, as xERA hints. But H% luck will always be a factor, and he won't help your WHIP. Floor with a limited ceiling, more valuable in the real game.

Yr	Tm	W	Sv	IP	K	ERA	WHIP	xERA	xWHIP	vL+	vR+	BF/G	BB%	K%	K-BB%	xBB%	SwK	Vel	G	L	F	H%	S%	HR/F	xHR/F	GS	APC	DOM%	DIS%	Sv%	LI	RAR	BPX	R$
18																																		
19																																		
20																																		
21	a/a	4	0	100	71	3.44	1.48	4.55				18.7	9%	16%	7%							33%	77%									10.2	65	-$2
22	STL	6	0	108	73	3.17	1.42	3.71	1.42	89	113	9.7	9%	16%	7%	9%	7.6%	95.2	64	19	17	31%	80%	15%	10%	10	37	10%	40%	0	1.07	10.7	68	$1
1st Half		2	0	59	38	3.03	1.40	3.84	1.43	79	116	10.5	9%	15%	6%	11%	8.2%	95.3	63	20	17	30%	82%	18%	8%	6	41	0%	33%	0	1.25	6.8	60	-$3
2nd Half		4	0	49	35	3.33	1.44	3.56	1.40	99	107	8.9	9%	17%	8%	8%	7.0%	95.1	66	17	17	32%	78%	12%	13%	4	34	25%	50%	0	0.90	3.8	78	-$2
Proj		**3**	**0**	**58**	**38**	**3.71**	**1.36**	**3.57**	**1.42**	**86**	**104**	**11.0**	**9%**	**16%**	**7%**	**9%**	**7.5%**	**95.2**	**64**	**18**	**17**	**30%**	**74%**	**13%**	**11%**	**2**						**1.8**	**69**	**-$3**

Patiño,Luis

Age: 23	Th: R	Role: RP	Health: F	LIMA Plan: C	
Ht: 6' 1"	Wt: 192	Type: Con/xFB	PT/Exp: D	Rand Var: 0	
			Consist: F	MM: 1101	

1-2, 8.10 ERA in 20 IP at TAM. Bookend disasters illustrated this lost season. Oblique strain in first start shelved him until mid-July; shoulder discomfort finished him after ugly (9 runs in 1 1/3 IP) Sept outing. Rushed once-elite prospect is too young, too good to give up on. But needs a third pitch and now health to stay in rotation consideration.

Yr	Tm	W	Sv	IP	K	ERA	WHIP	xERA	xWHIP	vL+	vR+	BF/G	BB%	K%	K-BB%	xBB%	SwK	Vel	G	L	F	H%	S%	HR/F	xHR/F	GS	APC	DOM%	DIS%	Sv%	LI	RAR	BPX	R$
18																																		
19																																		
20	SD	1	0	17	21	5.19	1.85	6.12	1.64	84	124	7.7	16%	25%	8%	11%	10.9%	96.8	35	16	49	35%	76%	13%	12%	1	32	0%	100%	0	0.64	-1.6	15	-$8
21	TAM *	8	0	107	111	4.12	1.26	3.99	1.33	115	79	16.9	9%	25%	16%	8%	12.2%	95.7	31	20	49	30%	71%	11%	12%	15	72	7%	40%	0	0.75	2.0	94	$4
22	TAM *	4	0	54	41	5.69	1.55	5.88	1.74	100	182	15.7	13%	11%	-2%	8%	9.8%	94.5	38	11	51	30%	68%	16%	10%	6	65	0%	83%			-11.5	24	-$8
1st Half		1	0	17	12	3.57	1.19	4.26	1.20		420	13.5	5%	19%	14%	5%	7.7%	94.7	33	33	33	29%	76%	0%	1%	1	13	0%	100%			0.8	98	-$8
2nd Half		3	0	39	30	6.26	1.61	6.05	1.57	105	177	17.5	12%	17%	4%	8%	9.9%	94.5	38	10	52	29%	65%	17%	10%	5	75	0%	80%			-11.2	14	-$13
Proj		**7**	**0**	**102**	**77**	**4.53**	**1.34**	**4.62**	**1.41**	**88**	**110**	**16.6**	**9%**	**18%**	**9%**	**8%**	**10.7%**	**95.0**	**35**	**14**	**51**	**28%**	**71%**	**11%**	**11%**	**17**						**-7.1**	**49**	**-$2**

Paxton,James

Age: 34	Th: L	Role: SP	Health: F	LIMA Plan: A+	
Ht: 6' 4"	Wt: 227	Type: Pwr/FB	PT/Exp: F	Rand Var: 0	
			Consist: F	MM: 5501	

Unable to answer the bell after April 2021 Tommy John surgery; torn lat in August rehab start—his first—left 2022 stillborn. Oft-injured SP was more than viable in 2019, but has logged 400+ IL days and tossed just 21 IP since then. Career-long injury track record (since 2013) is instructive. At his age, a flyer at best if healthy on Opening Day.

Yr	Tm	W	Sv	IP	K	ERA	WHIP	xERA	xWHIP	vL+	vR+	BF/G	BB%	K%	K-BB%	xBB%	SwK	Vel	G	L	F	H%	S%	HR/F	xHR/F	GS	APC	DOM%	DIS%	Sv%	LI	RAR	BPX	R$
18	SEA	11	0	160	208	3.76	1.10	3.22	1.05	119	86	23.0	7%	32%	26%	5%	14.8%	95.4	40	19	41	31%	71%	14%	13%	28	93	32%	18%			7.7	189	$16
19	NYY	15	0	151	186	3.82	1.28	4.08	1.22	88	101	21.8	9%	29%	21%	8%	14.7%	95.5	38	19	43	32%	76%	14%	13%	29	92	34%	31%			12.7	139	$14
20	NYY	1	0	20	26	6.64	1.48	4.46	1.18	116	118	18.0	8%	29%	21%	6%	14.3%	92.1	32	18	50	38%	58%	14%	16%	5	71	20%	60%			-5.5	151	-$7
21	SEA	0	0	1	2	6.75	0.75	0.00			33	5.0	20%	40%	20%		12.5%	94.1	50	50	0	0%	0%	0%		1	24	0%	0%			-0.4	97	-$6
22																																		
1st Half																																		
2nd Half																																		
Proj		**6**	**0**	**73**	**91**	**3.80**	**1.21**	**3.11**	**1.12**	**103**	**95**	**21.7**	**8%**	**31%**	**23%**	**6%**	**14.7%**	**95.4**	**39**	**19**	**42**	**32%**	**74%**	**15%**	**13%**	**13**						**1.5**	**156**	**$3**

Pearson,Nate

Age: 26	Th: R	Role: RP	Health: F	LIMA Plan: B	
Ht: 6' 6"	Wt: 250	Type: Pwr	PT/Exp: D	Rand Var: 0	
			Consist: D	MM: 3301	

Health a perennial struggle for once-elite prospect, who was limited to just 15 minor league IP this time around. Began 2022 with mononucleosis; lat strain during June rehab start shelved him again until Sept; finished with 9 IP (3 runs, 10/5 K/BB) all in relief. A big arm still young and skilled enough for a career, but he needs to stay on the field.

Yr	Tm	W	Sv	IP	K	ERA	WHIP	xERA	xWHIP	vL+	vR+	BF/G	BB%	K%	K-BB%	xBB%	SwK	Vel	G	L	F	H%	S%	HR/F	xHR/F	GS	APC	DOM%	DIS%	Sv%	LI	RAR	BPX	R$
18																																		
19	a/a	2	0	82	71	3.65	1.11	2.92				17.0	8%	22%	14%							26%	69%									8.7	99	$3
20	TOR	1	0	18	16	6.00	1.50	6.22	1.73	160	58	16.2	16%	20%	4%	10%	11.1%	96.4	38	17	44	21%	68%	22%	12%	4	65	0%	50%	0	0.62	-3.4	-18	-$7
21	TOR *	2	0	47	56	5.38	1.42	4.56	1.56	116	94	8.3	13%	28%	15%	12%	13.0%	97.9	41	13	46	30%	65%	11%	9%	1	25	0%	100%	0	0.31	-6.5	81	-$6
22																																		
1st Half																																		
2nd Half																																		
Proj		**3**	**0**	**87**	**92**	**4.65**	**1.30**	**3.75**	**1.35**			**18.3**	**11%**	**26%**	**15%**				**41**	**19**	**40**	**29%**	**67%**	**12%**	**0%**	**22**						**-7.3**	**87**	**-$3**

Pepiot,Ryan

Age: 25	Th: R	Role: RP	Health: A	LIMA Plan: B+	
Ht: 6' 3"	Wt: 215	Type: Pwr/xFB	PT/Exp: D	Rand Var: -5	
			Consist: C	MM: 1301	

3-0, 3.47 ERA in 36 IP at LA. Injuries rushed well-regarded prospect into May MLB debut after less than 80 Triple-A IP. More than held his own while riding the LA-Oklahoma City shuttle all season. Control remains a real obstacle; fortunate H% / S%, FB% tilt say this could have been much worse. Now an end-game flyer with the seeds for something good.

Yr	Tm	W	Sv	IP	K	ERA	WHIP	xERA	xWHIP	vL+	vR+	BF/G	BB%	K%	K-BB%	xBB%	SwK	Vel	G	L	F	H%	S%	HR/F	xHR/F	GS	APC	DOM%	DIS%	Sv%	LI	RAR	BPX	R$
18																																		
19																																		
20																																		
21	a/a	5	0	104	106	4.44	1.24	4.18				16.3	10%	25%	15%							27%	70%									-2.3	79	$1
22	LA *	12	0	128	135	2.49	1.11	2.80	1.58	123	77	18.0	17%	26%	9%	12%	11.3%	94.0	26	16	57	24%	84%	12%	12%	7	82	14%	14%	0	0.68	23.4	103	$17
1st Half		7	0	74	81	1.83	1.04	1.94	1.29	90	69	17.8	11%	27%	16%	12%	9.6%	94.3	27	19	54	24%	85%	5%	7%	4	83	25%	0%			19.4	128	$23
2nd Half		5	0	57	54	3.24	1.16	3.68	1.35	152	82	19.0	11%	24%	13%	10%	12.6%	93.8	26	14	60	23%	81%	17%	14%	3	81	0%	33%	0	0.61	5.1	71	$6
Proj		**8**	**0**	**102**	**97**	**3.64**	**1.33**	**4.39**	**1.44**	**124**	**78**	**19.8**	**12%**	**23%**	**11%**	**12%**	**11.4%**	**94.0**	**30**	**20**	**50**	**27%**	**79%**	**12%**	**12%**	**21**						**4.1**	**47**	**$3**

JOCK THOMPSON

Peralta,Freddy

Age: 27	Th: R	Role: SP	Health	F	LIMA Plan A+
Ht: 5' 11"	Wt: 199	Type: Pwr/xFB	PT/Exp	A	Rand Var -3
			Consist	A	MM 4503

Scuffled early before being IL'd by May lat strain; August return offered more upside flashes. But beyond K% and HR avoidance, warning signs abound. Velocity, SwK teetered, control hasn't improved, fortunate H% fueled 2nd half ERA. Shoulder woes shelved him again for 17 days in Sept. All about Health; with it ... UP: 160 IP, 180 K. DN: More IL time.

Yr Tm	W	Sv	IP	K	ERA	WHIP	xERA	xWHIP	vL+	vR+	BF/G	BB%	K%	K-BB%	xBB%	SwK	Vel	G	L	F	H%	S%	HR/F	xHR/F	GS	APC	DOM%	DIS%	Sv%	LI	RAR	BPX	R$
18 MIL *	12	0	139	173	3.72	1.18	2.61	1.33	118	55	19.2	12%	31%	19%	9%	11.5%	90.8	31	18	52	29%	69%	9%	11%	14	86	29%	14%	0	0.75	7.4	138	$12
19 MIL	7	1	85	115	5.29	1.46	4.34	1.25	90	114	9.8	10%	30%	20%	7%	13.9%	93.6	32	24	44	37%	68%	15%	15%	8	41	25%	38%	50	0.88	-8.3	134	-$1
20 MIL	3	0	29	47	3.99	1.16	3.22	1.08	77	93	8.3	10%	38%	28%	10%	16.6%	93.0	35	22	43	36%	66%	8%	14%	1	37	0%	100%	0	1.02	1.7	196	$6
21 MIL	10	0	144	195	2.81	0.97	3.52	1.14	75	78	20.7	10%	34%	24%	9%	15.1%	93.4	33	20	47	25%	75%	10%	8%	27	84	30%	15%	0	0.76	26.0	149	$24
22 MIL	4	0	78	86	3.58	1.04	3.64	1.20	71	87	17.6	9%	27%	19%	10%	12.6%	92.7	40	18	42	26%	67%	7%	7%	17	75	29%	24%	0	0.80	3.8	124	$4
1st Half	3	0	39	50	4.42	1.19	3.01	1.11	69	101	20.6	8%	30%	22%	9%	13.3%	92.7	46	23	30	35%	60%	3%	7%	8	88	50%	25%			-2.2	168	-$2
2nd Half	1	0	39	36	2.75	0.89	4.24	1.29	73	73	15.2	9%	24%	14%	10%	11.8%	92.6	34	13	53	18%	77%	9%	7%	9	65	11%	22%	0	0.81	5.9	81	$2
Proj	8	0	123	148	3.46	1.13	3.34	1.21	83	90	21.4	10%	30%	21%	9%	13.1%	92.8	35	19	45	28%	73%	10%	10%	23						7.7	125	$10

Peralta,Wandy

Age: 31	Th: L	Role: RP	Health	D	LIMA Plan A+
Ht: 6' 0"	Wt: 217	Type: /GB	PT/Exp	C	Rand Var -5
			Consist	A	MM 3110

Elite GB% and plus SwK% have kept him watchable. But it was H% luck, better control and dramatically improved HR containment that moved him up the bullpen pecking order and fueled his season to remember. Unfortunately these seem likely to regress, and his K% remains stubbornly sub-par. Rosterable in Sv+Holds leagues, otherwise fungible.

Yr Tm	W	Sv	IP	K	ERA	WHIP	xERA	xWHIP	vL+	vR+	BF/G	BB%	K%	K-BB%	xBB%	SwK	Vel	G	L	F	H%	S%	HR/F	xHR/F	GS	APC	DOM%	DIS%	Sv%	LI	RAR	BPX	R$
18 CIN *	3	0	60	39	5.04	1.88	5.84	1.73	110	107	3.9	14%	14%	0%	9%	10.1%	95.6	48	25	27	35%	72%	5%	7%	0	15			0	0.75	-6.6	40	-$11
19 2 NL	1	0	40	32	5.67	1.41	4.74	1.45	103	125	3.7	9%	19%	9%	10%	15.2%	95.3	51	19	30	27%	69%	31%	24%	0	14			0	0.79	-5.7	67	-$6
20 SF	1	0	27	25	3.29	1.21	4.23	1.37	78	96	4.6	10%	22%	12%	11%	13.1%	94.8	46	26	28	27%	77%	14%	15%	0	20			0	0.54	3.9	84	$0
21 2 TM	5	5	51	43	3.35	1.37	4.08	1.40	94	96	3.9	10%	20%	10%	8%	15.7%	95.2	58	19	23	30%	80%	17%	15%	1	14	0%	100%	83	1.25	5.7	80	$2
22 NYY	3	4	56	47	2.72	1.05	3.52	1.27	61	83	4.0	8%	21%	13%	8%	16.5%	95.5	54	16	30	26%	74%	4%	6%	0	15			44	1.16	8.7	103	$4
1st Half	2	1	29	22	2.15	0.99	3.78	1.35	36	82	4.3	9%	19%	10%	10%	16.3%	95.2	56	12	32	23%	79%	4%	8%	0	17			33	0.93	6.6	80	$1
2nd Half	1	3	27	25	3.33	1.11	3.25	1.19	80	84	3.7	7%	23%	17%	7%	16.8%	95.7	51	21	28	30%	69%	5%	4%	0	13			50	1.38	2.1	128	-$2
Proj	3	4	58	48	3.86	1.28	3.65	1.37	89	96	3.8	9%	20%	11%	8%	15.3%	95.4	53	19	28	28%	73%	13%	12%	0						0.8	80	$0

Pérez,Cionel

Age: 27	Th: L	Role: RP	Health	A	LIMA Plan A
Ht: 5' 11"	Wt: 162	Type: Pwr/GB	PT/Exp	D	Rand Var -5
			Consist	B	MM 3200

Lefty GBer with change of scenery and first extended MLB opportunity. Rode vastly improved BB% and fortunate S% (featuring some absurd HR/F luck) to late-inning relief prominence—and a nice little profit. But he needs more swing-and-miss in his repertoire to get us excited. It's regression waiting-to-happen; this is a ceiling.

Yr Tm	W	Sv	IP	K	ERA	WHIP	xERA	xWHIP	vL+	vR+	BF/G	BB%	K%	K-BB%	xBB%	SwK	Vel	G	L	F	H%	S%	HR/F	xHR/F	GS	APC	DOM%	DIS%	Sv%	LI	RAR	BPX	R$
18 HOU *	7	1	87	90	2.41	1.18	2.92	1.53	82	101	12.4	10%	26%	16%	11%	10.9%	95.4	58	12	31	29%	82%	38%	11%	0	28			50	0.13	18.6	121	$10
19 HOU *	3	0	56	44	6.60	1.69	6.27	1.30	127	118	14.0	10%	17%	8%	11%	9.8%	95.3	45	16	39	35%	63%	25%	14%	0	33			0	0.85	-14.5	31	-$10
20 HOU	1	0	6	8	2.84	2.05	5.01	1.71	43	118	4.6	19%	25%	6%	12%	13.3%	95.1	59	24	18	42%	85%	0%	0%	0	18			0	0.65	1.3	13	-$7
21 CIN *	2	2	55	60	5.16	1.59	4.91	1.74	105	112	4.3	14%	25%	10%	12%	11.2%	96.0	52	11	38	33%	69%	20%	14%	0	18			40	0.74	-6.1	76	-$7
22 BAL	7	1	58	55	1.40	1.16	3.53	1.28	77	82	3.5	9%	24%	15%	8%	11.9%	96.9	51	19	30	29%	89%	4%	12%	0	14			100	1.41	18.2	105	$8
1st Half	4	1	26	25	1.03	1.33	3.67	1.34	78	96	3.5	10%	23%	13%	8%	12.6%	96.4	51	19	29	32%	94%	5%	14%	0	13			100	1.61	9.6	90	$2
2nd Half	3	0	31	30	1.72	1.02	3.42	1.24	75	71	3.6	8%	24%	16%	8%	11.3%	97.3	51	18	31	26%	84%	4%	10%	0	14			0	1.24	8.7	118	$3
Proj	5	1	58	55	3.39	1.35	3.64	1.36	87	99	5.0	10%	23%	12%	8%	11.8%	97.0	51	18	30	31%	77%	9%	12%	0						4.1	86	$0

Pérez,Martín

Age: 32	Th: L	Role: SP	Health	C	LIMA Plan C+
Ht: 6' 0"	Wt: 200	Type:	PT/Exp	A	Rand Var -4
			Consist	B	MM 2105

Veteran reestablished sinker-first repertoire, regained GB% tilt. Increased change-up usage also helped slash Barrel% and HR damage, fueling career year. Poor SwK, K% are entrenched, control inconsistent; fortunes are too often H% dependent, and he's usually pitching with traffic. It's a game of adjustments; 2nd half dip warns against a repeat bet.

Yr Tm	W	Sv	IP	K	ERA	WHIP	xERA	xWHIP	vL+	vR+	BF/G	BB%	K%	K-BB%	xBB%	SwK	Vel	G	L	F	H%	S%	HR/F	xHR/F	GS	APC	DOM%	DIS%	Sv%	LI	RAR	BPX	R$
18 TEX	2	0	85	52	6.22	1.78	5.25	1.52	102	135	18.0	9%	13%	4%	9%	7.5%	92.7	51	20	29	35%	68%	18%	15%	15	64	0%	73%	0	0.83	-21.8	29	-$17
19 MIN	10	0	165	135	5.12	1.52	4.94	1.45	77	112	23.0	9%	18%	9%	7%	10.3%	94.1	48	23	29	33%	69%	15%	12%	29	87	21%	55%	0	0.73	-12.5	65	-$5
20 BOS	3	0	62	46	4.50	1.34	5.23	1.52	107	98	21.8	11%	18%	7%	11%	8.7%	92.1	38	26	35	27%	69%	13%	13%	12	86	25%	42%			-0.4	30	$1
21 BOS	7	0	114	97	4.74	1.51	4.56	1.31	92	117	14.1	7%	19%	12%	8%	8.5%	93.0	44	24	33	34%	73%	16%	17%	22	52	9%	45%	0	0.54	-6.6	91	-$6
22 TEX	12	0	196	169	2.89	1.26	3.79	1.31	80	93	25.7	8%	21%	12%	8%	8.6%	92.7	51	19	30	30%	78%	7%	8%	32	93	38%	13%			26.2	92	$16
1st Half	7	0	100	81	2.34	1.17	3.67	1.23	80	89	25.6	6%	20%	14%	8%	8.6%	92.7	53	16	31	30%	81%	4%	6%	16	92	50%	19%			20.1	111	$21
2nd Half	5	0	96	88	3.46	1.35	3.94	1.40	80	97	25.8	11%	21%	11%	8%	8.7%	92.7	50	21	28	30%	76%	9%	10%	16	95	25%	6%			6.1	72	$7
Proj	10	0	174	143	4.04	1.37	3.91	1.38	89	102	21.0	9%	20%	10%	8%	8.8%	92.7	47	22	31	31%	73%	11%	11%	35						-1.6	71	$2

Pérez,Eury

Age: 20	Th: R	Role: SP	Health	A	LIMA Plan A+
Ht: 6' 9"	Wt: 190	Type: Pwr/FB	PT/Exp	F	Rand Var +2
			Consist	F	MM 4500

Precocious MIA prospect jumped to Double-A after just 78 professional IP. Began slowly, then reeled off 50 IP of 1.98 ERA, 69/11 K/BB and a flash of his upside. Fell apart in late July, IL'd for 5 weeks with arm fatigue, tossed 6 scoreless IP in Sept out of the pen. Owns size, velocity, command; with health, he'll be somebody. But a IP-capped dart throw in 2023.

Yr Tm	W	Sv	IP	K	ERA	WHIP	xERA	xWHIP	vL+	vR+	BF/G	BB%	K%	K-BB%	xBB%	SwK	Vel	G	L	F	H%	S%	HR/F	xHR/F	GS	APC	DOM%	DIS%	Sv%	LI	RAR	BPX	R$
18																																	
19																																	
20																																	
21																																	
22 aa	3	0	75	97	4.17	1.14	3.24				17.5	7%	32%	25%							33%	65%									-1.9	158	$1
1st Half	3	0	56	71	3.28	0.95	2.19				17.6	5%	32%	26%							30%	67%									4.7	199	$9
2nd Half	0	0	19	27	6.78	1.70	6.31				17.2	11%	31%	20%							41%	62%									-6.6	89	-$14
Proj	1	0	58	69	3.71	1.21	3.42	1.23			21.0	10%	29%	19%				40	15	45	30%	73%	11%	11%	11						1.8	124	-$1

Peterson,David

Age: 27	Th: L	Role: RP	Health	D	LIMA Plan A+
Ht: 6' 6"	Wt: 240	Type: Pwr	PT/Exp	C	Rand Var +2
			Consist	B	MM 4301

7-5, 3.83 ERA in 106 IP at NYM. Spotty control still limits his upside. 2nd-half H%, LD% also contributed to basepath congestion that kept rotation work tenuous. But velocity, SwK continued to uptick, K% is now elite, and GB% limited HR damage. Inconsistency, poor BB% point to more bullpen work, but if he figures it out ... UP: 3.50 ERA, 160 K.

Yr Tm	W	Sv	IP	K	ERA	WHIP	xERA	xWHIP	vL+	vR+	BF/G	BB%	K%	K-BB%	xBB%	SwK	Vel	G	L	F	H%	S%	HR/F	xHR/F	GS	APC	DOM%	DIS%	Sv%	LI	RAR	BPX	R$
18																																	
19 aa	3	0	116	106	5.96	1.65	5.72				21.6	8%	20%	13%							39%	64%									-20.8	75	-$12
20 NYM	6	0	50	40	3.44	1.21	4.93	1.52	70	90	20.5	12%	20%	8%	12%	10.8%	92.1	44	19	36	24%	75%	10%	12%	9	81	11%	56%	0	0.79	6.2	40	$13
21 NYM	2	0	67	69	5.54	1.40	3.90	1.34	106	108	19.1	10%	24%	14%	8%	11.5%	92.6	49	23	27	31%	63%	22%	22%	15	75	7%	47%			-10.4	98	-$7
22 NYM *	9	0	132	154	3.99	1.41	4.21	1.27	92	101	16.4	11%	28%	17%	11%	13.0%	93.6	49	24	27	35%	73%	15%	14%	19	67	11%	21%	0	0.77	-0.4	108	$2
1st Half	7	0	76	76	3.30	1.23	3.44	1.27	101	91	20.4	9%	24%	15%	12%	11.7%	93.3	54	19	27	30%	76%	14%	11%	10	82	10%	20%	0	0.92	6.2	105	$10
2nd Half	2	0	58	78	4.73	1.59	4.92	1.27	77	112	13.6	11%	30%	18%	11%	14.4%	94.0	43	30	27	40%	71%	16%	19%	9	57	11%	22%	0	0.66	-5.5	115	-$8
Proj	8	0	116	122	3.84	1.30	3.44	1.34	84	98	19.8	11%	25%	15%	11%	12.5%	93.1	47	24	29	30%	73%	13%	15%	24						1.8	94	$4

Phillips,Evan

Age: 28	Th: R	Role: RP	Health	A	LIMA Plan B+
Ht: 6' 2"	Wt: 215	Type: Pwr	PT/Exp	D	Rand Var -5
			Consist	D	MM 5411

Journeyman became slider forward, added a cutter and was suddenly his team's most indispensable RP. Improved H%, S% luck helped, but legitimate gains were made almost across-the-board. K%, BB% were elite, GB% remained sturdy, velocity was near top-shelf. And he dominated hitters from both sides. Some confirmation needed, but ... UP: 25 Sv

Yr Tm	W	Sv	IP	K	ERA	WHIP	xERA	xWHIP	vL+	vR+	BF/G	BB%	K%	K-BB%	xBB%	SwK	Vel	G	L	F	H%	S%	HR/F	xHR/F	GS	APC	DOM%	DIS%	Sv%	LI	RAR	BPX	R$
18 2 TM *	4	8	64	66	4.86	1.30	3.83	1.91	110	176	5.5	11%	25%	14%	12%	8.2%	93.9	40	10	50	29%	64%	25%	16%	1	24	0%	100%	80	0.42	-5.6	93	$1
19 BAL *	1	1	69	75	5.32	1.61	4.66	1.47	111	108	5.9	12%	24%	12%	11%	12.0%	94.2	38	32	30	36%	66%	9%	12%	0	23			100	0.66	-7.0	90	-$7
20 BAL	1	0	14	20	5.02	1.67	4.27	1.45	68	105	4.9	14%	29%	14%	10%	10.6%	94.6	46	23	31	39%	70%	9%	7%	0	20			0	0.69	-1.0	91	-$6
21 2 TM *	2	1	42	42	5.36	1.49	5.25	1.37	52	106	6.5	11%	23%	11%	5%	11.1%	95.4	51	27	22	31%	68%	11%	9%	0	31			100	0.94	-5.7	58	-$7
22 LA	7	2	63	77	1.14	0.76	2.68	1.01	64	58	3.6	6%	33%	27%	6%	13.1%	96.1	46	17	38	24%	87%	4%	6%	0	14			50	1.12	22.0	181	$15
1st Half	2	0	33	39	1.65	0.86	2.83	1.04	63	77	3.9	6%	31%	25%	7%	14.7%	95.9	44	20	36	25%	85%	7%	7%	0	15			0	0.94	9.3	172	$5
2nd Half	5	2	30	38	0.59	0.66	2.51	0.98	66	37	3.4	6%	35%	29%	5%	11.4%	96.4	48	13	39	21%	90%	0%	6%	0	14			100	1.29	12.6	190	$14
Proj	5	10	65	74	2.84	1.05	3.00	1.14	88	80	4.4	8%	29%	22%	6%	12.7%	96.2	46	16	38	29%	75%	7%	6%	0						9.1	150	$10

JOCK THOMPSON

Pilkington,Konnor

Age: 25	Th: L	Role	SP	Health	A	LIMA Plan	C+
Ht: 6' 3"	Wt: 225	Type		PT/Exp	D	Rand Var	-1
				Consist	D	MM	2101

1-2, 3.88 ERA in 58 IP at CLE. Made debut in May, rode MLB-AAA shuttle all year in spot-start / swingman role. Wasn't overmatched, SwK held up reasonably well, and change-up looks promising. But eye-catching dominance from previous seasons faded at higher levels, and control has long been sub-par. A work-in-progress; too early to get excited about.

Yr Tm	W	Sv	IP	K	ERA	WHIP	xERA	xWHIP	vL+	vR+	BF/G	BB%	K%	K-BB%	xBB%	SwK	Vel	G	L	F	H%	S%	HR/F	xHR/F	GS	APC	DOM%	DIS%	Sv%	LI	RAR	BPX	R$
18																																	
19																																	
20																																	
21 aa	7	0	102	101	3.64	1.09	2.89				18.2	10%	25%	15%							24%	71%									7.8	99	$8
22 CLE *	4	0	116	98	4.41	1.43	4.39	1.52	95	99	17.6	12%	19%	7%	11%	11.7%	92.2	40	21	39	30%	71%	9%	11%	11	69	9%	55%	0	0.59	-6.3	65	-$5
1st Half	1	0	54	47	4.50	1.69	5.53	1.44	118	101	16.4	10%	19%	8%	11%	11.5%	92.2	39	24	37	37%	74%	5%	11%	7	66	0%	57%	0	0.55	-3.6	64	-$14
2nd Half	3	0	62	51	4.33	1.20	3.39	1.44	43	97	19.1	11%	19%	9%	11%	12.1%	92.0	41	17	42	23%	67%	15%	11%	4	76	25%	50%	0	0.68	-2.7	66	-$1
Proj	4	0	87	72	4.23	1.32	4.22	1.42	81	97	21.0	10%	20%	10%	11%	11.9%	92.1	40	20	40	28%	71%	10%	11%	13						-2.8	54	-$2

Pineda,Michael

Age: 34	Th: R	Role	RP	Health	F	LIMA Plan	B
Ht: 6' 7"	Wt: 280	Type	Con/FB	PT/Exp	B	Rand Var	0
				Consist	C	MM	2001

2-7, 5.79 ERA in 47 IP at DET. Visa issues delayed his 2022 start, broken finger quickly shelved him in mid-May. July return was interrupted by triceps tightness, DFA'd after final ugly start in early September. Not the first time health fueled a lost season, but now SwK, K% and velocity are all suspect. Even with elite control intact, outlook seems dubious.

Yr Tm	W	Sv	IP	K	ERA	WHIP	xERA	xWHIP	vL+	vR+	BF/G	BB%	K%	K-BB%	xBB%	SwK	Vel	G	L	F	H%	S%	HR/F	xHR/F	GS	APC	DOM%	DIS%	Sv%	LI	RAR	BPX	R$
18																																	
19 MIN	11	0	146	140	4.01	1.16	4.30	1.18	88	102	23.1	5%	23%	19%	5%	12.9%	92.6	36	23	41	30%	71%	13%	14%	26	88	27%	19%			9.0	134	$12
20 MIN	2	0	27	25	3.38	1.20	4.45	1.23	103	60	22.2	6%	23%	16%	7%	14.9%	92.1	38	21	41	33%	69%	0%	7%	5	91	20%	20%			3.5	118	$2
21 MIN	9	0	109	88	3.62	1.23	4.43	1.21	113	94	20.8	5%	19%	15%	5%	10.8%	90.7	40	22	38	31%	77%	13%	14%	21	78	5%	33%	0	0.77	8.7	112	$6
22 DET *	3	0	72	41	5.64	1.50	6.47	1.28	135	122	17.2	4%	13%	9%	6%	7.9%	89.9	39	17	43	33%	68%	18%	15%	11	66	0%	64%			-14.8	34	-$10
1st Half	1	0	41	21	4.13	1.32	5.30	1.32	125	93	17.1	5%	13%	8%	6%	9.0%	90.1	40	17	43	29%	76%	15%	12%	6	65	0%	33%			-0.8	29	-$8
2nd Half	2	0	33	20	7.15	1.63	7.30	1.23	147	157	18.1	4%	14%	11%	6%	6.7%	89.8	38	18	43	36%	59%	21%	18%	5	68	0%	100%			-12.8	51	-$16
Proj	5	0	102	71	4.91	1.37	4.17	1.23	116	111	19.0	4%	17%	12%	6%	9.3%	90.7	38	20	42	32%	70%	13%	15%	20						-11.8	95	-$5

Pivetta,Nick

Age: 30	Th: R	Role	SP	Health	A	LIMA Plan	B
Ht: 6' 5"	Wt: 214	Type	Pwr	PT/Exp	A	Rand Var	0
				Consist	A	MM	3305

Circuitous route to near-repeat of 2021. Awful April was followed by fine May / June (2.18 ERA, 75/19 K/BB over 78 IP) that disintegrated in the 2nd half. Some poor H% luck was part of it, but so was historically shaky control, entrenched hard contact. 5.74 ERA vs AL East teams last two years. He'll be facing them less often in 2023. Just sayin'.

Yr Tm	W	Sv	IP	K	ERA	WHIP	xERA	xWHIP	vL+	vR+	BF/G	BB%	K%	K-BB%	xBB%	SwK	Vel	G	L	F	H%	S%	HR/F	xHR/F	GS	APC	DOM%	DIS%	Sv%	LI	RAR	BPX	R$
18 PHI	7	0	164	188	4.77	1.30	3.53	1.17	107	99	21.0	7%	27%	20%	6%	12.5%	94.8	47	19	35	34%	67%	16%	14%	32	86	31%	38%	0	0.80	-12.6	156	$1
19 PHI *	9	1	135	138	4.89	1.43	4.85	1.40	114	116	14.7	11%	24%	13%	8%	10.7%	94.6	43	25	32	31%	70%	22%	21%	13	54	15%	46%	100	0.78	-6.3	66	$0
20 2 TM	2	0	16	17	6.89	1.53	5.16	1.30	148	109	14.2	8%	24%	15%	8%	10.0%	92.8	28	23	49	34%	60%	17%	17%	2	58	0%	0%	0	0.52	-4.7	100	-$6
21 BOS	9	1	155	175	4.53	1.30	4.29	1.29	102	97	21.3	10%	26%	17%	7%	11.1%	94.8	38	19	43	30%	70%	14%	12%	30	89	20%	43%	100	0.82	-5.0	106	$4
22 BOS	10	0	180	175	4.56	1.38	4.32	1.32	115	101	23.4	9%	23%	13%	8%	10.5%	93.5	38	20	42	31%	71%	12%	13%	33	93	18%	39%			-13.1	83	-$1
1st Half	8	0	100	95	3.68	1.16	4.10	1.26	92	92	24.2	8%	23%	15%	7%	10.1%	93.4	35	22	43	28%	71%	8%	12%	17	93	29%	24%			3.6	93	$15
2nd Half	2	0	79	80	5.67	1.66	4.61	1.39	140	112	22.6	11%	22%	11%	8%	10.9%	93.6	43	17	41	35%	71%	17%	15%	16	94	6%	56%			-16.7	71	-$17
Proj	9	0	167	172	4.54	1.35	3.72	1.29	109	98	22.3	9%	25%	15%	8%	10.9%	94.1	41	20	39	31%	70%	14%	15%	31						-11.8	99	$0

Plesac,Zach

Age: 28	Th: R	Role	SP	Health	C	LIMA Plan	B
Ht: 6' 3"	Wt: 220	Type	Con	PT/Exp	A	Rand Var	0
				Consist	B	MM	2101

Missed September with a fractured hand, but that clearly wasn't the problem. Typically good control wavered in 2nd half; K% and velocity look ingrained and sub-par. Allows too much solid contact without healthy GB%, and SwK buffers. Repertoire is still fronted by 4-seamer that yielded a .503 Slg. Without adjustments, it's a limited, unexciting ceiling.

Yr Tm	W	Sv	IP	K	ERA	WHIP	xERA	xWHIP	vL+	vR+	BF/G	BB%	K%	K-BB%	xBB%	SwK	Vel	G	L	F	H%	S%	HR/F	xHR/F	GS	APC	DOM%	DIS%	Sv%	LI	RAR	BPX	R$
18 aa	3	0	22	18	3.35	1.26	3.74				22.4	4%	20%	16%							33%	74%									2.2	131	-$2
19 CLE *	12	0	181	142	3.27	1.13	3.37	1.43	90	105	23.1	7%	20%	13%	7%	9.9%	94.0	39	22	39	27%	76%	15%	14%	21	90	19%	29%			27.6	85	$19
20 CLE	4	0	55	57	2.28	0.80	3.46	1.01	85	70	25.8	3%	28%	25%	5%	14.7%	92.8	39	20	41	23%	83%	14%	16%	8	97	75%	0%			14.9	178	$25
21 CLE	10	0	143	100	4.67	1.20	4.67	1.30	95	103	23.9	6%	17%	11%	6%	11.5%	92.9	45	17	38	27%	66%	13%	14%	25	88	16%	44%			-7.1	86	$3
22 CLE	3	0	132	100	4.31	1.32	4.49	1.30	118	92	22.7	7%	18%	11%	7%	10.6%	92.0	40	22	38	30%	72%	12%	14%	24	86	8%	46%	0	0.76	-5.5	78	-$3
1st Half	2	0	85	60	3.80	1.23	4.43	1.29	111	90	24.0	6%	17%	11%	6%	10.1%	92.0	40	22	38	28%	73%	11%	15%	15	89	0%	47%			1.8	76	$0
2nd Half	1	0	46	40	5.24	1.49	4.60	1.31	129	96	20.8	8%	19%	12%	8%	11.4%	92.0	41	20	39	33%	69%	14%	12%	9	82	22%	44%	0	0.71	-7.3	82	-$12
Proj	5	0	116	92	4.16	1.25	3.94	1.29	110	93	22.7	7%	19%	12%	6%	11.7%	92.5	41	20	39	29%	72%	13%	14%	21						-2.8	86	$1

Poche,Colin

Age: 29	Th: L	Role	RP	Health	F	LIMA Plan	A+
Ht: 6' 3"	Wt: 225	Type	Pwr/xFB	PT/Exp	D	Rand Var	-1
				Consist	F	MM	4510

Jumped into saves mix after Tommy John surgery shelved him for two years. Encouraging 1st half was fueled by fortunate H%, S%. But elite dominance was slow to return, BB% has long been volatile, and serious FB% tilt eventually came back to bite. 2nd-half K%, October oblique injury point to upside and issues. With Health, a flawed late-inning arm.

Yr Tm	W	Sv	IP	K	ERA	WHIP	xERA	xWHIP	vL+	vR+	BF/G	BB%	K%	K-BB%	xBB%	SwK	Vel	G	L	F	H%	S%	HR/F	xHR/F	GS	APC	DOM%	DIS%	Sv%	LI	RAR	BPX	R$
18 a/a	6	2	66	96	1.02	0.89	1.23				6.1	8%	39%	31%							29%	91%									25.5	221	$15
19 TAM *	7	2	80	113	5.71	1.25	4.14	1.16	82	89	4.6	9%	35%	26%	6%	17.6%	93.0	18	19	62	34%	57%	13%	11%	0	17			29	1.63	-11.8	132	$1
20																																	
21																																	
22 TAM	4	7	59	64	3.99	1.16	4.13	1.24	104	95	3.8	9%	26%	17%	7%	13.3%	93.3	32	19	49	26%	74%	14%	11%	0	15			54	1.19	-0.1	105	$3
1st Half	2	5	25	22	2.16	0.92	4.39	1.31	122	72	3.7	9%	22%	13%	6%	13.5%	93.6	33	15	52	16%	94%	14%	12%	0	14			83	1.12	5.6	73	$4
2nd Half	2	2	34	42	5.35	1.34	3.93	1.19	92	111	3.8	9%	29%	20%	8%	13.3%	93.1	31	22	47	33%	64%	14%	11%	0	16			29	1.24	-5.7	130	-$6
Proj	4	9	58	71	3.51	1.11	3.33	1.16	95	92	4.1	9%	31%	22%	6%	14.2%	93.2	29	19	52	28%	75%	13%	11%	0						3.3	132	$6

Pressly,Ryan

Age: 34	Th: R	Role	RP	Health	D	LIMA Plan	B
Ht: 6' 2"	Wt: 206	Type	Pwr	PT/Exp	A	Rand Var	0
				Consist	A	MM	5530

Lost almost a month early with a knee injury; sat almost three weeks late with a neck issue. Control wobbled in the 1st half, and xBB suggests it will always be his biggest issue. But velocity, GB% are fine, K% among the elites, and SwK was soaring by season-end. Carved up all comers in a 2nd half that allayed any fears. Still a premium saves source.

Yr Tm	W	Sv	IP	K	ERA	WHIP	xERA	xWHIP	vL+	vR+	BF/G	BB%	K%	K-BB%	xBB%	SwK	Vel	G	L	F	H%	S%	HR/F	xHR/F	GS	APC	DOM%	DIS%	Sv%	LI	RAR	BPX	R$
18 2 AL	2	2	71	101	2.54	1.11	2.71	1.05	70	92	3.8	8%	35%	27%	6%	18.0%	95.8	52	17	32	34%	81%	12%	11%	0	14			25	1.16	14.1	213	$7
19 HOU	2	3	54	72	2.32	0.90	2.56	1.01	48	96	3.8	6%	34%	29%	5%	18.0%	95.6	51	28	21	28%	81%	22%	20%	0	15			38	1.25	14.7	207	$8
20 HOU	1	12	21	29	3.43	1.33	3.25	1.11	97	101	4.0	8%	32%	24%	4%	17.8%	94.7	48	22	30	39%	77%	13%	5%	0	15			75	1.61	2.7	191	$14
21 HOU	5	26	64	81	2.25	0.97	2.66	1.00	72	76	3.9	5%	32%	27%	5%	15.2%	95.5	55	17	28	31%	79%	9%	15%	0	15			93	1.40	15.9	207	$21
22 HOU	3	33	48	65	2.98	0.89	2.45	1.00	74	72	3.6	7%	36%	29%	8%	18.3%	94.5	46	23	31	27%	69%	13%	14%	0	14			89	1.33	5.9	194	$18
1st Half	2	17	23	23	3.52	1.13	3.41	1.24	102	69	3.6	9%	26%	17%	8%	15.7%	94.2	42	26	32	28%	71%	11%	15%	0	13			85	1.26	1.3	108	$10
2nd Half	1	16	25	42	2.49	0.67	1.71	0.79	50	74	3.7	5%	46%	40%	8%	20.5%	95.0	51	18	31	25%	67%	14%	12%	0	15			94	1.40	4.6	276	$16
Proj	3	32	58	79	2.62	0.96	2.31	1.03	66	83	3.7	8%	36%	28%	6%	17.9%	95.1	49	22	29	28%	77%	14%	15%	0						9.6	192	$19

Price,David

Age: 37	Th: L	Role	RP	Health	F	LIMA Plan	B
Ht: 6' 5"	Wt: 215	Type	#DIV/0!	PT/Exp	C	Rand Var	-4
				Consist	C	MM	#DIV/0!

Old dog learns new role, new tricks near the end of the line. Used exclusively out of the pen, revamped pitch-mix produced elite BB%, career-best GB%. This ends with a quiet retirement announcement. 14-year career netted a 157-82 record, 3.32 ERA and 115 BPV over 2000+ innings of work. Happy trails to one of the most skilled pitchers of the century.

Yr Tm	W	Sv	IP	K	ERA	WHIP	xERA	xWHIP	vL+	vR+	BF/G	BB%	K%	K-BB%	xBB%	SwK	Vel	G	L	F	H%	S%	HR/F	xHR/F	GS	APC	DOM%	DIS%	Sv%	LI	RAR	BPX	R$
18 BOS	16	0	176	177	3.58	1.14	3.86	1.20	92	97	24.1	7%	25%	18%	7%	10.2%	92.7	40	21	39	28%	74%	13%	14%	30	91	43%	27%			12.4	129	$18
19 BOS	7	0	107	128	4.28	1.31	3.89	1.18	88	104	20.8	7%	28%	21%	6%	11.8%	92.0	41	24	35	35%	71%	14%	16%	22	85	23%	23%			3.0	152	$4
20																																	
21 LA	5	1	74	58	4.03	1.43	4.56	1.37	107	101	8.4	8%	18%	10%	6%	9.5%	92.9	50	20	30	32%	74%	11%	10%	11	30	9%	18%	100	0.59	2.1	77	-$2
22 LA	2	2	40	37	2.45	1.17	3.39	1.16	103	97	4.2	5%	22%	17%	5%	8.4%	92.3	56	15	29	29%	88%	17%	17%	0	15			50	0.59	7.5	141	$1
1st Half	0	0	20	24	3.20	1.32	3.15	1.03	96	124	4.4	5%	29%	24%	5%	9.9%	92.4	44	20	35	38%	83%	16%	13%	0	15			0	0.58	1.9	188	-$8
2nd Half	2	2	21	13	1.74	1.02	3.64	1.31	113	75	4.0	6%	15%	10%	6%	6.9%	92.2	65	11	24	22%	94%	19%	22%	0	14			67	0.61	5.7	95	$0
Proj																																	

JOCK THOMPSON

Puk,A.J.

Age: 28	Th: L	Role RP	Health D	LIMA Plan A+	
Ht: 6' 7"	Wt: 248	Type Pwr	PT/Exp D	Rand Var -1	
			Consist F	MM 5421	

Once-elite SP prospect finally stayed injury-free all season, found calling as a late-inning bullpen option. SwK and velocity look healthy; K% marched toward elite status for the duration. 2nd-half control wavered; xBB% suggests this was a blip. Return to GB tilt would help, and dominance vR remains sketchy. But with these skills ... UP: 30 Sv

Yr Tm	W	Sv	IP	K	ERA	WHIP	xERA	xWHIP	vL+	vR+	BF/G	BB%	K%	K-BB%	xBB%	SwK	Vel	G	L	F	H%	S%	HR/F	xHR/F	GS	APC	DOM%	DIS%	Sv%	LI	RAR	BPX	R$
18																																	
19 OAK *	6	0	31	37	4.64	1.27	4.50	1.33	117	73	5.1	9%	29%	20%	8%	14.4%	97.1	48	10	41	30%	70%	8%	2%	0	20			0	1.00	-0.5	95	-$1
20																																	
21 OAK *	2	1	64	62	5.94	1.70	6.84	1.29	95	105	7.0	8%	22%	13%	9%	10.3%	95.7	52	26	21	38%	69%	11%	8%	0	20			33	0.57	-13.1	53	-$12
22 OAK	4	4	66	76	3.12	1.15	3.39	1.18	73	105	4.5	8%	27%	19%	7%	13.5%	96.6	43	20	37	29%	77%	11%	12%	0	17			44	1.17	6.9	135	$5
1st Half	1	0	34	35	2.65	1.06	3.09	1.09	87	99	4.6	5%	25%	20%	6%	12.3%	96.5	46	24	30	30%	79%	11%	10%	0	18			0	1.06	5.5	155	-$1
2nd Half	3	4	32	41	3.62	1.24	3.72	1.28	53	111	4.4	11%	29%	18%	7%	14.8%	96.8	41	14	45	28%	75%	12%	14%	0	17			67	1.27	1.4	115	$2
Proj	**7**	**12**	**73**	**83**	**3.34**	**1.11**	**3.09**	**1.14**	**68**	**104**	**4.6**	**8%**	**29%**	**21%**	**7%**	**13.8%**	**96.7**	**43**	**18**	**39**	**29%**	**74%**	**12%**	**12%**	**0**						**5.6**	**146**	**$11**

Quantrill,Cal

Age: 28	Th: R	Role SP	Health A	LIMA Plan B+	
Ht: 6' 3"	Wt: 195	Type Con	PT/Exp A	Rand Var -2	
			Consist A	MM 2105	

Pitchability poster-boy again outperformed his peripherals. Beyond health, good control and consistency, nothing here jumps off the page. But he continues to induce chase and soft contact while avoiding issues with HR. Mediocre DOM/DIS%, xBB%, poorly trending SwK point to ever-present risk, which xERA trumpets loud and clear... DN: 4.00+ ERA

Yr Tm	W	Sv	IP	K	ERA	WHIP	xERA	xWHIP	vL+	vR+	BF/G	BB%	K%	K-BB%	xBB%	SwK	Vel	G	L	F	H%	S%	HR/F	xHR/F	GS	APC	DOM%	DIS%	Sv%	LI	RAR	BPX	R$
18 a/a	9	0	148	106	5.16	1.55	5.50				23.1	6%	16%	10%							36%	68%									-18.4	67	-$10
19 SD *	10	0	140	116	4.95	1.33	4.44	1.30	112	78	19.4	7%	20%	13%	8%	10.4%	94.5	44	21	35	32%	65%	14%	15%	18	77	11%	44%	0	0.83	-7.7	80	$2
20 2 TM	2	1	32	31	2.25	1.22	4.11	1.20	70	114	7.5	6%	23%	17%	8%	10.1%	94.9	44	19	37	31%	89%	12%	14%	3	28	0%	33%	50	1.39	8.7	134	$7
21 CLE	8	0	150	121	2.89	1.18	4.34	1.32	90	93	15.4	8%	20%	12%	8%	9.8%	94.3	43	22	35	27%	80%	11%	11%	22	59	14%	27%	0	0.60	25.5	83	$14
22 CLE	15	0	186	128	3.38	1.21	4.32	1.29	96	101	24.1	6%	17%	11%	8%	8.4%	93.6	42	20	38	28%	76%	10%	11%	32	91	13%	38%			13.5	77	$13
1st Half	4	0	89	55	3.86	1.30	4.68	1.38	108	102	24.9	7%	15%	8%	7%	8.2%	93.0	40	22	38	28%	74%	10%	11%	15	92	13%	33%			1.2	49	$0
2nd Half	11	0	98	73	2.95	1.13	4.00	1.22	85	99	23.4	5%	18%	13%	8%	8.6%	94.2	44	18	38	28%	78%	9%	11%	17	91	12%	41%			12.3	103	$23
Proj	**11**	**0**	**174**	**132**	**3.81**	**1.23**	**3.89**	**1.28**	**91**	**102**	**22.8**	**6%**	**19%**	**12%**	**8%**	**9.3%**	**94.2**	**42**	**20**	**38**	**29%**	**72%**	**10%**	**12%**	**31**						**3.4**	**88**	**$8**

Quintana,José

Age: 34	Th: L	Role RP	Health D	LIMA Plan B+	
Ht: 6' 1"	Wt: 220	Type	PT/Exp B	Rand Var -3	
			Consist B	MM 3203	

2016 had been his last season with a sub-4 ERA—so safe to say that few saw this coming after two seasons of shoulder woes. Improved health, control rebound were certainly factors. But better H%, S% luck that included near-immaculate HR management amidst retreating K% were the primary drivers. A perfect storm that is unlikely to gather again.

Yr Tm	W	Sv	IP	K	ERA	WHIP	xERA	xWHIP	vL+	vR+	BF/G	BB%	K%	K-BB%	xBB%	SwK	Vel	G	L	F	H%	S%	HR/F	xHR/F	GS	APC	DOM%	DIS%	Sv%	LI	RAR	BPX	R$
18 CHC	13	0	174	158	4.03	1.32	4.26	1.36	95	104	23.1	9%	21%	12%	9%	8.3%	91.6	43	22	34	29%	74%	15%	14%	32	91	28%	34%			2.6	84	$7
19 CHC	13	0	171	152	4.68	1.39	4.48	1.29	82	107	23.3	6%	20%	14%	9%	8.7%	91.4	44	25	31	34%	68%	12%	14%	31	88	23%	45%	0	0.80	-3.8	110	$4
20 CHC	0	0	10	12	4.50	1.30	3.28	1.14	151	79	10.3	7%	29%	22%	12%	10.9%	91.4	42	35	23	36%	67%	17%	12%	1	46	0%	100%	0	0.61	-0.1	160	-$6
21 2 TM	0	0	63	85	6.43	1.73	4.06	1.32	71	133	10.2	12%	29%	17%	10%	12.5%	91.6	47	21	32	40%	66%	21%	19%	10	43	0%	40%	0	0.82	-16.8	119	-$14
22 2 NL	6	0	166	137	2.93	1.21	3.80	1.26	80	93	21.2	7%	20%	13%	8%	11.0%	91.3	46	22	31	31%	76%	5%	8%	32	85	19%	25%			21.2	98	$11
1st Half	2	0	81	74	3.33	1.28	3.90	1.25	77	101	21.4	7%	22%	14%	9%	12.2%	91.1	43	24	33	32%	76%	9%	11%	16	86	13%	19%			6.4	104	$3
2nd Half	4	0	85	63	2.55	1.15	3.70	1.27	83	84	21.1	7%	19%	12%	8%	9.9%	91.5	50	21	29	30%	76%	1%	5%	16	84	25%	31%			14.8	94	$13
Proj	**7**	**0**	**160**	**147**	**3.97**	**1.34**	**3.59**	**1.28**	**82**	**102**	**18.0**	**8%**	**22%**	**14%**	**9%**	**10.4%**	**91.4**	**46**	**23**	**31**	**33%**	**72%**	**10%**	**12%**	**30**						**0.0**	**102**	**$3**

Ragans,Cole

Age: 25	Th: L	Role SP	Health B	LIMA Plan C+	
Ht: 6' 4"	Wt: 190	Type Con	PT/Exp D	Rand Var 0	
			Consist F	MM 2101	

0-3, 4.95 ERA in 40 IP at TEX. 2016 1st-round pick seemingly had career derailed by two Tommy John surgeries. But he marched through AA, AAA without resistance (3.04 ERA, 113/31 K/BB over 95 IP) prior to Aug MLB debut. TEX wasn't as welcoming, and the peripherals here are unimpressive. Pitchability gives him a chance, but let someone else take it.

Yr Tm	W	Sv	IP	K	ERA	WHIP	xERA	xWHIP	vL+	vR+	BF/G	BB%	K%	K-BB%	xBB%	SwK	Vel	G	L	F	H%	S%	HR/F	xHR/F	GS	APC	DOM%	DIS%	Sv%	LI	RAR	BPX	R$
18																																	
19																																	
20																																	
21 aa	3	0	37	27	7.07	1.82	7.56				19.1	12%	16%	3%							33%	66%									-12.8	-7	-$11
22 TEX *	8	0	136	118	3.42	1.21	3.58	1.45	74	119	20.3	9%	16%	6%	9%	11.2%	92.1	36	25	39	29%	75%	12%	8%	9	78	0%	22%			9.2	90	$7
1st Half	6	0	74	70	2.93	1.17	3.35				21.2	7%	23%	16%							30%	78%	0%		0	0					9.5	115	$12
2nd Half	2	0	64	48	3.87	1.21	3.62	1.38	74	119	19.9	9%	18%	10%	9%	11.2%	92.1	36	25	39	26%	72%	12%	8%	9	78	0%	22%			0.8	66	-$1
Proj	**5**	**0**	**94**	**76**	**4.04**	**1.34**	**4.10**	**1.36**	**74**	**117**	**21.2**	**9%**	**19%**	**11%**		**11.2%**	**92.1**	**36**	**25**	**39**	**30%**	**74%**	**13%**	**9%**	**18**						**-0.9**	**63**	**-$1**

Rainey,Tanner

Age: 30	Th: R	Role RP	Health F	LIMA Plan A+	
Ht: 6' 2"	Wt: 247	Type Pwr/xFB	PT/Exp C	Rand Var -3	
			Consist F	MM 4510	

Coming off injury-plagued 2021 (leg, side, COVID), hard-throwing, two-pitch reliever with big whiff upside was inserted into the closer role immediately. Navigated poor control, entrenched flyball / HR issues in passable 1st half. Strained UCL finished him in early July; Tommy John surgery might have finished him for 2023. Unrosterable on Opening Day.

Yr Tm	W	Sv	IP	K	ERA	WHIP	xERA	xWHIP	vL+	vR+	BF/G	BB%	K%	K-BB%	xBB%	SwK	Vel	G	L	F	H%	S%	HR/F	xHR/F	GS	APC	DOM%	DIS%	Sv%	LI	RAR	BPX	R$
18 CIN *	7	3	58	60	6.06	1.65	4.42	2.44	215	183	5.0	20%	23%	3%	12%	12.2%	97.8	31	23	46	27%	64%	33%	20%	0	24			50	0.41	-13.7	72	-$6
19 WAS *	4	2	66	99	4.20	1.54	4.06	1.49	124	70	4.3	18%	34%	17%	11%	17.7%	97.8	53	18	29	33%	75%	21%	22%	0	17			22	0.71	2.5	113	-$1
20 WAS	1	0	20	32	2.66	0.74	2.74	0.99	59	82	3.8	9%	43%	33%	8%	21.7%	96.6	31	23	46	14%	82%	25%	19%	0	15			0	1.34	4.5	204	$5
21 WAS	1	3	32	42	7.39	1.71	5.72	1.57	116	111	4.0	17%	28%	11%	10%	15.9%	96.4	25	15	60	33%	58%	12%	14%	0	18			50	1.09	-12.2	29	-$9
22 WAS	1	12	30	36	3.30	1.30	4.15	1.25	86	107	4.4	10%	28%	18%	8%	16.5%	97.0	32	18	51	30%	82%	13%	12%	0	18			75	1.30	2.5	109	$2
1st Half	1	11	27	34	3.67	1.37	4.20	1.27	87	113	4.4	11%	29%	18%	8%	16.4%	96.9	32	17	51	31%	81%	14%	9%	0	18			73	1.21	1.0	107	$3
2nd Half	0	1	3	2	0.00	0.67	3.55		72	47	5.0	0%	20%	20%	7%	18.4%	98.1	25	25	50	24%	100%	0%	41%	0	19			100	2.46	1.5	122	-$9
Proj	**0**	**2**	**7**	**9**	**2.79**	**1.13**	**3.33**	**1.22**	**92**	**92**	**3.8**	**11%**	**32%**	**21%**	**9%**	**16.5%**	**96.9**	**34**	**16**	**49**	**26%**	**84%**	**15%**	**13%**	**0**						**1.1**	**123**	**-$4**

Raley,Brooks

Age: 35	Th: L	Role RP	Health D	LIMA Plan A	
Ht: 6' 3"	Wt: 200	Type Pwr	PT/Exp C	Rand Var -2	
			Consist A	MM 4310	

Late blooming soft-tossing lefty stepped up vR, became one of TAM late-inning options. 1st-half SwK, K% fueled fast start; chase rate, ability to limit barrels were elite all season. Swing-and-miss skills fell off a cliff in 2nd half, but he was saved by HR management, improved control—both of which look unrepeatable. Age, late-season decline say this is a ceiling.

Yr Tm	W	Sv	IP	K	ERA	WHIP	xERA	xWHIP	vL+	vR+	BF/G	BB%	K%	K-BB%	xBB%	SwK	Vel	G	L	F	H%	S%	HR/F	xHR/F	GS	APC	DOM%	DIS%	Sv%	LI	RAR	BPX	R$
18 for	11	0	178	169	5.90	1.48	5.83				25.5	9%	22%	13%							32%	66%									-38.5	47	-$12
19 for	5	0	181	133	4.82	1.58	5.05				26.5	10%	17%	7%							33%	70%									-7.0	51	-$8
20 2 TM	0	1	20	27	4.95	0.95	3.27	1.08	56	108	4.0	7%	32%	25%	7%	14.3%	90.2	39	24	37	25%	50%	18%	16%	0	16			100	1.10	-1.2	184	-$1
21 HOU	2	2	49	65	4.78	1.20	3.06	1.10	67	106	3.5	8%	32%	24%	8%	14.9%	90.8	45	26	29	34%	62%	18%	22%	0	15			40	1.16	-3.1	174	-$2
22 TAM	1	6	54	61	2.68	0.97	3.21	1.12	69	80	3.7	7%	28%	21%	7%	12.2%	90.7	38	29	34	27%	73%	7%	5%	0	14			67	1.22	8.5	146	$5
1st Half	1	4	25	35	2.13	0.87	2.68	1.04	54	71	3.7	8%	34%	26%	9%	14.5%	91.0	38	29	33	28%	73%	0%	2%	0	15			80	1.28	5.7	180	$4
2nd Half	0	2	28	26	3.18	1.06	3.70	1.18	78	90	3.6	6%	23%	17%	5%	10.0%	90.5	37	28	35	27%	74%	11%	7%	0	14			50	1.17	2.8	114	-$3
Proj	**1**	**4**	**51**	**52**	**3.89**	**1.22**	**3.34**	**1.23**	**84**	**104**	**5.1**	**8%**	**26%**	**17%**	**7%**	**12.6%**	**90.7**	**39**	**28**	**33**	**30%**	**70%**	**12%**	**8%**	**0**						**0.5**	**112**	**$0**

Ramirez,Erasmo

Age: 33	Th: R	Role RP	Health C	LIMA Plan A	
Ht: 6' 0"	Wt: 220	Type Con	PT/Exp D	Rand Var -2	
			Consist B	MM 3101	

Modestly successful SP fell off the radar with sketchy health after 2017; resurfaced to eat relief innings for rebuilder. Started slowly but 2nd half piques our interest. Was never a big K guy, but both velocity, SwK are back. Elite control, sturdy GB% also returned, along with soft contact skills. Flyer only, but with move back to SP role... UP: 10 Wins, 3.75 ERA.

Yr Tm	W	Sv	IP	K	ERA	WHIP	xERA	xWHIP	vL+	vR+	BF/G	BB%	K%	K-BB%	xBB%	SwK	Vel	G	L	F	H%	S%	HR/F	xHR/F	GS	APC	DOM%	DIS%	Sv%	LI	RAR	BPX	R$
18 SEA *	2	0	70	51	5.23	1.28	5.23	1.32	132	122	17.9	5%	18%	13%	6%	8.9%	89.9	40	21	40	29%	66%	23%	19%	10	75	0%	50%			-9.3	60	-$5
19 BOS *	6	0	129	69	7.29	1.77	7.15		362	134	21.2	9%	12%	3%		9.8%	90.5	45	18	36	34%	61%	50%	46%	0	41			0	0.12	-44.3	-8	-$22
20 NYM	0	1	14	9	0.63	0.84	4.88	1.40	50	74	8.8	8%	17%	9%	10%	9.2%	90.4	38	18	45	18%	100%	6%	13%	0	33			100	0.25	6.8	56	$2
21 DET	1	0	27	20	5.74	1.09	4.77	1.23	131	70	6.4	5%	18%	14%	5%	8.2%	92.4	37	16	47	27%	48%	10%	11%	0	23			0	0.53	-4.8	100	-$5
22 WAS	4	0	86	61	2.92	1.08	3.83	1.19	84	103	5.8	4%	18%	14%	6%	10.7%	93.3	45	21	34	27%	79%	12%	8%	2	20	0%	50%	0	0.55	11.2	108	$5
1st Half	1	0	36	25	4.50	1.42	4.54	1.29	92	132	5.6	6%	16%	10%	8%	10.7%	92.6	42	20	38	31%	77%	18%	8%	1	20	0%	100%	0	0.51	-2.4	79	-$10
2nd Half	3	0	50	36	1.79	0.83	3.33	1.11	78	77	5.9	3%	19%	16%	4%	10.7%	93.8	48	21	31	24%	82%	7%	9%	1	21	0%	0%	0	0.59	13.5	130	$11
Proj	**3**	**0**	**80**	**60**	**4.17**	**1.23**	**3.70**	**1.24**	**103**	**108**	**8.0**	**5%**	**19%**	**13%**	**6%**	**10.3%**	**92.6**	**44**	**21**	**35**	**30%**	**69%**	**12%**	**10%**	**0**						**-2.0**	**102**	**-$1**

JOCK THOMPSON

Rasmussen,Drew

Age: 27	Th: R	Role	SP	Health	B	LIMA Plan	B
Ht: 6' 1"	Wt: 211	Type		PT/Exp	B	Rand Var	-2
				Consist	A	MM	4203

Introduced cutter as reliable 3rd pitch and thrived as full time SP. Velocity drop was minimal; SwK, GB% remained rock-solid. Hit another gear in 2nd half; K% perked up, better control, fewer HR got him deeper into games. ERA, WHIP pullbacks seem inevitable; two Tommy John surgeries are cautionary. But now a solid mid-range starter.

Yr Tm	W	Sv	IP	K	ERA	WHIP	xERA	xWHIP	vL+	vR+	BF/G	BB%	K%	K-BB%	xBB%	SwK	Vel	G	L	F	H%	S%	HR/F	xHR/F	GS	APC	DOM%	DIS%	Sv%	LI	RAR	BPX	R$
18																																	
19 aa	1	0	61	66	5.87	1.67	5.27				12.5	13%	24%	11%							36%	65%									-10.3	74	-$9
20 MIL	1	0	15	21	5.87	1.70	3.72	1.34	156	68	5.9	13%	30%	17%	8%	13.2%	97.7	54	24	22	39%	70%	33%	14%	0	25			0	0.52	-2.7	126	-$7
21 2 TM	4	1	76	73	2.84	1.08	3.80	1.26	76	78	8.8	8%	24%	16%	7%	11.2%	97.1	47	23	30	27%	75%	8%	9%	10	34	10%	20%	100	0.83	13.3	110	$7
22 TAM	11	0	146	125	2.84	1.04	3.60	1.17	77	94	20.9	5%	21%	16%	6%	12.6%	95.5	47	19	34	27%	76%	9%	11%	28	80	18%	29%			20.4	124	$17
1st Half	5	0	63	51	3.30	1.16	3.77	1.27	88	99	19.8	7%	20%	13%	7%	11.6%	95.4	47	24	29	28%	76%	13%	14%	13	78	15%	38%			5.1	96	$6
2nd Half	6	0	83	74	2.48	0.95	3.48	1.10	66	90	21.8	4%	23%	19%	5%	13.5%	95.5	46	16	38	27%	77%	7%	9%	15	82	20%	20%			15.3	143	$22
Proj	**9**	**0**	**160**	**148**	**3.60**	**1.18**	**3.37**	**1.24**	**85**	**101**	**21.5**	**7%**	**23%**	**16%**	**6%**	**12.4%**	**95.8**	**47**	**20**	**34**	**30%**	**71%**	**10%**	**10%**	**30**						**7.3**	**114**	**$11**

Ray,Robbie

Age: 31	Th: L	Role	SP	Health	C	LIMA Plan	B+
Ht: 6' 2"	Wt: 215	Type	Pwr/FB	PT/Exp	A	Rand Var	0
				Consist	C	MM	5505

Regression had been anticipated and most of the components fell into place. Elite K% backed off some as SwK returned to career norms. Pristine control was never going to hold up, though he kept most of the prior year's gains. S% fell, H% ticked up. A repeat seems likely, though history, inconsistency, 2nd half HR/F are mild warning signs.

Yr Tm	W	Sv	IP	K	ERA	WHIP	xERA	xWHIP	vL+	vR+	BF/G	BB%	K%	K-BB%	xBB%	SwK	Vel	G	L	F	H%	S%	HR/F	xHR/F	GS	APC	DOM%	DIS%	Sv%	LI	RAR	BPX	R$
18 ARI	6	0	124	165	3.93	1.35	3.75	1.34	62	109	21.9	13%	31%	18%	9%	13.2%	93.7	39	22	39	30%	76%	17%	12%	24	95	17%	25%			3.3	110	$3
19 ARI	12	0	174	235	4.34	1.34	3.90	1.28	85	108	22.6	11%	32%	20%	8%	14.1%	92.4	37	26	37	32%	74%	20%	20%	33	93	18%	12%			3.6	127	$9
20 2 TM	2	0	52	68	6.62	1.90	6.14	1.67	91	135	20.9	18%	27%	9%	12%	13.0%	93.7	24	24	51	34%	71%	19%	16%	11	89	0%	55%	0	0.76	-13.8	4	-$17
21 TOR	13	0	193	248	2.84	1.04	3.46	1.06	82	91	24.2	7%	32%	25%	6%	16.3%	94.8	37	19	44	28%	83%	16%	15%	32	98	38%	22%			34.0	173	$31
22 SEA	12	0	189	212	3.71	1.19	3.61	1.17	93	104	24.2	8%	27%	19%	8%	14.2%	93.4	39	19	42	29%	76%	16%	11%	32	95	31%	19%			5.9	131	$14
1st Half	7	0	104	117	3.62	1.12	3.60	1.19	91	97	24.9	9%	28%	19%	8%	15.8%	93.2	40	17	43	27%	74%	13%	11%	17	95	35%	18%			4.5	128	$18
2nd Half	5	0	85	95	3.83	1.28	3.64	1.16	95	112	23.5	7%	27%	20%	7%	12.4%	93.7	39	21	41	31%	79%	18%	12%	15	95	27%	20%			1.5	137	$7
Proj	**11**	**0**	**174**	**212**	**3.84**	**1.17**	**3.21**	**1.14**	**82**	**100**	**21.5**	**8%**	**31%**	**22%**	**8%**	**13.9%**	**93.6**	**36**	**21**	**43**	**30%**	**74%**	**15%**	**14%**	**32**						**2.8**	**145**	**$13**

Reyes,Alex

Age: 28	Th: R	Role	RP	Health	F	LIMA Plan	D+
Ht: 6' 4"	Wt: 220	Type	Pwr	PT/Exp	B	Rand Var	0
				Consist	A	MM	1510

Despite woeful control, he was coming off a successful season just in terms of staying on the field. But labrum surgery left 2022 stillborn; his only returns being another 188 IL days. Still had velocity, K%, SwK pre-surgery; now all this and Opening Day readiness are uncertain. Consistency grade is in part a reflection of his every-year health challenge.

Yr Tm	W	Sv	IP	K	ERA	WHIP	xERA	xWHIP	vL+	vR+	BF/G	BB%	K%	K-BB%	xBB%	SwK	Vel	G	L	F	H%	S%	HR/F	xHR/F	GS	APC	DOM%	DIS%	Sv%	LI	RAR	BPX	R$
18 STL *	2	0	20	23	0.00	0.55	-0.83		86	92	22.7	9%	34%	25%		4.1%	94.8	40	20	40	13%	100%	0%	1%	1	73	0%	0%			10.4	211	$3
19 STL *	1	0	31	31	9.49	2.05	7.08		38	192	10.8	20%	21%	1%		5.6%	96.8	30	20	50	33%	54%	20%	12%	0	18			0	1.00	-19.1	23	-$13
20 STL	2	1	20	27	3.20	1.42	4.63	1.48	80	84	5.7	16%	31%	15%	12%	14.9%	97.6	37	16	47	31%	78%	5%	11%	1	25	0%	0%	100	1.09	3.0	73	$1
21 STL	10	29	72	95	3.24	1.35	4.57	1.50	84	81	4.6	16%	30%	14%	12%	14.8%	96.7	37	19	44	25%	81%	12%	9%	0	18			85	1.22	9.2	58	$18
22																																	
1st Half																																	
2nd Half																																	
Proj	**4**	**2**	**44**	**52**	**3.70**	**1.59**	**4.52**	**1.66**	**102**	**104**	**5.9**	**19%**	**27%**	**8%**	**12%**	**14.8%**	**96.7**	**37**	**19**	**44**	**29%**	**79%**	**11%**	**8%**	**0**						**1.4**	**9**	**-$2**

Richards,Trevor

Age: 30	Th: R	Role	RP	Health	B	LIMA Plan	B
Ht: 6' 2"	Wt: 195	Type	Pwr/xFB	PT/Exp	C	Rand Var	+2
				Consist	C	MM	2401

Despite upticking velocity, speculative late-inning option was bombed early and often, courtesy of HR barrage and awful control. Regained some 2nd-half footing before losing the plate again in Sept (8 walks, 11 ER over 10 IP). Premium swing-and-miss keeps him watchable from afar, but checkered BB% history, FB lean make for a flammable speculation.

Yr Tm	W	Sv	IP	K	ERA	WHIP	xERA	xWHIP	vL+	vR+	BF/G	BB%	K%	K-BB%	xBB%	SwK	Vel	G	L	F	H%	S%	HR/F	xHR/F	GS	APC	DOM%	DIS%	Sv%	LI	RAR	BPX	R$
18 MIA *	7	0	166	161	3.92	1.29	3.99	1.34	91	116	22.1	8%	24%	15%	9%	11.2%	90.8	36	25	39	31%	73%	11%	12%	25	89	32%	32%			4.6	97	$5
19 2 TM	6	0	135	127	4.06	1.35	5.05	1.42	100	99	19.3	10%	22%	12%	8%	12.3%	90.9	35	22	43	30%	74%	12%	12%	23	76	22%	30%	0	0.78	7.5	70	$4
20 TAM	0	0	32	27	5.91	1.72	5.75	1.37	108	126	16.7	7%	18%	11%	7%	12.3%	90.5	32	25	43	38%	69%	13%	9%	4	64	0%	75%	0	0.71	-5.7	71	-$13
21 3 TM	7	1	64	78	3.50	0.96	3.84	1.16	82	83	4.7	9%	31%	22%	9%	14.7%	92.8	28	22	50	21%	74%	16%	15%	0	20			17	0.87	6.1	131	$8
22 TOR	3	0	64	82	5.34	1.44	4.12	1.32	101	105	4.5	12%	29%	17%	12%	15.4%	93.5	34	19	47	33%	65%	12%	13%	4	19	0%	50%	0	0.67	-10.9	96	-$6
1st Half	2	0	31	35	6.10	1.58	4.57	1.45	100	130	4.5	14%	25%	11%	12%	14.6%	93.4	38	19	43	30%	67%	19%	17%	0	18			0	0.84	-8.1	55	-$13
2nd Half	1	0	33	47	4.64	1.30	3.74	1.20	102	72	4.5	11%	33%	22%	11%	16.1%	93.6	29	19	51	35%	63%	5%	10%	4	19	0%	50%	0	0.50	-2.7	133	-$6
Proj	**3**	**0**	**65**	**75**	**4.51**	**1.40**	**3.87**	**1.30**	**99**	**104**	**6.1**	**11%**	**27%**	**17%**	**10%**	**14.2%**	**92.4**	**32**	**21**	**46**	**32%**	**72%**	**12%**	**12%**	**0**						**-4.3**	**96**	**-$4**

Robertson,David

Age: 38	Th: R	Role	RP	Health	F	LIMA Plan	B+
Ht: 5' 11"	Wt: 195	Type	Pwr	PT/Exp	D	Rand Var	-5
				Consist	A	MM	5520

Turned clock back in first full year after Tommy John surgery; found 9th-inning work for both CHC and PHI. Top-shelf K%, SwK were intact; early GB% trended toward historical peak. But some luck was also involved, as ballooning BB% was neutralized by lofty S% all season. Will get more high-leverage work; an age-based risk/reward fantasy play.

Yr Tm	W	Sv	IP	K	ERA	WHIP	xERA	xWHIP	vL+	vR+	BF/G	BB%	K%	K-BB%	xBB%	SwK	Vel	G	L	F	H%	S%	HR/F	xHR/F	GS	APC	DOM%	DIS%	Sv%	LI	RAR	BPX	R$
18 NYY	8	5	70	91	3.23	1.03	3.22	1.15	85	80	4.1	9%	32%	23%	9%	13.9%	92.3	45	17	37	27%	72%	12%	15%	0	17			56	1.20	7.9	166	$10
19 PHI	0	0	7	6	5.40	2.10	7.45	1.92	75	174	4.7	18%	18%	0%	12%	11.0%	91.7	33	24	43	35%	77%	11%	10%	0	19			0	1.24	-0.7	-67	-$6
20																																	
21 TAM	0	0	12	16	4.50	1.25	3.31	1.11	81	108	4.2	8%	32%	24%	8%	9.6%	92.0	40	27	33	34%	69%	20%	13%	1	17	0%	0%	0	0.87	-0.3	168	-$5
22 2 NL	4	20	64	81	2.40	1.16	3.53	1.33	79	88	4.6	13%	31%	17%	8%	14.2%		47	13	40	25%	84%	10%	9%	0	18			71	1.47	12.3	107	$13
1st Half	2	11	32	44	1.95	0.99	2.97	1.20	76	73	4.6	11%	33%	22%	7%	14.2%		52	10	38	23%	86%	12%	12%	0	18			73	1.60	8.1	152	$13
2nd Half	2	9	31	37	2.87	1.34	4.15	1.46	82	102	4.6	15%	28%	13%	9%	14.3%		41	16	43	27%	82%	9%	8%	0	19			69	1.34	4.2	61	$5
Proj	**4**	**14**	**58**	**70**	**3.45**	**1.16**	**3.16**	**1.23**	**88**	**95**	**4.5**	**10%**	**30%**	**20%**	**8%**	**14.2%**	**19.4**	**46**	**14**	**40**	**29%**	**73%**	**10%**	**10%**	**0**						**3.7**	**129**	**$8**

Rodón,Carlos

Age: 30	Th: L	Role	SP	Health	F	LIMA Plan	C+
Ht: 6' 3"	Wt: 245	Type	Pwr/FB	PT/Exp	A	Rand Var	-2
				Consist	C	MM	5505

Followed 2021 breakout by adding IP, avoiding shoulder/elbow issues for the first time since forever. ERA jump was a product of H% and S% normalization, the one blip in otherwise mirror image performance. Despite lack of GB% lean, HR management became pristine. Only health, regression candidacy keep him half a tick behind the most elite arms.

Yr Tm	W	Sv	IP	K	ERA	WHIP	xERA	xWHIP	vL+	vR+	BF/G	BB%	K%	K-BB%	xBB%	SwK	Vel	G	L	F	H%	S%	HR/F	xHR/F	GS	APC	DOM%	DIS%	Sv%	LI	RAR	BPX	R$
18 CHW	6	0	121	90	4.18	1.26	5.00	1.51	118	91	25.6	11%	18%	7%	11%	9.4%	93.0	41	16	43	25%	70%	10%	9%	20	98	30%	30%			-0.4	33	$2
19 CHW	3	0	35	46	5.19	1.44	4.26	1.31	49	101	22.6	11%	29%	18%	9%	12.6%	91.5	43	19	38	36%	65%	11%	14%	7	99	29%	14%			-2.9	127	-$4
20 CHW	0	0	8	6	8.22	1.57	5.95	1.45	161	118	8.8	9%	17%	9%	7%	10.5%	92.9	28	24	48	34%	45%	8%	12%	2	33	0%	100%	0	1.90	-3.6	43	-$9
21 CHW	13	0	133	185	2.37	0.96	3.20	1.02	82	73	22.3	7%	35%	28%	6%	15.7%	95.4	38	17	45	29%	81%	10%	10%	24	92	42%	21%			30.9	193	$27
22 SF	14	0	178	237	2.88	1.03	3.13	1.04	74	82	22.9	7%	33%	26%	6%	14.6%	95.6	34	21	45	31%	74%	7%	7%	31	96	42%	10%			23.9	173	$26
1st Half	7	0	91	112	2.87	1.11	3.32	1.13	73	85	23.0	8%	30%	22%	6%	14.0%	96.0	38	21	41	32%	74%	4%	6%	16	95	38%	13%			12.4	150	$21
2nd Half	7	0	87	125	2.90	0.94	2.95	0.96	75	78	22.8	6%	37%	30%	7%	15.2%	95.2	29	22	49	30%	73%	9%	9%	15	98	47%	7%			11.5	197	$27
Proj	**13**	**0**	**167**	**216**	**3.35**	**1.10**	**2.98**	**1.09**	**77**	**86**	**22.4**	**8%**	**33%**	**25%**	**8%**	**13.8%**	**94.2**	**37**	**20**	**43**	**31%**	**72%**	**9%**	**10%**	**29**						**12.7**	**161**	**$20**

Rodriguez,Eduardo

Age: 30	Th: L	Role	SP	Health	F	LIMA Plan	A
Ht: 6' 2"	Wt: 231	Type		PT/Exp	A	Rand Var	-1
				Consist	A	MM	3203

5-5, 4.05 ERA in 91 IP at DET. First season with new club didn't go as planned. Started slowly before rib-cage injury shelved him in mid-May. Unspecified personal issues interrupted June rehab, kept him on the restricted list until late August. A mulligan of sorts is in order, but sudden plunge in K%, SwK can't be ignored. Low-ceiling risk portfolio only.

Yr Tm	W	Sv	IP	K	ERA	WHIP	xERA	xWHIP	vL+	vR+	BF/G	BB%	K%	K-BB%	xBB%	SwK	Vel	G	L	F	H%	S%	HR/F	xHR/F	GS	APC	DOM%	DIS%	Sv%	LI	RAR	BPX	R$
18 BOS	13	0	130	146	3.82	1.26	3.97	1.22	94	95	20.5	8%	26%	18%	8%	11.5%	93.3	39	20	41	32%	74%	11%	12%	23	86	30%	26%	0	0.81	5.3	132	$9
19 BOS	19	0	203	213	3.81	1.33	4.10	1.30	103	93	25.3	9%	25%	16%	8%	12.1%	93.1	48	19	33	32%	75%	13%	15%	34	103	29%	21%			17.5	116	$17
20																																	
21 BOS	13	0	158	185	4.74	1.39	3.70	1.15	102	103	21.1	7%	27%	20%	7%	12.1%	92.6	43	22	34	37%	68%	13%	11%	31	85	13%	23%	0	0.79	-9.2	152	$2
22 DET *	6	0	106	91	3.58	1.25	3.84	1.37	130	94	21.6	9%	18%	10%	8%	7.8%	91.8	43	19	37	29%	75%	12%	11%	17	86	6%	41%			5.1	82	$3
1st Half	1	0	39	34	4.38	1.33	4.66	1.40	161	80	21.1	10%	20%	10%	8%	7.3%	92.0	38	21	41	29%	69%	8%	12%	8	84	0%	38%			-2.0	56	-$8
2nd Half	4	0	52	38	3.81	1.33	4.34	1.35	103	104	24.7	8%	17%	9%	8%	8.2%	91.6	48	18	35	29%	77%	14%	11%	9	89	11%	44%			1.0	71	-$1
Proj	**9**	**0**	**160**	**151**	**3.95**	**1.29**	**3.64**	**1.28**	**113**	**93**	**22.1**	**8%**	**23%**	**15%**	**8%**	**10.0%**	**92.3**	**44**	**20**	**36**	**30%**	**73%**	**12%**	**12%**	**30**						**0.4**	**102**	**$5**

JOCK THOMPSON

Rodriguez,Grayson

Age: 23	Th: R	Role: SP	Health	A	LIMA Plan B+
Ht: 6' 5"	Wt: 220	Type: Pwr	PT/Exp	D	Rand Var 0
			Consist	B	MM 4401

Elite BAL prospect lost three months to lat injury or he might've already erased all doubt whether he'll thrive in MLB. Work upon Sept return was predictably ragged, but was rounding into form as curtain came down on year. IP limit, further injury woes, or even service time manipulation may hold him back in 2022, but he's ready.

Yr	Tm	W	Sv	IP	K	ERA	WHIP	xERA	xWHIP	vL+	vR+	BF/G	BB%	K%	K-BB%	xBB%	SwK	Vel	G	L	F	H%	S%	HR/F	xHR/F	GS	APC	DOM%	DIS%	Sv%	LI	RAR	BPX	R$
18																																		
19																																		
20																																		
21	aa	6	0	81	100	2.71	0.87	1.94				16.7	7%	33%	27%							25%	74%									15.6	176	$13
22	a/a	6	0	77	90	2.51	0.92	1.37				18.1	8%	31%	23%							26%	72%									13.9	170	$10
1st Half		5	0	56	66	2.00	0.83	1.01				18.6	6%	31%	25%							26%	75%									13.6	210	$18
2nd Half		1	0	21	23	3.71	1.13	2.17				17.0	14%	29%	15%							25%	67%									0.7	120	-$6
Proj		7	0	109	118	3.56	1.17	3.27				22.1	9%	27%	18%				41	24	35	30%	72%	10%	9%	20						5.6	122	$7

Rodríguez,Manuel

Age: 26	Th: R	Role: RP	Health	F	LIMA Plan D+
Ht: 5' 11"	Wt: 210	Type: Pwr/GB	PT/Exp	D	Rand Var -5
			Consist	B	MM 2210

Rumored to be in closer mix to open season; instead, was demoted, strained elbow, and didn't return to majors until Aug 26. And while he did walk off IL into extra-inning save opp and more chances followed, shaky BB%, low SwK say he's still far from being potent late-inning weapon. GB% is skill to build on, but he'll need to do more to get our attention.

Yr	Tm	W	Sv	IP	K	ERA	WHIP	xERA	xWHIP	vL+	vR+	BF/G	BB%	K%	K-BB%	xBB%	SwK	Vel	G	L	F	H%	S%	HR/F	xHR/F	GS	APC	DOM%	DIS%	Sv%	LI	RAR	BPX	R$
18																																		
19																																		
20																																		
21	CHC *	4	6	40	38	3.47	1.46	4.14	1.63	154	61	4.3	14%	22%	8%	10%	10.7%	97.2	54	17	30	29%	79%	19%	15%	0	15			75	1.13	3.9	72	$0
22	CHC	2	4	14	8	3.29	1.39	4.90	1.79	172	76	4.1	16%	14%	-2%	11%	9.9%	95.8	53	25	23	23%	78%	11%	11%	0	15			67	1.42	1.1	-38	-$2
1st Half																																		
2nd Half		2	4	14	8	3.29	1.39	4.90	1.79	172	76	4.1	16%	14%	-2%	11%	9.9%	95.8	53	25	23	23%	78%	11%	11%	0	15			67	1.42	1.1	-38	-$4
Proj		4	2	58	50	3.98	1.39	4.22				4.7	15%	20%	5%				51	21	28	26%	73%	12%	12%	0						-0.1	17	-$2

Rogers,Taylor

Age: 32	Th: L	Role: RP	Health	D	LIMA Plan B+
Ht: 6' 3"	Wt: 190	Type: Pwr	PT/Exp	B	Rand Var +5
			Consist	B	MM 5520

Tempting to see near-identical half-season BPX and say, "Nothing a little S% regression won't fix." But with heavily-used slider failing to induce grounders in 2nd half, he again became vulnerable vR, who touched him for all 7 of his HR, 6 after trade to MIL. Until that turns around, closer gig may prove elusive. But sub-4 ERA, decent WHIP? That he can manage.

Yr	Tm	W	Sv	IP	K	ERA	WHIP	xERA	xWHIP	vL+	vR+	BF/G	BB%	K%	K-BB%	xBB%	SwK	Vel	G	L	F	H%	S%	HR/F	xHR/F	GS	APC	DOM%	DIS%	Sv%	LI	RAR	BPX	R$
18	MIN	1	2	68	75	2.63	0.95	2.98	1.10	58	90	3.6	6%	29%	23%	6%	11.6%	93.4	45	26	30	28%	73%	6%	10%	0	14			50	1.04	12.8	166	$7
19	MIN	2	30	69	90	2.61	1.00	2.85	0.98	88	82	4.6	4%	32%	28%	5%	11.3%	94.8	51	18	31	32%	80%	15%	16%	0	18			83	1.50	16.1	220	$21
20	MIN	2	9	20	24	4.05	1.50	3.73	1.08	89	111	4.3	4%	26%	22%	4%	11.5%	94.6	42	29	29	43%	75%	11%	12%	0	17			82	1.15	1.0	187	$9
21	MIN	2	9	40	59	3.35	1.14	2.59	0.93	73	95	4.2	5%	36%	31%	4%	13.6%	95.8	50	20	30	38%	74%	14%	11%	0	16			69	1.55	4.6	238	$4
22	2 NL	4	31	64	84	4.76	1.18	3.05	1.07	73	112	4.2	7%	31%	24%	6%	12.9%	94.3	42	20	37	34%	61%	12%	15%	0	16			76	1.36	-6.2	176	$12
1st Half		0	23	34	39	3.48	0.98	2.78	1.03	78	90	4.0	5%	29%	24%	6%	13.8%	94.6	47	22	31	31%	63%	4%	13%	0	16			85	1.35	2.1	179	$17
2nd Half		4	8	31	45	6.16	1.40	3.34	1.10	67	132	4.3	9%	32%	24%	6%	12.1%	94.0	37	19	44	38%	59%	18%	16%	0	17			57	1.37	-8.3	174	$1
Proj		3	12	58	77	3.50	1.13	2.61		75	102	4.0	6%	34%	27%	5%	12.4%	94.5	45	20	35	34%	73%	14%	14%	0						3.4	194	$7

Rogers,Trevor

Age: 25	Th: L	Role: SP	Health	D	LIMA Plan A
Ht: 6' 5"	Wt: 217	Type: Pwr	PT/Exp	A	Rand Var +3
			Consist	B	MM 4303

4-11, 5.47 ERA in 107 IP at MIA. Surface stats say "unmitigated disaster," but command and ground balls returned in 2nd half, along with 3.31 MLB xERA. Those skills are a reminder of considerable ceiling, leaving him looking a lot like guy who drew all that preseason buzz. No sure thing, but path to profit is clearer than many may appreciate.

Yr	Tm	W	Sv	IP	K	ERA	WHIP	xERA	xWHIP	vL+	vR+	BF/G	BB%	K%	K-BB%	xBB%	SwK	Vel	G	L	F	H%	S%	HR/F	xHR/F	GS	APC	DOM%	DIS%	Sv%	LI	RAR	BPX	R$
18																																		
19	aa	1	0	26	24	6.99	1.64	5.96				23.2	9%	21%	12%							37%	58%									-8.0	60	-$7
20	MIA	1	0	28	39	6.11	1.61	3.80	1.23	108	120	18.6	10%	30%	20%	8%	13.2%	93.6	47	21	32	40%	65%	21%	11%	7	81	0%	14%			-5.7	156	-$8
21	MIA	7	0	133	157	2.64	1.15	3.63	1.18	92	79	22.0	8%	29%	20%	6%	14.7%	94.6	40	24	36	32%	78%	5%	9%	25	87	40%	16%			26.7	137	$16
22	MIA *	5	0	123	126	5.64	1.48	5.22	1.33	84	124	19.6	9%	22%	13%	8%	11.6%	94.6	42	22	36	35%	64%	13%	13%	23	84	9%	39%			-25.4	79	-$11
1st Half		4	0	68	62	5.56	1.59	4.78	1.44	117	113	20.6	11%	20%	9%	9%	11.7%	94.7	39	23	38	33%	67%	13%	13%	15	86	0%	40%			-13.3	48	-$14
2nd Half		1	0	55	64	5.75	1.35	4.86	1.08	29	144	19.1	5%	27%	22%	5%	11.4%	94.5	48	20	32	37%	59%	14%	13%	8	81	25%	38%			-12.1	142	-$10
Proj		8	0	145	150	3.84	1.25	3.34		65	113	22.5	8%	25%	17%	6%	12.2%	94.6	43	22	35	32%	71%	11%	11%	26						2.3	121	$7

Romano,Jordan

Age: 30	Th: R	Role: RP	Health	B	LIMA Plan C+
Ht: 6' 5"	Wt: 225	Type: Pwr	PT/Exp	A	Rand Var -5
			Consist	A	MM 5431

Gastrointestinal illness may explain May-June skills swoon, but dominant 2nd half, buoyed by velocity uptick, allays any real concern. GB%, K%, K-BB% leaking in wrong direction, and xERA says to expect ERA closer to 3 than 2, leaving him notch below league's elite. Still, no reason to suspect that Sv chances will dry up or that he can't continue to get job done.

Yr	Tm	W	Sv	IP	K	ERA	WHIP	xERA	xWHIP	vL+	vR+	BF/G	BB%	K%	K-BB%	xBB%	SwK	Vel	G	L	F	H%	S%	HR/F	xHR/F	GS	APC	DOM%	DIS%	Sv%	LI	RAR	BPX	R$
18	a/a	12	0	143	103	5.55	1.44	4.96				23.5	8%	17%	9%							32%	63%									-24.7	54	-$7
19	TOR *	2	5	55	63	7.42	1.63	6.72	1.37	86	141	5.9	10%	26%	16%	10%	13.8%	94.6	53	20	28	36%	59%	36%	29%	0	18			100	0.70	-19.6	46	-$8
20	TOR	2	2	15	21	1.23	0.89	2.54	1.06	51	84	3.8	9%	37%	28%	8%	20.7%	96.6	58	16	26	23%	100%	25%	24%	0	16			67	1.80	5.8	209	$7
21	TOR	7	23	63	85	2.14	1.05	3.28	1.15	60	90	4.1	10%	34%	24%	7%	15.2%	97.6	47	13	40	27%	86%	13%	11%	0	17			96	1.14	16.5	161	$20
22	TOR	5	36	64	73	2.11	1.02	3.34	1.16	78	73	4.1	8%	28%	20%	5%	15.1%	96.9	44	17	39	27%	82%	6%	9%	0	16			86	1.58	14.7	140	$23
1st Half		2	17	29	32	2.79	1.24	3.77	1.30	69	101	4.0	11%	26%	16%	7%	14.9%	96.4	42	20	38	30%	79%	7%	9%	0	16			85	1.41	4.2	99	$12
2nd Half		3	19	35	41	1.54	0.83	3.00		85	46	4.2	6%	30%	24%	4%	15.2%	97.5	45	14	40	25%	85%	6%	9%	0	16			86	1.72	10.5	174	$25
Proj		5	33	73	82	3.01	1.06	3.01		89	88	4.6	8%	29%	22%	5%	15.1%	97.2	45	16	39	28%	77%	12%	9%	0						8.6	149	$21

Ruiz,José

Age: 28	Th: R	Role: RP	Health	A	LIMA Plan C+
Ht: 6' 1"	Wt: 245	Type: Pwr/FB	PT/Exp	C	Rand Var 0
			Consist	B	MM 2300

Exhibit A for "it takes more than velocity to thrive in MLB." Gave back control gains, and for past two seasons, few pitchers have given up more consistent hard contact. 2nd half ERA shows what happens when strand rate misfortune jumps on the pile. That fastball may keep buying him chances, but until something changes, he can be safely ignored.

Yr	Tm	W	Sv	IP	K	ERA	WHIP	xERA	xWHIP	vL+	vR+	BF/G	BB%	K%	K-BB%	xBB%	SwK	Vel	G	L	F	H%	S%	HR/F	xHR/F	GS	APC	DOM%	DIS%	Sv%	LI	RAR	BPX	R$
18	CHW *	3	14	50	53	4.36	1.41	3.88		73	131	5.5	12%	25%	13%		16.9%	96.2	42	25	33	32%	69%	25%	2%	0	15			88	0.45	-1.3	101	$3
19	CHW *	1	7	55	48	4.48	1.78	5.91		94	138	5.0	12%	19%	7%	8%	10.6%	96.4	37	22	40	36%	77%	11%	13%	1	19	0%	100%	78	0.55	0.2	48	-$4
20	CHW	0	0	4	5	2.25	0.50	3.08		99	38	2.8	0%	36%	36%		10.0%	96.8	33	11	56	14%	0%	20%	16%	0	12			0	1.41	1.1	241	-$4
21	CHW	1	0	65	63	3.05	1.17	4.35		104	76	4.6	9%	23%	14%	7%	11.2%	97.0	42	20	38	26%	79%	12%	14%	0	18			0	0.43	9.8	92	$1
22	CHW	1	0	61	68	4.60	1.42	4.24	1.39	97	108	4.2	12%	26%	13%	11%	12.6%	96.9	42	17	41	30%	71%	13%	14%	0	18			0	0.54	-4.7	76	-$6
1st Half		0	0	31	37	4.02	1.53	4.37	1.46	101	114	4.2	14%	27%	12%	12%	13.2%	96.9	44	13	43	31%	79%	14%	16%	0	19			0	0.67	-0.2	64	-$10
2nd Half		1	0	29	31	5.22	1.30	4.11		94	101	4.2	10%	25%	14%	11%	11.8%	96.9	40	21	39	29%	62%	13%	12%	0	17			0	0.40	-4.5	90	-$9
Proj		1	0	44	44	4.56	1.46	4.09		93	106	4.4	12%	24%	12%	10%	11.8%	96.8	41	19	40	31%	71%	11%	13%	0						-3.2	67	-$6

Ryan,Joe

Age: 27	Th: R	Role: SP	Health	B	LIMA Plan B+
Ht: 6' 2"	Wt: 205	Type: /xFB	PT/Exp	C	Rand Var -3
			Consist	D	MM 3305

Take out 10-ER, 5-HR shelling on July 29, ERA would be half-run lower. But not only are such blow-ups always in play with extreme fly ballers, xERA also suggests low-3 ERA is not his true talent level—not yet, anyway. On to-do list: bring K% vL (19%) more in line with vR (32%). Control, command provide strong foundation; small tweak could pay big dividends.

Yr	Tm	W	Sv	IP	K	ERA	WHIP	xERA	xWHIP	vL+	vR+	BF/G	BB%	K%	K-BB%	xBB%	SwK	Vel	G	L	F	H%	S%	HR/F	xHR/F	GS	APC	DOM%	DIS%	Sv%	LI	RAR	BPX	R$
18																																		
19																																		
20																																		
21	MIN *	6	0	93	105	4.22	0.89	2.62	1.04	83	69	18.1	5%	31%	25%	4%	12.1%	91.3	28	19	53	24%	57%	12%	15%	5	82	40%	20%			0.5	172	$9
22	MIN	13	0	147	151	3.55	1.10	4.21	1.21	91	97	22.4	8%	25%	17%	6%	12.0%	92.1	28	18	54	26%	73%	9%	9%	27	89	33%	30%			7.6	104	$14
1st Half		6	0	66	60	3.00	1.05	4.38	1.21	94	88	22.3	7%	22%	16%	6%	10.5%	91.8	28	16	55	26%	76%	7%	8%	12	87	33%	33%			7.9	96	$12
2nd Half		7	0	81	91	4.00	1.15	4.07	1.20	89	105	22.5	9%	27%	18%	6%	13.2%	92.3	27	20	53	27%	71%	12%	10%	15	90	33%	27%			-0.3	110	$11
Proj		13	0	167	168	3.70	1.13	3.81		93	101	23.7	7%	25%	18%	6%	12.1%	92.1	28	18	54	28%	73%	11%	10%	28						5.6	110	$15

KRIS OLSON

Ryu,Hyun-Jin

Age: 36	Th: L	Role: SP	Health: F	LIMA Plan: B	
Ht: 6' 3"	Wt: 255	Type: Con	PT/Exp: A	Rand Var: +4	
			Consist: A	MM: 4100	

What was already looking like steady decline turned into death spiral with mid-June Tommy John surgery, his second. We may not see a whole lot of him in 2023, and age adds uncertainty to recovery. Is it a good sign when what your team is most excited about is that the final year of your contract is fully insured? Probably not even worth a speculative stash.

Yr Tm	W	Sv	IP	K	ERA	WHIP	xERA	xWHIP	vL+	vR+	BF/G	BB%	K%	K-BB%	xBB%	SwK	Vel	G	L	F	H%	S%	HR/F	xHR/F	GS	APC	DOM%	DIS%	Sv%	LI	RAR	BPX	R$
18 LA	7	0	82	89	1.97	1.01	3.23	1.06	98	83	21.6	5%	27%	23%	6%	12.3%	90.2	46	19	35	29%	88%	12%	12%	15	83	40%	20%			22.2	178	$13
19 LA	14	0	183	163	2.32	1.01	3.47	1.13	71	87	24.9	3%	23%	19%	6%	11.8%	90.6	50	24	25	29%	82%	13%	12%	29	93	45%	7%			49.3	153	$31
20 TOR	5	0	67	72	2.69	1.15	3.49	1.15	79	87	22.9	6%	26%	20%	8%	12.3%	89.6	51	21	28	32%	80%	12%	9%	12	94	17%	17%			14.6	160	$21
21 TOR	14	0	169	143	4.37	1.22	4.09	1.21	95	99	22.6	5%	20%	15%	6%	10.1%	90.0	47	20	33	30%	68%	14%	15%	31	87	32%	29%			-2.1	119	$8
22 TOR	2	0	27	16	5.67	1.33	4.41	1.23	86	128	18.8	4%	14%	11%	8%	7.6%	89.3	46	17	37	31%	61%	15%	14%	6	66	0%	67%			-5.7	93	-$6
1st Half	2	0	27	16	5.67	1.33	4.41	1.23	85	128	18.8	4%	14%	11%	8%	7.6%	89.3	46	17	37	31%	61%	15%	14%	6	66	0%	67%			-5.7	92	-$11
2nd Half																																	
Proj	1	0	15	12	4.37	1.17	3.33	1.16	85	102	21.2	4%	21%	17%		10.4%	89.9	48	20	32	30%	66%	14%	13%	3						-0.7	131	-$4

Sadler,Casey

Age: 32	Th: R	Role: RP	Health: F	LIMA Plan: A+	
Ht: 6' 3"	Wt: 205	Type: Con/xGB	PT/Exp: D	Rand Var: 0	
			Consist: D	MM: 4100	

Late bloomer's encore did not go as planned, as shoulder surgery in late March cost him entire season. Even in breakout, he battled shoulder issue in 1st half, so it remains to be seen if he can recapture 2021 2nd half ground ball magic—and how long it will last before another injury intervenes. Even as a deep-league roster finisher, there may be safer plays.

Yr Tm	W	Sv	IP	K	ERA	WHIP	xERA	xWHIP	vL+	vR+	BF/G	BB%	K%	K-BB%	xBB%	SwK	Vel	G	L	F	H%	S%	HR/F	xHR/F	GS	APC	DOM%	DIS%	Sv%	LI	RAR	BPX	R$
18 PIT *	6	1	81	48	4.61	1.73	6.09		204	82	12.8	9%	13%	4%		7.0%	92.1	68	16	16	36%	75%	0%	21%	0	43			100	0.42	-4.7	32	-$8
19 2 TM *	5	3	87	71	2.89	1.23	4.20	1.39	94	82	7.6	5%	20%	15%	8%	9.6%	93.5	52	18	30	30%	83%	12%	10%	1	21	0%	100%	60	0.45	17.2	96	$7
20 2 TM	1	0	19	21	5.12	1.40	4.89	1.52	90	104	5.1	14%	24%	10%	10%	12.9%	92.9	40	27	33	26%	67%	18%	9%	0	20			0	0.81	-1.6	49	-$5
21 SEA	0	0	40	37	0.67	0.72	2.93	1.18	61	51	3.5	7%	26%	19%	7%	10.2%	93.1	63	11	26	19%	93%	4%	8%	0	14			0	1.09	17.9	142	$6
22																																	
1st Half																																	
2nd Half																																	
Proj	2	0	58	45	3.04	1.13	3.29	1.26	109	82	5.6	6%	20%	13%	8%	9.9%	93.3	58	14	27	28%	76%	11%	9%	0						6.7	110	$1

Sale,Chris

Age: 34	Th: L	Role: SP	Health: F	LIMA Plan: B	
Ht: 6' 6"	Wt: 183	Type: Pwr	PT/Exp: D	Rand Var: -3	
			Consist: C	MM: 5503	

Looked to be back from 2020 TJS, but year took one tragicomic turn after another. Workout (ribcage) got him early, then comebacker (finger), then bike mishap (wrist) finished him off. Tagged with "UP: Cy Young" last year, it'd be reckless to stick to our guns, right? Wellll, injuries WERE kinda fluky... aaand none WERE to arm/elbow. (This is a cry for help.)

Yr Tm	W	Sv	IP	K	ERA	WHIP	xERA	xWHIP	vL+	vR+	BF/G	BB%	K%	K-BB%	xBB%	SwK	Vel	G	L	F	H%	S%	HR/F	xHR/F	GS	APC	DOM%	DIS%	Sv%	LI	RAR	BPX	R$
18 BOS	12	0	158	237	2.11	0.86	2.40	0.90	58	77	22.9	6%	38%	33%	5%	16.4%	94.7	44	20	36	30%	79%	9%	13%	27	94	63%	11%			39.8	245	$34
19 BOS	6	0	147	218	4.40	1.09	2.98	1.00	88	94	24.5	6%	36%	30%	6%	14.6%	93.2	43	21	36	33%	65%	20%	18%	25	99	32%	16%			2.0	218	$12
20																																	
21 BOS *	6	0	62	74	2.77	1.29	4.21	1.11	48	110	19.6	7%	29%	22%	6%	13.0%	93.6	47	21	32	35%	84%	17%	12%	9	82	0%	22%			11.5	136	$4
22 BOS	0	0	6	5	3.18	1.06	3.15			109	12.5	4%	20%	16%	6%	4.9%	94.5	50	33	17	31%	67%	0%	4%	2	51	50%	50%			0.6	141	-$5
1st Half																																	
2nd Half	0	0	6	5	3.18	1.06	3.15			109	12.5	4%	20%	16%	6%	4.9%	94.5	50	33	17	31%	67%	0%	4%	2	51	50%	50%			0.6	141	-$10
Proj	9	0	138	176	3.31	1.08	2.58	1.02	63	97	21.7	6%	33%	26%		14.2%	93.7	45	21	34	32%	74%	15%	14%	25						11.2	187	$15

Sampson,Adrian

Age: 31	Th: R	Role: RP	Health: A	LIMA Plan: C+	
Ht: 6' 2"	Wt: 210	Type: Con	PT/Exp: C	Rand Var: -3	
			Consist: F	MM: 1003	

4-5, 3.11 ERA in 104 IP with CHC. Ended year with string of 8 GS of 2 ER or fewer (1.71 ERA in 42 IP), but xERA shows just how fluky that run was. With so few strikeouts, he will always be just one bad turn of HR/F back towards terrible career norms. If you pay for last year's stats, like Delilah, you'll wind up taking a haircut on return on your investment.

Yr Tm	W	Sv	IP	K	ERA	WHIP	xERA	xWHIP	vL+	vR+	BF/G	BB%	K%	K-BB%	xBB%	SwK	Vel	G	L	F	H%	S%	HR/F	xHR/F	GS	APC	DOM%	DIS%	Sv%	LI	RAR	BPX	R$
18 TEX *	8	0	151	79	4.89	1.52	5.85	1.26	99	136	17.3	5%	12%	7%	8%	8.3%	91.1	36	22	42	34%	71%	19%	19%	4	68	0%	50%	0	0.66	-13.9	39	-$9
19 TEX	6	0	125	101	5.89	1.53	5.27	1.35	105	137	16.1	6%	18%	12%	8%	10.2%	92.5	40	19	40	33%	67%	17%	19%	15	59	13%	53%	0	0.79	-21.4	86	-$9
20																																	
21 CHC *	5	0	119	72	4.95	1.59	6.78	1.24	102	105	20.1	9%	14%	5%	8%	10.1%	91.9	44	19	37	31%	77%	21%	18%	5	55	0%	60%	0	0.92	-10.0	-3	-$11
22 CHC *	4	0	133	86	3.31	1.27	4.24	1.29	88	107	18.8	6%	17%	11%	8%	9.7%	92.2	40	20	40	29%	78%	8%	10%	19	81	16%	37%	0	0.72	10.8	64	$3
1st Half	0	0	45	27	3.81	1.31	4.87	1.30	131	58	15.5	5%	14%	9%	8%	12.8%	92.9	46	21	33	30%	77%	6%	4%	2	64	0%	50%	0	0.51	0.9	52	-$8
2nd Half	4	0	88	59	3.06	1.25	4.56	1.32	81	117	21.4	7%	16%	10%	9%	9.1%	92.1	39	20	41	29%	79%	8%	11%	17	85	18%	35%			9.9	65	$7
Proj	5	0	131	87	4.38	1.41	4.34	1.34	113	117	17.7	7%	16%	9%	8%	10.5%	92.4	42	20	38	31%	74%	13%	12%	24						-6.5	66	-$5

Sánchez,Sixto

Age: 24	Th: R	Role: SP	Health: F	LIMA Plan: B	
Ht: 6' 0"	Wt: 234	Type: Con	PT/Exp: F	Rand Var: 0	
			Consist: F	MM: 3100	

Recovery from July 2021 shoulder surgery still continuing deep into year two—by June, he was essentially shut down for year. Received cortisone shot in late August, then went under knife again a month later. Once we buff off that rust, how much of his once-bright prospect sheen remains? Maybe we'll actually get to find out this year.

Yr Tm	W	Sv	IP	K	ERA	WHIP	xERA	xWHIP	vL+	vR+	BF/G	BB%	K%	K-BB%	xBB%	SwK	Vel	G	L	F	H%	S%	HR/F	xHR/F	GS	APC	DOM%	DIS%	Sv%	LI	RAR	BPX	R$
18																																	
19 aa	8	0	103	85	3.90	1.29	3.89				23.5	5%	20%	15%							34%	70%									7.8	121	$4
20 MIA	3	0	39	33	3.46	1.21	3.89	1.28	73	99	22.6	7%	21%	14%	6%	12.9%	97.6	58	13	29	30%	73%	9%	11%	7	80	43%	43%			4.8	118	$6
21																																	
22																																	
1st Half																																	
2nd Half																																	
Proj	3	0	51	43	3.83	1.30	3.52	1.30	87	116	23.2	8%	20%	13%	6%	12.9%	97.6	55	13	32	32%	71%	8%	10%	9						0.9	101	-$2

Sandoval,Patrick

Age: 26	Th: L	Role: RP	Health: C	LIMA Plan: A	
Ht: 6' 3"	Wt: 190	Type: Pwr	PT/Exp: A	Rand Var: -4	
			Consist: A	MM: 4303	

No huge step up, but a worthy follow-up to 2021's "breakout-ish" season. Skills held up very well, with remarkable consistency from xERA, xWHIP, and though GB% is leaking, it remains quite high. Could stand to find a more reliable way to get out RHB, but there is enough here to continue to get the job done.

Yr Tm	W	Sv	IP	K	ERA	WHIP	xERA	xWHIP	vL+	vR+	BF/G	BB%	K%	K-BB%	xBB%	SwK	Vel	G	L	F	H%	S%	HR/F	xHR/F	GS	APC	DOM%	DIS%	Sv%	LI	RAR	BPX	R$
18 aa	1	0	21	24	1.58	1.02	1.49				20.4	10%	29%	20%							28%	83%									6.7	163	-$1
19 LAA *	4	0	120	127	5.70	1.67	5.61	1.41	135	89	18.0	11%	24%	12%	11%	13.7%	93.0	47	26	27	37%	67%	21%	18%	9	71	11%	56%	0	0.72	-17.8	71	-$11
20 LAA	1	0	37	33	5.65	1.34	4.21	1.30	117	107	17.7	8%	21%	13%	8%	12.9%	92.8	55	18	27	28%	67%	32%	26%	6	66	0%	83%	0	0.87	-5.4	112	-$6
21 LAA	3	1	87	94	3.62	1.21	3.73	1.29	71	93	21.4	10%	26%	16%	9%	15.2%	93.3	51	19	30	28%	74%	16%	12%	14	85	21%	29%	100	0.75	6.9	114	$3
22 LAA	6	0	149	151	2.91	1.34	3.74	1.30	55	102	23.6	9%	24%	14%	8%	13.6%	93.2	47	22	31	33%	79%	6%	10%	27	91	26%	30%			19.5	101	$7
1st Half	3	0	70	74	3.09	1.41	4.01	1.33	66	100	23.9	10%	24%	14%	8%	13.0%	93.1	46	20	34	34%	79%	6%	9%	13	90	15%	15%			7.6	93	$2
2nd Half	3	0	79	77	2.75	1.27	3.50	1.27	44	103	23.4	9%	24%	15%	7%	14.2%	93.4	49	24	28	32%	79%	7%	12%	14	92	36%	43%			11.9	109	$8
Proj	6	0	160	159	3.62	1.27	3.33	1.27	87	98	19.8	9%	24%	16%	8%	13.7%	93.1	50	21	29	30%	76%	16%	15%	32						6.8	112	$6

Sanmartin,Reiver

Age: 27	Th: L	Role: RP	Health: A	LIMA Plan: B	
Ht: 6' 2"	Wt: 160	Type: /GB	PT/Exp: D	Rand Var: +5	
			Consist: F	MM: 2200	

4-4, 6.32 ERA in 57 IP in CIN. Began year as SP, but when he failed to escape 1st inning in Coors on May 1, ERA climbed to 13.78, and it was time to yell, "Mayday!" After time in minors to lick wounds, returned as RP, which went better, though control still an issue (20 BB in 40.2 IP). Ineffectiveness vR cements that he'll be a reliever, and not a very intriguing one.

Yr Tm	W	Sv	IP	K	ERA	WHIP	xERA	xWHIP	vL+	vR+	BF/G	BB%	K%	K-BB%	xBB%	SwK	Vel	G	L	F	H%	S%	HR/F	xHR/F	GS	APC	DOM%	DIS%	Sv%	LI	RAR	BPX	R$
18																																	
19 aa	2	0	58	48	5.84	1.60	5.92				21.4	7%	19%	11%							36%	65%									-9.5	59	-$8
20																																	
21 CIN *	12	0	113	107	3.99	1.35	4.15	1.12	64	106	17.4	7%	23%	16%	7%	11.0%	89.4	47	21	32	35%	71%	0%	3%	2	91	50%	0%			3.8	111	$5
22 CIN *	6	0	76	68	6.98	1.69	6.18	1.49	103	131	6.6	11%	18%	7%	9%	11.2%	90.7	54	15	30	37%	59%	15%	14%	4	23	0%	100%	0	0.88	-28.2	52	-$14
1st Half	2	0	44	39	9.39	1.92	7.63	1.34	110	151	10.5	8%	19%	11%	10%	9.1%	90.1	52	22	26	42%	50%	17%	15%	4	37	0%	100%	0	0.82	-29.5	43	-$30
2nd Half	4	0	32	29	3.66	1.38	4.11	1.45	98	109	4.2	12%	21%	10%	9%	13.0%	91.4	57	8	35	28%	78%	13%	14%	0	17			0	0.90	1.2	66	-$3
Proj	4	0	51	45	4.81	1.56	3.87	1.36	98	125	8.0	9%	20%	11%	9%	11.3%	90.9	55	14	31	35%	72%	13%	14%	0						-5.3	88	-$6

KRIS OLSON

Santana,Dennis

Age: 27	Th: R	Role RP	Health D	LIMA Plan C
Ht: 6' 2"	Wt: 190	Type Pwr	PT/Exp C	Rand Var +2
			Consist B	MM 2200

A fitting first name, as our game's version of the Menace wrecked his ratios in 2nd half. Little hope per their "x" counterparts, as shaky control seems entrenched and below-average SwK doesn't bode well for strikeouts. Unlikely to mature into late-inning gig; let him wreak all the havoc he wants on your waiver wire.

Yr	Tm	W	Sv	IP	K	ERA	WHIP	xERA	xWHIP	vL+	vR+	BF/G	BB%	K%	K-BB%	xBB%	SwK	Vel	G	L	F	H%	S%	HR/F	xHR/F	GS	APC	DOM%	DIS%	Sv%	LI	RAR	BPX	R$
18	LA *	2	0	55	61	3.24	1.08	2.54		150	133	19.5	7%	28%	21%		14.3%	92.9	25	67	8	31%	70%	0%	1%	0	70			0	0.69	6.2	163	$2
19	LA *	5	0	99	97	7.25	1.79	6.60		201	96	15.2	11%	21%	10%	11%	13.5%	92.7	40	33	27	37%	61%	25%	7%	0	35			0	0.67	-33.6	43	-$17
20	LA	1	0	17	18	5.29	1.29	4.37	1.33	81	117	6.1	10%	25%	15%	6%	12.0%	94.4	33	31	36	27%	67%	25%	17%	0	24			0	1.04	-1.8	93	-$4
21	2 TM	2	0	55	46	4.28	1.46	4.83	1.59	100	89	4.3	14%	19%	6%	10%	11.9%	95.4	50	20	30	29%	71%	9%	14%	0	17			0	0.90	-0.1	24	-$5
22	TEX	3	1	59	54	5.22	1.33	4.10	1.42	88	91	4.0	11%	21%	10%	9%	11.6%	96.9	48	21	30	30%	58%	4%	5%	1	16	0%	0%	33	1.22	-9.0	65	-$5
1st Half		3	1	32	24	2.25	0.88	3.76	1.26	66	65	3.7	6%	19%	13%	8%	11.8%	96.6	50	16	34	23%	71%	0%	5%	0	14			50	1.56	6.8	98	$4
2nd Half		0	0	27	30	8.78	1.88	4.54	1.58	109	118	4.4	16%	23%	8%	11%	11.4%	97.1	46	28	26	38%	50%	10%	5%	1	18	0%	0%	0	0.82	-15.8	27	-$21
Proj		2	0	51	45	4.45	1.43	4.03	1.49	102	102	5.4	12%	21%	9%	10%	11.6%	96.6	47	22	30	30%	69%	10%	6%	0						-3.0	48	-$5

Santillan,Tony

Age: 26	Th: R	Role RP	Health F	LIMA Plan C+
Ht: 6' 3"	Wt: 240	Type Pwr/FB	PT/Exp D	Rand Var +1
			Consist B	MM 2310

Picked up a clean save on Opening Day, but it was all downhill from there as ratios unraveled before June back strain shelved him for rest of season. Small-sample caveats aside, velocity uptick had adverse effect on whiffs and Ks, while wildness remains a major obstacle to the ninth inning. Plenty of better save speculations elsewhere.

Yr	Tm	W	Sv	IP	K	ERA	WHIP	xERA	xWHIP	vL+	vR+	BF/G	BB%	K%	K-BB%	xBB%	SwK	Vel	G	L	F	H%	S%	HR/F	xHR/F	GS	APC	DOM%	DIS%	Sv%	LI	RAR	BPX	R$
18	aa	4	0	63	55	4.54	1.46	5.56				24.6	6%	20%	14%							35%	74%									-3.0	78	-$4
19	aa	2	0	103	84	6.32	1.84	6.19				22.9	12%	17%	5%							37%	65%									-23.1	43	-$17
20																																		
21	CIN *	2	2	81	101	2.84	1.25	3.96	1.28	108	92	8.5	11%	31%	19%	10%	12.6%	95.0	33	24	43	28%	86%	16%	12%	4	29	0%	50%	100	0.76	14.3	99	$5
22	CIN	0	4	20	21	5.49	1.78	4.94	1.47	145	99	4.6	13%	22%	9%	11%	11.3%	96.2	30	30	40	39%	68%	4%	4%	0	19			57	1.66	-3.7	36	-$6
1st Half		0	4	20	21	5.49	1.78	4.94	1.47	145	99	4.6	13%	22%	9%	11%	11.3%	96.2	30	30	40	39%	68%	4%	4%	0	19			57	1.66	-3.7	36	-$11
2nd Half																																		
Proj		2	2	58	59	4.26	1.42	4.12	1.39	123	93	7.5	11%	24%	13%		11.8%	95.7	31	28	41	32%	73%	10%	8%	0						-2.1	64	-$3

Sborz,Josh

Age: 29	Th: R	Role RP	Health D	LIMA Plan B
Ht: 6' 3"	Wt: 215	Type Pwr	PT/Exp C	Rand Var +1
			Consist B	MM 5500

1-0, 6.45 ERA in 22 IP at TEX. IL-bound in April and September (elbow) as he buoyed between AAA and MLB. Tiny sample, but brutal luck in majors (40/63% H%/S%) hid some decent skills, as strong K% ticked higher with plenty of whiffs and primo velocity. There's a path to higher leverage; just see if he can tame those walks (and stay healthy) first.

Yr	Tm	W	Sv	IP	K	ERA	WHIP	xERA	xWHIP	vL+	vR+	BF/G	BB%	K%	K-BB%	xBB%	SwK	Vel	G	L	F	H%	S%	HR/F	xHR/F	GS	APC	DOM%	DIS%	Sv%	LI	RAR	BPX	R$
18	a/a	4	6	54	59	4.29	1.38	3.60				4.9	8%	26%	18%							37%	66%									-0.9	139	$0
19	LA *	4	3	59	62	5.67	1.55	5.10	1.52	165	89	4.9	7%	24%	17%	6%	10.3%	95.3	38	28	34	40%	62%	20%	23%	0	26			38	0.37	-8.5	116	-$4
20	LA	0	0	4	2	2.08	0.69	5.52		69	86	4.0	6%	13%	6%		13.6%	95.9	38	8	54	9%	100%	14%	18%	0	11			0	0.26	1.3	39	-$5
21	TEX	4	1	59	69	3.97	1.42	4.35	1.39	116	84	4.1	12%	27%	14%	9%	15.3%	96.8	42	21	37	32%	75%	12%	11%	0	17			25	0.88	2.2	85	-$2
22	TEX *	4	1	45	54	3.95	1.30	3.80	1.21	116	122	4.9	11%	32%	21%	10%	14.6%	97.0	30	30	40	30%	73%	17%	16%	1	22	0%	100%	100	0.46	0.1	102	-$1
1st Half		1	1	27	32	3.28	1.18	2.53	1.38	129	131	4.8	13%	29%	15%	12%	13.0%	97.0	22	33	44	25%	74%	17%	17%	0	21			100	0.33	2.3	117	-$4
2nd Half		3	0	18	22	4.97	1.48	5.74	1.20	108	112	5.2	9%	29%	19%	7%	16.1%	97.1	37	27	37	36%	73%	18%	14%	1	23	0%	100%	0	0.61	-2.2	85	-$7
Proj		5	0	51	61	4.24	1.25	3.18	1.23	122	88	4.6	10%	30%	19%	9%	15.3%	96.8	42	21	37	31%	69%	14%	10%	0						-1.7	126	-$1

Scherzer,Max

Age: 38	Th: R	Role SP	Health F	LIMA Plan C+
Ht: 6' 3"	Wt: 208	Type Pwr/xFB	PT/Exp A	Rand Var -4
			Consist A	MM 5505

A pair of oblique strains (May, Sept) cost him two months, had little effect on his on-field dominance. Second-highest K-BB% among starters (min. 140 IP) says it all, as xERA/xWHIP were carbon copies of 2021. Perhaps some HR/F regression with all those FBs pushes ERA up a bit, but we're nitpicking. You're at least another year away, Father Time.

Yr	Tm	W	Sv	IP	K	ERA	WHIP	xERA	xWHIP	vL+	vR+	BF/G	BB%	K%	K-BB%	xBB%	SwK	Vel	G	L	F	H%	S%	HR/F	xHR/F	GS	APC	DOM%	DIS%	Sv%	LI	RAR	BPX	R$
18	WAS	18	0	221	300	2.53	0.91	3.10	0.99	83	76	26.2	6%	35%	29%	5%	16.7%	94.4	34	18	48	28%	78%	10%	10%	33	106	67%	6%			44.1	203	$44
19	WAS	11	0	172	243	2.92	1.03	3.04	0.97	100	70	25.7	5%	35%	30%	5%	17.1%	94.9	41	21	38	34%	76%	12%	12%	27	103	52%	7%			33.6	219	$27
20	WAS	5	0	67	92	3.74	1.38	3.86	1.13	119	82	24.6	8%	31%	23%	7%	15.3%	94.7	33	27	40	38%	78%	14%	16%	12	101	25%	33%			5.9	169	$12
21	2 NL	15	0	179	236	2.46	0.86	3.22	0.97	83	72	23.1	5%	34%	29%	6%	16.6%	94.3	34	18	48	26%	80%	12%	13%	30	94	57%	7%			40.0	192	$39
22	NYM	11	0	145	173	2.29	0.91	3.23	0.97	89	75	24.6	4%	31%	26%	5%	15.3%	94.1	31	19	50	29%	80%	7%	10%	23	94	52%	4%			30.1	178	$26
1st Half		5	0	56	70	2.26	0.88	2.98	0.97	93	60	23.8	5%	33%	28%	6%	15.4%	93.8	34	20	46	28%	80%	8%	10%	9	93	44%	0%			11.7	185	$16
2nd Half		6	0	90	103	2.31	0.93	3.38	0.97	86	83	25.1	4%	29%	26%	5%	15.3%	94.2	29	19	51	29%	80%	7%	10%	14	95	57%	7%			18.4	175	$27
Proj		13	0	174	222	2.68	1.01	2.86	0.99	96	75	23.5	6%	33%	28%	6%	15.8%	94.3	33	21	46	31%	79%	10%	12%	28						27.6	183	$28

Schmidt,Clarke

Age: 27	Th: R	Role RP	Health F	LIMA Plan A+
Ht: 6' 1"	Wt: 209	Type	PT/Exp D	Rand Var -1
			Consist D	MM 3201

5-5, 3.12 ERA in 58 IP at NYY. A year of change with multiple AAA recalls, spot starts, and multi-inning relief gigs. Some nice gains: SwK drove uptick in Ks, 2nd half xERA/xWHIP looked great, and xBB% hints he can tame those walks. Needs stable rotation spot to be viable (and skills would need to play up); worth a stab to find out if it happens.

Yr	Tm	W	Sv	IP	K	ERA	WHIP	xERA	xWHIP	vL+	vR+	BF/G	BB%	K%	K-BB%	xBB%	SwK	Vel	G	L	F	H%	S%	HR/F	xHR/F	GS	APC	DOM%	DIS%	Sv%	LI	RAR	BPX	R$
18																																		
19	aa	2	0	19	16	3.21	0.96	2.65				23.9	1%	22%	21%							30%	68%									3.0	373	-$2
20	NYY	0	0	6	7	7.11	1.89	5.89	1.66	100	109	11.0	15%	21%	6%	12%	9.5%	95.0	44	17	39	39%	58%	0%	20%	1	42	0%	100%	0	1.18	-2.1	10	-$9
21	NYY *	0	0	41	37	3.32	1.53	6.01	1.64	189	76	17.7	9%	21%	12%	8%	9.1%	93.0	60	20	20	33%	87%	20%	13%	1	72	0%	100%	0	0.48	4.7	46	-$5
22	NYY *	7	2	91	94	3.28	1.18	3.02	1.31	114	77	9.8	10%	24%	14%	7%	12.2%	94.9	42	20	38	30%	73%	9%	10%	3	32	33%	0%	67	1.18	7.7	120	$6
1st Half		4	0	29	26	3.16	1.34	3.45	1.47	95	85	7.5	12%	21%	9%	10%	13.4%	94.8	45	16	39	28%	78%	8%	10%	1	27	100%	0%	0	1.16	2.9	83	-$3
2nd Half		3	2	62	68	3.34	1.11	2.81	1.13	126	71	11.5	7%	27%	20%	5%	11.3%	94.9	40	23	38	31%	71%	9%	10%	2	37	0%	0%	67	1.19	4.8	148	$8
Proj		6	0	87	79	3.42	1.24	3.77	1.31	123	81	11.0	9%	22%	14%	7%	12.1%	94.9	42	20	38	29%	76%	11%	11%	3						5.9	89	$3

Schreiber,John

Age: 29	Th: R	Role RP	Health A	LIMA Plan B+
Ht: 6' 2"	Wt: 210	Type Pwr/xGB	PT/Exp A	Rand Var -4
			Consist C	MM 5310

A shining light in otherwise dark BOS bullpen. Fewer four-seamers helped fuel skills explosion, as slider-driven SwK surge and newfound velocity drove elite K%, sinker produced ground balls galore (80% GB%), and he did it all with improved BB%. Limited track record, and came back to earth in 2nd half, but color us intrigued... UP: 25 Sv.

Yr	Tm	W	Sv	IP	K	ERA	WHIP	xERA	xWHIP	vL+	vR+	BF/G	BB%	K%	K-BB%	xBB%	SwK	Vel	G	L	F	H%	S%	HR/F	xHR/F	GS	APC	DOM%	DIS%	Sv%	LI	RAR	BPX	R$
18	aa	3	18	58	47	3.20	1.32	3.51				4.9	8%	20%	11%							32%	75%									6.8	99	$7
19	DET *	8	4	80	83	3.79	1.27	3.84	1.09	105	116	5.0	9%	25%	16%	8%	12.7%	91.8	37	31	31	30%	74%	27%	18%	0	19			50	0.77	7.1	95	$6
20	DET	0	0	16	14	6.32	1.47	4.96	1.26	136	97	4.7	6%	20%	14%	8%	7.8%	89.8	32	28	40	36%	57%	10%	10%	0	19			0	0.91	-3.6	105	-$9
21	BOS *	3	1	70	56	3.52	1.57	4.83		69	142	9.1	9%	18%	9%		10.7%	92.2	43	43	14	35%	77%	0%	0%	0	56			50	0.51	6.4	73	-$4
22	BOS	4	8	65	74	2.22	0.98	2.86	1.12	97	73	4.0	7%	29%	21%	8%	14.1%	94.0	56	13	31	28%	79%	6%	9%	0	16			80	1.47	14.1	162	$10
1st Half		2	3	27	32	0.66	0.66	2.42	1.02	55	55	3.6	6%	32%	26%	7%	16.1%	94.0	57	13	30	20%	94%	6%	9%	0	15			100	1.36	11.2	189	$9
2nd Half		2	5	38	42	3.35	1.22	3.19	1.19	115	88	4.3	8%	27%	19%	9%	12.8%	93.9	56	12	32	33%	73%	6%	9%	0	17			71	1.55	2.9	144	$3
Proj		4	10	58	60	2.94	1.18	3.11	1.23	120	86	4.7	8%	26%	17%	8%	14.0%	94.0	56	13	31	29%	79%	12%	10%	0						7.4	131	$6

Scott,Tanner

Age: 28	Th: L	Role RP	Health B	LIMA Plan A+
Ht: 6' 0"	Wt: 235	Type Pwr	PT/Exp C	Rand Var +3
			Consist A	MM 4511

A nice stretch of 18 Sv from June through Aug, but inability to hit water from a boat eventually knocked him from role. Walks aside, plenty of swing-and-miss backed elite K%, xGB% tilt returned in 2nd half, and H% was unkind. Perhaps xBB% hints at better control, but BB% history is skeptical. Don't expect a prolonged shot at saves like this again.

Yr	Tm	W	Sv	IP	K	ERA	WHIP	xERA	xWHIP	vL+	vR+	BF/G	BB%	K%	K-BB%	xBB%	SwK	Vel	G	L	F	H%	S%	HR/F	xHR/F	GS	APC	DOM%	DIS%	Sv%	LI	RAR	BPX	R$
18	BAL	3	0	53	76	5.40	1.56	3.26	1.26	87	122	4.5	12%	32%	20%	8%	17.5%	97.1	47	27	25	40%	66%	18%	14%	0	18			0	0.87	-8.2	148	-$6
19	BAL *	4	7	72	82	4.03	1.44	4.16	1.48	90	133	5.3	11%	27%	15%	12%	15.1%	95.9	50	27	23	34%	73%	27%	22%	0	17			58	0.56	4.2	99	$3
20	BAL	0	1	21	23	1.31	1.06	3.53	1.35	79	61	3.4	12%	27%	15%	12%	13.9%	96.5	58	18	24	24%	90%	8%	12%	0	14			50	1.77	8.0	112	$3
21	BAL	5	0	54	70	5.17	1.57	4.02	1.46	81	103	4.0	15%	28%	13%	11%	15.7%	96.8	51	23	26	34%	68%	17%	16%	0	17			0	1.17	-6.0	80	-$5
22	MIA	4	20	63	90	4.31	1.61	3.57	1.44	109	97	4.3	16%	31%	15%	9%	15.8%	96.9	46	28	26	37%	74%	13%	11%	0	19			74	0.99	-2.6	86	$4
1st Half		4	10	33	50	4.36	1.33	3.20	1.28	79	95	4.1	14%	34%	21%	9%	16.7%	96.8	38	32	31	33%	68%	14%	10%	0	18			83	0.92	-1.6	125	$6
2nd Half		0	10	30	40	4.25	1.92	4.03	1.60	141	99	4.6	18%	28%	10%	10%	14.8%	97.0	55	24	21	40%	78%	13%	13%	0	20			67	1.08	-1.0	42	-$4
Proj		4	5	65	82	4.18	1.37	3.29	1.41	87	87	4.2	15%	30%	15%	9%	16.0%	96.9	48	27	25	30%	71%	15%	13%	0						-1.7	87	$1

RYAN BLOOMFIELD

Sears,JP

Age: 27	Th: L	Role	RP	Health	A	LIMA Plan	C+
Ht: 5' 11"	Wt: 180	Type	Con/FB	PT/Exp	D	Rand Var	-2
				Consist	C	MM	2001

6-3, 3.86 ERA in 70 IP at NYY/OAK. Spent much of 1st half dominating AAA (1.70 ERA in 47 IP) before trade sent him to OAK's rotation. MLB returns were shaky: batters hardly ever whiffed, K-BB% was well below average, didn't post a single DOMinant start in 11 tries. Not the catalog you want to be shopping in, even late in drafts.

Yr	Tm	W	Sv	IP	K	ERA	WHIP	xERA	xWHIP	vL+	vR+	BF/G	BB%	K%	K-BB%	xBB%	SwK	Vel	G	L	F	H%	S%	HR/F	xHR/F	GS	APC	DOM%	DIS%	Sv%	LI	RAR	BPX	R$
18																																		
19																																		
20																																		
21	a/a	10	1	106	113	4.15	1.25	4.05				17.3	7%	26%	19%							32%	70%									1.6	116	$6
22	2 AL *	7	0	119	99	2.79	1.03	2.64	1.35	98	101	15.8	8%	18%	10%	7%	8.4%	93.2	40	18	41	26%	76%	9%	11%	11	63	0%	45%	0	0.72	17.4	117	$12
1st Half		4	0	55	49	1.16	0.75	0.95	1.10	127	58	13.2	4%	24%	19%	6%	8.6%	93.8	48	16	36	22%	87%	0%	7%	2	44	0%	0%	0	0.87	19.2	191	$19
2nd Half		3	0	64	50	4.20	1.26	4.10	1.31	92	114	18.6	8%	19%	11%	7%	8.4%	93.1	39	19	43	29%	70%	11%	12%	9	71	0%	56%	0	0.66	-1.8	73	-$2
Proj		**6**	**0**	**116**	**84**	**4.47**	**1.29**	**4.19**	**1.36**	**107**	**100**	**18.1**	**8%**	**18%**	**10%**	**7%**	**8.5%**	**93.4**	**42**	**18**	**40**	**29%**	**69%**	**11%**	**10%**	**21**						**-7.2**	**67**	**-$1**

Senga,Koudai

Age: 30	Th: R	Role	SP	Health	A	LIMA Plan	B
Ht: 6'0"	Wt: 178	Type	Pwr	PT/Exp	A	Rand Var	-3
				Consist	B	MM	4403

Top international free agent should make stateside debut in 2023, and you should be interested. Over 1,000 career innings of a 2.59 ERA in Nippon Professional Baseball with an upper-90s fastball and split-finger to drive excellent recent K%. Has the experience, workload, and stuff to be a mid-rotation starter. Watch his landing spot closely.

Yr	Tm	W	Sv	IP	K	ERA	WHIP	xERA	xWHIP	vL+	vR+	BF/G	BB%	K%	K-BB%	xBB%	SwK	Vel	G	L	F	H%	S%	HR/F	xHR/F	GS	APC	DOM%	DIS%	Sv%	LI	RAR	BPX	R$
18	for	13	0	141	155	4.36	1.39	5.24				27.0	12%	26%	14%							27%	79%									-3.7	52	$3
19	for	13	0	180	215	3.48	1.32	4.14				28.6	12%	29%	16%							28%	81%									22.8	84	$15
20	for	8	0	99	117	3.27	1.49	3.85				28.4	15%	27%	12%							32%	79%									14.4	105	$19
21	for	10	0	85	85	3.29	1.15	2.51				26.0	10%	25%	15%							28%	71%									10.3	121	$9
22	for	11	0	144	148	2.41	1.19	2.98				26.2	11%	26%	15%							28%	83%									27.8	107	$16
1st Half																																		
2nd Half																																		
Proj		**11**	**0**	**145**	**159**	**3.58**	**1.25**	**3.47**	**1.31**			**26.8**	**11%**	**27%**	**16%**				**44**	**20**	**36**	**29%**	**75%**	**13%**	**11%**	**22**						**7.0**	**102**	**$10**

Senzatela,Antonio

Age: 28	Th: R	Role	SP	Health	F	LIMA Plan	C+
Ht: 6' 1"	Wt: 236	Type	Con/GB	PT/Exp	A	Rand Var	+3
				Consist	A	MM	2001

Injury-riddled campaign with IL stints in May (back) and July (shoulder) before torn ACL finished him off in August. Velocity held firm, though SwK going from bad to awful might have been health-related. Combo of GB% and BB% stayed intact and sets a decent floor, but until he can miss or bats or get Ks—he's yet to do either—this is a matchup play only.

Yr	Tm	W	Sv	IP	K	ERA	WHIP	xERA	xWHIP	vL+	vR+	BF/G	BB%	K%	K-BB%	xBB%	SwK	Vel	G	L	F	H%	S%	HR/F	xHR/F	GS	APC	DOM%	DIS%	Sv%	LI	RAR	BPX	R$
18	COL *	9	0	130	102	3.77	1.30	3.88	1.36	95	114	17.2	8%	19%	11%	9%	8.8%	93.7	46	21	33	30%	73%	11%	11%	13	66	15%	38%	0	0.73	6.1	85	$5
19	COL *	12	0	160	85	6.61	1.74	6.66	1.58	124	113	22.8	9%	12%	2%	11%	7.7%	93.7	54	22	24	34%	64%	18%	19%	25	89	8%	68%			-41.5	2	-$19
20	COL	5	0	73	41	3.44	1.21	4.76	1.38	100	94	25.3	6%	14%	8%	8%	8.4%	94.4	51	20	29	27%	76%	13%	13%	12	95	25%	50%			9.2	68	$13
21	COL	4	0	157	105	4.42	1.34	4.27	1.27	108	96	23.9	5%	16%	11%	7%	9.2%	94.6	51	22	27	33%	67%	9%	12%	28	86	14%	39%			-3.1	96	-$3
22	COL	3	0	92	54	5.07	1.69	4.38	1.34	122	132	21.7	6%	13%	8%	9%	7.4%	94.2	49	26	25	38%	71%	11%	10%	19	80	5%	58%			-12.5	67	-$13
1st Half		3	0	60	34	4.95	1.80	4.74	1.35	126	133	21.2	5%	12%	7%	8%	7.5%	93.9	45	28	27	39%	73%	8%	11%	13	78	0%	62%			-7.3	59	-$18
2nd Half		0	0	32	20	5.29	1.48	3.70	1.32	113	129	22.8	6%	15%	9%	10%	7.3%	94.6	59	22	19	34%	66%	20%	10%	6	84	17%	50%			-5.3	85	-$13
Proj		**4**	**0**	**116**	**70**	**4.77**	**1.49**	**4.03**	**1.35**	**113**	**115**	**22.6**	**6%**	**14%**	**8%**	**9%**	**7.9%**	**94.3**	**52**	**23**	**25**	**33%**	**70%**	**13%**	**12%**	**22**						**-11.5**	**71**	**-$8**

Severino,Luis

Age: 29	Th: R	Role	SP	Health	F	LIMA Plan	B+
Ht: 6' 2"	Wt: 218	Type		PT/Exp	D	Rand Var	-2
				Consist	B	MM	4303

First extended action since 2018 was a success, though he did miss nearly two months (lat) in 2nd half. Both K% and BB% snapped right back to 2018 form, and despite some H% fortune, "x" ratios were both in great shape. Not out of the woods durability-wise and post-injury whiffs dropped a bit, but looks like an effective SP2.

Yr	Tm	W	Sv	IP	K	ERA	WHIP	xERA	xWHIP	vL+	vR+	BF/G	BB%	K%	K-BB%	xBB%	SwK	Vel	G	L	F	H%	S%	HR/F	xHR/F	GS	APC	DOM%	DIS%	Sv%	LI	RAR	BPX	R$
18	NYY	19	0	191	220	3.39	1.14	3.30	1.10	94	90	24.4	6%	28%	22%	6%	12.8%	97.6	41	26	33	33%	74%	11%	13%	32	99	41%	9%			18.0	169	$23
19	NYY	1	0	12	17	1.50	1.00	3.59	1.26	61	53	16.0	13%	35%	23%	6%	11.4%	96.1	42	13	46	26%	83%	0%	5%	3	73	33%	0%			4.4	139	-$2
20																																		
21	NYY	1	0	6	8	0.00	0.50	2.58		161	23	5.5	5%	36%	32%		13.3%	95.3	42	17	42	18%	100%	0%	2%	0	25			0	0.63	3.2	214	-$3
22	NYY	7	0	102	112	3.18	1.00	3.35	1.14	90	85	21.3	7%	28%	20%	7%	12.6%	96.3	44	16	40	25%	75%	14%	10%	19	86	32%	16%			10.0	142	$10
1st Half		4	0	78	91	3.35	1.05	3.35	1.12	106	82	22.5	7%	29%	22%	8%	13.4%	96.2	41	17	42	27%	75%	14%	9%	14	91	29%	14%			6.0	151	$13
2nd Half		3	0	24	21	2.63	0.83	3.33	1.24	53	100	18.0	8%	23%	16%	6%	9.6%	96.8	53	15	32	18%	76%	15%	14%	5	73	40%	20%			4.0	113	$1
Proj		**11**	**0**	**160**	**155**	**3.43**	**1.11**	**3.34**	**1.19**	**88**	**104**	**21.7**	**7%**	**25%**	**18%**	**6%**	**11.5%**	**96.8**	**43**	**18**	**40**	**28%**	**73%**	**12%**	**12%**	**29**						**10.7**	**125**	**$15**

Sewald,Paul

Age: 33	Th: R	Role	RP	Health	B	LIMA Plan	B
Ht: 6' 3"	Wt: 207	Type	Pwr/xFB	PT/Exp	B	Rand Var	-5
				Consist	F	MM	4421

Would've nailed last year's "UP: 30 Sv" if it wasn't for that stinkin' SEA committee. Whiffs and Ks both fell back from the stratosphere, and while he ran lucky with lowest H% of any pitcher (min. 50 IP), can't complain about K-BB% and BPX encore. At the whims of home run gods given FB tilt, but looks like a fine mid-tier stopper once again.

Yr	Tm	W	Sv	IP	K	ERA	WHIP	xERA	xWHIP	vL+	vR+	BF/G	BB%	K%	K-BB%	xBB%	SwK	Vel	G	L	F	H%	S%	HR/F	xHR/F	GS	APC	DOM%	DIS%	Sv%	LI	RAR	BPX	R$
18	NYM	0	2	56	58	6.07	1.51	4.84	1.33	118	110	5.5	9%	23%	14%	6%	9.8%	90.3	30	23	46	35%	61%	10%	8%	0	23			50	0.97	-13.4	87	-$9
19	NYM *	4	4	71	63	4.51	1.57	5.85	1.09	80	103	5.3	6%	20%	14%	7%	9.7%	91.1	17	21	62	37%	75%	9%	9%	0	19			100	0.61	0.0	73	-$2
20	NYM	0	0	6	2	13.50	2.67	8.99	1.84	207	117	7.0	11%	6%	-6%	12%	6.2%	91.8	32	39	29	42%	47%	13%	11%	0	26			0	0.56	-6.7	-111	-$14
21	SEA	10	11	65	104	3.06	1.02	3.28	1.03	90	73	4.3	9%	40%	30%	6%	17.2%	92.4	26	21	53	29%	79%	14%	15%	0	18			69	1.60	9.6	191	$15
22	SEA	5	20	64	72	2.67	0.77	3.42	1.09	85	67	3.7	7%	30%	23%	6%	15.8%	92.6	31	18	51	17%	77%	13%	8%	0	15			80	1.36	10.2	140	$17
1st Half		3	9	31	34	2.64	0.72	3.27	1.06	74	70	3.7	6%	29%	23%	6%	14.8%	92.5	36	17	47	16%	76%	15%	7%	0	15			82	1.59	5.0	153	$12
2nd Half		2	11	33	38	2.70	0.81	3.56	1.12	93	63	3.7	8%	30%	22%	7%	16.8%	92.7	25	20	55	18%	77%	12%	9%	0	15			79	1.16	5.2	127	$13
Proj		**5**	**17**	**65**	**74**	**2.83**	**1.08**	**3.45**	**1.15**	**97**	**82**	**4.2**	**8%**	**29%**	**21%**	**6%**	**14.4%**	**92.0**	**29**	**20**	**50**	**28%**	**80%**	**10%**	**9%**	**0**						**9.2**	**129**	**$13**

Silseth,Chase

Age: 23	Th: R	Role	SP	Health	A	LIMA Plan	C+
Ht: 6' 0"	Wt: 217	Type	Con	PT/Exp	F	Rand Var	+1
				Consist	F	MM	2101

1-3, 6.59 ERA in 29 IP at LAA. Impressive AA returns (26% K-BB%, 2.28 ERA) bookended far less successful mid-year MLB stint. Lofty HR/F certainly didn't help, but average sub-indicators (xBB%, SwK) and mid-4.00s xERA say it wasn't all bad luck. Just a pup so he'll get another shot; be ready to pounce if you see an uptick in strikeouts.

Yr	Tm	W	Sv	IP	K	ERA	WHIP	xERA	xWHIP	vL+	vR+	BF/G	BB%	K%	K-BB%	xBB%	SwK	Vel	G	L	F	H%	S%	HR/F	xHR/F	GS	APC	DOM%	DIS%	Sv%	LI	RAR	BPX	R$
18																																		
19																																		
20																																		
21																																		
22	LAA *	8	0	112	120	3.25	1.08	3.29	1.39	160	101	19.8	9%	19%	9%	8%	11.4%	95.3	46	23	31	26%	78%	25%	17%	7	72	0%	57%			9.9	109	$10
1st Half		3	0	57	58	2.93	1.05	3.08	1.19	165	98	18.3	8%	26%	18%	8%	10.9%	95.5	48	24	29	26%	79%	28%	18%	5	70	0%	40%			7.3	114	$7
2nd Half		5	0	55	62	3.58	1.11	3.51	1.19	151	111	21.6	9%	28%	19%	12%	12.4%	94.7	43	21	36	26%	76%	20%	15%	2	77	0%	100%			2.7	105	$7
Proj		**5**	**0**	**73**	**55**	**4.17**	**1.30**	**3.89**	**1.40**	**138**	**91**	**21.2**	**9%**	**18%**	**9%**	**8%**	**10.9%**	**95.5**	**45**	**24**	**31**	**28%**	**71%**	**15%**	**17%**	**14**						**-1.8**	**62**	**-$1**

Sims,Lucas

Age: 29	Th: R	Role	RP	Health	F	LIMA Plan	B
Ht: 6' 2"	Wt: 225	Type	Pwr/xFB	PT/Exp	C	Rand Var	+5
				Consist	C	MM	4510

Elbow issues pushed his debut to late April, pitched in six games, then had season-ending back surgery. This was a skill set on the rise in last year's book given concurrent K% and BB% trends, whiffs galore, and closer-worthy BPX. Still owns those skills and age is on his side, but firmly in the "wait-and-see" bucket pending spring reports.

Yr	Tm	W	Sv	IP	K	ERA	WHIP	xERA	xWHIP	vL+	vR+	BF/G	BB%	K%	K-BB%	xBB%	SwK	Vel	G	L	F	H%	S%	HR/F	xHR/F	GS	APC	DOM%	DIS%	Sv%	LI	RAR	BPX	R$
18	2 NL *	4	0	118	114	4.42	1.47	4.88	1.73	112	115	17.4	11%	23%	12%	12%	11.5%	92.5	37	22	41	32%	74%	16%	12%	0	35			0	0.52	-3.9	69	-$4
19	CIN *	7	0	122	145	5.56	1.44	4.80	1.27	88	99	13.0	12%	28%	16%	8%	15.6%	93.6	25	19	57	33%	65%	15%	12%	4	31	25%	50%	0	0.66	-15.9	82	-$4
20	CIN	3	0	26	34	2.45	0.94	3.62	1.21	75	77	5.2	11%	33%	22%	12%	13.1%	94.0	42	13	45	21%	81%	12%	4%	0	23			0	1.20	6.3	147	$9
21	CIN	5	7	47	76	4.40	1.11	3.12	1.03	101	81	4.1	9%	39%	30%	8%	15.3%	95.1	26	26	47	33%	63%	13%	11%	0	17			70	1.47	-0.8	190	$4
22	CIN	1	1	7	5	9.45	1.65	5.58	1.96	73	111	5.2	19%	16%	-3%	12%	7.0%	93.5	53	21	26	27%	36%	0%	7%	0	22			100	0.82	-4.5	-73	-$6
1st Half		1	1	7	5	9.45	1.65	5.58	1.96	73	110	5.2	19%	16%	-3%	12%	7.0%	93.5	53	21	26	27%	36%	0%	7%	0	22			100	0.82	-4.5	-73	-$12
2nd Half																																		
Proj		**4**	**7**	**58**	**74**	**3.75**	**1.26**	**3.50**	**1.24**	**104**	**96**	**6.8**	**11%**	**31%**	**20%**		**15.4%**	**94.5**	**30**	**22**	**48**	**30%**	**75%**	**12%**	**11%**	**0**						**1.6**	**116**	**$3**

RYAN BLOOMFIELD

Singer,Brady

Age: 26 | Th: R | Role: SP | Health: B | LIMA Plan: B+
Ht: 6' 5" | Wt: 215 | Type: /GB | PT/Exp: A | Rand Var: 0
Consist: A | MM: 4205

10-5, 3.23 ERA in 153 IP at KC. Started season with bullpen blow-up (6.35 ERA) and demotion, then righted ship with best work of career. Primary driver of success was BB% growth, giving him second plus skill along with GB%, and while S% aided 2nd half numbers, xERA and xWHIP were nearly as strong. He's capable of a repeat, ideally over more IP.

Yr	Tm	W	Sv	IP	K	ERA	WHIP	xERA	xWHIP	vL+	vR+	BF/G	BB%	K%	K-BB%	xBB%	SwK	Vel	G	L	F	H%	S%	HR/F	xHR/F	GS	APC	DOM%	DIS%	Sv%	LI	RAR	BPX	R$
18																																		
19	aa	7	0	92	70	4.75	1.46	4.87				24.7	7%	18%	11%							34%	69%									-2.7	68	-$2
20	KC	4	0	64	61	4.06	1.17	3.98	1.31	93	83	21.9	9%	23%	14%	7%	9.8%	93.4	53	17	30	27%	69%	15%	15%	12	89	33%	50%			3.1	110	$11
21	KC	5	0	128	131	4.91	1.55	4.17	1.32	112	97	21.7	9%	22%	13%	8%	10.5%	93.7	50	22	28	36%	70%	13%	14%	27	85	22%	37%			-10.2	102	-$9
22	KC *	11	0	169	158	3.20	1.11	3.45	1.14	103	90	22.1	6%	24%	19%	7%	9.6%	93.8	49	20	31	29%	76%	14%	14%	24	88	42%	21%	0	0.69	16.0	123	$16
1st Half		4	0	74	66	4.01	1.13	3.96	1.17	118	93	19.4	6%	22%	17%	7%	9.9%	93.8	47	17	35	28%	71%	17%	15%	9	77	22%	22%	0	0.60	-0.4	103	$4
2nd Half		7	0	95	92	2.57	1.10	3.10	1.14	93	88	25.2	6%	24%	19%	7%	9.4%	93.8	50	22	28	30%	80%	11%	13%	15	97	53%	20%			16.4	143	$22
Proj		12	0	189	176	3.56	1.17	3.23	1.21	98	87	24.6	7%	23%	17%	7%	9.8%	93.7	50	20	30	30%	73%	13%	14%	31						9.4	125	$15

Skubal,Tarik

Age: 26 | Th: L | Role: SP | Health: D | LIMA Plan: A
Ht: 6' 3" | Wt: 240 | Type: Pwr/FB | PT/Exp: A | Rand Var: -1
Consist: B | MM: 4401

Flexor tendon surgery ended season in Aug, and will keep him out of action for at least nine months. Prior to that, took another solid step forward, with shift in GB%, FB% enough to move needle on xERA even with other skills remaining static. Return from injury makes 2023 outlook a little cloudy, but long-term, he's growing nicely into mid-rotation upside.

Yr	Tm	W	Sv	IP	K	ERA	WHIP	xERA	xWHIP	vL+	vR+	BF/G	BB%	K%	K-BB%	xBB%	SwK	Vel	G	L	F	H%	S%	HR/F	xHR/F	GS	APC	DOM%	DIS%	Sv%	LI	RAR	BPX	R$
18																																		
19	aa	2	0	43	67	3.09	1.19	2.67				19.2	12%	39%	27%							35%	75%									7.5	165	$1
20	DET	1	0	32	37	5.63	1.22	4.58	1.22	48	120	16.8	8%	28%	19%	8%	13.4%	94.5	28	18	54	26%	63%	20%	17%	7	74	14%	43%	0	0.80	-4.6	124	-$4
21	DET	8	0	149	164	4.34	1.26	4.11	1.20	93	107	20.5	7%	26%	18%	7%	12.1%	94.4	39	20	41	29%	76%	20%	21%	29	82	17%	31%	0	0.76	-1.4	129	$5
22	DET	7	0	118	117	3.52	1.16	3.52	1.17	89	94	22.7	7%	25%	18%	6%	12.2%	94.4	46	19	35	31%	71%	8%	10%	21	91	43%	24%			6.5	131	$7
1st Half		5	0	89	90	4.06	1.20	3.45	1.16	97	97	22.6	7%	25%	18%	6%	12.1%	94.3	47	18	35	32%	67%	10%	9%	16	91	50%	31%			-1.0	137	$7
2nd Half		2	0	29	27	1.86	1.03	3.73	1.20	71	83	23.2	7%	23%	16%	6%	12.4%	94.9	41	22	37	28%	83%	3%	11%	5	90	20%	0%			7.5	113	$1
Proj		6	0	102	111	3.74	1.16	3.36	1.18	74	100	20.7	8%	27%	19%	7%	12.5%	94.6	39	20	41	29%	73%	13%	13%	20						2.9	128	$5

Small,Ethan

Age: 26 | Th: L | Role: RP | Health: A | LIMA Plan: B
Ht: 6' 3" | Wt: 214 | Type: Pwr | PT/Exp: D | Rand Var: +1
Consist: C | MM: 3201

0-0, 7.11 ERA in 6 IP at MIL. Two brief starts of poor quality probably isn't how he envisioned MLB career kicking off—unfortunately, shaky minor-league BB%, K-BB% suggest it wasn't unexpected. Gets by on deception and movement that make up for ordinary velocity, but lacks third pitch. Too flawed for 2023 investment; needs more time to develop.

Yr	Tm	W	Sv	IP	K	ERA	WHIP	xERA	xWHIP	vL+	vR+	BF/G	BB%	K%	K-BB%	xBB%	SwK	Vel	G	L	F	H%	S%	HR/F	xHR/F	GS	APC	DOM%	DIS%	Sv%	LI	RAR	BPX	R$
18																																		
19																																		
20																																		
21	a/a	4	0	77	78	2.19	1.30	3.07				18.7	13%	25%	12%							28%	85%									19.7	101	$5
22	MIL *	7	0	109	103	4.72	1.48	4.09	2.09	96	159	16.2	24%	21%	-3%	12%	12.1%	91.0	33	33	33	30%	68%	17%	22%	2	66	0%	100%			-10.2	77	-$5
1st Half		5	0	67	62	3.45	1.31	3.11	1.48	287	126	19.7	13%	22%	9%	12%	15.9%	91.3	57	29	14	27%	74%	0%	0%	1	69	0%	100%			4.3	92	$3
2nd Half		2	0	45	41	6.38	1.67	5.18	1.62		187	13.4	15%	21%	6%	12%	7.9%	90.6	18	36	45	32%	62%	20%	26%	1	63	0%	100%			-13.3	57	-$16
Proj		5	0	87	78	4.39	1.41	3.74				16.4	13%	21%	8%							28%	69%		0%	14						-4.5	158	-$3

Smeltzer,Devin

Age: 27 | Th: L | Role: RP | Health: F | LIMA Plan: C+
Ht: 6' 3" | Wt: 195 | Type: Con/FB | PT/Exp: D | Rand Var: 0
Consist: C | MM: 1001

5-2, 3.71 ERA in 70 IP at MIN. As in 2019, low MLB ERA might make it look like he's got upside, but 4.91 xERA should quickly disabuse you of that notion. As should lousy K-BB% and SwK, and high FB% for pitcher who allows a lot of balls in play. 2nd half meltdown that landed him on outright waivers is final warning to stay away; things could get ugly fast.

Yr	Tm	W	Sv	IP	K	ERA	WHIP	xERA	xWHIP	vL+	vR+	BF/G	BB%	K%	K-BB%	xBB%	SwK	Vel	G	L	F	H%	S%	HR/F	xHR/F	GS	APC	DOM%	DIS%	Sv%	LI	RAR	BPX	R$
18	aa	5	4	97	68	5.45	1.51	5.45				12.7	5%	16%	11%							36%	64%									-15.6	80	-$7
19	MIN *	6	1	154	123	3.81	1.26	4.59	1.32	114	101	20.3	6%	20%	14%	6%	9.7%	89.1	39	22	40	30%	77%	14%	16%	6	67	17%	17%	100	0.64	13.3	77	$8
20	MIN	2	0	16	15	6.75	1.50	5.04	1.30	118	109	10.3	7%	21%	14%	9%	10.1%	87.6	34	24	42	36%	55%	10%	10%	1	38	0%	0%	0	0.55	-4.5	99	-$6
21	MIN	0	0	5	3	0.00	0.43	3.80		54	30	17.0	6%	18%	12%		13.5%	85.6	45	9	45	9%	100%	0%	2%	0	52			0	0.90	2.5	82	-$4
22	MIN *	8	0	120	77	5.25	1.42	5.50	1.37	130	100	17.0	7%	14%	7%	7%	7.5%	89.5	39	16	46	30%	67%	13%	11%	12	75	25%	50%	0	0.80	-19.0	34	-$8
1st Half		5	0	77	48	3.24	1.12	3.60	1.30	87	99	20.3	6%	16%	10%	6%	7.8%	89.5	39	14	48	26%	77%	12%	8%	10	86	30%	40%			7.0	69	$8
2nd Half		3	0	43	29	8.87	1.96	8.92	1.43	231	105	13.7	8%	14%	6%	9%	6.6%	89.4	38	23	40	38%	58%	14%	21%	2	54	0%	100%	0	0.82	-26.0	-19	-$26
Proj		4	0	80	55	5.83	1.54	4.65	1.35	130	125	15.3	7%	16%	9%	6%	8.6%	89.3	39	17	45	34%	65%	11%	11%	12						-18.3	64	-$11

Smith,Will

Age: 33 | Th: L | Role: RP | Health: B | LIMA Plan: B
Ht: 6' 5" | Wt: 255 | Type: Pwr/FB | PT/Exp: A | Rand Var: -1
Consist: A | MM: 4510

Even with unlucky H% trying to sink 2nd half, he recovered nicely after deadline trade to HOU (3.27 ERA, 3.45 xERA). xBB% suggests that past two seasons of shaky control were fluky, and K% should rebound with SwK still holding strong. Leverage Index took a hit, but knowing how much managers love guys with closing experience, can't rule out more saves.

Yr	Tm	W	Sv	IP	K	ERA	WHIP	xERA	xWHIP	vL+	vR+	BF/G	BB%	K%	K-BB%	xBB%	SwK	Vel	G	L	F	H%	S%	HR/F	xHR/F	GS	APC	DOM%	DIS%	Sv%	LI	RAR	BPX	R$
18	SF	2	14	53	71	2.55	0.98	2.99	1.05	60	81	3.9	7%	34%	27%	5%	15.1%	92.7	42	20	38	30%	76%	7%	9%	0	15			78	1.44	10.5	194	$10
19	SF	6	34	65	96	2.76	1.03	2.95	1.05	52	95	4.1	8%	37%	29%	6%	15.8%	92.7	42	22	36	29%	82%	20%	16%	0	17			89	1.58	14.1	196	$24
20	ATL	2	0	16	18	4.50	0.94	4.12	1.13	102	109	3.4	6%	29%	23%	10%	17.5%	92.6	30	18	53	13%	88%	33%	24%	0	14			0	1.24	-0.1	146	$1
21	ATL	3	37	68	87	3.44	1.13	3.94	1.21	97	92	4.0	10%	31%	21%	7%	14.7%	92.8	31	21	47	27%	77%	14%	10%	0	15			86	1.33	6.9	127	$20
22	2 TM	0	5	59	65	3.97	1.41	4.28	1.28	91	120	4.0	10%	25%	15%	6%	15.4%	92.2	35	20	45	33%	77%	12%	9%	0	15			63	0.85	0.0	98	-$2
1st Half		0	5	32	34	3.09	1.34	4.52	1.44	103	89	4.1	13%	24%	11%	7%	14.3%	92.3	39	18	43	26%	84%	14%	10%	0	16			63	1.06	3.5	58	-$2
2nd Half		0	0	27	31	5.00	1.48	4.02	1.11	80	162	3.9	6%	26%	20%	5%	16.9%	92.0	31	22	47	39%	69%	11%	8%	0	14			0	0.60	-3.4	145	-$11
Proj		3	6	58	73	3.58	1.24	3.24	1.16	80	109	3.9	9%	31%	22%	6%	15.6%	92.4	36	21	43	32%	77%	14%	11%	0						2.8	142	$3

Smyly,Drew

Age: 34 | Th: L | Role: SP | Health: F | LIMA Plan: A+
Ht: 6' 2" | Wt: 188 | Type: Con/FB | PT/Exp: A | Rand Var: -2
Consist: B | MM: 2203

Injuries seem like a given at this point, as he missed six weeks with oblique, shoulder issues. When healthy, has been gradually making his way back to deep league value after lost seasons of 2017-18, with elite BB% helping to offset high FB% and lack of Ks. High S% gave 2022 ERA a boost, so regression back over 4.00 seems likely.

Yr	Tm	W	Sv	IP	K	ERA	WHIP	xERA	xWHIP	vL+	vR+	BF/G	BB%	K%	K-BB%	xBB%	SwK	Vel	G	L	F	H%	S%	HR/F	xHR/F	GS	APC	DOM%	DIS%	Sv%	LI	RAR	BPX	R$
18																																		
19	2 TM	4	1	114	120	6.24	1.59	5.31	1.44	142	116	20.6	11%	23%	13%	9%	11.0%	91.2	33	22	45	32%	68%	21%	20%	21	85	19%	48%	100	0.73	-24.3	70	-$11
20	SF	0	0	26	42	3.42	1.10	2.97	1.03	37	96	15.9	8%	38%	30%	6%	15.1%	93.8	42	23	35	36%	70%	10%	15%	5	69	20%	20%	0	0.74	3.4	221	$1
21	ATL	11	0	127	117	4.48	1.37	4.55	1.29	117	105	18.8	8%	21%	14%	6%	12.1%	92.1	39	22	39	31%	76%	18%	17%	23	74	4%	26%	0	0.74	-3.3	97	$1
22	CHC	7	0	106	91	3.47	1.19	4.19	1.21	87	105	20.3	6%	20%	15%	6%	12.7%	92.6	40	18	42	29%	77%	12%	11%	22	82	18%	36%			6.5	107	$5
1st Half		2	0	43	34	3.80	1.27	4.14	1.23	102	113	20.0	6%	19%	13%	6%	12.3%	92.0	48	13	39	29%	78%	15%	16%	9	80	0%	33%			0.9	108	-$4
2nd Half		5	0	64	57	3.25	1.15	4.21	1.20	74	99	20.5	6%	21%	15%	5%	13.0%	92.8	35	21	45	29%	77%	9%	8%	13	84	31%	38%			5.6	107	$8
Proj		7	0	131	111	4.18	1.27	3.95	1.27	105	105	20.6	7%	21%	14%	6%	12.2%	92.1	38	19	42	28%	75%	15%	14%	26						-3.4	92	$2

Snell,Blake

Age: 30 | Th: L | Role: SP | Health: F | LIMA Plan: A
Ht: 6' 4" | Wt: 225 | Type: Pwr | PT/Exp: A | Rand Var: -1
Consist: B | MM: 5503

Groin tightness delayed start of season until mid-May, and kept him from finding groove until 2nd half. That performance shows that former ace skills are alive and well, but recent injury history makes it way too risky to pay anything close to ace prices for potential upside. Set your sights on 130 IP of good work, and pray that health gods look favorably upon him.

Yr	Tm	W	Sv	IP	K	ERA	WHIP	xERA	xWHIP	vL+	vR+	BF/G	BB%	K%	K-BB%	xBB%	SwK	Vel	G	L	F	H%	S%	HR/F	xHR/F	GS	APC	DOM%	DIS%	Sv%	LI	RAR	BPX	R$
18	TAM	21	0	181	221	1.89	0.97	3.17	1.16	56	82	22.6	9%	32%	22%	9%	15.3%	95.8	45	19	36	25%	86%	11%	13%	31	94	55%	19%			50.3	156	$39
19	TAM	6	0	107	147	4.29	1.27	3.49	1.16	118	89	19.2	9%	33%	24%	8%	18.2%	95.6	39	25	36	35%	70%	15%	12%	23	82	26%	48%			2.8	162	$5
20	TAM	4	0	50	63	3.24	1.20	3.27	1.17	96	98	18.5	9%	31%	22%	9%	15.6%	95.1	49	23	28	29%	84%	29%	21%	11	79	9%	27%			7.5	162	$13
21	SD	7	0	129	170	4.20	1.32	3.85	1.31	63	101	20.4	13%	31%	18%	10%	13.4%	95.2	40	23	37	31%	71%	14%	20%	27	87	26%	37%			1.1	112	$4
22	SD	8	0	128	171	3.38	1.20	3.41	1.15	91	89	22.3	10%	32%	22%	9%	15.2%	95.9	37	21	43	33%	74%	8%	10%	24	98	21%	13%			9.4	148	$10
1st Half		0	0	40	50	5.13	1.46	4.07	1.36	90	103	22.4	13%	28%	15%	11%	14.8%	95.5	43	15	42	33%	65%	9%	10%	8	85	0%	25%			-5.8	92	-$11
2nd Half		8	0	88	121	2.57	1.08	3.13	1.05	91	82	22.3	8%	34%	26%	8%	15.4%	96.0	33	24	43	32%	80%	8%	10%	16	99	31%	6%			15.2	174	$26
Proj		8	0	131	171	3.60	1.23	3.07	1.19	88	93	20.3	10%	32%	22%	9%	15.3%	95.6	40	21	38	32%	75%	14%	14%	26						6.0	142	$9

BRANDON KRUSE

Soroka,Mike

Age: 25	Th: R	Role	SP	Health	F	LIMA Plan	B
Ht: 6' 5"	Wt: 225	Type	Con	PT/Exp	F	Rand Var	+5
				Consist	C	MM	4001

Nearly three-year absence from MLB with only small samples in interim leaves us grasping at straws for what to expect. Important to remember that 2019 ERA, WHIP were aided by H%, S%, so keep visions of that $20 pitcher out of your head. If BB%, GB% skills return intact, should have solid floor, but with IP likely limited, might be best to sit this one out.

Yr	Tm	W	Sv	IP	K	ERA	WHIP	xERA	xWHIP	vL+	vR+	BF/G	BB%	K%	K-BB%	xBB%	SwK	Vel	G	L	F	H%	S%	HR/F	xHR/F	GS	APC	DOM%	DIS%	Sv%	LI	RAR	BPX	R$
18	ATL *	4	0	53	48	2.91	1.23	3.15	1.28	86	120	21.3	6%	22%	16%	8%	10.6%	92.6	44	32	24	34%	75%	5%	12%	5	81	20%	40%			8.1	146	$2
19	ATL	13	0	175	142	2.68	1.11	3.87	1.27	99	72	24.2	6%	20%	14%	7%	10.7%	92.5	51	23	25	28%	79%	11%	13%	29	88	34%	17%			39.3	113	$23
20	ATL	0	0	14	8	3.95	1.32	4.60	1.64	100	55	19.0	12%	14%	2%	9%	10.6%	92.1	61	24	15	26%	67%	0%	12%	3	66	0%	33%			0.8	11	-$6
21																																		
22	aaa	0	0	21	14	8.22	1.51	5.71				18.2	0%	0%	0%							31%	45%									-11.0	29	-$9
1st Half																																		
2nd Half		0	0	21	14	8.22	1.51	5.71				18.2	8%	16%	8%							31%	45%									-11.0	29	-$16
Proj		3	0	87	63	4.53	1.24	3.51	1.30	132	91	20.9	7%	18%	11%	7%	10.7%	92.5	51	23	25	29%	66%	16%	11%	17						-6.0	89	-$3

Soto,Gregory

Age: 28	Th: L	Role	RP	Health	A	LIMA Plan	C+
Ht: 6' 1"	Wt: 234	Type	Pwr	PT/Exp	A	Rand Var	-4
				Consist	A	MM	2321

xERA, xWHIP spent year and a half warning of regression that finally arrived in 2nd half, as fading K%, K-BB% caught up with him. Volatile SwK suggests strikeouts can't be counted on, and walks have yet to fall in line with xBB%, leaving GB% as only dependable skill. Hasn't truly been closer-worthy these last two years, so next step could be... DN: 10 Sv

Yr	Tm	W	Sv	IP	K	ERA	WHIP	xERA	xWHIP	vL+	vR+	BF/G	BB%	K%	K-BB%	xBB%	SwK	Vel	G	L	F	H%	S%	HR/F	xHR/F	GS	APC	DOM%	DIS%	Sv%	LI	RAR	BPX	R$
18																																		
19	DET *	0	0	96	78	6.28	1.77	6.30	1.63	89	129	10.5	12%	18%	6%	9%	8.5%	95.4	48	19	34	35%	66%	14%	18%	7	34	0%	86%	0	0.67	-21.0	33	-$16
20	DET	0	2	23	29	4.30	1.26	3.62	1.37	54	90	3.6	13%	30%	16%	11%	11.4%	97.3	54	20	26	28%	67%	14%	13%	0	15			67	0.69	0.4	112	-$1
21	DET	6	18	64	76	3.39	1.35	4.35	1.46	68	93	4.5	14%	28%	13%	8%	13.5%	98.3	45	18	37	27%	78%	12%	12%	0	18			95	1.49	6.9	70	$10
22	DET	2	30	60	60	3.28	1.38	4.22	1.47	107	89	4.1	13%	23%	10%	9%	11.7%	98.4	48	16	36	30%	75%	3%	9%	0	17			91	1.42	5.1	55	$11
1st Half		2	16	29	30	2.48	1.14	4.00	1.37	100	77	4.0	12%	25%	13%	9%	13.1%	98.3	42	13	45	26%	78%	3%	10%	0	18			89	1.39	5.3	78	$12
2nd Half		0	14	31	30	4.02	1.60	4.44	1.56	113	97	4.2	14%	21%	7%	9%	10.4%	98.5	53	18	29	33%	73%	4%	6%	0	17			93	1.45	-0.2	34	$2
Proj		2	24	65	64	4.11	1.49	4.14	1.50	95	99	4.8	13%	23%	9%	9%	11.0%	97.7	48	17	35	31%	73%	7%	11%	0						-1.1	49	$6

Springs,Jeffrey

Age: 30	Th: L	Role	SP	Health	F	LIMA Plan	B
Ht: 6' 3"	Wt: 218	Type	Pwr/FB	PT/Exp	C	Rand Var	-5
				Consist	B	MM	4403

Late bloomer answered question of whether he'd be able to carry newfound skills over from relief to rotation with a resounding yes. Dip in velocity, SwK was to be expected, and he made up for it with fewer walks, more grounders while maintaining surprising effectiveness vR. Even with ERA regression likely, should be able to sustain mid-rotation value.

Yr	Tm	W	Sv	IP	K	ERA	WHIP	xERA	xWHIP	vL+	vR+	BF/G	BB%	K%	K-BB%	xBB%	SwK	Vel	G	L	F	H%	S%	HR/F	xHR/F	GS	APC	DOM%	DIS%	Sv%	LI	RAR	BPX	R$
18	TEX *	5	2	90	107	4.71	1.47	4.40	1.38	116	98	7.6	9%	28%	18%	9%	11.7%	91.3	32	24	44	38%	68%	10%	9%	2	31	0%	0%	33	0.68	-6.3	122	-$3
19	TEX	4	0	32	32	6.40	1.89	6.56	1.70	120	116	6.2	15%	21%	6%	9%	12.6%	92.1	23	31	45	36%	67%	9%	9%	0	27			0	0.49	-7.6	-13	-$7
20	BOS	0	0	20	28	7.08	1.82	4.18	1.16	122	138	6.2	7%	28%	21%	7%	17.0%	92.1	35	29	35	46%	66%	23%	23%	0	25			0	0.75	-6.6	172	-$12
21	TAM	5	2	45	63	3.43	1.10	3.22	1.05	117	87	4.2	8%	35%	27%	8%	16.5%	93.4	34	23	42	29%	80%	21%	15%	0	17			50	1.07	4.6	180	$3
22	TAM	9	0	135	144	2.46	1.07	3.48	1.10	107	82	16.6	6%	26%	21%	6%	14.1%	91.5	41	20	40	30%	82%	10%	10%	25	65	12%	8%	0	0.89	25.2	150	$17
1st Half		3	0	64	70	2.53	1.05	3.34	1.09	96	89	13.3	6%	28%	22%	6%	14.5%	91.6	41	19	40	28%	86%	15%	11%	11	54	0%	9%	0	0.98	11.3	154	$11
2nd Half		6	0	71	74	2.40	1.09	3.61	1.11	118	76	21.1	5%	25%	20%	6%	13.7%	91.4	41	20	39	31%	80%	5%	8%	14	81	21%	7%			13.8	146	$17
Proj		12	0	152	169	3.51	1.11	3.30	1.16	104	81	20.6	8%	28%	21%	7%	13.7%	91.9	35	24	42	29%	72%	11%	10%	26						8.6	131	$16

Staumont,Josh

Age: 29	Th: R	Role	RP	Health	D	LIMA Plan	C
Ht: 6' 3"	Wt: 200	Type	Pwr/xFB	PT/Exp	C	Rand Var	+3
				Consist	B	MM	1410

Neck strain, biceps tendinitis ruined 2nd half, ended season in Aug. But even when we set aside lousy 2nd half stats, we're still left with xERAs saying he's not as good as he's looked. It's mostly because poor control, high FB% are an incendiary combination just waiting for a match. Maybe you won't get burned like 2022, but do you really want to play with fire?

Yr	Tm	W	Sv	IP	K	ERA	WHIP	xERA	xWHIP	vL+	vR+	BF/G	BB%	K%	K-BB%	xBB%	SwK	Vel	G	L	F	H%	S%	HR/F	xHR/F	GS	APC	DOM%	DIS%	Sv%	LI	RAR	BPX	R$
18	aaa	2	1	75	81	4.45	1.68	4.51				8.2	16%	24%	8%							34%	73%									-2.8	91	-$7
19	KC *	1	2	71	72	3.81	1.51	4.17	1.60	101	130	6.4	16%	23%	7%	11%	9.2%	95.9	34	24	42	28%	78%	15%	16%	0	20			33	0.45	6.1	70	-$2
20	KC	2	0	26	37	2.45	1.40	4.40	1.37	109	68	4.3	14%	33%	19%	8%	15.7%	98.1	29	20	52	34%	85%	7%	7%	0	18			0	0.77	6.3	101	$3
21	KC	4	5	66	72	2.88	1.07	4.13	1.29	85	71	4.1	10%	27%	17%	9%	11.0%	96.6	38	17	45	25%	77%	8%	11%	0	17			100	1.00	11.2	103	$8
22	KC	3	3	38	43	6.45	1.75	5.19	1.60	129	102	4.2	16%	24%	8%	12%	11.1%	96.4	30	25	44	35%	62%	7%	9%	0	17			50	0.95	-11.5	6	-$8
1st Half		2	3	26	32	3.81	1.46	4.64	1.45	74	107	4.0	15%	28%	13%	11%	13.5%	96.7	23	29	48	33%	73%	3%	11%	0	17			50	1.19	0.5	45	-$4
2nd Half		1	0	12	11	12.34	2.40	6.57	1.92	248	91	4.6	20%	18%	-2%	12%	6.2%	95.9	44	19	36	39%	46%	15%	5%	0	19			0	0.42	-12.1	-82	-$19
Proj		3	2	58	65	3.73	1.43	4.29	1.49	83	98	4.9	15%	27%	12%	10%	12.6%	96.6	29	24	47	30%	74%	6%	11%	0						1.7	43	-$1

Steele,Justin

Age: 27	Th: L	Role	RP	Health	D	LIMA Plan	A+
Ht: 6' 2"	Wt: 205	Type	Pwr	PT/Exp	C	Rand Var	-2
				Consist	A	MM	4303

Back issues ended season in late Aug, cutting short year of quiet growth. Since moving from RP to SP at mid-season 2021, last three half-season xERA marks have been 4.69, 3.86, 3.07. That last one hinges on K% that probably isn't sustainable for him, but if he continues to limit walks, increases IP total, could have a shot at reaching double-digit R$.

Yr	Tm	W	Sv	IP	K	ERA	WHIP	xERA	xWHIP	vL+	vR+	BF/G	BB%	K%	K-BB%	xBB%	SwK	Vel	G	L	F	H%	S%	HR/F	xHR/F	GS	APC	DOM%	DIS%	Sv%	LI	RAR	BPX	R$
18																																		
19	aa	0	0	40	35	7.70	1.99	6.92				17.6	12%	18%	6%							40%	60%									-15.8	44	-$13
20																																		
21	CHC *	6	0	85	82	3.33	1.25	3.84	1.38	65	112	11.9	12%	24%	12%	9%	11.8%	93.1	50	20	30	25%	80%	26%	15%	9	48	11%	67%	0	0.90	9.9	71	$4
22	CHC	4	0	119	126	3.18	1.35	3.56	1.30	88	94	21.3	10%	25%	15%	8%	10.7%	92.1	51	21	28	33%	78%	9%	9%	24	85	29%	25%			11.6	108	$3
1st Half		3	0	76	76	4.13	1.43	3.86	1.37	91	96	20.9	11%	23%	12%	8%	9.9%	92.2	51	22	27	33%	71%	8%	7%	16	82	31%	31%			-1.5	84	-$4
2nd Half		1	0	43	50	1.48	1.22	3.07	1.15	81	92	22.1	8%	28%	20%	8%	12.1%	92.0	51	18	30	33%	92%	9%	13%	8	90	25%	13%			13.1	154	$3
Proj		9	0	145	148	3.57	1.26	3.25	1.28	80	97	17.2	9%	25%	16%	8%	11.3%	92.3	51	20	29	31%	74%	12%	11%	25						7.1	113	$8

Stephan,Trevor

Age: 27	Th: R	Role	RP	Health	A	LIMA Plan	A
Ht: 6' 5"	Wt: 225	Type	Pwr	PT/Exp	C	Rand Var	-1
				Consist	D	MM	5511

Reasons breakout looks legit: SwK backed K% increase, driven by more splitters (27.7% usage, 28.3% SwK); BB% growth mirrored by xBB%; hidden gains against LHB (23% K-BB% obscured by 43% H%). High GB% isn't new skill, but we haven't seen it since High-A ball in 2018-19. If those elite 2nd half skills—and LI gain they inspired—hold up... UP: 20 Sv

Yr	Tm	W	Sv	IP	K	ERA	WHIP	xERA	xWHIP	vL+	vR+	BF/G	BB%	K%	K-BB%	xBB%	SwK	Vel	G	L	F	H%	S%	HR/F	xHR/F	GS	APC	DOM%	DIS%	Sv%	LI	RAR	BPX	R$
18	aa	3	0	84	79	5.99	1.52	4.90				21.5	8%	22%	13%							36%	60%									-19.1	90	-$10
19	aa	2	0	47	48	7.13	1.92	6.51				18.6	12%	21%	9%							41%	62%									-15.3	62	-$11
20																																		
21	CLE	3	1	63	75	4.41	1.41	4.60	1.33	103	111	6.6	11%	27%	16%	9%	13.4%	96.2	33	22	45	29%	78%	19%	18%	0	28			100	0.57	-1.1	92	-$3
22	CLE	6	3	64	82	2.69	1.18	2.93	1.06	104	78	4.0	7%	31%	24%	6%	16.7%	96.6	48	19	33	36%	78%	6%	6%	0	16			60	1.22	10.1	183	$6
1st Half		3	1	30	32	3.30	1.23	3.70	1.18	128	66	4.1	7%	25%	18%	7%	14.1%	96.6	44	19	38	33%	74%	6%	5%	0	16			50	1.06	2.5	134	-$2
2nd Half		3	2	34	50	2.14	1.13	2.28	0.96	84	89	4.0	6%	36%	29%	6%	19.0%	96.5	53	19	28	38%	81%	5%	6%	0	15			67	1.36	7.6	228	$6
Proj		4	5	65	77	2.95	1.14	2.93	1.15	98	84	5.6	8%	30%	22%	7%	16.1%	96.5	46	19	35	31%	77%	11%	9%	0						8.2	149	$6

Strahm,Matt

Age: 31	Th: L	Role	RP	Health	F	LIMA Plan	A+
Ht: 6' 2"	Wt: 190	Type	Pwr/FB	PT/Exp	D	Rand Var	-1
				Consist	C	MM	3310

1.88 ERA through first 14 IP got him some save opps, then 6.97 ERA, three blown saves in next 10 IP took them away. That kind of inconsistency, on top of yearly health issues, have kept him from fantasy relevance, but even when he posts a decent xERA, like in 2022, it's easy to find flaws (SwK doesn't support K%). LIMA grade does not consider risk.

Yr	Tm	W	Sv	IP	K	ERA	WHIP	xERA	xWHIP	vL+	vR+	BF/G	BB%	K%	K-BB%	xBB%	SwK	Vel	G	L	F	H%	S%	HR/F	xHR/F	GS	APC	DOM%	DIS%	Sv%	LI	RAR	BPX	R$
18	SD *	4	0	76	86	2.27	1.07	2.67	1.20	106	66	6.0	8%	29%	21%	6%	12.8%	93.5	35	21	44	28%	84%	9%	14%	5	24	20%	40%	0	0.91	17.8	139	$9
19	SD	6	0	115	118	4.71	1.25	4.26	1.16	106	105	10.6	5%	24%	20%	4%	11.1%	91.5	37	23	41	33%	69%	16%	18%	16	39	13%	25%	0	0.90	-2.9	147	$2
20	SD	0	0	21	15	2.61	0.87	4.19	1.25	57	116	4.4	5%	18%	13%	7%	9.1%	92.9	44	20	36	20%	80%	14%	15%	0	16			0	1.12	4.7	105	$1
21	SD	0	0	7	4	8.10	2.40	5.36	1.28	138	144	6.0	3%	11%	8%	4%	11.0%	93.2	48	31	21	50%	63%	0%	2%	1	23	0%	100%	0	0.41	-3.2	95	-$8
22	BOS	4	4	45	52	3.83	1.23	3.86	1.21	99	92	3.9	9%	27%	18%	6%	10.5%	94.2	37	18	45	31%	72%	9%	11%	0	15			44	1.30	0.8	122	$1
1st Half		3	3	25	27	4.01	1.22	4.05	1.15	93	93	3.6	7%	26%	19%	5%	11.2%	94.3	32	18	50	33%	68%	6%	7%	0	14			50	1.51	-0.1	131	-$2
2nd Half		1	1	20	25	3.60	1.25	3.62	1.29	105	89	4.2	11%	28%	17%	7%	9.6%	94.0	43	18	39	28%	77%	16%	17%	0	17			33	1.00	0.9	112	-$5
Proj		4	2	58	59	3.99	1.16	3.59	1.23	104	87	4.5	8%	25%	17%	6%	11.0%	93.6	37	20	43	28%	69%	11%	13%	0						-0.2	110	$1

BRANDON KRUSE

Strasburg,Stephen

Age: 34	Th: R	Role SP	Health F	LIMA Plan B	
Ht: 6' 5"	Wt: 240	Type Pwr	PT/Exp D	Rand Var +5	
			Consist B	MM 5301	

Recovery from July 2021 thoracic outlet surgery did not go well, as he was shut down with stress reaction in ribs after three rehab games and one MLB start. And even his own GM has admitted that 2023 status is "a mystery." You can roll the dice on a comeback if he winds up in your league's bargain bin; anything more than that is wishful thinking.

Yr	Tm	W	Sv	IP	K	ERA	WHIP	xERA	xWHIP	vL+	vR+	BF/G	BB%	K%	K-BB%	xBB%	SwK	Vel	G	L	F	H%	S%	HR/F	xHR/F	GS	APC	DOM%	DIS%	Sv%	LI	RAR	BPX	R$
18	WAS	10	0	130	156	3.74	1.20	3.34	1.13	99	97	24.7	7%	29%	22%	8%	12.5%	94.5	44	22	34	32%	74%	16%	17%	22	98	36%	5%			6.6	167	$10
19	WAS	18	0	209	251	3.32	1.04	3.18	1.12	77	86	25.5	7%	30%	23%	7%	13.9%	93.9	51	20	29	29%	73%	16%	14%	33	103	52%	9%			30.7	173	$31
20	WAS	0	0	5	2	10.80	1.80	6.24		152	107	11.5	4%	9%	4%		10.6%	91.7	37	26	37	37%	38%	14%	5%	2	43	0%	100%			-3.9	35	-$10
21	WAS	1	0	22	21	4.57	1.38	5.17	1.59	122	78	19.0	15%	22%	7%	12%	10.2%	91.9	36	27	37	23%	73%	18%	18%	5	72	20%	20%			-0.8	15	-$5
22	WAS	0	0	5	5	13.50	2.14	4.34		287	118	23.0	9%	22%	13%	8%	6.0%	90.4	38	23	38	46%	33%	20%	17%	1	83	0%	100%			-5.5	94	-$8
1st Half		0	0	5	5	13.50	2.14	4.34		287	118	23.0	9%	22%	13%	8%	6.0%	90.4	38	23	38	46%	33%	20%	17%	1	83	0%	100%			-5.5	95	-$15
2nd Half																																		
Proj		**7**	**0**	**87**	**89**	**4.00**	**1.19**	**3.18**	**1.21**	**96**	**96**	**21.7**	**8%**	**26%**	**18%**		**13.4%**	**94.1**	**48**	**21**	**31**	**30%**	**70%**	**15%**	**15%**	**16**						**-0.4**	**128**	**$3**

Stratton,Chris

Age: 32	Th: R	Role RP	Health B	LIMA Plan B	
Ht: 6' 2"	Wt: 205	Type Pwr	PT/Exp B	Rand Var 0	
			Consist A	MM 3300	

Deadline trade to STL led to 2.78 ERA over final two months, but 1.50 WHIP during same stretch was giveaway that success was more luck than skill. And while xERA, K-BB% histories confirm he can be good for brief periods, when those brief periods will happen is a dart throw. It's telling that LI indicates PIT has been only team to consider him saves-worthy.

Yr	Tm	W	Sv	IP	K	ERA	WHIP	xERA	xWHIP	vL+	vR+	BF/G	BB%	K%	K-BB%	xBB%	SwK	Vel	G	L	F	H%	S%	HR/F	xHR/F	GS	APC	DOM%	DIS%	Sv%	LI	RAR	BPX	R$
18	SF *	13	0	169	130	4.85	1.45	4.90	1.40	114	103	22.5	9%	18%	9%	8%	9.0%	91.1	43	25	32	32%	69%	13%	15%	26	88	23%	38%	0	0.80	-14.6	59	-$3
19	2 TM	1	0	76	69	5.57	1.66	5.16	1.44	117	115	9.8	10%	20%	10%	8%	10.8%	92.2	40	26	34	36%	70%	16%	10%	5	39	0%	60%	0	0.53	-9.9	65	-$9
20	PIT	2	0	30	39	3.90	1.30	3.76	1.24	82	93	4.9	10%	30%	20%	8%	15.7%	93.3	47	22	32	34%	72%	12%	14%	0	20			0	1.28	2.0	147	$2
21	PIT	7	8	79	86	3.63	1.30	4.20	1.30	103	82	5.0	10%	26%	16%	8%	12.7%	93.0	41	21	38	31%	76%	11%	12%	0	20			62	0.90	6.2	103	$7
22	2 NL	10	2	63	60	4.26	1.53	4.17	1.32	129	96	4.7	9%	22%	13%	8%	11.9%	92.9	44	21	35	36%	72%	6%	10%	1	18	0%	0%	29	1.08	-2.3	88	-$1
1st Half		4	2	33	32	5.13	1.44	3.85	1.20	143	88	4.4	6%	22%	16%	6%	13.4%	92.5	45	22	33	36%	66%	12%	12%	0	18			29	1.39	-4.8	125	-$6
2nd Half		6	0	30	28	3.30	1.63	4.57	1.46	104	102	4.9	12%	21%	9%	10%	10.2%	93.3	43	20	36	37%	78%	0%	8%	1	19	0%	0%	0	0.71	2.5	47	-$2
Proj		**7**	**0**	**58**	**59**	**4.14**	**1.47**	**3.78**	**1.33**	**110**	**96**	**5.2**	**10%**	**24%**	**14%**	**8%**	**12.4%**	**92.9**	**44**	**22**	**35**	**35%**	**73%**	**9%**	**11%**	**0**						**-1.2**	**93**	**-$2**

Strider,Spencer

Age: 24	Th: R	Role SP	Health B	LIMA Plan C+	
Ht: 6' 0"	Wt: 195	Type Pwr	PT/Exp C	Rand Var -1	
			Consist D	MM 5503	

Just an incredible debut, with eye-popping skills to match, including elite xBB% that suggests 2nd half control improvement could stick. Still some question about whether change-up can become usable third pitch, but early returns were encouraging (4.8% usage, 17.4% SwK). He did this as rookie with two pitches; follow-up could lead to... UP: Cy Young

Yr	Tm	W	Sv	IP	K	ERA	WHIP	xERA	xWHIP	vL+	vR+	BF/G	BB%	K%	K-BB%	xBB%	SwK	Vel	G	L	F	H%	S%	HR/F	xHR/F	GS	APC	DOM%	DIS%	Sv%	LI	RAR	BPX	R$
18																																		
19																																		
20																																		
21	ATL *	4	0	66	81	5.90	1.38	4.21		138	66	16.4	11%	29%	18%		13.2%	97.9	25	13	63	33%	57%	20%	4%	0	19			0	1.05	-13.3	105	-$6
22	ATL	11	0	132	202	2.67	0.99	2.60	1.01	78	69	17.0	9%	38%	30%	6%	16.4%	98.2	40	23	37	32%	74%	7%	10%	20	73	35%	10%	0	0.82	21.2	202	$22
1st Half		4	0	60	90	2.87	1.01	2.70	1.06	69	77	13.3	10%	38%	28%	7%	17.1%	98.4	40	22	38	30%	72%	6%	11%	7	57	43%	14%	0	0.86	8.1	186	$13
2nd Half		7	0	72	112	2.50	0.99	2.51	0.97	85	63	22.2	8%	39%	31%	6%	15.8%	98.1	40	23	36	33%	76%	7%	8%	13	97	31%	8%			13.0	216	$24
Proj		**13**	**0**	**160**	**220**	**3.04**	**1.01**	**2.57**	**1.05**	**80**	**70**	**20.6**	**8%**	**36%**	**28%**	**6%**	**16.3%**	**98.2**	**40**	**23**	**37**	**30%**	**71%**	**8%**	**10%**	**27**						**18.3**	**181**	**$24**

Stripling,Ross

Age: 33	Th: R	Role RP	Health D	LIMA Plan B	
Ht: 6' 3"	Wt: 220	Type Con	PT/Exp A	Rand Var -2	
			Consist B	MM 3201	

Rebounds in BB%, GB% helped set table, but real heroes of most valuable season of career were H%, super-low HR/F, and staying relatively healthy. (And even so, still spent 15 days on IL with hip strain.) History suggests HR prevention will backslide, which might be enough to push ERA back over 4.00. Add in risk of IP decline, and he's likely to be overvalued.

Yr	Tm	W	Sv	IP	K	ERA	WHIP	xERA	xWHIP	vL+	vR+	BF/G	BB%	K%	K-BB%	xBB%	SwK	Vel	G	L	F	H%	S%	HR/F	xHR/F	GS	APC	DOM%	DIS%	Sv%	LI	RAR	BPX	R$
18	LA	8	0	122	136	3.02	1.19	3.27	1.06	90	110	15.2	4%	27%	23%	6%	11.7%	91.7	45	22	33	34%	82%	16%	12%	21	61	29%	19%	0	0.83	16.9	184	$11
19	LA	4	0	91	93	3.47	1.15	3.66	1.16	93	92	11.6	5%	25%	20%	6%	10.6%	90.5	50	19	31	31%	74%	14%	14%	15	45	13%	27%	0	0.73	11.5	153	$6
20	2 TM	3	1	49	40	5.84	1.50	5.20	1.39	102	137	18.3	8%	18%	10%	7%	7.5%	91.7	40	24	36	30%	69%	23%	22%	9	68	11%	78%	100	0.69	-8.4	69	-$6
21	TOR	5	0	101	94	4.80	1.27	4.66	1.26	102	110	18.0	7%	22%	15%	8%	10.5%	91.9	36	20	45	28%	71%	17%	15%	19	70	11%	37%	0	0.73	-6.6	101	-$2
22	TOR	10	1	134	111	3.01	1.02	3.75	1.13	81	92	16.8	4%	21%	17%	5%	11.5%	91.6	44	17	39	28%	74%	8%	8%	24	64	13%	33%	100	0.98	15.8	132	$15
1st Half		4	1	62	49	3.32	1.12	3.79	1.20	73	99	13.3	5%	19%	14%	6%	10.7%	91.6	49	17	34	29%	72%	8%	7%	11	54	9%	55%	100	1.14	5.0	115	$6
2nd Half		6	0	72	62	2.75	0.93	3.71	1.06	85	84	21.8	2%	22%	19%	5%	12.3%	91.5	39	17	44	27%	75%	8%	9%	13	78	15%	15%			10.8	146	$17
Proj		**7**	**0**	**102**	**89**	**3.87**	**1.17**	**3.55**	**1.19**	**91**	**104**	**16.1**	**5%**	**22%**	**16%**	**6%**	**10.5%**	**91.5**	**42**	**19**	**39**	**29%**	**73%**	**14%**	**13%**	**15**						**1.2**	**119**	**$4**

Stroman,Marcus

Age: 32	Th: R	Role SP	Health D	LIMA Plan A	
Ht: 5' 7"	Wt: 180	Type Con/GB	PT/Exp A	Rand Var 0	
			Consist A	MM 4203	

9-ER debacle on June 3 contributed to bloated 1st half ERA, and can likely be blamed on shoulder inflammation that sent him to IL for a month immediately afterward. H%, S% helped him make up difference in 2nd half, but xERA shows 2022 ERA is closer to true skill level than 2021, and xWHIP hints at possibility of further regression. Be cautious with valuation.

Yr	Tm	W	Sv	IP	K	ERA	WHIP	xERA	xWHIP	vL+	vR+	BF/G	BB%	K%	K-BB%	xBB%	SwK	Vel	G	L	F	H%	S%	HR/F	xHR/F	GS	APC	DOM%	DIS%	Sv%	LI	RAR	BPX	R$
18	TOR	4	0	102	77	5.54	1.48	3.93	1.38	102	108	23.6	8%	17%	9%	9%	9.3%	92.4	62	18	20	33%	62%	14%	18%	19	90	16%	42%			-17.6	88	-$9
19	2 TM	10	0	184	159	3.22	1.31	4.14	1.33	102	82	24.2	8%	21%	13%	9%	10.6%	92.5	54	20	26	31%	78%	13%	12%	32	95	25%	28%			29.2	104	$14
20																																		
21	NYM	10	0	179	158	3.02	1.15	3.65	1.21	89	88	22.1	6%	22%	16%	7%	11.9%	92.0	51	23	26	29%	77%	13%	17%	33	83	36%	30%			27.6	123	$19
22	CHC	6	0	139	119	3.50	1.15	3.53	1.22	102	86	22.8	6%	21%	15%	7%	9.8%	92.1	52	20	28	28%	73%	14%	13%	25	87	32%	20%			7.9	117	$7
1st Half		2	0	47	45	5.32	1.23	3.70	1.18	111	96	22.0	6%	23%	17%	6%	10.0%	92.0	42	25	33	30%	60%	17%	14%	9	86	22%	33%			-7.9	124	-$7
2nd Half		4	0	91	74	2.56	1.11	3.44	1.25	96	82	23.2	6%	20%	13%	8%	9.6%	92.2	57	17	26	27%	81%	12%	11%	16	88	38%	13%			15.8	113	$16
Proj		**8**	**0**	**160**	**137**	**3.65**	**1.17**	**3.23**	**1.22**	**99**	**85**	**22.1**	**6%**	**21%**	**15%**	**8%**	**10.3%**	**92.2**	**53**	**20**	**27**	**29%**	**72%**	**14%**	**14%**	**29**						**6.4**	**120**	**$9**

Suarez,José

Age: 25	Th: L	Role RP	Health A	LIMA Plan A+	
Ht: 5' 10"	Wt: 225	Type	PT/Exp B	Rand Var 0	
			Consist F	MM 3203	

8-8, 3.96 ERA in 109 IP at LAA. 6.35 ERA in first 4 GS had him riding AAA/MLB shuttle for May/June; after final recall on June 26, put up stats similar to 2021, this time with skill support. BB% growth has come in lockstep with xBB%, and while he hasn't tamed RHB, has at least reached a truce. Could be ready to turn 2nd half line into full-season results.

Yr	Tm	W	Sv	IP	K	ERA	WHIP	xERA	xWHIP	vL+	vR+	BF/G	BB%	K%	K-BB%	xBB%	SwK	Vel	G	L	F	H%	S%	HR/F	xHR/F	GS	APC	DOM%	DIS%	Sv%	LI	RAR	BPX	R$
18	a/a	3	0	110	113	4.00	1.41	3.99				19.4	8%	24%	16%							36%	70%									2.0	123	-$2
19	LAA *	4	0	114	100	5.93	1.49	5.82	1.44	87	140	18.9	10%	20%	11%	9%	11.2%	91.8	35	22	43	30%	66%	21%	15%	15	78	7%	60%	0	0.81	-20.0	33	-$9
20	LAA	0	0	2	2	38.57	6.43	19.69		254	199	11.5	22%	9%	-13%		13.6%	93.3	53	33	13	66%	36%	50%	81%	2	44	0%	100%			-9.8	-396	-$17
21	LAA	8	0	98	85	3.75	1.23	4.30	1.35	133	79	18.0	9%	21%	12%	8%	11.5%	92.7	48	19	33	28%	73%	12%	10%	14	72	7%	50%	0	0.79	6.2	85	$5
22	LAA *	9	0	127	117	4.36	1.26	4.11	1.23	87	104	20.0	7%	22%	15%	6%	12.1%	92.5	41	22	37	30%	69%	12%	10%	20	81	20%	30%	0	0.89	-6.1	89	$2
1st Half		2	0	56	52	5.08	1.48	5.15	1.36	100	116	18.5	10%	21%	11%	8%	12.1%	92.5	34	28	38	32%	69%	14%	9%	7	74	0%	43%	0	1.04	-7.7	62	-$11
2nd Half		7	0	71	65	3.79	1.09	3.72	1.17	81	96	22.7	5%	22%	17%	5%	12.1%	92.5	45	18	37	28%	69%	10%	11%	13	86	31%	23%			1.6	128	$11
Proj		**8**	**0**	**131**	**119**	**4.06**	**1.20**	**3.62**	**1.24**	**86**	**98**	**18.7**	**7%**	**23%**	**16%**	**8%**	**11.8%**	**92.4**	**40**	**22**	**38**	**29%**	**70%**	**12%**	**11%**	**24**						**-1.4**	**106**	**$5**

Suárez,Ranger

Age: 27	Th: L	Role RP	Health B	LIMA Plan A+	
Ht: 6' 1"	Wt: 217	Type Con/xGB	PT/Exp A	Rand Var 0	
			Consist F	MM 4103	

About that huge drop in value... expected ERA, WHIP regression combined with slides in BB%, K%, SwK that arose from switch to full-time SP, so it's less worrisome than it might appear. That said, still has work to do vR (10% BB%, 13 of 15 HR allowed in 2022). While rotation spot looks secure, seems more likely to tread water than take big step forward.

Yr	Tm	W	Sv	IP	K	ERA	WHIP	xERA	xWHIP	vL+	vR+	BF/G	BB%	K%	K-BB%	xBB%	SwK	Vel	G	L	F	H%	S%	HR/F	xHR/F	GS	APC	DOM%	DIS%	Sv%	LI	RAR	BPX	R$
18	PHI *	7	0	140	87	3.46	1.35	4.00	1.44	78	157	23.4	7%	15%	8%	8%	8.0%	91.8	51	18	31	31%	75%	19%	15%	3	56	0%	67%	0	0.58	12.0	72	$3
19	PHI *	8	0	87	70	4.69	1.40	5.37	1.26	75	110	8.3	6%	19%	13%	9%	10.0%	92.4	55	22	22	32%	72%	18%	17%	0	21			0	1.00	-2.0	64	$0
20	PHI	0	0	4	1	20.25	3.50	11.55		152	187	8.7	15%	4%	-12%		8.5%	91.2	45	20	35	47%	38%	14%	10%	0	31			0	0.64	-7.8	-203	-$15
21	PHI	8	4	106	107	1.36	1.00	3.21	1.21	43	80	10.7	8%	26%	18%	8%	11.7%	93.2	59	15	26	26%	88%	6%	6%	12	41	42%	8%	57	1.01	38.0	137	$23
22	PHI	10	0	155	129	3.65	1.33	3.87	1.35	77	106	22.8	9%	19%	11%	9%	9.2%	92.8	55	17	27	30%	75%	12%	12%	29	88	21%	38%			6.1	85	$5
1st Half		6	0	79	64	4.33	1.46	4.10	1.40	89	112	22.9	10%	19%	9%	9%	7.9%	92.8	55	17	28	31%	73%	13%	13%	15	92	27%	40%			-3.5	69	-$4
2nd Half		4	0	76	65	2.95	1.21	3.63	1.29	59	100	22.7	8%	20%	13%	8%	10.8%	92.7	56	18	27	29%	78%	10%	10%	14	85	14%	36%			9.6	102	$8
Proj		**11**	**0**	**152**	**127**	**3.47**	**1.29**	**3.43**	**1.31**	**73**	**105**	**14.0**	**8%**	**20%**	**12%**	**9%**	**9.9%**	**92.7**	**56**	**18**	**26**	**30%**	**76%**	**14%**	**12%**	**18**						**9.4**	**100**	**$8**

BRANDON KRUSE

Suarez,Robert

Age: 32	Th: R	Role RP	Health D
Ht: 6' 2"	Wt: 210	Type Pwr	PT/Exp A
LIMA Plan A+	Rand Var -5	MM 5411	Consist D

Found way to MLB after spending entire career in Mexico and Japan, and used electric fastball, elite change-up (20.2% SwK) to make strong first impression. H%/S% helped, but 2nd half gains in BB%, SwK, and GB% show there's genuine skill here, and 2nd half xERA, xWHIP highlight terrific upside. With previous closer experience, he's a good bet for... UP: 25 Sv

Yr	Tm	W	Sv	IP	K	ERA	WHIP	xERA	xWHIP	vL+	vR+	BF/G	BB%	K%	K-BB%	xBB%	SwK	Vel	G	L	F	H%	S%	HR/F	xHR/F	GS	APC	DOM%	DIS%	Sv%	LI	RAR	BPX	R$
18	for	2	1	25	25	4.90	1.51	5.07				4.4	10%	23%	13%							34%	70%									-2.3	73	-$5
19	for	2	0	80	61	4.61	1.44	5.11				16.2	12%	18%	6%							26%	75%									-1.0	24	-$4
20	for	3	25	52	47	2.79	1.19	2.81				4.1	11%	22%	11%							26%	78%									10.7	99	$42
21	for	1	42	62	55	1.44	0.85	1.19				3.7	4%	24%	20%							26%	81%									21.6	197	$27
22	SD	5	1	48	61	2.27	1.05	3.07	1.21	81	80	4.2	11%	32%	21%	8%	12.1%	97.7	43	22	35	25%	83%	11%	10%	0	18			25	1.35	10.0	134	$5
1st Half		2	1	23	29	3.09	1.07	3.52	1.35	47	119	4.3	14%	31%	17%	10%	10.0%	97.3	40	20	40	18%	81%	20%	14%	0	18			33	1.48	2.5	93	-$2
2nd Half		3	0	24	32	1.48	1.03	2.67	1.08	117	47	4.2	8%	33%	25%	6%	14.2%	98.1	46	24	30	32%	84%	0%	5%	0	17			0	1.23	7.5	174	$2
Proj		**5**	**5**	**65**	**76**	**2.57**	**1.05**	**2.95**	**1.18**	**89**	**76**	**4.3**	**9%**	**30%**	**21%**	**8%**	**13.2%**	**97.8**	**44**	**22**	**34**	**27%**	**78%**	**9%**	**8%**	**0**						**11.3**	**137**	**$8**

Suter,Brent

Age: 33	Th: L	Role RP	Health D
Ht: 6' 4"	Wt: 213	Type Con	PT/Exp B
LIMA Plan A+	Rand Var -1	MM 4201	Consist B

Elite relief potential that he teased in 2020 small sample has faded as BB% normalized and he's struggled to sustain that year's strong K%, SwK. Which makes 2022 GB%/FB% shift a concern, as xERA, xWHIP illustrate what happens when his skills land closer to league average. Subpar LI history rules out saves speculation, leaving fantasy value stagnant.

Yr	Tm	W	Sv	IP	K	ERA	WHIP	xERA	xWHIP	vL+	vR+	BF/G	BB%	K%	K-BB%	xBB%	SwK	Vel	G	L	F	H%	S%	HR/F	xHR/F	GS	APC	DOM%	DIS%	Sv%	LI	RAR	BPX	R$
18	MIL	8	0	101	84	4.44	1.19	4.22	1.20	93	108	21.2	4%	20%	15%	6%	10.4%	86.7	33	29	38	29%	69%	16%	14%	18	82	22%	22%	0	0.83	-3.6	115	$3
19	MIL *	4	0	35	31	0.26	0.59	0.07	1.06	85	48	7.8	4%	26%	22%	5%	14.2%	87.5	52	15	33	18%	100%	6%	7%	0	26			0	0.84	18.1	224	$7
20	MIL	2	0	32	38	3.13	1.11	2.94	1.01	99	81	8.1	4%	29%	26%	8%	14.1%	85.6	51	24	25	34%	77%	19%	18%	4	32	25%	0%	0	0.83	5.2	209	$6
21	MIL	12	1	73	69	3.07	1.31	3.95	1.27	91	99	5.1	8%	22%	14%	7%	9.3%	87.4	53	19	29	31%	82%	15%	13%	1	20	0%	100%	11	0.99	10.8	114	$7
22	MIL	5	0	67	53	3.78	1.20	4.07	1.32	100	101	5.0	8%	19%	11%	8%	12.1%	86.6	45	19	36	27%	73%	13%	8%	0	20			0	0.62	1.6	79	$0
1st Half		1	0	33	24	4.36	1.27	4.25	1.39	80	104	5.4	9%	18%	9%	10%	10.5%	86.7	45	22	33	28%	67%	9%	4%	0	22			0	0.63	-1.6	58	-$8
2nd Half		4	0	34	29	3.21	1.13	3.90	1.26	122	98	4.7	7%	21%	14%	8%	13.6%	86.4	45	16	39	25%	81%	16%	12%	0	18			0	0.61	3.2	100	$1
Proj		**5**	**0**	**73**	**62**	**3.54**	**1.20**	**3.50**	**1.24**	**98**	**96**	**5.8**	**7%**	**21%**	**15%**	**8%**	**12.1%**	**86.4**	**47**	**21**	**33**	**29%**	**75%**	**13%**	**12%**	**0**						**3.8**	**109**	**$2**

Swanson,Erik

Age: 29	Th: R	Role RP	Health D
Ht: 6' 3"	Wt: 220	Type Pwr/xFB	PT/Exp D
LIMA Plan A	Rand Var -5	MM 5411	Consist B

Breakout season was fueled by highest S%, lowest HR/F of career, but real driver of success was career-best K%, SwK, as slider (15.6% SwK) became third plus pitch in repertoire. Odds are HR prevention won't stick with high FB% ways, so ERA is likely heading back over 3.00. But 2nd half LI leap suggests improved skills were duly noted... UP: 25 Sv

Yr	Tm	W	Sv	IP	K	ERA	WHIP	xERA	xWHIP	vL+	vR+	BF/G	BB%	K%	K-BB%	xBB%	SwK	Vel	G	L	F	H%	S%	HR/F	xHR/F	GS	APC	DOM%	DIS%	Sv%	LI	RAR	BPX	R$
18	a/a	8	0	117	110	3.44	1.18	3.67				21.3	7%	23%	17%							29%	75%									10.2	111	$8
19	SEA *	1	2	83	75	5.85	1.35	5.78	1.23	121	95	9.4	7%	22%	15%	7%	10.0%	92.7	38	20	42	29%	65%	23%	20%	8	36	0%	63%	100	0.57	-13.7	46	-$6
20	SEA	0	0	8	9	12.91	1.70	4.57	1.16	127	169	4.1	5%	24%	19%	6%	13.4%	95.6	29	29	42	39%	20%	30%	26%	0	17			0	1.02	-8.0	151	-$12
21	SEA	0	1	35	35	3.31	1.08	4.57	1.21	96	86	4.4	7%	24%	17%	6%	14.0%	94.8	32	15	53	26%	76%	10%	9%	2	17	0%	50%	33	0.93	4.2	112	-$2
22	SEA	3	3	54	70	1.68	0.91	2.97	0.94	74	78	3.6	5%	34%	29%	5%	15.9%	93.7	33	20	47	31%	85%	5%	5%	1	15	0%	0%	60	1.04	15.2	195	$8
1st Half		0	1	23	32	0.79	0.88	2.90	0.94	65	81	3.8	6%	36%	31%	4%	17.3%	93.9	29	24	47	29%	100%	8%	6%	0	17			100	0.75	8.9	201	$1
2nd Half		3	2	31	38	2.32	0.94	3.02	0.95	80	75	3.5	4%	32%	28%	6%	14.7%	93.5	35	18	47	32%	75%	3%	4%	1	14	0%	0%	50	1.24	6.3	190	$5
Proj		**3**	**7**	**65**	**77**	**3.16**	**1.07**	**3.14**	**1.06**	**93**	**88**	**4.9**	**6%**	**30%**	**24%**	**6%**	**14.6%**	**93.6**	**34**	**20**	**47**	**30%**	**76%**	**11%**	**9%**	**0**						**6.5**	**160**	**$6**

Syndergaard,Noah

Age: 30	Th: R	Role SP	Health F
Ht: 6' 6"	Wt: 242	Type Con	PT/Exp D
LIMA Plan A+	Rand Var -2	MM 3103	Consist A

Post-TJS version of Thor was less god-like, as fastball hammer has yet to regain previous thunder. Struggles were especially apparent vL, where he fell to 12% K%. Not every pitcher bounces back right away from TJS, but also, not every pitcher bounces back. Despite the nickname, he's as mortal as the rest of us, so keep expectations earthbound.

Yr	Tm	W	Sv	IP	K	ERA	WHIP	xERA	xWHIP	vL+	vR+	BF/G	BB%	K%	K-BB%	xBB%	SwK	Vel	G	L	F	H%	S%	HR/F	xHR/F	GS	APC	DOM%	DIS%	Sv%	LI	RAR	BPX	R$
18	NYM	13	0	154	155	3.03	1.21	3.40	1.17	90	90	25.8	6%	24%	18%	6%	14.0%	97.4	49	24	27	33%	76%	8%	6%	25	96	36%	16%			21.3	148	$16
19	NYM	10	0	198	202	4.28	1.23	3.90	1.20	99	91	25.8	6%	24%	18%	5%	12.9%	97.7	48	20	32	32%	68%	13%	12%	32	97	41%	16%			5.5	142	$11
20																																		
21	NYM	0	0	2	2	9.00	1.50	4.08		138	186	4.0	0%	25%	25%		11.5%	94.7	17	33	50	35%	50%	33%	33%	2	13	0%	50%			-1.2	172	-$6
22	2 TM	10	0	135	95	3.94	1.25	4.34	1.26	107	97	22.6	5%	17%	11%	6%	9.5%	93.8	43	19	38	30%	71%	9%	11%	24	81	13%	29%	0	0.77	0.4	87	$4
1st Half		5	0	70	55	3.84	1.17	4.05	1.23	105	91	22.5	5%	19%	13%	5%	11.1%	94.1	46	17	37	29%	70%	10%	11%	13	82	23%	15%			1.1	105	$4
2nd Half		5	0	64	40	4.06	1.35	4.67	1.31	110	103	22.8	5%	15%	9%	6%	7.7%	93.3	40	21	39	32%	72%	7%	11%	11	80	0%	45%	0	0.78	-0.7	68	-$1
Proj		**11**	**0**	**145**	**119**	**4.09**	**1.25**	**3.65**	**1.23**	**102**	**94**	**23.1**	**6%**	**20%**	**14%**	**6%**	**10.9%**	**95.2**	**45**	**21**	**34**	**31%**	**69%**	**10%**	**10%**	**26**						**-2.2**	**107**	**$5**

Taillon,Jameson

Age: 31	Th: R	Role SP	Health F
Ht: 6' 5"	Wt: 230	Type Con	PT/Exp A
LIMA Plan B+	Rand Var 0	MM 4203	Consist B

Second season after Tommy John surgery resulted in BB%, GB% both rebounding from 2021 declines, and while those kinds of subtle changes aren't as sexy as more strikeouts, xERA and xWHIP show they're plenty effective. (Getting 5.7 runs per start of support doesn't hurt, either.) Wins, walks may regress a bit, but most of this looks very sustainable.

Yr	Tm	W	Sv	IP	K	ERA	WHIP	xERA	xWHIP	vL+	vR+	BF/G	BB%	K%	K-BB%	xBB%	SwK	Vel	G	L	F	H%	S%	HR/F	xHR/F	GS	APC	DOM%	DIS%	Sv%	LI	RAR	BPX	R$
18	PIT	14	0	191	179	3.20	1.18	3.66	1.19	101	86	24.5	6%	23%	17%	6%	11.0%	95.2	46	22	31	31%	77%	12%	11%	32	93	25%	16%			22.3	135	$19
19	PIT	2	0	37	30	4.10	1.13	4.17	1.26	88	93	22.6	5%	19%	14%	5%	12.1%	94.8	50	23	27	28%	66%	13%	16%	7	79	14%	29%			1.9	116	-$1
20																																		
21	NYY	8	0	144	140	4.30	1.21	4.60	1.25	101	95	20.8	7%	23%	16%	6%	12.9%	94.0	33	19	48	28%	70%	12%	11%	29	82	17%	28%			-0.7	103	$6
22	NYY	14	0	177	151	3.91	1.13	3.90	1.15	102	100	22.8	4%	21%	16%	6%	10.6%	94.2	40	21	39	29%	71%	12%	12%	32	88	25%	34%			1.3	124	$12
1st Half		9	0	89	74	3.63	1.15	3.81	1.11	112	97	23.1	3%	20%	17%	6%	10.4%	94.1	40	22	37	32%	72%	10%	9%	16	87	25%	25%			3.8	135	$13
2nd Half		5	0	88	77	4.19	1.10	4.00	1.19	93	103	22.4	6%	22%	16%	8%	10.7%	94.2	40	19	41	26%	69%	15%	16%	16	89	25%	44%			-2.4	112	$8
Proj		**11**	**0**	**160**	**138**	**3.97**	**1.14**	**3.50**	**1.19**	**98**	**96**	**21.5**	**6%**	**22%**	**16%**	**6%**	**11.4%**	**94.4**	**42**	**21**	**37**	**29%**	**70%**	**13%**	**13%**	**29**						**-0.1**	**118**	**$10**

Tate,Dillon

Age: 29	Th: R	Role RP	Health C
Ht: 6' 2"	Wt: 195	Type Con/xGB	PT/Exp B
LIMA Plan A	Rand Var -2	MM 4111	Consist B

In three seasons since his debut, has turned lack of strikeouts into non-issue by steadily decreasing walks, increasing ground balls to point where he's now deserving of high-leverage work. However, with this many balls in play - especially with shift restrictions and normalizing H% - hits will be higher and xWHIP history reflects that. Caution is warranted.

Yr	Tm	W	Sv	IP	K	ERA	WHIP	xERA	xWHIP	vL+	vR+	BF/G	BB%	K%	K-BB%	xBB%	SwK	Vel	G	L	F	H%	S%	HR/F	xHR/F	GS	APC	DOM%	DIS%	Sv%	LI	RAR	BPX	R$
18	aa	7	0	124	77	4.80	1.33	4.26				23.4	7%	15%	8%							31%	64%									-9.9	65	-$3
19	BAL *	4	7	65	49	4.82	1.24	4.10	1.40	100	96	7.2	8%	18%	11%	9%	8.3%	93.7	59	14	27	28%	64%	19%	14%	0	22			88	1.03	-2.5	64	$2
20	BAL	1	0	17	14	3.24	0.84	3.65	1.29	125	37	5.3	8%	22%	14%	12%	9.8%	94.4	51	22	27	20%	62%	9%	17%	0	24			0	0.98	2.5	104	$1
21	BAL	0	3	68	49	4.39	1.24	4.12	1.38	106	91	4.6	8%	17%	9%	7%	10.0%	95.5	60	15	25	28%	66%	13%	15%	0	17			60	1.10	-1.0	80	-$3
22	BAL	4	5	74	60	3.05	0.99	3.14	1.19	117	73	4.4	5%	21%	15%	5%	10.8%	94.0	57	19	23	26%	72%	12%	11%	0	16			83	1.09	8.3	126	$7
1st Half		0	2	39	34	2.52	1.07	3.23	1.16	92	83	4.7	5%	21%	16%	5%	11.1%	94.0	53	22	24	30%	76%	4%	9%	0	17			100	0.94	7.0	135	$1
2nd Half		4	3	34	26	3.67	0.90	3.02	1.23	169	64	4.0	6%	20%	14%	6%	10.3%	94.0	62	15	23	20%	65%	24%	14%	0	15			75	1.25	1.3	117	$5
Proj		**4**	**7**	**65**	**49**	**3.67**	**1.16**	**3.25**	**1.28**	**132**	**84**	**5.3**	**7%**	**19%**	**12%**	**6%**	**10.5%**	**94.4**	**59**	**17**	**24**	**28%**	**69%**	**12%**	**12%**	**0**						**2.4**	**105**	**$3**

Tepera,Ryan

Age: 35	Th: R	Role RP	Health D
Ht: 6' 1"	Wt: 195	Type	PT/Exp C
LIMA Plan A+	Rand Var -3	MM 3210	Consist A

2020-21 xERA, K%, and SwK all stand as outliers in his career, though 2022 K% looks like it should have been higher. xBB% fluctuations add risk for a guy who tends to lean fly-ball-heavy; wouldn't take much for ERA to balloon again. Given the flaws, LI increase is likely to be short-lived, and this skill set minus saves just isn't of much interest.

Yr	Tm	W	Sv	IP	K	ERA	WHIP	xERA	xWHIP	vL+	vR+	BF/G	BB%	K%	K-BB%	xBB%	SwK	Vel	G	L	F	H%	S%	HR/F	xHR/F	GS	APC	DOM%	DIS%	Sv%	LI	RAR	BPX	R$
18	TOR	5	7	65	68	3.62	1.22	3.81	1.27	110	97	3.9	9%	26%	17%	9%	14.3%	94.9	44	17	39	29%	76%	14%	13%	0	15			47	1.29	4.2	118	$5
19	TOR	0	0	22	14	4.98	1.29	5.37	1.51	145	86	4.0	9%	15%	7%	9%	12.9%	93.7	41	24	35	24%	70%	21%	21%	1	15	0%	100%	0	0.97	-1.3	37	-$5
20	CHC	0	0	21	31	3.92	1.40	3.34	1.28	88	96	4.2	13%	35%	21%	12%	19.5%	94.0	40	36	24	35%	74%	18%	10%	0	18			0	1.05	1.4	135	-$4
21	2 TM	0	2	61	74	2.79	0.88	3.42	1.13	61	74	3.7	8%	31%	23%	8%	16.9%	93.3	44	13	43	24%	70%	7%	9%	0	15			40	1.09	11.2	156	$6
22	LAA	5	6	57	47	3.61	1.08	4.16	1.33	90	86	3.9	9%	20%	12%	11%	13.5%	92.7	41	20	39	23%	71%	11%	10%	0	15			55	1.44	2.5	74	$4
1st Half		1	1	32	26	4.18	1.05	4.22	1.33	102	73	4.0	8%	20%	11%	12%	12.5%	92.7	38	23	39	23%	63%	11%	8%	0	16			20	1.54	-0.8	70	-$4
2nd Half		4	5	25	21	2.88	1.12	4.07	1.33	76	104	3.9	9%	21%	12%	9%	14.8%	92.8	45	16	39	24%	80%	11%	12%	0	14			83	1.33	3.4	79	$4
Proj		**5**	**3**	**58**	**54**	**3.84**	**1.18**	**3.66**	**1.29**	**94**	**94**	**3.8**	**9%**	**23%**	**15%**	**10%**	**14.4%**	**93.4**	**43**	**17**	**40**	**27%**	**71%**	**11%**	**11%**	**0**						**0.9**	**96**	**$2**

BRANDON KRUSE

Thielbar,Caleb

Age: 36 Th: L Role: RP Ht: 6' 0" Wt: 205 Type: Pwr/xFB
Health: C PT/Exp: C Consist: B
LIMA Plan: A+ Rand Var: 0 MM: 4400

Steady xERA, xWHIP improvement has come in lockstep with BB%, K% growth, which in turn has been backed by gains in xBB%, SwK, and velocity. FB% has been lone stubborn holdout, but BPX confirms that other skills have blossomed enough to offset it. vR+, LI show he's now a legit late-inning arm, though at 36, saves will likely remain elusive.

Yr	Tm	W	Sv	IP	K	ERA	WHIP	xERA	xWHIP	vL+	vR+	BF/G	BB%	K%	K-BB%	xBB%	SwK	Vel	G	L	F	H%	S%	HR/F	xHR/F	GS	APC	DOM%	DIS%	Sv%	LI	RAR	BPX	R$
18	a/a	7	0	57	35	3.10	1.27	4.22				6.0	3%	15%	12%							33%	77%									7.4	154	$2
19	aaa	2	5	79	68	4.79	1.55	5.63				6.8	5%	20%	14%							38%	71%									-2.8	89	-$4
20	MIN	2	0	20	22	2.25	1.15	4.63	1.35	52	74	4.8	11%	27%	16%	7%	13.5%	89.8	27	27	47	29%	78%	0%	6%	0	22			0	0.88	5.4	83	$3
21	MIN	7	0	64	77	3.23	1.17	4.01	1.15	89	96	4.5	8%	29%	21%	6%	12.3%	91.3	32	19	49	31%	78%	10%	14%	0	19			0	1.00	8.1	141	$5
22	MIN	4	1	59	80	3.49	1.16	3.41	1.06	82	89	3.7	7%	33%	25%	4%	15.7%	92.9	29	23	48	35%	72%	7%	8%	0	15			50	1.30	3.5	167	$2
1st Half		2	1	30	40	5.46	1.35	3.68	1.19	76	104	3.7	10%	31%	21%	5%	15.7%	92.6	34	20	46	35%	59%	9%	9%	0	15			100	1.19	-5.5	137	-$7
2nd Half		2	0	30	40	1.52	0.98	3.16	0.92	89	74	3.6	4%	34%	30%	4%	15.6%	93.2	25	25	50	34%	89%	6%	6%	0	14			0	1.42	9.0	199	$3
Proj		**4**	**0**	**58**	**66**	**3.70**	**1.12**	**3.33**	**1.11**	**90**	**94**	**4.2**	**6%**	**29%**	**22%**	**5%**	**14.9%**	**92.6**	**29**	**22**	**49**	**31%**	**70%**	**10%**	**8%**	**0**						**1.9**	**141**	**$2**

Thompson,Keegan

Age: 28 Th: R Role: RP Ht: 6' 1" Wt: 210 Type:
Health: D PT/Exp: C Consist: A
LIMA Plan: B+ Rand Var: 0 MM: 2201

League-average strikeout skills, slightly high FB% continue to hold him back, so when control problems flared up in 2nd half, it was enough to sink value into negative territory. Only lasted 4.6 IP per start while earning a PQS-DIS in half of them; 1.47 ERA, 30% K% in 12 relief appearances adds to feeling that role change is in order. Probably best to wait for it.

Yr	Tm	W	Sv	IP	K	ERA	WHIP	xERA	xWHIP	vL+	vR+	BF/G	BB%	K%	K-BB%	xBB%	SwK	Vel	G	L	F	H%	S%	HR/F	xHR/F	GS	APC	DOM%	DIS%	Sv%	LI	RAR	BPX	R$
18	aa	6	0	62	46	5.15	1.62	5.22				21.2	8%	17%	8%							37%	67%									-7.6	70	-$7
19																																		
20																																		
21	CHC *	3	1	70	68	2.59	1.29	3.73	1.49	111	92	7.9	13%	24%	11%	9%	10.7%	93.9	43	22	35	26%	86%	17%	18%	6	30	0%	50%	50	0.94	14.4	75	$3
22	CHC	10	1	115	108	3.76	1.27	4.11	1.30	100	106	16.7	9%	22%	13%	8%	10.4%	93.5	41	19	40	29%	75%	12%	13%	17	65	29%	53%	50	1.12	3.0	88	$5
1st Half		7	0	71	66	3.28	1.22	3.91	1.27	90	106	16.3	8%	22%	14%	8%	10.2%	93.8	43	18	39	29%	76%	9%	10%	10	62	30%	50%	0	1.24	6.1	98	$9
2nd Half		3	1	44	42	4.53	1.35	4.44	1.35	113	107	17.4	10%	22%	12%	9%	10.6%	93.1	38	20	42	28%	74%	17%	17%	7	69	29%	57%	50	0.93	-3.0	73	-$4
Proj		**6**	**0**	**116**	**104**	**4.07**	**1.38**	**4.03**	**1.37**	**111**	**106**	**14.9**	**10%**	**21%**	**12%**	**8%**	**10.5%**	**93.5**	**41**	**20**	**40**	**31%**	**74%**	**12%**	**14%**	**16**						**-1.4**	**72**	**-$1**

Thompson,Zach

Age: 29 Th: R Role: SP Ht: 6' 7" Wt: 230 Type:
Health: B PT/Exp: C Consist: A
LIMA Plan: C+ Rand Var: +1 MM: 1101

This is Zach with an "H" Thompson, a righty who pitches for PIT, not to be confused with Zack with a "K" Thompson, a lefty who pitches for STL, and a former first-rounder with back-end SP upside. Why are we devoting Zach with an H's write-up to discussing Zack with a K's potential? To distract you from the horror of these stats. No, don't look. We beg you.

Yr	Tm	W	Sv	IP	K	ERA	WHIP	xERA	xWHIP	vL+	vR+	BF/G	BB%	K%	K-BB%	xBB%	SwK	Vel	G	L	F	H%	S%	HR/F	xHR/F	GS	APC	DOM%	DIS%	Sv%	LI	RAR	BPX	R$
18	aa	4	1	40	33	1.93	1.42	4.14				8.1	12%	19%	7%							29%	92%									10.9	65	$1
19	a/a	5	0	77	69	7.16	1.74	7.62				7.8	8%	20%	12%							37%	64%									-25.3	22	-$13
20																																		
21	MIA *	3	1	90	82	4.17	1.35	4.45	1.35	112	74	11.0	8%	22%	14%	8%	12.1%	92.2	43	17	40	32%	72%	7%	9%	14	46	14%	29%	50	0.75	1.1	84	-$2
22	PIT	3	0	122	90	5.18	1.51	4.62	1.40	113	111	18.7	8%	17%	8%	8%	10.8%	92.3	45	22	33	32%	69%	15%	14%	22	72	9%	64%	0	0.67	-18.1	56	-$12
1st Half		3	0	59	43	4.42	1.39	4.61	1.43	100	116	18.3	9%	17%	7%	9%	9.8%	92.3	47	19	34	27%	76%	19%	15%	13	72	8%	62%	0	0.78	-3.3	48	-$7
2nd Half		0	0	63	47	5.89	1.63	4.63	1.36	126	107	19.1	8%	16%	9%	8%	11.7%	92.2	44	25	31	36%	64%	10%	12%	9	71	11%	67%	0	0.57	-14.8	64	-$20
Proj		**4**	**0**	**102**	**80**	**5.26**	**1.57**	**4.33**	**1.41**	**128**	**115**	**20.3**	**9%**	**18%**	**9%**	**8%**	**11.2%**	**92.2**	**43**	**22**	**35**	**33%**	**70%**	**16%**	**12%**	**22**						**-16.2**	**56**	**-$10**

Treinen,Blake

Age: 35 Th: R Role: RP Ht: 6' 5" Wt: 225 Type: Pwr
Health: F PT/Exp: C Consist: B
LIMA Plan: B Rand Var: +5 MM: 5410

Made three appearances in April before torn capsule in shoulder shut him down until September, when he logged two more games before hitting IL again. Off-season examination found extensive damage that will likely require surgery and could cause him to miss entire 2023 season. Wait for further updates, but given his age, outlook is awfully murky.

Yr	Tm	W	Sv	IP	K	ERA	WHIP	xERA	xWHIP	vL+	vR+	BF/G	BB%	K%	K-BB%	xBB%	SwK	Vel	G	L	F	H%	S%	HR/F	xHR/F	GS	APC	DOM%	DIS%	Sv%	LI	RAR	BPX	R$
18	OAK	9	38	80	100	0.78	0.83	2.61	1.06	63	52	4.6	7%	32%	25%	5%	18.6%	97.4	52	24	24	26%	92%	4%	7%	0	17			88	1.60	33.3	194	$36
19	OAK	6	16	59	59	4.91	1.62	5.26	1.59	104	103	4.7	14%	22%	8%	8%	12.6%	96.7	43	24	33	32%	73%	16%	17%	0	18			76	1.40	-2.9	33	$3
20	LA	3	1	26	22	3.86	1.21	3.43	1.29	92	79	4.0	7%	21%	13%	6%	11.4%	96.9	64	21	15	30%	67%	9%	8%	0	15			50	1.25	1.9	119	$4
21	LA	6	7	72	85	1.99	0.98	3.16	1.17	69	70	4.0	9%	30%	21%	7%	13.4%	97.5	53	17	30	26%	83%	10%	7%	0	15			64	1.41	20.3	151	$15
22	LA	1	0	5	6	1.80	0.40	1.92			90	3.4	6%	35%	29%	6%	11.6%	96.4	60	20	20	0%	0%	50%	34%	0	14			0	0.86	1.3	203	-$4
1st Half		1	0	3	5	3.00	0.33	1.41			140	3.3	0%	50%	50%	6%	17.1%	96.2	60	0	40	0%	0%	50%	34%	0	14			0	1.34	0.4	340	-$8
2nd Half		0	0	2	1	0.00	0.50	0.00			28	3.5	14%	14%	0%	5%	3.6%	96.6	60	40	0	0%	0%	0%		0	14			0	0.15	1.0	-3	-$10
Proj		**1**	**2**	**15**	**16**	**3.15**	**1.09**	**3.06**	**1.27**	**83**	**78**	**4.3**	**10%**	**28%**	**17%**	**7%**	**14.1%**	**97.2**	**49**	**21**	**30**	**26%**	**74%**	**12%**	**9%**	**0**						**1.5**	**116**	**-$2**

Trivino,Lou

Age: 31 Th: R Role: RP Ht: 6' 5" Wt: 235 Type: Pwr
Health: B PT/Exp: A Consist: B
LIMA Plan: B Rand Var: +5 MM: 4410

Ugly finish to 2021 (5.63 ERA, 1.42 WHIP after 8/1) carried over to 1st half of 2022, but unlike 2021, this time it was mostly bad luck (a 52% H%?!). Even outperforming xERA in 2nd half wasn't enough to bring full-season ERA and WHIP in line with skills. There could be a nice buy-low opportunity here, especially if xBB% is right about control upside.

Yr	Tm	W	Sv	IP	K	ERA	WHIP	xERA	xWHIP	vL+	vR+	BF/G	BB%	K%	K-BB%	xBB%	SwK	Vel	G	L	F	H%	S%	HR/F	xHR/F	GS	APC	DOM%	DIS%	Sv%	LI	RAR	BPX	R$
18	OAK	8	4	74	82	2.92	1.14	3.50	1.29	88	79	4.3	10%	27%	17%	8%	14.9%	97.6	47	23	31	26%	79%	14%	12%	1	16	0%	0%	44	1.18	11.2	118	$9
19	OAK	4	0	60	57	5.25	1.53	5.21	1.51	105	102	4.4	12%	21%	10%	8%	12.7%	97.5	45	16	39	32%	67%	10%	8%	0	16			0	1.08	-5.5	56	-$5
20	OAK	0	0	23	26	3.86	1.11	4.07	1.31	106	65	4.7	11%	28%	17%	10%	12.4%	95.5	40	21	39	25%	70%	14%	17%	0	19			0	0.39	1.7	107	-$2
21	OAK	7	22	74	67	3.18	1.25	4.36	1.42	111	66	4.4	11%	22%	11%	9%	10.5%	95.8	48	19	33	27%	76%	8%	15%	0	17			85	1.22	9.9	67	$14
22	2 AL	2	11	54	67	4.53	1.64	3.45	1.25	142	98	3.9	10%	27%	17%	8%	12.7%	95.7	53	20	28	41%	74%	14%	16%	0	15			79	1.43	-3.7	137	-$2
1st Half		1	6	23	35	6.94	2.01	3.41	1.22	134	121	3.9	10%	30%	19%	8%	13.0%	95.7	48	26	26	52%	64%	11%	14%	0	15			86	1.34	-8.6	159	-$12
2nd Half		1	5	30	32	2.67	1.35	3.45	1.27	149	78	3.9	9%	24%	15%	8%	12.4%	95.8	57	14	29	32%	86%	17%	18%	0	15			71	1.51	4.9	121	$0
Proj		**3**	**5**	**58**	**64**	**3.81**	**1.30**	**3.29**	**1.27**	**110**	**82**	**3.8**	**10%**	**27%**	**17%**	**8%**	**12.6%**	**96.4**	**50**	**19**	**32**	**31%**	**74%**	**13%**	**14%**	**0**						**1.2**	**117**	**$1**

Turnbull,Spencer

Age: 30 Th: R Role: SP Ht: 6' 3" Wt: 210 Type:
Health: F PT/Exp: C Consist: C
LIMA Plan: A+ Rand Var: 0 MM: 3203

Tommy John surgery cost him all of 2022, but should be ready to go come spring training. Important to remember that 2020-21 successes were aided by low HR/F marks, and even 2021's career-best xERA relied on BB% that might not be fully sustainable. Too many risk factors and unknowns for a guy who has yet to crack double digits in value.

Yr	Tm	W	Sv	IP	K	ERA	WHIP	xERA	xWHIP	vL+	vR+	BF/G	BB%	K%	K-BB%	xBB%	SwK	Vel	G	L	F	H%	S%	HR/F	xHR/F	GS	APC	DOM%	DIS%	Sv%	LI	RAR	BPX	R$
18	DET *	5	0	131	110	5.76	1.50	4.43	1.21	89	94	22.6	9%	19%	10%	7%	9.9%	94.1	46	28	26	35%	59%	8%	13%	3	71	0%	33%	0	0.89	-25.9	87	-$12
19	DET	3	0	148	146	4.61	1.44	4.46	1.36	107	95	21.9	9%	22%	13%	10%	11.1%	93.8	48	19	32	34%	69%	10%	15%	30	89	7%	33%			-1.9	97	-$2
20	DET	4	0	57	51	3.97	1.34	4.59	1.49	90	90	22.0	12%	21%	9%	12%	11.8%	94.1	50	22	28	29%	69%	5%	17%	11	88	18%	18%			3.4	56	$6
21	DET	4	0	50	44	2.88	0.98	3.47	1.20	74	77	22.3	6%	22%	16%	8%	11.2%	94.2	57	15	28	27%	70%	5%	10%	9	86	33%	11%			8.5	131	$4
22																																		
1st Half																																		
2nd Half																																		
Proj		**8**	**0**	**131**	**113**	**4.14**	**1.29**	**3.64**	**1.37**	**99**	**96**	**23.6**	**10%**	**21%**	**12%**	**9%**	**11.4%**	**94.1**	**51**	**19**	**30**	**30%**	**67%**	**6%**	**12%**	**23**						**-2.7**	**81**	**$2**

Uelmen,Erich

Age: 27 Th: R Role: RP Ht: 6' 3" Wt: 185 Type:
Health: A PT/Exp: D Consist: F
LIMA Plan: C Rand Var: 0 MM: 1100

2-1, 4.67 ERA in 27 IP at CHC. Not considered much of a prospect, but managed to draw two save opps, three holds during brief time in majors. 4.59 MLB-only xERA, lackluster skills make it seem unlikely he'll get much more high-leverage work in future. Between size and churn, modern bullpens evoke Andy Warhol: everybody gets their 15 minutes of fame.

Yr	Tm	W	Sv	IP	K	ERA	WHIP	xERA	xWHIP	vL+	vR+	BF/G	BB%	K%	K-BB%	xBB%	SwK	Vel	G	L	F	H%	S%	HR/F	xHR/F	GS	APC	DOM%	DIS%	Sv%	LI	RAR	BPX	R$
18																																		
19	aa	0	0	29	22	10.89	2.16	8.38				24.1	15%	15%	0%							37%	49%									-22.8	-8	-$15
20																																		
21	a/a	2	2	93	71	6.27	1.49	5.43				13.0	10%	18%	7%							30%	60%									-23.2	34	-$13
22	CHC *	5	7	69	63	3.54	1.31	3.35	1.44	122	93	5.4	10%	17%	7%	12%	11.2%	93.6	48	16	37	28%	74%	10%	10%	0	19			58	0.88	3.7	87	$3
1st Half		3	4	39	37	3.03	1.31	3.05				6.4	13%	22%	10%							28%	77%	0%		0	0					4.5	97	$2
2nd Half		2	3	30	26	4.20	1.30	3.74	1.40	121	93	4.4	10%	20%	10%	12%	11.2%	93.6	48	16	37	28%	69%	10%	10%	0	19			75	0.88	-0.9	76	-$3
Proj		**2**	**1**	**51**	**40**	**4.40**	**1.43**	**4.35**	**1.51**	**133**	**101**	**6.3**	**11%**	**19%**	**7%**		**11.2%**	**93.6**	**45**	**17**	**38**	**29%**	**72%**	**11%**	**9%**	**0**						**-2.7**	**36**	**-$5**

BRANDON KRUSE

Urías,Julio

Age: 26	Th: L	Role SP	PT/Exp A	Rand Var -5	Health C
Ht: 6' 0"	Wt: 225	Type /FB	Consist B	MM 3205	LIMA Plan C

Early-career durability concerns are distant memory after another workhorse season, and ERA, WHIP tell us he's a bona fide ace. Combination of low HR/F, high FB%, and elite BB% conspire to keep H%, WHIP at better-than-expected levels, helping to offset pedestrian K%, SwK. Lengthy track record of beating xERA should continue, but remains risky.

Yr Tm	W	Sv	IP	K	ERA	WHIP	xERA	xWHIP	vL+	vR+	BF/G	BB%	K%	K-BB%	xBB%	SwK	Vel	G	L	F	H%	S%	HR/F	xHR/F	GS	APC	DOM%	DIS%	Sv%	LI	RAR	BPX	R$
18 LA	0	0	4	7	0.00	0.25	1.23			28	4.3	0%	54%	54%		22.4%	93.1	50	17	33	19%	0%	0%	1%	0	19			0	0.00	2.0	359	-$3
19 LA	4	4	80	85	2.49	1.08	4.14	1.27	89	76	8.8	8%	26%	18%	8%	14.4%	95.2	39	22	39	27%	81%	9%	9%	8	36	38%	25%	80	0.96	19.9	117	$10
20 LA	3	0	55	45	3.27	1.15	5.04	1.36	68	86	20.4	8%	20%	12%	6%	12.5%	94.2	33	22	46	27%	74%	7%	10%	10	80	10%	20%	0	0.74	8.0	72	$10
21 LA	20	0	186	195	2.96	1.02	3.73	1.10	88	80	23.3	5%	26%	21%	4%	11.9%	94.1	40	19	41	29%	75%	9%	11%	32	87	34%	19%			30.0	152	$32
22 LA	17	0	175	166	2.16	0.96	3.76	1.15	79	86	22.2	6%	24%	18%	5%	11.5%	93.1	40	15	45	24%	87%	11%	8%	31	85	29%	23%			39.0	126	$32
1st Half	7	0	88	83	2.57	1.03	3.86	1.16	89	91	21.8	6%	24%	18%	5%	12.2%	92.8	37	16	46	25%	84%	12%	8%	16	82	25%	31%			15.2	122	$22
2nd Half	10	0	87	83	1.75	0.89	3.65	1.14	67	80	22.7	6%	24%	18%	5%	10.9%	93.4	42	14	44	23%	90%	10%	8%	15	88	33%	13%			23.9	131	$34
Proj	15	0	181	171	3.00	1.10	3.58	1.20	84	90	22.8	7%	24%	17%	5%	12.1%	93.8	38	18	44	28%	78%	9%	9%	31						21.8	116	$22

Urquidy,José

Age: 28	Th: R	Role SP	PT/Exp A	Rand Var 0	Health D
Ht: 6' 0"	Wt: 217	Type Con/xFB	Consist A	MM 3203	LIMA Plan A

Profile based heavily on inducing soft contact and limiting mistakes thanks to excellent control. While high FB% helps create easy outs, keeping H% and WHIP low in sustainable fashion, it also leads to home run problems (1.6 HR/9) and creates downside risk illustrated by xERA. He's a mid-rotation starter capable of eating innings; just don't expect more.

Yr Tm	W	Sv	IP	K	ERA	WHIP	xERA	xWHIP	vL+	vR+	BF/G	BB%	K%	K-BB%	xBB%	SwK	Vel	G	L	F	H%	S%	HR/F	xHR/F	GS	APC	DOM%	DIS%	Sv%	LI	RAR	BPX	R$
18																																	
19 HOU *	9	0	144	153	5.20	1.26	4.76	1.16	70	110	20.2	5%	26%	21%	8%	12.3%	93.3	37	18	45	33%	63%	12%	14%	7	77	29%	29%	0	0.93	-12.4	130	$3
20 HOU	1	0	30	17	2.73	1.01	5.15	1.42	52	114	23.2	7%	15%	8%	5%	10.0%	93.1	36	23	41	21%	81%	11%	12%	5	86	20%	60%			6.3	47	$3
21 HOU	8	0	107	90	3.62	0.99	4.35	1.17	79	97	21.2	4%	21%	17%	5%	12.5%	92.6	32	22	46	25%	71%	12%	12%	20	82	35%	25%			8.6	113	$11
22 HOU	13	0	164	134	3.94	1.17	4.31	1.22	97	109	23.5	6%	20%	14%	5%	10.6%	93.6	36	19	45	28%	74%	13%	13%	28	91	21%	32%	0	0.78	0.5	99	$9
1st Half	7	0	80	63	4.15	1.33	4.60	1.24	104	117	23.1	5%	18%	13%	5%	10.9%	93.8	36	20	44	31%	76%	13%	14%	15	88	7%	40%			-1.7	93	$2
2nd Half	6	0	84	71	3.75	1.01	4.05	1.19	90	99	23.9	6%	21%	16%	5%	10.3%	93.4	36	19	46	24%	70%	13%	11%	13	95	38%	23%	0	0.77	2.3	105	$13
Proj	12	0	160	141	4.08	1.15	3.72	1.18	90	109	21.6	5%	22%	17%	6%	11.3%	93.3	36	19	45	28%	71%	13%	13%	29						-2.1	115	$10

Valdez,Framber

Age: 29	Th: L	Role SP	PT/Exp A	Rand Var 0	Health D
Ht: 5' 11"	Wt: 239	Type /xGB	Consist A	MM 5205	LIMA Plan C+

Belongs in a different era: one of eight pitchers to reach 200 IP, completed at least seven innings nine times, and posted 25 consecutive quality starts. Core profile of elite GB% and limiting HR remained, while velocity growth, career-best SwK illustrated complementary skills to sustain success. Average K% enhanced by IP volume, and ratios will buoy value.

Yr Tm	W	Sv	IP	K	ERA	WHIP	xERA	xWHIP	vL+	vR+	BF/G	BB%	K%	K-BB%	xBB%	SwK	Vel	G	L	F	H%	S%	HR/F	xHR/F	GS	APC	DOM%	DIS%	Sv%	LI	RAR	BPX	R$
18 HOU *	10	1	142	140	3.95	1.35	3.83	1.62	58	91	19.8	9%	24%	14%	12%	8.5%	92.0	70	13	16	32%	71%	20%	13%	5	79	0%	20%	50	0.93	3.5	104	$5
19 HOU *	9	1	116	124	5.05	1.47	4.31	1.57	87	112	13.8	12%	25%	12%	11%	10.8%	93.0	62	21	17	32%	67%	26%	19%	8	45	25%	50%	100	0.46	-7.7	83	-$1
20 HOU	5	0	71	76	3.57	1.12	2.96	1.11	85	85	26.2	6%	26%	21%	7%	10.5%	93.1	60	21	19	32%	69%	14%	21%	10	95	50%	10%	0	0.77	7.7	178	$18
21 HOU	11	0	135	125	3.14	1.25	3.31	1.37	99	83	26.0	10%	22%	12%	10%	10.7%	92.5	70	15	15	28%	78%	21%	20%	22	95	36%	23%			18.7	103	$12
22 HOU	17	0	201	194	2.82	1.16	2.83	1.25	72	87	26.7	8%	23%	15%	7%	11.6%	94.0	67	17	16	29%	77%	13%	16%	31	97	42%	10%			28.6	132	$24
1st Half	8	0	101	93	2.67	1.14	2.91	1.31	76	84	25.7	9%	23%	13%	7%	10.5%	94.1	67	18	15	27%	78%	15%	13%	16	96	31%	6%			16.1	113	$22
2nd Half	9	0	100	101	2.96	1.18	2.75	1.19	69	90	27.7	7%	24%	17%	8%	12.8%	93.9	66	17	17	32%	75%	10%	18%	15	99	53%	13%			12.5	151	$22
Proj	15	0	189	176	3.31	1.21	2.84	1.28	80	89	23.2	9%	23%	15%	8%	11.0%	93.4	66	18	17	30%	74%	15%	18%	33						15.4	122	$17

Verlander,Justin

Age: 40	Th: R	Role SP	PT/Exp C	Rand Var -5	Health F
Ht: 6' 5"	Wt: 235	Type /xFB	Consist B	MM 4303	LIMA Plan C

Return from Tommy John surgery went pretty well, wouldn't you say? ERA, WHIP were both better than Cy Young 2019 campaign. DOM%, DIS% suggest there's little risk of decline, however, he benefitted from H%/S% support. SwK drop hints at potential K% regression. xERA offers more realistic expectation. But for him, 40 may be the new 20.

Yr Tm	W	Sv	IP	K	ERA	WHIP	xERA	xWHIP	vL+	vR+	BF/G	BB%	K%	K-BB%	xBB%	SwK	Vel	G	L	F	H%	S%	HR/F	xHR/F	GS	APC	DOM%	DIS%	Sv%	LI	RAR	BPX	R$
18 HOU	16	0	214	290	2.52	0.90	3.16	0.93	80	86	24.5	4%	35%	30%	5%	15.3%	95.1	29	20	51	29%	81%	11%	8%	34	101	62%	3%			42.9	212	$42
19 HOU	21	0	223	300	2.58	0.80	3.18	0.98	74	80	24.9	5%	35%	30%	5%	16.8%	94.7	36	19	45	23%	80%	16%	14%	34	101	59%	6%			52.9	203	$50
20 HOU	1	0	6	7	3.00	0.67	2.73		83	95	21.0	5%	33%	29%		12.3%	94.9	62	0	38	9%	100%	40%	33%	1	73	0%	0%			1.1	213	-$2
21																																	
22 HOU	18	0	175	185	1.75	0.83	3.26	1.03	63	78	23.8	4%	28%	23%	5%	12.1%	95.1	38	19	44	25%	83%	6%	9%	28	93	54%	0%			47.9	162	$40
1st Half	10	0	97	90	2.03	0.83	3.49	1.10	64	83	24.8	5%	24%	20%	5%	11.6%	94.9	39	19	42	22%	84%	10%	11%	15	94	47%	0%			23.2	137	$38
2nd Half	8	0	78	95	1.39	0.82	2.98	0.94	63	68	22.6	4%	32%	28%	5%	12.7%	95.3	36	17	46	29%	83%	1%	6%	13	92	62%	0%			24.7	193	$34
Proj	14	0	160	166	3.03	1.06	3.32	1.09	87	99	24.3	5%	27%	22%	5%	12.1%	95.0	35	19	46	29%	78%	11%	11%	25						18.5	147	$21

Vesia,Alex

Age: 27	Th: L	Role RP	PT/Exp D	Rand Var -5	Health A
Ht: 6' 1"	Wt: 209	Type Pwr/xFB	Consist F	MM 5500	LIMA Plan A

Backed 2021 breakout with another effective season, though path to that success differed. GB% ticked up and LD% normalized, helping him drastically cut back HR, and even after step back, SwK%, K% were well above average. BB% could hold him back from save chances, but if xBB% is right and he can carry over 2nd half improvement... UP: 15 Sv

Yr Tm	W	Sv	IP	K	ERA	WHIP	xERA	xWHIP	vL+	vR+	BF/G	BB%	K%	K-BB%	xBB%	SwK	Vel	G	L	F	H%	S%	HR/F	xHR/F	GS	APC	DOM%	DIS%	Sv%	LI	RAR	BPX	R$
18																																	
19 aa	2	1	17	21	0.00	0.69	0.50				6.7	2%	35%	33%							28%	100%									9.5	513	$2
20 MIA	0	0	4	5	18.69	3.23	12.30		171	186	5.4	26%	19%	-7%	12%	12.0%	91.8	20	20	60	36%	45%	33%	23%	0	27			0	0.56	-7.6	-235	-$14
21 LA	3	1	40	54	2.25	0.98	4.30	1.32	63	85	3.9	14%	34%	20%	8%	18.1%	93.9	25	11	64	16%	88%	11%	11%	0	16			50	1.16	9.9	97	$4
22 LA	5	1	54	79	2.15	1.12	3.19	1.14	50	87	3.6	11%	35%	24%	8%	15.7%	94.2	35	23	43	32%	81%	4%	9%	0	15			33	0.98	12.2	156	$6
1st Half	1	0	26	33	3.16	1.52	4.06	1.32	57	112	3.7	12%	28%	16%	8%	14.0%	93.6	36	25	39	38%	79%	4%	10%	0	15			0	0.75	2.6	99	-$7
2nd Half	4	1	29	46	1.26	0.77	2.50	0.96	42	63	3.5	9%	42%	33%	7%	17.4%	94.7	33	20	47	24%	86%	4%	8%	0	15			33	1.21	9.6	206	$10
Proj	5	0	58	80	2.74	1.08	3.03	1.16	58	96	3.7	11%	35%	24%	8%	16.4%	94.2	33	19	48	28%	79%	10%	10%	0						8.8	142	$5

Vest,Will

Age: 28	Th: R	Role RP	PT/Exp D	Rand Var 0	Health B
Ht: 6' 0"	Wt: 180	Type	Consist D	MM 3210	LIMA Plan B

There were positives in first full season in majors, as xERA, xWHIP suggest he deserved better results spurred by growth in velocity, K%, and GB%. Despite that, SwK and strikeouts aren't approaching rate of traditional closer, or even high-leverage reliever. Hard to see how it gets much better, meaning fantasy usefulness is likely to be limited.

Yr Tm	W	Sv	IP	K	ERA	WHIP	xERA	xWHIP	vL+	vR+	BF/G	BB%	K%	K-BB%	xBB%	SwK	Vel	G	L	F	H%	S%	HR/F	xHR/F	GS	APC	DOM%	DIS%	Sv%	LI	RAR	BPX	R$
18																																	
19 a/a	2	5	35	22	6.55	1.77	7.22				7.0	7%	14%	6%							36%	66%									-8.9	12	-$7
20																																	
21 SEA *	2	2	62	46	6.32	1.60	5.35	1.54	107	112	5.0	10%	17%	7%	9%	10.2%	93.6	43	26	30	34%	60%	6%	8%	0	19			50	1.02	-15.8	52	-$12
22 DET	3	1	63	63	4.00	1.33	3.56	1.25	99	97	4.6	8%	23%	15%	8%	10.9%	95.2	50	23	28	33%	72%	12%	15%	2	18	0%	100%	100	0.69	-0.2	116	-$2
1st Half	1	1	29	32	3.41	1.14	3.31	1.23	92	82	4.5	9%	27%	18%	8%	12.5%	94.9	48	21	32	28%	73%	13%	17%	0	18			100	0.72	2.0	124	-$3
2nd Half	2	0	34	31	4.50	1.50	3.79	1.27	103	108	4.7	7%	20%	13%	8%	9.6%	95.4	51	24	25	36%	71%	11%	13%	2	18	0%	100%	0	0.66	-2.2	108	-$8
Proj	3	2	58	50	4.27	1.41	3.69	1.33	107	108	4.9	8%	20%	12%	8%	10.6%	94.9	48	23	28	33%	72%	13%	13%	0						-2.1	87	-$3

Voth,Austin

Age: 31	Th: R	Role SP	PT/Exp B	Rand Var 0	Health D
Ht: 6' 2"	Wt: 211	Type /FB	Consist B	MM 2201	LIMA Plan B

Took off after role shifted to SP in BAL, maintaining 3.04 ERA across 83 IP; however, there wasn't any meaningful change in skill. His FB% remained high and K% low, which over a larger sample is likely to result in a lot of hard contact and runs against. Second half results could earn him longer look in rotation, but he's safe to ignore in our game.

Yr Tm	W	Sv	IP	K	ERA	WHIP	xERA	xWHIP	vL+	vR+	BF/G	BB%	K%	K-BB%	xBB%	SwK	Vel	G	L	F	H%	S%	HR/F	xHR/F	GS	APC	DOM%	DIS%	Sv%	LI	RAR	BPX	R$
18 WAS *	7	0	140	103	6.04	1.53	5.50	1.46	100	114	21.7	8%	17%	9%	8%	7.9%	91.4	43	14	43	33%	62%	19%	6%	2	54	0%	50%	0	0.44	-32.5	48	-$14
19 WAS *	6	0	118	105	5.11	1.43	5.04	1.26	101	79	20.9	6%	21%	15%	8%	13.0%	92.8	35	24	42	35%	66%	11%	11%	8	76	25%	13%	0	0.74	-8.8	85	-$3
20 WAS	2	0	50	44	6.34	1.51	5.65	1.37	122	127	20.5	8%	20%	12%	8%	9.6%	92.1	29	22	49	31%	66%	18%	16%	11	81	18%	73%			-11.6	71	-$11
21 WAS	4	0	57	59	5.34	1.48	4.59	1.40	120	103	5.1	11%	24%	13%	8%	11.7%	94.2	38	24	38	31%	68%	17%	18%	1	21	0%	0%	0	0.94	-7.6	70	-$6
22 2 TM	5	0	102	90	4.34	1.40	4.48	1.26	109	107	10.8	7%	20%	13%	8%	11.3%	93.5	34	22	43	33%	73%	10%	10%	17	43	12%	35%	0	0.52	-4.6	90	-$3
1st Half	0	0	35	33	7.20	1.80	4.55	1.28	118	125	6.4	7%	20%	13%	9%	10.6%	93.9	38	28	34	41%	60%	12%	11%	4	26	0%	25%	0	0.40	-13.9	94	-$21
2nd Half	5	0	67	57	2.84	1.19	4.43	1.25	100	99	18.4	7%	21%	14%	8%	11.8%	93.3	33	19	48	28%	83%	9%	10%	13	73	15%	38%	0	0.74	9.3	88	$9
Proj	5	0	109	98	4.76	1.41	4.16	1.31	113	109	21.4	8%	21%	13%	8%	11.0%	93.2	34	23	43	32%	71%	13%	13%	15						-10.6	81	-$5

DANIEL MARCUS

Wacha,Michael

Age: 32	Th: R	Role	SP	Health	F	LIMA Plan	B+
Ht: 6' 6"	Wt: 215	Type	Con	PT/Exp	A	Rand Var	-2
				Consist	A	MM	3203

Enjoyed surface-level success in 1st half mostly because H%, S%, and HR/F covered for missing skills, so 2nd half crash wasn't a surprise. However, rebound in BB%, K%, SwK over final months gives us glimmer of hope. Despite mixed signals, xERA and xWHIP are your reality check, and DOM%/DIS% track record is your sanity check.

Yr Tm	W	Sv	IP	K	ERA	WHIP	xERA	xWHIP	vL+	vR+	BF/G	BB%	K%	K-BB%	xBB%	SwK	Vel	G	L	F	H%	S%	HR/F	xHR/F	GS	APC	DOM%	DIS%	Sv%	LI	RAR	BPX	R$
18 STL	8	0	84	71	3.20	1.23	4.24	1.42	80	99	23.7	10%	20%	10%	10%	10.2%	93.5	43	29	27	26%	78%	14%	16%	15	95	40%	33%			9.9	62	$5
19 STL	6	0	127	104	4.76	1.56	4.99	1.48	107	120	19.4	10%	19%	9%	9%	10.1%	93.1	48	22	30	32%	76%	22%	23%	24	76	8%	58%	0	0.80	-4.0	58	-$5
20 NYM	1	0	34	37	6.62	1.56	4.53	1.14	112	143	19.5	4%	24%	19%	7%	12.0%	93.6	36	23	41	39%	64%	20%	15%	7	76	0%	71%	0	0.70	-9.1	158	-$11
21 TAM	3	0	125	121	5.05	1.31	4.09	1.19	99	110	18.2	6%	23%	17%	5%	11.8%	93.8	39	25	35	32%	66%	18%	20%	23	68	22%	39%	0	0.76	-12.1	125	-$5
22 BOS	11	0	127	104	3.32	1.12	3.99	1.22	86	107	22.4	6%	20%	14%	6%	10.0%	93.0	41	20	39	27%	77%	12%	15%	23	85	9%	35%			10.2	102	$11
1st Half	6	0	70	50	2.69	1.11	4.29	1.34	69	102	21.8	8%	18%	10%	8%	9.0%	93.2	41	22	36	25%	80%	9%	12%	13	84	8%	38%			11.1	64	$12
2nd Half	5	0	57	54	4.11	1.12	3.65	1.08	109	111	23.1	4%	23%	19%	6%	11.2%	92.7	41	18	41	29%	72%	16%	18%	10	86	10%	30%			-1.0	148	$4
Proj	9	0	145	133	4.05	1.25	3.60	1.20	95	111	22.3	6%	22%	16%	7%	10.9%	93.2	40	22	38	30%	74%	15%	15%	26						-1.5	115	$5

Wainwright,Adam

Age: 41	Th: R	Role	SP	Health	D	LIMA Plan	A
Ht: 6' 7"	Wt: 230	Type	Con	PT/Exp	A	Rand Var	-2
				Consist	A	MM	3105

Self-disclosed a late Aug knee injury that disrupted delivery and caused 7.22 ERA, 10% K% across final six starts. While that inflated surface stats, H% luck also ran out and was partial reason why gap between ERA/xERA and WHIP/xWHIP closed. Career-lows in GB%, SwK are further warning signs that final season may not be the great send-off he's hoping for.

Yr Tm	W	Sv	IP	K	ERA	WHIP	xERA	xWHIP	vL+	vR+	BF/G	BB%	K%	K-BB%	xBB%	SwK	Vel	G	L	F	H%	S%	HR/F	xHR/F	GS	APC	DOM%	DIS%	Sv%	LI	RAR	BPX	R$
18 STL *	4	0	59	54	3.03	1.34	3.94	1.37	102	105	19.0	9%	22%	13%	10%	9.3%	89.3	49	18	33	32%	80%	13%	13%	8	92	25%	38%			8.2	94	$1
19 STL	14	0	172	153	4.19	1.43	4.48	1.38	116	94	24.0	9%	21%	12%	9%	8.0%	89.9	49	22	29	32%	74%	15%	15%	31	93	16%	39%			6.6	88	$6
20 STL	5	0	66	54	3.15	1.05	4.21	1.24	92	82	26.2	6%	21%	15%	6%	11.0%	89.3	43	22	34	26%	77%	14%	15%	10	93	40%	20%			10.5	112	$19
21 STL	17	0	206	174	3.05	1.06	3.85	1.23	91	79	25.9	6%	21%	15%	7%	8.5%	89.1	47	22	30	26%	75%	12%	11%	32	96	41%	28%			30.9	113	$29
22 STL	11	0	192	143	3.71	1.28	4.16	1.30	101	97	25.1	7%	18%	11%	7%	7.0%	88.5	43	24	33	31%	73%	8%	11%	32	98	28%	28%			6.1	81	$7
1st Half	6	0	97	81	3.26	1.27	3.79	1.25	97	106	24.9	7%	20%	14%	7%	7.1%	88.6	46	24	30	31%	77%	10%	11%	16	97	31%	13%			8.5	101	$10
2nd Half	5	0	95	62	4.17	1.29	4.54	1.34	104	89	25.3	7%	15%	9%	8%	6.8%	88.3	41	24	35	30%	68%	6%	10%	16	99	25%	44%			-2.3	61	$1
Proj	10	0	174	137	3.98	1.25	3.73	1.29	102	93	24.5	7%	19%	13%	8%	8.1%	88.9	45	23	33	30%	71%	11%	12%	29						-0.1	91	$6

Waldichuk,Ken

Age: 25	Th: L	Role	SP	Health	A	LIMA Plan	A+
Ht: 6' 4"	Wt: 220	Type		PT/Exp	D	Rand Var	0
				Consist	F	MM	3201

2-2, 4.93 ERA in 35 IP at OAK. Well-regarded prospect rode three plus pitches, highlighted by fastball, through NYY system before being dealt at deadline. High FB% could lead to HR issues, even with league average HR/F, but K rate was elite in minors and appears likely to translate. Still a flyer at this point, with potential to be mid-round selection by 2024.

Yr Tm	W	Sv	IP	K	ERA	WHIP	xERA	xWHIP	vL+	vR+	BF/G	BB%	K%	K-BB%	xBB%	SwK	Vel	G	L	F	H%	S%	HR/F	xHR/F	GS	APC	DOM%	DIS%	Sv%	LI	RAR	BPX	R$
18																																	
19																																	
20																																	
21 aa	4	0	80	93	4.91	1.39	4.85				21.1	12%	28%	16%							31%	70%									-6.4	77	-$4
22 OAK *	8	0	132	147	2.95	1.08	2.77	1.21	53	126	18.4	7%	23%	16%	8%	12.5%	94.1	35	21	43	29%	76%	12%	13%	7	84	29%	43%			16.6	138	$14
1st Half	6	0	65	79	1.56	0.91	1.37				18.8	8%	31%	22%							25%	85%	0%		0	0					19.4	167	$24
2nd Half	2	0	67	68	4.31	1.24	4.14	1.17	52	126	18.0	6%	24%	18%	8%	12.5%	94.1	35	21	43	32%	69%	12%	13%	7	84	29%	43%			-2.8	111	-$1
Proj	6	0	116	104	3.78	1.17	3.74	1.27	53	124	20.8	8%	23%	15%		12.5%	94.1	35	21	43	28%	71%	10%	12%	22						2.8	90	$5

Walker,Taijuan

Age: 30	Th: R	Role	SP	Health	D	LIMA Plan	B+
Ht: 6' 4"	Wt: 235	Type		PT/Exp	A	Rand Var	-1
				Consist	A	MM	3203

Results tailed off in 2nd half for second straight season, but this wasn't business as usual. GB% rose to best mark since 2017 and HR/F was better than average even after second-half spike, giving him skills to fall back on to offset lack of strikeouts. Still not a workhorse, but has shown improved durability in recent seasons, making double-digit R$ repeat likely.

Yr Tm	W	Sv	IP	K	ERA	WHIP	xERA	xWHIP	vL+	vR+	BF/G	BB%	K%	K-BB%	xBB%	SwK	Vel	G	L	F	H%	S%	HR/F	xHR/F	GS	APC	DOM%	DIS%	Sv%	LI	RAR	BPX	R$
18 ARI	0	0	13	9	3.46	1.54	4.72	1.45	132	73	18.7	9%	16%	7%	8%	6.7%	93.7	43	28	30	34%	79%	8%	18%	3	75	0%	67%			1.1	46	-$5
19 ARI	0	0	1	1	0.00	1.00	4.79			201	4.0	0%	25%	25%		13.3%	93.3	33	0	67	35%	0%	0%	9%	1	15	0%	100%			0.6	188	-$5
20 2 AL	4	0	53	50	2.70	1.16	4.65	1.33	120	68	20.5	8%	22%	14%	9%	8.1%	93.2	39	21	40	26%	85%	13%	15%	11	80	27%	36%			11.5	93	$14
21 NYM	7	0	159	146	4.47	1.18	4.40	1.31	89	98	21.8	8%	22%	14%	7%	10.1%	94.2	42	17	41	26%	67%	14%	15%	29	85	21%	28%	0	0.77	-4.0	93	$5
22 NYM	12	0	157	132	3.49	1.19	3.88	1.26	101	89	22.4	7%	20%	13%	8%	10.4%	93.5	46	20	34	29%	73%	10%	12%	29	86	21%	38%			9.3	100	$11
1st Half	7	0	79	61	2.86	1.14	3.74	1.28	95	80	22.6	7%	19%	12%	7%	10.5%	93.8	50	21	29	28%	76%	6%	9%	14	88	14%	36%			10.8	94	$13
2nd Half	5	0	79	71	4.12	1.25	4.01	1.24	106	98	22.2	7%	21%	14%	8%	10.3%	93.3	43	19	38	30%	71%	12%	14%	15	85	27%	40%			-1.5	106	$4
Proj	11	0	160	141	3.50	1.19	3.66	1.28	104	86	21.0	8%	22%	14%	8%	9.8%	93.5	43	20	37	28%	75%	12%	13%	30						9.2	97	$12

Wantz,Andrew

Age: 27	Th: R	Role	RP	Health	A	LIMA Plan	C+
Ht: 6' 4"	Wt: 235	Type	Pwr/xFB	PT/Exp	D	Rand Var	-5
				Consist	A	MM	2300

2-1, 3.22 ERA in 50 IP at LAA. Useful bullpen arm that has performed well against same-handed hitters in both stints at the major-league level, though that has been fueled by 21% H%. Once that normalizes, high FB% is likely to sink currently effective surface stats. Best-case scenario is serviceable middle-relief arm, which doesn't help in most fantasy formats.

Yr Tm	W	Sv	IP	K	ERA	WHIP	xERA	xWHIP	vL+	vR+	BF/G	BB%	K%	K-BB%	xBB%	SwK	Vel	G	L	F	H%	S%	HR/F	xHR/F	GS	APC	DOM%	DIS%	Sv%	LI	RAR	BPX	R$
18																																	
19 aa	0	0	48	46	9.72	2.12	9.66				18.2	12%	19%	7%							39%	59%									-30.9	-25	-$19
20																																	
21 LAA *	2	0	58	62	3.16	1.07	3.02	1.16	125	79	6.9	7%	27%	20%	7%	13.7%	93.3	30	16	54	28%	75%	14%	11%	0	23			0	0.92	7.9	129	$2
22 LAA *	3	0	68	65	3.00	1.07	3.21	1.30	104	86	5.1	10%	25%	15%	8%	13.6%	93.8	30	18	52	23%	81%	12%	10%	1	20	0%	0%	0	0.74	8.1	90	$3
1st Half	2	0	36	30	3.11	0.97	3.56	1.19	132	91	5.7	6%	22%	16%	8%	11.7%	93.6	28	17	56	22%	82%	17%	7%	1	21	0%	0%	0	0.52	3.8	91	$0
2nd Half	1	0	31	35	2.87	1.18	4.14	1.36	89	83	4.5	13%	28%	15%	9%	14.7%	94.0	31	19	50	25%	79%	8%	12%	0	19			0	0.85	4.2	73	-$3
Proj	2	0	58	58	3.96	1.30	4.20	1.35	117	96	6.5	10%	24%	14%	8%	13.5%	93.8	30	18	52	27%	77%	14%	10%	0						0.1	72	-$2

Watkins,Spenser

Age: 30	Th: R	Role	RP	Health	B	LIMA Plan	C
Ht: 6' 2"	Wt: 185	Type	Con	PT/Exp	C	Rand Var	-1
				Consist	D	MM	1000

Got first extended shot in majors, serving primarily as a starter. GB% and BB% give solid foundation to work from—however, he doesn't miss any bats, which allows hitters from both sides of the plate to excel and make hard contact against him. Ultimately, DOM% and DIS% paint an accurate picture of the skills and leave little hope of future relevance.

Yr Tm	W	Sv	IP	K	ERA	WHIP	xERA	xWHIP	vL+	vR+	BF/G	BB%	K%	K-BB%	xBB%	SwK	Vel	G	L	F	H%	S%	HR/F	xHR/F	GS	APC	DOM%	DIS%	Sv%	LI	RAR	BPX	R$
18 a/a	2	0	26	18	6.71	1.68	5.93				23.6	11%	15%	4%							33%	61%									-8.3	27	-$8
19 a/a	8	0	121	80	9.92	1.98	9.16				24.3	8%	14%	6%							38%	52%									-81.0	-24	-$35
20																																	
21 BAL *	3	0	92	56	6.64	1.54	6.61	1.44	120	141	16.7	8%	14%	6%	9%	7.7%	90.8	34	26	40	30%	62%	18%	17%	10	60	10%	70%	0	0.58	-26.9	2	-$16
22 BAL	5	0	105	63	4.70	1.41	4.81	1.37	110	105	20.0	7%	14%	7%	7%	8.8%	91.4	42	23	36	32%	68%	9%	11%	20	71	15%	50%	0	0.72	-9.5	53	-$7
1st Half	1	0	41	23	4.61	1.49	5.45	1.52	98	125	18.2	9%	13%	3%	8%	9.1%	91.9	38	21	41	30%	71%	9%	13%	10	67	10%	60%			-3.2	7	-$12
2nd Half	4	0	64	40	4.76	1.37	4.41	1.28	117	90	21.3	5%	14%	10%	6%	8.5%	91.1	44	24	32	33%	66%	8%	9%	10	75	20%	40%	0	0.69	-6.2	81	-$6
Proj	3	0	58	36	4.90	1.41	4.45	1.41	112	113	19.2	7%	15%	7%	8%	8.5%	91.3	40	24	37	30%	69%	13%	12%	12						-6.7	45	-$6

Webb,Logan

Age: 26	Th: R	Role	SP	Health	D	LIMA Plan	C+
Ht: 6' 1"	Wt: 220	Type	/xGB	PT/Exp	A	Rand Var	-2
				Consist	C	MM	5205

Showed that formula of breakout 2021 season was repeatable, as both BB% and GB% remained elite and kept his floor extremely high, though step back in K%, SwK suggests he won't have ceiling of other elite starters. Also seems to have put past shoulder issues behind him, and is now a legitimate candidate to reach 200 IP with mid-3.00 ERA.

Yr Tm	W	Sv	IP	K	ERA	WHIP	xERA	xWHIP	vL+	vR+	BF/G	BB%	K%	K-BB%	xBB%	SwK	Vel	G	L	F	H%	S%	HR/F	xHR/F	GS	APC	DOM%	DIS%	Sv%	LI	RAR	BPX	R$
18 aa	1	0	32	22	4.38	1.40	4.61				22.7	8%	16%	8%							31%	71%									-0.9	58	-$5
19 SF *	3	0	89	82	3.82	1.45	4.65	1.34	92	123	22.3	7%	22%	14%	9%	9.8%	92.9	49	28	23	36%	75%	18%	20%	8	85	13%	38%			7.5	97	-$1
20 SF	3	0	54	46	5.47	1.56	4.49	1.44	109	110	18.9	10%	19%	9%	10%	9.3%	92.7	52	26	22	35%	64%	11%	13%	11	77	9%	55%	0	0.82	-6.8	68	-$7
21 SF	11	0	148	158	3.03	1.11	2.81	1.12	94	75	22.1	6%	27%	20%	7%	12.8%	92.9	61	21	19	31%	74%	13%	12%	26	82	46%	23%	0	0.79	22.5	167	$19
22 SF	15	0	192	163	2.90	1.16	3.31	1.22	105	77	24.6	6%	21%	15%	6%	10.9%	91.9	57	20	24	30%	76%	8%	12%	32	94	41%	13%			25.3	122	$20
1st Half	7	0	98	86	3.13	1.13	3.20	1.19	116	72	24.8	6%	22%	16%	6%	11.4%	92.1	57	19	24	30%	73%	9%	12%	16	95	44%	6%			10.1	133	$17
2nd Half	8	0	95	77	2.66	1.19	3.42	1.26	97	84	24.4	7%	20%	13%	6%	10.4%	91.7	56	20	23	30%	79%	8%	12%	16	93	38%	19%			15.3	110	$19
Proj	13	0	189	165	3.44	1.22	3.19	1.26	98	88	21.6	7%	22%	14%	8%	10.5%	92.3	55	22	23	30%	73%	11%	13%	35						12.3	112	$14

DANIEL MARCUS

Wells,Tyler

Age: 28	Th: R	Role: SP	Health: D	LIMA Plan: A	
Ht: 6' 8"	Wt: 255	Type: Con/xFB	PT/Exp: C	Rand Var: -2	
			Consist: A	MM: 2103	

Shifted back to SP, then shoulder, oblique injuries cost him two months. Decent control pitcher supported by marginal skills otherwise, his 1st half success was driven by fortunate H% and fewer balls going yard. The correction came calling by summer, though 2nd half SwK rebound offers sliver of hope of a higher ceiling. Probably better suited to relief role.

Yr Tm	W	Sv	IP	K	ERA	WHIP	xERA	xWHIP	vL+	vR+	BF/G	BB%	K%	K-BB%	xBB%	SwK	Vel	G	L	F	H%	S%	HR/F	xHR/F	GS	APC	DOM%	DIS%	Sv%	LI	RAR	BPX	R$
18 aa	2	1	34	31	1.97	1.21	2.69				23.0	10%	22%	12%							29%	84%									9.2	112	$1
19																																	
20																																	
21 BAL	2	4	57	65	4.11	0.91	4.08	1.07	65	90	5.1	5%	29%	24%	5%	14.4%	95.2	21	22	57	24%	60%	11%	12%	0	20			57	0.85	1.1	145	$4
22 BAL	7	0	104	76	4.25	1.14	4.56	1.29	81	111	18.4	7%	18%	11%	6%	11.9%	93.6	37	17	47	25%	68%	11%	11%	23	72	4%	43%			-3.6	75	$2
1st Half	7	0	76	50	3.09	1.00	4.54	1.28	82	92	18.8	6%	17%	11%	6%	11.1%	93.8	36	16	48	23%	75%	8%	9%	16	74	6%	38%			8.2	73	$14
2nd Half	0	0	28	26	7.39	1.50	4.58	1.33	78	155	17.6	9%	21%	12%	8%	14.2%	93.1	38	19	43	31%	54%	19%	17%	7	68	0%	57%			-11.8	79	-$16
Proj	**6**	**0**	**138**	**112**	**4.50**	**1.21**	**4.13**	**1.33**	**75**	**118**	**21.1**	**8%**	**20%**	**12%**	**6%**	**12.9%**	**93.8**	**34**	**19**	**47**	**27%**	**67%**	**11%**	**13%**	**23**						**-9.1**	**71**	**$1**

Wentz,Joey

Age: 25	Th: L	Role: SP	Health: A	LIMA Plan: A	
Ht: 6' 5"	Wt: 210	Type: /FB	PT/Exp: D	Rand Var: -3	
			Consist: D	MM: 2101	

2-2, 3.03 ERA in 33 IP at DET. Lost 2020 season to Tommy John surgery, then shoulder issue, to finally make big-league debut. Lack of K%, high BB% will put pressure on ability to limit hard contact, particularly with above-average FB% (MLB xERA was 4.50). Had some prospect pedigree, so don't dismiss, but has narrow path to success.

Yr Tm	W	Sv	IP	K	ERA	WHIP	xERA	xWHIP	vL+	vR+	BF/G	BB%	K%	K-BB%	xBB%	SwK	Vel	G	L	F	H%	S%	HR/F	xHR/F	GS	APC	DOM%	DIS%	Sv%	LI	RAR	BPX	R$
18																																	
19 aa	7	0	130	114	6.02	1.46	5.15				22.3	9%	20%	11%							31%	61%									-24.2	53	-$8
20																																	
21 aa	0	0	54	46	4.48	1.50	4.73				18.0	14%	20%	6%							27%	74%									-1.4	47	-$7
22 DET *	4	0	82	69	3.15	1.17	3.02	1.38	76	90	17.2	10%	20%	10%	10%	8.8%	92.4	37	20	43	26%	76%	5%	9%	7	79	14%	29%			8.3	87	$3
1st Half	0	0	35	32	5.29	1.30	3.86	1.31	24	128	16.0	9%	23%	14%	11%	8.6%	93.0	45	27	27	30%	59%	0%	17%	2	64	0%	50%			-5.7	86	-$11
2nd Half	4	0	49	37	1.48	1.02	2.14	1.41	84	78	18.9	10%	19%	9%	10%	8.9%	92.2	34	18	48	21%	91%	6%	7%	5	85	20%	20%			15.1	88	$10
Proj	**5**	**0**	**116**	**97**	**4.04**	**1.27**	**4.27**	**1.42**	**128**	**106**	**21.1**	**10%**	**21%**	**10%**	**10%**	**8.9%**	**92.2**	**34**	**18**	**48**	**27%**	**71%**	**10%**	**8%**	**22**						**-1.1**	**50**	**$1**

Wesneski,Hayden

Age: 25	Th: R	Role: SP	Health: A	LIMA Plan: A	
Ht: 6' 3"	Wt: 210	Type: Con	PT/Exp: D	Rand Var: -1	
			Consist: D	MM: 4103	

3-2, 2.18 ERA in 33 IP at CHC. Dealt from NYY at deadline and was promoted to majors shortly thereafter. Despite mediocre velocity, has gotten strikeouts at every level, and SwK backed K% in first MLB test. BB%, GB% should also help limit mistakes, paving path to becoming mid-rotation starter. Should get chance to show what he has in 2023.

Yr Tm	W	Sv	IP	K	ERA	WHIP	xERA	xWHIP	vL+	vR+	BF/G	BB%	K%	K-BB%	xBB%	SwK	Vel	G	L	F	H%	S%	HR/F	xHR/F	GS	APC	DOM%	DIS%	Sv%	LI	RAR	BPX	R$
18																																	
19																																	
20																																	
21 a/a	10	0	94	88	4.71	1.36	4.76				21.8	7%	22%	15%							33%	68%									-5.1	89	$0
22 CHC *	9	0	144	120	3.46	1.13	3.06	1.11	57	96	19.0	5%	25%	20%	6%	12.3%	92.7	47	11	41	28%	71%	8%	5%	4	83	75%	25%	0	0.73	9.0	104	$10
1st Half	3	0	70	52	4.07	1.20	3.46				18.8	7%	18%	10%							28%	67%	0%		0	0					-0.8	83	-$1
2nd Half	6	0	74	67	2.89	1.05	2.68	1.19	57	96	19.1	6%	23%	16%	6%	12.3%	92.7	47	11	41	27%	75%	8%	5%	4	83	75%	25%	0	0.73	9.8	126	$15
Proj	**7**	**0**	**131**	**107**	**3.76**	**1.16**	**3.50**	**1.26**	**72**	**120**	**21.4**	**7%**	**21%**	**14%**		**12.3%**	**92.7**	**45**	**21**	**34**	**28%**	**70%**	**11%**	**8%**	**24**						**3.4**	**100**	**$7**

Wheeler,Zack

Age: 33	Th: R	Role: SP	Health: C	LIMA Plan: C+	
Ht: 6' 4"	Wt: 195	Type:	PT/Exp: A	Rand Var: -1	
			Consist: A	MM: 5305	

Shoulder issue delayed start of season, forearm tendinitis cost him month in Aug/Sep, leading to diminished velocity. Didn't hamper results in 1st half, with SwK, K% matching career-best marks of 2021, and even when whiffs declined in 2nd half, xERA didn't suffer, showing safety in his floor. Hope for clean bill of health in spring; with it, he's a good investment.

Yr Tm	W	Sv	IP	K	ERA	WHIP	xERA	xWHIP	vL+	vR+	BF/G	BB%	K%	K-BB%	xBB%	SwK	Vel	G	L	F	H%	S%	HR/F	xHR/F	GS	APC	DOM%	DIS%	Sv%	LI	RAR	BPX	R$
18 NYM	12	0	182	179	3.31	1.12	3.74	1.23	93	77	25.7	7%	24%	17%	6%	11.3%	95.9	44	20	35	29%	72%	8%	9%	29	99	45%	28%			18.9	124	$19
19 NYM	11	0	195	195	3.96	1.26	4.22	1.23	102	85	26.7	6%	24%	18%	6%	11.0%	96.7	43	21	35	33%	71%	11%	12%	31	102	45%	19%			13.1	131	$13
20 PHI	4	0	71	53	2.92	1.17	3.67	1.26	90	90	26.2	6%	18%	13%	6%	11.1%	96.9	56	25	19	30%	75%	8%	9%	11	98	27%	18%			13.5	113	$16
21 PHI	14	0	213	247	2.78	1.01	2.98	1.06	82	77	26.5	5%	29%	24%	5%	12.9%	97.1	50	23	28	30%	75%	11%	11%	32	100	63%	6%			39.0	179	$35
22 PHI	12	0	153	163	2.82	1.04	3.11	1.09	88	90	23.3	6%	27%	21%	6%	11.8%	95.8	46	21	33	29%	76%	10%	10%	26	91	38%	8%			21.6	157	$20
1st Half	7	0	88	99	2.66	1.07	3.07	1.07	88	90	23.7	6%	28%	22%	6%	12.7%	95.8	45	22	33	32%	76%	7%	7%	15	91	40%	7%			14.2	166	$22
2nd Half	5	0	65	64	3.05	1.00	3.18	1.11	86	89	22.9	6%	25%	20%	6%	10.5%	95.9	47	20	33	26%	75%	14%	13%	11	90	36%	9%			7.4	146	$12
Proj	**13**	**0**	**181**	**180**	**3.01**	**1.08**	**2.98**	**1.13**	**89**	**87**	**24.1**	**6%**	**25%**	**20%**	**6%**	**11.5%**	**96.3**	**48**	**22**	**30**	**30%**	**75%**	**10%**	**11%**	**29**						**21.5**	**145**	**$22**

White,Mitch

Age: 28	Th: R	Role: RP	Health: B	LIMA Plan: C+	
Ht: 6' 3"	Wt: 210	Type: Con	PT/Exp: D	Rand Var: +1	
			Consist: D	MM: 2101	

1-7, 5.45 ERA in 99 IP at LA/TOR. Finally freed from LA rotation purgatory to get more consistent shot with TOR in final months of season. Results didn't follow, as already middling skills crumbled, encapsulated by DIS%. Strand rate, 4.95 MLB xERA in 2nd half show there was some bad luck, but without more strikeouts, he's just not a viable starter.

Yr Tm	W	Sv	IP	K	ERA	WHIP	xERA	xWHIP	vL+	vR+	BF/G	BB%	K%	K-BB%	xBB%	SwK	Vel	G	L	F	H%	S%	HR/F	xHR/F	GS	APC	DOM%	DIS%	Sv%	LI	RAR	BPX	R$
18 aa	6	0	106	74	4.84	1.47	5.12				20.7	7%	16%	9%							34%	69%									-9.0	62	-$6
19 a/a	4	0	95	87	6.09	1.45	5.55				17.7	7%	21%	14%							33%	61%									-18.6	60	-$7
20 LA	1	0	3	2	0.00	0.67	5.96		23	53	5.5	9%	18%	9%		11.4%	93.6	13	13	75	13%	100%	0%	0%	0	22			0	0.03	1.6	20	-$3
21 LA *	2	0	79	80	2.90	1.24	3.54	1.26	94	79	10.3	9%	25%	16%	6%	10.8%	94.5	48	18	34	31%	80%	14%	9%	4	36	0%	25%	0	0.69	13.3	107	$3
22 2 TM *	3	0	117	89	5.38	1.39	4.51	1.35	106	110	17.6	8%	18%	10%	8%	8.6%	93.8	43	21	36	32%	61%	8%	8%	18	69	6%	44%	0	0.69	-20.4	71	-$10
1st Half	3	0	48	41	2.84	0.98	2.32	1.23	92	95	13.9	7%	22%	15%	10%	9.5%	93.6	41	21	38	24%	74%	11%	10%	6	52	17%	33%	0	0.57	6.6	114	$5
2nd Half	0	0	70	49	7.11	1.67	6.01	1.39	112	117	20.8	8%	15%	8%	6%	8.2%	93.9	44	21	35	36%	56%	6%	6%	12	82	0%	50%	0	0.78	-27.0	46	-$28
Proj	**3**	**0**	**102**	**81**	**4.95**	**1.43**	**4.10**	**1.37**	**110**	**110**	**16.4**	**9%**	**19%**	**10%**	**8%**	**9.1%**	**93.9**	**44**	**20**	**36**	**32%**	**67%**	**12%**	**8%**	**17**						**-12.2**	**68**	**-$7**

White,Owen

Age: 23	Th: R	Role: RP	Health: A	LIMA Plan: B	
Ht: 6' 3"	Wt: 170	Type:	PT/Exp: F	Rand Var: -1	
			Consist: F	MM: 4300	

Has flown under the radar since being selected 55th overall by TEX in 2018 draft. Did not pitch in affiliated ball until 2021 due to bevy of injuries and lost 2020 season. Still has to prove durability after throwing only 79 IP in 2022, only 22 at AA. With time and patience, minor-league skills and scouting reports suggest he has tools to succeed in majors.

Yr Tm	W	Sv	IP	K	ERA	WHIP	xERA	xWHIP	vL+	vR+	BF/G	BB%	K%	K-BB%	xBB%	SwK	Vel	G	L	F	H%	S%	HR/F	xHR/F	GS	APC	DOM%	DIS%	Sv%	LI	RAR	BPX	R$
18																																	
19																																	
20																																	
21																																	
22 aa	3	0	23	19	2.15	1.02	2.30				22.3	5%	22%	18%							28%	79%									5.2	150	-$1
1st Half	2	0	12	10	1.36	0.71	0.87				21.6	8%	25%	18%							18%	87%									3.9	144	-$3
2nd Half	1	0	11	9	3.02	1.35	3.89				23.0	4%	20%	16%							38%	75%									1.3	165	-$8
Proj	**2**	**0**	**29**	**28**	**4.03**	**1.24**	**3.46**	**1.24**			**16.8**	**8%**	**24%**	**16%**				**44**	**22**	**34**	**30%**	**72%**	**15%**	**11%**	**5**						**-0.2**	**113**	**-$3**

Whitlock,Garrett

Age: 27	Th: R	Role: SP	Health: D	LIMA Plan: A	
Ht: 6' 5"	Wt: 225	Type:	PT/Exp: B	Rand Var: 0	
			Consist: A	MM: 4201	

Starter, closer, multi-inning reliever—he did it all in 2022. Looks to be SP in 2023, a role in which he posted just a 23 K% in 2022. Would benefit from a return to GB% lean from 2021, though he did have significant IFFB% to offset HR risk, and has skills to succeed with elite BB%, xBB%. Only nine career GS makes him a lottery ticket, but one worth scratching.

Yr Tm	W	Sv	IP	K	ERA	WHIP	xERA	xWHIP	vL+	vR+	BF/G	BB%	K%	K-BB%	xBB%	SwK	Vel	G	L	F	H%	S%	HR/F	xHR/F	GS	APC	DOM%	DIS%	Sv%	LI	RAR	BPX	R$
18																																	
19 aa	3	0	71	49	4.12	1.53	5.16				22.1	6%	16%	9%							35%	74%									3.4	66	-$4
20																																	
21 BOS	8	2	73	81	1.96	1.10	3.30	1.10	114	69	6.5	6%	27%	21%	5%	13.2%	96.0	50	20	30	32%	87%	10%	7%	0	25			40	1.20	20.8	165	$12
22 BOS	4	6	78	82	3.45	1.02	3.37	1.07	80	98	10.0	5%	26%	22%	5%	14.2%	95.3	41	20	39	28%	71%	12%	10%	9	38	11%	33%	75	0.95	5.0	157	$7
1st Half	2	1	49	49	3.51	1.13	3.61	1.13	77	107	15.3	6%	25%	19%	6%	12.8%	95.1	43	18	39	30%	73%	11%	12%	9	59	11%	33%	50	0.88	2.7	142	$1
2nd Half	2	5	30	33	3.34	0.84	2.99	0.97	87	83	6.2	4%	29%	26%	4%	16.7%	95.6	37	24	39	25%	67%	14%	7%	0	22			83	1.00	2.3	180	$5
Proj	**7**	**0**	**116**	**111**	**3.70**	**1.17**	**3.37**	**1.18**	**100**	**99**	**20.1**	**6%**	**24%**	**18%**	**5%**	**14.6%**	**95.6**	**42**	**21**	**37**	**30%**	**72%**	**11%**	**8%**	**23**						**3.9**	**124**	**$6**

DANIEL MARCUS

Wick,Rowan

Age: 30	Th: R	Role	RP	Health	F	LIMA Plan	B
Ht: 6' 3"	Wt: 234	Type	Pwr	PT/Exp	C	Rand Var	+3
				Consist	A	MM	3310

It's not often that you see a near 80% strand rate in tandem with a 4.00-plus ERA. Blame his 39% hit rate, in part. But also note his extreme gopheritis, especially in the 2nd half, declining SwK and K%, and control issues that really aren't going away. He was equally poor against RHB and LHB. The biggest head-scratcher is the fact that he got 9 saves.

Yr Tm	W	Sv	IP	K	ERA	WHIP	xERA	xWHIP	vL+	vR+	BF/G	BB%	K%	K-BB%	xBB%	SwK	Vel	G	L	F	H%	S%	HR/F	xHR/F	GS	APC	DOM%	DIS%	Sv%	LI	RAR	BPX	R$
18 SD *	4	14	65	59	3.38	1.38	3.61	1.15	99	158	4.6	12%	22%	10%	4%	11.3%	94.6	39	14	46	30%	76%	8%	11%	0	13			88	0.76	6.1	90	$6
19 CHC *	3	8	68	69	2.44	1.18	2.72	1.41	84	59	4.7	10%	25%	16%	8%	12.1%	95.9	54	15	31	29%	81%	0%	13%	0	19			100	0.98	17.4	116	$9
20 CHC	0	4	17	20	3.12	1.38	4.10	1.22	103	92	3.9	8%	27%	19%	7%	11.5%	95.0	38	27	35	37%	78%	6%	14%	0	16			100	1.23	2.9	134	$1
21 CHC	0	5	23	29	4.30	1.35	4.26	1.41	67	91	4.5	14%	29%	15%	10%	11.8%	94.7	35	27	38	31%	67%	5%	8%	0	18			63	1.14	-0.1	76	-$3
22 CHC	4	9	64	69	4.22	1.69	4.04	1.32	131	110	4.6	10%	23%	14%	7%	10.6%	94.9	44	26	30	39%	79%	16%	19%	0	18			64	1.00	-2.0	95	-$2
1st Half	1	4	35	35	4.63	1.69	4.32	1.38	125	109	4.9	10%	22%	11%	8%	11.2%	94.7	44	26	30	38%	73%	9%	13%	0	19			80	1.03	-2.8	73	-$9
2nd Half	3	5	29	34	3.72	1.69	3.70	1.25	138	111	4.3	9%	26%	17%	6%	9.9%	95.0	45	25	30	39%	86%	24%	27%	0	17			56	0.96	0.9	124	-$2
Proj	4	2	58	60	4.14	1.53	3.67	1.34	125	99	4.5	10%	24%	14%	7%	10.7%	95.1	46	23	30	35%	76%	14%	19%	0						-1.2	93	-$3

Williams,Devin

Age: 28	Th: R	Role	RP	Health	B	LIMA Plan	B
Ht: 6' 2"	Wt: 200	Type	Pwr	PT/Exp	C	Rand Var	-4
				Consist	C	MM	5531

Trusted back-end bullpen arm that got promotion to full-time closer at trade deadline. Largely performed as would be expected, piling up Ks while generating high GB%—a formula often found in top-end closers. SwK remained elite, even with velocity loss, and also drastically cut HR/F, xHR/F, clearing path to be one of most valuable relievers in the game.

Yr Tm	W	Sv	IP	K	ERA	WHIP	xERA	xWHIP	vL+	vR+	BF/G	BB%	K%	K-BB%	xBB%	SwK	Vel	G	L	F	H%	S%	HR/F	xHR/F	GS	APC	DOM%	DIS%	Sv%	LI	RAR	BPX	R$
18																																	
19 MIL *	7	4	73	83	3.13	1.41	3.77	1.40	107	129	6.6	13%	27%	14%	9%	10.7%	96.2	41	23	36	32%	80%	13%	12%	0	21			100	0.32	12.4	99	$6
20 MIL	4	0	27	53	0.33	0.63	1.40	0.80	48	43	4.5	9%	54%	44%	9%	22.3%	96.5	61	11	28	23%	100%	10%	17%	0	20			0	1.16	13.7	312	$21
21 MIL	8	3	54	87	2.50	1.19	2.99	1.16	93	66	3.9	12%	38%	26%	8%	19.0%	95.4	45	18	37	32%	83%	13%	10%	0	17			50	1.36	11.8	173	$8
22 MIL	6	15	61	96	1.93	1.01	2.34	1.12	89	51	3.7	13%	40%	28%	8%	18.7%	94.0	51	20	29	28%	81%	6%	5%	0	16			88	1.58	15.3	182	$16
1st Half	2	5	32	54	1.99	1.07	2.30	1.15	82	54	3.7	14%	42%	28%	8%	19.5%	94.4	45	29	25	31%	79%	0%	1%	0	17			100	1.30	7.7	178	$8
2nd Half	4	10	29	42	1.86	0.93	2.38	1.10	95	48	3.7	11%	38%	27%	9%	17.8%	93.4	57	11	32	25%	84%	11%	8%	0	16			83	1.91	7.5	187	$15
Proj	5	32	65	95	2.29	1.12	2.54	1.19	104	60	4.1	13%	37%	24%	8%	18.6%	94.1	51	18	31	29%	82%	10%	6%	0						13.5	159	$21

Williams,Trevor

Age: 31	Th: R	Role	RP	Health	D	LIMA Plan	A+
Ht: 6' 3"	Wt: 235	Type		PT/Exp	C	Rand Var	-3
				Consist	A	MM	3201

Ongoing transition to swing role as low-leverage reliever and spot starter once again helped him post better ERA, WHIP, but there was no significant change in underlying skill. HR/F, xHR/F improved, but rate of HR increased slightly due to FB% hike. Useful pitcher for big-league clubs, but without realistic path to wins or saves, value in our game is very limited.

Yr Tm	W	Sv	IP	K	ERA	WHIP	xERA	xWHIP	vL+	vR+	BF/G	BB%	K%	K-BB%	xBB%	SwK	Vel	G	L	F	H%	S%	HR/F	xHR/F	GS	APC	DOM%	DIS%	Sv%	LI	RAR	BPX	R$
18 PIT	14	0	171	126	3.11	1.18	4.51	1.37	87	95	22.6	8%	18%	10%	8%	8.4%	90.5	41	22	37	27%	76%	8%	10%	31	88	16%	32%			21.9	69	$17
19 PIT	7	0	146	113	5.38	1.41	5.26	1.38	125	104	24.5	7%	18%	11%	7%	10.8%	91.3	37	23	40	31%	66%	15%	15%	26	90	19%	31%			-15.6	73	-$5
20 PIT	2	0	55	49	6.18	1.57	4.99	1.37	103	148	22.9	8%	19%	11%	9%	10.9%	91.3	45	20	35	32%	68%	24%	16%	11	92	9%	55%			-11.8	84	-$12
21 2 NL *	6	0	110	102	3.85	1.38	4.60	1.27	109	111	17.1	7%	22%	15%	6%	10.7%	91.1	46	23	31	34%	75%	13%	13%	15	67	20%	40%	0	0.61	5.6	92	$1
22 NYM	3	1	90	84	3.21	1.23	3.99	1.19	126	87	12.4	6%	23%	16%	8%	11.0%	90.9	36	21	42	31%	80%	11%	11%	9	47	11%	56%	50	0.67	8.4	114	$3
1st Half	1	0	46	42	4.34	1.34	4.27	1.25	122	102	13.1	7%	21%	14%	8%	11.5%	90.7	37	21	42	30%	75%	16%	13%	7	51	0%	57%	0	0.81	-2.1	98	-$7
2nd Half	2	1	44	42	2.05	1.11	3.71	1.12	130	73	11.7	5%	24%	19%	7%	10.4%	91.0	36	21	43	31%	85%	6%	10%	2	43	50%	50%	100	0.54	10.4	131	$5
Proj	4	0	87	78	3.99	1.32	3.81	1.25	114	100	15.3	7%	22%	15%	8%	10.7%	91.0	40	22	39	31%	75%	13%	13%	10						-0.2	102	-$1

Wilson,Bryse

Age: 25	Th: R	Role	SP	Health	B	LIMA Plan	B
Ht: 6' 2"	Wt: 225	Type	Con	PT/Exp	C	Rand Var	0
				Consist	B	MM	2101

3-9, 5.52 ERA in 116 IP at PIT. Previously well-regarded prospect has struggled to put skills together at highest level, and there were few positives to be found in largest MLB sample yet. HR remains biggest problem, and even increased GB% couldn't offset bloated HR/F. Until that's corrected, or he finds a way to generate more whiffs, he's safe to ignore.

Yr Tm	W	Sv	IP	K	ERA	WHIP	xERA	xWHIP	vL+	vR+	BF/G	BB%	K%	K-BB%	xBB%	SwK	Vel	G	L	F	H%	S%	HR/F	xHR/F	GS	APC	DOM%	DIS%	Sv%	LI	RAR	BPX	R$
18 ATL *	7	0	106	107	5.35	1.44	4.73	1.85	118	124	19.7	8%	24%	16%	9%	15.6%	95.0	29	48	24	36%	63%	0%	14%	1	45	0%	0%	0	0.35	-15.7	107	-$6
19 ATL *	11	0	141	116	4.77	1.44	5.14	1.57	149	130	22.2	6%	19%	13%	6%	9.0%	94.7	31	26	43	35%	69%	18%	17%	4	59	0%	50%	0	0.58	-4.6	79	$0
20 ATL	1	1	16	15	4.02	1.72	5.42	1.53	139	99	12.2	12%	21%	8%	8%	9.3%	94.0	42	23	35	35%	80%	12%	24%	2	52	50%	50%	100	0.26	0.8	40	-$5
21 2 NL *	8	0	130	80	5.33	1.51	6.07	1.40	116	113	21.7	7%	14%	7%	6%	9.2%	93.0	37	25	38	32%	69%	16%	17%	16	71	6%	63%			-17.1	24	-$10
22 PIT *	8	0	153	106	4.90	1.34	5.03	1.32	128	108	20.5	6%	16%	9%	7%	8.2%	92.4	43	22	35	30%	68%	15%	13%	20	73	5%	65%	0	0.83	-17.5	56	-$5
1st Half	5	0	72	54	5.54	1.48	5.70	1.31	149	118	20.6	7%	17%	10%	8%	8.6%	92.9	42	25	33	33%	66%	16%	11%	7	71	0%	86%	0	0.91	-13.9	50	-$12
2nd Half	3	0	81	52	4.33	1.21	4.44	1.27	116	101	20.4	5%	15%	10%	6%	8.0%	92.0	44	20	36	28%	70%	14%	14%	13	74	8%	54%	0	0.77	-3.7	64	-$1
Proj	5	0	102	75	4.76	1.39	4.01	1.30	124	107	21.0	6%	18%	11%	7%	8.4%	92.5	42	23	36	32%	70%	14%	13%	20						-9.9	84	-$5

Wilson,Steven

Age: 28	Th: R	Role	RP	Health	B	LIMA Plan	A
Ht: 6' 3"	Wt: 185	Type	Pwr/xFB	PT/Exp	D	Rand Var	-5
				Consist	F	MM	1300

Made MLB debut at 27, with development slowed by Tommy John surgery in final year of college. Late June hamstring injury seemed to crush strong skills start, but never saw correction in results as indicated by gap between xERA/ERA, xWHIP/WHIP. Strong fastball/slider combo is classic relief profile, and he could stick in middle innings once settled in.

Yr Tm	W	Sv	IP	K	ERA	WHIP	xERA	xWHIP	vL+	vR+	BF/G	BB%	K%	K-BB%	xBB%	SwK	Vel	G	L	F	H%	S%	HR/F	xHR/F	GS	APC	DOM%	DIS%	Sv%	LI	RAR	BPX	R$
18																																	
19 aaa	1	0	35	34	4.24	1.42	4.02				5.9	14%	23%	9%							27%	73%									1.1	67	-$4
20																																	
21 aaa	4	0	40	49	3.09	0.91	2.21				5.3	9%	33%	23%							22%	73%									5.8	139	$3
22 SD	4	1	53	53	3.06	1.06	4.42	1.28	80	92	4.3	9%	25%	15%	8%	13.2%	95.1	24	18	58	23%	78%	9%	6%	1	17	0%	0%	33	0.89	6.0	80	$3
1st Half	4	1	27	29	3.62	0.95	4.03	1.19	63	104	4.1	8%	27%	19%	8%	15.3%	95.4	24	18	58	20%	71%	13%	7%	0	17			33	1.11	1.2	104	$1
2nd Half	0	0	26	24	2.45	1.17	4.85	1.36	99	82	4.5	10%	22%	12%	8%	11.1%	94.8	23	19	59	26%	82%	5%	4%	1	18	0%	0%	0	0.65	4.8	53	-$5
Proj	3	0	58	59	3.79	1.26	4.29	1.35	95	97	4.8	11%	25%	14%	8%	12.7%	95.0	23	18	58	28%	73%	8%	6%	0						1.3	67	-$1

Winckowski,Josh

Age: 25	Th: R	Role	SP	Health	A	LIMA Plan	C
Ht: 6' 4"	Wt: 202	Type	Con/GB	PT/Exp	D	Rand Var	0
				Consist	A	MM	1000

5-7, 5.89 ERA in 70 IP at BOS. First taste of majors began with significant success, and drew some attention as a result. While BB%, GB% were bankable skills in minors, found it harder to fill zone against big-league hitters without ability to generate whiffs—leading to 2nd half crash. Gained velocity in recent years, but not enough to portend MLB success.

Yr Tm	W	Sv	IP	K	ERA	WHIP	xERA	xWHIP	vL+	vR+	BF/G	BB%	K%	K-BB%	xBB%	SwK	Vel	G	L	F	H%	S%	HR/F	xHR/F	GS	APC	DOM%	DIS%	Sv%	LI	RAR	BPX	R$
18																																	
19																																	
20																																	
21 a/a	9	0	117	87	4.69	1.38	4.58				20.5	7%	18%	11%							33%	67%									-6.2	75	-$2
22 BOS *	7	0	132	94	4.99	1.44	4.83	1.45	122	120	20.2	9%	14%	5%	8%	7.2%	94.0	52	18	30	32%	66%	14%	13%	14	80	0%	57%	0	0.70	-16.8	60	-$8
1st Half	5	0	70	54	3.32	1.13	2.94	1.21	97	102	19.8	5%	19%	14%	7%	8.4%	94.1	56	18	26	30%	70%	5%	8%	5	81	0%	20%			5.6	126	$7
2nd Half	2	0	65	40	6.63	1.73	6.60	1.52	133	131	21.0	10%	14%	4%	9%	6.6%	93.9	50	18	32	33%	64%	18%	15%	9	79	0%	78%	0	0.68	-21.2	11	-$23
Proj	3	0	58	38	4.64	1.45	4.29	1.45	106	104	21.5	9%	15%	7%	8%	7.3%	94.0	50	18	31	31%	70%	11%	12%	12						-4.8	48	-$6

Winder,Josh

Age: 26	Th: R	Role	RP	Health	C	LIMA Plan	C
Ht: 6' 5"	Wt: 210	Type	Con/xFB	PT/Exp	D	Rand Var	0
				Consist	C	MM	1000

4-6, 4.70 ERA in 67 IP at MIN. Contact-heavy pitcher saw his K% shrivel and HR/F balloon with each step he took up organizational ladder. First sample in majors followed same pattern, and heavy FB% lean creates further risk of him being sunk by long ball. Likely innings filler at best, with shift to long or middle relief also a potential outcome.

Yr Tm	W	Sv	IP	K	ERA	WHIP	xERA	xWHIP	vL+	vR+	BF/G	BB%	K%	K-BB%	xBB%	SwK	Vel	G	L	F	H%	S%	HR/F	xHR/F	GS	APC	DOM%	DIS%	Sv%	LI	RAR	BPX	R$
18																																	
19																																	
20																																	
21 a/a	4	0	74	65	3.05	1.05	3.38				20.6	5%	23%	18%							27%	77%									11.2	130	$6
22 MIN *	4	0	83	56	4.42	1.26	4.48	1.31	103	116	16.9	6%	16%	10%	8%	10.1%	94.1	35	20	45	27%	70%	11%	12%	11	74	18%	64%	0	0.72	-4.6	50	-$3
1st Half	4	0	48	32	3.32	1.24	3.90	1.39	87	108	16.4	8%	16%	8%	7%	10.8%	94.1	37	23	40	27%	78%	8%	9%	5	70	40%	40%	0	0.70	3.9	57	$0
2nd Half	0	0	35	24	5.95	1.27	5.29	1.27	120	127	17.7	5%	16%	11%	8%	9.3%	94.0	32	16	52	28%	59%	15%	15%	6	81	0%	83%			-8.5	45	-$13
Proj	2	0	44	30	4.50	1.34	4.63	1.40	101	110	19.2	8%	16%	8%	8%	9.9%	94.0	34	18	47	28%	72%	11%	13%	9						-2.9	46	-$5

DANIEL MARCUS

Winn,Cole

Age: 23	Th: R	Role SP	Health A	LIMA Plan C	
Ht: 6' 2"	Wt: 190	Type Pwr/xFB	PT/Exp D	Rand Var +2	
			Consist F	MM 1200	

Former first-round pick has three potentially plus pitches, but stumbled on control problems in first prolonged exposure to AAA. 2021 skills showcase the upside, with plenty of strikeouts on tap, and long-term outlook as a frontline SP. While one bad season doesn't change the trajectory, it does increase likelihood TEX debut won't come until later in 2023.

Yr	Tm	W	Sv	IP	K	ERA	WHIP	xERA	xWHIP	vL+	vR+	BF/G	BB%	K%	K-BB%	xBB%	SwK	Vel	G	L	F	H%	S%	HR/F	xHR/F	GS	APC	DOM%	DIS%	Sv%	LI	RAR	BPX	R$
18																																		
19																																		
20																																		
21	a/a	4	0	86	92	2.74	0.90	1.68				15.3	9%	29%	19%							21%	73%									16.2	134	$11
22	aaa	9	0	123	103	5.57	1.60	4.69				19.5	13%	18%	5%							31%	65%									-24.3	61	-$12
1st Half		5	0	66	46	4.24	1.32	2.97				19.6	12%	16%	4%							26%	66%									-2.2	74	-$2
2nd Half		4	0	57	57	7.11	1.93	6.68				19.3	14%	20%	6%							38%	63%									-22.1	47	-$22
Proj		**4**	**0**	**58**	**54**	**4.70**	**1.39**	**4.53**	**1.45**			**20.5**	**12%**	**22%**	**10%**				**29**	**22**	**49**	**28%**	**71%**	**11%**	**12%**	**12**						**-5.2**	**41**	**-$4**

Wood,Alex

Age: 32	Th: L	Role SP	Health F	LIMA Plan B	
Ht: 6' 4"	Wt: 215	Type	PT/Exp A	Rand Var +5	
			Consist C	MM 5301	

Injuries are a given, as he's missed time every year since 2016—this time it was a shoulder impingement that shut him down in early September. But main difference between $10 season in 2021 and negative value in 2022 was S% plunge, with xERA, xWHIP, and BPX all holding remarkably stable. Could get these innings at a discount if shoulder checks out.

Yr	Tm	W	Sv	IP	K	ERA	WHIP	xERA	xWHIP	vL+	vR+	BF/G	BB%	K%	K-BB%	xBB%	SwK	Vel	G	L	F	H%	S%	HR/F	xHR/F	GS	APC	DOM%	DIS%	Sv%	LI	RAR	BPX	R$
18	LA	9	0	152	135	3.68	1.21	3.75	1.24	81	97	19.3	6%	21%	15%	6%	11.3%	89.9	49	22	29	31%	72%	11%	10%	27	74	19%	26%	0	0.81	8.8	123	$9
19	CIN	1	0	36	30	5.80	1.40	4.65	1.30	120	124	21.9	6%	20%	14%	8%	11.4%	90.0	38	28	34	30%	69%	30%	22%	7	84	14%	43%			-5.7	99	-$6
20	LA	0	0	13	15	6.39	1.82	5.29	1.34	106	133	7.2	9%	23%	14%	9%	12.8%	91.2	39	17	44	42%	67%	11%	9%	2	31	0%	100%	0	0.68	-3.0	106	-$10
21	SF	10	0	139	152	3.83	1.18	3.34	1.16	93	91	22.5	7%	26%	19%	6%	13.0%	91.8	51	22	27	32%	70%	14%	14%	26	84	31%	23%			7.5	152	$10
22	SF	8	0	131	131	5.10	1.24	3.40	1.14	67	112	21.3	5%	24%	18%	6%	11.6%	92.4	48	21	31	33%	61%	14%	15%	26	86	23%	27%			-18.2	146	-$1
1st Half		5	0	78	75	4.83	1.33	3.46	1.18	71	112	20.8	6%	23%	17%	6%	10.8%	92.5	49	24	27	34%	65%	13%	14%	16	85	13%	31%			-8.3	132	-$3
2nd Half		3	0	52	56	5.50	1.11	3.33	1.07	61	112	22.2	5%	25%	21%	7%	12.8%	92.4	47	16	37	30%	53%	17%	16%	10	88	40%	20%			-9.9	168	-$3
Proj		**6**	**0**	**116**	**113**	**4.00**	**1.20**	**3.22**	**1.16**	**79**	**102**	**20.4**	**6%**	**24%**	**18%**	**6%**	**11.9%**	**91.5**	**46**	**22**	**32**	**31%**	**71%**	**15%**	**15%**	**23**						**-0.5**	**136**	**$4**

Woodford,Jake

Age: 26	Th: R	Role RP	Health A	LIMA Plan C	
Ht: 6' 4"	Wt: 215	Type Con	PT/Exp D	Rand Var -4	
			Consist B	MM 2000	

4-0, 2.23 ERA in 48 IP at STL. A high S% and allowing only 1 HR will do wonders for your ERA, but 4.05 MLB xERA and declining K%, K-BB% show he's the same mediocre pitcher he's always been. That said, 2nd half gains in BB%, GB% suggest he might be on the verge of better results, though lack of strikeouts puts hard cap on value and role.

Yr	Tm	W	Sv	IP	K	ERA	WHIP	xERA	xWHIP	vL+	vR+	BF/G	BB%	K%	K-BB%	xBB%	SwK	Vel	G	L	F	H%	S%	HR/F	xHR/F	GS	APC	DOM%	DIS%	Sv%	LI	RAR	BPX	R$
18	a/a	8	0	145	85	5.22	1.56	5.34				22.7	9%	13%	4%							32%	68%									-19.1	33	-$11
19	aaa	9	0	153	109	4.75	1.38	4.40				24.8	11%	17%	6%							27%	69%									-4.6	41	$0
20	STL	1	0	21	16	5.57	1.19	4.58	1.28	74	142	7.1	6%	19%	13%	9%	8.3%	92.9	45	17	38	23%	67%	29%	24%	1	30	0%	0%	0	0.41	-2.9	100	-$5
21	STL *	5	0	102	70	4.16	1.43	4.76	1.41	120	83	13.1	8%	16%	8%	10%	8.4%	91.7	41	24	35	31%	73%	10%	9%	8	44	13%	50%	0	0.68	1.3	55	-$3
22	STL *	6	0	91	54	2.57	1.22	3.06	1.36	100	81	9.7	6%	13%	7%	7%	8.2%	92.1	52	20	28	29%	78%	2%	8%	1	26	0%	0%	0	0.37	15.8	78	$5
1st Half		1	0	41	25	3.62	1.47	4.18	1.52	78	99	10.3	10%	14%	4%	8%	8.8%	91.9	47	17	36	31%	75%	4%	13%	0	28			0	0.35	1.7	59	-$9
2nd Half		5	0	51	28	1.72	1.02	2.17	1.30	118	67	9.3	5%	14%	9%	6%	7.7%	92.3	56	22	23	26%	83%	0%	2%	1	24	0%	0%	0	0.39	14.1	104	$10
Proj		**3**	**0**	**44**	**27**	**3.78**	**1.32**	**4.11**	**1.44**	**125**	**93**	**13.0**	**9%**	**15%**	**7%**	**7%**	**8.2%**	**92.0**	**50**	**21**	**30**	**29%**	**72%**	**9%**	**7%**	**4**						**1.0**	**47**	**-$3**

Woodruff,Brandon

Age: 30	Th: R	Role SP	Health D	LIMA Plan B	
Ht: 6' 4"	Wt: 243	Type Pwr	PT/Exp A	Rand Var -1	
			Consist A	MM 5505	

Ankle sprain and scary case of numbness in pitching hand took a bite out of 1st half value; after that, it was business as usual. Continuing growth in SwK is great to see, and you could set your watch to his xERA, xWHIP from last four seasons. Health grade can't be ignored, but skill-wise, he's become one of the most dependable SP options around.

Yr	Tm	W	Sv	IP	K	ERA	WHIP	xERA	xWHIP	vL+	vR+	BF/G	BB%	K%	K-BB%	xBB%	SwK	Vel	G	L	F	H%	S%	HR/F	xHR/F	GS	APC	DOM%	DIS%	Sv%	LI	RAR	BPX	R$
18	MIL *	6	1	114	103	3.95	1.34	4.11	1.20	85	92	13.2	9%	22%	12%	8%	11.1%	95.3	53	18	29	31%	73%	12%	14%	4	39	0%	50%	100	0.51	2.7	84	$2
19	MIL	11	0	122	143	3.62	1.14	3.43	1.12	100	74	22.4	6%	29%	23%	6%	12.4%	96.3	45	23	32	33%	71%	12%	12%	22	90	32%	9%			13.2	167	$13
20	MIL	3	0	74	91	3.05	0.99	3.22	1.06	82	83	22.5	6%	31%	25%	6%	13.1%	96.5	49	15	36	28%	75%	14%	15%	13	93	31%	0%			12.7	189	$23
21	MIL	9	0	179	211	2.56	0.96	3.18	1.07	75	80	23.6	6%	30%	24%	5%	13.6%	96.5	41	26	32	28%	79%	13%	12%	30	94	47%	10%			37.7	166	$30
22	MIL	13	0	153	190	3.05	1.07	3.27	1.07	82	99	23.0	7%	31%	24%	6%	14.8%	96.2	38	19	43	30%	77%	11%	11%	27	94	33%	7%			17.3	165	$20
1st Half		7	0	55	71	3.95	1.13	3.22	1.02	76	113	20.5	6%	31%	26%	6%	15.0%	96.0	37	19	45	34%	69%	11%	9%	11	89	18%	9%			0.1	184	$7
2nd Half		6	0	99	119	2.55	1.03	3.31	1.10	85	90	24.6	7%	30%	23%	6%	14.7%	96.2	38	19	43	28%	81%	11%	11%	16	97	44%	6%			17.2	155	$26
Proj		**12**	**0**	**174**	**210**	**3.11**	**1.06**	**2.88**	**1.07**	**83**	**91**	**22.6**	**7%**	**31%**	**24%**	**6%**	**13.9%**	**96.2**	**42**	**20**	**38**	**30%**	**76%**	**12%**	**12%**	**30**						**18.4**	**166**	**$22**

Wright,Kyle

Age: 27	Th: R	Role SP	Health A	LIMA Plan C+	
Ht: 6' 4"	Wt: 215	Type /GB	PT/Exp B	Rand Var 0	
			Consist C	MM 4205	

Long-awaited breakout was driven by greater emphasis on killer curveball (34.1% usage, 15.7% SwK, 60% GB), massive swing from 53% FB to 56% GB, which suppressed HR (for half a season, anyway). Everything here came with skill support, including career-best BB% and improvement vL (backed by 15% K-BB%). Slight regression likely, but he's arrived.

Yr	Tm	W	Sv	IP	K	ERA	WHIP	xERA	xWHIP	vL+	vR+	BF/G	BB%	K%	K-BB%	xBB%	SwK	Vel	G	L	F	H%	S%	HR/F	xHR/F	GS	APC	DOM%	DIS%	Sv%	LI	RAR	BPX	R$
18	ATL *	8	0	146	116	4.33	1.37	3.98		178	65	19.8	9%	19%	10%	12%	10.2%	94.0	41	18	41	31%	69%	29%	19%	0	32			0	0.21	-3.3	79	$0
19	ATL *	11	0	133	112	5.98	1.54	5.46	1.66	134	123	20.7	9%	19%	11%	12%	9.4%	94.6	42	27	32	34%	63%	21%	23%	4	50	0%	75%	0	0.46	-24.1	56	-$7
20	ATL	2	0	38	30	5.21	1.55	5.64	1.67	128	84	21.0	14%	18%	4%	11%	10.0%	94.3	45	23	32	27%	71%	19%	23%	8	80	13%	50%			-3.5	-3	-$7
21	ATL *	10	0	143	114	4.27	1.44	4.59	1.69	171	116	23.5	9%	19%	10%	12%	9.8%	93.2	42	5	53	33%	71%	20%	28%	2	67	0%	50%			0.0	70	-$1
22	ATL	21	0	180	174	3.19	1.16	3.23	1.21	100	83	24.6	7%	24%	16%	6%	12.3%	94.7	56	18	27	29%	76%	14%	15%	30	90	23%	13%			17.2	131	$21
1st Half		9	0	96	98	2.91	1.14	3.26	1.21	83	89	24.4	8%	25%	17%	7%	12.3%	94.9	53	17	30	29%	76%	8%	11%	16	91	31%	13%			12.6	130	$22
2nd Half		12	0	84	76	3.52	1.19	3.20	1.21	116	75	24.8	6%	22%	16%	5%	12.3%	94.6	59	19	23	29%	77%	23%	21%	14	89	14%	14%			4.7	131	$19
Proj		**16**	**0**	**174**	**162**	**3.61**	**1.27**	**3.28**	**1.28**	**115**	**87**	**22.2**	**8%**	**23%**	**15%**	**7%**	**11.8%**	**94.6**	**54**	**19**	**27**	**30%**	**76%**	**18%**	**17%**	**32**						**7.6**	**111**	**$13**

Yarbrough,Ryan

Age: 31	Th: L	Role RP	Health D	LIMA Plan B	
Ht: 6' 5"	Wt: 205	Type Con	PT/Exp A	Rand Var -1	
			Consist B	MM 2101	

3-8, 4.50 ERA in 80 IP at TAM. April groin injury seemed to be cause of rough 1st half, and when you factor in multiple trips to AAA, shift to bulk relief role, it's clear his standing took a hit. 2nd half restoration of skills offers hope that there's still a path back to relevance, though his slowly fading K% caps his value.

Yr	Tm	W	Sv	IP	K	ERA	WHIP	xERA	xWHIP	vL+	vR+	BF/G	BB%	K%	K-BB%	xBB%	SwK	Vel	G	L	F	H%	S%	HR/F	xHR/F	GS	APC	DOM%	DIS%	Sv%	LI	RAR	BPX	R$
18	TAM	16	0	147	128	3.91	1.29	4.41	1.33	89	106	16.5	8%	20%	12%	7%	9.2%	89.4	38	25	37	30%	73%	11%	11%	6	63	0%	50%	0	1.21	4.4	86	$9
19	TAM *	13	0	168	146	4.25	1.04	3.11	1.18	93	84	19.6	4%	23%	19%	6%	10.6%	88.2	44	20	36	29%	61%	10%	11%	14	73	50%	29%	0	0.90	5.2	171	$16
20	TAM	1	0	56	44	3.56	1.19	4.23	1.25	95	92	21.3	5%	19%	14%	5%	13.7%	87.4	42	29	29	30%	72%	10%	11%	9	76	33%	33%	0	0.84	6.2	108	$5
21	TAM	9	0	155	117	5.11	1.23	4.61	1.21	86	106	21.8	4%	18%	14%	6%	9.6%	86.5	36	24	40	30%	62%	13%	11%	21	83	14%	29%	0	0.77	-16.1	103	$0
22	TAM *	5	0	109	81	4.56	1.47	5.28	1.29	74	122	17.3	6%	17%	11%	6%	10.4%	86.8	38	21	41	33%	72%	12%	11%	9	68	33%	22%	0	0.66	-8.0	55	-$6
1st Half		1	0	53	34	5.60	1.73	6.48	1.44	101	126	18.6	8%	14%	6%	8%	8.6%	86.2	34	22	44	36%	69%	9%	12%	6	74	17%	33%	0	0.78	-10.6	27	-$20
2nd Half		4	0	56	47	3.58	1.22	4.15	1.22	59	118	16.2	6%	20%	14%	5%	11.8%	87.1	41	21	38	29%	76%	14%	11%	3	64	67%	0%	0	0.58	2.7	90	$3
Proj		**5**	**0**	**102**	**79**	**4.27**	**1.30**	**3.92**	**1.26**	**83**	**109**	**18.3**	**6%**	**19%**	**13%**	**6%**	**10.9%**	**87.1**	**39**	**23**	**37**	**31%**	**70%**	**11%**	**11%**	**19**						**-3.8**	**91**	**-$1**

Zimmermann,Bruce

Age: 28	Th: L	Role SP	Health D	LIMA Plan C+	
Ht: 6' 1"	Wt: 215	Type Con	PT/Exp D	Rand Var +1	
			Consist B	MM 1000	

2-5, 5.99 ERA in 74 IP at BAL. Career 3.95 ERA in AAA, 5.65 ERA in MLB makes him look like classic Four-A player, and skills aren't doing much to disabuse that notion. BB% is all he's got to hang his hat on, and putting ball over plate has only led to hitters teeing off to .303 BA, 2.3 HR/9. Biggest fantasy contribution might be helping batters on your roster succeed.

Yr	Tm	W	Sv	IP	K	ERA	WHIP	xERA	xWHIP	vL+	vR+	BF/G	BB%	K%	K-BB%	xBB%	SwK	Vel	G	L	F	H%	S%	HR/F	xHR/F	GS	APC	DOM%	DIS%	Sv%	LI	RAR	BPX	R$
18	aa	4	0	50	34	4.50	1.63	5.36				20.2	11%	15%	4%							32%	74%									-2.2	39	-$6
19	a/a	7	0	142	108	4.11	1.51	4.96				24.7	9%	18%	8%							33%	75%									7.0	56	-$1
20	BAL	0	0	7	7	7.71	1.14	4.21	1.22	90	108	15.5	6%	23%	16%	6%	8.4%	91.5	50	10	40	24%	33%	25%	20%	1	54	0%	100%	0	0.43	-2.8	136	-$7
21	BAL *	5	0	82	70	4.85	1.45	5.74	1.33	127	109	18.5	8%	20%	12%	8%	11.2%	91.5	40	26	34	32%	73%	20%	23%	13	79	0%	69%	0	0.74	-5.9	47	-$5
22	BAL *	7	0	151	105	4.91	1.45	5.97	1.22	158	130	22.2	4%	15%	12%	6%	9.6%	90.6	40	20	41	34%	71%	20%	19%	13	75	23%	46%	0	0.76	-17.6	63	-$9
1st Half		4	0	85	61	5.67	1.46	6.27	1.23	152	130	22.7	5%	17%	12%	6%	9.8%	90.6	38	20	41	33%	67%	19%	19%	13	79	23%	46%			-17.8	57	-$15
2nd Half		3	0	66	44	3.94	1.44	5.58	1.25	182	130	21.7	5%	15%	11%	9%	6.8%	90.2	52	15	33	34%	77%	33%	15%	0	52			0	0.77	0.2	70	-$5
Proj		**2**	**0**	**44**	**32**	**4.92**	**1.49**	**4.36**	**1.34**	**125**	**110**	**21.8**	**7%**	**17%**	**10%**	**7%**	**10.4%**	**91.0**	**39**	**22**	**38**	**33%**	**71%**	**12%**	**21%**	**9**						**-5.1**	**69**	**-$6**

BRANDON KRUSE

THE NEXT TIER

Pitchers

The preceding section provided player boxes and analysis for 413 pitchers. As we know, far more than 413 pitchers will play in the major leagues in 2023. Many of those additional pitchers are covered in the minor league section, but that still leaves a gap: established major leaguers who don't play enough, or well enough, to merit a player box.

This section looks to fill that gap. Here, you will find "The Next Tier" of pitchers who are mostly past their growth years, but who are likely to see some playing time in 2023. We are including their 2021-22 statlines here for reference for you to do your own analysis. (Years that include MLEs are marked by an asterisk.) This way, if Matt Bush again gets some late-game chatter at some point in 2023, you can confirm that even at 38 years of age, he's had recent high-skills seasons. Or if Aaron Sanchez latches on with a team and throws a good first start, you can deftly wait for him to "prove it" before rushing to the waiver wire.

Pitcher	T	Yr	Age	W	Sv	IP	K	ERA	xERA	WHIP	vL+	vR+	BB%	K%	K-BB	xBB%	SwK	G/L/F	H%	S%	BPX
Abreu, Albert	R	21*	26	3	3	55	60	4.87	3.65	1.27	121	92	12	22	10	10	11.1	45/18/36	25	65	83
		22	27	2	0	39	38	3.26	4.15	1.47	90	112	13	22	9	12	10.5	52/19/30	30	83	56
Banks, Tanner	L	21*	30	3	0	61	53	5.35	6.81	1.63	0	0	0	0	0		-	-	38	71	72
		22*	31	2	0	70	67	2.97	3.40	1.21	105	76	8	23	14	5	9.3	47/23/30	30	78	106
Baumann, Mike	R	21*	26	5	0	77	55	5.06	4.23	1.38	100	150	12	10	-2	12	8.1	37/21/42	27	65	48
		22*	27	3	1	94	85	4.50	4.77	1.45	104	122	6	15	9	9	6.9	51/18/32	34	70	81
Bradley, Archie	R	21	29	7	2	51	40	3.71	4.52	1.43	97	106	10	18	8	8	7.5	56/17/27	31	76	62
		22	30	0	2	19	15	4.82	3.83	1.29	74	101	9	19	10	8	8.5	57/16/27	30	61	82
Brebbia, John	R	21*	32	3	0	34	42	4.60	4.83	1.31	93	150	5	25	21	4	10.8	28/28/45	35	70	128
		22	33	6	0	68	54	3.18	4.59	1.31	111	102	6	19	13	6	11.5	36/17/46	32	77	86
Bush, Matt	R	21	36	0	0	4	5	6.75	4.81	1.25	23	214	6	29	24		13.0	27/0/73	14	100	161
		22	37	2	3	60	74	3.47	3.33	1.02	99	84	7	30	23	6	12.9	40/16/44	25	76	160
Castellanos, Humberto	R	21*	24	8	0	105	79	4.35	4.34	1.21	115	105	8	15	7	7	6.3	42/19/40	28	69	70
		22	25	3	0	44	32	5.68	4.67	1.40	114	120	6	17	10	7	8.2	33/26/40	32	62	68
Cishek, Steve	R	21	36	0	0	68	64	3.42	4.89	1.49	90	92	13	21	7	10	8.1	50/17/33	31	76	37
		22	37	1	1	66	74	4.21	3.70	1.22	132	85	9	26	16	9	10.6	41/20/39	28	71	111
Colome, Alex	R	21	33	4	17	65	58	4.15	4.25	1.40	121	87	8	20	12	8	13.0	54/18/29	32	73	99
		22	34	2	4	47	32	5.74	4.73	1.68	110	130	10	15	5	11	9.2	56/17/28	34	66	34
Diekman, Jake	L	21	35	3	7	61	83	3.86	4.03	1.34	97	98	13	32	19	10	14.1	35/21/44	30	77	108
		22	36	5	1	58	79	4.99	4.10	1.63	102	121	16	29	14	11	13.7	40/22/38	34	73	69
Duffey, Tyler	R	21	31	3	3	62	61	3.18	4.11	1.22	106	73	11	24	13	9	9.7	46/21/34	28	75	81
		22	32	2	2	44	39	4.91	3.75	1.36	124	107	8	21	13	8	11.5	45/29/26	30	69	92
Edwards, Carl	R	21*	30	1	3	23	26	5.19	5.20	1.30	173	178	10	19	10	12	12.6	32/23/45	31	68	83
		22*	31	7	5	77	68	2.35	2.76	1.09	89	97	10	22	12	8	11.0	48/16/37	24	84	93
Foster, Matt	R	21*	27	2	1	55	59	5.52	5.31	1.34	105	116	7	23	16	8	10.7	29/21/50	33	64	94
		22	28	1	1	45	42	4.40	4.58	1.33	110	94	9	22	13	8	10.3	31/23/46	30	70	75
Garrett, Amir	L	21	30	0	7	48	61	6.04	4.15	1.57	95	122	13	28	15	8	14.7	51/15/35	34	65	97
		22	31	3	0	45	49	4.96	4.45	1.32	55	100	16	25	9	11	10.9	39/22/39	26	58	23
Green, Chad	R	21	31	10	6	84	99	3.12	3.64	0.88	85	85	5	31	26	6	15.9	27/20/53	24	75	162
		22	32	1	1	15	16	3.00	4.24	1.20	111	82	8	26	18	4	14.9	25/20/55	31	76	104
Hernandez, Carlos	R	21*	25	8	0	113	94	3.93	3.93	1.30	77	99	11	21	9	10	11.4	40/20/40	28	73	71
		22*	26	2	0	106	69	5.62	5.02	1.51	99	145	12	13	2	10	10.8	38/21/41	30	64	37
Jefferies, Daulton	R	21*	26	6	0	92	62	4.69	5.08	1.33	82	91	7	14	7	6	8.2	44/22/33	33	68	94
		22	27	1	0	39	28	5.72	4.40	1.37	88	127	5	16	12	8	9.7	47/16/38	34	58	100
Kittredge, Andrew	R	21	32	9	8	72	77	1.88	3.07	0.98	88	78	5	27	22	4	16.4	54/18/28	28	87	170
		22	33	3	5	20	14	3.15	3.73	0.85	94	89	3	19	16	4	13.3	46/14/41	21	77	125
Krehbiel, Joey	R	21*	29	3	4	51	47	5.66	5.63	1.39	30	107	15	21	6	12	10.5	59/9/32	31	65	60
		22	30	5	1	58	45	3.90	4.31	1.23	105	105	7	18	11	8	9.9	42/21/37	27	74	78
Leiter, Mark	R	21*	31	10	0	116	101	5.39	5.07	1.38	0	0	0	0	0		-	-	32	64	70
		22*	32	2	3	90	97	4.44	3.91	1.20	81	112	9	26	17	9	12.0	49/18/33	29	68	99
Leone, Dominic	R	21	30	4	2	54	50	1.51	4.25	1.10	68	80	10	23	13	9	13.4	48/14/38	26	88	85
		22	31	4	3	49	52	4.01	4.39	1.60	158	91	11	23	13	7	19.0	39/23/38	36	78	77
Littell, Zack	R	21	26	4	2	62	63	2.92	4.01	1.14	106	82	10	25	15	7	13.9	47/16/38	26	79	105
		22	27	3	1	44	39	5.08	4.23	1.38	102	121	7	21	14	6	13.1	43/16/40	32	68	102
Long, Sam	L	21*	26	3	0	83	80	4.06	3.17	1.17	69	119	9	22	13	7	9.6	39/17/44	29	66	109
		22*	27	2	1	61	46	3.67	4.26	1.33	180	77	8	18	10	8	11.6	39/15/45	25	79	43
Luetge, Lucas	L	21	35	4	1	72	78	2.74	3.74	1.13	70	97	5	26	21	9	13.6	42/20/38	33	79	158
		22	36	4	2	57	60	2.67	4.05	1.40	98	105	7	24	17	10	12.3	35/23/42	37	83	122

THE NEXT TIER

Pitchers

Pitcher	T	Yr	Age	W	Sv	IP	K	ERA	xERA	WHIP	vL+	vR+	BB%	K%	K-BB	xBB%	SwK	G/L/F	H%	S%	BPX
May, Trevor	R	21	32	7	4	63	83	3.59	3.95	1.26	106	88	9	31	22	7	16.0	36/15/48	32	78	149
		22	33	2	1	25	30	5.04	4.12	1.44	105	110	8	27	19	9	13.3	29/25/46	36	69	126
Mayers, Mike	R	21	30	5	2	75	90	3.84	3.88	1.29	102	102	8	29	20	8	13.5	37/21/42	33	76	137
		22*	31	1	0	84	70	5.81	5.89	1.43	125	116	8	20	12	9	11.7	38/16/46	28	67	22
McGee, Jake	L	21	35	3	31	60	58	2.72	4.03	0.91	67	82	4	24	20	4	10.6	36/19/45	25	77	143
		22	36	1	3	37	25	6.81	5.66	1.43	123	112	7	15	8	6	9.1	27/17/56	31	53	39
Merryweather, Julian	R	21	30	0	2	13	12	4.85	4.47	1.31	161	90	7	22	15	5	10.6	41/16/43	27	77	103
		22*	31	2	0	42	36	4.31	3.55	1.22	115	121	6	19	13	4	11.0	48/12/40	29	66	93
Minor, Mike	L	21	34	8	0	159	149	5.05	4.37	1.24	96	105	6	22	16	7	11.1	38/20/41	30	63	116
		22*	35	5	0	117	92	6.26	7.02	1.60	92	140	9	17	8	8	8.6	34/21/44	32	68	12
Moronta, Reyes	R	21*	29	0	0	22	16	10.15	8.15	2.39	0	86	0	15	15		6.3	55/0/45	33	57	6
		22	30	2	2	38	38	4.30	4.68	1.27	87	102	11	24	12	9	11.5	32/15/53	27	70	63
Nelson, Nick	R	21*	26	3	1	66	72	5.61	6.02	1.85	109	124	21	28	8	12	13.0	35/38/27	37	70	65
		22	27	3	1	69	69	4.85	4.47	1.49	93	105	12	23	11	11	12.6	40/22/38	34	64	59
Payamps, Joel	R	21	28	1	0	50	38	3.40	4.62	1.15	73	102	7	19	12	8	10.4	44/15/41	27	75	84
		22	29	3	0	56	41	3.23	4.12	1.37	93	114	7	17	10	9	10.0	53/17/31	31	81	89
Peralta, Wily	R	21*	33	5	0	115	73	3.22	4.38	1.35	83	119	9	14	5	11	8.8	51/19/31	27	81	40
		22	34	2	0	38	32	2.58	4.79	1.51	85	104	14	19	5	12	8.5	46/21/33	30	84	8
Peters, Dillon	L	21*	29	4	0	81	68	4.15	5.78	1.48	100	101	9	20	11	6	12.0	48/18/34	31	80	40
		22	30	5	0	39	26	4.58	4.90	1.32	72	117	10	16	5	8	8.4	43/17/40	26	68	25
Phelps, David	R	21	35	0	0	10	15	0.87	3.01	1.16	50	90	10	36	26	12	10.6	41/23/36	36	92	176
		22	36	0	1	64	64	2.83	4.21	1.30	86	91	11	24	12	11	7.1	36/26/38	30	78	64
Pruitt, Austin	R	21*	32	2	0	25	18	4.96	5.07	1.29	142	81	0	17	17	6	11.8	36/18/45	31	66	75
		22*	33	1	2	77	53	3.80	3.46	1.03	96	102	4	17	13	6	11.9	45/14/40	26	68	119
Ramirez, Noe	R	21	32	0	1	36	29	3.00	5.02	0.97	80	70	8	20	12	7	10.4	30/18/52	22	72	63
		22	33	5	0	50	51	5.22	4.35	1.42	123	109	12	24	12	8	12.4	38/20/42	29	68	60
Richards, Garrett	R	21	34	7	3	137	115	4.87	4.87	1.60	99	123	10	19	9	8	10.3	47/21/32	34	72	60
		22	35	1	1	43	36	5.27	3.88	1.34	87	116	7	19	12	7	12.6	53/17/30	33	59	103
Rodriguez, Joely	L	21	30	2	1	46	47	4.66	3.70	1.53	76	114	9	23	14	7	13.9	58/20/21	37	70	116
		22	31	2	0	50	57	4.47	3.48	1.35	91	90	12	26	14	8	11.5	54/20/26	31	66	99
Rogers, Tyler	R	21	31	7	13	81	55	2.22	3.77	1.07	62	103	4	17	13	4	7.8	58/16/26	28	82	117
		22	32	3	0	76	49	3.57	3.97	1.27	120	81	7	15	8	6	8.6	56/18/26	30	71	72
Sanchez, Aaron	R	21*	30	2	0	53	34	4.82	5.35	1.60	93	87	10	17	7	11	8.2	52/17/31	32	71	36
		22*	31	7	0	123	73	5.19	5.41	1.48	94	143	6	15	10	7	8.1	53/18/29	32	67	39
Sandlin, Nick	R	21	25	1	0	34	48	2.94	3.43	1.13	85	78	12	34	22	10	12.3	42/18/40	29	75	141
		22	26	5	0	44	41	2.25	3.83	1.16	90	72	13	23	9	9	12.3	56/14/31	23	82	58
Shaw, Bryan	R	21	34	6	2	77	71	3.49	4.56	1.38	87	108	11	21	10	9	11.8	46/24/31	29	79	57
		22	35	6	1	58	52	5.40	4.29	1.44	102	112	10	20	10	9	9.9	50/18/32	30	65	71
Stanek, Ryne	R	21	30	3	2	68	83	3.42	4.37	1.21	110	67	13	29	16	10	14.5	34/20/47	26	76	85
		22	31	2	1	55	62	1.15	3.96	1.23	71	85	14	28	14	11	15.9	39/21/40	27	92	69
Stephenson, Robert	R	21	29	2	1	46	52	3.13	4.10	1.30	100	98	9	26	17	7	12.3	38/24/38	32	80	114
		22	30	2	0	58	55	5.43	4.33	1.33	111	122	6	22	17	5	14.2	29/24/47	33	63	112
Sulser, Cole	R	21	32	5	8	63	73	2.70	3.82	1.12	74	89	9	28	19	7	14.8	41/19/40	29	79	129
		22	33	1	2	34	38	5.29	3.98	1.62	69	165	11	26	15	7	13.7	40/24/36	36	71	93
Thompson, Ryan	R	21	30	3	0	34	37	2.38	3.35	1.03	95	87	7	28	21	4	12.8	48/18/34	28	81	151
		22	31	3	3	43	39	3.80	3.61	1.17	78	99	6	22	15	6	10.6	51/18/31	30	70	126
Thornton, Trent	R	21	28	1	0	49	52	4.78	4.21	1.43	100	130	7	24	17	8	10.2	40/23/37	33	76	121
		22*	29	2	3	74	59	3.96	4.40	1.39	98	102	9	20	11	7	9.0	34/24/42	30	74	64
Underwood Jr., Duane	R	21	27	2	0	73	65	4.33	4.47	1.43	121	94	8	20	12	8	10.5	44/26/31	33	73	83
		22	28	1	1	57	57	4.40	3.91	1.45	102	89	10	22	12	8	12.8	49/24/27	35	67	90
Weaver, Luke	R	21	28	3	0	66	62	4.25	4.35	1.19	113	98	7	23	15	6	11.5	38/22/40	28	70	104
		22	29	1	0	36	38	6.56	4.19	1.82	120	120	7	22	14	7	11.1	40/30/30	45	61	112
Wisler, Matthew	R	21	29	3	1	49	62	3.70	3.68	1.07	95	90	6	32	26	7	14.0	25/26/50	32	70	169
		22	30	3	1	44	35	2.25	4.83	1.00	78	96	8	20	12	8	11.1	25/18/58	21	87	60

Five-Year Injury Log

The following chart details the injured list stints for all players during the past five years. Use this as a supplement to our health grades in the player profile boxes as well as the "Risk Management" charts that start on page 264. It's also where to turn when in April you want to check whether, say, a Freddy Peralta shoulder injury should be concerning (tip: yes), or where you might realize that Eloy Jiménez missed nearly 200 days in the past two seasons combined.

For each injury, the number of days the player missed during the season is listed. A few IL stints are for fewer than 10 days; these are either cases when a player was placed on the IL prior to Opening Day or less than 10 days before the end of the season (only in-season time lost is listed) or when players went on the temporary "COVID-related" list for contact tracing or vaccination side effects.

Abbreviations:
Lt, L = left
Rt, R = right
fx = fractured
R/C = rotator cuff
str = strained
surg = surgery
TJS = Tommy John surgery (ulnar collateral ligament reconstruction)
x 2 = two occurrences of the same injury
x 3 = three occurrences of the same injury

Throughout the spring and all season long, BaseballHQ.com has comprehensive injury coverage.

FIVE-YEAR INJURY LOG — Hitters

Batter	Yr	Days	Injury
Abreu, Jose	18	20	Surg to repair ABD
Acuna, Ronald	18	32	L knee & ACL strain
	20	11	Strn L wrist
	21	68	Torn ACL R knee
	22	25	Recovery from knee surgery
Adames, Willy	21	12	Strn L quad
	22	25	High L ankle sprain
Adams, Matt	18	15	Fractured L index finger
	19	18	L shoulder strain
	20	12	Strn L hamstring
	21	49	Bruised R shin; Strn R elbow
Adrianza, Ehire	18	11	Strn L hamstring
	19	11	Strn ab
	21	7	Covid-19
	22	82	Covid-19; strained L quad x2
Aguilar, Jesus	21	9	Inflammation L knee
	22	5	Covid-19
Ahmed, Nick	21	8	Inflam R knee; inflam R shoulder
	22	166	Covid-19; inflam R shoulder
Akiyama, Shogo	21	37	Strn R hamstring; strn L ham
Alberto, Hanser	18	11	R hamstring strain
Albies, Ozzie	20	35	Wrist
	22	116	Fx L foot; fx R pinky
Alfaro, Jorge	19	8	Concussion
	20	29	Covid-19
	21	34	Strn L hamstring
	22	11	Inflammation in knee
Alford, Anthony	20	20	Fractured R elbow, Covid-19
	21	9	Strn lower back
	22	18	Sprained R wrist
Allen, Austin	22	4	Covid-19
Allen, Greg	22	110	Strained R hamstring
Almora, Albert	21	39	Bruised L shoulder
	22	39	Covid-19; bruised R shoulder
Alonso, Pete	21	13	Sprained R hand
Altuve, Jose	18	24	R knee discomfort
	19	39	Strn L hamstring
	20	12	Sprained R knee
	21	13	Covid-19
	22	13	Strained L hamstring
Alvarez, Yordan	20	67	Surg repair ligament dam R knee
	21	10	Covid-19
	22	15	Covid-19; inflammation R hand

FIVE-YEAR INJURY LOG — Hitters

Batter	Yr	Days	Injury
Anderson, Brian	19	38	Fx L finger
	21	88	Strn L oblique; sublux L shoulder
	22	59	Covid-19; R shoulder inflam
Anderson, Tim	19	34	Sprained R ankle
	20	11	Strn R groin
	21	25	Strn L hamstring x2
	22	82	Strnd groin; torn tend. L mid fing
Andrus, Elvis	18	67	Fractured R elbow
	19	11	Strn R hamstring
	20	30	Strn lower back
Andujar, Miguel	19	175	Surg repair torn labrum R should
	21	97	Strn L wrist
Aquino, Aristides	21	59	Fractured hamate bone L hand
	22	51	Strained L calf
Arauz, Jonathan	21	7	Covid-19
	22	53	Covid-19; fx finger R hand
Arcia, Orlando	22	23	Strained L hamstring
Arenado, Nolan	20	9	Bone bruise L shoulder
Arozarena, Randy	20	39	Covid-19
	21	5	Covid-19
Arraez, Luis	20	19	Tendinitis L knee
	21	39	Concuss; inflam R shldr; R knee
	22	8	Covid-19
Arroyo, Christian	18	30	Strn L oblique
	19	109	Strn R forearm
	20	2	Covid-19
	21	91	Covid; R knee contusion
	22	32	Covid-19; strained L groin
Astudillo, Williams	19	82	Strn R hamstring
	20	20	Covid-19
Avila, Alex	18	11	Strn R hamstring
	19	51	Strn L calf
	20	12	Tightness lower back
	21	67	Covid-19; bilateral calf strains
Baddoo, Akil	21	13	Concussion
Bader, Harrison	19	11	Strn R hamstring
	21	68	Strn R forearm; fx R side rib
	22	86	Plantar fasciitis in R foot
Baez, Javier	21	11	Strn lower back
	22	12	Sore R thumb
Barnes, Austin	19	11	Strn L groin
Barnhart, Tucker	19	32	Strn R oblique
Barrera, Luis	19	22	R shoulder surgery

FIVE-YEAR INJURY LOG — Hitters

Batter	Yr	Days	Injury
Barrero,Jose	22	64	Surg repair hamate bone L hand
Barreto,Franklin	20	25	Subluxation L shoulder, Covid-19
	21	169	Strn R elbow
Bart,Joey	22	8	Concussion
Baty,Brett	22	39	Torn UCL R thumb
Beaty,Matt	19	11	Strn L hip flexor
	22	100	Impingement L shoulder
Bell,Josh	18	12	Strn L oblique
	21	7	Covid-19
Bellinger,Cody	21	63	L hamstring strain; fx L fibula
Belt,Brandon	18	35	Appendectomy; hyperexnd R knee
	20	9	Tendinitis R Achilles
	21	57	Str L obliq;R knee infl;Fx L thumb
	22	79	Covid; Inflammation/surg R knee
Bemboom,Anthony	19	61	Sprained L knee
Benintendi,Andrew	20	47	Strn R ribcage
	21	21	Fx R rib
	22	36	Inflammation R wrist
Berti,Jon	19	72	Strn L oblique
	20	11	Laceration R index finger
	21	56	Concussion
	22	50	Covid-19; strained L groin
Betts,Mookie	18	11	Pulled abdominal
	21	24	Inflammation R hip x2
	22	15	Fractured rib R side
Bichette,Bo	20	28	Sprained R knee
Biggio,Cavan	21	66	Sprn cervical spine;midback tight
	22	22	Covid-19
Blackmon,Charlie	19	12	Strn R calf
	22	11	Torn meniscus L knee
Bogaerts,Xander	18	19	Stress fracture L ankle
	21	10	Covid-19
Bohm,Alec	21	13	Covid-19
	22	4	Covid-19
Bolt,Skye	22	102	Strn oblique, ham; Sublux R knee
Bote,David	21	69	Dislocate L shldr; sprain R ankle
	22	82	Recovery from L shoulder surgery
Bouchard,Sean	22	20	Strained L oblique
Bradley,Bobby	21	21	Strn L knee
Brantley,Michael	18	9	Recovery R ankle surgery
	20	8	Strn R quad
	21	17	Tightness R ham; sore R knee
	22	47	Surgery on R shoulder
Bregman,Alex	20	20	Sore R hamstring
	21	77	Covid; L quad strain
Bride,Jonah	22	28	Strained R shoulder
Brinson,Lewis	18	60	L hip inflammation
	20	12	Bone bruise R hip
	21	17	Sprained index finger L hand
Brosseau,Michael	21	13	Strn R oblique
	22	39	Sprnd R ankle; strained R oblique
Brown,Seth	21	15	Covid-19
Bruce,Jay	18	66	Sore R hip
	19	47	Strn R oblique
	20	23	Sprained flexor tendon L elbow
Bryant,Kris	18	54	L shoulder inflammation x 2
	20	14	Sprained ring finger L hand
	22	127	Strn low back; fasciitis L foot
Burger,Jake	22	28	Bone bruise R hand
Buxton,Byron	18	57	Fractured great L toe; migraines
	19	73	Concus;L shldr sublux;brse R wrist
	20	12	Inflammation L shoulder
	21	111	Strn R hip; fx L hand
	22	47	Strained R hip

FIVE-YEAR INJURY LOG — Hitters

Batter	Yr	Days	Injury
Cabrera,Asdrubal	21	38	Strn R hamstring
Cabrera,Miguel	18	140	R ham. strn; Rup L biceps tendon
	21	15	Strn L biceps
	22	17	Biceps tendinitis L arm
Cain,Lorenzo	18	13	L groin strain
	21	77	Strn R hamstring; Strn L quad
Calhoun,Kole	18	17	R oblique strain
	21	119	Torn menisc R knee; str L ham x2
	22	18	R heel inflammation
Calhoun,Willie	19	27	Strn L quadriceps
	20	27	Strn L hamstring
	21	98	Strn L groin; fx ulna L forearm
Camargo,Johan	18	21	Strn R oblique
	19	18	Fx shin R lower leg
	22	36	Strained R knee
Cameron,Daz	20	48	Covid-19
	21	46	Sprained R big toe
	22	17	Covid-19
Campusano,Luis	20	16	Sprained L wrist
Candelario,Jeimer	18	12	L wrist tendinitis
	19	71	Sprained L thumb; L shldr inflam
	21	4	Covid-19
	22	14	Sprained L shoulder
Canha,Mark	19	16	Sprain R wrist
	21	23	Strn L hip
	22	6	Covid-19
Cano,Robinson	18	93	Fractured R hand
	19	52	Strn L quadriceps
	20	11	Strn L adductor
Capra,Vinny	22	4	Concussion
Caratini,Victor	19	35	Fx hamate bone L hand
	22	6	Covid-19
Carlson,Dylan	21	10	Sprained R wrist
	22	30	Strnd L ham; sprained L thumb
Carpenter,Kerry	22	10	Strained Lumbar spine
Carpenter,Matt	19	33	Bruised R foot
	22	61	Fx L foot; fx R pinky finger
Casali,Curt	19	40	Sprained R knee
	21	12	Strn L wrist
	22	46	Concussion; strained R oblique
Castellanos,Nick	21	14	Sprained R wrist
	22	24	Strained R oblique
Castillo,Welington	18	11	R shoulder inflammation
	19	37	Concussion; Strn L oblique
Castro,Harold	20	31	Strn L hamstring
Castro,Jason	18	149	Torn meniscus - R knee
	21	37	Sore R Achilles; sore R knee
	22	100	Torn meniscus R knee
Castro,Starlin	20	46	Fx R wrist
Castro,Willi	20	1	Sore R shoulder
	22	9	Strained L hamstring
Cave,Jake	21	71	Strn lower back
Celestino,Gilberto	22	9	Covid-19
Chang,Yu	22	29	Covid-19
Chapman,Matt	18	18	R hand soreness
	20	17	Strn R hip, Covid-19
Chavis,Michael	19	49	Sprained AC joint L shoulder
	21	19	Strn R elbow
Chirinos,Robinson	20	14	Sprained R ankle
Chisholm,Jazz	21	38	Covid-19; Strn L hamstring
	22	102	Stress Fx R lower back

FIVE-YEAR INJURY LOG — Hitters

Batter	Yr	Days	Injury
Choi,Ji-Man	19	11	Sprained L ankle
	20	16	Strn L hamstring
	21	73	Surg R knee; Strn groin; str L ham
	22	8	Loose bodies in R elbow
Clement,Ernie	21	22	Covid-19
Collins,Zack	22	7	Covid-19
Conforto,Michael	18	8	Recovery from L shoulder surgery
	19	10	Concussion
	20	5	Tightness L hamstring
	21	38	Strn R hamstring
	22	188	Shoulder (unsigned FA)
Contreras,Willson	19	42	Strn R foot; Strn R hamstring
	21	24	Sprained R knee
	21	26	Sprained R knee; inflam R hip
	22	22	Sprained L ankle
Cooper,Garrett	18	163	R wrist contusion
	19	42	Strn L calf
	20	34	Covid-19
	21	79	Covid; sprn L elbow; lumbar strn
	22	30	Brs R wrist;Conc.;Fx L metacarp 5
Cordero,Franchy	18	140	L abductor strain; bone spur R elb
	19	176	Sprained R elb; stress reax R elb
	20	46	Fractured hamate bone R wrist
	22	32	Sprained R ankle
Correa,Carlos	18	43	Lower back soreness
	19	87	Fx ribs; lower back strain
	21	7	Covid-19
	22	18	Bruised middle finger; covid-19
Crawford,Brandon	21	11	Strn L oblique
	22	32	Inflamed L knee; inflamed R knee
Crawford,J.P.	18	91	Strn R elbow
	19	17	Sprained L ankle
Cron,C.J.	19	25	R thumb inflammation
	20	49	Sprained L knee
	21	12	Strn lower back
Cruz,Nelson	18	12	Sprained R ankle
	19	29	L wrist sprain
	21	2	Covid-19
Dahl,David	18	123	Fractured R foot
	19	10	Strn abdominal
	20	42	Sore lower back, strnd R shoulder
	21	37	Bruised L rib cage
d'Arnaud,Travis	18	174	TJS
	19	11	TJS
	20	6	Covid-19
	21	102	Sprained L thumb
Davidson,Matthew	18	8	Back spasms
	20	7	Covid-19
Davis,Henry	22	144	Non-displaced fracture L wrist
Davis,J.D.	21	84	Bruised & sprained R hand
Davis,Jaylin	21	155	L patellar tendonitis; Strn L ham.
Davis,Jonathan	19	28	Sprained R ankle
	20	11	Sprained R ankle
	22	30	R elbow impingement
Daza,Yonathan	18	28	Strn L shoulder
	21	40	Covid-19; laceration L thumb
	22	26	Separated L shoulder
Dean,Austin	20	44	Strn R elbow, Covid-19
DeJong,Paul	18	50	Fractured L hand
	20	20	Covid-19
	21	30	Fx rib R side
DeShields,Delino	18	48	Fx R fing; concussion; Fx L hamate
	20	15	Covid-19

FIVE-YEAR INJURY LOG — Hitters

Batter	Yr	Days	Injury
Devers,Jose	21	95	Impingement R shoulder
	22	40	Impingement R shoulder
Devers,Rafael	18	40	L should. inflam; Strn L ham.
	22	11	Strained R hamstring
Diaz,Aledmys	18	25	Sprained L ankle
	19	67	Dizziness; Strn L hamstring
	20	36	Strn R groin
	21	51	Fx L hand
	22	27	Strained L groin
Diaz,Elias	19	25	Viral infection
	22	10	Sprained L wrist
Diaz,Isan	20	14	Strn L groin
	21	3	Undisclosed inj
Diaz,Yandy	19	91	Strn R ham; bruised L foot
	20	28	Strn R hamstring
	22	2	Covid-19
Dickerson,Alex	18	187	TJS
	19	28	Strn R oblique; strn R wrist
	21	37	Impinge R shldr;up back;R hamstr
Dickerson,Corey	18	8	Strn L hamstring
	19	80	Strn R shoulder; Fx L foot
	21	50	Bruised L foot
	22	35	Strained R calf
Donaldson,Josh	18	125	R shoulder inflam; tight L calf x 2
	20	27	Strn R calf
	21	12	Strn R hamstring
	22	12	Inflammation in R shoulder
Dozier,Hunter	19	22	Bruised chest
	20	18	Covid-19
	21	15	Concussion
Drury,Brandon	18	94	Migraines; fractured L hand
	22	11	Concussion
Duffy,Matt	18	11	Strn R hamstring
	19	118	Tightness L hamstring
	21	66	Strn lower back; Covid-19
	22	47	Covid-19; lower back spasms
Duggar,Steven	18	34	Torn labrum - L shoulder
	19	67	Strn low back;sprn AC joint L shld
	22	63	Strained L oblique
Duran,Jarren	21	15	Covid-19
Duvall,Adam	22	77	Recovery from L wrist surgery
Encarnacion,Edwin	18	11	L biceps inflammation
	19	32	Fx R wrist
Engel,Adam	20	3	Covid-19
	21	119	Strn R hamstring
	22	12	Strained R hamstring
Escobar,Alcides	22	21	Strained R hamstring
Escobar,Eduardo	21	12	Strn R hamstring
	22	11	Strained L oblique
Espinal,Santiago	21	19	Strn R hip flexor
	22	14	Strained L oblique
Espinoza,Anderson	20	68	TJS
Estrada,Thairo	19	22	Strn R hamstring
	22	13	Concussion; covid-19
Evans,Phillip	18	61	Fractured L tibia
	20	51	Fractured jaw, concussion
	21	38	Concussion; Strn L hamstring
Fairchild,Stuart	21	20	Covid-19
Fargas,Johneshwy	21	51	Sprained A/C joint L shoulder
Farmer,Kyle	19	27	Strn L oblique; concussion
Fisher,Derek	18	15	Gastrointestinal discomfort
	20	34	Strn L quad, bruised R knee
	21	78	Strn L hamstring

FIVE-YEAR INJURY LOG — Hitters

Batter	Yr	Days	Injury
Fletcher,David	20	13	Sprained L ankle
	22	113	Str L hip x2;Surg grn/hip;Brs R hip
Flores,Wilmer	18	19	Lower back soreness
	19	59	Fx R foot
	21	22	Strn R hamstring
Flowers,Tyler	18	29	L oblique strain
	20	7	Covid-19
Ford,Mike	22	9	Strained neck
Forsythe,Logan	18	31	R shoulder inflammation
	20	32	Strn R oblique
Fraley,Jake	20	6	Strn R quad
	21	89	Covid; Strn L hamstr;inflam R shld
	22	90	Inflammation R knee
France,Ty	21	10	Inflammation L wrist
	22	13	Sprnd L elbow; Strnd flexor L elb.
Franco,Maikel	21	17	Sprained R ankle
Franco,Wander	21	6	Tightness R hamstring
	22	89	Strained R quad; sore R wrist
Frazier,Clint	18	113	Concussion
	19	12	Sprained L ankle
	21	78	Medical Illness
	22	37	Appendix surgery
Friedl,T.J.	22	5	Screen R hamstring
Gallagher,Cameron	19	25	Strn L oblique
	20	11	Covid-19
	21	54	Concuss; R shldr imping; L knee
	22	51	Strained L hamstring
Gallo,Joey	19	92	Strn L oblique
	22	4	Covid-19
Galvis,Freddy	21	59	Strn R quad
Gamel,Ben	20	10	Strn L quad
	21	11	Strn R hamstring
	22	38	Strained L hamstring
Garcia,Aramis	20	68	Torn labrum L hip
	21	9	Medical Illness
	22	90	Fx L middle finger
Garcia,Avisail	18	72	Strn R hamstring x 2
	19	11	Strn R oblique
	22	55	Covid-19; strained L hamstring
Garcia,Leury	18	75	Strn L hamstring x 2; spr. L knee
	20	49	Sprained L thumb
	21	12	Concussion
	22	11	Strained lower back
Garcia,Luis (WAS)	21	2	Strn oblique
Garcia,Robel	21	7	Covid-19
Gardner,Brett	19	12	L knee inflammation
Garlick,Kyle	20	13	Strn R oblique
	21	110	Sports hernia; Covid-19
	22	75	Str Rcalf, Lham;Brsd rib;Spr. L wrst
Garver,Mitch	19	19	High ankle sprain L ankle
	20	30	Strn R intercostal
	21	69	Surg groin; lower back tightness
	22	111	Strnd flex R forearm;Covid
Gimenez,Andres	20	7	Tight R oblique
Gittens,Chris	21	20	Sprained R ankle
Gomes,Yan	21	24	Covid-19; Strn L oblique
	22	17	Strained L oblique
Gonzalez,Erik	19	105	Fx L clavicle
	21	37	Strn R oblique
Gonzalez,Luis	21	45	R shoulder surgery
	22	32	Strained lower back x2
Gonzalez,Marwin	19	11	Strn R hamstring
	21	22	Strn R hamstring
Gonzalez,Oscar	22	32	Strained R intercostal

FIVE-YEAR INJURY LOG — Hitters

Batter	Yr	Days	Injury
Goodrum,Niko	19	38	Strn L groin
	20	11	Strn R oblique
	21	67	Spr L hand; bruised L calf; groin
Gordon,Nick	20	68	Covid-19
Grandal,Yasmani	21	53	Torn tendon L knee
	22	51	Low back spasms; strained L knee
Graterol,Juan	19	44	Concussion
Gregorius,Didi	18	18	Bruised L heel
	19	72	TJS
	21	52	Covid-19; impingement R elbow
	22	32	Sprained R knee
Greiner,Grayson	19	70	Strn lower back
	21	38	Strn L hamstring
Grichuk,Randal	18	32	R knee sprain
Grisham,Trent	21	29	Strn R hamstring; bruised L heel
Grossman,Robbie	18	14	Strn R hamstring
	22	12	Strained neck
Guillorme,Luis	21	75	Strn R oblique; Strn L hamstring
	22	29	Strained L groin
Gurriel,Lourdes	18	32	Concussion; sprained L knee/ank
	19	43	Appendectomy; Strn L quad
	21	3	Covid-19
	22	30	Strained L hamstring
Gurriel,Yulieski	18	11	Recov hamate surgery, L hand
	21	12	Strn neck
Gutierrez,Kelvin	19	19	Fx toe R foot
	20	52	Strn R elbow
Guzman,Ronald	18	8	Concussion
	19	32	Strn R hamstring
	21	157	Torn lateral meniscus R knee
Haase,Eric	21	12	Strn abdominal
Haggerty,Sam	20	22	Strn L forearm
	21	116	Inflamed R shoulder
	22	5	Strained L groin
Hamilton,Billy	21	73	Strn L ham; Strn R oblique x2
Hampson,Garrett	22	20	Bruised R hand; covid-19
Haniger,Mitch	19	116	Ruptured testicle
	20	67	Strn ab
	22	113	High R ankle sprain; covid-19
Happ,Ian	21	12	Bruised ribs
Harper,Bryce	21	14	Bruised L forearm
	22	63	Fx L thumb
Harrison,Josh	18	35	Fractured metacarpal - L hand
	19	91	Strn L ham tendon; L shldr inflam
	21	8	Covid-19
Haseley,Adam	19	23	Strn L groin
	20	10	Sprained R wrist
	21	55	Covid-19
Hayes,Ke'Bryan	21	61	Sore L wrist
	22	8	Back spasms; strained lower back
Hays,Austin	18	8	Sprained R ankle
	20	31	Non-displaced fx rib L side
	21	35	Strn R & L hamstring
Healy,Ryon	18	18	Sprained R ankle
	19	133	Lower back inflammation
Hedges,Austin	21	9	Concussion
	22	11	Concussion
Heim,Jonah	21	8	Covid-19
Heineman,Tyler	22	24	Strained R groin; concussion
Heredia,Guillermo	21	16	Inflammation R hamstring
Hermosillo,Michael	19	187	Abdominal injury
	21	9	Strn L forearm
	22	122	Strnd L quad x2; covid-19

FIVE-YEAR INJURY LOG — Hitters

Batter	Yr	Days	Injury
Hernandez,Enrique	19	23	Sprained L hand
	21	24	Covid; Strn R hamstring
	22	72	Covid-19; strained R hip flexor
Hernandez,Marco	18	187	Recovery from L shoulder surgery
	19	29	Recovery from L shoulder surgery
Hernandez,Teoscar	20	10	Strn L oblique
	21	22	Covid-19
	22	24	Strained L oblique
Hernandez,Yadiel	22	50	Strained L calf
Hernandez,Yonny	22	34	Strained L calf
Herrera,Jose	22	6	Covid-19
Herrera,Odubel	19	16	Strn R hamstring
	21	14	Tendinitis L ankle
	22	19	Strained R oblique
Heyward,Jason	18	28	Concussion; R hamstring tight
	21	30	Concus;str L ham;infl L index fing
	22	117	Covid; inflam R knee and surgery
Hicks,Aaron	18	14	R intercostal strain
	19	105	Strn L lower back
	21	127	Sprained L wrist
Hicks,John	18	55	Strn R groin
Higashioka,Kyle	20	25	Strn R oblique
	21	12	Covid-19
	22	3	Covid-19
Higgins,P.J.	21	98	Strn R forearm
Hill,Derek	21	31	Sprain R shldr; brsd ribs; L knee
	22	18	Strained R hamstring
Hiura,Keston	19	12	Strn L hamstring
	21	15	Covid-19
Hoerner,Nico	21	101	Str L forearm;str L ham;str R obliq
	22	15	Sprained R ankle
Holt,Brock	18	12	Strn L hamstring
	19	52	Scratched cornea R eye
	21	51	Covid-19; Strn R hamstring
Hoskins,Rhys	18	10	Facial injury
	20	16	Strn L elbow
	21	38	Strn L groin; ab surgery
Hosmer,Eric	20	20	Gastritis, fx index finger L hand
	21	8	Covid-19
	22	42	Inflamed lower back
Huff,Sam	21	108	Strn L hamstring
Hummel,Cooper	22	9	Covid-19
Hundley,Nick	19	46	Back spasms
Iannetta,Chris	19	19	Strn R lat
Ibanez,Andy	21	19	Strn L hamstring
Iglesias,Jose	18	33	Lower abdominal strain
	20	12	Strn L quad
	21	11	Strn L hamstring
	22	23	Bruised R hand
Inciarte,Ender	19	109	Strn lumbar region; str. R hammy
	21	34	Strn L hamstring; Covid
India,Jonathan	21	3	Undisclosed
	22	52	Strained R hamstring x2
Isbel,Kyle	22	5	Covid-19
Jackson,Alex	19	26	Sprained L knee
	21	81	Strn L hamstring
	22	121	Sprnd mid finger; L wrist Inflam
Jackson,Drew	22	11	Covid-19
Jankowski,Travis	19	117	Fx L wrist
	21	6	Covid-19; bruised R foot
	22	46	Fx 4th metacarpal L hand
Jansen,Danny	21	67	Strn R hamstring
	22	70	Strain L oblique; fx finger L hand
Jay,Jon	19	121	Sore L shoulder

FIVE-YEAR INJURY LOG — Hitters

Batter	Yr	Days	Injury
Jeffers,Ryan	22	74	Fx R thumb
Jimenez,Eloy	19	36	Brse uln nerve R elb;R ankle sprn
	21	117	Surgery - torn L pectoral tendon
	22	74	Strained R hamstring
Joe,Connor	21	13	Strn R hamstring
	22	10	Strained serratus in R side
Jones,JaCoby	18	15	R hamstring strain
	19	82	Sprn R shldr; strn back; Fx L wrist
	20	27	Fractured L hand
Jones,Taylor	21	19	Covid-19
	22	81	Sore lower back
Joyce,Matt	18	74	Lumbar strain x 2
	20	12	Covid-19
	21	102	Strn R calf; Strn lower back
Judge,Aaron	18	50	Chip fracture, R wrist
	19	62	Strn L oblique
	20	34	Strn R calf x2
	21	12	Covid-19
Kang,Jung Ho	19	26	Strn L oblique
Kelly,Carson	18	10	R hamstring strain
	21	52	Fx L big toe; fx R wrist
	22	38	Strained L oblique
Kepler,Max	20	10	Strn L adductor
	21	30	Covid-19; Strn L hamstring
	22	37	Covid; Sprnd R wrist; fx R 5th toe
Kieboom,Carter	20	7	Contusion L wrist
	22	188	TJS
Kieboom,Spencer	19	23	R elbow inflammation
Kiermaier,Kevin	18	65	Torn ligament R rhumb
	19	11	Sprained L thumb
	21	23	Strn L quad; Covid-19; spr R wrist
	22	102	L hip inflammation x2
Kiner-Falefa,Isiah	19	44	Sprained ligament R middle finger
Kingery,Scott	19	30	Strn R hamstring
	20	15	Back spasms
	21	22	Concussion
Kipnis,Jason	19	19	Strn R calf
Kirilloff,Alex	21	77	Torn ligament R wrist
	22	92	Inflammation R wrist x2
Kirk,Alejandro	21	80	Strn L hip flexor
Knapp,Andrew	21	25	Covid-19; concussion
Kramer,Kevin	20	67	Recovery from R hip surgery
Lagares,Juan	18	137	L toe surgery
	21	18	Strn R calf
LaMarre,Ryan	21	28	Strn R hamstring
Lamb,Jake	18	113	Sprained L AC joint
	19	83	Strn L quad
	21	40	Strn R quad
Larnach,Trevor	22	121	Strnd R groin; Strnd AB
LaStella,Tommy	19	87	Fx tibia L leg
	21	93	Strn L hamstring
	22	86	Covid;Inflam R Achilles;Neck spas
Laureano,Ramon	19	38	R lower leg stress reaction
	21	19	Strn R hip
	22	44	Strnd L oblique; Strnd R ham
LeMahieu,D.J.	18	40	Strn R ham; L thumb; L oblique
	20	14	Sprained L thumb, Covid-19
	21	2	Sports hernia
LeMahieu,DJ	22	23	Inflammation toe R foot
Leon,Sandy	22	12	Surg repair torn meniscus R knee
Lewis,Kyle	21	128	Bone brs R knee;torn menisc R kn
	22	103	Concus; Surg torn menisc R knee
Lewis,Royce	22	132	Bone bruise R knee
Lin,Tzu-Wei	19	150	Sprained L knee

FIVE-YEAR INJURY LOG — Hitters

Batter	Yr	Days	Injury
Lindor,Francisco	19	24	Strn R calf
	21	39	Strn R oblique
Lobaton,Jose	21	79	Strn R shoulder
Locastro,Tim	21	78	Torn ACL R knee
	22	28	Strained L lat
Long,Shed	20	20	Stress fracture L tibia
	21	114	Stress Fx R shin
Longoria,Evan	18	42	Fractured L hand
	19	21	Plantar fasciitis L foot
	20	9	Strn R oblique
	21	83	Sprain R shldr; brse R hand; Covid
	22	68	St ham;Fx R thm;St oblq;Fing surg
Lopes,Timmy	19	12	Concussion
	21	61	Strn R oblique
Lowe,Brandon	19	83	Bone bruise R shin
	22	86	Stress reax low back; Brsd R tricps
Lowrie,Jed	19	164	Sprained L knee capsule
	20	68	Capsule injury L knee
	22	46	Covid-19; sprained R shoulder
Luplow,Jordan	19	28	Strn R hamstring
	21	76	Sprained L ankle
	22	22	Strained R oblique
Lux,Gavin	21	41	Strn L hamstring; sore R wrist
Madrigal,Nick	20	23	Separated L shoulder
	21	98	Surgery R hamstring
	22	100	Strnd low back; strained R groin
Maile,Luke	19	53	L oblique strain
	20	68	Fractured R index finger
	22	22	Strained L hamstring
Maldonado,Martin	21	7	Covid-19
Mancini,Trey	20	67	Recovery from colon cancer
Marcano,Tucupita	22	14	Covid-19
Marchan,Rafael	22	68	Strained L hamstring
Margot,Manuel	18	11	Bruised ribs
	21	21	Strn L hamstring
	22	72	Sprnd R ham; Sprained R knee
Marisnick,Jake	18	22	L groin discomfort
	20	39	Strn L hamstring
	21	29	Strn R hamstring
	22	76	Covid; Lig L thm; Spr R big toe
Marsh,Brandon	22	10	Sprained L ankle
Marte,Ketel	20	14	Inflammation L wrist
	21	77	Strn R & L hamstrings
	22	9	Covid-19
Marte,Starling	18	9	Strn R oblique
	19	11	Bruised abdominal wall
	21	39	Fx rib
	22	26	Fx R middle finger
Martin,Jason	19	28	Dislocated L shoulder
	20	8	Strn upper back
Martin,Richie	20	68	Fractured R wrist
	21	64	Fx L wrist
Martin,Russell	19	18	Lower back inflam
Martinez,J.D.	21	4	Covid-19
Martinez,Jose	19	21	Sprained AC joint R shoulder
	21	169	Torn meniscus L knee
Martini,Nick	19	62	Sprained R knee
Mateo,Jorge	20	22	Covid-19
	21	10	Strn lower back; Covid-19
Mathias,Mark	21	169	Torn labrum R shoulder
Maton,Nick	22	126	Sprained R shoulder

FIVE-YEAR INJURY LOG — Hitters

Batter	Yr	Days	Injury
Mazara,Nomar	18	28	Sprained R thumb
	19	13	Strn L oblique
	20	12	Covid-19
	21	25	Strn L ab
McCann,James	21	19	Strn lower back
	22	69	Fx hamate L hand; Strnd L oblique
McCormick,Chas	21	12	Sore L hand
McCutchen,Andrew	19	119	Torn ACL L knee
	21	11	Inflammation L knee
	22	14	Covid-19
McKinney,Billy	18	55	L AC shoulder sprain
	21	7	R hip impingement
McKinstry,Zach	21	38	Strn R oblique
	22	9	Strained neck
McMahon,Ryan	19	13	Sprained L elbow
McNeil,Jeff	19	29	Strn L ham; Fx R wrist
	21	36	Strn L hamstring
Meadows,Austin	19	20	Sprained R thumb
	20	24	Strn L oblique, Covid-19
	22	140	Concus; Strnd R/L Achilles; Covid
Mejia,Francisco	19	41	Strn R oblique; sore L knee
	20	31	Thumb
	21	9	L intercostal injury
	22	25	Covid-19; impingement R should
Mendick,Danny	22	108	Torn ACL R knee
Mercedes,Yermin	22	38	Fx hamate bone L hand
Mercer,Jordy	18	14	Strn L calf
	19	73	Strn R quad
	21	75	Covid-19; Strn R quad; str L calf
Meyers,Jake	22	82	Surg repair torn labrum L should
Miller,Brad	18	12	Groin strain
	19	12	Strn R hip flexor
	22	58	R hip impingement; strained neck
Miller,Owen	22	5	Covid-19
Molina,Yadier	18	31	Pelvic injury
	19	48	Strn tendon R thumb
	20	17	Covid-19
	21	12	Strn tendon R foot
	22	46	Inflammation R knee
Moncada,Yoan	18	10	Tight L hamstring
	19	23	Strn R hamstring
	22	56	Strnd R oblq; Str R ham; Str L ham
Mondesi,Adalberto	18	33	R shoulder impingement
	19	61	Strn R groin
	21	140	Strn R oblique; L ham; L oblique
	22	166	Torn ACL L knee
Moniak,Mickey	22	94	Fx R hand; bruised L hand
Moore,Dylan	19	12	Bruised R wrist
	20	22	Concussion, sprained R wrist
	21	25	Strn L calf
	22	30	Back spasms; strained R oblique
Moran,Colin	20	5	Concussion
	21	69	Strn L groin; fx L wrist
Moreland,Mitch	19	59	Strn R quad
	21	47	Inflam cartilage L rib; L wrist
Moroff,Max	21	113	L shoulder subluxation
Mountcastle,Ryan	21	11	Concussion
	22	11	Strained L forearm/wrist
Moustakas,Mike	20	15	Bruised L quad, Covid-19
	21	91	Covid-19; bruised R heel
	22	79	Str R biceps; str L calf; covid-19
Muncy,Max	19	16	Fx R wrist
	21	11	Strn R oblique
	22	13	L elbow inflammation

FIVE-YEAR INJURY LOG — Hitters

Batter	Yr	Days	Injury
Munoz,Yairo	18	12	Sprained R wrist
	20	11	Lower back strain
	21	16	Covid-19
Murphy,Tom	20	68	Fractured metatarsal L foot
	22	156	Dislocated L shoulder
Muzziotti,Simon	22	44	Partially torn R patellar tendon
Myers,Wil	18	81	Nerve irrit;bone bruise L Ft;L obliq
	20	2	Recovery from bone spur surgery
	21	12	Covid-19
	22	76	Brsd R thumb; inflam L knee
Naquin,Tyler	18	101	R hip strain; Strn L ham.
	19	53	Torn ACL R knee; Strn L calf
	20	18	Hairline fx L big toe
	22	44	Covid-19 x2; strained L quad
Narvaez,Omar	21	13	Strn L hamstring
	22	26	Covid-19; strained L quad x2
Naylor,Josh	21	81	Fx R ankle
	22	20	Surgery R ankle; covid-19
Newman,Kevin	19	24	Lacerated R middle finger
	20	9	Bruised peroneal nerve L knee
	22	73	Strained L groin
Nido,Tomas	19	9	Concussion
	20	35	Covid-19
	21	42	Bruised R wrist; sprnd L thumb x2
	22	8	Covid-19
Nimmo,Brandon	18	9	Bruised L index finger
	19	132	Stiff neck
	21	72	Bruised L index fing; Strn R ham
	22	5	Covid-19
Nogowski,John	21	29	Bone bruise L hand
Nola,Austin	21	88	Fx L middle finger; Sprnd L knee
Nottingham,Jacob	21	22	Sprained L thumb
Odor,Rougned	18	32	Strn L hamstring
	19	14	Sprained R knee
	20	10	Infection R eye
	21	14	Covid-19; sprained L knee
O'Hearn,Ryan	20	6	Covid-19
Ohtani,Shohei	18	26	Sprained UCL, R elbow
	19	41	Recovery from TJS
Olivares,Edward	22	104	Strained R quad; strained L quad
Olson,Matt	19	41	R hand surgery
Ona,Jorge	21	169	Strn R elbow
O'Neill,Tyler	18	22	Inflammation groin area
	19	41	Ulnar nerve subluxation R elbow
	21	24	Strn R groin; fx L middle finger
	22	66	R shoulr impinge; Str L ham x2
Ortega,Rafael	22	25	Fx L ring finger
Owings,Chris	20	40	Strn L hamstring
	21	134	Spr L thumb;mallet fing L thumb
Ozuna,Marcell	18	11	R shoulder inflammation
	19	94	Fx middle finger on R hand
	21	108	Fx L index finger
Pache,Cristian	21	31	Strn L groin; inflammation R ham
Panik,Joe	18	59	Sprnd L thumb; L groin strain
	21	37	Covid-19
Paredes,Isaac	20	17	Covid-19
	21	30	Strn R hip
Parra,Gerardo	21	12	Inflammation R knee
Pasquantino,Vinnie	22	18	Tendinitis R shoulder
Pederson,Joc	21	12	Tendinitis L wrist
	22	9	Concussion
Pena,Jeremy	22	12	Sore L thumb
Peralta,David	19	70	R shoulder AC joint inflammation
Peraza,Jose	21	58	Fx R middle finger

FIVE-YEAR INJURY LOG — Hitters

Batter	Yr	Days	Injury
Perez,Michael	18	32	L hamstring strain
	19	34	Strn R oblique
Perez,Roberto	20	21	Strn R shoulder
	21	102	Inflam R shldr; fx finger R hand
	22	155	Strained L hamstring
Perez,Salvador	18	27	Sprained R MCL
	19	187	Recovery from TJS
	20	25	CSC L eye
	22	48	Torn UCL L thumb
Peterson,Jace	21	40	Covid-19; sprained L thumb
	22	38	Strained L elbow
Pham,Tommy	18	14	Fractured R foot
	20	33	Fractured hamate bone R hand
Phegley,Josh	18	24	Fractured R hand
	19	17	L thumb contusion
Phillips,Brett	20	8	Covid-19
	21	23	Strn L hamstring; sprained R ank
Pillar,Kevin	18	20	Sprained R shoulder
	21	14	Multiple facial fractures
	22	129	Fracture in L shoulder
Pina,Manny	18	22	R calf strain; L biceps strain
	19	17	Strn R hamstring
	20	32	Torn meniscus R knee
Pina,Manuel	21	25	Strn L oblique; fx big toe L foot
	22	168	Inflammation L wrist
Pinder,Chad	18	20	Hyperext. L knee; L elb laceration
	20	15	Strn R hamstring
	21	85	Sprained L knee; Strn R ham
	22	10	Covid-19
Piscotty,Stephen	19	68	Sprained R knee; R ankle
	21	46	Sprained L wrist x2
	22	62	Covid-19; tight L calf
Plawecki,Kevin	18	46	Hairline fracture - L hand
	21	19	Strn L hamstring
	22	11	Covid-19
Polanco,Gregory	18	14	Surgery to stabilize L shoulder
	19	127	L shoulder inflammation
	20	5	Covid-19
	21	20	Covid-19; sore R shoulder
Polanco,Jorge	22	48	Sore low back; inflam L knee
Pollock,A.J.	18	49	Fractured L thumb
	19	74	R elbow inflammation
	21	32	L hamstring; R hamstring
	22	11	Strained R hamstring
Profar,Jurickson	21	22	Covid-19
	22	8	Concussion
Pujols,Albert	18	44	L knee surgery
Quinn,Roman	19	181	Strn R groin; Strn R oblique
	20	26	Concussion, Covid-19
	21	133	Covid-19: torn L Achilles
	22	50	Bruised L knee
Ramirez,Harold	20	64	Strn L hamstring, Covid-19
	21	21	Strn R hamstring
	22	30	Fx R shoulder
Ramirez,Jose	19	31	Fx hamate bone R hand
Ramos,Wilson	18	29	Strn L hamstring
	21	51	Torn ACL L knee;
Realmuto,J.T.	18	20	Lower back bruise
	21	14	Covid-19; bone bruise L wrist
	22	3	Covid-19
Refsnyder,Rob	21	61	Concussion; Strn L hamstr; R elb
	22	21	Sprnd R knee; Low back spasms

FIVE-YEAR INJURY LOG — Hitters

Batter	Yr	Days	Injury
Rendon,Anthony	18	13	L toe contusion
	19	11	Bruised L elbow
	21	98	Groin strn;L ham strn;L knee brse
	22	118	Inflam R wrist; surgery R wrist
Renfroe,Hunter	18	38	R elbow inflammation
	22	32	Strained R ham; strained R calf
Rengifo,Luis	19	13	Fx hamate bone L hand
	20	9	Strn R hamstring
Reyes,Franmil	21	41	Strn abdominal
	22	27	Tight R hamstring
Reyes,Victor	21	37	Strn intercostal; Strn R groin
	22	52	Strained L quad; strained R quad
Reynolds,Bryan	22	17	Covid-19; strained R oblique
Reynolds,Matt	22	18	L hip pain
Rickard,Joey	20	29	Inflammation L elbow
Riddle,J.T.	18	36	Recovery from L shoulder surgery
	19	75	Strn R forearm
	20	14	Strn ab
Riley,Austin	19	33	Torn LCL R knee
Rios,Edwin	20	16	Strn L hamstring
	21	135	Partially torn R rotator cuff
	22	128	Strained R hamstring
Rivera,Emmanuel	21	36	Fx hamate bone R hand
	22	7	Fractured L wrist
Rivera,Rene	18	88	R knee inflammation
	20	58	Hyperextended L elbow
	21	46	Bruised R elbow
Rizzo,Anthony	18	9	Lower back tightness
	21	11	Covid-19
	22	12	Medical illness
Robert,Luis	21	101	Covid; torn flexor tendon R hip
	22	35	Covid; Blur vision; Sprnd L wrist
Robertson,Daniel	18	71	Sprnd L thumb; strnd L hamstring
	19	39	Recov R knee surgery (meniscus)
	21	26	Concussion
Robles,Victor	21	12	Sprained R ankle
Rodgers,Brendan	19	98	R shoulder impingement
	20	29	Strn capsule R shoulder
	21	51	Strn R hamstring
	22	11	Strained L hamstring
Rodriguez,Julio	22	23	Brsd R wrist; Strained lower back
Rogers,Jake	21	31	Strn pronator R arm
	22	188	Tommy John surg
Rojas,Jose	22	16	Covid-19
Rojas,Josh	20	7	Lower back inflammation
	21	20	Dislocated R pinkie finger
	22	33	Strained R oblique
Rojas,Miguel	19	26	Strn R hamstring
	20	17	Covid-19
	21	22	Dislocation index finger L hand
Romine,Austin	21	123	Sprain R knee;spr L wrist; undisc
Rooker,Brent	20	16	Fx R forearm
	21	14	Strn neck
Rortvedt,Ben	22	97	Strn R oblq;Surg menisc L knee
Rosario,Eddie	19	19	Sprained L ankle
	21	52	Strn abdominal
	22	70	Blurred vision R eye
Ruf,Darin	21	26	Strn R hamstring
	22	6	Strained cervical neck
Ruiz,Keibert	22	30	Testicular contusion
Sanchez,Gary	18	65	R groin strain
	19	32	Strn L groin
	21	13	Covid-19

FIVE-YEAR INJURY LOG — Hitters

Batter	Yr	Days	Injury
Sanchez,Jesus	21	52	Covid; Strn R groin
	22	5	Covid-19
Sandoval,Pablo	18	63	R hamstring strain
	19	50	R elbow inflammation
Sano,Miguel	18	24	Strn L hamstring
	19	49	Laceration on R heel
	21	15	Strn R hamstring
	22	157	Surg repair torn meniscus L knee
Santana,Carlos	22	12	Bursitis R ankle
Santana,Danny	20	48	Strn R forearm
	21	64	Covid; L groin strain; L quad strn
Santander,Anthony	20	24	Strn R oblique
	21	41	Covid; sprained R knee
Schoop,Jonathan	18	25	R oblique strain
	20	16	Sprained R wrist
	22	17	Sprained R ankle
Schrock,Max	21	38	Strn L calf
	22	74	Strained L calf
Schwarber,Kyle	21	50	Covid-19; Strn R hamstring
Schwindel,Frank	22	27	Strained lower back
Seager,Corey	18	154	UCL strain - R elbow
	19	29	Strn L hamstring
	21	76	Fx R hand
Seager,Kyle	19	58	Recovery from surgery L hand
Segura,Jean	19	11	Strn L hamstring
	21	30	Strn R quad; Strn L groin
	22	65	Fx R index finger
Senzel,Nick	20	27	Covid-19
	21	87	Inflammation & surgery L knee
	22	42	Covid-19
Shaw,Travis	19	21	Strn R wrist
	21	66	Dislocated L shoulder
Sierra,Magneuris	20	32	Strn R hamstring
Simmons,Andrelton	18	11	Grade 2 R ankle sprain
	19	60	Sprained L ankle
	20	25	Sprained L ankle
	21	13	Covid-19
	22	66	Strained R shoulder
Slater,Austin	20	14	Strn L groin
	21	8	Concussion
	22	28	Inflamed L wrist; sprained L hand
Smith,Dominic	19	62	Stress reaction L foot
	22	26	Sprained R ankle
Smith,Josh	22	19	Sprained L shoulder
Smith,Kevan	18	24	Sprained L ankle
	19	55	Concuss; sprn L hand; back spasm
	20	2	Covid-19
Smith,Kevin	22	10	Bone bruise in L ankle
Smith,Pavin	21	7	Covid-19
Smith,Will	20	24	Neck inflammation, Covid-19
Smith-Njigba,Canaan	22	114	Fx R wrist
Sogard,Eric	21	11	Bruised L thumb
Solak,Nick	22	18	Fx R foot
Solano,Donovan	21	50	Covid-19; Strn R calf
	22	79	Strained L hamstring
Soler,Jorge	18	107	Fractured L toe
	20	15	Strn R oblique
	22	93	Pelvis inflam; lower back spasms
Sosa,Edmundo	20	24	Covid-19
	22	30	Covid-19; strained R hamstring
Soto,Juan	19	11	Back spasms
	20	12	Covid-19
	21	15	Strn L shoulder

FIVE-YEAR INJURY LOG — Hitters

Batter	Yr	Days	Injury
Souza,Steven	18	81	Strn R pectoral
	19	186	Recovery from torn ACL,PCL,LCL
	20	16	Strn R hamstring
Springer,George	18	12	Sprained L thumb
	19	31	Strn L hamstring
	21	95	Strn L obliq;str R quad;spr L knee
	22	9	R elbow inflammation
Stallings,Jacob	20	1	Concussion
Stanton,Giancarlo	19	164	Sprained PCL R knee
	20	38	Strn L hamstring
	21	15	Strn L quad
	22	42	Strained R calf; strained L Achilles
Stassi,Max	19	27	Sore L knee
	20	17	Strn R quad
	21	43	Concussion; sprained L thumb
	22	14	Covid-19
Stephenson,Tyler	22	122	Fx R thumb; fFx R clavicle; Concus
Stevenson,Andrew	19	16	Back spasms
	21	33	Strn oblique
Stewart,Christin	19	45	Concussion; Strn R quad
Stewart,D.J.	19	50	Concussion; sprained R ankle
	21	10	R Knee osteocondral defect
Stokes,Troy	20	51	Fx bone R hand
Story,Trevor	19	13	Sprained R thumb
	21	14	Inflammation R elbow
	22	63	Bruised R hand
Strange-Gordon,Dee	18	10	Fractured R great toe
	19	41	Strn L quad; bruised R wrist
	22	19	Covid-19
Suarez,Eugenio	18	18	Fractured R thumb
	22	11	Fx R index finger
Suzuki,Kurt	22	15	Covid-19
Suzuki,Seiya	22	40	Sprained L ring finger
Swanson,Dansby	18	16	L wrist inflammation
	19	34	Bruised R heel
Tapia,Raimel	19	11	Bruised L hand
	21	21	Sprained big toe R foot
Tatis Jr.,Fernando	19	86	Strn L ham; stress reax low back
	21	36	Covid; L shoulder subluxation x2
	22	131	Fx L wrist
Tauchman,Mike	19	22	Strn L calf
	21	17	Sprained R knee
Taylor,Chris	19	37	Fx L forearm
	22	31	Fx L foot; fx R pinky finger
Taylor,Michael	19	12	Sprained L knee
	22	16	Covid-19
Taylor,Tyrone	21	39	Strn R oblique; Strn R shoulder
	22	21	Concussion
Tellez,Rowdy	20	21	Knee
	21	5	Strn patella tendon R knee
Thomas,Lane	19	34	Fx R wrist
	20	23	Covid-19
Tillo,Daniel	20	68	TJS L elbow surg 8/20
Tom,Ka'Ai	21	92	Covid; brse L wrist; low back strn
Toro,Abraham	22	11	Sprained L shoulder
Torrens,Luis	20	2	Back spasms-lumbar area
	22	20	Covid-19; L shoulder soreness
Torres,Gleyber	18	22	Strn R hip
	20	16	Strn L quad, L hamstring
	21	33	Covid-19; sprained L thumb
Torreyes,Ronald	21	30	Covid-19
Trammell,Taylor	22	46	Strained R hamstring
Trevino,Jose	20	16	Sprained L wrist
	21	25	Bruised R forearm

FIVE-YEAR INJURY LOG — Hitters

Batter	Yr	Days	Injury
Tromp,Chadwick	20	7	Strn R shoulder
	22	54	Strained L quad
Trout,Mike	18	15	R wrist inflammation
	21	122	Strn R calf
	22	33	Inflammation L rib cage
Tsutsugo,Yoshitomo	21	31	Strn R calf
	22	41	Lumbar strain
Tucker,Cole	20	12	Concussion
	22	5	Covid-19
Tucker,Kyle	21	19	Covid-19
Turner,Justin	18	59	Recover fr fx L wrist; groin strain
	20	18	Strn L hamstring
	22	8	Strained ab
Turner,Trea	19	45	Fx R index finger
	21	10	Covid-19
Upton,Justin	18	10	L index finger laceration
	19	82	Turf toe L foot
	21	42	Strn lower back
Urias,Luis	20	20	Covid-19
	22	29	Strained L quad
Urias,Ramon	22	36	Strained L oblique
Urshela,Giovanny	18	37	Strn R hamstring
	19	11	Tightness L groin
	20	12	Bone spur R elbow
	21	35	Covid-19; Strn L hamstring
VanMeter,Josh	22	25	Fx L ring finger
Vargas,Ildemaro	20	8	Strn R hamstring
Vaughn,Andrew	21	113	Strn lower back; Covid-19
	22	12	Bruised R hand
Vazquez,Christian	18	56	R fifth finger fx
	22	2	Covid-19
Velazquez,Andrew	22	25	Torn meniscus in R knee
Verdugo,Alex	19	56	Strn R oblique
Villar,Jonathan	18	19	Sprained R thumb
	21	13	Strn R calf
	22	12	Major dental work
Vogelbach,Dan	21	71	Strn L hamstring
	22	11	Strained L hamstring
Vogt,Stephen	18	187	R shoulder strain
	21	7	R hip inflammation
	22	48	Sprained R knee
Voit,Luke	19	45	Strn ab; sports hernia
	21	96	Torn menisc L knee; Strn R obliq
	22	17	Biceps tendinitis R arm
Votto,Joey	18	14	R lower leg contusion
	19	13	Lower back strain
	21	34	Sprained L thumb
	22	69	Covid; Inflam/surg rot cuff L shldr
Wade,LaMonte	19	57	Dislocated R thumb
	21	30	Strn L oblique
	22	71	Inflammation L knee
Walker,Christian	18	3	Sinus bone fracture
	21	50	Strn R oblique x2
Walker,Steele	22	6	Covid-19
Wallach,Chad	19	132	Concussion
	20	26	Covid-19
Walls,Taylor	21	11	R wrist tendonitis
Walsh,Jared	21	16	Intercostal strain
	22	45	Thorac outlet synd L shoulder
Walton,Donnie	22	49	Inflammation in R shoulder
Ward,Taylor	21	2	Strn adductor R groin
	22	20	Strnd R groin; Strnd R hamstring
Wendle,Joe	19	98	Strn L hamstring; Fx L wrist
	22	57	Strned R ham x2; inflam L ham

FIVE-YEAR INJURY LOG — Hitters

Batter	Yr	Days	Injury
White,Eli	21	44	Strn R elbow
	22	118	Fx R wrist
White,Evan	21	125	Covid-19; Strn L hip
	22	148	Sports hernia
Williams,Justin	19	187	Fx second metacarpal R hand
	21	16	Strn neck
Williams,Lucas	21	21	Covid-19
Winker,Jesse	18	68	R shoulder subluxation
	19	43	Strn cervical spine
	21	32	Intercostal ligament strain
	22	4	Herniated disc cervical spine
Wisdom,Patrick	22	15	Sprained L ring finger
Wong,Kolten	18	21	L knee inflammation
	21	44	Strn R calf; Strn L oblique
	22	18	Strained R calf
Wynns,Austin	19	21	Strn L oblique
Yastrzemski,Mike	21	21	Strn L oblique; sprained R thumb
	22	11	Covid-19
Yelich,Christian	18	10	Strn R oblique
	21	47	Covid-19; Strn lower back
Yepez,Juan	22	34	Strained R forearm
Zagunis,Mark	18	28	R shoulder inflammation
Zavala,Seby	22	12	Concussion
Zimmer,Bradley	18	18	L rib contusion
	19	156	Recovery from surgery (July 2018)
Zimmerman,Ryan	18	71	Strn R oblique
	19	106	Plantar fasciitis R foot
Zunino,Mike	18	39	Strn L oblique
	19	22	Strn L quadriceps
	20	23	Strn L oblique, Covid-19
	22	121	Inflammation L shoulder

FIVE-YEAR INJURY LOG — Pitchers

Pitchers	Yr	Days	Injury
Abreu,Albert	22	71	Sprained L ankle; inflam R elbow
Abreu,Bryan	21	39	Strained R calf
Adam,Jason	21	3	Undisclosed inj
Adams,Austin	19	60	Strained R shoulder
	20	60	Strained L hamstring
	21	10	Strained R elbow
	22	179	Surgery to repair R flexor tendon
Akin,Keegan	21	12	Covid-19
Alaniz,Ruben	21	25	Strained R calf
Alcala,Jorge	21	19	Tendinitis R biceps
	22	179	R elbow inflammation
Alcantara,Sandy	18	35	R axillary/armpit infection
	20	27	Covid-19
Alexander,Scott	19	115	L forearm inflam
	21	123	Inflammation L shoulder x2
Alexander,Tyler	22	47	Sprained L elbow
Almonte,Yency	21	32	Covid-19; bruised R hand
	22	53	Tightness R elbow
Altavilla,Dan	18	95	R AC joint inflam; R UCL sprain
	19	58	Strained R forearm
	21	168	Strained R calf; inflam R elbow
Alvarado,Jose	19	75	Strained R oblique muscle
	20	45	Inflammation L shoulder
	21	27	Covid-19; impingement L shoulder
Alvarez,Jose	20	16	Testicular contusion
	21	11	Sprained R ankle
	22	109	Sore back; L elbow inflammation
Alzolay,Adbert	21	33	Strn L hamstring; blist R index fing
	22	167	Strained R lat muscle
Anderson,Brett	18	68	Strn L shoulder
	20	10	Blister L index finger
	21	46	Strn R ham; bruised R knee; L shld
Anderson,Chase	18	9	Food poisoning
	19	17	Lacerated R middle finger
	20	17	Strn R oblique
	21	60	Covid-19; tendinitis R triceps
Anderson,Ian	21	48	Inflammation R shoulder
Anderson,Nick	20	16	Inflam R forearm
	21	165	Sprained R elbow; Strn lower back
	22	159	UCL tear R elb; plant fasciitis R ft
Anderson,Shaun	19	17	Blister on R middle finger
	21	28	Strn L quad; blister R hand
Anderson,Tanner	21	3	Bruised R foot
Anderson,Tyler	19	148	Recovery from L knee surgery
Andriese,Matt	19	23	L foot contusion
	21	39	Strn R hamstring
Antone,Tejay	21	99	Inflamm R forearm; surgery R elb
	22	188	Tommy John surg
Appel,Mark	22	27	R elbow inflammation
Arano,Victor	18	18	Strn R rotator cuff
	19	165	R elbow inflammation
	22	83	Sprn R shldr; inflam L knee
Archer,Chris	18	35	L abdominal strain
	19	60	R thumb inflammation
	20	67	Recovery from neck surgery
	21	140	Strn R forearm; Strn L hip
	22	41	Tight R pectoral; tight L hip
Armstrong,Shawn	19	27	Strn R forearm
	20	25	Inflm S.I. joint R shld; sor low back
	21	2	Covid-19
Arrieta,Jake	19	48	Bone spur R elbow
	20	13	Strn R hamstring
	21	51	Strn L ham; abrasion R thumb
Ashby,Aaron	22	46	Inflamed L shldr; inflam R forearm

FIVE-YEAR INJURY LOG — Pitchers

Pitchers	Yr	Days	Injury
Ashcraft,Graham	22	33	Sore R biceps
Avilan,Luis	19	60	Sore L elbow
	20	8	Inflammation L shoulder
	21	154	Tommy John surgery
Baez,Michel	21	169	Tommy John surgery
	22	64	Tommy John surg
Baez,Pedro	18	42	R biceps tendinitis
	20	24	Strn R groin
	21	149	Sore R shoulder
Bailey,Brandon	21	169	Tommy John surgery recovery
Banda,Anthony	19	180	TJS
	21	2	Covid-19
	22	8	Medical illness
Baragar,Caleb	21	14	Inflammation L elbow
Bard,Luke	19	12	Bruised R triceps
	21	169	Inflammation R hip
Barlow,Joe	21	11	Blister R middle finger
	22	72	Blister index finger x2
Barnes,Matt	21	20	Covid-19
	22	66	Inflammation R shoulder
Bass,Anthony	18	34	Viral illness; R mid-thoracic strain
Bassitt,Chris	19	19	R lower leg contusion
	21	30	Head injury
	22	8	Covid-19
Bauer,Trevor	18	39	Stress fracture, R fibula
Bautista,Felix	22	8	Discomfort L knee
Baz,Shane	22	156	R elbow surgery; Sprnd R elbow
Bazardo,Eduard	21	71	Strn lower back
Bednar,David	21	5	Strn R oblique
	22	54	inflamed lower back
Bedrosian,Cam	19	33	Strn R forearm
	20	28	Strn R adductor muscle
Beede,Tyler	20	67	TJS
	21	128	Tommy John surgery
Beeks,Jalen	20	34	Sprained L elbow
	21	169	Tommy John surgery
	22	29	Tightness lower R leg
Bello,Brayan	22	20	Strnd L groin
Bender,Anthony	22	126	Low back sore; Tommy John surg
Bergen,Travis	19	81	Strn L shoulder
	21	24	Impingement L shoulder
Betances,Dellin	19	184	R shldr impinge; torn Achilles ten
	20	25	Tight R lat muscle
	21	162	Impingement R shoulder
Bickford,Phil	22	11	R shoulder fatigue
Bieber,Shane	21	95	Strn subscapularis R shoulder
Blach,Ty	22	17	Strnd L wrist
Black,Ray	20	54	Strn R rotator cuff
Blackburn,Paul	18	157	Strn R forearm
	22	60	Inflammation R middle finger
Bleier,Richard	18	109	Torn upper lat; L shoulder surg
	19	36	L shoulder tendinitis
	20	14	Strn L triceps muscle
	22	19	Covid-19
Bolanos,Ronald	21	94	Strn flexor R forearm
	22	3	Covid-19
Borucki,Ryan	19	182	Surg remove bone spur R elbow
	21	69	Covid; Strn flex tendon L forearm
	22	86	Blist L hand; Str L flex; Str R ham
Boyd,Matt	21	84	Tendinitis L triceps; Strn L elbow
	22	151	Surgery to repair L flexor tendon
Brach,Brad	20	20	Covid-19
	21	29	R shoulder impingement

FIVE-YEAR INJURY LOG — Pitchers

Pitchers	Yr	Days	Injury
Bracho,Silvino	19	186	Recovery from TJS
	20	64	TJS
Bradish,Kyle	22	36	Inflammation in R shoulder
Bradley,Archie	21	38	Strn L & R oblique
	22	126	Strnd ab; fx R elbow
Brasier,Ryan	21	154	Strn L calf muscle
Brault,Steven	19	32	Strn L shoulder
	21	132	Strn L lat x2
	22	63	Covid-19; Strnd L shoulder
Brebbia,John	20	67	TJS
	21	81	Tommy John surgery
Brentz,Jake	21	10	Impingement R shoulder
	22	162	Strnd L flexor tendon
Brice,Austin	18	11	Mid-back strain
	19	79	Gastroenteritis
	20	20	Strn R Lat muscle
Brieske,Beau	22	80	Tendinitis R biceps
Brigham,Jeff	20	56	Covid-19
	21	169	Covid-19
Britton,Zack	18	75	Ruptured R Achilles
	20	13	Strn L hamstring
	21	104	Bone spur L elbow; Strn L ham
	22	180	Tommy John surg recovery
Brogdon,Connor	21	37	Covid; tend. R elbow; str R groin
	22	21	Covid-19
Brubaker,JT	21	23	Bilateral adductor strain, R hip
	22	17	Strnd R lat
Buchter,Ryan	18	60	Strn L shoulder
Buehler,Walker	18	32	R rib microfracture
	20	23	Blister R hand
	22	120	Tommy John surg
Bukauskas,J.B.	21	48	Strn R flexor
	22	109	Strnd teres major in R shoulder
Bumgarner,Madison	18	69	Fractured L hand
	20	26	Mid-back strain
	21	44	Inflammation L shoulder
Bummer,Aaron	20	48	Strn L biceps
	21	18	Strn R hamstring
	22	101	Strnd R knee; Strnd R lat
Bundy,Dylan	18	11	L ankle sprain
	19	11	R knee tendinitis
	21	23	Strn R ankle
	22	13	Covid-19
Burke,Brock	20	67	Torn L labrum surgery
	21	24	Recovery from L shoulder surgery
Burnes,Corbin	19	17	R shoulder irritation
	21	15	Covid-19
Burr,Ryan	19	141	R shldr AC joint inflam; str R elb
	22	26	Strnd R shoulder
Bush,Matt	21	162	Inflamed R shoulder
	22	19	R forearm soreness
Cabrera,Edward	22	57	Tendinitis R elbow; Sprnd R ankle
Cabrera,Genesis	22	14	Covid-19
Canning,Griffin	19	55	Inflammation R elbow
	22	188	Sore lower back
Carrasco,Carlos	18	20	R elbow contusion
	19	89	Leukemia
	21	121	Strn R hamstring
	22	20	Strnd L oblique
Castano,Daniel	21	74	Impingement L shoulder
	22	71	Concussion
Castellanos,Humberto	22	130	Strnd R elbow

FIVE-YEAR INJURY LOG — Pitchers

Pitchers	Yr	Days	Injury
Castillo,Diego	19	19	R shoulder inflam/impingement
	21	28	Covid; inflam R shldr; tight groin
	22	14	Inflammation R shoulder
Castillo,Jose	18	22	R hamstring strain
	19	187	Torn L finger tendon
	20	68	Strn lat muscle
	21	169	Tommy John surgery
Castillo,Luis M.	22	36	Sore R shoulder
Castro,Anthony	21	73	Strn R forearm; ulnar nerve irritat
	22	12	Covid-19
Castro,Miguel	21	2	Covid-19
	22	80	Strnd R shoulder
Cavalli,Cade	22	40	Inflammation R shoulder
Cease,Dylan	21	3	Covid-19
Cederlind,Blake	21	169	Tommy John surgery
	22	188	Tommy John surg
Cessa,Luis	18	64	L oblique strain
	20	15	Covid-19
	22	27	Strnd lower back
Chacin,Jhoulys	19	84	Strn lower back; oblique
	21	13	Covid-19
	22	25	Toe sesamoiditis/inflammation
Chafin,Andrew	20	32	Sprained finger L hand
	22	23	Strnd L groin
Chapman,Aroldis	18	29	L knee tendinitis
	20	26	Covid-19
	21	13	Impingement L elbow
	22	60	Tndonitis L Achilles; infect low leg
Chargois,J.T.	18	35	Nerve irritation neck
	22	134	Tightness L oblique
Chatwood,Tyler	18	12	L hip tightness
	20	39	Strn lower back
	21	63	Strn cervical spine
Chavez,Jesse	19	49	Strn R groin
	20	15	Sprained L big toe
Chirinos,Yonny	18	35	R forearm strain
	19	48	R middle finger inflammation
	20	54	TJS
	21	169	Tommy John surgery
	22	156	Tommy John surg
Cishek,Steve	19	10	L hip inflammation
Cisnero,Jose	21	3	Laceration R elbow
	22	103	Strnd R shoulder
Civale,Aaron	21	76	Sprained finger R hand
	22	75	Str. L glute R wrist; inflam R 4-arm
Clarke,Taylor	19	17	Lower L back inflammation
	21	52	Strn teres major muscle R shldr
	22	56	Strnd L oblique x2
Cleavinger,Garrett	21	72	L forearm inflam; R oblique strain
Clevinger,Mike	19	81	Strn R upper back; sprained R ank
	21	169	Tommy John surgery
	22	57	Sprnd R knee; Str R triceps; covid
Clippard,Tyler	21	119	Covid; Strn R shoulder
	22	32	Strnd R groin
Cobb,Alex	19	176	Strn R groin; R hip impinge surg
	20	9	Covid-19
	21	65	Inflammation R wrist; blist R hand
	22	26	Strnd R adductor; Strnd neck
Cole,A.J.	18	13	L neck strain
	19	52	R shoulder impingement
	21	110	Cervical spine inflammation
Cole,Gerrit	21	14	Covid-19
Cole,Taylor	19	12	Strn R shoulder
Colina,Edwar	21	169	Inflammation R elbow

FIVE-YEAR INJURY LOG — Pitchers

Pitchers	Yr	Days	Injury
Colome,Alex	22	16	R lateral epicondylitis
Coonrod,Sam	20	27	Strn R lat muscle
	21	61	Tendinitis R forearm
	22	134	Sore R shoulder
Corbin,Patrick	21	6	Covid-19
Cordero,Jimmy	21	169	Tommy John surgery
Cortes,Nestor	20	45	Impingement L elbow
	21	9	Covid-19
	22	15	Strnd L groin
Coulombe,Daniel	22	151	L hip impingement x2
Cousins,Jake	21	11	Covid-19
	22	116	Effusion R elbow
Crawford,Kutter	22	35	Impingement R shoulder
Crick,Kyle	19	30	Tight R triceps; surg R index fing
	20	50	Strn R shoulder, lat muscle
	21	26	Covid-19; Strn R triceps
	22	116	R elbow inflammation
Criswell,Cooper	22	104	Sore R shoulder
Crochet,Garrett	21	12	Strn lower back
	22	188	Tommy John surg
Crouse,Hans	22	86	Biceps tendinitis R arm
Crowe,Wil	22	8	Inflammation R elbow
Cueto,Johnny	18	133	Spr R ankle; R elb inflam x 3; TJS
	19	167	TJS
	21	59	Covid; Strn lat muscle; str. R elb
Curtiss,John	21	51	Torn UCL R elbow
	22	186	Tommy John surg
Danish,Tyler	22	54	Strnd R forearm
Darvish,Yu	18	138	Viral infection; R triceps tendinitis
	21	25	Inflam L hip; Strn lower back
Davidson,Tucker	21	93	Inflammation L forearm
Davies,Zach	18	106	R rotator cuff inflammation
	19	57	Back spasms
Davies,Zachary	22	37	Inflammation in R shoulder
Davis,Austin	18	17	Lower back tightness
	21	67	Tommy John surgery
Davis,Wade	19	17	Strn L oblique
	20	42	Strn R shoulder
	21	26	Strn R forearm; R shoulder inflam
Dayton,Grant	18	187	TJS
	19	67	Fractured R big toe
	21	115	L shoulder inflam; L quad inflam.
De Leon,Jose	18	187	TJS
	19	98	TJS
	20	13	Strn R groin
De Los Santos,Yerry	22	62	Covid-19; Strnd R lat
deGrom,Jacob	18	8	Hyperextended R elbow
	19	11	Sore R elbow
	21	77	Low back tight; tight R forearm
	22	118	Stress FX in scapula in R shoulder
DeJong,Chase	21	16	Inflammation L knee
	22	17	Tendinitis L knee
Delaplane,Sam	21	108	Tommy John surgery
	22	110	R forearm strain
DelPozo,Miguel	21	7	Covid-19
DeSclafani,Anthony	18	69	L oblique strain
	20	11	Strn R teres major muscle
	21	21	Covid;Fatig R shldr;R ankle inflam
	22	68	Inflammation R ankle
Detmers,Reid	21	23	Covid-19
Detwiler,Ross	22	21	Strnd lower back
Devenski,Chris	18	27	L hamstring tightness
	20	57	Elbow/undisclosed
	21	125	Sprained UCL R elbow

FIVE-YEAR INJURY LOG — Pitchers

Pitchers	Yr	Days	Injury
Diaz,Alexis	22	20	Biceps tendinitis R arm
Diaz,Jhonathan	22	35	Concussion
Diaz,Miguel	19	162	Recov R knee surgery (meniscus)
Dobnak,Randy	21	82	Strn R index finger
	22	164	Sprnd R middle finger
Dolis,Rafael	21	29	Strn R calf; sprained finger R hand
Dominguez,Seranthon	19	117	Torn UCL R elbow
	20	67	TJS
	21	154	Tommy John surgery
	22	22	Strnd R triceps
Doolittle,Sean	18	60	L toe inflammation
	19	15	Tendonitis R knee
	20	31	Inflam R knee, str R oblique
	22	172	Sprnd L elbow
Drake,Oliver	20	38	Tendinitis R biceps
	21	169	Strn flexor tendon in R elbow
Duarte,Daniel	22	162	Inflammation R elbow
Duffy,Danny	18	11	L shoulder impingement
	19	59	L shoulder impinge; strn L ham
	21	100	Strn flexor L forearm
	22	188	Strnd L forearm
Dugger,Robert	20	26	Covid-19
	21	2	Covid-19
	22	58	Sore R shoulder
Dunn,Justin	21	100	Inflamed R shoulder x2
	22	139	Covid;subscapularis infl R shldr
Dunning,Dane	21	28	Covid-19; impingement R ankle
	22	28	Impingement R ankle
Duplantier,Jon	19	38	R shoulder inflammation
	21	44	Sprained R middle finger
Dyson,Sam	19	10	R biceps tendinitis
Edwards,Carl	18	38	R shoulder fatigue
	19	89	Strn R shoulder
	20	50	Strn R forearm
	21	75	Strn L oblique
Effross,Scott	22	31	Strnd R shoulder
Eflin,Zach	18	9	Blister - R middle finger
	19	11	Tightness lower back
	21	59	Covid; patellar tendinitis R knee
	22	87	Covid-19; bruised R knee
Eickhoff,Jerad	18	159	R lat strain
	19	106	R biceps tendinitis
Elias,Roenis	18	20	Strn L triceps
	19	27	Strn R hamstring
	20	67	Strn L flexor tendon, Covid-19
Ellis,Chris	22	167	Inflam R shoulder, surgery
Emanuel,Kent	21	114	Sore L elbow
	22	121	L elb impinge; Strnd L shoulder
Eovaldi,Nathan	18	63	Loose bodies R elbow
	19	92	R elbow surg remve loose bodies
	20	14	Strn R calf
	22	75	Low back inflam; R shldr inflam
Estevez,Carlos	18	109	Strn L oblique
	21	23	Strn R middle finger
	22	12	Covid-19
Evans,Demarcus	21	24	Strn R lat muscle
Fairbanks,Pete	21	57	Strn R/C R shoulder
	22	105	Strnd lower back
Falter,Bailey	21	32	Covid-19
Familia,Jeurys	18	10	Sore R shoulder
	19	27	Bennett lesion R shoulder
	21	12	Impingement R hip
Farmer,Buck	20	10	Strn L groin

FIVE-YEAR INJURY LOG — Pitchers

Pitchers	Yr	Days	Injury
Farrell,Luke	19	150	Fractured jaw
	20	49	Covid-19
	21	75	Strn R oblique
Fedde,Erick	18	62	R shoulder inflammation
	21	38	Covid-19; Strn oblique muscle
	22	25	Inflammation R shoulder
Feliz,Michael	18	14	R shoulder inflammation
	20	58	Strn R forearm
	21	99	Covid-19; sprained R elbow
Ferguson,Caleb	19	19	Strn L oblique
	20	13	Torn UCL L elbow
	21	169	L elbow TJS
	22	59	Tommy John surg
Fernandez,Junior	20	24	Covid-19
	21	15	Torn lat muscle R shoulder area
Festa,Matt	22	16	Sprnd R elbow
Feyereisen,J.P.	21	41	Discomfort R shoulder
	22	128	Impingement R shoulder
Fiers,Michael	18	11	R lumbar strain
	21	159	Strn lower back; Strn R elbow
File,Dylan	21	99	Surgery R elbow
Finnegan,Kyle	21	17	Strn L hamstring
Flaherty,Jack	21	97	Strn L oblique; Strn R shoulder
	22	144	Rec R shldr surgery; sore R shdlr
Fleming,Josh	21	12	Strn R calf
	22	48	Tightness R oblique
Floro,Dylan	19	25	Neck inflam; strn L intercostal lig
	22	36	Tendinitis R R/C
Foltynewicz,Mike	18	10	R triceps tightness
	19	31	Bone spur R elbow
	21	25	Covid-19
Font,Wilmer	18	94	R lat strain
	20	16	Bruised R shin
Frankoff,Seth	21	104	Strn R forearm x2
Freeland,Kyle	19	40	Blister L middle finger
	21	55	Strn L shoulder
Fried,Max	18	43	Blist L index finger; L groin strain
	19	12	Blister on L index finger
	20	12	Back spasms-lumbar area
	21	34	Blist L index fing;Strn R index fing
	22	8	Concussion
Fry,Jace	19	11	Sore L shoulder
	20	11	Back spasms-lumbar area
	21	87	Strn lower back
Fuentes,Steven	21	77	Strn R shoulder
Fulmer,Carson	19	30	Strn R hamstring
Fulmer,Michael	18	47	Strn L obliq; torn meniscs R knee
	19	187	Recovery from TJS
	21	43	Strn cervical spine
Funkhouser,Kyle	22	188	Strnd R shoulder
Gallegos,Giovanny	20	16	Strn R groin x2
Gallen,Zac	21	67	Fx R forearm;sprn R elb;str R ham
Gant,John	20	3	Tightness R groin
	21	15	Strn L ab muscle; str R groin
Garcia,Jarlin	18	12	R ankle contusion
	20	18	Covid-19
	21	14	Strn L groin
Garcia,Luis	18	36	Strn R wrist
	22	12	Strnd R oblique; Strnd L groin
	22	12	Strnd R oblique; Strnd L groin
Garcia,Rico	21	169	Tommy John surgery
Garcia,Rony	21	115	Strn L ab muscle; sprained L knee
	22	98	Sore R shoulder x2

FIVE-YEAR INJURY LOG — Pitchers

Pitchers	Yr	Days	Injury
Garcia,Yimi	18	49	R forearm inflammation
	20	25	Covid-19
	22	15	Strnd lower back
Garrett,Amir	18	13	Strn L Achilles
	19	17	Strn lat L shoulder
	22	18	Covid-19
Garrett,Braxton	22	24	Strnd R oblique
Garrett,Reed	22	32	Biceps tendinitis R arm
Gausman,Kevin	19	50	R foot plant fasc;tendinitis R shldr
	21	9	Covid-19
German,Domingo	19	26	Strn L hip flexor
	21	47	Inflamed R shoulder
	22	109	Impingement R shoulder
Gibson,Kyle	19	10	Ulcerative colitis
	21	14	Strn R groin
	22	4	Covid-19
Gil,Luis	22	42	Tommy John surg
Gilbert,Tyler	21	2	Inflammation L elbow
	22	72	Sprnd L elbow
Gilbreath,Lucas	22	56	Covid-19; Strnd flexor L elbow
Giles,Ken	19	9	Inflammation R elbow
	20	55	Strn R forearm x2
	21	169	Tommy John surgery
	22	112	Spr. R mid fing; tight R shldr
Ginkel,Kevin	21	2	Inflammation R elbow
Giolito,Lucas	19	32	Strn L hammy; strn R muscle
	21	13	Strn R hamstring
	22	21	Strnd L abdominal; covid-19
Givens,Mychal	21	20	Strn lower back
	22	19	Covid-19
Glasnow,Tyler	19	121	Strn R forearm
	21	94	Sprained UCL in R elbow
	22	178	Tommy John surg
Godley,Zack	20	22	Strn flexor mass R elbow
	21	13	Bruised R index finger
Gomber,Austin	20	7	Covid-19
	21	45	L forearm tight stress fx low back
Gomez,Yoendrys	21	51	Covid-19; Strn lower back
Gonsolin,Anthony	21	111	R shoulder inflammation
	22	39	Strnd R forearm
Gonzales,Marco	18	16	Cervical neck muscle strain
	21	34	Strn L forearm
Gonzalez,Chi Chi	20	23	Tendinitis R biceps
	21	31	Covid-19; Strn R oblique
Gonzalez,Gio	19	50	L arm fatigue
	20	13	Strn R groin
Gonzalez,Victor	21	30	Plant fasciitis L ft; inflam R knee
	22	188	L elbow inflammation
Gore,MacKenzie	22	75	L elbow inflammation
Gose,Anthony	22	98	Strnd L triceps
Gott,Trevor	19	47	Strn R elbow
	20	16	Inflammation R elbow
	22	59	Strnd R groin; R forearm
Graterol,Brusdar	21	56	R forearm strain
	22	62	R shoulder and elbow inflam
Graveman,Kendall	18	31	TJS
	19	187	Recovery from TJS
	20	29	Neck spasms
	21	20	Covid-19
Gray,Jon	19	41	Fractured L foot
	20	27	Inflammation R shoulder
	21	29	Strn R flexor
	22	64	Str L oblq x2; Blist R mid fing

FIVE-YEAR INJURY LOG — Pitchers

Pitchers	Yr	Days	Injury
Gray,Sonny	20	10	Strn back
	21	52	Strn back; Str R groin; str rib cage
	22	57	Strnd R hamstring; str. pectoral
Green,Chad	22	141	Tommy John surg
Greene,Hunter	22	47	Strnd R shoulder
Greene,Shane	18	12	R shoulder strain
Greinke,Zack	21	15	Covid-19
	22	44	Strnd R flexor
Griffin,Foster	20	63	Strn L forearm
Grove,Michael	22	7	Bruised L knee
Gsellman,Robert	19	48	Tightness R tightness
	20	35	Fractured rib L side
	21	89	Strn lower back
Guduan,Reymin	21	29	Sprained L thumb; Strn R groin
Guenther,Sean	21	1	Strn upper back
	22	188	Tommy John surg
Guerra,Deolis	22	188	Tommy John surg
Guerra,Javier	20	16	Covid-19
	21	169	Sprained UCL R elbow
Guerra,Javy	20	27	Strn L hamstring
Guerra,Junior	18	11	R forearm tightness
	21	12	Strn R groin; Strn L forearm
Guerrero,Tayron	18	27	Strn L lumbar spine
	19	44	Blister R middle finger
Gustave,Jandel	18	187	TJS
	21	36	Covid-19
	22	110	Strnd R hamstring; sore R forearm
Gutierrez,Vladimir	22	126	Tommy John surg
Guzman,Jorge	21	133	Strn R elbow
Hader,Josh	21	11	Covid-19
Hahn,Jesse	18	187	Sprained R UCL
	19	160	Recovery from TJS
	21	158	Inflammation R shoulder
Hale,David	19	60	Strn lumbar spine
	21	3	Covid-19
Hamels,Cole	19	35	Strn L oblique
	20	67	Tend. L triceps, fatigue L shoulder
	21	32	Strn L rotator cuff
Hammer,JD	21	8	Covid-19
Hand,Brad	21	4	Covid-19
	22	11	Tendinitis L elbow
Happ,J.A.	18	8	Viral infection
Harris,Will	20	14	Strn R groin
	21	151	Blood clot R arm; TOS surgery
	22	185	Surgery to repair R pec
Hartman,Ryan	21	17	Covid-19
Harvey,Hunter	20	39	Strn R elbow
	21	143	Strn R triceps
	22	81	Strnd pronatorR forearm
Harvey,Joe	20	39	Strn R elbow
Harvey,Matt	19	50	Upper back strain
	20	13	Strn R lat muscle
	21	8	Strn R triceps
Hatch,Thomas	21	97	Impingement R elbow x2
Head,Louis	22	20	Impingement L shoulder
Heaney,Andrew	18	16	L elbow inflammation
	19	83	L elbow inflam; L shoulder inflam
	22	95	Inflammation L shoulder
Hearn,Taylor	19	158	Tightness L elbow
Heasley,Jon	22	21	Tendinitis R shoulder
Helsley,Ryan	19	21	R shoulder impingement
	20	21	Covid-19
	21	31	Stress reaction R elbow

FIVE-YEAR INJURY LOG — Pitchers

Pitchers	Yr	Days	Injury
Hembree,Heath	19	74	Strn R elbow extensor
	20	8	Strn R elbow
	22	22	Strnd R calf
Hendricks,Kyle	19	17	R shoulder inflammation
	22	95	Strnd R shoulder
Hendriks,Liam	18	53	R groin strain
	22	24	Strnd R flexor tendon
Herget,Jimmy	22	39	Impingement R shoulder
Hernandez,Darwinzon	20	48	Sprained A/C joint L shldr, Covid
	21	43	Strn R oblique
Hernandez,Elieser	18	55	Finger blister; dental surg
	20	27	Strn R late
	21	133	Inflammation R biceps
	22	16	Covid-19
Hernandez,Jonathan	21	169	Tommy John surgery
	22	104	Tommy John surg
Heuer,Codi	22	188	Tommy John surg
Hicks,Jordan	19	98	Torn UCL R elbow
	21	136	Inflammation R elbow
	22	57	Sprain flexor R arm; R arm fatigue
Hill,Cam	21	119	Surgery R wrist
Hill,Rich	18	52	Blisters L hand x 2
	19	117	Strn L forearm; sprained L knee
	20	16	Shoulder fatigue L shoulder
	21	2	Covid-19
	22	40	Covid-19; Sprnd R knee
Hill,Tim	22	17	InflammationL shoulder
Hoffman,Jeff	21	56	R shoulder impingement
	22	83	Stiffness R forearm; covid-19
Holder,Jonathan	19	52	R shoulder inflammation
	21	169	Strn R shoulder
Holderman,Colin	22	51	Impinge R shldr; sore R shoulder
Holland,Derek	19	22	Bruise L wrist; bruise L index fing
	21	50	Strn L shoulder; inflam L shldr
Holland,Greg	18	25	R hip impingement
	21	28	Covid; impingement R shoulder
Holloway,Jordan	20	56	Strn R groin
	21	118	Strn R groin
	22	73	R elbow impingement
Holmes,Clay	19	31	R triceps inflammation
	20	63	Strn R forearm
	21	13	Covid-19
	22	13	L lower back spasms
Honeywell,Brent	22	161	Stress reaction R elbow
Houck,Tanner	22	60	Inflamed lower back
Houser,Adrian	21	16	Covid-19
	22	67	Strnd R flexor; Strnd R groin
Howard,Sam	21	61	Tendinitis R knee; Strn R oblique
	22	17	Strndmid-back
Howard,Spencer	20	12	Stiffness R shoulder
	21	12	Covid-19
	22	62	R shoulder impinge; Blist R hand
Hudson,Dakota	20	11	Strn R forearm
	21	169	Tommy John surgery
	22	16	Strnd neck
Hudson,Daniel	18	49	R forearm tightness
	21	43	Covid-19; inflammation R elbow
	22	106	Torn ACL L knee
Hunter,Tommy	18	25	Strn R hamstring
	19	172	R forearm surgery
	21	121	Strn lower back
	22	34	Tight lower back
Iglesias,Raisel	18	8	Strn L biceps
Irvin,Cole	22	21	Sore L shoulder

FIVE-YEAR INJURY LOG — Pitchers

Pitchers	Yr	Days	Injury
Ivey,Tyler	21	46	Inflammation R elbow
Jackson,Edwin	19	27	Lower back strain
Jackson,Jay	21	2	Covid-19
	22	90	Strnd R lat
Jackson,Luke	22	188	Tommy John surg
Jackson,Zach	22	40	Separated L shoulder
James,Josh	19	41	Inflammation R shoulder
	20	19	Sore L hip
	21	123	L hip surgery
	22	108	Strnd R lat
Jansen,Kenley	18	11	Irregular heartbeat
	22	16	Irregular heartbeat
Jefferies,Daulton	22	133	Strnd cervical spine
Jimenez,Dany	22	86	Strnd R shoulder
Jimenez,Joe	21	10	Covid-19
	22	15	Strnd lumbar spine
Johnson,D.J.	21	38	Sprained R shoulder
Johnson,Pierce	21	38	Strn R groin; inflam R triceps tndn
	22	143	R forearm tendinitis
Jones,Damon	22	104	Impingement L shoulder
Junis,Jake	18	14	Lower back inflammation
	20	26	Lower back spasms/Covid-19
	21	16	Impingement R shoulder
	22	36	Strnd L hamstring
Kahnle,Tommy	18	39	R shoulder tendinitis
	20	59	TJS
	21	169	Tommy John surgery
	22	148	Tommy John surg
Kaprielian,James	21	9	Impingement R shoulder
	22	28	Inflammation AC joint R shoulder
Karinchak,James	22	90	Strnd upper back R side
Kay,Anthony	21	22	Covid-19; blister L hand
Kela,Keone	19	79	Shoulder, elbow inflammation
	20	54	Tight R forearm, Covid-19
	21	143	Inflam R shoulder; R forearm
Keller,Brad	20	14	Covid-19
	21	21	Strn R Lat
Keller,Mitch	20	44	Strn L oblique
	21	3	Covid-19
Kelly,Joe	20	32	Inflammation R shoulder
	21	52	R shoulder inflammation x2
	22	56	Strn L ham; nerve injury R biceps
Kelly,Merrill	20	36	Impingement R shoulder
	21	36	Covid-19; undisclosed inj
Kennedy,Ian	18	68	Strn L oblique
	20	29	Strn L calf
	21	8	Strn L hamstring
	22	18	R calf inflammation
Kershaw,Clayton	18	49	L biceps tndinitis; low back strain
	19	19	L shoulder inflammation
	20	11	Lower back stiffness
	21	69	L forearm inflammation x2
	22	57	SI joint inflm L shld; Low bck sore
Keuchel,Dallas	20	13	Back spasms
Kikuchi,Yusei	21	2	Covid-19
	22	24	Strnd cervical spine
Kim,Kwang-hyun	20	13	Kidney ailment
	21	43	Tight lower back; inflam L elbow
Kimbrel,Craig	19	30	R knee inflam; R elbow inflam
King,John	21	72	Inflamed L shoulder
King,Michael	21	68	Bruised R middle finger
	22	78	Fx R elbow
Kinley,Tyler	22	119	Torn flex tend, UCL nrve inj R elb

FIVE-YEAR INJURY LOG — Pitchers

Pitchers	Yr	Days	Injury
Kintzler,Brandon	18	16	Flexor muscle strain - R arm
	19	10	R pectoral muscle inflammation
	21	24	Strn neck
Kittredge,Andrew	20	48	Sprained UCL R elbow
	22	137	Low back sore; Tommy John surg
Kluber,Corey	19	151	Fractured ulna R forearm
	20	63	Torn teres major muscle R shldr
	21	97	Strn R shoulder
Knebel,Corey	18	34	L hamstring strain
	19	187	Recovery from TJS
	20	20	Strn L hamstring
	21	109	Strn R Lat
	22	9	Strnd R lat; covid-19
Kopech,Michael	18	24	TJS
	19	187	Recovery from TJS
	21	34	Strn L hamstring
	22	38	Strnd L knee; inflamed R shoulder
Kranick,Max	22	132	Tommy John surg
Krehbiel,Joey	22	16	InflammationR shoulder
Kremer,Dean	22	57	Strnd L oblique
Kuhl,Chad	18	95	Strn R forearm
	19	187	TJS
	21	59	Covid-19; sore R shoulder
	22	27	Strnd R hip flexor; Strnd R triceps
Lakins,Travis	21	79	Stress Fx R elbow
	22	53	InflammationR elbow
Lambert,Peter	20	68	TJS
	21	169	Tommy John surgery
	22	188	Recovery from Tommy John surg
Lamet,Dinelson	18	187	Recovery from TJS
	19	99	Recovery from TJS
	21	101	Strn UCL R elbow; Strn R forearm
Lange,Alex	21	23	Strn R shoulder
Lauer,Eric	18	32	L forearm strain
	20	3	Covid-19
	21	12	Covid-19
	22	14	L elbow inflammation
Law,Derek	21	62	Impingement R shoulder
LeBlanc,Wade	19	35	Strn R oblique
	20	35	Stress reaction L elbow
	21	35	L elbow inflammation
Leclerc,Jose	20	60	Strn teres major muscle R shldr
	21	169	Tommy John surgery
	22	74	Tommy John surg
Lee,Evan	22	113	Strnd L flexor tendon
Leibrandt,Brandon	20	22	Ulnar neuritis L elbow
Leone,Dominic	18	114	R upper arm nerve irritation
	22	39	Covid-19; R elbow inflamm
Lester,Jon	19	17	Strn L hamstring
	21	26	Covid-19
Lindblom,Josh	21	20	R knee effusion
Littell,Zack	20	30	Strn L elbow, inflam R elbow
	22	50	Covid-19; Strnd L oblique
Llovera,Mauricio	22	85	Strnd R flexor tendon
Loaisiga,Jonathan	19	93	Strn R shoulder
	20	14	Undisclosed medical condition
	21	26	Covid-19; Strn R/C R shoulder
	22	51	Inflammation R shoulder
Lodolo,Nick	22	69	Strnd lower back
Long,Sam	21	24	Strn lower back
	22	44	Strnd R oblique
Lopez,Jorge	20	6	Covid-19
	21	10	Sprained R ankle

FIVE-YEAR INJURY LOG — Pitchers

Pitchers	Yr	Days	Injury
Lopez,Pablo	18	31	R shoulder strain
	19	69	Strn R shoulder
	21	65	Strn R rotator cuff
Lopez,Reynaldo	20	27	Strn R shoulder
	22	13	Strnd lower back
Lorenzen,Michael	18	56	R shoulder strain
	21	120	Strn R shoulder; Strn R hamstring
	22	68	Strnd R shoulder
Loup,Aaron	18	34	Strn L forearm
	19	176	Strn L elbow
Lovelady,Richard	21	19	Sprained UCL L elbow
Lucchesi,Joey	18	37	R hip strain
	21	90	Inflammation L elbow; surgery
	22	188	Tommy John surg
Lugo,Seth	19	12	R shoulder tendinitis
	21	61	Recovery from R elbow surgery
Luzardo,Jesus	21	29	Fx L hand
	22	79	Strnd L flexor tendon
Lyles,Jordan	18	36	R elbow inflammation
	19	29	Strn L ham; Strn L oblique
Lynch,Daniel	22	33	Blister R index finger x2
Lynn,Lance	21	27	Strn R trap muscle; inflam R knee
	22	71	Surg repair torn tendon knee
Lyons,Tyler	18	52	Mid-back strain; sprained L elbow
Maeda,Kenta	18	15	R hip strain
	19	10	Bruised L adductor muscle
	21	49	Strn R adductor; tight R forearm
	22	188	Tommy John surg
Mahle,Tyler	19	32	Strn L hamstring
	22	71	Strnd R shoulder
Manaea,Sean	18	37	L shoulder impingement
	19	158	R shoulder surgery rehab
Manning,Matt	22	118	InflammationR shoulder
Manoah,Alek	21	16	Strn lower back
Mantiply,Joe	21	17	Covid-19
Maples,Dillon	21	70	Strn R biceps; blist R index finger
Margevicius,Nick	21	144	Inflamed L shoulder
Marinaccio,Ron	22	27	InflammationR shoulder
Marquez,German	19	39	R arm inflammation
Marshall,Evan	18	50	R elbow inflammation
	20	11	Inflammation R shoulder
	21	79	Strn R flexor pronator muscle
Marte,Jose	21	26	Covid-19
Martin,Brett	20	26	RC inflam L shoulder, Covid-19
	21	9	Strn lower back
	22	22	Covid-19
Martin,Chris	18	54	R forearm irrit;str R calf;str L groin
	20	14	Esophageal constriction
	21	51	Inflam R shoulder; R elbow inflam
Martin,Corbin	20	68	TJS
Martinez,Carlos	18	59	R lat strain; R oblique strain
	19	51	Strn R shoulder cuff
	20	41	Strn L oblique
	21	85	Sprn R ankle; torn ligament R thm
Maton,Phil	18	40	R lat strain
Matz,Steven	18	14	L flexor pronator strain
	19	10	Sore L elbow
	20	15	Impingement L shoulder
	21	18	Covid-19
	22	112	Imping L shldr; torn MCL L knee
Matzek,Tyler	22	52	InflammationL shoulder
May,Dustin	21	138	Tommy John surgery
	22	153	Tommy John surg

FIVE-YEAR INJURY LOG — Pitchers

Pitchers	Yr	Days	Injury
May,Trevor	18	71	TJS
	22	103	inflammation R triceps
Mayers,Mike	18	17	R shoulder inflammation
	19	99	Strn lat R shoulder
	21	3	Covid-19
Mayza,Tim	19	26	Ulnar neuritis L 4arm; TJS
	21	13	Inflammation L elbow
	22	17	Dislocated R shoulder
Mazza,Chris	21	132	Inflamed R shoulder
	22	60	Covid-19
McArthur,James	22	102	Stress reaction R elbow
McClanahan,Shane	21	8	Strn lower back
	22	16	Impingement L shoulder
McCullers,Lance	18	51	R elbow discomfort
	19	187	Recovery from TJS
	20	10	Neck irritation
	21	24	Sore R shoulder
	22	132	Strnd R forearm
McFarland,T.J.	18	12	L neck strain
	19	34	Inflammation L shoulder
	22	20	Covid-19
McGee,Jake	19	46	Sprained L knee
	21	3	Covid-19; Strn R oblique
	22	16	Tight lower back
McGowin,Kyle	21	57	Strn R biceps; sprained UCL R elb
McHugh,Collin	19	66	R elbow pain
	21	33	Covid;Strn lower back;R arm fatig
	22	10	Covid-19
McKay,Brendan	20	19	Sore L shoulder, Covid-19
	22	172	Tommy John surg
McKenzie,Triston	21	8	Fatigue R shoulder
Means,John	19	26	Strn L biceps; Strn L shldr
	20	14	Covid-19, L shoulder fatigue
	21	45	Strn L shoulder
	22	176	Strnd L elbow
Mears,Nick	22	139	Tommy John surg recovery
Megill,Trevor	21	34	Strn R forearm
	22	29	Strnd L oblique; covid-19
Megill,Tylor	22	127	Tnditis R biceps; Str R shldr; Covid
Melancon,Mark	18	65	R elbow flexor strain
	22	8	Covid-19
Mengden,Daniel	18	18	L shoulder impingement
	20	19	Covid-19
Merryweather,Julian	20	8	Tendinitis R elbow
	21	148	Strn L oblique
	22	84	Strain L abdominal
Meyer,Max	22	77	Sprnd R elbow
Middleton,Keynan	18	151	R elbow inflammation
	19	153	Recovery from TJS
	21	17	Strn R biceps tendon
	22	77	R elb inflam; spr R ank; Sprnd toe
Mikolas,Miles	20	63	Strn flexor tendon R forearm
	21	142	Rec fr TJS; tightness R forearm
Miley,Wade	18	101	Strn R oblique x 2
	20	40	Strn L groin, Strn L shoulder
	21	11	Sprained L foot
	22	138	L elb inflam; Strnd L shoulder
Miller,Andrew	18	99	L shld; R knee inflam x2; str L ham
	20	13	Fatigue L shoulder
	21	46	Blist big toe; ulnar nerv irrit R elb
Miller,Justin	19	88	Low back strain; strn AC R shldr
	21	25	Ulnar nerve irritation R elbow
Miller,Shelby	18	169	Recovery from TJS - R elbow
	21	35	Strn lower back

FIVE-YEAR INJURY LOG — Pitchers

Pitchers	Yr	Days	Injury
Miller,Tyson	21	35	Covid-19
Mills,Alec	21	24	Strn lower back
	22	160	Strnd lower back
Milner,Hoby	19	20	Bruised cervical nerve
	20	10	Lower back spasms
Milone,Tom	18	14	L shoulder soreness
	20	19	Inflammation L elbow
	21	101	Inflamed L shoulder
	22	71	Strnd cervical spine
Minor,Mike	21	2	Impingement R shoulder
	22	77	Sore L shoulder
Minter,A.J.	19	26	L shoulder inflammation x2
Misiewicz,Anthony	21	18	Covid-19; Strn L forearm
Mize,Casey	22	176	Sprnd R elbow; Tommy John surg
Moll,Sam	22	26	Covid-19; Strnd L shoulder
Montas,Frankie	22	19	Inflammation R shoulder
Montero,Rafael	18	187	TJS
	20	16	Tendinitis R elbow
	21	38	Discomfort R shoulder
Montes de Oca,Bryce	22	27	Tight L hamstring
Montgomery,Jordan	18	151	TJS
	19	172	TJS
	21	15	Covid-19
Moore,Matt	18	12	R knee soreness
	19	178	Recovery meniscus surgery R knee
	21	42	Strn lower back; Covid-19
Morejon,Adrian	19	55	L shoulder impingement
	21	158	Strn L forearm
	22	92	Covid-19; Tommy John surg
Moreta,Dauri	22	5	Covid-19
Morgan,Adam	18	11	Back strain
	19	85	Strn L forearm
	20	12	Fatigue L shoulder
Moronta,Reyes	19	27	Torn labrum R shoulder
	20	68	Recov labrum surgery R shldr
	21	134	Strn R flexor mass
Morris,Cody	22	151	Strnd R shoulder
Morton,Charlie	18	11	R shoulder discomfort
	20	24	Inflammation R shoulder
Mujica,Jose	18	29	R forearm strain
Munoz,Andres	20	68	TJS
	21	169	Tommy John surgery
Murphy,Patrick	21	77	Sprained A/C joint R shoulder
Musgrove,Joe	18	62	Strnd R shldr; infect R index fing
	20	23	Inflam R triceps
	22	7	Covid-19
Mushinski,Parker	22	45	Discomfort L elbow
Nance,Tommy	21	3	Covid-19
	22	36	Covid-19; Strnd R groin
Neidert,Nick	20	41	Covid-19
	21	33	Inflammation R biceps
Nelson,Jimmy	18	187	Recovery from R rotator cuff surg
	19	126	Labrum surg R shldr; effusn R elb
	20	68	Recovery from lower back surgery
	21	85	Inflam R forearm;Low back str; TJS
	22	188	Tommy John surg
Nelson,Kyle	22	61	Covid; low back str; L elb inflam
Nelson,Ryne	22	18	Inflammation R scapula
Newcomb,Sean	19	7	Concussion
	21	13	Covid-19
	22	33	Sprnd L ankle
Newsome,Ljay	21	133	Inflamed R elbow
Nogosek,Steve	21	48	Impingement R shoulder
	22	28	Strnd L oblique

FIVE-YEAR INJURY LOG — Pitchers

Pitchers	Yr	Days	Injury
Nola,Aaron	21	10	Covid-19
	22	4	Covid-19
Norris,Daniel	18	125	L groin strain
	20	11	Covid-19
	22	21	Strnd L index finger
Nunez,Darien	21	9	Undisclosed arm injury
Nunez,Dedniel	21	169	Sprained R elbow
Ober,Bailey	22	125	Strnd R groin x2
Oberg,Scott	18	18	Back strain
	19	45	Blood clot R arm
	20	68	Strnd low back, blood clot R arm
	21	169	Blood clots R arm
	22	188	Medical illness
O'Day,Darren	18	129	Hyperext R elbow; str L hamstring
	19	162	Strn R forearm
	21	133	Strn rotator cuff R shoulder
	22	88	Strnd L calf
Odorizzi,Jake	19	11	Blister R index finger
	20	55	Strn R intercost;brsed chest;R fing
	21	37	Strn R pronator; sore R foot
	22	49	Strnd lower L leg
Ohtani,Shohei	18	26	Sprained UCL, R elbow
	19	41	Recovery from TJS
Okert,Steven	22	10	Tight L triceps
Olivarez,Helcris	22	134	Strnd L shoulder
Oller,Adam	22	25	R rib costochondritis
Osich,Josh	18	14	Strn R hip
Oswalt,Corey	20	23	Tendinitis R biceps
	21	74	Inflammation R knee
Ottavino,Adam	18	18	L oblique strain
Otto,Glenn	22	16	Covid-19
Overton,Connor	22	123	Stress Fx lower back
Oviedo,Johan	20	7	Covid-19
Oviedo,Luis	21	47	Strn L quad
	22	15	Sprnd R ankle
Paddack,Chris	21	46	Strn L oblique; inflam R elbow
	22	152	Inflammation R elbow
Pagan,Emilio	20	11	Tendinitis R biceps
	22	4	Covid-19
Paredes,Enoli	21	121	Strn R shoulder; R oblique
Patino,Luis	21	12	laceration R middle finger
	22	95	Strnd L oblique
Patton,Spencer	22	18	Strnd R oblique
Paxton,James	18	36	Low back inflam; L forearm bruise
	19	26	L knee inflammation
	20	39	Strn flexor muscle L forearm
	21	163	Strn L forearm
	22	188	Tommy John surg
Payamps,Joel	21	3	Covid-19
	22	36	Covid-19
Peacock,Matt	22	19	Covid-19
Pearson,Nate	20	37	Strn flexor tendon R elbow
	21	29	Strn R adductor muscle
	22	185	Medical illness
Pena,Felix	19	58	Torn ACL R knee
	21	36	Strn R hamstring
Peralta,Freddy	19	17	Sore AC joint R shoulder
	21	16	Inflammation R shoulder
	22	90	Sprnd R lat; fatigue R shoulder
Peralta,Wandy	19	28	Strn R hip flexor
	21	27	Covid-19; Strn lower back
	22	20	TightnessL thoracic spine
Peralta,Wily	21	11	Blister index finger R hand
	22	29	Strnd L hamstring

FIVE-YEAR INJURY LOG — Pitchers

Pitchers	Yr	Days	Injury
Perdomo,Angel	21	70	Strn lower back
Perdomo,Luis	18	38	R shoulder strain
	20	8	R forearm inflam
	22	81	R elbow effusion; Strnd R calf
Perez,Martin	18	84	R elbow discomfort
	21	16	Covid-19
Peters,Dillon	20	42	Covid-19
	21	11	Strn lower back
	22	79	Str low back; L elbow inflam
Peterson,David	20	11	Fatigued R shoulder
	21	78	Sore R side
Phelps,David	18	187	TJS
	19	82	Recovery from TJS
	21	134	Strn R lat muscle
Phillips,Evan	20	6	Inflammation R elbow
	21	11	Strn R quad
Pineda,Michael	18	187	TJS
	19	25	R knee tendinitis; strn R triceps
	21	59	Abscess leg;R elb infl;Str L oblique
	22	88	Fx R mid fing; tightness R triceps
Pivetta,Nick	21	10	Covid-19
Plesac,Zach	21	45	Fx R thumb
	22	30	Fx 5th metacarpal R hand
Poche,Colin	20	68	Torn UCL L elbow
	21	169	Recovery from surgery L elbow
	22	4	Strnd R oblique
Pomeranz,Drew	18	73	L forearm strn; L biceps tendinitis
	19	11	Strn L Lat
	20	13	Strn L shoulder
	21	99	Tight L lat; inflam L forearm
	22	188	Surgery L flexor tendon
Ponce,Cody	21	18	Tightness R forearm
Poncedeleon,Daniel	21	68	Inflamed R shoulder
Pop,Zach	21	18	Inflammation index finger R hand
Poppen,Sean	19	30	R elbow contusion
	22	27	Inflammation R shoulder
Poteet,Cody	21	98	Sprained R knee; Strn R MCL
	22	126	Inflammation R elbow
Pressly,Ryan	19	41	Sore R knee
	22	38	Inflamm R knee; neck spasms
Price,David	19	46	TFCC cyst L wrist; L elb tendinitis
	21	22	Strn R hamstring
	22	48	Covid-19; inflammation L wrist
Pruitt,Austin	20	68	Sore R elbow
	21	107	Recovery from surgery on R elbow
Puk,A.J.	20	68	Strn L shoulder
	21	51	Strn L biceps
	22	3	Covid-19
Quantrill,Cal	22	4	Covid-19
Quijada,Jose	20	32	Covid-19
	22	50	Strnd R oblique
Quintana,Jose	20	57	Laceration R thumb, Strn L lat
	21	22	Inflamed L shoulder
Ragans,Cole	22	19	Strnd L calf
Rainey,Tanner	20	17	Strn flexor muscle R forearm
	21	40	Covid-19; stress reaction R tibia
	22	87	Tommy John surg
Raley,Brooks	21	71	Covid-19
Ramirez,Erasmo	18	129	R shld/lat strn; R teres major strn
	20	1	Tightness R groin
	21	56	Strn R pectoral muscle
Ramirez,Nick	21	19	Inflamed R/C L shoulder
Ramirez,Noe	19	19	Viral infection
	21	21	Covid-19

FIVE-YEAR INJURY LOG — Pitchers

Pitchers	Yr	Days	Injury
Ramos, A.J.	18	127	R shoulder surg
Rasmussen, Drew	22	18	Strnd R hamstring
Ray, Robbie	18	59	Strn R oblique
	19	10	Lower R back spasms
	21	12	Bruised R elbow
Reed, Cody	20	12	Laceration L index finger
	21	136	sprained L thumb
Reed, Jake	21	27	Strn R forearm
	22	17	Strnd L oblique
Reid-Foley, Sean	21	78	Inflammation R elbow
	22	161	Partially torn UCLR elbow
Reyes, Alex	18	187	Recovery from TJS; back surg
	22	188	Frayed labrum R shoulder
Richards, Garrett	18	103	Strn L hamstring; TJS
	19	173	Recovery from TJS
	22	10	Blister index finger
Richards, Trevor	22	17	Strnd neck
Riddle, J.T.	21	9	Covid-19
Ridings, Stephen	22	188	Impingement R shoulder
Rios, Yacksel	20	45	Inflammation L shoulder
Roberts, Ethan	22	163	Inflammation R shoulder
Robertson, David	19	169	Strn R shoulder
	20	68	TJS
	22	10	Covid-19
Robles, Hansel	18	29	Sprained R knee
	22	13	Back spasms
Rodon, Carlos	18	73	Surg on L shoulder
	19	152	L elbow inflammation
	20	52	Sore L shoulder
	21	19	L shoulder fatigue
	22	5	Covid-19
Rodriguez, Chris	21	29	Inflammation R shoulder
	22	188	Rec surgery on R shoulder
Rodriguez, Eduardo	18	90	Recov fr R knee surg.; spr. R ankle
	20	68	Covid-19, myocarditis
	21	7	Inflammation L elbow
	22	26	Strnd L rib cage
Rodriguez, Jefry	19	98	Strn R shoulder
	20	20	Strnd R shldr, strnd L hamstring
Rodriguez, Joely	20	37	Strn L lat, str L hamstring
	21	16	Sprained L ankle
Rodriguez, Manuel	20	3	Strn R biceps
	22	87	Strnd R elbow
Rodriguez, Richard	18	11	R shoulder discomfort
	19	11	R shoulder inflammation
Rodriguez, Sean	20	43	Covid-19
Roe, Chaz	18	38	R groin strain
	19	9	Strn R flexor
	20	40	Sore R elbow
	21	164	Strn R shoulder
Rogers, Josh	19	96	Sprained L elbow
	21	3	Strn R hamstring
	22	51	Impingement L shoulder
Rogers, Taylor	21	52	Sprained index finger L hand
Rogers, Trevor	21	13	Strn lower Back; Covid-19
	22	55	Back spasms; Strnd L lat
Rolison, Ryan	22	188	Recovery R shoulder surgery
Romano, Jordan	20	31	Strn R middle finger
	21	9	Ulnar neuritis R elbow
Romero, Jhon	22	172	Biceps tendinitis R arm
Romero, JoJo	21	134	Strn L elbow
	22	103	Tommy John surg
Romero, Seth	20	36	Fractured R hand
	22	143	Strnd L calf

FIVE-YEAR INJURY LOG — Pitchers

Pitchers	Yr	Days	Injury
Romo, Sergio	22	32	Inflammation R shoulder
Rosario, Randy	20	30	Tightness L forearm
Rosenthal, Trevor	19	44	Viral infection
	21	169	Inflamed R shoulder
	22	80	Strnd L hamstring
Ross, Joe	18	160	TJS
	21	56	Inflammation R elbow; torn UCL
	22	188	Surgery rem bone spurs R elbow
Rucker, Michael	22	14	Turf toe L foot
Ruiz, Jose	20	18	Covid-19
Ryan, Joe	22	21	Covid-19
Ryu, Hyun-Jin	18	105	L groin strain
	19	23	Strn L groin; neck stiffness
	21	9	Strn R glute; tightness neck
	22	157	Tommy John surg
Sadler, Casey	21	84	Inflamed R shoulder
	22	188	Rec R shoulder surgery
Sale, Chris	18	38	Inflamed L shoulder x 2
	19	44	L elbow inflammation
	20	67	TJS
	21	143	Covid-19; recovery from TJS
	22	182	Stress Fx R rib cage; fx R wrist
Samardzija, Jeff	18	141	Strnd R pec muscle; R shldr tight .
	20	52	Impingement R shoulder
Sampson, Adrian	19	14	Lower back spasms
Sanchez, Aaron	18	64	R index finger contusion
	19	41	Stained R pectoral muscle
	21	86	Tightness R biceps
Sanchez, Anibal	18	42	R hamstring strain
	19	13	Strn L hamstring
	22	102	Cervical nerve impingement
Sanchez, Miguel	22	109	L elbow pain
Sanchez, Ricardo	20	54	Sore L elbow, Covid-19
Sanchez, Sixto	22	188	Rec from surgery on R shoulder
Sanders, Phoenix	22	16	Lower back spasms
Sandlin, Nick	21	36	Strn R shoulder
Sandoval, Patrick	21	33	Strn lower back
Sands, Cole	22	16	Bruised R elbow
Santana, Dennis	18	116	Strn R rotator cuff
	21	3	Covid-19
	22	31	Sprnd L ankle; covid-19
Santana, Edgar	19	187	TJS
	21	3	Strn R intercostal lig
Santillan, Tony	22	114	Strnd lower back
Santos, Gregory	22	47	Strnd R groin
Saucedo, Tayler	22	163	Sore R hip
Sawamura, Hirokazu	21	25	Covid; inflammation R triceps
Sborz, Josh	19	11	Sore lower back
	22	56	Sore R elbow
Sceroler, Mac	21	56	Tendinitis R shoulder
Scherzer, Max	19	42	Inflamed bursa sac back/shoulder
	21	11	Strn R groin
	22	60	Strnd R & L oblique
Schmidt, Clarke	21	133	Strn extensor R elbow
Scott, Tanner	21	14	Sprained R knee
Scott, Tayler	22	28	Laceration R index finger
Scrubb, Andre	21	91	Sore R shoulder; R shoulder strain
Seabold, Connor	22	18	Strnd extensorR forearm
Senzatela, Antonio	18	24	Finger blister; R shoulder inflam
	19	19	Infected blister on R heel
	21	33	Covid-19; Strn R groin
	22	88	Str low back; infl L shld; ACL L kn.

FIVE-YEAR INJURY LOG — Pitchers

Pitchers	Yr	Days	Injury
Severino,Luis	19	174	Inflammation R/C R shoulder
	20	67	TJS
	21	169	Tommy John surgery
	22	72	Covid; Strnd R lat
Sewald,Paul	22	8	Covid-19
Shaw,Bryan	18	18	R calf strain
Sheffield,Jordan	21	92	Strn R lat muscle
Sheffield,Justus	21	57	L forearm strain
Sherfy,Jimmie	21	55	Inflammation R elbow
Sherriff,Ryan	18	27	R big toe fracture
	22	120	Strnd biceps; Strnd L shoulder
Shoemaker,Matt	18	154	R forearm strain
	19	163	Torn ACL L knee
	20	31	Strnd R lat, inflam R shldr
Sims,Lucas	21	47	Sprained R elbow
	22	170	Lower back spasms
Singer,Brady	21	35	Covid; R shldr fatigue; R biceps inj
Skubal,Tarik	22	67	Fatigue L arm
Smeltzer,Devin	21	128	Inflammation L elbow
Smith,Burch	20	44	Strn R forearm
	21	35	Strn R groin
Smith,Caleb	18	99	L lat surg
	19	30	L hip inflammation
	20	39	Covid-19
	22	29	Fx R hand
Smith,Drew	19	187	TJS
	21	59	Impingement R shoulder
	22	55	Strnd R lat
Smith,Joe	18	24	R elbow soreness
	19	107	Recovery surgery L Achilles
	21	29	Sore R elbow
	22	18	Tight upper trapezius
Smith,Josh	20	5	Torn fingernail
Smith,Riley	21	7	Covid-19
Smith,Will	18	34	TJS
	19	11	Concussion
	20	15	Covid-19
Smyly,Drew	18	187	Recovery from L elbow surg
	19	16	Tightness L arm
	20	40	Strn L index finger
	21	9	Inflammation L forearm
	22	41	Strnd R oblique
Snead,Kirby	22	6	Covid-19
Snell,Blake	18	13	L shoulder fatigue
	19	69	Fx R big toe; loose bodies L elbow
	21	19	Gastroenteritis x2; Str L adductor
	22	38	Strnd L adductor
Snyder,Nick	21	13	R shoulder fatigue
Sobotka,Chad	19	27	Strn L ab muscle
Soria,Joakim	18	15	R thigh strain
	21	53	Covid-19; sprained R middle fing
Soriano,Jose	21	169	Tommy John surgery
Soroka,Michael	18	130	R shoulder strain
	20	56	Torn R Achilles tendon
	21	169	Recovery from R Achilles injury
	22	151	Torn R Achilles
Sparkman,Glenn	20	54	Strn R forearm
Speier,Gabe	22	19	Covid-19
Springs,Jeffrey	19	77	L biceps tendinitis
	21	47	Sprained R knee
	22	17	Covid-19; tightness lower R leg
Stammen,Craig	22	65	Inflammation R shoulder
Stanek,Ryne	19	17	Bruised R hip
	20	32	Covid-19

FIVE-YEAR INJURY LOG — Pitchers

Pitchers	Yr	Days	Injury
Stashak,Cody	20	25	Lower back inflammation
	21	101	Strn lower back
	22	154	Tndnitis R bicep; impinge R shldr
Staumont,Josh	21	15	Covid-19
	22	66	Biceps tendinitis R arm; Str neck
Steckenrider,Drew	19	147	R elbow inflammation
	20	68	Tendinitis R triceps
	21	16	Covid-19
Steele,Justin	21	49	Strn R hamstring
	22	34	Strnd lower back
Stephens,Jackson	22	9	Concussion
Stephenson,Robert	18	33	R shoulder tendinitis
	19	17	Strn cervical spine
	20	28	Strn mid-back
	21	38	Strn lower back
	22	19	Covid-19
Stewart,Brock	18	30	R oblique strain
Stewart,Kohl	21	73	Inflammation R elbow
Stiever,Jonathan	22	188	Surgical repair R lat
Stock,Robert	19	77	Inflammation R biceps
	21	58	Strn R hamstring
Stout,Eric	22	17	Sore lower back
Strahm,Matthew	18	40	Torn L patellar tendon
	19	9	Strn L rib ligament
	20	10	Inflammation R knee
	20	10	Inflammation R knee
	21	155	Rec fr patellar tendon surg R knee
Strahm,Matthew	22	40	Covid-19; bruised L wrist
Strasburg,Stephen	18	71	R shoulder inflammation
	20	45	Carpal tunnel syndrome R hand
	21	144	Inflamed R shoulder; TOS surgery
	22	184	Surgery TOS; stress reaction ribs
Stratton,Chris	19	45	Inflammation R ribcage
Strickland,Hunter	18	61	Fractured R hand
	19	121	Strn R lat muscle
	21	9	Covid-19
Strider,Spencer	22	15	Strnd L oblique
Stripling,Ross	18	35	Low back inflam; R big toe inflam.
	19	39	R biceps tendinitis
	21	48	Str flexor R forearm; Str L oblique
	22	15	Strnd R hip
Stroman,Marcus	18	60	R shldr fatigue; fing blisters
	20	19	Strn L calf
	22	42	Covid-19; inflam R shoulder
Strop,Pedro	19	36	Strn L hamstring; neck tightness
	20	16	Strn R groin
Suarez,Jose	20	20	Covid-19
Suarez,Ranger	20	40	Covid-19
	22	17	Lower back spasms
Suarez,Robert	22	61	Surg remove loose bodies L knee
Suero,Wander	20	13	Covid-19
	21	25	Strn L oblique
Sulser,Cole	22	63	Strnd R lat
Suter,Brent	18	80	Torn UCL - TJS
	19	158	Recovery from TJS
Swanson,Erik	20	29	Strn R forearm
	21	40	Strn R groin
	22	28	R elbow inflammation
Swarzak,Anthony	18	100	Strn L oblique; R shldr inflam
	19	20	R shoulder inflammation
Syndergaard,Noah	18	57	Strn R index finger; viral infect
	19	15	Strn R hamstring
	20	68	TJS
	21	188	Covid-19; recovery from TJS

FIVE-YEAR INJURY LOG — Pitchers

Pitchers	Yr	Days	Injury
Szapucki,Thomas	22	6	Strain R hip
Taillon,Jameson	19	150	Strn flexor R elbow
	20	68	TJS
	21	10	Tendon injury R ankle
Tanaka,Masahiro	18	32	Strn R and L hamstrings
	20	10	Concussion
Tarpley,Stephen	19	33	L shoulder impingement
	20	33	Strn R oblique
Tate,Dillon	20	34	Bruised R elbow, sprained R fing
	21	20	Strn L hamstring
Taylor,Blake	20	12	Sore L elbow
	21	45	Sprained R ankle
	22	102	DiscomfortL elbow
Taylor,Josh	20	43	Tendinitis L shldr, Covid-19
	21	10	Covid-19
	22	188	Strnd lower back
Teheran,Julio	18	12	R thumb contusion
	20	14	Covid-19
	21	163	Strn R shoulder
Tepera,Ryan	18	16	R elbow inflammation
	19	126	R elbow inflammation
	21	17	Laceration R index finger
Tetreault,Jackson	22	97	Stress fracturescapulaR shoulder
Thielbar,Caleb	21	19	Covid-19; Strn L groin
	22	17	Covid-19; Strnd L hamstring
Thompson,Keegan	21	14	Inflammation R shoulder
	22	33	Tight lower back
Thompson,Mason	22	83	Biceps tendinitis R arm
Thompson,Ryan	21	79	Inflamed R shoulder
	22	40	Stress reaction R elbow
Thompson,Zach	22	16	Inflammation w/nerve R forearm
Thornburg,Tyler	18	98	recovery from R shoulder surg
	19	49	R hip impingement
	20	17	Sprained R elbow
Thornton,Trent	19	11	Inflammation R elbow
	20	51	Inflammation R elbow
Thorpe,Lewis	21	29	Impingement L shoulder
Tillo,Daniel	21	137	Tommy John surgery
Tomlin,Josh	18	45	Strn R hamstring
	21	19	Strn neck
Topa,Justin	21	146	Strn R elbow
	22	138	Strnd R forearm; Sprnd L ankle
Toussaint,Touki	21	107	Strn R shoulder
Treinen,Blake	19	12	Strn R shoulder
	22	163	Inflam, tightness R shoulder
Triggs,Andrew	18	137	Blood clot, L calf
	20	15	R radial nerve irritation
Trivino,Lou	22	16	Covid-19
Tropeano,Nicholas	18	105	R shoulder inflammation
	19	63	Strn R shoulder
Turnbull,Spencer	19	34	Strn upr back; R shoulder fatigue
	21	125	Covid-19; Strn R forearm
	22	188	Tommy John surg
Uceta,Edwin	21	53	Strn R lower back
Underwood,Duane	21	23	Sore R oblique; inflam R shoulder
	22	54	Strnd R ham; covid-19
Urena,Jose	18	13	R shoulder impingement
	19	86	Strn L lower back
	20	44	Covid-19
	21	53	Strn R forearm; Strn R groin
Urias,Julio	18	150	Recovery from L shoulder surg
	21	11	Contusion L calf
Urquidy,Jose	20	45	Covid-19
	21	80	Sore R shoulder x2

FIVE-YEAR INJURY LOG — Pitchers

Pitchers	Yr	Days	Injury
Valdez,Cesar	21	14	Strn lower back
Valdez,Framber	21	58	Fractured L index finger
Valdez,Jose	18	133	R elbow inflammation
Valdez,Phillips	21	5	Covid-19
Vargas,Carlos	22	106	Tommy John surg
Vargas,Jason	18	65	Fractured R hand; Strn calf
	19	20	Strn L hamstring
Vasquez,Andrew	22	54	Sprnd R ankle
Velasquez,Vincent	18	11	Bruised R forearm
	19	18	Strn R forearm
	21	43	Blister R middle finger
	22	57	Strnd L groin; blister R index fing
Venditte,Pat	20	41	Strn R oblique
VerHagen,Drew	18	20	Fractured nose
	19	11	Strn R forearm
	22	126	R hip impingement; hip surgery
Verlander,Justin	20	64	Strn R forearm/TJS
	21	169	Tommy John surgery
	22	18	Strnd R calf
Vesia,Alex	20	26	Covid-19
Vest,Will	21	9	Covid-19
	22	12	Covid-19
Vincent,Nick	18	27	Strn R groin
	19	62	Strn R pectoral muscle
Vizcaino,Arodys	18	73	R shoulder inflammation
	19	173	Surgery to repair torn labrum
Volquez,Edinson	19	150	Sprained R elbow
	20	46	Strn R oblique
Voth,Austin	19	43	Sprained AC joint R shoulder
	21	37	Covid-19; broken nose
Wacha,Michael	18	103	L oblique strain
	19	11	Patellar tendinitis L knee
	20	19	Inflammation R shoulder
	21	20	Strn R hamstring
	22	54	L intercost inflam; inflam R shldr
Waddell,Brandon	21	30	Covid-19
Wahl,Bobby	18	46	Strn R hamstring
	19	187	Torn ACL R knee
	21	61	Strn R oblique
Wainwright,Adam	18	150	R elbow inflam x 2; str L ham
	19	10	Strn L hamstring
	21	4	Covid-19
	22	10	Covid-19
Walker,Jeremy	20	67	Impingement R shoulder
Walker,Taijuan	18	170	R elbow surg
	19	186	Recovery from TJS
	21	11	Tightness L oblique
	22	19	Bursitis R shoulder
Warren,Art	21	67	Stained L oblique
	22	59	Strnd R flexor pronator
Warren,Austin	21	23	Covid-19
	22	67	Fx nose; Strnd R triceps
Watkins,Spenser	22	17	Bruised R elbow
Watson,Tony	19	16	Fx L wrist
	21	11	Strn L calf
Weathers,Ryan	21	12	Fx R ankle
Weaver,Luke	19	118	Tightness R forearm
	21	107	Strn R shoulder
	22	66	R elbow inflammation
Webb,Jacob	19	65	R elbow impingement
	20	48	Shoulder
Webb,Logan	21	54	Strn R shoulder
	22	7	Strnd lower back x2
Webster,Allen	19	143	Radial nerve inflammation R arm

FIVE-YEAR INJURY LOG — Pitchers

Pitchers	Yr	Days	Injury
Weems,Jordan	20	11	Shoulder
Wells,Alex	22	141	Strnd L elbow
Wells,Tyler	21	24	Inflammation R shoulder
	22	58	R shoulder inflam; Strnd L obliq
Wendelken,J.B.	20	5	Undisclosed medical condition
	21	59	Strn L oblique
	22	10	Covid-19
Wheeler,Zack	19	15	R shoulder fatigue
	22	36	Tendinitis R forearm; covid-19
White,Mitchell	21	3	Covid-19
	22	18	Covid-19
Whitley,Kodi	20	50	Covid-19
	21	46	Strn lower back
Whitlock,Garrett	21	2	R pectoral strain
	22	53	R hip inflam; R hip impingement
Wick,Rowan	20	12	Strn L oblique
	21	132	Strn L oblique
Widener,Taylor	20	20	Strn R ribcage muscle
	21	80	Covid; Strn R groin x2
Wieck,Brad	20	65	Strn R hamstring
	21	72	Irregular heartbeat
	22	188	Strnd L elbow
Wiles,Collin	22	9	Strnd R shoulder
Williams,Austen	19	165	Strn L hamstring
Williams,Devin	21	11	Strn R elbow
Williams,Taylor	18	11	R elbow soreness
	21	140	Inflammation R knee
Williams,Trevor	19	34	Strn R side
	21	40	Appendix surgery
Wilson,Bryse	21	11	Fatigue R arm; Strn R hamstring
Wilson,Justin	19	67	Sore R elbow
	21	42	Inflam L shldr; Strn R hamstring
	22	165	Sore L elbow
Wilson,Steven	22	19	L hamstring tendinitis
Winckowski,Josh	22	13	Covid-19
Winder,Josh	22	37	Impingement R shoulder
Wingenter,Trey	19	15	Strn R shoulder
	20	68	TJS
	21	169	Tommy John surgery
Winkler,Daniel	21	18	Covid; R triceps tendinitis
Wisler,Matt	21	32	Inflamed R middle finger
	22	37	Strnd neck
Wittgren,Nick	18	21	Bruised middle finger - R hand
Wood,Alex	18	11	L wrist inflammation
	19	123	Lower back strain
	20	36	Inflammation R shoulder
	21	36	Covid-19; Strn lower back
	22	36	Impingement L shoulder
Wood,Hunter	19	17	R shoulder inflammation
	21	117	Sprained UCL R elbow
Woodruff,Brandon	19	58	Strn L oblique
	22	32	Sprnd R ankle
Workman,Brandon	21	6	Covid exposure
Yacabonis,Jimmy	22	15	Strnd L groin
Yajure,Miguel	21	84	Sore R forearm
Yamamoto,Jordan	19	25	Strn R forearm
	21	116	Sore R shoulder
Yarbrough,Ryan	20	10	Tightness L groin
	21	11	Covid-19
	22	39	Strnd L groin; Strnd R oblique
Yardley,Eric	21	26	Strn R shoulder

FIVE-YEAR INJURY LOG — Pitchers

Pitchers	Yr	Days	Injury
Yates,Kirby	18	12	R ankle tendinitis
	20	45	Bone chips R elbow
	21	169	Tommy John surgery
	22	152	Tommy John surg
Ynoa,Huascar	21	93	Fx R Hand
	22	11	Tommy John surg
Zerpa,Angel	22	74	Strnd L knee; sore R knee
Zeuch,T.J.	21	12	Tendinitis R shoulder
	22	21	Strnd upper back
Zimmer,Kyle	20	6	Neuritis R elbow
	21	38	Strn lower back; Strn neck
Zimmermann,Bruce	21	91	Tendinitis L biceps tendon
Zuber,Tyler	22	188	Impingement R shoulder

Top 75 Impact Prospects for 2023

1.	Corbin Carroll (OF, ARI)	21.	Hayden Wesneski (RHP, CHC)
2.	Gunnar Henderson (IF, BAL)	22.	Ken Waldichuk (RHP, OAK)
3.	Josh Jung (3B, TEX)	23.	Eury Perez (RHP, MIA)
4.	Triston Casas (1B, BOS)	24.	Alec Burleson (OF, STL)
5.	Grayson Rodriguez (RHP, BAL)	25.	Michael Toglia (1B, COL)
6.	Royce Lewis (SS, MIN)	26.	Bobby Miller (RHP, LA)
7.	Brett Baty (3B, NYM)	27.	Brennen Davis (OF, CHC)
8.	Ezequiel Tovar (SS, COL)	28.	Ryan Pepiot (RHP, LA)
9.	Miguel Vargas (3B/OF, LA)	29.	Yainer Díaz (C/1B, HOU)
10.	Hunter Brown (RHP, HOU)	30.	Garrett Mitchell (OF, MIL)
11.	Will Brennan (OF, CLE)	31.	Matt Mervis (1B, CHC)
12.	Anthony Volpe (SS, NYY)	32.	Cade Cavalli (RHP, WAS)
13.	Oswald Peraza (SS, NYY)	33.	Colton Cowser (OF, BAL)
14.	Jordan Walker (OF, STL)	34.	Taj Bradley (RHP, TAM)
15.	Francisco Álvarez (C, NYM)	35.	DL Hall (LHP, BAL)
16.	Bo Naylor (C, CLE)	36.	Esteury Ruiz (UT, MIL)
17.	Sal Frelick (OF, MIL)	37.	Matt Wallner (OF, MIN)
18.	Kyle Stowers (OF, BAL)	38.	Cody Morris (RHP, CLE)
19.	Spencer Steer (UT, CIN)	39.	Curtis Mead (IF, TAM)
20.	Kerry Carpenter (OF, DET)	40.	Ryne Nelson (RHP, ARI)

Ji-Hwan Bae (2B/OF, PIT)	Drey Jameson (RHP, ARI)	Endy Rodriguez (C, PIT)
Michael Busch (2B, LA)	Caleb Kilian (RHP, CHC)	Sixto Sánchez (RHP, MIA)
Diego Cartaya (C, LA)	Jack Leiter (RHP, TEX)	Tyler Soderstrom (C/1B, OAK)
Jackson Chourio (OF, MIL)	Matthew Liberatore (LHP, STL)	Gavin Stone (RHP, LA)
Oscar Colás (OF, CHW)	Marco Luciano (SS, SF)	George Valera (OF, CLE)
Elly De La Cruz (SS, CIN)	Kyle Manzardo (1B, TAM)	Zac Veen (OF, COL)
Daniel Espino (RHP, CLE)	Kyle Muller (LHP, ATL)	Joey Wentz (LHP, DET)
Wilmer Flores (RHP, DET)	Logan O'Hoppe (C, LAA)	Jordan Westburg (IF, BAL)
Jordan Groshans (IF, MIA)	Luis Ortiz (RHP, PIT)	Owen White (RHP, TEX)
Kyle Harrison (LHP, SF)	James Outman (OF, LAD)	Gavin Williams (RHP, CLE)
Robert Hassell III (OF, WAS)	Andrew Painter (RHP, PHI)	Masyn Winn (SS, STL)
Iván Herrera (C, STL)	Quinn Priester (RHP, PIT)	

by Chris Blessing, Rob Gordon and Jeremy Deloney

Let's be honest, you've come to this part of the *Forecaster* to grab a sneak peek at the rookies you'll be spending most of your FAB on this year. As in past years, in the following pages you'll find skills and narrative profiles of the 75 rookie-eligible prospects most likely to have an impact in 2023.

Above, we've ranked the Top 40 prospects in terms of projected 2023 Rotisserie value. Beyond those 40, we list 35 more, presented in alphabetical order, who could see time in the majors in 2023, but whose raw skill or later timeline might be less polished or a step below others in terms of potential 2023 impact. Keep in mind, this is just a pre-season snapshot. Prospects develop at

different paces and making that one adjustment or finding opportunity when one doesn't seem to exist can make all the difference.

Starting on the next page, each of the 75 has his own narrative capsule, presented in alphabetical order. It's a primer on each player's strengths and weaknesses that attempts to balance raw skill, readiness for the majors and likelihood of 2023 playing time.

For even more detail, including profiles of over 900 prospects, statistics and our overall HQ100 top prospect list, see our sister publication, the *2023 Minor League Baseball Analyst*—as well as the weekly scouting reports and minor league information at BaseballHQ.com. Happy Prospecting!

Francisco Álvarez (C, NYM) was called up for the last week of the season after a .260/.375/.511 slash line with 27 HR, split between upper level affiliates. The 21-year-old struggled with whiff issues throughout the season, which could keep him in the minors longer than anticipated. However, it's power for days with a chance to grab playing time at C and DH this year.

Ji-hwan Bae (2B/OF, PIT) could have an inside track to a starting job in the Pirates infield with a strong spring. The 22-year-old made his big league in 2022 and hit .333/.405/.424 in 33 AB. He finished 2nd in the organization with 30 SB and has the speed to steal 30+ bags on an annual basis. He plays all over the diamond, including SS and CF. A contact over power prospect, he only hit 8 HR in 2022.

Brett Baty (3B, NYM) showed flashes of what he can bring to the table in a short-sample MLB debut before being lost for the season due to a thumb injury. Baty slashed .315/.410/.533 with 19 HR in 362 minor league AB. He consistently gets to hard contact but not as much loft, depressing present power to below average. The 23-year-old will battle Eduardo Escobar for 3B reps.

Taj Bradley (RHP, TAM) is a four-pitch pitcher who is on the verge of his big-league debut. The 21-year-old had a 2.57 ERA, a 1.035 WHIP and a 9.5 K/9 rate between two upper levels last year. Bradley throws four pitches. The most notable offerings are a mid-90s 4-seam FB and a mid-to-high 80s SL, both plus pitches.

Will Brennan (OF, CLE) has catapulted himself into top position player prospect status in the Guardians organization after a stellar 2022, including a late-season stint on the major league roster. After slashing .314/.371/.479 with 13 HR and 20 SB in the upper minors, the 24-year-old Brennan started for Cleveland into the playoffs. There is a good chance he's a starting OF on Opening Day.

Hunter Brown (RHP, HOU) has the versatility and arm strength to be a contributor as a starter or reliever. In 2022, the large-framed righty posted a 2.55 ERA and 11.9 K/9 while holding opponents to a .186 oppBA, even earning a late-season call-up. He has premium velocity and one of the better curveballs in the entire organization.

Alec Burleson (OF, STL) has a pure left-handed stroke, a good understanding of the strike zone, and finds barrels on a regular basis. After a solid pro debut in 2021, Burleson exploded in 2022, slashing .331/.372/.532 with 20 home runs and an excellent 14% K rate at Triple-A. He struggled in a brief MLB debut and will need to prove he can handle premium velocity.

Michael Busch (2B, LA) is a strong, physically mature hitter who put together another impressive season, slashing .274/.365/.514 with 32 HR between Double and Triple-A. Busch uses a slightly open stance with a quick LH stroke and good barrel awareness as he hunts for pitches he can drive. He does have some swing-and-miss that will prevent him from being a plus hitter, but understands the zone and is willing to take his walks (12% BB rate).

Kerry Carpenter (OF, DET) had a surprisingly productive season, slashing .331/.420/.644 at Triple-A and then holding his own in his MLB debut. Carpenter retooled his swing to get more loft off the bat. He does most of his damage against fastballs (.672 SLG% in the majors), leaving him vulnerable to breaking balls down and away. Below-average speed limits him to LF or DH.

Corbin Carroll (OF, ARI) could be a generational talent if he can remain healthy. In a 104 AB MLB sample, the 22-year-old hit .260/.330/.500 with 4 HR, after slugging 24 HR in the minor leagues. Carroll is a double-plus runner who stole 33 bases across multiple levels. He's likely to break camp Opening Day and would be the favorite for NL Rookie of the Year.

Diego Cartaya (C, LA) has a good understanding of the strike zone and an advanced approach at the plate, laying off pitches out of the zone and hunting fastballs. There is some swing-and-miss to his game, but he draws plenty of walks (14% BB rate). His best tool is his above-average power. He's played 162 games as a professional with 38 doubles and 36 home runs.

Triston Casas (1B, BOS) showed off his wares in a 76 AB trial with the Red Sox at the tail-end of 2022. He only hit .197, but smashed 5 HR while getting on base at a high clip (.358 oppBA). The 22-year-old could evolve into a 35+ HR monster with middle-of-the-order skills. He uses the entire field and has a keen understanding of the strike zone. Add in quality defensive skills and Casas is Boston's 1B of the future. He will battle Eric Hosmer for the starting job.

Cade Cavalli (RHP, WAS) made one start with the Nationals late in 2022 only to be shut down shortly thereafter due to shoulder inflammation. All reports indicate that his prized arm is fully healthy. The 24-year-old has a solid chance of winning a rotation spot to begin the year, thanks to his plus fastball and two breaking balls. There's work to be done with his change-up and pitch sequencing, but he has all the requisite goods to be a big contributor.

Jackson Chourio (OF, MIL) has evolved into an elite prospect and reached Double-A at age 18 in 2022. His explosive athleticism appears in his swing mechanics, CF defense and running game. He hit .288/.342/.538 with 30 doubles, 20 HR and 16 SB on three levels in the minors in 2022. Not on the 40-man roster, he could force his way to Milwaukee by mid-season.

Oscar Colás (OF, CHW) is a 24-year-old Cuban prospect who made his U.S. debut last season after playing in Japan. Colas slashed .314/.371/.524 with 23 HR, split across the top three levels of the minors. Colas struggled with spin and chased out of the zone often, which was not unexpected since he last saw pro pitching in 2019.

Colton Cowser (OF, BAL) reached Triple-A in his first full season as a pro after his selection as the 5th overall pick in 2021. The 22-year-old hit .278/.406/.469 with 19 HR and 18 SB on three levels in 2022, produces plus power potential and also brings average speed and baserunning skill to the table. He'll need to close up some holes in his swing, but he could become an above-average regular who could surface fairly early in 2023.

Brennen Davis (OF, CHC) struggled with health and production all season, missing several months with a back injury that required surgery. When healthy, Davis flashes plus speed and power and has the tools to be a 20/20 player in the majors. He has plus bat speed, but because of his size, his swing can get long, and he struggles against elite velocity.

Elly De La Cruz (SS, CIN) is the most exciting player in the minor leagues. Splitting 2022 between High-A and Double-A, De La Cruz slashed .304/.359/.586 with 28 HR and stole 47 bases. The 20-year-old struck out a lot, mostly due to his issues identifying breaking ball spin, especially in Double-A. He might see MLB towards the end of the season.

Yainer Díaz (C/1B, HOU) was another breakout performer in 2022 when he hit .306/.356/.542 and a career-high 25 HR between Double-A and Triple-A. He earned a trip to the majors and had 8 AB. He will get an opportunity to compete for a roster spot given his offensive talent. There is work to be done defensively to earn significant time, but the bat will play. He makes easy, loud contact and can play multiple positions, including the outfield corners.

Daniel Espino (RHP, CLE) is a 21-year-old pitching phenom who missed most of last season with a knee injury. He only started 4 games in Double-A but looked dirty, sporting a 17.2 K/9 rate. Espino commands well a high-90s FB with exceptional riding action and complements it with a whiff-inducing SL. He also throws a CB and CU and has SP1 upside.

Wilmer Flores (RHP, DET) is the younger brother of current major leaguer Wilmer Flores. Flores had a breakout season, going 7-4 with a 2.79 ERA and 23 BB/130 K in 103.1 IP between High-A and Double-A. His fastball now sits in the mid-90s, topping at 98 with good spin and late life up in the zone. His best offering is a plus 12-6 curveball that generates plenty of swing-and-miss. He also mixes in a change-up that needs refinement.

Sal Frelick (OF, MIL) finished 4th in the entire minor leagues in BA when he hit .331/403/480 with 28 doubles and 11 HR between Double-A and Triple-A. That also came with 24 SB. One of the most difficult hitters to fan in the minors, the 22-year-old uses all fields and leverages his double-plus speed to his advantage on base and in CF. He will battle with Garrett Mitchell for CF time. Though he offers little HR pop now, he could get to 20 HR at peak.

Jordan Groshans (IF, MIA) made his MLB debut after being acquired in a mid-season trade with Toronto for Anthony Bass and Zach Pop. Once a top prospect, Groshans has struggled in 2022. In the minors, he slashed .263/.359/.331 with 3 HR. Receiving starting reps with the Marlins, he wasn't much better. Lauded for his hit tool until last year, there is hope he can at least hit for a high BA again.

DL Hall (LHP, BAL) could be a valuable arm for the Orioles for the entirety of 2023. He pitched 13.2 innings with Baltimore in 2022, mostly out of the bullpen. Though he's considered a starter long-term, his versatility and pure arm strength could be leveraged as a reliever. His lack of command has been a hindrance

(career 5.1 BB/9), but he induces an inordinate number of swings-and-misses (14.6 K/9 in 2022).

Kyle Harrison (LHP, SF) has been simply dominant at each rung of the minor league ladder. He posted the highest K/9 in the organization due to his outstanding pure stuff and natural deception from his lower arm slot. He misses bats with both his mid-90s fastball and big-breaking slider. He could be ready for his MLB debut by mid-season.

Robert Hassell III (OF, WAS) was part of the return the Nationals received from San Diego in the Juan Soto deal. The 21-year-old made it to Double-A in 2022 and hit .273/.357/.407 with 11 HR and 24 SB in 450 AB. With improved power and above-average speed, he could evolve into a top-of-the-order producer who hits for a .300+ BA with 25+ HR and 20+ SB. He broke the hamate bone in his right wrist in the AFL, but he'll be ready for spring training.

Gunnar Henderson (INF, BAL) may very well be the leading candidate for AL Rookie of the Year in 2023. The 21-year-old performed well in 116 AB with the Orioles in 2022: .259/.348/.440 with 4 HR. Given his advanced hitting aptitude and improved plate discipline, there is nothing he can't do well. He can play any infield position, including his natural shortstop, with a cannon arm and ideal athleticism. He should be an Opening Day starter.

Iván Herrera (C, STL) is an underrated backstop who should get a chance to win a part-time role this spring. Herrera doesn't have any standout tools, but all of them are average or above. After five minor league seasons, he owns a .276/.375/.415 slash line. Herrera should eventually hit double-digit home runs and each year continues to get better behind the plate.

Drey Jameson (RHP, ARI) had a wonderful MLB debut, sporting a 1.48 ERA and a 1.11 WHIP in 24.1 innings. Jameson's overall minor-league line was ugly, mostly due to command issues for half of the season. Those command issues and his smaller stature have always capped his ceiling, despite featuring premium stuff. The 25-year-old could open the season in the D-Backs rotation.

Josh Jung (3B, TEX) made his MLB debut in September after missing much of the season recovering from a torn labrum. The 24-year-old Jung controls the strike zone and has excellent bat-to-ball skills, which should enable him to hit for both power and average. He should be able to stick at the hot corner, too. With a strong spring, Jung will likely emerge as the Rangers' everyday 3B and be a leading contender for AL ROY in 2023.

Caleb Kilian (RHP, CHC) showed improved velocity in his second full season and made three starts with the Cubs. The improved velocity was offset by surprising struggles with command (5.0 BB/9 at Triple-A Iowa). His fastball sits at 93-95, topping out at 97, and he throws a sinker, cutter, and four-seamer. Kilian also mixes in a couple of fringe off-speed pitches, working primarily off the heater. He will likely be used in a swing role in 2023.

Jack Leiter (RHP, TEX) has seen his prospect status drop since dominating as a draft-eligible sophomore at Vanderbilt. The 22-year-old has struggled with control, too often falling behind in counts and walking 5.4/9 in his pro debut. Leiter still has a dynamic four-pitch mix highlighted by a plus mid-90s fastball that tops out at 98 mph with high spin. His slider, curve, and change-up all flash plus at times.

Royce Lewis (SS, MIN) likely wouldn't be on this list if he didn't suffer another knee injury that ended his season. The 23-year-old is likely to return in June 2023. When healthy, he is an exceptional athlete who hit .300 with 2 HR in 40 AB with the Twins prior to the injury. He was even dominant in Triple-A. His power is really starting to emerge due to his polished swing mechanics and bat speed. He could play either SS or CF.

Matthew Liberatore (LHP, STL) made 7 starts for the Cardinals in 2022. Liberatore profiles as a mid-rotation innings-eater SP. His fastball sits in the low-90s with good late movement. Liberatore struck out just 28 batters in 34.2 IP after posting a 5.17 ERA in 22 Triple-A starts. Still, Liberatore showed enough in his big-league debut that he should contend for a spot in the Cardinals starting rotation next spring.

Marco Luciano (SS, SF) spent all of 2022 in High-A and showed improvement across the board. He is an electric prospect who can be a highlight reel with his elite bat speed and incredible brute power. He only had 205 AB in 2022, hitting .263/.339/.459 with 10 HR. Luciano has a high baseball IQ and may be able to stick at SS for the long-term.

Kyle Manzardo (1B, TAM) hit his way into top prospect consideration last year. Between two levels, Manzardo slashed .327/.426/.617 with 22 HR in 93 games. The 22-year-old has an advanced approach and feel for the zone. A swing adjustment has allowed the double-plus hit tool Manzardo to get to lofted contact more often, too. He is close and could be up in the second half.

Curtis Mead (IF, TAM) seemingly hits the ball hard all the time, especially when he gets to lofted contact. The 22-year-old slashed .298/.390/.532 in 76 games last year with an average exit velocity over 90 mph. Getting to loft more often has allowed for the power projection to play up. Is he ready for the big leagues? Mead doesn't have a defensive position, and the Rays are often slow to work young players into the lineup.

Matt Mervis (1B, CHC) is one of the more buzzworthy prospects this offseason after slashing .309/.379/.606 and hitting 36 HR across three levels. A longer-limbed hitter, the 24-year-old has a high contact rate too, even though he'll chase on breaking balls too often. This could be the Cubs' 1B relatively soon.

Bobby Miller (RHP, LA) is the top arm in the Dodgers system. The 23-year-old has two plus fastballs. His four-seamer sits at 96-98, topping out at 100 mph, and his two-seamer works in the mid-to-upper-90s. Miller also has a plus slider that sits at 89-91, a plus change-up with late fade and sink, and low-80s curve that also show plus potential.

Garrett Mitchell (OF, MIL) continues to hear critiques about his lack of over-the-wall power. The 23-year-old left-handed hitter produces in several ways. He hit over .326 in each month from July thru October and earned 61 AB in the big leagues. He hit .311/.373/.459 with 2 HR and 8 SB. Mitchell is a premium athlete with double-plus speed and above-average CF qualities.

Cody Morris (RHP, CLE) is a four-pitch pitcher, relying mostly on his FB/CT. Despite missing most of 2022 with a shoulder strain, the 26-year-old found himself in the Guardians' rotation during the pennant race. Though he posted a 2.28 ERA. he struggled throwing strikes, which was out of character for him, given his minor-league track record. He could start this season in the Guardians' rotation.

Kyle Muller (LHP, ATL) is still a rookie, which seems impossible but is reality. Muller made three starts on the big-league level and got bounced around last year. Command has always plagued the big-bodied, 25-year-old ever since he entered pro ball. It's hard to see a path forward not involving a role change to the bullpen.

Bo Naylor (C, CLE) is the Guardians' catcher of the future and possibly even the Guardians' catcher of now. He didn't record a hit in 8 MLB AB. In the minors, the 22-year-old slashed .263/.392/.496 with 21 HR in 118 games. He's a patient hitter with a power approach. Naylor is a strong pitch framer, which should help him get into the MLB lineup sooner rather than later.

Ryne Nelson (RHP, ARI) made his MLB debut and pitched well until taking a liner off of his forearm. The 24-year-old pitched much better than his stats indicated in Triple-A, where his ERA was 5.43 and his WHIP was 1.39. Nelson throws his low-to-mid 90s four-seam FB at a high rate. Unfortunately, Nelson's fastball command comes and goes, causing inconsistencies.

Logan O'Hoppe (C, LAA) was acquired from Philadelphia in the Brandon Marsh deal last summer. O'Hoppe is more known for his glove than his bat. However, the bat has steadily improved, including a .283/.416/.544 line with 26 HR last year, though the underlying analytics don't support this level of performance. However, the 22-year-old should be a solid offensive catcher, even as a rookie.

Luis Ortiz (RHP, PIT) could be a benefactor of the current Pirates roster makeup. He exceeded expectations in 2022, starting four games with Pittsburgh at the end of the season. In the minors, he posted a 4.56 ERA while finishing 2nd in the organization in Ks. He got better as the season progressed and leveraged his large frame and premium fastball to dominate hitters. His slider also misses bats and hitters have trouble barreling his heavy fastball.

James Outman (OF, LA) worked hard to retool his LH stroke and became more selective at the plate. His approach paid off to the tune of a .294/.392/.585 slash line between Double and Triple-A, earning him a brief stint in the majors. Outman hunts for balls he can punish to all fields and has above-average speed and power. Outman has the tools to be a 20/20 threat if he finds his way to full-time AB.

Andrew Painter (RHP, PHI) checks all the boxes of a true ace. Given he's only 19, his quick ascension has been a revelation. Across three minor league levels in 2022, the 6'7" righty posted a 1.56 ERA, 2.2 BB/9 and 13.5 K/9 in 22 starts covering 103.2 innings. Further, he held hitters to a .181 oppBA. Though he hasn't pitched at Triple-A, he'll be a closely-monitored arm in spring training.

Ryan Pepiot (RHP, LA) spent much of the year on the shuttle between OKC and LA. Pepiot owns a mid-90s heater with high spin and plus horizontal movement. His change-up is widely considered the best in the minors. Pepiot's slider lags the other offerings, and he occasionally struggles with control. Pepiot has the stuff to be a solid mid-rotation starter and could see significant innings in 2023.

Oswald Peraza (SS, NYY) was a breath of fresh air for the Yankees during a September call-up last year. He slashed .306/.404/.429 in a 49 AB MLB sample after hitting 18 HR and stealing 38 bases in the minors. The 22-year-old is a dark horse candidate to start at SS on Opening Day for the Yankees. He's more likely to stick defensively at SS than fellow Yankees prospect Anthony Volpe.

Eury Perez (RHP, MIA) is a long-levered power pitcher known for exceptional command of a double-plus four-seam FB. The 19-year-old sits 94-98 mph with his FB and features three secondary offerings, including a hard SL he introduced last season that is already a plus offering. Perez has overpowering stuff and will be up for Miami some point early in the season.

Quinn Priester (RHP, PIT) will be given ample opportunity to win a job in spring training. He began 2022 in Double-A before a much-needed promotion to Triple-A in August. He has the repertoire, athleticism and moxie to thrive in the majors. The 21-year-old had a 3.29 ERA and 8.9 K/9 in 19 starts. He induces a ton of ground balls with a quality fastball and his terrific curveball is a legitimate swing-and-miss pitch.

Grayson Rodriguez (RHP, BAL) likely would have already made his big-league debut if not for a right lat strain in early June. The 22-year-old was downright dominant in 2022, mostly in Triple-A. He held hitters to a .176 oppBA while posting a 2.62 ERA and 109 Ks in 75.2 innings. He has an exceptional fastball that sits in the mid-to-high 90s and knocks out hitters with a fantastic slider. He also has excellent control and command.

Endy Rodriguez (C, PIT) was one of the Pirates' major success stories in 2022. He finished 4th in the minors in OPS and set personal bests in HR and each of the triple-slash categories. The 22-year-old hit .323/.407/.590 with 39 doubles and 25 HR in 458 AB on three levels. He mostly played catcher, but also saw time at 2B, LF and 1B. He is a sound hitter from both sides and should hit for a high BA.

Esteury Ruiz (UT, MIL) made his MLB debut and was traded to the Brewers as part of the Josh Hader deal. The 23-year-old has always been an intriguing prospect due to his power/speed combination. Last year, in the minors, he started to hit some after

tweaking his approach, slashing .332/.447/.526, renewing interest in the skill set. Still, concerns remain Ruiz can hit enough to make up for a potential low OBP.

Sixto Sánchez (RHP, MIA) missed his second straight season with arm issues. He's had two surgeries on his shoulder since his sparkling MLB debut during the pandemic-shortened 2020 season. The 24-year-old is the hardest player to rank on a list like this with his 2023 outcome ranging from an MLB SP to a guy struggling to get back on the mound from injury.

Tyler Soderstrom (C, OAK) has quickly climbed the minor league ladder. Split between three levels in 2022, he smashed the most HR (29) in the organization. Soderstrom could emerge in the majors by mid-season. The question will be at what position, catcher or 1B. His bat will play anywhere. He owns a picturesque swing from the left side and can hit for BA and power.

Spencer Steer (IF, CIN) made his MLB debut last season after a trade with Minnesota for Tyler Mahle. Steer has a .274/.364/.515 slash line in the minors but struggled getting to hard contact in his big-league sample. The 25-year-old hit 25 HR last year, hunting for middle-in pitches to drive out of the park. Steer's versatility figures to find him playing time this season.

Gavin Stone (RHP, LA) had a breakout season that saw him dominate across three levels, going 9-6 with a 1.48 ERA. Stone added velocity since being drafted and now features an above-average 93-95 mph fastball that he locates to all quadrants. His best offering is a mid-80 change-up that he will throw in any count. What separates Stone from others in the system is his advanced ability to pound the zone and hit his spots.

Kyle Stowers (OF, BAL) could win an Opening Day roster spot and possibly a starting role if the Orioles decide to trade one or both of Cedric Mullins and Anthony Santander. The 24-year-old doesn't get as much hype and publicity as some of the other young Orioles prospects, but he shouldn't be ignored. He has very good power, particularly to the pull side, and can steal bases with average speed. There will be strikeouts, but his overall skill set is solid.

Michael Toglia (1B/OF, COL) has the best power in the Rockies system and smashed 30 longballs between Double and Triple-A, earning him a late-season call-up. At 6'5", 230 Toglia is a below-average runner and is best suited at 1B where he is a plus defender. Toglia is a true three-outcome player who will draw plenty of walks with plus power, but his all-or-nothing approach makes it unlikely he will ever hit for average.

Ezequiel Tovar (SS, COL) is the Rockies' top prospect and had a breakout campaign at the plate, posting a .927 OPS en route to making his MLB debut. Already an elite defender, Tovar showed a more aggressive approach at the plate and sacrificed some plate discipline for power. The trade-off worked as he posted his first .500+ SLG. Tovar will likely get every chance to win the starting SS job in Colorado this spring.

George Valera (OF, CLE) is a power-hitting prospect who struggled with whiffs but still hit for a bunch of power. The 22-year-old hit 24 HR in 132 games and got to hard contact often. He also doesn't expand the zone either, which should help keep his OBP above water if his BA tanks.

Miguel Vargas (3B/OF, LA) posted a .915 OPS at Triple-A Oklahoma City, which earned him a big-league call-up. The 22-year-old has an advanced hit tool with a quick bat and excellent bat-to-ball skills. The uptick in power raised his profile and he now owns a career slash line of .313/.390/.488. He's a below-average defender and split time between 1B, 3B, and LF, both in the majors and the minors.

Zac Veen (OF, COL) swiped 55 bases between High-A and Double-A and then stole another 16 in the Arizona Fall League. Veen has a good understanding of the strike zone. To reach his tremendous potential, Veen needs to hunt for pitches he can drive into the spacious gaps in Coors Field. If the speed and OBP stick at the MLB level, he has plenty of value.

Anthony Volpe (SS, NYY) is the top prospect in the Yankees organization. The 21-year-old recovered from a slow start to slash .249/.342/.460 with 21 HR, split between two levels. Volpe is a well-rounded offensive machine, producing plus power angles off the bat. There are some questions whether Volpe is a SS due to below-average arm strength. However, his bat should carry him to the Yankees lineup sometime early in the season.

Ken Waldichuk (LHP, OAK) was a key acquisition from the Yankees at the trade deadline. Shortly thereafter, the 24-year-old was promoted to the majors, starting seven games. He posted a 4.93 ERA while showing good control. Waldichuk operates with a funky, deceptive delivery and an ability to vary his arm angle and slots to the plate. With a plus fastball and solid-average slider, he is particularly stingy against left-handed hitters.

Jordan Walker (OF, STL) is an impressive mix of power and hit tool, slashing .310/.388/.525 for his career. Walker has continued to add size and strength to his 6'5" frame. He has elite bat speed and some of the best exit velocity in the minors. He stands upright at the plate before coiling and unleashing a vicious stroke with an uncanny ability to find the barrel, mostly to the pull side. This fall, Walker was moved to the OF full-time.

Matt Wallner (OF, MIN) is a prototypical slugging RF with incredible arm strength and significant power. While he only hit .228 with 25 K in 57 AB with the Twins, he finished 7th in the minors in walks. He established new career highs in both HR and doubles. The drawback to his power, of course, is the propensity

to swing and miss. Breaking balls have proven to be problematic. He could battle for the starting RF job, particularly if Max Kepler is dealt.

Joey Wentz (LHP, DET) was impressive in his MLB debut, going 2-2 with a 3.03 ERA in 32.2 IP. While he lacks elite stuff, his four-pitch mix gives him the tools to be an effective back-end starter. Wentz showed an improved fastball with run up in the zone. He also has a plus 82-84 change-up that is well located and particularly effective vs RHB. Wentz also added a cutter to go along with a fringe-average curve.

Hayden Wesneski (RHP, CHC) attacks hitters with a diverse arsenal that is highlighted by a 92-94 mph four-seamer and low-90s sinker that has late break. He also mixes in a plus slider, a change-up, and a recently-added cutter. He used the four-seamer and slider to great effect in his MLB debut, posting a 2.18 ERA over 33 IP and limiting opposing hitters to a .198 batting average against.

Jordan Westburg (INF, BAL) is among many Orioles farmhands who could have a significant impact in their 2023 campaign. His versatility may be the ticket for him to the big leagues as he can play all over the diamond. The 23-year-old hit .265/.355/.496 with 39 doubles, 27 HR and 12 SB between Double-A and Triple-A. He struggles with contact at times, but his bat speed, power, hitting acumen and defensive skills should give him a lasting career.

Owen White (RHP, TEX) was a 2nd round pick in 2018, but Tommy John surgery in early 2019 meant he didn't make his pro debut until last year. White is an athletic hurler with an above-average mid-90s fastball. He mixes in a 12-6 curveball, a slider, and a change-up. That four-pitch mix allows him to keep hitters off-balance and enables his fastball to play up.

Gavin Williams (RHP, CLE) had a great start to his pro career, split between High-A and Double-A. In 115 innings, the 23-year-old struck out 149 batters, mostly on the back of his mid-90s four-seam FB and his two-plane breaking mid-80s SL. There is a good chance the Guardians count on Williams for some late-season starts.

Masyn Winn (SS, STL) had a breakout campaign in 2022, slashing .283/.364/.468 with 36 doubles, 12 HR, and 43 SB. Winn was a two-way player when drafted and has the tools to be an elite defender at short with the ability to hit 100 mph on his throws to first. Winn's production and uptick in power changed his profile from a glove-first prospect to a potential five-category fantasy stud.

Top Players from East Asia for 2023 and Beyond

by Tom Mulhall

After a disappointing 2021 signing period, Seiya Suzuki made some waves with one of the more successful debuts by a Japanese hitter. Usually pitchers make more impact, and several experienced and skilled starting pitchers should be available soon. But we may be entering an era where more hitters will successfully make the transition to MLB. For dynasty players, there are many exciting names to follow.

With Japanese teams offering their free agent stars better contracts with opt-out provisions, MLB teams can no longer simply outbid Japanese teams. Still, with labor and COVID-19 restrictions more or less behind us, players from Japan may be more willing to test out MLB. One has to wonder if MLB teams regret their decision to low-ball their offers to Tomoyuki Sugano last year, causing him to stay in Japan. Korean teams will still be easily outbid by MLB teams.

As always, we are looking for a combination of skill, opportunity, and desire to play in MLB.

NOTES: For more general background about East Asia baseball style of play and the posting systems, see the Encyclopedia article beginning on page 49. The Sawamura Award for starting pitchers is roughly equivalent to the Cy Young Award but is not given every year. It emphasizes complete games and wins over other stats. Names are sometimes difficult to translate so the official NPB or KBO designation is used.

Shintaro Fujinami (RHP, Hanshin Tigers) was in the same draft class as Shohei Ohtani and there was some debate as to who was the better pitcher. But he began to struggle with his control in 2016 and has spent the rest of his career bouncing between the majors and minors, as well as starting and relieving. Fujinami seemed to correct his control issues in 2022 when he walked only 21 batters in 66.2 innings. He will be posted, but it seems like his team may be trying to sell high and it would be a surprise if any MLB team took a chance on him. A real dart-throw at the end of your draft.
Possible ETA: 2023

Shota Imanaga (LHP, Yokohama DeNA Baystars) has been a competent and consistent SP over the past four seasons and is expressing a desire to play in MLB "in the near future." He picked a good time to announce that decision, coming off a career year in 2022 with a 2.26 ERA and 0.94 WHIP. Not as dominating as Sugano or Senga, he could be an acceptable end-of-the-rotation MLB pitcher.
Possible ETA: 2024

Jung-hoo Lee (OF, Kiwoom Heroes) is a hitting machine who won the 2021 KBO batting title with a .360 BA nearly 30 years after his father it. In 2022, he "slumped" to a mere .349 BA/.421 OBP. He did have a career-high 23 HR so his power may be developing. Lee is a good defender but he probably projects as an average fourth OF in the majors. Although he is just 24, he is nearing free agency and Korean teams will post their younger stars.
Possible ETA: 2024

Raidel Martinez (RHP, Chunichi Dragons) continues to be one of the top closers in Japan. The 6'3", 205-pound Cuban has now had five solid seasons in a row, capped with a 0.97 ERA and 0.75 WHIP in 2022. Martinez has a plus fastball that is consistently in the upper 90s, complemented with a nice splitter. Closers coming from Japan have a decent track record when making the move to MLB, and the 25-year-old could continue that trend.
Possible ETA: 2023

Yuki Matsui (LHP, Tohoku Rakuten Golden Eagles) doesn't have the overwhelming fastball that most closers possess, and at 5'8" and 163 pounds, he isn't going to overpower hitters. What he does have is four solid pitches with a splitter, curve, change-up, and slider. As a result, he has an excellent K% and minimizes home runs. But control is a problem; he's logged a 10% BB% over the past two seasons. In MLB, he projects as an above-average middle reliever rather than a closer.
Possible ETA: 2024

Hiroya Miyagi (LHP, Orix Buffaloes) continues to play in the shadow of his amazing teammate, Yoshinobu Yamamoto, who is the best young pitcher in the NPB. Miyagi had a slight drop-off to a 3.16 ERA in 2022 but has many years to fully develop before he leaves Japan. For dynasty players who missed out on Yamamoto and Roki Sasaki, Miyagi may be worth stashing away.
Possible ETA: 2026

Munetaka Murakami (1B/3B, Tokyo Yakult Swallows) had a career year in 2022, to put it mildly. He not only became the youngest Triple Crown winner at age 22 and the first since 2004, but he broke Sadaharu Oh's all-time record for HR in a season by a Japanese-born player. Just how dominant was Murakami? The entire roster of the Chunichi Dragons had 62 HR; Murakami had 56. He led the entire NPB in walks, HR, RBI, OBP and OPS, and led the Central League in BA. Murakami has power to all three fields and a little speed, with double-digit SB the past two seasons. While he wishes to play in MLB one day, he's a long way from international free agency.
Possible ETA: 2026

Roki Sasaki (RHP, Chiba Lotte Marines) almost broke social media when he was pulled from his second straight perfect game in the eighth inning. That's right, he almost pitched two perfect games in a row. Sasaki threw the first perfect game in NPB in 28 years, tying the record for strikeouts (19) and setting the record for most consecutive strikeouts (13). One week later, he had 19 strikeouts when his manager pulled the 20-year old in the eighth inning after 102 pitches. Sasaki has a fastball consistently in the high 90s, occasionally touching 100. He's also got a nasty splitter and an improving slider. Sasaki is reportedly learning English, which is a sure sign that he wants to test out MLB.
Possible ETA: 2026

Koudai Senga (RHP, Fukuoka SoftBank Hawks) picked the perfect time to have a career year, just as he achieved international free agency. His 1.94 ERA in 2022 lowered his career ERA to 2.59, and he walked only 49 batters in 144 IP. Senga has a 98-mph fastball that he couples with an excellent forkball/splitter. One of the most experienced pitchers in Japan, Senga projects to be a solid mid-level starting pitcher in MLB if he can stay healthy.
Probable ETA: 2023

Tomoyuki Sugano (RHP, Yomiuri Giants) failed to attract sufficient offers from any MLB team when he was posted in 2021, and he re-signed with his home team. His contract has an opt-out provision, so at age 33, it's now or never for Sugano. Sugano has plus command of up to seven pitches including a deadly slider and curveball, which complement an average fastball in the low to mid-90s. Despite battling minor health issues in 2022, he managed a 3.12 ERA and 1.11 WHIP. It's worrisome, however, that his strikeouts were down.
Probable ETA: 2023

Yoshinobu Yamamoto (RHP, Orix Buffaloes) picked up where he left off with a 1.68 ERA and 0.92 WHIP in 2022, becoming the first pitcher in NPB history to win a second straight Sawamura Award. He also won the pitching Triple Crown (ERA, Wins and Strikeouts) for the second year in a row. Yamamoto has a mid-90s fastball, complemented with a splitter and a knee-buckling curveball. Yamamoto is just 5'8" so there will be questions about his durability, but he pitched 193.2 innings in 2021 and 193 innings in 2022. There are rumors he could be posted early, so if you are a dynasty player, here is your #1 prospect.
Possible ETA: 2025 with a slight possibility of 2024

Yasuaki Yamasaki (RHP, Yokahama DeNA Baystars) was the youngest player in Japan to reach 200 career saves. After struggling mightily the previous two seasons, Yamazaki rebounded in 2022 with 37 saves and a 1.33 ERA. His control returned as he walked just 9 batters in 54.1 innings and compiled a 0.69 WHIP. Yamazaki expects to negotiate his release this off-season and attempt to sign with an MLB team. He isn't a big strikeout pitcher and will probably start in middle relief.
Probable ERA: 2023

Masataka Yoshida (OF, Orix Buffaloes) is, per Adam Jones, "an on-base machine". Yoshida has asked his team to post him and with a .327 lifetime BA, he may draw some interest. He does have some power, hitting 21 HR each of the past two years. Yoshida is not a great defender, so unless his power holds up, he probably projects as an average #4 OF in MLB.
Possible ETA: 2023

Conclusion

For immediate help: Koudai Senga, Raidel Martinez, Tomoyuki Sugano, Yasuaki Yamazaki and Masataka Yoshida.

For Dynasty players: Yoshinobu Yamamoto, Roki Sasaki, Munetaka Murakami; a gap; and then Hiroya Miyagi.

Forget it: Masahiro Tanaka (another solid season in Japan but now age 34); Sung-Bum Na (.320 BA with power but now 33 and a new long-term contract); Haruki Nishikawa (continued decline); Yuki Yanagita (still solid but is now 34).

MAJOR LEAGUE EQUIVALENTS

In his 1985 *Baseball Abstract*, Bill James introduced the concept of major league equivalencies. His assertion was that, with the proper adjustments, a minor leaguer's statistics could be converted to an equivalent major league level performance with a great deal of accuracy.

Because of wide variations in the level of play among different minor leagues, it is difficult to get a true reading on a player's potential. For instance, a .300 batting average achieved in the high-offense Pacific Coast League is not nearly as much of an accomplishment as a similar level in the Eastern League. MLEs normalize these types of variances, for all statistical categories.

The actual MLEs are not projections. They represent how a player's previous performance might look at the major league level. However, the MLE stat line can be used in forecasting future performance in just the same way as a major league stat line would.

The model we use contains a few variations to James' version and updates all of the minor league and ballpark factors. In addition, we designed a module to convert pitching statistics, which is something James did not originally do.

Players are listed if they spent at least part of 2021 or 2022 in Triple-A or Double-A and had at least 150 AB or 45 IP within those two levels (players who split a season at both levels are indicated as a/a) in 2022. Major league and Single-A (and lower) stats are excluded. Each player is listed in the organization with which they finished the season. Some players over age 30 with major-league experience have been omitted for space.

These charts also provide the unique perspective of looking at two seasons' worth of data—even when the span is over three years. These are only short-term trends, for sure. But even here we can find small indications of players improving their skills, or struggling, as they rise through more difficult levels of competition. Since players—especially those with any modicum of talent —are promoted rapidly through major league systems, a two-season scan is often all we get to spot any trends. Five-year trends do appear in the *Minor League Baseball Analyst*.

Used correctly, MLEs are excellent indicators of potential. But, just like we cannot take traditional major league statistics at face value, the same goes for MLEs. The underlying measures of base skill—contact rates, pitching command ratios, BPV, etc.—are far more accurate in evaluating future talent than raw home runs, batting averages or ERAs. This chart format focuses more on those underlying gauges.

Here are some things to look for as you scan these charts:

Target players who...
- had a full season's worth of playing time in AA and then another full year in AAA
- had consistent playing time from one year to the next
- improved their base skills as they were promoted

Raise the warning flag for players who...
- were stuck at the same level both years, or regressed
- displayed marked changes in playing time from one year to the next
- showed large drops in BPIs from one year to the next

BATTER	yr	b	age	pos	lvl	org	ab	hr	sb	ba	bb%	ct%	px	sx	bpv
Abrams,CJ	21	L	21	SS	aa	SD	162	1	10	259	7	76	78	97	10
	22	L	22	SS	aaa	WAS	171	5	10	268	4	79	77	132	26
Abreu,Wilyer	22	L	23	CF	aa	BOS	457	12	21	213	14	63	119	103	10
Acuna,Jose	22	R	20	SS	aa	TEX	152	2	8	187	7	75	59	124	-1
Adams,Jordyn	22	R	23	CF	aa	LAA	209	3	9	199	6	61	62	127	-52
Adell,Jo	21	R	22	CF	aaa	LAA	311	14	5	229	4	63	132	95	-4
	22	R	23	LF	aaa	LAA	155	8	2	182	7	58	193	69	23
Adolfo,Micker	21	R	25	RF	a/a	CHW	367	19	3	202	6	55	167	70	-12
	22	R	26	RF	aaa	CHW	338	10	5	169	4	53	118	61	-65
Adolph,Ross	21	L	25	LF	aa	HOU	216	8	2	204	8	58	117	90	-31
	22	L	26	LF	aa	HOU	183	3	5	185	14	48	92	109	-71
Aguilar,Ryan	21	L	27	CF	aa	MIL	213	4	6	115	11	48	69	105	-99
	22	L	28	RF	aa	LAA	291	9	6	197	12	54	117	87	-37
Aiello,John	22	B	25	1B	a/a	TOR	309	7	1	240	8	69	91	46	-20
Alexander,Blaze	22	R	23	SS	a/a	ARI	344	10	6	236	6	66	105	78	-14
Alexander,C.J.	21	L	25	3B	aa	ATL	304	8	12	174	6	61	111	131	-13
	22	L	26	3B	aaa	KC	455	13	11	203	3	72	84	97	-7
Allen,Austin	21	L	27	C	aaa	OAK	281	12	0	240	3	75	100	27	-3
	22	L	28	C	aaa	STL	195	4	0	203	6	64	94	18	-48
Allen,Nick	21	R	23	SS	a/a	OAK	339	4	8	241	6	74	60	85	-15
	22	R	24	SS	aaa	OAK	173	1	5	193	8	77	49	80	-13
Alu,Jake	21	L	24	3B	aa	WAS	197	4	4	233	5	76	79	75	0
	22	L	25	3B	a/a	WAS	502	15	11	249	7	76	110	86	33
Alvarez,Andres	22	R	25	3B	aa	PIT	368	12	13	170	10	61	100	106	-20
Alvarez,Armando	21	R	27	3B	aaa	NYY	360	8	1	187	7	76	75	44	-7
	22	R	28	3B	aaa	NYY	299	12	3	206	4	69	119	57	-1
Alvarez,Francisco	22	R	21	C	a/a	NYM	408	19	0	211	10	65	132	25	-5
Alvarez,Roberto	22	R	23	C	aa	TAM	222	0	1	201	5	77	39	72	-26
Amaya,Jacob	21	R	23	SS	aa	LA	417	9	3	177	8	72	59	68	-27
	22	R	24	SS	a/a	LA	476	12	4	203	9	72	75	69	-11
Amburgey,Trey	21	R	27	RF	aaa	NYY	257	6	1	220	7	61	120	64	-26
	22	R	28	LF	aaa	SEA	197	5	1	141	5	56	78	66	-83
Anchia,Jake	22	R	25	C	a/a	SEA	293	2	1	163	4	64	45	37	-87
Andujar,Miguel	22	R	27	LF	aaa	NYY	277	9	3	217	4	84	84	67	33
Antico,Mike	22	L	24	CF	aa	STL	240	4	16	165	6	68	64	116	-27
Aranda,Jonathan	21	L	23	1B	aa	TAM	274	8	3	280	8	73	106	102	26
	22	L	24	1B	aaa	TAM	403	12	4	257	7	69	107	73	2
Arcia,Orlando	21	R	27	SS	aaa	ATL	287	12	4	233	7	84	93	62	47
Arias,Bryan	22	R	25	1B	aa	HOU	291	4	7	166	8	59	78	68	-62
Arias,Diosbel	21	R	25	1B	aa	TEX	379	4	2	230	7	78	47	42	-21
	22	R	26	2B	a/a	TEX	300	4	1	190	6	70	65	37	-42
Arias,Gabriel	21	R	21	SS	aaa	CLE	436	10	4	250	6	72	92	75	-2
	22	R	22	SS	aaa	CLE	288	8	3	189	5	69	74	62	-35
Ashford,Zach	22	L	25	RF	aa	NYM	320	3	6	191	6	69	65	78	-34
Astudillo,Williams	22	R	31	DH	aaa	MIA	283	9	2	222	4	92	78	45	55
Auerbach,Brett	22	R	24	2B	aa	SF	372	11	8	181	8	58	105	68	-45
Avans,Drew	21	L	25	CF	aaa	LA	233	3	13	217	10	70	79	132	4
	22	L	26	CF	aaa	LA	432	4	22	204	7	63	63	147	-40
Avelino,Abiatal	21	R	26	SS	aaa	CHC	380	4	10	212	7	78	51	88	-5
	22	R	27	3B	aa	LA	209	5	5	173	4	77	67	86	-1
Aviles Jr.,Luis	21	R	26	2B	a/a	LAA	269	9	8	176	4	67	100	104	-12
	22	R	27	3B	a/a	MIA	363	9	9	198	3	66	110	107	-8
Bae,Ji-Hwan	21	L	22	2B	aa	PIT	320	5	15	244	8	72	64	126	-3
	22	L	23	2B	aaa	PIT	419	5	20	240	7	79	71	130	27
Baker,Darren	22	L	23	2B	aa	WAS	169	1	4	257	7	80	49	65	-3
Baker,Luken	21	R	24	1B	a/a	STL	353	16	0	193	6	66	120	19	-20
	22	R	25	1B	aaa	STL	464	12	0	170	5	68	68	19	-56
Baldoquin,Roberto	22	R	28	3B	a/a	STL	195	0	1	156	6	76	22	43	-51
Ball,Brycelin	22	L	24	1B	aa	CHC	485	7	1	204	8	71	74	46	-27
Banks,Nick	21	L	27	LF	a/a	WAS	335	6	0	187	6	61	72	19	-77
	22	L	28	RF	aaa	WAS	272	7	2	200	5	59	100	78	-47
Bannon,Rylan	21	R	25	3B	aaa	BAL	289	12	7	149	11	73	91	74	10
	22	R	26	3B	aaa	ATL	342	10	7	209	12	65	105	87	-4
Banuelos,David	21	R	25	C	a/a	MIN	144	2	0	171	4	58	87	87	-63
	22	R	26	C	aaa	MIN	181	4	0	151	5	59	86	41	-69
Barger,Addison	22	L	23	SS	a/a	TOR	207	9	1	271	7	70	127	37	9
Barrera,Luis	21	L	26	CF	aaa	OAK	341	2	6	213	7	76	52	103	-8
	22	L	27	CF	aaa	OAK	312	4	5	179	4	72	65	108	-16
Barrera,Tres	21	R	27	C	aaa	WAS	169	2	0	166	9	70	44	12	-61
	22	R	28	C	aaa	WAS	177	4	0	192	6	71	76	47	-25
Barrero,Jose	21	R	23	SS	a/a	CIN	330	17	13	274	8	70	130	93	31
	22	R	24	SS	aaa	CIN	220	8	4	181	4	53	123	83	-55
Barreto,Franklin	22	R	26	2B	aaa	HOU	241	4	6	118	7	48	71	92	-107
Barrosa,Jorge	22	B	21	CF	aa	ARI	434	7	14	226	8	80	78	94	28
Basabe,Luis Alejandro	21	B	25	3B	aa	ARI	283	6	5	181	6	56	97	94	-56
Basabe,Osleivis	22	R	22	3B	aa	TAM	228	0	10	281	7	87	77	129	64
Bastidas,Jesus	22	R	24	2B	aa	NYY	396	13	8	194	7	66	101	76	-19
Batten,Matt	21	R	26	SS	a/a	SD	440	4	18	224	7	65	44	103	-57
	22	R	27	SS	aaa	SD	325	6	9	195	7	70	68	89	-22
Baty,Brett	21	L	22	3B	aa	NYM	153	4	1	219	9	65	81	35	-45
	22	L	23	3B	a/a	NYM	362	13	1	254	8	65	119	42	-13
Bauers,Jake	22	L	27	1B	aaa	NYY	202	5	5	137	11	53	93	70	-68
Bechina,Marty	21	R	25	LF	a/a	OAK	261	6	3	161	3	54	109	85	-63
	22	R	26	LF	a/a	OAK	303	4	4	152	6	54	72	64	-92
Bechtold,Andrew	21	R	25	3B	aa	MIN	351	12	1	198	8	57	133	36	-37
	22	R	26	C	a/a	MIN	438	11	1	174	8	62	80	35	-58
Beer,Seth	21	L	25	1B	aaa	ARI	362	8	0	209	6	74	91	33	-7
	22	L	26	1B	aaa	ARI	331	7	0	170	6	75	75	44	-12
Bell,Chad	21	L	24	3B	aa	NYY	107	4	4	153	7	56	84	46	-78
	22	L	25	1B	a/a	NYY	315	11	0	189	8	52	116	25	-75
Beltre,Michael	21	L	26	CF	aa	NYY	398	13	28	211	9	67	105	156	17
	22	B	27	RF	a/a	NYY	225	6	19	181	10	56	111	136	-27

BATTER	yr	b	age	pos	lvl	org	ab	hr	sb	ba	bb%	ct%	px	sx	bpv
Benson,Will	21	L	23	LF	a/a	CLE	355	13	10	177	14	54	141	125	-7
	22	L	24	CF	aaa	CLE	316	10	9	213	12	65	117	99	10
Berman,Stevie	21	R	27	C	a/a	MIN	143	1	0	140	9	77	48	13	-31
	22	R	28	C	aaa	TOR	212	6	1	165	10	63	111	35	-26
Berryhill,Luke	22	R	24	C	aa	HOU	352	8	3	199	10	58	93	58	-52
Bethancourt,Christian	21	R	30	C	aaa	PIT	331	8	3	209	5	72	78	57	-19
Biggers,Jax	21	L	24	2B	a/a	TEX	303	3	11	183	6	79	45	94	-7
	22	L	25	3B	aa	TEX	217	1	3	217	5	79	56	75	-5
Binelas,Alex	22	L	22	3B	aa	BOS	211	7	0	144	7	61	124	48	-26
Bins,Carter	22	R	24	C	a/a	PIT	291	6	3	157	6	54	125	102	-41
Bird,Corey	21	L	26	RF	aaa	MIA	280	4	12	194	9	71	74	123	2
Bird,Gregory	21	L	29	1B	aaa	COL	393	16	0	204	8	67	111	26	-17
	22	L	30	1B	aaa	NYY	206	4	1	155	9	60	71	43	-69
Bishop,Braden	21	R	28	LF	aaa	SF	305	7	6	237	5	75	83	110	11
	22	R	29	LF	aaa	MIN	256	3	7	161	5	67	51	103	-50
Bissonette,Josh	21	R	25	3B	aa	PIT	231	1	1	188	7	75	36	41	-43
	22	R	26	3B	a/a	PIT	170	0	1	154	9	73	43	46	-43
Blanco,Dairon	21	R	28	CF	a/a	KC	422	9	28	220	5	73	68	138	3
	22	R	29	CF	aaa	KC	366	7	24	218	5	67	84	123	-16
Blankenhorn,Travis	21	L	25	2B	aaa	NYM	195	6	2	185	9	58	108	37	-51
	22	L	26	LF	aaa	NYM	329	9	6	198	6	66	100	66	-24
Bleday,J.J.	21	L	24	RF	aa	MIA	397	9	4	180	12	71	83	76	-1
	22	L	25	CF	aaa	MIA	302	12	1	178	12	61	121	39	-22
Bohanek,Cody	22	R	27	3B	aaa	NYM	239	1	5	128	8	50	64	98	-101
Boldt,Ryan	21	L	27	LF	aaa	TAM	300	9	10	214	8	59	121	103	-18
	22	L	28	CF	aaa	TAM	250	4	5	172	4	59	83	102	-57
Bonifacio,Jorge	21	R	28	RF	a/a	PHI	325	12	3	202	9	68	118	71	6
	22	R	29	LF	aaa	PHI	380	9	5	173	7	59	89	60	-61
Boswell,Bret	22	L	28	3B	aaa	COL	287	6	3	181	6	60	97	69	-48
Bouchard,Sean	21	R	25	LF	aa	COL	342	10	5	235	6	68	132	95	20
	22	R	26	LF	aaa	COL	260	11	6	236	8	70	139	124	44
Bradley,Bobby	22	L	26	1B	aaa	CLE	167	4	0	124	6	46	127	45	-88
Bradley,Tucker	22	L	24	LF	aa	KC	396	6	12	240	7	77	77	97	15
Breaux,Josh	21	R	24	C	aa	NYY	100	5	1	205	3	70	138	53	14
	22	R	25	C	a/a	NYY	370	14	1	173	6	63	105	56	-33
Brennan,Will	21	L	23	CF	aa	CLE	150	2	2	249	9	78	45	61	-14
	22	L	24	CF	a/a	CLE	528	9	13	253	6	84	78	87	39
Brigman,Bryson	21	R	26	SS	aaa	MIA	376	4	8	232	9	78	54	98	5
	22	R	27	2B	aaa	MIA	382	5	6	192	4	70	57	101	-33
Brinson,Lewis	22	R	28	RF	aaa	SF	339	11	3	215	4	59	129	72	-27
Brito,Daniel	21	L	23	2B	a/a	PHI	276	6	2	267	6	78	78	79	12
Brodey,Quinn	21	L	26	RF	a/a	NYM	222	2	9	132	6	50	60	126	-102
	22	L	27	RF	a/a	NYM	176	3	6	138	3	52	109	143	-53
Brooks,Trenton	21	L	26	1B	a/a	CLE	360	9	2	208	9	71	92	61	-2
	22	L	27	1B	aaa	CLE	293	6	1	195	7	76	83	39	-2
Brosseau,Michael	21	R	27	3B	aaa	TAM	170	6	2	179	10	63	78	78	-39
Brown,Logan	22	L	26	C	aa	ATL	182	1	0	161	6	69	29	49	-72
Brujan,Vidal	21	R	23	2B	aaa	TAM	389	10	38	234	10	80	95	137	58
	22	R	24	SS	aaa	TAM	257	4	18	236	7	77	72	144	25
Burdick,Peyton	21	R	24	CF	a/a	MIA	401	18	7	190	14	58	133	87	-4
	22	R	25	CF	aaa	MIA	364	9	9	170	9	61	103	144	-10
Burleson,Alec	21	L	23	RF	a/a	STL	414	11	1	214	5	77	66	34	-18
	22	L	24	LF	aaa	STL	432	12	3	259	4	82	79	58	19
Burt,D.J.	21	R	26	2B	aa	MIN	215	2	14	244	9	68	64	103	-27
	22	R	27	3B	a/a	CHW	305	2	26	189	8	75	40	122	-14
Burt,Max	21	R	25	3B	a/a	NYY	269	5	5	182	7	68	74	84	-30
	22	R	26	3B	aaa	NYY	268	8	13	158	4	61	95	119	-35
Busch,Michael	21	L	24	2B	aa	LA	409	14	1	217	10	63	117	49	-17
	22	L	25	2B	a/a	LA	552	21	2	211	7	63	131	57	-8
Byrd,Grayson	21	L	25	1B	aa	CHC	184	1	1	184	7	63	58	38	-75
Cabrera,Daniel	22	L	24	RF	aa	DET	355	3	4	169	7	75	52	93	-14
Cabrera,Leobaldo	21	R	23	LF	aa	MIN	170	8	4	203	10	57	136	102	-8
	22	R	24	LF	aa	MIN	256	4	4	174	7	60	77	78	-60
Cabrera,Oswaldo	21	B	22	2B	a/a	NYY	467	25	17	243	7	70	139	97	35
	22	B	23	2B	aaa	NYY	183	6	7	216	7	65	127	127	15
Calabuig,Chase	21	L	26	LF	aa	OAK	323	3	1	167	8	77	38	45	-29
	22	L	27	LF	aa	OAK	380	3	2	233	7	81	59	49	3
Calhoun,Willie	22	L	28	DH	aaa	SF	231	5	0	188	6	80	62	34	-5
Calixte,Orlando	21	R	29	3B	aaa	NYM	196	1	8	160	6	69	41	87	-53
Call,Alex	21	R	27	CF	a/a	CLE	386	10	10	209	9	79	75	81	22
	22	R	28	CF	aaa	WAS	257	8	6	222	11	73	108	92	30
Camargo,Jair	22	R	23	C	aa	MIN	176	7	3	190	6	57	123	52	-43
Camargo,Johan	21	B	28	1B	aaa	ATL	386	14	0	265	8	77	100	54	23
	22	B	29	DH	a/a	PHI	156	1	0	170	8	79	40	29	-27
Cameron,Daz	21	R	24	CF	aaa	DET	162	5	6	269	7	74	108	128	38
	22	R	25	CF	aaa	DET	383	6	12	191	6	63	91	117	-25
Campbell,Noah	22	B	23	LF	aa	MIL	195	1	4	212	10	65	83	80	-28
Campusano,Luis	21	R	23	C	aaa	SD	292	9	1	229	6	74	99	59	5
	22	R	24	C	aaa	SD	319	7	0	215	6	76	70	38	-17
Canario,Alexander	22	R	22	CF	a/a	CHC	375	19	13	198	8	66	144	109	31
Cancel,Gabriel	21	R	25	2B	aaa	KC	206	9	8	194	6	63	130	111	6
	22	R	26	2B	aaa	KC	267	2	3	170	5	59	76	62	-72
Canzone,Dominic	21	L	24	LF	aa	ARI	130	5	1	296	7	75	103	69	19
	22	L	25	RF	a/a	ARI	386	11	8	224	5	75	96	93	16
Capel,Conner	21	L	24	RF	a/a	STL	369	8	4	201	7	75	70	75	-6
	22	L	25	RF	a/a	OAK	353	5	11	186	7	76	64	87	-3
Capra,Vinny	21	R	25	3B	a/a	TOR	256	8	3	274	7	65	124	96	5
	22	R	26	SS	aaa	TOR	191	4	4	231	9	82	56	77	17
Cardenas,Ruben	21	R	24	LF	aa	TAM	290	11	2	219	3	65	96	88	-27
	22	R	25	RF	aaa	TAM	287	10	3	162	7	59	125	86	-21
Carpenter,Kerry	21	L	24	LF	aa	DET	416	11	4	227	5	76	84	58	-1
	22	L	25	LF	a/a	DET	358	19	2	249	6	71	152	49	34

BATTER	yr	b	age	pos	lvl	org	ab	hr	sb	ba	bb%	ct%	px	sx	bpv
Carpio,Luis	21	R	24	2B	aa	NYM	305	5	4	195	7	64	77	52	-50
	22	R	25	2B	aa	DET	243	1	5	172	7	69	56	72	-43
Carrasco,Dennicher	21	R	26	3B	aa	KC	151	3	0	177	6	52	98	32	-89
Carroll,Corbin	22	L	22	CF	a/a	ARI	356	13	18	244	10	67	134	150	41
Casas,Triston	21	L	21	1B	a/a	BOS	310	10	6	257	13	75	99	94	35
	22	L	22	1B	aaa	BOS	264	7	0	240	10	72	120	35	18
Casey,Donovan	21	R	25	CF	a/a	WAS	484	13	16	233	5	60	101	99	-36
	22	R	26	RF	aaa	WAS	287	5	4	169	5	60	72	92	-63
Castellano,Angelo	21	R	26	2B	a/a	KC	297	6	6	190	5	71	52	70	-40
	22	R	27	SS	a/a	KC	268	1	4	149	6	74	44	71	-33
Castellanos,Pedro	21	R	24	LF	aa	BOS	325	9	1	251	7	78	79	76	13
	22	R	25	1B	a/a	BOS	467	8	1	227	2	75	84	49	-13
Castillo,Ivan	21	B	26	2B	aaa	SD	404	2	7	210	4	77	33	74	-35
	22	B	27	SS	aaa	KC	392	3	5	183	6	84	52	61	11
Castillo,Moises	22	R	23	SS	aa	CHW	233	2	5	187	9	77	49	78	-9
Castro,Luis	21	R	26	1B	a/a	MIL	237	6	2	170	7	52	110	68	-68
Castro,Rodolfo	21	B	22	3B	a/a	PIT	320	10	5	215	5	72	98	78	3
	22	B	23	3B	aaa	PIT	272	7	4	201	7	65	101	80	-19
Cecchini,Gavin	21	R	28	SS	a/a	LAA	344	3	4	187	3	77	46	54	-32
Cedeno,Leandro	22	R	24	1B	a/a	ARI	481	17	1	234	5	69	96	39	-24
Cedrola,Lorenzo	21	R	23	CF	a/a	CIN	441	9	8	284	4	86	64	102	35
	22	R	24	CF	aaa	CIN	475	3	11	230	2	79	48	104	-7
Celestino,Gilberto	21	R	22	CF	a/a	MIN	267	5	3	250	10	73	86	50	-5
Cerda,Allan	22	R	23	RF	aa	CIN	207	8	3	168	12	57	130	56	-23
Cervenka,Martin	21	R	29	C	aaa	NYM	186	4	1	123	7	61	68	48	-71
Cespedes,Yoelqui	22	R	25	CF	aa	CHW	458	13	21	199	4	60	113	98	-31
Chaparro,Andres	22	R	23	3B	aa	NYY	239	15	2	241	7	73	150	45	44
Chatham,C.J.	21	R	27	SS	aaa	PHI	155	2	0	227	5	78	47	44	-24
Chavez,Santiago	21	R	26	C	a/a	MIA	164	1	1	133	5	57	43	59	-105
	22	R	27	C	a/a	MIA	178	2	0	140	4	64	57	35	-80
Chinea,Chris	21	R	27	1B	a/a	MIA	157	4	0	198	6	73	64	20	-36
Cintron,Jancarlos	21	R	27	2B	a/a	ARI	309	4	7	173	4	78	39	77	-25
	22	R	28	2B	a/a	ARI	400	3	7	240	3	81	71	86	14
Citta,Brendt	21	R	25	DH	aa	PIT	160	1	0	244	4	74	62	53	-26
	22	R	26	1B	a/a	PIT	348	5	1	184	7	63	81	56	-52
Clarke,Philip	22	L	24	C	aa	TOR	248	3	1	183	8	80	42	43	-16
Clemens,Kody	21	L	25	2B	aaa	DET	369	14	3	220	7	72	105	117	25
	22	L	26	2B	aaa	DET	241	8	3	221	5	66	127	115	11
Clementina,Hendrik	21	R	24	C	aa	ATL	141	7	0	184	6	62	105	24	-48
	22	R	25	C	a/a	ATL	332	10	1	191	5	56	95	46	-72
Cluff,Jackson	21	L	25	SS	aa	WAS	126	2	2	163	5	65	55	66	-65
	22	L	26	SS	aa	WAS	356	4	6	160	6	58	88	84	-56
Coca,Yeison	22	B	23	3B	a/a	MIL	232	1	7	169	8	62	55	93	-63
Colas,Oscar	22	L	24	RF	a/a	CHW	237	12	1	253	4	67	131	52	-2
Collins,Isaac	22	B	25	2B	aa	COL	375	3	18	183	8	74	73	133	13
Conine,Griffin	21	L	24	RF	aa	MIA	159	10	0	148	6	41	201	26	-52
	22	L	25	RF	aa	MIA	414	16	1	173	11	48	145	53	-51
Conley,Jack	21	R	24	C	a/a	PHI	160	3	1	128	7	59	76	76	-62
	22	R	25	C	a/a	PHI	250	4	2	183	8	67	70	68	-39
Connell,Justin	22	R	23	RF	aa	WAS	318	9	6	202	10	62	114	88	-13
Contreras,Mark	21	L	26	RF	a/a	MIN	410	14	11	209	7	60	136	106	-3
	22	L	27	CF	aaa	MIN	376	8	14	173	6	59	98	115	-39
Cook,Zac	22	L	24	CF	aa	TOR	333	10	9	148	4	49	117	102	-70
Cope,Daniel	22	R	25	C	aa	COL	151	4	1	207	5	68	99	58	-21
Cordell,Ryan	21	R	29	RF	aaa	PHI	197	8	5	157	7	43	142	73	-77
Corredor,Aldrem	21	L	26	1B	aa	WAS	323	7	1	217	7	72	80	34	-24
	22	L	27	1B	aa	PHI	393	9	0	186	8	69	62	24	-48
Cortes,Carlos	21	L	24	LF	aa	NYM	307	10	1	204	7	66	117	51	-10
	22	L	25	LF	a/a	NYM	439	8	0	168	6	65	76	45	-53
Costes,Marty	21	R	26	RF	a/a	HOU	330	4	8	243	10	74	59	79	-11
	22	R	27	LF	aaa	HOU	213	3	6	187	6	72	66	80	-20
Cottam,Kole	22	R	25	C	a/a	BOS	274	1	0	213	6	66	85	46	-40
Coulter,Clint	21	R	28	RF	aaa	STL	128	5	0	169	5	56	98	26	-79
	22	R	29	LF	aaa	STL	182	5	0	205	4	77	91	45	5
Cowser,Colton	22	L	22	CF	a/a	BAL	281	12	1	251	10	63	135	54	-2
Craig,Will	21	R	27	1B	aaa	PIT	122	5	0	226	7	73	112	30	6
Cribbs,Galli	21	L	29	SS	a/a	MIA	168	1	3	144	4	50	58	91	-116
Crim,Blaine	21	R	24	DH	aa	TEX	139	7	0	254	4	71	116	35	-1
	22	R	25	1B	a/a	TEX	515	14	2	224	6	78	78	53	4
Crook,Narciso	21	R	26	RF	a/a	CIN	295	12	6	206	10	59	131	59	-18
	22	R	27	RF	aaa	CHC	362	11	8	193	6	57	127	105	-25
Cruz,Michael	21	L	25	C	aa	LAA	179	6	0	176	8	60	90	31	-61
Cruz,Oneil	21	L	23	SS	a/a	PIT	271	12	14	267	7	72	126	142	48
	22	L	24	SS	aaa	PIT	211	5	7	185	9	70	82	121	1
Cuadrado,Romer	21	R	24	RF	aa	LA	278	7	0	183	6	51	66	21	-122
Cullen,Greg	22	L	26	2B	a/a	BAL	184	5	1	211	11	69	79	51	-22
Cumana,Grenny	21	R	26	RF	aa	PHI	147	1	0	215	5	87	31	22	-10
Curry,Michael	21	R	24	DH	aa	SD	252	5	2	188	10	62	73	40	-59
Cuthbert,Cheslor	21	R	29	1B	aaa	NYM	302	9	1	151	8	69	77	48	-29
Czinege,Todd	21	R	27	RF	aa	COL	123	3	1	154	6	49	87	25	-112
Dahl,David	21	L	27	RF	a/a	MIL	144	3	1	275	5	79	93	76	26
	22	L	28	RF	aaa	WAS	319	6	2	211	6	67	89	72	-24
Dalesandro,Nick	22	R	26	C	aa	ARI	280	1	20	205	4	71	41	122	-34
Dalton,Wil	22	R	25	LF	aa	BOS	192	4	4	160	6	53	124	102	-45
Daniel,Clayton	21	R	26	DH	a/a	LA	169	1	1	178	6	76	31	47	-45
Daschbach,Andrew	21	R	24	1B	aa	BAL	102	6	0	182	8	53	154	31	-37
	22	R	25	1B	aa	BAL	329	11	1	153	9	43	135	40	-87
Datres,Kyle	22	R	26	DH	aa	COL	308	9	13	208	6	67	97	92	-12
Davidson,Logan	21	B	24	SS	aa	OAK	448	5	3	174	9	61	67	53	-68
	22	B	25	SS	aa	OAK	424	8	3	192	7	62	82	64	-49
Davidson,Matthew	21	R	30	1B	aaa	LA	313	18	0	213	6	62	151	24	-11
	22	R	31	1B	aaa	OAK	323	14	0	199	6	57	121	34	-52

BATTER	yr	b	age	pos	lvl	org	ab	hr	sb	ba	bb%	ct%	px	sx	bpv
Davis,Brendon	21	R	24	SS	a/a	LAA	230	11	5	239	8	67	123	104	15
	22	R	25	3B	aaa	DET	503	12	5	186	9	69	94	80	-4
Davis,Henry	22	R	23	C	aa	PIT	116	2	2	169	7	72	95	77	1
Davis,Jaylin	21	R	27	RF	aaa	SF	161	6	2	170	6	55	126	118	-30
	22	R	28	CF	aaa	BOS	340	5	2	164	7	57	85	78	-65
Davis,Jonah	21	L	24	CF	aa	PIT	190	5	3	175	9	45	130	106	-65
	22	L	25	CF	aa	STL	164	4	1	98	7	37	123	126	-101
Davis,Zach	21	B	27	LF	a/a	CHC	166	1	12	184	7	67	36	103	-57
	22	B	28	CF	a/a	CHC	177	0	20	181	7	64	35	150	-57
Dawkins,Ian	21	R	26	LF	aa	CHW	209	4	9	212	5	67	65	116	-33
	22	R	27	LF	aa	CHW	225	4	6	172	5	71	71	88	-23
Dawson,Ronnie	21	L	26	CF	aaa	HOU	353	5	10	190	8	71	62	85	-25
	22	L	27	LF	aaa	CIN	393	9	7	205	7	65	93	71	-30
De Goti,Alex	21	R	27	SS	aaa	HOU	383	3	4	172	7	65	62	99	-47
	22	R	28	SS	aaa	HOU	494	5	5	180	8	72	60	75	-22
De La Cruz,Carlos	22	R	23	LF	aa	PHI	151	5	1	232	4	66	135	62	0
De La Cruz,Elly	22	B	20	SS	aa	CIN	190	7	14	274	6	63	167	142	40
De La Guerra,Chad	21	L	29	3B	aaa	BOS	152	2	4	159	9	53	108	105	-48
De La Rosa,Eric	22	R	25	RF	aa	DET	191	2	6	182	5	53	91	142	-60
De La Trinidad,Ernie	21	L	25	RF	aa	MIN	289	6	3	222	5	67	74	70	-39
De Leon,Michael	21	B	24	3B	a/a	CIN	294	7	0	229	5	71	80	20	-34
	22	B	25	1B	a/a	CIN	330	4	0	203	5	71	70	18	-44
De Los Santos,Luis	22	R	24	SS	a/a	TOR	421	8	5	210	5	72	71	69	-21
Dean,Austin	22	R	29	RF	aaa	SF	392	8	5	188	5	68	80	100	-20
Dean,Justin	21	R	25	CF	aa	ATL	363	6	24	210	9	60	79	144	-33
	22	R	26	CF	a/a	ATL	328	2	17	189	9	59	66	134	-50
Dearden,Tyler	22	L	24	LF	aa	BOS	316	5	0	222	9	63	86	30	-48
DeCarlo,Joe	21	R	28	1B	a/a	CHW	162	2	0	152	8	58	40	31	-106
Dedelow,Craig	21	L	27	RF	aa	CHW	366	14	2	185	9	54	132	61	-41
	22	L	28	RF	a/a	CHW	469	18	9	159	8	42	162	104	-53
Deichmann,Greg	21	L	26	RF	aaa	CHC	329	5	7	220	11	65	88	106	-15
	22	L	27	CF	aaa	CHC	257	4	5	156	4	56	70	63	-90
DeJong,Paul	22	R	29	SS	aaa	STL	201	9	1	168	5	67	113	47	-13
Delgado,Raynel	22	L	22	3B	aa	CLE	210	2	8	198	9	73	52	99	-14
Delgado,Riley	22	R	27	3B	aa	ATL	371	1	2	218	6	81	32	59	-19
DeLoach,Zach	21	L	23	RF	aa	SEA	185	4	1	193	11	63	90	74	-31
	22	L	24	RF	aa	SEA	418	9	3	199	10	65	73	74	-36
DeLuzio,Ben	21	R	27	CF	a/a	ARI	241	2	9	214	4	68	79	144	-14
	22	R	28	CF	aaa	STL	364	5	17	197	5	69	63	133	-20
DeShields Jr.,Delino	21	R	29	LF	aaa	BOS	309	4	15	201	12	65	63	109	-30
	22	R	30	CF	aaa	ATL	337	1	24	169	14	56	40	101	-85
Destino,Alex	22	L	27	1B	aa	CHW	222	4	0	175	10	53	78	32	-95
Devanney,Cam	21	R	24	2B	aa	MIL	291	4	1	148	8	62	55	28	-81
	22	R	25	SS	a/a	MIL	451	15	3	205	7	70	114	55	2
Devers,Jose	22	L	23	2B	aa	MIA	233	1	2	181	4	78	55	126	4
Diaz,Brent	21	R	25	C	a/a	MIL	182	4	1	168	5	54	78	49	-93
	22	R	26	C	a/a	MIL	192	5	3	198	5	65	77	50	-51
Diaz,Eduardo	22	R	25	LF	aa	ARI	426	6	8	199	4	68	84	95	-24
Diaz,Edwin	21	R	26	3B	a/a	OAK	198	6	1	159	6	51	100	35	-92
	22	R	27	SS	a/a	HOU	259	7	1	140	5	48	103	70	-90
Diaz,Isan	21	L	25	3B	aaa	MIA	103	4	0	200	8	66	128	76	6
	22	L	26	2B	aaa	SF	291	12	4	199	8	63	124	83	-7
Diaz,Jordan	22	R	22	DH	a/a	OAK	491	11	0	259	3	82	82	25	10
Diaz,Lewin	21	L	25	1B	aaa	MIA	278	15	2	204	7	75	116	64	26
	22	L	26	1B	aaa	MIA	325	12	0	195	6	72	107	45	1
Diaz,Yainer	22	R	24	C	a/a	HOU	445	16	1	242	5	78	96	69	22
Diaz,Yusniel	21	R	25	RF	a/a	BAL	230	4	1	132	5	61	59	62	-78
	22	R	26	RF	aaa	BAL	247	4	5	191	8	68	57	65	-44
Didder,Ray-Patrick	21	R	27	SS	aa	LAA	329	3	11	187	7	68	72	121	-16
	22	R	28	SS	a/a	MIA	390	7	17	181	5	61	61	107	-61
Dillard,Thomas	22	B	25	1B	aa	MIL	425	8	9	180	11	55	109	85	-44
Dingler,Dillon	21	R	23	C	aa	DET	188	3	1	181	3	66	56	105	-52
	22	R	24	C	aa	DET	387	9	1	194	7	59	112	77	-35
Dini,Nick	22	R	29	C	aaa	NYM	177	6	1	160	6	72	78	47	-19
Dirden,Justin	22	L	25	CF	a/a	HOU	477	15	7	233	6	65	135	97	12
Dorow,Ryan	21	R	26	SS	a/a	TEX	369	11	2	209	8	64	116	72	-12
	22	R	27	SS	aaa	TEX	371	3	1	169	6	68	55	67	-50
Dorrian,Patrick	21	L	25	3B	a/a	BAL	414	17	3	202	11	62	121	63	-15
	22	L	26	1B	a/a	MIL	314	9	3	154	8	56	109	68	-52
Downs,Jeter	21	R	23	SS	aaa	BOS	357	10	14	170	8	60	81	83	-54
	22	R	24	SS	aaa	BOS	284	10	12	162	8	61	113	124	-10
Doyle,Brenton	22	R	24	CF	a/a	COL	507	16	13	211	3	64	109	121	-13
Drury,Brandon	21	R	29	3B	aaa	NYM	214	5	0	177	5	69	80	23	-43
Duarte,Osvaldo	21	R	25	2B	aa	WAS	217	1	4	162	5	56	64	116	-79
Dubon,Mauricio	21	R	27	SS	aaa	SF	247	5	6	253	7	81	63	82	14
Dunand,Joe	21	R	26	3B	aaa	MIA	204	6	0	162	6	59	94	39	-63
	22	R	27	3B	aaa	ATL	295	4	4	175	8	57	98	91	-48
Dungan,Clay	21	L	25	2B	aa	KC	444	6	21	250	6	82	52	114	19
	22	L	26	2B	aaa	KC	452	4	9	159	5	75	59	107	-8
Dunham,Elijah	22	L	24	LF	aa	NYY	415	13	27	200	9	70	104	124	23
Dunlap,Alex	21	R	27	C	a/a	WAS	149	2	1	149	5	61	67	53	-74
Dunn,Jack	22	R	26	CF	a/a	WAS	390	2	7	196	8	72	48	56	-40
Dunn,Nick	21	L	24	2B	aa	STL	324	3	2	199	6	79	42	43	-23
	22	L	25	2B	aa	STL	399	3	3	190	7	88	44	67	23
Duran,Ezequiel	22	R	23	SS	a/a	TEX	328	10	9	240	4	72	129	84	28
Duran,Jarren	21	L	25	CF	aaa	BOS	244	11	12	223	9	69	122	120	28
	22	L	26	CF	aaa	BOS	279	6	11	229	5	69	103	138	14
Duran,Rodolfo	21	R	23	C	a/a	PHI	129	5	0	176	3	75	95	14	-11
	22	R	24	C	aa	NYY	203	7	0	178	4	69	103	16	-27
Duzenack,Camden	21	R	26	2B	a/a	ARI	221	5	2	189	3	61	90	91	-47
	22	R	27	LF	aaa	ARI	318	6	5	182	3	71	83	96	-13
Eaton,Nate	22	R	26	RF	a/a	KC	340	7	13	221	5	74	73	111	0

BATTER	yr	b	age	pos	lvl	org	ab	hr	sb	ba	bb%	ct%	px	sx	bpv
Eden,Cameron	22	R	24	CF	aa	TOR	274	7	20	169	5	55	106	110	-49
Edwards,Evan	22	L	25	1B	aa	TAM	214	7	4	167	11	48	122	76	-65
Edwards,Xavier	21	R	22	2B	aa	TAM	291	0	15	264	9	83	36	103	13
	22	R	23	2B	aaa	TAM	349	3	5	201	8	74	60	71	-15
Eierman,Jeremy	21	R	25	3B	aa	OAK	223	7	6	200	6	52	131	93	-46
	22	R	26	SS	aa	OAK	290	8	2	149	4	57	99	55	-68
Ellis,Drew	21	R	26	3B	aaa	ARI	296	10	1	212	8	63	138	72	3
	22	R	27	3B	aaa	SEA	385	11	3	156	10	61	113	60	-28
Encarnacion,Jerar	21	R	24	RF	aa	MIA	230	7	4	189	8	51	124	70	-59
	22	R	25	RF	a/a	MIA	384	14	4	237	7	62	109	56	-32
Encarnacion-Strand,Christian	22	R	23	3B	aa	CIN	190	9	1	272	4	68	131	48	0
English,Tristin	22	R	25	3B	aa	ARI	230	3	1	207	7	76	54	41	-27
Enriquez,Roby	22	L	25	RF	aa	ARI	264	4	3	250	4	80	64	63	0
Erceg,Lucas	21	L	26	DH	aa	MIL	103	2	2	183	5	74	82	62	-9
Escobedo,Julian	22	L	24	CF	aa	CLE	377	5	11	178	7	74	62	99	-11
Espino,Sebastian	22	R	22	RF	aa	TOR	354	10	3	148	4	49	137	75	-62
Estevez,Omar	21	R	23	SS	aaa	LA	361	6	0	163	7	67	56	34	-62
	22	R	24	LF	aaa	LA	162	2	1	160	4	71	64	56	-39
Estrada,Thairo	21	R	25	SS	aaa	SF	210	5	4	265	6	80	82	73	21
Evans,Phillip	21	R	29	1B	aaa	PIT	127	0	0	191	7	72	56	31	-42
	22	R	30	RF	aaa	NYY	361	6	1	173	5	79	53	42	-17
Fabian,Sandro	21	R	23	RF	aa	SF	296	11	0	227	3	78	85	41	2
	22	R	24	RF	a/a	TEX	343	9	1	188	4	77	90	64	11
Fairchild,Stuart	21	R	25	RF	aaa	ARI	156	5	4	222	7	70	95	108	3
	22	R	26	RF	aaa	CIN	190	9	5	216	7	62	140	87	1
Fargas,Johneshwy	21	R	27	CF	a/a	CHC	128	2	11	191	5	64	69	148	-30
	22	R	28	CF	a/a	NYM	259	5	18	150	5	62	63	134	-49
Feduccia,Hunter	21	L	24	C	aa	LA	284	7	0	205	8	75	61	37	-24
	22	L	25	C	a/a	LA	294	10	0	181	7	66	117	33	-15
Feliciano,Mario	21	R	23	C	aaa	MIL	105	2	1	170	3	71	45	49	-58
	22	R	24	C	aaa	MIL	285	4	1	217	4	78	56	36	-23
Fermin,Freddy	21	R	26	DH	a/a	KC	282	6	1	228	7	78	71	54	0
	22	R	27	C	aaa	KC	296	7	1	202	8	76	85	30	-4
Fermin,Jose	21	R	22	3B	a/a	CLE	306	5	3	231	6	85	62	69	22
	22	R	23	3B	aaa	CLE	270	4	5	164	8	80	48	88	4
Fernandez,Juan	21	R	22	C	aa	SD	257	6	2	193	8	74	64	60	-15
	22	R	23	1B	a/a	SD	405	1	7	214	5	77	29	66	-35
Fernandez,Vince	21	L	26	LF	aa	SF	249	9	2	186	8	53	133	117	-27
	22	L	27	RF	aaa	OAK	311	7	2	167	6	51	118	102	-57
Fernandez,Xavier	21	R	26	C	aa	CHW	195	7	0	241	8	73	77	23	-22
	22	R	27	C	a/a	CHW	287	3	1	194	5	81	46	37	-18
Filia,Eric	21	L	29	LF	aaa	SEA	149	2	3	190	12	77	54	65	-4
Fitzgerald,Ryan	21	L	27	SS	a/a	BOS	365	11	3	224	7	73	121	75	25
	22	L	28	3B	aaa	BOS	452	9	4	168	6	64	98	70	-32
Fitzgerald,Tyler	22	R	25	SS	aa	SF	455	13	14	186	5	56	118	130	-31
Fletcher,Dominic	21	L	24	RF	aa	ARI	402	10	2	219	4	69	84	85	-31
	21	L	24	RF	aa	ARI	402	10	2	219	4	69	84	85	-22
Fletcher,Dominic	22	L	25	CF	a/a	ARI	523	6	5	237	5	74	80	93	1
Flores,Jecksson	21	R	28	SS	a/a	WAS	215	1	1	188	9	79	54	48	-7
	22	R	29	2B	a/a	WAS	273	3	1	182	6	76	51	54	-24
Florial,Estevan	21	L	24	CF	a/a	NYY	347	14	10	186	10	60	123	100	-11
	22	L	25	CF	aaa	NYY	403	11	27	224	9	57	131	115	-11
Fontana,Shayne	22	L	25	LF	a/a	BAL	194	6	2	196	9	60	97	54	-47
Forbes,Tl'Quan	21	R	25	1B	a/a	CHW	303	5	5	222	5	64	72	92	-45
	22	R	26	3B	aaa	ARI	352	5	4	193	3	67	58	79	-55
Foscue,Justin	22	R	23	2B	aa	TEX	400	9	2	231	7	81	90	43	25
Fowler,Dustin	21	L	27	RF	aaa	MIA	142	6	2	233	6	58	124	93	-30
Fox,Lucius	21	B	24	2B	aaa	KC	215	3	13	204	10	69	72	107	-12
	22	B	25	SS	aaa	WAS	206	3	8	183	6	66	60	109	-42
Foyle,Devin	21	L	25	LF	aa	OAK	362	8	6	210	7	71	78	109	-6
	22	L	26	LF	aa	OAK	189	1	0	181	9	76	43	27	-36
Fraizer,Matt	21	L	23	CF	aa	PIT	132	2	1	250	7	72	111	89	19
	22	L	24	CF	aa	PIT	439	4	12	176	5	71	60	130	-18
Frank,Tyler	22	L	25	2B	aa	TAM	182	1	4	151	4	59	39	88	-95
Frazier,Clint	22	R	28	LF	aaa	CHC	232	3	3	135	6	50	70	64	-111
Free,James	22	B	24	C	a/a	CIN	228	6	0	216	4	70	79	18	-43
Freeman,Isaac	21	R	23	2B	aa	CLE	122	1	0	165	8	60	43	57	-89
Freeman,Tyler	21	R	22	SS	aa	CLE	164	2	3	295	4	86	79	93	43
	22	R	23	SS	aaa	CLE	297	4	4	218	5	87	32	64	5
Frelick,Sal	22	L	22	CF	a/a	MIL	413	7	13	286	6	86	66	108	44
Frick,Patrick	21	R	24	SS	aa	SEA	137	2	1	202	8	77	31	53	-32
	22	R	25	2B	aa	SEA	294	1	1	170	7	68	31	66	-67
Friedl,T.J.	21	L	26	CF	aaa	CIN	386	10	10	224	8	79	71	97	21
	22	L	27	LF	aaa	CIN	205	6	7	226	9	71	96	105	11
Friscia,Vito	22	R	26	DH	a/a	PHI	298	7	0	181	11	62	91	27	-47
Fry,David	21	R	26	3B	a/a	MIL	314	9	1	203	8	65	100	61	-24
	22	R	27	3B	aaa	CLE	422	9	1	182	5	72	84	53	-17
Gamboa,Arquimedes	21	B	24	SS	a/a	PHI	324	8	7	202	11	66	76	76	-28
	22	B	25	SS	aaa	SF	255	2	4	183	8	68	61	80	-39
Garcia,David	22	B	22	C	aa	TEX	237	3	0	185	5	69	64	40	-48
Garcia,Dermis	21	R	23	1B	aa	NYY	385	26	8	185	10	51	178	79	-8
	22	R	24	1B	aaa	OAK	239	6	2	190	7	59	114	76	-37
Garcia,Maikel	22	R	22	SS	a/a	KC	487	6	24	243	7	78	80	112	25
Garrett,Stone	21	R	26	LF	a/a	ARI	412	14	10	206	3	65	94	82	-34
	22	R	27	RF	aaa	ARI	389	13	8	192	4	66	112	104	-5
Gasper,Mickey	22	B	27	1B	aa	NYY	214	6	2	202	12	68	97	60	-4
Gatewood,Jacob	21	R	26	CF	aaa	LAA	450	16	3	162	4	53	118	65	-65
	22	R	27	1B	aaa	LAA	394	12	1	146	3	55	111	62	-63
Gelof,Zack	22	R	23	2B	a/a	OAK	389	10	6	206	7	64	89	79	-33
Genoves,Ricardo	22	R	23	C	a/a	SF	311	6	0	176	7	65	82	27	-53
Gentry,Tyler	22	R	23	RF	aa	KC	274	9	5	268	8	74	106	61	17
George,Max	21	R	25	C	aa	COL	199	7	7	168	11	52	117	113	-43

BATTER	yr	b	age	pos	lvl	org	ab	hr	sb	ba	bb%	ct%	px	sx	bpv
Gettys,Michael	21	R	26	RF	aaa	BOS	149	3	5	171	6	53	102	101	-63
Giambrone,Trent	21	R	28	2B	aaa	CHC	235	2	3	131	8	59	46	71	-89
	22	R	29	2B	aaa	CHC	256	2	6	131	6	63	46	97	-69
Gigliotti,Michael	22	L	26	CF	aa	SF	251	4	16	171	12	63	62	138	-30
Gilliam,Isiah	21	B	25	RF	aa	NYY	328	9	20	195	10	58	112	91	-28
	22	B	26	DH	a/a	CIN	387	14	9	223	8	55	150	105	-11
Gimenez,Andres	21	L	23	SS	aaa	CLE	209	7	6	245	4	70	108	81	-1
Gittens,Chris	21	R	27	1B	a/a	NYY	154	12	0	248	15	61	178	31	29
Givin,Chris	22	R	25	SS	aa	BAL	154	2	1	179	7	73	67	51	-22
Glendinning,Robbie	22	R	27	1B	aa	KC	428	10	6	191	9	55	105	75	-56
Godoy,Jose	21	L	27	C	aaa	SEA	298	5	1	218	4	75	57	55	-28
	22	L	28	C	aaa	PIT	176	3	0	165	5	66	63	22	-66
Gold,Ryan	22	L	25	C	aa	TOR	173	7	0	166	7	65	114	24	-25
Golden,Casey	21	R	27	RF	aa	COL	140	4	1	198	5	43	178	71	-50
Gomez,Jose	21	R	25	SS	a/a	COL	303	3	4	199	4	67	55	76	-57
	22	R	26	3B	a/a	LAA	383	4	4	183	4	68	70	69	-39
Gomez,Moises	21	R	23	RF	aa	TAM	269	6	4	142	7	51	97	69	-83
	22	R	24	RF	a/a	STL	442	21	6	218	6	55	161	79	-14
Gonzales,Nick	22	R	23	2B	aa	PIT	259	4	3	218	10	61	114	75	-18
Gonzalez,Norel	21	L	27	1B	a/a	HOU	316	11	3	213	7	73	92	45	-4
	22	L	28	DH	a/a	MIA	339	9	1	192	6	68	93	42	-26
Gonzalez,Oscar	21	R	23	RF	a/a	CLE	478	24	1	255	3	73	115	36	4
	22	R	24	RF	a/a	CLE	189	6	0	215	3	81	85	41	12
Gonzalez,Yariel	21	B	27	3B	a/a	DET	315	13	1	228	7	69	91	49	-21
	22	B	28	SS	a/a	ATL	364	6	4	182	6	72	64	58	-29
Gorman,Nolan	21	L	21	2B	a/a	STL	480	16	5	230	5	74	81	62	-9
	22	L	22	2B	aaa	STL	171	10	2	219	5	56	151	68	-23
Govern,Jimmy	21	R	25	3B	a/a	KC	170	5	2	187	5	76	83	56	-1
	22	R	26	3B	aaa	KC	216	3	2	167	3	73	77	82	-14
Granberg,Devlin	21	R	26	RF	aa	BOS	263	7	3	242	3	76	87	83	5
	22	R	27	CF	a/a	BOS	312	2	5	223	6	75	77	101	5
Granite,Zack	21	L	29	CF	aa	CHW	195	4	6	179	12	68	68	110	-17
Gray,Tristan	21	L	25	SS	aaa	TAM	248	6	1	213	7	61	109	96	-24
	22	L	26	SS	aaa	TAM	458	20	3	170	4	56	139	61	-36
Green,Zach	21	R	27	3B	aaa	MIL	327	10	0	160	7	42	140	21	-96
	22	R	28	1B	aaa	SEA	339	10	1	153	4	56	121	46	-56
Greiner,Grayson	21	R	29	C	aaa	DET	119	1	0	161	7	51	63	17	-123
	22	R	30	C	aaa	ARI	151	3	0	150	5	42	96	35	-134
Grenier,Cadyn	21	R	25	SS	a/a	BAL	389	7	9	183	9	60	77	80	-54
	22	R	26	SS	aaa	BAL	316	3	7	150	10	63	71	89	-41
Groshans,Jordan	21	R	22	SS	aa	TOR	278	6	0	255	8	76	92	30	4
	22	R	23	SS	aaa	MIA	353	2	2	221	10	79	40	47	-17
Guldberg,Michael	22	R	23	CF	aa	OAK	166	0	3	222	7	76	36	80	-29
Gushue,Taylor	21	B	28	C	aaa	CHC	247	5	0	168	6	59	85	21	-77
	22	B	29	C	a/a	WAS	235	7	0	163	11	58	102	14	-59
Guthrie,Dalton	21	R	26	SS	a/a	PHI	295	4	3	221	4	70	67	65	-36
	22	R	27	CF	aaa	PHI	338	7	13	228	4	73	90	107	7
Gutierrez,Kelvin	21	R	27	3B	aaa	BAL	126	3	1	206	3	74	79	52	-16
	22	R	28	1B	aaa	BAL	211	4	3	176	6	70	64	83	-30
Guzman,Jonathan	22	R	23	SS	aa	PHI	404	2	6	138	4	70	36	95	-54
Guzman,Ronald	22	L	28	1B	aaa	NYY	322	11	1	188	8	60	129	48	-26
Hager,Jake	21	R	28	SS	aaa	ARI	308	7	3	161	5	67	86	62	-33
	22	R	29	SS	aaa	ARI	260	2	4	174	5	70	65	61	-38
Haggerty,Sam	22	B	28	2B	aaa	SEA	152	3	9	194	6	70	93	130	7
Hair,Trey	22	L	27	3B	aa	TEX	234	10	1	177	4	67	121	47	-11
Haley,Jim	21	R	26	3B	a/a	TAM	340	10	14	165	5	57	109	132	-33
	22	R	27	1B	aaa	TAM	373	11	10	172	6	57	107	138	-32
Hall,Adam	22	R	23	DH	a/a	BAL	185	1	10	207	6	65	63	102	-44
Hall,Darick	21	L	26	1B	aaa	PHI	400	11	0	193	9	69	89	16	-27
	22	L	27	1B	aaa	PHI	389	18	4	191	6	69	127	52	9
Hamilton,Caleb	21	R	26	C	a/a	MIN	232	6	3	148	12	55	93	62	-63
	22	R	27	C	aaa	MIN	206	6	1	169	11	60	103	35	-44
Hamilton,David	21	L	24	SS	aa	MIL	133	2	8	213	8	72	76	132	5
	22	L	25	2B	aa	BOS	463	7	45	207	7	71	72	167	7
Handley,Maverick	22	R	24	C	aa	BAL	259	8	4	192	8	72	91	72	2
Hanson,Alen	21	B	29	2B	aaa	SEA	138	1	3	202	6	73	62	129	-4
Harris II,Michael	22	L	21	CF	aa	ATL	174	4	9	277	7	75	124	128	55
Harris,Brett	22	R	24	3B	aa	OAK	315	6	7	224	6	77	68	88	2
Harris,Dustin	22	L	23	LF	aa	TEX	331	11	12	205	8	75	91	100	19
Harris,Dylan	22	L	25	LF	a/a	BAL	186	4	2	151	9	58	108	64	-45
Harris,Trey	21	R	25	RF	aa	ATL	364	6	3	219	6	78	56	55	-15
	22	R	26	RF	aa	WAS	332	4	5	199	5	73	50	70	-36
Harrison,KJ	21	R	25	1B	aa	WAS	300	11	0	210	6	62	126	21	-30
	22	R	26	1B	aa	WAS	152	3	1	168	6	63	87	42	-54
Harrison,Monte	21	R	26	CF	aaa	MIA	269	11	19	196	8	46	134	129	-51
	22	R	27	CF	aaa	LAA	288	5	14	164	7	50	89	123	-75
Haseley,Adam	21	L	25	CF	aaa	PHI	156	2	5	197	5	75	30	67	-44
	22	L	26	CF	aaa	CHW	418	10	11	175	4	77	71	98	5
Haskin,Hudson	22	R	23	CF	aa	BAL	387	12	3	220	7	71	103	68	3
Hatch,LJ	21	R	27	2B	a/a	COL	124	1	1	200	4	53	81	95	-84
	22	R	28	SS	aaa	COL	161	4	1	206	4	59	94	78	-55
Hearn,Matt	21	L	25	CF	aa	COL	245	0	18	172	6	74	19	100	-46
Heineman,Tyler	21	B	30	C	aaa	PHI	129	0	0	208	7	70	30	26	-71
Helman,Michael	22	R	26	CF	a/a	MIN	512	11	24	194	7	73	74	126	6
Henderson,Gunnar	22	L	21	SS	a/a	BAL	407	15	15	256	11	69	124	136	41
Hensley,David	21	R	25	2B	aa	HOU	396	7	8	244	8	69	81	84	-18
	22	R	26	SS	aaa	HOU	379	6	12	224	11	65	100	108	-1
Hernandez,Elier	21	R	27	RF	a/a	TEX	385	11	4	185	5	62	86	55	-56
	22	R	28	RF	aaa	TEX	319	7	6	211	4	74	86	109	9
Hernandez,Marco	21	L	29	2B	aaa	CHW	334	3	1	193	2	76	48	50	-37
Hernandez,Ronaldo	21	R	24	C	a/a	BOS	365	11	0	250	2	76	112	35	12
	22	R	25	C	aaa	BOS	410	10	0	215	3	74	98	23	-9

BATTER	yr	b	age	pos	lvl	org	ab	hr	sb	ba	bb%	ct%	px	sx	bpv
Hernandez,Yonny	21	B	23	SS	aaa	TEX	192	1	16	214	16	74	39	117	-1
	22	B	24	2B	aaa	ARI	253	0	16	181	7	78	32	157	2
Herrera,Dilson	21	R	27	2B	aaa	TOR	174	9	0	184	8	58	129	58	-30
Herrera,Ivan	21	R	21	C	a/a	STL	367	11	1	186	10	72	71	30	-26
	22	R	22	C	aaa	STL	235	4	3	219	9	76	58	74	-7
Herron,Jimmy	22	R	26	LF	a/a	COL	328	8	8	207	7	76	82	98	16
Heyward,Jacob	21	R	26	LF	aa	SF	202	8	2	165	11	58	129	54	-23
	22	R	27	RF	aa	SF	318	7	1	155	8	53	79	62	-89
Hicklen,Brewer	21	R	25	LF	aa	KC	362	11	31	209	10	60	104	149	-10
	22	R	26	RF	aaa	KC	480	14	20	189	6	52	146	130	-21
Hill,Darius	21	L	24	LF	aa	CHC	249	4	1	239	6	79	34	48	-30
	22	L	25	LF	a/a	CHC	528	6	4	244	4	82	66	80	15
Hill,Derek	21	R	26	CF	aaa	DET	125	3	3	282	6	65	99	117	-11
	22	R	27	CF	aaa	SEA	227	4	5	158	5	61	77	116	-47
Hilliard,Sam	21	L	27	CF	aaa	COL	188	9	3	193	7	63	146	95	12
	22	L	28	CF	aaa	COL	133	7	2	230	7	65	141	92	17
Hinojosa,C.J.	21	R	27	2B	aaa	HOU	414	7	3	239	3	76	78	53	-8
	22	R	28	SS	aaa	SD	460	8	4	192	5	75	75	62	-11
Hiura,Keston	21	R	25	1B	aaa	MIL	172	5	1	202	10	51	139	33	-54
	22	R	26	2B	aaa	MIL	47	4	0	249	11	59	191	25	22
Hoese,Kody	21	R	24	3B	aa	LA	229	1	1	150	4	72	31	57	-59
	22	R	25	3B	aa	LA	289	4	1	181	4	69	52	53	-58
Holder,Kyle	21	L	27	SS	aaa	NYY	250	1	1	171	7	67	36	50	-73
	22	L	28	2B	aaa	COL	152	1	0	143	4	67	38	45	-77
Hollins,Bubba	22	R	27	3B	a/a	MIA	232	1	2	182	6	70	43	61	-55
Hollis,Connor	22	R	28	3B	a/a	SD	487	5	12	228	8	70	65	81	-25
Holt,Gabe	22	L	24	2B	aa	MIL	288	0	7	160	5	90	23	80	12
Honeyman,Bobby	21	L	25	1B	aa	SEA	304	3	2	196	8	76	50	46	-26
Hoover,Connor	22	L	26	3B	aa	SEA	239	3	3	126	8	61	57	66	-72
Hopkins,T.J.	21	R	24	LF	aa	CIN	257	4	2	235	8	67	92	112	-8
	22	R	25	LF	a/a	CIN	467	17	5	216	7	63	122	61	-19
Horwitz,Spencer	22	L	25	1B	a/a	TOR	403	9	5	222	10	72	102	75	17
Huff,Samuel	21	R	23	1B	a/a	TEX	195	10	0	210	7	51	147	22	-56
	22	R	24	C	aaa	TEX	246	12	0	198	6	60	114	28	-48
Hulsizer,Niko	21	R	24	RF	aa	TAM	173	6	1	201	8	46	151	91	-49
	22	R	25	RF	a/a	TAM	289	12	11	209	8	50	177	87	-14
Humphreys,Zach	22	R	25	C	aa	LAA	230	5	5	190	12	70	59	73	-24
Hunt,Blake	22	R	24	C	aa	TAM	273	3	1	193	5	69	68	57	-41
Hunter Jr.,Torii	21	R	26	CF	a/a	LAA	309	5	8	175	6	54	76	77	-86
	22	R	27	LF	a/a	LAA	263	5	13	183	4	57	82	139	-54
Hurst,Scott	21	L	25	CF	aaa	STL	266	2	3	157	7	59	57	78	-77
	22	L	26	CF	aaa	STL	311	6	11	213	9	74	59	88	-9
Hurtubise,Jacob	22	L	25	RF	aa	CIN	156	1	10	200	9	68	25	125	-50
Ibanez,Andy	21	R	28	3B	aaa	TEX	114	5	1	267	7	80	122	61	51
	22	R	29	1B	aaa	TEX	282	3	3	174	5	78	58	59	-12
Infante,Diego	22	R	23	LF	a/a	TAM	159	1	4	215	8	60	71	76	-62
Isabel,Ibandel	21	R	26	DH	aa	LAA	219	9	0	155	7	47	135	42	-75
Isola,Alex	22	R	24	DH	aa	MIN	210	6	0	226	9	75	80	25	-9
Jackson,Drew	21	R	28	2B	aaa	NYM	243	5	15	177	12	57	82	105	-50
	22	R	29	LF	aaa	SF	178	2	4	163	7	48	65	72	-120
Jackson,Jeremiah	22	R	22	2B	aa	LAA	307	10	4	174	7	72	93	58	-3
Jarrett,Zach	21	R	27	CF	a/a	BAL	346	7	8	184	8	59	81	83	-58
Jenista,Greyson	21	L	25	1B	aa	ATL	273	15	6	189	13	51	158	93	-12
	22	L	26	RF	aaa	ATL	321	11	1	171	6	54	116	53	-63
Johnson Jr.,Daniel	21	L	26	RF	aaa	CLE	279	9	5	176	8	54	130	84	-38
	22	L	27	DH	a/a	WAS	222	5	1	159	4	59	69	60	-81
Johnson,Bryce	21	B	26	CF	aaa	SF	353	5	20	222	8	63	70	138	-33
	22	B	27	CF	aaa	SF	307	3	17	215	6	63	58	124	-51
Johnson,Ivan	22	B	24	2B	aa	CIN	180	3	3	215	5	57	115	112	-37
Johnston,Troy	22	L	25	1B	a/a	MIA	426	9	3	209	8	73	82	60	-5
Jones,Greg	22	B	24	SS	aa	TAM	319	5	25	188	5	51	111	161	-45
Jones,Nolan	21	L	23	3B	aaa	CLE	341	9	7	201	11	59	122	83	-17
	22	L	24	RF	aaa	CLE	214	5	2	211	8	64	93	72	-31
Jones,Ryder	21	L	27	1B	a/a	ARI	251	6	1	210	4	70	94	50	-21
	22	L	28	3B	aaa	CHW	214	5	0	137	5	53	68	25	-114
Jones,Taylor	21	R	28	1B	aaa	HOU	178	7	0	247	10	68	117	30	-3
	22	R	29	1B	aaa	SF	298	6	0	183	7	62	99	34	-47
Jones,Thomas	22	R	25	CF	aa	MIA	193	5	4	141	9	45	151	112	-46
Jones,Travis	21	R	26	3B	a/a	KC	195	3	4	177	12	63	60	99	-45
Jordan,Levi	21	R	26	3B	a/a	CHC	247	5	1	202	6	63	85	41	-54
	22	R	27	3B	a/a	CHC	357	8	6	199	5	77	77	89	10
Julien,Edouard	22	L	23	2B	aa	MIN	400	11	12	244	14	64	100	86	-8
Julks,Corey	21	R	25	LF	aa	HOU	338	11	11	239	7	70	105	112	14
	22	R	26	3B	aaa	HOU	523	19	13	202	6	69	98	105	1
Justus,Connor	21	R	27	3B	a/a	MIA	282	1	2	161	8	62	42	57	-82
Kaiser,Connor	21	R	25	SS	a/a	PIT	158	3	0	154	8	67	69	43	-45
	22	R	26	SS	a/a	SD	187	4	5	142	7	59	73	92	-63
Katoh,Gosuke	21	L	27	2B	aaa	SD	350	4	5	220	7	69	77	80	-20
	22	L	28	2B	aaa	NYM	289	5	4	152	6	67	74	88	-33
Keirsey,DaShawn	22	L	25	CF	aa	MIN	425	4	26	210	5	70	71	127	-15
Kelenic,Jarred	21	L	22	LF	aaa	SEA	125	7	5	274	9	79	128	104	69
	22	L	23	RF	aaa	SEA	352	11	6	227	6	72	125	83	25
Kelly,Dalton	21	L	27	1B	aaa	TAM	377	21	14	200	11	57	156	87	4
	22	L	28	LF	aaa	OAK	310	7	3	142	6	51	91	78	-85
Kendall,Jeren	21	L	25	CF	aa	LA	201	7	10	165	7	46	128	103	-66
	22	L	26	CF	aa	LA	234	4	16	122	8	49	89	144	-70
Kennedy,Buddy	21	R	23	3B	aa	ARI	237	11	5	235	10	65	110	96	0
	22	R	24	3B	aaa	ARI	330	3	4	194	8	73	54	81	-23
Kerrigan,Jimmy	21	R	27	RF	a/a	MIN	362	13	7	210	6	54	126	101	-39
Kessinger,Grae	21	R	24	SS	aa	HOU	297	7	10	176	6	69	62	92	-34
	22	R	25	SS	aa	HOU	421	10	14	160	9	67	70	98	-24
Kieboom,Carter	21	R	24	3B	aaa	WAS	148	4	1	209	12	77	75	46	6

BATTER	yr	b	age	pos	lvl	org	ab	hr	sb	ba	bb%	ct%	px	sx	bpv
Kingery,Scott	22	R	28	2B	aaa	PHI	301	4	10	168	10	55	81	130	-54
Kirwer,Tanner	21	R	25	LF	aa	TOR	159	4	13	169	9	63	67	116	-40
	22	R	26	LF	aa	SEA	312	3	14	177	7	61	43	106	-75
Knight,Nash	21	B	29	3B	aaa	TOR	212	6	1	151	12	56	96	60	-57
	22	B	30	2B	a/a	MIN	269	3	0	168	8	51	88	56	-91
Kohlwey,Taylor	21	L	27	1B	a/a	SD	409	5	7	233	8	70	62	74	-32
	22	L	28	LF	aaa	SD	501	5	5	196	7	75	60	70	-15
Kopach,Connor	21	R	27	SS	aa	SEA	147	3	6	116	10	33	95	103	-141
Koperniak,Matt	21	L	23	RF	aa	STL	133	2	1	213	4	83	50	46	-4
	22	L	24	LF	a/a	STL	388	7	7	216	6	76	56	79	-15
Koss,Christian	22	R	24	SS	aa	BOS	488	11	11	220	3	69	90	103	-14
Kramer,Kevin	21	L	28	SS	aaa	MIL	232	2	0	151	8	60	51	52	-86
Kreidler,Ryan	21	R	24	SS	a/a	DET	482	17	12	237	8	65	103	83	-15
	22	R	25	SS	aaa	DET	202	5	10	170	10	60	115	132	-7
Kroon,Matt	21	R	25	CF	aa	PHI	163	4	4	258	5	67	75	85	-36
Kwan,Steven	21	L	24	CF	a/a	CLE	296	9	4	281	8	88	77	93	59
Labour,Franklin	22	R	24	RF	aa	SF	209	4	3	147	8	46	133	101	-62
Lagrange,Wagner	21	R	26	RF	a/a	NYM	284	5	2	200	4	72	59	46	-42
Langeliers,Shea	21	R	24	C	a/a	ATL	340	18	1	227	9	66	126	45	-1
	22	R	25	C	aaa	OAK	353	9	3	201	6	69	88	68	-18
Lantigua,Rafael	22	R	24	2B	a/a	TOR	489	5	10	224	7	75	74	71	-3
Lara,Gilbert	21	R	24	SS	a/a	WAS	241	4	1	212	3	72	82	29	-31
	22	R	25	SS	aa	WAS	290	5	0	183	4	65	59	22	-78
Large,Cullen	21	B	25	RF	aaa	TOR	403	7	3	230	10	71	79	66	-11
	22	B	26	RF	aaa	TOR	411	5	5	194	7	64	83	89	-35
Larsen,Jack	21	L	26	CF	aa	SEA	173	8	1	224	11	66	107	68	-5
	22	L	27	RF	aa	SEA	450	6	5	194	9	69	66	92	-24
Lavastida,Bryan	21	R	23	C	a/a	CLE	122	3	2	235	8	64	99	74	-23
	22	R	24	C	a/a	CLE	321	6	4	164	5	71	62	99	-25
Lavigne,Grant	22	L	23	1B	aa	COL	208	3	0	211	8	67	69	57	-41
Leblanc,Charles	21	R	25	3B	aaa	TEX	332	12	4	187	8	54	130	87	-36
	22	R	26	3B	aaa	MIA	318	9	4	236	7	62	112	77	-23
Lee,Braxton	21	L	28	LF	a/a	CIN	263	0	2	179	7	66	43	76	-64
Lee,Khalil	21	L	23	RF	aaa	NYM	292	9	6	216	14	52	137	83	-26
	22	L	24	CF	aaa	NYM	353	6	8	162	8	52	114	77	-60
Lee,Korey	21	R	23	C	a/a	HOU	220	6	2	209	6	77	82	63	6
	22	R	24	C	aaa	HOU	404	16	7	184	5	62	122	104	-9
Leon,Pedro	21	R	23	SS	a/a	HOU	246	7	12	183	10	58	88	97	-45
	22	R	24	CF	aaa	HOU	413	11	24	176	10	58	120	118	-15
Lester,Josh	21	L	27	1B	a/a	DET	395	24	2	219	6	63	163	99	26
	22	L	28	1B	aaa	DET	557	16	4	181	5	70	107	73	0
Lewis,Brandon	22	R	24	1B	aa	LA	397	17	0	169	4	57	138	35	-40
Leyba,Domingo	21	B	26	2B	aaa	TEX	208	9	1	253	3	82	97	59	31
	22	B	27	2B	a/a	SD	404	6	7	177	8	78	59	74	2
Liberato,Luis	21	L	26	CF	aaa	SEA	298	5	2	218	7	66	72	100	-33
	22	L	27	CF	aaa	SD	329	10	3	174	7	60	129	80	-15
Lien,Connor	21	R	27	CF	aa	SEA	147	3	1	116	11	27	142	111	-120
Lindsly,Brady	22	L	24	C	aa	WAS	221	5	0	163	5	60	74	33	-79
Lipcius,Andre	21	R	23	3B	aa	DET	341	7	3	207	8	75	74	80	0
	22	R	24	3B	a/a	DET	462	7	9	227	11	78	82	83	28
Listi,Austin	21	R	28	3B	aaa	PHI	190	1	0	180	6	69	31	16	-79
Lockridge,Brandon	21	R	24	CF	aa	NYY	174	8	10	285	6	61	136	97	-5
	22	R	25	CF	aa	NYY	418	10	13	181	6	64	83	103	-34
Loehr,Trace	21	L	26	2B	a/a	TEX	163	0	1	202	4	65	53	76	-64
Loftin,Nick	22	R	24	CF	a/a	KC	516	9	17	204	6	79	65	106	15
Longhi,Nick	21	R	26	LF	aaa	COL	219	3	0	196	7	65	63	21	-65
Lopes,Christian	21	R	29	2B	aaa	ARI	181	4	2	181	7	55	102	74	-58
	22	R	30	2B	aaa	OAK	187	1	2	165	5	60	70	67	-72
Lopes,Tim	21	R	27	3B	aaa	MIL	327	7	6	170	6	64	81	102	-34
	22	R	28	2B	aaa	COL	266	5	5	201	4	69	83	104	-15
Lopez,Alejo	21	B	25	2B	a/a	CIN	356	5	7	276	9	89	66	75	52
	22	B	26	2B	aaa	CIN	160	2	1	212	7	84	57	35	8
Lopez,Irving	21	L	26	3B	a/a	STL	232	2	1	174	4	71	47	72	-48
	22	L	27	3B	a/a	STL	230	1	3	178	6	78	45	59	-20
Lopez,Otto	21	R	23	2B	a/a	TOR	451	4	18	283	7	78	74	125	25
	22	R	24	2B	aaa	TOR	340	2	11	254	8	80	65	120	24
Lowe,Josh	21	L	23	CF	aaa	TAM	402	19	23	262	12	65	145	125	37
	22	L	24	RF	aaa	TAM	302	9	18	255	9	53	173	122	8
Lugbauer,Drew	21	L	25	1B	aa	ATL	300	15	0	196	10	51	163	35	-34
	22	L	26	1B	aa	ATL	474	20	0	174	10	47	176	23	-43
Lukes,Nathan	21	L	27	RF	aaa	TAM	294	3	2	249	5	82	83	69	30
	22	L	28	CF	aaa	TOR	428	8	14	223	7	74	76	90	0
Lund,Brennon	21	L	27	CF	aaa	LAA	286	6	2	157	3	62	82	60	-61
Lutz,Tristen	21	R	23	RF	aa	MIL	240	6	2	189	6	59	96	53	-58
	22	R	24	LF	aa	MIL	255	8	1	207	8	58	107	24	-55
Machin,Vimael	21	L	28	3B	aaa	OAK	336	7	1	219	8	73	74	84	-7
	22	L	29	3B	aaa	OAK	256	2	0	215	6	84	50	45	4
MacIver,Willie	21	R	25	C	a/a	COL	196	3	6	136	5	64	48	78	-70
	22	R	26	C	a/a	COL	367	9	5	175	5	65	86	53	-41
MacKinnon,David	21	R	27	1B	aa	LAA	366	9	1	223	9	72	96	35	-6
	22	R	28	1B	aaa	OAK	289	7	1	215	8	71	104	60	3
Madris,Bligh	21	L	25	RF	a/a	PIT	360	6	1	220	9	76	76	39	-4
	22	L	26	RF	aaa	TAM	296	7	3	231	7	68	111	87	3
Maitan,Kevin	22	B	22	3B	aa	LAA	399	8	2	213	6	60	87	49	-60
Maldonado,Nelson	21	R	25	DH	aa	CHC	245	4	1	254	6	76	83	66	6
	22	R	26	DH	a/a	CHC	373	7	4	208	4	71	93	63	-11
Malloy,Justyn-Henry	22	R	22	LF	a/a	ATL	215	6	2	243	16	67	102	50	-3
Manea,Scott	21	R	26	C	aa	HOU	210	7	0	233	12	70	87	22	-19
	22	R	27	C	aaa	HOU	285	2	0	141	8	59	48	55	-90
Mangum,Jake	21	B	25	CF	aa	NYM	305	5	10	231	3	76	73	117	6
	22	B	26	CF	a/a	NYM	276	3	9	229	4	74	62	115	-11

BATTER	yr	b	age	pos	lvl	org	ab	hr	sb	ba	bb%	ct%	px	sx	bpv
Mann,Devin	21	R	24	1B	aa	LA	369	10	4	197	8	68	100	54	-12
	22	R	25	2B	a/a	LA	375	11	1	202	9	72	92	51	-2
Marabell,Connor	21	L	27	LF	aaa	CLE	337	5	3	228	3	76	70	57	-15
Marcano,Tucupita	21	L	22	2B	aaa	PIT	355	5	9	218	10	82	45	91	15
	22	L	23	LF	a/a	PIT	200	3	3	245	10	77	80	81	19
Marchan,Rafael	21	B	22	C	a/a	PHI	242	0	1	184	6	79	22	44	-40
	22	B	23	C	aaa	PHI	230	3	0	189	5	88	63	23	23
Maris,Peter	21	L	28	2B	a/a	SF	180	5	1	215	6	64	95	74	-34
Marlowe,Cade	22	L	25	CF	a/a	SEA	499	14	26	214	7	61	98	117	-28
Marmolejos,Jose	21	L	28	1B	aaa	SEA	293	17	0	256	11	68	137	45	20
Marrero,Elih	22	B	25	C	aa	BOS	246	1	12	171	9	66	49	86	-51
Martin,Austin	21	R	22	CF	aa	MIN	330	4	10	240	12	72	66	100	-1
	22	R	23	SS	aa	MIN	336	1	22	194	8	82	38	132	16
Martin,Jason	21	L	26	LF	aaa	TEX	129	7	1	199	13	69	119	83	23
	22	L	27	RF	aaa	LA	470	19	4	204	7	63	123	72	-11
Martin,Mason	21	L	22	1B	a/a	PIT	439	17	0	210	6	59	145	43	-22
	22	L	23	1B	aaa	PIT	481	11	8	172	7	56	128	106	-27
Martin,Richie	21	R	27	SS	a/a	BAL	111	1	5	171	9	71	62	114	-14
	22	R	28	SS	aaa	BAL	292	1	16	181	6	72	65	148	-2
Martinez,Braxton	22	R	28	1B	a/a	LAA	286	5	0	140	8	57	81	27	-80
Martinez,J.P.	21	L	25	CF	aa	TEX	285	4	16	209	11	55	86	144	-46
	22	L	26	CF	a/a	TEX	395	8	23	180	9	61	85	142	-26
Martinez,Orelvis	22	R	21	SS	aa	TOR	433	22	3	169	5	65	124	44	-14
Martinez,Orlando	21	L	23	LF	aa	LAA	400	12	4	219	6	66	101	71	-21
	22	L	24	RF	a/a	LAA	385	6	5	207	5	72	68	76	-24
Martorano,Brandon	21	R	23	C	a/a	SF	120	5	1	149	11	59	101	45	-44
	22	R	24	C	aa	SF	323	6	8	182	8	57	108	126	-28
Massey,Michael	22	L	24	2B	a/a	KC	346	9	8	255	5	72	114	71	12
Masters,Dave	21	R	28	SS	a/a	SEA	123	5	1	159	7	54	106	38	-72
Mastrobuoni,Miles	21	L	26	SS	a/a	TAM	382	4	6	244	9	70	71	94	-13
	22	L	27	2B	aaa	TAM	507	10	15	227	8	75	80	106	15
Matheny,Shane	21	L	25	SS	aa	SF	174	3	2	172	13	56	93	82	-51
	22	L	26	CF	a/a	SF	362	8	2	186	10	54	94	68	-69
Matheny,Tate	21	R	27	CF	a/a	BOS	240	7	6	200	8	54	135	106	-27
Mathias,Mark	22	R	28	2B	aaa	TEX	199	5	7	229	8	63	89	76	-36
Matias,Seuly	22	R	24	RF	aa	KC	347	9	4	180	7	57	108	82	-45
Matijevic,J.J.	21	L	26	1B	a/a	HOU	402	18	4	201	8	59	136	82	-12
	22	L	27	1B	aaa	HOU	246	10	6	209	7	64	130	98	7
Maton,Nick	21	L	24	SS	aaa	PHI	207	4	2	173	11	66	79	71	-28
	22	L	25	SS	aaa	PHI	211	3	2	203	9	69	104	68	1
Mauricio,Ronny	22	B	21	SS	aa	NYM	509	18	14	214	3	71	104	86	3
Mazeika,Patrick	21	L	28	C	aaa	NYM	157	4	0	199	6	84	66	21	8
	22	L	29	C	aaa	SF	162	2	0	176	6	81	34	19	-28
McAfee,Quincy	21	R	24	2B	aa	CIN	122	2	4	206	13	69	61	96	-21
	22	R	25	2B	aa	CIN	254	4	1	174	8	61	77	53	-59
McCann,Kyle	21	L	24	C	aa	OAK	320	5	1	135	9	51	75	41	-103
	22	L	25	C	a/a	OAK	394	11	1	169	7	53	113	46	-65
McCarthy,Joe	21	L	27	1B	aaa	SF	275	8	3	230	7	72	95	63	0
McCoy,Mason	21	R	26	SS	aaa	BAL	408	7	9	181	7	63	82	108	-34
	22	R	27	SS	aaa	SEA	442	12	13	178	6	61	99	114	-27
McDonald,Mickey	21	L	26	CF	a/a	OAK	364	1	12	240	8	70	48	123	-25
	22	L	27	CF	a/a	OAK	272	1	6	198	7	67	48	81	-52
McDowell,Max	21	R	27	C	a/a	NYY	143	1	2	171	11	63	52	83	-58
	22	R	28	C	aaa	NYY	187	1	2	139	8	66	52	50	-64
McGarry,Alex	22	L	24	1B	a/a	CIN	262	13	6	215	5	65	143	95	13
McGovern,Keegan	21	L	26	RF	aa	SEA	143	3	4	150	12	41	87	111	-109
McIlwain,Brandon	22	R	24	CF	aa	NYM	192	3	2	170	6	60	66	60	-76
McIntosh,Paul	22	R	25	C	aa	MIA	318	9	7	210	11	72	111	96	30
McKenna,Alex	21	R	24	CF	aa	HOU	131	2	1	173	9	52	71	59	-100
	22	R	25	CF	a/a	HOU	367	4	10	176	8	57	74	100	-63
McKinney,Billy	22	L	28	RF	aaa	OAK	251	5	1	197	7	56	102	87	-51
McKinstry,Zach	21	L	26	SS	aaa	LA	147	5	3	211	8	78	88	113	35
	22	L	27	SS	aaa	LA	191	2	0	241	7	78	58	63	-9
McLain,Matt	22	R	23	SS	aa	CIN	371	13	18	196	11	61	134	126	12
McLaughlin,Matt	21	R	25	3B	aa	COL	279	2	1	183	6	75	44	45	-35
Mead,Curtis	22	R	22	3B	a/a	TAM	282	9	5	249	9	74	128	61	36
Meadows,Parker	22	L	23	CF	aa	DET	425	10	12	234	8	77	90	127	35
Means,Jake	22	R	26	3B	aa	KC	375	6	6	161	7	64	83	76	-38
Mejia,Erick	21	B	27	3B	aaa	KC	203	4	1	194	7	77	67	43	-11
	22	B	28	3B	aaa	SEA	464	8	11	178	6	70	75	91	-19
Melean,Kelvin	21	R	23	2B	a/a	SD	136	1	1	133	6	80	20	46	-35
	22	R	24	3B	a/a	SD	186	1	1	183	6	70	60	78	-35
Melendez Jr.,MJ	21	L	23	C	a/a	KC	448	29	2	251	11	73	143	63	49
	22	L	24	C	aaa	KC	78	1	2	132	8	70	68	52	-32
Melendez,Manuel	21	L	24	RF	aa	COL	266	4	3	176	6	74	64	44	-26
Mendoza,Evan	21	R	25	SS	aaa	STL	396	1	10	189	5	69	29	83	-62
	22	R	26	SS	aaa	STL	360	2	10	182	8	82	37	81	0
Meneses,Joey	21	R	29	RF	a/a	BOS	334	9	0	227	5	72	121	50	12
	22	R	30	1B	aaa	WAS	374	12	1	210	5	69	88	34	-31
Mercado,Oscar	21	R	27	CF	aaa	CLE	171	3	6	168	8	77	81	106	22
	22	R	28	CF	aaa	CLE	167	3	5	197	5	78	60	98	2
Mercedes,Yermin	21	R	28	DH	aaa	CHW	222	7	2	205	3	77	67	65	-10
	22	R	29	1B	aaa	SF	229	6	4	176	7	67	82	54	-35
Mervis,Matt	22	L	24	1B	a/a	CHC	412	18	1	234	6	77	127	59	40
Mesa,Victor Victor	22	R	26	CF	a/a	MIA	301	2	24	179	4	79	28	126	-14
Meyer,Nick	21	R	24	C	a/a	NYM	220	2	4	198	7	74	34	60	-41
	22	R	25	C	a/a	NYM	246	4	9	175	10	70	59	92	-22
Mieses,Johan	21	R	26	DH	a/a	BOS	283	13	2	194	7	65	118	70	-6
	22	R	27	RF	aaa	BOS	192	7	3	214	9	61	153	58	3
Millas,Drew	22	B	24	C	aa	WAS	152	2	1	181	7	61	57	31	-85
Miller,Anderson	21	L	27	RF	aaa	KC	219	7	6	166	7	65	79	80	-38

BATTER	yr	b	age	pos	lvl	org	ab	hr	sb	ba	bb%	ct%	px	sx	bpv
Miller,Brian	21	L	26	CF	aaa	MIA	396	1	28	220	6	73	38	127	-24
	22	L	27	LF	aaa	MIA	408	4	17	227	6	76	65	146	15
Miller,Jalen	21	R	25	2B	aa	ATL	229	7	2	177	7	63	108	60	-27
	22	R	26	DH	aa	ATL	327	6	12	193	9	69	92	105	2
Miller,Luke	21	R	25	1B	aa	PHI	277	9	0	178	5	58	109	20	-64
Miller,Owen	21	R	25	2B	aaa	CLE	182	5	0	244	7	66	102	33	-29
Milligan,Cody	22	L	24	CF	aa	ATL	273	1	10	232	8	76	37	102	-20
Milone,Thomas	21	L	26	LF	a/a	NYY	311	8	12	230	10	63	94	92	-24
	22	L	27	CF	a/a	SD	405	5	8	175	7	57	74	96	-69
Miroglio,Dominic	21	R	26	C	aa	ARI	296	7	1	195	8	67	84	65	-27
	22	R	27	C	aaa	ARI	214	5	1	179	5	82	77	59	20
Misner,Kameron	22	L	24	CF	aa	TAM	416	10	22	197	12	55	117	105	-30
Mitchell,Calvin	21	L	22	RF	a/a	PIT	402	8	4	244	4	80	67	45	-2
	22	L	23	RF	aaa	PIT	236	6	5	284	5	82	100	84	44
Mitchell,Garrett	21	L	23	CF	aa	MIL	129	2	4	161	10	64	40	70	-71
	22	L	24	CF	a/a	MIL	239	3	11	238	7	64	86	126	-20
Monasterio,Andruw	21	R	24	3B	a/a	CLE	376	6	5	245	9	65	93	95	-18
	22	R	25	SS	a/a	MIL	377	6	10	211	9	70	73	90	-14
Mondou,Nate	21	L	26	2B	aaa	OAK	308	5	0	218	8	78	68	42	-3
	22	L	27	2B	aaa	OAK	385	3	1	194	6	72	71	50	-25
Montano,Daniel	22	L	23	LF	aa	COL	305	9	3	216	9	65	105	62	-16
Montero,Elehuris	21	R	23	3B	a/a	COL	431	20	0	248	8	73	113	35	10
	22	R	24	3B	aaa	COL	255	9	2	251	5	73	95	67	1
Montes,Coco	21	R	25	2B	aa	COL	431	10	2	227	5	70	112	60	-2
	22	R	26	2B	a/a	COL	469	12	8	214	6	66	105	109	-6
Morales,Jonathan	21	R	26	C	aaa	ATL	152	1	0	121	1	78	37	25	-46
	22	R	27	C	aaa	COL	308	5	0	233	6	78	50	9	-30
Morales,Roy	21	R	26	1B	aa	MIN	333	1	3	251	7	83	32	53	-10
	22	R	27	1B	a/a	MIN	184	2	2	226	9	82	47	54	2
Moreno,Gabriel	21	R	21	C	a/a	TOR	135	7	1	332	8	81	128	67	63
	22	R	22	C	aaa	TOR	238	3	6	280	7	79	70	72	11
Moritz,Andrew	22	L	26	LF	aa	ATL	302	1	4	234	8	72	53	79	-27
Morris,Tanner	22	L	24	3B	a/a	TOR	252	4	1	211	12	75	48	44	-21
Mottice,Kyle	21	L	25	2B	aa	SF	110	0	5	215	8	80	37	93	-5
Mount,Drew	21	L	25	RF	a/a	CIN	205	9	1	236	6	65	105	71	-22
Mulrine,Anthony	21	R	23	C	a/a	LAA	183	3	0	165	7	69	56	24	-56
	22	R	24	C	a/a	LAA	207	1	1	118	6	63	33	46	-96
Mundy,J.D.	22	L	24	1B	aa	BAL	234	6	0	176	7	59	112	11	-54
Muno,JJ	21	L	28	3B	aa	CHW	186	5	11	170	8	57	82	142	-48
	22	L	29	3B	aa	CHW	278	3	17	163	8	64	47	117	-55
Munoz,Yairo	21	R	26	3B	aaa	BOS	351	6	13	264	3	82	62	107	19
	22	R	27	3B	aaa	PHI	277	4	8	236	2	78	60	92	-5
Muzziotti,Simon	22	L	24	CF	a/a	PHI	159	4	5	217	8	75	75	124	17
Myers,Dane	22	R	26	LF	a/a	DET	450	15	14	207	3	65	106	105	-14
Navigato,Andrew	22	R	24	2B	aa	DET	361	11	10	203	5	78	81	97	17
Nay,Mitch	21	R	28	3B	aa	LAA	367	15	1	180	10	61	120	35	-28
Naylor,Bo	21	L	21	C	aa	CLE	313	8	8	171	9	61	90	96	-36
	22	L	22	C	a/a	CLE	415	14	13	218	11	67	123	103	21
Neslony,Tyler	21	L	27	LF	aa	CHW	176	7	1	245	11	63	153	63	18
	22	L	28	RF	a/a	CHW	352	9	12	223	6	73	102	91	16
Neustrom,Robert	21	L	25	LF	a/a	BAL	453	13	8	215	8	74	94	81	12
	22	L	26	LF	aaa	BAL	368	10	8	176	4	78	77	72	6
Nevin,Tyler	21	R	24	1B	aaa	BAL	401	13	1	196	7	75	81	27	-9
	22	R	25	3B	aaa	BAL	165	5	2	230	7	74	87	76	7
Nieporte,Quincy	22	R	28	1B	aa	DET	459	18	1	201	5	77	102	64	22
Nishioka,Tanner	21	R	27	2B	aa	BOS	150	4	1	205	4	64	81	58	-54
Noda,Ryan	21	L	25	1B	aa	LA	384	20	2	199	11	61	130	53	-14
	22	L	26	1B	aaa	LA	464	15	11	188	9	57	114	75	-39
Noel,Jhonkensy	22	R	21	RF	a/a	CLE	257	9	1	198	7	69	121	75	14
Nogowski,John	21	R	28	1B	aaa	SF	209	3	4	152	8	74	45	61	-31
	22	R	29	1B	a/a	WAS	395	5	8	187	10	79	57	65	3
Nolan,Nate	21	R	27	C	aaa	CHW	154	4	0	115	5	35	132	44	-132
Noll,Jake	21	R	27	2B	aaa	WAS	438	13	3	251	4	80	88	61	19
	22	R	28	2B	aaa	WAS	390	6	4	194	3	75	78	81	-3
Norby,Connor	22	R	22	2B	a/a	BAL	291	16	7	262	8	76	135	93	57
Nottingham,Jacob	22	R	27	C	aaa	BAL	301	10	6	172	7	61	101	71	-40
Nunez,Dom	22	L	27	C	aaa	COL	247	3	1	168	6	68	70	74	-36
Nunez,Malcom	21	R	20	3B	aa	STL	202	4	1	212	6	77	44	43	-31
	22	R	21	1B	aa	PIT	416	14	3	219	11	73	92	50	4
Nunez,Renato	21	R	27	1B	aaa	MIL	332	14	1	204	7	64	112	65	-20
O Grady,Brian	21	L	29	RF	aaa	SD	285	8	5	191	7	61	112	92	-25
O Hoppe,Logan	22	R	22	C	aa	LAA	360	18	5	234	11	77	109	59	36
O Keefe,Brian	22	R	29	C	aaa	SEA	316	7	1	169	5	65	86	49	-43
Ockimey,Josh	21	L	26	1B	aaa	BOS	293	10	0	189	14	53	117	12	-61
	22	L	27	1B	a/a	PHI	395	11	2	174	12	58	109	62	-35
O'Keefe,Brian	21	R	28	C	a/a	SEA	406	16	3	204	8	57	107	50	-54
Oliva,Jared	21	R	26	CF	aaa	PIT	225	1	7	201	6	66	64	112	-40
	22	R	27	CF	aaa	PIT	319	4	13	203	5	71	86	127	1
Ona,Jorge	22	R	25	RF	aa	SD	250	5	0	166	6	50	87	34	-108
Orimoloye,Demi	21	R	24	RF	aa	TOR	283	5	9	197	3	62	81	98	-50
Ornelas,Jonathan	22	R	22	SS	aa	TEX	525	9	9	247	5	74	60	76	-20
Ornelas,Tirso	22	L	22	LF	aa	SD	455	4	4	223	6	77	62	67	-7
Orr,J.D.	22	L	26	LF	a/a	MIA	264	1	27	198	11	73	42	131	-14
Ortega,Dennis	21	R	24	C	aaa	STL	160	1	0	183	6	65	47	27	-79
	22	R	25	1B	aa	MIN	168	1	2	184	5	64	59	72	-62
Ortiz,Jhailyn	22	R	24	RF	aa	PHI	448	12	6	192	6	58	114	91	-37
Ortiz,Joey	22	R	24	SS	a/a	BAL	539	14	5	230	5	79	91	88	29
Osborne,J.D.	22	R	27	DH	a/a	MIA	152	3	0	187	5	59	95	48	-60
Ostberg,Erik	22	L	27	DH	aa	TAM	162	3	2	159	9	55	91	83	-61
Outman,James	21	L	24	CF	aa	LA	166	6	1	236	7	64	115	83	-12
	22	L	25	RF	a/a	LA	473	21	8	227	8	61	151	99	12
Overstreet,Kyle	21	R	28	1B	aa	SD	361	3	1	182	10	70	40	31	-60

BATTER	yr	b	age	pos	lvl	org	ab	hr	sb	ba	bb%	ct%	px	sx	bpv
Pache,Cristian	21	R	23	CF	aaa	ATL	321	9	7	238	7	67	87	68	-26
	22	R	24	CF	aaa	OAK	157	2	1	179	4	71	62	47	-45
Padlo,Kevin	21	R	25	3B	aaa	SEA	357	14	4	177	8	60	106	89	-30
	22	R	26	3B	aaa	PIT	306	7	8	196	6	65	93	103	-19
Pages,Andy	22	R	22	RF	aa	LA	487	20	4	198	8	68	125	62	7
Pages,Pedro	22	R	24	C	a/a	STL	291	5	1	165	7	60	79	35	-69
Palacios,Jermaine	21	R	25	SS	aa	MIN	410	13	12	214	8	69	85	73	-17
	22	R	26	SS	aaa	MIN	392	8	7	214	5	68	94	69	-19
Palacios,Joshua	22	L	27	LF	aaa	WAS	296	6	13	228	7	77	64	96	5
Palacios,Richard	21	L	24	2B	a/a	CLE	357	5	15	254	11	77	94	118	42
	22	L	25	LF	aaa	CLE	179	2	7	209	7	70	78	134	0
Palensky,Aaron	21	R	23	LF	aa	NYY	111	2	0	186	13	61	102	69	-24
Palma,Alexander	21	R	26	DH	aa	MIL	320	10	0	205	4	77	75	20	-17
Palmeiro,Preston	21	L	26	1B	aaa	LAA	399	8	3	175	4	71	63	57	-39
	22	L	27	DH	aa	LAA	407	5	1	193	6	75	72	30	-20
Palomaki,Jake	21	B	26	SS	aa	TAM	217	0	10	158	11	72	22	109	-40
	22	B	27	SS	aaa	LAA	316	1	5	215	6	77	33	68	-30
Papierski,Michael	21	B	25	C	aaa	HOU	333	5	1	192	11	69	64	36	-37
	22	B	26	C	aaa	CIN	190	5	0	192	9	75	69	18	-19
Park,Hoy Jun	21	L	25	SS	a/a	PIT	224	7	8	238	16	71	88	85	16
	22	L	26	3B	aaa	PIT	316	6	9	171	10	63	67	85	-47
Pasquantino,Vinnie	21	L	24	1B	aa	KC	200	8	2	273	11	86	110	46	69
	22	L	25	DH	aaa	KC	264	9	2	216	8	83	102	71	54
Paul,Ethan	21	L	25	2B	a/a	PIT	150	1	3	168	10	56	35	60	-108
Payne,Tyler	21	R	29	C	aa	CHC	213	3	1	175	5	61	79	62	-64
	22	R	30	C	aaa	CHC	151	1	0	211	3	68	59	38	-61
Peguero,Liover	22	R	21	SS	aa	PIT	483	6	19	220	4	75	67	119	0
Pena,Jeremy	21	R	24	SS	aaa	HOU	122	7	3	234	3	66	132	111	11
Peraza,Jose	22	R	28	2B	aaa	BOS	237	3	2	182	3	84	57	44	3
Peraza,Oswald	21	R	21	SS	a/a	NYY	354	11	18	266	6	73	86	102	4
	22	R	22	SS	aaa	NYY	386	15	25	219	6	70	98	104	6
Perdomo,Geraldo	21	B	22	SS	a/a	ARI	298	4	5	197	9	69	53	104	-28
Pereda,Jhonny	21	R	25	C	a/a	BOS	203	0	1	215	10	85	52	48	17
	22	R	26	C	aaa	SF	206	2	0	204	9	75	53	18	-30
Perez,Carlos	21	R	25	C	a/a	CHW	422	10	1	214	5	87	63	40	22
	22	R	26	C	aaa	CHW	418	14	1	188	5	88	71	28	29
Perez,Delvin	21	R	23	SS	aa	STL	389	2	15	209	4	72	31	113	-44
	22	R	24	3B	a/a	STL	296	3	12	163	6	67	43	115	-47
Perez,Joe	21	R	22	3B	aa	HOU	281	7	2	235	6	68	93	41	-26
	22	R	23	3B	a/a	HOU	286	5	2	229	7	68	77	44	-36
Perez,Wenceel	22	B	23	2B	aa	DET	150	3	3	269	6	83	109	121	72
Perkins,Blake	21	B	25	CF	aa	KC	238	5	7	172	11	63	70	92	-40
	22	B	26	LF	a/a	NYY	329	11	14	190	10	65	106	124	6
Perlaza,Yonathan	22	B	24	RF	aa	CHC	470	14	9	196	8	68	116	89	10
Peterson,Cole	21	L	26	SS	a/a	DET	184	0	5	183	6	82	44	138	18
Peterson,Dustin	21	R	27	LF	aaa	MIL	291	6	0	205	6	81	59	28	-8
	22	R	28	RF	aaa	PHI	396	6	4	177	6	68	71	67	-36
Pinder,Chase	22	R	26	LF	a/a	STL	238	6	3	183	12	70	87	47	-11
Pinto,Rene	21	R	25	C	a/a	TAM	354	15	3	228	5	61	127	51	-28
	22	R	26	C	aaa	TAM	282	9	1	205	5	63	145	60	-2
Plummer,Nick	21	L	25	LF	a/a	STL	386	9	8	216	10	62	92	97	-28
	22	L	26	LF	aaa	NYM	235	4	5	175	6	57	81	61	-76
Podkul,Nick	21	R	24	1B	aa	TOR	181	5	3	170	8	68	90	78	-14
	22	R	25	1B	aaa	TOR	175	4	2	175	12	60	79	49	-57
Polcovich,Kaden	21	B	22	2B	aa	SEA	128	2	3	113	9	63	47	74	-66
	22	B	23	2B	aa	SEA	451	8	12	188	8	69	71	110	-17
Pompey,Dalton	21	B	29	LF	a/a	LAA	127	3	1	196	7	70	66	80	-29
Pompey,Tristan	21	B	24	LF	a/a	MIA	164	1	0	167	13	54	44	71	-99
Porter,Logan	22	R	27	1B	a/a	KC	372	6	0	230	11	68	93	21	-25
Potts,Hudson	21	R	23	3B	aa	BOS	282	8	0	192	4	61	116	26	-47
	22	R	24	1B	a/a	BOS	274	9	1	196	6	62	132	36	-22
Pozo,Yohel	21	R	24	C	aaa	TEX	315	17	0	286	2	85	109	32	40
	22	R	25	C	aaa	TEX	253	3	0	243	3	85	71	32	12
Prato,Anthony	22	R	24	LF	aa	MIN	296	2	6	235	9	72	77	98	-1
Pratto,Nick	21	L	23	1B	a/a	KC	445	25	9	232	12	63	173	120	52
	22	L	24	1B	aaa	KC	303	9	5	179	10	59	102	97	-31
Pries,Micah	22	L	24	1B	aa	CLE	448	13	14	223	6	69	114	114	18
Prieto,Cesar	22	L	23	3B	aa	BAL	368	3	1	211	3	83	53	41	-8
Proctor,Ford	21	L	25	C	aa	TAM	308	9	3	198	13	61	91	81	-33
	22	L	26	C	aaa	SF	384	6	2	169	9	58	60	31	-91
Pruitt,Reggie	21	R	24	LF	a/a	TOR	200	2	10	147	7	49	74	138	-88
Qsar,Jordan	22	L	27	LF	a/a	TAM	361	10	7	169	7	44	149	129	-50
Quintana,Nick	22	R	25	3B	aa	CIN	189	3	0	188	9	69	75	32	-32
Rabago,Chris	21	R	28	C	aaa	COL	154	2	2	181	7	67	45	50	-64
	22	R	29	C	a/a	DET	157	1	1	139	5	55	59	80	-98
Rafaela,Ceddanne	22	R	22	CF	aa	BOS	284	8	10	246	4	76	106	131	39
Raley,Luke	21	L	27	RF	aaa	LA	272	13	5	225	6	66	120	90	0
	22	L	28	1B	aaa	TAM	227	8	5	221	7	57	114	79	-41
Ramos,Heliot	21	R	22	CF	a/a	SF	449	9	11	218	7	66	88	106	-18
	22	R	23	CF	aaa	SF	427	6	4	179	6	70	61	62	-40
Ramos,Henry	21	B	29	RF	aaa	ARI	256	6	2	256	5	74	73	62	-13
Raposo,Nick	21	R	23	C	aa	STL	116	1	1	211	8	74	40	80	-30
	22	R	24	C	aa	STL	204	3	1	192	6	69	93	47	-23
Rave,John	22	L	25	CF	a/a	KC	430	8	13	200	8	67	70	94	-31
Ray,Corey	21	L	27	CF	aaa	MIL	146	4	1	208	4	60	119	77	-30
	22	L	28	CF	a/a	MIL	288	8	6	158	4	55	117	87	-50
Read,Raudy	22	R	29	DH	a/a	CHW	307	12	0	215	8	71	117	17	-1
Redmond,Chandler	21	L	24	1B	aa	STL	122	3	0	235	5	52	121	19	-76
	22	L	25	1B	aa	STL	327	10	0	162	6	61	93	50	-55
Reed,Tyreque	21	R	24	LF	aa	BOS	138	2	0	209	9	56	101	29	-68
	22	R	25	1B	aa	BOS	167	4	0	161	6	57	95	19	-77

BATTER	yr	b	age	pos	lvl	org	ab	hr	sb	ba	bb%	ct%	px	sx	bpv
Reetz,Jakson	21	R	25	C	a/a	WAS	259	5	1	163	7	63	83	48	-50
	22	R	26	C	a/a	KC	367	15	1	202	5	66	133	52	-1
Refsnyder,Rob	22	R	31	RF	a/a	BOS	151	4	2	241	11	65	147	64	18
Reinheimer,Jack	21	R	29	SS	aaa	SEA	327	3	12	175	6	65	44	105	-60
Remillard,Zach	21	R	27	SS	a/a	CHW	313	9	10	163	8	63	79	104	-34
	22	R	28	SS	aaa	CHW	418	6	11	197	7	66	61	90	-43
Reyes,Pablo	21	R	28	2B	aaa	MIL	132	3	1	167	7	76	61	66	-11
	22	R	29	2B	aaa	MIL	385	7	9	194	6	76	75	90	6
Reyes,Ripken	22	B	25	RF	aa	SD	191	0	4	182	9	81	26	95	-6
Rijo,Wendell	21	R	26	2B	aa	ATL	322	12	7	204	8	70	99	74	0
	22	R	27	3B	aa	PHI	342	8	15	203	7	69	93	101	-2
Rincones,Diego	21	R	22	RF	aa	SF	186	7	1	257	7	78	92	67	21
	22	R	23	DH	aa	SF	334	7	0	218	3	84	56	19	-6
Rios,Edwin	22	L	28	3B	aaa	LA	189	5	0	180	5	55	139	37	-47
Ripken,Ryan	21	L	28	1B	aaa	BAL	150	1	1	130	5	60	41	59	-98
Ritter,Luke	22	R	25	3B	a/a	NYM	457	10	6	153	8	55	93	81	-63
Rivas,Leonardo	21	B	24	2B	aa	CIN	190	0	7	237	12	71	35	108	-28
	22	B	25	2B	a/a	CIN	311	5	12	188	8	69	68	92	-25
Rivera,Jeremy	21	B	26	LF	a/a	BOS	217	1	3	190	8	72	44	72	-38
Rivera,Laz	21	R	27	3B	a/a	CHW	218	5	7	219	4	68	77	96	-27
	22	R	28	2B	aaa	CHW	232	5	5	166	5	66	65	79	-47
Rivero,Sebastian	21	R	23	C	aaa	KC	150	2	1	225	5	68	66	73	-42
	22	R	24	C	aa	KC	156	3	1	179	5	74	110	47	10
Rizzo,Joe	21	L	23	3B	aa	SEA	380	9	3	216	8	67	79	54	-32
	22	L	24	3B	aa	SEA	488	14	1	214	6	74	89	48	-4
Roberts,Cody	22	R	26	C	a/a	BAL	266	6	0	209	6	64	96	20	-48
Robertson,Daniel	22	R	28	SS	aaa	PHI	197	3	0	150	7	67	77	45	-42
Robertson,Kramer	21	R	27	2B	aaa	STL	391	7	7	189	9	75	66	99	2
	22	R	28	SS	aaa	STL	410	6	17	167	10	69	53	98	-28
Robertson,Will	22	L	25	LF	aa	TOR	307	8	1	166	5	64	108	37	-36
Robinson,Chuckie	21	R	27	C	aa	CIN	210	6	1	202	9	72	74	57	-15
	22	R	28	C	a/a	CIN	203	4	3	206	4	69	73	61	-37
Robson,Jake	21	L	27	LF	a/a	DET	305	5	14	248	12	53	115	122	-32
	22	L	28	CF	aaa	DET	151	2	8	145	10	47	114	141	-57
Roby,Sean	22	R	24	3B	aa	SF	320	16	1	178	6	49	155	51	-49
Rocchio,Brayan	21	B	20	SS	aa	CLE	184	5	6	275	6	76	110	128	43
	22	B	21	SS	a/a	CLE	510	12	9	215	7	77	80	72	11
Rodriguez,Alfredo	21	R	27	2B	aaa	CIN	410	2	2	234	5	76	40	42	-41
	22	R	28	2B	a/a	WAS	150	1	1	153	2	63	49	28	-97
Rodriguez,Eric	22	R	24	C	a/a	CLE	151	1	0	145	4	63	52	23	-90
Rodriguez,Jose	22	R	21	SS	aa	CHW	440	9	28	232	6	83	68	132	40
Rodriguez,Julio	21	R	24	C	aa	STL	107	2	1	148	4	76	35	37	-49
	21	R	21	RF	aa	SEA	174	6	13	325	12	75	95	87	29
Rodriguez,Julio	22	R	25	C	aa	STL	218	5	1	175	10	66	68	34	-51
Rodriguez,Yorman	21	R	24	1B	a/a	SD	148	4	0	236	3	79	68	26	-16
	22	R	25	1B	aa	SD	491	9	3	214	5	79	64	51	-5
Roederer,Cole	22	L	23	LF	aa	CHC	181	5	2	189	5	65	82	49	-47
Rojas,Johan	22	R	22	CF	aa	PHI	235	3	20	222	6	79	58	170	29
Rojas,Jose	21	L	28	3B	aaa	LAA	216	4	2	179	6	77	60	62	-13
	22	L	29	1B	aaa	SF	274	10	3	192	6	69	113	86	7
Roller,Chris	21	R	25	LF	aa	CLE	246	1	11	172	7	66	51	110	-48
	22	R	26	CF	a/a	CLE	265	2	4	162	7	66	64	82	-44
Roman,Mitch	21	R	26	2B	aa	CHW	218	1	13	175	10	56	37	116	-88
Romero,Yoel	21	R	23	2B	aa	NYM	231	3	0	204	6	63	70	25	-72
Rooker,Brent	21	R	27	LF	aaa	MIN	220	14	1	201	12	56	168	52	0
	22	R	28	LF	aaa	KC	308	13	3	212	7	60	174	60	13
Rortvedt,Ben	21	L	24	C	aaa	MIN	122	4	0	223	6	68	94	30	-31
	22	L	25	C	aaa	NYY	154	4	0	173	8	55	116	28	-60
Rosa,Dylan	21	R	25	RF	a/a	DET	207	6	1	201	3	59	128	86	-27
	22	R	26	LF	a/a	DET	164	5	3	143	8	38	129	69	-107
Rosario,Eguy	21	R	22	SS	aa	SD	420	9	23	243	9	71	94	104	11
	22	R	23	2B	aaa	SD	490	12	12	211	7	73	93	92	9
Rosario,Jeisson	21	L	22	CF	aa	BOS	346	2	8	212	10	65	56	75	-52
	22	L	23	CF	aa	NYY	362	8	9	200	12	74	83	83	11
Ruiz,Esteury	21	R	22	LF	aa	SD	309	7	28	214	7	74	78	138	15
	22	R	23	CF	a/a	MIL	437	11	59	273	10	74	102	150	44
Ruiz,Keibert	21	R	23	C	aaa	WAS	284	17	0	282	8	87	135	21	80
Ruiz,Rio	21	L	27	2B	aaa	COL	224	4	2	245	5	80	90	62	22
Ruta,Ben	21	L	27	LF	a/a	SD	270	3	4	129	7	69	58	65	-42
Rutherford,Blake	21	L	24	LF	aaa	CHW	448	8	3	201	3	68	81	79	-29
	22	L	25	LF	aaa	CHW	439	9	5	203	3	75	75	64	-14
Sabol,Blake	22	L	24	C	a/a	PIT	447	11	7	230	8	67	109	102	4
Salazar,Cesar	21	L	25	C	a/a	HOU	111	6	1	212	5	74	127	61	29
	22	L	26	C	a/a	HOU	366	10	5	198	5	76	77	64	-6
Sanchez,Ali	21	R	24	C	aaa	STL	251	3	0	220	4	79	40	20	-37
	22	R	25	C	aaa	DET	252	4	1	207	8	65	75	49	-47
Sanchez,Jesus	21	L	24	RF	aaa	MIA	141	8	1	303	7	76	124	85	44
	22	L	25	RF	aaa	MIA	159	4	3	246	8	70	76	65	-20
Sanchez,Lolo	22	R	23	LF	aa	PIT	212	3	5	187	10	79	44	59	-9
Sanchez,Yolbert	21	R	24	2B	aa	CHW	143	3	3	307	3	87	58	51	18
	22	R	25	2B	a/a	CHW	494	2	7	218	5	81	29	50	-27
Sanchez,Yolmer	21	B	29	2B	aaa	ATL	310	6	4	170	7	65	64	79	-49
	22	B	30	2B	aaa	NYM	322	6	3	167	9	63	72	60	-50
Sands,Donny	21	R	25	C	a/a	NYY	341	15	2	219	7	80	88	39	19
	22	R	26	C	aaa	PHI	201	3	1	239	11	73	60	44	-22
Santana,Cristian	21	R	24	3B	aaa	LA	331	6	0	254	2	76	67	24	-30
	22	R	25	3B	aaa	CIN	457	9	1	230	5	71	75	21	-38
Santos,Jhonny	21	R	25	CF	aa	OAK	322	9	1	196	7	69	83	36	-29
Scheffler,Matt	22	R	24	C	aa	SEA	244	1	7	191	10	71	32	108	-37
Scheiner,Jake	21	R	26	1B	aa	SEA	395	13	1	203	8	57	113	75	-39
	22	R	27	1B	aa	SEA	477	13	2	181	9	68	100	44	-17

BATTER	yr	b	age	pos	lvl	org	ab	hr	sb	ba	bb%	ct%	px	sx	bpv
Schneemann,Daniel	22	L	25	3B	a/a	CLE	387	4	12	155	7	69	43	109	-42
Schneider,Davis	22	R	23	2B	a/a	TOR	226	6	8	227	10	67	105	121	11
Schuemann,Max	21	R	24	2B	a/a	OAK	245	1	12	255	7	75	56	112	-6
	22	R	25	2B	a/a	OAK	325	5	14	202	9	63	73	112	-37
Schunk,Aaron	22	R	25	3B	aa	COL	450	9	4	211	4	72	93	62	-8
Schuyler,Jay	21	R	24	C	a/a	CIN	127	2	0	157	7	52	79	18	-107
Schwarz,JJ	21	R	25	C	aa	OAK	254	4	0	194	9	68	64	34	-45
	22	R	26	C	a/a	OAK	276	5	1	212	8	64	82	32	-50
Schwecke,Trevor	22	R	25	1B	a/a	TOR	206	4	1	183	6	58	93	88	-52
Scott,Connor	22	L	23	RF	aa	PIT	380	4	7	205	6	73	82	87	-2
Scott,Stephen	22	L	25	C	aa	BOS	206	4	5	197	12	72	86	90	11
Seagle,Chandler	21	R	25	C	aa	SD	158	1	0	152	3	67	51	71	-62
	22	R	26	C	aa	SD	239	2	1	154	6	62	57	50	-77
Selman,Shane	22	R	26	RF	aa	OAK	270	6	1	155	5	57	95	69	-62
Senger,Hayden	21	R	24	C	aa	NYM	181	2	0	199	6	58	85	48	-72
	22	R	25	C	a/a	NYM	288	3	2	181	4	54	80	72	-87
Shackelford,Aaron	22	L	26	1B	a/a	PIT	413	15	7	177	6	61	125	86	-15
Sharpe,Chris	21	R	25	CF	aaa	PIT	317	3	4	161	8	61	90	66	-46
	22	R	26	CF	a/a	PHI	232	3	6	158	9	58	88	101	-45
Shenton,Austin	22	L	24	3B	aa	TAM	195	5	0	185	9	56	105	46	-57
Shewmake,Braden	21	L	24	SS	aa	ATL	324	10	3	206	4	74	86	86	3
	22	L	25	SS	aaa	ATL	278	5	7	222	6	76	77	104	11
Short,Zack	21	R	26	SS	aaa	DET	157	7	1	202	14	67	112	45	0
	22	R	27	SS	aaa	DET	459	6	7	173	11	61	88	76	-38
Siani,Mike	22	L	23	CF	a/a	CIN	492	11	37	217	9	78	73	131	28
Sierra,Magneuris	22	L	26	CF	aaa	LAA	279	4	12	216	5	77	52	113	-5
Sierra,Miguelangel	21	R	24	2B	aaa	HOU	207	7	2	153	6	54	106	113	-51
Simoneit,Will	22	R	26	C	a/a	OAK	250	3	1	190	9	64	77	54	-44
Sims,Demetrius	21	R	26	SS	aa	MIA	276	3	13	159	8	51	58	91	-102
	22	R	27	SS	a/a	MIA	199	2	7	198	6	48	91	109	-87
Skoug,Evan	22	L	27	C	aa	CHW	215	8	1	173	10	56	140	48	-28
Slaughter,Jake	22	R	26	3B	aa	CHC	328	12	16	217	6	68	104	98	1
Smith,Armani	22	R	24	LF	aa	SF	263	1	2	191	9	61	60	51	-73
Smith,Dominic	22	L	27	1B	aaa	NYM	218	6	2	207	7	76	78	64	2
Smith,Josh	21	L	24	SS	aa	TEX	102	2	6	260	13	78	70	62	13
	22	L	25	3B	aaa	TEX	221	3	5	219	8	71	80	110	-2
Smith,Kevin	21	R	25	SS	aaa	TOR	355	19	16	259	10	69	161	126	64
	22	R	26	SS	aaa	OAK	332	6	3	185	4	58	84	67	-71
Smith-Njigba,Canaan	21	L	22	LF	a/a	PIT	240	4	10	225	13	67	70	76	-26
	22	L	23	LF	aaa	PIT	184	1	5	233	11	69	92	111	5
Soderstrom,Tyler	22	L	21	C	a/a	OAK	170	5	0	222	4	69	69	44	-45
Sogard,Nick	22	B	25	3B	a/a	BOS	402	2	12	210	9	75	60	93	-6
Solak,Nick	22	R	27	LF	aaa	TEX	223	5	3	200	7	71	91	76	-2
Sosa,Lenyn	21	R	21	SS	aa	CHW	117	1	0	198	2	74	45	43	-51
	22	R	22	SS	a/a	CHW	483	18	2	260	5	80	89	44	18
Soto,Livan	22	L	22	SS	aa	LAA	456	4	12	230	9	75	44	69	-25
Spanberger,Chad	21	L	26	RF	a/a	MIL	302	9	1	160	7	53	114	61	-65
Stankiewicz,Drew	21	B	28	2B	aaa	MIN	146	1	1	206	9	68	85	68	-20
	22	B	29	2B	a/a	ARI	342	6	3	153	6	60	88	82	-53
Steer,Spencer	21	R	24	3B	aa	MIN	249	10	3	204	6	67	109	97	-4
	22	R	25	3B	a/a	CIN	427	18	3	229	8	75	125	60	35
Stefanic,Michael	21	R	25	2B	a/a	LAA	491	11	4	265	7	81	64	42	2
	22	R	26	2B	aaa	LAA	287	2	2	228	9	90	42	65	33
Stephen,Josh	21	L	24	LF	a/a	PHI	325	6	3	176	8	68	68	62	-36
Stevenson,Andrew	22	L	28	CF	aaa	WAS	545	10	24	212	5	69	87	131	-4
Stevenson,Cal	21	L	25	CF	aa	TAM	295	6	12	206	12	68	76	95	-13
	22	L	26	CF	aaa	OAK	257	3	8	198	8	74	47	103	-18
Stewart,Christin	21	L	28	RF	aaa	DET	303	16	2	212	7	62	145	96	9
	22	L	29	LF	aaa	BOS	338	11	5	176	9	52	124	60	-54
Stokes Jr.,Troy	21	R	25	RF	aaa	MIL	207	3	6	147	8	67	55	115	-35
Stokes,Madison	21	R	25	1B	aa	PHI	342	8	1	201	6	63	89	52	-47
	22	R	26	CF	a/a	PHI	162	3	4	131	6	45	106	99	-91
Stovall,Hunter	22	R	26	SS	aa	COL	393	6	6	216	5	74	82	78	-3
Stowers,Josh	21	R	24	RF	aa	TEX	305	16	17	193	9	61	135	139	14
	22	R	25	CF	aa	TEX	356	6	14	168	8	61	85	110	-36
Stowers,Kyle	21	L	23	RF	a/a	BAL	318	16	4	245	10	61	142	46	-8
	22	L	24	CF	aaa	BAL	349	14	2	212	7	66	145	58	14
Strahm,Kellen	22	R	25	RF	aa	TEX	354	6	7	213	10	68	66	79	-28
Strumpf,Chase	21	R	23	3B	aa	CHC	214	5	1	180	12	67	98	30	-20
	22	R	24	2B	aa	CHC	393	13	1	178	10	51	137	63	-44
Stubbs,Garrett	21	L	28	C	aaa	HOU	113	1	2	194	14	67	49	67	-44
Sugilio,Andy	21	L	25	RF	aa	SF	152	1	4	209	5	69	33	68	-66
Sullivan,Brett	21	L	27	C	aaa	TAM	309	7	6	182	7	78	75	77	13
	22	L	28	C	aaa	SD	421	4	1	187	4	81	58	75	5
Susnara,Tim	21	L	25	C	aa	CHC	112	2	0	201	9	52	86	41	-92
Suwinski,Jack	21	L	23	RF	aa	PIT	367	13	8	223	13	63	113	87	-5
	22	L	24	RF	a/a	PIT	168	5	1	206	6	57	150	64	-17
Swaggerty,Travis	22	L	25	CF	aaa	PIT	398	5	13	201	9	66	72	121	-23
Swihart,Blake	21	B	29	C	aaa	WAS	178	4	1	155	9	64	69	80	-46
Talley,L.J.	21	L	24	1B	aa	TOR	296	6	2	206	7	75	72	64	-8
	22	L	25	1B	a/a	TOR	394	9	8	212	6	74	76	95	-1
Taveras,Leody	21	B	23	CF	aaa	TEX	322	13	10	209	10	67	117	95	12
	22	B	24	CF	aaa	TEX	204	4	4	227	4	72	85	99	-3
Tawa,Tim	22	R	23	2B	aa	ARI	218	3	2	152	6	71	47	50	-51
Taylor,Carson	22	B	23	C	aa	LA	269	3	0	207	6	71	51	22	-52
Taylor,Chandler	21	L	25	RF	a/a	HOU	199	6	5	120	10	40	99	65	-120
Taylor,Samad	21	R	23	2B	aa	TOR	319	12	22	254	9	61	122	112	-5
	22	R	24	2B	aaa	TOR	244	7	17	220	8	71	91	133	15
Tejeda,Anderson	21	B	23	SS	a/a	TEX	274	9	8	158	7	48	120	90	-69
Tena,Jose	22	L	21	SS	a/a	CLE	535	10	5	224	3	70	81	87	-20
Tenerowicz,Robbie	21	R	26	3B	aa	CIN	303	11	2	221	6	63	118	66	-18
	22	R	27	1B	a/a	CIN	193	5	1	206	10	67	97	52	-17
Teodosio,Bryce	22	R	23	CF	aa	LAA	369	9	17	152	7	49	93	94	-86
Terry,Curtis	21	R	25	1B	aaa	TEX	364	16	2	226	5	70	122	63	8
	22	R	26	1B	aaa	MIN	296	6	0	188	8	77	79	38	0
Thaiss,Matt	21	L	26	C	aaa	LAA	379	10	1	203	8	69	86	61	-17
	22	L	27	C	aaa	LAA	284	6	4	188	8	73	75	82	-8
Theroux,Collin	21	R	27	C	a/a	OAK	192	3	0	100	6	42	67	36	-154
Thomas,Lane	21	R	26	CF	aaa	WAS	126	4	2	236	6	66	102	96	-12
Thompson,Bubba	21	R	23	CF	aa	TEX	429	13	21	248	5	69	110	150	21
	22	R	24	CF	aaa	TEX	346	8	30	235	4	68	73	161	-13
Thompson,David	21	R	28	1B	aaa	NYM	219	8	6	160	6	59	105	98	-39
Thompson,Trayce	22	R	31	LF	aaa	DET	154	9	1	219	5	60	192	87	32
Tilson,Charlie	21	L	29	CF	aaa	PHI	203	1	8	235	5	70	56	132	-25
Tocci,Carlos	21	R	26	CF	a/a	WAS	120	1	0	168	6	75	34	13	-56
Toerner,Justin	21	L	25	CF	a/a	STL	271	5	2	162	8	61	69	58	-64
	22	L	26	CF	a/a	STL	277	3	5	157	10	58	65	77	-71
Toffey,Will	21	L	26	3B	a/a	SF	175	5	5	168	11	41	110	86	-98
	22	L	27	3B	aaa	PHI	322	6	6	181	8	54	118	108	-38
Toglia,Michael	21	B	23	1B	aa	COL	143	4	2	199	10	63	121	72	-8
	22	B	24	1B	a/a	COL	429	19	5	203	7	63	129	64	-10
Tolman,Mitchell	21	L	27	3B	a/a	SF	296	6	3	202	6	67	84	93	-22
	22	L	28	2B	aaa	CLE	358	6	3	175	7	69	82	65	-24
Tom,Ka ai	22	L	28	LF	aaa	SF	268	5	3	170	7	62	92	55	-47
Torres,Bryan	21	L	24	C	aa	SF	132	0	5	242	4	73	46	105	-29
Tostado,Frankie	21	L	23	1B	aa	SF	366	10	1	216	6	72	87	64	-10
	22	L	24	1B	aa	SF	292	7	2	238	5	71	93	57	-12
Tovar,Ezequiel	22	R	21	SS	a/a	COL	285	9	10	279	5	76	103	105	31
Tovar,Wilfredo	21	R	30	SS	aaa	NYM	355	4	8	189	7	82	39	66	-5
Travis,Sam	21	R	28	1B	aaa	SEA	277	7	1	190	5	58	105	48	-59
Trejo,Alan	21	R	25	SS	aaa	COL	334	11	1	238	4	74	140	87	45
	22	R	26	SS	aaa	COL	274	9	1	228	2	73	112	56	6
Triolo,Jared	22	R	24	3B	aa	PIT	425	5	16	229	9	77	67	112	14
Tromp,Chadwick	21	R	26	C	aaa	ATL	209	4	0	185	3	71	78	29	-35
	22	R	27	C	aaa	ATL	249	9	0	208	5	73	95	33	-11
Tucker,Cole	21	B	25	SS	aaa	PIT	220	4	6	182	12	70	73	91	-8
	22	B	26	SS	aaa	ARI	151	1	3	148	5	62	39	63	-88
Turang,Brice	21	L	22	SS	a/a	MIL	431	5	15	222	9	78	54	90	3
	22	L	23	SS	aaa	MIL	532	9	23	233	8	74	64	111	-3
Turchin,Doran	21	R	24	RF	aa	BAL	161	6	3	155	8	55	118	61	-51
Twine,Justin	21	R	26	2B	a/a	MIA	237	4	9	184	2	51	92	169	-67
Unroe,Riley	21	B	26	2B	a/a	ATL	121	2	2	176	7	74	48	97	-20
	22	B	27	SS	aaa	SEA	368	5	15	190	9	70	62	112	-17
Urbaez,Francisco	22	R	25	2B	aa	CIN	164	2	1	228	8	77	74	66	5
Valdez,Enmanuel	22	L	24	2B	a/a	BOS	500	18	5	251	8	72	127	68	28
Valente,John	21	R	26	DH	aa	DET	229	3	7	254	6	83	68	98	30
	22	R	27	3B	aaa	DET	249	1	9	227	6	88	47	112	36
Valera,Breyvic	21	B	29	LF	aaa	TOR	150	3	6	259	11	84	73	95	48
Valera,George	22	L	22	RF	a/a	CLE	484	16	2	207	9	66	111	63	-8
Valera,Leonel	22	R	23	SS	aa	LA	321	10	15	239	6	57	111	140	-26
Valerio,Felix	22	R	22	2B	aa	MIL	417	9	21	188	8	78	59	109	9
Vance,Cobie	22	R	25	3B	aa	MIA	395	3	1	198	5	80	47	38	-19
Vargas,Miguel	21	R	22	3B	aa	LA	327	12	5	275	7	80	86	75	28
	22	R	23	3B	aaa	LA	438	11	9	236	8	79	91	92	37
Vasquez,Jeremy	21	L	25	1B	aa	NYM	105	1	0	129	9	62	40	27	-94
	22	L	26	1B	aa	NYM	365	2	0	178	7	75	46	12	-42
Vavra,Terrin	21	L	24	2B	aa	BAL	149	4	4	207	12	69	96	92	7
	22	L	25	2B	aaa	BAL	173	1	3	255	9	75	74	80	5
Vazquez,Luis	22	R	23	SS	a/a	CHC	409	6	6	178	4	72	60	78	-30
Velazquez,Andrew	21	B	27	SS	aaa	NYY	264	5	21	217	10	59	108	132	-17
Velazquez,Nelson	21	R	23	RF	aa	CHC	124	6	4	253	6	69	149	97	36
	22	R	24	CF	a/a	CHC	203	9	8	187	8	52	167	105	-10
Vicuna,Kevin	21	R	23	SS	a/a	TOR	290	2	10	217	4	73	48	78	-36
	22	R	24	2B	aa	PHI	312	1	6	223	4	76	53	98	-17
Vientos,Mark	21	R	22	3B	a/a	NYM	312	17	0	227	7	62	147	25	-12
	22	R	23	3B	aaa	NYM	378	16	0	223	7	61	123	37	-30
Vilade,Ryan	21	R	22	LF	aaa	COL	468	5	8	255	5	80	67	100	14
	22	R	23	RF	aaa	COL	368	3	6	205	7	81	49	92	5
Villar,David	21	R	24	3B	aa	SF	385	14	4	233	9	67	124	67	5
	22	R	25	3B	aaa	SF	298	15	1	210	10	62	158	54	14
Viloria,Meibrys	21	L	24	C	a/a	KC	281	5	2	208	12	62	84	52	-45
	22	L	25	C	aaa	TEX	175	3	1	210	12	67	88	53	-22
Vinsky,David	21	R	23	LF	aa	STL	210	2	2	163	9	58	47	82	-88
Volpe,Anthony	22	R	21	SS	a/a	NYY	511	16	38	210	9	74	110	144	47
Vosler,Jason	21	L	28	3B	aaa	SF	261	8	0	216	8	78	81	41	7
	22	L	29	3B	aaa	SF	360	9	2	167	5	64	79	62	-52
Waddell,Luke	22	L	24	SS	aa	ATL	162	2	2	233	10	84	58	48	19
Wagner,Brandon	21	L	26	1B	a/a	NYY	155	3	1	137	12	42	68	39	-138
Wagner,Will	22	L	24	2B	aa	HOU	251	4	3	196	8	73	66	83	-13
Walker,Jordan	22	R	20	3B	aa	STL	461	10	13	238	7	73	90	102	8
Walker,Steele	21	L	25	RF	a/a	TEX	423	11	8	202	6	75	73	82	-2
	22	L	26	RF	aaa	SF	280	5	5	201	5	78	65	73	-4
Wall,Forrest	21	L	26	CF	aaa	TOR	297	1	30	234	8	66	62	166	-19
	22	L	27	CF	aaa	SEA	412	3	30	178	5	60	53	129	-65
Wallner,Matt	22	L	25	RF	a/a	MIN	458	16	6	215	12	56	153	78	-6
Walls,Taylor	21	B	25	SS	aaa	TAM	178	7	8	213	16	61	116	110	3
Ward,Drew	21	L	27	1B	aa	DET	275	11	1	194	8	56	118	60	-45
Ward,Ryan	22	L	24	LF	aa	LA	459	20	3	207	5	71	109	55	-2
Warmoth,Logan	21	R	26	CF	aaa	TOR	342	8	14	201	12	54	99	108	-48
	22	R	27	RF	aaa	TOR	293	5	10	182	8	62	97	100	-28
Waters,Drew	21	R	23	LF	aaa	ATL	404	9	23	216	9	62	93	113	-26
	22	R	24	CF	aaa	KC	313	6	11	212	6	66	84	134	-15
Watson,Zach	21	R	24	CF	aa	BAL	183	9	4	207	3	66	123	78	-7
	22	R	25	CF	aa	BAL	331	6	3	158	4	58	77	89	-72

BATTER	yr	b	age	pos	lvl	org	ab	hr	sb	ba	bb%	ct%	px	sx	bpv
Weber,Andy	21	L	24	SS	aa	CHC	131	0	0	182	7	56	97	64	-65
	22	L	25	SS	aa	CHC	280	2	4	228	5	68	51	80	-53
Wells,Austin	22	L	23	C	aa	NYY	211	9	5	217	9	68	110	88	7
Wendzel,Davis	21	R	24	SS	a/a	TEX	187	5	1	201	9	69	89	43	-20
	22	R	25	SS	aaa	TEX	314	9	1	152	6	65	79	40	-50
Westbrook,Jamie	21	R	26	2B	a/a	MIL	320	9	3	225	6	79	74	79	13
	22	R	27	DH	aaa	DET	429	6	1	192	7	78	59	32	-16
Westburg,Jordan	21	R	22	SS	aa	BAL	112	3	2	202	8	70	97	96	5
	22	R	23	SS	a/a	BAL	544	20	8	219	8	70	125	82	22
Whalen,Seaver	21	R	26	1B	aa	TAM	187	4	4	168	3	72	82	89	-11
Whatley,Matt	21	R	25	C	aa	TEX	227	3	6	173	11	60	50	57	-81
	22	R	26	C	a/a	TEX	189	2	1	167	5	70	48	64	-50
Whitcomb,Shay	22	R	24	2B	aa	HOU	461	12	13	170	5	57	103	111	-43
Whitefield,Aaron	21	R	25	CF	aa	MIN	397	4	25	214	7	67	49	124	-39
	22	R	26	LF	aa	LAA	301	6	17	197	7	62	93	126	-24
Whitley,Garrett	21	R	24	LF	a/a	TAM	293	10	9	195	9	59	130	136	0
	22	R	25	RF	a/a	MIL	291	7	12	169	12	52	112	101	-48
Wiemer,Joey	22	R	23	RF	a/a	MIL	484	15	21	207	7	64	120	118	4
Williams,Chris	22	R	26	1B	a/a	MIN	422	16	1	184	8	59	127	39	-34
Williams,Nick	21	L	28	RF	aaa	CHW	154	0	5	105	8	62	26	109	-81
Wilson,Cody	21	R	25	CF	a/a	WAS	154	0	5	105	8	62	26	109	-81
Wilson,Izzy	21	L	24	RF	aa	LAA	296	16	19	209	9	61	121	95	-13
	22	L	24	RF	a/a	BOS	314	8	8	179	8	65	106	110	-5
Wilson,Marcus	21	R	25	RF	aaa	SEA	363	10	11	190	12	50	114	104	-52
	22	R	26	RF	aaa	SEA	293	9	8	154	9	45	155	108	-41
Wilson,Weston	21	R	27	1B	aaa	MIL	217	10	5	203	8	66	120	72	0
	22	R	28	3B	aaa	MIL	416	7	10	164	6	59	76	87	-65
Wilson,William	21	R	23	SS	aa	SF	196	3	1	161	8	54	79	40	-89
	22	R	24	SS	a/a	SF	224	7	1	173	8	59	102	48	-50

BATTER	yr	b	age	pos	lvl	org	ab	hr	sb	ba	bb%	ct%	px	sx	bpv
Winaker,Matt	21	L	26	1B	a/a	NYM	189	1	1	189	10	67	50	63	-51
	22	L	27	1B	aa	NYM	202	2	1	117	9	64	45	82	-63
Windham,Bryce	22	L	26	C	aa	CHC	253	2	1	145	9	79	39	52	-18
Winn,Masyn	22	R	20	SS	aa	STL	345	6	17	197	7	73	81	109	8
Wisely,Brett	22	L	23	2B	a/a	TAM	451	10	22	223	9	71	92	134	17
Wiseman,Rhett	21	L	24	RF	aa	WAS	286	7	1	179	4	55	108	51	-69
Witherspoon,Grant	22	L	26	RF	a/a	TAM	415	10	10	202	7	66	100	97	-12
Witt Jr.,Bobby	21	R	21	SS	a/a	KC	497	24	23	263	7	73	138	123	55
Wong,Connor	21	R	25	C	aaa	BOS	199	6	5	224	3	67	108	69	-18
	22	R	26	C	aaa	BOS	323	9	4	232	5	71	103	54	-6
Wong,Kean	21	L	26	2B	aaa	LAA	189	2	6	250	4	78	54	89	-7
	22	L	27	3B	aaa	LAA	497	2	21	181	6	68	36	106	-53
Workman,Gage	22	B	23	SS	aa	DET	475	9	21	193	5	53	139	150	-20
Wrenn,Stephen	21	R	27	LF	aa	SEA	308	5	17	191	7	55	77	124	-66
Yang,Eric	22	R	24	C	a/a	CIN	151	2	1	172	8	62	71	47	-62
Yanqui,Yoel	21	L	25	1B	aa	CIN	272	6	3	200	9	63	71	80	-48
Yepez,Juan	21	R	23	1B	a/a	STL	367	17	1	228	8	75	122	31	24
	22	R	24	1B	aaa	STL	188	9	0	211	5	72	118	29	5
Yerzy,Andy	22	L	24	1B	aa	ARI	290	6	1	168	9	66	86	48	-32
Young,Andy	21	R	27	2B	aaa	ARI	194	5	1	215	5	49	169	93	-30
	22	R	28	LF	a/a	WAS	318	9	2	162	8	54	110	34	-68
Young,Chavez	21	B	24	CF	aa	TOR	279	5	14	222	8	67	80	108	-19
	22	B	25	CF	aaa	TOR	214	4	15	194	9	69	63	142	-12
Young,Jared	21	L	26	1B	a/a	CHC	256	6	3	234	7	74	81	78	2
	22	L	27	1B	aaa	CHC	400	10	2	170	6	66	91	72	-29
Young,Wyatt	22	L	23	2B	a/a	NYM	445	5	5	216	9	72	61	79	-18
Yurchak,Justin	21	L	25	1B	aa	LA	115	1	0	311	7	77	66	28	-17
	22	L	26	1B	aa	LA	393	6	1	218	8	81	58	35	-2

PITCHER	yr	t	age	lvl	org	ip	era	whip	bf/g	k%	bb%	k-bb	hr/9	h%	s%	bpv
Abbott,Andrew	22	L	23	aa	CIN	91	5.05	1.44	19.4	27	10	17	0.8	35	65	95
Abbott,Cory	21	R	26	aaa	CHC	96	6.57	1.72	23.0	23	13	11	1.9	35	65	38
Acton,Garrett	22	R	24	a/a	OAK	72	3.93	1.32	5.9	25	8	17	1.2	33	75	90
Adames,Jose	21	R	28	a/a	BOS	37	5.05	1.61	4.7	21	13	8	0.8	33	69	62
	22	R	29	a/a	LA	47	4.69	1.71	5.3	25	17	8	0.4	34	71	87
Adams,Derrick	21	L	24	aa	KC	51	10.14	2.34	12.0	14	13	1	1.8	41	57	-11
Adams,Mike	21	R	27	aaa	PHI	37	4.39	1.68	5.6	14	12	2	0.3	34	72	47
	22	R	28	a/a	PHI	64	6.09	1.79	7.6	16	11	5	1.7	34	69	9
Alexy,A.J.	21	R	23	a/a	TEX	67	1.86	1.05	16.3	25	10	14	0.8	23	88	94
	22	R	24	aaa	TEX	96	5.22	1.64	13.8	19	11	8	1.8	32	74	27
Allard,Kolby	22	L	25	aaa	TEX	89	4.20	1.31	18.4	24	9	15	1.7	29	75	66
Alldred,Cam	21	L	25	a/a	PIT	68	2.30	1.18	8.3	17	11	6	0.9	23	85	57
	22	L	26	aaa	PIT	67	4.17	1.46	6.8	17	9	8	0.6	33	71	61
Allen,Logan	22	L	25	aaa	COL	53	7.21	1.76	9.0	14	7	7	2.0	36	62	5
	22	L	24	a/a	CLE	134	4.45	1.28	20.4	27	8	19	1.0	33	67	104
Allgeyer,Nick	21	L	25	aaa	TOR	90	7.50	1.98	19.6	15	13	2	2.0	35	65	-8
	22	L	26	aaa	TOR	101	6.53	1.60	12.7	17	9	7	1.8	32	62	19
Amaya,Luis	21	L	23	aa	SF	54	6.29	1.66	7.3	24	13	11	1.4	34	64	57
Anderson,Grant	22	R	25	a/a	TEX	70	3.10	1.23	6.1	25	7	19	0.8	33	78	115
Arias,Jaime	22	L	23	a/a	CLE	48	5.73	1.59	14.1	15	7	7	1.1	34	65	38
Armbruester,Justin	22	R	24	aa	BAL	64	3.77	1.06	17.7	20	6	14	2.0	23	76	65
Ashby,Aaron	21	L	23	aaa	MIL	64	4.36	1.36	12.8	33	11	22	0.5	37	67	127
Assad,Javier	21	R	24	aa	CHC	94	5.98	1.69	19.3	15	8	7	1.2	36	66	30
	22	R	25	a/a	CHC	111	2.45	1.21	19.5	20	7	13	0.7	30	83	89
Avila,Pedro	21	R	24	a/a	SD	76	3.96	1.34	8.8	21	11	11	0.5	30	70	83
	22	R	25	aaa	SD	112	3.67	1.22	15.1	22	9	13	0.9	28	73	83
Bachar,Lake	22	R	27	aa	SD	46	6.35	1.57	7.5	17	9	8	1.8	32	63	24
Bachman,Sam	22	R	23	aa	LAA	45	3.54	1.43	16.0	13	12	1	0.7	27	77	38
Bain,Jeff	21	R	25	a/a	ARI	63	4.97	1.54	9.8	18	7	11	0.9	36	69	61
	22	R	26	a/a	ARI	71	3.13	1.12	6.2	21	6	15	1.3	27	79	90
Baird,Michael	22	R	27	aa	COL	68	4.78	1.35	16.7	19	7	12	2.4	28	76	29
Baker,Dylan	21	R	29	a/a	CIN	51	7.98	2.29	16.4	11	11	0	1.5	41	66	-12
Balazovic,Jordan	21	R	23	aa	MIN	97	3.96	1.50	21.0	21	9	12	0.8	35	75	70
	22	R	24	aaa	MIN	72	6.65	1.88	15.4	18	9	9	2.0	38	69	17
Baldonado,Alberto	21	L	28	a/a	WAS	42	3.69	1.21	5.0	21	6	15	0.6	31	70	106
	22	L	29	aaa	WAS	64	4.30	1.29	4.7	23	11	12	0.7	29	67	81
Banda,Anthony	21	L	28	aaa	NYM	51	6.32	1.69	17.8	18	8	10	1.4	37	64	39
Barker,Luke	21	R	29	aaa	MIL	62	2.65	0.92	4.4	26	5	21	1.4	24	82	140
Barria,Jaime	21	R	25	aaa	LAA	49	3.99	1.27	20.0	14	4	10	1.5	30	75	67
Bash,Andrew	22	R	26	a/a	TOR	97	4.55	1.29	11.8	14	9	5	0.4	28	63	59
Battenfield,Peyton	21	R	24	aa	CLE	72	3.65	0.98	19.5	25	5	20	1.3	26	68	128
	22	R	25	aaa	CLE	155	3.10	1.20	22.3	14	8	6	0.8	26	77	53
Baumann,Mike	21	R	26	a/a	BAL	67	4.34	1.30	17.3	18	12	6	1.0	26	69	53
	22	R	27	aaa	BAL	60	4.37	1.41	12.7	24	9	14	1.0	33	71	82
Baz,Shane	21	R	22	a/a	TAM	80	2.27	0.84	17.3	35	4	30	1.0	27	81	224
Bazardo,Eduard	22	R	27	aaa	BOS	58	3.84	1.63	7.0	18	8	10	0.8	37	78	62
Beck,Tristan	22	R	26	a/a	SF	112	5.34	1.44	20.8	19	7	12	0.8	34	63	74
Beede,Tyler	21	R	28	aaa	SF	50	6.98	2.05	15.3	16	19	-3	1.1	33	66	23
Beeter,Clayton	22	R	24	aa	NYY	77	4.78	1.48	13.2	32	13	19	1.3	35	71	98
Belen,Carlos	21	R	25	aa	SD	55	4.67	1.60	6.3	13	7	7	0.3	36	69	56
	22	R	26	a/a	SD	59	3.46	1.25	5.9	14	7	7	0.6	28	73	58
Bello,Brayan	21	R	22	aa	BOS	65	5.09	1.46	18.6	27	8	19	0.7	38	65	110
	22	R	23	a/a	BOS	98	2.40	1.04	21.1	28	9	19	0.5	27	79	126
Bellomy,Bear	22	R	26	aa	PIT	55	7.30	1.64	7.9	14	4	9	1.8	36	58	31
Bennett,Nick	21	L	24	aa	MIL	47	5.51	1.44	20.1	18	12	6	2.2	25	69	15
	22	L	25	a/a	MIL	126	5.31	1.45	20.7	19	9	11	1.4	32	66	51
Bergner,Austin	22	R	25	a/a	DET	122	3.53	1.18	18.1	19	9	10	1.1	25	74	64
Bermudez,Jonathan	21	L	26	a/a	HOU	113	3.55	1.24	18.4	26	7	18	0.9	32	74	109
	22	L	27	aaa	SF	81	8.67	1.86	15.8	16	11	5	2.1	35	55	2
Biasi,Dante	22	L	25	aa	KC	85	3.99	1.47	16.6	18	13	5	0.6	29	73	59
Bibee,Tanner	22	R	23	aa	CLE	75	1.90	0.91	21.6	25	5	20	0.5	26	81	162
Bido,Osvaldo	21	R	26	a/a	PIT	104	5.77	1.53	19.7	17	8	8	1.2	33	64	40
	22	R	27	aaa	PIT	112	4.77	1.62	15.6	18	13	5	1.3	31	74	38
Bielak,Brandon	22	R	26	aaa	HOU	90	3.03	1.43	16.7	18	11	8	0.5	31	79	68
Bilous,Jason	21	R	24	aa	CHW	65	8.88	1.86	17.9	22	11	12	1.3	40	51	50
	22	R	25	a/a	CHW	107	5.99	1.74	15.8	21	15	6	1.2	33	67	49
Black,Grant	21	R	27	a/a	STL	60	4.90	1.65	8.9	18	12	6	0.6	34	70	53
	22	R	28	a/a	STL	79	3.43	1.33	7.3	12	9	3	0.9	27	77	34
Blackburn,Paul	21	R	28	aaa	OAK	90	5.10	1.73	24.1	15	7	8	0.7	39	71	50
Blackwood,Nolan	21	R	26	aaa	DET	61	6.84	1.71	7.5	14	9	5	0.9	35	59	30
	22	R	27	aaa	DET	51	3.99	1.48	5.0	13	9	5	1.4	30	78	18
Blanco,Ronel	21	R	28	aaa	HOU	45	3.70	1.10	4.2	25	9	16	1.5	24	74	80
	22	R	29	aaa	HOU	46	3.67	1.28	4.3	24	10	14	1.5	27	79	63
Blewett,Scott	21	R	25	aaa	KC	69	7.18	1.76	14	16	10	6	2.3	33	64	-5
	22	R	26	a/a	CHW	123	5.69	1.66	20	16	8	7	1.3	35	68	31
Bolton,Cody	22	R	24	aaa	PIT	77	3.01	1.28	11	21	12	9	0.4	27	76	83
Boushley,Caleb	21	R	28	a/a	SD	117	5.38	1.62	22	16	6	10	1.8	35	72	31
	22	R	29	aaa	MIL	128	3.63	1.34	21	14	9	5	0.9	28	76	38
Boyle,Sean	21	R	25	a/a	NYY	41	1.33	0.98	16	22	5	17	0.3	28	87	147
	22	R	26	a/a	NYY	156	4.02	1.22	23	21	5	15	1.5	30	73	84
Bradford,Cody	21	L	23	aa	TEX	36	4.63	1.44	22	23	3	20	0.3	41	66	212
	22	L	24	aa	TEX	120	4.66	1.23	19	20	6	14	1.1	30	64	87
Bradley,Taj	22	R	21	a/a	TAM	134	2.31	0.99	18	24	5	19	0.7	27	80	137
Brash,Matt	21	R	23	aa	SEA	55	2.39	1.06	21	34	11	23	0.5	28	79	140
	22	R	24	aaa	SEA	26	3.00	1.18	4.7	33	11	22	1.1	29	80	117
Bravo,Jose	22	R	25	aa	HOU	109	4.33	1.40	19	18	7	11	1.2	32	73	58
Bremer,Noah	21	R	25	aa	TEX	69	5.73	1.53	14	18	9	9	1.2	33	64	43
Brennan,Tim	22	R	26	aa	TEX	75	2.72	1.05	15	14	4	10	0.9	26	79	84
Brettell,Michael	21	R	24	aa	STL	70	7.06	1.70	14	15	7	7	1.5	36	59	24
	22	R	25	aa	STL	71	4.25	1.43	6.7	14	8	6	0.4	32	69	58
Brigden,Trevor	22	R	27	a/a	TAM	61	2.98	0.99	6.3	28	4	25	1.0	30	75	191
Brill,Matt	22	R	28	a/a	WAS	50	4.87	1.69	5.1	16	17	-1	0.4	29	70	54
Bristo,Braden	22	R	28	aaa	NYY	54	5.10	1.74	6.0	21	13	7	1.1	35	72	48
Brito,Jhony	21	R	23	aa	NYY	48	5.74	1.37	25.3	19	5	15	1.7	33	62	78
	22	R	24	a/a	NYY	114	3.05	1.20	17.7	17	7	10	0.7	28	77	71
Brnovich,Kyle	21	R	24	aa	BAL	62	4.16	1.20	16.7	24	6	18	1.6	30	72	94
Broadway,Taylor	22	R	25	aa	BOS	56	4.78	1.45	5.7	28	6	22	1.4	39	71	121
Broom,Robert	21	R	25	aaa	CLE	50	5.80	1.47	4.8	20	11	9	1.6	30	64	39
	22	R	26	a/a	CLE	65	4.36	1.39	6.3	14	11	3	0.5	28	68	50
Brown,Hunter	21	R	23	a/a	HOU	101	4.20	1.44	17.9	26	11	15	1.1	34	74	82
	22	R	24	aaa	HOU	106	2.39	1.06	17.9	27	10	17	0.4	27	78	122
Brown,Tyler	22	R	24	aa	HOU	65	6.45	1.62	17.0	20	9	12	2.0	35	64	36
Brown,Zack	22	R	28	aaa	MIL	51	4.25	1.32	4.3	19	9	10	0.7	29	68	68
Bugg,Parker	21	R	27	aaa	MIA	68	5.67	1.63	9.5	22	16	6	1.5	28	68	43
	22	R	28	a/a	MIA	50	3.80	1.57	7.4	20	16	4	0.7	29	77	56
Burch,Tyler	22	R	25	aa	BAL	45	5.69	1.46	5.8	18	8	10	2.2	30	68	21
Burke,Brock	21	L	25	aaa	TEX	79	6.34	1.49	16.3	23	9	14	1.5	34	59	60
Burke,Sean	22	R	23	a/a	CHW	80	4.99	1.47	16.4	26	9	16	1.3	35	69	79
Burns,Tanner	22	R	24	aa	CLE	90	3.77	1.39	18.1	20	11	9	1.4	28	79	49
Burrows,Beau	21	R	25	aaa	MIN	66	6.34	1.55	13.1	18	11	8	2.1	30	65	14
	22	R	26	aaa	LA	101	6.03	1.71	14.8	16	11	5	1.4	34	67	26
Burrows,Mike	22	R	23	a/a	PIT	95	3.87	1.21	16.0	23	7	16	0.6	31	68	107
Bush,Ky	22	L	23	aa	LAA	103	3.44	1.17	19.6	20	6	14	1.1	29	75	86
Bush,Nick	21	L	25	aa	COL	35	6.83	2.12	24.7	13	7	6	1.3	43	69	12
	22	L	26	aa	COL	101	4.16	1.30	21.9	18	4	14	1.7	31	75	84
Butto,Jose	21	R	23	aa	NYM	41	2.90	1.01	19.7	28	5	23	1.1	29	77	153
	22	R	24	a/a	NYM	129	3.18	1.18	19.2	22	7	15	0.9	29	77	92
Byrne,Michael	21	R	24	a/a	CIN	51	4.03	1.40	6.3	15	12	4	0.4	28	71	56
	22	R	25	a/a	CIN	64	5.07	1.60	6.8	22	11	11	1.2	35	71	56
Cabrera,Edward	21	R	23	a/a	MIA	56	3.89	1.30	21.0	30	11	19	1.2	31	74	97
Camarena,Daniel	21	L	29	aaa	SD	84	4.53	1.46	16.3	13	9	4	1.0	30	71	31
Campos,Yeizo	21	R	25	a/a	NYM	59	3.51	1.28	7.8	18	8	10	0.9	29	75	63
	22	R	26	aa	NYM	49	5.88	1.44	7.2	19	11	7	1.2	29	60	47
Cantillo,Joey	22	L	23	aa	CLE	62	1.99	1.08	17.3	31	11	20	0.3	28	82	134
Caracci,Parker	22	R	26	a/a	TOR	51	4.43	1.65	5.3	20	13	6	0.8	33	74	57
Carlton,Drew	21	R	26	aaa	DET	53	4.05	1.32	6.7	17	5	12	1.1	32	72	75
	22	R	27	aaa	DET	59	5.11	1.30	5.3	21	4	16	1.2	33	63	104
Carr,Tyler	21	R	25	aa	PHI	52	5.92	1.63	7.0	16	9	7	1.5	33	66	24
Carrera,Faustino	21	L	22	aa	TAM	49	3.25	1.08	12.0	15	7	8	0.7	25	72	67
Carrillo,Gerardo	21	R	23	aa	WAS	97	5.63	1.56	18.5	21	12	9	1.5	32	67	44
Case,Brad	21	R	25	aa	PIT	67	5.74	1.66	10.7	15	7	8	1.6	35	69	22
	22	R	26	a/a	PIT	72	4.65	1.52	8.7	16	8	8	0.7	34	70	54
Castaneda,Victor	22	R	24	a/a	MIL	122	4.10	1.38	19.8	19	10	10	1.2	30	74	55
Castellanos,Humberto	21	R	23	aaa	ARI	59	3.91	1.08	19.3	22	5	17	1.5	27	71	99
Castillo,Jesus	21	R	26	a/a	MIL	107	5.61	1.51	17.9	13	5	8	1.7	33	67	26
Castillo,Luis	21	R	26	a/a	ARI	35	4.44	1.89	5.7	17	11	6	0.9	39	78	39
	22	R	27	a/a	DET	46	1.70	1.25	4.4	18	6	11	0.4	31	88	89
Castillo,Max	22	R	23	a/a	KC	79	3.41	1.20	17.7	20	8	12	0.7	28	73	86
Castillo,Maximo	21	R	22	aa	TOR	102	5.06	1.41	20.6	18	7	10	1.1	32	66	58
Castro,Kervin	21	R	22	aaa	SF	44	2.73	1.16	5.8	30	11	18	0.5	29	77	120
	22	R	23	aaa	CHC	46	4.08	1.44	5.3	21	14	8	0.7	29	72	72
Cate,Tim	21	L	24	aa	WAS	98	6.35	1.73	21.3	15	8	6	1.3	36	65	25
	22	L	25	aa	WAS	57	7.29	1.65	23.2	16	8	7	1.6	34	57	24
Cavalli,Cade	21	R	23	a/a	WAS	84	4.86	1.55	21.7	24	13	11	0.5	34	68	82
	22	R	24	aaa	WAS	97	3.77	1.19	19.5	21	9	12	0.3	29	67	99
Cecconi,Slade	22	R	23	aa	ARI	131	3.77	1.24	20.5	19	5	14	1.1	31	74	95
Chacin,Jose	22	R	25	aa	NYM	103	5.32	1.41	19.0	18	7	11	1.2	33	64	60
Chaidez,Adrian	22	R	23	aa	HOU	79	5.82	1.57	15.8	20	14	6	1.7	29	67	33
Chentouf,Yaya	21	R	24	aa	DET	45	4.89	1.61	8.0	17	11	6	1.5	32	74	24
	22	R	25	aa	DET	59	3.03	1.19	4.8	21	6	15	0.9	30	78	98
Chirino,Harold	22	R	24	aa	MIL	52	3.35	1.37	5.0	19	11	8	0.7	29	77	68
Clarke,Chris	22	R	23	aa	CHC	98	4.26	1.42	20.8	17	4	13	0.7	36	71	105
Clarkin,Ian	21	L	26	a/a	COL	70	9.36	2.09	16.4	7	12	-5	2.2	34	57	-50
Cobb,Trey	21	R	27	a/a	NYM	45	8.20	2.04	8.1	13	10	3	2.3	38	63	-24
	22	R	28	a/a	NYM	72	3.85	1.30	7.4	18	9	8	0.7	29	71	65
Cohen,Chase	22	R	25	aa	OAK	58	3.13	1.32	5.5	22	11	11	0.6	29	78	83
Coleman,Dylan	21	R	25	a/a	KC	59	3.78	1.13	5.2	31	10	21	0.6	30	67	128
Conine,Brett	21	R	25	aaa	HOU	100	5.67	1.53	17.5	16	9	7	1.8	31	68	18
	22	R	26	aaa	HOU	107	6.67	1.91	17.5	14	10	4	1.5	37	67	9
Conley,Bryce	21	R	27	aa	OAK	95	4.88	1.44	14.0	17	11	6	0.6	30	65	58
	22	R	28	a/a	OAK	56	4.25	1.73	6.2	16	10	6	0.7	36	76	46
Conn,Devin	21	R	24	aa	HOU	35	2.96	1.09	6.6	19	7	12	1.4	24	82	64
	22	R	25	a/a	HOU	67	2.98	1.20	5.9	16	11	5	0.8	24	79	53
Conroy,Ryan	22	R	25	a/a	BAL	55	5.84	1.77	7.5	18	11	7	1.2	36	69	34
Contreras,Luis	22	R	26	a/a	MIL	51	4.10	1.42	6.2	27	14	13	0.7	31	72	94
Contreras,Roansy	21	R	22	a/a	PIT	60	2.61	0.92	17	30	5	25	0.7	28	74	173
	22	R	23	aaa	PIT	35	2.99	1.20	16	27	9	18	0.8	31	78	108
Correa,Danis	22	R	23	a/a	CHC	58	3.24	1.23	6.2	22	11	11	0.6	27	75	86
Cosgrove,Tom	22	L	26	a/a	SD	57	3.30	1.07	4.6	29	11	18	1.1	23	75	102
Cox,Austin	21	L	24	a/a	KC	68	4.76	1.50	17	16	10	6	1.4	30	72	29
	22	L	25	aaa	KC	148	4.03	1.44	22	12	7	6	0.9	31	74	37
Criswell,Jeff	22	R	23	a/a	OAK	71	3.20	1.22	21	18	7	10	0.5	29	74	81
Cronin,Declan	22	R	25	a/a	CHW	51	3.57	1.41	4.4	14	8	5	0.7	30	76	44
Cronin,Matthew	22	L	25	a/a	WAS	54	2.56	1.12	4.5	22	10	11	0.5	25	79	88
Crouse,Hans	21	R	23	a/a	PHI	87	3.40	1.07	17	25	10	16	1.0	24	72	94
Crow,Coleman	22	R	22	aa	LAA	128	4.46	1.28	22	20	6	14	1.3	31	69	85
Cruz,Omar	21	L	22	aa	PIT	72	3.46	1.31	21	17	7	10	0.7	31	75	70
	22	L	23	aa	PIT	64	4.78	1.39	12	20	9	11	1.0	31	67	66
Cruz,Steven	22	R	23	aa	MIN	56	4.71	1.53	5.3	24	12	11	0.5	34	68	88
Cuello,Edward	21	R	23	a/a	LA	30	7.20	1.56	6.6	12	8	3	2.2	29	58	-14
Curlis,Connor	21	L	25	aa	CIN	99	6.35	1.60	22	17	12	5	2.4	28	67	0
	22	L	26	aa	CIN	112	7.08	1.61	16	21	8	13	2.4	34	61	25
Curry,Xzavion	22	R	24	a/a	CLE	122	3.84	1.20	20	22	7	15	1.2	29	72	85
Cushing,Jack	22	R	26	a/a	OAK	132	4.49	1.42	22	16	6	10	0.9	33	70	64
Dabovich,R.J.	22	R	23	a/a	SF	54	3.18	1.09	4.7	28	11	16	0.3	26	69	119

PITCHER	yr	t	age	lvl	org	ip	era	whip	bf/g	k%	bb%	k-bb	hr/9	h%	s%	bpv
Damron,Ty	21	L	27	aa	OAK	90	6.61	1.81	19	16	7	9	1.1	39	64	39
	22	L	28	a/a	OAK	118	3.76	1.48	19	14	8	6	1.0	32	78	37
Daniel,Davis	21	R	24	a/a	LAA	68	5.01	1.37	20	27	5	22	1.3	38	66	140
	22	R	25	aaa	LAA	103	3.86	1.17	20	16	7	9	1.0	26	70	61
Danielak,Michael	22	R	28	aa	OAK	76	3.81	1.44	7.9	15	8	7	0.8	32	75	49
Daniels,Brett	21	R	25	aa	HOU	91	7.70	1.76	19	22	12	11	1.3	37	56	49
	22	R	26	a/a	CLE	63	3.94	1.42	6.9	20	12	7	0.5	30	72	70
Danish,Tyler	21	R	27	a/a	LAA	71	4.03	1.35	9.3	21	5	16	1.2	34	74	97
Darnell,Dugan	22	R	25	aa	COL	49	5.71	1.69	5.8	23	14	9	1.8	33	71	38
Dashwood,Jack	22	L	25	aa	LAA	61	4.75	1.25	8	27	8	19	1.3	31	65	101
Davidson,Tucker	22	L	26	aaa	ATL	81	5.94	1.57	24	22	8	15	1.9	36	67	50
Davila,Garrett	22	L	25	aa	CHW	90	4.91	1.62	14	18	11	7	0.7	34	70	52
Davis,Noah	22	R	25	a/a	COL	140	5.58	1.49	22	19	9	10	1.7	31	67	36
De Jesus,Angel	21	R	24	a/a	DET	66	4.18	1.26	6.1	23	14	9	1.1	23	70	69
	22	R	25	aaa	DET	49	4.17	1.14	4.4	17	10	8	0.6	24	63	70
De Jesus,Enmanuel	21	L	25	a/a	BOS	64	4.83	1.73	13	21	10	11	0.6	40	72	71
	22	L	26	aaa	SF	103	4.19	1.57	13	20	10	10	0.8	35	74	66
De La Cruz,Oscar	21	R	26	a/a	NYM	72	7.92	1.82	16	18	9	9	0.7	40	54	53
Deal,Hayden	21	L	27	aa	ATL	89	5.42	1.62	17	14	10	4	0.6	34	66	40
	22	L	28	aa	ATL	59	5.29	1.66	8.5	16	11	5	0.4	35	66	52
Deason,Cody	22	R	26	aa	HOU	79	5.98	1.79	17	16	12	4	0.5	36	65	47
Del Bonta-Smith,Finn	22	R	25	aa	COL	50	4.42	1.18	5.7	20	6	15	2.2	26	73	62
Del Rosario,Yefri	21	R	22	aa	KC	72	6.89	1.71	13	20	11	9	1.5	36	61	37
	22	R	23	a/a	KC	73	4.16	1.42	6.6	13	8	6	0.8	31	72	42
Demurias,Eddy	21	R	24	a/a	CIN	44	3.36	1.27	5.7	20	13	7	0.5	25	74	76
	22	R	25	aaa	CIN	56	4.77	1.73	4.7	20	15	6	1.1	34	74	44
Dennis,Matt	21	R	26	aa	COL	96	7.52	1.77	19	14	5	9	1.5	38	58	31
	22	R	27	aaa	COL	81	7.10	1.86	12	10	9	1	1.7	34	64	-15
Denoyer,Noah	22	R	24	aa	BAL	53	2.62	0.80	14	29	5	23	1.5	20	80	147
Detmers,Reid	21	L	22	a/a	LAA	62	3.05	1.13	17	39	7	32	1.2	36	80	172
Diaz,Indigo	22	R	24	aa	ATL	51	3.51	1.27	4.3	25	15	10	0.8	24	74	85
Diaz,Jhonathan	21	L	25	a/a	LAA	77	4.04	1.16	19	25	6	19	0.5	32	65	128
	22	L	26	aaa	LAA	47	4.41	1.34	20	18	9	9	0.7	30	67	69
Diaz,Miguel	22	R	28	aaa	DET	65	4.75	1.53	4.9	18	11	7	0.6	33	69	59
Dipoto,Jonah	22	R	26	aa	KC	65	3.65	1.58	6.8	21	16	5	0.7	30	78	68
Dodd,Dylan	22	L	24	a/a	ATL	55	3.75	1.34	23	24	7	17	0.7	35	73	104
Dollard,Taylor	22	R	23	aa	SEA	144	2.06	0.93	20	20	5	15	0.5	25	80	133
Donato,Chad	21	R	26	a/a	HOU	56	5.03	1.35	16	18	6	12	1.4	31	66	58
	22	R	27	aaa	HOU	126	5.28	1.53	19	15	11	4	1.3	29	68	24
Dowdy,Kyle	21	R	28	aaa	CLE	60	5.71	1.81	7.1	18	15	2	1.5	32	71	23
	22	R	29	aaa	CIN	53	5.28	1.84	5.2	18	16	3	0.7	35	71	43
Doxakis,John	22	L	24	aa	TAM	83	5.26	1.41	18	17	11	6	0.9	28	63	51
Dubin,Shawn	21	R	26	aaa	HOU	51	3.47	1.11	13	28	9	19	0.7	28	70	115
	22	R	27	aaa	HOU	59	4.73	1.49	11	26	12	13	0.4	35	67	93
Dugger,Robert	21	R	26	aaa	SEA	70	6.67	1.55	20	18	8	10	1.5	34	58	38
	22	R	27	aaa	CIN	67	5.73	1.70	16	15	13	2	1.3	31	68	15
Dunshee,Parker	21	R	26	aaa	OAK	44	6.52	1.54	19	16	8	7	1.3	33	58	34
	22	R	27	aaa	OAK	112	7.20	1.63	16	13	9	5	2.0	31	59	2
Duplantier,Jon	22	R	28	aaa	LA	95	4.18	1.45	12	20	12	8	1.5	28	77	42
DuRapau,Montana	21	R	29	aa	OAK	55	4.60	1.28	6.1	13	8	6	0.7	28	64	49
Duron,Nick	21	R	25	a/a	SEA	44	4.79	1.34	4.9	20	13	7	1.2	25	67	52
	22	R	26	aaa	PHI	49	2.86	1.57	4.2	23	14	10	0.6	34	83	75
Dye,Josh	21	L	25	a/a	KC	67	3.01	1.28	6.9	20	7	13	0.8	31	79	86
	22	L	26	aaa	KC	63	4.34	1.43	5.6	16	5	11	1.6	33	76	49
Eastman,Colton	21	R	25	a/a	PHI	54	3.70	1.30	15	18	10	8	0.9	27	74	57
	22	R	26	a/a	PHI	101	4.93	1.55	18	15	15	1	1.1	27	70	32
Eckelman,Matt	21	R	28	aaa	PIT	66	5.72	1.70	8.3	13	5	8	1.6	37	70	26
	22	R	29	a/a	PIT	45	6.62	1.96	7.7	11	11	0	1.5	36	68	-8
Eder,Jacob	21	L	23	aa	MIA	72	2.15	1.08	19	30	10	20	0.4	28	81	131
Effross,Scott	21	R	28	a/a	CHC	62	3.99	1.12	7.9	20	7	14	1.2	26	69	78
Eickhoff,Jerad	21	R	31	aaa	NYM	81	4.93	1.37	21	18	6	12	1.7	31	70	51
	22	R	32	aaa	PIT	115	5.53	1.34	17	16	7	9	1.2	30	60	49
Eisert,Brandon	22	L	24	aaa	TOR	62	3.83	1.22	5.6	25	6	20	1.3	32	74	112
Elder,Bryce	21	R	22	a/a	ATL	94	3.49	1.10	23	23	10	13	0.9	24	71	86
	22	R	23	aaa	ATL	105	5.46	1.34	24	19	8	11	1.4	30	62	56
Elledge,Seth	21	R	25	aaa	STL	37	6.28	1.80	5.7	21	12	10	0.6	39	64	66
	22	R	26	aaa	ATL	47	4.99	1.29	4.5	27	9	18	0.7	33	61	104
Elliott,Jake	21	R	26	aa	CHW	57	5.15	1.50	8.2	16	10	6	1.6	30	70	23
	22	R	27	a/a	TOR	59	4.60	1.38	6	20	8	12	1.5	30	72	52
Elliott,Jensen	22	R	25	aa	BAL	52	4.73	1.78	7.5	12	6	6	1.4	38	77	19
Endersby,Jimmy	21	R	23	aa	HOU	68	3.89	1.49	18	20	13	7	0.7	30	75	61
	22	R	24	a/a	HOU	118	4.96	1.55	18	16	11	5	1.3	30	71	29
Engler,Scott	21	R	25	a/a	TEX	56	4.25	1.38	6.4	22	10	11	1.1	30	72	67
Enlow,Blayne	22	R	23	aa	MIN	58	3.98	1.50	10	21	10	11	0.5	34	73	79
Enright,Nic	21	R	24	aa	CLE	41	5.05	1.04	6.9	30	6	23	1.2	28	53	134
	22	R	25	a/a	CLE	67	2.72	0.96	5.3	28	5	23	0.8	28	76	163
Erceg,Lucas	21	R	26	aa	MIL	49	6.42	1.70	10	17	17	0	1.1	28	62	34
	22	R	27	a/a	MIL	62	4.85	1.79	5.8	20	14	6	0.9	36	74	49
Erla,Mason	22	R	25	aa	LAA	82	4.18	1.36	21	15	5	10	0.9	32	71	65
Ernst,Nick	22	R	26	aa	NYY	61	4.67	1.49	6.8	22	13	9	1.2	29	72	56
Escobar,Edgar	21	R	24	aa	STL	42	5.11	1.11	6.6	26	8	18	1.9	25	60	79
	22	R	25	aa	STL	125	5.10	1.40	19	14	7	7	1.0	30	65	42
Eshelman,Tom	21	R	27	aaa	BAL	30	9.99	1.84	9.3	10	2	7	2.3	38	46	22
	22	R	28	a/a	SD	116	5.38	1.58	19	10	2	8	1.2	36	68	64
Espinal,Carlos	22	R	26	a/a	NYY	63	3.71	1.33	7.1	20	13	7	1.0	26	75	56
Espinoza,Anderson	22	R	24	a/a	CHC	71	6.94	1.58	15	21	12	8	1.8	31	59	32
Falter,Bailey	21	L	24	aaa	PHI	32	1.89	1.05	16	30	6	24	1.0	30	89	145
	22	L	25	aaa	PHI	47	1.96	0.70	18	23	3	20	0.8	20	78	189
Feigl,Brady	21	R	26	a/a	OAK	123	4.89	1.41	21	19	9	10	1.2	31	68	53
Felipe,Angel	22	R	25	a/a	SD	64	3.12	1.29	5.2	26	12	14	0.1	30	74	112
Feltman,Durbin	21	R	24	a/a	BOS	53	3.45	1.16	5.4	24	7	18	1.4	29	77	94
	22	R	25	aaa	BOS	49	8.12	1.67	5.5	20	10	10	2.1	34	53	23

PITCHER	yr	t	age	lvl	org	ip	era	whip	bf/g	k%	bb%	k-bb	hr/9	h%	s%	bpv
Feltner,Ryan	22	R	26	aaa	COL	53	3.76	1.31	20	20	7	13	0.8	31	73	80
Fernandez,Julian Antonio	21	R	26	a/a	COL	44	2.97	1.33	4.2	17	9	8	1.0	28	82	52
	22	R	27	aaa	COL	57	6.85	1.57	4.3	18	11	7	2.4	28	62	7
Fernandez,Junior	22	R	25	aaa	PIT	45	4.86	1.67	4.9	20	11	9	0.7	36	71	62
File,Dylan	21	R	25	aaa	MIL	44	5.31	1.57	22	16	6	10	1.4	35	69	41
	22	R	26	aaa	MIL	115	4.76	1.33	18	16	7	9	1.0	30	66	56
Fillmyer,Heath	21	R	27	aaa	CLE	83	7.19	1.67	18	17	10	7	2.0	32	60	11
Finnegan,Brandon	21	L	28	aaa	CIN	56	7.72	2.13	6.9	17	16	1	1.8	37	66	3
	22	L	29	aaa	CHW	41	5.97	1.88	6.2	18	15	3	0.7	36	67	44
Fishman,Jake	21	L	26	aaa	MIA	57	4.62	1.26	6.9	18	8	10	1.2	28	66	54
	22	L	27	aaa	MIA	56	2.51	1.16	6.8	18	9	10	0.6	26	81	78
Fleming,Josh	22	L	26	aaa	TAM	66	3.02	1.41	19	15	5	10	0.5	34	79	72
Flores,Wilmer	22	R	21	aa	DET	85	2.89	1.02	17	23	5	18	0.7	28	74	131
Flowers,J.C.	22	R	24	aa	PIT	70	2.80	1.19	8.5	18	8	10	0.6	27	78	74
Fox,Mason	21	R	24	a/a	SD	34	9.80	2.21	7.2	22	14	8	1.7	43	55	26
	22	R	25	a/a	SD	54	5.18	1.57	6.6	18	12	7	0.9	32	68	50
France,J.P.	21	R	26	a/a	HOU	116	4.15	1.38	20	26	11	16	1.2	32	73	81
	22	R	27	aaa	HOU	112	3.85	1.41	14	23	10	12	1.1	31	76	69
Francis,Bowden	21	R	25	a/a	TOR	134	4.84	1.26	22	20	9	11	1.9	25	69	41
	22	R	26	aaa	TOR	99	7.86	1.72	12	19	9	10	2.5	34	59	7
Fraze,Nick	22	R	25	aa	TOR	60	4.69	1.10	18	17	3	14	1.0	29	59	127
Frias,Luis	21	R	23	a/a	ARI	103	4.71	1.21	20	23	9	14	1.2	28	64	77
	22	R	24	aaa	ARI	48	3.17	1.31	7.4	29	10	19	0.8	34	78	113
Frisbee,Matt	21	R	25	a/a	SF	114	6.05	1.46	22	18	6	13	1.8	33	63	51
	22	R	26	aa	SF	141	5.71	1.49	23	17	6	11	1.4	34	64	50
Fuentes,Steven	22	R	25	aa	WAS	92	5.56	1.70	15	14	12	2	0.7	33	66	37
Fulmer,Carson	21	R	28	aaa	CIN	41	6.53	2.02	5.4	21	15	6	1.2	39	69	38
	22	R	29	aaa	LA	58	2.52	1.20	4.8	19	13	6	0.6	23	81	74
Funderburk,Kody	22	L	26	aa	MIN	107	2.87	1.36	14	18	9	9	0.6	31	80	70
Gaddis,Hunter	22	R	24	a/a	CLE	122	3.77	1.06	20	27	7	20	1.1	27	68	115
Gaddis,Will	21	R	25	aa	COL	67	7.48	1.85	8.5	12	7	5	2.1	36	63	-10
	22	R	26	a/a	COL	62	5.87	1.56	6.4	11	7	4	0.8	34	61	29
Gamboa,Alec	22	L	25	aa	LA	89	5.71	1.50	13	15	11	4	1.1	30	63	33
Garabito,Gerson	21	R	26	a/a	SF	86	5.04	1.68	15	16	11	6	0.9	34	71	40
Garcia,Carlos	22	R	24	a/a	TAM	64	4.01	1.22	6.5	24	10	14	1.0	28	70	85
Garcia,Deivi	21	R	22	aaa	NYY	92	7.70	1.96	18	19	15	4	2.2	34	65	4
	22	R	23	a/a	NYY	66	6.81	1.42	14	23	10	12	1.7	30	54	53
Garcia,Pedro	22	R	27	a/a	CIN	59	3.70	1.42	5.1	22	10	12	0.8	33	76	73
Garcia,Robert	21	L	25	aa	KC	48	7.04	1.73	6.6	21	11	10	1.4	37	60	46
	22	L	26	a/a	MIA	65	4.03	1.34	5.9	20	11	8	0.6	28	70	67
Garrett,Braxton	21	L	24	aaa	MIA	87	4.66	1.36	20	20	9	11	1.1	30	68	61
	22	L	25	aaa	MIA	35	3.28	1.13	20	17	6	11	0.7	27	73	81
Gasser,Robert	22	L	23	a/a	MIL	48	3.33	1.34	22	25	11	14	0.5	31	76	95
Gau,Chris	22	R	25	a/a	TAM	58	3.15	1.09	6	22	7	15	0.9	27	75	100
Gavin,Grant	21	R	26	aaa	KC	75	4.95	1.38	6.6	22	11	11	1.3	29	67	60
	22	R	27	a/a	SD	56	4.49	1.69	5.5	19	13	6	0.8	34	74	55
German,Frank	21	R	24	aa	BOS	85	5.91	1.68	16	16	8	8	1.3	36	66	33
	22	R	25	a/a	BOS	51	2.88	0.93	4.5	26	9	16	0.3	23	68	123
German,Osiris	22	R	24	aa	MIN	46	3.11	1.34	5.2	20	8	13	0.8	32	79	81
Gilbert,Tyler	21	L	28	aaa	ARI	53	3.03	1.23	20	18	8	10	0.5	29	76	75
	22	L	29	aaa	ARI	44	6.83	1.83	19	9	11	-1	1.7	32	65	-19
Gillies,Darin	21	R	29	a/a	SEA	47	3.27	1.30	4.9	21	12	9	1.0	26	79	63
Gipson-Long,Sawyer	22	R	25	aa	DET	74	6.12	1.42	21	17	5	13	1.3	34	58	77
Gold,Brandon	21	R	27	aaa	COL	87	7.17	1.68	22	14	6	8	1.5	36	58	28
	22	R	28	aaa	COL	108	7.66	1.93	18	10	8	2	2.6	35	66	-42
Gomez,Michael	21	R	25	aa	NYY	49	3.85	1.23	6.4	21	8	13	0.9	29	71	84
	22	R	26	a/a	NYY	66	4.90	1.69	6.5	16	12	4	0.6	34	70	48
Gomez,Moises	21	R	24	a/a	SEA	48	3.08	1.24	5.4	19	6	14	0.7	31	77	96
Gonsalves,Step	21	L	27	aaa	BOS	73	6.19	1.90	16	23	16	7	1.8	35	71	33
Goody,Nicholas	21	R	30	aaa	NYY	49	5.90	1.41	5.3	21	10	11	1.9	29	63	40
Gordon,Cole	21	R	26	aa	NYM	83	3.71	1.04	16	22	10	12	1.1	21	69	75
Gordon,Tanner	22	R	25	aa	ATL	99	6.33	1.64	21	19	9	10	1.6	35	64	32
Gore,Jordan	22	R	28	a/a	MIN	47	5.40	1.96	5.4	14	17	-3	0.7	33	72	30
Gotsis,Noah	22	R	26	aa	COL	80	6.15	1.41	15	14	6	8	1.1	31	56	42
Graceffo,Gordon	22	R	22	aa	STL	95	2.78	0.89	20	18	5	13	0.9	22	74	108
Green,Josh	21	R	26	aaa	ARI	100	6.23	1.75	18	11	6	5	1.4	36	66	10
	22	R	27	a/a	ARI	61	6.10	1.64	7.2	12	9	3	0.9	33	63	25
Green,Nick	21	R	26	a/a	NYY	73	4.61	1.64	11	16	15	1	0.7	30	72	43
Greene,Hunter	21	R	22	a/a	CIN	107	4.00	1.30	21	29	9	20	1.3	32	74	96
Greene,Zach	21	R	25	aa	NYY	40	4.43	1.32	6.6	29	8	21	1.1	35	69	110
	22	R	26	aaa	NYY	69	3.68	1.30	5.9	27	11	16	1.5	28	78	78
Grey,Connor	21	R	27	aa	NYM	33	4.46	1.21	19	23	4	18	0.7	33	63	138
	22	R	28	aaa	NYM	105	6.20	1.76	19	15	9	6	0.9	37	65	33
Griffin,David	22	R	26	a/a	NYM	72	5.84	1.64	15	15	9	6	1.2	34	66	28
Griffin,Foster	21	L	26	a/a	KC	39	4.16	1.56	19	14	7	7	0.2	36	72	61
	22	L	27	aaa	TOR	52	2.55	1.22	5.5	21	7	14	0.6	30	82	93
Groome,Jay	22	L	24	a/a	SD	146	2.95	1.25	21	19	9	10	0.8	28	79	72
Gross,Andrew	22	R	26	aa	TAM	58	4.07	1.40	6.8	14	10	4	1.3	28	75	29
Grove,Michael	21	R	25	aa	LA	71	8.00	1.82	16	22	11	11	2.3	36	60	18
	22	R	26	a/a	LA	78	3.37	1.17	16	22	7	15	1.2	28	77	88
Guasch,Richard	22	R	24	aa	WAS	48	8.02	1.75	12	21	16	5	1.0	32	52	55
Gudino,Norwith	21	R	26	a/a	SF	60	4.37	1.28	7.7	28	9	18	1.2	31	69	95
	22	R	27	aaa	SF	49	8.28	1.62	8.4	22	14	8	1.9	30	50	29
Guillen,Alexander	21	R	26	a/a	MIA	49	4.72	1.55	7.7	13	8	5	1.2	32	73	23
Hagenman,Justin	21	R	25	aa	LA	64	3.42	1.16	6.7	25	6	18	0.8	31	73	118
	22	R	26	a/a	LA	65	4.92	1.36	5.9	19	7	12	1.2	32	66	66
Hall,DL	21	L	23	aa	BAL	33	3.23	0.98	18	36	12	24	1.2	21	73	126
	22	L	24	a/a	BAL	83	4.54	1.38	15	29	13	17	1.2	31	70	93
Hamilton,Ian	21	R	26	aaa	MIN	59	5.30	1.70	7	26	16	9	0.9	34	69	73
	22	R	27	aaa	CLE	48	3.20	1.07	4.9	24	9	16	0.9	25	74	98
Hancock,Emerson	22	R	23	aa	SEA	99	3.41	1.14	19	20	8	12	1.2	25	76	70
Hardy,Matt	21	R	26	aa	MIL	43	4.71	1.46	6.8	23	11	12	2.0	30	75	42

PITCHER	yr	t	age	lvl	org	ip	era	whip	bf/g	k%	bb%	k-bb	hr/9	h%	s%	bpv
Harris,Hobie	22	R	29	aaa	MIL	53	2.29	1.22	4	21	15	6	0.9	22	86	65
Harris,Hogan	22	L	26	a/a	OAK	62	3.18	1.23	16	26	12	14	0.6	28	76	102
Harris,Nate	21	R	27	aa	COL	70	11.22	2.32	15	11	11	0	3.3	38	55	-67
Harrison,Kyle	22	L	21	aa	SF	84	3.17	1.19	19	32	11	21	1.0	30	78	118
Hatch,Thomas	21	R	27	aaa	TOR	66	5.83	1.49	19	19	8	11	1.9	32	66	35
	22	R	28	aaa	TOR	131	5.87	1.50	20	15	7	8	1.4	33	63	35
Hejka,Josh	22	R	25	a/a	NYM	48	4.87	1.58	7.9	18	9	9	1.0	35	71	53
Henderson,Layne	21	R	25	aa	HOU	51	4.36	1.48	8.5	23	13	10	1.0	30	73	66
	22	R	26	a/a	HOU	54	3.44	1.18	6.4	26	11	15	0.8	27	73	97
Hennigan,Jonathan	21	L	27	aa	PHI	39	7.72	2.04	5.9	17	15	3	0.8	39	61	38
	22	L	28	aaa	PHI	58	3.90	1.51	5.7	16	16	1	0.7	27	75	50
Henriquez,Ronny	21	R	21	aa	TEX	71	5.94	1.27	18	23	6	18	2.1	30	59	75
	22	R	22	aaa	MIN	96	4.96	1.30	17	22	7	15	1.4	31	65	80
Henry,Henry	21	R	23	aa	SD	67	4.12	1.38	7.4	18	11	7	0.4	30	69	69
	22	R	24	aa	SD	81	5.01	1.76	11	19	14	5	0.5	35	71	59
Henry,Thomas	21	L	24	aa	ARI	117	5.41	1.51	22	22	10	12	1.7	32	69	47
	22	L	25	aaa	ARI	113	3.09	1.22	22	17	8	10	0.6	28	76	75
Henzman,Lincoln	22	R	27	a/a	CHW	74	4.52	1.77	6.8	14	11	4	0.9	35	76	28
Herb,Tyler	21	R	29	a/a	SEA	90	5.53	1.57	22	17	4	13	1.4	37	68	75
	22	R	30	a/a	MIL	127	4.52	1.70	21	17	7	11	1.0	38	75	52
Herget,Kevin	21	R	30	aaa	CLE	81	5.47	1.57	13	18	7	11	2.2	33	73	21
	22	R	31	a/a	TAM	198	3.12	1.41	20	19	4	14	1.1	35	82	94
Hernandez,Aaron	21	R	25	aa	LAA	45	8.11	2.03	20	22	14	7	1.4	40	60	37
	22	R	26	aa	LAA	49	5.29	1.43	6	19	9	10	1.4	30	66	46
Hernandez,Arnaldo	22	R	26	aa	MIL	50	7.24	2.01	6.2	23	13	10	1.4	42	65	42
Hernandez,Carlos	22	R	25	aaa	KC	50	3.63	1.15	17	16	8	8	1.0	25	72	60
Hernandez,Daysbel	21	R	25	a/a	ATL	45	4.78	1.39	5.3	24	13	11	0.9	29	67	76
Hernandez,Jakob	21	L	25	a/a	PHI	54	5.17	1.43	5.5	25	9	16	0.9	35	65	89
	22	L	26	aaa	PHI	49	4.41	1.24	4.3	28	9	18	1.9	28	72	75
Hernandez,Kenny	21	L	23	a/a	ARI	62	5.22	1.51	19	12	5	7	1.2	33	68	33
	22	L	24	aa	ARI	46	5.57	1.78	9.2	16	8	8	1.3	38	71	30
Hernandez,Nick	21	R	27	a/a	HOU	56	1.84	1.15	6.7	25	14	10	0.9	21	90	83
	22	R	28	a/a	HOU	66	3.64	1.11	5.1	26	12	14	1.0	23	71	86
Hernandez,Osvaldo	21	L	23	aa	SD	101	5.36	1.53	20	17	6	11	1.6	35	69	45
	22	L	24	aa	SD	57	4.18	1.30	6.6	16	10	6	0.9	27	70	50
Herrin,Tim	22	L	26	a/a	CLE	70	3.93	1.27	6.2	28	7	20	0.8	35	71	122
Hess,David	21	R	28	aaa	TAM	46	4.86	1.38	9.7	21	6	15	2.6	30	77	40
Higginbotham,Jake	22	L	26	aa	ATL	52	5.72	1.72	4.9	17	8	9	1.0	38	67	43
Highberger,Nick	21	R	28	aa	OAK	40	7.20	2.01	6	13	13	0	1.4	36	65	4
	22	R	29	aa	OAK	56	6.44	2.02	7	14	16	-2	0.5	35	67	32
Hill,Adam	21	R	24	aa	SEA	61	7.28	1.74	20	21	11	10	2.1	35	62	22
Hill,David	21	R	27	aa	COL	75	6.80	1.76	22	14	6	8	2.6	35	68	-10
Hill,Garrett	22	R	26	a/a	DET	71	3.37	1.13	19	26	9	18	0.8	28	72	110
Hillman,Juan	21	L	24	a/a	CLE	111	4.47	1.48	22	15	7	8	1.4	32	74	37
Hintzen,J.T.	21	R	25	aa	MIL	58	4.76	1.35	6.7	28	8	20	2.0	32	73	79
	22	R	26	aa	DET	47	6.13	1.51	6.2	15	13	2	1.2	27	60	29
Hitt,Robbie	21	R	25	aa	MIL	43	3.59	1.40	5	22	12	10	1.0	30	77	67
	22	R	26	aa	MIL	52	4.95	1.58	5.5	19	11	8	0.5	34	68	66
Hjelle,Sean	21	R	24	a/a	SF	121	4.54	1.53	22	16	9	8	0.9	33	72	48
	22	R	25	aaa	SF	97	4.54	1.56	19	15	8	7	0.8	34	72	47
Hock,Colton	21	R	25	a/a	MIA	53	4.27	1.36	5.1	20	7	13	0.9	33	70	78
	22	R	26	a/a	MIA	61	3.98	1.28	5.5	17	6	11	0.8	31	70	74
Hoeing,Bryan	22	R	26	a/a	MIA	121	4.52	1.46	24	12	8	4	1.0	31	71	28
Holder,Heath	21	R	29	aaa	COL	47	11.99	2.46	6.7	13	16	-3	2.1	39	51	-26
Hollowell,Gavin	22	R	25	aa	COL	50	3.40	0.94	4.5	26	7	19	0.6	25	64	128
Holmes,Grant	21	R	25	aaa	OAK	67	7.73	2.11	9.2	17	11	6	1.3	42	64	24
Holton,Tyler	21	L	25	a/a	ARI	65	6.24	1.57	11	22	6	16	0.8	40	59	97
	22	L	26	aaa	ARI	46	3.61	1.15	7.7	18	8	11	0.7	27	70	77
Honeywell,Brent	21	R	26	aaa	TAM	83	5.15	1.42	11	16	7	8	1.7	30	69	29
	22	R	27	aaa	OAK	18	5.86	1.83	7.7	19	7	12	2.3	39	75	25
Hovis,Reilly	21	R	28	aa	TOR	51	7.74	1.90	20	12	7	4	3.2	35	68	-50
Howard,Brian	21	R	26	aaa	OAK	112	5.77	1.55	20	16	8	8	1.6	33	66	26
	22	R	27	aaa	OAK	71	5.17	1.51	7.3	16	9	7	1.1	32	68	41
Howard,Spencer	22	R	26	aaa	TEX	59	4.36	1.32	17	23	9	14	0.7	32	68	88
Hudson,Bryan	21	L	24	a/a	CHC	60	5.10	1.37	7.2	18	12	6	0.7	28	62	58
	22	L	25	a/a	CHC	59	3.48	1.30	6.2	24	10	15	0.6	32	74	98
Hughes,Brandon	21	L	26	aa	CHC	32	1.98	1.31	7.4	25	10	15	0.9	31	90	89
	22	L	27	a/a	CHC	18	0.00	0.45	6	30	5	25	0.0	14	##	215
Hunley,Sean	22	R	23	aa	TAM	92	3.22	1.21	14	16	4	12	0.3	32	72	106
Ingram,Kolton	22	L	26	aa	LAA	62	2.60	0.94	4.7	25	7	18	0.8	24	77	116
Irvin,Jake	22	R	25	aa	WAS	74	5.60	1.31	20	20	7	14	1.2	31	58	76
Jackson,Andre	21	R	25	a/a	LA	91	3.80	1.13	17	22	7	15	1.7	25	75	71
	22	R	26	aaa	LA	77	4.14	1.54	16	17	14	3	1.0	27	76	45
Jacob,Alek	22	R	24	a/a	SD	50	2.65	1.15	5.1	25	7	19	0.7	31	80	123
Jameson,Drey	21	R	24	aa	ARI	47	4.22	1.24	24	30	9	21	1.0	32	69	110
	22	R	25	a/a	ARI	134	5.39	1.42	22	18	7	11	1.0	33	63	66
Jarvis,Bryce	21	R	24	aa	ARI	35	5.95	1.46	19	22	11	11	1.9	30	64	41
	22	R	25	aa	ARI	108	7.41	1.82	20	18	10	7	1.7	36	61	18
Javier,Odalvi	21	R	25	aa	ATL	76	4.44	1.39	13	20	11	9	0.7	30	69	68
	22	R	26	a/a	ATL	61	3.16	1.18	5.2	23	10	13	0.3	28	73	99
Jefferies,Daulton	21	R	26	aaa	OAK	77	4.90	1.40	22	17	3	13	1.4	34	68	99
Jennings,Steven	21	R	23	aa	PIT	31	6.66	1.72	11	12	8	4	1.0	35	61	19
	22	R	24	aa	NYY	68	4.29	1.19	5.9	21	5	16	0.9	31	65	110
Jensen,Ryan	22	R	25	aa	CHC	60	3.83	1.33	15	19	13	6	0.6	25	72	69
Jewell,Jake	21	R	28	aaa	SF	45	3.68	1.32	5.6	20	10	10	0.7	29	73	73
	22	R	29	aaa	MIN	56	3.30	1.21	5	21	9	11	0.1	29	71	99
Jimenez,Dany	21	R	28	aaa	TOR	46	3.24	1.49	5.1	28	15	13	1.4	30	85	71
Johnston,Kyle	21	R	25	a/a	TOR	71	1.88	1.27	8.3	15	10	5	0.5	27	87	60
	22	R	26	aaa	TOR	64	6.40	1.74	6	16	10	6	1.3	35	65	26
Johnstone,Connor	21	R	27	aaa	ATL	75	6.49	1.37	9.5	12	4	8	2.2	30	57	27
	22	R	28	aaa	ATL	67	4.57	1.62	9.3	11	9	1	0.8	32	73	17
Jones,Connor	21	R	27	aaa	STL	57	6.08	1.96	5.8	14	11	3	0.4	39	67	38
	22	R	28	aa	SEA	75	7.09	1.79	20	15	14	1	0.9	33	59	29
Jones,Stephen	22	R	25	aa	COL	58	2.94	1.15	4.9	21	9	12	1.0	25	79	76
Joyner,Tyler	21	R	25	a/a	BAL	46	7.06	1.66	9.5	13	9	4	2.3	31	62	-11
Juenger,Hayden	22	R	22	a/a	TOR	90	3.71	1.08	9.3	24	9	15	1.8	22	76	67
Junk,Janson	21	R	25	aa	LAA	93	3.26	1.23	20	21	7	14	1.1	29	78	80
	22	R	26	aaa	LAA	75	4.02	1.26	19	18	5	12	0.9	31	70	83
Jurado,Ariel	22	R	26	aaa	MIN	54	3.35	0.99	15	17	6	12	1.0	24	70	82
Karcher,Ricky	22	R	25	a/a	CIN	58	4.16	1.61	5	29	17	13	0.6	35	74	95
Kasowski,Marshall	22	R	27	aaa	LA	56	3.20	1.27	4.9	22	14	8	0.4	25	75	89
Kauffmann,Karl	21	R	24	aa	COL	82	9.11	2.30	22	12	10	2	2.5	41	64	-38
	22	R	25	a/a	COL	143	5.14	1.58	23	17	11	6	1.3	31	70	34
Keel,Jerry	21	L	28	a/a	SD	97	6.48	1.90	18	12	9	4	1.6	37	69	-2
Keller,Brian	21	R	27	aaa	NYY	56	3.46	1.85	10	20	19	0	0.6	32	82	58
	22	R	28	aaa	BOS	113	3.77	1.33	15	20	12	8	0.6	28	72	71
Kellogg,Ryan	21	L	27	a/a	CHC	67	5.17	1.64	15	11	6	4	1.1	34	70	18
Kelly,Kevin	22	R	25	a/a	CLE	58	1.95	1.11	4.8	25	8	17	0.1	30	82	131
Kelly,Zack	21	R	26	a/a	BOS	48	2.56	1.17	5.4	28	10	19	0.4	30	79	122
	22	R	27	aaa	BOS	51	2.97	1.26	4.8	26	12	14	0.3	30	76	105
Kennedy,Brett	21	R	27	a/a	SD	44	9.83	2.27	16	14	11	3	1.4	42	56	2
	22	R	28	a/a	BOS	78	4.43	1.53	14	14	9	5	0.9	32	73	32
Kennedy,Nick	21	L	25	aa	COL	44	8.28	1.99	5.4	21	11	10	2.4	40	62	12
	22	L	26	a/a	COL	52	7.57	1.92	4.9	12	11	1	1.4	36	61	-2
Kent,Zak	21	R	23	aa	TEX	30	6.29	1.62	22	25	7	18	3.0	36	72	35
	22	R	24	a/a	TEX	111	3.55	1.26	19	20	8	11	0.8	29	74	74
Kerr,Ray	21	L	27	a/a	SEA	41	3.59	1.16	4.6	30	10	20	0.5	30	68	126
	22	L	28	aaa	SD	45	4.27	1.77	4.5	26	16	9	0.6	37	76	79
Kerry,Brett	22	R	23	aa	LAA	103	4.18	1.37	17	23	6	17	1.5	34	75	83
Kilian,Caleb	21	R	24	aa	CHC	80	3.06	1.08	21	21	4	17	0.6	30	73	145
	22	R	25	aaa	CHC	108	4.11	1.57	18	21	11	10	0.5	35	74	75
Kilkenny,Mitchell	22	R	25	aa	COL	102	6.20	1.62	19	13	7	6	2.2	32	68	-7
Kilome,Franklyn	21	R	26	aaa	NYM	46	3.74	1.36	9.2	17	14	4	0.8	25	74	53
	22	R	27	a/a	WAS	93	6.37	1.66	21	18	10	8	1.5	34	64	33
King,Zach	22	L	24	aa	MIA	46	9.18	2.10	21	17	13	4	1.3	40	55	22
Kingham,Nolan	21	R	25	a/a	ATL	95	6.09	1.58	22	12	6	6	1.3	34	63	21
	22	R	26	a/a	ATL	98	5.80	1.53	13	14	4	10	1.5	35	65	45
Kirby,Chance	21	R	26	aa	DET	48	6.93	1.50	19	13	10	3	2.2	27	58	-5
	22	R	27	aa	DET	127	2.87	1.04	17	18	6	12	0.9	25	77	83
Kisena,Alec	22	R	27	a/a	NYM	66	5.70	1.37	17	16	8	8	1.7	28	62	26
Klein,Will	22	R	23	aa	KC	45	9.69	2.21	7.6	19	19	0	0.9	38	54	40
Kloffenstein,Adam	22	R	22	aa	TOR	86	5.59	1.57	20	19	9	10	1.2	34	66	53
Knack,Landon	22	R	25	aa	LA	66	4.77	1.38	16	23	9	15	1.1	33	68	80
Knarr,Brandon	22	L	24	aa	MIL	89	3.71	1.43	24	19	9	11	1.0	32	77	64
Knehr,Reiss	21	R	25	a/a	SD	77	3.42	1.16	16	17	10	8	0.7	25	72	67
	22	R	26	aaa	SD	89	5.54	1.53	12	19	12	7	1.3	30	66	42
Knight,Blaine	21	R	25	a/a	BAL	70	7.07	1.64	17	14	9	5	1.3	33	57	19
	22	R	26	aaa	BAL	72	7.51	2.08	10	15	10	5	1.5	40	65	11
Kober,Collin	21	R	27	aa	SEA	41	4.01	1.52	5.6	22	12	10	0.7	33	75	72
	22	R	28	aa	SEA	48	3.45	1.21	4.4	25	11	14	1.0	26	75	87
Koenig,Jared	21	L	27	aa	OAK	122	3.64	1.38	21	15	9	7	1.0	29	77	42
	22	L	28	aaa	OAK	107	3.79	1.28	22	18	6	12	0.7	32	72	84
Kolek,Stephen	22	R	25	aa	SEA	145	4.26	1.42	23	18	9	9	0.5	32	70	71
Komar,Brandon	21	R	22	aa	SD	51	5.11	1.53	12	21	12	9	0.9	32	67	59
	22	R	23	aa	SD	75	5.77	1.61	21	14	9	6	1.0	34	65	33
Kopps,Kevin	22	R	25	aa	SD	55	4.10	1.46	5.6	21	14	7	0.6	29	72	72
Kowar,Jackson	21	R	25	aaa	KC	82	3.81	1.32	20	26	10	16	0.7	32	72	98
	22	R	26	aaa	KC	84	5.99	1.67	19	17	10	7	1.2	35	65	38
Kranick,Max	21	R	24	a/a	PIT	72	4.26	1.26	20	17	6	11	0.9	30	68	69
Krauth,Ben	21	L	27	a/a	CLE	38	5.23	1.46	6.5	22	12	11	1.3	30	67	56
	22	L	28	a/a	SD	60	5.69	1.60	9.9	16	11	5	1.4	32	67	27
Kremer,Dean	21	R	25	aaa	BAL	63	5.94	1.47	16	20	8	12	1.6	33	63	51
Krook,Matt	21	L	27	a/a	NYY	108	3.61	1.37	19	23	15	8	0.5	27	74	83
	22	L	28	aaa	NYY	140	4.59	1.56	21	20	13	7	1.3	31	74	43
Kuhn,Travis	22	R	24	aa	SEA	60	3.78	1.25	4.9	24	12	12	0.4	28	69	99
Kuzia,Nick	21	R	25	a/a	SD	54	3.25	1.17	5.3	27	12	15	0.7	26	74	99
	22	R	26	a/a	DET	58	5.10	1.50	6.1	16	12	5	0.8	30	66	46
Labosky,Jack	21	R	25	aa	TAM	80	4.63	1.20	12	20	5	15	1.7	29	68	81
Lambert,Jimmy	21	R	27	aaa	CHW	65	5.38	1.39	14	24	12	12	1.6	28	65	57
Latz,Jake	21	L	25	a/a	TEX	97	5.17	1.51	19	23	11	12	1.4	33	69	56
	22	L	26	aaa	TEX	53	5.33	1.70	13	19	12	7	1.6	33	73	29
Laweryson,Cody	22	R	23	aa	MIN	61	0.94	0.89	12	26	6	20	0.2	26	91	152
Lawson,Brandon	21	R	27	aa	HOU	96	5.08	1.43	16	15	7	7	0.6	32	63	56
Lawson,Reggie	22	R	25	aa	SD	63	5.59	1.73	17	16	17	-1	1.4	28	70	22
Leahy,Kyle	21	R	24	aa	STL	88	7.14	1.89	17	12	9	3	1.3	37	63	7
	22	R	25	a/a	STL	146	4.35	1.47	22	17	9	8	1.0	32	72	53
Leal,David	22	L	25	aa	OAK	116	4.40	1.33	24	13	3	10	0.7	33	67	108
Leasher,Aaron	21	L	25	a/a	SD	66	3.59	1.36	17	18	9	9	0.7	30	75	66
	22	L	26	aaa	SD	88	3.43	1.35	11	20	9	11	0.7	31	76	74
Leasure,Jordan	22	R	24	aa	LA	50	3.43	1.12	4.5	26	8	18	1.4	26	77	93
Lebron,David	21	R	28	a/a	BAL	76	4.29	1.58	12	23	14	9	2.2	29	83	27
Ledo,Luis	21	R	26	aa	CHW	41	5.94	1.66	5.4	23	12	11	0.6	37	63	77
	22	R	27	a/a	LAA	46	3.18	1.24	5.1	19	13	7	1.3	22	81	51
Lee,Andrew	21	R	28	a/a	WAS	68	7.03	1.65	12	18	11	7	1.7	32	60	24
	22	R	29	a/a	WAS	49	4.86	1.65	7.1	20	14	6	1.5	31	75	37
Lee,Chase	22	R	24	a/a	TEX	56	3.66	1.31	4.5	24	7	17	0.3	36	71	123
Leeper,Ben	21	R	24	a/a	CHC	37	1.33	0.80	5	32	10	23	0.5	19	87	146
	22	R	25	aaa	CHC	46	4.45	1.19	4.4	24	9	15	1.9	25	71	64
Legumina,Casey	22	R	25	aa	MIN	73	4.71	1.53	11	19	9	10	1.1	33	72	54
Leiter,Jack	22	R	22	aa	TEX	94	4.93	1.44	17	22	12	10	0.8	31	66	74
Leiter,Mark	21	R	30	a/a	DET	116	5.39	1.38	20	21	7	13	1.4	32	64	64
	22	R	31	aaa	CHC	22	5.81	1.40	15	25	7	19	1.6	35	62	90
Lemieux,Mack	21	L	25	a/a	ARI	47	3.05	1.42	5.6	24	13	11	0.2	32	77	95
	22	L	26	a/a	ARI	45	3.87	1.62	4.8	16	12	4	1.3	31	81	24
Leverett,Adam	21	R	23	a/a	PHI	45	5.54	1.45	19	20	8	12	1.5	32	65	53
	22	R	24	aa	PHI	76	5.65	1.53	11	21	8	13	1.7	34	67	50

PITCHER	yr	t	age	lvl	org	ip	era	whip	bf/g	k%	bb%	k-bb	hr/9	h%	s%	bpv
Lewis,Justin	21	R	26	aa	ARI	34	10.46	1.79	6.5	21	12	9	2.3	35	41	16
	22	R	27	a/a	ARI	50	4.53	1.41	5.4	18	12	6	2.3	24	79	12
Leyer,Robinson	21	R	28	aaa	MIN	46	9.19	1.98	6.3	18	17	1	2.6	31	57	-14
Liberatore,Matthew	21	L	22	aaa	STL	126	3.75	1.20	23	20	6	15	1.1	30	73	93
	22	L	23	aaa	STL	115	4.54	1.31	22	19	7	12	0.9	31	67	77
Lillie,Ryan	22	R	26	a/a	SD	52	5.16	1.74	11	14	12	2	1.2	32	73	16
Lindgren,Jeff	21	R	25	aa	MIA	106	4.90	1.47	23	15	7	8	1.6	31	72	29
	22	R	26	a/a	MIA	138	4.70	1.45	22	16	9	7	1.1	31	70	41
Lindow,Ethan	22	L	24	aa	PHI	97	4.33	1.28	21	14	5	8	1.1	29	69	51
Lingos,Eli	22	L	26	a/a	CLE	66	2.95	1.04	6.8	17	7	10	0.7	24	75	73
Little,Brendon	21	L	25	a/a	CHC	43	3.51	1.47	7.1	23	10	12	0.8	34	79	76
	22	L	26	aaa	CHC	51	4.27	1.54	6.2	18	11	7	0.6	33	73	56
Lodolo,Nicholas	21	L	23	a/a	CIN	52	2.79	1.08	16	34	6	29	0.6	35	76	187
Loeprich,Conner	22	R	25	aa	BAL	72	4.74	1.47	9.7	20	8	11	1.4	33	72	52
Logue,Zach	21	L	25	a/a	TOR	127	4.49	1.27	21	22	5	17	1.3	32	68	101
	22	L	26	aaa	OAK	80	6.13	1.80	22	12	8	4	1.8	35	70	-2
Lopez,Diomar	21	R	25	a/a	CIN	46	3.04	1.25	7	19	11	8	1.2	24	82	52
Lopez,Jose	22	L	23	a/a	TAM	58	2.31	1.17	5.7	34	14	20	0.1	29	79	145
Loseke,Barrett	22	R	26	aa	NYY	65	3.78	1.43	7.5	22	9	13	1.1	33	77	66
Loutos,Ryan	22	R	23	a/a	STL	50	3.30	1.43	5.8	20	8	12	0.5	35	77	87
Lowther,Zac	21	L	25	a/a	BAL	35	6.63	1.74	18	18	11	7	1.2	36	63	37
	22	L	26	aaa	BAL	45	10.14	2.29	14	16	10	6	2.2	44	57	-11
Lucas,Easton	22	L	26	aa	BAL	58	4.99	1.38	7.6	21	10	11	1.1	30	65	63
Lugo,Luis	21	L	27	a/a	CHC	97	5.75	1.67	17	18	13	5	1.5	32	68	27
Lugo,Moises	22	R	23	a/a	SD	74	2.70	1.14	7.5	28	11	16	0.5	27	78	113
Luna,Carlos	21	R	25	aa	MIL	30	3.67	1.20	20	18	3	15	1.4	30	76	108
	22	R	26	aa	MIL	110	5.65	1.59	17	19	8	11	1.4	35	67	47
Lunn,Connor	22	R	24	aa	STL	83	4.84	1.37	17	17	5	12	1.0	33	66	77
Lynch,Daniel	21	L	25	aaa	KC	57	6.56	1.79	22	18	7	11	1.5	40	65	44
MacGregor,Travis	21	R	24	aa	PIT	92	6.59	1.53	18	18	10	8	1.2	32	57	42
	22	R	25	a/a	PIT	81	5.30	1.54	9.3	22	13	9	0.9	32	66	67
Madero,Luis	21	R	24	aaa	MIA	57	3.47	1.38	14	20	10	10	0.7	31	76	72
Maese,Justin	22	R	26	aa	ATL	55	5.60	1.68	5	23	10	13	1.3	38	69	57
Maldonado,Anthony	22	R	24	a/a	MIA	65	3.12	1.07	6.1	29	8	21	1.1	27	76	117
Manning,Matt	21	R	23	aaa	DET	33	10.41	1.77	22	19	7	12	3.6	35	44	-14
	22	R	24	aaa	DET	21	2.60	1.40	15	21	11	11	0.0	33	79	93
Marciano,Joey	21	L	26	aa	SF	48	3.64	1.29	5.1	24	8	15	0.7	32	73	95
	22	L	27	aaa	SF	59	3.97	1.60	4.7	18	12	6	0.7	33	76	54
Marconi,Brian	21	L	24	a/a	PHI	49	3.58	1.43	5.5	24	13	11	1.0	30	78	71
	22	L	25	a/a	PHI	59	4.41	1.78	5.3	20	16	4	0.9	33	77	49
Margevicius,Nick	22	L	26	aaa	SEA	49	6.81	1.99	7.1	17	7	10	1.2	43	66	44
Marinaccio,Ron	21	R	26	a/a	NYY	69	2.43	1.03	6.7	32	11	21	0.6	25	79	128
Marman,Kyle	22	R	25	a/a	CLE	55	4.42	1.28	5.1	25	12	13	1.2	27	69	77
Marsh,Alec	22	R	24	a/a	KC	125	6.54	1.58	20	21	9	12	1.6	35	61	52
Marte,Jose	21	R	25	a/a	LAA	35	4.14	1.57	5.4	26	14	12	0.0	37	71	104
	22	R	26	aaa	LAA	36	4.62	1.34	4.4	24	14	10	0.9	27	67	79
Martin,Corbin	22	R	27	aaa	ARI	77	5.24	1.47	19	18	8	10	1.3	33	67	51
Martin,Davis	22	R	25	a/a	CHW	77	4.96	1.44	18	24	7	17	1.8	35	72	72
Martinez,Adrian	21	R	25	a/a	SD	127	3.25	1.26	20	19	8	11	0.6	30	75	81
	22	R	26	aaa	OAK	91	4.33	1.28	21	20	7	13	1.5	29	72	67
Martinez,Henry	21	R	27	a/a	DET	57	7.09	1.64	6.7	19	10	9	1.0	36	56	51
Martinez,Jose	21	R	22	aa	LA	34	6.79	2.01	18	12	6	6	1.7	40	69	-1
	22	R	23	a/a	LA	61	4.44	1.39	9.2	14	10	4	0.7	29	68	50
Martinez,Marcelo	21	L	25	a/a	KC	114	5.97	1.47	20	18	8	11	2.0	31	65	29
	22	L	26	a/a	KC	110	6.12	1.51	16	17	10	8	1.5	31	62	34
Marvel,James	21	R	28	aaa	PIT	133	6.06	1.74	24	12	10	2	1.4	33	67	5
	22	R	29	aaa	PHI	94	6.72	1.76	13	11	8	3	0.8	36	61	19
Mason,Ryan	21	R	27	a/a	MIN	56	3.20	1.53	6.5	20	13	7	0.7	32	81	62
Mata,Bryan	22	R	23	a/a	BOS	74	2.41	1.26	20	24	12	13	0.4	28	82	95
Matson,Zach	21	L	26	aa	COL	33	7.41	1.54	4.1	30	11	18	2.1	35	55	62
	22	L	27	a/a	PIT	58	4.58	1.40	5.9	14	11	3	0.9	27	69	36
McArthur,James	21	R	25	aa	PHI	75	4.75	1.39	17	21	7	14	1.2	33	69	73
	22	R	26	aa	PHI	57	5.48	1.76	20	20	10	10	1.7	37	73	33
McCambley,Zach	21	R	22	aa	MIA	40	6.24	1.67	20	23	11	12	2.6	33	71	18
	22	R	23	aa	MIA	94	6.19	1.50	21	21	12	9	1.0	31	59	59
McCarty,Kirk	21	L	26	aaa	CLE	124	5.70	1.45	22	16	8	8	1.9	29	66	19
	22	L	27	aaa	CLE	66	3.19	1.29	15	16	8	8	1.4	28	82	42
McCaughan,Darren	21	R	25	a/a	SEA	123	4.92	1.22	24	18	3	15	1.5	30	63	107
	22	R	26	aaa	SEA	155	4.09	1.17	22	18	6	12	1.0	28	68	80
McClure,Kade	21	R	25	a/a	CHW	106	5.93	1.57	19	20	8	12	1.5	35	65	52
	22	R	26	aaa	CHW	87	4.70	1.46	8.5	20	7	13	1.8	33	74	52
McGee,Easton	21	R	24	a/a	TAM	86	4.40	1.22	17	19	4	15	1.1	31	66	114
	22	R	25	aaa	TAM	109	5.30	1.36	17	15	4	11	1.6	32	66	58
McGreevy,Michael	22	R	22	aa	STL	99	3.32	1.16	20	15	5	11	0.8	29	74	84
McKendry,Evan	22	R	24	a/a	TAM	96	3.74	1.06	16	21	3	18	1.3	29	70	163
McLarty,Griffin	22	R	24	aa	BAL	46	6.03	1.63	7.3	20	14	6	1.7	29	67	28
McLaughlin,Sean	21	R	27	aa	ATL	36	7.61	1.99	6	17	8	9	1.3	42	62	32
	22	R	28	aa	LAA	59	5.08	1.34	6.5	19	8	12	1.2	30	65	61
McMahan,Pearson	21	R	25	a/a	WAS	48	5.38	1.55	6.6	14	15	-1	0.7	27	65	40
McRae,Alex	21	R	28	aaa	CHW	90	6.19	1.86	16	16	11	5	1.2	37	68	24
McSweeney,Morgan	22	R	25	a/a	BAL	48	4.02	1.43	5.4	17	12	5	1.2	27	76	37
Medina,Adonis	21	R	25	aaa	PHI	69	5.69	1.56	18	15	9	7	1.5	32	67	23
	22	R	26	aaa	NYM	31	4.35	1.73	7.8	18	11	8	1.0	36	77	49
Medina,Luis	21	R	22	aa	NYY	75	4.16	1.51	22	22	13	10	0.9	32	74	66
	22	R	23	aa	OAK	94	4.53	1.41	17	22	13	9	0.5	30	67	82
Mejia,Enmanuel	22	R	24	aa	PIT	51	5.59	1.61	5.7	18	13	5	0.9	32	65	48
Melendez,Jaime	22	R	21	aa	HOU	75	4.44	1.36	14	29	14	16	0.7	31	68	104
Mella,Keury	21	R	28	aaa	PIT	48	6.34	1.64	5.9	18	11	7	1.1	34	62	41
Mellen,Sean	22	L	24	aa	TOR	55	3.14	1.25	7	22	9	13	0.8	29	77	84
Mendez,Sal	21	L	26	a/a	TEX	66	5.89	1.44	10	18	11	7	0.9	30	59	51
Mercado,Michael	22	R	23	aa	TAM	104	4.43	1.29	18	23	7	16	1.1	32	69	89
Meyer,Max	21	R	22	a/a	MIA	111	2.70	1.30	21	25	9	16	0.7	32	82	98
	22	R	23	aaa	MIA	58	3.81	1.02	19	24	8	17	0.7	26	63	113

PITCHER	yr	t	age	lvl	org	ip	era	whip	bf/g	k%	bb%	k-bb	hr/9	h%	s%	bpv
Mikolajchak,Nick	21	R	24	aa	CLE	41	3.72	1.19	5.5	29	6	24	1.7	32	78	126
	22	R	25	aaa	CLE	51	2.58	1.23	4.4	20	12	8	0.4	26	80	79
Milburn,Matt	21	R	28	a/a	OAK	93	6.53	1.61	17	10	3	7	2.0	35	64	29
	22	R	29	aa	OAK	100	6.03	1.76	16	12	7	5	1.0	37	66	20
Miller,Bobby	22	R	23	a/a	LA	113	3.62	1.08	18	26	6	20	0.8	30	69	130
Miller,Bryce	22	R	24	aa	SEA	52	2.90	0.99	20	26	8	18	0.4	25	71	124
Miller,Erik	22	L	24	a/a	PHI	49	3.55	1.45	6.5	24	14	10	0.7	30	77	80
Miller,Evan	21	R	26	aaa	SD	79	4.70	1.53	8.4	20	7	12	0.5	37	68	81
	22	R	27	aaa	SD	55	6.98	1.59	5.3	16	10	6	1.1	32	55	38
Miller,Tyson	21	R	26	aaa	TEX	62	3.71	1.33	11	20	10	10	1.1	29	76	61
	22	R	27	aaa	TEX	91	4.19	1.47	14	22	9	13	1.1	33	75	67
Minnick,Matt	22	L	26	a/a	NYY	63	2.02	0.79	6.3	23	8	14	0.9	16	82	100
Misiaszek,Andrew	22	L	25	a/a	CLE	63	1.93	1.18	6	30	9	21	0.5	32	86	127
Mlodzinski,Carmen	22	R	23	aa	PIT	106	4.63	1.42	17	20	8	12	0.7	34	67	78
Moats,Dalton	21	L	26	a/a	TAM	30	6.58	1.82	7	19	7	12	1.3	41	65	52
	22	L	27	aaa	TAM	55	3.72	1.19	4.3	22	5	17	1.4	30	75	96
Molina,Cristopher	21	R	24	aa	LAA	41	3.99	1.11	20	21	9	12	0.9	25	66	81
	22	R	25	a/a	LAA	58	5.96	1.60	12	19	9	10	2.1	33	68	23
Montes de Oca,Bryce	22	R	26	a/a	NYM	52	3.12	1.38	5.1	28	15	13	0.0	31	75	120
Montgomery,Mason	22	L	22	aa	TAM	55	2.20	0.97	19	22	6	16	0.6	25	80	115
Moore,McKinley	22	R	24	aa	PHI	51	4.38	1.54	5.7	26	11	15	0.5	37	71	96
Morales,Francisco	21	R	22	a/a	PHI	93	6.45	1.61	17	25	15	10	1.1	32	60	67
	22	R	23	a/a	PHI	53	4.55	1.43	5	26	18	8	0.2	27	65	103
Moreno,Gerson	21	R	26	a/a	DET	51	5.87	1.48	6	25	14	11	1.9	28	65	46
	22	R	27	aa	DET	57	3.64	1.24	4.8	31	14	17	0.7	27	72	110
Moreta,Dauri	21	R	25	a/a	CIN	55	1.27	0.86	4.9	24	5	20	1.0	23	97	138
	22	R	26	aaa	CIN	28	4.87	1.81	4.7	19	11	8	2.6	35	83	-6
Morimando,Shawn	21	L	29	aaa	MIA	91	5.78	1.68	23	16	9	7	2.0	34	71	9
Moseley,Ryan	21	R	27	aaa	LA	49	7.70	2.02	6	13	12	1	1.3	37	62	5
Mosqueda,Oddanier	22	L	23	aa	BOS	60	4.43	1.14	5.3	26	8	18	1.2	28	64	100
Mota,Juan	21	R	25	a/a	CLE	51	5.99	1.67	5.7	27	15	11	0.9	35	64	76
Moyers,Steven	21	L	28	aa	SEA	54	3.54	1.25	10	18	7	11	0.6	30	72	79
	22	L	29	a/a	CHW	73	6.48	1.94	15	13	8	5	2.1	38	71	-12
Muckenhirn,Zach	21	L	26	aa	CHW	42	2.43	1.43	6	19	12	7	0.8	29	87	59
	22	L	27	aaa	CHW	55	3.01	1.41	4.9	19	10	9	1.5	29	87	41
Mujica,Jose	21	R	25	aaa	COL	92	9.79	1.87	18	15	6	9	3.0	37	51	-16
	22	R	26	a/a	NYY	62	4.43	1.13	6	19	7	12	2.4	22	74	34
Muller,Chris	22	R	26	aaa	TAM	60	4.84	1.62	5.2	23	12	11	0.8	36	70	73
Muller,Kyle	21	L	24	aaa	ATL	81	4.22	1.51	21	22	12	9	1.1	31	75	58
	22	L	25	aaa	ATL	136	4.31	1.37	25	24	8	16	1.1	33	71	83
Murfee,Penn	21	R	27	a/a	SEA	80	4.88	1.52	13	23	11	12	1.3	34	71	61
Murphy,Chris	21	L	23	aa	BOS	33	6.22	1.40	20	29	9	20	1.1	36	55	102
	22	L	24	a/a	BOS	154	4.24	1.32	21	19	11	8	0.8	28	69	65
Murphy,Luke	22	R	23	aa	LAA	46	2.37	1.06	4.9	25	13	11	0.0	23	75	114
Murray,Jayden	21	R	24	aa	TAM	39	3.01	0.77	18	26	5	22	1.3	19	70	146
	22	R	25	a/a	HOU	110	3.31	1.21	19	18	7	11	1.0	28	76	72
Murray,Shea	21	R	28	aa	PIT	45	4.66	1.99	5.9	17	19	-2	0.6	34	77	46
Myers,Tobias	21	R	23	a/a	TAM	119	4.42	1.18	19	27	6	21	1.5	31	68	117
	22	R	24	aaa	CHW	76	7.09	1.97	16	12	12	0	1.7	34	66	-9
Naile,James	21	R	28	aaa	OAK	63	4.17	1.62	5.5	14	5	9	0.9	37	76	49
	22	R	29	aaa	STL	74	3.28	1.48	7.2	14	6	8	0.5	34	78	61
Nardi,Andrew	22	L	24	a/a	MIA	53	2.37	0.92	5.4	32	9	23	0.6	25	77	144
Navarro,Edgar	22	R	24	a/a	CHW	47	3.79	1.50	5.4	22	16	5	0.6	27	75	79
Navilhon,Joe	21	R	28	a/a	DET	65	4.43	1.51	7.4	19	7	12	0.7	36	71	74
	22	R	29	a/a	DET	56	5.83	1.54	6.3	20	8	11	1.8	33	67	35
Neff,Zach	21	L	25	aa	MIN	54	5.31	1.23	7.1	20	9	11	1.5	26	60	52
Neidert,Nick	21	R	25	aaa	MIA	70	4.48	1.53	22	14	7	7	1.1	33	73	35
	22	R	26	aaa	MIA	46	2.13	1.15	13	21	5	16	1.1	30	88	109
Nelson,Nick	21	R	26	aaa	NYY	52	4.73	1.76	8.2	21	13	8	1.2	36	76	46
Nelson,Ryne	21	R	23	aa	ARI	77	3.61	1.23	22	28	8	20	1.4	31	77	103
	22	R	24	aaa	ARI	136	4.38	1.28	21	18	6	11	1.1	30	69	68
Nicolas,Kyle	21	R	22	aa	MIA	40	2.97	1.28	21	26	15	11	0.7	25	79	92
	22	R	23	aa	PIT	92	3.80	1.28	16	21	11	10	0.7	27	71	78
Nordlin,Seth	22	R	25	a/a	TEX	78	3.33	1.27	10	16	7	9	0.7	30	75	69
Nunez,Andres	21	R	26	a/a	KC	76	4.71	1.42	6.9	20	8	12	0.9	33	68	68
	22	R	27	aaa	KC	63	3.58	1.36	4.9	19	6	13	0.6	34	74	93
Nunez,Darien	21	L	28	a/a	LA	53	2.57	1.05	6.4	31	9	22	0.7	28	79	130
Nunez,Oddy	21	L	25	aa	PIT	45	8.96	2.02	7.8	18	17	1	0.9	36	54	38
Nutof,Ryan	22	R	27	a/a	CIN	61	3.59	1.67	6.4	20	14	6	0.6	34	79	61
Ogando,Cristofer	21	R	28	a/a	TAM	41	4.44	1.27	7.7	25	11	14	1.2	27	68	77
	22	R	29	aaa	TAM	54	4.86	1.38	5.5	18	12	6	1.2	27	67	45
Olczak,Jon	21	R	28	a/a	HOU	50	3.13	1.01	5.4	21	5	16	0.6	27	70	120
	22	R	29	aaa	HOU	67	4.77	1.53	6.2	20	7	13	1.8	34	75	45
Olivero,Deyni	22	R	24	a/a	ARI	125	4.75	1.42	21	14	7	7	1.1	31	69	40
Oller,Adam	21	R	27	a/a	NYM	120	3.46	1.22	21	23	9	14	0.6	29	72	95
	22	R	28	aaa	OAK	33	2.83	1.31	20	17	11	7	0.0	29	76	82
Olson,J.B.	21	R	26	aa	CHW	43	8.94	1.87	6.7	13	4	9	1.3	41	51	45
	22	R	27	a/a	CHW	71	5.85	1.65	6.4	14	10	4	1.5	32	67	14
Olson,Reese	22	R	23	aa	DET	121	4.11	1.24	19	27	7	20	0.9	33	69	121
Olthoff,Braden	22	R	23	a/a	LAA	63	4.54	1.40	19	9	8	2	0.9	28	69	20
Onyshko,Ben	22	L	26	aa	SEA	55	4.14	1.38	5.4	15	10	5	1.3	27	74	33
OReilly,John	22	R	27	aaa	PIT	63	6.04	1.64	6.9	8	9	-1	0.9	32	63	5
Ortiz,Luis	21	R	26	aaa	TEX	43	5.36	1.60	6.8	18	9	9	1.5	34	70	35
	22	R	27	aaa	SF	68	4.33	1.26	7.9	20	4	15	0.9	33	67	112
Ortiz,Luis	22	R	23	a/a	PIT	125	4.41	1.15	19	22	7	15	1.2	28	64	90
Orze,Eric	21	R	24	a/a	NYM	31	2.17	0.85	5.5	31	6	25	0.7	25	79	164
	22	R	25	aaa	NYM	48	4.63	1.16	6	28	7	21	1.7	29	67	105
Otanez,Michel	22	R	25	a/a	NYM	46	4.37	1.72	4.7	23	18	5	0.7	32	75	72
Otto Jr.,Glenn	21	R	25	a/a	TEX	97	3.81	1.14	23	28	6	22	0.6	32	67	142
Overton,Connor	21	R	28	aaa	PIT	60	2.26	1.23	11	16	5	11	0.4	31	83	90
	22	R	29	aaa	CIN	28	3.46	1.22	19	22	5	17	1.8	29	82	77
Oviedo,Johan	21	R	23	aaa	STL	55	5.79	1.48	20	21	11	10	0.9	32	61	62
	22	R	24	aaa	PIT	62	4.61	1.27	17	20	10	10	1.7	26	70	47

PITCHER	yr	t	age	lvl	org	ip	era	whip	bf/g	k%	bb%	k-bb	hr/9	h%	s%	bpv
Oviedo,Luis	22	R	23	a/a	CLE	60	4.97	1.51	10	19	14	5	1.3	27	70	45
Ozuna,Fernery	21	R	26	aa	TEX	47	6.81	1.50	6.4	20	9	11	2.5	30	61	15
	22	R	27	a/a	TEX	63	4.72	1.38	5.5	21	8	13	0.7	33	66	83
Pacheco,Freddy	22	R	24	a/a	STL	64	2.39	0.90	4.8	27	9	18	0.6	21	76	123
Padilla,Nicholas	22	R	26	a/a	CHW	45	2.15	1.22	5.7	21	14	7	0.2	25	82	88
Pallante,Neil	21	R	23	a/a	STL	100	3.44	1.48	19	17	9	7	0.6	33	77	59
Pannone,Thomas	21	L	27	aaa	LAA	119	6.64	1.75	23	12	7	5	1.5	36	64	8
	22	L	28	aaa	BOS	63	5.27	1.47	19	20	3	17	1.0	38	65	138
Paredes,Enoli	21	R	26	a/a	HOU	33	3.95	1.60	4.9	26	14	12	2.0	31	85	43
	22	R	27	aaa	HOU	56	2.56	1.20	4.5	28	13	15	0.6	26	81	107
Parke,John	21	L	26	a/a	CHW	114	5.14	1.44	19	14	8	6	1.1	31	66	38
	22	L	27	aaa	CHW	135	6.64	1.73	22	13	7	6	1.7	36	64	10
Parrish,Drew	21	L	24	aa	KC	83	4.12	1.23	19	22	8	14	0.9	30	68	88
	22	L	25	a/a	KC	130	3.99	1.21	19	14	9	4	1.1	24	70	40
Parsons,Tommy	21	R	26	aaa	STL	75	5.86	1.52	14	17	7	10	2.0	32	67	26
	22	R	27	aaa	STL	137	4.08	1.17	14	15	9	5	1.5	22	72	31
Patino,Luis	21	R	22	aaa	TAM	30	3.64	1.24	17	30	9	21	0.6	33	72	124
	22	R	23	aaa	TAM	34	4.27	1.31	16	21	8	13	1.3	30	71	68
Paulino,David	21	R	27	a/a	PHI	82	4.83	1.51	11	20	11	9	1.2	32	70	50
Paulino,Felix	21	R	26	a/a	CHW	46	8.99	1.64	9.9	18	10	8	2.2	32	46	13
	22	R	27	aa	CHW	69	3.42	1.16	8.3	19	7	12	1.2	27	76	71
Payano,Pedro	21	R	27	a/a	DET	124	6.36	1.70	22	15	13	2	1.3	31	64	23
	22	R	28	aaa	CIN	62	4.22	1.82	5.8	18	17	1	1.2	32	80	27
Pearson,Nate	21	R	25	aaa	TOR	32	5.94	1.27	11	27	11	16	1.5	28	56	76
Peek,Zach	22	R	24	aa	BAL	46	3.63	1.22	17	18	7	11	0.6	30	71	79
Peguero,Elvis	22	R	25	aaa	LAA	45	2.42	1.01	4.5	23	6	16	0.3	27	76	126
Peguero,Francis	22	R	27	aa	WAS	57	6.05	1.41	6.9	17	12	6	1.3	27	58	39
Peguero,Joel	21	R	24	a/a	TAM	58	4.90	1.44	6.2	18	9	9	0.3	33	64	75
	22	R	25	aaa	COL	58	4.59	1.65	5.2	15	12	3	1.0	32	74	30
Peluse,Colin	22	R	24	a/a	OAK	123	4.60	1.28	21	15	5	10	0.9	31	65	73
Pennington,Walter	22	L	24	aa	KC	62	5.52	1.67	8.4	15	9	5	0.5	36	65	48
Pepiot,Ryan	21	R	24	a/a	LA	104	4.44	1.24	16	25	10	15	1.5	27	70	72
	22	R	25	aaa	LA	92	2.11	0.98	18	25	8	17	0.8	24	84	114
Peralta,Sammy	22	L	24	a/a	CHW	62	3.56	1.25	7.4	24	8	17	0.9	31	74	100
Perez,Andrew	21	L	24	aa	CHW	45	4.61	1.39	6.1	27	7	20	1.5	35	71	96
	22	L	25	aaa	CHW	64	5.20	1.36	4.5	22	9	12	1.8	29	67	49
Perez,Eury	22	R	19	aa	MIA	75	4.17	1.14	17	31	7	24	0.9	33	65	143
Perez,Francisco	21	L	24	a/a	CLE	53	2.15	1.15	7	33	14	19	0.4	27	82	130
	22	L	25	aaa	WAS	48	4.84	1.39	4.5	24	15	9	0.5	28	64	85
Perkins,Jack	21	R	24	a/a	PHI	85	4.94	1.54	21	17	7	10	1.5	34	72	39
	22	R	25	a/a	PHI	63	7.86	1.84	11	16	11	5	1.6	36	58	15
Peters,Dillon	21	L	29	aaa	PIT	54	4.36	1.54	18	19	9	10	2.4	31	83	17
Pfaadt,Brandon	21	R	23	aa	ARI	34	4.62	1.35	24	21	5	17	2.8	30	81	58
	22	R	24	a/a	ARI	169	3.20	1.08	23	26	4	22	1.1	31	76	167
Phillips,Connor	22	R	21	aa	CIN	47	4.91	1.75	18	25	15	10	0.6	37	72	78
Phillips,Zack	22	L	24	aa	KC	46	6.10	1.53	10	14	9	5	1.1	31	60	32
Pidich,Matt	21	R	27	a/a	CIN	51	9.29	2.01	7.5	19	7	12	1.6	44	53	36
	22	R	28	a/a	CIN	52	9.05	1.98	6	18	12	6	1.8	38	55	12
Pike,Tyler	21	L	27	aa	STL	70	4.48	1.42	20	17	5	13	0.5	36	68	94
	22	L	28	aa	STL	63	4.06	1.38	7.4	21	10	10	0.8	30	72	74
Pilkington,Konnor	21	L	24	aa	CLE	102	3.64	1.09	18	25	10	15	1.1	24	71	90
	22	L	25	aaa	CLE	58	4.93	1.39	19	19	9	10	1.0	31	66	62
Pint,Riley	22	R	25	a/a	COL	47	4.60	1.39	4.8	22	14	8	0.8	27	67	70
Pinto,Aaron	21	R	25	aa	CLE	43	2.86	1.18	6.9	32	8	24	1.2	32	82	128
	22	R	26	a/a	CLE	55	4.98	1.75	6.5	22	12	10	1.0	38	73	58
Pinto,Julio	21	R	26	aa	CIN	34	3.42	1.54	5.1	20	20	0	1.0	22	81	56
	22	R	27	a/a	CIN	49	6.68	1.95	5.8	21	15	5	1.2	37	67	37
Plassmeyer,Michael	21	L	25	aa	SF	110	5.56	1.47	21	21	5	16	1.2	37	63	98
	22	L	26	aaa	PHI	129	4.37	1.32	20	19	8	10	1.9	27	75	36
Politi,Andrew	21	R	25	aa	BOS	75	7.56	1.71	16	21	11	10	1.3	36	56	47
	22	R	26	a/a	BOS	70	2.58	1.05	5.4	24	8	16	0.7	26	79	103
Ponce,Gabriel	22	R	23	a/a	TOR	59	3.73	1.21	6.6	21	12	9	1.1	24	73	64
Ponticelli,Thomas	21	R	24	aa	CLE	88	3.73	1.35	14	18	9	9	0.9	29	75	57
	22	R	25	a/a	CLE	72	3.86	1.37	7.7	17	10	7	0.9	28	74	53
Poulin,PJ	22	L	26	a/a	COL	62	4.34	1.44	4.8	22	9	13	1.2	33	73	67
Priester,Charles	22	R	22	a/a	PIT	86	2.79	1.17	20	20	8	13	0.4	29	76	97
Puckett,A.J.	21	R	26	aa	ATL	35	4.36	1.61	19	16	11	5	0.3	34	71	57
	22	R	27	aa	ATL	60	9.00	2.12	9	21	10	11	1.2	45	56	41
Puk,A.J.	21	L	26	aaa	OAK	50	5.90	1.67	7.8	20	8	12	1.9	37	70	37
Quinones,Luis	21	R	24	aa	TOR	37	5.53	1.41	20	27	16	11	1.0	27	61	80
	22	R	25	aa	TOR	71	5.34	1.44	16	23	14	9	0.9	29	63	74
Rackoski,Sean	21	R	26	aa	TOR	31	5.26	1.57	5.4	12	4	8	0.6	36	66	59
	22	R	27	a/a	TOR	46	6.96	1.76	5.6	18	10	8	1.1	37	60	39
Ragan,Mitch	22	R	25	aa	NYM	52	5.44	1.64	9.3	18	13	6	1.5	31	70	31
Ragans,Cole	21	L	24	aa	TEX	37	7.07	1.82	19	16	12	4	2.2	33	66	-6
	22	L	25	a/a	TEX	96	2.79	1.10	21	24	7	16	0.8	28	78	106
Rangel,Alan	21	R	24	aa	ATL	34	6.12	1.18	19	25	4	21	1.0	33	46	159
	22	R	25	a/a	ATL	119	6.45	1.72	20	22	10	12	1.3	38	64	53
Record,Joe	21	R	26	aa	HOU	63	3.95	1.42	14	16	14	2	0.8	26	74	46
	22	R	27	a/a	HOU	61	4.60	1.60	6	19	12	7	0.4	34	70	66
Remy,Peyton	21	R	25	aa	CHC	35	7.45	1.71	20	13	7	6	1.6	35	58	12
	22	R	26	a/a	CHC	96	6.45	1.51	14	21	10	10	1.5	32	59	51
Reyes,Denyi	21	R	25	aa	BOS	59	4.88	1.45	13	20	4	16	1.5	36	71	90
	22	R	26	aaa	BAL	54	7.30	1.64	16	17	3	14	2.3	38	60	74
Reyes,Luis	21	R	27	a/a	WAS	128	6.68	1.72	23	14	11	3	1.7	32	64	7
	22	R	28	a/a	WAS	123	6.72	1.70	21	16	13	3	1.4	31	62	20
Reyes,Samuel	22	R	26	a/a	CHC	54	4.66	1.39	8.5	23	10	13	1.4	31	71	61
Rivera,Blake	22	R	24	aa	SF	48	2.81	1.16	6.9	21	12	9	0.3	25	76	88
Roach,Dalton	21	R	25	aa	STL	116	5.05	1.52	21	19	8	11	1.6	33	72	42
	22	R	26	a/a	STL	101	3.55	1.14	9.8	18	5	13	1.3	27	74	80
Robaina,Julio	22	L	21	aa	HOU	82	6.04	1.76	16	19	14	6	1.0	34	66	47
Roberts,Austin	22	R	24	aa	PIT	49	4.19	1.49	5.7	21	8	12	1.4	34	77	60

PITCHER	yr	t	age	lvl	org	ip	era	whip	bf/g	k%	bb%	k-bb	hr/9	h%	s%	bpv
Robertson,Nick	22	R	24	a/a	LA	69	3.76	1.25	5.3	25	8	16	0.8	31	72	100
Robles,Domingo	21	L	23	aa	STL	93	5.20	1.42	17	16	5	11	1.3	33	66	62
	22	L	24	aa	STL	110	4.58	1.35	15	11	7	5	0.6	30	66	45
Rodriguez,Elvin	21	R	23	a/a	DET	79	7.00	1.40	18	20	9	11	2.3	28	55	25
	22	R	24	aaa	DET	100	5.02	1.56	19	17	8	9	1.3	34	71	41
Rodriguez,Grayson	21	R	22	aa	BAL	81	2.71	0.87	17	33	7	27	0.9	25	74	161
	22	R	23	a/a	BAL	77	2.51	0.92	18	31	8	23	0.2	26	72	155
Rodriguez,Jefry	21	R	28	aaa	WAS	47	6.40	1.69	18	16	13	4	1.0	33	62	35
	22	R	29	aaa	WAS	65	8.29	1.86	13	17	13	3	1.2	35	54	25
Rodriguez,Jose	21	R	26	a/a	ATL	102	6.03	1.48	19	17	6	10	1.8	32	63	33
	22	R	27	aaa	NYM	76	4.74	1.56	12	17	11	6	1.5	31	74	26
Rodriguez,Nivaldo	21	R	24	aaa	DET	62	7.24	1.92	13	12	10	2	1.9	35	65	-16
	22	R	25	aaa	DET	65	7.17	2.05	17	12	9	3	1.9	38	68	-15
Rodriguez,Yerry	21	R	24	a/a	TEX	83	5.39	1.44	13	23	9	14	0.9	34	63	79
	22	R	25	aaa	TEX	59	3.86	1.52	5.2	22	11	11	1.1	33	78	65
Rogers,Josh	21	L	27	aaa	WAS	91	5.82	1.65	23	12	6	5	1.8	34	69	4
	22	L	28	a/a	MIA	71	7.44	1.76	23	11	9	2	2.1	32	61	-20
Rom,Drew	21	L	22	aa	BAL	40	4.06	1.15	18	25	5	19	1.4	30	70	113
	22	L	23	a/a	BAL	122	4.27	1.45	20	22	8	15	0.8	36	72	88
Romero,Miguel	21	R	27	aaa	OAK	76	6.27	1.68	12	12	10	3	1.6	32	66	2
	22	R	28	aaa	OAK	54	6.16	1.80	6.6	10	10	-1	1.0	34	66	6
Romero,Tommy	21	R	24	a/a	TAM	111	3.04	1.05	19	29	7	22	0.8	29	75	132
	22	R	25	aaa	WAS	86	3.37	1.26	12	16	9	7	1.6	25	82	33
Rondon,Angel	21	R	24	aaa	STL	78	4.39	1.39	17	17	6	11	1.4	32	73	52
	22	R	25	aaa	SF	53	3.90	1.48	11	20	15	5	1.1	27	77	52
Rooney,John	21	L	24	aa	LA	30	3.86	1.48	16	27	14	13	0.8	32	76	85
	22	L	25	aa	LA	98	6.00	1.57	18	18	10	9	1.7	32	66	30
Roper,Kaleb	22	R	27	aa	CHW	84	8.08	2.06	14	17	11	6	1.9	40	63	1
Rosenberg,Kenny	21	L	26	a/a	TAM	37	2.96	1.36	9.7	26	10	16	1.3	31	85	79
	22	L	27	aaa	LAA	64	2.79	1.21	18	18	10	9	1.1	25	83	58
Ruppenthal,Matt	22	R	27	a/a	HOU	65	4.87	1.47	6.2	24	15	10	0.5	30	66	87
Russ,Addison	21	R	27	a/a	NYY	45	4.59	1.62	5.7	22	15	7	1.2	31	75	51
Ryan,Joe	21	R	25	aaa	MIN	66	4.29	0.93	18	30	5	25	1.4	25	58	153
Ryan,Ryder	21	R	26	aaa	TEX	45	6.52	1.68	5.3	22	10	12	1.5	37	63	49
	22	R	27	aaa	TEX	60	3.39	1.39	5.4	20	10	9	0.9	30	78	65
Salazar,Eduardo	22	R	24	aa	CIN	127	5.60	1.63	21	17	11	6	0.9	33	66	43
Salinas,Ricky	21	R	25	aa	CIN	77	5.93	1.74	21	22	10	12	1.8	37	70	38
	22	R	26	aa	CIN	72	6.21	1.84	11	14	15	0	1.5	32	69	9
Sammons,Bryan	21	L	26	a/a	MIN	109	7.87	1.79	19	16	13	3	2.2	31	59	-5
	22	L	27	aa	MIN	50	5.75	1.38	5.7	21	8	13	2.2	29	65	41
Sampen,Caleb	22	R	26	aa	TAM	45	4.28	1.45	14	12	4	7	1.1	33	74	41
Sampson,Adrian	21	R	30	aaa	CHC	83	5.86	1.81	24	12	10	2	2.2	33	74	-23
	22	R	31	aaa	CHC	29	4.05	1.42	15	11	6	5	1.8	29	80	6
Sanchez,Cristopher	21	L	25	aaa	PHI	73	5.39	1.58	17	23	15	8	0.6	32	65	77
	22	L	26	aaa	PHI	58	3.23	1.25	16	19	8	11	0.2	31	72	94
Sanchez,Mario	21	R	27	a/a	WAS	116	5.35	1.33	20	18	5	13	1.6	31	64	66
	22	R	28	aaa	MIN	92	4.22	1.22	13	14	7	7	1.0	27	68	49
Sanchez,Ricardo	22	L	25	aaa	DET	117	5.10	1.57	20	16	8	8	0.9	35	68	49
Sanders,Cam	21	R	25	aa	CHC	91	6.06	1.44	22	22	12	10	1.6	29	61	46
	22	R	26	a/a	CHC	99	4.76	1.30	12	21	13	8	0.9	25	65	67
Sands,Cole	21	R	24	aa	MIN	81	2.73	1.26	17	24	11	13	0.7	29	81	90
	22	R	25	aaa	MIN	63	5.08	1.63	15	21	8	13	1.0	38	70	66
Sanmartin,Reiver	21	L	25	a/a	CIN	101	4.27	1.37	17	23	7	15	0.7	35	69	96
	22	L	26	aaa	CIN	19	8.95	1.76	13	26	5	21	1.3	45	47	108
Santos,Antonio	21	R	25	aaa	COL	46	8.79	1.93	6.4	11	13	-1	2.2	32	57	-28
	22	R	26	a/a	NYM	45	5.10	1.56	7.1	18	9	9	1.2	34	70	45
Santos,Victor	21	R	21	aa	BOS	66	3.02	1.13	19	20	4	16	0.9	30	77	136
	22	R	22	a/a	BOS	147	5.02	1.28	22	17	5	12	1.3	31	63	74
Schmidt,Clarke	21	R	25	a/a	NYY	34	2.89	1.34	18	21	7	14	1.8	30	90	55
	22	R	26	aaa	NYY	33	3.56	1.16	16	27	7	21	0.3	34	68	147
Scholtens,Jesse	21	R	27	aaa	SD	103	4.57	1.38	21	18	8	11	1.0	32	69	63
	22	R	28	aaa	SD	84	3.48	1.34	9.5	20	8	12	1.0	31	78	70
Schreiber,John	21	R	27	aaa	BOS	67	3.54	1.57	8.9	17	10	8	0.5	35	77	62
Schulfer,Austin	21	R	26	aa	MIN	110	5.06	1.63	20	17	11	6	0.6	35	68	53
	22	R	27	a/a	MIN	57	3.11	1.07	5.1	21	7	14	0.5	27	72	100
Schultz,Paxton	22	R	24	aa	TOR	106	3.82	1.40	18	18	10	8	1.2	29	77	47
Scott,Adam	21	L	26	a/a	CLE	61	4.78	1.47	19	22	11	11	1.1	32	70	63
	22	L	27	aaa	CLE	76	5.65	1.61	9.1	19	12	7	1.3	32	67	43
Scott,Braden	22	L	24	aa	TOR	47	6.41	1.79	7.8	22	12	10	2.0	35	69	32
Seabold,Connor	21	R	25	aaa	BOS	54	4.43	1.33	20	19	9	10	1.1	29	69	59
	22	R	26	aaa	BOS	88	3.60	1.23	19	19	5	14	0.7	32	72	102
Sears,JP	21	L	25	a/a	NYY	106	4.15	1.25	17	26	7	19	1.1	32	70	106
	22	L	26	aaa	OAK	49	1.27	0.66	14	26	3	23	0.3	21	83	238
Sedlock,Cody	21	R	26	a/a	BAL	95	5.33	1.64	18	18	10	8	1.9	32	73	19
	22	R	27	aaa	DET	80	5.24	1.62	13	17	12	5	0.7	32	67	49
Seelinger,Matt	21	R	26	aa	SF	41	3.75	1.70	5.1	27	18	10	1.3	33	82	68
	22	R	27	a/a	PHI	64	3.66	1.49	6	22	13	8	0.9	30	78	64
Seminaris,Adam	22	L	24	a/a	LAA	67	4.33	1.60	17	15	9	6	0.6	34	73	49
Senga,Koudai	22	R	29	for	JAP	144	2.41	1.19	26	32	13	19	0.7	28	83	97
Sharp,Sterling	21	R	26	a/a	WAS	88	5.45	1.71	21	12	12	0	1.5	30	72	0
	22	R	27	a/a	BOS	102	6.12	1.77	19	15	10	6	0.9	37	65	34
Sheffield,Justus	22	L	26	aaa	SEA	103	6.32	1.79	20	15	9	6	1.3	37	66	22
Shook,TJ	22	R	24	aa	MIL	81	5.77	1.71	20	17	12	5	1.9	32	71	13
Shore,Logan	21	R	27	aaa	DET	73	5.67	1.63	20	15	10	4	1.0	33	66	32
	22	R	28	aaa	DET	53	6.19	1.84	9.9	12	10	2	1.9	34	71	-13
Short,Wyatt	21	L	27	aa	CHC	41	6.38	1.61	7	19	13	7	1.9	30	65	23
	22	L	28	a/a	CHC	81	3.49	1.42	12	16	11	5	0.7	29	77	50
Shortridge,Aaron	22	R	25	aa	PIT	56	4.89	1.72	18	12	12	0	0.8	32	72	21
Shugart,Chase	22	R	26	a/a	BOS	64	5.78	1.54	6.2	18	8	10	1.1	35	63	53
Shuster,Jared	22	L	24	a/a	ATL	142	3.91	1.16	21	22	7	15	1.3	27	71	80
Silseth,Chase	22	R	22	aa	LAA	83	2.09	0.92	21	30	8	22	1.1	23	86	132
Silven,Yoelvin	22	R	23	aa	CHW	48	7.19	1.70	6	20	8	13	2.5	36	63	21
Simpson,Josh	22	L	25	a/a	MIA	70	4.24	1.13	5.6	33	12	21	0.6	28	62	128

PITCHER	yr	t	age	lvl	org	ip	era	whip	bf/g	k%	bb%	k-bb	hr/9	h%	s%	bpv
Sisk,Evan	21	L	24	aa	MIN	41	4.65	1.79	6.5	22	15	8	0.9	36	75	60
	22	L	25	a/a	MIN	65	1.44	0.97	5	24	11	14	0.2	22	86	114
Skirrow,Noah	22	R	24	a/a	PHI	121	4.39	1.39	20	21	8	14	1.0	34	70	80
Slaten,Justin	22	R	25	aa	TEX	52	6.47	1.84	9.7	21	18	3	0.9	33	64	54
Small,Ethan	21	L	24	a/a	MIL	77	2.19	1.30	19	25	13	12	0.5	28	85	92
	22	L	25	aaa	MIL	103	4.58	1.42	16	22	13	9	0.7	30	68	74
Smith,Chad	21	R	26	aaa	COL	34	3.34	1.33	3.9	20	14	6	0.3	26	74	78
Smith,Kevin	21	L	24	a/a	BAL	83	5.24	1.71	17	22	15	7	1.9	31	75	31
	22	L	25	aaa	BAL	49	4.57	1.62	11	16	14	2	1.7	27	78	13
Smith,Ryan	21	L	24	a/a	LAA	58	5.68	1.57	23	19	7	12	1.5	36	67	50
	22	L	25	aaa	LAA	80	5.73	1.51	11	19	9	10	1.6	32	66	39
Solomon,Jared	22	R	25	a/a	CIN	48	8.76	1.86	4.9	19	14	5	2.8	31	57	-13
Solomon,Peter	21	R	25	aaa	HOU	99	4.71	1.37	20	22	9	13	1.4	30	70	61
	22	R	26	aaa	PIT	111	5.71	1.59	18	15	11	4	1.5	30	67	20
Soriano,George	22	R	23	a/a	MIA	76	2.88	1.29	7.8	22	12	11	0.4	29	78	91
Sotillet,Andres	21	R	24	a/a	KC	47	6.19	1.82	6.4	18	13	5	0.7	36	65	47
	22	R	25	a/a	KC	69	1.40	0.95	5.5	17	8	10	0.3	22	87	91
Spacke,Dylan	22	R	24	aa	BOS	66	6.03	1.66	9.3	16	12	4	1.0	32	64	36
Spence,Mitch	22	R	24	a/a	NYY	131	4.88	1.45	21	19	7	12	1.1	34	69	64
Spiers,Carson	22	R	25	a/a	CIN	123	6.15	1.70	21	16	9	8	2.4	33	71	-4
Spitzbarth,Shea	21	R	27	aaa	PIT	48	2.34	1.31	4.7	16	11	4	0.7	26	85	51
	22	R	28	a/a	DET	55	3.09	1.31	5.2	15	15	1	0.6	23	78	51
Sprinkle,Jonathan	22	R	24	aa	HOU	49	5.59	1.56	5.5	26	14	13	0.7	35	63	92
St. John,Locke	21	L	28	aaa	DET	60	3.74	1.66	7.5	20	11	10	0.8	36	79	61
	22	L	29	aaa	NYM	49	5.88	1.60	6.4	15	13	2	1.5	28	66	18
Stallings,Garrett	22	R	25	aa	BAL	119	6.61	1.53	20	19	5	13	2.3	34	62	43
Stambaugh,Dalton	22	L	25	aa	CHC	69	5.59	1.63	14	15	10	5	1.2	33	67	29
Stauffer,Adam	22	R	23	aa	BAL	64	3.41	1.35	11	23	10	12	0.9	30	78	76
Sterner,Justin	22	R	26	a/a	TAM	48	3.91	1.45	5.4	26	11	15	1.1	33	76	82
Stewart,Will	21	L	24	aa	MIA	101	5.36	1.52	22	16	9	7	0.9	33	65	47
	22	L	25	a/a	MIA	97	5.72	1.71	14	16	10	5	0.6	36	65	45
Stockton,Spencer	22	R	26	aa	CIN	49	4.57	1.45	8.4	20	11	9	1.3	30	72	48
Stone,Gavin	22	R	24	a/a	LA	98	1.29	1.06	19	30	8	22	0.2	31	88	151
Stoudt,Levi	22	R	25	a/a	CIN	111	5.50	1.46	19	18	7	11	1.3	33	65	54
Stratton,Hunter	21	R	25	a/a	PIT	51	2.49	1.30	5.6	26	12	14	0.5	30	82	100
	22	R	26	aaa	PIT	63	5.93	1.57	5.9	23	14	9	1.0	32	62	64
Strider,Spencer	21	R	23	a/a	ATL	64	5.97	1.38	18	30	11	19	1.0	34	56	103
Strotman,Drew	21	R	25	aaa	MIN	113	6.61	1.83	21	16	13	3	1.1	35	64	28
	22	R	26	aaa	TEX	54	5.67	1.68	5.8	20	13	6	0.8	34	66	56
Stryffeler,Michael	21	R	25	aa	SEA	43	2.45	1.21	4.2	35	21	14	0.7	17	82	125
	22	R	26	a/a	SF	53	3.98	1.35	4.2	29	16	13	0.7	27	72	99
Sullivan,Billy	22	R	23	aa	PHI	51	4.67	1.70	5.2	27	14	13	0.9	38	74	85
Sulser,Beau	21	R	27	aaa	PIT	124	6.36	1.86	22	13	10	4	1.5	36	68	6
	22	R	28	aaa	BAL	58	4.28	1.49	13	18	6	12	0.9	36	73	76
Swarmer,Matt	21	R	28	a/a	CHC	114	5.67	1.45	20	19	8	10	1.9	31	66	34
	22	R	29	aaa	CHC	82	4.14	1.40	16	19	10	9	1.0	30	73	57
Sweet,Devin	21	R	25	aa	SEA	81	5.45	1.52	14	23	8	14	2.1	34	71	44
	22	R	26	aa	SEA	58	5.15	1.35	5.6	23	9	14	1.2	31	64	75
Szapucki,Thomas	21	L	25	aaa	NYM	43	3.70	1.59	19	18	13	5	0.9	31	79	50
	22	L	26	aaa	SF	73	2.90	1.30	12	27	10	17	0.5	33	78	109
Tabor,Matt	21	R	23	a/a	ARI	84	5.99	1.35	19	18	8	9	1.8	28	60	32
Tamarez,Misael	22	R	22	a/a	HOU	122	3.88	1.17	17	25	12	13	1.2	23	72	79
Tapani,Ryan	21	R	27	aa	WAS	48	5.34	1.39	8.4	19	10	9	2.1	26	69	23
Tarnok,Freddy	21	R	23	aa	ATL	45	3.46	1.29	21	28	9	19	0.5	35	73	120
	22	R	24	a/a	ATL	108	4.84	1.41	18	23	10	13	1.4	31	70	61
Taveras,Willy	22	R	24	aa	NYM	45	5.04	1.50	8.1	15	4	11	2.1	34	74	47
Taylor,Curtis	21	R	26	a/a	TOR	36	6.95	1.70	5.5	20	11	9	1.5	35	61	36
Teel,Carson	21	L	26	a/a	WAS	92	5.47	1.49	12	15	7	8	2.1	31	70	16
	22	L	27	a/a	WAS	64	6.65	1.78	8.9	16	8	8	1.2	38	63	31
Teng,Kai-Wei	22	R	24	aa	SF	137	5.57	1.60	22	23	14	9	0.8	33	65	69
Tetreault,Jackson	21	R	25	a/a	WAS	67	4.52	1.52	24	15	8	7	1.5	32	75	28
	22	R	26	aaa	WAS	58	4.44	1.38	20	16	9	7	1.5	28	73	33
Thomas,Connor	21	L	23	a/a	STL	124	3.03	1.30	20	19	5	13	0.9	32	80	86
	22	L	24	aaa	STL	135	4.91	1.53	21	14	6	9	0.8	35	68	58
Thomas,Tahnaj	22	R	23	aa	PIT	52	2.85	1.23	5.7	20	9	11	0.6	29	78	84
Thompson,Jake	22	R	28	a/a	BOS	51	3.88	1.53	6.8	19	15	4	0.2	31	73	72
Thompson,Riley	22	R	26	aa	CHC	57	4.13	1.37	13	21	12	9	1.1	28	73	62
Thompson,Zack	21	L	24	aaa	STL	93	6.91	1.83	20	15	12	4	1.5	35	64	15
	22	L	25	aaa	STL	54	4.27	1.17	11	23	8	15	0.8	29	64	99
Tiedemann,Tai	22	R	26	aa	TEX	61	6.10	1.77	6.5	8	10	-2	1.5	31	68	-17
Todd,Reagan	21	L	26	a/a	COL	53	5.35	1.58	4.8	22	10	12	1.7	34	71	46
	22	L	27	aaa	COL	47	5.33	1.59	4.2	21	12	9	1.0	33	67	58
Toribio,Noe	21	R	22	aa	PIT	50	4.45	1.22	14	17	6	10	0.8	29	64	73
	22	R	23	a/a	PIT	83	4.33	1.40	9.5	17	11	6	0.5	29	68	65
Torres,Eric	22	L	23	aa	LAA	51	1.49	0.91	4.5	34	10	23	0.5	23	87	153
Torres,Jojanse	22	R	27	a/a	HOU	45	9.25	2.50	6.2	16	19	-3	2.4	39	66	-24
Toussaint,Touki	22	R	26	aaa	LAA	56	4.97	1.59	11	20	13	7	1.4	30	72	41
Troop,Alex	22	L	26	a/a	WAS	115	5.29	1.42	17	21	7	15	1.7	33	68	61
Tully,Tanner	21	L	27	a/a	CLE	113	4.30	1.62	19	15	7	9	0.9	36	75	49
	22	L	28	aaa	CLE	122	4.35	1.43	22	14	5	10	0.8	34	70	71
Uceta,Edwin	21	R	23	aaa	LA	30	4.32	1.29	12	26	9	17	1.1	31	69	93
	22	R	24	aaa	ARI	50	3.93	1.16	7.1	27	11	15	1.1	25	70	95
Ueckert,Cayne	22	R	26	aaa	CHC	50	7.81	2.16	6.4	20	19	1	2.0	35	66	14
Vallimont,Chris	21	R	24	aa	MIN	91	6.74	1.80	20	26	15	11	1.5	37	64	54
	22	R	25	a/a	BAL	104	5.76	1.56	18	18	10	8	1.2	32	65	43
Valverde,Alex	21	R	25	aa	TAM	72	5.43	1.48	10	25	9	16	0.7	36	63	92
	22	R	26	aa	NYM	87	5.64	1.57	17	21	9	12	1.7	34	68	46
Van Belle,Brian	22	R	26	aa	BOS	80	5.19	1.41	21	19	4	15	1.8	34	69	92
Vargas,Emilio	21	R	25	aa	CHW	85	3.97	1.39	17	23	9	14	1.2	33	75	74
	22	R	26	a/a	CHW	115	5.38	1.51	19	19	11	8	1.5	31	68	37
Vargas,Jesus	22	R	24	a/a	NYM	74	6.20	1.43	17	15	5	10	1.5	33	59	51
Varland,Gus	21	R	25	aa	LA	36	5.56	1.43	9.6	12	10	1	1.7	26	65	3
	22	R	26	aa	LA	72	5.96	1.65	7.9	21	10	11	1.4	35	66	47
Varland,Louie	22	R	25	a/a	MIN	127	2.88	1.27	22	22	7	15	0.9	31	81	92
Vasquez,Randy	22	R	24	aa	NYY	116	4.07	1.33	19	21	8	13	0.8	32	71	80
Velez,Antonio	22	L	25	aa	BAL	49	6.37	1.42	19	20	6	14	2.5	31	62	36
Veneziano,Anthony	22	L	25	aa	KC	124	5.62	1.62	21	17	10	7	1.4	33	68	34
Vennaro,Zach	21	R	25	aa	MIL	38	8.96	2.09	5.1	22	13	10	2.2	41	59	18
	22	R	26	a/a	MIL	55	5.69	1.73	5.1	19	14	4	0.6	34	66	53
Vieaux,Cam	21	L	28	a/a	PIT	74	6.10	1.72	13	16	12	4	1.3	33	66	23
	22	L	29	aaa	PIT	50	3.39	1.19	5.7	17	8	9	1.2	26	77	55
Villalobos,Eli	22	R	25	a/a	MIA	80	3.09	1.08	6	27	9	18	1.0	26	76	100
Vines,Darius	22	R	24	a/a	ATL	142	4.53	1.38	22	22	8	14	1.2	33	70	74
Waldichuk,Ken	21	L	23	aa	NYY	80	4.91	1.39	21	28	11	16	1.6	31	70	70
	22	L	24	a/a	OAK	97	2.25	1.03	18	29	7	21	0.6	28	81	139
Waldron,Matt	21	R	25	aa	SD	32	7.10	1.74	21	17	11	6	0.5	36	57	53
	22	R	26	a/a	SD	115	5.62	1.52	20	15	7	8	0.9	34	63	51
Walker,Ryan	22	R	27	a/a	SF	55	3.75	1.45	4.7	21	11	10	0.1	33	72	89
Wallace,Jacob	22	R	24	aa	BOS	58	4.01	1.47	5.3	25	19	6	1.0	24	75	71
Walston,Blake	22	L	21	aa	ARI	107	4.33	1.32	21	21	7	14	1.0	32	69	84
Walter,Brandon	22	L	26	a/a	BOS	59	3.90	0.99	20	25	3	22	0.9	30	62	211
Walters,Nash	22	R	25	a/a	LAA	55	4.19	1.25	4.4	25	8	17	0.7	32	67	108
Warner,Austin	21	L	27	aaa	STL	74	3.42	1.14	7.2	19	7	12	0.9	27	73	81
	22	L	28	aaa	SEA	87	4.89	1.53	11	15	8	7	1.2	33	71	34
Warren,Will	22	R	23	aa	NYY	94	4.13	1.34	22	18	8	10	0.7	31	70	70
Washington,Mark	21	R	25	aa	LA	63	2.04	1.15	6.8	21	10	12	1.4	24	93	63
	22	R	26	a/a	LA	59	3.33	1.26	5.8	18	9	8	0.7	28	75	64
Watson,Nolan	21	R	24	aa	KC	69	7.02	1.92	13	10	10	0	1.6	35	65	-14
	22	R	25	aa	SD	91	5.86	1.67	14	18	11	8	0.7	36	64	58
Watson,Ryan	22	R	25	a/a	BAL	108	3.50	1.14	16	19	6	13	1.5	27	77	73
Weathers,Ryan	22	L	23	aaa	SD	123	5.18	1.61	18	14	8	5	1.5	32	72	16
Weems,Avery	22	L	25	aa	TEX	91	4.95	1.44	15	21	7	14	1.2	34	68	75
Weigel,Patrick	21	R	27	aaa	MIL	44	7.79	2.09	6	18	18	0	1.3	36	63	26
	22	R	28	aaa	SEA	62	3.98	1.44	5	18	13	5	0.7	28	73	59
Weiman,Blake	21	L	26	aaa	PIT	46	5.22	1.19	5.3	19	7	12	2.0	25	63	44
	22	L	27	a/a	SEA	45	4.21	1.07	5.2	19	3	16	1.0	29	63	142
Weiss,Ryan	21	R	25	a/a	ARI	79	4.28	1.21	9.4	22	9	14	1.1	28	68	77
	22	R	26	a/a	KC	63	6.84	1.73	6.1	15	7	8	1.5	37	62	25
Weissert,Greg	21	R	26	a/a	NYY	52	1.93	1.23	5.3	23	14	9	0.4	25	86	89
	22	R	27	aaa	NYY	48	1.87	0.98	4.3	29	10	19	0.6	24	84	127
Wentz,Joey	21	L	24	aa	DET	54	4.48	1.50	18	20	14	5	1.3	27	74	43
	22	L	25	aaa	DET	49	3.23	1.21	16	21	10	12	0.9	27	77	73
Wesneski,Hayden	21	R	24	a/a	NYY	94	4.71	1.36	22	22	7	15	1.2	33	68	81
	22	R	25	aaa	CHC	111	3.84	1.18	19	19	7	12	0.7	28	68	83
West,Derek	22	R	26	aa	HOU	48	4.63	1.56	6.6	20	13	7	0.5	32	70	68
White,Brendan	22	R	24	aa	DET	68	2.72	0.93	5.3	22	6	16	0.3	25	70	129
White,Mitchell	21	R	27	aaa	LA	32	1.78	1.33	13	23	8	15	0.3	34	87	105
	22	R	28	aaa	TOR	18	4.96	0.99	23	18	5	13	1.2	24	51	83
Whitley,Forrest	22	R	25	aaa	HOU	33	6.80	1.72	15	19	15	4	0.5	34	58	64
Whitney,Blake	22	R	26	a/a	CHC	69	4.05	1.34	8.2	20	9	12	1.0	31	72	70
Widener,Taylor	22	R	28	aaa	ARI	38	4.57	1.37	5.9	22	7	16	0.9	34	68	92
Wiles,Collin	21	R	27	aaa	TEX	86	4.98	1.45	16	17	6	12	1.4	34	69	58
	22	R	28	aaa	OAK	144	4.32	1.37	23	13	4	9	1.1	32	71	65
Willeman,Zach	21	R	25	aa	LA	49	3.72	1.34	6.2	24	10	14	0.7	31	73	87
	22	R	26	a/a	KC	62	5.62	1.54	5.4	17	13	5	1.2	29	65	38
Williams,Garrett	21	L	27	a/a	STL	53	5.20	1.59	6.3	20	17	3	0.6	29	66	65
	22	L	28	a/a	STL	79	4.94	1.45	12	21	12	10	0.9	31	67	66
Williams,Gavin	22	R	23	aa	CLE	70	2.45	1.02	17	25	9	16	1.1	23	84	98
Williamson,Brandon	21	L	23	aa	SEA	68	3.86	1.34	22	30	8	22	0.9	37	74	120
	22	L	24	a/a	CIN	124	4.65	1.68	21	19	14	5	0.8	33	73	51
Wilson,Bryse	21	R	24	aaa	ATL	56	5.30	1.59	25	14	7	7	1.4	34	70	25
	22	R	25	aaa	PIT	37	2.95	1.09	24	18	4	14	1.2	28	80	104
Winans,Allan	22	R	27	a/a	ATL	60	4.26	1.46	21	18	6	12	0.7	35	71	77
Winckowski,Josh	21	R	23	a/a	BOS	117	4.69	1.38	21	18	7	11	0.8	33	67	68
	22	R	24	aaa	BOS	62	3.98	1.27	20	20	7	13	0.5	32	68	93
Winn,Cole	21	R	22	a/a	TEX	86	2.74	0.90	15	29	9	19	0.8	21	73	122
	22	R	23	aaa	TEX	123	5.57	1.60	19	18	13	5	0.7	31	65	55
Withrow,Matt	21	R	28	aa	ATL	51	4.19	1.58	9	17	16	1	0.5	29	73	58
Wolf,Adam	22	L	26	aa	DET	90	2.89	1.39	11	18	9	9	0.5	31	80	71
Wolfram,Grant	22	L	26	aa	TEX	57	4.35	1.64	6.5	21	16	6	0.4	32	73	75
Woods Richardson,Simeon	21	R	21	aa	MIN	54	6.19	1.55	16	28	14	14	0.8	35	59	91
	22	R	22	a/a	MIN	110	2.40	0.97	18	23	7	16	0.4	25	76	119
Woods,Stephen	21	R	26	aa	KC	48	9.33	2.50	12	14	19	-5	1.0	40	61	12
	22	R	27	a/a	KC	61	4.37	1.97	7.1	18	15	3	0.6	37	78	50
Workman,Blake	21	R	24	aa	ARI	31	8.24	1.61	6.9	26	6	20	2.7	39	53	71
	22	R	25	a/a	ARI	51	3.80	1.28	5.3	21	6	15	1.0	32	74	94
Wright,Chris	22	L	24	aa	SF	56	4.14	1.49	5.9	26	14	12	0.7	32	73	86
Wright,Kyle	21	R	26	aaa	ATL	137	4.01	1.42	24	19	8	10	0.7	33	73	68
Wynne,Randy	21	R	28	aa	CIN	90	6.65	1.65	16	13	3	10	1.7	37	62	53
	22	R	29	aaa	CIN	134	6.36	1.78	24	11	7	4	2.7	34	73	-35
Yajure,Miguel	21	R	23	aaa	PIT	45	3.12	1.06	20	19	7	12	1.1	24	76	74
	22	R	24	aaa	PIT	56	5.89	1.50	15	18	9	9	0.9	33	61	53
Yamamoto,Jordan	22	R	26	a/a	NYM	50	5.29	1.54	10	19	7	11	1.6	34	70	45
Yan,Jefry	22	L	26	aa	MIA	57	5.71	1.84	7	27	18	9	0.5	38	67	87
Ynoa,Huascar	22	R	24	aaa	ATL	79	6.97	1.56	19	22	11	11	1.8	32	58	35
Zamora,Daniel	21	L	28	aaa	SEA	45	7.36	1.89	6.7	20	13	8	1.6	37	63	29
	22	L	29	aaa	LA	63	3.49	1.37	5.2	19	9	11	0.7	31	76	75
Zanghi,Joe	22	R	28	a/a	NYM	50	3.23	1.32	5.8	23	14	9	1.0	25	79	73
Zavolas,Noah	21	R	25	aa	MIL	122	5.34	1.36	23	20	6	14	1.5	32	65	64
	22	R	26	aa	MIL	63	6.81	1.64	20	17	9	8	1.9	33	62	17
Zerpa,Angel	21	L	22	a/a	KC	48	6.85	1.60	15	21	9	12	1.4	36	58	54
	22	L	23	a/a	KC	73	3.69	1.29	16	18	7	11	0.6	31	72	78
Zimmermann,Bruce	22	L	27	aaa	BAL	77	3.89	1.43	23	17	5	12	0.8	35	74	79
Zuniga,Guillerm	21	R	23	aa	LA	36	2.92	1.02	6	30	8	22	1.2	26	78	122

LEADERBOARDS & INSIGHTS

This section provides rankings of projected skills indicators for 2023. Rather than take shots in the dark predicting league leaders in the exact number of home runs, or stolen bases, or strikeouts, the Forecaster's Leaderboards focus on the component elements of each skill.

For batters, we've ranked the top players in terms of pure power, speed, and batting average skill, breaking each down in a number of different ways. For pitchers, we rank some of the key base skills, differentiating between starters and relievers, and provide a few interesting cuts that might uncover some late round sleepers.

In addition, the section examines some potential gainers/faders for 2023 based on 2022 results and supporting skills (or lack thereof), and a format-specific leaderboard for DFS play.

These are clearly not exhaustive lists of sorts and filters—drop us a note if you see something we should consider for next year's book. Also, the database at BaseballHQ.com allows you to construct your own custom sorts and filters. Finally, remember that these are just tools. Some players will appear on multiple lists—even mutually exclusive lists—so you have to assess what makes most sense and make decisions for your specific application.

Power

Top PX, 400+ AB: Top power skills among projected full-time players.

Top PX, –300 AB: Top power skills among projected part-time players; possible end-game options are here.

Position Scarcity: See which positions have deepest power options.

Top PX, ct% over 75%: Top power skills among the top contact hitters. Best pure power options here.

Top PX, ct% under 70%: Top power skills among the worst contact hitters; free-swingers who might be prone to streakiness and lower BAs.

Top PX, FB% over 40%: Top power skills among the most extreme fly ball hitters. Most likely to convert their power into home runs.

Top PX, FB% under 35%: Top power skills among those with lesser fly ball tendencies. There may be more downside to their home run potential.

Speed

Top Spd, 400+ AB: Top speed skills among projected full-time players.

Top Spd, -300 AB: Top speed skills among projected part-time players; possible end-game options here.

Position Scarcity: See which positions have deepest speed options.

Top Spd, OB% .330 and above: Top speed skills among those who get on base most often. Best opportunities for stolen bases here.

Top Spd, OB% under .300: Top speed skills among those who have trouble getting on base; worth watching if they can improve OB%.

Top Spd, SBA% over 15%: Top speed skills among those who get the green light most often. Most likely to convert their speed into stolen bases.

Top Spd, SBA% under 10%: Top speed skills among those who are currently not running; sleeper SBs here if given more opportunities.

Batting Average

Top ct%, 400+ AB: Top contact skills among projected full-time players. Contact is strongly correlated to higher BAs.

Top ct%, -300 AB: Top contact skills among projected part-time players; possible end-gamers here.

Low ct%, 400+ AB: The poorest contact skills among projected full-time players. Potential BA killers.

Top ct%, bb% over 9%: Top contact skills among the most patient hitters. Best batting average upside here.

Top ct%, bb% under 6%: Top contact skills among the least patient hitters; free-swingers who might be prone to streakiness or lower BAs.

Top ct%, GB% over 50%: Top contact skills among the most extreme ground ball hitters. A ground ball has a higher chance of becoming a hit than a non-HR fly ball so there may be some batting average upside here.

Top ct%, GB% under 40%: Top contact skills from those with lesser ground ball tendencies. These players make contact but hit more fly balls, which tend to convert to hits at a lower rate than GB.

Potential Skills Gainers/Faders
Expected Stats vs. Actual

These charts look to identify upcoming changes in performance by highlighting 2022 results that were in conflict with their corresponding skill indicators as well as our own set of expected statistics (xBA, xHR, xSB for hitters; xW, xERA, xWHIP for pitchers). Use these as a check on recency bias, as players here could compile stats in the upcoming season that look every different than the one just completed. Additional details are provided on the page in which the charts appear.

Pitching Skills

Top K-BB%: Leaders in projected K-BB% rates.

Top BB%: Leaders in fewest projected walks allowed.

Top K%: Leaders in projected strikeout rate.

Top Ground Ball Rate: GB pitchers tend to have lower ERAs (and higher WHIP) than fly ball pitchers.

Top Fly Ball Rate: FB pitchers tend to have higher ERAs (and lower WHIP) than ground ball pitchers.

High GB, Low K%: GB pitchers tend to have lower K rates, but these are the most extreme examples.

High GB, High K%: The best at dominating hitters and keeping the ball down. These are the pitchers who keep runners off the bases and batted balls in the park, a skills combination that is the most valuable a pitcher can own.

Lowest xERA: Leaders in projected skills-based ERA.

Top BPX: Two lists of top skilled pitchers. For starters, those projected to be rotation regulars (160+ IP) and fringe starters with skill (<120 IP). For relievers, those projected to be frontline closers (10+ saves) and high-skilled bullpen fillers (<10 saves).

Risk Management

These lists include players who've accumulated the most days on the injured list over the past five years (Grade "F" in Health) and whose performance was the most consistent over the past three years. Also listed are the most reliable batters and pitchers overall, with a focus on positional and skills reliability. As a reminder, reliability in this context is not tied to skill level; it is a gauge of which players manage to accumulate playing time and post consistent output from year to year, whether that output is good or bad.

Daily Fantasy Indicators

Players splits, teams and park factors designed to give you an edge in DFS.

BATTER SKILLS RANKINGS — Power

TOP PX, 400+ AB

NAME	POS	PX
Trout,Mike	8	227
Judge,Aaron	0 8 9	209
Alvarez,Yordan	0 7	188
Schwarber,Kyle	7	183
Ohtani,Shohei	0	176
Tatis Jr.,Fernando	0	171
Harper,Bryce	0	171
Suarez,Eugenio	5	165
Wisdom,Patrick	5	165
Hernández,Teoscar	9	161
Olson,Matt	3	160
Stanton,Giancarlo	0 9	159
Hoskins,Rhys	3	158
Riley,Austin	5	158
Chapman,Matt	5	156
Lowe,Brandon	4	155
Cruz,Oneil	6	154
Alonso,Pete	0 3	153
Renfroe,Hunter	9	153
Adames,Willy	6	151
Brown,Seth	3 7 9	151
Goldschmidt,Paul	0 3	150
Muncy,Max	0 4 5	150
Springer,George	0 8 9	150
Rodríguez,Julio	8	149
Perez,Salvador	0 2	149
Acuña Jr.,Ronald	0 9	148
Devers,Rafael	5	147
Betts,Mookie	9	147
Story,Trevor	4	147
Yastrzemski,Mike	8 9	145
Chisholm,Jazz	4	145
Haniger,Mitch	9	145
Voit,Luke	0 3	145
Garcia,Adolís	0 8 9	143
Meneses,Joey	3 9	143
Tellez,Rowdy	3	142
Ramírez,José	0 5	142
Ward,Taylor	9	142
Bryant,Kris	7	142

TOP PX, 300 or fewer AB

NAME	POS	PX
Ríos,Edwin	0	207
Carpenter,Matt	0	189
Sanó,Miguel	3	178
Hiura,Keston	0 3	166
Villar,David	5	165
Hall,Darick	0	158
Dalbec,Bobby	3 5	156
Garlick,Kyle	7 9	149
Maton,Nick	O	146
Aquino,Aristides	9	146
Cordero,Franchy	3 9	144
Jansen,Danny	2	142
Lewis,Royce	6	139
Garcia,Dermis	3	136
Jeffers,Ryan	2	136
Moore,Dylan	6 9	130
Sánchez,Jesús	8	130
Zavala,Seby	2	129
Bote,David	4	127
Jones,Nolan	9	126
Velazquez,Nelson	8 9	125
Hilliard,Sam	7	123
Alvarez,Francisco	2	123

POSITIONAL SCARCITY

NAME	POS	PX
Judge,Aaron	DH	209
Ríos,Edwin	2	207
Buxton,Byron	3	201
Carpenter,Matt	4	189
Alvarez,Yordan	5	188
Ohtani,Shohei	6	176
Raleigh,Cal	CA	181
Zunino,Mike	2	164
Perez,Salvador	3	149
Haase,Eric	4	143
Jansen,Danny	5	142
Contreras,William	6	141
Smith,Will	7	139
Contreras,Willson	8	137
Sanó,Miguel	1B	178
Hiura,Keston	2	166
Olson,Matt	3	160
Hoskins,Rhys	4	158
Dalbec,Bobby	5	156
Alonso,Pete	6	153
Brown,Seth	7	151
Goldschmidt,Paul	8	150
Belt,Brandon	9	145
Voit,Luke	10	145
Lowe,Brandon	2B	155
Muncy,Max	2	150
Story,Trevor	3	147
Chisholm,Jazz	4	145
Gorman,Nolan	5	136
Castro,Rodolfo	6	135
Taylor,Chris	7	131
Morel,Christopher	8	129
Suarez,Eugenio	3B	165
Villar,David	2	165
Wisdom,Patrick	3	165
Riley,Austin	4	158
Dalbec,Bobby	5	156
Chapman,Matt	6	156
Muncy,Max	7	150
Devers,Rafael	8	147
Ramírez,José	9	142
Henderson,Gunnar	10	142
Cruz,Oneil	SS	154
Adames,Willy	2	151
Lewis,Royce	3	139
Moore,Dylan	4	130
Bichette,Bo	5	126
Witt Jr.,Bobby	6	124
Seager,Corey	7	124
Bogaerts,Xander	8	122
Trout,Mike	OF	227
Judge,Aaron	2	209
Buxton,Byron	3	201
Gallo,Joey	4	191
Alvarez,Yordan	5	188
Schwarber,Kyle	6	183
Hernández,Teoscar	7	161
Duvall,Adam	8	160
Stanton,Giancarlo	9	159
Soler,Jorge	10	157
Renfroe,Hunter	11	153
Brown,Seth	12	151
Springer,George	13	150
Rodríguez,Julio	14	149
Garlick,Kyle	15	149
Acuña Jr.,Ronald	16	148

TOP PX, ct% over 75%

NAME	Ct%	PX
Alonso,Pete	77	153
Goldschmidt,Paul	75	150
Springer,George	78	150
Perez,Salvador	76	149
Devers,Rafael	77	147
Betts,Mookie	82	147
Tellez,Rowdy	77	142
Jansen,Danny	78	142
Ramírez,José	85	142
Bryant,Kris	75	142
Tucker,Kyle	81	141
Santander,Anthony	78	141
Smith,Will	78	139
Lewis,Royce	75	139
Castellanos,Nick	75	139
Machado,Manny	79	139
Walker,Christian	75	138
Arenado,Nolan	86	134
Soto,Juan	81	134
Guerrero Jr.,Vladimir	82	133
Meadows,Austin	75	131
Realmuto,J.T.	75	130
Rizzo,Anthony	80	127
d'Arnaud,Travis	75	126
Bichette,Bo	78	126
Torres,Gleyber	76	125
Altuve,Jose	84	125
Freeman,Freddie	83	124
Witt Jr.,Bobby	76	124
Reynolds,Bryan	75	124
Seager,Corey	82	124
Robert,Luis	76	124
Sheets,Gavin	75	123
Escobar,Eduardo	76	123
Bogaerts,Xander	80	122
Grichuk,Randal	76	121
Polanco,Jorge	78	120
Marte,Ketel	82	120
Albies,Ozzie	79	120
Hays,Austin	78	118

TOP PX, ct% under 70%

NAME	Ct%	PX
Trout,Mike	69	227
Judge,Aaron	69	209
Ríos,Edwin	55	207
Buxton,Byron	68	201
Gallo,Joey	55	191
Carpenter,Matt	69	189
Schwarber,Kyle	67	183
Raleigh,Cal	69	181
Sanó,Miguel	58	178
Ohtani,Shohei	69	176
Tatis Jr.,Fernando	69	171
Hiura,Keston	56	166
Suarez,Eugenio	66	165
Villar,David	65	165
Wisdom,Patrick	59	165
Zunino,Mike	61	164
Hernández,Teoscar	70	161
Duvall,Adam	68	160
Stanton,Giancarlo	66	159
Hall,Darick	68	158
Soler,Jorge	67	157
Dalbec,Bobby	63	156
Chapman,Matt	66	156

Top PX, FB% over 40%

NAME	FB%	PX
Trout,Mike	50	227
Judge,Aaron	40	209
Ríos,Edwin	43	207
Buxton,Byron	47	201
Gallo,Joey	53	191
Carpenter,Matt	50	189
Schwarber,Kyle	46	183
Raleigh,Cal	52	181
Sanó,Miguel	47	178
Suarez,Eugenio	46	165
Villar,David	45	165
Wisdom,Patrick	48	165
Zunino,Mike	54	164
Olson,Matt	43	160
Duvall,Adam	53	160
Hoskins,Rhys	45	158
Hall,Darick	47	158
Soler,Jorge	40	157
Dalbec,Bobby	42	156
Chapman,Matt	49	156
Lowe,Brandon	42	155
Alonso,Pete	43	153
Renfroe,Hunter	46	153
Adames,Willy	41	151
Brown,Seth	46	151
Muncy,Max	46	150
Springer,George	41	150
Perez,Salvador	43	149
Suwinski,Jack	42	147
Carpenter,Kerry	44	147
Betts,Mookie	46	147
Story,Trevor	42	147
Maton,Nick	40	146
Aquino,Aristides	47	146
Yastrzemski,Mike	46	145
Belt,Brandon	49	145
Chisholm,Jazz	42	145
Haniger,Mitch	43	145
Trammell,Taylor	41	144
Garver,Mitch	44	144

Top PX, FB% under 35%

NAME	FB%	PX
Meneses,Joey	30	143
Henderson,Gunnar	32	142
Contreras,William	32	141
Harris II,Michael	29	139
Happ,Ian	34	139
Reyes,Franmil	35	139
Contreras,Willson	33	137
Castro,Rodolfo	33	135
Waters,Drew	34	134
Soto,Juan	33	134
Jung,Josh	34	134
Arozarena,Randy	33	134
Guerrero Jr.,Vladimir	32	133
Davis,J.D.	32	133
McMahon,Ryan	34	129
Choi,Ji-Man	34	129
Morel,Christopher	33	129
Jiménez,Eloy	31	128
Bote,David	31	127
d'Arnaud,Travis	34	126
Bichette,Bo	31	126
Freeman,Freddie	34	124
Reynolds,Bryan	35	124

BATTER SKILLS RANKINGS — Speed

TOP Spd, 400+ AB

NAME	POS	Spd
Carroll,Corbin	7	157
Kwan,Steven	7 9	148
McCarthy,Jake	7 9	147
Chisholm,Jazz	4	146
Morel,Christopher	4 8	145
Rosario,Amed	6	145
Mateo,Jorge	6	145
Greene,Riley	8	144
Nimmo,Brandon	8	144
Lux,Gavin	4 7	140
Straw,Myles	8	140
Cruz,Oneil	6	138
Turner,Trea	6	137
Henderson,Gunnar	5	137
Giménez,Andrés	4	137
Witt Jr.,Bobby	5 6	135
Taveras,Leody	8	133
Mullins,Cedric	8	131
Rodríguez,Julio	8	131
Abrams,CJ	6	129
Marte,Starling	9	128
Marsh,Brandon	7 8	128
Anderson,Tim	6	128
Tatis Jr.,Fernando	0	128
Thomas,Alek	8	126
Reynolds,Bryan	8	126
Yelich,Christian	0 7	124
Albies,Ozzie	4	123
Garcia,Adolís	0 8 9	123
Suzuki,Seiya	9	123
Pena,Jeremy	6	122
Stott,Bryson	4 6	122
Franco,Wander	6	122
Ohtani,Shohei	0	121
Thomas,Lane	7 8 9	121
Cronenworth,Jake	3 4	119
Betts,Mookie	9	119
Frazier,Adam	4 9	119
Báez,Javier	6	118
Berti,Jon	4 5	117

TOP Spd, 300 or fewer AB

NAME	POS	Spd
Thompson,Bubba	7	183
Eaton,Nate	9	160
Baddoo,Akil	7	150
Siri,Jose	8	144
Hampson,Garrett	6 8	142
Marcano,Tucupita	4 7	141
Azocar,Jose	7 8 9	140
Alcantara,Sergio	4 5 6	139
Vavra,Terrin	4	138
Mondesi,Adalberto	6	138
Lopez,Nicky	4 5 6	138
Tapia,Raimel	7 8 9	137
Fairchild,Stuart	7 8	135
Williams,Luke	5 7	135
Haggerty,Sam	7 9	133
Isbel,Kyle	7 8 9	133
Friedl,T.J.	7 8	131
Moniak,Mickey	8	130
Sosa,Edmundo	5 6	128
Kiermaier,Kevin	8	128
Garcia,Maikel	6	126
Cabrera,Oswaldo	9	126
Benson,Will	O	125

POSITIONAL SCARCITY

NAME	POS	Spd
Buxton,Byron	DH	130
Tatis Jr.,Fernando	2	128
Yelich,Christian	3	124
Garcia,Adolís	4	123
Ohtani,Shohei	5	121
Smith,Pavin	6	117
Contreras,William	CA	117
Herrera,Iván	2	111
Wong,Connor	3	110
Moreno,Gabriel	4	108
Melendez,MJ	5	107
Fortes,Nick	6	105
Realmuto,J.T.	7	103
Naylor,Bo	8	102
Cronenworth,Jake	1B	119
Garcia,Dermis	2	115
Arraez,Luis	3	111
Dozier,Hunter	4	110
Vargas,Miguel	5	108
Toglia,Michael	6	107
Rivas III,Alfonso	7	105
Lowe,Nate	8	104
Dalbec,Bobby	9	102
Biggio,Cavan	10	101
Chisholm,Jazz	2B	146
Morel,Christopher	2	145
Marcano,Tucupita	3	141
Lux,Gavin	4	140
Alcantara,Sergio	5	139
Vavra,Terrin	6	138
Lopez,Nicky	7	138
Giménez,Andrés	8	137
Alcantara,Sergio	3B	139
Lopez,Nicky	2	138
Henderson,Gunnar	3	137
Williams,Luke	4	135
Witt Jr.,Bobby	5	135
Sosa,Edmundo	6	128
Kreidler,Ryan	7	124
Freeman,Tyler	8	120
Berti,Jon	9	117
Smith,Josh	10	117
Rosario,Amed	SS	145
Mateo,Jorge	2	145
Hampson,Garrett	3	142
Alcantara,Sergio	4	139
Mondesi,Adalberto	5	138
Cruz,Oneil	6	138
Lopez,Nicky	7	138
Turner,Trea	8	137
Thompson,Bubba	OF	183
Eaton,Nate	2	160
Carroll,Corbin	3	157
Baddoo,Akil	4	150
Kwan,Steven	5	148
McCarthy,Jake	6	147
Morel,Christopher	7	145
Greene,Riley	8	144
Siri,Jose	9	144
Nimmo,Brandon	10	144
Hampson,Garrett	11	142
Marcano,Tucupita	12	141
Azocar,Jose	13	140
Lux,Gavin	14	140
Straw,Myles	15	140
Tapia,Raimel	16	137

TOP Spd, .330+ OBP

NAME	OBP	Spd
Carroll,Corbin	353	157
Kwan,Steven	361	148
Nimmo,Brandon	378	144
Lux,Gavin	338	140
Turner,Trea	343	137
Henderson,Gunnar	338	137
Giménez,Andrés	337	137
Mullins,Cedric	330	131
Rodríguez,Julio	366	131
Marte,Starling	348	128
Anderson,Tim	330	128
Madrigal,Nick	337	128
Tatis Jr.,Fernando	351	128
Reynolds,Bryan	356	126
Yelich,Christian	362	124
Suzuki,Seiya	365	123
Franco,Wander	354	122
Ohtani,Shohei	355	121
Betts,Mookie	357	119
Smith,Josh	330	117
Arozarena,Randy	342	116
Hoerner,Nico	333	115
Moore,Dylan	337	115
Lowe,Josh	338	114
Lindor,Francisco	338	112
McNeil,Jeff	361	111
Ward,Taylor	347	111
Arraez,Luis	362	111
Springer,George	349	109
Crawford,J.P.	342	109
Hicks,Aaron	330	109
Moreno,Gabriel	344	108
Davis,J.D.	346	106
Kemp,Tony	337	106
Daza,Yonathan	333	106
Canha,Mark	363	105
Altuve,Jose	365	105
Lowe,Nate	358	104
Slater,Austin	353	104
Segura,Jean	331	103

TOP Spd, OBP under .300

NAME	OBP	Spd
Thompson,Bubba	275	183
Eaton,Nate	286	160
Morel,Christopher	293	145
Mateo,Jorge	278	145
Siri,Jose	278	144
Hampson,Garrett	288	142
Marcano,Tucupita	295	141
Azocar,Jose	276	140
Alcantara,Sergio	291	139
Mondesi,Adalberto	271	138
Cruz,Oneil	295	138
Williams,Luke	294	135
Taveras,Leody	290	133
Haggerty,Sam	300	133
Isbel,Kyle	278	133
Moniak,Mickey	255	130
Thomas,Alek	296	126
Garcia,Maikel	295	126
Perdomo,Geraldo	299	126
Cabrera,Oswaldo	278	126
Kreidler,Ryan	273	124
Castro,Willi	292	123
Garcia,Adolís	290	123

Top Spd, SBA% over 15%

NAME	SBA%	Spd
Thompson,Bubba	37%	183
Eaton,Nate	25%	160
Carroll,Corbin	21%	157
Baddoo,Akil	23%	150
McCarthy,Jake	24%	147
Chisholm,Jazz	27%	146
Morel,Christopher	17%	145
Mateo,Jorge	36%	145
Siri,Jose	19%	144
Hampson,Garrett	22%	142
Azocar,Jose	17%	140
Mondesi,Adalberto	35%	138
Cruz,Oneil	19%	138
Williams,Luke	39%	135
Witt Jr.,Bobby	23%	135
Grissom,Vaughn	17%	135
Taveras,Leody	17%	133
Haggerty,Sam	23%	133
Isbel,Kyle	22%	133
Mullins,Cedric	22%	131
Rodríguez,Julio	19%	131
Moniak,Mickey	18%	130
Abrams,CJ	18%	129
Sosa,Edmundo	16%	128
Marte,Starling	17%	128
Garcia,Maikel	22%	126
Cabrera,Oswaldo	16%	126
Kreidler,Ryan	16%	124
Garcia,Adolís	19%	123
Allen,Greg	27%	122
Volpe,Anthony	31%	121
Garrett,Stone	16%	120
Mitchell,Garrett	20%	120
Duran,Jarren	18%	119
Capel,Conner	20%	119
Berti,Jon	32%	117

Top Spd, SBA% under 10%

NAME	SBA%	Spd
Greene,Riley	8%	144
Nimmo,Brandon	7%	144
Lux,Gavin	9%	140
Alcantara,Sergio	9%	139
Vavra,Terrin	8%	138
Reyes,Victor	9%	135
Buxton,Byron	9%	130
Madrigal,Nick	7%	128
Tatis Jr.,Fernando	9%	128
Reynolds,Bryan	8%	126
Perdomo,Geraldo	9%	126
Taylor,Michael A.	7%	122
Franco,Wander	10%	122
Leblanc,Charles	9%	121
Thomas,Lane	10%	121
Freeman,Tyler	8%	120
Cronenworth,Jake	5%	119
Betts,Mookie	10%	119
Báez,Javier	9%	118
Smith,Pavin	5%	117
Contreras,William	5%	117
Fletcher,David	6%	117
Rengifo,Luis	8%	116
Nootbaar,Lars	7%	115
Garcia,Dermis	6%	115
Dubon,Mauricio	9%	114
Blackmon,Charlie	6%	114

BATTER SKILLS RANKINGS— Batting Average

TOP ct%, 400+ AB

NAME	ct%	BA
Arraez,Luis	91	306
Fletcher,David	90	264
Kwan,Steven	89	291
Franco,Wander	88	297
McNeil,Jeff	87	300
Kirk,Alejandro	87	274
Frazier,Adam	86	263
Rojas,Miguel	86	253
Arenado,Nolan	86	280
Hoerner,Nico	86	276
Pasquantino,Vinnie	86	272
Bregman,Alex	86	272
Kemp,Tony	85	252
LeMahieu,DJ	85	278
Kiner-Falefa,Isiah	85	264
Ramírez,José	85	283
Diaz,Yandy	84	283
Altuve,Jose	84	287
Verdugo,Alex	83	288
Merrifield,Whit	83	270
Segura,Jean	83	269
Freeman,Freddie	83	315
Flores,Wilmer	83	248
Guerrero Jr.,Vladimir	82	291
Seager,Corey	82	286
Naylor,Josh	82	255
Profar,Jurickson	82	241
Crawford,J.P.	82	256
Betts,Mookie	82	275
Edman,Tommy	82	264
Marte,Ketel	82	271
Turner,Justin	82	273
Miranda,Jose	82	278
Ramirez,Harold	82	286
Straw,Myles	81	246
Tucker,Kyle	81	277
Kepler,Max	81	242
Soto,Juan	81	281
Turner,Trea	81	293
Margot,Manuel	81	260
Benintendi,Andrew	81	270
France,Ty	81	272
Wong,Kolten	81	261
Estrada,Thairo	81	262
Rizzo,Anthony	80	260
Cronenworth,Jake	80	247
Blackmon,Charlie	80	265
Rosario,Amed	80	278
Gurriel Jr.,Lourdes	80	286
Paredes,Isaac	80	244
Semien,Marcus	80	253
Kim,Ha-Seong	80	254
Lindor,Francisco	80	265
Rengifo,Luis	80	238
Rutschman,Adley	80	267
Bogaerts,Xander	80	301
Anderson,Tim	80	297
Machado,Manny	79	289
Pollock,A.J.	79	266
Rodgers,Brendan	79	272
Bell,Josh	79	276
Marte,Starling	79	288
Albies,Ozzie	79	262
Urshela,Giovanny	79	276
Vaughn,Andrew	79	255
Farmer,Kyle	79	251

LOW ct%, 400+ AB

NAME	ct%	BA
Wisdom,Patrick	59	211
Bart,Joey	60	224
Marsh,Brandon	63	249
Morel,Christopher	64	225
Suarez,Eugenio	66	235
Gorman,Nolan	66	233
Chapman,Matt	66	235
Stanton,Giancarlo	66	243
Voit,Luke	66	242
Jung,Josh	66	241
Schwarber,Kyle	67	238
Langeliers,Shea	67	220
O Neill,Tyler	68	241
Cruz,Oneil	68	232
Chisholm,Jazz	68	250
Garcia,Adolís	68	246
Tatis Jr.,Fernando	69	278
Adames,Willy	69	250
Trout,Mike	69	290
Judge,Aaron	69	299
Brown,Seth	69	238
Laureano,Ramón	69	231
Moncada,Yoán	69	241
Walsh,Jared	69	248
Grisham,Trent	69	226
Ohtani,Shohei	69	263
McMahon,Ryan	70	245
Báez,Javier	70	249
Greene,Riley	70	253
Happ,Ian	70	256
Hernández,Teoscar	70	275
García,Avisaíl	70	236
Taveras,Leody	70	232
Story,Trevor	70	255
Henderson,Gunnar	71	251
Mateo,Jorge	71	233

TOP ct%, 300 or fewer AB

NAME	ct%	BA
Gurriel,Yuli	87	271
Newman,Kevin	87	255
Lopez,Alejo	86	253
Freeman,Tyler	86	249
Vargas,Ildemaro	86	221
Frelick,Sal	85	282
Lopez,Nicky	85	250
Andrus,Elvis	83	244
Guillorme,Luis	83	259
Dubon,Mauricio	83	236
Díaz,Jordan	83	269
Nola,Austin	83	258
Hosmer,Eric	82	267
Díaz,Aledmys	82	252
Dickerson,Corey	82	267
Tapia,Raimel	81	274
Moreno,Gabriel	81	291
Gomes,Yan	80	247
Burleson,Alec	80	245
Mitchell,Calvin	79	253
Toro,Abraham	79	226
Jansen,Danny	78	256
Smith,Pavin	78	252
Machin,Vimael	78	217
Bruján,Vidal	78	222
Marcano,Tucupita	78	221
Groshans,Jordan	78	245

TOP ct%, bb% over 9%

NAME	bb%	ct%
Kwan,Steven	9	89
Kirk,Alejandro	11	87
Pasquantino,Vinnie	10	86
Bregman,Alex	13	86
Kemp,Tony	10	85
LeMahieu,DJ	11	85
Ramírez,José	11	85
Diaz,Yandy	14	84
Altuve,Jose	10	84
Guillorme,Luis	11	83
Freeman,Freddie	13	83
Flores,Wilmer	9	83
Guerrero Jr.,Vladimir	9	82
Seager,Corey	10	82
Rendon,Anthony	13	82
Profar,Jurickson	11	82
Crawford,J.P.	11	82
Betts,Mookie	10	82
Turner,Justin	10	82
Straw,Myles	9	81
Tucker,Kyle	9	81
Kepler,Max	10	81
Soto,Juan	21	81
Benintendi,Andrew	9	81
Rizzo,Anthony	10	80
Santana,Carlos	14	80
Cronenworth,Jake	10	80
Donovan,Brendan	11	80
Paredes,Isaac	12	80
Lindor,Francisco	9	80
Rutschman,Adley	14	80
Bogaerts,Xander	9	80
Machado,Manny	10	79
Bell,Josh	12	79
Hernández,Kiké	9	79
Jansen,Danny	10	78
Springer,George	10	78
Smith,Pavin	10	78
Winker,Jesse	14	78
Marcano,Tucupita	9	78

TOP ct%, bb% under 6%

NAME	bb%	ct%
Madrigal,Nick	6	90
Fletcher,David	5	90
Newman,Kevin	5	87
Iglesias,José	4	86
Freeman,Tyler	4	86
Vargas,Ildemaro	4	86
Kiner-Falefa,Isiah	6	85
Dubon,Mauricio	5	83
Díaz,Jordan	3	83
Daza,Yonathan	6	83
Andujar,Miguel	4	83
Harrison,Josh	5	82
Díaz,Aledmys	6	82
Miranda,Jose	6	82
Wendle,Joe	5	82
Ramirez,Harold	4	82
Vázquez,Christian	6	82
Dickerson,Corey	5	82
Tapia,Raimel	5	81
Trevino,Jose	4	81
Rosario,Amed	4	80
Gurriel Jr.,Lourdes	6	80
Gomes,Yan	4	80

Top ct%, GB% over 50%

NAME	GB%	ct%
Madrigal,Nick	60	90
Freeman,Tyler	52	86
Vargas,Ildemaro	54	86
LeMahieu,DJ	53	85
Kiner-Falefa,Isiah	55	85
Lopez,Nicky	56	85
Diaz,Yandy	52	84
Guillorme,Luis	53	83
Segura,Jean	54	83
Díaz,Jordan	67	83
Daza,Yonathan	56	83
Hosmer,Eric	55	82
Brennan,Will	53	82
Wendle,Joe	52	82
Ramirez,Harold	53	82
Tapia,Raimel	59	81
Estrada,Thairo	50	81
Donovan,Brendan	53	80
Rosario,Amed	52	80
Anderson,Tim	55	80
Rodgers,Brendan	52	79
Bell,Josh	52	79
Marte,Starling	51	79
Abrams,CJ	50	79
García,Luis	54	79
Thomas,Alek	55	78
García,Leury	52	77
Hayes,Ke'Bryan	52	77
Allen,Nick	51	76
Cabrera,Miguel	50	76
Ahmed,Nick	51	75
Caratini,Victor	51	75
Celestino,Gilberto	55	74
Berti,Jon	55	74
Harris II,Michael	53	74
Baty,Brett	50	74
Azocar,Jose	50	74
Jiménez,Eloy	50	73
McCarthy,Jake	52	73
Casas,Triston	57	73

Top ct%, GB% under 40%

NAME	GB%	ct%
Ruiz,Keibert	39	88
Arenado,Nolan	32	86
Bregman,Alex	35	86
Kemp,Tony	39	85
Ramírez,José	33	85
Dubon,Mauricio	39	83
Freeman,Freddie	39	83
Flores,Wilmer	35	83
Rendon,Anthony	34	82
Betts,Mookie	34	82
Turner,Justin	33	82
Tucker,Kyle	34	81
Rizzo,Anthony	36	80
Cronenworth,Jake	35	80
Semien,Marcus	33	80
Rutschman,Adley	39	80
Vargas,Miguel	34	79
Machado,Manny	38	79
Heim,Jonah	39	79
Albies,Ozzie	38	79
Hernández,Kiké	39	79
Jansen,Danny	33	78
Mejía,Francisco	39	78

POTENTIAL SKILLS GAINERS AND FADERS — Batters

Power Gainers

Batters whose 2022 Power Index (PX) fell significantly short of their underlying power skill (xPX). If they show the same xPX skill in 2023, they are good candidates for more power output.

Power Faders

Batters whose 2022 Power Index (PX) noticeably outpaced their underlying power skill (xPX). If they show the same xPX skill in 2023, they are good candidates for less power output.

BA Gainers

Batters who had strong Hard Contact Index levels in 2022, but lower hit rates (h%). Since base hits come most often on hard contact, if these batters can make hard contact at the same strong rate again in 2023, they may get better results in terms of hit rate, resulting in a batting average improvement.

BA Faders

Batters who had weak Hard Contact Index levels in 2022, but higher hit rates (h%). Since base hits come most often on hard contact, if these batters only make hard contact at the same weak rate again in 2023, they may get worse results in terms of hit rate, resulting in a batting average decline.

PX GAINERS

NAME	PX	xPX
Massey,Michael	93	159
Vogt,Stephen	99	141
Belt,Brandon	97	140
Pasquantino,Vinnie	86	134
Higashioka,Kyle	97	126
Hernandez,Yadiel	96	124
Chang,Yu	83	123
Fortes,Nick	92	122
Calhoun,Kole	100	121
Aguilar,Jesus	95	120
McKenna,Ryan	93	120
Ruf,Darin	95	117
Wade,LaMonte	93	117
Nido,Tomas	68	116
Taylor,Michael	66	114
Rojas,Josh	85	110
Kelly,Carson	86	108
McCann,James	61	108
Hilliard,Sam	63	107
Velazquez,Andrew	82	107
Diaz,Lewin	84	106
Grossman,Robert	80	106
Merrifield,Whit	80	104
Kirk,Alejandro	74	103
Alberto,Hanser	77	102
Brantley,Michael	78	100
VanMeter,Josh	68	100
Walls,Taylor	83	100

PX FADERS

NAME	PX	xPX
Trout,Mike	234	160
Stanton,Giancarlo	164	125
Cruz,Oneil	159	119
Harris II,Michael	144	110
Meneses,Joey	151	110
Morel,Christopher	147	110
Cron,C.J.	139	104
Ramirez,Jose	134	100
Altuve,Jose	140	99
Garlick,Kyle	128	97
Paredes,Isaac	135	96
Sanchez,Jesus	126	95
Castro,Rodolfo	122	90
Springer,George	118	90
Naylor,Josh	119	89
Arozarena,Randy	128	88
Haase,Eric	131	88
Adell,Jo	121	85
Pinder,Chad	112	84
Gimenez,Andres	108	79
Marte,Starling	108	75
Aquino,Aristides	135	74
Siri,Jose	99	72
Andrus,Elvis	97	71
Bogaerts,Xander	102	71
Barnes,Austin	98	70
Mejia,Francisco	101	67
Rengifo,Luis	95	67
Dickerson,Corey	85	64
Duran,Ezequiel	90	63
Higgins,P.J.	110	56
Herrera,Odubel	92	51
Haggerty,Sam	106	40

BA GAINERS

NAME	h%	HctX
Tellez,Rowdy	22	136
Seager,Corey	25	134
Walker,Christian	25	129
Muncy,Max	23	125
Santana,Carlos	21	122
Buxton,Byron	24	120
Santander,Anthony	25	120
Higashioka,Kyle	25	118
Castillo,Diego	24	116
Nootbaar,Lars	25	116
Caratini,Victor	23	115
Fortes,Nick	25	113
Heim,Jonah	25	112
Stanton,Giancarlo	23	112
Rizzo,Anthony	22	111
Schwarber,Kyle	24	110
Kepler,Max	25	108
Raleigh,Cal	23	108
Luplow,Jordan	19	106
Flores,Wilmer	25	105
Garver,Mitch	23	105
Soto,Juan	25	105
Suwinski,Jack	24	105
Vogt,Stephen	17	103
Bride,Jonah	25	101
McCann,James	25	101
Kelly,Carson	25	100
Paredes,Isaac	20	98

BA FADERS

NAME	h%	HctX
McGuire,Reese	34	57
Adell,Jo	34	65
Thompson,Bubba	39	66
Rivas III,Alfonso	35	70
Meyers,Jake	35	72
Kwan,Steven	33	74
Lowe,Josh	34	74
Mazara,Nomar	34	74
Haggerty,Sam	34	75
Cabrera,Miguel	33	76
Azocar,Jose	33	79
Alfaro,Jorge	37	84
Bart,Joey	33	84
Iglesias,Jose	33	84
McKenna,Ryan	35	84
Gimenez,Andres	36	86
Reyes,Victor	33	87
Reynolds,Matt	35	87
Taylor,Chris	34	87
Marte,Starling	34	88
McCarthy,Jake	35	88
Hiura,Keston	36	89
Margot,Manuel	33	89
Zavala,Seby	41	89
Castellanos,Nick	33	91
Daza,Yonathan	35	91
Marsh,Brandon	36	91
Slater,Austin	36	94
Burger,Jake	33	95
Donovan,Brendan	33	95
Rosario,Amed	33	95
McNeil,Jeff	36	96
Taveras,Leody	35	96
Lux,Gavin	34	97
Davis,J.D.	36	98
Greene,Riley	36	98
Leblanc,Charles	37	98

EXPECTED STATS vs. ACTUAL — Batters

BA Underperformers (min. 250 AB)

NAME	BA	xBA	Diff
Paredes,Isaac	205	251	-46
Rizzo,Anthony	224	265	-41
Tellez,Rowdy	219	257	-38
Toro,Abraham	185	223	-38
Walls,Taylor	172	209	-37
Schoop,Jonathan	202	238	-36
Nootbaar,Lars	228	263	-35
Raleigh,Cal	211	246	-35
Santana,Carlos	202	237	-35
Bradley,Jackie	203	234	-31
Caratini,Victor	199	230	-31
Seager,Corey	245	275	-30
Castillo,Diego	206	235	-29
Soto,Juan	242	271	-29
Buxton,Byron	224	252	-28
Hedges,Austin	163	191	-28
Muncy,Max	196	224	-28
Contreras,Willson	243	269	-26
Schwarber,Kyle	218	244	-26
Sanchez,Jesus	214	239	-25
Gallo,Joey	160	184	-24

HR Underperformers

NAME	HR	xHR	Diff
Freeman,Freddie	21	32	-11
Ohtani,Shohei	34	45	-11
Acuna,Ronald	15	25	-10
Gordon,Nick	9	19	-10
Martinez,J.D.	16	26	-10
Mountcastle,Ryan	22	32	-10
Abreu,Jose	15	24	-9
Greene,Riley	5	13	-8
Sanchez,Gary	16	24	-8
Davis,J.D.	12	19	-7
Alvarez,Yordan	37	43	-6
Benintendi,Andrew	5	11	-6
Cooper,Garrett	9	15	-6
Cruz,Nelson	10	16	-6
Swanson,Dansby	25	31	-6
Berti,Jon	4	9	-5
Garcia,Luis	7	12	-5
Hernandez,Teoscar	25	30	-5
Judge,Aaron	62	67	-5
Lux,Gavin	6	11	-5
Massey,Michael	4	9	-5

SB Underperformers

NAME	SB	xSB	Diff
Donovan,Brendan	2	17	-15
Abrams,CJ	7	20	-13
Ohtani,Shohei	11	22	-11
Taylor,Michael	4	15	-11
Gordon,Nick	6	16	-10
Nimmo,Brandon	3	13	-10
Profar,Jurickson	5	14	-9
Greene,Riley	1	9	-8
Marte,Starling	18	26	-8
Bohm,Alec	2	9	-7
Azocar,Jose	5	11	-6
Benintendi,Andrew	8	14	-6
Crawford,Brandon	1	7	-6
Lowe,Nate	2	8	-6
Rengifo,Luis	6	12	-6
Reyes,Victor	2	8	-6
Smith,Josh	4	10	-6
Baez,Javier	9	14	-5
Canha,Mark	3	8	-5
Crawford,J.P.	3	8	-5
Cronenworth,Jake	3	8	-5

BA Overperformers (min. 250 AB)

NAME	BA	xBA	Diff
Arraez,Luis	316	284	32
Marsh,Brandon	245	214	31
Daza,Yonathan	301	271	30
Gonzalez,Luis	254	224	30
Solano,Donovan	284	254	30
Alfaro,Jorge	246	217	29
Davis,J.D.	248	219	29
Diaz,Yandy	296	267	29
Acuna,Ronald	266	238	28
Anderson,Tim	301	273	28
Contreras,William	278	250	28
Greene,Riley	253	225	28
Kirk,Alejandro	285	257	28
Margot,Manuel	274	246	28
Rivas III,Alfonso	235	207	28
Gonzalez,Oscar	296	269	27
Lux,Gavin	276	249	27
Robert,Luis	284	257	27
Hosmer,Eric	268	242	26
McCarthy,Jake	283	257	26
Segura,Jean	277	251	26

HR Overperformers

NAME	HR	xHR	Diff
Machado,Manny	32	22	10
Paredes,Isaac	20	10	10
Ramirez,Jose	29	19	10
Arenado,Nolan	30	21	9
Drury,Brandon	28	19	9
Altuve,Jose	28	20	8
Betts,Mookie	35	27	8
Guerrero Jr.,Vladimir	32	25	7
Rizzo,Anthony	32	25	7
Andrus,Elvis	17	11	6
Bregman,Alex	23	17	6
Carpenter,Matt	15	9	6
France,Ty	20	14	6
Heim,Jonah	16	10	6
Pena,Jeremy	22	16	6
Pujols,Albert	24	18	6
Alonso,Pete	40	35	5
Castro,Willi	8	3	5
Estrada,Thairo	14	9	5
Profar,Jurickson	15	10	5
Renfroe,Hunter	29	24	5

SB Overperformers

NAME	SB	xSB	Diff
Berti,Jon	41	12	29
Mateo,Jorge	35	18	17
Arozarena,Randy	32	16	16
Tucker,Kyle	25	9	16
Rojas,Josh	23	8	15
Harris II,Michael	20	6	14
Mullins II,Cedric	34	21	13
Semien,Marcus	25	13	12
Altuve,Jose	18	7	11
Andrus,Elvis	18	7	11
Edman,Tommy	32	21	11
Judge,Aaron	16	5	11
Acuna,Ronald	29	19	10
Estrada,Thairo	21	11	10
Garcia,Adolis	25	15	10
Hayes,KeBryan	20	10	10
Kiner-Falefa,Isiah	22	12	10
Realmuto,JT	21	11	10
Bader,Harrison	17	8	9
Bellinger,Cody	14	5	9
Hamilton,Billy	10	1	9

PITCHER SKILLS RANKINGS — Starting Pitchers

Top K-BB%

NAME	K-BB%
deGrom,Jacob	34
Cole,Gerrit	28
Scherzer,Max	28
Strider,Spencer	28
Sale,Chris	26
Glasnow,Tyler	26
Heaney,Andrew	26
Burnes,Corbin	26
Gausman,Kevin	25
Nola,Aaron	25
Rodón,Carlos	25
Ohtani,Shohei	25
Woodruff,Brandon	24
Greene,Hunter	24
Kershaw,Clayton	24
Baz,Shane	24
Paxton,James	23
Alzolay,Adbert	23
Darvish,Yu	22
Ray,Robbie	22
Snell,Blake	22
Javier,Cristian	22
Miller,Bobby	22
Verlander,Justin	22
Kirby,George	21
Musgrove,Joe	21
Castillo,Luis	21
Lodolo,Nick	21
Morton,Charlie	21
McClanahan,Shane	21
Springs,Jeffrey	21

Top BB%

NAME	BB%
Paddack,Chris	4
Pineda,Michael	4
Ryu,Hyun-Jin	4
Kirby,George	4
Greinke,Zack	5
Kershaw,Clayton	5
Falter,Bailey	5
Mikolas,Miles	5
Means,John	5
Gausman,Kevin	5
Irvin,Cole	5
Verlander,Justin	5
Eflin,Zach	5
Hendricks,Kyle	5
Bradley,Taj	5
Urquidy,José	5
deGrom,Jacob	5
Fried,Max	5
Eovaldi,Nathan	5
Stripling,Ross	5
Scherzer,Max	6
Taillon,Jameson	6
Civale,Aaron	6
Chirinos,Yonny	6
Montgomery,Jordan	6
Bieber,Shane	6
Nola,Aaron	6
Ober,Bailey	6
Wheeler,Zack	6
Syndergaard,Noah	6
Kluber,Corey	6

Top K%

NAME	K%
deGrom,Jacob	40
Strider,Spencer	36
Glasnow,Tyler	36
Cole,Gerrit	34
Scherzer,Max	33
Heaney,Andrew	33
Rodón,Carlos	33
Sale,Chris	33
Ohtani,Shohei	33
Burnes,Corbin	33
Snell,Blake	32
Javier,Cristian	32
Greene,Hunter	32
Paxton,James	31
Nola,Aaron	31
Woodruff,Brandon	31
Baz,Shane	31
Lodolo,Nick	31
Ray,Robbie	31
Gausman,Kevin	30
Peralta,Freddy	30
Alzolay,Adbert	30
Hall,DL	30
Pérez,Eury	29
Morton,Charlie	29
Cease,Dylan	29
Castillo,Luis	29
Darvish,Yu	29
Miller,Bobby	28
Kershaw,Clayton	28
Springs,Jeffrey	28

Top Ground Ball Rate

NAME	GB%
Valdez,Framber	66
Cobb,Alex	57
Ashby,Aaron	57
Jameson,Drey	56
Bello,Brayan	56
Webb,Logan	55
Sánchez,Sixto	55
Ashcraft,Graham	55
Hudson,Dakota	54
Wright,Kyle	54
Stroman,Marcus	53
McCullers Jr.,Lance	52
Senzatela,Antonio	52
Alcantara,Sandy	52
Fried,Max	52
Houser,Adrian	52
Dunning,Dane	52
Castillo,Luis	51
Miley,Wade	51
Soroka,Mike	51
Steele,Justin	51
Turnbull,Spencer	51
May,Dustin	51
Alexander,Jason	51
Winckowski,Josh	50
Brown,Hunter	50
Singer,Brady	50
Sandoval,Patrick	50
Anderson,Ian	49
Elder,Bryce	49
McClanahan,Shane	49

Top Fly Ball Rate

NAME	FB%
Javier,Cristian	54
Ryan,Joe	54
Ober,Bailey	51
Patino,Luis	51
Logue,Zach	51
Oller,Adam	51
Gray,Josiah	50
Pepiot,Ryan	50
Winn,Cole	49
McKenzie,Triston	48
Wentz,Joey	48
García,Rony	48
Crawford,Kutter	48
Winder,Josh	47
Wells,Tyler	47
Nelson,Ryne	47
Means,John	47
Liberatore,Matthew	47
Cortes,Nestor	47
Verlander,Justin	46
Kopech,Michael	46
Scherzer,Max	46
Odorizzi,Jake	46
Heasley,Jon	45
Peralta,Freddy	45
Urquidy,José	45
Pérez,Eury	45
Faedo,Alex	45
Hill,Garrett	45
Kaprielian,James	44
Greene,Hunter	44

High GB, Low K%

NAME	GB%	K%
Ashcraft,Graham	55	17
Hudson,Dakota	54	16
Senzatela,Antonio	52	14
Houser,Adrian	52	16
Miley,Wade	51	18
Soroka,Mike	51	18
Alexander,Jason	51	15
Winckowski,Josh	50	15
Elder,Bryce	49	19
Adon,Joan	48	19
Mize,Casey	48	20
Pérez,Martín	47	20
Mikolas,Miles	47	19
Fedde,Erick	47	16
Blackburn,Paul	46	18
Silseth,Chase	45	18
Freeland,Kyle	45	18
Davidson,Tucker	45	19
Castillo,Max	45	19
Wainwright,Adam	45	19
Mills,Alec	44	17
Corbin,Patrick	44	19
White,Mitch	44	19
Chirinos,Yonny	43	19
Otto Jr.,Glenn	43	20
Thompson,Zach	43	18
Greinke,Zack	43	18
Davies,Zach	42	18
Sears,JP	42	18
Quantrill,Cal	42	19
Wilson,Bryse	42	18

High GB, High K%

NAME	GB%	K%
Ashby,Aaron	57	27
Castillo,Luis	51	29
McClanahan,Shane	49	27
Kershaw,Clayton	49	28
Burnes,Corbin	47	33
Gray,Sonny	47	27
Lodolo,Nick	46	31
Kikuchi,Yusei	46	27
Glasnow,Tyler	46	36
Alzolay,Adbert	45	30
Sale,Chris	45	33
Nola,Aaron	45	31
Miller,Bobby	45	28
Musgrove,Joe	45	28
Gallen,Zac	45	27
Baz,Shane	44	31
Hall,DL	44	30
Senga,Koudai	44	27
Morton,Charlie	43	29
deGrom,Jacob	43	40
Megill,Tylor	43	27
Woodruff,Brandon	42	31
Ohtani,Shohei	42	33
Rodriguez,Grayson	41	27
Cole,Gerrit	41	34
Snell,Blake	40	32
Strider,Spencer	40	36
Pérez,Eury	40	29
Luzardo,Jesús	40	28
Gausman,Kevin	40	30
Lynn,Lance	40	26

Lowest xERA

NAME	xERA
deGrom,Jacob	2.16
Strider,Spencer	2.57
Sale,Chris	2.58
Glasnow,Tyler	2.59
Burnes,Corbin	2.60
Cole,Gerrit	2.67
Nola,Aaron	2.68
Baz,Shane	2.70
Ohtani,Shohei	2.71
Kershaw,Clayton	2.75
Gausman,Kevin	2.80
Alzolay,Adbert	2.81
Castillo,Luis	2.81
McClanahan,Shane	2.83
Valdez,Framber	2.84
Scherzer,Max	2.86
Woodruff,Brandon	2.88
Cobb,Alex	2.90
Miller,Bobby	2.91
Heaney,Andrew	2.94
Fried,Max	2.97
Wheeler,Zack	2.98
Rodón,Carlos	2.98
Lodolo,Nick	2.98
Paxton,James	2.99
Musgrove,Joe	3.00
Bieber,Shane	3.01
May,Dustin	3.01
Ashby,Aaron	3.06
Paddack,Chris	3.07
Snell,Blake	3.07

Top BPX, 160+ IP

NAME	BPX
Cole,Gerrit	192
Scherzer,Max	183
Burnes,Corbin	181
Nola,Aaron	179
Gausman,Kevin	179
Woodruff,Brandon	166
Ohtani,Shohei	164
Kirby,George	163
Rodón,Carlos	161
Castillo,Luis	154
Darvish,Yu	153
Musgrove,Joe	151
Ray,Robbie	145
Wheeler,Zack	145
Morton,Charlie	144
Bieber,Shane	143
Fried,Max	142
Montgomery,Jordan	138
Alcantara,Sandy	131
Cortes,Nestor	130
McKenzie,Triston	126
Singer,Brady	125
Giolito,Lucas	124
Valdez,Framber	122
Gilbert,Logan	116
Urías,Julio	116
Berríos,José	115
Bassitt,Chris	115
Bello,Brayan	114
Webb,Logan	112
Wright,Kyle	111

Top BPX, <120 IP

NAME	BPX
Kershaw,Clayton	176
Heaney,Andrew	174
Alzolay,Adbert	167
Baz,Shane	160
Small,Ethan	158
Paxton,James	156
Miller,Bobby	156
Paddack,Chris	150
Civale,Aaron	140
Megill,Tylor	139
Wood,Alex	136
Buehler,Walker	132
Ryu,Hyun-Jin	131
Bradley,Taj	130
Eflin,Zach	129
Strasburg,Stephen	128
Skubal,Tarik	128
Whitlock,Garrett	124
Pérez,Eury	124
Rodriguez,Grayson	122
Stripling,Ross	119
Falter,Bailey	115
Germán,Domingo	114
Means,John	114
White,Owen	113
Hall,DL	111
Jameson,Drey	110
Ober,Bailey	109
Ortiz,Luis	106
Kikuchi,Yusei	103
Garrett,Braxton	103

PITCHER SKILLS RANKINGS — Relief Pitchers

Top K-BB%

NAME	K-BB%
Díaz,Edwin	38
Hader,Josh	33
Alvarado,José	32
Hendriks,Liam	31
Muñoz,Andrés	30
Fairbanks,Peter	29
Pressly,Ryan	28
Martin,Christopher	28
Rogers,Taylor	27
Iglesias,Raisel	27
Kahnle,Tommy	26
Karinchak,James	25
Neris,Hector	25
Gallegos,Giovanny	25
Lee,Dylan	25
Williams,Devin	24
Jiménez,Joe	24
Swanson,Erik	24
Vesia,Alex	24
Duran,Jhoan	24
Anderson,Nick	24
Pagan,Emilio	24
Jansen,Kenley	24
Minter,A.J.	24
Bednar,David	24
Hudson,Daniel	23
Clase,Emmanuel	23
Hentges,Sam	22
Poche,Colin	22
Thielbar,Caleb	22
Bautista,Félix	22

Top BB%

NAME	BB%
Martin,Christopher	2
Mantiply,Joe	5
Clase,Emmanuel	5
Ramirez,Erasmo	5
Clarke,Taylor	6
Akin,Keegan	6
Foley,Jason	6
Anderson,Nick	6
Acevedo,Domingo	6
Alexander,Tyler	6
Cimber,Adam	6
Swanson,Erik	6
Garcia,Yimi	6
Milner,Hoby	6
Lee,Dylan	6
Espino,Paolo	6
Hendriks,Liam	6
Kuhnel,Joel	6
Barria,Jaime	6
Rogers,Taylor	6
Duran,Jhoan	6
Bickford,Phil	6
Morgan,Elijah	6
López,Reynaldo	6
Sadler,Casey	6
Thielbar,Caleb	6
King,John	7
Smeltzer,Devin	7
Iglesias,Raisel	7
Suter,Brent	7
Price,David	7

Top K%

NAME	K%
Díaz,Edwin	46
Hader,Josh	43
Alvarado,José	42
Karinchak,James	38
Hendriks,Liam	38
Williams,Devin	37
Muñoz,Andrés	37
Fairbanks,Peter	36
Pressly,Ryan	36
Vesia,Alex	35
Chapman,Aroldis	34
Kahnle,Tommy	34
Rogers,Taylor	34
Abreu,Bryan	33
Neris,Hector	33
Jiménez,Joe	33
Iglesias,Raisel	33
Jansen,Kenley	33
Moran,Jovani	32
Brash,Matt	32
Bautista,Félix	32
Gallegos,Giovanny	32
Lamet,Dinelson	32
Pagan,Emilio	32
Leclerc,José	32
Rainey,Tanner	32
Díaz,Alexis	32
Bednar,David	31
Poche,Colin	31
Sims,Lucas	31
Lee,Dylan	31

Top Ground Ball Rate

NAME	GB%
Holmes,Clay	70
Britton,Zack	70
Bummer,Aaron	66
Clase,Emmanuel	65
Pallante,Andre	64
King,John	64
Duran,Jhoan	62
Graterol,Brusdar	60
Hill,Tim	60
Tate,Dillon	59
Hentges,Sam	59
Sadler,Casey	58
Hicks,Jordan	58
Doval,Camilo	58
Kelly,Joe	58
Foley,Jason	57
Schreiber,John	56
Suárez,Ranger	56
Mayza,Tim	56
Hernández,Jonathan	56
Sanmartin,Reiver	55
Graveman,Kendall	54
Loáisiga,Jonathan	54
Alvarado,José	54
Muñoz,Andrés	54
Lange,Alex	53
Montero,Rafael	53
López,Jorge	53
Peralta,Wandy	53
Keller,Brad	52
Martin,Brett	52

Top Fly Ball Rate

NAME	FB%
Jackson,Zach	59
Wilson,Steven	58
Díaz,Alexis	54
Wantz,Andrew	52
Morejon,Adrian	52
Poche,Colin	52
Gallegos,Giovanny	52
Morgan,Elijah	51
Hernandez,Elieser	51
Sewald,Paul	50
Jansen,Kenley	50
Rainey,Tanner	49
Leclerc,José	49
Hader,Josh	49
Bellatti,Andrew	49
Thielbar,Caleb	49
Murfee,Penn	49
Sims,Lucas	48
Vesia,Alex	48
Hendriks,Liam	48
Karinchak,James	48
Helsley,Ryan	47
Garcia,Yimi	47
Staumont,Josh	47
Swanson,Erik	47
Pagan,Emilio	47
Jiménez,Joe	47
Richards,Trevor	46
Kimbrel,Craig	46
Okert,Steven	46
Kennedy,Ian	46

High GB, Low K%

NAME	GB%	K%
Britton,Zack	70	20
Pallante,Andre	64	16
King,John	64	18
Graterol,Brusdar	60	21
Hill,Tim	60	18
Tate,Dillon	59	19
Sadler,Casey	58	20
Foley,Jason	57	16
Suárez,Ranger	56	20
Hernández,Jonathan	56	21
Sanmartin,Reiver	55	20
López,Jorge	53	22
Peralta,Wandy	53	20
Keller,Brad	52	18
Martin,Brett	52	19
Kuhnel,Joel	52	22
Rodríguez,Manuel	51	20
Mantiply,Joe	50	22
Woodford,Jake	50	15
Cessa,Luis	49	20
Oviedo,Johan	49	22
Vest,Will	48	20
Crowe,Wil	48	19
Floro,Dylan	48	22
Melancon,Mark	48	18
Santana,Dennis	47	21
Martinez,Nick	47	20
Cimber,Adam	47	20
Suter,Brent	47	21
Cuas,Jose	46	18
Uelmen,Erich	45	19

High GB, High K%

NAME	GB%	K%
Duran,Jhoan	62	30
Kelly,Joe	58	30
Alvarado,José	54	42
Muñoz,Andrés	54	37
Williams,Devin	51	37
Brash,Matt	51	32
Kahnle,Tommy	50	34
Fairbanks,Peter	49	36
Pressly,Ryan	49	36
Abreu,Bryan	49	33
Moran,Jovani	48	32
Antone,Tejay	48	30
Martin,Christopher	48	30
Robertson,David	46	30
Rogers,Taylor	45	34
Bautista,Félix	44	32
Suarez,Robert	44	30
Díaz,Edwin	43	46
Marinaccio,Ron	42	30
Hudson,Daniel	41	30
Neris,Hector	40	33
Minter,A.J.	39	31
Chapman,Aroldis	39	34
Lamet,Dinelson	37	32
Smith,Will	36	31
Bednar,David	36	31
Lee,Dylan	36	31
Kimbrel,Craig	35	30
Helsley,Ryan	35	30
Pagan,Emilio	35	32
Iglesias,Raisel	34	33

Lowest xERA

NAME	xERA
Díaz,Edwin	1.91
Alvarado,José	1.94
Muñoz,Andrés	2.25
Clase,Emmanuel	2.26
Duran,Jhoan	2.29
Pressly,Ryan	2.31
Fairbanks,Peter	2.35
Kahnle,Tommy	2.43
Holmes,Clay	2.46
Hentges,Sam	2.50
Hader,Josh	2.51
Martin,Christopher	2.53
Williams,Devin	2.54
Rogers,Taylor	2.61
Hendriks,Liam	2.65
Kelly,Joe	2.72
Abreu,Bryan	2.79
Bummer,Aaron	2.81
Doval,Camilo	2.84
Neris,Hector	2.85
Iglesias,Raisel	2.86
Brash,Matt	2.86
Stephan,Trevor	2.93
Ottavino,Adam	2.95
Bautista,Félix	2.95
Suarez,Robert	2.95
Moran,Jovani	2.96
Karinchak,James	2.96
King,Michael	2.97
Hudson,Daniel	2.98
Phillips,Evan	3.00

Top BPX, 10+ Saves

NAME	BPX
Díaz,Edwin	253
Muñoz,Andrés	210
Hendriks,Liam	205
Hader,Josh	203
Fairbanks,Peter	203
Rogers,Taylor	194
Pressly,Ryan	192
Clase,Emmanuel	181
Iglesias,Raisel	174
Williams,Devin	159
Holmes,Clay	153
Gallegos,Giovanny	152
Bednar,David	151
Romano,Jordan	149
Puk,A.J.	146
Jansen,Kenley	144
Bautista,Félix	143
Barlow,Scott	139
Adam,Jason	136
Robertson,David	129
Sewald,Paul	129
Helsley,Ryan	121
Doval,Camilo	121
Hughes,Brandon	113
Leclerc,José	111
Díaz,Alexis	108
Kimbrel,Craig	107
Floro,Dylan	106
Finnegan,Kyle	106
Bard,Daniel	105
Domínguez,Seranthony	104

Top BPX, <10 Saves

NAME	BPX
Alvarado,José	222
Martin,Christopher	210
Duran,Jhoan	187
Kahnle,Tommy	183
Hentges,Sam	171
Lee,Dylan	167
Anderson,Nick	165
Neris,Hector	165
Swanson,Erik	160
Pagan,Emilio	155
Jiménez,Joe	155
Hudson,Daniel	150
Stephan,Trevor	149
King,Michael	146
Milner,Hoby	145
Mantiply,Joe	143
McHugh,Collin	143
Chafin,Andrew	142
Ottavino,Adam	142
Smith,Will	142
Vesia,Alex	142
López,Reynaldo	141
Lugo,Seth	141
Kelly,Joe	141
Thielbar,Caleb	141
Brogdon,Connor	138
Karinchak,James	138
Suarez,Robert	137
Lamet,Dinelson	137
Festa,Matt	137
Poche,Colin	132

POTENTIAL SKILLS GAINERS AND FADERS — Pitchers

K% Gainers

From a pitcher's swinging-strike rate (SwK), we can establish a typical range in which we would expect to find their K%. The pitchers on this list posted a 2022 K% that was in the bottom of the expected range based on their SwK. The names above the break line are in the bottom 10% of that range, and are the strongest candidates for K% gains. The names below the break line are in the bottom 25%, and are also good candidates for K% gains.

K% Faders

From a pitcher's swinging-strike rate (SwK), we can establish a typical range in which we would expect to find their K%. The pitchers on this list posted a 2022 K% that was in the top of that expected range based on their SwK. The names above the break line are in the top 10% of that range, and are the strongest candidates for a K% fade. The names below the break line are in the top 25%, and are also good candidates for a K% fade.

BB% Gainers

A pitcher's xBB% is a skills-based representation of what their BB% should be. Assuming the same underlying skills across seasons, a pitcher's actual BB% should move in the direction of their xBB%. Therefore, by ordering pitchers with the biggest gap between actual BB% and xBB% in 2022 in the chart below, we can identify those whose walk rates should improve (Gainers) in 2023.

BB% Faders

A pitcher's xBB% is a skills-based representation of what their BB% should be. Assuming the same underlying skills across seasons, a pitcher's actual BB% should move in the direction of their xBB%. Therefore, by ordering pitchers with the biggest gap between xBB% and actual BB% in 2022 in the chart below, we can identify those whose walk rates should get worse (Faders) in 2023.

K% GAINERS

NAME	SwK	K%
Montgomery, Jordan	13	21.8
Contreras, Roansy	13	21.1
Smyly, Drew	13	20.4
Anderson, Ian	13	19.7
Anderson, Tyler	12	19.5
Crowe, Wil	12	20.5
Wells, Tyler	12	18.0
Barria, Jaime	11	17.1
Clevinger, Mike	11	18.8
Thompson, Zach	11	16.6
Odorizzi, Jake	11	19.0
Ramirez, Erasmo	11	17.6
Plesac, Zach	11	17.6
Sandoval, Patrick	14	23.7
Carrasco, Carlos	14	23.6
McKenzie, Triston	13	25.6
Montas, Frankie	13	23.4
Lopez, Pablo	13	23.6
Eovaldi, Nathan	13	22.4
Rasmussen, Drew	13	21.4
Fried, Max	13	23.2
Suarez, Jose	12	22.3
Martinez, Nick	12	21.2
Velasquez, Vince	12	21.6
Lynch, Daniel	12	20.3
Kluber, Corey	12	20.2
Lorenzen, Michael	12	20.7
Stripling, Ross	12	20.7
Voth, Austin	11	20.4
Gibson, Kyle	11	20.1
Quintana, Jose	11	20.2
Marquez, German	11	19.3
Urquidy, Jose	11	19.7

K% FADERS

NAME	SwK	K%
Gallen, Zac	10	26.9
Burke, Brock	11	27.4
Lodolo, Nick	13	29.7
Javier, Cristian	14	33.2
Rodriguez, Eduardo	8	18.4
Perez, Martin	9	20.6
Mikolas, Miles	9	19.0
Keller, Mitch	9	20.1
Gray, Sonny	10	24.0
Singer, Brady	10	24.2
Kirby, George	10	24.5
Lauer, Eric	10	23.8
Steele, Justin	11	24.6
Civale, Aaron	11	24.1
Cobb, Alex	11	23.9
Musgrove, Joe	11	24.9
Wheeler, Zack	12	26.9
Cortes, Nestor	12	26.5
Verlander, Justin	12	27.8
Severino, Luis	13	27.7
Morton, Charlie	13	28.2
Luzardo, Jesus	14	30.0
Rodon, Carlos	15	33.4

BB% GAINERS

NAME	xBB%	BB%
Kikuchi, Yusei	8.7	12.8
Kopech, Michael	8.7	11.5
Akin, Keegan	4.1	6.1
Hill, Rich	5.0	7.0
Gray, Jon	5.9	7.5
Manaea, Sean	5.9	7.5
Ryan, Joe	5.9	7.8
Strider, Spencer	6.1	8.5
Contreras, Roansy	7.2	9.6
Martinez, Nick	7.2	9.2
Ashby, Aaron	7.6	9.9
Hearn, Taylor	7.6	9.6
Pivetta, Nick	7.6	9.4
Rogers, Trevor	7.6	9.4
Sandoval, Patrick	7.6	9.4
Bubic, Kris	8.3	10.7
Kaprielian, James	8.3	10.1
Cease, Dylan	8.7	10.4
Lorenzen, Michael	8.7	10.7

BB% FADERS

NAME	xBB%	BB%
Fried, Max	7.2	4.4
Espino, Paolo	7.6	4.9
Greinke, Zack	7.6	4.6
Senzatela, Antonio	8.7	5.6
Ramirez, Erasmo	5.9	4.0
Lynn, Lance	6.1	3.7
Taillon, Jameson	6.1	4.4
Cueto, Johnny	7.2	5.1
Eflin, Zach	7.2	4.8
Singer, Brady	7.2	5.6
Civale, Aaron	7.6	5.4
Burnes, Corbin	8.3	6.4
Lyles, Jordan	8.3	6.7
Sampson, Adrian	8.3	6.3
Blackburn, Paul	8.7	6.4

EXPECTED STATS vs. ACTUAL — Pitchers

ERA Underperformers (min. 75 IP)

NAME	ERA	xERA	Diff
Corbin,Patrick	6.31	4.51	1.80
Wood,Alex	5.10	3.40	1.70
Feltner,Ryan	5.83	4.46	1.37
Civale,Aaron	4.92	3.65	1.27
Rogers,Trevor	5.47	4.22	1.25
Gomber,Austin	5.56	4.32	1.24
Kikuchi,Yusei	5.19	3.96	1.23
Ashby,Aaron	4.44	3.29	1.15
Gibson,Kyle	5.05	3.98	1.07
Giolito,Lucas	4.90	3.86	1.04
Crawford,Kutter	5.47	4.45	1.02
Wilson,Bryse	5.52	4.54	0.98
Berrios,Jose	5.23	4.27	0.96
Bradish,Kyle	4.90	4.00	0.90
Marquez,German	5.00	4.12	0.88
White,Mitchell	5.45	4.58	0.87
Manaea,Sean	4.96	4.10	0.86
Bubic,Kris	5.58	4.73	0.85
Morton,Charlie	4.34	3.50	0.84
Ashcraft,Graham	4.89	4.09	0.80
Greene,Hunter	4.44	3.65	0.79

WHIP Underperformers (min. 75 IP)

NAME	WHIP	xWHIP	Diff
Corbin,Patrick	1.70	1.30	0.40
Senzatela,Antonio	1.69	1.34	0.35
Bubic,Kris	1.70	1.45	0.25
Lynch,Daniel	1.57	1.33	0.24
Gausman,Kevin	1.24	1.00	0.24
Minor,Mike	1.63	1.41	0.22
Giolito,Lucas	1.44	1.24	0.20
Brubaker,Jonathan	1.47	1.27	0.20
Berrios,Jose	1.42	1.23	0.19
Rogers,Trevor	1.50	1.33	0.17
Espino,Paolo	1.37	1.20	0.17
Ashby,Aaron	1.43	1.26	0.17
Fedde,Erick	1.63	1.47	0.16
Carrasco,Carlos	1.33	1.18	0.15
Hearn,Taylor	1.50	1.35	0.15
Kirby,George	1.21	1.07	0.14
Crawford,Kutter	1.42	1.28	0.14
Voth,Austin	1.40	1.26	0.14
Kuhl,Chad	1.55	1.41	0.14
Kikuchi,Yusei	1.50	1.37	0.13
Thompson,Zach	1.51	1.40	0.11

Wins Underperformers (SP)

NAME	W	xW	Diff
Quintana,Jose	6	16	-10
Davies,Zachary	2	10	-8
Archer,Chris	2	9	-7
Greinke,Zack	4	10	-6
Montas,Frankie	5	11	-6
Sandoval,Patrick	6	12	-6
Steele,Justin	4	10	-6
Dunning,Dane	4	10	-6
Cobb,Alex	7	12	-5
Montgomery,Jordan	9	14	-5
Kopech,Michael	5	10	-5
Brubaker,Jonathan	3	8	-5
Stroman,Marcus	6	10	-4
Nola,Aaron	11	15	-4
Musgrove,Joe	10	14	-4
Castillo,Luis	8	12	-4
Gallen,Zac	12	16	-4
Burnes,Corbin	12	16	-4

ERA Overperformers (min. 75 IP)

NAME	ERA	xERA	Diff
Barria,Jaime	2.61	4.27	-1.66
Urias,Julio	2.16	3.76	-1.60
Manoah,Alek	2.24	3.81	-1.57
Burke,Brock	1.97	3.53	-1.56
Verlander,Justin	1.75	3.26	-1.51
Gonsolin,Tony	2.14	3.56	-1.42
Anderson,Tyler	2.57	3.98	-1.41
Flexen,Chris	3.73	5.11	-1.38
Cease,Dylan	2.20	3.54	-1.34
Sampson,Adrian	3.11	4.41	-1.30
Cortes,Nestor	2.44	3.68	-1.24
Kopech,Michael	3.54	4.70	-1.16
Kremer,Dean	3.23	4.37	-1.14
Greinke,Zack	3.68	4.72	-1.04
Springs,Jeffrey	2.46	3.48	-1.02
Cueto,Johnny	3.35	4.35	-1.00
Javier,Cristian	2.54	3.52	-0.98
Scherzer,Max	2.29	3.23	-0.94
Quantrill,Cal	3.38	4.32	-0.94
Ramirez,Erasmo	2.92	3.83	-0.91
Alcantara,Sandy	2.28	3.18	-0.90

WHIP Overperformers (min. 75 IP)

NAME	WHIP	xWHIP	Diff
Gonsolin,Tony	0.87	1.20	-0.33
Barria,Jaime	1.03	1.28	-0.25
Kopech,Michael	1.19	1.44	-0.25
Gallen,Zac	0.91	1.12	-0.21
Manoah,Alek	0.99	1.19	-0.20
Cortes,Nestor	0.92	1.12	-0.20
Verlander,Justin	0.83	1.03	-0.20
Urias,Julio	0.96	1.15	-0.19
Anderson,Tyler	1.00	1.19	-0.19
McKenzie,Triston	0.95	1.12	-0.17
Alcantara,Sandy	0.98	1.15	-0.17
Mikolas,Miles	1.03	1.20	-0.17
Brieske,Beau	1.20	1.36	-0.16
Peralta,Freddy	1.04	1.20	-0.16
Javier,Cristian	0.95	1.10	-0.15
Wells,Tyler	1.14	1.29	-0.15
Archer,Chris	1.31	1.45	-0.14
Severino,Luis	1.00	1.14	-0.14
Rasmussen,Drew	1.04	1.17	-0.13
Lorenzen,Michael	1.28	1.41	-0.13
Darvish,Yu	0.95	1.08	-0.13

Wins Overperformers (SP)

NAME	W	xW	Diff
Wright,Kyle	21	14	7
Carrasco,Carlos	15	12	3
Garcia,Luis	15	12	3
Verlander,Justin	18	16	2
Darvish,Yu	16	14	2
Giolito,Lucas	11	9	2
Lorenzen,Michael	8	6	2
Anderson,Ian	10	8	2
Valdez,Framber	17	15	2
Gonsolin,Tony	16	14	2
Ryan,Joe	13	11	2
Lyles,Jordan	12	11	1
Wacha,Michael	11	10	1
Bassitt,Chris	15	14	1
Berrios,Jose	12	11	1

RISK MANAGEMENT

GRADE "F" in HEALTH (R$>0)

Pitchers		Batters
Alzolay,Adbert	Loáisiga,Jonathan	Ahmed,Nick
Antone,Tejay	Lorenzen,Michael	Albies,Ozzie
Barnes,Matt	Luzardo,Jesús	Andujar,Miguel
Beeks,Jalen	Lynn,Lance	Arroyo,Christian
Blackburn,Paul	Maeda,Kenta	Bader,Harrison
Carrasco,Carlos	Manning,Matt	Belt,Brandon
Chirinos,Yonny	Matz,Steven	Benintendi,Andrew
Civale,Aaron	May,Dustin	Berti,Jon
Clarke,Taylor	McCullers Jr.,Lance	Bote,David
Clevinger,Mike	Megill,Tylor	Bryant,Kris
Cobb,Alex	Miley,Wade	Buxton,Byron
Cueto,Johnny	Montero,Rafael	Calhoun,Kole
deGrom,Jacob	Moore,Matt	Chisholm,Jazz
Domínguez,Seranthor	Morejon,Adrian	Cooper,Garrett
Eflin,Zach	Morris,Cody	Cordero,Franchy
Eovaldi,Nathan	Muñoz,Andrés	d'Arnaud,Travis
Fairbanks,Peter	Ober,Bailey	Díaz,Aledmys
Flaherty,Jack	Paxton,James	Fletcher,David
Germán,Domingo	Peralta,Freddy	Fraley,Jake
Glasnow,Tyler	Poche,Colin	García,Leury
Gonsolin,Tony	Robertson,David	Garlick,Kyle
Graterol,Brusdar	Rodón,Carlos	Garver,Mitch
Gray,Jon	Rodriguez,Eduardo	Haggerty,Sam
Gray,Sonny	Sadler,Casey	Haniger,Mitch
Harvey,Hunter	Sale,Chris	Hicks,Aaron
Heaney,Andrew	Scherzer,Max	Jansen,Danny
Hendricks,Kyle	Schmidt,Clarke	Jiménez,Eloy
Hernández,Jonathan	Severino,Luis	Kieboom,Carter
Hill,Rich	Sims,Lucas	Kiermaier,Kevin
Hudson,Daniel	Smyly,Drew	Kirilloff,Alex
Kahnle,Tommy	Snell,Blake	Larnach,Trevor
Karinchak,James	Springs,Jeffrey	Lewis,Kyle
Kelly,Joe	Strahm,Matt	Lewis,Royce
Kershaw,Clayton	Strasburg,Stephen	Longoria,Evan
King,Michael	Syndergaard,Noah	Madrigal,Nick
Kluber,Corey	Taillon,Jameson	Maton,Nick
Knebel,Corey	Turnbull,Spencer	Meadows,Austin
Kopech,Michael	Verlander,Justin	Mondesi,Adalberto
Lamet,Dinelson	Wacha,Michael	Naquin,Tyler
Leclerc,José		Ramirez,Harold
		Rendon,Anthony
		Ríos,Edwin
		Rosario,Eddie
		Sanó,Miguel
		Senzel,Nick
		Solano,Donovan
		Soler,Jorge
		Stanton,Giancarlo
		Stephenson,Tyler
		Tatis Jr.,Fernando
		Trout,Mike
		Voit,Luke
		White,Evan
		Zunino,Mike

Highest Reliability-Health/Experience/Consistency (Min. Grade BBB)

CA	Rel
Realmuto,J.T.	AAA
Murphy,Sean	AAB
Varsho,Daulton	AAB
Vázquez,Christian	AAB
Rutschman,Adley	ABA
Stallings,Jacob	ABA
Heim,Jonah	ABB
Langeliers,Shea	ABB
Sánchez,Gary	BAB

1B/DH	Rel
Alonso,Pete	AAA
Blackmon,Charlie	AAA
France,Ty	AAA
Santana,Carlos	AAA
Vaughn,Andrew	AAA
Murphy,Sean	AAB
Bell,Josh	AAB
Cronenworth,Jake	AAB
Goldschmidt,Paul	AAB
Lowe,Nate	AAB
Mountcastle,Ryan	AAB
Rutschman,Adley	ABA
Hall,Darick	ABA
Meneses,Joey	ABA
Miller,Owen	ABA
Paredes,Isaac	ABB
Pasquantino,Vinnie	ABB
Dozier,Hunter	BAA
Rizzo,Anthony	BAA
Yelich,Christian	BAA
Sánchez,Gary	BAB
Aguilar,Jesús	BAB
Cron,C.J.	BAB
Longoria,Evan	BAB
Flores,Wilmer	BAB
Ramírez,José	BAB
Tellez,Rowdy	BAB
Walker,Christian	BAB
Chavis,Michael	BBA

2B	Rel
Edman,Tommy	AAA
Merrifield,Whit	AAA
Cronenworth,Jake	AAB
Hernández,César	AAB
Rengifo,Luis	AAB
Miller,Owen	ABA
Allen,Nick	ABA
Castro,Rodolfo	ABA
García,Luis	ABA
Gorman,Nolan	ABA
Stott,Bryson	ABA
Paredes,Isaac	ABB
Aranda,Jonathan	ABB
Donovan,Brendan	ABB
Gordon,Nick	ABB
Leblanc,Charles	ABB
Morel,Christopher	ABB
Walls,Taylor	ABB
Harrison,Josh	BAA
Odor,Rougned	BAA
Torres,Gleyber	BAA
Flores,Wilmer	BAB
Lux,Gavin	BAB
Polanco,Jorge	BAB
Schoop,Jonathan	BAB
Taylor,Chris	BAB

3B	Rel
Farmer,Kyle	AAA
Devers,Rafael	AAA
Witt Jr.,Bobby	AAB
Rengifo,Luis	AAB
Arenado,Nolan	AAB
McMahon,Ryan	AAB
Suarez,Eugenio	AAB
Castro,Rodolfo	ABA
Machin,Vimael	ABA
Montero,Elehuris	ABA
Steer,Spencer	ABA
Vargas,Ildemaro	ABA
Villar,David	ABA
Walls,Taylor	ABB
Paredes,Isaac	ABB
Donovan,Brendan	ABB
Harrison,Josh	BAA
Dozier,Hunter	BAA
Chapman,Matt	BAA
Flores,Wilmer	BAB
Ramírez,José	BAB

OF	Rel
Merrifield,Whit	AAA
Blackmon,Charlie	AAA
Vaughn,Andrew	AAA
Kwan,Steven	AAA
Taylor,Michael A.	AAA
Ward,Taylor	AAA
Varsho,Daulton	AAB
Grichuk,Randal	AAB
Grisham,Trent	AAB
Grossman,Robbie	AAB
Happ,Ian	AAB
Profar,Jurickson	AAB
Tapia,Raimel	AAB
Taveras,Leody	AAB
Verdugo,Alex	AAB
Meneses,Joey	ABA
Bleday,J.J.	ABA
Garrett,Stone	ABA
Kelenic,Jarred	ABA
Marsh,Brandon	ABA
McCormick,Chas	ABA
Robles,Victor	ABA
Suwinski,Jack	ABA
Thompson,Bubba	ABA
Donovan,Brendan	ABB
Gordon,Nick	ABB
Morel,Christopher	ABB
Mitchell,Calvin	ABB
Thomas,Alek	ABB
Dozier,Hunter	BAA
Yelich,Christian	BAA
Canha,Mark	BAA
Gonzalez,Oscar	BAA
Peralta,David	BAA
Lux,Gavin	BAB
Taylor,Chris	BAB
Betts,Mookie	BAB
Gurriel Jr.,Lourdes	BAB
Hernández,Teoscar	BAB
Renfroe,Hunter	BAB
Yepez,Juan	BBA
Taylor,Tyrone	BBB

SS	Rel
Edman,Tommy	AAA
Bogaerts,Xander	AAA
Crawford,J.P.	AAA
Farmer,Kyle	AAA
Kiner-Falefa,Isiah	AAA
Swanson,Dansby	AAA
Mateo,Jorge	AAB
Rosario,Amed	AAB
Turner,Trea	AAB
Witt Jr.,Bobby	AAB
Allen,Nick	ABA
García,Luis	ABA
Stott,Bryson	ABA
Pena,Jeremy	ABA
Perdomo,Geraldo	ABA
Walls,Taylor	ABB
Adames,Willy	BAA
Bichette,Bo	BAA
Lindor,Francisco	BAA
DeJong,Paul	BBB

SP	Rel
Alcantara,Sandy	AAA
Bassitt,Chris	BAA
Berríos,José	AAB
Bubic,Kris	AAB
Burnes,Corbin	BAA
Cole,Gerrit	BAA
Corbin,Patrick	AAA
Espino,Paolo	AAA
Flexen,Chris	AAB
Garcia,Luis H.	AAA
Gibson,Kyle	BAA
Gilbert,Logan	AAA
Irvin,Cole	BAB
Javier,Cristian	AAB
Lyles,Jordan	BAB
Márquez,Germán	BAA
McClanahan,Shane	BAB
McKenzie,Triston	ABA
Montas,Frankie	BAA
Montgomery,Jordan	BAA
Nola,Aaron	AAB
Pivetta,Nick	AAA
Quantrill,Cal	AAA
Rasmussen,Drew	BBA
Senga,Koudai	AAB
Singer,Brady	BAA

RP	Rel
Bard,Daniel	AAB
Barlow,Scott	AAA
Clase,Emmanuel	AAA
Finnegan,Kyle	BBB
Gallegos,Giovanny	BAA
Hader,Josh	AAB
Hand,Brad	BAB
Iglesias,Raisel	AAA
Jansen,Kenley	BAA
Kimbrel,Craig	BAB
López,Jorge	BAB
Neris,Hector	ABB
Romano,Jordan	BAA
Smith,Will	BAA
Soto,Gregory	AAA
Stratton,Chris	BBA
Trivino,Lou	BAB

RISK MANAGEMENT

GRADE "A" in CONSISTENCY

Pitchers (min 80 IP)

Alcantara,Sandy	Scherzer,Max
Alexander,Tyler	Senzatela,Antonio
Archer,Chris	Singer,Brady
Ashby,Aaron	Steele,Justin
Bassitt,Chris	Stroman,Marcus
Bieber,Shane	Syndergaard,Noah
Boyd,Matt	Thompson,Keegan
Brubaker,Jonathan	Thompson,Zach
Burnes,Corbin	Urquidy,José
Canning,Griffin	Valdez,Framber
Civale,Aaron	Wacha,Michael
Clevinger,Mike	Wainwright,Adam
Cole,Gerrit	Walker,Taijuan
Corbin,Patrick	Wells,Tyler
Cueto,Johnny	Wheeler,Zack
Darvish,Yu	Whitlock,Garrett
deGrom,Jacob	Williams,Trevor
Detmers,Reid	

Batters (min 400 AB)

Dunning,Dane	Adames,Willy
Eflin,Zach	Allen,Nick
Eovaldi,Nathan	Alonso,Pete
Falter,Bailey	Bart,Joey
Flaherty,Jack	Bichette,Bo
Freeland,Kyle	Blackmon,Charlie
Fried,Max	Bogaerts,Xander
Garcia,Luis H.	Bregman,Alex
Gausman,Kevin	Canha,Mark
Gibson,Kyle	Casas,Triston
Gilbert,Logan	Chapman,Matt
Giolito,Lucas	Contreras,Willson
Glasnow,Tyler	Crawford,J.P.
Gomber,Austin	De La Cruz,Bryan
Gore,MacKenzie	Devers,Rafael
Gray,Josiah	Edman,Tommy
Gray,Sonny	Farmer,Kyle
Greinke,Zack	France,Ty
Heasley,Jon	García,Luis
Hendricks,Kyle	Gonzalez,Oscar
Hill,Garrett	Gorman,Nolan
Hill,Rich	Hays,Austin
Houck,Tanner	Hoskins,Rhys
Houser,Adrian	Kepler,Max
Kelly,Merrill	Kiner-Falefa,Isiah
Kershaw,Clayton	Kwan,Steven
Kikuchi,Yusei	Lindor,Francisco
Kirby,George	Mancini,Trey
Kuhl,Chad	Margot,Manuel
Lodolo,Nick	Marsh,Brandon
López,Pablo	McCutchen,Andrew
Lynn,Lance	Meneses,Joey
Mahle,Tyler	Merrifield,Whit
Manaea,Sean	Montero,Elehuris
Márquez,Germán	Naylor,Josh
Matz,Steven	Nimmo,Brandon
McCullers Jr.,Lance	Pena,Jeremy
McKenzie,Triston	Pham,Tommy
Montas,Frankie	Realmuto,J.T.
Montgomery,Jordan	Rizzo,Anthony
Musgrove,Joe	Rutschman,Adley
Nelson,Ryne	Springer,George
Ober,Bailey	Stott,Bryson
Odorizzi,Jake	Swanson,Dansby
Peralta,Freddy	Torres,Gleyber
Pivetta,Nick	Turner,Justin
Quantrill,Cal	Vaughn,Andrew
Rasmussen,Drew	Ward,Taylor
Rodriguez,Eduardo	Wong,Kolten
Sandoval,Patrick	Yelich,Christian

TOP COMBINATION OF SKILLS AND RELIABILITY
Maximum of one "C" in Reliability Grade

BATTING POWER (Min. 400 AB)

PX 110+	PX	Rel
Suarez,Eugenio	165	AAB
Hernández,Teoscar	161	BAB
Hoskins,Rhys	158	CAA
Riley,Austin	158	AAC
Chapman,Matt	156	BAA
Alonso,Pete	153	AAA
Renfroe,Hunter	153	BAB
Adames,Willy	151	BAA
Goldschmidt,Paul	150	AAB
Rodríguez,Julio	149	AAC
Devers,Rafael	147	AAA
Betts,Mookie	147	BAB
Story,Trevor	147	CAB
Meneses,Joey	143	ABA
Tellez,Rowdy	142	BAB
Ramírez,José	142	BAB
Ward,Taylor	142	AAA
Cron,C.J.	141	BAB
Martinez,J.D.	141	AAC
Tucker,Kyle	141	AAC
Santander,Anthony	141	CAB
Smith,Will	139	BAC
Machado,Manny	139	AAC
Happ,Ian	139	AAB
Walker,Christian	138	BAB
Contreras,Willson	137	CAA
Gorman,Nolan	136	ABA
Arenado,Nolan	134	AAB
Arozarena,Randy	134	AAC
Casas,Triston	133	ACA
Varsho,Daulton	131	AAB
Realmuto,J.T.	130	AAA
McMahon,Ryan	129	AAB
Murphy,Sean	129	AAB
Morel,Christopher	129	ABB
Rizzo,Anthony	127	BAA
Mountcastle,Ryan	127	AAB
Bichette,Bo	126	BAA
Torres,Gleyber	125	BAA
Laureano,Ramón	125	CBB
Witt Jr.,Bobby	124	AAB
Langeliers,Shea	124	ABB
Escobar,Eduardo	123	AAC
Bogaerts,Xander	122	AAA
Carlson,Dylan	122	BAC
Swanson,Dansby	122	AAA
Grisham,Trent	121	AAB
Grichuk,Randal	121	AAB
Polanco,Jorge	120	BAB
Hays,Austin	118	CAA
Rutschman,Adley	118	ABA
Abreu,José	118	AAC
Naylor,Josh	118	CAA
Melendez,MJ	117	AAC
Lowe,Nate	117	AAB
Báez,Javier	117	AAC
McCutchen,Andrew	116	CAA
Suzuki,Seiya	116	BAC
Marsh,Brandon	116	ABA
Correa,Carlos	116	CAB
Gurriel Jr.,Lourdes	115	BAB
Turner,Trea	115	AAB
Pasquantino,Vinnie	113	ABB
Thomas,Lane	111	AAC
Candelario,Jeimer	111	BAC

RUNNER SPEED (Min. 400 AB)

Spd 100+	Spd	Rel
Kwan,Steven	148	AAA
Morel,Christopher	145	ABB
Rosario,Amed	145	AAB
Mateo,Jorge	145	AAB
Lux,Gavin	140	BAB
Straw,Myles	140	AAC
Turner,Trea	137	AAB
Giménez,Andrés	137	AAC
Witt Jr.,Bobby	135	AAB
Taveras,Leody	133	AAB
Rodríguez,Julio	131	AAC
Abrams,CJ	129	ACB
Marsh,Brandon	128	ABA
Anderson,Tim	128	CAB
Thomas,Alek	126	ABB
Yelich,Christian	124	BAA
Suzuki,Seiya	123	BAC
Pena,Jeremy	122	ABA
Stott,Bryson	122	ABA
Thomas,Lane	121	AAC
Cronenworth,Jake	119	AAB
Betts,Mookie	119	BAB
Báez,Javier	118	AAC
Arozarena,Randy	116	AAC
Rengifo,Luis	116	AAB
Blackmon,Charlie	114	AAA
Gonzalez,Oscar	114	BAA
Edman,Tommy	113	AAA
Lindor,Francisco	112	BAA
Ward,Taylor	111	AAA
Kiner-Falefa,Isiah	111	AAA
Arraez,Luis	111	CAB
Profar,Jurickson	110	AAB
De La Cruz,Bryan	109	ACA
Crawford,J.P.	109	AAA
Estrada,Thairo	107	AAC
Melendez,MJ	107	AAC
Allen,Nick	106	ABA
Canha,Mark	105	BAA
Hays,Austin	105	CAA
Carlson,Dylan	104	BAC
Lowe,Nate	104	AAB
Realmuto,J.T.	103	AAA
Kim,Ha-Seong	103	AAC
Merrifield,Whit	103	AAA
Ramírez,José	102	BAB
Verdugo,Alex	102	AAB
Goldschmidt,Paul	101	AAB
Wong,Kolten	101	CAA
India,Jonathan	100	BAC
Swanson,Dansby	100	AAA
Bichette,Bo	100	BAA
Varsho,Daulton	100	AAB

OVERALL PITCHING SKILL

BPX 100+	BPX	Rel
Díaz,Edwin	253	AAC
Hendriks,Liam	205	CAA
Hader,Josh	203	AAB
Cole,Gerrit	192	BAA
Burnes,Corbin	181	BAA
Clase,Emmanuel	181	AAA
Nola,Aaron	179	AAB
Gausman,Kevin	179	CAA
Iglesias,Raisel	174	AAA
Neris,Hector	165	ABB
Minter,A.J.	159	ACB
Pagan,Emilio	155	BCB
Castillo,Luis	154	CAB
Darvish,Yu	153	CAA
Gallegos,Giovanny	152	BAA
Musgrove,Joe	151	CAA
McClanahan,Shane	150	BAB
Romano,Jordan	149	BAA
Wheeler,Zack	145	CAA
Jansen,Kenley	144	BAA
Morton,Charlie	144	CAB
Ottavino,Adam	142	BBC
Smith,Will	142	BAA
Barlow,Scott	139	AAA
Montgomery,Jordan	138	BAA
Alcantara,Sandy	131	AAA
Bickford,Phil	130	ACA
McKenzie,Triston	126	ABA
Singer,Brady	125	BAA
Garcia,Yimi	124	CBA
Giolito,Lucas	124	CAA
Castillo,Diego	121	CBB
Doval,Camilo	121	ACB
Javier,Cristian	120	AAB
Maton,Phil	118	ACB
Crismatt,Nabil	118	ACB
Trivino,Lou	117	BAB
Gilbert,Logan	116	AAA
Urías,Julio	116	CAB
Berríos,José	115	AAB
Bassitt,Chris	115	BAA
Rasmussen,Drew	114	BBA
Sandoval,Patrick	112	CAA
Montas,Frankie	111	BAA
Bass,Anthony	110	BCB
Manoah,Alek	109	ABC
Detmers,Reid	108	BCA
Boxberger,Brad	108	ACB
Kimbrel,Craig	107	BAB
Finnegan,Kyle	106	BBB
Cease,Dylan	106	AAC
Bard,Daniel	105	AAB
Garcia,Luis H.	105	AAA
Tate,Dillon	105	CBB
Cimber,Adam	104	ACB
Márquez,Germán	104	BAA
Kikuchi,Yusei	103	CAA
Garrett,Braxton	103	BCB
Senga,Koudai	102	AAB

DAILY FANTASY INDICATORS

Top OPS v LHP, 2021-22

Hitter	OPS
Goldschmidt, Paul	1194
Zunino, Mike	1100
Hernandez, Teoscar	1080
Robert, Luis	1052
Posey, Buster	1051
Pujols, Albert	1039
Turner, Trea	1012
Judge, Aaron	999
Trout, Mike	983
Marte, Ketel	968
Tatis Jr., Fernando	968
Buxton, Byron	951
Contreras, William	948
Drury, Brandon	941
Hoskins, Rhys	938
Arenado, Nolan	935
Alvarez, Yordan	934
Bryant, Kris	932
Riley, Austin	930
Franco, Wander	929
Perez, Salvador	928
Rodgers, Brendan	928
Story, Trevor	926
Betts, Mookie	926
Arozarena, Randy	922
Longoria, Evan	919
Altuve, Jose	917
Abreu, Jose	916
O Neill, Tyler	911
Grandal, Yasmani	910
D Arnaud, Travis	908
Bogaerts, Xander	907
McCormick, Chas	906
Pollock, A.J.	903
Rizzo, Anthony	897
McCutchen, Andrew	895
Martinez, J.D.	891
Correa, Carlos	886
Haniger, Mitch	884
Carlson, Dylan	884
Baez, Javier	883

450+ PA, 2021-2022

Top OPS v RHP, 2021-22

Hitter	OPS
Harper, Bryce	1059
Trout, Mike	1029
Judge, Aaron	1025
Soto, Juan	1007
Tatis Jr., Fernando	978
Alvarez, Yordan	954
Devers, Rafael	953
Freeman, Freddie	953
Schwarber, Kyle	938
Ohtani, Shohei	937
Guerrero Jr., Vladimir	926
Ramirez, Jose	909
Votto, Joey	898
Rutschman, Adley	889
Tucker, Kyle	884
Brantley, Michael	882
Belt, Brandon	881
Machado, Manny	880
Buxton, Byron	878
Riley, Austin	875
Alonso, Pete	864
Jansen, Danny	863
Reynolds, Bryan	863
Goldschmidt, Paul	862
Altuve, Jose	861
Rodriguez, Julio	860
Lowe, Brandon	858
Acuna, Ronald	856
Mullins II, Cedric	853
Winker, Jesse	850
Cron, C.J.	849
Olson, Matt	849
Springer, George	847
Vogelbach, Daniel	843
Betts, Mookie	842
Naylor, Josh	841
Fraley, Jake	840
Walsh, Jared	840
Meadows, Austin	838
Smith, Will	837
Polanco, Jorge	836

Top L-R Splits, 2021-22

Hitter	OPS vL-vR
Zunino, Mike	498
Pujols, Albert	394
Goldschmidt, Paul	332
Hernandez, Teoscar	304
Robert, Luis	284
Bohm, Alec	265
Hampson, Garrett	265
Slater, Austin	244
Rodgers, Brendan	242
Marte, Ketel	235
Dubon, Mauricio	234
McCutchen, Andrew	226
Grossman, Robert	225
McCormick, Chas	219
Farmer, Kyle	217
Pinder, Chad	216
Franco, Wander	211
Jeffers, Ryan	210
Turner, Trea	208

Top R-L Splits, 2021-22

Hitter	OPS vR-vL
Wade, LaMonte	480
Vogelbach, Daniel	441
Phillips, Brett	430
Sheets, Gavin	380
Rutschman, Adley	337
Ortega, Rafael	336
Naylor, Josh	329
Fraley, Jake	324
Meadows, Austin	275
Harper, Bryce	271
Walsh, Jared	265
Naquin, Tyler	260
Brantley, Michael	256
Brown, Seth	248
Yastrzemski, Mike	246
Narvaez, Omar	237
Dickerson, Corey	237
Gordon, Nick	222
Moustakas, Mike	221

Best Parks - LH HR

Ballpark	Factor
CHW	45%
LAA	32%
NYY	19%
COL	10%
CLE	9%
MIN	9%
CIN	7%

Worst Parks - LH HR

Ballpark	Factor
DET	-39%
BAL	-24%
KC	-23%
TOR	-18%
OAK	-17%
TAM	-15%
BOS	-9%

Best Parks - Runs

Ballpark	Factor
COL	37%
CIN	23%
BOS	19%

Worst Parks - Runs

Ballpark	Factor
TAM	-15%
SD	-15%
NYM	-13%
SEA	-13%
STL	-11%
OAK	-10%

Best Parks - BB

Ballpark	Factor
NYM	9%
MIL	8%
SF	7%
TAM	6%
CHW	6%

Best Parks - RH HR

Ballpark	Factor
LA	44%
CIN	39%
COL	26%
CHW	22%
LAA	15%
PHI	12%
NYY	10%
BOS	10%

Worst Parks-RH HR

Ballpark	Factor
OAK	-28%
ARI	-27%
SF	-23%
PIT	-20%
BAL	-18%
DET	-17%
MIN	-17%
KC	-16%
TAM	-14%

Best Parks - Ks

Ballpark	Factor
SD	9%
TAM	8%
NYM	7%
SEA	7%

Worst Parks - Ks

Ballpark	Factor
COL	-16%
KC	-12%
PIT	-7%
BOS	-7%

Worst Parks - BB

Ballpark	Factor
TOR	-19%
COL	-12%
SEA	-11%

Note: for Runs, the best parks for hitters are also the worst for pitchers and vice versa

Consistent Hi-PQS SP

Pitcher	QC*
Verlander, Justin	107
Scherzer, Max	87
Darvish, Yu	73
Cole, Gerrit	73
McKenzie, Triston	67
Nola, Aaron	63
Alcantara, Sandy	63
Bieber, Shane	58
Gausman, Kevin	52
Ohtani, Shohei	50
Wheeler, Zack	46
Rodon, Carlos	45
Valdez, Framber	45
Castillo, Luis	40
Fried, Max	40
Woodruff, Brandon	37
Burnes, Corbin	30
Strider, Spencer	30

20+ Starts, 2021-2022
*Quality-Consistency score

Consistent Low-PQS SP

Pitcher	QC*
Fedde, Erick	(252)
Wilson, Bryse	(250)
Alexander, Tyler	(218)
Zimmermann, Bruce	(215)
Howard, Spencer	(214)
Patino, Luis	(209)
Crowe, Wil	(207)
Bumgarner, Madison	(200)
Hernandez, Carlos	(200)
Watkins, Spenser	(200)
Feltner, Ryan	(200)
Heasley, Jon	(200)
Kuhl, Chad	(200)
Hudson, Dakota	(192)
Keller, Brad	(191)
Gonzales, Marco	(188)
Corbin, Patrick	(187)
Gutierrez, Vladimir	(187)
Hearn, Taylor	(183)
Akin, Keegan	(183)

Most DOMinant SP

Pitcher	DOM
Alcantara, Sandy	56%
Ohtani, Shohei	54%
Verlander, Justin	54%
Scherzer, Max	52%
Manoah, Alek	50%
Darvish, Yu	50%
Cole, Gerrit	48%
Bieber, Shane	48%
Burnes, Corbin	45%
Gallen, Zac	45%
Castillo, Luis	44%
Mikolas, Miles	44%
Nola, Aaron	44%
Rodon, Carlos	42%
Valdez, Framber	42%
Manoah, Alek	41%
Musgrove, Joe	40%
McKenzie, Triston	40%
Gausman, Kevin	39%
Wheeler, Zack	38%

Most DISastrous SP

Pitcher	DIS
Fedde, Erick	67%
Wilson, Bryse	65%
Zimmermann, Bruce	59%
Alexander, Tyler	59%
Crowe, Wil	59%
Hernandez, Carlos	57%
Feltner, Ryan	57%
Bumgarner, Madison	57%
Watkins, Spenser	57%
Howard, Spencer	55%
Keller, Brad	55%
Patino, Luis	55%
Akin, Keegan	54%
Heasley, Jon	54%
Hudson, Dakota	54%
Gutierrez, Vladimir	53%
Gonzales, Marco	53%
Thompson, Keegan	52%
Kuhl, Chad	52%
Corbin, Patrick	52%

Universal Draft Grid

Most publications and websites provide cheat sheets with ranked player lists for different fantasy draft formats. The biggest problem with these tools is that they perpetuate the myth that players can be ranked in a linear fashion.

Since rankings are based on highly variable projections, it is foolhardy to draw conclusions that a $24 player is better than a $23 player is better than a $22 player. Yes, a first round pick is better than a 10th round pick, but within most rounds, all players are pretty much interchangeable commodities.

But typical cheat sheets don't reflect that reality. Auction sheets rank players by dollar value. Snake draft sheets rank players within round, accounting for position and categorical scarcity. But just as ADPs have a ridiculously low success rate, these cheat sheets are similarly flawed.

We have a tool at BaseballHQ.com called the Rotisserie Grid. It is a chart—that can be customized to your league parameters—which organizes players into pockets of skill, by position. It is one of the most popular tools on the site. One of the best features of this grid is that its design provides immediate insight into position scarcity.

So in the *Forecaster*, we have transitioned to this format as a sort of Universal Draft Grid.

How to use the chart

Across the top of the grid, players are sorted by position. First and third base, and second and shortstop are presented side-by-side for easy reference when considering corner and middle infielders, respectively.

The vertical axis separates each group of players into tiers based on potential fantasy impact. At the top are the Elite players; at the bottom are the Fringe players.

Auction leagues: The tiers in the grid represent rough break-points for dollar values. Elite players could be considered those that are purchased for $30 and up. Each subsequent tier is a step down of approximately $5.

Snake drafters: Tiers can be used to rank players similarly, though most tiers will encompass more than one round. Any focus on position scarcity will bump some players up a bit. In recent years, Catcher has been the only position to exhibit any real positional scarcity effect. As such, one might opt to draft Will Smith (from the Stars tier) before the Gold level Jake McCarthy.

To build the best foundation, try to stay balanced in the first 10 rounds of your draft: 2 MI, 2 CI, 3 OF, and 3 SP (likely one closer) is a foundation target that will set you up for maximum flexibility in the mid- and end-games.

The **players** are listed at the position where they both qualify and provide the most fantasy value. Additional position eligibility (20 games) is listed in parentheses. (NOTE: check out our new Multiposition Eligiblity Chart on page 274 for additional eligibility detail.) Listings in bold are players with high reliability grades (minimum "B" across the board).

Each player is presented with his 7-character Mayberry score. The first four digits (all on a 0-5 scale) represent skill: power, speed, batting average and playing time for batters; ERA, dominance, saves potential and playing time for pitchers. The last three alpha characters are the reliability grade (A-F): health, experience and consistency.

Within each tier, players are sorted by the first character of their Mayberry score. This means that batters are sorted by power; pitchers by ERA potential. If you need to prospect for the best skill sets among players in a given tier, target those with 4s and 5s in whatever skill you need.

CAVEATS and DISCLAIMERS

The placement of players in tiers does not represent average draft positions (ADP) or average auction values (AAV). It represents where each player's true value may lie. It is the variance between this true value and the ADP/AAV market values—or better, the value that your league-mates place on each player—where you will find your potential for profit or loss.

That means *you cannot take this chart right into your draft with you*. You have to compare these rankings with your ADPs and AAVs, and build your draft list from there. In other words, if we project Nolan Arenado as a "Elite" level pick but you know the other owners (or your ADPs) see him as a fourth-rounder, you can probably wait to pick him up in round three. If you are in an auction league with owners who overvalue young players and Jazz Chisholm (projected at $27) gets bid past $30, you will likely take a loss should you decide to chase the bidding, especially given the depth of second baseman in in that tier for 2023.

Finally, this chart is intended as a preliminary look based on current factors. For Draft Day, you will need to make your own adjustments based upon many different criteria that will impact the world between now and then. Daily updates appear online at BaseballHQ.com. A free projections update is available in March at **http://www.baseballhq.com/bf2023**

Simulation League Cheat Sheet
Using Runs Above Replacement creates a more real-world ranking of player value, which serves simulation gamers well. Batters and pitchers are integrated, and value break-points are delineated.

Multi-Position Eligiblity Chart
The default position eligibility requirements throughout this book is 20 games in the previous season. This chart serves those who play in leagues where the eligiblity requirements are 10 or 5 games at a position in the preceeding year.

Playing Time Measurement Charts
Based on the research article on page 67, these charts offer a snapshot view of our new playing time metrics. Charts are presented by position, with each chart sorted by Plate Appearances per Active Week (PAAW). This entirely new language for measuring playing time will have an adoption curve, but presenting all of the data here should make the transition smoother.

Universal Draft Grid

TIER	FIRST BASE		THIRD BASE		SECOND BASE		SHORTSTOP	
Elite	Alonso,Pete	(4145 AAA)	Arenado,Nolan	(4155 AAB)			Bichette,Bo	(4345 BAA)
	Goldschmidt,Paul	(4445 AAB)	Devers,Rafael	(4145 AAA)			Bogaerts,Xander	(4345 AAA)
	Freeman,Freddie	(4255 AAD)	Ramírez,José	(4355 BAB)			Witt Jr.,Bobby (5)	(4525 AAB)
	Guerrero Jr.,Vladimir	(4155 AAF)	Machado,Manny	(4245 AAC)			Lindor,Francisco	(3335 BAA)
			Riley,Austin	(4145 AAC)			Turner,Trea	(3545 AAB)
Gold	Olson,Matt	(4135 AAD)	Bregman,Alex	(3145 DAA)	Torres,Gleyber	(4235 BAA)	Swanson,Dansby	(4325 AAA)
	Abreu,José	(3245 AAC)			Altuve,Jose	(4355 CAD)	Seager,Corey	(4255 CAC)
					Chisholm,Jazz	(4515 FCC)	Edman,Tommy (4)	(2435 AAA)
					Story,Trevor	(4325 CAB)	Franco,Wander	(2455 DCB)
					Albies,Ozzie	(3335 FBB)	Rosario,Amed	(1535 AAB)
					Semien,Marcus	(3435 AAD)	Anderson,Tim	(1545 CAB)
					Giménez,Andrés	(2525 AAC)	Hoerner,Nico	(1445 DAB)
Stars	Cron,C.J.	(4135 BAB)	Henderson,Gunnar	(4535 ACF)	Polanco,Jorge	(4135 BAB)	Adames,Willy	(4225 BAA)
	Mountcastle,Ryan	(4225 AAB)	Miranda,Jose (3)	(3035 AAC)	Lowe,Brandon	(4335 DBC)	Cruz,Oneil	(4525 ABD)
	Tellez,Rowdy	(4045 BAB)	Bohm,Alec	(2235 AAD)	Cronenworth,Jake (3)	(3325 AAB)	Báez,Javier	(3415 AAC)
	Walker,Christian	(4135 BAB)			Marte,Ketel	(3355 DAD)	Correa,Carlos	(3035 CAB)
	Hoskins,Rhys	(4135 CAA)			Wong,Kolten	(3335 CAA)	Kiner-Falefa,Isiah	(1435 AAA)
	Bell,Josh	(3035 AAB)			Merrifield,Whit (o)	(2335 AAA)	Abrams,CJ	(1515 ACB)
	Lowe,Nate	(3335 AAB)			Rojas,Josh (5)	(2325 CAC)		
	Pasquantino,Vinnie	(3245 ABB)			Arraez,Luis (3)	(1255 CAB)		
					McNeil,Jeff (o)	(1345 BAD)		
					Segura,Jean	(1335 DBB)		
Regulars	Rizzo,Anthony	(4145 BAA)	Suarez,Eugenio	(5115 AAB)	Drury,Brandon (53)	(4025 AAD)	Moore,Dylan (o)	(4403 DCC)
	Brown,Seth (o)	(4225 AAD)	Chapman,Matt	(4115 BAA)	Muncy,Max (5)	(4225 CAD)	Mateo,Jorge	(3515 AAB)
	Casas,Triston	(4125 ACA)	McMahon,Ryan	(4225 AAB)	Flores,Wilmer (53)	(3335 BAB)	Pena,Jeremy	(3425 ABA)
	Voit,Luke	(4015 FAC)	Escobar,Eduardo	(4125 AAC)	Gordon,Nick (o)	(3433 ABB)	Stott,Bryson (4)	(2415 ABA)
	Walsh,Jared	(4225 BAD)	Jung,Josh	(4115 AFF)	India,Jonathan	(3225 BAC)	Estrada,Thairo (4)	(2335 AAC)
	France,Ty	(3045 AAA)	Rendon,Anthony	(3245 FDC)	Lux,Gavin (o)	(2425 BAB)	Kim,Ha-Seong (5)	(2325 AAC)
	Mancini,Trey (o)	(3025 DAA)	Díaz,Yandy	(2145 CAB)	Arroyo,Christian	(2333 FDB)	Mondesi,Adalberto	(2503 FFB)
	Naylor,Josh	(3045 CAA)	Hayes,Ke'Bryan	(2325 CAF)	Grissom,Vaughn	(2533 AFF)	Wendle,Joe (45)	(2343 DAA)
			Turner,Justin	(2335 CAA)	Rodgers,Brendan	(2235 CAD)		
			Urshela,Giovanny	(2335 CAC)	Berti,Jon (5)	(1515 FBB)		
					Frazier,Adam (o)	(1335 AAD)		
					LeMahieu,DJ (53)	(1235 CAD)		
Mid-Level	Hiura,Keston	(5103 ACB)	Wisdom,Patrick	(5205 AAD)	Castro,Rodolfo (5)	(4223 ABA)	Urías,Luis (45)	(3125 AAC)
	Meneses,Joey (o)	(4245 ABA)	Davis,J.D.	(4313 CBB)	Gorman,Nolan	(4205 ABA)	Farmer,Kyle (5)	(2125 AAA)
	Belt,Brandon	(4225 FBD)	Donaldson,Josh	(4115 DAB)	Morel,Christopher (o)	(4405 ABB)	García,Luis (4)	(2145 ABA)
	Myers,Wil (o)	(4213 DBC)	Longoria,Evan	(4123 FCB)	Taylor,Chris (o)	(4403 BAB)	Andrus,Elvis	(2233 CAA)
	Vaughn,Andrew (o)	(3125 AAA)	Montero,Elehuris	(3215 ABA)	Paredes,Isaac (53)	(3025 ABB)	Crawford,Brandon	(2213 BAD)
	Cooper,Garrett	(3023 FBA)	Baty,Brett	(3023 BCA)	Massey,Michael	(3205 ACF)	Hampson,Garrett (o)	(2503 ACA)
	Votto,Joey	(3215 DAD)	Candelario,Jeimer	(3125 BAC)	Urías,Ramón (5)	(3223 BBD)	Sosa,Edmundo (5)	(2423 BDB)
	Ramírez,Harold (o)	(2133 FBC)	Moncada,Yoán	(3215 CAC)	Rengifo,Luis (5)	(2225 AAB)	Crawford,J.P.	(1225 AAA)
	Vargas,Miguel	(1303 ABC)			Donovan,Brendan (5o)	(1133 ABB)	Iglesias,José	(1143 CAD)
					Harrison,Josh (5)	(1223 BAA)	Peraza,Oswald	(1403 ACA)
					Espinal,Santiago	(1233 BBC)	Rojas,Miguel	(1335 BAD)
					Kemp,Tony (o)	(1325 AAD)	Tovar,Ezequiel	(1315 AFF)
					Madrigal,Nick	(0353 FDB)	Fletcher,David (4)	(0435 FBC)
							Lopez,Nicky (45)	(0533 AAD)
Bench	Cordero,Franchy (o)	(4201 FCA)	Villar,David	(5111 ABA)	Aranda,Jonathan	(3303 ABB)	DeJong,Paul	(3103 BBB)
	Díaz,Lewin	(4303 ABC)	Dalbec,Bobby (3)	(4311 ABC)	Odor,Rougned	(3203 BAA)	Castillo,Diego (4o)	(3133 ACB)
	Garcia,Dermis	(4303 ACB)	Dozier,Hunter (3o)	(3313 BAA)	Schoop,Jonathan	(2223 BAB)	Volpe,Anthony	(3511 ABF)
	Pratto,Nick	(4203 ABD)	Steer,Spencer	(3213 ABA)	Díaz,Aledmys (o)	(2133 FCA)	Walls,Taylor (45)	(2303 ABB)
	Aguilar,Jesús	(3021 BAB)	Brosseau,Michael	(3301 BDF)	McKinstry,Zach (5)	(2313 BDA)	Barrero,Jose	(2403 CCF)
	Wade Jr.,LaMonte (o)	(3223 DDC)	Burger,Jake	(3003 CDA)	Toro,Abraham (5)	(2211 ACD)	Velazquez,Andrew	(2401 ACB)
	Santana,Carlos	(2013 AAA)	Anderson,Brian (o)	(2303 DCB)	Villar,Jonathan (5)	(2311 BBC)	Allen,Nick (4)	(1205 ABA)
	Gurriel,Yuli	(2233 AAD)	Peterson,Jace	(2313 CCA)	Hernández,César	(1223 BAA)	Perdomo,Geraldo	(1303 ABA)
	Hosmer,Eric	(2131 CAB)	Rivera,Emmanuel	(2221 BCA)	Miller,Owen (3)	(1313 ABA)	Dubon,Mauricio (o)	(1221 ACB)
	Joe,Connor (o)	(2223 BBD)	Castro,Harold (3)	(1133 BBC)	Brujáan,Vidal (o)	(1411 ACB)	Newman,Kevin (4)	(1333 DBB)
	Solano,Donovan	(2143 FCB)	Groshans,Jordan	(1313 ACF)	Díaz,Jordan	(1013 ACF)		
	Torkelson,Spencer	(2005 ABD)	Kieboom,Carter	(1113 FFB)	Lopez,Alejo	(1341 ADC)		
			Smith,Josh (o)	(1301 ACC)	Vavra,Terrin	(1411 ADA)		
			Williams,Luke (o)	(1501 AFA)	Guillorme,Luis (5)	(0033 CCD)		
			Freeman,Tyler	(0321 ADD)				
Fringe	Sanó,Miguel	(5201 FDC)	Duran,Ezequiel	(3221 ACF)	Bote,David	(4311 FDA)	Lewis,Royce	(4421 FFF)
	Choi,Ji-Man	(4013 DBA)	Smith,Kevin	(2301 ACF)	Leblanc,Charles	(3301 ABB)	Trejo,Alan	(3021 ACA)
	Chavis,Michael	(3101 BBA)	Vargas,Ildemaro	(1331 ABA)	Biggio,Cavan (3)	(3301 CCB)	Ahmed,Nick	(2221 FDB)
	White,Evan	(3001 FFB)	Kreidler,Ryan	(1501 ACC)	Neuse,Sheldon (5)	(2201 ACA)	Alcantara,Sergio (45)	(2301 ADB)
	Toglia,Michael (o)	(2303 ACA)	Machin,Vimael	(0213 ABA)	García,Leury (o)	(1311 FBC)	Garcia,Maikel	(1421 ACF)
	Rivas III,Alfonso	(1301 ADA)			Marcano,Tucupita (o)	(1301 ACA)		
					Bride,Jonah (5)	(0303 ADA)		

Universal Draft Grid

Elite

TIER	CATCHER	DH	OUTFIELD	OUTFIELD
Elite	Realmuto,J.T. (4435 AAA)	Harper,Bryce (5255 CAD)	Hernández,Teoscar (5235 BAB)	Harris II,Michael (4545 ACF)
		Ohtani,Shohei (5345 AAD)	Alvarez,Yordan (5155 CAD)	Robert,Luis (4335 DBD)
		Tatis Jr.,Fernando (5435 FDB)	Judge,Aaron (5155 DAD)	Rodríguez,Julio (4545 AAC)
			Trout,Mike (5355 FAD)	Soto,Juan (4255 BAF)
			Betts,Mookie (4455 BAB)	Tucker,Kyle (4345 AAC)
			Acuña Jr.,Ronald (4335 DAC)	Marte,Starling (3445 CAC)
			Arozarena,Randy (4435 AAC)	Mullins,Cedric (2525 AAD)

Gold

TIER	CATCHER	DH	OUTFIELD	OUTFIELD
Gold			Schwarber,Kyle (5125 BAD)	Santander,Anthony (4045 CAB)
			Castellanos,Nick (4345 BAF)	Springer,George (4355 DAA)
			Garcia,Adolís (4415 AAD)	McCarthy,Jake (3515 ACC)
			O Neill,Tyler (4315 DAF)	Suzuki,Seiya (3325 BAC)
			Reynolds,Bryan (4335 AAD)	

Stars

TIER	CATCHER	DH	OUTFIELD	OUTFIELD
Stars	Varsho,Daulton (o) (4325 AAB)	Conforto,Michael (4135 BFD)	Buxton,Byron (5543 FBF)	Yelich,Christian (3425 BAA)
	Perez,Salvador (4145 DAC)	Martinez,J.D. (4235 AAC)	Happ,Ian (4225 AAB)	Bader,Harrison (3415 FCB)
	Smith,Will (4335 BAC)		Renfroe,Hunter (4135 BAB)	Hays,Austin (3135 CAA)
	Rutschman,Adley (3245 ABA)		Ward,Taylor (4335 AAA)	Nimmo,Brandon (3335 DAA)
			Bryant,Kris (4235 FCC)	Verdugo,Alex (2245 FAD)
			Carroll,Corbin (4535 ADF)	Benintendi,Andrew (2235 FAD)
			Gurriel Jr.,Lourdes (3145 BAB)	Kwan,Steven (1535 AAA)

Regulars

TIER	CATCHER	DH	OUTFIELD	OUTFIELD
Regulars	Murphy,Sean (4235 AAB)	Garver,Mitch (4123 FDD)	Grichuk,Randal (4225 AAB)	Greene,Riley (3415 ABD)
	Contreras,Willson (4135 CAA)	Cruz,Nelson (3213 BAD)	Haniger,Mitch (4225 FCB)	McCutchen,Andrew (3125 CAA)
	Melendez,MJ (o) (3115 AAC)	Lewis,Kyle (3403 FDC)	Jiménez,Eloy (4025 FCC)	Pollock,A.J. (3235 DAC)
	Stephenson,Tyler (3343 FDC)	Vogelbach,Daniel (3013 CBA)	Laureano,Ramón (4215 CBB)	Winker,Jesse (3235 CAD)
	Kirk,Alejandro (2035 CAD)		Pederson,Joc (4223 AAC)	Blackmon,Charlie (2335 AAA)
			Stanton,Giancarlo (4215 FAB)	Canha,Mark (2325 BAA)
			Yastrzemski,Mike (4325 BAD)	Gonzalez,Oscar (2135 BAA)
			Marsh,Brandon (3405 ABA)	Brantley,Michael (2253 DBA)
			Bellinger,Cody (3415 BAD)	Pham,Tommy (2215 CAA)
			De La Cruz,Bryan (3235 ACA)	Margot,Manuel (1325 DBA)
			Fraley,Jake (3213 FDC)	Straw,Myles (0515 AAC)

Mid-Level

TIER	CATCHER	DH	OUTFIELD	OUTFIELD
Mid-Level	Raleigh,Cal (5123 ACB)		Carpenter,Kerry (4023 ABB)	Thomas,Lane (3315 AAC)
	Contreras,William (4523 ACD)		Grisham,Trent (4215 AAB)	Profar,Jurickson (2335 AAB)
	d'Arnaud,Travis (4133 FBD)		Taylor,Tyrone (4323 BBB)	Taveras,Leody (2405 AAB)
	Haase,Eric (4213 ACC)		Carlson,Dylan (4235 BAC)	Taylor,Michael A. (2303 AAA)
	Jansen,Danny (4033 FDB)		Duvall,Adam (4113 CBB)	Castro,Willi (2423 ABD)
	Fortes,Nick (3323 ADA)		Lowe,Josh (4501 ABC)	Friedl,T.J. (2403 ACA)
	Grandal,Yasmani (3113 DBD)		Meadows,Austin (4125 FCC)	Hernández,Kiké (2125 DAC)
	Ruiz,Keibert (2143 BBC)		Naquin,Tyler (4223 FBC)	Kepler,Max (2235 CAA)
	Vázquez,Christian (1023 AAB)		Sheets,Gavin (4013 ACA)	Reyes,Victor (2433 CCB)
			Soler,Jorge (4023 FBA)	Rosario,Eddie (2313 FCB)
			Trammell,Taylor (4313 BDB)	Ruiz,Esteury (2511 ABC)
			McCormick,Chas (3213 ABA)	Brennan,Will (1233 ABA)
			García,Avisaíl (3215 CBD)	Robles,Victor (1403 ABA)
			Haggerty,Sam (3501 FDC)	Thompson,Bubba (1503 ABA)
			Nootbaar,Lars (3223 ADA)	Daza,Yonathan (1143 CBA)
			Olivares,Edward (3233 DDB)	Eaton,Nate (1503 ADF)
			Slater,Austin (3423 BCC)	

Bench

TIER	CATCHER	DH	OUTFIELD	OUTFIELD
Bench	Zunino,Mike (5003 FDD)	Carpenter,Matt (5231 CDD)	Gallo,Joey (5303 BAC)	Grossman,Robbie (2203 AAB)
	Langeliers,Shea (4215 ABB)	Ríos,Edwin (5001 FFF)	Kelenic,Jarred (4213 ABA)	Mitchell,Calvin (2133 ABB)
	Sánchez,Gary (4103 BAB)	Hall,Darick (4121 ABA)	Suwinski,Jack (4103 ABA)	Thomas,Alek (2235 ABB)
	Alvarez,Francisco (4003 ADF)	Reyes,Franmil (4113 BAC)	Adell,Jo (4303 ABC)	Baddoo,Akil (2503 ACD)
	Jeffers,Ryan (4123 CDB)	Vientos,Mark (3003 ACA)	Cabrera,Oswaldo (4403 ACA)	Calhoun,Kole (2103 FBC)
	Bart,Joey (3105 ADA)	Cabrera,Miguel (1113 CAA)	Jones,Nolan (4301 ADA)	Dickerson,Corey (2233 DBA)
	Díaz,Elias (3023 ABC)		Sánchez,Jesús (4223 BBF)	Duran,Jarren (2401 ACA)
	Mejía,Francisco (3133 DCD)		Stowers,Kyle (4203 ACA)	Hicks,Aaron (2303 FBB)
	Naylor,Bo (3301 ACC)		Velazquez,Nelson (4403 ADD)	Isbel,Kyle (2403 ACB)
	Heim,Jonah (2113 ABB)		Waters,Drew (4303 ACA)	Kiermaier,Kevin (2423 FCA)
	Alfaro,Jorge (2203 DCA)		Garrett,Stone (3303 ABA)	Meyers,Jake (2213 DCC)
	Caratini,Victor (2113 ACA)		Peralta,David (3133 BAA)	Ortega,Rafael (2313 BCB)
	Gomes,Yan (2333 BCB)		Yepez,Juan (3003 BBA)	Vierling,Matt (2423 ACB)
	Kelly,Carson (2313 CBC)		Benson,Will (3303 ACA)	Tapia,Raimel (1443 AAB)
	McCann,James (2203 DDC)		Fairchild,Stuart (3401 ADA)	Allen,Greg (1501 DFD)
	McGuire,Reese (2321 ADC)		Gamel,Ben (3223 CBA)	Andujar,Miguel (1223 FCB)
	Campusano,Luis (1203 ACF)		Kirilloff,Alex (3123 FDA)	Azocar,Jose (1311 ACA)
	Diaz,Yainer (1433 ADF)		Larnach,Trevor (3303 FFA)	Frelick,Sal (1331 ACF)
	Moreno,Gabriel (1221 ADF)		Ozuna,Marcell (3123 CAF)	Mitchell,Garrett (1501 BDD)
	Trevino,Jose (1123 BCA)		Siri,Jose (3501 ACA)	Senzel,Nick (1223 FCA)
			Walker,Jordan (3311 ACF)	

Fringe

TIER	CATCHER	DH	OUTFIELD	OUTFIELD
Fringe	Molina,Yadier (0000 DBA)	Beer,Seth (3011 ACB)	Aquino,Aristides (4201 DDA)	Pache,Cristian (1103 ACB)
	Zavala,Seby (4003 ADD)		Garlick,Kyle (4021 FFD)	Palacios,Richard (1411 ADC)
	Adams,Riley (3001 AFB)		Hilliard,Sam (4401 ACA)	
	Bethancourt,Christian (: (3323 ACB)		Maton,Nick (4221 FDA)	
	Stassi,Max (3003 DBC)		Wallner,Matt (4201 ACF)	
	Wong,Connor (3301 ADA)		Bleday,J.J. (3203 ABA)	
	Higgins,P.J. (3) (2121 DFC)		Moniak,Mickey (3401 DDA)	
	Huff,Sam (2303 CDF)		Pinder,Chad (3213 DCA)	
	Stallings,Jacob (1003 ABA)		Capel,Conner (2331 ACA)	
	Barnhart,Tucker (1003 ACA)		Cowser,Colton (2001 ADF)	
	Delay,Jason (1101 AFB)		Davis,Brennen (2101 ADD)	
	Hedges,Austin (1203 ACA)		Madris,Bligh (2001 ACA)	
	Herrera,Iván (1301 ADA)		Smith,Pavin (2411 ACA)	
	Knizner,Andrew (1003 ADA)		Burleson,Alec (1321 ABB)	
	Narváez,Omar (1003 BBD)		Ramos,Heliot (1201 ABB)	
	Nido,Tomás (1311 BDD)		Celestino,Gilberto (1311 ACA)	
	Nola,Austin (1123 CBB)		González,Luis (1303 ADC)	
	Serven,Brian (1203 ADA)		McKenna,Ryan (1201 AFB)	

Universal Draft Grid

STARTING PITCHERS

TIER				
Elite				
Gold	Bieber,Shane	(5305 DAA)	Ohtani,Shohei	(5505 BAF)
	Burnes,Corbin	**(5505 BAA)**	Scherzer,Max	(5505 FAA)
Stars	**Alcantara,Sandy**	**(5205 AAA)**	Strider,Spencer	(5503 BCD)
	Castillo,Luis	(5405 CAB)	Wheeler,Zack	(5305 CAA)
	Cole,Gerrit	**(5505 BAA)**	Woodruff,Brandon	(5505 DAA)
	deGrom,Jacob	(5503 FBA)	**Javier,Cristian**	**(4503 AAB)**
	Fried,Max	(5205 DAA)	**McKenzie,Triston**	**(4305 ABA)**
	Gausman,Kevin	(5505 CAA)	Verlander,Justin	(4303 FCB)
	Nola,Aaron	**(5505 AAB)**	Urías,Julio	(3205 CAB)
Regulars	Darvish,Yu	(5405 CAA)	Rodón,Carlos	(5505 FAC)
	Gallen,Zac	(5403 DAB)	Valdez,Framber	(5205 DAA)
	Glasnow,Tyler	(5503 FBA)	Cease,Dylan	(4405 AAC)
	Kershaw,Clayton	(5401 FAA)	Cortes,Nestor	(4305 DCF)
	Kirby,George	(5305 ADA)	Springs,Jeffrey	(4403 FCB)
	McClanahan,Shane	**(5303 BAB)**	**Garcia,Luis H.**	**(3203 AAA)**
	Musgrove,Joe	(5405 CAA)	Manoah,Alek	(3205 ABC)
Mid-Level	Gray,Sonny	(5403 FAA)	Peralta,Freddy	(4503 FAA)
	Greene,Hunter	(5503 DCB)	**Rasmussen,Drew**	**(4203 BBA)**
	May,Dustin	(5303 FDC)	Severino,Luis	(4303 FDB)
	Montgomery,Jordan	**(5305 BAA)**	**Singer,Brady**	**(4205 BAA)**
	Morton,Charlie	(5405 CAB)	Detmers,Reid	(3303 BCA)
	Ray,Robbie	(5505 CAC)	Wright,Kyle	(4205 ABC)
	Sale,Chris	(5503 FDC)	Gonsolin,Tony	(3303 FBC)
	Webb,Logan	(5205 DAC)	Kelly,Merrill	(3205 DAA)
	Bassitt,Chris	**(4205 BAA)**	Mikolas,Miles	(3103 CCB)
	Gilbert,Logan	**(4305 AAA)**	Ryan,Joe	(3305 BCD)
	Giolito,Lucas	(4405 CAA)	Walker,Taijuan	(3203 DAA)
	Lynn,Lance	(4303 FAA)	Anderson,Tyler	(2105 DAB)
Bench	Ashby,Aaron	(5403 DCA)	**Senga,Koudai**	**(4403 AAB)**
	Bello,Brayan	(5305 BDC)	Skubal,Tarik	(4401 DAB)
	Cobb,Alex	(5303 FAB)	Steele,Justin	(4303 DCA)
	Gray,Jon	(5303 FDC)	Stroman,Marcus	(4203 DAA)
	Heaney,Andrew	(5501 FAB)	Taillon,Jameson	(4203 FAB)
	Lodolo,Nick	(5503 DDA)	Wesneski,Hayden	(4103 ADD)
	Snell,Blake	(5503 FAB)	Whitlock,Garrett	(4201 DBA)
	Brown,Hunter	(4203 ADF)	**Berríos,José**	**(3305 AAB)**
	Carrasco,Carlos	(4303 FBB)	Cabrera,Edward	(3303 DDF)
	Civale,Aaron	(4301 FAA)	Clevinger,Mike	(3203 FDA)
	Eovaldi,Nathan	(4303 FAA)	Contreras,Roansy	(3203 ADD)
	Flaherty,Jack	(4303 FCA)	Mahle,Tyler	(3303 DAA)
	López,Pablo	(4303 DAA)	**Montas,Frankie**	**(3305 BAA)**
	Luzardo,Jesús	(4403 FCF)	Rodriguez,Eduardo	(3203 FAA)
	Maeda,Kenta	(4303 FBC)	Syndergaard,Noah	(3103 FDA)
	Matz,Steven	(4303 DAA)	Urquidy,José	(3203 DAA)
	McCullers Jr.,Lance	(4303 FAA)	Wacha,Michael	(3203 FAA)
	Rodriguez,Grayson	(4401 ADB)	Wainwright,Adam	(3105 DAA)
	Rogers,Trevor	(4303 DAB)	Lauer,Eric	(2203 BAD)
	Sandoval,Patrick	(4303 CAA)	**Quantrill,Cal**	**(2105 AAA)**
Fringe	Alzolay,Adbert	(5501 FBB)	Suarez,José	(3203 ABF)
	Miller,Bobby	(5400 AFF)	Turnbull,Spencer	(3203 FCC)
	Morris,Cody	(5401 FFA)	Waldichuk,Ken	(3201 ADF)
	Paxton,James	(5501 FFF)	Cueto,Johnny	(2103 FAA)
	Strasburg,Stephen	(5301 FDB)	Gray,Josiah	(2305 ACA)
	Wood,Alex	(5301 FAC)	Hendricks,Kyle	(2103 FAA)
	Bradley,Taj	(4200 AFF)	**Irvin,Cole**	**(2003 BAB)**
	Eflin,Zach	(4201 FAA)	Kopech,Michael	(2303 FBC)
	Garrett,Braxton	(4201 BCB)	Kremer,Dean	(2103 DCD)
	Hall,DL	(4501 ADD)	Manning,Matt	(2103 FDF)
	Márquez,Germán	**(4205 BAA)**	Miley,Wade	(2103 FAB)
	Megill,Tylor	(4301 FCB)	Nelson,Ryne	(2101 BDA)
	Ortiz,Luis	(4201 AFF)	Pepiot,Ryan	(2301 ADC)
	Peterson,David	(4301 DCB)	Pérez,Martín	(2105 CAB)
	Anderson,Ian	(3301 CCB)	Plesac,Zach	(2101 CAB)
	Blackburn,Paul	(3103 FCF)	Smyly,Drew	(2203 FAB)
	Bradish,Kyle	(3203 CDB)	Wells,Tyler	(2103 DCA)
	Cavalli,Cade	(3201 CDD)	Wentz,Joey	(2101 ADD)
	Chirinos,Yonny	(3101 FFD)		
	Falter,Bailey	(3201 BDA)		
	Germán,Domingo	(3301 FBC)		
	Gibson,Kyle	**(3205 BAA)**		
	Gore,MacKenzie	(3301 DFA)		
	Greinke,Zack	(3003 DAA)		
	Hill,Rich	(3201 FAA)		
	Keller,Mitch	(3205 BBC)		
	Kluber,Corey	(3203 FBB)		
	Lorenzen,Michael	(3201 FCB)		
	Manaea,Sean	(3203 DAA)		
	Ober,Bailey	(3201 FDA)		
	Pivetta,Nick	**(3305 AAA)**		
	Quintana,José	(3203 DBB)		
	Stripling,Ross	(3201 DAB)		

RELIEF PITCHERS

TIER				
Gold	Clase,Emmanuel	**(5331 AAA)**		
Stars	Díaz,Edwin	(5531 AAC)		
	Hendriks,Liam	(5531 CAA)		
	Romano,Jordan	**(5431 BAA)**		
	Williams,Devin	(5531 BCC)		
Regulars	**Barlow,Scott**	**(5431 AAA)**	Pressly,Ryan	(5530 DAA)
	Bautista,Félix	(5531 ADC)	**Bard,Daniel**	**(4330 AAB)**
	Bednar,David	(5531 DCD)	Helsley,Ryan	(4431 DCD)
	Doval,Camilo	(5431 ACB)		
	Hader,Josh	**(5530 AAB)**		
	Iglesias,Raisel	(5531 AAA)		
	Jansen,Kenley	**(5530 BAA)**		
Mid-Level	Adam,Jason	(5421 ADA)		
	Gallegos,Giovanny	**(5521 BAA)**		
	Holmes,Clay	(5321 DBB)		
	Muñoz,Andrés	(5521 FDF)		
	Puk,A.J.	(5421 DDF)		
	Kimbrel,Craig	**(4520 BAB)**		
	Leclerc,José	(4520 FDD)		
	Sewald,Paul	(4421 BBF)		
	Díaz,Alexis	(3521 BDA)		
	Hughes,Brandon	(3321 AFC)		
	López,Jorge	**(3230 BAB)**		
Bench	Alvarado,José	(5510 DCC)	Floro,Dylan	(4221 DBA)
	Duran,Jhoan	(5410 ADF)	Houck,Tanner	(4311 DCA)
	Fairbanks,Peter	(5520 FCC)	Poche,Colin	(4510 FDF)
	Hudson,Daniel	(5410 FCC)	Suárez,Ranger	(4103 BAF)
	Karinchak,James	(5511 FCB)	Herget,Jimmy	(3221 CDC)
	Lange,Alex	(5511 BDF)	**Soto,Gregory**	**(2321 AAA)**
	McHugh,Collin	(5401 DCA)		
	Montero,Rafael	(5311 FBB)		
	Neris,Hector	**(5511 ABB)**		
	Ottavino,Adam	(5411 BBC)		
	Phillips,Evan	(5411 ADD)		
	Robertson,David	(5520 FDA)		
	Rogers,Taylor	(5520 DBB)		
	Schreiber,John	(5310 ADC)		
	Stephan,Trevor	(5511 ACD)		
	Suarez,Robert	(5411 DAD)		
	Swanson,Erik	(5411 DDB)		
	Vesia,Alex	(5500 ADF)		
	Domínguez,Seranthony	(4421 FDF)		
	Finnegan,Kyle	**(4321 BBB)**		
Fringe	Abreu,Bryan	(5510 CDF)	Givens,Mychal	(4410 CCB)
	Akin,Keegan	(5211 ABD)	Jax,Griffin	(4311 ACF)
	Antone,Tejay	(5510 FDB)	Kuhnel,Joel	(4210 ADD)
	Beeks,Jalen	(5401 FDA)	Marinaccio,Ron	(4501 BDD)
	Brash,Matt	(5511 ADD)	Sadler,Casey	(4100 FDA)
	Castillo,Diego	(5310 CBB)	Scott,Tanner	(4511 BCA)
	Chafin,Andrew	(5400 DCA)	Sims,Lucas	(4510 FCC)
	De Los Santos,Enyel	(5400 ADC)	**Smith,Will**	**(4510 BAA)**
	García,Luis A.	(5310 CDD)	Suter,Brent	(4201 DBB)
	Graterol,Brusdar	(5110 FDA)	Tate,Dillon	(4111 CBB)
	Graveman,Kendall	(5311 CBC)	Thielbar,Caleb	(4400 CCB)
	Hentges,Sam	(5401 ACF)	**Trivino,Lou**	**(4410 BAB)**
	Jiménez,Joe	(5510 BCC)	Acevedo,Domingo	(3211 ADC)
	Kahnle,Tommy	(5500 FFF)	Barnes,Matt	(3420 FBC)
	Kelly,Joe	(5510 FCB)	Burke,Brock	(3301 DDD)
	King,Michael	(5410 FCC)	Cimber,Adam	(3101 ACB)
	Lamet,Dinelson	(5511 FCB)	Clarke,Taylor	(3211 CBA)
	Lee,Dylan	(5510 ADA)	Coleman,Dylan	(3311 ADD)
	Loáisiga,Jonathan	(5210 FCB)	Estévez,Carlos	(3211 DBA)
	Lugo,Seth	(5411 DCA)	Garcia,Yimi	(3310 CBA)
	Mantiply,Joe	(5210 BDF)	Harvey,Hunter	(3210 FDB)
	Martin,Christopher	(5410 DCC)	Hearn,Taylor	(3301 DBA)
	Mayza,Tim	(5300 CCA)	Hernández,Jonathan	(3211 FFA)
	Minter,A.J.	(5510 ACB)	Knebel,Corey	(3410 FDD)
	Moran,Jovani	(5510 ADB)	Moore,Matt	(3311 FCF)
	Pagan,Emilio	(5511 BCB)	Morgan,Elijah	(3201 ACC)
	Baker,Bryan	(4311 ADD)	Murfee,Penn	(3300 ADD)
	Bass,Anthony	(4210 BCB)	Pérez,Cionel	(3200 ADB)
	Bickford,Phil	(4301 ACA)	Schmidt,Clarke	(3201 FDD)
	Brogdon,Connor	(4411 DCB)	Strahm,Matt	(3310 FDC)
	Chapman,Aroldis	(4510 DAC)	Tepera,Ryan	(3210 DCA)
	Crismatt,Nabil	(4301 ACB)	Martinez,Nick	(2213 AAF)
	Festa,Matt	(4400 BDA)	Morejon,Adrian	(2301 FDB)

Universal Draft Grid

TIER	STARTING PITCHERS				RELIEF PITCHERS			
Below Fringe	Baz,Shane	(5500 FDD)	Liberatore,Matthew	(2101 ADB)	Anderson,Nick	(5510 FFF)	Cuas,Jose	(2100 AFA)
	Buehler,Walker	(5300 FAA)	Lyles,Jordan	**(2105 BAB)**	Bummer,Aaron	(5300 FCA)	Effross,Scott	(2110 CDA)
	Jameson,Drey	(5101 ADB)	Lynch,Daniel	(2103 CCF)	King,John	(5100 DDD)	Espino,Paolo	**(2101 AAA)**
	Paddack,Chris	(5200 FBA)	Martin,Davis	(2200 ADA)	Milner,Hoby	(5300 BDB)	Fulmer,Michael	(2210 FBC)
	Kikuchi,Yusei	(4401 CAA)	Martinez,Adrian	(2100 ADD)	Sborz,Josh	(5500 DCB)	García,Jarlín	(2100 ACB)
	Pérez,Eury	(4500 AFF)	Mills,Alec	(2001 FBB)	Treinen,Blake	(5410 FCB)	Hernandez,Elieser	(2301 FDB)
	Ryu,Hyun-Jin	(4100 FAA)	Leiter,Jack	(2300 AFF)	Britton,Zack	(4200 FDF)	Heuer,Codi	(2100 FCB)
	Soroka,Mike	(4001 FFC)	Muller,Kyle	(2200 ACB)	Hicks,Jordan	(4310 FDC)	Keller,Brad	(2100 CAA)
	White,Owen	(4300 AFF)	Otto Jr.,Glenn	(2101 BCB)	Hill,Tim	(4000 BCA)	Kennedy,Ian	(2300 DBC)
	Ashcraft,Graham	(3103 CDD)	Pilkington,Konnor	(2101 ADD)	Kinley,Tyler	(4310 FCB)	Melancon,Mark	(2110 CAC)
	Brubaker,Jonathan	(3303 DAA)	Pineda,Michael	(2001 FBC)	López,Reynaldo	(4400 BCC)	Richards,Trevor	(2401 BCC)
	DeSclafani,Anthony	(3203 FAC)	Ragans,Cole	(2101 BDF)	Loup,Aaron	(4200 DCB)	Rodríguez,Manuel	(2210 FDB)
	Dunning,Dane	(3203 DAA)	Sears,JP	(2001 ADC)	Maton,Phil	(4400 ACB)	Ruiz,José	(2300 ACB)
	Elder,Bryce	(3101 ADC)	Senzatela,Antonio	(2001 FAA)	Megill,Trevor	(4300 DDB)	Sanmartin,Reiver	(2200 ADF)
	Junis,Jakob	(3203 DCD)	Silseth,Chase	(2101 AFF)	Pallante,Andre	(4000 ADA)	Santana,Dennis	(2200 DCB)
	Means,John	(3101 FAA)	Voth,Austin	(2201 DBB)	Price,David	(4200 FCC)	Santillan,Tony	(2310 FDB)
	Mize,Casey	(3100 FAC)	White,Mitch	(2101 BDD)	Rainey,Tanner	(4510 FCF)	Thompson,Keegan	(2201 DCA)
	Pearson,Nate	(3301 FDD)	Wilson,Bryse	(2101 BCB)	Raley,Brooks	(4310 DCA)	Wantz,Andrew	(2300 ADA)
	Sánchez,Sixto	(3100 FFF)	Yarbrough,Ryan	(2101 DAB)	Boxberger,Brad	(3400 ACB)	Woodford,Jake	(2000 ADB)
	Small,Ethan	(3201 ADC)	Adon,Joan	(1200 ADB)	Boyd,Matt	(3301 FCA)	Jackson,Zach	(1510 CDF)
	Alexander,Jason	(2001 ADC)	Assad,Javier	(1101 ADF)	Cabrera,Génesis	(3210 ACA)	Reyes,Alex	(1510 FBA)
	Archer,Chris	(2201 FDA)	Brieske,Beau	(1000 DDC)	Cessa,Luis	(3101 DCB)	Smeltzer,Devin	(1001 FDC)
	Bubic,Kris	**(2203 AAB)**	Davidson,Tucker	(1101 DDF)	Crochet,Garrett	(3400 FDD)	Staumont,Josh	(1410 DCB)
	Bumgarner,Madison	(2103 DAB)	Fedde,Erick	(1003 DAB)	Foley,Jason	(3000 ADF)	Uelmen,Erich	(1100 ADF)
	Bundy,Dylan	(2103 DAB)	Flexen,Chris	**(1101 AAB)**	**Hand,Brad**	**(3310 BAB)**	Wilson,Steven	(1300 BDF)
	Canning,Griffin	(2301 FCA)	Heasley,Jon	(1001 BCA)	Jiménez,Dany	(3300 DDF)		
	Castillo,Max	(2101 ADC)	Hill,Garrett	(1101 ADA)	Martin,Brett	(3110 CCC)		
	Corbin,Patrick	**(2103 AAA)**	Kaprielian,James	(1103 CAC)	Martinez,Seth	(3300 ADA)		
	Crawford,Kutter	(2201 CDB)	Kuhl,Chad	(1201 FBA)	Okert,Steven	(3410 BDC)		
	Davies,Zach	(2103 DAB)	Odorizzi,Jake	(1101 FBA)	Oviedo,Johan	(3200 ACB)		
	Faedo,Alex	(2100 AFF)	Patino,Luis	(1101 FDF)	Peralta,Wandy	(3110 DCA)		
	Feltner,Ryan	(2103 ADB)	Sampson,Adrian	(1003 ACF)	Ramirez,Erasmo	(3101 CDB)		
	Freeland,Kyle	(2105 DAA)	Thompson,Zach	(1101 BCA)	**Stratton,Chris**	**(3300 BBA)**		
	García,Rony	(2200 FDC)	Watkins,Spenser	(1000 BCD)	Vest,Will	(3210 BDD)		
	Gomber,Austin	(2101 DAA)	Winckowski,Josh	(1000 ADA)	Wick,Rowan	(3310 FCA)		
	Gonzales,Marco	(2003 CAB)	Winder,Josh	(1000 CDC)	Williams,Trevor	(3201 DCA)		
	Hancock,Emerson	(2100 CFD)	Winn,Cole	(1200 ADF)	Alexander,Tyler	(2001 DAA)		
	Henry,Thomas	(2101 ADD)	Zimmermann,Bruce	(1000 DDB)	Barlow,Joe	(2210 DDF)		
	Houser,Adrian	(2003 DAA)	Logue,Zach	(0001 ADF)	Barria,Jaime	(2001 ACB)		
	Howard,Spencer	(2200 DDB)	Oller,Adam	(0000 BDF)	Bellatti,Andrew	(2510 ADC)		
	Hudson,Dakota	(2001 FDF)			Crowe,Wil	(2101 ABF)		

SIMULATION LEAGUE DRAFT   TOP 500+

NAME	POS	RAR
Judge,Aaron	89	78.0
Trout,Mike	8	63.8
Soto,Juan	9	57.8
Freeman,Freddie	3	57.4
Alvarez,Yordan	7	53.9
Goldschmidt,Paul	3	52.6
Ramírez,José	5	51.3
Harper,Bryce	0	49.6
Machado,Manny	5	46.3
Rodríguez,Julio	8	43.8
Guerrero Jr.,Vladimir	3	43.1
Bogaerts,Xander	6	43.1
Altuve,Jose	4	41.3
Riley,Austin	5	40.5
Betts,Mookie	9	40.4
Devers,Rafael	5	40.1
Arenado,Nolan	5	39.8
Tucker,Kyle	9	39.3
Turner,Trea	6	39.1
Alonso,Pete	3	38.0
Seager,Corey	6	36.9
Springer,George	89	36.5
Bichette,Bo	6	35.3
Rutschman,Adley	2	35.2
Smith,Will	2	34.8
Acuña Jr.,Ronald	9	34.7
Realmuto,J.T.	2	34.3
Ohtani,Shohei	0	33.8
Bregman,Alex	5	33.6
Schwarber,Kyle	7	31.0
Bryant,Kris	7	30.5
Reynolds,Bryan	8	30.2
Robert,Luis	8	29.6
Franco,Wander	6	29.5
Olson,Matt	3	29.3
Correa,Carlos	6	29.1
Lowe,Nate	3	28.3
Hernández,Teoscar	9	28.2
Kirk,Alejandro	2	27.8
Abreu,José	3	27.7
Scherzer,Max	P	27.6
Nimmo,Brandon	8	27.4
Fried,Max	P	26.5
Tatis Jr.,Fernando	0	26.4
Ohtani,Shohei	P	26.3
Alcantara,Sandy	P	26.1
Harris II,Michael	8	26.1
Ward,Taylor	9	26.0
Bell,Josh	3	25.6
Perez,Salvador	2	25.4
Castellanos,Nick	9	25.3
Suzuki,Seiya	9	25.3
Muncy,Max	45	25.1
Pasquantino,Vinnie	3	24.5
Burnes,Corbin	P	24.4
Lowe,Brandon	4	24.2
Diaz,Yandy	5	24.2
Buxton,Byron	8	23.7
Marte,Ketel	4	23.6
Contreras,Willson	2	23.6
Bieber,Shane	P	23.3
McNeil,Jeff	47	23.3
Henderson,Gunnar	5	22.7

NAME	POS	RAR
Semien,Marcus	4	22.1
Urías,Julio	P	21.8
Rendon,Anthony	5	21.5
Wheeler,Zack	P	21.5
Happ,Ian	7	21.2
Lindor,Francisco	6	21.0
Martinez,J.D.	0	21.0
Santander,Anthony	79	20.9
Gurriel Jr.,Lourdes	7	20.8
Arozarena,Randy	79	20.8
Hoskins,Rhys	3	20.5
Verdugo,Alex	79	20.2
Story,Trevor	4	20.2
Torres,Gleyber	4	20.1
Carroll,Corbin	7	20.1
Suarez,Eugenio	5	19.7
Castillo,Luis	P	19.6
Stephenson,Tyler	2	18.6
Polanco,Jorge	4	18.6
Yelich,Christian	7	18.6
Walker,Christian	3	18.5
Verlander,Justin	P	18.5
Woodruff,Brandon	P	18.4
Winker,Jesse	7	18.3
Strider,Spencer	P	18.3
Jansen,Danny	2	18.3
Kwan,Steven	79	18.2
Contreras,William	2	18.2
Clase,Emmanuel	P	18.1
deGrom,Jacob	P	18.0
Murphy,Sean	2	18.0
Turner,Justin	5	17.9
Marte,Starling	9	17.8
Chisholm,Jazz	4	17.5
Conforto,Michael	0	17.4
Nola,Aaron	P	17.0
Rizzo,Anthony	3	17.0
Mullins,Cedric	8	16.9
Adames,Willy	6	16.7
Cron,C.J.	3	16.7
Gausman,Kevin	P	16.6
Grandal,Yasmani	2	16.5
Albies,Ozzie	4	16.5
Swanson,Dansby	6	16.4
Javier,Cristian	P	16.3
Raleigh,Cal	2	16.3
Musgrove,Joe	P	16.2
Chapman,Matt	5	16.2
McClanahan,Shane	P	16.0
Anderson,Tim	6	15.8
McKenzie,Triston	P	15.4
Valdez,Framber	P	15.4
Renfroe,Hunter	9	15.1
Arraez,Luis	34	15.1
Kershaw,Clayton	P	15.0
France,Ty	3	14.9
Rodgers,Brendan	4	14.8
d'Arnaud,Travis	2	14.8
Lux,Gavin	47	14.7
India,Jonathan	4	14.7
Tellez,Rowdy	3	14.6
Cronenworth,Jake	34	14.2
Manoah,Alek	P	14.1

NAME	POS	RAR
Bohm,Alec	5	14.1
Pollock,A.J.	78	14.1
Wong,Kolten	4	14.0
Witt Jr.,Bobby	56	13.9
Urshela,Giovanny	5	13.9
Belt,Brandon	3	13.8
Kirby,George	P	13.8
Cole,Gerrit	P	13.7
Williams,Devin	P	13.5
Muñoz,Andrés	P	13.4
Melendez,MJ	27	13.3
Stanton,Giancarlo	9	13.2
Ruiz,Keibert	2	13.2
Brantley,Michael	7	13.1
Miranda,Jose	35	13.1
Rojas,Josh	45	13.1
LeMahieu,DJ	345	13.0
Pederson,Joc	7	12.9
McMahon,Ryan	5	12.9
Cease,Dylan	P	12.9
Giménez,Andrés	4	12.7
Rodón,Carlos	P	12.7
May,Dustin	P	12.6
Díaz,Edwin	P	12.6
Casas,Triston	3	12.5
Gallen,Zac	P	12.4
Webb,Logan	P	12.3
Haniger,Mitch	9	12.2
Carpenter,Matt	0	12.1
Gallo,Joey	79	12.1
Benintendi,Andrew	7	12.0
O Neill,Tyler	78	12.0
Mountcastle,Ryan	3	11.8
Longoria,Evan	5	11.8
Escobar,Eduardo	5	11.6
Edman,Tommy	46	11.6
Duran,Jhoan	P	11.4
Suarez,Robert	P	11.3
Sale,Chris	P	11.2
Paredes,Isaac	345	11.2
Bednar,David	P	11.1
Jiménez,Eloy	7	11.0
Glasnow,Tyler	P	11.0
Flores,Wilmer	345	10.7
Severino,Luis	P	10.7
Garcia,Luis H.	P	10.6
Varsho,Daulton	289	10.5
Darvish,Yu	P	10.4
Gonsolin,Tony	P	10.2
Canha,Mark	7	10.2
Hays,Austin	79	10.2
Cortes,Nestor	P	10.2
Merrifield,Whit	49	10.1
Slater,Austin	8	10.1
Adam,Jason	P	10.1
Grissom,Vaughn	4	10.0
Bassitt,Chris	P	9.9
Montgomery,Jordan	P	9.9
Pressly,Ryan	P	9.6
Greene,Hunter	P	9.6
Cooper,Garrett	3	9.6
Moreno,Gabriel	2	9.4
Singer,Brady	P	9.4

NAME	POS	RAR
Soler,Jorge	7	9.4
Suárez,Ranger	P	9.4
Vogelbach,Daniel	0	9.3
Baty,Brett	5	9.3
Grichuk,Randal	89	9.2
Karinchak,James	P	9.2
Walker,Taijuan	P	9.2
Sewald,Paul	P	9.2
Greene,Riley	8	9.1
Naylor,Josh	3	9.1
Phillips,Evan	P	9.1
Lodolo,Nick	P	9.1
Iglesias,Raisel	P	9.1
Helsley,Ryan	P	9.0
Fraley,Jake	7	8.9
Meadows,Austin	O	8.9
Rosario,Amed	6	8.9
Gray,Sonny	P	8.8
Vesia,Alex	P	8.8
Cruz,Oneil	6	8.8
Arroyo,Christian	4	8.7
Romano,Jordan	P	8.6
Bautista,Félix	P	8.6
Lee,Dylan	P	8.6
Springs,Jeffrey	P	8.6
Barlow,Scott	P	8.5
Stott,Bryson	46	8.5
Hendriks,Liam	P	8.5
Hentges,Sam	P	8.5
Brown,Hunter	P	8.5
Carlson,Dylan	89	8.4
Hoerner,Nico	6	8.4
Stephan,Trevor	P	8.2
Wade Jr.,LaMonte	39	8.2
Haase,Eric	2	8.1
Nootbaar,Lars	9	7.9
De La Cruz,Bryan	789	7.8
Doval,Camilo	P	7.8
Brown,Seth	379	7.8
Drury,Brandon	345	7.7
Myers,Wil	39	7.7
Montero,Rafael	P	7.7
Taylor,Chris	47	7.7
Peralta,Freddy	P	7.7
Donaldson,Josh	5	7.7
Estrada,Thairo	46	7.6
Wright,Kyle	P	7.6
Ottavino,Adam	P	7.5
McCormick,Chas	78	7.5
McCullers Jr.,Lance	P	7.5
Hughes,Brandon	P	7.5
Vázquez,Christian	2	7.4
Segura,Jean	4	7.4
Detmers,Reid	P	7.4
Schreiber,John	P	7.4
Garver,Mitch	0	7.4
Chafin,Andrew	P	7.4
Rasmussen,Drew	P	7.3
Montero,Elehuris	5	7.3
Montas,Frankie	P	7.3
McHugh,Collin	P	7.2
Urías,Luis	456	7.2
Steele,Justin	P	7.1

SIMULATION LEAGUE DRAFT

TOP 500+

NAME	POS	RAR
Fairbanks,Peter	P	7.1
Walsh,Jared	3	7.1
Holmes,Clay	P	7.0
Senga,Koudai	P	7.0
Hudson,Daniel	P	6.9
Díaz,Alexis	P	6.9
Kim,Ha-Seong	56	6.9
Fortes,Nick	2	6.9
Alvarez,Francisco	2	6.8
Sandoval,Patrick	P	6.8
Díaz,Elias	2	6.8
Yastrzemski,Mike	89	6.8
Lynn,Lance	P	6.7
Voit,Luke	3	6.7
Sadler,Casey	P	6.7
Cobb,Alex	P	6.6
Morton,Charlie	P	6.6
Swanson,Erik	P	6.5
Peralta,David	7	6.5
Daza,Yonathan	78	6.4
Mejía,Francisco	2	6.4
Stroman,Marcus	P	6.4
Floro,Dylan	P	6.3
Garcia,Adolís	89	6.3
Jeffers,Ryan	2	6.3
Taylor,Tyrone	789	6.3
Cimber,Adam	P	6.3
Mikolas,Miles	P	6.2
Vaughn,Andrew	379	6.2
Domínguez,Seranthony	P	6.2
Kepler,Max	9	6.1
Votto,Joey	3	6.1
Brash,Matt	P	6.1
Snell,Blake	P	6.0
Schmidt,Clarke	P	5.9
Kelly,Carson	2	5.9
Alvarado,José	P	5.9
Mancini,Trey	37	5.8
Santana,Carlos	3	5.8
Kemp,Tony	47	5.8
Bellinger,Cody	8	5.8
Giolito,Lucas	P	5.7
Bass,Anthony	P	5.6
Morris,Cody	P	5.6
Ryan,Joe	P	5.6
Puk,A.J.	P	5.6
Rodriguez,Grayson	P	5.6
Ashby,Aaron	P	5.5
Castillo,Diego	P	5.5
Meneses,Joey	39	5.4
Nola,Austin	2	5.4
Davis,J.D.	5	5.4
Flaherty,Jack	P	5.3
Naylor,Bo	2	5.3
Jansen,Kenley	P	5.3
Jax,Griffin	P	5.3
Grisham,Trent	8	5.2
Sánchez,Gary	2	5.1
Gallegos,Giovanny	P	5.1
Minter,A.J.	P	5.1
Gilbert,Logan	P	5.1
Candelario,Jeimer	5	5.1
Anderson,Tyler	P	5.0

NAME	POS	RAR
Lowe,Josh	9	5.0
Houck,Tanner	P	5.0
Aranda,Jonathan	4	4.9
Bummer,Aaron	P	4.9
Sheets,Gavin	9	4.9
Graterol,Brusdar	P	4.9
Joe,Connor	37	4.8
Trammell,Taylor	9	4.8
King,Michael	P	4.8
McCarthy,Jake	79	4.8
Moncada,Yoán	5	4.7
Graveman,Kendall	P	4.7
Hader,Josh	P	4.7
Beeks,Jalen	P	4.7
Marinaccio,Ron	P	4.7
García,Luis A.	P	4.6
Urías,Ramón	45	4.6
Coleman,Dylan	P	4.6
Moore,Matt	P	4.6
Sánchez,Jesús	8	4.6
Leclerc,José	P	4.5
Gordon,Nick	478	4.5
Eovaldi,Nathan	P	4.5
Blackmon,Charlie	9	4.5
Carrasco,Carlos	P	4.4
Cabrera,Edward	P	4.4
Wendle,Joe	456	4.4
Kahnle,Tommy	P	4.4
Luzardo,Jesús	P	4.2
Narváez,Omar	2	4.2
Pérez,Cionel	P	4.1
Marsh,Brandon	78	4.1
Martin,Christopher	P	4.1
Pepiot,Ryan	P	4.1
Bello,Brayan	P	4.1
Kelly,Joe	P	4.1
Akin,Keegan	P	4.0
Brennan,Will	O	4.0
Gorman,Nolan	4	4.0
Lange,Alex	P	3.9
Festa,Matt	P	3.9
Lewis,Royce	6	3.9
Whitlock,Garrett	P	3.9
Abreu,Bryan	P	3.9
Bard,Daniel	P	3.9
Suter,Brent	P	3.8
Finnegan,Kyle	P	3.8
McGuire,Reese	2	3.8
Crismatt,Nabil	P	3.8
López,Jorge	P	3.8
Profar,Jurickson	7	3.7
Robertson,David	P	3.7
Heaney,Andrew	P	3.7
Loáisiga,Jonathan	P	3.7
Duvall,Adam	78	3.7
Hayes,Ke'Bryan	5	3.7
Herget,Jimmy	P	3.6
Kelly,Merrill	P	3.6
Kinley,Tyler	P	3.6
Gomes,Yan	2	3.5
Dickerson,Corey	7	3.5
Sanó,Miguel	3	3.5
Neris,Hector	P	3.5

NAME	POS	RAR
Quantrill,Cal	P	3.4
Gray,Jon	P	3.4
Rogers,Taylor	P	3.4
García,Luis	46	3.4
Wesneski,Hayden	P	3.4
Loup,Aaron	P	3.3
Caratini,Victor	2	3.3
Tapia,Raimel	789	3.3
Baker,Bryan	P	3.3
De Los Santos,Enyel	P	3.3
Villar,David	5	3.3
Poche,Colin	P	3.3
Madrigal,Nick	4	3.2
Cruz,Nelson	0	3.2
Antone,Tejay	P	3.2
Hosmer,Eric	3	3.2
Castro,Rodolfo	45	3.2
Civale,Aaron	P	3.0
McCutchen,Andrew	7	2.9
Kimbrel,Craig	P	2.9
Skubal,Tarik	P	2.9
Donovan,Brendan	459	2.8
Gurriel,Yuli	3	2.8
Ray,Robbie	P	2.8
Smith,Will	P	2.8
Brogdon,Connor	P	2.8
Waldichuk,Ken	P	2.8
Chapman,Aroldis	P	2.8
Frazier,Adam	49	2.7
Ober,Bailey	P	2.7
Garrett,Braxton	P	2.6
Morgan,Elijah	P	2.6
Burke,Brock	P	2.5
Bader,Harrison	8	2.5
Ramirez,Harold	39	2.5
Miller,Bobby	P	2.4
Chirinos,Yonny	P	2.4
Gonzalez,Oscar	9	2.4
Moran,Jovani	P	2.4
Mayza,Tim	P	2.4
Baz,Shane	P	2.4
Tate,Dillon	P	2.4
Crawford,Brandon	6	2.4
Lorenzen,Michael	P	2.4
Thomas,Lane	789	2.3
Martinez,Nick	P	2.3
Rogers,Trevor	P	2.3
Frelick,Sal	8	2.3
Garcia,Yimi	P	2.2
Iglesias,José	6	2.2
Solano,Donovan	3	2.2
Díaz,Aledmys	47	2.2
Contreras,Roansy	P	2.2
Báez,Javier	6	2.2
Jung,Josh	5	2.1
Choi,Ji-Man	3	2.1
Hernández,Kiké	8	2.0
Acevedo,Domingo	P	2.0
Kirilloff,Alex	7	2.0
Crochet,Garrett	P	2.0
Mantiply,Joe	P	2.0
Thielbar,Caleb	P	1.9
Pham,Tommy	7	1.9

NAME	POS	RAR
Carpenter,Kerry	O	1.9
Langeliers,Shea	2	1.9
Naquin,Tyler	9	1.8
Pallante,Andre	P	1.8
Pérez,Eury	P	1.8
Peterson,David	P	1.8
Martinez,Seth	P	1.8
Lewis,Kyle	0	1.8
Ortiz,Luis	P	1.8
Lugo,Seth	P	1.8
Heuer,Codi	P	1.8
Hearn,Taylor	P	1.8
Staumont,Josh	P	1.7
Gamel,Ben	79	1.7
Anderson,Nick	P	1.7
Tovar,Ezequiel	6	1.7
Zunino,Mike	2	1.7
Fulmer,Michael	P	1.7
Crawford,J.P.	6	1.7
Givens,Mychal	P	1.7
López,Reynaldo	P	1.6
López,Pablo	P	1.6
Bradley,Taj	P	1.6
Anderson,Brian	59	1.6
Sims,Lucas	P	1.6
Paxton,James	P	1.5
Massey,Michael	4	1.5
Treinen,Blake	P	1.5
Smith,Pavin	9	1.5
Reyes,Alex	P	1.4
Price,David	P	1.4
Wilson,Steven	P	1.3
Britton,Zack	P	1.2
Hill,Tim	P	1.2
Buehler,Walker	P	1.2
Falter,Bailey	P	1.2
Grossman,Robbie	79	1.2
Stripling,Ross	P	1.2
Trivino,Lou	P	1.2
Espinal,Santiago	4	1.2
Lamet,Dinelson	P	1.1
Volpe,Anthony	6	1.1
Hernández,Jonathan	P	1.1
Gore,MacKenzie	P	1.1
Rainey,Tanner	P	1.1
Ortega,Rafael	8	1.0
Friedl,T.J.	78	1.0
Woodford,Jake	P	1.0
Guillorme,Luis	45	1.0
Olivares,Edward	9	0.9
Heim,Jonah	2	0.9
Kuhnel,Joel	P	0.9
Tepera,Ryan	P	0.9
Harvey,Hunter	P	0.9
Sánchez,Sixto	P	0.9
Hiura,Keston	3	0.9
Bradish,Kyle	P	0.8
Lauer,Eric	P	0.8
Maeda,Kenta	P	0.8
Peralta,Wandy	P	0.8
Aguilar,Jesús	3	0.8
Harrison,Josh	45	0.7
Jones,Nolan	9	0.7

MULTI-POSITION ELIGIBLITY

*Position player eligibility for leagues that use 5 games, 10 games and 20 games as their requirements. *Qualified based on the position played the most.*

NAME	5-Gm	10-Gm	20-Gm
Abrams,CJ	2B SS	2B SS	SS
Adrianza,Ehire	2B 3B OF	3B	3B *
Alberto,Hanser	2B 3B SS	2B 3B	2B 3B
Alcantara,Sergio	2B 3B SS	2B 3B SS	2B 3B SS
Allen,Nick	2B SS	2B SS	2B SS
Alvarez,Eddy	3B OF	OF	OF*
Anderson,Brian	3B OF	3B OF	3B OF
Aranda,Jonathan	1B 2B 3B	1B 2B	2B *
Arcia,Orlando	2B OF	2B	2B
Arraez,Luis	1B 2B 3B	1B 2B	1B 2B
Arroyo,Christian	1B 2B 3B SS OF	2B 3B SS OF	2B
Astudillo,Willians	2B 3B	3B	3B *
Batten,Matt	2B 3B	3B *	3B *
Berti,Jon	2B 3B SS OF	2B 3B SS OF	2B 3B
Bethancourt,Christian	CA 1B	CA 1B	CA 1B
Betts,Mookie	2B OF	OF	OF
Biggio,Cavan	1B 2B OF	1B 2B	1B 2B
Bohm,Alec	1B 3B	1B 3B	3B
Bote,David	1B 2B 3B	2B 3B	2B *
Bride,Jonah	1B 2B 3B	2B 3B	2B 3B
Brown,Seth	1B OF	1B OF	1B OF
Brujan,Vidal	2B SS OF	2B OF	2B OF
Burleson,Alec	OF	OF	OF *
Camargo,Johan	1B 2B 3B SS	3B SS	SS
Carpenter,Matt	1B OF	OF	OF *
Castillo,Diego	1B 2B SS OF	2B SS OF	2B SS OF
Castro,Harold	1B 2B 3B SS	1B 2B 3B SS	1B 3B
Castro,Rodolfo	2B 3B SS	2B 3B SS	2B 3B
Castro,Willi	2B SS OF	2B SS OF	OF
Chang,Yu	1B 2B 3B SS	2B SS	2B
Chavis,Michael	1B 2B 3B	1B 2B	1B
Clemens,Kody	1B 2B 3B OF	1B 3B	3B *
Clement,Ernie	1B 2B 3B OF	2B 3B OF	3B
Collins,Zack	CA 1B	CA	CA *
Cordero,Franchy	1B OF	1B OF	1B OF
Cronenworth,Jake	1B 2B SS	1B 2B	1B 2B
Culberson,Charlie	2B 3B OF	2B 3B OF	3B
Dalbec,Bobby	1B 3B	1B 3B	1B 3B
Davis,J.D.	1B 3B	1B 3B	3B
Diaz,Aledmys	1B 2B 3B SS OF	2B 3B SS OF	2B OF
Diaz,Yandy	1B 3B	3B	3B
Donovan,Brendan	1B 2B 3B SS OF	1B 2B 3B OF	2B 3B OF
Downs,Jeter	2B 3B	2B *	2B *
Dozier,Hunter	1B 3B OF	1B 3B OF	1B 3B OF
Drury,Brandon	1B 2B 3B	1B 2B 3B	1B 2B 3B
Dubon,Mauricio	2B SS OF	2B SS OF	SS OF
Duffy,Matt	1B 2B 3B	1B 3B	1B 3B
Duran,Ezequiel	2B 3B	3B	3B
Eaton,Nate	3B OF	3B OF	OF
Edman,Tommy	2B 3B SS	2B SS	2B SS
Espinal,Santiago	2B 3B SS	2B 3B SS	2B
Estrada,Thairo	2B SS OF	2B SS OF	2B SS
Farmer,Kyle	3B SS	3B SS	3B SS
Fletcher,David	2B SS	2B SS	2B SS
Flores,Wilmer	1B 2B 3B	1B 2B 3B	1B 2B 3B
France,Ty	1B 3B	1B	1B
Frazier,Adam	2B OF	2B OF	2B OF
Freeman,Tyler	3B SS	3B	3B *
Gamel,Ben	1B OF	OF	OF
Garcia,Aramis	CA 1B	CA	CA
Garcia,Leury	2B 3B SS OF	2B SS OF	2B OF
Garcia,Luis	2B SS	2B SS	2B SS

NAME	5-Gm	10-Gm	20-Gm
Gimenez,Andres	2B SS	2B SS	2B
Gonzalez,Erik	3B SS	SS *	SS *
Gonzalez,Marwin	1B 3B SS OF	1B 3B SS OF	SS OF
Gordon,Nick	2B SS OF	2B SS OF	2B OF
Gosselin,Phil	2B 3B	2B 3B	3B *
Grandal,Yasmani	CA 1B	CA	CA
Guillorme,Luis	2B 3B SS	2B 3B SS	2B 3B
Gurriel,Lourdes	1B OF	OF	OF
Haase,Eric	CA OF	CA OF	CA
Hager,Jake	2B 3B	2B	2B *
Hamilton,Caleb	CA 1B	CA	CA *
Hampson,Garrett	2B 3B SS OF	2B SS OF	SS OF
Harrison,Josh	2B 3B	2B 3B	2B 3B
Henderson,Gunnar	3B SS	3B	3B
Hernandez,Cesar	2B 3B OF	2B 3B OF	2B
Hernandez,Enrique	2B SS OF	2B SS OF	OF
Higgins,P.J.	CA 1B	CA 1B	CA 1B
Hiura,Keston	1B 2B OF	1B 2B	1B
Huff,Samuel	CA 1B	CA	CA
Hummel,Cooper	CA OF	CA OF	OF
Ibanez,Andy	1B 3B	3B	3B
Joe,Connor	1B OF	1B OF	1B OF
Kemp,Anthony	2B OF	2B OF	2B OF
Kim,Ha-Seong	3B SS	3B SS	3B SS
Kiner-Falefa,Isiah	3B SS	SS	SS
Kirilloff,Alex	1B OF	1B OF	OF
Knizner,Andrew	CA 1B	CA	CA
Leblanc,Charles	1B 2B 3B	2B 3B	2B
LeMahieu,DJ	1B 2B 3B	1B 2B 3B	1B 2B 3B
Lopez,Alejo	2B 3B OF	2B	2B
Lopez,Nicky	2B 3B SS	2B 3B SS	2B 3B SS
Lux,Gavin	2B SS OF	2B OF	2B OF
MacKinnon,David	1B 3B	1B	1B *
Madris,Bligh	1B OF	OF	OF
Mancini,Trey	1B OF	1B OF	1B OF
Marcano,Tucupita	2B OF	2B OF	2B OF
Maton,Nick	2B OF	2B OF	OF
Mayfield,Jack	2B 3B OF	2B	2B *
McKinney,Billy	1B OF	OF	OF*
McKinstry,Zach	2B 3B SS	2B 3B SS	2B 3B
McMahon,Ryan	2B 3B	2B 3B	3B
McNeil,Jeff	2B OF	2B OF	2B OF
Melendez Jr.,MJ	CA OF	CA OF	CA OF
Mendick,Danny	2B SS	SS	SS
Meneses,Joey	1B OF	1B OF	1B OF
Merrifield,Whit	2B OF	2B OF	2B OF
Miller,Bradley	3B OF	3B OF	3B OF
Miller,Owen	1B 2B	1B 2B	1B 2B
Miranda,Jose	1B 3B	1B 3B	1B 3B
Montero,Elehuris	1B 3B	1B 3B	3B
Moore,Dylan	1B 2B SS OF	2B SS OF	SS OF
Moran,Colin	1B 3B	1B 3B	1B
Morel,Christopher	2B 3B SS OF	2B 3B SS OF	2B OF
Moustakas,Mike	1B 3B	1B 3B	1B 3B
Muncy,Max	2B 3B	2B 3B	2B 3B
Munoz,Yairo	2B 3B	2B	2B *
Myers,Wil	1B OF	1B OF	1B OF
Naylor,Josh	1B OF	1B	1B
Neuse,Sheldon	1B 2B 3B	1B 2B 3B	2B 3B
Nevin,Tyler	1B 3B	3B	3B
Newman,Kevin	2B SS	2B SS	2B SS
O'Hearn,Ryan	1B OF	1B OF	1B * OF *

NAME	5-Gm	10-Gm	20-Gm
Owings,Chris	2B SS	2B	2B *
Padlo,Kevin	1B 3B	1B *	1B *
Palacios,Jermaine	2B SS	2B SS	SS *
Paredes,Isaac	1B 2B 3B	1B 2B 3B	1B 2B 3B
Park,Hoy Jun	2B 3B	2B	2B *
Perdomo,Geraldo	3B SS	SS	SS
Peterson,Jace	1B 3B OF	3B OF	3B
Pinder,Chad	3B OF	OF	OF
Polanco,Jorge	2B SS	2B	2B
Pratto,Nick	1B OF	1B	1B
Ramirez,Harold	1B OF	1B OF	1B OF
Rengifo,Luis	2B 3B SS OF	2B 3B SS	2B 3B
Reynolds,Matt	1B 2B 3B SS OF	1B 2B 3B SS OF	2B SS
Rivera,Emmanuel	1B 3B	3B	3B
Rojas,Jose	3B OF	3B	3B *
Rojas,Josh	2B 3B	2B 3B	2B 3B
Rojas,Miguel	1B SS	1B SS	SS
Rosario,Amed	SS OF	SS	SS
Ruf,Darin	1B OF	1B OF	1B OF
Semien,Marcus	2B SS	2B SS	2B
Sheets,Gavin	1B OF	1B OF	OF
Simmons,Andrelton	2B SS	2B SS	2B *SS *
Smith,Josh	3B SS OF	3B OF	3B OF
Smith,Kevin	3B SS	3B SS	3B
Smith,Pavin	1B OF	1B OF	OF
Solano,Donovan	1B 2B 3B	1B 3B	1B
Sosa,Edmundo	3B SS	3B SS	3B SS
Sosa,Lenyn	2B SS	2B *	2B *
Steer,Spencer	1B 2B 3B	3B	3B *
Stott,Bryson	2B SS	2B SS	2B SS
Strange-Gordon,Dee	SS OF	SS	SS *
Taylor,Chris	2B OF	2B OF	2B OF
Thaiss,Matt	CA 1B	CA 1B	CA *
Toglia,Michael	1B OF	1B OF	OF*
Toro,Abraham	2B 3B	2B 3B	2B 3B
Torres,Gleyber	2B SS	2B	2B
Trejo,Alan	2B SS	2B SS	SS
Tucker,Cole	2B OF	OF	OF*
Urias,Luis	2B 3B SS	2B 3B SS	2B 3B SS
Urias,Ramon	2B 3B SS	2B 3B	2B 3B
VanMeter,Josh	1B 2B	1B 2B	1B 2B
Vargas,Ildemaro	3B SS	3B SS	3B
Vargas,Miguel	1B OF	1B *	1B *
Varsho,Daulton	CA OF	CA OF	CA OF
Vaughn,Andrew	1B OF	1B OF	1B OF
Vavra,Terrin	2B OF	2B OF	2B *
Vazquez,Christian	CA 1B	CA	CA
Vierling,Matt	3B OF	OF	OF
Villar,David	1B 2B 3B	1B 3B	3B
Villar,Jonathan	2B 3B	2B 3B	2B 3B
Vogt,Stephen	CA 1B	CA 1B	CA *
Wade,LaMonte	1B OF	1B OF	1B OF
Wade,Tyler	2B 3B SS OF	2B 3B SS	2B
Walls,Taylor	2B 3B SS	2B 3B SS	2B 3B SS
Walton,Donnie	2B SS	2B SS	2B *
Wendle,Joe	2B 3B SS	2B 3B SS	2B 3B SS
Williams,Luke	2B 3B OF	2B 3B OF	3B OF
Wisdom,Patrick	1B 3B OF	1B 3B	3B
Witt Jr.,Bobby	3B SS	3B SS	3B SS
Yepez,Juan	1B 3B OF	1B OF	OF

2022 PLAYING TIME MEASURMENT CHARTS BY POSITION

See research article on page 67 for column descriptions, benchmarks and usage tips. Players are sorted in each chart by Plate Appearances per Active Week (PAAW).

First Base

Name	PA	AW	PAAW	SAW	PAS	EAW	GPA%	Multi
Freeman, Freddie	708	27	26.2	5.9	4.45	0.0	0%	
Guerrero Jr., Vlad	706	27	26.1	5.9	4.45	0.1	0%	
Olson, Matt	699	27	25.9	6.0	4.34	0.0	0%	
Alonso, Pete	685	27	25.4	5.9	4.28	0.0	0%	
Cronenworth, Jake	684	27	25.3	5.7	4.39	0.1	0%	4
Abreu, Jose	679	27	25.1	5.8	4.32	0.0	0%	
Hoskins, Rhys	672	27	24.9	5.7	4.35	0.1	0%	
Walker, Christian	667	27	24.7	5.8	4.23	0.1	0%	
Goldschmidt, Paul	651	26	24.5	5.6	4.33	0.0	2%	
Meneses, Joey	240	9	24.3	5.6	4.35	0.1	9%	o
Bell, Josh	647	27	24.0	5.6	4.25	0.2	0%	
France, Ty	613	25	23.9	5.4	4.43	0.1	2%	
Lowe, Nate	645	27	23.9	5.7	4.15	0.1	0%	
Cron, C.J.	632	27	23.4	5.5	4.26	0.1	0%	
Mountcastle, Ryan	609	26	23.1	5.5	4.22	0.0	1%	
LeMahieu, DJ	541	23	23.1	4.9	4.59	0.4	2%	45
Arraez, Luis	603	26	22.7	4.8	4.49	0.9	2%	4
Flores, Wilmer	602	27	22.3	4.9	4.31	1.2	0%	45
Tellez, Rowdy	599	27	22.2	5.0	4.25	0.9	0%	
Drury, Brandon	568	25	22.2	5.1	4.28	0.3	2%	45
Pasquantino, Vinnie	298	13	22.0	5.3	4.14	0.0	4%	
Vaughn, Andrew	555	25	21.8	5.1	4.22	0.2	2%	o
Rizzo, Anthony	548	25	21.8	4.9	4.36	0.3	1%	
Mancini, Trey	587	27	21.7	5.0	4.25	0.3	0%	o
Gurriel, Yulieski	584	27	21.6	5.2	4.11	0.1	0%	
Walsh, Jared	454	21	21.6	5.0	4.11	0.9	0%	
Voit, Luke	568	26	21.1	4.9	4.27	0.1	3%	
Miranda, Jose	483	23	21.0	5.0	4.09	0.3	0%	5
Brown, Seth	555	26	20.9	5.0	4.04	0.8	2%	o
Votto, Joey	376	18	20.3	4.9	4.17	0.1	3%	

Second Base

Name	PA	AW	PAAW	SAW	PAS	EAW	GPA%	Multi
Semien, Marcus	724	27	26.8	6.0	4.50	0.0	0%	
Cronenworth, Jake	684	27	25.3	5.7	4.39	0.1	0%	3
Edman, Tommy	630	27	23.3	5.3	4.37	0.4	0%	6
Altuve, Jose	604	26	23.2	5.3	4.38	0.2	0%	
LeMahieu, DJ	541	23	23.1	4.9	4.59	0.4	2%	35
Rengifo, Luis	511	22	23.0	5.4	4.18	0.6	1%	5
Hernandez, Cesar	617	27	22.9	5.3	4.31	0.2	0%	
Rojas, Josh	510	22	22.7	5.1	4.34	0.5	2%	5
Rodgers, Brendan	581	25	22.7	5.3	4.27	0.0	2%	
Arraez, Luis	603	26	22.7	4.8	4.49	0.9	2%	3
Flores, Wilmer	602	27	22.3	4.9	4.31	1.2	0%	35
Frazier, Adam	602	27	22.3	5.2	4.12	0.9	0%	o
Castro, Rodolfo	278	11	22.2	5.4	4.04	0.2	12%	5
Drury, Brandon	568	25	22.2	5.1	4.28	0.3	2%	35
McNeil, Jeff	589	26	22.1	5.3	4.13	0.1	2%	o
Albies, Ozzie	269	11	22.1	5.2	4.24	0.2	10%	
Muncy, Max	565	25	22.1	5.1	4.28	0.4	2%	5
Garcia, Luis	377	16	21.9	5.3	4.12	0.1	7%	6
Polanco, Jorge	445	19	21.6	5.0	4.30	0.1	8%	
India, Jonathan	431	19	21.6	4.9	4.35	0.3	5%	
Torres, Gleyber	572	27	21.2	4.9	4.28	0.4	0%	
Estrada, Thairo	541	25	21.1	5.0	4.09	0.5	3%	6
Marte, Ketel	558	26	21.0	4.8	4.27	0.4	2%	
Story, Trevor	396	18	20.9	4.9	4.27	0.2	5%	
Segura, Jean	387	18	20.8	5.2	4.00	0.2	3%	
Schoop, Jonathan	510	24	20.7	5.2	3.94	0.1	2%	
Kemp, Anthony	558	27	20.7	4.8	4.12	0.8	0%	o
Gimenez, Andres	557	27	20.6	5.0	4.07	0.4	0%	
Urias, Luis	472	23	20.5	4.7	4.16	0.8	0%	56
Merrifield, Whit	550	27	20.4	4.8	4.20	0.3	0%	o

Shortstop

Name	PA	AW	PAAW	SAW	PAS	EAW	GPA%	Multi
Turner, Trea	708	27	26.2	5.9	4.43	0.0	0%	
Lindor, Francisco	706	27	26.1	6.0	4.39	0.0	0%	
Adames, Willy	617	23	26.0	5.8	4.46	0.0	3%	
Bichette, Bo	697	27	25.8	5.9	4.41	0.0	0%	
Swanson, Dansby	696	27	25.8	6.0	4.30	0.0	0%	
Rosario, Amed	670	27	24.8	5.6	4.42	0.1	0%	
Seager, Corey	663	27	24.6	5.6	4.39	0.0	0%	
Witt Jr., Bobby	632	27	23.4	5.5	4.25	0.1	0%	5
Bogaerts, Xander	631	27	23.4	5.5	4.25	0.1	0%	
Edman, Tommy	630	27	23.3	5.3	4.37	0.4	0%	4
Correa, Carlos	590	24	23.1	5.2	4.41	0.2	6%	
Baez, Javier	590	26	22.5	5.4	4.14	0.1	1%	
Cruz, Oneil	361	16	22.5	5.3	4.22	0.1	0%	
Anderson, Tim	351	15	22.4	5.0	4.44	0.0	4%	
Crawford, J.P.	603	27	22.3	5.3	4.21	0.0	0%	
Franco, Wander	344	15	21.9	5.1	4.25	0.3	4%	
Garcia, Luis	377	16	21.9	5.3	4.12	0.1	7%	4
Farmer, Kyle	583	27	21.6	5.3	4.08	0.1	0%	5
Kim, Ha-Seong	582	27	21.6	5.3	4.05	0.3	0%	5
Andrus, Elvis	577	27	21.4	5.3	3.99	0.2	0%	
Pena, Jeremy	558	26	21.3	5.0	4.20	0.1	1%	
Estrada, Thairo	541	25	21.1	5.0	4.09	0.5	3%	4
Urias, Luis	472	23	20.5	4.7	4.16	0.8	0%	45
Hoerner, Nico	517	25	20.1	5.0	3.97	0.2	3%	
Mateo, Jorge	533	27	19.7	5.3	3.72	0.2	0%	
Crawford, Brandon	458	22	19.7	4.9	4.00	0.3	5%	
Kiner-Falefa, Isiah	531	27	19.7	5.0	3.88	0.3	0%	
Iglesias, Jose	467	24	18.8	4.8	3.96	0.0	3%	
Rojas, Miguel	507	27	18.8	4.9	3.78	0.3	0%	
Perdomo, Geraldo	500	27	18.5	5.1	3.59	0.1	0%	

Third Base

Name	PA	AW	PAAW	SAW	PAS	EAW	GPA%	Multi
Riley, Austin	693	27	25.7	5.9	4.38	0.0	0%	
Ramirez, Jose	685	27	25.4	5.8	4.36	0.0	0%	
Bregman, Alex	656	26	24.4	5.7	4.27	0.1	3%	
Suarez, Eugenio	629	25	24.3	5.7	4.24	0.2	3%	
Machado, Manny	644	27	23.9	5.5	4.34	0.1	0%	
Devers, Rafael	614	25	23.7	5.4	4.37	0.1	3%	
Witt Jr., Bobby	632	27	23.4	5.5	4.25	0.1	0%	6
Bohm, Alec	631	27	23.4	5.4	4.27	0.3	0%	
Arenado, Nolan	620	26	23.3	5.5	4.21	0.0	2%	
LeMahieu, DJ	541	23	23.1	4.9	4.59	0.4	2%	34
Rengifo, Luis	511	22	23.0	5.4	4.18	0.6	1%	4
Chapman, Matt	621	27	23.0	5.6	4.07	0.1	0%	
Henderson, Gunnar	132	5	23.0	5.2	4.13	1.4	13%	
Jung, Josh	102	4	22.9	5.8	3.92	0.4	10%	
Rojas, Josh	510	22	22.7	5.1	4.34	0.5	2%	4
Flores, Wilmer	602	27	22.3	4.9	4.31	1.2	0%	34
Castro, Rodolfo	278	11	22.2	5.4	4.04	0.2	12%	4
Drury, Brandon	568	25	22.2	5.1	4.28	0.3	2%	34
McMahon, Ryan	597	27	22.1	5.3	4.20	0.0	0%	
Muncy, Max	565	25	22.1	5.1	4.28	0.4	2%	4
Moncada, Yoan	433	19	21.6	4.9	4.37	0.3	5%	
Hayes, KeBryan	560	25	21.6	5.0	4.28	0.2	3%	
Farmer, Kyle	583	27	21.6	5.3	4.08	0.1	0%	6
Kim, Ha-Seong	582	27	21.6	5.3	4.05	0.3	0%	6
Donaldson, Josh	546	25	21.4	4.9	4.32	0.2	2%	
Wisdom, Patrick	534	25	21.1	5.0	4.12	0.4	1%	
Miranda, Jose	483	23	21.0	5.0	4.09	0.3	0%	3
Diaz, Yandy	558	27	20.7	4.7	4.35	0.4	0%	
Escobar, Eduardo	542	26	20.6	4.9	4.11	0.3	1%	
Turner, Justin	532	25	20.5	4.9	4.18	0.0	3%	

2022 PLAYING TIME MEASURMENT CHARTS BY POSITION

See research article on page 67 for column descriptions, benchmarks and usage tips. Players are sorted in each chart by Plate Appearances per Active Week (PAAW).

Outfield

Name	PA	AW	PAAW	SAW	PAS	EAW	GPA%	Multi
Judge, Aaron	696	27	25.8	5.7	4.52	0.1	0%	
Greene, Riley	418	16	25.6	5.7	4.49	0.0	2%	
Betts, Mookie	639	25	25.4	5.5	4.61	0.1	1%	
Nimmo, Brandon	673	26	25.0	5.5	4.55	0.0	3%	
Mullins II, Cedric	672	27	24.9	5.3	4.57	0.5	0%	
Profar, Jurickson	658	26	24.9	5.6	4.43	0.3	2%	
Yelich, Christian	671	27	24.9	5.5	4.48	0.1	0%	
Schwarber, Kyle	669	27	24.8	5.7	4.36	0.1	0%	
Soto, Juan	664	27	24.6	5.6	4.36	0.0	0%	
Gonzalez, Oscar	382	14	24.5	5.7	4.26	0.2	10%	
Reynolds, Bryan	614	25	24.5	5.8	4.25	0.1	0%	
Santander, Anthony	647	26	24.4	5.7	4.30	0.1	2%	
Garcia, Adolis	657	27	24.3	5.7	4.25	0.1	0%	
Meneses, Joey	240	9	24.3	5.6	4.35	0.1	9%	3
Arozarena, Randy	645	27	23.9	5.6	4.27	0.2	0%	
Verdugo, Alex	644	27	23.9	5.6	4.29	0.0	0%	
Happ, Ian	641	27	23.7	5.6	4.15	0.4	0%	
Kwan, Steven	638	27	23.6	5.1	4.50	0.5	0%	
Soler, Jorge	306	13	23.5	5.4	4.33	0.2	0%	
Castellanos, Nick	558	23	23.3	5.6	4.15	0.1	4%	
Ward, Taylor	564	23	23.3	5.4	4.28	0.3	5%	
Melendez Jr., MJ	534	23	23.2	5.4	4.26	0.3	0%	2
Brantley, Michael	277	12	23.1	5.3	4.33	0.0	0%	
Benintendi, Andrew	521	22	23.0	5.3	4.30	0.2	3%	
Pham, Tommy	622	27	23.0	5.3	4.34	0.1	0%	
Laureano, Ramon	383	15	22.9	5.5	4.12	0.2	10%	
Harris II, Michael	441	19	22.8	5.9	3.87	0.0	2%	
McCutchen, Andrew	580	25	22.8	5.1	4.40	0.2	2%	
Rodriguez, Julio	560	24	22.7	5.3	4.27	0.0	3%	
Acuna, Ronald	533	23	22.6	4.9	4.59	0.2	3%	
Tucker, Kyle	609	27	22.6	5.5	4.10	0.1	0%	
Hernandez, Enrique	402	17	22.4	5.1	4.38	0.2	5%	
Springer, George	583	26	22.4	4.8	4.56	0.3	0%	
Frazier, Adam	602	27	22.3	5.2	4.12	0.9	0%	4
Trout, Mike	499	22	22.2	5.2	4.24	0.1	2%	
McNeil, Jeff	589	26	22.1	5.3	4.13	0.1	2%	4
Straw, Myles	596	27	22.1	5.3	4.05	0.5	0%	
Cabrera, Oswaldo	171	7	22.1	5.3	4.05	0.6	10%	
Marte, Starling	505	22	22.0	5.1	4.34	0.0	4%	
Hernandez, Teoscar	535	24	22.0	5.3	4.15	0.2	1%	
Varsho, Daulton	592	27	21.9	5.0	4.24	0.6	0%	2
Renfroe, Hunter	522	22	21.9	5.2	4.18	0.0	8%	
Winker, Jesse	547	25	21.8	5.1	4.16	0.6	0%	
Vaughn, Andrew	555	25	21.8	5.1	4.22	0.2	2%	3
Mancini, Trey	587	27	21.7	5.0	4.25	0.3	0%	3

Outfield, cont.

Name	PA	AW	PAAW	SAW	PAS	EAW	GPA%	Multi
Yastrzemski, Mike	558	25	21.7	4.9	4.10	1.6	3%	
Blackmon, Charlie	577	26	21.7	4.8	4.44	0.3	2%	
Hays, Austin	582	27	21.6	5.1	4.15	0.2	0%	
Alvarez, Yordan	561	26	21.5	5.1	4.20	0.1	0%	
McCarthy, Jake	354	16	21.3	4.9	4.17	0.7	4%	
Suzuki, Seiya	446	20	21.3	5.0	4.20	0.2	5%	
Bleday, J.J.	238	11	21.0	4.9	4.05	1.0	3%	
Bader, Harrison	313	14	21.0	5.2	3.95	0.6	6%	
Gurriel, Lourdes	493	23	20.9	5.0	4.13	0.1	3%	
Brown, Seth	555	26	20.9	5.0	4.04	0.8	2%	3
Suwinski, Jack	372	17	20.7	5.1	3.87	1.1	5%	
Pollock, A.J.	527	25	20.7	4.8	4.20	0.4	2%	
Kemp, Anthony	558	27	20.7	4.8	4.12	0.8	0%	4
Haniger, Mitch	247	11	20.7	4.8	4.33	0.0	8%	
Stanton, Giancarlo	452	21	20.6	4.7	4.32	0.3	4%	
Carlson, Dylan	488	23	20.5	4.6	4.24	0.9	3%	
Bellinger, Cody	550	27	20.4	5.0	3.99	0.4	0%	
Merrifield, Whit	550	27	20.4	4.8	4.20	0.3	0%	4
Toglia, Michael	120	5	20.4	5.1	3.97	0.2	15%	
Morel, Christopher	425	20	20.3	5.0	3.97	0.4	4%	4
Thomas, Lane	548	27	20.3	4.6	4.22	0.8	0%	
Canha, Mark	542	26	20.3	4.6	4.21	0.7	3%	
Friedl, T.J.	258	10	20.1	4.5	4.16	1.4	22%	
Taveras, Leody	341	17	20.0	5.1	3.85	0.4	0%	
Larnach, Trevor	180	8	20.0	4.8	3.86	1.6	11%	
Margot, Manuel	363	17	20.0	4.7	4.22	0.2	6%	
O Neill, Tyler	383	17	19.9	4.6	4.28	0.3	11%	
Grichuk, Randal	538	27	19.9	4.8	4.12	0.3	0%	
Thomas, Alek	411	20	19.8	4.9	3.97	0.3	4%	
Duvall, Adam	315	16	19.7	5.0	3.91	0.1	0%	
Wallner, Matt	65	3	19.6	5.1	3.76	0.3	10%	
Jimenez, Eloy	327	16	19.5	4.8	4.04	0.2	5%	
Donovan, Brendan	468	24	19.5	4.5	4.20	0.6	0%	45
Grisham, Trent	524	27	19.4	4.6	4.02	1.0	0%	
Taylor, Chris	454	23	19.3	4.7	3.98	0.7	2%	4
Gamel, Ben	423	21	19.3	4.7	4.02	0.4	4%	
Aquino, Aristides	276	13	19.2	4.9	3.74	1.0	10%	
Anderson, Brian	383	19	19.1	4.6	4.09	0.4	5%	5
Carroll, Corbin	115	6	19.1	4.3	4.12	1.3	1%	
Ramirez, Harold	435	22	19.0	4.3	4.13	1.3	4%	3
Thompson, Bubba	181	9	18.8	5.3	3.55	0.0	6%	
Dozier, Hunter	500	26	18.8	4.5	4.08	0.2	2%	35
Ozuna, Marcell	507	27	18.8	4.6	4.09	0.0	0%	
Grossman, Robert	477	25	18.7	4.6	3.96	0.6	2%	
Bryant, Kris	181	8	18.7	4.3	4.31	0.0	17%	

2022 PLAYING TIME MEASURMENT CHARTS BY POSITION

See research article on page 67 for column descriptions, benchmarks and usage tips. Players are sorted in each chart by Plate Appearances per Active Week (PAAW).

Catcher

Name	PA	AW	PAAW	SAW	PAS	EAW	GPA%	Multi
Melendez Jr., MJ	534	23	23.2	5.4	4.26	0.3	0%	o
Rutschman, Adley	470	20	23.1	5.3	4.32	0.4	2%	
Murphy, Sean	612	27	22.7	5.4	4.18	0.1	0%	
Varsho, Daulton	592	27	21.9	5.0	4.24	0.6	0%	o
Perez, Salvador	473	21	21.6	5.2	4.15	0.0	4%	
Smith, Will	578	27	21.4	4.8	4.38	0.3	0%	
Realmuto, JT	562	27	20.8	4.9	4.18	0.4	0%	
Contreras, Willson	487	23	20.4	4.6	4.37	0.1	4%	
Kirk, Alejandro	541	27	20.0	4.6	4.25	0.7	0%	
Grandal, Yasmani	376	19	18.6	4.5	4.02	0.3	6%	
Ruiz, Keibert	433	23	18.3	4.1	4.23	0.8	3%	
Sanchez, Gary	471	27	17.4	4.1	4.06	0.6	0%	
Heim, Jonah	450	27	16.7	3.9	4.07	0.7	0%	
Stephenson, Tyler	183	10	16.0	4.0	3.89	0.4	13%	
Kelly, Carson	354	22	15.9	3.9	3.90	0.5	1%	
Vazquez, Christian	426	27	15.8	3.8	4.03	0.6	0%	
D Arnaud, Travis	426	27	15.8	3.9	4.07	0.1	0%	
Raleigh, Cal	415	26	15.8	3.8	3.90	1.0	1%	
Nola, Austin	397	27	14.7	3.7	3.94	0.3	0%	
Contreras, William	376	25	14.7	3.5	4.11	0.4	2%	
Diaz, Elias	381	26	14.6	3.6	3.95	0.4	1%	
Stassi, Max	375	26	14.4	3.6	3.88	0.5	0%	
Stallings, Jacob	384	27	14.2	3.9	3.63	0.2	0%	
Maldonado, Martin	379	27	14.0	4.1	3.45	0.0	0%	
Jeffers, Ryan	236	16	14.0	3.7	3.69	0.4	5%	
Perez, Roberto	69	5	13.8	3.8	3.53	0.4	0%	
Jansen, Danny	248	17	13.6	3.3	3.97	0.3	7%	
Hedges, Austin	338	25	13.3	3.8	3.44	0.2	2%	
Molina, Yadier	270	19	13.1	3.5	3.76	0.1	8%	
Bethancourt, Christia	333	25	13.1	3.3	3.76	0.7	2%	3

Designated Hitter

Name	PA	AW	PAAW	SAW	PAS	EAW	GPA%	Multi
Ohtani, Shohei	666	27	24.7	5.7	4.33	0.1	0%	
Harper, Bryce	426	18	23.0	5.3	4.34	0.1	3%	
Martinez, J.D.	596	27	22.1	5.1	4.29	0.0	0%	
Reyes, Franmil	473	23	19.8	4.7	4.16	0.3	4%	
Langeliers, Shea	153	7	19.4	4.8	3.97	0.3	11%	
Cruz, Nelson	507	27	18.8	4.5	4.13	0.1	0%	
Vogelbach, Daniel	461	26	17.4	4.2	3.94	0.9	2%	
Cabrera, Miguel	433	25	17.3	4.4	3.94	0.1	0%	
Garver, Mitch	215	11	16.9	3.8	4.27	0.5	14%	
Lowrie, Jed	184	11	14.8	3.4	4.19	0.7	12%	
Carpenter, Matt	154	11	14.0	3.2	4.06	1.1	0%	
Hall, Darick	142	9	13.7	3.3	3.97	0.7	13%	
Beer, Seth	126	9	13.0	3.4	3.67	0.5	7%	
La Stella, Tommy	195	14	12.5	3.0	3.72	1.3	10%	
Calhoun, Willie	62	5	12.3	3.4	3.12	1.8	1%	
Mercedes, Yermin	83	6	11.8	2.8	3.45	2.1	15%	
Lewis, Kyle	62	3	11.1	2.7	3.93	0.6	46%	
Vientos, Mark	41	4	9.6	1.6	4.14	2.9	6%	
Vogt, Stephen	191	20	9.2	2.2	3.58	1.5	4%	
Dickerson, Alex	36	4	9.0	2.5	3.40	0.5	0%	
Rios, Edwin	92	9	8.9	1.9	4.20	0.8	13%	
Frazier, Clint	45	5	8.4	1.8	3.60	1.7	7%	
O Hearn, Ryan	145	27	5.4	1.0	3.71	1.5	0%	
Matijevic, J.J.	71	10	5.2	1.0	3.57	1.8	26%	
Mathias, Mark	91	18	4.7	1.1	3.62	0.8	6%	
Hensley, David	34	7	4.7	1.0	3.43	1.4	4%	
Upton, Justin	57	16	3.5	0.9	3.67	0.1	3%	
Dawson, Ronnie	3	1	0.4	0.1	3.00	0.0	87%	

Get Forecaster Insights Every Single Day.

The **Baseball Forecaster** provides the core concepts in player evaluation and gaming strategy. You can maintain that edge all season long.

From spring training to the season's last pitch, **BaseballHQ.com** covers all aspects of what's happening on and off the field—all with the most powerful fantasy slant on the Internet:

- Nationally-renowned baseball analysts.
- MLB news analysis; including anticipating the **next** move.
- Dedicated columns on starting pitching, relievers, batters, and our popular Fact or Fluke? player profiles.
- Minor-league coverage beyond just scouting and lists.
- FAB targets, starting pitcher reports, strategy articles, daily game resources, call-up profiles and more!

Plus, **BaseballHQ.com** gets personal, with customizable tools and valuable resources:

- Team Stat Tracker and Power Search tools
- Custom Draft Guide for YOUR league's parameters
- Sortable and downloadable stats and projection files
- Subscriber forums, the friendliest on the baseball Internet

Visit **www.baseballhq.com/subscribe**
to lock down your path to a 2023 championship!

Full Season subscription **$89**
(prorated at the time of order; auto-renews each October)
Draft Prep subscription **$39**
(complete access from January through April 30, 2023)
Please read our Terms of service at www.baseballhq.com/terms.html

Baseball Forecaster & BaseballHQ.com: Your season-long championship lineup.

Where else to find Ron Shandler these days

Save the date!

March 3-5, 2023

Interactive sessions • Player analysis

Injury updates • Current ADP feedback

Gaming strategies • Live drafts

Spring training games

Plus the LABR experts drafts in-person

.... and a whole lot more!

Details: www.baseballhq.com/first-pitch-florida

BONUS DATE: First Pitch Arizona at the Arizona Fall League • November 2-5, 2023

2023 CHEATER'S BOOKMARK

BATTING STATISTICS

Abbrv	Term	Formula / Desc.	BAD UNDER	'22 LG AVG AL	'22 LG AVG NL	BEST OVER
Avg	Batting Average	h/ab	225	242	243	275
xBA	Expected Batting Average	*See glossary*		252	252	
OB	On Base Average	(h+bb)/(ab+bb)	285	304	308	330
Slg	Slugging Average	total bases/ab	350	392	398	450
OPS	On Base plus Slugging	OB+Slg	650	696	706	800
bb%	Walk Rate	bb/(ab+bb)	6%	8%	9%	10%
ct%	Contact Rate	(ab-k) / ab	73%	75%	75%	83%
Eye	Batting Eye	bb/k	0.30	0.36	0.37	0.50
PX	Power Index	Normalized power skills	80	100	100	120
Spd	Speed Score	Normalized speed skills	80	100	100	120
SBA	Stolen Base Attempt Rate %	(sb+cs)/(singles+bb+hbp)		7.7%	7.7%	
G	Ground Ball Per Cent	gb / balls in play		43%	43%	
L	Line Drive Per Cent	ld / balls in play		20%	20%	
F	Fly Ball Per Cent	fb / balls in play		38%	37%	
HR/F	Home runs per fly ball	HR/FB		11%	12%	
Brl%	Barrel rate	barrels/batted ball event		7.9%	7.2%	
RAR	Runs Above Replacement	*See glossary*	0.0			10.0

PITCHING STATISTICS

Abbrv	Term	Formula / Desc.	BAD OVER	'22 LG AVG AL	'22 LG AVG NL	BEST UNDER
ERA	Earned Run Average	er*9/ip	5.00	3.89	4.05	3.50
xERA	Expected ERA	*See glossary*		3.93	3.87	
WHIP	Baserunners per Inning	(h+bb)/ip	1.45	1.25	1.28	1.15
PC	Pitch Counts per Start		100	84	86	
H%	BatAvg on balls in play	(h-hr)/((ip*2.82)+h-k-hr)		29%	29%	
BB%	Walk percentage	BB/total batters faced	11%	8%	8%	7%
Ball%	Ball%	Balls/total pitches	38%	36%	36%	34%
HR/F	Homerun per Fly ball	HR/FB		11%	12%	
S%	Strand Rate	(h+bb-er)/(h+bb-hr)		72%	72%	
DIS%	PQS Disaster Rate	% GS that are PQS 0/1		34%	34%	15%

Abbrv	Term	Formula / Desc.	BAD UNDER	'22 LG AVG AL	'22 LG AVG NL	BEST OVER
RAR	Runs Above Replacement	*See glossary*	-0.0			+10
K%	Strikeout percentage	K/total batters faced	20%	22%	23%	28%
K-BB%	K rate minus BB rate	K%-BB%	10%	14%	14%	18%
SwK	Swinging Strike Percentage	swinging strikes/pitches		11.7%	11.5%	13.0%
DOM%	PQS Dominance Rate	% GS that are PQS 4/5		20%	22%	50%
Sv%	Saves Conversion Rate	(saves / save opps)		65%	64%	80%

NOTES